NEW PERSPECTIVES ON

Microsoft® Excel® 2010

COMPREHENSIVE

Important Information About This Printing

This printing of this book was approved to meet the official standards for the Microsoft Office Specialist Excel 2010 Expert exam. This printing includes a new Appendix E that provides:

- Information on Microsoft Office Specialist certification
- Coverage of additional skills related to the exam that are not covered in the main tutorials of this text
- A table that lists the skills for the exam and identifies where each is covered in the text

The information about the Microsoft Office Specialist exams on page ii is also new to this printing. Otherwise, the book contains the exact page-for-page content of previous printings.

What is the Microsoft® Office Specialist Program?

The Microsoft Office Specialist Program enables candidates to show that they have something exceptional to offer – proven expertise in certain Microsoft programs. Recognized by businesses and schools around the world, over 4 million certifications have been obtained in over 100 different countries. The Microsoft Office Specialist Program is the only Microsoft-approved certification program of its kind.

What is the Microsoft Office Specialist Certification?

The Microsoft Office Specialist certification validates through the use of exams that you have obtained specific skill sets within the applicable Microsoft Office programs and other Microsoft programs included in the Microsoft Office Specialist Program. The candidate can choose which exam(s) they want to take according to which skills they want to validate.

The available Microsoft Office Specialist Program exams include*:

- Using Windows Vista®
- Using Microsoft® Office Word 2007
- Using Microsoft® Office Word 2007 – Expert
- Using Microsoft® Office Excel® 2007
- Using Microsoft® Office Excel® 2007 – Expert
- Using Microsoft® Office PowerPoint® 2007
- Using Microsoft® Office Access® 2007
- Using Microsoft® Office Outlook® 2007
- Using Microsoft SharePoint® 2007

The Microsoft Office Specialist Program 2010 exams will include*:

- Microsoft Word 2010
- Microsoft Word 2010 Expert
- Microsoft Excel® 2010
- Microsoft Excel® 2010 Expert
- Microsoft PowerPoint® 2010
- Microsoft Access® 2010
- Microsoft Outlook® 2010
- Microsoft SharePoint® 2010

What does the Microsoft Office Specialist Approved Courseware logo represent?

The logo indicates that this courseware has been approved by Microsoft to cover the course objectives that will be included in the relevant exam. It also means that after utilizing this courseware, you may be better prepared to pass the exams required to become a certified Microsoft Office Specialist.

For more information:

To learn more about Microsoft Office Specialist exams, visit www.microsoft.com/learning/msbc

To learn about other Microsoft approved courseware from Cengage Learning, visit www.cengagebrain.com

The availability of Microsoft Office Specialist certification exams varies by Microsoft program, program version and language. Visit www.microsoft.com/learning for exam availability.

NEW PERSPECTIVES ON

Microsoft® Excel® 2010

COMPREHENSIVE

June Jamrich Parsons
Dan Oja
Roy Ageloff
Patrick Carey

COURSE TECHNOLOGY
CENGAGE Learning™

Australia • Brazil • Japan • Korea • Mexico • Singapore • Spain • United Kingdom • United States

New Perspectives on Microsoft Excel 2010, Comprehensive

Vice President, Publisher: Nicole Jones Pinard

Executive Editor: Marie L. Lee

Associate Acquisitions Editor: Brandi Shailer

Senior Product Manager: Kathy Finnegan

Product Manager: Leigh Hefferon

Associate Product Manager: Julia Leroux-Lindsey

Editorial Assistant: Jacqueline Lacaire

Director of Marketing: Cheryl Costantini

Senior Marketing Manager: Ryan DeGrote

Marketing Coordinator: Kristen Panciocco

Developmental Editor: Robin M. Romer

Senior Content Project Manager: Jennifer Goguen McGrail

Composition: GEX Publishing Services

Art Director: Marissa Falco

Text Designer: Althea Chen

Cover Designer: Roycroft Design

Cover Art: © David Jordan Williams/Corbis

Copyeditor: Suzanne Huizenga

Proofreader: Andrea Schein

Indexer: Alexandra Nickerson

Library of Congress Control Number: 2010936136

ISBN-13: 978-0-538-74291-7

ISBN-10: 0-538-74291-7

Course Technology
20 Channel Center Street
Boston, MA 02210
USA

Cengage Learning is a leading provider of customized learning solutions with office locations around the globe, including Singapore, the United Kingdom, Australia, Mexico, Brazil, and Japan. Locate your local office at:
international.cengage.com/global

Cengage Learning products are represented in Canada by Nelson Education, Ltd.

To learn more about Course Technology, visit **www.cengage.com/course technology**

To learn more about Cengage Learning, visit **www.cengage.com**

Purchase any of our products at your local college store or at our preferred online store **www.cengagebrain.com**

Printed in the United States of America
2 3 4 5 6 7 8 9 14 13 12 11

Preface

The New Perspectives Series' critical-thinking, problem-solving approach is the ideal way to prepare students to transcend point-and-click skills and take advantage of all that Microsoft Office 2010 has to offer.

In developing the New Perspectives Series, our goal was to create books that give students the software concepts and practical skills they need to succeed beyond the classroom. We've updated our proven case-based pedagogy with more practical content to make learning skills more meaningful to students.

With the New Perspectives Series, students understand *why* they are learning *what* they are learning, and are fully prepared to apply their skills to real-life situations.

"The new Visual Overviews give students valuable insight into what they will learn in each tutorial session. Clearly seeing what's ahead will engage students from the start."
— Diane Shingledecker
Portland Community College

About This Book

This book provides complete coverage of Microsoft Excel 2010, and includes the following:

- Detailed, hands-on instruction of Excel 2010, including creating and formatting a workbook; working with formulas and functions; creating charts, tables, and PivotTables; managing multiple workbooks; developing an Excel application; working with VBA; and consolidating data from various sources
- Coverage of important spreadsheet concepts, including order of precedence in formulas, function syntax, absolute and relative cell references, what-if analysis, and data validation
- Exploration of the exciting new features in Excel 2010, including working in Backstage view, adding sparklines for compact graphing, using a slicer to filter a PivotTable, and sharing files on SkyDrive

New for this edition!

- Each session begins with a Visual Overview, a new two-page spread that includes colorful, enlarged screenshots with numerous callouts and key term definitions, giving students a comprehensive preview of the topics covered in the session, as well as a handy study guide.
- New ProSkills boxes provide guidance for how to use the software in real-world, professional situations, and related ProSkills exercises integrate the technology skills students learn with one or more of the following soft skills: decision making, problem solving, teamwork, verbal communication, and written communication.
- Important steps are highlighted in yellow with attached margin notes to help students pay attention to completing the steps correctly and avoid time-consuming rework.

System Requirements

This book assumes a typical installation of Microsoft Excel 2010 and Microsoft Windows 7 Ultimate using an Aero theme. (You can also complete the material in this text using another version of Windows 7, such as Home Premium, or earlier versions of the Windows operating system. You will see only minor differences in how some windows look.) The browser used for any steps that require a browser is Internet Explorer 8.

"The clear step-by-step instructions, real-world data files, and helpful figures make New Perspectives texts excellent for courses taught in the classroom, the hybrid/blended format, or entirely online."
—Sylvia Amito'elau
Coastline Community College

The New Perspectives Approach

Context
Each tutorial begins with a problem presented in a "real-world" case that is meaningful to students. The case sets the scene to help students understand what they will do in the tutorial.

Hands-on Approach
Each tutorial is divided into manageable sessions that combine reading and hands-on, step-by-step work. Colorful screenshots help guide students through the steps. **Trouble?** tips anticipate common mistakes or problems to help students stay on track and continue with the tutorial.

VISUAL OVERVIEW

Visual Overviews
New for this edition! Each session begins with a Visual Overview, a new two-page spread that includes colorful, enlarged screenshots with numerous callouts and key term definitions, giving students a comprehensive preview of the topics covered in the session, as well as a handy study guide.

PROSKILLS

ProSkills Boxes and Exercises
New for this edition! ProSkills boxes provide guidance for how to use the software in real-world, professional situations, and related ProSkills exercises integrate the technology skills students learn with one or more of the following soft skills: decision making, problem solving, teamwork, verbal communication, and written communication.

KEY STEP

Key Steps
New for this edition! Important steps are highlighted in yellow with attached margin notes to help students pay close attention to completing the steps correctly and avoid time-consuming rework.

INSIGHT

InSight Boxes
InSight boxes offer expert advice and best practices to help students achieve a deeper understanding of the concepts behind the software features and skills.

TIP

Margin Tips
Margin Tips provide helpful hints and shortcuts for more efficient use of the software. The Tips appear in the margin at key points throughout each tutorial, giving students extra information when and where they need it.

REVIEW
APPLY

Assessment
Retention is a key component to learning. At the end of each session, a series of Quick Check questions helps students test their understanding of the material before moving on. Engaging end-of-tutorial Review Assignments and Case Problems have always been a hallmark feature of the New Perspectives Series. Colorful bars and brief descriptions accompany the exercises, making it easy to understand both the goal and level of challenge a particular assignment holds.

REFERENCE
TASK REFERENCE
GLOSSARY/INDEX

Reference
Within each tutorial, Reference boxes appear before a set of steps to provide a succinct summary and preview of how to perform a task. In addition, a complete Task Reference at the back of the book provides quick access to information on how to carry out common tasks. Finally, each book includes a combination Glossary/Index to promote easy reference of material.

www.cengage.com/ct/newperspectives

Our Complete System of Instruction

BRIEF

INTRODUCTORY

COMPREHENSIVE

Coverage To Meet Your Needs

Whether you're looking for just a small amount of coverage or enough to fill a semester-long class, we can provide you with a textbook that meets your needs.

- Brief books typically cover the essential skills in just 2 to 4 tutorials.
- Introductory books build and expand on those skills and contain an average of 5 to 8 tutorials.
- Comprehensive books are great for a full-semester class, and contain 9 to 12+ tutorials.

So if the book you're holding does not provide the right amount of coverage for you, there's probably another offering available. Go to our Web site or contact your Course Technology sales representative to find out what else we offer.

CourseCasts – Learning on the Go. Always available...always relevant.

Want to keep up with the latest technology trends relevant to you? Visit our site to find a library of podcasts, CourseCasts, featuring a "CourseCast of the Week," and download them to your mp3 player at http://coursecasts.course.com.

Our fast-paced world is driven by technology. You know because you're an active participant—always on the go, always keeping up with technological trends, and always learning new ways to embrace technology to power your life.

Ken Baldauf, host of CourseCasts, is a faculty member of the Florida State University Computer Science Department where he is responsible for teaching technology classes to thousands of FSU students each year. Ken is an expert in the latest technology trends; he gathers and sorts through the most pertinent news and information for CourseCasts so your students can spend their time enjoying technology, rather than trying to figure it out. Open or close your lecture with a discussion based on the latest CourseCast.

Visit us at http://coursecasts.course.com to learn on the go!

Instructor Resources

We offer more than just a book. We have all the tools you need to enhance your lectures, check students' work, and generate exams in a new, easier-to-use and completely revised package. This book's Instructor's Manual, ExamView testbank, PowerPoint presentations, data files, solution files, figure files, and a sample syllabus are all available on a single CD-ROM or for downloading at http://www.cengage.com/coursetechnology.

SAM: Skills Assessment Manager

SAM is designed to help bring students from the classroom to the real world. It allows students to train and test on important computer skills in an active, hands-on environment.

SAM's easy-to-use system includes powerful interactive exams, training, and projects on the most commonly used Microsoft Office applications. SAM simulates the Office application environment, allowing students to demonstrate their knowledge and think through the skills by performing real-world tasks, such as bolding text or setting up slide transitions. Add in live-in-the-application projects, and students are on their way to truly learning and applying skills to business-centric documents.

Designed to be used with the New Perspectives Series, SAM includes handy page references, so students can print helpful study guides that match the New Perspectives textbooks used in class. For instructors, SAM also includes robust scheduling and reporting features.

WebTUTOR™

Content for Online Learning

Course Technology has partnered with the leading distance learning solution providers and class-management platforms today. To access this material, visit www.cengage.com/webtutor and search for your title. Instructor resources include the following: additional case projects, sample syllabi, PowerPoint presentations, and more. For students to access this material, they must have purchased a WebTutor PIN-code specific to this title and your campus platform. The resources for students might include (based on instructor preferences): topic reviews, review questions, practice tests, and more. For additional information, please contact your sales representative.

Acknowledgments

We would like to thank the many people whose invaluable contributions made this book possible. First, sincere thanks go to our reviewers: Carol DesJardins, St. Clair County Community College; Kristen Hockman, University of Missouri–Columbia; Dana Hooper, The University of Alabama; Ahmed Kamel, Concordia College; Peter Ross, University at Albany; Diane Shingledecker, Portland Community College; Kelly Swain, Humber College; Karen Toreson, Shoreline Community College; Mary Voehl, Caldwell College; Raymond Yu, Douglas College; and Violet Zhang, George Brown College. At Course Technology we would like to thank Marie Lee, Executive Editor; Kathy Finnegan, Senior Product Manager; Brandi Shailer, Associate Acquisitions Editor; Julia Leroux-Lindsey, Associate Product Manager; Jacqueline Lacaire, Editorial Assistant; Jennifer Goguen McGrail, Senior Content Project Manager; Christian Kunciw, Manuscript Quality Assurance Supervisor; and John Freitas, Serge Palladino, Susan Pedicini, Danielle Shaw, and Susan Whalen, MQA Testers. Special thanks to Robin Romer, Developmental Editor, for her exceptional efforts, keeping us focused and providing guidance and encouragement as we worked to complete this text.

– June Jamrich Parsons
– Dan Oja
– Roy Ageloff
– Patrick Carey

BRIEF CONTENTS

FILE MANAGEMENT

Managing Your Files . . . . . FM 1
Organizing Files and Folders with Windows 7

OFFICE

Getting Started with Microsoft Office 2010 . . . . . OFF 1
Preparing a Meeting Agenda

EXCEL

Level I Tutorials

Tutorial 1 Getting Started with Excel . . . . . EX 1
Creating an Order Report

Tutorial 2 Formatting a Workbook . . . . . EX 57
Designing a Financial Report

Tutorial 3 Working with Formulas and Functions . . . . . EX 115
Developing a Family Budget

Tutorial 4 Enhancing a Workbook with Charts and Graphics . . . . . EX 169
Charting Financial Data

Level II Tutorials

Tutorial 5 Working with Excel Tables, PivotTables, and PivotCharts . . . . . EX 233
Tracking Museum Art Objects

Tutorial 6 Managing Multiple Worksheets and Workbooks . . . . . EX 301
Summarizing Ticket Sales

Tutorial 7 Using Advanced Functions and Conditional Formatting . . . . . EX 363
Calculating Employee Benefits

Tutorial 8 Developing an Excel Application . . . . . EX 419
Creating an Invoice

Level III Tutorials

Tutorial 9 Working with Financial Tools and Functions. . . . . . EX 489
Developing a Financial Analysis

Tutorial 10 Performing What-If Analyses . . . . . EX 551
Analyzing the Cost-Volume-Profit Relationship

Tutorial 11 Connecting to External Data . . . . . EX 613
Retrieving Financial Information from Different Data Sources

Tutorial 12 Enhancing Excel with Visual Basic for Applications . . . . . EX 683
Creating a Climate Report Application

Additional Cases . . . . ADD 1

Appendix A Working with Text Functions and Creating Custom Formats . . . EX A1
Cleaning Data in a Spreadsheet

Appendix B Advanced Filters, Database, and Summary IFS Functions . . . . . EX B1
Generating a List of Eligible Employee Candidates

Appendix C Creating a Shared Workbook . . . . EX C1
Collaborating on a Financial Report

Appendix D Working with Enhanced Formatting Tools . . . . EX D1
Formatting a Chemistry Report

Appendix E Microsoft Office Specialist Certification Skills. . . . . EX E1

Glossary/Index **REF 1**

Task Reference **REF 15**

TABLE OF CONTENTS

Preface v

MANAGING YOUR FILES

Organizing Files and Folders with Windows 7 .... **FM 1**

Organizing Files and Folders .... FM 4

Understanding the Need for Organizing Files and Folders .... FM 4

Developing Strategies for Organizing Files and Folders .... FM 5

Exploring Files, Folders, and Libraries .... FM 6

Using Libraries and Folders .... FM 7

Navigating to Your Data Files .... FM 9

Managing Folders and Files .... FM 11

Creating Folders .... FM 11

Moving and Copying Files and Folders .... FM 12

Naming and Renaming Files .... FM 15

Deleting Files and Folders .... FM 17

Working with Compressed Files .... FM 17

Quick Check .... FM 19

Review Assignments .... FM 20

Case Problems .... FM 20

ProSkills Exercise: Decision Making .... FM 23

GETTING STARTED WITH MICROSOFT OFFICE 2010

Preparing a Meeting Agenda .... **OFF 1**

Exploring Microsoft Office 2010 .... OFF 4

Starting Office Programs .... OFF 5

Switching Between Open Programs and Files .... OFF 7

Exploring Common Window Elements .... OFF 8

Resizing the Program Window and Workspace ... OFF 8

Switching Views .... OFF 9

Zooming and Scrolling .... OFF 9

Using the Ribbon .... OFF 11

Clicking Buttons .... OFF 12

Using Galleries and Live Preview .... OFF 14

Opening Dialog Boxes and Task Panes .... OFF 14

Using Contextual Tools .... OFF 16

Displaying Contextual Tabs .... OFF 16

Accessing the Mini Toolbar .... OFF 16

Opening Shortcut Menus .... OFF 17

Working with Files .... OFF 18

Saving a File .... OFF 19

Closing a File .... OFF 22

Opening a File .... OFF 22

Sharing Files Using Windows Live SkyDrive .... OFF 24

Getting Help .... OFF 25

Viewing ScreenTips .... OFF 25

Using the Help Window .... OFF 26

Printing a File .... OFF 28

Exiting Programs .... OFF 30

Quick Check .... OFF 30

Review Assignments .... OFF 31

ProSkills Exercise: Teamwork .... OFF 32

EXCEL LEVEL I TUTORIALS

Tutorial 1 Getting Started with Excel
Creating an Order Report . . . . **EX 1**

SESSION 1.1 . . . . **EX 2**

Introducing Excel. . . . . EX 4
Understanding Spreadsheets . . . . EX 4
Exploring the Excel Window . . . . EX 4
Navigating Between Worksheets . . . . EX 5
Navigating Within a Worksheet . . . . EX 6
Planning a Workbook. . . . . EX 8
Entering Text, Numbers, and Dates. . . . . . . EX 9
Entering Text. . . . . EX 9
Entering Multiple Lines of Text Within a Cell . . . . . EX 11
Entering Dates . . . . EX 12
Entering Numbers. . . . . EX 13
Working with Columns and Rows . . . . EX 15
Setting Column Widths. . . . . EX 15
Setting Row Heights . . . . EX 17
Inserting a Column or Row . . . . EX 18
Deleting and Clearing a Row or Column. . . . . EX 20
Session 1.1 Quick Check. . . . . EX 21

SESSION 1.2 . . . . **EX 22**

Working with Cells and Ranges. . . . . EX 24
Selecting a Range . . . . EX 24
Moving and Copying a Range. . . . . EX 26
Inserting and Deleting a Range . . . . EX 28
Working with Formulas . . . . EX 30
Entering a Formula . . . . EX 30
Copying and Pasting Formulas. . . . . EX 33
Introducing Functions . . . . EX 34
Entering a Function. . . . . EX 34
Entering Functions with the AutoSum Feature . . . . EX 35
Working with Worksheets . . . . EX 37
Inserting or Deleting a Worksheet . . . . EX 37
Renaming a Worksheet. . . . . EX 38
Moving and Copying a Worksheet . . . . EX 38
Editing Worksheet Content . . . . EX 38
Undoing and Redoing an Action. . . . . EX 40
Using Find and Replace . . . . EX 40
Using the Spelling Checker. . . . . EX 41
Previewing and Printing a Workbook . . . . . . EX 43
Changing Worksheet Views . . . . EX 43
Working with Portrait and Landscape Orientation . . . . EX 44
Printing the Workbook . . . . EX 45
Viewing and Printing Worksheet Formulas. . . . . . EX 46
Session 1.2 Quick Check . . . . EX 48
Review Assignments . . . . EX 49
Case Problems. . . . . EX 50

Tutorial 2 Formatting a Workbook
Designing a Financial Report . . . . **EX 57**

SESSION 2.1 . . . . **EX 58**

Formatting Cell Text . . . . EX 60
Applying Fonts and Font Styles . . . . EX 61

Applying a Font Color . . . . . EX 62

Formatting Text Selections . . . . . EX 63

Working with Colors and Backgrounds . . . . . EX 64

Applying a Fill Color . . . . . EX 64

Adding a Background Image . . . . . EX 65

Formatting Calculated Values . . . . . EX 66

Creating Formulas to Add, Subtract, and Divide Values . . . . . EX 66

Applying Number Formats . . . . . EX 68

Formatting Dates and Times . . . . . EX 71

Formatting Worksheet Cells . . . . . EX 72

Aligning Cell Content . . . . . EX 72

Indenting Cell Content . . . . . EX 73

Merging Cells . . . . . EX 74

Rotating Cell Contents . . . . . EX 75

Adding Cell Borders . . . . . EX 76

Exploring Options in the Format Cells Dialog Box . . . . EX 77

Copying and Pasting Formats . . . . . EX 79

Copying Formats with the Format Painter . . . . . EX 79

Copying Formats with the Paste Options Button . . EX 80

Copying Formats with Paste Special . . . . . EX 81

Session 2.1 Quick Check . . . . . EX 81

SESSION 2.2 . . . . . EX 82

Applying Cell Styles . . . . . EX 84

Working with Themes . . . . . EX 86

Creating Formulas to Add and Subtract Values . . . . . EX 88

Creating Formulas to Calculate Totals . . . . . EX 88

Creating Formulas to Subtract Values . . . . . EX 89

Working with Table Styles . . . . . EX 91

Selecting Table Style Options . . . . . EX 93

Highlighting Cells with Conditional Formats . . . . . EX 95

Hiding Worksheet Data . . . . . EX 101

Formatting the Worksheet for Printing . . . . . EX 101

Defining the Print Area . . . . . EX 102

Inserting Page Breaks . . . . . EX 103

Adding Print Titles . . . . . EX 104

Creating Page Headers and Footers . . . . . EX 105

Defining the Page Margins . . . . . EX 107

Session 2.2 Quick Check . . . . . EX 107

Review Assignments . . . . . EX 108

Case Problems . . . . . EX 109

Tutorial 3 Working with Formulas and Functions

Developing a Family Budget . . . . . **EX 115**

SESSION 3.1 . . . . . EX 116

Understanding Cell References . . . . . EX 118

Using Relative References . . . . . EX 120

Using Absolute References . . . . . EX 121

Using Mixed References . . . . . EX 125

Working with Functions . . . . . EX 127

Understanding Function Syntax . . . . . EX 127

Inserting a Function . . . . . EX 131

Typing a Function . . . . . EX 134

Session 3.1 Quick Check . . . . . EX 137

SESSION 3.2 . . . . . EX 138

Entering Data and Formulas with AutoFill . . . . . EX 140

Using the Fill Handle . . . . . EX 141

Using the Auto Fill Options Button . . . . EX 143
Filling a Series . . . . EX 143
Developing a Savings Plan . . . . EX 147
Working with Logical Functions . . . . EX 151
Using the IF Function . . . . EX 151
Working with Date Functions . . . . EX 155
Working with Financial Functions . . . . EX 156
Using the PMT Function . . . . EX 158
Session 3.2 Quick Check . . . . EX 162
Review Assignments . . . . EX 163
Case Problems . . . . EX 164

Tutorial 4 Enhancing a Workbook with Charts and Graphs
Charting Financial Data . . . . **EX 169**

SESSION 4.1 . . . . EX 170
Creating an Excel Chart . . . . EX 172
Selecting a Data Source . . . . EX 173
Selecting a Chart Type . . . . EX 173
Moving a Chart to a Different Worksheet . . . . EX 175
Moving and Resizing Charts . . . . EX 176
Designing a Pie Chart . . . . EX 177
Choosing a Chart Style . . . . EX 177
Choosing a Chart Layout . . . . EX 178
Formatting the Chart Title . . . . EX 179
Formatting the Chart Legend . . . . EX 180
Formatting Data Labels . . . . EX 182
Defining Pie Slice Colors . . . . EX 183
Creating a Column Chart . . . . EX 184
Inserting a Column Chart . . . . EX 185
Formatting a Column Chart Title and Legend . . . EX 186
Editing the Axis Scale and Text . . . . EX 187
Formatting the Chart Columns . . . . EX 189
Session 4.1 Quick Check . . . . EX 191

SESSION 4.2 . . . . EX 192
Creating a Line Chart . . . . EX 194
Formatting Date Labels . . . . EX 195
Setting Label Units . . . . EX 198
Overlaying a Chart Legend . . . . EX 199
Adding Gridlines . . . . EX 201
Adding an Axis Title . . . . EX 201
Editing and Revising Chart Data . . . . EX 202
Changing a Data Value . . . . EX 202
Adding a Data Series to an Existing Chart . . . . . . EX 203
Creating a Combination Chart . . . . EX 205
Creating a 3-D Chart . . . . EX 209
Adding Sparklines and Data Bars . . . . EX 211
Creating Sparklines . . . . EX 211
Adding and Formatting Sparkline Markers . . . . . EX 214
Creating Data Bars . . . . EX 216
Modifying a Data Bar Rule . . . . EX 217
Creating a Chart Sheet . . . . EX 219
Session 4.2 Quick Check . . . . EX 222
Review Assignments . . . . EX 223

Case Problems . . . . EX 224

ProSkills Exercise: Decision Making . . . . EX 229

EXCEL LEVEL II TUTORIALS

Tutorial 5 Working with Excel Tables, PivotTables, and PivotCharts

Tracking Museum Art Objects . . . . **EX 233**

SESSION 5.1 . . . . EX 234

Planning a Structured Range of Data . . . . EX 236

Freezing Rows and Columns . . . . EX 238

Creating an Excel Table . . . . EX 239

Renaming an Excel Table . . . . EX 240

Formatting an Excel Table . . . . EX 241

Maintaining Data in an Excel Table . . . . EX 241

Adding Records . . . . EX 242

Finding and Editing Records . . . . EX 243

Deleting a Record . . . . EX 244

Sorting Data . . . . EX 244

Sorting One Column Using the Sort Buttons . . . . EX 244

Sorting Multiple Columns Using the Sort Dialog Box . . . . EX 245

Sorting Using a Custom List . . . . EX 247

Session 5.1 Quick Check . . . . EX 249

SESSION 5.2 . . . . EX 250

Filtering Data . . . . EX 252

Filtering Using One Column . . . . EX 252

Filtering Using Multiple Columns . . . . EX 254

Clearing Filters . . . . EX 255

Selecting Multiple Filter Items . . . . EX 255

Creating Criteria Filters to Specify More Complex Criteria . . . . EX 256

Using the Total Row to Calculate Summary Statistics . . . . EX 259

Splitting the Worksheet Window into Panes . . . . . EX 261

Inserting Subtotals . . . . EX 263

Using the Subtotal Outline View . . . . EX 266

Session 5.2 Quick Check . . . . EX 267

SESSION 5.3 . . . . EX 268

Analyzing Data with PivotTables . . . . EX 270

Creating a PivotTable . . . . EX 272

Adding Fields to a PivotTable . . . . EX 274

Applying PivotTable Styles . . . . EX 276

Formatting PivotTable Values Fields . . . . EX 276

Rearranging a PivotTable . . . . EX 277

Changing the PivotTable Report Layout Options . . . . EX 278

Adding a Report Filter to a PivotTable . . . . EX 279

Filtering PivotTable Fields . . . . EX 281

Collapsing and Expanding Items . . . . EX 282

Sorting PivotTable Fields . . . . EX 283

Adding a Second Values Field to a PivotTable . . . . EX 283

Removing a Field, Field Headers, and Buttons from a PivotTable . . . . EX 284

Using a Slicer to Filter a PivotTable . . . . EX 285

Refreshing a PivotTable . . . . EX 287

Grouping PivotTable Items. EX 288

Grouping Date Fields . . . . EX 290

Creating a PivotChart . . . . EX 291

Session 5.3 Quick Check . . . . EX 293

Review Assignments . . . . EX 294

Case Problems. . . . . EX 294

Tutorial 6 Managing Multiple Worksheets and Workbooks
Summarizing Ticket Sales. . . . . **EX 301**

SESSION 6.1 . . . . EX 302

Grouping Worksheets . . . . EX 304

Entering Formulas in a Worksheet Group . . . . EX 306

Formatting a Worksheet Group . . . . EX 308

Ungrouping Worksheets. EX 308

Working with Multiple Worksheets . . . . EX 309

Copying Worksheets. . . . . EX 309

Referencing Cells and Ranges in Other Worksheets . . . . EX 310

Using 3-D References to Add Values Across Worksheets . . . . EX 312

Printing a Worksheet Group . . . . EX 317

Session 6.1 Quick Check. . . . . EX 319

SESSION 6.2. . . . . EX 320

Linking Workbooks . . . . EX 322

Navigating Multiple Workbooks. . . . . EX 323

Arranging Multiple Workbooks. . . . . EX 324

Creating Formulas with External References . . . . EX 325

Updating Linked Workbooks. . . . . EX 329

Updating a Destination Workbook with Source Workbooks Open. . . . . EX 329

Updating a Destination Workbook with Source Workbooks Closed. . . . . EX 330

Managing Links. . . . . EX 332

Creating an Excel Workspace . . . . EX 333

Session 6.2 Quick Check . . . . EX 335

SESSION 6.3. . . . . EX 336

Creating a Hyperlink . . . . EX 338

Inserting a Hyperlink . . . . EX 338

Editing a Hyperlink . . . . EX 340

Creating Templates . . . . EX 340

Creating a Workbook Based on an Existing Template . . . . EX 341

Creating a Custom Workbook Template. . . . . EX 344

Creating a New Workbook from a Template . . . . EX 346

Using the Excel Web App and SkyDrive . . . . EX 348

Obtaining a Windows Live ID . . . . EX 349

Saving a Workbook to SkyDrive . . . . EX 349

Editing a Workbook with the Excel Web App . . . . EX 350

Session 6.3 Quick Check . . . . EX 352

Review Assignments . . . . EX 353

Case Problems. . . . . EX 354

Tutorial 7 Using Advanced Functions and Conditional Formatting
Calculating Employee Benefits. . . . . **EX 363**

SESSION 7.1 . . . . EX 364

Working with Logical Functions. . . . . EX 366

Inserting Calculated Columns in an Excel Table . . . . EX 366

Using the IF Function . . . . EX 367

Using the AND Function . . . . EX 370

Using the OR Function . . . . EX 374

Using Structured References to Create Formulas in Excel Tables . . . . EX 376

Section 7.1 Quick Check . . . . EX 379

SESSION 7.2 . . . . EX 380

Creating Nested IFs . . . . EX 382

Using Lookup Tables and Functions . . . . EX 387

Using the VLOOKUP Function to Find an Exact Match . . . . EX 388

Using the VLOOKUP Function to Find an Approximate Match . . . . EX 390

Looking Up Values Using the HLOOKUP Function . . . . EX 394

Using the IFERROR Function . . . . EX 394

Session 7.2 Quick Check . . . . EX 397

SESSION 7.3 . . . . EX 398

Conditional Formatting . . . . EX 400

Highlighting Duplicate Values . . . . EX 400

Using the Conditional Formatting Rules Manager . . . . EX 402

Summarizing Data Conditionally . . . . EX 404

Using the COUNTIF Function . . . . EX 405

Using the SUMIF Function . . . . EX 407

Using the AVERAGEIF Function . . . . EX 408

Session 7.3 Quick Check . . . . EX 411

Review Assignments . . . . EX 412

Case Problems . . . . EX 413

Tutorial 8 Developing an Excel Application

Creating an Invoice . . . . **EX 419**

SESSION 8.1 . . . . EX 420

Planning an Excel Application . . . . EX 422

Naming Cells and Ranges . . . . EX 423

Creating Defined Names . . . . EX 424

Using the Paste Names Command . . . . EX 428

Using Defined Names in Formulas . . . . EX 429

Adding Defined Names to Existing Formulas . . . . EX 433

Session 8.1 Quick Check . . . . EX 435

SESSION 8.2 . . . . EX 436

Validating Data Entry . . . . EX 438

Specifying Validation Criteria . . . . EX 438

Creating an Input Message . . . . EX 440

Creating an Error Alert Style and Message . . . . . EX 440

Creating a List Validation Rule . . . . EX 442

Protecting a Worksheet and a Workbook . . . . EX 445

Locking and Unlocking Cells . . . . EX 445

Protecting a Worksheet . . . . EX 445

Protecting a Workbook . . . . EX 447

Unprotecting a Worksheet and a Workbook . . . . . EX 448

Inserting Comments . . . . EX 449

Session 8.2 Quick Check . . . . EX 451

SESSION 8.3 . . . . EX 452

Automating Tasks with Macros . . . . EX 454

Protecting Against Macro Viruses . . . . EX 455

Macro Security Settings . . . . EX 455

Recording a Macro . . . . . EX 457

Running a Macro . . . . . EX 460

Creating the TransferData Macro . . . . . EX 462

Fixing Macro Errors . . . . . EX 464

Working with the Visual Basic Editor . . . . . EX 464

Understanding the Structure of Macros . . . . . EX 466

Editing a Macro Using the Visual Basic Editor . . . EX 466

Creating Macro Buttons . . . . . EX 468

Saving Workbooks with Macros . . . . . EX 471

Opening a Workbook with Macros . . . . . EX 472

Customizing the Ribbon . . . . . EX 472

Minimize the Ribbon . . . . . EX 473

Removing a Tab from the Ribbon . . . . . EX 473

Expanding the Ribbon . . . . . EX 473

Session 8.3 Quick Check . . . . . EX 474

Review Assignments . . . . . EX 475

Case Problems . . . . . EX 477

ProSkills Exercise: Problem Solving . . . . . EX 486

EXCEL LEVEL III TUTORIALS

Tutorial 9 Working with Financial Tools and Functions
Developing a Financial Analysis . . . . . **EX 489**

SESSION 9.1 . . . . . EX 490

Evaluating Investment Options . . . . . EX 492

Calculating a Periodic Payment with the PMT Function . . . . . EX 492

Calculating a Future Value with the FV Function . . . . . EX 494

Calculating an Investment's Length with the NPER Function . . . . . EX 495

Calculating an Investment's Present Value with the PV Function . . . . . EX 496

Calculating an Investment's Interest Rate with the RATE Function . . . . . EX 497

Working with Loans and Mortgages . . . . . EX 498

Calculating a Loan Payment . . . . . EX 499

Creating an Amortization Schedule . . . . . EX 500

Calculating Cumulative Interest and Principal Payments . . . . . EX 502

Session 9.1 Quick Check . . . . . EX 505

SESSION 9.2 . . . . . EX 506

Projecting Future Income and Expenses . . . . . EX 508

Exploring Linear and Growth Trends . . . . . EX 509

Interpolating within a Series of Values . . . . . EX 509

Projecting Future Expenses . . . . . EX 511

Extrapolating from a Series of Values . . . . . EX 512

Calculating Depreciation of Assets . . . . . EX 514

Straight-Line Depreciation . . . . . EX 516

Declining Balance Depreciation . . . . . EX 517

Completing the Income Statement . . . . . EX 520

Session 9.2 Quick Check . . . . . EX 523

SESSION 9.3 . . . . . EX 524

Calculating the Payback Period of an Investment . . . . . EX 526

Calculating Net Present Value . . . EX 527
The Time Value of Money . . . EX 527
Using the NPV Function . . . EX 528
Choosing a Rate of Return . . . EX 529
Calculating the Internal Rate of Return . . . EX 530
Using the IRR Function . . . EX 531
Exploring the XNPV and XIRR Functions . . . EX 533
Auditing a Workbook . . . EX 534
Tracing an Error . . . EX 535
Evaluating a Formula . . . EX 538
Using the Watch Window . . . EX 540
Session 9.3 Quick Check . . . EX 542
Review Assignments . . . EX 543
Case Problems . . . EX 544

Tutorial 10 Performing What-If Analyses
Analyzing the Cost-Volume-Profit Relationship . . . **EX 551**

SESSION 10.1 . . . EX 552
Understanding Cost-Volume-Profit Relationships . . . EX 554
Comparing Expenses and Revenue . . . EX 554
Determining the Break-Even Point . . . EX 556
Performing a What-If Analysis with Goal Seek . . . EX 558
Working with Data Tables . . . EX 561
Creating a One-Variable Data Table . . . EX 562
Charting a One-Variable Data Table . . . EX 564
Creating a Two-Variable Data Table . . . EX 566
Charting a Two-Variable Data Table . . . EX 570
Session 10.1 Quick Check . . . EX 573

SESSION 10.2 . . . EX 574
Using the Scenario Manager . . . EX 576
Defining a Scenario . . . EX 577
Viewing Scenarios . . . EX 580
Editing a Scenario . . . EX 582
Creating a Scenario Summary Report . . . EX 583
Creating a Scenario PivotTable Report . . . EX 585
Session 10.2 Quick Check . . . EX 587

SESSION 10.3 . . . EX 588
Understanding Price Elasticity of Demand . . . EX 590
Maximizing Net Income Through Trial and Error . . . EX 591
Finding an Optimal Solution Using Solver . . . EX 593
Activating Solver . . . EX 593
Setting Up Solver to Find a Solution . . . EX 595
Creating a Solver Answer Report . . . EX 600
Saving and Loading Solver Models . . . EX 602
Session 10.3 Quick Check . . . EX 606
Review Assignments . . . EX 607
Case Problems . . . EX 608

Tutorial 11 Connecting to External Data
Retrieving Financial Information from Different Data Sources . . . **EX 613**

SESSION 11.1 . . . EX 614
Exploring External Data Sources . . . EX 616
Importing Data from Text Files . . . EX 617
Understanding Text File Formats . . . EX 618

Starting the Text Import Wizard. . . . . EX 619
Specifying the Starting Row. . . . . EX 620
Editing Column Breaks . . . . EX 620
Formatting and Trimming Incoming Data . . . . . . EX 621
Exploring Connections and Data Ranges . . . . EX 624
Understanding External Data Ranges. . . . . EX 625
Refreshing an External Data Range . . . . EX 626
Defining a Trusted Location. . . . . EX 629
Session 11.1 Quick Check . . . . EX 631

SESSION 11.2 . . . . EX 632

Introducing Databases and Queries . . . . EX 634
Understanding Tables, Fields, and Records . . . . . EX 634
Understanding Queries. . . . . EX 635
Using Microsoft Query. . . . . EX 636
Connecting to a Data Source . . . . EX 637
Choosing Tables and Columns . . . . EX 638
Filtering and Sorting Data . . . . EX 640
Saving a Query . . . . EX 642
Importing Data from Microsoft Query . . . . EX 643
Editing a Query. . . . . EX 645
Importing Data into PivotTables and PivotCharts . . . EX 648
Session 11.2 Quick Check. . . . . EX 655

SESSION 11.3 . . . . EX 656

Creating a Web Query. . . . . EX 658
Formatting a Web Query . . . . EX 661
Saving a Web Query . . . . EX 662
Importing Data from the Web. . . . . EX 662
Retrieving Multiple Stock Quotes . . . . EX 662
Importing Data from XML. EX 666
Loading an XML Data Map . . . . EX 668
Binding XML Elements to a Worksheet. . . . . EX 670
Importing XML Data. . . . . EX 671
Understanding Real-Time Data Acquisition. . . . . . . EX 673
Session 11.3 Quick Check. EX 674
Review Assignments . . . . EX 675
Case Problems. . . . . EX 677

Tutorial 12 Enhancing Excel with Visual Basic for Applications
Creating a Climate Report Application . . . . **EX 683**

SESSION 12.1 . . . . EX 684

Developing an Excel Application. . . . . EX 686
Working with the Visual Basic Editor. . . . . EX 688
Examining Project Explorer . . . . EX 689
Using the Properties Window. . . . . EX 690
Naming Modules. . . . . EX 692
Viewing the Code Window . . . . EX 692
Working with Sub Procedures . . . . EX 693
Introducing Sub Procedures. . . . . EX 693
Creating a Sub Procedure Using Copy and Paste . . . . EX 694
Running a Sub Procedure . . . . EX 696
Session 12.1 Quick Check. EX 699

SESSION 12.2 . . . . .EX 700

Introducing Visual Basic for Applications . . . . EX 702

Using the Immediate Window to Learn VBA. . . . . EX 702

Referring to VBA Objects . . . . EX 703

Modifying Properties . . . . EX 705

Applying Methods . . . . EX 709

Working with Variables and Values . . . . EX 711

Declaring a Variable . . . . EX 712

Assigning a Value to a Variable. . . . . EX 712

Writing a Sub Procedure . . . . EX 714

Creating a Sub Procedure to Switch Defined Names . . . . EX 715

Creating a Variable to Store a Defined Name . . . EX 717

Retrieving Information from the User . . . . EX 718

Session 12.2 Quick Check . . . . EX 721

SESSION 12.3 . . . . .EX 722

Working with Conditional Statements. . . . . EX 724

Using the If Statement . . . . EX 725

Using the If-Then-Else Control Structure . . . . EX 725

Using Comparison and Logical Operators . . . . . . EX 727

Using the If-Then-ElseIf Control Structure . . . . . . EX 728

Creating a Message Box . . . . EX 730

Customizing the Quick Access Toolbar . . . . EX 732

Adding Commands to the Quick Access Toolbar . . . . EX 732

Customizing a Quick Access Toolbar Button. . . . . EX 734

Customizing Excel Screen Elements . . . . EX 736

Saving a Worksheet as a PDF. . . . . EX 739

Introducing Custom Functions . . . . EX 740

Session 12.3 Quick Check . . . . EX 741

Review Assignments . . . . EX 742

Case Problems. . . . . EX 743

ProSkills Exercise: Teamwork. . . . . EX 749

Additional Case 1 Creating a Grading Workbook . . . . ADD 1

Additional Case 2 Calculating the Optimal Price. . . . . ADD 4

Additional Case 3 Creating an Interactive Order Form . . . . ADD 6

Additional Case 4 Analyzing Housing Prices. . . . . ADD 9

Appendix A Working with Text Functions and Creating Custom Formats
Cleaning Data in a Spreadsheet. . . . . **EX A1**

Opening and Saving Workbooks Created in Earlier Versions of Excel . . . . .EX A2

Using Text Functions . . . . .EX A3

Using the LEN and LEFT Functions . . . . .EX A4

Using the Paste Values Command . . . . .EX A5

Using the PROPER Function and the & Operator . .EX A6

Using the Text to Columns Command . . . . .EX A7

Using the UPPER Function to Convert Case . . . . . .EX A8

Using the SUBSTITUTE Function. . . . . .EX A9

Using Special Formats . . . . EX A10

Creating Custom Formats . . . . EX A11

Creating a Custom Number Format . . . . EX A11

Creating a Custom Date Format . . . . EX A13

Using the Compatibility Checker . . . . EX A14

Review Assignments . . . . EX A15

Case Problems . . . . EX A15

Appendix B Advanced Filters, Database, and Summary IFS Functions

Generating a List of Eligible Employee Candidates . . . . **EX B1**

Using Advanced Filters . . . . EX B2

Understanding the Criteria Range . . . . EX B2

Creating a Criteria Range . . . . EX B3

Using Database Functions to Summarize Data . . . . . . EX B5

Summarizing Data Using the COUNTIFS, SUMIFS, and AVERAGEIFS Functions. . . . . EX B9

Review Assignments . . . . EX B15

Case Problems . . . . EX B15

Appendix C Creating a Shared Workbook

Collaborating on a Financial Report . . . . **EX C1**

Sharing a Workbook with Multiple Users . . . . EX C2

Setting Privacy Options . . . . EX C2

Enable Workbook Sharing. EX C2

Resolving Conflicts . . . . EX C3

Tracking Changes in a Workbook . . . . EX C5

Reviewing Changes Using the Tracking Log . . . . . EX C6

Accepting and Rejecting Edits . . . . EX C8

Merge and Compare Workbooks. . . . . EX C10

Preparing the Final Workbook. . . . . EX C12

Setting Document Properties. . . . . EX C12

Inspecting a Workbook . . . . EX C14

Encrypting a Workbook . . . . EX C16

Marking a Workbook as Final . . . . EX C17

Providing a Digital Signature . . . . EX C18

Ensuring Backward Compatibility in a Workbook . . . . EX C20

Integrating Excel with other Office Applications. . . . . EX C21

Copying and Pasting Data . . . . EX C22

Object Linking and Embedding . . . . EX C22

Linking Excel and Word Files . . . . EX C24

Updating a Linked Object. . . . . EX C25

Embedding an Object. . . . . EX C25

Modifying an Embedded Object. . . . . EX C26

Review Assignments . . . . EX C28

Case Problems. . . . . EX C29

Appendix D Working with Enhanced Formatting Tools

Formatting a Chemistry Report . . . . **EX D1**

Creating a Custom Cell Style. . . . . EX D2

Creating a Custom Table Style . . . . EX D5

Working with Conditional Formats . . . . EX D7

Highlighting Cells . . . . EX D7

Modifying a Conditional Formatting Rule. . . . . . . EX D10

Working with Color Scales . . . . EX D11

Working with Icon Sets. . . . . EX D15

Conditional Formatting with Formulas. . . . . EX D17

Working with Pictures and SmartArt Graphics . . . . . EX D18

Inserting Text Labels . . . . EX D19

Applying SmartArt Quick Styles. . . . . EX D20

Editing a Picture . . . . EX D22

Working with Themes . . . . EX D24

Applying a Theme. . . . . EX D24

Creating and Saving a Custom Theme . . . . EX D25

Review Assignments . . . . EX D27

Case Problems. . . . . EX D28

Appendix E Microsoft Office Specialist Certification Skills E1

What Is Microsoft Office Specialist Certification?. . . . EX E2

Benefits of Achieving Certification. . . . . EX E2

Certification Process. . . . . EX E3

Inserting Multiple Worksheets at One Time . . . . EX E4

Printing Cell Gridlines . . . . EX E4

Printing Row and Column Headers . . . . EX E5

Printing Columns to Repeat on Each Printed Page . . . EX E6

Working with Advanced Header and Footer Print Options . . . . EX E8

Creating a Custom View . . . . EX E9

Using the Percent Symbol in a Formula. . . . . EX E11

Editing a Defined Name . . . . EX E11

Hiding and Unhiding Worksheets . . . . EX E12

Changing the Default Font and Font Size . . . . EX E12

Customizing Ribbon Groups . . . . EX E13

Setting AutoSave and Managed Version. . . . . EX E14

Enabling or Disabling Automatic Workbook Calculation. . . . . EX E15

Setting the Iterative Calculations Option . . . . EX E16

Applying Advanced Chart Features Using Trendlines . . . . EX E17

Applying Advanced Chart Features Using Dual Axes. . . . . EX E18

Using Slicers with Data Sets from External Data Connections. . . . . EX E19

Restricting Permissions to a Workbook . . . . EX E22

Introducing CUBE Functions . . . . EX E23

Inserting and Modifying a Screenshot . . . . EX E24

Microsoft Office Specialist: Excel 2010 Core Certification Skills Reference . . . . EX E25

Microsoft Office Specialist: Excel 2010 Expert Certification Skills Reference. . . . . EX E31

GLOSSARY/INDEX . . . . REF 1

TASK REFERENCE. . . . . REF 15

OBJECTIVES

- Develop file management strategies
- Explore files, folders, and libraries
- Create, name, copy, move, and delete folders
- Name, copy, move, and delete files
- Work with compressed files

Managing Your Files

Organizing Files and Folders with Windows 7

Case | *Distance Learning Company*

The Distance Learning Company specializes in distance-learning courses for people who want to gain new skills and stay competitive in the job market. Distance learning is formalized education that typically takes place using a computer and the Internet, replacing normal classroom interaction with modern communications technology. The head of the Customer Service Department, Shannon Connell, interacts with the Distance Learning Company's clients on the phone and from her computer. Shannon, like all other employees, is required to learn the basics of managing files on her computer.

In this tutorial, you'll work with Shannon to devise a strategy for managing files. You'll learn how Windows 7 organizes files and folders, and you'll examine Windows 7 file management tools. You'll create folders and organize files within them. You'll also explore options for working with compressed files.

STARTING DATA FILES

Tutorial	Review	Case1
Flyer.docx	Album.pptx	Art-Agenda.docx
Map.png	Bills.xlsx	Art-Eval.docx
Members.htm	Brochure.docx	Art-Notes.docx
Paris.jpg	Budget.xlsx	Garden.jpg
Proposal.docx	Photo.jpg	Inv01.xlsx
Resume.docx	Plan.xlsx	Inv02.xlsx
Rome.jpg	Receipt.xlsx	Inv03.xlsx
Stationery.docx	Sales.xlsx	Sculpture.jpg

VISUAL OVERVIEW

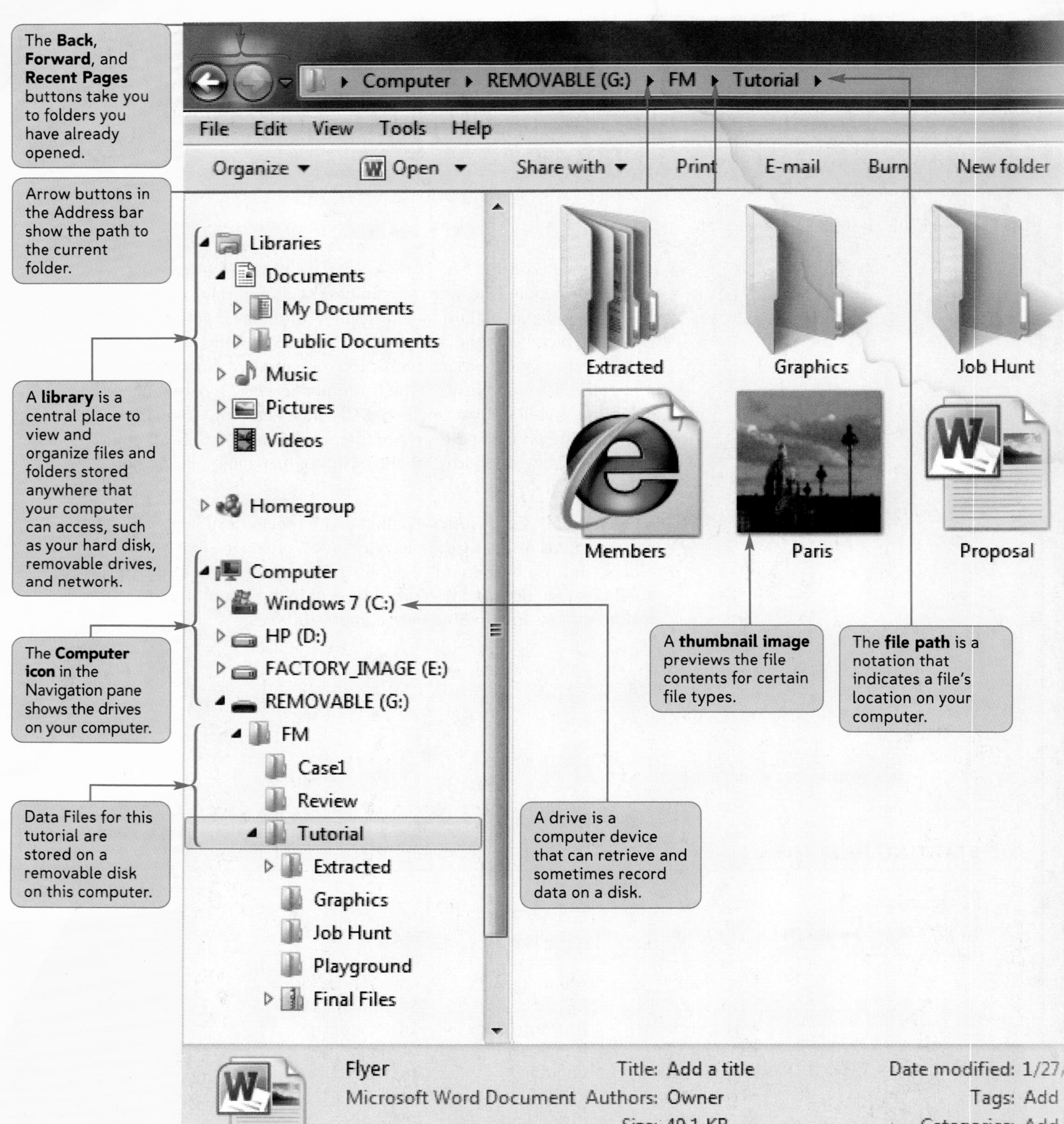

FILES IN A FOLDER WINDOW

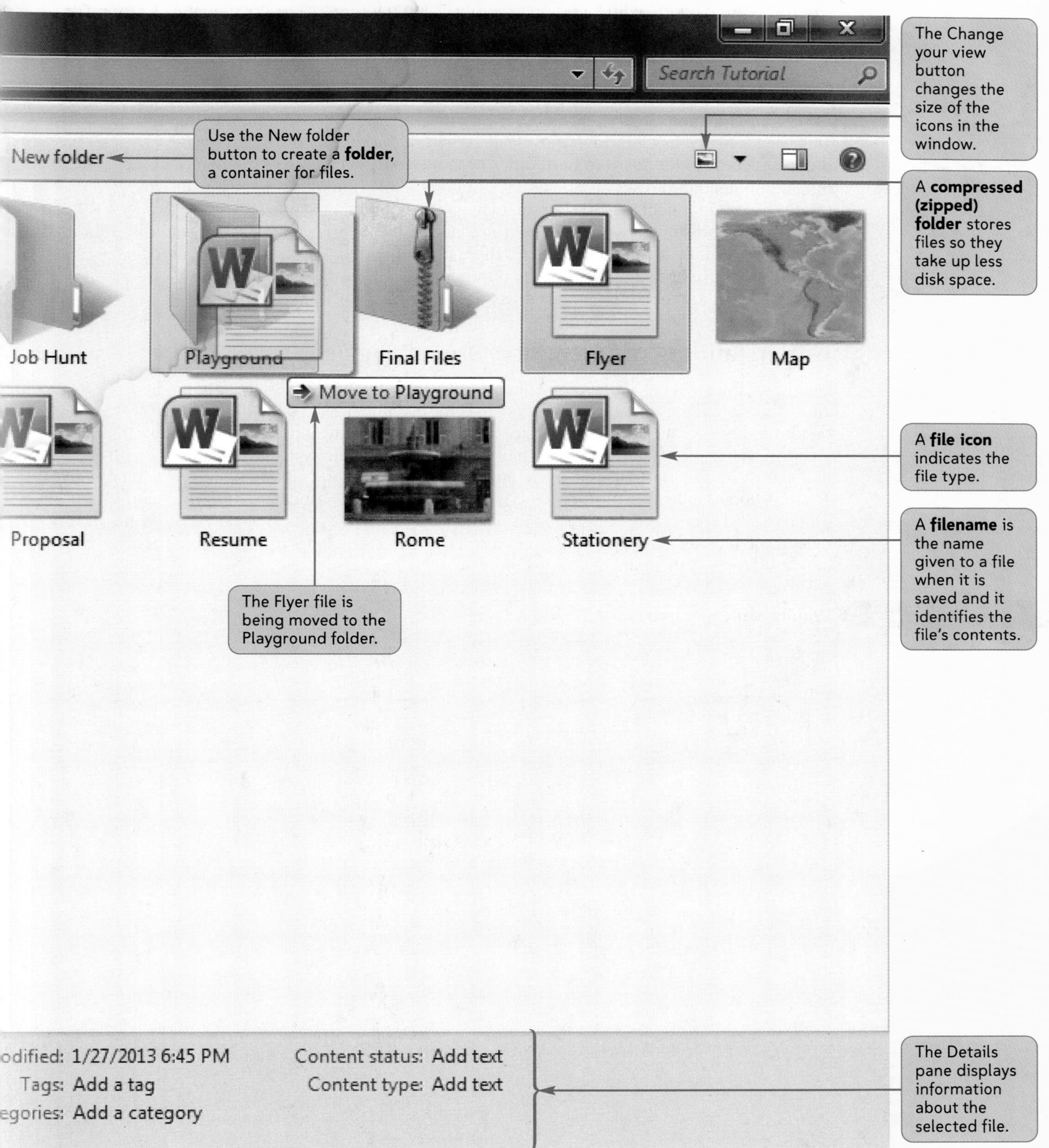

Organizing Files and Folders

Knowing how to save, locate, and organize computer files makes you more productive when you are working with a computer. A **file**, often referred to as a document, is a collection of data that has a name and is stored on a computer. After you create a file, you can open it, edit its contents, print it, and save it again—usually using the same program you used to create it. You organize files by storing them in folders. You need to organize files so that you can find them easily and work efficiently.

A computer can store folders and files on different types of disks, ranging from removable media—such as USB drives (also called USB flash drives), compact discs (CDs), and digital video discs (DVDs)—to **hard disks**, or fixed disks, which are permanently stored on a computer. Hard disks are the most popular type of computer storage because they provide an economical way to store many gigabytes of data.

A computer distinguishes one drive from another by assigning each a drive letter. The hard disk is usually assigned to drive C. The remaining drives can have any other letters, but are usually assigned in the order that the drives were installed on the computer—so your USB drive might be drive D or drive G.

Understanding the Need for Organizing Files and Folders

Windows 7 stores thousands of files in many folders on the hard disk of your computer. These are system files that Windows 7 needs to display the desktop, use drives, and perform other operating system tasks. To ensure system stability and to find files quickly, Windows 7 organizes the folders and files in a hierarchy, or **file system**. At the top of the hierarchy, Windows 7 stores folders and files that it needs when you turn on the computer. This location is called the **root directory**, and is usually drive C (the hard disk). The term *root* refers to a popular metaphor for visualizing a file system—an upside-down tree, which reflects the file hierarchy that Windows 7 uses. In Figure 1, the tree trunk corresponds to the root directory, the branches to the folders, and the leaves to the files.

Figure 1 **Windows file hierarchy**

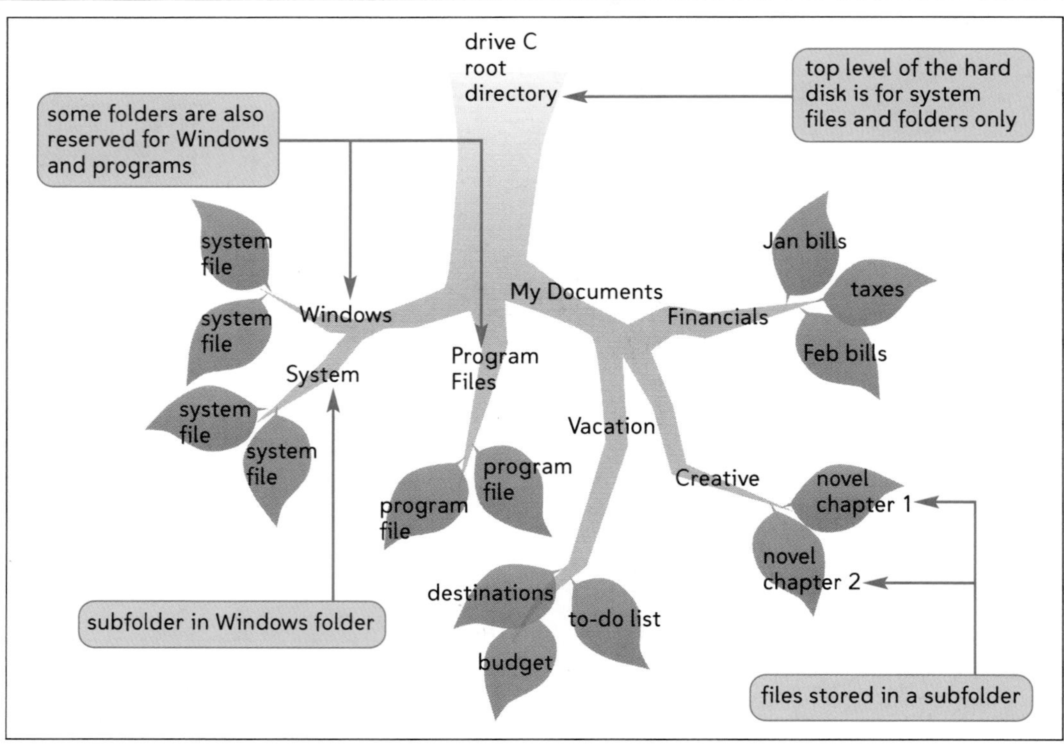

Note that some folders contain other folders. An effectively organized computer contains a few folders in the root directory, and those folders contain other folders, also called **subfolders**.

The root directory, or top level, of the hard disk is for system files and folders only—you should not store your own work here because it could interfere with Windows or a program. (If you are working in a computer lab, you might not be allowed to access the root directory.)

Do not delete or move any files or folders from the root directory of the hard disk—doing so could disrupt the system so that you can't run or start the computer. In fact, you should not reorganize or change any folder that contains installed software because Windows 7 expects to find the files for specific programs within certain folders. If you reorganize or change these folders, Windows 7 cannot locate and start the programs stored in that folder. Likewise, you should not make changes to the folder (usually named Windows) that contains the Windows 7 operating system.

Developing Strategies for Organizing Files and Folders

The type of disk you use to store files determines how you organize those files. Figure 2 shows how you could organize your files on a hard disk if you were taking a full semester of distance-learning classes. To duplicate this organization, you would open the main folder for your documents, create four folders—one each for the Basic Accounting, Computer Concepts, Management Skills II, and Professional Writing courses—and then store the writing assignments you complete in the Professional Writing folder.

Figure 2 **Organizing folders and files on a hard disk**

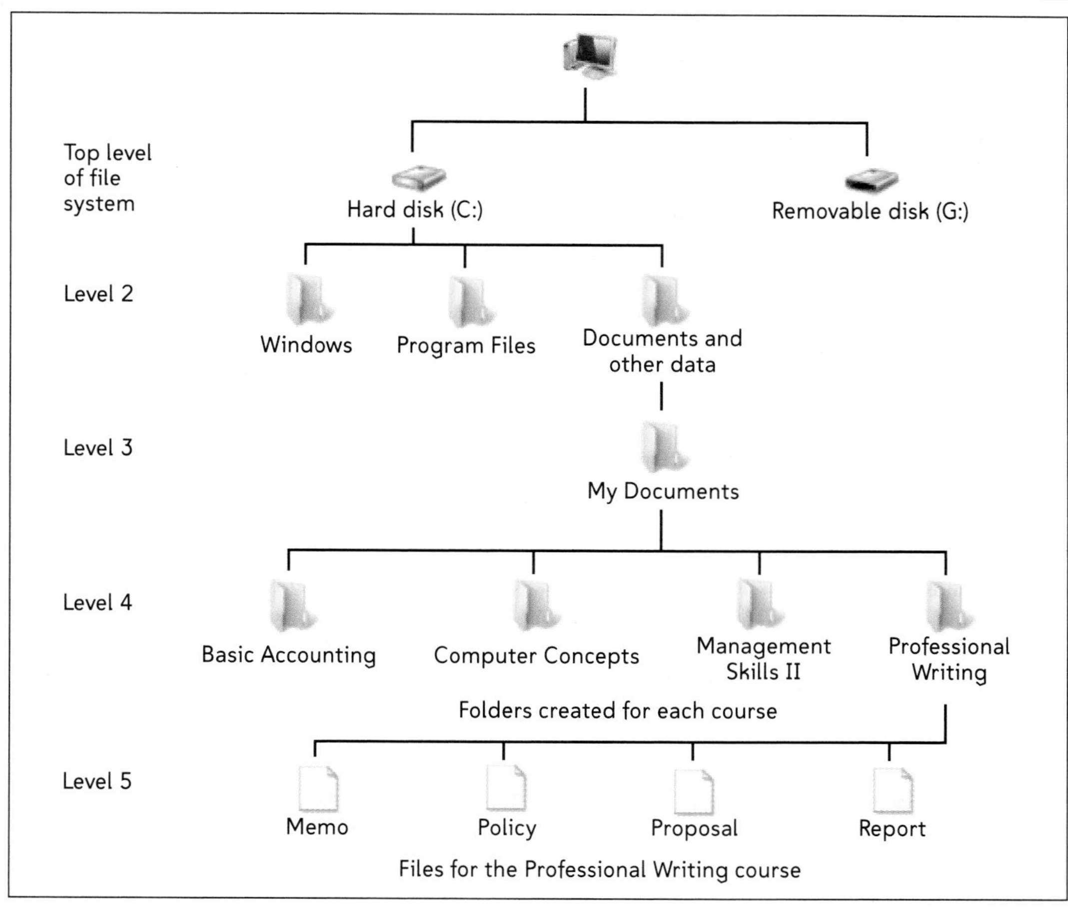

If you store your files on removable media, such as a USB drive or rewritable CD, you can use a simpler organization because you do not have to account for system files. In general, the larger the medium, the more levels of folders you should use because large media can store more files, and, therefore, need better organization. For example, if you are organizing your files on a USB drive, you could create folders in the top level of the USB drive for each general category of documents you store—one each for Courses, Creative, Financials, and Vacation. The Courses folder could then include one folder for each course, and each of those folders could contain the appropriate files.

INSIGHT

Duplicating Your Folder Organization

If you work on two computers, such as one computer at an office or school and another computer at home, you can duplicate the folders you use on both computers to simplify transferring files from one computer to another. For example, if you have four folders in your My Documents folder on your work computer, you would create these same four folders on your removable medium as well as in the My Documents folder of your home computer. If you change a file on the hard disk of your home computer, you can copy the most recent version of the file to the corresponding folder on your removable disk so the file is available when you are at work. You also then have a **backup**, or duplicate copy, of important files.

Exploring Files, Folders, and Libraries

Windows 7 provides two tools for exploring the files and folders on your computer—Windows Explorer and the Computer window. Both display the contents of your computer, using icons to represent drives, folders, and files. However, by default, each presents a slightly different view of your computer. **Windows Explorer** opens to show the contents of the Windows default libraries, making it easy to find the files you work with often, such as documents and pictures. The **Computer window** shows the drives on your computer and makes it easy to perform system tasks, such as viewing system information. You can use either tool to open a **folder window** that displays the files and subfolders in a folder.

Folder windows are divided into two sections, called panes. The left pane is the Navigation pane, which contains icons and links to locations you use often. The right pane lists the contents of your folders and other locations. If you select a folder in the Navigation pane, the contents of that folder appear in the right pane. To display the hierarchy of the folders and other locations on your computer, you select the Computer icon in the Navigation pane, and then select the icon for a drive, such as Local Disk (C:) or Removable Disk (G:). You can then open and explore folders on that drive.

TIP

Move the mouse pointer into the Navigation pane to display the expand and collapse icons.

If the Navigation pane showed all the folders on your computer at once, it could be a very long list. Instead, you open drives and folders only when you want to see what they contain. If a folder contains undisplayed subfolders, an expand icon ▷ appears to the left of the folder icon. (The same is true for drives.) To view the folders contained in an object, you click the expand icon. A collapse icon ◢ then appears next to the folder icon; click the collapse icon to hide the folder's subfolders. To view the files contained in a folder, you click the folder icon, and the files appear in the right pane. See Figure 3.

Figure 3 **Viewing files in a folder window**

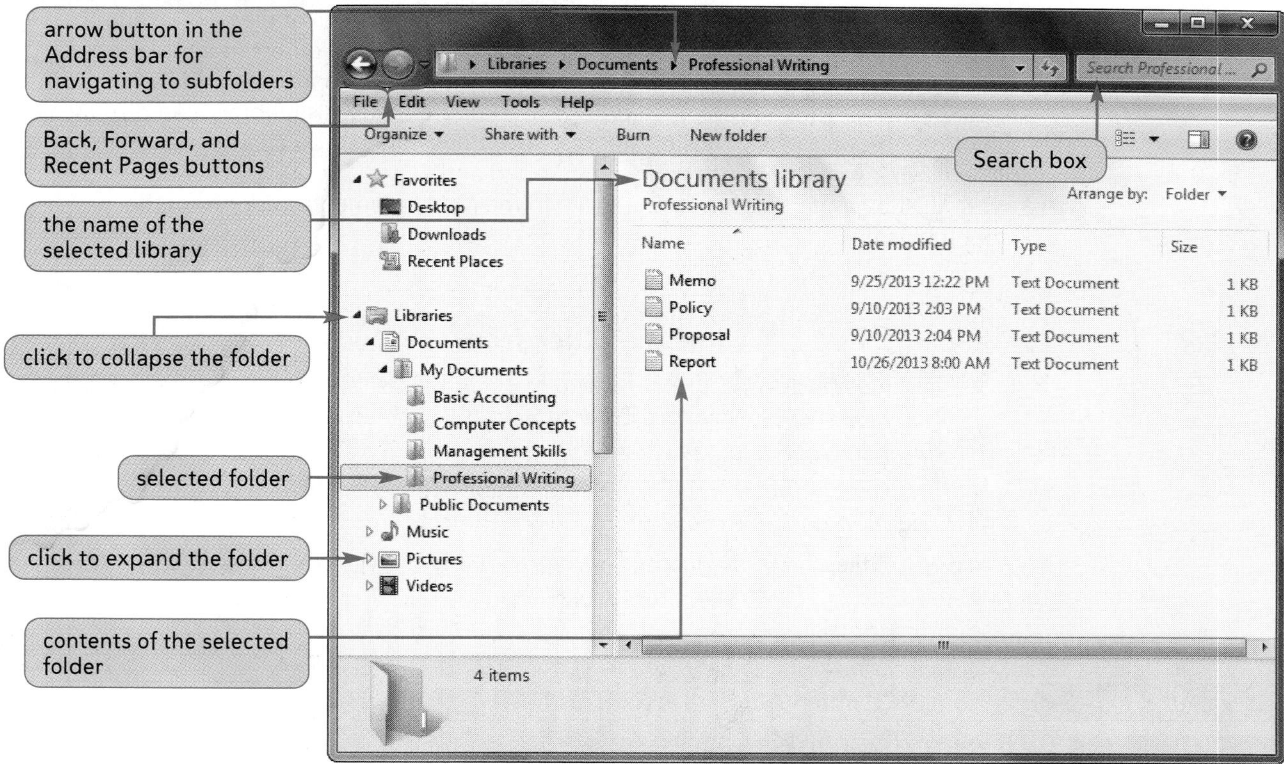

Using the Navigation pane helps you explore your computer and orients you to your current location. As you move, copy, delete, and perform other tasks with the files in the right pane of a folder window, you can refer to the Navigation pane to see how your changes affect the overall organization.

In addition to using the Navigation pane, you can use folder windows and many dialog boxes to explore your computer in the following ways:

- Opening drives and folders in the right pane: To view the contents of a drive or folder, double-click the drive or folder icon in the right pane of a folder window.
- Using the Address bar: Use the Address bar to navigate to a different folder. The Address bar displays your current folder as a series of locations separated by arrows. Click a folder name or an arrow button to navigate to a different location.
- Clicking the Back, Forward, and Recent Pages buttons: Use the Back, Forward, and Recent Pages buttons to navigate to other folders you have already opened. After you change folders, use the Back button to return to the original folder or click the Recent Pages button to navigate to a location you've visited recently.
- Using the Search box: To find a file or folder stored in the current folder or its subfolders, type a word or phrase in the Search box. The search begins as soon as you start typing. Windows finds files based on text in the filename, text within the file, and other characteristics of the file, such as tags (descriptive words or phrases you add to your files) or the author.

Using Libraries and Folders

When you open Windows Explorer, it shows the contents of the Windows built-in libraries by default. A library displays similar types of files together, no matter where they are stored. In contrast, a folder stores files in a specific location, such as in the Professional Writing subfolder of the My Documents folder on the Local Disk (C:) drive. When you want to open the Report file stored in the Professional Writing folder, you must navigate to the Local Disk (C:) drive, then the My Documents folder, and finally the Professional Writing folder. A library makes it easier to access similar types of files. For example, you might store some music files in the My Music folder and others in a folder named Albums on your hard disk. You might also store music files in a Tunes folder on a USB drive. If the USB drive is connected to your computer, the Music library can display all the music files in the My Music, Albums, and Tunes folders. You can then arrange the files to quickly find the ones you want to open and play.

You'll show Shannon how to navigate to the My Documents folder from the Documents library.

To open the My Documents folder from the Documents library:

1. Click the **Windows Explorer** button on the taskbar. The Windows Explorer window opens, displaying the contents of the default libraries.
2. In the Libraries section of the Navigation pane, click the **expand** icon next to the Documents icon. The folders in the Documents library appear in the Navigation pane, as shown in Figure 4. The contents of your computer will differ.

   Trouble? If your window displays icons in a view different from the one shown in Figure 4, you can still explore files and folders. The same is true for all the figures in this tutorial.

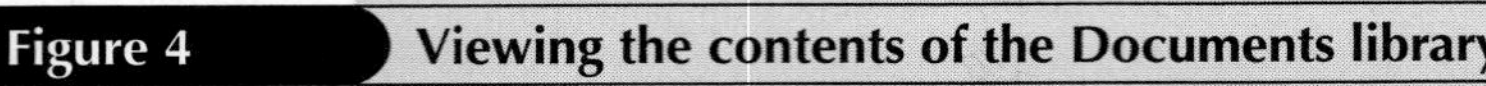

Figure 4 Viewing the contents of the Documents library

TIP

By default, the Documents library shows all the documents located in the My Documents folder.

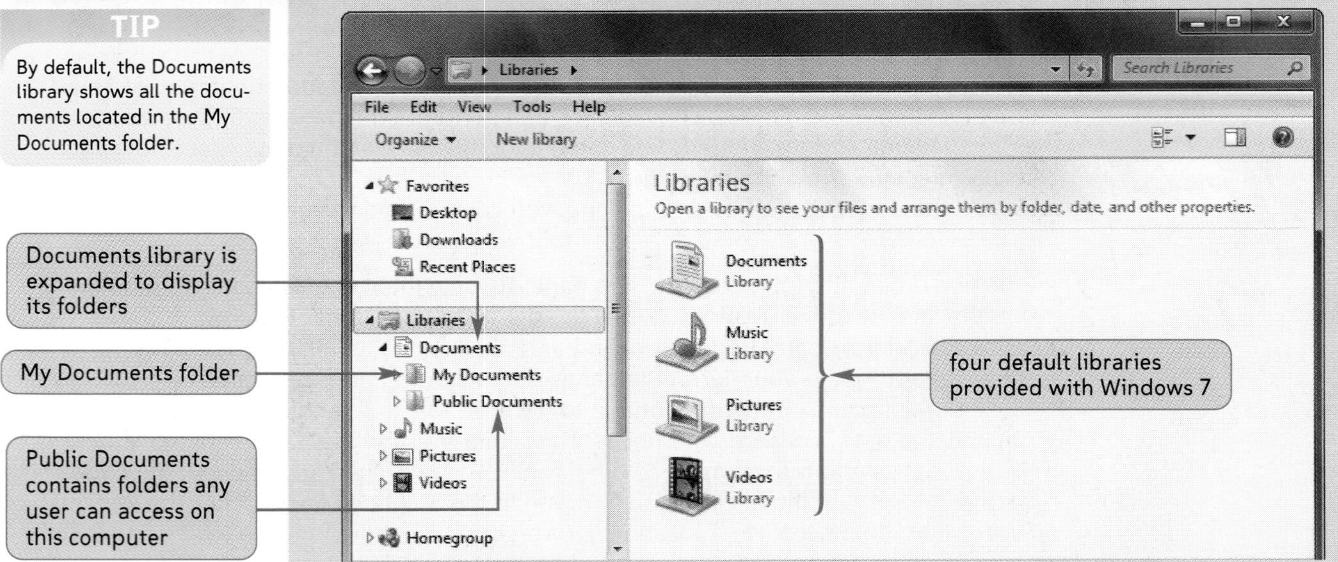

3. Click the **My Documents** folder in the Navigation pane to display its contents in the right pane.

Navigating to Your Data Files

To navigate to the files you want, it helps to know the file path, which leads you through the file and folder organization to your file. For example, the Map file is stored in the Tutorial subfolder of the FM folder. If you are working on a USB drive, for example, the path to this file might be as follows:

G:\FM\Tutorial\Map.png

This path has four parts, and each part is separated by a backslash (\ ):

- G: The drive name; for example, drive G might be the name for the USB drive. (If this file were stored on the hard disk, the drive name would be C.)
- FM: The top-level folder on drive G
- Tutorial: A subfolder in the FM folder
- Map.png: The full filename, including the file extension

If someone tells you to find the file G:\FM\Tutorial\Map.png, you know you must navigate to your USB drive, open the FM folder, and then open the Tutorial folder to find the Map file.

You can use any folder window to navigate to the Data Files you need for the rest of this tutorial. In the following steps, the Data Files are stored on drive G, a USB drive. If necessary, substitute the appropriate drive on your system when you perform the steps.

To navigate to your Data Files:

1. Make sure your computer can access your Data Files for this tutorial. For example, if you are using a USB drive, insert the drive into the USB port.

   Trouble? If you don't have the starting Data Files, you need to get them before you can proceed. Your instructor will either give you the Data Files or ask you to obtain them from a specified location (such as a network drive). In either case, make a backup copy of the Data Files before you start so that you will have the original files available in case you need to start over. If you have any questions about the Data Files, see your instructor or technical support person for assistance.

2. In the open folder window, click the **expand** icon ▷ next to the Computer icon to display the drives on your computer, if necessary.
3. Click the **expand** icon ▷ next to the drive containing your Data Files, such as Removable Disk (G:). A list appears below the drive name showing the folders on that drive.
4. If the list of folders does not include the FM folder, continue clicking the **expand** icon ▷ to navigate to the folder that contains the FM folder.
5. Click the **expand** icon ▷ next to the FM folder, and then click the **FM** folder. Its contents appear in the Navigation pane and in the right pane of the folder window. The FM folder contains the Case1, Review, and Tutorial folders, as shown in Figure 5. The other folders on your system might vary.

Figure 5 Navigating to the FM folder

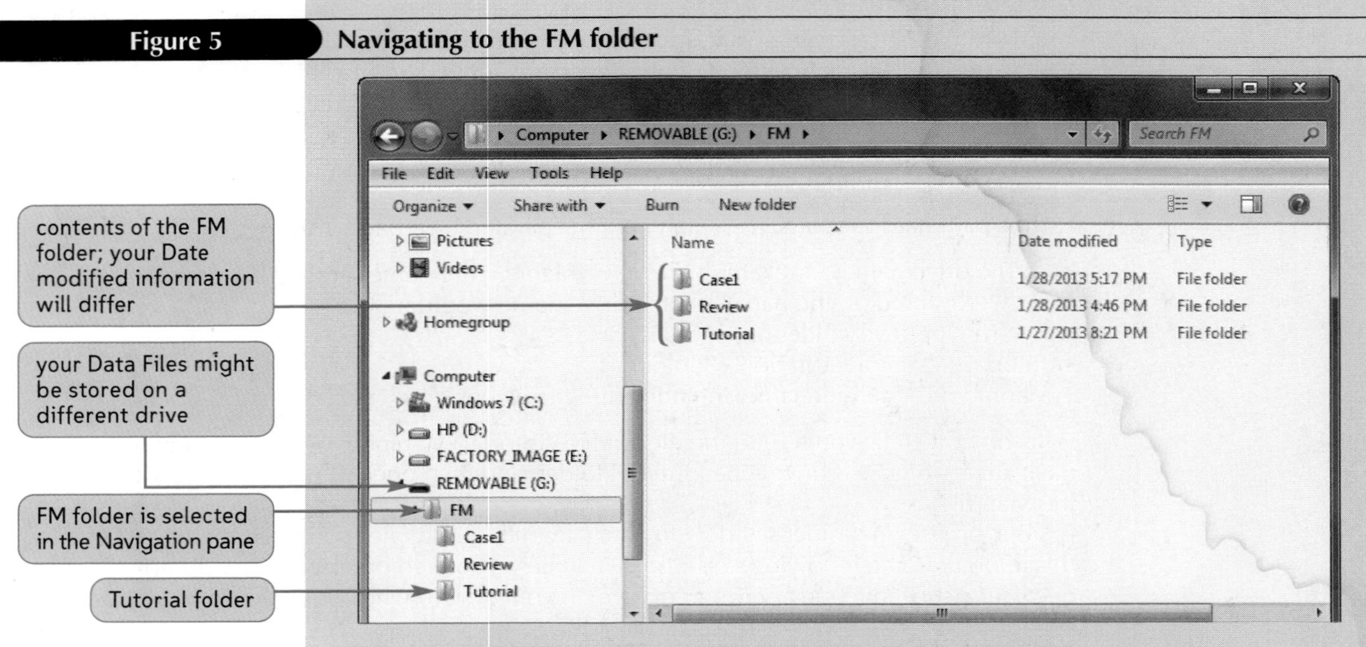

6. In the Navigation pane, click the **Tutorial** folder. The files it contains appear in the right pane. To view the contents of the graphics files, you can display the files as large icons.
7. If necessary, click the **Change your view button arrow** 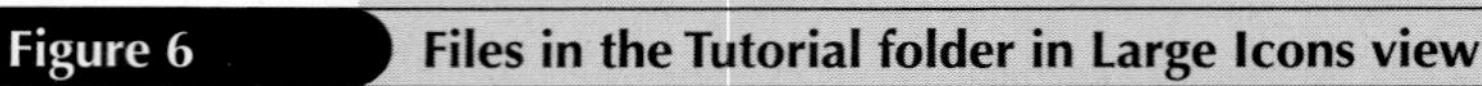 on the toolbar, and then click **Large Icons**. The files appear in Large Icons view in the folder window. See Figure 6.

Figure 6 Files in the Tutorial folder in Large Icons view

TIP

If you change the view of one folder, other folders continue to display files in the default Details view.

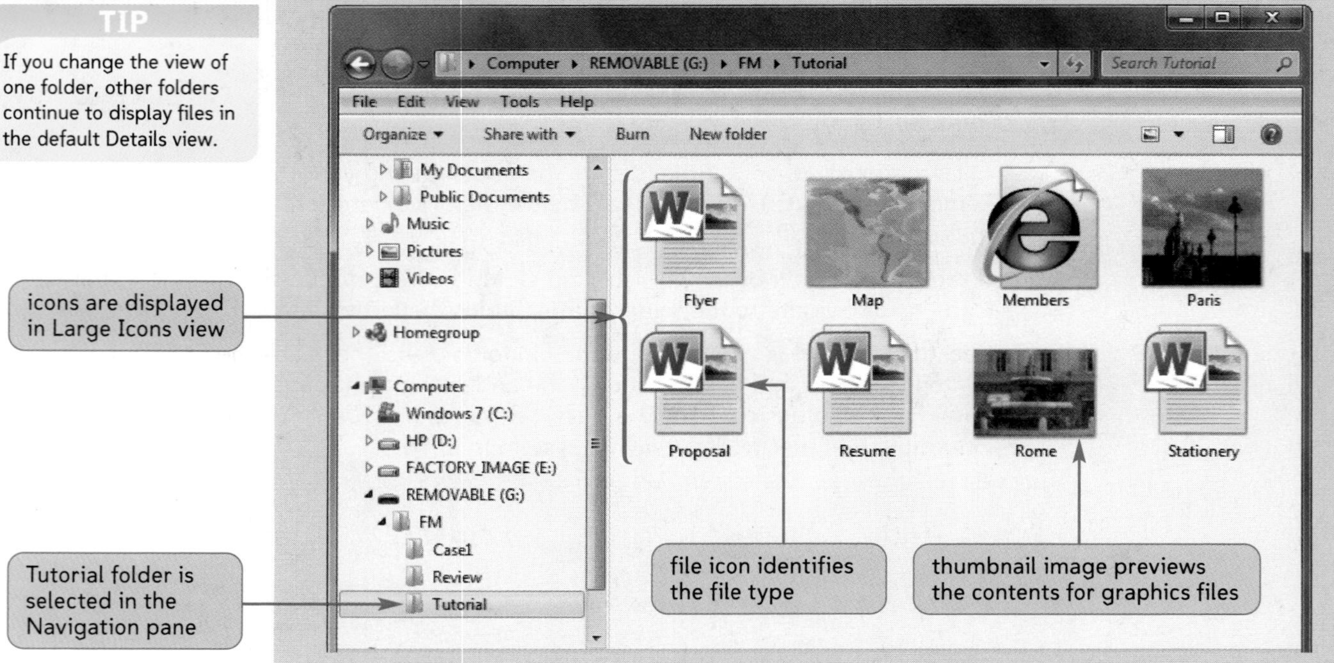

The file icons in your window depend on the programs installed on your computer, so they might be different from the ones shown in Figure 6.

Managing Folders and Files

After you devise a plan for storing your files, you are ready to get organized by creating folders that will hold your files. For this tutorial, you'll create folders in the Tutorial folder. When you are working on your own computer, you usually create folders within the My Documents folder and other standard folders, such as My Music and My Pictures.

Examine the files shown in Figure 6 again and determine which files seem to belong together. Map, Paris, and Rome are all graphics files containing pictures or photos. The Resume and Stationery files were created for a summer job hunt. The other files were created for a neighborhood association trying to update a playground.

One way to organize these files is to create three folders—one for graphics, one for the job hunt files, and another for the playground files. When you create a folder, you give it a name, preferably one that describes its contents. A folder name can have up to 255 characters, except / \ : * ? " < > or |. Considering these conventions, you could create three folders as follows:

- Graphics folder: Map, Paris, and Rome files
- Job Hunt folder: Resume and Stationery files
- Playground folder: Flyer, Proposal, and Members files

INSIGHT

Guidelines for Creating Folders

- Keep folder names short and familiar: Long names can be cut off in a folder window, so use names that are short but clear. Choose names that will be meaningful later, such as project names or course numbers.
- Develop standards for naming folders: Use a consistent naming scheme that is clear to you, such as one that uses a project name as the name of the main folder, and includes step numbers in each subfolder name, such as 01Plan, 02Approvals, 03Prelim, and so on.
- Create subfolders to organize files: If a file listing in a folder window is so long that you must scroll the window, consider organizing those files into subfolders.

Creating Folders

You've already seen folder icons in the windows you've examined. Now, you'll show Shannon how to create folders in the Tutorial folder.

REFERENCE

Creating a Folder in a Folder Window

- In the Navigation pane, click the drive or folder in which you want to create a folder.
- Click New folder on the toolbar.
- Type a name for the folder, and then press the Enter key.

or

- Right-click a folder in the Navigation pane or right-click a blank area in the folder window, point to New, and then click Folder.
- Type a name for the folder, and then press the Enter key.

You'll create the Graphics, Job Hunt, and Playground folders in your Tutorial folder.

To create folders in a folder window:

1. Click the **New folder** button on the toolbar. A folder icon with the label *New folder* appears in the right pane. See Figure 7.

Figure 7 Creating a folder in the Tutorial folder

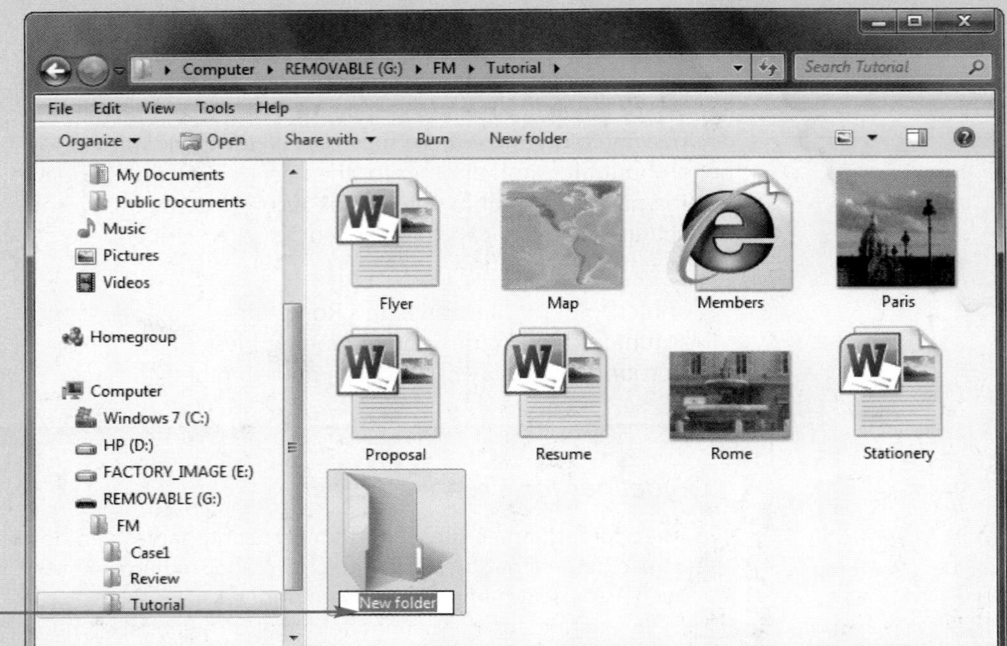

Trouble? If the *New folder* name is not selected, right-click the new folder, click Rename, and then continue with Step 2.

Windows 7 uses *New folder* as a placeholder, and selects the text so that you can replace it with the name you want.

2. Type **Graphics** as the folder name, and then press the **Enter** key. The new folder is named Graphics and is the selected item in the right pane. You'll create a second folder using a shortcut menu.
3. Right-click a blank area near the Graphics folder, point to **New** on the shortcut menu, and then click **Folder**. A folder icon with the label *New folder* appears in the right pane with the *New folder* text selected.
4. Type **Job Hunt** as the name of the new folder, and then press the **Enter** key.
5. Using the toolbar or the shortcut menu, create a folder named **Playground**. The Tutorial folder contains three new subfolders.

Moving and Copying Files and Folders

If you want to place a file into a folder from another location, you can move the file or copy it. **Moving** a file removes it from its current location and places it in a new location you specify. **Copying** also places the file in a new location that you specify, but does not remove it from its current location. Windows 7 provides several techniques for moving and copying files, which you can also use to move and copy folders.

REFERENCE

Moving a File or Folder in a Folder Window

- Right-click and drag the file or folder you want to move to the destination folder.
- Click Move here on the shortcut menu.

or

- Right-click the file or folder you want to move, and then click Cut on the shortcut menu. (You can also click the file or folder and then press the Ctrl+X keys.)
- Navigate to and right-click the destination folder, and then click Paste on the shortcut menu. (You can also click the destination folder and then press the Ctrl+V keys.)

Next, you'll move the Flyer, Proposal, and Members files to the Playground folder.

To move a file using the right mouse button:

1. Point to the **Flyer** file in the right pane, and then press and hold the *right* mouse button.
2. With the right mouse button still pressed down, drag the **Flyer** file to the **Playground** folder. When the *Move to Playground* ScreenTip appears, release the button. A shortcut menu opens.
3. With the left mouse button, click **Move here** on the shortcut menu. The Flyer file is removed from the main Tutorial folder and stored in the Playground subfolder.

   Trouble? If you release the mouse button before dragging the Flyer file to the Playground folder, the shortcut menu opens, letting you move the file to a different folder. Press the Esc key to close the shortcut menu without moving the file, and then repeat Steps 1–3.
4. In the right pane, double-click the **Playground** folder. The Flyer file is in the Playground folder.
5. In the left pane, click the **Tutorial** folder to see its contents. The Tutorial folder no longer contains the Flyer file.

The advantage of moving a file or folder by dragging with the right mouse button is that you can efficiently complete your work with one action. However, this technique requires polished mouse skills so that you can drag the file comfortably. Another way to move files and folders is to use the **Clipboard**, a temporary storage area for files and information that you have copied or moved from one place and plan to use somewhere else. You can select a file and use the Cut or Copy commands to temporarily store the file on the Clipboard, and then use the Paste command to insert the file elsewhere. Although using the Clipboard takes more steps, some users find it easier than dragging with the right mouse button.

You'll move the Resume file to the Job Hunt folder next by using the Clipboard.

To move files using the Clipboard:

1. Right-click the **Resume** file, and then click **Cut** on the shortcut menu. Although the file icon is still displayed in the folder window, Windows 7 removes the Resume file from the Tutorial folder and stores it on the Clipboard.
2. In the right pane, right-click the **Job Hunt** folder, and then click **Paste** on the shortcut menu. Windows 7 pastes the Resume file from the Clipboard to the Job Hunt folder. The Resume file icon no longer appears in the folder window.

3. In the right pane, double-click the **Job Hunt** folder to display its contents. The Job Hunt folder now contains the Resume file.

   Next, you'll move the Stationery file from the Tutorial folder to the Job Hunt folder.

TIP

To use keyboard shortcuts to move files, click the file you want to move, press Ctrl+X to cut the file, navigate to a new location, and then press Ctrl+V to paste the file.

4. Click the **Back** button on the Address bar to return to the Tutorial folder, right-click the **Stationery** file in the folder window, and then click **Cut** on the shortcut menu.
5. Right-click the **Job Hunt** folder, and then click **Paste** on the shortcut menu.
6. Click the **Forward** button on the Address bar to return to the Job Hunt folder. It now contains the Resume and Stationery files. See Figure 8.

Figure 8 Moving files

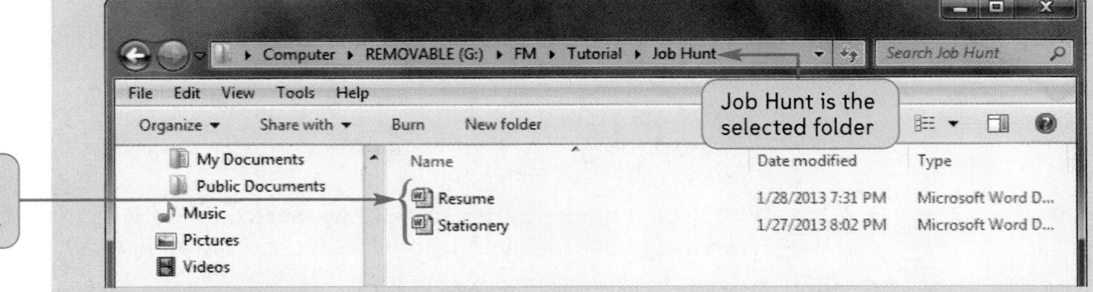

7. Click the **Back** button to return to the Tutorial folder.

You can also copy a file using the same techniques as when you move a file—by dragging with the right mouse button or by using the Clipboard. You can copy more than one file at the same time by selecting all the files you want to copy, and then clicking them as a group. To select files that are listed together in a window, click the first file in the list, hold down the Shift key, click the last file in the list, and then release the Shift key. To select files that are not listed together, click one file, hold down the Ctrl key, click the other files, and then release the Ctrl key.

REFERENCE

Copying a File or Folder in a Folder Window

- Right-click and drag the file or folder you want to move to the destination folder.
- Click Copy here on the shortcut menu.

or

- Right-click the file or folder you want to copy, and then click Copy on the shortcut menu. (You can also click the file or folder and then press the Ctrl+C keys.)
- Navigate to and right-click the destination folder, and then click Paste on the shortcut menu. (You can also click the destination folder and then press the Ctrl+V keys.)

You'll copy the three graphics files from the Tutorial folder to the Graphics folder now.

To copy files using the shortcut menu:

1. In the Tutorial window, click the **Map** file.
2. Hold down the **Ctrl** key, click the **Paris** file, click the **Rome** file, and then release the **Ctrl** key. Three files are selected in the Tutorial window.
3. Right-click a selected file, and then click **Copy** on the shortcut menu.
4. Right-click the **Graphics** folder, and then click **Paste** on the shortcut menu. Windows copies the three files to the Graphics folder.

Now you can use a different technique to copy the Proposal and Members files to the Playground folder.

To copy two files by right-dragging:

1. Click the background of the folder window to remove the selection from the three files, hold down the **Ctrl** key, click the **Members** file, click the **Proposal** file, and then release the **Ctrl** key. The two files are selected in the Tutorial window.
2. Point to a selected file, and then press and hold the *right* mouse button.
3. With the right mouse button still pressed down, drag the **Members** and **Proposal** files to the **Playground** folder, and then release the mouse button. A shortcut menu opens.
4. With the left mouse button, click **Copy here** on the shortcut menu to copy the files to the Playground subfolder.

You can move and copy folders in the same way that you move and copy files. When you do, you move or copy all the files contained in the folder.

Decision Making: Determining Where to Store Files

When you create and save files on your computer's hard disk, you should store them in subfolders. The top level of the hard disk is off-limits for your files because they could interfere with system files. If you are working on your own computer, store your files within the My Documents folder, which is where many programs save your files by default. When you use a computer on the job, your employer might assign a main folder to you for storing your work. In either case, if you simply store all your files in one folder, you will soon have trouble finding the files you want. Instead, you should create subfolders within a main folder to separate files in a way that makes sense for you.

Even if you store most of your files on removable media, such as USB drives, you still need to organize those files into folders and subfolders. Before you start creating folders, whether on a hard disk or removable disk, you need to plan the organization you will use.

Naming and Renaming Files

As you work with files, pay attention to filenames—they provide important information about the file, including its contents and purpose. A filename such as Car Sales.docx has three parts:

- Main part of the filename: The name you provide when you create a file, and the name you associate with a file

- Dot: The period (.) that separates the main part of the filename from the file extension
- File extension: Usually three or four characters that follow the dot in the filename

The main part of a filename can have up to 255 characters—this gives you plenty of room to name your file accurately enough so that you'll know the contents of the file just by looking at the filename. You can use spaces and certain punctuation symbols in your filenames. Like folder names, however, filenames cannot contain the symbols \ / ? : * " < > | because these characters have special meaning in Windows 7.

A filename might display an **extension**—three or more characters following a dot—to help you identify files. For example, in the filename Car Sales.docx, the extension *docx* identifies the file as one created by Microsoft Office Word, a word-processing program. You might also have a file called Car Sales.jpg—the *jpg* extension identifies the file as one created in a graphics program, such as Paint. Though the main parts of these filenames are identical, their extensions distinguish them as different files. You usually do not need to add extensions to your filenames because the program that you use to create the file adds the file extension automatically. Also, although Windows 7 keeps track of extensions, not all computers are set to display them.

Be sure to give your files and folders meaningful names that help you remember their purpose and contents. You can easily rename a file or folder by using the Rename command on the file's shortcut menu.

INSIGHT

Guidelines for Naming Files

The following are a few suggestions for naming your files:

- Use common names: Avoid cryptic names that might make sense now, but could cause confusion later, such as nonstandard abbreviations or imprecise names like Stuff2013.
- Don't change the file extension: When renaming a file, don't change the file extension. If you do, Windows might not be able to find a program that can open it.
- Find a comfortable balance between too short and too long: Use filenames that are long enough to be meaningful, but short enough to read easily on the screen.

Next, you'll rename the Flyer file to give it a more descriptive name.

To rename the Flyer file:

1. In the Tutorial folder window, double-click the **Playground** folder to open it.
2. Right-click the **Flyer** file, and then click **Rename** on the shortcut menu. The filename is highlighted and a box appears around it.
3. Type **Raffle Flyer**, and then press the **Enter** key. The file now appears with the new name.

   Trouble? If you make a mistake while typing and you haven't pressed the Enter key yet, press the Backspace key until you delete the mistake, and then complete Step 3. If you've already pressed the Enter key, repeat Steps 2 and 3 to rename the file again.

   Trouble? If your computer is set to display file extensions, a message might appear asking if you are sure you want to change the file extension. Click the No button, right-click the Flyer file, click Rename on the shortcut menu, type *Raffle Flyer*, and then press the Enter key.

All the files in the Tutorial folder are now stored in appropriate subfolders. You can streamline the organization of the Tutorial folder by deleting the duplicate files you no longer need.

Deleting Files and Folders

TIP

A file deleted from removable media, such as a USB drive, does not go into the Recycle Bin. Instead, it is deleted when Windows 7 removes its icon, and cannot be recovered.

You should periodically delete files and folders you no longer need so that your main folders and disks don't get cluttered. In a folder window, you delete a file or folder by deleting its icon. When you delete a file from a hard disk, Windows 7 removes the file from the folder but stores the file contents in the Recycle Bin. The **Recycle Bin** is an area on your hard disk that holds deleted files until you remove them permanently; an icon on the desktop allows you easy access to the Recycle Bin. When you delete a folder from the hard disk, the folder and all of its files are stored in the Recycle Bin. If you change your mind and want to retrieve a file or folder deleted from your hard disk, you can use the Recycle Bin to recover it and return it to its original location. However, after you empty the Recycle Bin, you can no longer recover the files it contained.

Shannon reminds you that because you copied the Map, Paris, Proposal, Members, and Rome files to the Graphics and Playground folders, you can safely delete the original files in the Tutorial folder. As with moving, copying, and renaming files and folders, you can delete a file or folder in many ways, including using a shortcut menu.

To delete files in the Tutorial folder:

1. Use any technique you've learned to navigate to and open the **Tutorial** folder.
2. Click the **first file** in the file list, hold down the **Shift** key, click the **last file** in the file list, and then release the **Shift** key. All the files in the Tutorial folder are now selected. None of the subfolders should be selected.
3. Right-click the selected files, and then click **Delete** on the shortcut menu. Windows 7 asks if you're sure you want to delete these files.

   Make sure you have copied the selected files to the Graphics folder before completing this step.
4. Click the **Yes** button to confirm that you want to delete five files.

So far, you've moved, copied, renamed, and deleted files, but you haven't viewed any of their contents. To view file contents, you can preview or open the file. When you double-click a file in a folder window, Windows 7 starts the associated program and opens the file. To preview the file contents, you can select the file in a folder window, and then click the Show the preview pane button on the toolbar to open the Preview pane, if necessary.

Working with Compressed Files

If you transfer files from one location to another, such as from your hard disk to a removable disk or vice versa, or from one computer to another via e-mail, you can store the files in a compressed (zipped) folder so that they take up less disk space. You can then transfer the files more quickly. When you create a compressed folder, Windows 7 displays a zipper on the folder icon.

You compress a folder so that the files it contains use less space on the disk. Compare two folders—a folder named Photos that contains about 8.6 MB of files, and a compressed folder containing the same files but requiring only 6.5 MB of disk space. In this case, the compressed files use about 25 percent less disk space than the uncompressed files.

You can create a compressed folder using the Send to Compressed (zipped) folder command on the shortcut menu of one or more selected files or folders. Then you can compress additional files or folders by dragging them into the compressed folder. You can open a file directly from a compressed folder, although you cannot modify the file. To edit and save a compressed file, you must extract it first. When you **extract** a file, you create an uncompressed copy of the file in a folder you specify. The original file remains in the compressed folder.

If a different compression program, such as WinZip, has been installed on your computer, the Send to Compressed (zipped) folder command might not appear on the shortcut menu. Instead, it might be replaced by the name of your compression program. In this case, refer to your compression program's Help system for instructions on working with compressed files.

Shannon suggests that you compress the files and folders in the Tutorial folder so you can more quickly transfer them to another location.

To compress the folders and files in the Tutorial folder:

1. Select all the folders in the Tutorial folder, right-click the selected folders, point to **Send to**, and then click **Compressed (zipped) folder**. After a few moments, a new compressed folder with a zipper icon appears in the Tutorial window.

   Trouble? If the Compressed (zipped) folder command does not appear on the Send to submenu of the shortcut menu, this means that a different compression program is probably installed on your computer. Click a blank area of the Tutorial window to close the shortcut menu, and then read but do not perform the remaining steps.

2. Type **Final Files** and then press the **Enter** key to rename the compressed folder. See Figure 9.

   Trouble? If the filename is not selected after you create the compressed folder, right-click the compressed folder, click Rename on the shortcut menu, and then complete Step 2.

Figure 9 **Creating a compressed folder**

When you compress the folders in the Tutorial folder, the original folders remain in the Tutorial folder—only copies are stored in the new compressed folder.

You open a compressed folder by double-clicking it. You can then move and copy files and folders in a compressed folder, although you cannot rename them. When you extract files, Windows 7 uncompresses and copies them to a location that you specify, preserving the files in their folders as appropriate.

To extract the compressed files:

1. Right-click the **Final Files** compressed folder, and then click **Extract All** on the shortcut menu. The Extract Compressed (Zipped) Folders dialog box opens.
2. Press the **End** key to deselect the path in the text box, press the **Backspace** key as many times as necessary to delete *Final Files*, and then type **Extracted**. The final three parts of the path in the text box should be *\FM\Tutorial\Extracted*. See Figure 10.

Figure 10 Extracting compressed files

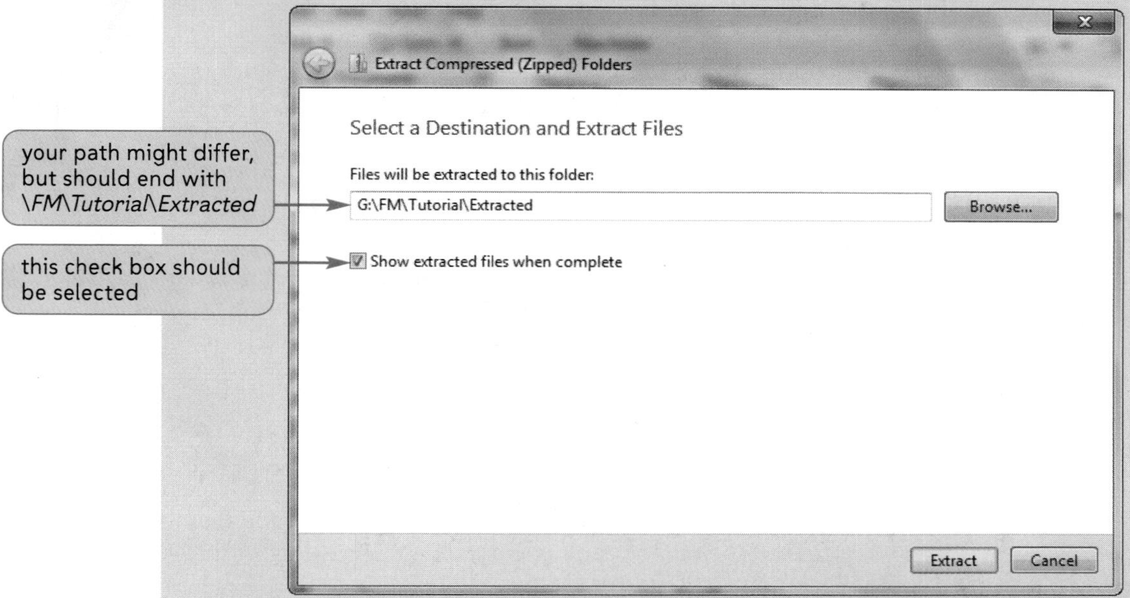

3. Make sure the **Show extracted files when complete** check box is checked, and then click the **Extract** button. The Extracted folder opens, showing the Graphics, Job Hunt, and Playground folders.
4. Open each folder to make sure it contains the files you worked with in this tutorial.
5. Close all open windows.

REVIEW

Quick Check

1. What do you call a named collection of data stored on a disk?
2. The letter C is typically used for the ______________ drive of a computer.
3. The term ______________ refers to any window that displays the contents of a folder.
4. Describe the difference between the left and right panes of the Windows Explorer window.
5. What does the file path tell you?
6. True or False. The advantage of moving a file or folder by dragging with the right mouse button is that you can efficiently complete your work with one action.
7. What does a filename indicate?
8. Is a file deleted from a compressed folder when you extract it?

Practice the skills you learned in the tutorial.

PRACTICE

Review Assignments

For a list of Data Files in the Review folder, see page FM 1.

Complete the following steps, recording your answers to any questions:

1. Use a folder window as necessary to find the following information:
   - Where are you supposed to store the files you use in the Review Assignments for this tutorial?
   - Describe the method you will use to navigate to the location where you save your files for this book.
   - Do you need to follow any special guidelines or conventions when naming the files you save for this book? For example, should all the filenames start with your course number or tutorial number? If so, describe the conventions.
   - When you are instructed to open a file for this book, what location are you supposed to use?
   - Describe the method you will use to navigate to this location.
2. Use a folder window to navigate to and open the **FM\Review folder** provided with your Data Files.
3. In the Review folder, create three folders: **Business**, **Marketing**, and **Project**.
4. Move the **Bills**, **Budget**, **Plan**, **Receipt**, and **Sales** files from the Review folder to the Business folder.
5. Move the **Brochure** file to the Marketing folder.
6. Copy the remaining files to the Project folder.
7. Delete the files in the Review folder (do *not* delete any folders).
8. Rename the Photo file in the Project folder as **Pond**.
9. Create a compressed (zipped) folder in the Review folder named **Final Review** that contains all the files and folders in the Review folder.
10. Extract the contents of the Final Review folder to a new folder named **Extracted**. (*Hint*: The file path will end with *\FM\Review\Extracted*.)
11. Locate all copies of the Budget file in the subfolders of the Review folder. In which locations did you find this file?
12. Close all open windows.
13. Submit the results of the preceding steps to your instructor, either in printed or electronic form, as requested.

Use your skills to manage files and folders for an arts organization.

APPLY

Case Problem 1

For a list of Data Files in the Case1 folder, see page FM 1.

Jefferson Street Fine Arts Center Rae Wysnewski owns the Jefferson Street Fine Arts Center (JSFAC) in Pittsburgh, and offers classes and gallery, studio, and practice space for young artists, musicians, and dancers. Rae opened JSFAC two years ago, and this year the center has a record enrollment in its classes. She hires you to teach a painting class and to show her how to manage her files on her new Windows 7 computer. Complete the following steps:

1. In the FM\Case1 folder in your Data Files, create two folders: **Invoices** and **Art Class**.
2. Move the **Inv01**, **Inv02**, and **Inv03** files from the Case1 folder to the Invoices folder.
3. In the Invoices folder, rename the Inv01 file as **Jan**, the Inv02 file as **Feb**, and the Inv03 file as **March**.
4. Move the three text documents from the Case1 folder to the Art Class folder. Rename the three documents, using shorter but still descriptive names.

5. Copy the remaining files in the Case1 folder to the Art Class folder.
6. Switch to Details view, if necessary, and then answer the following questions:
   - What is the largest file in the Art Class folder?
   - How many files in the Art Class folder are JPEG images?
7. Delete the Garden and Sculpture files from the Case1 folder.
8. Open the Recycle Bin folder by double-clicking the Recycle Bin icon on the desktop. Do the Garden and Sculpture files appear in the Recycle Bin folder? Explain why or why not. Close the Recycle Bin window.
9. Make a copy of the Art Class folder in the Case1 folder. The duplicate folder appears as Art Class – Copy. Rename the Art Class – Copy folder as **Images**.
10. Delete the text files from the Images folder.
11. Delete the Garden and Sculpture files from the Art Class folder.
12. Close all open windows, and then submit the results of the preceding steps to your instructor, either in printed or electronic form, as requested.

Use your skills to manage files for a social service organization.

CHALLENGE

Case Problem 2

There are no Data Files needed for this Case Problem.

First Call Outreach Victor Crillo is the director of a social service organization named First Call Outreach in Toledo, Ohio. Its mission is to connect people who need help from local and state agencies to the appropriate service. Victor has a dedicated staff, but they are all relatively new to Windows 7. Because of this, they often have trouble finding files that they have saved on their hard disks. He asks you to demonstrate how to find files in Windows 7. Complete the following:

EXPLORE

1. Windows 7 Help and Support includes topics that explain how to search for files on a disk without looking through all the folders. Click the Start button, click Help and Support, and then use one of the following methods to locate topics on searching for files:
   - In the Windows Help and Support window, click the Learn about Windows Basics link. Click the Working with files and folders link.
   - In the Windows Help and Support window, click the Browse Help topics link. (If necessary, click the Home icon first, and then click the Browse Help topics link.) Click the Files, folders, and libraries link, and then click Working with files and folders.
   - In the Search Help box, type **searching for files**, and then press the Enter key. Click the Working with files and folders link.

EXPLORE

2. In the *In this article* section, click Finding files. Read the topic and click any *See also* or *For more information* links, if necessary, to provide the following information:
   a. Where is the Search box located?
   b. Do you need to type the entire filename to find the file?
   c. What does it mean to filter the view?

EXPLORE

3. Use the Windows 7 Help and Support window to locate topics related to using libraries. Read the topics to answer the following questions:
   a. What are the names of the four default libraries?
   b. When you move, copy, or save files in the Pictures library, in what folder are they actually stored?
   c. What can you click to play all the music files in the Music library?
4. Submit the results of the preceding steps to your instructor, either in printed or electronic form, as requested.

ASSESS

SAM: Skills Assessment Manager

For current SAM information, including versions and content details, visit SAM Central (http://samcentral.course.com). If you have a SAM user profile, you may have access to hands-on instruction, practice, and assessment of the skills covered in this tutorial. Since various versions of SAM are supported throughout the life of this text, check with your instructor for the correct instructions and URL/Web site for accessing assignments.

ENDING DATA FILES

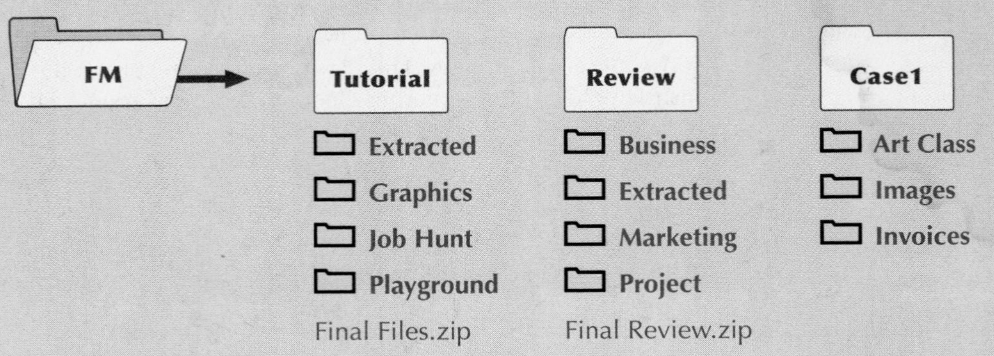

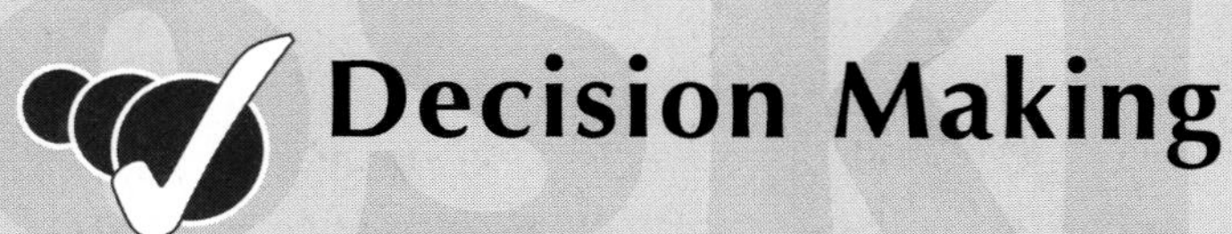

Choosing the Most Efficient Organization for Your Computer Files

Decision making is choosing the best option from many possible alternatives. The alternative you select is your decision. When making a decision, you typically complete the following steps:

1. Gather information.
2. Make predictions.
3. Select the best alternative.
4. Prepare an action plan.
5. Perform tasks and monitor results.
6. Verify the accuracy of the decision.

If you are involved in making a complex decision that affects many people, you perform all six steps in the process. If you are making a simpler decision that does not affect many people, you can perform only those steps that relate to your decision.

Gather Information and Select the Best Alternative

Start by gathering information to identify your alternatives. For example, when organizing your files, you could store most of your work on your computer hard disk or on removable media, such as a USB drive or an external hard drive. Ask questions that quantify information, or use numbers to compare the alternatives. For example, how much space do you need for your files? In how many locations do you need to access the files? How often do you work with your files?

Next, ask questions that compare the qualities of the alternatives. For example, is one alternative easier to perform or maintain than another? After testing each alternative by asking both types of questions, one alternative should emerge as the best choice for you. If one option does not seem like the best alternative, continue comparing alternatives by listing the pros and cons of each.

Prepare an Action Plan

After you make a decision, prepare an action plan by identifying the steps you need to perform to put the decision into practice. One way to do this is to work backward from your final goal. If you are determining how best to manage your computer files, your final goal might be a set of folders and files organized so that you can find any file quickly. Start by listing the tasks you need to perform to meet your goal. Be as specific as possible to avoid confusion later. For example, instead of listing *Create folders* as a task, identify each folder and subfolder by name and indicate which files or types of files each folder should contain.

Next, estimate how long each task will take, and assign the task to someone. For simple decisions, you assign most tasks to yourself. If you need to use outside resources, include those in the action plan. For example, if you decide to store your files on USB drives, include a step to purchase the drives you need. If someone else needs to approve any of your tasks, be sure to include that step in the action plan. If appropriate, the action plan can also track your budget. For example, you could track expenses for a new hard disk or backup media.

ProSkills

Complete the Tasks and Monitor the Results

After you prepare an action plan and receive any necessary approvals, perform the tasks outlined in the plan. For example, create or rename the folders you identified in your action plan, and then move existing files into each folder. As you perform each step, mark its status as complete or pending, for example.

When you complete all the tasks in the action plan, monitor the results. For example, after reorganizing your files, did you meet your goal of being able to quickly find any file when you need it? If so, continue to follow your plan as you add files and folders to your computer. If not, return to your plan and determine where you could improve it.

PROSKILLS

Organize Your Files

Now that you have reviewed the fundamentals of managing files, organize the files and folders you use for course work or for other projects on your own computer. Be sure to follow the guidelines presented in this tutorial for developing an organization strategy, creating folders, naming files, and moving, copying, deleting, and compressing files. To manage your own files, complete the following tasks:

1. Use a program such as Word, WordPad, or Notepad to create a plan for organizing your files. List the types of files you work with, and then determine whether you want to store them on your hard disk or on removable media. Then sketch the folders and subfolders you will use to manage these files. If you choose a hard disk as your storage medium, make sure you plan to store your work files and folders in a subfolder of the Documents folder.
2. Use Windows Explorer or the Computer window to navigate to your files. Determine which tool you prefer for managing files, if you have a preference.
3. Create or rename the main folders you want to use for your files. Then create or rename the subfolders you will use.
4. Move and copy files to the appropriate folders according to your plan, and rename and delete files as necessary.
5. Create a backup copy of your work files by creating a compressed file and then copying the compressed file to a removable disk, such as a USB flash drive.
6. Submit your finished plan to your instructor, either in printed or electronic form, as requested.

Getting Started with Microsoft Office 2010

Preparing a Meeting Agenda

OBJECTIVES

- Explore the programs in Microsoft Office
- Start programs and switch between them
- Explore common window elements
- Minimize, maximize, and restore windows
- Use the Ribbon, tabs, and buttons
- Use the contextual tabs, the Mini toolbar, and shortcut menus
- Save, close, and open a file
- Learn how to share files using SkyDrive
- Use the Help system
- Preview and print a file
- Exit programs

Case | *Recycled Palette*

Recycled Palette, a company in Oregon founded by Ean Nogella in 2006, sells 100 percent recycled latex paint to both individuals and businesses in the area. The high-quality recycled paint is filtered to industry standards and tested for performance and environmental safety. The paint is available in both 1 gallon cans and 5 gallon pails, and comes in colors ranging from white to shades of brown, blue, green, and red. The demand for affordable recycled paint has been growing each year. Ean and all his employees use Microsoft Office 2010, which provides everyone in the company with the power and flexibility to store a variety of information, create consistent files, and share data. In this tutorial, you'll review how the company's employees use Microsoft Office 2010.

STARTING DATA FILES

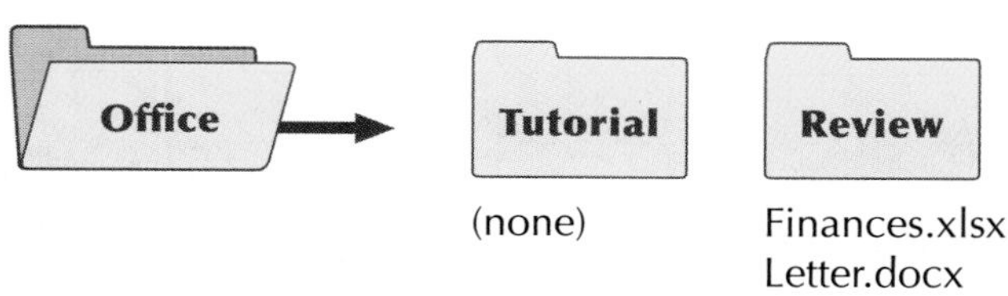

VISUAL OVERVIEW

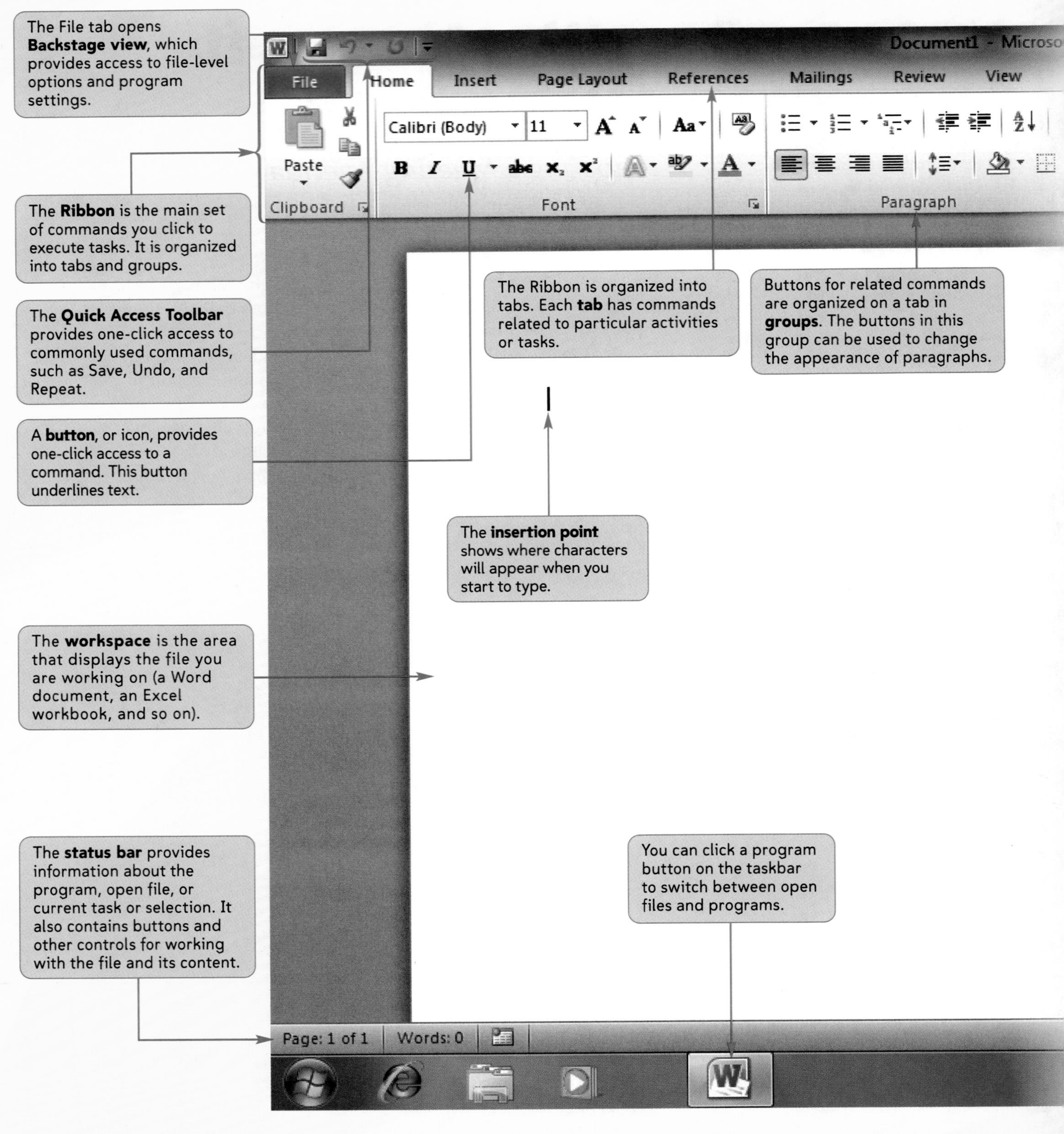

COMMON WINDOW ELEMENTS

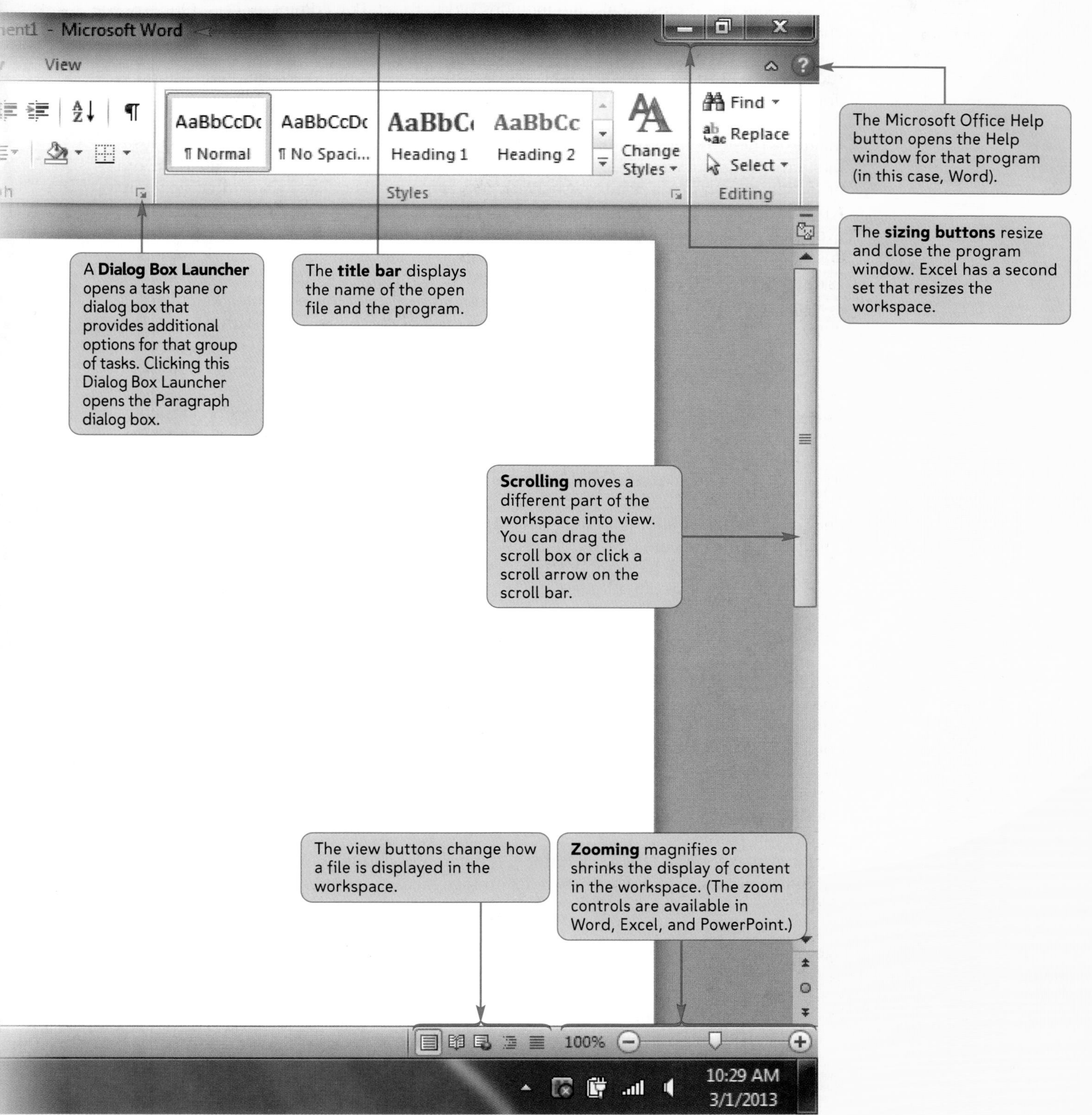

Exploring Microsoft Office 2010

TIP

For additional information about the available suites, go to the Microsoft Web site.

Microsoft Office 2010, or **Office**, is a collection of Microsoft programs. Office is available in many suites, each of which contains a different combination of these programs. For example, the Professional suite includes Word, Excel, PowerPoint, Access, Outlook, Publisher, and OneNote. Other suites are available and can include more or fewer programs. Each Office program contains valuable tools to help you accomplish many tasks, such as composing reports, analyzing data, preparing presentations, compiling information, sending email, planning schedules, and compiling notes.

Microsoft Word 2010, or **Word**, is a computer program you use to enter, edit, and format text. The files you create in Word are called **documents**, although many people use the term *document* to refer to any file created on a computer. Word, often called a word-processing program, offers many special features that help you compose and update all types of documents, ranging from letters and newsletters to reports, brochures, faxes, and even books, in attractive and readable formats. You can also use Word to create, insert, and position figures, tables, and other graphics to enhance the look of your documents. For example, the Recycled Palette employees create business letters using Word.

Microsoft Excel 2010, or **Excel**, is a computer program you use to enter, calculate, analyze, and present numerical data. You can do some of this in Word with tables, but Excel provides many more tools for recording and formatting numbers as well as performing calculations. The graphics capabilities in Excel also enable you to display data visually. You might, for example, generate a pie chart or a bar chart to help people quickly see the significance of and the connections between information. The files you create in Excel are called **workbooks** (commonly referred to as spreadsheets), and Excel is often called a spreadsheet program. The Recycled Palette accounting department uses a line chart in an Excel workbook to visually track the company's financial performance.

Microsoft Access 2010, or **Access**, is a computer program used to enter, maintain, and retrieve related information (or data) in a format known as a database. The files you create in Access are called **databases**, and Access is often referred to as a database or relational database program. With Access, you can create forms to make data entry easier, and you can create professional reports to improve the readability of your data. The Recycled Palette operations department tracks the company's inventory in an Access database.

Microsoft PowerPoint 2010, or **PowerPoint**, is a computer program you use to create a collection of slides that can contain text, charts, pictures, sound, movies, multimedia, and so on. The files you create in PowerPoint are called **presentations**, and PowerPoint is often called a presentation graphics program. You can show these presentations on your computer monitor, project them onto a screen as a slide show, print them, share them over the Internet, or display them on the Web. You can also use PowerPoint to generate presentation-related documents such as audience handouts, outlines, and speakers' notes. The Recycled Palette marketing department uses a PowerPoint slide presentation to promote its paints.

Microsoft Outlook 2010, or **Outlook**, is a computer program you use to send, receive, and organize email; plan your schedule; arrange meetings; organize contacts; create a to-do list; and record notes. You can also use Outlook to print schedules, task lists, phone directories, and other documents. Outlook is often referred to as an information management program. The Recycled Palette staff members use Outlook to send and receive email, plan their schedules, and create to-do lists.

Although each Office program individually is a strong tool, their potential is even greater when used together.

PROSKILLS

Teamwork: Integrating Office Programs

One of the main advantages of Office is **integration**, the ability to share information between programs. Integration ensures consistency and accuracy, and it saves time because you don't have to reenter the same information in several Office programs. It also means that team members can effortlessly share Office files. Team members can create files based on their skills and information that can be used by others as needed. The staff at Recycled Palette uses the integration features of Office every day, as described in the following examples:

- The accounting department created an Excel bar chart on fourth-quarter results for the previous two years, and inserted it into the quarterly financial report created in Word. The Word report includes a hyperlink that employees can click to open the Excel workbook and view the original data.
- The operations department included an Excel pie chart of sales percentages by paint colors on a PowerPoint slide, which is part of a presentation to stockholders.
- The marketing department produced a mailing to promote its recycled paints to local contractors and designers by combining a form letter created in Word with an Access database that stores the names and addresses of these potential customers.
- A sales representative merged the upcoming promotion letter that the marketing department created in Word with an Outlook contact list containing the names and addresses of prospective customers.

Even these few examples of how information from one Office program can be integrated with another illustrate how integration can save time and effort. Each team member can focus on creating files in the program best suited to convey the information he or she is responsible for. Yet, everyone can share the files, using them as needed for their specific purpose.

Starting Office Programs

You can start any Office program from the Start menu on the taskbar. As soon as the program starts, you can immediately begin to create new files or work with existing ones.

REFERENCE

Starting an Office Program

- On the taskbar, click the Start button.
- On the Start menu, click All Programs, click Microsoft Office, and then click the name of the program to start.

or

- Click the name of the program to start in the left pane of the Start menu.

You'll start Word using the Start button.

To start Word and open a new, blank document:

1. Make sure your computer is on and the Windows desktop appears on your screen.

   Trouble? If your screen varies slightly from those shown in the figures, your computer might be set up differently. The figures in this book were created while running Windows 7 with the Aero feature turned on, but how your screen looks depends on the version of Windows you are using, the resolution of your screen, and other settings.

2. On the taskbar, click the **Start** button, and then click **All Programs** to display the All Programs list.

3. Click **Microsoft Office**, and then point to **Microsoft Word 2010**. Depending on how your computer is set up, your desktop and menu might contain different icons and commands. See Figure 1.

Figure 1 **Start menu with All Programs list displayed**

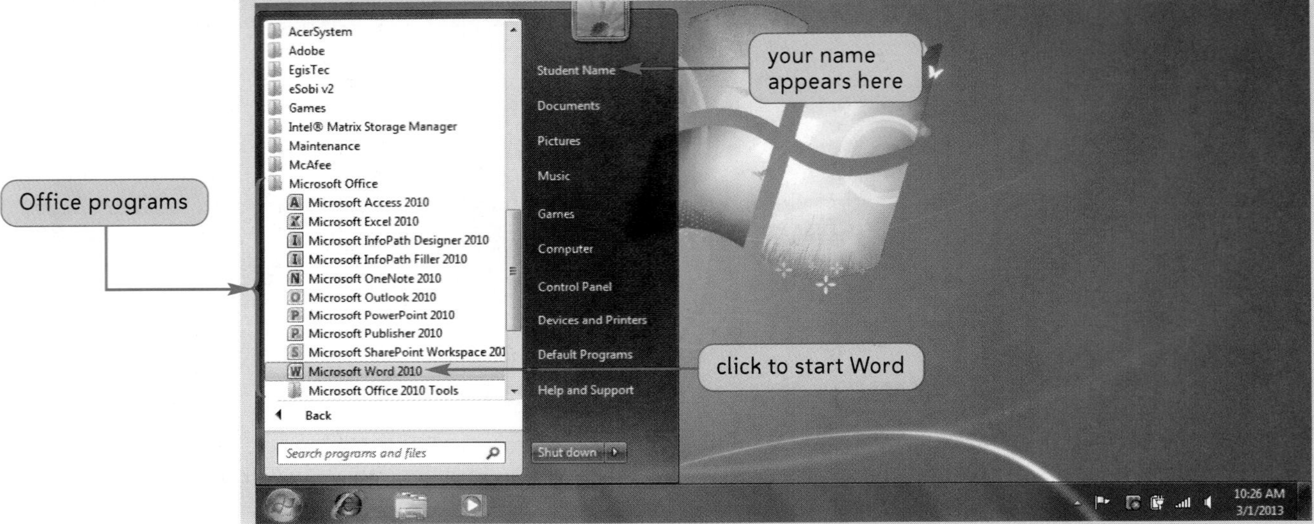

   Trouble? If you don't see Microsoft Office on the All Programs list, point to Microsoft Word 2010 on the All Programs menu. If you still don't see Microsoft Word 2010, ask your instructor or technical support person for help.

4. Click **Microsoft Word 2010**. Word starts and a new, blank document opens. Refer to the Visual Overview to review the common program window elements.

   Trouble? If the Word window doesn't fill your entire screen as shown in the Visual Overview, the window is not maximized, or expanded to its full size. You'll maximize the window shortly.

You can have more than one Office program open at once. You'll use this same method to start Excel and open a new, blank workbook.

To start Excel and open a new, blank workbook:

1. On the taskbar, click the **Start** button, click **All Programs** to display the All Programs list, and then click **Microsoft Office**.

   Trouble? If you don't see Microsoft Office on the All Programs list, point to Microsoft Excel 2010 on the All Programs list. If you still don't see Microsoft Excel 2010, ask your instructor or technical support person for help.

2. Click **Microsoft Excel 2010**. Excel starts and a new, blank workbook opens. See Figure 2.

Figure 2 New, blank Excel workbook

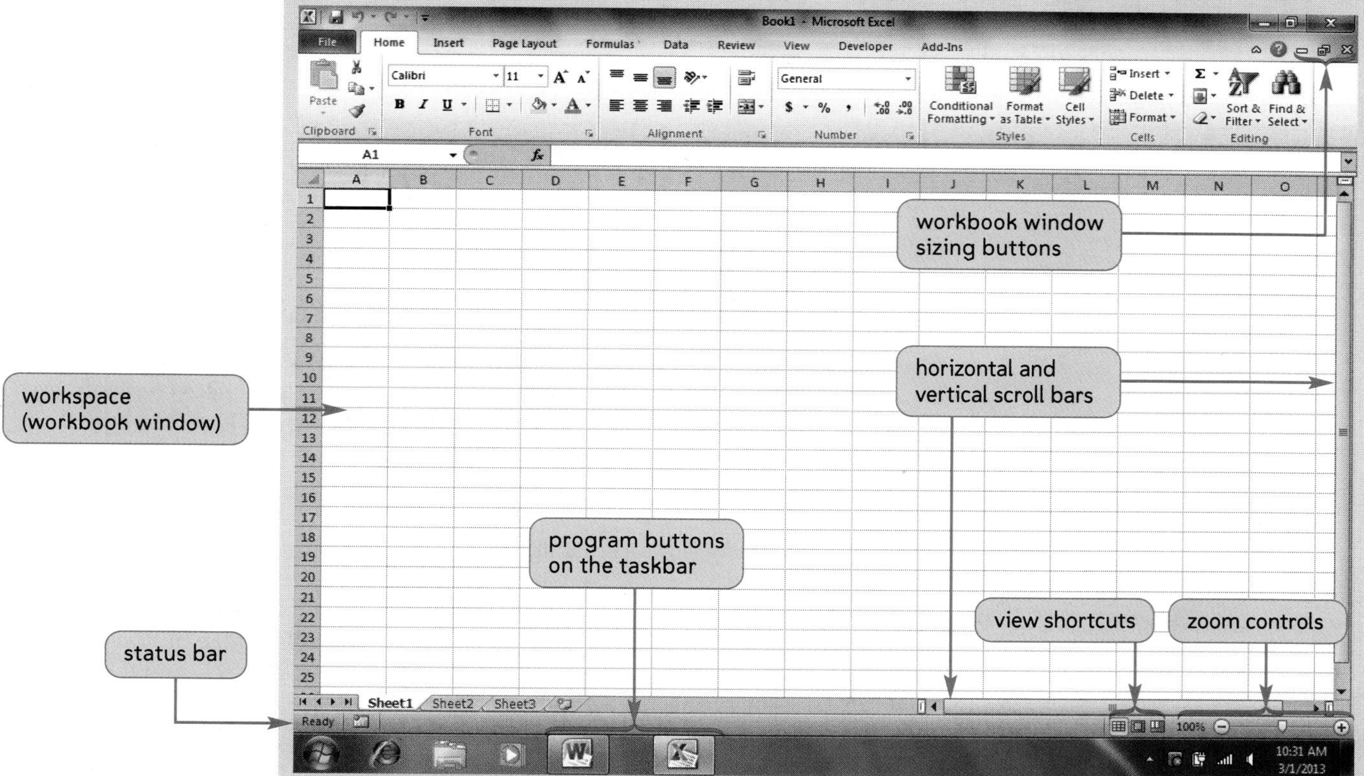

Trouble? If the Excel window doesn't fill your entire screen, the window is not maximized, or expanded to its full size. You'll maximize the window shortly.

Switching Between Open Programs and Files

Two programs are running at the same time—Word and Excel. The taskbar contains buttons for both programs. When you have two or more programs running or two files within the same program open, you can click the program buttons on the taskbar to switch from one program or file to another. When you point to a program button, a thumbnail (or small picture) of each open file in that program is displayed. You can then click the thumbnail of the file you want to make active. The employees at Recycled Palette often work in several programs and files at once.

To switch between the open Word and Excel files:

1. On the taskbar, point to the **Microsoft Word** program button. A thumbnail of the open Word document appears. See Figure 3.

Figure 3 Thumbnail of the open Word document

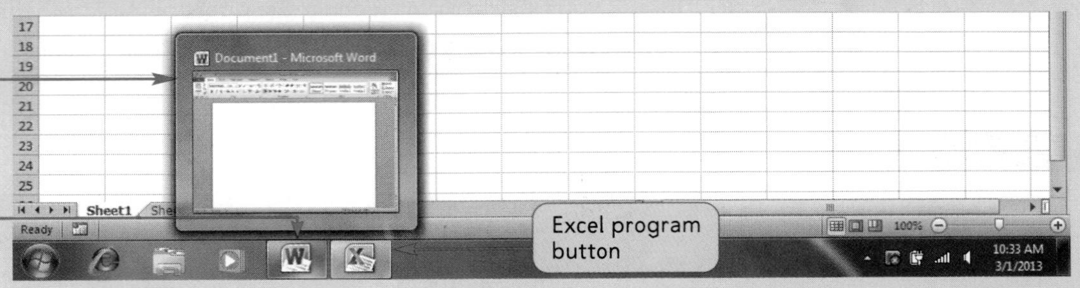

2. Click the **Document1 - Microsoft Word** thumbnail. The active program switches from Excel to Word.

Exploring Common Window Elements

As you can see, many elements in both the Word and Excel program windows are the same. In fact, most Office programs have these same elements. Because these elements are the same in each program, after you've learned one program, it's easy to learn the others.

Resizing the Program Window and Workspace

TIP

Excel has two sets of sizing buttons. The top set controls the program window and the bottom set controls the workspace.

There are three different sizing buttons that appear on the right side of a program window's title bar. The Minimize button, which is the left button, hides a window so that only its program button is visible on the taskbar. The middle button changes name and function depending on the status of the window—the Maximize button expands the window to the full screen size or to the program window size, and the Restore Down button returns the window to a predefined size. The Close button, on the right, exits the program or closes the file.

The sizing buttons give you the flexibility to arrange the program and file windows to best fit your needs. Most often, you'll want to maximize the program window and workspace to take advantage of the full screen size you have available. If you have several files open, you might want to restore down their windows so that you can see more than one window at a time, or you might want to minimize programs or files you are not working on at the moment.

To resize the windows and workspaces:

1. On the Word title bar, click the **Minimize** button. The Word program window is reduced to a taskbar button. The Excel program window is visible again.
2. On the Excel title bar, click the **Maximize** button to expand the Excel program window to fill the screen, if necessary.

3. In the bottom set of Excel sizing buttons, click the **Restore Window** button. The workspace is resized smaller than the full program window. See Figure 4.

Figure 4 **Resized Excel window and workspace**

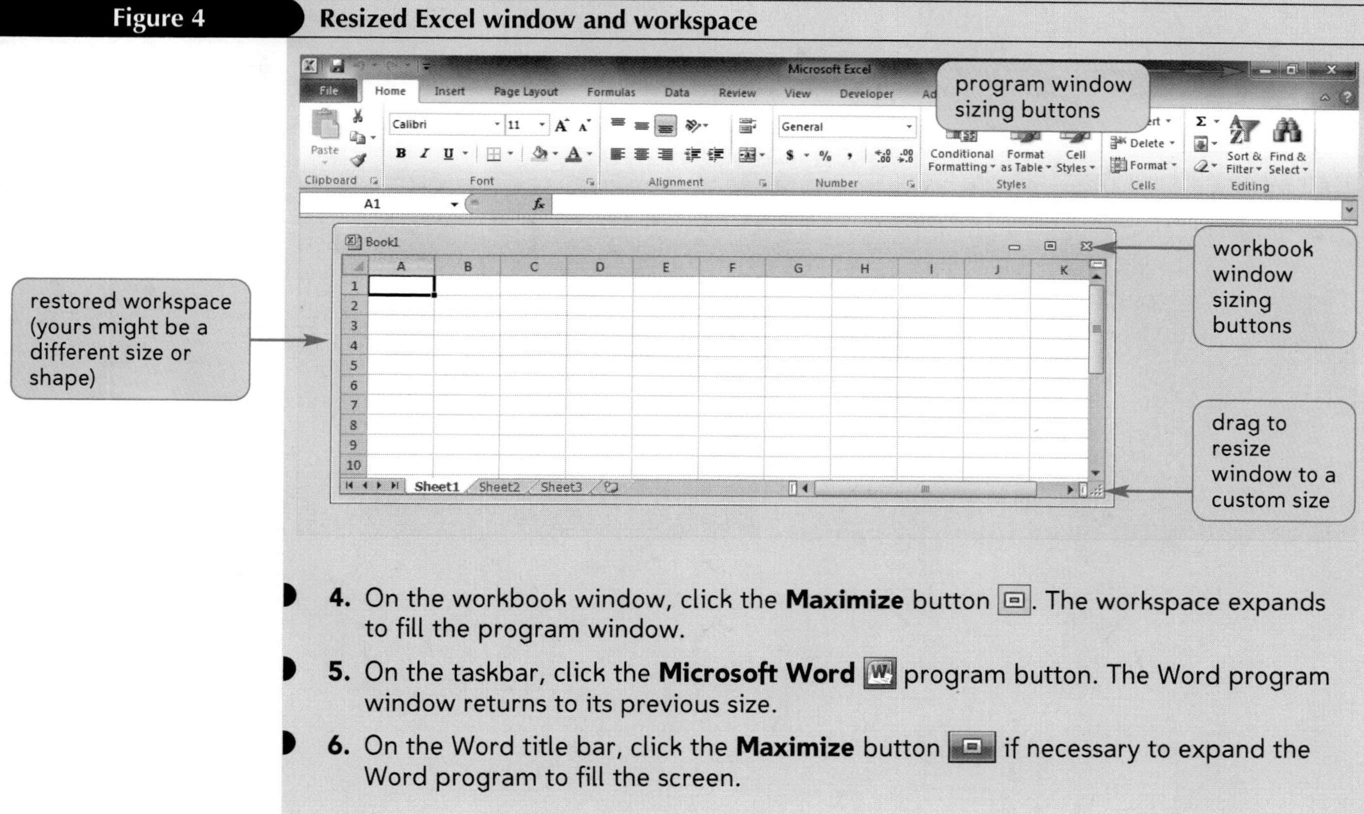

4. On the workbook window, click the **Maximize** button. The workspace expands to fill the program window.
5. On the taskbar, click the **Microsoft Word** program button. The Word program window returns to its previous size.
6. On the Word title bar, click the **Maximize** button if necessary to expand the Word program to fill the screen.

Switching Views

TIP

You can quickly switch between views using the view buttons on the status bar or options on the View tab on the Ribbon.

Each program has a variety of views, or ways to display the file in the workspace. For example, Word has five views: Print Layout, Full Screen Reading, Web Layout, Outline, and Draft. The content of the file doesn't change from view to view, although the presentation of the content does. In Word, for example, Print Layout view shows how the document would appear as a printed page, whereas Web Layout view shows how the document would appear as a Web page. You'll change views in later tutorials.

Zooming and Scrolling

You can zoom in to get a closer look at the content of an open document, worksheet, slide, or database report. Likewise, you can zoom out to see more of the content at a smaller size. You can select a specific percentage or size based on your file. The zoom percentage can range from 10 percent to 400 percent (Excel and PowerPoint) or 500 percent (Word). The figures shown in these tutorials show the workspace zoomed in to enhance readability. Zooming can shift part of the workspace out of view. To change which area of the workspace is visible in the program window, you can use the scroll bars. A scroll bar has arrow buttons that you can click to shift the workspace a small amount in the specified direction and a scroll box that you can drag to shift the workspace a larger amount in the direction you drag. Depending on the program and zoom level, you might see a vertical scroll bar, a horizontal scroll bar, or both.

To zoom and scroll in Word and Excel:

1. On the Word status bar, drag the **Zoom slider** to the left until the percentage is **10%**. The document is reduced to its smallest size, which makes the entire page visible but unreadable. See Figure 5.

Figure 5 Word zoom level set to 10%

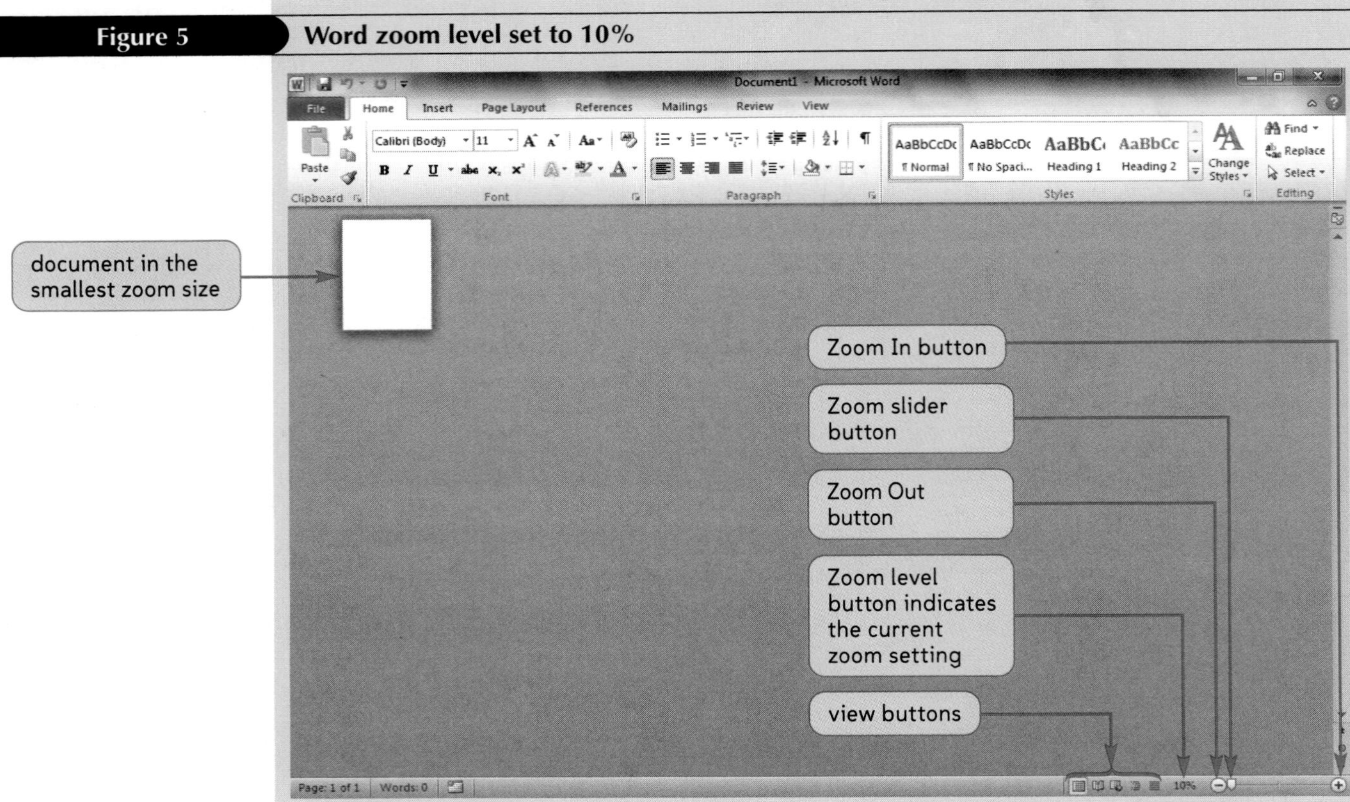

2. On the Word status bar, click the **Zoom level** button . The Zoom dialog box opens. See Figure 6.

Figure 6 Zoom dialog box

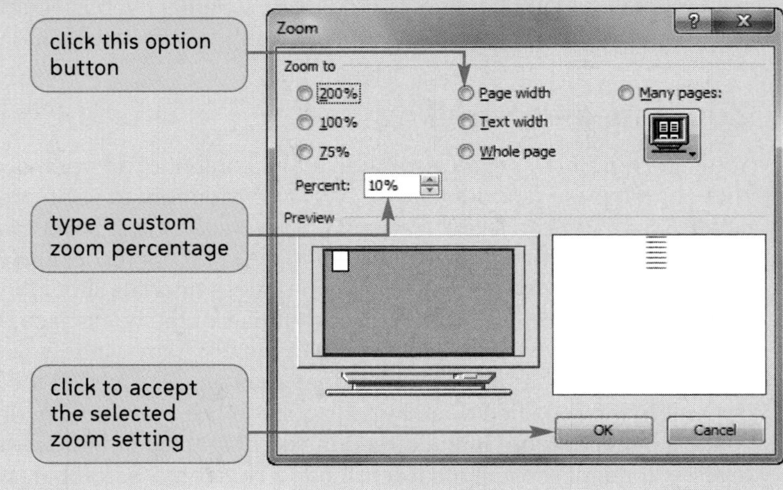

3. Click the **Page width** option button, and then click the **OK** button. The Word document is magnified to its page width, which matches how the Word figures appear in the tutorials.
4. On the taskbar, click the **Microsoft Excel** program button. The Excel program window is displayed.
5. On the status bar, click the **Zoom In** button twice. The worksheet is magnified to 120%, which is the zoom level that matches the Excel figures shown in the tutorials.
6. On the horizontal scroll bar, click the **right arrow** button twice. The worksheet shifts two columns to the right. Columns A and B (labeled by letter at the top of the columns) shift out of view and two other columns shift into view.
7. On the horizontal scroll bar, drag the **scroll box** all the way to the left. The worksheet shifts left to display columns A and B again.
8. On the taskbar, click the **Microsoft Word** program button. The Word program window is displayed.

Using the Ribbon

TIP

To view more workspace, click the Minimize the Ribbon button, located below the sizing buttons, to reduce the Ribbon to a single line. Click the Expand the Ribbon button to redisplay the full Ribbon.

Although the tabs on the Ribbon differ from program to program, each program has two tabs in common. The first tab on the Ribbon, the File tab, opens Backstage view. Backstage view provides access to file-level features, such as creating new files, opening existing files, saving files, printing files, and closing files, as well as the most common program options. The second tab in each program—called the Home tab—contains the commands for the most frequently performed activities, including cutting and pasting, changing fonts, and using editing tools. In addition, the Insert, Review, and View tabs appear on the Ribbon in all Office programs except Access, although the commands they include might differ from program to program. Other tabs are program specific, such as the Design tab in PowerPoint and the Datasheet Tools tab in Access.

To use the Ribbon tabs:

1. In Word, point to the **Insert** tab on the Ribbon. The Insert tab is highlighted, though the Home tab with the options for using the Clipboard and formatting text remains visible.
2. Click the **Insert** tab. The Insert tab is displayed on the Ribbon. This tab provides access to all the options for adding objects such as shapes, pages, tables, illustrations, text, and symbols to a document. See Figure 7.

Figure 7 Insert tab on the Ribbon in Word

Insert tab selected

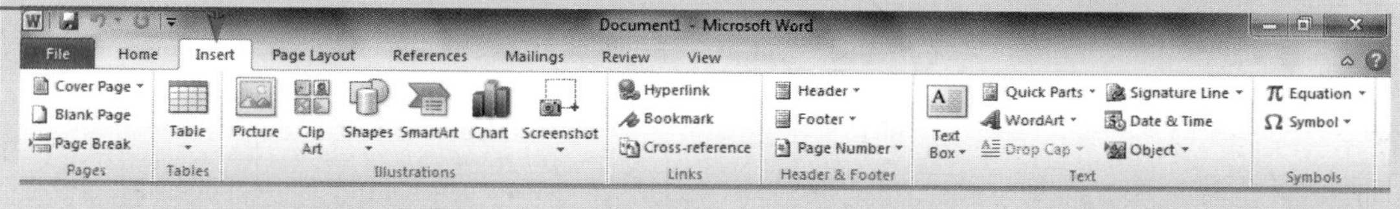

3. Click the **Home** tab. The Home tab options appear on the Ribbon.

Clicking Buttons

TIP

You can point to a button on the Ribbon to display a ScreenTip with that button's name and a brief description of what the button does when you click it.

For the most part, when you click a button, something happens in the file. For example, the Clipboard group on the Home tab includes the Cut, Copy, Paste, and Format Painter buttons, which you can click to move or copy text, objects, and formatting.

Buttons can be **toggles**: one click turns the feature on and the next click turns the feature off. While the feature is on, the button remains colored or highlighted. For example, on the Home tab in Word, the Show/Hide ¶ button in the Paragraph group displays the nonprinting characters when toggled on and hides them when toggled off.

Some buttons have two parts: a button that accesses a command, and an arrow that opens a menu of all the commands or options available for that task. For example, the Paste button in the Clipboard group on the Home tab includes the Paste command and an arrow to access all the Paste commands and options. To select one of these commands or options, you click the button arrow and then click the command or option.

INSIGHT

How Buttons and Groups Appear on the Ribbon

The buttons and groups on the Ribbon change based on your monitor size, your screen resolution, and the size of the program window. With smaller monitors, lower screen resolutions, and reduced program windows, buttons can appear as icons without labels and a group can be condensed into a button that you click to display the group options. The figures in these tutorials were created using a screen resolution of 1024 × 768 and, unless otherwise specified, the program and workspace windows are maximized. If you are using a different screen resolution or window size, the buttons on the Ribbon might show more or fewer button names, and some groups might be reduced to a button.

You'll type text in the Word document, and then use the buttons on the Ribbon.

To use buttons on the Ribbon:

1. Type **Meeting Agenda** and then press the **Enter** key. The text appears in the first line of the document and the insertion point moves to the second line.

   Trouble? If you make a typing error, press the Backspace key to delete the incorrect letters, and then retype the text.

2. In the Paragraph group on the Home tab, click the **Show/Hide ¶** button ¶. The nonprinting characters appear in the document, and the Show/Hide ¶ button remains toggled on. See Figure 8.

TIP

The **default** (original setting) for the Show/Hide ¶ button is for the button to be toggled off.

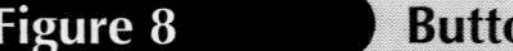

Figure 8 **Button toggled on**

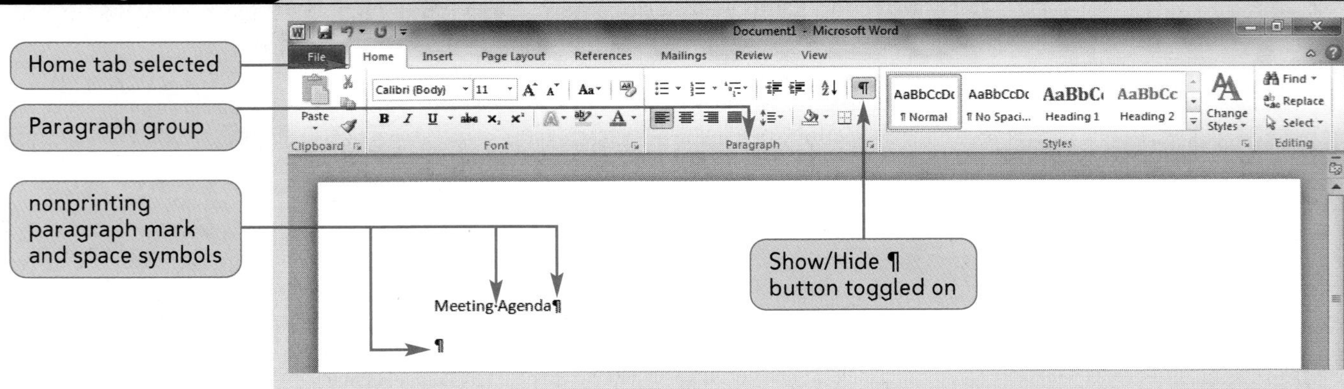

Trouble? If the nonprinting characters disappear from your screen, the Show/Hide ¶ button was already on. Repeat Step 2 to show nonprinting characters.

3. Position the insertion point to the left of the word "Meeting," press and hold the left mouse button, drag the pointer across the text of the first line but not the paragraph mark to highlight the text, and then release the mouse button. All the text in the first line of the document (but not the paragraph mark ¶) is selected.
4. In the Clipboard group on the Home tab, click the **Copy** button. The selected text is copied to the Clipboard.
5. Press the ↓ key. The text is deselected (no longer highlighted), and the insertion point moves to the second line in the document.
6. In the Clipboard group on the Home tab, point to the top part of the **Paste** button. Both parts of the Paste button are outlined in yellow, but the icon at the top is highlighted to indicate that it will be selected if you click the mouse button.
7. Point to the **Paste button arrow**. The button is outlined and the button arrow is highlighted.
8. Click the **Paste button arrow**. The paste commands and options are displayed. See Figure 9.

Figure 9 Two-part Paste button

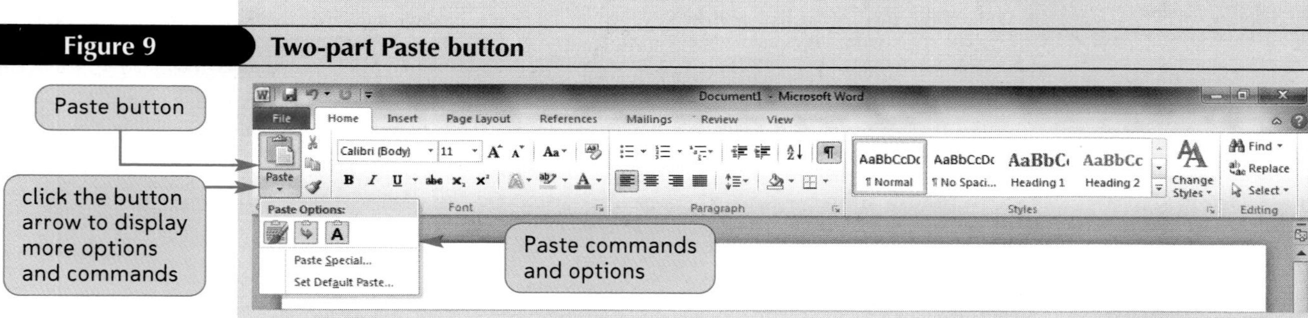

9. On the Paste Options menu, click the **Keep Text Only** button. The menu closes, and the text is duplicated in the second line of the document. The Paste Options button (Ctrl) appears below the duplicated text, providing access to the same paste commands and options.

INSIGHT

Using Keyboard Shortcuts and Key Tips

Keyboard shortcuts can help you work faster and more efficiently. A **keyboard shortcut** is a key or combination of keys you press to access a feature or perform a command. You can use these shortcuts to access options on the Ribbon, on the Quick Access Toolbar, and in Backstage view without removing your hands from the keyboard. To access the options on the Ribbon, press the Alt key. A label, called a Key Tip, appears over each tab. To select a tab, press the corresponding key. The tab is displayed on the Ribbon and Key Tips appear over each available button or option on that tab. Press the appropriate key or keys to select a button.

You can also press combinations of keys to perform specific commands. For example, Ctrl+S is the keyboard shortcut for the Save command (you press and hold the Ctrl key while you press the S key). This type of keyboard shortcut appears in ScreenTips next to the command's name. Not all commands have this type of keyboard shortcut. Identical commands in each Office program use the same keyboard shortcut.

Using Galleries and Live Preview

Galleries and Live Preview let you quickly see how your file will be affected by a selection. A **gallery** is a menu or grid that shows a visual representation of the options available for a button. For example, the Bullet Library gallery in Word shows an icon of each bullet style you can select. Some galleries include a More button that you click to expand the gallery to see all the options it contains. When you point to an option in a gallery, **Live Preview** shows the results that would occur in your file if you clicked that option. To continue the bullets example, when you point to a bullet style in the Bullet Library gallery, the selected text or the paragraph in which the insertion point is located appears with that bullet style. By moving the pointer from option to option, you can quickly see the text set with different bullet styles; you can then click the style you want.

To use the Bullet Library gallery and Live Preview:

1. In the Paragraph group on the Home tab, click the **Bullets button arrow**. The Bullet Library gallery opens.
2. Point to the **check mark bullet** style ✓. Live Preview shows the selected bullet style in your document. See Figure 10.

Figure 10 Live Preview of bullet icon

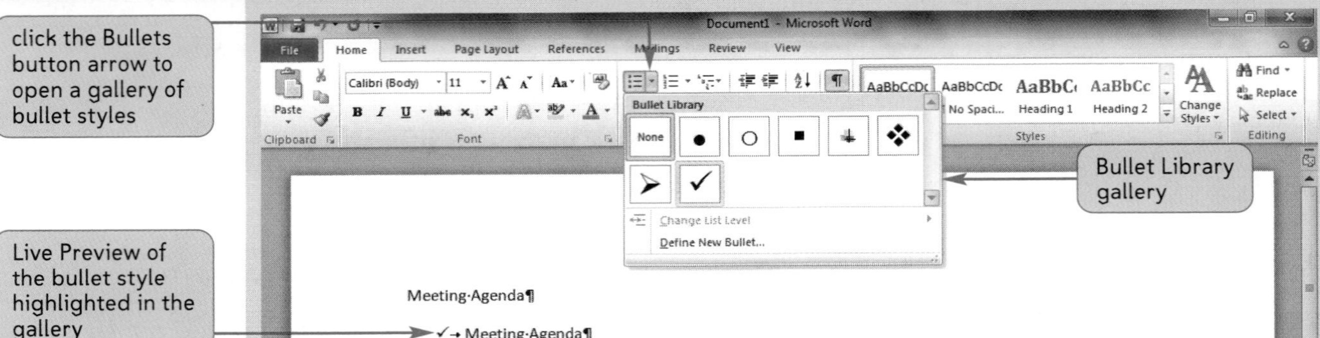

3. Place the pointer over each of the remaining bullet styles and preview them in your document.
4. Click the **check mark bullet** style ✓. The Bullet Library gallery closes, and the check mark bullet is added to the line, which is indented. The Bullets button remains toggled on when the insertion point is in the line with the bullet.
5. On the second line, next to the check mark bullet, select **Meeting Agenda**. The two words are highlighted to indicate they are selected.
6. Type **Brainstorm names for the new paint colors.** to replace the selected text with an agenda item.
7. Press the **Enter** key twice to end the bulleted list.

TIP

You can press the Esc key to close a gallery without making a selection.

Opening Dialog Boxes and Task Panes

The button to the right of some group names is the Dialog Box Launcher, which opens a task pane or dialog box related to that group of tasks. A **task pane** is a window that helps you navigate through a complex task or feature. For example, you can use the Clipboard task pane to paste some or all of the items that were cut or copied from any Office program during the current work session. A **dialog box** is a window from which you enter or choose settings for how you want to perform a task. For example, the Page Setup dialog box in Word contains options to change how the document looks. Some dialog boxes organize related information into tabs, and related options and settings are organized into groups, just as they are on the Ribbon. You select settings in a dialog box using option buttons, check boxes, text boxes, and lists to specify how you want to perform a task. In Excel, you'll use the Dialog Box Launcher to open the Page Setup dialog box.

To open the Page Setup dialog box using the Dialog Box Launcher:

1. On the taskbar, click the **Microsoft Excel** program button to switch from Word to Excel.
2. On the Ribbon, click the **Page Layout** tab. The page layout options appear on the Ribbon.
3. In the Page Setup group, click the **Dialog Box Launcher**. The Page Setup dialog box opens with the Page tab displayed. See Figure 11.

Figure 11 **Page tab in the Page Setup dialog box**

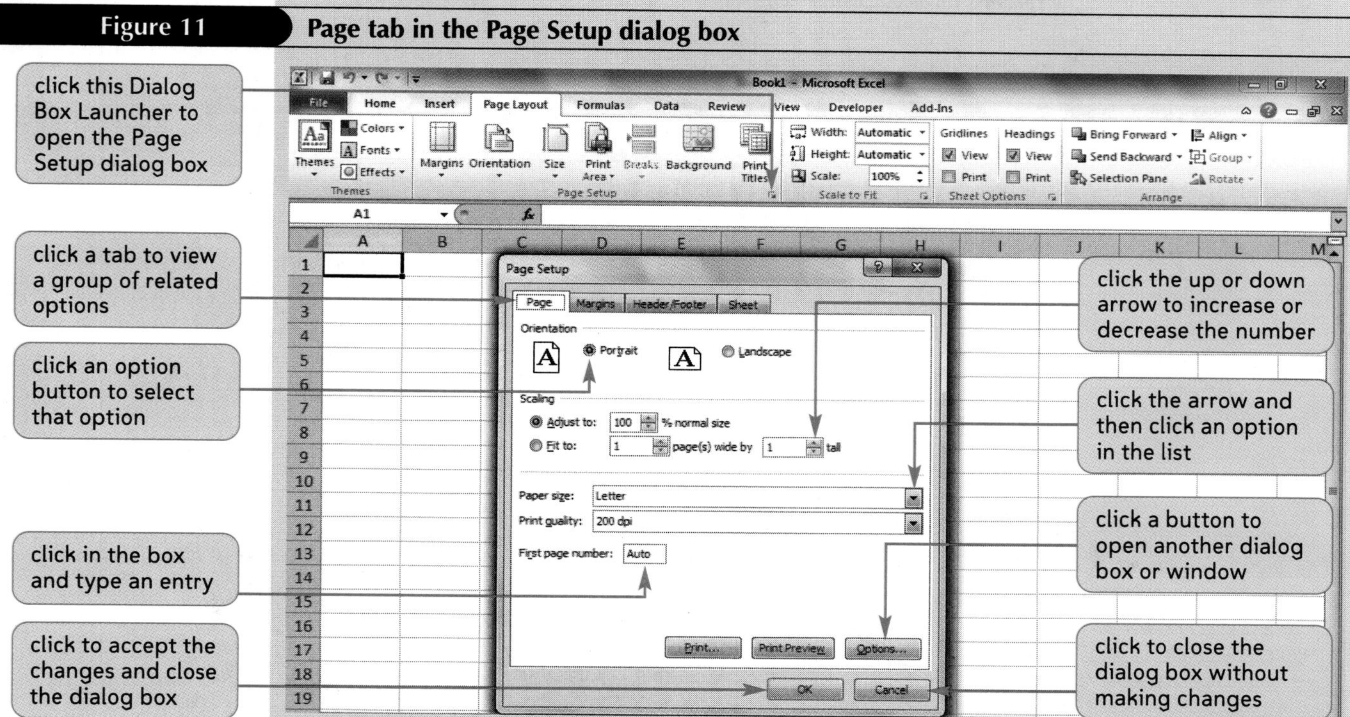

4. Click the **Landscape** option button. The workbook's page orientation changes to a page wider than it is long.
5. Click the **Sheet** tab. The dialog box displays options related to the worksheet. You can click a check box to turn an option on (checked) or off (unchecked).
6. In the Print section of the dialog box, click the **Gridlines** check box and the **Row and column headings** check box. Check marks appear in both check boxes, indicating that these options are selected.
7. Click the **Cancel** button. The dialog box closes without making any changes to the page setup.

TIP

You can check more than one check box in a group, but you can select only one option button in a group.

Using Contextual Tools

Some tabs, toolbars, and menus come into view as you work. Because these tools become available only as you might need them, the workspace remains less cluttered. However, tools that appear and disappear as you work can take some getting used to.

Displaying Contextual Tabs

Any object that you can select in a file has a related contextual tab. An **object** is anything that appears on your screen that can be selected and manipulated, such as a table, a picture, a shape, a chart, or an equation. A **contextual tab** is a Ribbon tab that contains commands related to the selected object so you can manipulate, edit, and format that object. Contextual tabs appear to the right of the standard Ribbon tabs just below a title label. For example, Figure 12 shows the Table Tools contextual tabs that appear when you select a table in a Word document. Although contextual tabs appear only when you select an object, they function in the same way as standard tabs on the Ribbon. Contextual tabs disappear when you click elsewhere on the screen, deselecting the object. Contextual tabs can also appear as you switch views. You'll use contextual tabs in later tutorials.

Figure 12 **Table Tools contextual tabs**

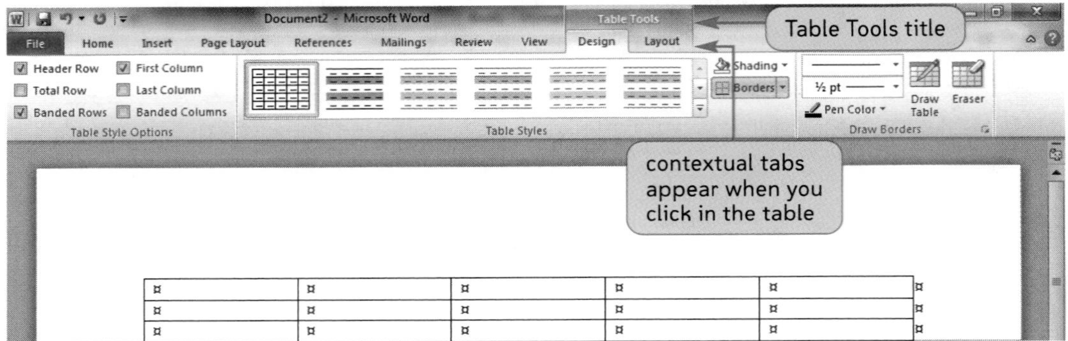

Accessing the Mini Toolbar

TIP

To turn off the Mini toolbar and Live Preview in Word, Excel, and PowerPoint, click the File tab, click the Options command, uncheck their check boxes in the Options dialog box, and then click the OK button.

The **Mini toolbar**, which appears next to the pointer whenever you select text, contains buttons for the most commonly used formatting commands, such as font, font size, styles, color, alignment, and indents. The Mini toolbar buttons differ in each program. A transparent version of the Mini toolbar appears immediately after you select text. When you move the pointer over the Mini toolbar, it comes into full view so you can click the appropriate formatting button or buttons. The Mini toolbar disappears if you move the pointer away from the toolbar, press a key, or click in the workspace. The Mini toolbar can help you format your text faster, but initially you might find that the toolbar disappears unexpectedly. All the commands on the Mini toolbar are also available on the Ribbon. Note that Live Preview does not work with the Mini toolbar.

You'll use the Mini toolbar to format text you enter in the workbook.

To use the Mini toolbar to format text:

1. If necessary, click cell **A1** (the rectangle in the upper-left corner of the worksheet).
2. Type **Budget**. The text appears in the cell.

3. Press the **Enter** key. The text is entered in cell A1 and cell A2 is selected.
4. Type **2013** and then press the **Enter** key. The year is entered in cell A2 and cell A3 is selected.
5. Double-click cell **A1** to place the insertion point in the cell. Now you can select the text you typed.
6. Double-click **Budget** in cell A1. The selected text appears white with a black background, and the transparent Mini toolbar appears directly above the selected text. See Figure 13.

Figure 13 **Transparent Mini toolbar**

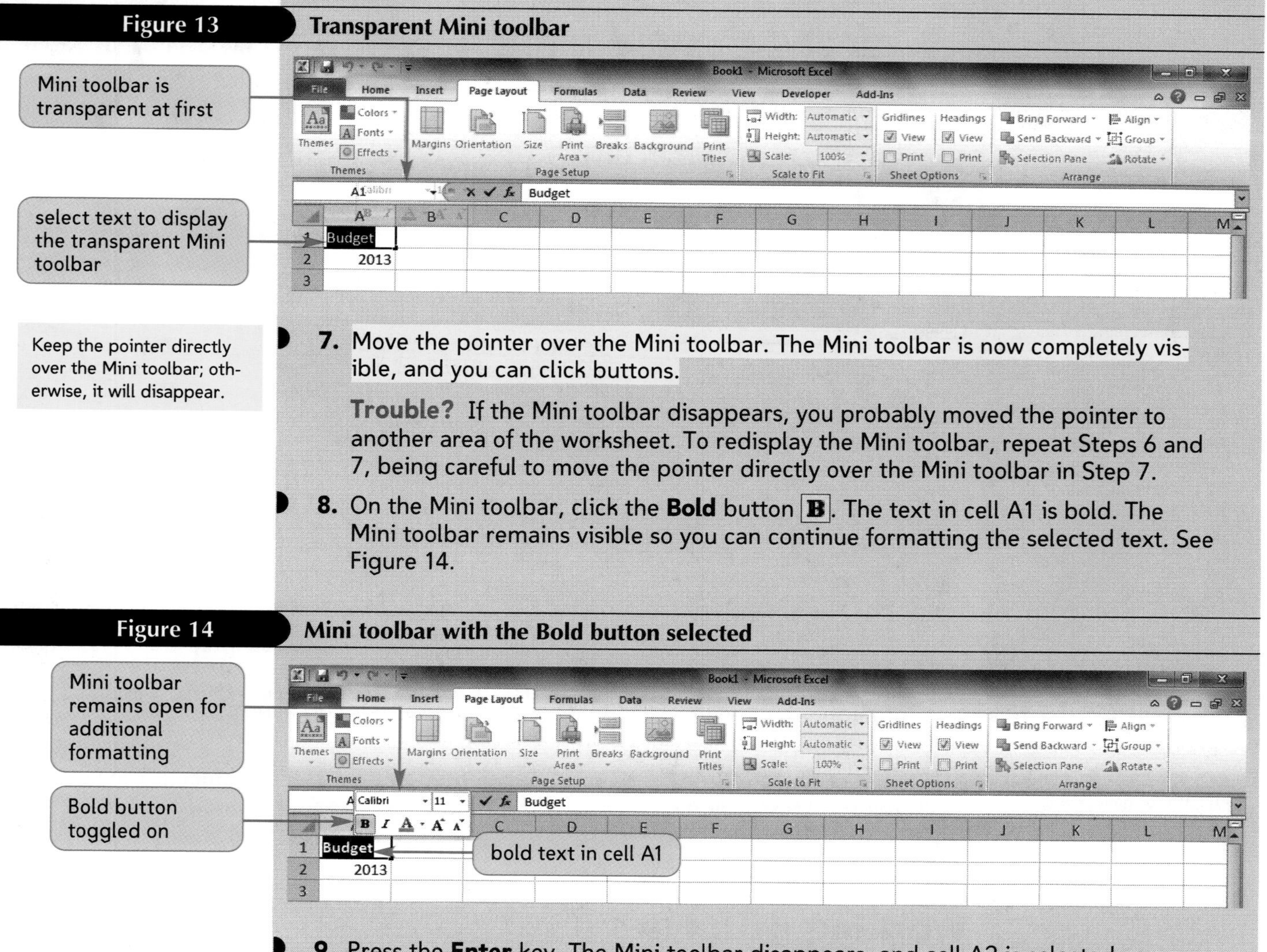

Keep the pointer directly over the Mini toolbar; otherwise, it will disappear.

7. Move the pointer over the Mini toolbar. The Mini toolbar is now completely visible, and you can click buttons.

   Trouble? If the Mini toolbar disappears, you probably moved the pointer to another area of the worksheet. To redisplay the Mini toolbar, repeat Steps 6 and 7, being careful to move the pointer directly over the Mini toolbar in Step 7.
8. On the Mini toolbar, click the **Bold** button **B**. The text in cell A1 is bold. The Mini toolbar remains visible so you can continue formatting the selected text. See Figure 14.

Figure 14 **Mini toolbar with the Bold button selected**

9. Press the **Enter** key. The Mini toolbar disappears, and cell A2 is selected.

Opening Shortcut Menus

A **shortcut menu** is a list of commands related to a selection that opens when you click the right mouse button. Shortcut menus enable you to quickly access commands that you're most likely to need in the context of the task you're performing without using the tabs on the Ribbon. The shortcut menu includes commands that perform actions, commands that open dialog boxes, and galleries of options that provide Live Preview. The Mini toolbar also opens when you right-click. If you click a button on the Mini toolbar, the rest of the shortcut menu closes while the Mini toolbar remains open so you can continue formatting the selection. For example, you can right-click selected text to open a shortcut menu with a Mini toolbar; the menu will contain text-related commands such as Cut, Copy, and Paste, as well as other program-specific commands.

You'll use a shortcut menu to delete the content you entered in cell A1.

To use a shortcut menu to delete content:

1. Right-click cell **A1**. A shortcut menu opens, listing commands related to common tasks you'd perform in a cell, along with the Mini toolbar. See Figure 15.

Figure 15 **Shortcut menu with Mini toolbar**

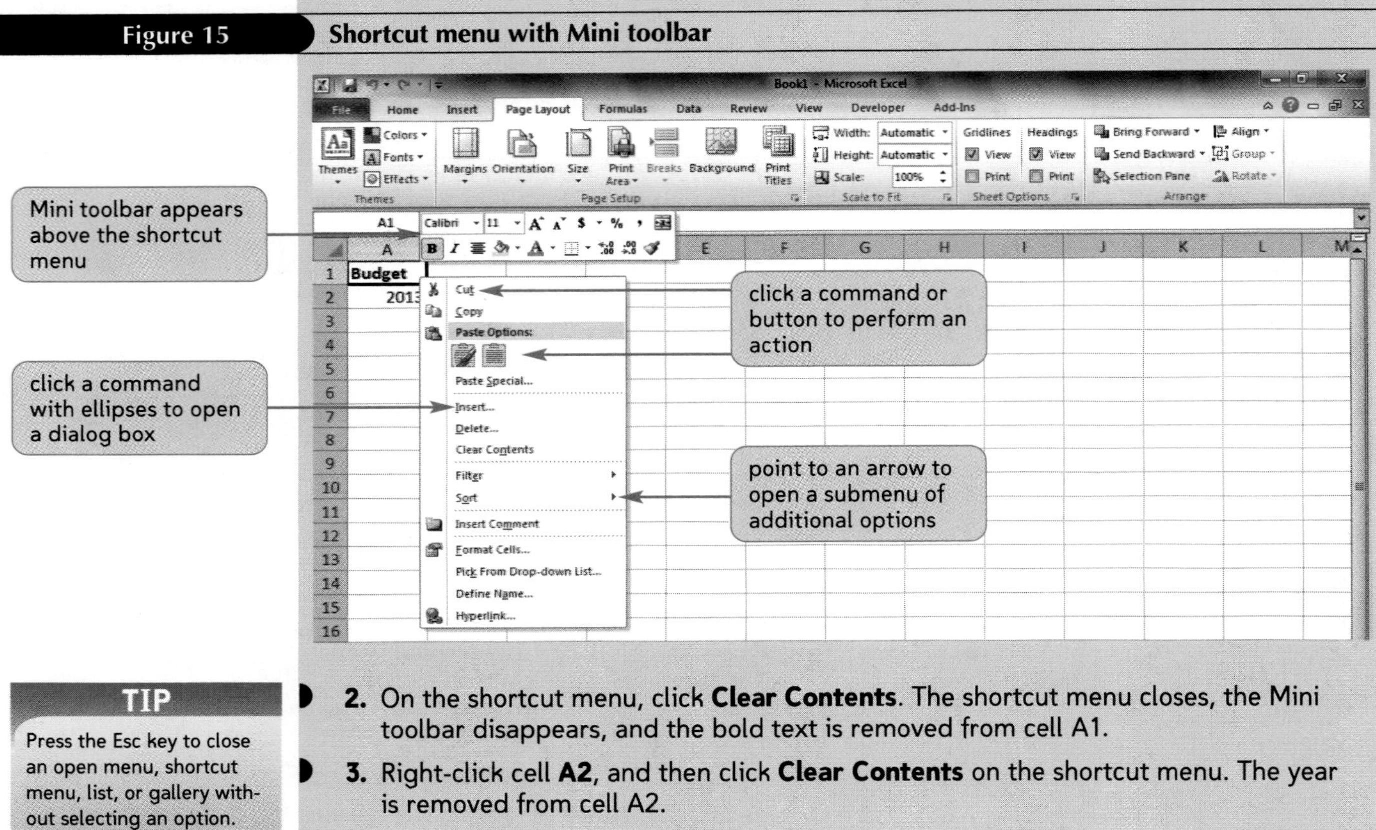

TIP

Press the Esc key to close an open menu, shortcut menu, list, or gallery without selecting an option.

2. On the shortcut menu, click **Clear Contents**. The shortcut menu closes, the Mini toolbar disappears, and the bold text is removed from cell A1.
3. Right-click cell **A2**, and then click **Clear Contents** on the shortcut menu. The year is removed from cell A2.

Working with Files

The most common tasks you perform in any Office program are to create, open, save, and close files. All of these tasks can be done from Backstage view, and the processes for these tasks are basically the same in all Office programs. To begin working in a program, you need to create a new file or open an existing file. When you start Word, Excel, or PowerPoint, the program opens along with a blank file—ready for you to begin working on a new document, workbook, or presentation. When you start Access, the New tab in Backstage view opens, displaying options for creating a new database or opening an existing one.

Saving a File

As you create and modify an Office file, your work is stored only in the computer's temporary memory, not on a hard drive. If you were to exit the program without saving, turn off your computer, or experience a power failure, your work would be lost. To prevent losing work, save your file frequently—at least every 10 minutes. You can save files to the hard drive located inside your computer, an external hard drive, a network storage drive, or a portable storage drive such as a USB flash drive.

To save a file, you can click either the Save button on the Quick Access Toolbar or the Save command in Backstage view. If it is the first time you are saving a file, the Save As dialog box will open so that you can specify save options. You can also click the Save As command in Backstage view to open the Save As dialog box, in which you can name the file you are saving and specify a location to save it.

TIP

Office 2003 and earlier files use the extensions .doc (Word), .xls (Excel), .mdb (Access), and .ppt (PowerPoint). To save in an earlier format, click the Save as type button in the Save As dialog box and click the 97-2003 format. When you open an earlier version file in Office 2010, you can save it in the same format or the Office 2010 format.

The first time you save a file, you need to name it. This **filename** includes a title you specify and a file extension assigned by Office to indicate the file type. You should specify a descriptive title that accurately reflects the content of the document, workbook, presentation, or database, such as "Shipping Options Letter" or "Fourth Quarter Financial Analysis." Your descriptive title can include uppercase and lowercase letters, numbers, hyphens, and spaces in any combination, but not the special characters ? " / \ < > * | and :. Each filename ends with a **file extension**, which is a period followed by several characters that Office adds to your descriptive title to identify the program in which that file was created. The default file extensions for Office 2010 are .docx for Word, .xlsx for Excel, .pptx for PowerPoint, and .accdb for Access. Filenames (the descriptive title and extension) can include a maximum of 255 characters. You might see file extensions depending on how Windows is set up on your computer. The figures in these tutorials do not show file extensions.

You also need to decide where to save the file—on which drive and in what folder. A **folder** is a container for your files. Just as you organize paper documents within folders stored in a filing cabinet, you can organize your files within folders stored on your computer's hard drive or on a removable drive such as a USB flash drive. Store each file in a logical location that you will remember whenever you want to use the file again. The default storage location for Office files is the Documents folder; you can create additional storage folders within that folder or navigate to a new location.

REFERENCE

Saving a File

To save a file the first time or with a new name or location:
- Click the File tab to open Backstage view, and then click the Save As command in the navigation bar (for an unnamed file, click the Save command or click the Save button on the Quick Access Toolbar).
- In the Save As dialog box, navigate to the location where you want to save the file.
- Type a descriptive title in the File name box, and then click the Save button.

To resave a named file to the same location with the same name:
- On the Quick Access Toolbar, click the Save button.

The text you typed in the Word window needs to be saved.

To save a file for the first time:

1. On the taskbar, click the **Microsoft Word** program button. Word becomes the active program.
2. On the Ribbon, click the **File** tab. Backstage view opens with commands and tabs for creating new files, opening existing files, and saving, printing, and closing files. See Figure 16.

Figure 16 **Backstage view**

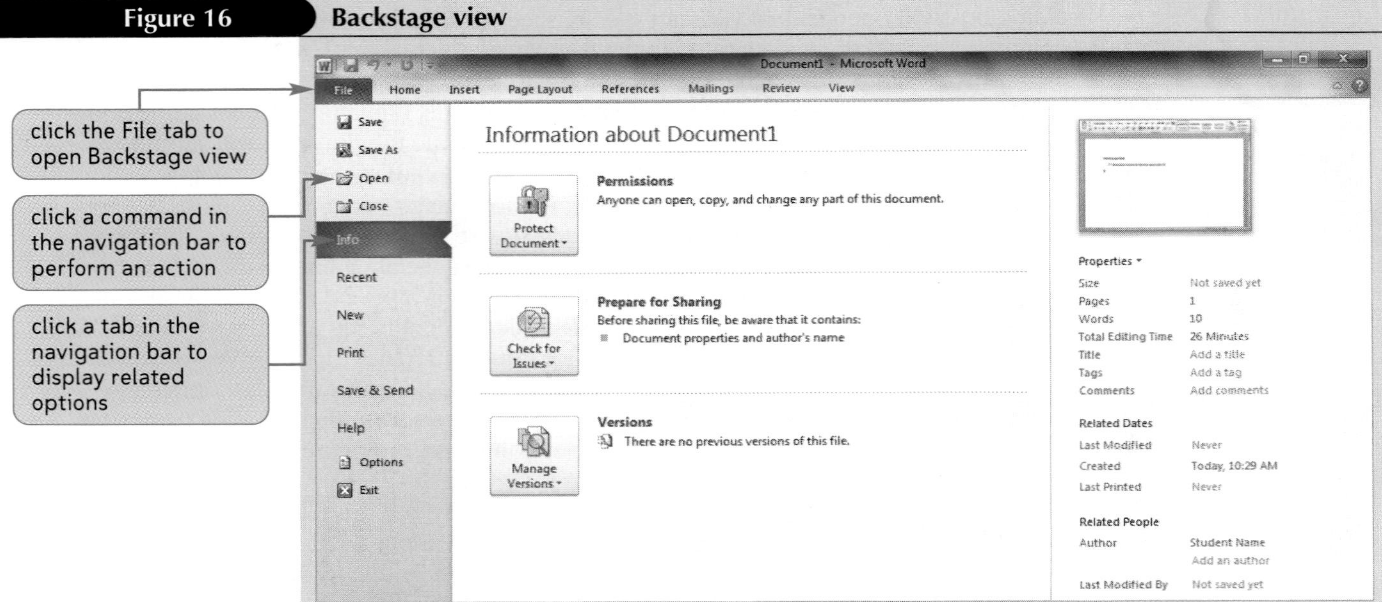

3. In the navigation bar, click the **Save As** command. The Save As dialog box opens because you have not yet saved the file and need to specify a storage location and filename. The default location is set to the Documents folder, and the first few words of the first line appear in the File name box as a suggested title.
4. In the Navigation pane along the left side of the dialog box, click the link for the location that contains your Data Files, if necessary.

   Trouble? If you don't have the starting Data Files, you need to get them before you can proceed. Your instructor will either give you the Data Files or ask you to obtain them from a specified location (such as a network drive). In either case, make a backup copy of the Data Files before you start so that you will have the original files available in case you need to start over. If you have any questions about the Data Files, see your instructor or technical support person for assistance.

5. In the file list, double-click the **Office** folder, and then double-click the **Tutorial** folder. This is the location where you want to save the document.
6. Type **Agenda** in the File name box. This descriptive filename will help you more easily identify the file. See Figure 17 (your file path may differ).

Figure 17 **Completed Save As dialog box**

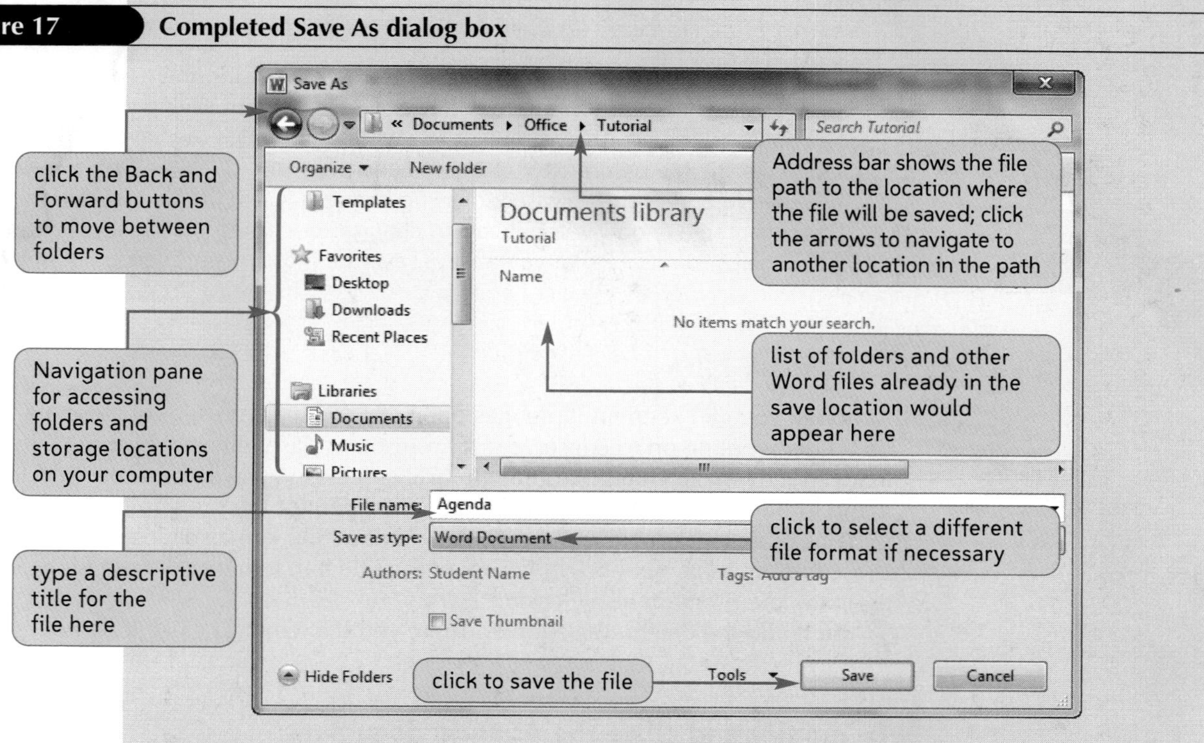

Trouble? If the .docx extension appears after the filename, your computer is configured to show file extensions. Continue with Step 7.

7. Click the **Save** button. The Save As dialog box closes, and the name of your file appears in the Word window title bar.

The saved file includes everything in the document at the time you last saved it. Any new edits or additions you make to the document exist only in the computer's memory and are not saved in the file on the drive. As you work, remember to save frequently so that the file is updated to reflect the latest content.

Because you already named the document and selected a storage location, you don't need to use the Save As dialog box unless you want to save a copy of the file with a different filename or to a different location. If you do, the previous version of the file remains on your drive as well.

You need to add your name to the agenda. Then, you'll save your changes.

To modify and save the Agenda document:

1. Type your name, and then press the **Enter** key. The text you typed appears on the next line.
2. On the Quick Access Toolbar, click the **Save** button. The changes you made to the document are saved in the file stored on the drive.

INSIGHT

Saving Files Before Closing

As a standard practice, you should save files before closing them. However, Office has an added safeguard: if you attempt to close a file without saving your changes, a dialog box opens, asking whether you want to save the file. Click the Save button to save the changes to the file before closing the file and program. Click the Don't Save button to close the file and program without saving changes. Click the Cancel button to return to the program window without saving changes or closing the file and program. This feature helps to ensure that you always save the most current version of any file.

Closing a File

Although you can keep multiple files open at one time, you should close any file you are no longer working on to conserve system resources as well as to ensure that you don't inadvertently make changes to the file. You can close a file by clicking the Close command in Backstage view. If that's the only file open for the program, the program window remains open and no file appears in the window. You can also close a file by clicking the Close button in the upper-right corner of the title bar. If that's the only file open for the program, the program also closes.

You'll add the date to the agenda. Then, you'll attempt to close it without saving.

To modify and close the Agenda document:

1. Type today's date, and then press the **Enter** key. The text you typed appears below your name in the document.
2. On the Ribbon, click the **File** tab to open Backstage view, and then click the **Close** command in the navigation bar. A dialog box opens, asking whether you want to save the changes you made to the document.
3. Click the **Save** button. The current version of the document is saved to the file, and then the document closes. Word is still open, so you can create additional new files in the open program or you can open previously created and saved files.

Opening a File

When you want to open a blank document, workbook, presentation, or database, you create a new file. When you want to work on a previously created file, you must first open it. Opening a file transfers a copy of the file from the storage location (either a hard drive or a portable drive) to the computer's memory and displays it on your screen. The file is then in your computer's memory and on the drive.

REFERENCE

Opening an Existing File

- Click the File tab to open Backstage view, and then click the Open command in the navigation bar.
- In the Open dialog box, navigate to the storage location of the file you want to open.
- Click the filename of the file you want to open.
- Click the Open button.
- If necessary, click the Enable Editing button in the Information Bar.

or

- Click the File tab, and then click the Recent tab in the navigation bar.
- Click a filename in the Recent list.

Any file you open that was downloaded from the Internet, accessed from a shared network, or received as an email attachment might open in a read-only format, called **Protected View**. In Protected View, you can see the file contents, but you cannot edit, save, or print them until you enable editing. To do so, click the Enable Editing button on the Information Bar, as shown in Figure 18.

Figure 18 **Protected View warning**

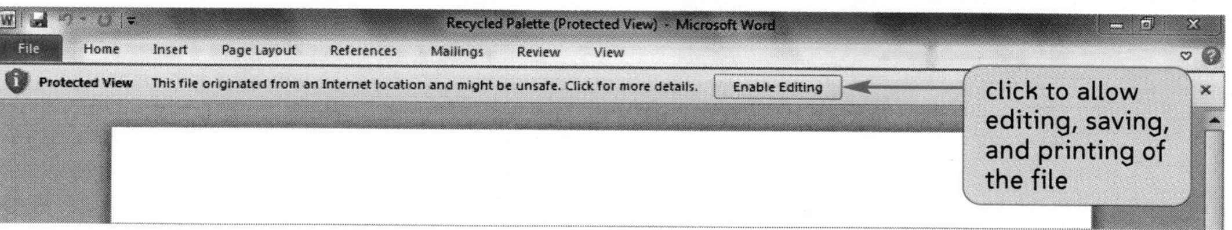

You need to print the meeting agenda you typed for Ean. To do that, you'll reopen the Agenda document.

To open the Agenda document:

1. On the Ribbon, click the **File** tab to display Backstage view.
2. In the navigation bar, click the **Open** command. The Open dialog box, which works similarly to the Save As dialog box, opens.
3. In the Open dialog box, use the Navigation pane or the Address bar to navigate to the **Office\Tutorial** folder included with your Data Files. This is the location where you saved the Agenda document.
4. In the file list, click **Agenda**. See Figure 19.

Figure 19 Open dialog box

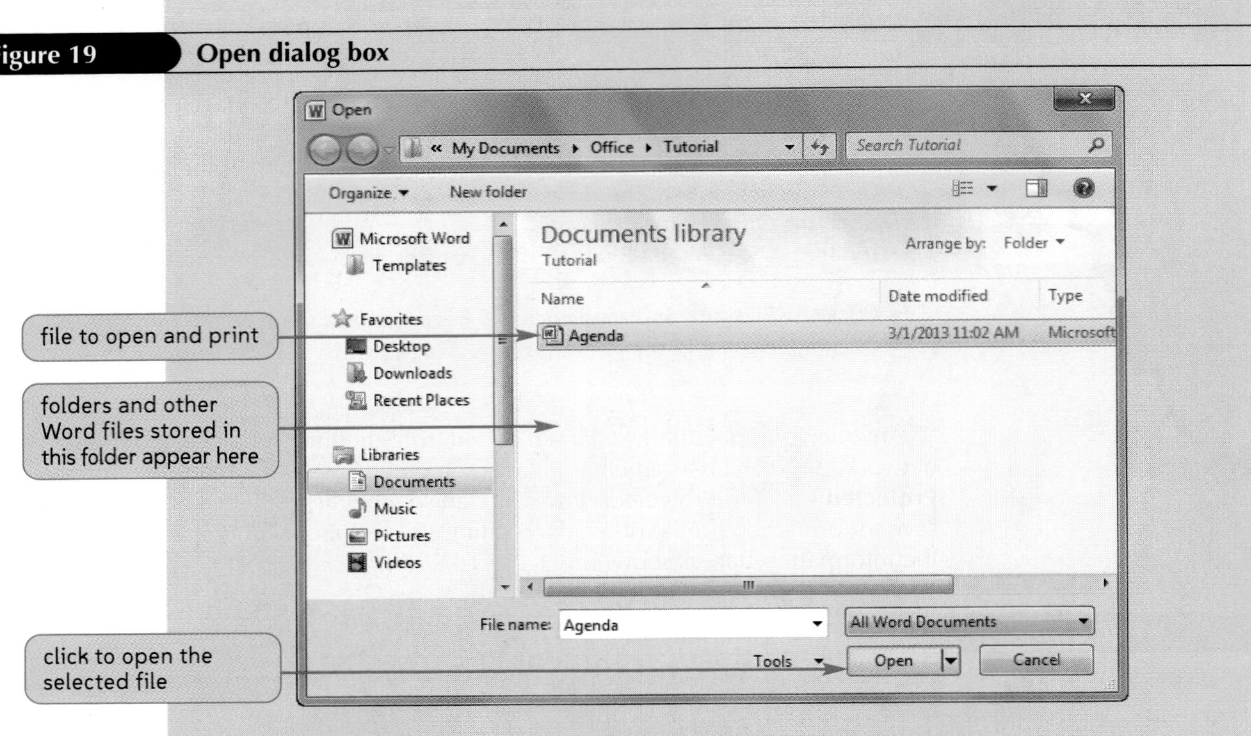

5. Click the **Open** button. The Agenda file opens in the Word program window.

Sharing Files Using Windows Live SkyDrive

Often the purpose of creating a file is to share it with other people—sending it attached to an email message for someone else to read or use, collaborating with others on the same document, or posting it as a blog for others to review. You can do all of these things in Backstage view from the Save & Send tab.

When you send a file using email, you can attach a copy of the file, send a link to the file, or attach a copy of the file in a PDF or another file format. You can also save to online workspaces where you can make the file available to others for review and collaboration. The Save to Web option on the Save & Send tab in Backstage view gives you access to **Windows Live SkyDrive**, which is an online workspace provided by Microsoft; your personal workspace comes with a Public folder for saving files to share as well as a My Documents folder for saving files you want to keep private. (SkyDrive is not available for Access.) Figure 20 shows the Save to Web options on the Save & Send tab in Backstage view of Word. SharePoint is an online workspace set up by an organization, such as a school, business, or nonprofit group.

> **TIP**
> To use SkyDrive, you need a Windows Live ID, which you can sign up for at no cost. After you sign in, you can create new folders and save files into the folders.

Files saved to an online workspace can be worked on by more than one person at the same time. The changes are recorded in the files with each author's name and the date of the change. A Web browser is used to access and edit the files. You choose who can have access to the files.

Figure 20 Save to Web options on the Save & Send tab

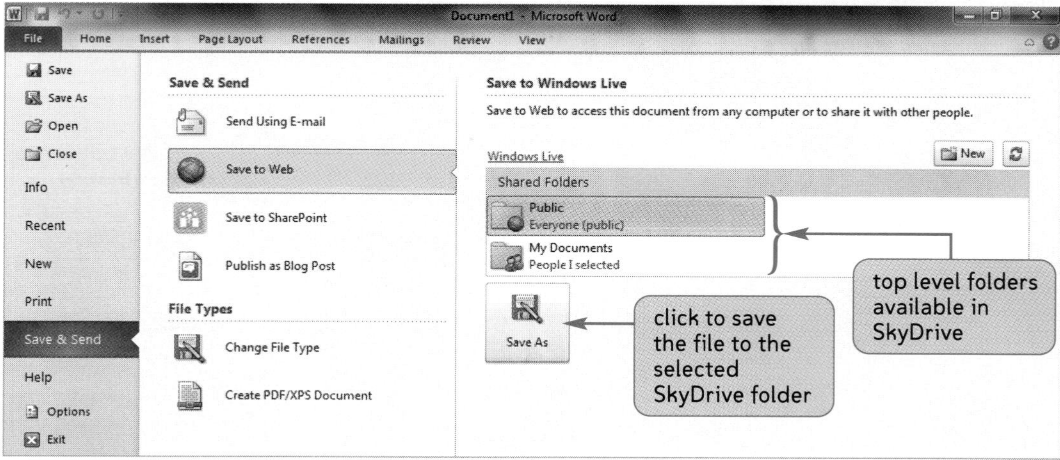

REFERENCE

Saving a File to SkyDrive

- Click the File tab to open Backstage view, and then click the Save & Send tab in the navigation bar.
- In the center pane, click Save to Web.
- In the right pane, click the Sign In button, and then use your Windows Live ID to log on to your Windows Live SkyDrive account.

Getting Help

If you don't know how to perform a task or want more information about a feature, you can turn to Office itself for information on how to use it. This information is referred to simply as **Help**. You can get Help in ScreenTips and from the Help window.

Viewing ScreenTips

ScreenTips are a fast and simple method you can use to get information about objects you see on the screen. A **ScreenTip** is a box with descriptive text about an object or button. Just point to a button or object to display its ScreenTip. In addition to the button's name, a ScreenTip might include the button's keyboard shortcut if it has one, a description of the command's function, and, in some cases, a link to more information so that you can press the F1 key while the ScreenTip is displayed to open the Help window with the relevant topic displayed.

To view ScreenTips:

1. Point to the **Microsoft Office Word Help** button. The ScreenTip shows the button's name, its keyboard shortcut, and a brief description. See Figure 21.

Figure 21 **ScreenTip for the Help button**

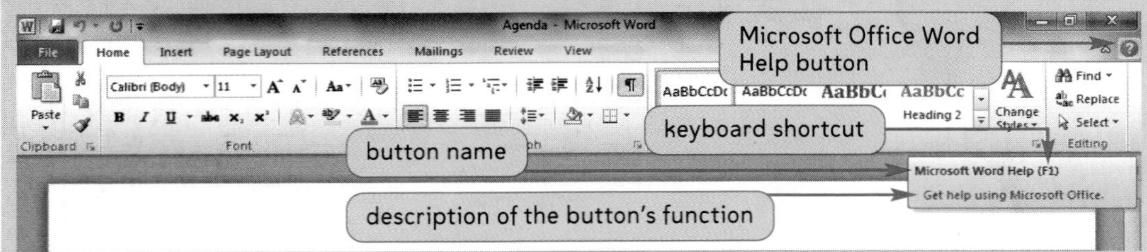

2. Point to other buttons on the Ribbon to display their ScreenTips.

Using the Help Window

For more detailed information, you can use the **Help window** to access all the Help topics, templates, and training installed on your computer with Office and available on Office.com. **Office.com** is a Web site maintained by Microsoft that provides access to the latest information and additional Help resources. For example, you can access current Help topics and training for Office. To connect to Office.com, you need to be able to access the Internet from your computer. Otherwise, you see only topics that are stored on your computer.

Each program has its own Help window from which you can find information about all of the Office commands and features as well as step-by-step instructions for using them. There are two ways to find Help topics—the search function and a topic list.

The Type words to search for box enables you to search the Help system for a task or a topic you need help with. You can click a link to open a Help topic with explanations and step-by-step instructions for a specific procedure. The Table of Contents pane displays the Help system content organized by subjects and topics, similar to a book's table of contents. You click main subject links to display related topic links. You click a topic link to display that Help topic in the Help window.

REFERENCE

Getting Help

- Click the Microsoft Office Help button (the button name depends on the Office program).
- Type a keyword or phrase in the Type words to search for box, click the Search button, and then click a Help topic in the search results list.
  or
  In the Table of Contents pane, click a "book," and then click a Help topic.
- Read the information in the Help window and then click other topics or links.
- On the Help window title bar, click the Close button.

You'll use Help to get information about printing a document in Word.

To search Help for information about printing:

1. Click the **Microsoft Office Word Help** button. The Word Help window opens.

2. If the Table of Contents pane is not open on the left side of the Help window, click the **Show Table of Contents** button on the toolbar to display the pane.
3. Click the **Type words to search for** box, if necessary, and then type **print document**. You can specify where you want to search.
4. Click the **Search button arrow**. The Search menu shows the online and local content available.
5. If your computer is connected to the Internet, click **All Word** in the Content from Office.com list. If your computer is not connected to the Internet, click **Word Help** in the Content from this computer list.
6. Click the **Search** button. The Help window displays a list of topics related to the keywords "print document" in the left pane. See Figure 22.

Figure 22 **Search results displaying Help topics**

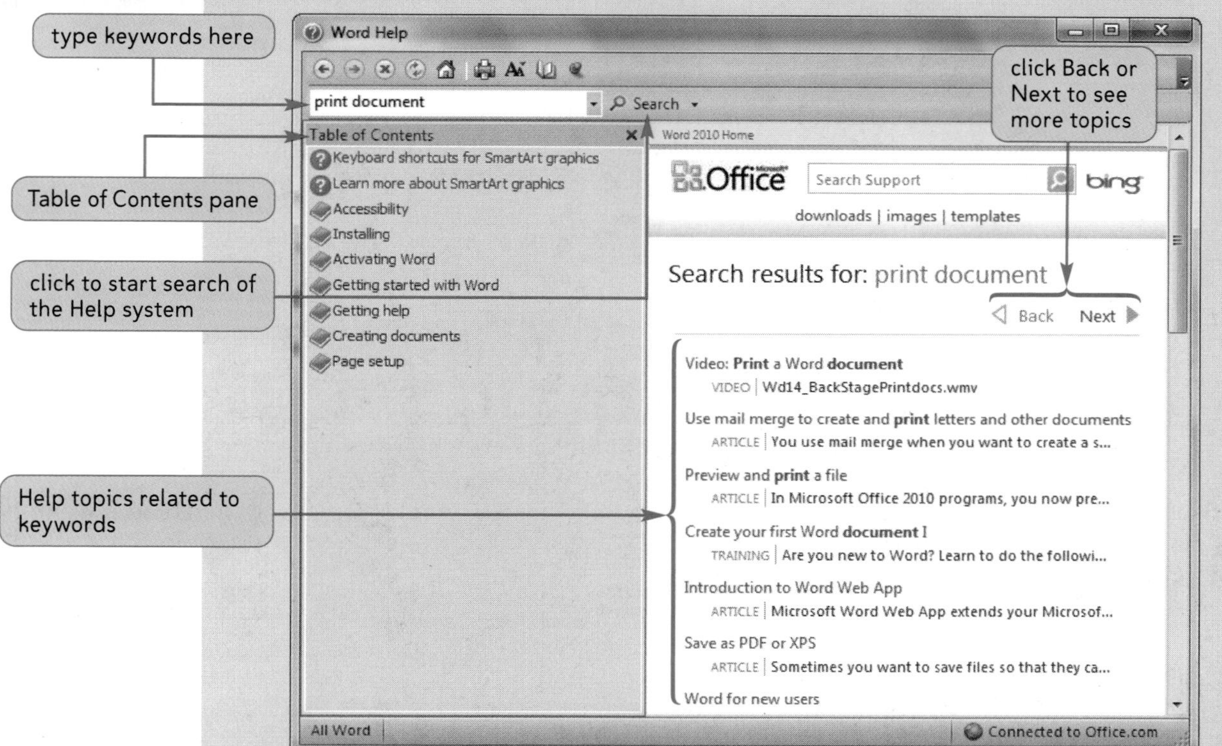

Trouble? If your search results list differs from the one shown in Figure 22, your computer is not connected to the Internet or Microsoft has updated the list of available Help topics since this book was published. Continue with Step 7.

7. Scroll through the list to review the Help topics.
8. Click **Preview and print a file**. The topic content is displayed in the Help window so you can learn more about how to print a document. See Figure 23.

Figure 23 Preview and print a file Help topic

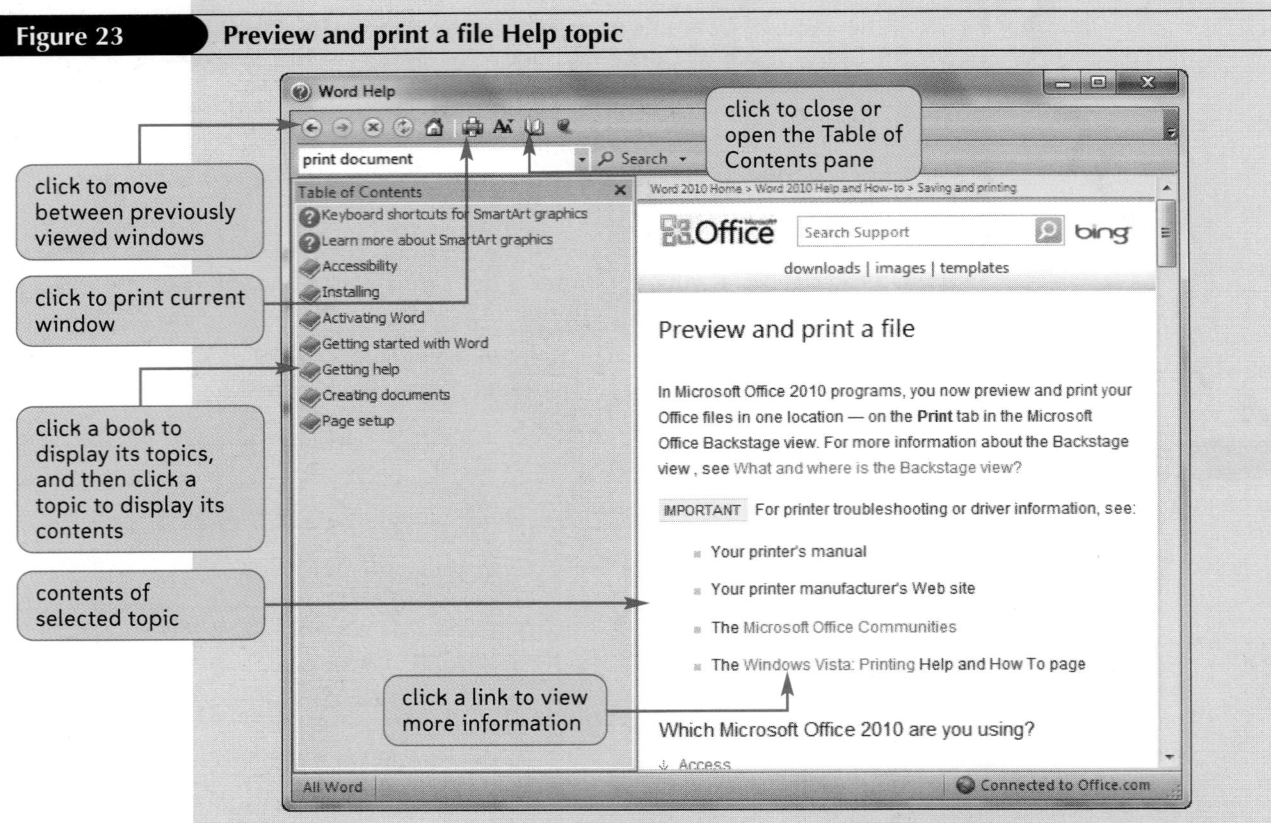

Trouble? If you don't see the Preview and print a file Help topic on page 1, its current location might be on another page. Click the Next link to move to the next page, and then scroll down to find the topic. Repeat as needed to search additional pages until you locate the topic.

9. Read the information, click the links within this topic, and then read the additional information.
10. On the Help window title bar, click the **Close** button [X] to close the window.

Printing a File

At times, you'll want a paper copy of Office files. Whenever you print, you should review and adjust the printing settings as needed. You can select the number of copies to print, the printer, the portion of the file to print, and so forth; the printing settings vary slightly from program to program. You should also check the file's print preview to ensure that the file will print as you intended. This simple review will help you to avoid reprinting, which requires additional paper, ink, and energy resources.

REFERENCE

Printing a File

- On the Ribbon, click the File tab to open Backstage view.
- In the navigation bar, click the Print tab.
- Verify the print settings and review the print preview.
- Click the Print button.

You will print the agenda for Ean.

To print the Agenda document:

1. Make sure your printer is turned on and contains paper.
2. On the Ribbon, click the **File** tab to open Backstage view.
3. In the navigation bar, click the **Print** tab. The print settings and preview appear. See Figure 24.

Figure 24 Print tab in Backstage view

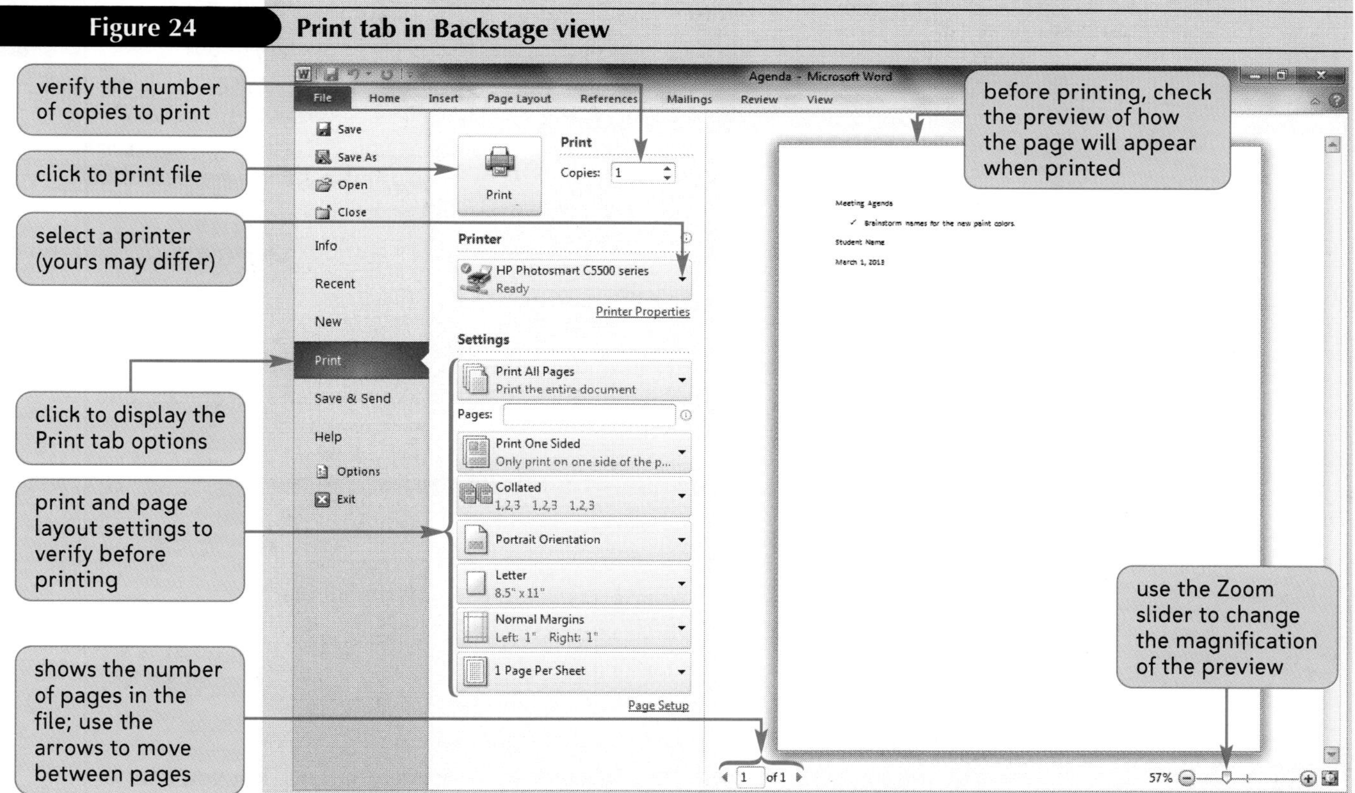

4. Verify that **1** appears in the Copies box.
5. Verify that the correct printer appears on the Printer button. If it doesn't, click the **Printer** button, and then click the correct printer from the list of available printers.
6. Click the **Print** button to print the document.

Trouble? If the document does not print, see your instructor or technical support person for help.

Exiting Programs

When you finish working with a program, you should exit it. As with many other aspects of Office, you can exit programs with a button or a command. You'll use both methods to exit Word and Excel. You can use the Exit command to exit a program and close an open file in one step. If you haven't saved the final version of the open file, a dialog box opens, asking whether you want to save your changes. Clicking the Save button in this dialog box saves the open file, closes the file, and then exits the program.

To exit the Word and Excel programs:

1. On the Word title bar, click the **Close** button [X]. Both the Word document and the Word program close. The Excel window is visible again.

   Trouble? If a dialog box opens asking if you want to save the document, you might have inadvertently made a change to the document. Click the Don't Save button.

2. On the Ribbon, click the **File** tab to open Backstage view, and then click the **Exit** command in the navigation bar. A dialog box opens asking whether you want to save the changes you made to the workbook. If you click the Save button, the Save As dialog box opens and Excel exits after you finish saving the workbook. This time, you don't want to save the workbook.
3. Click the **Don't Save** button. The workbook closes without saving a copy, and the Excel program closes.

Exiting programs after you are done using them keeps your Windows desktop uncluttered for the next person using the computer, frees up your system's resources, and prevents data from being lost accidentally.

REVIEW

Quick Check

1. What Office program would be best to use to write a letter?
2. How do you start an Office program?
3. What is the purpose of Live Preview?
4. What is Backstage view?
5. Explain the difference between Save and Save As.
6. True or False. In Protected View, you can see file contents, but you cannot edit, save, or print them until you enable editing.
7. What happens if you open a file, make edits, and then attempt to close the file or exit the program without saving the current version of the file?
8. What are the two ways to get Help in Office?

PRACTICE

Practice the skills you learned in the tutorial.

Review Assignments

Data Files needed for the Review Assignments: Finances.xlsx, Letter.docx

You need to prepare for an upcoming meeting at Recycled Palette. You'll open and print documents for the meeting. Complete the following:

1. Start PowerPoint, and then start Excel.
2. Switch to the PowerPoint window, and then close the presentation but leave the PowerPoint program open. (*Hint*: Use the Close command in Backstage view.)
3. Open a blank PowerPoint presentation from the New tab in Backstage view. (*Hint*: Make sure Blank presentation is selected in the Available Templates and Themes section, and then click the Create button.)
4. Close the PowerPoint presentation and program using the Close button on the PowerPoint title bar; do not save changes if asked.
5. Open the **Finances** workbook located in the Office\Review folder. If the workbook opens in Protected View, click the Enable Editing button.
6. Use the Save As command to save the workbook as **Recycled Palette Finances** in the Office\Review folder.
7. In cell A1, type your name, press the Enter key to insert your name at the top of the worksheet, and then save the workbook.
8. Preview and print one copy of the worksheet using the Print tab in Backstage view.
9. Exit Excel using the Exit command in Backstage view.
10. Start Word, and then open the **Letter** document located in the Office\Review folder. If the document opens in Protected View, click the Enable Editing button.
11. Use the Save As command to save the document with the filename **Recycled Palette Letter** in the Office\Review folder.
12. Press and hold the Ctrl key, press the End key, and then release both keys to move the insertion point to the end of the letter, and then type your name.
13. Use the Save button to save the change to the Recycled Palette Letter document.
14. Preview and print one copy of the document using the Print tab in Backstage view.
15. Close the document, and then exit the Word program.
16. Submit the finished files to your instructor.

ASSESS

SAM: Skills Assessment Manager

For current SAM information, including versions and content details, visit SAM Central (http://samcentral.course.com). If you have a SAM user profile, you may have access to hands-on instruction, practice, and assessment of the skills covered in this tutorial. Since various versions of SAM are supported throughout the life of this text, check with your instructor for the correct instructions and URL/Web site for accessing assignments.

ENDING DATA FILES

ProSkills

Teamwork

Working on a Team

Teams consist of individuals who have skills, talents, and abilities that complement each other and, when joined, produce synergy—results greater than those a single individual could achieve. It is this sense of shared mission and responsibility for results that makes a team successful in its efforts to reach its goals. Teams are everywhere. In the workplace, a team might develop a presentation to introduce products. In the classroom, a team might complete a research project.

Teams meet face to face or virtually. A virtual team rarely, if ever, meets in person. Instead, technology makes it possible for members to work as if everyone was in the same room. Some common technologies used in virtual teamwork are corporate networks, email, teleconferencing, and collaboration and integration tools, such as those found in Office 2010.

Even for teams in the same location, technology is a valuable tool. For example, teams commonly collaborate on a copy of a file posted to an online shared storage space, such as SkyDrive. In addition, team members can compile data in the program that best suits the information related to their part of the project. Later, that information can be integrated into a finished report, presentation, email message, and so on.

PROSKILLS

Collaborate with Others

At home, school, or work, you probably collaborate with others to complete many types of tasks—such as planning an event, creating a report, or developing a presentation. You can use Microsoft Office to streamline many of these tasks. Consider a project that you might need to work on with a team. Complete the following steps:

1. Start Word, and open a new document, if necessary.
2. In the document, type a list of all the tasks the team needs to accomplish. If you are working with a team, identify which team member would complete each task.
3. For each task, identify the type of Office file you would create to complete that task. For example, you would create a Word document to write a letter.
4. For each file, identify the Office program you would use to create that file, and explain why you would use that program.
5. Save the document with an appropriate filename in an appropriate folder location.
6. Use a Web browser to visit the Microsoft site at *www.microsoft.com* and research the different Office 2010 suites available. Determine which suite includes all the programs needed for the team to complete the tasks on the list.
7. In the document, type which Office suite you selected and a brief explanation of why.
8. Determine how the team can integrate the different programs in the Office suite you selected to create the files that complete the team's goal or task. Include this information at the end of the Word document. Save the document.
9. Develop an efficient way to organize the files that the team will create to complete the goal or task. Add this information at the end of the Word document.
10. If possible, sign in to SkyDrive, and then save a copy of the file in an appropriate subfolder within your Public folder. If you are working with a team, have your teammates access your file, review your notes, and add a paragraph with their comments and name.
11. Preview and print the finished document, and then submit it to your instructor.

TUTORIAL 1

Getting Started with Excel

Creating an Order Report

EXCEL

OBJECTIVES

Session 1.1

- Understand the use of spreadsheets and Excel
- Learn the parts of the Excel window
- Scroll through a worksheet and navigate between worksheets
- Create and save a workbook file
- Enter text, numbers, and dates into a worksheet
- Resize, insert, and remove columns and rows

Session 1.2

- Select and move cell ranges
- Insert formulas and functions
- Insert, delete, move, and rename worksheets
- Work with editing tools
- Preview and print a workbook

Case | *RipCity Digital*

When Amanda Dunn purchased a DVD burner a few years ago, one of her first tasks was to convert her home videos into DVDs. After she saw how simple it was, she upgraded her hardware and software, and proceeded to create DVDs from home movies and slides for her parents and friends. Based on her success, Amanda decided to make a business out of her hobby and founded RipCity Digital, an online service specializing in creating DVDs from the home movies, photos, and slides sent to her from customers. Amanda wants to list the weekly orders from her customers, tracking the names and addresses of her clients, the number of DVDs that she creates, and finally the cost of creating and shipping the DVDs.

Amanda is so busy creating DVDs that she asks you to record her orders. You'll do this in **Microsoft Excel 2010** (or **Excel**), a computer program used to enter, analyze, and present quantitative data. You'll also enter the latest orders she received for her new business.

STARTING DATA FILES

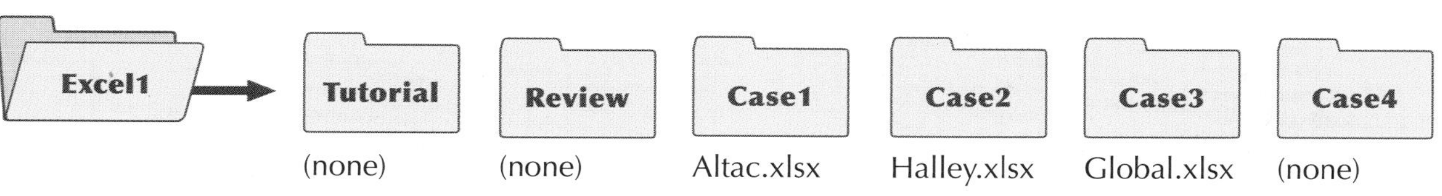

SESSION 1.1 VISUAL OVERVIEW

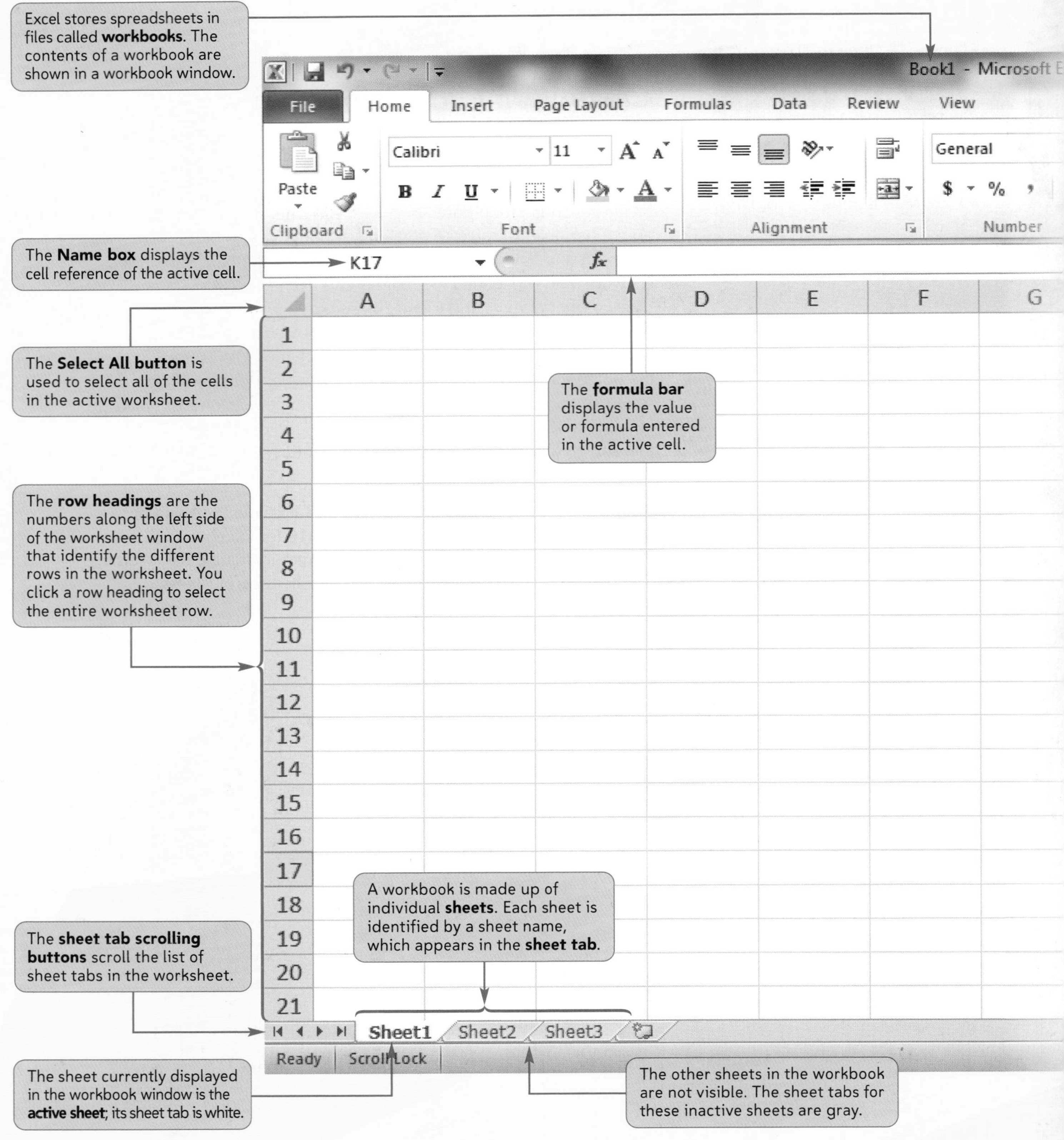

THE EXCEL WINDOW

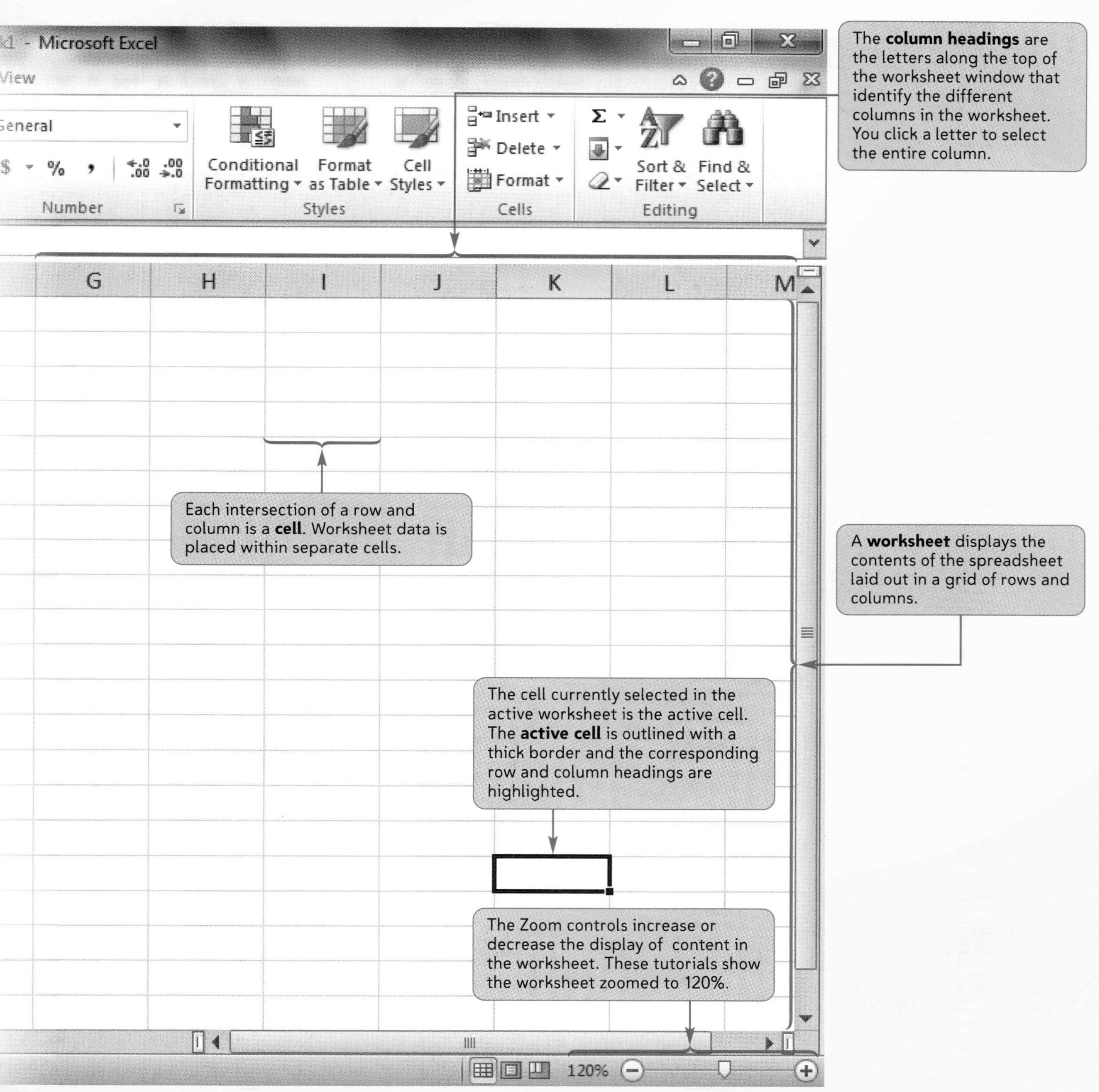

Introducing Excel

Before you begin working in Excel, you will review some of the features, key terms, and concepts associated with spreadsheets.

Understanding Spreadsheets

A **spreadsheet** is a collection of text and numbers laid out in a rectangular grid. Spreadsheets are often used in business for budgeting, inventory management, and decision making. They can also be used to manage personal budgets and track household assets. Excel is a computer program used to create electronic versions of spreadsheets. For example, the spreadsheet in Figure 1-1 shows a cash flow report. The spreadsheet records the estimated and actual cash flow for the month of January. Each line, or row, displays a different value, such as the starting cash balance or cash sales for the month. Each column displays the budgeted or actual numbers, or text that describes those values. The total cash expenditures, net cash flow, and closing cash balance for the month are not entered directly, but calculated from other numbers in the spreadsheet. For example, the total cash expenditure is equal to the expenditures on advertising, wages, and supplies. This allows you to use Excel to perform a **what-if analysis** in which you change one or more values in a spreadsheet and then assess the effect those changes have on the calculated values. You can also use Excel to store data, generate reports, and analyze data values using a variety of statistical tools.

Figure 1-1 **Spreadsheet data in Excel**

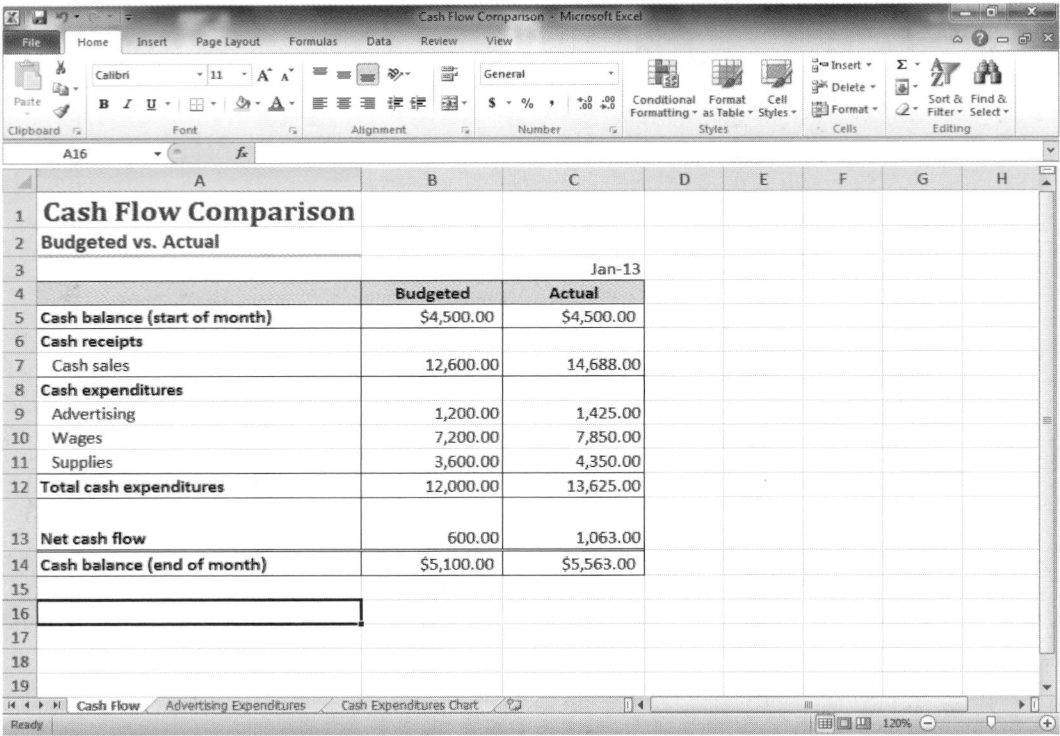

	A	B	C
1	Cash Flow Comparison		
2	Budgeted vs. Actual		
3			Jan-13
4		Budgeted	Actual
5	Cash balance (start of month)	$4,500.00	$4,500.00
6	Cash receipts		
7	Cash sales	12,600.00	14,688.00
8	Cash expenditures		
9	Advertising	1,200.00	1,425.00
10	Wages	7,200.00	7,850.00
11	Supplies	3,600.00	4,350.00
12	Total cash expenditures	12,000.00	13,625.00
13	Net cash flow	600.00	1,063.00
14	Cash balance (end of month)	$5,100.00	$5,563.00

Exploring the Excel Window

Before entering Amanda's data, you'll review the different parts of the Excel window. The Excel window contains many of the elements that you find in other Office 2010 programs, including a title bar, the Ribbon, scroll bars, and a status bar. The Excel window also contains features that are unique to Excel.

To start Excel:

1. Click the **Start** button on the taskbar, click **All Programs**, click **Microsoft Office**, and then point to **Microsoft Excel 2010**.

   Trouble? If you don't see Microsoft Excel 2010 on the Microsoft Office submenu, look for it on a different submenu or on the All Programs menu. If you still cannot find Microsoft Excel 2010, ask your instructor or technical support person for help.

2. Click **Microsoft Excel 2010**. The Excel window opens.

   All the figures showing the Excel window in these tutorials are zoomed to 120% for better readability. If you want to zoom your Excel window to match the figures, complete Step 3. If you prefer to work in the default zoom of 100% or at another zoom level, continue with Step 4; you might see more or less of the worksheet on your screen, but this does not affect your work in the tutorials.

3. If you want your Excel window zoomed to match the figures, click the **Zoom In** button on the status bar twice to increase the zoom level to 120%. The 120% magnification increases the screen size of each cell, but reduces the number of worksheet cells visible in the workbook window.

4. If necessary, click the **Maximize** button on the Excel window title bar. The Excel window fills the screen.

By default, Excel starts with a blank workbook maximized to fill the Excel window. The name of the active workbook, Book1, appears in the title bar. You can open more than one workbook window at a time to display the contents of different workbooks. You can also open multiple workbook windows for one workbook to display different views of the workbook's contents.

Navigating Between Worksheets

A workbook can have two kinds of sheets: worksheets and chart sheets. A worksheet contains a grid of rows and columns into which the user enters data values and formulas. A **chart sheet** contains an Excel chart that provides a visual representation of worksheet data. Charts can also be embedded within worksheets, displaying both the data and charts in one sheet. By default, all new Excel workbooks are created with three worksheets named Sheet1, Sheet2, and Sheet3. The Sheet1 worksheet is the active sheet.

Multiple sheets enable you to better organize data in the workbook. For example, a sales report workbook might have a different worksheet for each sales region and another worksheet that summarizes the results from all the regions.

Some workbooks contain so many sheets that their sheet tabs cannot all be displayed at the same time in the workbook window. For these workbooks, you can scroll through the sheet tabs using the sheet tab scrolling buttons. Scrolling through the sheet tabs does not change the active sheet. To change the active sheet, you must click a sheet tab.

TIP

You can also move to the previous or next sheet by pressing the Ctrl+Page Up or Ctrl+Page Down keys.

To change the active sheet:

1. Click the **Sheet2** sheet tab. The Sheet2 worksheet, which is also blank, becomes the active worksheet. The Sheet2 tab is white, indicating this worksheet is active.
2. Click the **Sheet3** sheet tab. The Sheet3 worksheet becomes the active worksheet.
3. Click the **Sheet1** sheet tab to return to the first worksheet.

Navigating Within a Worksheet

Each cell within a worksheet is identified by a **cell reference**, which indicates its column and row location. For example, the cell reference B6 refers to the cell located where column B intersects row 6. The column letter always appears before the row number in any cell reference. Row numbers range from 1 to 1,048,576. The first 26 column letters range in alphabetical order from A to Z. After Z, the next column headings are labeled AA, AB, AC, and so forth. Excel allows a maximum of 16,385 columns in a worksheet (the last column has the heading XFD). When Excel starts, cell A1 is the active cell.

As you work, you'll need to change which cell is the active cell. You can use your mouse to click a cell to make it the active cell, or you can use the keyboard to move between cells, as described in Figure 1-2.

Figure 1-2 **Excel navigation keys**

Press	To move the active cell
↑ ↓ ← →	Up, down, left, or right one cell
Home	To column A of the current row
Ctrl+Home	To cell A1
Ctrl+End	To the last cell in the worksheet that contains data
Enter	Down one row or to the start of the next row of data
Shift+Enter	Up one row
Tab	One column to the right
Shift+Tab	One column to the left
Page Up, Page Down	Up or down one screen
Ctrl+Page Up, Ctrl+Page Down	To the previous or next sheet in the workbook

You'll use both your mouse and your keyboard to change the active cell in the Sheet1 worksheet.

To change the active cell:

1. Move your pointer over cell **A5**, and then click the mouse button. The active cell moves from cell A1 to cell A5, and the cell reference in the Name box changes from A1 to A5. The column heading for column A and the row heading for row 5 are both highlighted.
2. Press the → key on your keyboard. The active cell moves one cell to the right to cell B5.
3. Press the **Page Down** key. The active cell moves down one full screen.
4. Press the **Page Up** key. The active cell moves up one full screen, back to cell B5.
5. Press the **Ctrl+Home** keys. The active cell returns to the first cell in the worksheet, cell A1.

The mouse and keyboard provide quick ways to navigate the active worksheet. For larger worksheets that span several screens, you can move directly to a specific cell using the Go To dialog box or by typing a cell reference in the Name box. You'll try both of these methods.

To use the Go To dialog box and Name box:

1. Click the **Home** tab on the Ribbon, if necessary. The button to open the Go To dialog box is in the Editing group.
2. In the Editing group, click the **Find & Select** button, and then click **Go To** on the menu that opens. The Go To dialog box opens.
3. Type **C14** in the Reference box. See Figure 1-3.

TIP

You can also open the Go To dialog box by pressing the F5 key or the Ctrl+G keys.

Figure 1-3 Go To dialog box

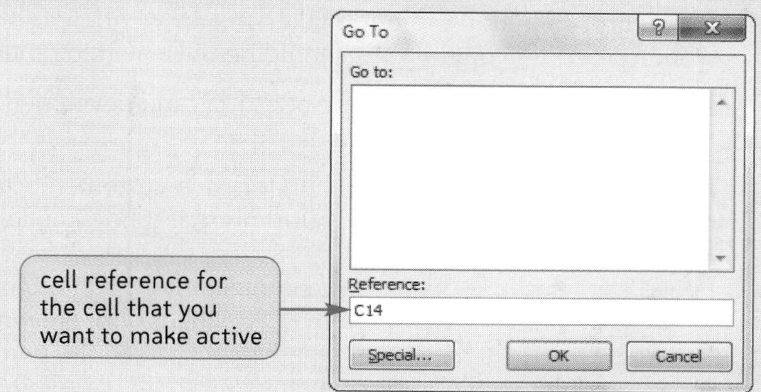

Trouble? If your screen varies slightly from those shown in the figures, your computer might be set up differently. The figures in this book were created while running Windows 7 using the default Windows 7 settings, but how your screen looks depends on a variety of things, including the version of Windows, background settings, monitor resolution, and so forth.

4. Click the **OK** button. Cell C14 is the active cell and its cell reference appears in the Name box. You'll use the Name box to make a different cell active.
5. Click in the **Name** box, type **A1**, and then press the **Enter** key. Cell A1 is once again the active cell.

To view more of the active worksheet, you can use the horizontal and vertical scroll bars, located at the bottom and right side of the workbook window, respectively, to move through the worksheet horizontally and vertically. You can scroll one row or column at a time, or you can scroll several rows and columns. Scrolling through the worksheet does not change the location of the active cell.

To scroll through the worksheet:

1. Click the **down arrow** on the vertical scroll bar three times. The worksheet scrolls down three rows, but the active cell remains cell A1.
2. Click the **right arrow** on the horizontal scroll bar twice. The worksheet scrolls two columns to the right. The active cell still remains cell A1, although that cell is scrolled out of view.
3. Drag the vertical scroll box up until you can see the first row in the worksheet.
4. Drag the horizontal scroll box to the left until you can see the first column in the worksheet.

Planning a Workbook

Before you begin to enter data into a workbook, you should develop a plan. You can do this by using a **planning analysis sheet**, which includes the following questions that help you think about the workbook's purpose and how to achieve your desired results:

1. **What problems do I want to solve?** The answer defines the goal or purpose of the workbook.
2. **What data do I need?** The answer defines the type of data that you need to collect and enter into the workbook.
3. **What calculations do I need to enter?** The answer defines the formulas you need to apply to the data you've collected and entered.
4. **What form should my solution take?** The answer defines the appearance of the workbook content and how it should be presented to others.

Amanda carefully considered these questions and developed the following plan as a guide for entering data in her workbook:

1. I need to know contact information for each customer, how many DVDs I create for customers, how much I charge customers, and how much revenue RipCity Digital is generating.
2. I need each customer's name and contact information, the order date, the number of DVDs created for each customer, and the cost of creating each DVD.
3. I need to calculate the total charge for each order, the total number of DVDs for all orders, and the total revenue generated from all orders.
4. Customer orders should be placed in a table with each row containing data on a different customer. Information about each customer should be placed in separate columns. The last column should contain the total charge for each customer. The last row should contain the total number of DVDs created and the total revenue from all customer orders.

PROSKILLS

Written Communication: Creating Effective Workbooks

Workbooks convey information in written form. As with any writing, the final product creates an impression and provides an indicator of your interest, knowledge, and attention to detail. To create the best impression, all workbooks—especially those you intend to share with others such as coworkers and clients—should be well planned, well organized, and well written.

A well-designed workbook should clearly identify its overall goal and present information in an organized format. The data it includes should be accurate both in the entered values and calculated values. Developing an effective workbook includes the following steps:

- Determine the workbook's purpose, content, and organization before you start.
- Create a list of the sheets used in the workbook, making note of each sheet's purpose.
- Insert a documentation sheet that describes the workbook's purpose and organization. Include the name of the workbook author, the date the workbook was created, and any additional information that will help others to track the workbook to its source.
- Enter all of the data in the workbook. Add text to indicate what the values represent and, if possible, where they originated so others can view the source of your data.
- Enter formulas for calculated items rather than entering the calculated values into the workbook. For more complicated calculations, provide documentation explaining them.
- Test the workbook with a variety of values; edit the data and formulas to correct errors.
- Save the workbook and create a backup copy when the project is completed. Print the workbook's contents if you need to provide a hard-copy version to others or for your files.
- Maintain a history of your workbook as it goes through different versions, so that you and others can quickly see how the workbook has changed during revisions.

By including clearly written documentation, explanatory text, a logical organization, and accurate data and formulas, you'll create effective workbooks that others can use easily.

Entering Text, Numbers, and Dates

Worksheet cells can contain text, numbers, or dates and times. **Text data** is any combination of letters, numbers, and symbols that form words and sentences. Text data is often referred to as a **text string** because it contains a string of text characters. **Number data** is any numerical value that can be used in a mathematical calculation. **Date** and **time data** are commonly recognized formats for date and time values. For example, Excel interprets the cell entry April 15, 2013 as a date and not as text. By default, text is left-aligned in cells, whereas numbers, dates, and times are right-aligned.

Entering Text

New data values are placed into the cell that is currently active in the worksheet. As you enter data, the entry appears in both the active cell and the formula bar. Amanda wants you to enter some of the information from the planning analysis sheet into the first sheet of the workbook. This worksheet will document the workbook's purpose and content.

To enter the text for the documentation sheet:

1. Press the **Ctrl+Home** keys to make cell A1 the active cell on the Sheet1 worksheet, if necessary.
2. Type **RipCity Digital Customer Orders** in cell A1. As you type, the text appears both in cell A1 and in the formula bar.
3. Press the **Enter** key twice. Excel enters the text into cell A1 and moves the active cell down two cells to cell A3.
4. Type **Author** in cell A3, and then press the **Tab** key. The text is entered and the active cell moves one cell to the right to cell B3.
5. Type your name in cell B3, and then press the **Enter** key. The text is entered and the active cell moves one cell down and to the left to cell A4.
6. Type **Date** in cell A4, and then press the **Tab** key. The text is entered and the active cell moves one cell to the right to cell B4, where you would enter the date you created the worksheet. For now, you'll leave the cell for the date blank.
7. Click cell **A5** to make it the active cell, type **Purpose** in the cell, and then press the **Tab** key. The active cell moves one cell to the right to cell B5.
8. Type **To record orders from RipCity Digital customers** in cell B5, and then press the **Enter** key. Figure 1-4 shows the text entered in the Sheet1 worksheet.

Figure 1-4 Documentation sheet

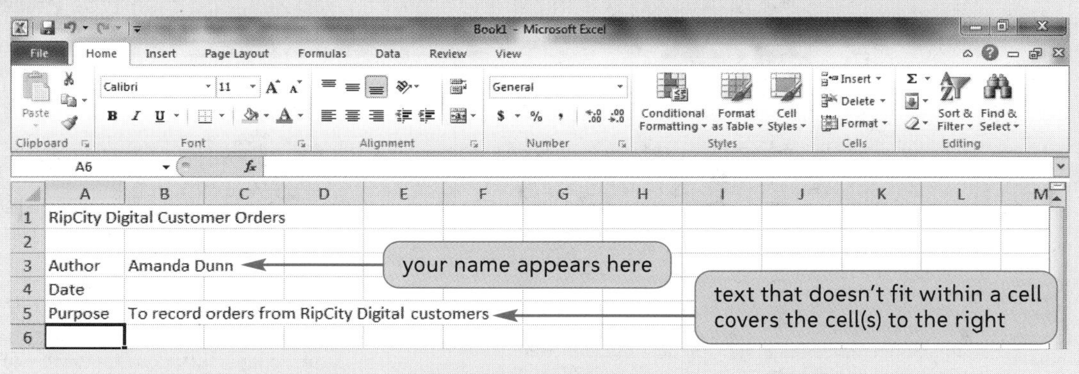

The text you entered in cell A1 is so long that it appears to flow into cells B1 and C1. The same is true for the text you entered in cells B3 and B5. Any text you enter in a cell that doesn't fit within that cell covers the adjacent cells to the right as long as they are empty. If the adjacent cells contain text or data, only the text that fits into the cell is displayed. The rest of the text entry is hidden, or **truncated**, from the view. The text itself is not affected. The complete text is still entered in the cell; it's just not displayed. To display all of the text, you must increase the cell's width, which you'll learn how to do in the next session.

Next, you'll enter the RipCity Digital customer orders. As shown in Figure 1-5, the orders will contain the name and address of each customer, the order date, the number of DVDs created from the customer's home videos, and the price per DVD. Amanda's price per DVD decreases for larger orders.

Figure 1-5 **Customer orders**

Last	First	Address	Date	DVDs	Price per DVD
Dawes	Gregory	402 Elm St. Merrill, MI 48637	3/13/2013	7	$17.29
Garcia	Susan	1025 Drake Ave. Exeter, NH 03833	3/14/2013	25	$15.79
Torbet	Dr. Lilla	5 North Ln. Oswego, NY 13126	3/17/2013	32	$12.99
Rhoden	Tony	24 Mountain Dr. Auburn, ME 04210	3/24/2013	20	$15.79

You'll enter this data in the Sheet2 worksheet.

To enter the text labels and customer names:

1. Click the **Sheet2** sheet tab. Sheet2 becomes the active worksheet. You'll enter the column labels in cells A1, B1, C1, D1, E1, and F1.
2. Type **Last** in cell A1, and then press the **Tab** key. The label is entered in cell A1 and the active cell moves to cell B1.
3. Type **First** in cell B1, and then press the **Tab** key. The label is entered in cell B1 and the active cell moves to cell C1.
4. Type **Address** in cell C1, and then press the **Tab** key.
5. Type **Date** in cell D1, and then press the **Tab** key.
6. Type **DVDs** in cell E1, press the **Tab** key, and then type **Price per DVD** in cell F1. You've typed all the labels for the customer orders.
7. Press the **Enter** key. The active cell moves to cell A2, the start of the next row where you want to begin entering the customer data.
8. Type **Dawes** in cell A2, press the **Tab** key, type **Gregory** in cell B2, and then press the **Tab** key. You've entered the first customer's name and moved the active cell to cell C2. Figure 1-6 shows the text you've entered so far.

Figure 1-6 Text entered for customer orders

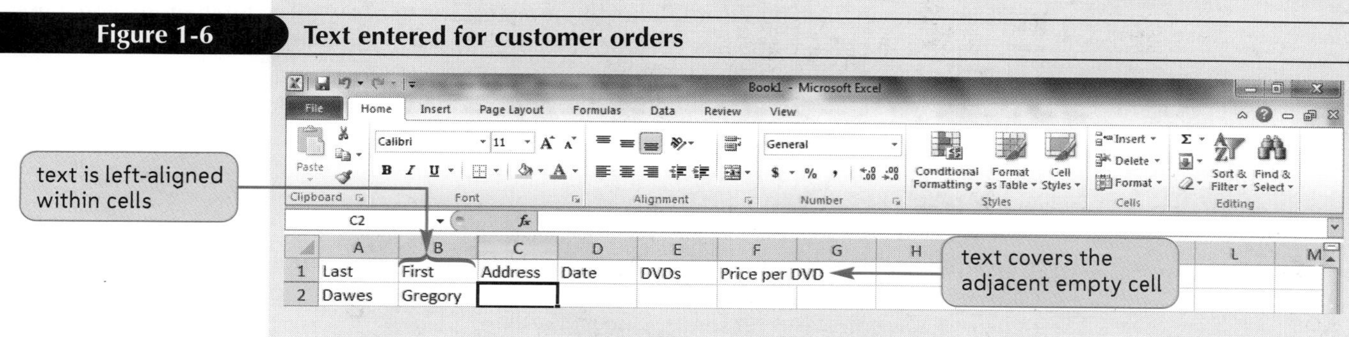

As you type text into the active cell, Excel tries to anticipate the remaining characters by displaying text that begins with the same letters as a previous entry in the same column. This feature, known as **AutoComplete**, helps make entering repetitive text easier. To accept the suggested text, press the Tab or Enter key. To override the suggested text, continue to type the text you want to enter in the cell. AutoComplete does not work with dates or numbers, or when a blank cell is between the previous entry and the text you're typing.

Entering Multiple Lines of Text Within a Cell

Addresses are often entered on two or more separate lines. Amanda wants you to follow that convention with her customers' addresses. To place text on separate lines within the same cell, you press and hold the Alt key while you press the Enter key. This creates a line break within the cell.

You'll enter the address for the first RipCity Digital customer, which will occupy two lines within the same cell.

To enter multiple lines of text within a cell:

1. Type **402 Elm St.** in cell C2, but do not press the Tab or Enter key. Instead, you'll insert a new line break.
2. Hold down the **Alt** key and press the **Enter** key, and then release both keys. The insertion point moves to a new line within cell C2.
3. Type **Merrill, MI 48637** on the new line, and then press the **Tab** key. The two lines of text are entered in cell C2, and cell D2 becomes the active cell. See Figure 1-7.

Be sure to hold down the Alt key as you press Enter; otherwise, only the first address line will be entered in cell C2.

Figure 1-7 Multiple lines of text entered in cell C2

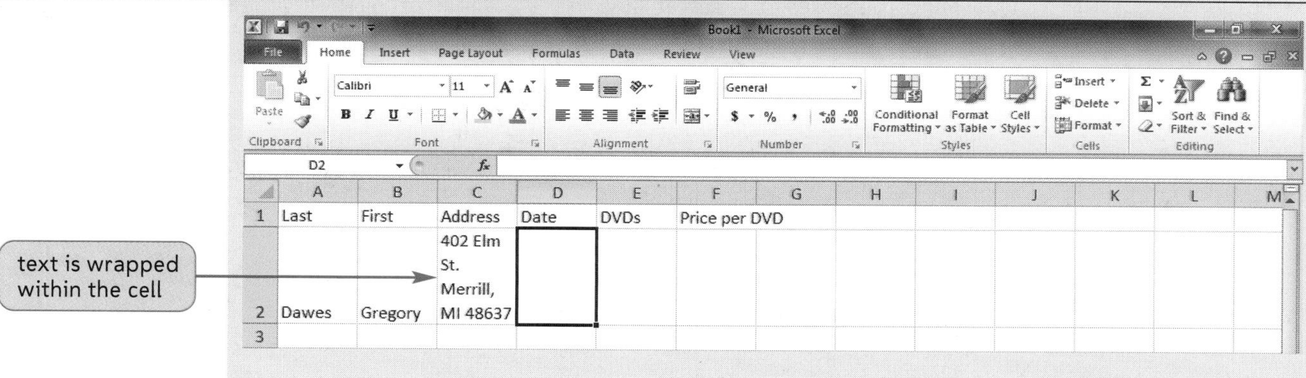

TIP

To force text that extends beyond a cell's border to fit within the cell, click the Wrap Text button in the Alignment group on the Home tab. The row height increases as needed to wrap all the text within the cell.

When you enter multiple lines of text within a cell, Excel confines the text within the cell's borders, increasing the cell's height, if necessary, to show all of the text. As you can see, the text in cell C2 appears on four lines even though you entered the address on two lines. The automatic reflow of text within a cell is referred to as wrapping. If the cell's width were increased, the text would then appear on two lines as Amanda wants. You'll do this in the next session.

Entering Dates

You can enter dates in any of the standard date formats. For example, you can enter the date April 6, 2013 in any of the following date formats (and many others) and Excel recognizes each entry as representing the same date:

- 4/6/2013
- 4/6/13
- 4-6-2013
- April 6, 2013
- 6-Apr-13

Even though you enter a date as text, Excel stores the date as a numeric value equal to the number of days between the specified date and January 0, 1900. This means that the date January 1, 1900 has a value of 1 and so forth. Times are also entered as text and are stored as fractional parts of a 24-hour day. Storing dates and times as numeric values allows Excel to perform date and time calculations, such as determining the elapsed time between one date and another.

Based on the default date format your computer uses, Excel might alter the date format you type. For example, if you enter the date 4/6/13 into the active cell, Excel might display the date with the four-digit year value, 4/6/2013; if you enter the text April 6, 2013, Excel might convert the date format to 6-Apr-13. Changing the date or time format doesn't affect the underlying date or time value.

For Amanda's workbook, you'll enter the dates in the format *m/d/yyyy*, where *m* is the 1- or 2-digit month number, *d* is the 1- or 2-digit day number, and *yyyy* is the 4-digit year number. You will enter the order date on the Sheet2 worksheet and the current date in the Sheet1 worksheet.

To enter the dates for the customer orders:

1. Type **3/13/2013** in cell D2, and then press the **Tab** key to move to cell E2. The date of Gregory Dawes's order appears in cell D2, and cell E2 becomes the active cell. The width of column D expands to display the full date.
2. Click the **Sheet1** sheet tab. The Sheet1 worksheet is the active worksheet.
3. Click cell **B4** to make it active, insert the current date using the format *m/d/yyyy*, and then press the **Enter** key.
4. Click the **Sheet2** sheet tab. The Sheet2 worksheet is the active worksheet, and cell E2 is still the active cell.

INSIGHT

International Date Formats

As business transactions become more international in scope, you may need to adopt international standards for expressing dates, times, and currency values in your workbooks. For example, a worksheet cell might contain 06/05/12. This format could represent any of the following dates:

- The 5th of June, 2012
- The 6th of May, 2012
- The 12th of May, 2006

The date depends on which country the workbook has been designed for. You can avoid this problem by entering the full date as in the example June 5, 2012. However, this will not work with documents written in foreign languages such as Japanese that use different character symbols.

To solve this problem, many international businesses adopt ISO (International Organization for Standardization) dates in the format *yyyy-mm-dd*, where *yyyy* is the four-digit year value, *mm* is the two-digit month value, and *dd* is the two-digit day value. So, a date such as June 5, 2012 is entered as 2012/06/05. If you choose to use this international date format, make sure that people using your workbook understand this format so they do not misinterpret the dates. You can include information about the date format in the documentation sheet.

Entering Numbers

TIP

If a number exceeds its cell size, you see ###### for the truncated numeric value. You can display the entire number by increasing the column width.

In Excel, numbers can be integers such as 378, decimals such as 1.95, or negatives such as –5.2. In the case of currency and percentages, you can include the currency symbol and percent sign when you enter the value. Excel treats a currency value such as $87.25 as the number 87.25, and a percentage such as 95% as the decimal 0.95. Currency and percentages, like dates, are formatted in a convenient way for you to read. Excel right-aligns numbers within each cell.

You'll complete the information for Gregory Dawes's order by entering the number of DVDs Amanda created for him and the price she charged him for each DVD.

To enter numbers for the first customer order:

1. Type **7** in cell E2, and then press the **Tab** key. The order quantity for Gregory Dawes is entered and the active cell is cell F2.
2. Type **$17.29** in cell F2, and then press the **Enter** key. The currency value is entered in cell F2. Note that Excel enters the number 17.29 in the cell and formats it as currency.
3. Click cell **A3**, which is where you want to enter the information for the next customer. See Figure 1-8.

Figure 1-8 **First customer order data**

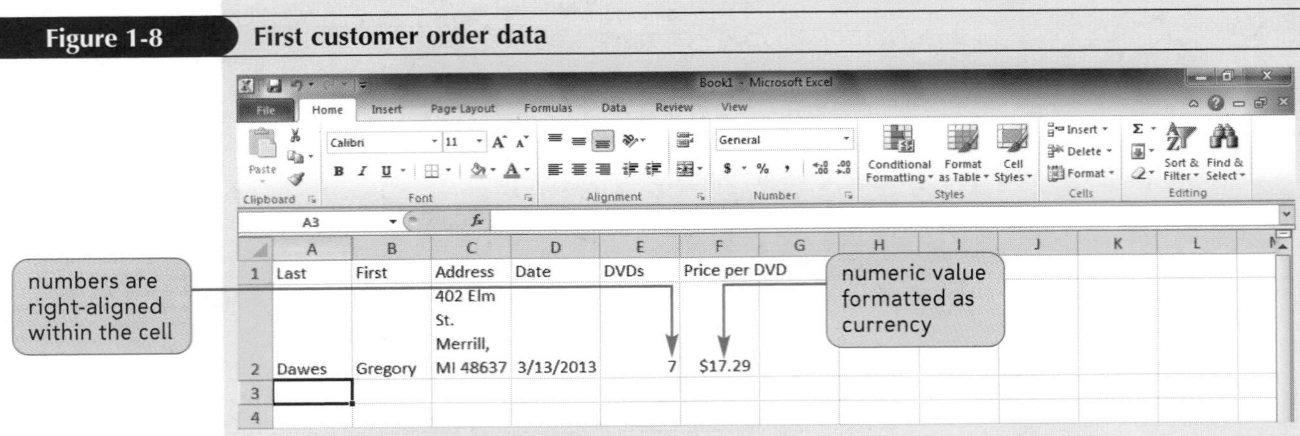

You've completed the data entry for Amanda's first customer. You still need to enter the data for three more customers into the worksheet. You'll use the same techniques you used to enter Gregory Dawes's order to enter their data.

To enter the remaining customer order data:

1. Type **Garcia** in cell A3, press the **Tab** key, type **Susan** in cell B3, and then press the **Tab** key. The second customer name is entered.
2. Type **1025 Drake Ave.** in cell C3, press the **Alt+Enter** keys, type **Exeter, NH 03833** on the next line, and then press the **Tab** key. The second customer's address is entered in the cell on two lines.
3. Type **3/14/2013** in cell D3, press the **Tab** key, type **25** in cell E3, press the **Tab** key, type **$15.79** in cell F3, and then press the **Enter** key. The rest of the second customer's data is entered.
4. Enter the following data for the remaining two customers in rows 4 and 5, making sure that you press the Alt+Enter keys to enter the addresses on two lines. Because column C is not wide enough to display the entire address text, it wraps within the cell and the zip code may be hidden. You'll correct this shortly. See Figure 1-9.

   Torbet, Dr. Lilla
   5 North Ln.
   Oswego, NY 13126
   3/17/2013, 32, $12.99

   Rhoden, Tony
   24 Mountain Dr.
   Auburn, ME 04210
   3/24/2013, 20, $15.79

Figure 1-9 Customer orders for RipCity Digital

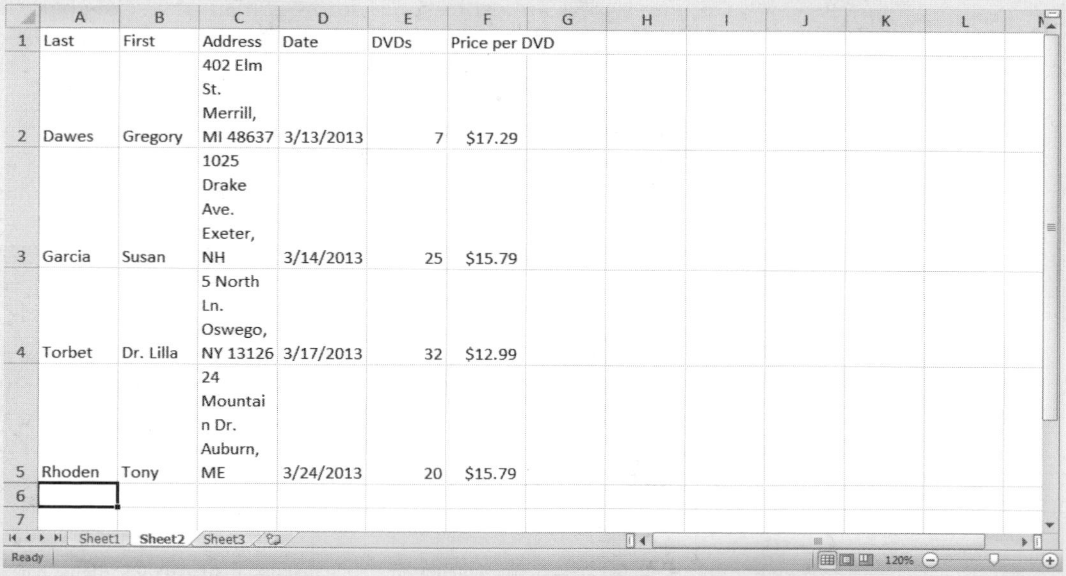

	A	B	C	D	E	F	G	H	I	J	K	L
1	Last	First	Address	Date	DVDs	Price per DVD						
2	Dawes	Gregory	402 Elm St. Merrill, MI 48637	3/13/2013	7	$17.29						
3	Garcia	Susan	1025 Drake Ave. Exeter, NH	3/14/2013	25	$15.79						
4	Torbet	Dr. Lilla	5 North Ln. Oswego, NY 13126	3/17/2013	32	$12.99						
5	Rhoden	Tony	24 Mountai n Dr. Auburn, ME	3/24/2013	20	$15.79						
6												
7												

Sheet1 Sheet2 Sheet3

Ready 120%

Working with Columns and Rows

Amanda has reviewed the customer order data you entered in the worksheet. She asks you to make the data easier to read. You can do this by modifying the size of the columns and rows in the worksheet.

REFERENCE

Changing the Column Width or Row Height

- Drag the right border of the column heading left to decrease the column width or right to increase the column width.
- Drag the bottom border of the row heading up to decrease the row height or down to increase the row height.

or

- Double-click the right border of a column heading or the bottom border of a row heading to autofit the column or row to the cell contents (or select one or more columns or rows, click the Home tab on the Ribbon, click the Format button in the Cells group, and then click AutoFit Column Width or AutoFit Row Height).

or

- Select one or more columns or rows.
- Click the Home tab on the Ribbon, click the Format button in the Cells group, and then click Column Width or Row Height.
- Enter the column width or row height you want, and then click the OK button.

Setting Column Widths

The default sizes of the columns and rows in a worksheet might not always accommodate the information you need to enter. This is what happened with the addresses you entered in the worksheet when Excel wrapped the text in ways that made the text difficult to read. Other times, long cell content might be truncated, hiding text or numeric values from the user. To make the cell content easier to read, you can resize the columns and rows in the worksheet.

Column widths are expressed in terms of the number of characters the column can contain. The default column width is 8.43 standard-sized characters. This means that, in general, you can type eight characters in a cell before that entry is truncated, overlaps the adjacent cell, or is wrapped to a new line within the cell. If the font size of the text in the cell is reduced, you can insert more characters within the cell.

Column widths are also expressed in terms of pixels. A **pixel** is a single point on a computer monitor or printout. A column width of 8.43 characters equals 64 pixels.

INSIGHT

Setting Column Widths

Pixel size is based on screen resolution. As a result, cell contents that look fine on one screen might be truncated when viewed on a screen with different resolution. If you work on multiple computers or share your workbooks with others, you should set column widths based on the maximum number of characters you want to display in the cells rather than pixel size. This ensures that everyone sees the cell contents the way you intended.

You will increase the width of the Address column to allow the addresses to appear on two lines in the cells without additional line wrapping.

To increase the width of column C:

1. Move the pointer over the right border of the column C heading until the pointer changes to ↔.
2. Click and drag to the right until the width of the column heading reaches **20** characters, but do not release the mouse button. The ScreenTip that appears as you resize the column shows the measurements of the new column width first as the number of characters and second in parentheses as pixels.
3. Release the mouse button. The width of column C expands to 20 characters and all the addresses fit on two lines with no extra line wrapping. See Figure 1-10.

Figure 1-10 **Increased column width**

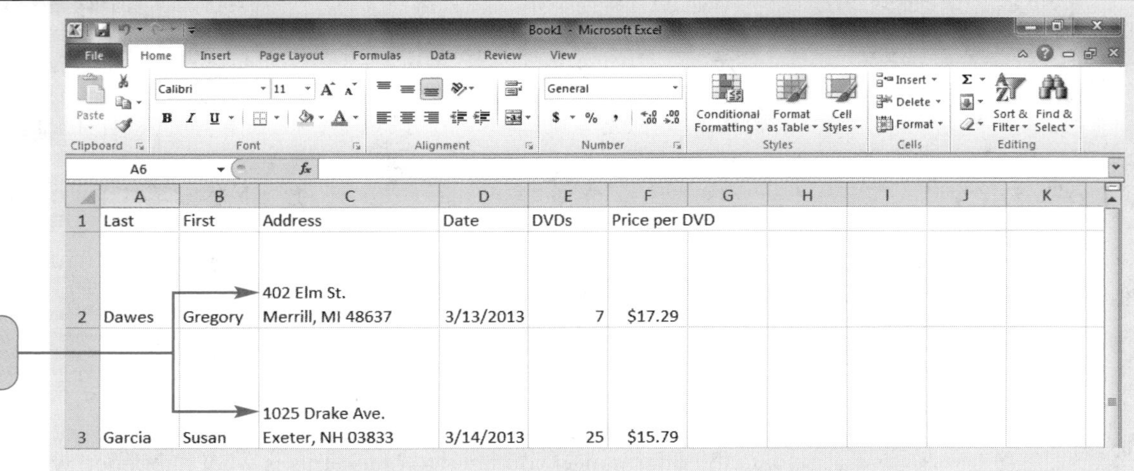

Amanda also wants you to increase the widths of columns A and B to 15 characters to accommodate longer names. Rather than resizing each column separately, you can select both columns and adjust their widths at the same time.

TIP

To select multiple columns, you can also click and drag the pointer over multiple column headings.

To increase the widths of columns A and B:

1. Click the **column A** heading. The entire column is selected.
2. Hold down the **Ctrl** key, click the **column B** heading, and then release the **Ctrl** key. Both columns A and B are selected.
3. Move the pointer to the right border of the column B heading until the pointer changes to ✛.
4. Drag to the right until the column width changes to **15** characters, and then release the mouse button. Both columns are wide enough to display longer names.

The text in cell F1, Price per DVD, overflows the cell borders. This column would look better if you increased the width of column F to 12 characters. You can set the column width using the Format command on the Home tab. The Format command gives you precise control in setting column widths and row heights.

To set the width of column F to 12 characters:

1. Click the **column F** heading. The entire column is selected.
2. In the Cells group on the Home tab, click the **Format** button, and then click **Column Width**. The Column Width dialog box opens.
3. Type **12** in the Column width box, and then click the **OK** button. The width of column F changes to 12 characters, placing the text in cell F1 entirely within the borders of the cell.

Setting Row Heights

The height of an Excel row is measured in points or pixels. A **point** is approximately 1/72 of an inch. The default row height is 15 points or 20 pixels. Row heights are set in the same way as column widths. You can drag the bottom border of the row to a new row height or define a specific row height using the Format command. Another option is to autofit the row's height (or the column's width) to match its content. **Autofitting** eliminates empty space by matching the row height or column width to its tallest or longest cell entry. If the row or column is blank, Excel restores its default height or width.

The row heights didn't change after you resized the columns, which leaves a lot of blank space in the four rows of customer data. This extra blank space makes the data difficult to read and extends the content out of view. Amanda wants you to autofit the heights of these rows to remove that empty space.

To autofit the second row to match its contents:

1. Move the pointer over the bottom border of the row 2 heading until the pointer changes to ✚.
2. Double-click the bottom border of row 2. The height of row 2 shrinks to match the content of cell C2, which is the tallest entry in the row, with two lines of text.

You could continue to resize the remaining rows one at a time, but a quicker way is to select the rows you want to resize and then autofit all the selected rows simultaneously.

To autofit rows 3 through 5:

1. Drag the pointer across the row headings for rows 3, 4, and 5. The contents of rows 3 through 5 are selected.
2. In the Cells group on the Home tab, click the **Format** button. A menu of commands opens.
3. Click **AutoFit Row Height**. The height of each of the three rows autofits to its contents, and all the empty space is removed.
4. Click cell **A1** to make it the active cell. The other cells in the worksheet are deselected. Figure 1-11 shows the worksheet with the revised row heights.

Figure 1-11 Row heights after autofitting to contents

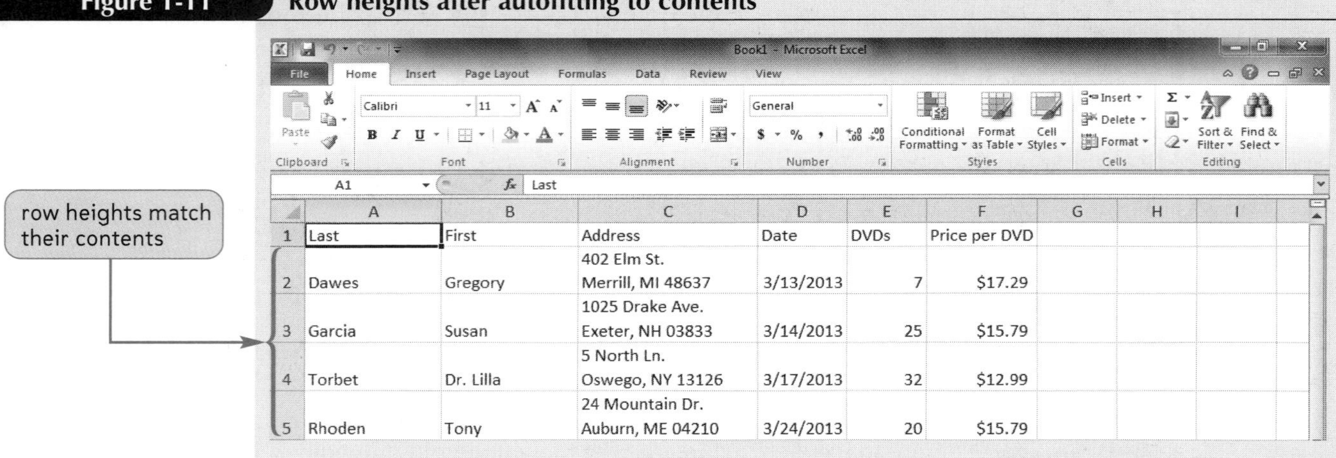

Inserting a Column or Row

You can insert a new column or row anywhere within a worksheet. When you insert a new column, the existing columns are shifted to the right and the new column has the same width as the column directly to its left. When you insert a new row, the existing rows are shifted down and the new row has the same height as the row above it.

REFERENCE

Inserting a Column or Row

- Select the column(s) or row(s) where you want to insert the new column(s) or row(s); Excel will insert the same number of columns or rows as you select to the left of the selected columns or above the selected rows.
- In the Cells group on the Home tab, click the Insert button (or right-click a column or row heading or selected column and row headings, and then click Insert on the shortcut menu).

You will insert a column for customer phone numbers between the Address column and the Date column, and then enter the customer phone numbers in the new column.

To insert the new column:

1. Click the **column D** heading to select the entire column.
2. In the Cells group on the Home tab, click the **Insert** button. A new column D is inserted into the worksheet and the rest of the columns shift to the right. The new column has the same width as column C.
3. Reduce the width of column D to **15** characters.
4. Click cell **D1** to make it the active cell, type **Phone** as the label, and then press the **Enter** key. The new column label is entered in cell D1, and cell D2 becomes the active cell.
5. Enter the phone numbers in cells D2, D3, D4, and D5, as shown in Figure 1-12, pressing the **Enter** key after each entry.

Figure 1-12 New column inserted into the worksheet

	A	B	C	D	E	F	G
1	Last	First	Address	Phone	Date	DVDs	Price per DVD
2	Dawes	Gregory	402 Elm St. Merrill, MI 48637	(989) 555-3433	3/13/2013	7	$17.29
3	Garcia	Susan	1025 Drake Ave. Exeter, NH 03833	(603) 555-1091	3/14/2013	25	$15.79
4	Torbet	Dr. Lilla	5 North Ln. Oswego, NY 13126	(315) 555-7823	3/17/2013	32	$12.99
5	Rhoden	Tony	24 Mountain Dr. Auburn, ME 04210	(207) 555-9915	3/24/2013	20	$15.79

new column content

inserted column

existing columns shifted to the right

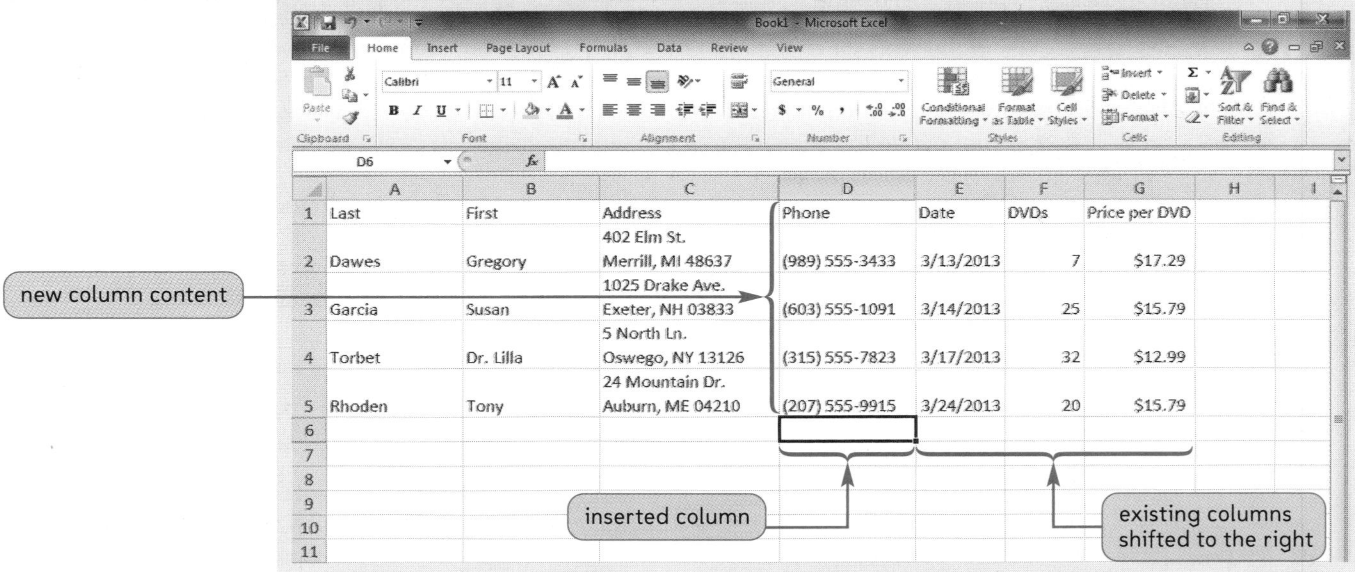

Amanda neglected to include a customer order. Because the customer was RipCity Digital's first customer, Amanda wants this order inserted at the top of the list. To add this new order, you need to insert a new row in the worksheet below the column labels.

To insert the new row:

1. Click the **row 2** heading. The entire second row is selected.
2. In the Cells group on the Home tab, click the **Insert** button. A new row 2 is inserted, and the remaining rows shift down.
3. Enter the new customer order shown in Figure 1-13 into row 2.

Figure 1-13 New row inserted into the worksheet

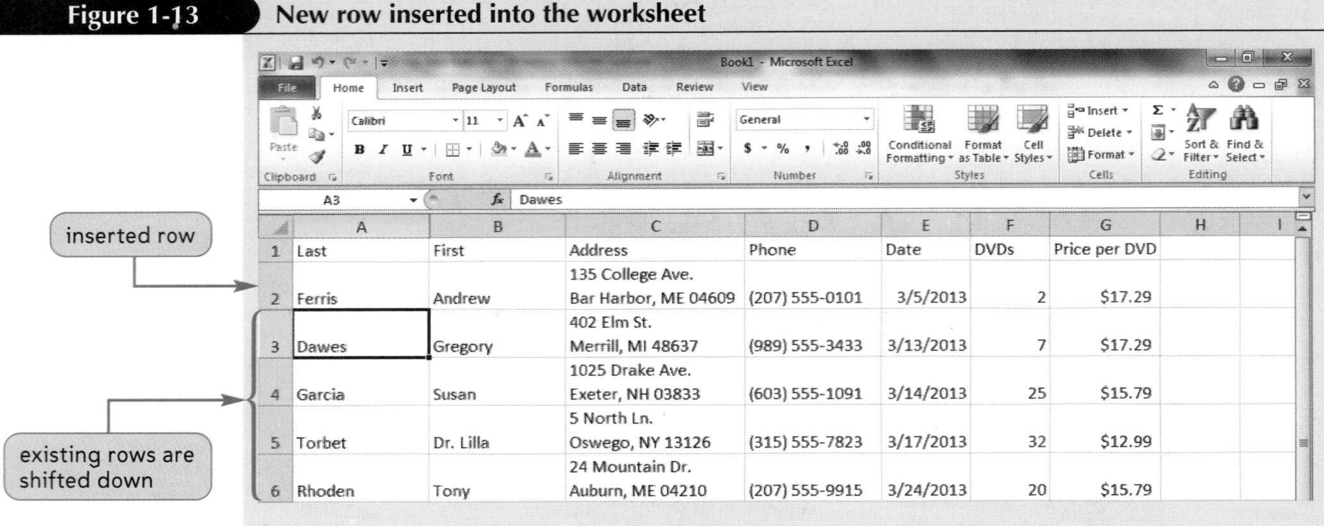

Deleting and Clearing a Row or Column

You can remove data in two ways: clearing and deleting. **Clearing** data from a worksheet removes the data, leaving blank cells where the data had been. **Deleting** data from the worksheet removes both the data and the cells. When a cell is deleted, the remaining cells in the worksheet shift into the deleted location. For example, when you delete a column, the columns to the right shift left to fill the vacated space. Similarly, the rows below a deleted row shift up to fill the vacated space. Note that pressing the Delete key does not *delete* the selected row or column; instead, it *clears* the contents, leaving the row or column in place.

Gregory Dawes just canceled his order. Amanda wants you to remove this order from the worksheet. You'll first clear Gregory Dawes's data from the worksheet and then delete the row that contained the data. Usually, you would do this in one step by simply deleting the row, but this will highlight the difference between clearing and deleting.

To clear and delete the third row:

1. Click the **row 3** heading. The entire row 3 with Gregory Dawes's order is selected.
2. Right-click the **row 3** heading, and then click **Clear Contents** on the shortcut menu. Excel clears the values in the third row, but leaves the blank row in that space.
3. Verify that the third row is still selected.
4. In the Cells group on the Home tab, click the **Delete** button. The third row is deleted, and the rows below it shift up. Only four customer orders remain in the worksheet.

Before continuing, you'll save your workbook with a descriptive name.

To save the current workbook:

1. Click the **File** tab on the Ribbon to display Backstage view.
2. Click the **Save** command in the navigation bar. The Save As dialog box opens because this is the first time you are saving this workbook.
3. Navigate to the **Excel1\Tutorial** folder included with your Data Files.

   Trouble? If you don't have the starting Data Files, you need to get them before you can proceed. Your instructor will either give you the Data Files or ask you to obtain them from a specified location (such as a network drive). In either case, make a backup copy of the Data Files before you start so that you will have the original files available in case you need to start over. If you have any questions about the Data Files, see your instructor or technical support person for assistance.
4. Verify that **Excel Workbook** appears in the Save as type box.

   Trouble? If your computer is set up to show filename extensions, you will see the Excel file extension .xlsx in the Save as type box as well.
5. Select **Book1** in the File name box, and then type **RipCity Digital Orders**. The default filename Book1 is replaced with the name you entered.
6. Click the **Save** button. The Save As dialog box closes and the workbook file is saved with its descriptive filename.

TIP

You can click the Save As command in the navigation bar to save a previously saved workbook with a new filename, to a different location, or in another file format.

So far, you have entered the customer order data. In the process, you worked with rows and columns. In the next session, you'll learn how to work with individual cells and groups of cells. You will also add calculations to the worksheet to determine how much revenue Amanda will generate from these orders.

REVIEW

Session 1.1 Quick Check

1. What are the two types of sheets used in a workbook?
2. List two ways of identifying the active cell in the worksheet.
3. What is the cell reference for the cell located in the fourth column and third row of a worksheet?
4. What keyboard shortcut changes the active cell to cell A1?
5. What is text data?
6. What keys do you press to start a new line of text within a cell?
7. Cell A4 contains May 3, 2013; why doesn't Excel consider this entry a text string?
8. Explain the difference between clearing a row and deleting a row.

SESSION 1.2 VISUAL OVERVIEW

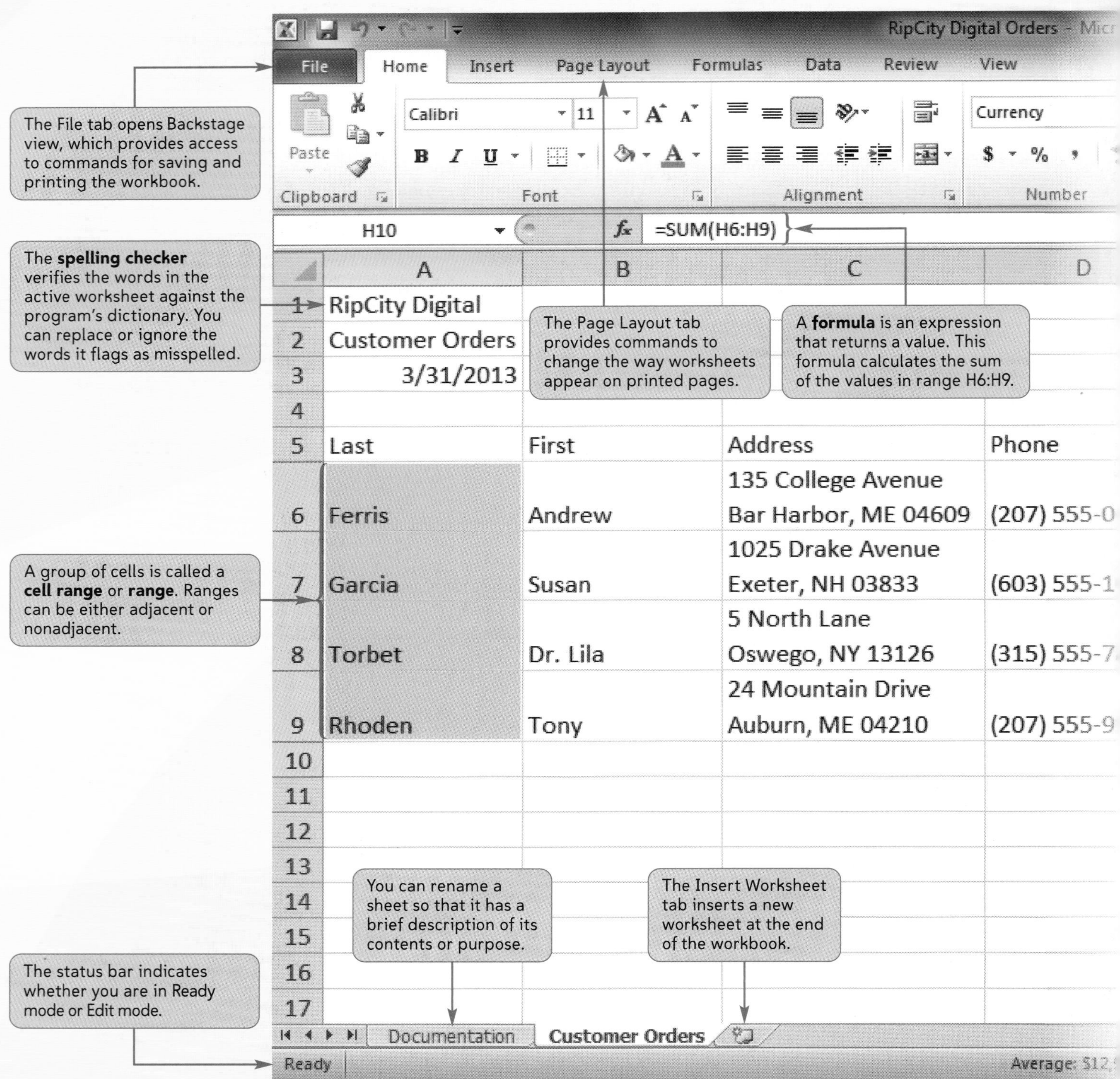

WORKSHEET DATA

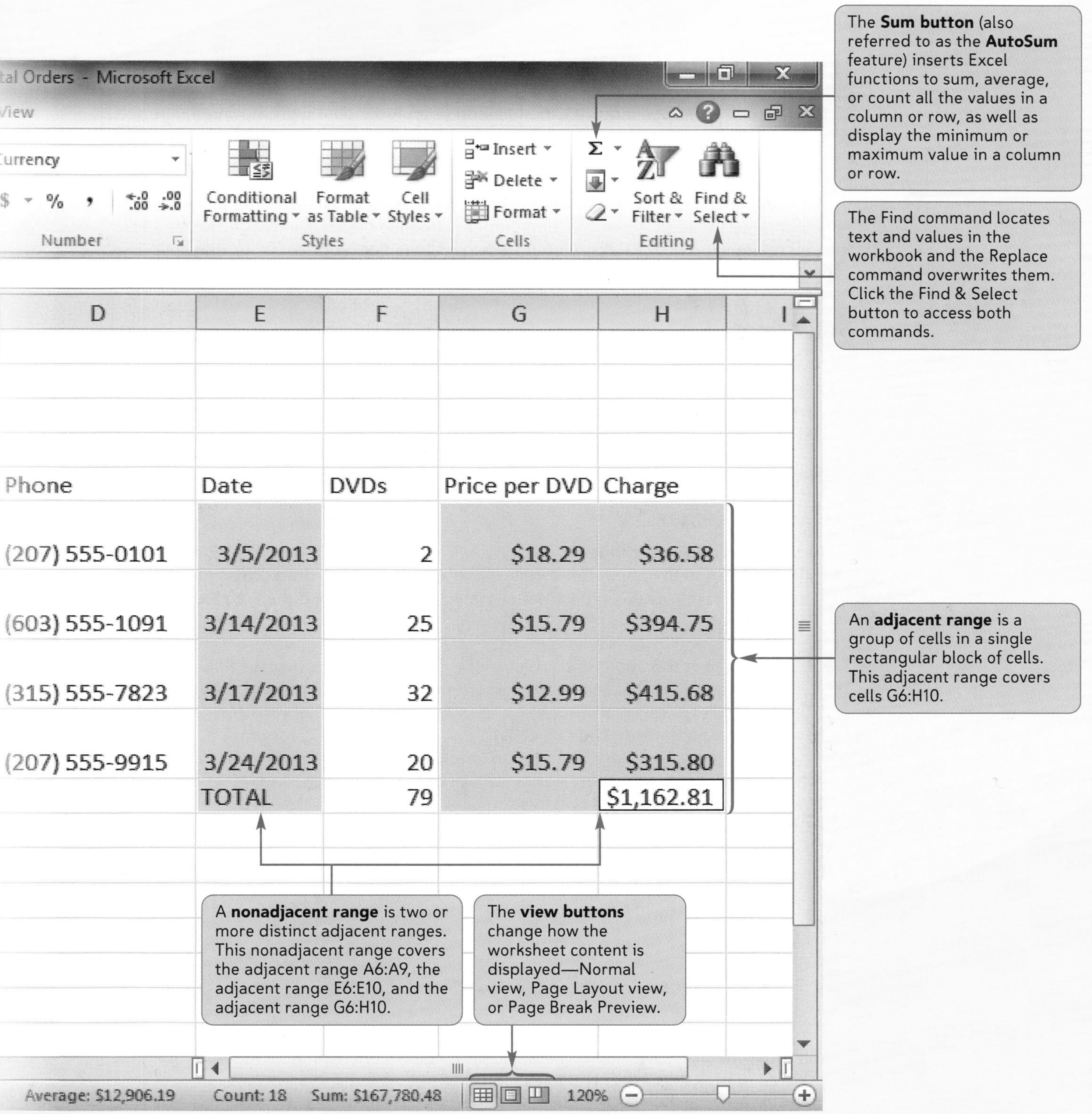

Working with Cells and Ranges

In the previous session, you worked with entire columns or rows of cells. In this session you'll work with groups of worksheet cells, or ranges. The customer order data you entered in cells A1 through G5 forms an adjacent range because it covers one rectangular block of cells. All the last names in cells A1 through A5 and all the numbers in cells F1 through G5 together form a nonadjacent range because they are two distinct rectangular blocks of cells.

Just as a cell reference indicates the location of an individual worksheet cell, a **range reference** indicates the location and size of a cell range. For adjacent ranges, the range reference includes the cell reference of the upper-left and lower-right cells in the rectangular block separated by a colon. For example, the range reference A1:G5 refers to all the cells in the rectangular block from cells A1 through G5. The range reference for nonadjacent ranges separates each adjacent range reference by a semicolon. For example, the cell reference A1:A5;F1:G5 references two rectangular blocks of cells: one covering cells A1 through A5 and the other covering cells F1 through G5.

Selecting a Range

You can select adjacent and nonadjacent ranges of cells with your mouse, just as you selected individual cells. Selecting a range enables you to work with all of the cells in the range as a group. This means you can move the groups of cells, delete them, or clear all their contents at the same time.

REFERENCE

Selecting Ranges

To select an adjacent range:
- Click the cell in the upper-left corner of the adjacent range, drag the pointer to the cell in the lower-right corner of the adjacent range, and then release the mouse button.

or
- Click the cell in the upper-left corner of the adjacent range, press the Shift key as you click the cell in the lower-right corner of the adjacent range, and then release the Shift key.

To select a nonadjacent range of cells:
- Select a cell or an adjacent range, press the Ctrl key as you select each additional cell or adjacent range, and then release the Ctrl key.

To select all the cells in a worksheet:
- Click the Select All button located at the intersection of the row and column headings (or press the Ctrl+A keys).

To select an entire row or entire rows:
- Click a row heading to select a single row. To select multiple rows, click and drag the pointer over multiple row headings.

To select an entire column or entire columns:
- Click a column heading to select a single column. To select multiple columns, click and drag the pointer over multiple column headings.

You'll use the pointer to select the adjacent range A1:G5, which includes all the content you entered in the orders worksheet.

To select the adjacent range A1:G5:

1. If you took a break at the end of the previous session, make sure the RipCity Digital Orders workbook is open and the Sheet2 worksheet is active.
2. Click cell **A1** to select that cell, and then with the mouse button still pressed, drag the pointer to cell **G5**, which is the cell in the lower-right corner of the range A1:G5.
3. Release the mouse button. As shown in Figure 1-14, all the cells in the adjacent range A1:G5 are selected. The selected cells are highlighted with color and surrounded by a black border. The first cell you selected, cell A1, is still the active cell in the worksheet.

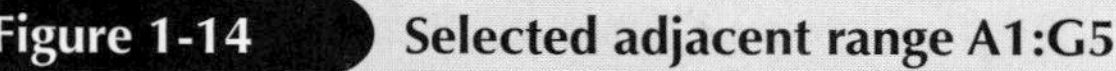

Figure 1-14 Selected adjacent range A1:G5

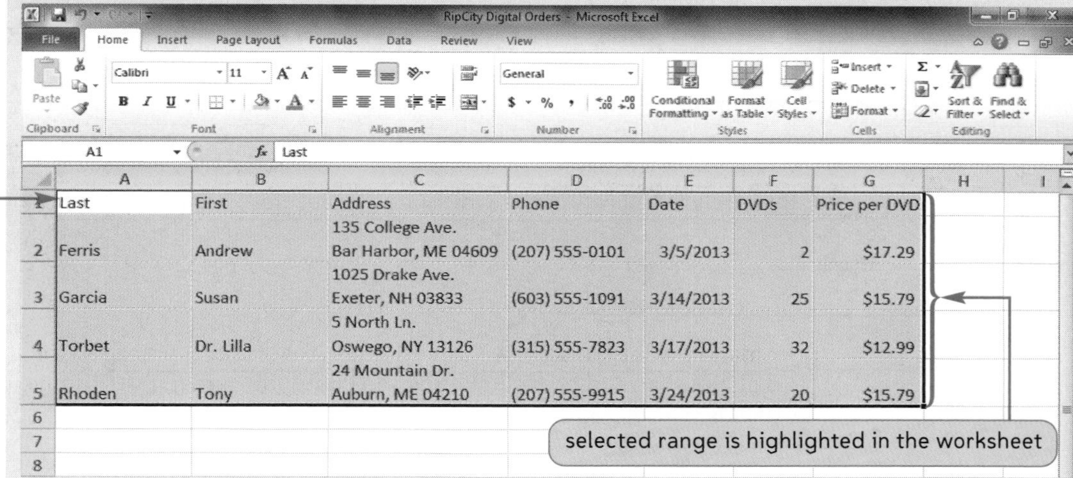

4. Click any cell in the worksheet to deselect the range.

Next, you'll use the pointer to select the nonadjacent range A1:A5;F1:G5.

To select the nonadjacent range A1:A5;F1:G5:

1. Select the adjacent range **A1:A5** with your mouse.
2. Hold down the **Ctrl** key, and then select the adjacent range **F1:G5**.
3. Release the **Ctrl** key. As shown in Figure 1-15, all the cells in the nonadjacent range A1:A5;F1:G5 are selected.

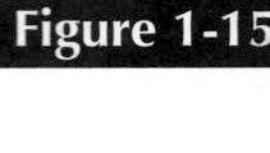

Figure 1-15 **Selected nonadjacent range A1:A5;F1:G5**

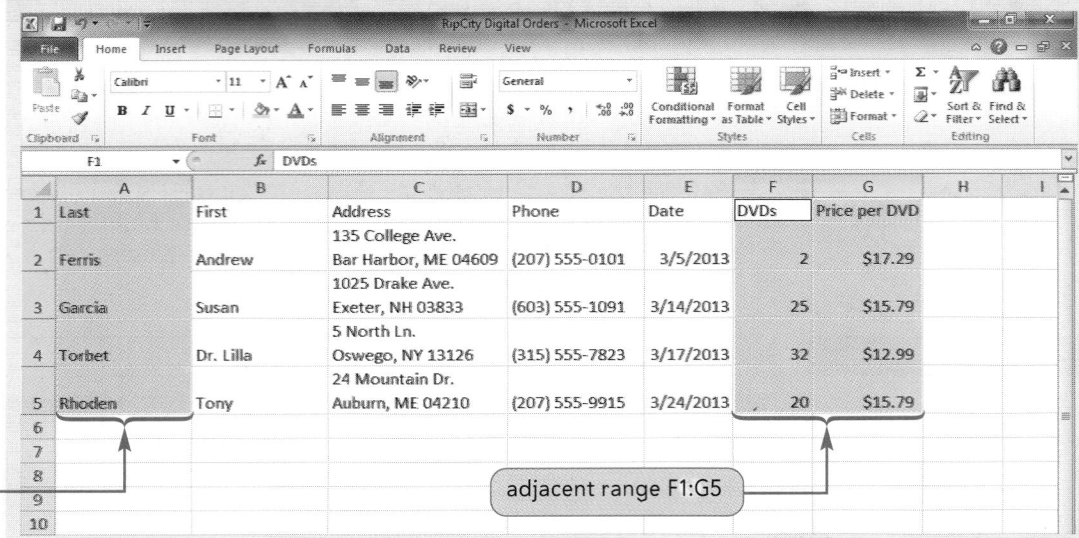

4. Click any cell in the worksheet to deselect the range.

Moving and Copying a Range

Amanda wants you to insert titles into the worksheet that describe the customer order data you have entered. Including the company name, a descriptive title, and the current date is part of good worksheet design, enabling others to quickly see the *who, what,* and *when* of the data. The current worksheet has no space to add this information. You could insert several blank rows at the top of the worksheet for this information. Another option is to select and then move the customer data lower in the worksheet, freeing up the rows at the top for the new text.

REFERENCE

Moving or Copying a Cell or Range

- Select the cell or range you want to move or copy.
- Move the pointer over the border of the selection until the pointer changes shape.
- To move the range, click the border and drag the selection to a new location (or to copy the range, hold down the Ctrl key and drag the selection to a new location).

or

- Select the cell or range you want to move or copy.
- In the Clipboard group on the Home tab, click the Cut button or the Copy button (or right-click the selection, and then click Cut or Copy on the shortcut menu).
- Select the cell or upper-left cell of the range where you want to move or copy the content.
- In the Clipboard group, click the Paste button (or right-click the selection, and then click Paste on the shortcut menu).

TIP

To move to a location that is not visible, drag the selection to the edge of the worksheet window until it scrolls down or across, and then drop the selection into the new location.

One way to move a cell or range is to select it, position the pointer over the bottom border of the selection, and then drag the selection to a new location. This technique is called **drag and drop** because you are dragging the range and dropping it in a new location. You can also use the drag-and-drop technique to copy cells by pressing the Ctrl key as you drag the selected range to its new location. A copy of the original range is placed in the new location without removing the original range from the worksheet.

You'll use the drag-and-drop method to move the customer order data to a new location in the worksheet.

To drag and drop the customer order data:

1. Select the range **A1:G5**.
2. Move the pointer over the bottom border of the selected range so that the pointer changes to ✥.
3. Press and hold the mouse button to change the pointer to ↖, and then drag the selection down three rows. Do not release the mouse button. A ScreenTip appears, indicating the new range reference of the selected cells. See Figure 1-16.

Figure 1-16 Selected range being moved

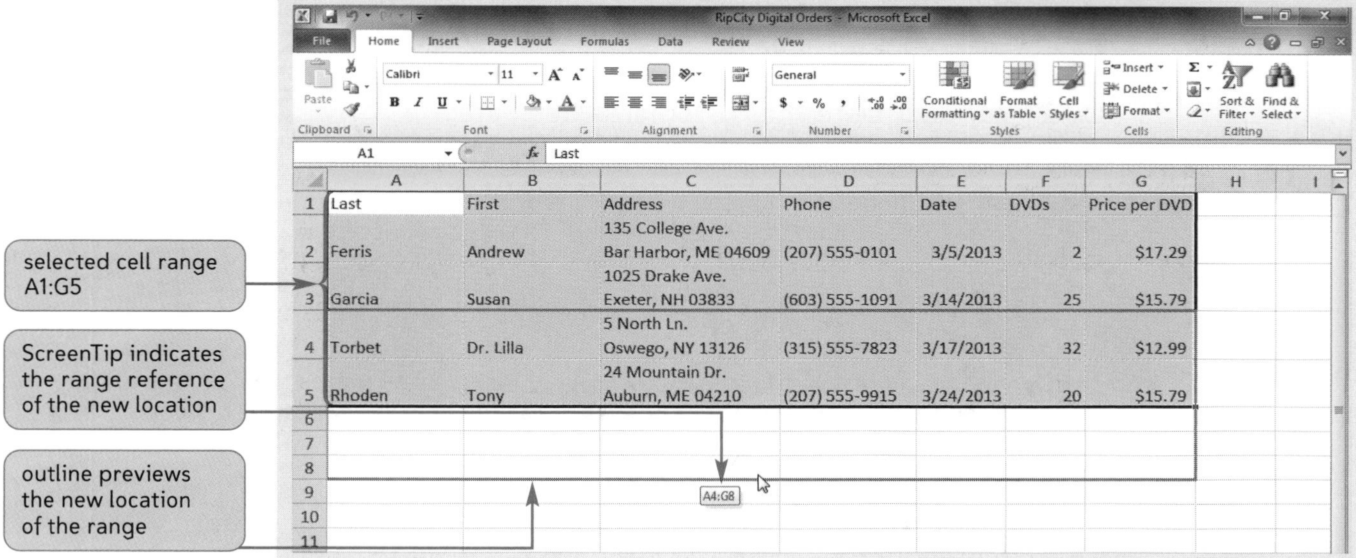

	A	B	C	D	E	F	G
1	Last	First	Address	Phone	Date	DVDs	Price per DVD
2	Ferris	Andrew	135 College Ave. Bar Harbor, ME 04609	(207) 555-0101	3/5/2013	2	$17.29
3	Garcia	Susan	1025 Drake Ave. Exeter, NH 03833	(603) 555-1091	3/14/2013	25	$15.79
4	Torbet	Dr. Lilla	5 North Ln. Oswego, NY 13126	(315) 555-7823	3/17/2013	32	$12.99
5	Rhoden	Tony	24 Mountain Dr. Auburn, ME 04210	(207) 555-9915	3/24/2013	20	$15.79

4. When the ScreenTip displays the range A4:G8, release the mouse button. The selected cells move to their new location.
5. Enter the title information shown in Figure 1-17 in the range A1:A3, pressing the **Enter** key after each entry.

Figure 1-17 **Titles added to the worksheet**

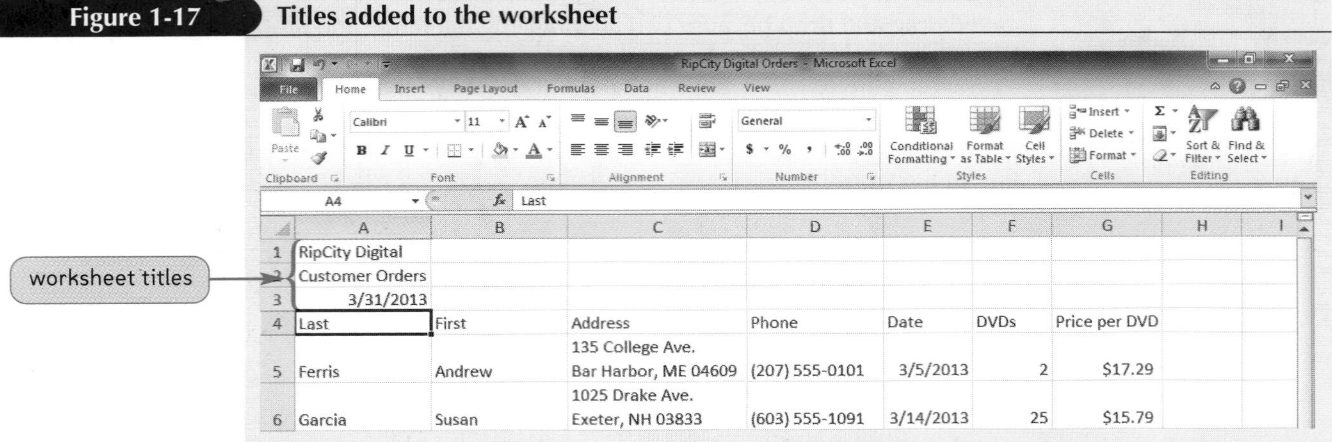

Some people find dragging and dropping a difficult and awkward way to move a selection, particularly if the worksheet is large and complex. In those situations, it's often more efficient to cut and paste the cell contents. **Cutting** places the cell contents into computer memory or on the Clipboard. The contents can then be pasted from the Clipboard into a new location in the worksheet. You'll cut and paste a range now.

To cut and paste the customer order data:

1. Select the range **A4:G8**.
2. In the Clipboard group on the Home tab, click the **Cut** button. The selected range is surrounded by a blinking border, which indicates that its contents are stored on the Clipboard.
3. Click cell **A11**. This cell is the upper-left corner of the range where you want to paste the data.
4. In the Clipboard group, click the **Paste** button. Excel pastes the contents of the range A4:G8 into the new range A11:G15. The blinking border disappears as a visual clue that the Clipboard is now empty.
5. With the range **A11:G15** still selected, click the **Cut** button in the Clipboard group.
6. Click cell **A4**, and then click the **Paste** button in the Clipboard group. The customer order data is pasted into its original location in the range A4:G8.

Inserting and Deleting a Range

Amanda wants more space between the three title rows you just entered and the table of customer orders. You could simply move the range A4:G8 down one more row, but another way is to insert new cells between the titles and the order data.

When you insert a new range of cells with the Insert button, the existing cells shift down when the selected range is wider than it is long, and they shift right when the selected range is longer than it is wide (as shown in Figure 1-18). When you use the Insert Cells command, you specify whether the existing cells shift right or down, or whether to insert an entire row or column into the new range.

Figure 1-18 **Cells being inserted into a worksheet**

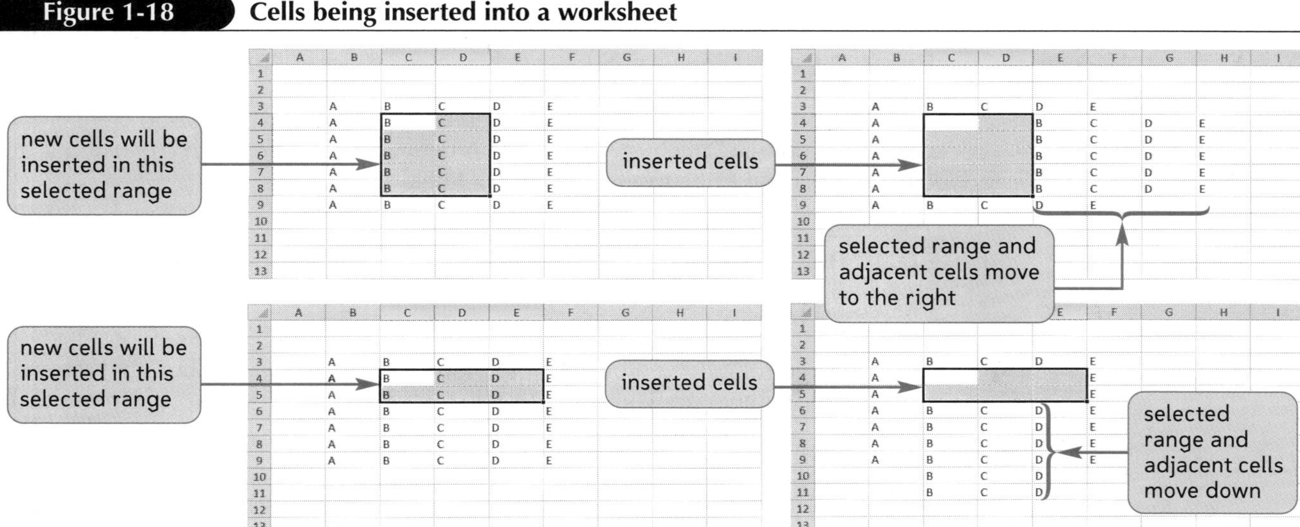

The process works in reverse when you delete a range. As with deleting a row or column, the cells adjacent to the deleted range either move up or left to fill in the space left by the deleted cells. The Delete Cells command lets you specify whether you want to shift the adjacent cells left or up, or whether to delete the entire column or row.

REFERENCE

Inserting or Deleting a Range

- Select a range that matches the range you want to insert or delete.
- In the Cells group on the Home tab, click the Insert button or the Delete button.

or

- Select the range that matches the range you want to insert or delete.
- In the Cells group on the Home tab, click the Insert button arrow and then click Insert Cells, or click the Delete button arrow and then click Delete Cells (or right-click the selected range, and then click Insert or Delete on the shortcut menu).
- Click the option button for the direction to shift the cells, columns, or rows.
- Click the OK button.

You will insert a blank range of cells between the worksheet titles and the table of customer orders.

To insert the cell range:

1. Select the range **A4:G4**. You want to insert blank cells in this range.
2. In the Cells group on the Home tab, click the **Insert button arrow**, and then click **Insert Cells**. The Insert dialog box opens.
3. Verify that the **Shift cells down** option button is selected.
4. Click the **OK** button. The existing cells shift down and the new cells are inserted into the range A4:G4.

Working with Formulas

So far you have entered only text, numbers, and dates in the worksheet. However, the main reason for using Excel is to display values calculated from data. For example, Amanda wants the workbook to determine the number of DVDs she has to create for her customers and how much revenue these orders will generate. Such calculations are added to a worksheet using formulas and functions.

Entering a Formula

A formula is an expression that returns a value. In most cases, this is a numeric value though it could also be a text string, a yes/no value, or a date. Every Excel formula begins with an equal sign (=) followed by an expression describing the operation that returns the value. Note that if you don't begin the formula with the equal sign, Excel assumes that you are entering text and will not treat the cell contents as a formula.

A formula is written using **operators** that combine different values, resulting in a single value that is then displayed within the cell. The most commonly used operators are **arithmetic operators** that perform addition, subtraction, multiplication, division, and exponentiation. For example, the following formula adds 5 and 7, returning a value of 12:

```
=5+7
```

Most Excel formulas contain references to cells rather than specific values. This allows you to change the values being used in the calculation without having to modify the formula itself. For example, the following formula returns the result of adding the values stored in cells A1 and B2:

```
=A1+B2
```

If the value 5 is stored in cell A1 and the value 7 is stored in cell B2, this formula would also return a value of 12. If you then changed the value in cell A1 to 10, the formula returns a value of 17. Figure 1-19 describes the different arithmetic operators and provides examples of formulas.

Figure 1-19 **Excel arithmetic operators**

Operation	Arithmetic Operator	Example	Description
Addition	+	=10+A1	Adds 10 to the value in cell A1
		=B1+B2+B3	Adds the values in cells B1, B2, and B3
Subtraction	–	=C9–B2	Subtracts the value in cell B2 from the value in cell C9
		=1–D2	Subtracts the value in cell D2 from 1
Multiplication	*	=C9*B9	Multiplies the values in cells C9 and B9
		=E5*0.06	Multiplies the value in cell E5 by 0.06
Division	/	=C9/B9	Divides the value in cell C9 by the value in cell B9
		=D15/12	Divides the value in cell D15 by 12
Exponentiation	^	=B5^3	Raises the value of cell B5 to the third power
		=3^B5	Raises 3 to the value in cell B5

If a formula contains more than one arithmetic operator, Excel performs the calculation using the same order of precedence you might have already seen in math classes. The **order of precedence** is a set of predefined rules used to determine the sequence in which operators are applied in a calculation. Excel first calculates the value of any operation within parentheses, then it applies exponentiation (^), multiplication (*), and division (/), and finally it performs addition (+) and subtraction (–). For example, the following formula returns the value 23 because multiplying 4 by 5 takes precedence over adding 3:

```
=3+4*5
```

If a formula contains two or more operators with the same level of precedence, the operators are applied in order from left to right. In the following formula, Excel first multiplies 4 by 10 and then divides that result by 8 to return the value 5:

```
=4*10/8
```

When parentheses are used, the value inside them is calculated first. In the following formula, Excel calculates the (3+4) and then multiplies that result by 5 to return the value 35:

```
=(3+4)*5
```

Figure 1-20 shows how slight changes in a formula affect the order of precedence and the result of the formula.

Figure 1-20 **Order of precedence applied to Excel formulas**

Formula	Application of the Order of Precedence	Result
=50+10*5	10*5 calculated first and then 50 is added	100
=(50+10)*5	(50+10) calculated first and then multiplied by 5	300
=50/10–5	50/10 calculated first and then 5 is subtracted	0
=50/(10–5)	(10–5) calculated first and then 50 is divided by that value	10
=50/10*5	Two operators at same precedence level, so the calculation is done left to right in the expression	25
=50/(10*5)	(10*5) calculated first and then 50 is divided by that value	1

REFERENCE

Inserting a Formula

- Click the cell in which you want the formula results to appear.
- Type = and a formula that calculates a value using cell references and arithmetic operators.
- Press the Enter key or press the Tab key to complete the formula.

Amanda wants the worksheet to include the total amount she charged for creating each customer's DVDs. The charge is equal to the number of DVDs created multiplied by the price per DVD. You've already entered this information for each customer in columns F and G. You'll enter a formula to calculate the charge for each customer in column H.

To enter the formula into the worksheet:

1. Click cell **H5** to make it the active cell, type **Charge** for the column label, and then press the **Enter** key. The column label is entered in cell H5. Cell H6, where you want to enter the formula, is the active cell.
2. Type **=F6*G6** (the number of DVDs created multiplied by the price per DVD). As you type the formula, a list of Excel function names appears in a ScreenTip, which provides a quick method for entering functions. The list will close when you complete the formula. You'll learn more about Excel functions shortly.
3. Press the **Enter** key. The formula is entered in cell H6, which displays the value $34.58. The result is displayed as currency because cell G6 referenced in the formula contains a currency value.

After a formula has been entered into a cell, the worksheet displays the value returned by the formula. If the results are not what you expect, you might have entered the formula incorrectly. You can view the formula by selecting the cell and reviewing the expression displayed in the formula bar. One challenge with formulas, particularly long formulas, is interpreting the cell references. Excel makes this simpler by color coding each cell reference in the formula and its corresponding cell in the worksheet. You'll see this when you view the formula you just entered.

To view the formula:

1. Click cell **H6** to make it the active cell. The formula you entered appears in the formula bar, whereas the value returned by the formula appears in the cell.
2. Click in the formula bar. Each cell used in the formula has a different colored border that matches the color of its cell reference in the formula. This provides a visual cue to the formula, so you can quickly match cell references with their locations in the worksheet. See Figure 1-21.

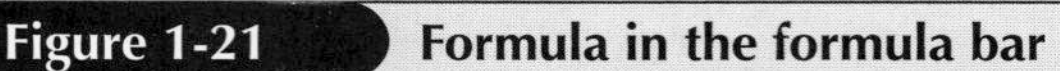

Figure 1-21 Formula in the formula bar

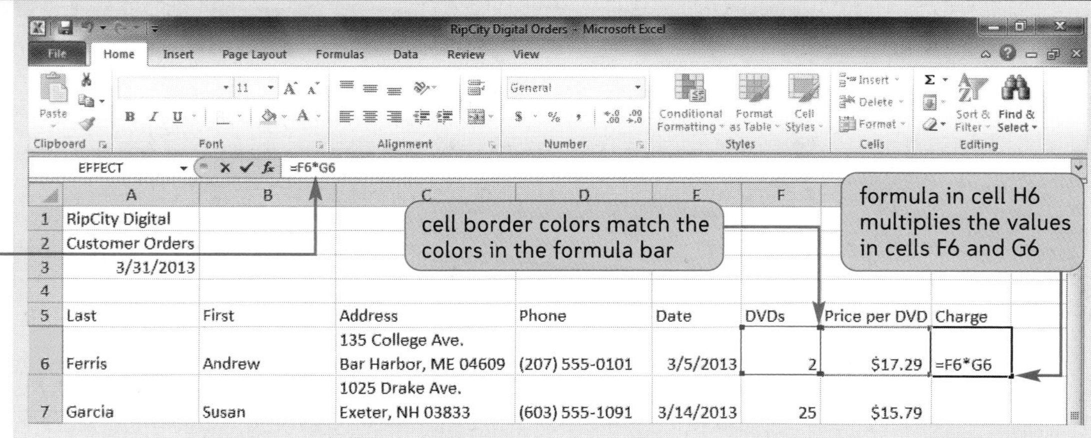

For Amanda's first customer, you entered the formula by typing each cell reference in the expression. You can also insert a cell reference by clicking the cell as you type the formula. This technique reduces the possibility of error caused by typing an incorrect cell reference. You'll use this method to enter the formula to calculate the charge for the second customer.

TIP

Be sure to type = as the first part of the entry in any cell containing a formula; otherwise, Excel will not interpret the entry as a formula.

To enter a cell reference using the mouse:

1. Click cell **H7** to make it the active cell, and then type =. When you type the equal sign, Excel knows that you're entering a formula. Any cell that you click from now on causes Excel to insert the cell reference of the selected cell into the formula until you complete the formula by pressing the Enter or Tab key.
2. Click cell **F7**. The cell reference is inserted into the formula in the formula bar. At this point, any cell you click changes the cell reference used in the formula. The cell reference isn't locked until you type an operator.
3. Type * to enter the multiplication operator. The cell reference for cell F7 is locked in the formula, and the next cell you click will be inserted after the operator.
4. Click cell **G7** to enter its cell reference in the formula, and then press the **Enter** key. Cell H7 displays the value $394.75, which is the total charge for the second customer.

Copying and Pasting Formulas

Sometimes you'll need to repeat the same formula throughout your worksheet. Rather than retyping the formula, you can copy a formula from one cell and paste it into another cell. Pasting a formula is different from pasting a value. With formulas, Excel adjusts the formula's cell references to reflect the new location of the formula in the worksheet. This is because you usually want to copy the actions of a formula rather than the specific value the formula generates. In this case, the formula's action is to multiply the number of DVDs Amanda created for a customer by the price she is charging for creating each DVD. By copying and pasting the formula, you can quickly repeat that action for every customer in the worksheet.

You will see how this works as you copy the formula you just entered in cell H7 to cells H8 and H9 to calculate Amanda's charges to the two remaining customers listed in the worksheet.

To copy and paste the formula that calculates charges:

1. Click cell **H7** to select the cell that contains the formula you want to copy.
2. In the Clipboard group on the Home tab, click the **Copy** button. Excel copies the formula to the Clipboard. The cell from which the formula was copied has a dotted border to remind you that cell is being copied.
3. Select the range **H8:H9**. These are the cells in which you want to paste the formula.
4. In the Clipboard group, click the **Paste** button. Excel pastes the formula into the selected range. A shortcut button appears below the selected range, providing options for pasting formulas and values. See Figure 1-22.

Figure 1-22 Formula copied and pasted

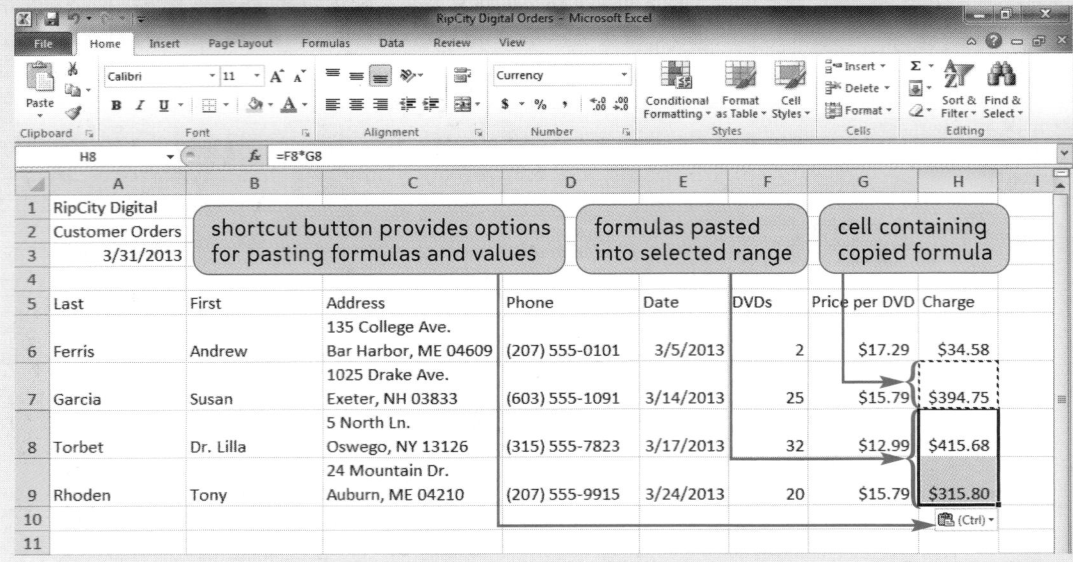

5. Click cell **H8** and verify that the formula =F8*G8 appears in the formula bar.
6. Click cell **H9** and verify that the formula =F9*G9 appears in the formula bar.

When you pasted the formulas into cells H8 and H9, Excel automatically adjusted the formulas so that the total charges calculated for the customers in rows 8 and 9 use the cell values from rows 8 and 9. By copying and pasting the formula, you have saved time and avoided potential mistakes in retyping the same formula again and again.

Introducing Functions

In addition to cell references and operators, formulas can also contain functions. A **function** is a named operation that returns a value. Functions are used to simplify formulas, reducing what might be a long formula into a compact statement. For example, to add the values in the range A1:A10, you could enter the following long formula:

```
=A1+A2+A3+A4+A5+A6+A7+A8+A9+A10
```

Or, you could use the SUM function to calculate the sum of cell values found within a specified range. In this case, the formula would appear as:

```
=SUM(A1:A10)
```

In both instances, Excel adds the values in cells A1 through A10, but the SUM function is faster and simpler to enter and less prone to a typing error. You should always use a function, if one is available, in place of a long, complex formula.

Excel supports more than 300 different functions from the fields of finance, business, science, and engineering. Excel provides functions that work with numbers, text, and dates.

Entering a Function

Amanda wants to calculate the total number of DVDs she needs to create for her customers. To do that, you'll use the SUM function to add the values in the range F6:F9.

TIP

You can also insert a range reference into a function by selecting the range with the pointer.

To enter the SUM function to add the values in the range F6:F9:

1. Click cell **E10**, type **TOTAL** in all uppercase letters as the label, and then press the **Tab** key. The label is entered in cell E10, and cell F10 is the active cell.
2. Type **=SUM(F6:F9** in cell F10. As you begin to type the function, a ScreenTip lists the names of all functions that start with the letter "S." When you type the cell references, Excel highlights all the cells in the specified range to provide a visual reminder of exactly which cells the SUM function is using. See Figure 1-23.

Figure 1-23 SUM function being entered

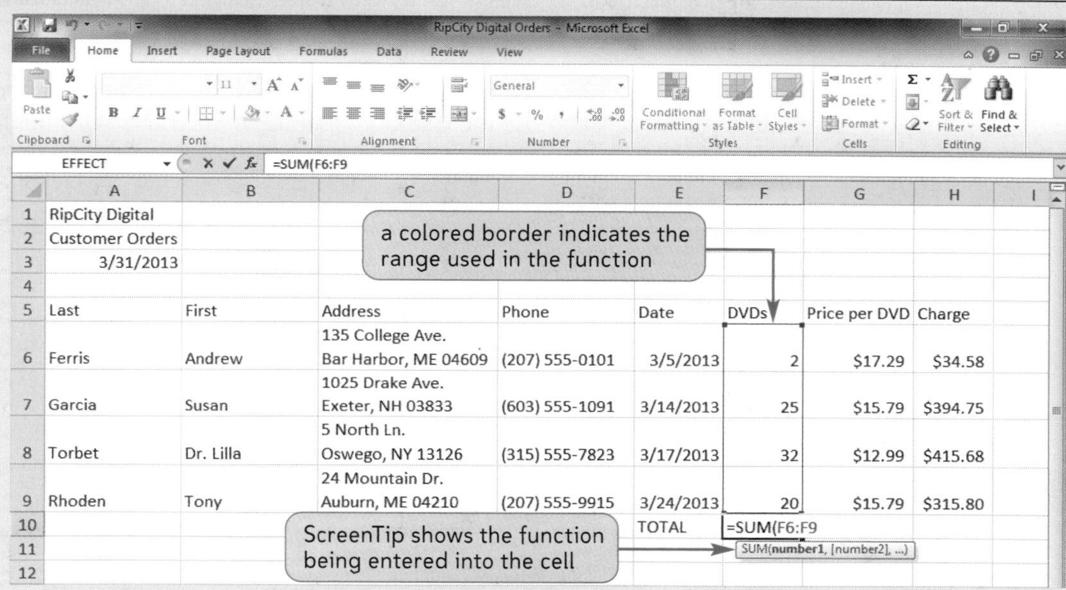

3. Type **)** to complete the function, and then press the **Tab** key. The value of the SUM function appears in cell F10, indicating that Amanda has to create 79 DVDs to complete all of her current orders.

Entering Functions with the AutoSum Feature

A fast and convenient way to enter commonly used functions is with the AutoSum feature. The AutoSum feature includes buttons to quickly insert the SUM, AVERAGE, COUNT, MIN, and MAX functions to generate the following:

- Sum of the values in the column or row
- Average value in the column or row
- Total count of numeric values in the column or row
- Minimum value in the column or row
- Maximum value in the column or row

The Sum button automatically inserts both the function name and the range reference to the row or column of data to which the summary function is being applied.

INSIGHT

How AutoSum Works

Excel determines the range reference needed for the function being inserted by the AutoSum feature by examining the layout of the data and choosing what seems to be the most likely range. When you use the Sum button, Excel highlights the range it thinks you want to use. For example, if you use the Sum button in a cell that is below a column of numbers, Excel assumes that you want to summarize the values in the column. You can change that range by typing a different range reference or selecting a different range.

Make sure to always verify the range AutoSum selected, especially when a worksheet's column or row titles contain numbers. AutoSum cannot differentiate between numbers used as titles (such as years) and numbers used as data for the calculation.

Amanda wants to calculate the total revenue she'll generate after she fulfills her customer orders. You'll use the AutoSum feature to enter the SUM function.

To calculate the total revenue using the AutoSum feature:

1. Click cell **H10** to make it the active cell.
2. In the Editing group on the Home tab, click the **Sum button arrow** Σ ▾. The button's menu opens and displays five common summary functions: Sum, Average, Count Numbers, Max (for maximum), and Min (for minimum).
3. Click **Sum** to enter the SUM function. See Figure 1-24.

Figure 1-24 SUM function being entered with AutoSum

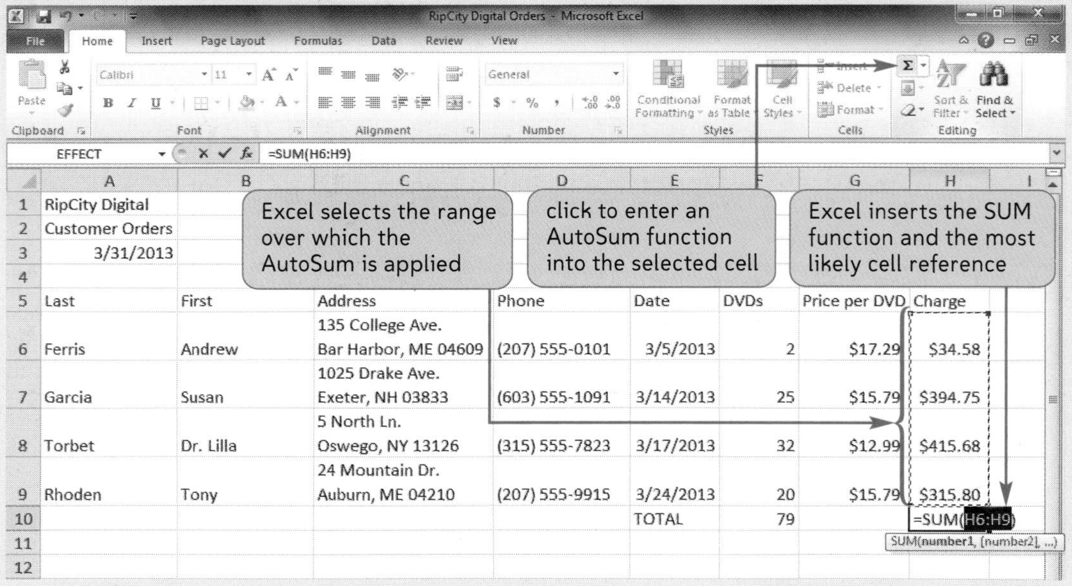

4. Verify that the range **H6:H9** appears in the SUM function and is highlighted with a dotted border. The dotted border shows what will be included in the SUM function.
5. Press the **Enter** key to accept the automatically generated formula. The total charge for all of Amanda's customers, shown in cell H10, is $1,160.81.

PROSKILLS

Problem Solving: Writing Effective Formulas

You can use formulas to quickly perform calculations and solve problems. First, identify the problem you need to solve. Then, gather the data needed to solve the problem. Finally, create accurate and effective formulas that use the data to answer or resolve the problem. Follow these guidelines:

- **Keep formulas simple.** Use functions in place of long, complex formulas whenever possible. For example, use the SUM function instead of entering a formula that adds individual cells, which makes it easier to confirm that the formula is making an accurate calculation as it provides answers needed to evaluate the problem.
- **Do not hide data values within formulas.** The worksheet displays formula results, not the actual formula. For example, to calculate a 5% interest rate on a currency value in cell A5, you could enter the formula =0.05*A5. However, this doesn't show how the value is calculated. A better approach places the value 0.05 in a cell accompanied by a descriptive label and uses the cell reference in the formula. If you place 0.05 in cell A6, the formula =A6*A5 would calculate the interest value. Other people can then easily see the interest rate as well as the resulting interest, ensuring that the formula is solving the right problem.
- **Break up formulas to show intermediate results.** When a worksheet contains complex computations, other people can more easily comprehend how the formula results are calculated when different parts of the formula are distinguished. For example, the formula =SUM(A1:A10)/SUM(B1:B10) calculates the ratio of two sums, but hides the two sum values. Instead, enter each SUM function in a separate cell, such as cells A11 and B11, and use the formula =A11/B11 to calculate the ratio. Other people can see both sums and the value of their ratio in the worksheet and better understand the final result, which makes it more likely that the best problem resolution will be selected.

Finding a solution to a problem requires accurate data and analysis. With workbooks, this means using formulas that are easy to understand, clearly show the data being used in the calculations, and demonstrate how the results are calculated. Only then can you be confident that you are choosing the best problem resolution.

Working with Worksheets

You've seen that new workbooks are created with three initial worksheets labeled Sheet1, Sheet2, and Sheet3. If needed, you can add new worksheets to a workbook and remove unused sheets. You can also give worksheets more descriptive and meaningful names.

Inserting or Deleting a Worksheet

TIP

To insert a new worksheet to the left of the active sheet, right-click a sheet tab, click Insert on the shortcut menu, select a sheet type, and then click the OK button.

When you insert a new worksheet in a workbook, the new sheet is named based on the number and names of the other sheets in the workbook. For example, if a workbook has four worksheets named Sheet1 through Sheet4, the next inserted worksheet is named Sheet5. You'll add a new, blank worksheet to the RipCity Digital Orders workbook.

To insert a new worksheet:

1. Locate the three sheet tabs in the lower-left corner of the worksheet window.
2. To the right of the Sheet3 sheet tab, click the **Insert Worksheet** tab. A new worksheet named Sheet4 appears at the end of the workbook and is active.

The workbook now includes two empty worksheets: Sheet3 and Sheet4. Because you don't plan to use these sheets, it's a good idea to remove them.

To delete the Sheet3 and Sheet4 worksheets:

1. Right-click the **Sheet3** sheet tab, and then click **Delete** on the shortcut menu. The Sheet3 worksheet is removed from the workbook.
2. If necessary, click the **Sheet4** sheet tab to make it the active sheet.
3. In the Cells group on the Home tab, click the **Delete button arrow**, and then click **Delete Sheet**. The Sheet4 worksheet is removed from the workbook.

Renaming a Worksheet

The remaining worksheets, Sheet1 and Sheet2, do not have very descriptive names. You can rename them so that they better describe their contents. Keep in mind that sheet names cannot exceed 31 characters in length, including blank spaces. The width of the sheet tab adjusts to the length of the name you enter. You'll rename Sheet1 and Sheet2.

TIP

You can also rename a sheet by right-clicking the sheet tab and clicking Rename on the shortcut menu.

To rename the two worksheets:

1. Double-click the **Sheet2** sheet tab. The sheet name is selected in the sheet tab.
2. Type **Customer Orders** and then press the **Enter** key. The width of the sheet tab expands to match the longer sheet name.
3. Double-click the **Sheet1** sheet tab, type **Documentation**, and then press the **Enter** key. Both sheets are renamed.

Moving and Copying a Worksheet

You can change the placement of the worksheets in a workbook. A good practice is to place the most important worksheets at the beginning of the workbook (the leftmost sheet tabs) and less important worksheets toward the end (the rightmost tabs). You'll move the Documentation sheet to the end of the workbook and then return it to the beginning.

TIP

To copy a worksheet, hold down the Ctrl key as you drag and drop the sheet tab. The copy appears where you drop the sheet tab; the original remains in its initial position.

To move the Documentation sheet:

1. If necessary, click the **Documentation** sheet tab to make that worksheet active.
2. Press and hold the mouse button so the pointer changes to and a small triangle appears in the upper-left corner of the tab.
3. Drag the pointer to the right of the Customer Orders sheet tab, and then release the mouse button. The Documentation worksheet is now the second sheet in the workbook.
4. Drag the **Documentation** worksheet back to be the first sheet in the workbook.

Editing Worksheet Content

As you work, you might make mistakes that you want to correct or undo, or you might need to replace a value based on more current information. The price per DVD for Andrew Ferris's order should be $18.29, not $17.29 as entered in cell G6. You could simply clear the value in the cell and then type the correct value. However, sometimes you need to edit only a portion of an entry rather than change the entire contents of a cell, especially if the cell contains a large block of text or a complex formula. To edit the cell contents, you can work in **Edit mode**.

When you work in Edit mode, some of the keyboard shortcuts you've been using work differently because they apply only to the text within the selected cell. For example, the Home, End, Backspace, Delete, and arrow keys move the insertion point to different locations within the cell. The Home key moves the insertion point to the beginning of the cell's content. The End key moves the insertion point to the end of the cell's content. The left and right arrow keys move the insertion point backward and forward through the cell's content. The Backspace key deletes the character immediately to the left of the insertion point, and the Delete key deletes the character to the right of the insertion point. You'll change one digit of the value in cell G6 to correct the price per DVD.

To edit the value in cell G6:

TIP

To change the active cell to Edit mode, press the F2 key or click in the formula bar. To cancel all changes made in Edit mode, press the Esc key or click the Cancel button in the formula bar.

1. Click the **Customer Orders** sheet tab to make it the active worksheet.
2. Double-click cell **G6**. The mode indicator on the status bar switches from Ready to Edit, indicating that you are in Edit mode.
3. Press the **End** key. The insertion point moves to the end of the cell.
4. Press the ← key three times. The insertion point moves to the right of the 7.
5. Press the **Backspace** key to delete the 7, and then type **8**. The value in cell G6 changes to 18.29. See Figure 1-25.

Figure 1-25 **Cell being edited in Edit mode**

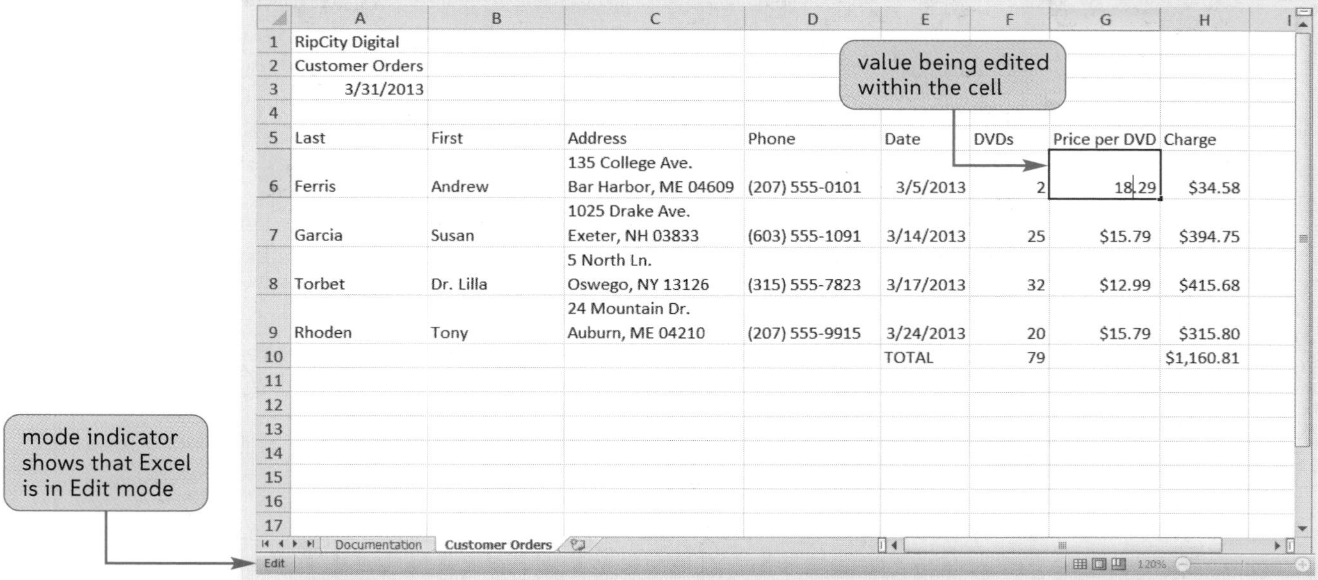

	A	B	C	D	E	F	G	H
1	RipCity Digital							
2	Customer Orders							
3	3/31/2013							
4								
5	Last	First	Address	Phone	Date	DVDs	Price per DVD	Charge
6	Ferris	Andrew	135 College Ave. Bar Harbor, ME 04609	(207) 555-0101	3/5/2013	2	18.29	$34.58
7	Garcia	Susan	1025 Drake Ave. Exeter, NH 03833	(603) 555-1091	3/14/2013	25	$15.79	$394.75
8	Torbet	Dr. Lilla	5 North Ln. Oswego, NY 13126	(315) 555-7823	3/17/2013	32	$12.99	$415.68
9	Rhoden	Tony	24 Mountain Dr. Auburn, ME 04210	(207) 555-9915	3/24/2013	20	$15.79	$315.80
10					TOTAL	79		$1,160.81
11								
12								
13								
14								
15								
16								
17								

6. Press the **Enter** key to accept the edit in cell G6. The value $18.29 appears in cell G6, the active cell is cell G7, and the mode indicator on the status bar changes from Edit to Ready to indicate that you are no longer in Edit mode.

Undoing and Redoing an Action

As you revise a workbook, you might need to undo a previous action. Excel maintains a list of the actions you perform in a workbook during the current session, so you can undo most of these actions. You can reverse the most recent action or you can reverse more than one action. If you undo more than one action, all actions subsequent to the earliest action you select are also undone. You'll undo the edit to cell G6.

To undo the edit to cell G6:

1. On the Quick Access Toolbar, click the **Undo** button.
2. Verify that $17.29 appears again in cell G6, indicating that your last action—editing the value of this cell—has been undone.

If you find that you have gone too far in undoing previous actions, you can go forward in the action list and redo those actions. As with the Undo feature, you can redo more than one action at a time. You'll use Redo to restore the value of cell G6.

To redo the edit to cell G6:

1. On the Quick Access Toolbar, click the **Redo** button.
2. Verify that the value in cell G6 returns to $18.29.

Using Find and Replace

Amanda wants you to replace all the street title abbreviations with their full names. Specifically, "Ave." should be "Avenue," "Ln." should be "Lane," and "Dr." should be "Drive." Although you could read through the worksheet to locate each occurrence, this can be time-consuming with larger workbooks. For greater speed and accuracy, you can use the Find command to locate a string of characters known as a **search string** and replace that text with a **replacement string** of new text characters.

You can limit the search to the current worksheet or search the entire workbook. You can specify whether to match the capitalization in the Find what box and whether the search text should match the entire cell contents or part of the cell contents. You can choose to review each occurrence of the search value and decide whether to replace it, or you can replace all occurrences at once.

You'll use the Find and Replace commands to replace each street title abbreviation.

To find and replace the street title abbreviations:

1. In the Editing group on the Home tab, click the **Find & Select** button, and then click **Replace**. The Find and Replace dialog box opens.
2. Type **Ave.** in the Find what box, press the **Tab** key, and then type **Avenue** in the Replace with box.
3. Click the **Options** button. The dialog box expands to display additional Find and Replace options. See Figure 1-26.

Figure 1-26 **Find and Replace dialog box**

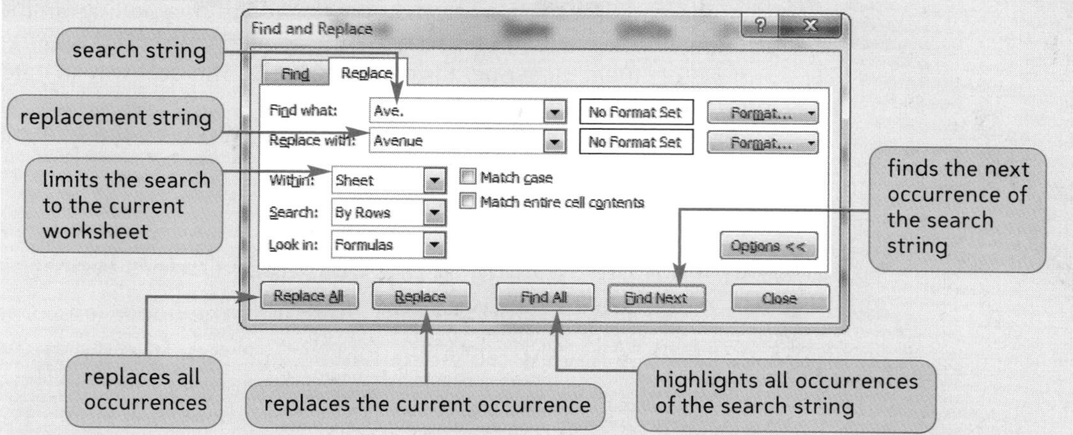

4. Verify that **Sheet** appears in the Within box to limit the find and replace to the current worksheet only.
5. Click the **Replace All** button. Excel finds and replaces the search string wherever it appears in the current worksheet. A dialog box opens, indicating that Excel has completed its search and made two replacements.
6. Click the **OK** button to close the dialog box.
7. Select the text in the Find what box, type **Ln.** as the new search string, press the **Tab** key, and then type **Lane** in the Replace with box. You want to replace all instances of this search string.
8. Click the **Replace All** button to make the replacement wherever it appears in the worksheet, and then click the **OK** button to close the dialog box that indicates Excel has completed its search and made one replacement.
9. Select the text in the Find what box, type **Dr.** as the new search string, press the **Tab** key, and then type **Drive** in the Replace with box. Because "Dr." is also the abbreviation for "Doctor," you must review each "Dr." abbreviation and replace only the ones within an address.
10. Click the **Find Next** button. The next occurrence of "Dr." in the worksheet occurs in cell B8 with the text, "Dr. Lilla."
11. Click the **Find Next** button to ignore this occurrence. The next occurrence of "Dr." is in the mailing address for Tony Rhoden.
12. Click the **Replace** button to replace this text. The only other occurrence of "Dr." in the worksheet—"Dr. Lilla"—is highlighted again. You've finished finding and replacing text in the worksheet.
13. Click the **Close** button to close the Find and Replace dialog box.

Using the Spelling Checker

Another editing tool is the spelling checker. Although the spelling checker's dictionary includes a large number of words, as well as common first and last names and places, many words you use in workbooks might not be included. If the spelling checker finds a word that is not in its dictionary, the word appears in a dialog box along with a list of suggested replacements. You can replace the word with one from the list, or you can ignore the word and go to the next possible misspelling. You can also add words to the dictionary to prevent them from being flagged as misspellings in the future. Note that the spelling checker will not find a correctly spelled word used incorrectly, such as "there" instead of "their" or "your" instead of "you're." The best way to catch these types of errors is to proofread your worksheets.

Before giving the workbook to Amanda, you'll check the spelling in the Customer Orders worksheet.

To check the spelling in the Customer Orders worksheet:

1. Click cell **A1** to start the spell check from the upper-left corner of the sheet.
2. Click the **Review** tab on the Ribbon, and then click the **Spelling** button in the Proofing group. The Spelling dialog box opens and flags "RipCity" as a possible spelling error. Excel suggests two alternatives. See Figure 1-27.

Figure 1-27 Spelling dialog box

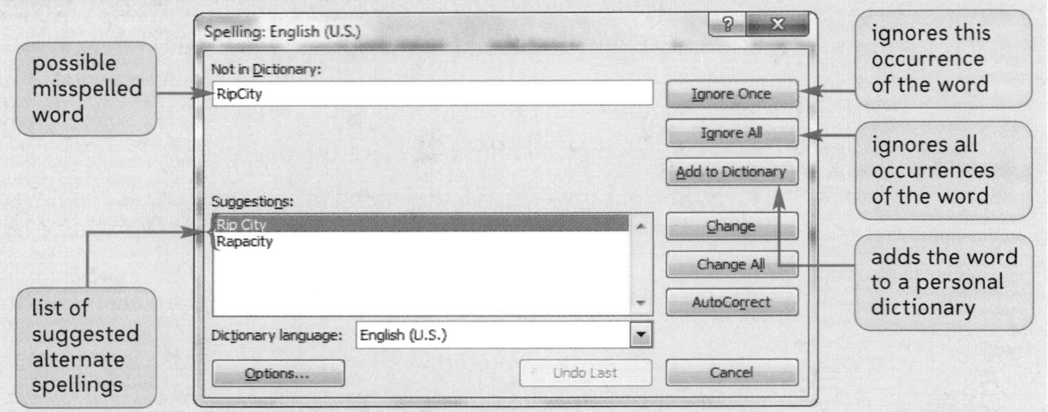

3. Click the **Ignore All** button. You ignored all the occurrences of this spelling because "RipCity" is the name of Amanda's company. The spelling checker flags "Torbet," a last name that is not in the program's dictionary.
4. Click the **Ignore All** button to ignore the spelling of this name. The next potential spelling error is the name "Lilla" in cell B8. The name should have been entered as "Lila," a first name that the spelling checker recognizes.
5. Click **Lila** in the Suggestions box, if necessary, and then click the **Change** button. The text is changed within the cell. The spelling checker is finished.

   Trouble? If the spelling checker finds another error, you might have another typing error in your worksheet. Use the spelling checker to find and correct any other errors in your workbook, and then continue with Step 6.
6. Click the **OK** button to close the Microsoft Excel dialog box.
7. Proofread the worksheet and correct any other spelling errors you find. You do not have to check the spelling in the Documentation worksheet at this time.

Previewing and Printing a Workbook

Now that you have finished the final edit of the workbook, you are ready to print a hard copy of the customer orders list for Amanda. However, before you print the workbook, you should preview it to ensure that it will print correctly.

Changing Worksheet Views

> **TIP**
> To view the workbook in the full screen space, which hides the Ribbon, click the Full Screen button in the Workbook Views group on the View tab. Press the Esc key to exit the view.

You can view a worksheet in three ways. **Normal view**, which you've been using throughout this tutorial, shows the contents of the worksheet. **Page Layout view** shows how the worksheet will appear when printed. **Page Break Preview** displays the location of the different page breaks within the worksheet. This is useful when a worksheet will span several printed pages and you need to control what content appears on each page.

You'll switch between these views to see how the Customer Orders worksheet will appear on printed pages.

To switch the worksheet views:

1. Click the **Page Layout** button on the status bar. The page layout of the worksheet appears in the program window. You want to see the rest of the data, which extends to a second page.
2. Use the Zoom slider to reduce the zoom level to **60%**. See Figure 1-28.

Figure 1-28 **Worksheet displayed in Page Layout view**

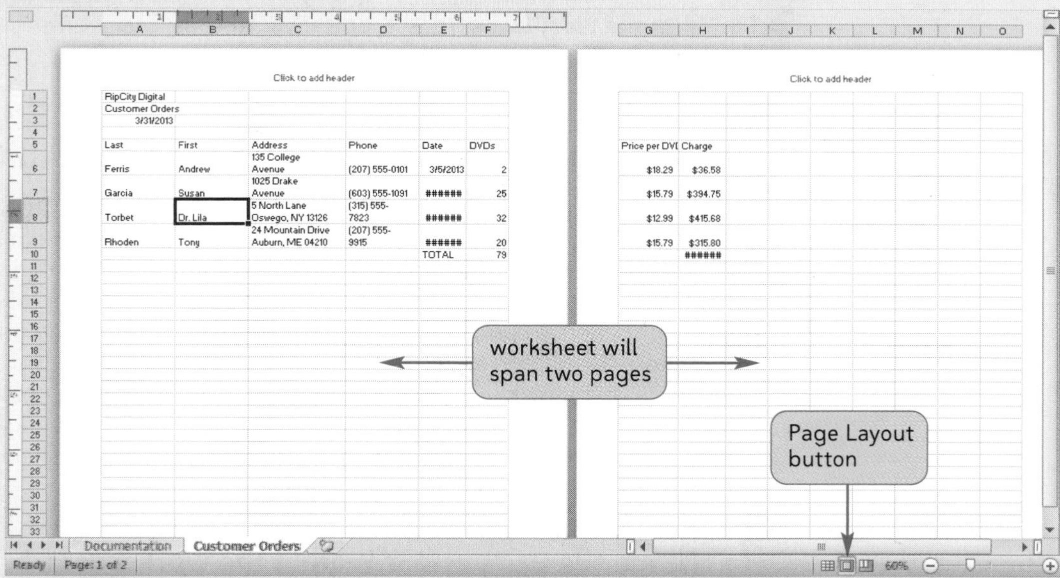

3. Click the **Page Break Preview** button on the status bar. The view switches to Page Break Preview, which shows only those parts of the current worksheet that will print. A dotted blue border separates one page from another.

   Trouble? If the Welcome to Page Break Preview dialog box opens, this is the first time you've switched to Page Break Preview. Click the OK button to close the dialog box and continue with Step 4.

4. Zoom the worksheet to **120%** so that you can more easily read the contents of the worksheet. See Figure 1-29.

Figure 1-29 Worksheet displayed in Page Break Preview

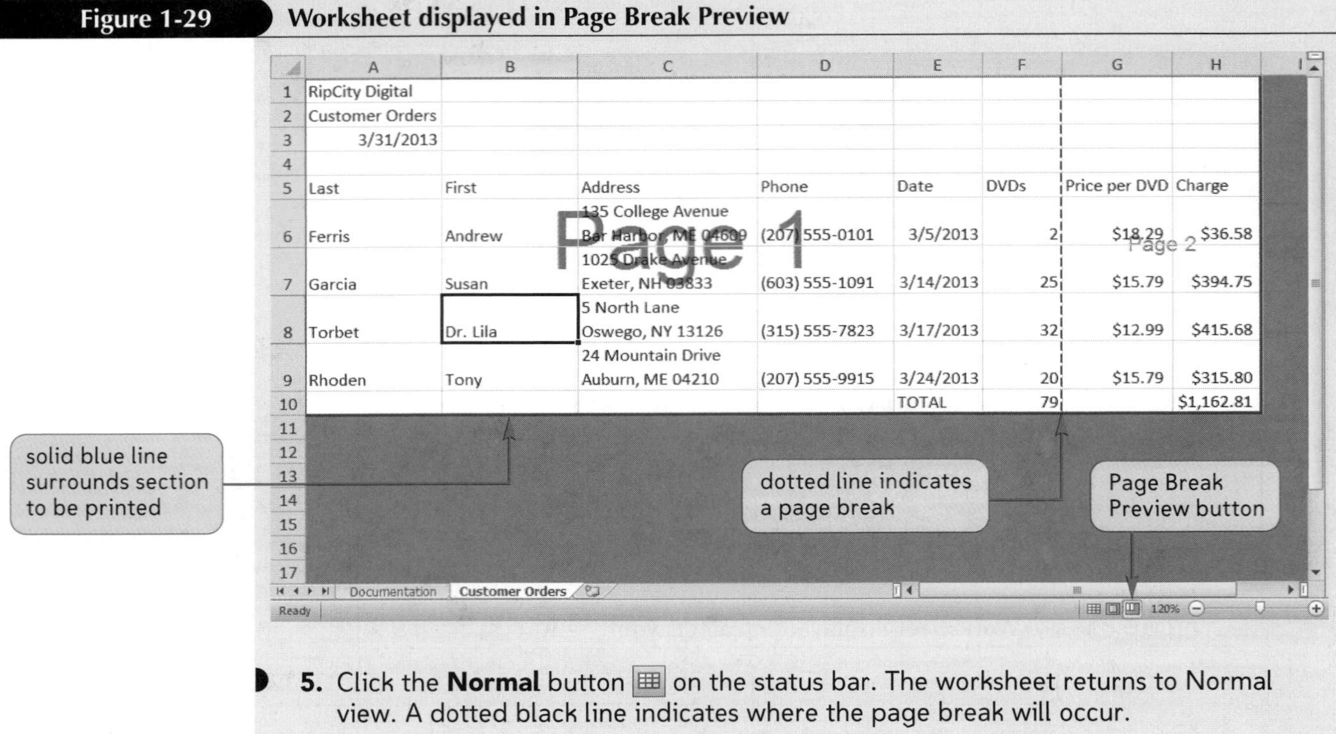

5. Click the **Normal** button on the status bar. The worksheet returns to Normal view. A dotted black line indicates where the page break will occur.

Working with Portrait and Landscape Orientation

As you saw in Page Layout view and Page Break Preview, the Customer Orders worksheet will print on two pages—columns A through F will print on one page and columns G and H will print on a second page. Amanda wants the entire worksheet printed on a single page. One way to accomplish this is to change the page orientation from portrait to landscape. In **portrait orientation**, the page is taller than it is wide. In **landscape orientation**, the page is wider than it is tall. By default, Excel displays pages in portrait orientation. In many cases, however, you will want to print the page in landscape orientation. Changing the page orientation affects only the active worksheet.

You'll change the orientation of the Customer Orders worksheet to landscape.

To change the page orientation of the worksheet:

1. Click the **Page Layout** tab on the Ribbon.
2. In the Page Setup group, click the **Orientation** button, and then click **Landscape**. The orientation switches to landscape, and the worksheet contents fit on one page.
3. Click the **Page Layout** button on the status bar, and then verify that all the worksheet contents fit on one page.
4. Click the **Documentation** sheet tab, and then click the **Page Layout** button. The Documentation sheet remains in portrait orientation.
5. Verify that the entire contents of the Documentation worksheet fit on one page.

Printing the Workbook

You can print the contents of a workbook by using the Print tab in Backstage view. The Print tab provides options for choosing what to print and how to print. For example, you can specify the number of copies to print, which printer to use, and what to print. You can choose to print only the selected cells, the active sheets, or all worksheets in the workbook that contain data. The printout will include only the data in the worksheet. The other elements in the worksheet, such as the row and column headings and the gridlines around the worksheet cells, will not print by default. You also see a preview of the workbook so you can see exactly how printed pages will look with the settings you've chosen before you print. A good practice is to always review the print preview before printing to ensure that the printout looks exactly as you intended and avoid unnecessary reprinting.

You'll preview and print the RipCity Digital Orders workbook now.

To preview and print the workbook:

1. Click the File tab on the Ribbon to display Backstage view.
2. Click the **Print** tab in the navigation bar to display the print options and preview of the first sheet in the workbook (the Documentation worksheet). See Figure 1-30.

Figure 1-30 **Print tab in Backstage view**

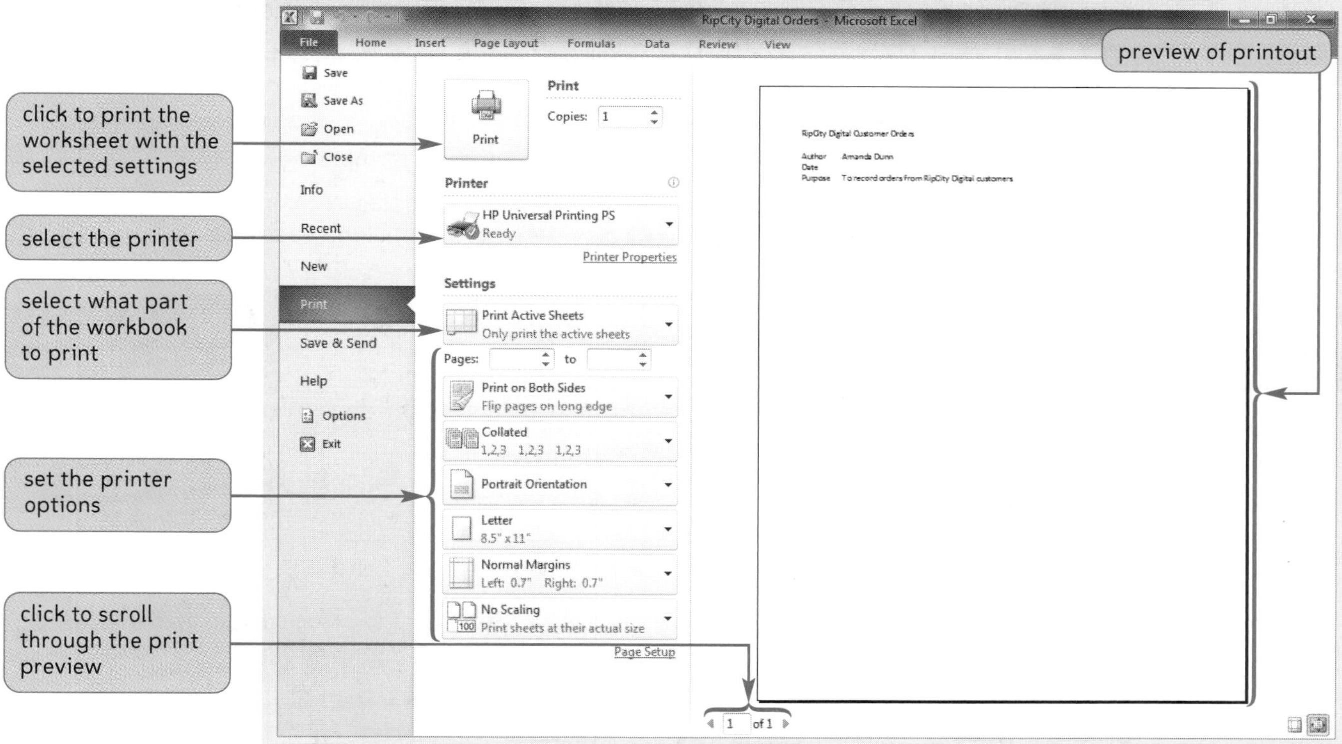

3. Click the **Printer** button, and then click the printer to which you want to print if it is not already selected.
4. In the Settings group, click the top button, and then click **Print Entire Workbook**. This will print both the Documentation worksheet and the Customer Orders worksheet.

5. Below the preview, click the **Next Page** button ▶. The first page of the print job contains the contents of the Documentation worksheet in portrait orientation, and the second page contains the Customer Orders worksheet in landscape orientation.
6. Click the **Print** button. The worksheet prints.

Viewing and Printing Worksheet Formulas

The printout of the Customer Orders worksheet displays only the worksheet values and none of the formulas. Most of the time, you will be interested in only the final results of the worksheet, not the formulas used to calculate those results. However, in some cases, you might want to view the formulas used to develop the workbook. This is particularly useful when you encounter unexpected results and you want to examine the underlying formulas, or you want to discuss your formulas with a colleague. You can view the formulas in a workbook by switching to **formula view**, a view of the worksheet contents that displays formulas instead of the resulting values.

You'll look at the Customer Orders worksheet in formula view now.

TIP

To toggle in and out of formula view, press the Ctrl+` keys. The ` grave accent symbol is usually located above the Tab key on your keyboard.

To view the formulas in the Customer Orders worksheet:

1. Click the **Customer Orders** sheet tab, if necessary, and then click the **Normal** button on the status bar. The Customer Orders worksheet is active and displayed in Normal view.
2. Press the **Ctrl+`** keys. The worksheet changes to formula view.
3. Scroll the worksheet to the right to view the formulas in columns F and H. The column widths are wider to display the entire formula in each cell. As long as you don't resize the column widths while in formula view, they remain unchanged in other views. See Figure 1-31.

Figure 1-31 Worksheet in formula view

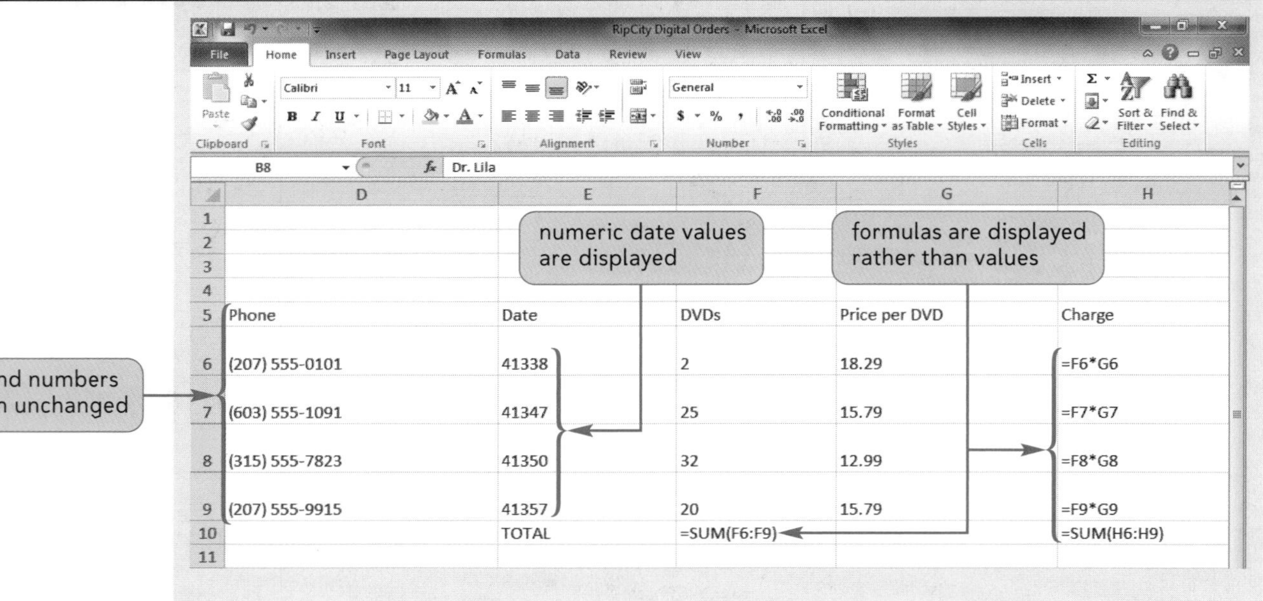

Amanda wants a printout of the formula view. The Customer Orders worksheet will not fit on one page because of the expanded column widths. You can scale the worksheet to force the contents to fit on a single page. **Scaling** a printout reduces the width and the height of the printout to fit the number of pages you specify by shrinking the text size as needed. You can also scale a printout proportionally to a percentage of its actual size. You'll scale the Customer Orders worksheet to a width and height of one page.

To scale the worksheet formulas to print on one page:

1. Click the **Page Layout** tab on the Ribbon.
2. In the Scale to Fit group, click the **Width arrow**, and then click **1 page**.
3. In the Scale to Fit group, click the **Height arrow**, and then click **1 page**. You'll verify that the worksheet formula view fits on a single page.
4. Click the **Page Layout** button on the status bar, and then zoom the worksheet to **50%**. The formula view of the worksheet fits on one page. See Figure 1-32.

Figure 1-32 Printout scaled to one page

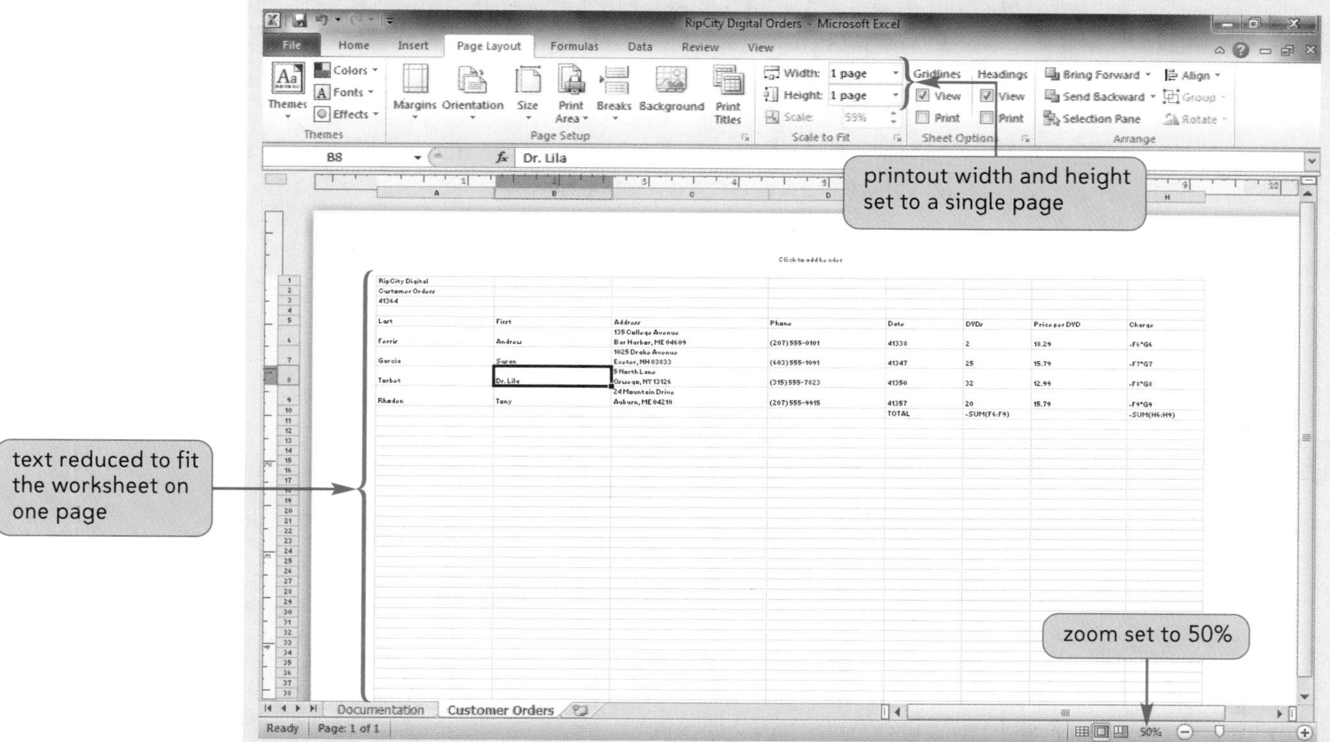

5. Click the **File** tab on the Ribbon to display Backstage view, and then click the **Print** tab in the navigation bar to view the print options.
6. In the Settings group, click the top button, and then click **Print Active Sheets** to print only the Customer Orders worksheet.
7. Click the **Print** button. The active sheet, the Customer Orders worksheet, prints.

At this point, you've completed your work for Amanda. Before closing the workbook, you'll change the view of the workbook contents back to Normal view.

To save and close the workbook:

1. Press the **Ctrl+`** keys to switch the worksheet out of formula view.
2. Click the **Normal** button on the status bar to return the worksheet to Normal view.
3. Save your changes to the workbook, and then close it.

Amanda is pleased with the workbook you created for her. All the customers and orders appear on one worksheet, and she can easily add new customers and orders. The formulas quickly update the calculations that show her income from burning DVDs.

REVIEW

Session 1.2 Quick Check

1. Describe the two types of ranges in Excel.
2. What is the range reference for cells A3 through G5 and J3 through M5?
3. What formula would you enter to add the values in cells B4, B5, and B6? What function would you enter to achieve the same result?
4. How do you rename a worksheet?
5. Describe four ways of viewing the content of an Excel workbook.
6. How are page breaks indicated in Page Break Preview?
7. How do you display the formulas used in a worksheet?
8. Why would you scale a worksheet?

Practice the skills you learned in the tutorial using the same case scenario.

PRACTICE

Review Assignments

There are no Data Files needed for the Review Assignments.

Amanda has another set of orders for you to enter on the Customer Orders worksheet. In addition to calculating the charge for creating the DVDs, Amanda also wants to include the cost of shipping in the total charged to each customer. Complete the following:

1. Open a blank workbook, and then save the workbook as **Order Report** in the Excel1\Review folder.
2. Rename the Sheet1 worksheet as **Documentation**, and then enter the following data into the specified cells:
   Cell A1: **RipCity Digital**
   Cell A3: **Author** Cell B3: your name
   Cell A4: **Date** Cell B4: the current date
   Cell A5: **Purpose** Cell B5: **To track customer orders for RipCity Digital**
3. Rename the Sheet2 worksheet as **Customer Orders**.
4. Delete the Sheet3 worksheet.
5. On the Customer Orders worksheet, enter the following data into the specified cells:
   Cell A1: **RipCity Digital**
   Cell A3: **Customer Orders Report**
   Cell A4: **March 27 to April 17, 2013**
6. In cells A5 through H10, enter the column titles and data from Figure 1-33. The address text in column D should be set on two lines within each cell.

Figure 1-33 **New customer order data**

Date	Last	First	Address	Phone	DVDs	Price per DVD	Shipping Charge
3/27/2013	Fleming	Doris	25 Lee St. Bedford, VA 24523	(540) 555-5681	7	$18.29	$7.49
4/4/2013	Ortiz	Thomas	28 Ridge Ln. Newfane, VT 05345	(802) 555-7710	13	$16.55	$9.89
4/8/2013	Dexter	Kay	150 Main St. Greenbelt, MD 20770	(301) 555-8823	25	$15.79	$7.23
4/9/2013	Sisk	Norman	250 East Maple Ln. Cranston, RI 02910	(401) 555-3350	15	$16.55	$10.55
4/17/2013	Romano	June	207 Jackston Ave. Westport, IN 47283	(812) 555-2681	22	$15.79	$13.95

7. Set the width of column A to 10 characters, columns B and C to 12 characters, column D to 20 characters, and columns E, G, and H to 16 characters.
8. Autofit all of the rows in the worksheet to the cell contents.
9. In cell I5, enter **Total Charge**. In cell I6, insert a formula that calculates the total charge for the first customer (the number of DVDs multiplied by the price per DVD and then added to the shipping charge). Increase the width of column I to 11 characters.
10. Copy the formula in cell I6 and paste it into the range I7:I10.

11. In cell E11, enter **Total DVDs**. In cell F11, use the SUM function to calculate the total number of DVDs created for all customers. In cell I11, use the AutoSum feature to insert the SUM function to calculate the total charges for all of the customer orders.
12. Use Edit mode to make the following corrections:
    a. In cell D6, change the street address from "25 Lee St." to **2500 Lee St.**
    b. In cell F9, change the number of DVDs from "15" to **17**.
    c. In cell H8, change the shipping charge from "$7.23" to **$8.23**.
13. Use the Find and Replace commands to replace all occurrences of "St." with **Street**, "Ln." with **Lane**, and "Ave." with **Avenue**.
14. Change the page layout of the Customer Orders worksheet to print in landscape orientation on a single page.
15. Preview and print the contents of the entire workbook.
16. Change the Customer Orders worksheet to formula view, landscape orientation, and scaled to fit on a single page. Preview and print the Customer Orders worksheet.
17. Return the view of the Customer Orders worksheet to Normal view, save your changes to the Order Report workbook, and then save the current workbook as **Revised Report** in the Excel1\Review folder. (*Hint*: Use the Save As command in Backstage view to save the existing workbook with a new name.)
18. Remove Kay Dexter's order from the Customer Orders worksheet.
19. Add the following order directly after the order placed by June Romano: date **4/22/2013**; name **Patrick Crawford**; address **200 Valley View Road, Rome, GA 30161**; phone **(706) 555-0998**; DVDs **14**; price per DVD **$16.55**; shipping charge **$12.45**.
20. Use Edit mode to change the ending date of the report in cell A4 from "April 17" to **April 22**.
21. Save the workbook, preview and print the contents and formulas of the revised Customer Orders worksheet, close the workbook, and then submit the finished workbooks and printouts to your instructor.

APPLY

Case Problem 1

If you have a SAM 2010 user profile, your instructor may have assigned an autogradable version of this assignment. If so, log into the SAM 2010 Web site at www.cengage.com/sam2010 to download the instructions and start files.

Data File needed for this Case Problem: Altac.xlsx

Altac Bicycles Deborah York is a financial consultant for Altac Bicycles, an online seller of bicycles and bicycle equipment based in Silver City, New Mexico. She has entered some financial information in an Excel workbook for an income statement she is preparing for the company. You will enter the remaining data and formulas. Complete the following:

1. Open the **Altac** workbook located in the Excel1\Case1 folder, and then save the workbook as **Altac Bicycles** in the same folder.
2. Insert three new rows at the top of the Sheet1 worksheet, and then enter the following text on two lines within cell A1:
   Altac Bicycles
   Income Statement*
3. In cell A2, enter **For the Years Ended December 31, 2011 through December 31, 2013**.
4. In the range C6:E7, enter the following net sales and cost of sales figures:

	2013	2012	2011
Net Sales	**13,520**	**10,981**	**9,034**
Cost of Sales	**4,140**	**3,960**	**3,011**

5. In the range C11:E14, enter the following expense figures (expand the column widths as necessary to show the text and data values):

	2013	2012	2011
Salaries and Wages	**1,632**	**1,481**	**1,392**
Sales and Marketing	**2,631**	**2,112**	**1,840**
Administrative	**521**	**410**	**375**
Research and Development	**501**	**404**	**281**

6. In the nonadjacent range C18:E18;C20:E20;C24:E24, enter the following values for Other Income, Income Taxes, and Shares, pressing the Enter or Tab key to navigate from cell to cell in the selected range:

	2013	2012	2011
Other Income	**341**	**302**	**239**
Income Taxes	**1,225**	**1,008**	**821**
Shares	**3,621**	**3,001**	**2,844**

7. In the range C8:E8, enter a formula to calculate the gross margin for each year, where the gross margin is equal to the net sales minus the cost of sales.
8. In the range C15:E15, enter the SUM function to calculate the total operating expenses for each year, where the total operating expenses equal the sum of the four expense categories.
9. In the range C17:E17, enter a formula to calculate the operating income for each year, where operating income is equal to the gross margin minus the total operating expenses.
10. In the range C19:E19, enter a formula to calculate the pretax income for each year, where pretax income is equal to the operating income plus other income.
11. In the range C22:E22, enter a formula to calculate the company's net income for each year, where net income is equal to the pretax income minus income taxes.
12. In the range C25:E25, enter a formula to calculate the earnings per share for each year, where earnings per share is equal to the net income divided by the number of shares.
13. Use the spelling checker to correct and replace any spelling errors in the worksheet. Ignore the spelling of "Altac."
14. In cell A18, use Edit mode to capitalize the word "income."
15. Increase the width of column A to 18 characters and increase the width of column B to 25 characters. Autofit the height of row 1.
16. Rename the Sheet1 worksheet as **Income Statement**, rename the Sheet2 worksheet as **Documentation** and move it to the beginning of the workbook, and then delete the Sheet3 worksheet.
17. In the Documentation worksheet, enter the following text and values:

Cell A1: **Altac Bicycles**	
Cell A3: **Author**	Cell B3: your name
Cell A4: **Date**	Cell B4: the current date
Cell A5: **Purpose**	Cell B5: **Income statement for Altac Bicycles for 2011 through 2013**

18. Save the workbook, preview the workbook and make sure each worksheet in portrait orientation fits on one page in the printout, and then print the entire workbook. Close the workbook, and then submit the finished workbook and printouts to your instructor.

Use the skills you learned to complete a balance sheet for a food retailer.

APPLY

Case Problem 2

Data File needed for this Case Problem: Halley.xlsx

Halley Foods Michael Li is working on the annual financial report for Halley Foods of Norman, Oklahoma. One part of the financial report will be the company's balance sheet for the previous three years. Michael has entered some of the labels for the balance sheet. You will finish the job by entering the actual values and formulas. Complete the following:

1. Open the **Halley** workbook located in the Excel1\Case2 folder, and then save the workbook as **Halley Foods** in the same folder.
2. Rename the Sheet1 worksheet as **Balance Sheet**, and then delete the Sheet2 and Sheet3 worksheets.
3. Insert two new rows at the top of the worksheet, and then enter the following text on four lines within cell A1:
   Halley Foods
   Balance Sheet
   As of December 31
   For the years 2011 through 2013
4. Change the width of column A to 30 characters, the width of column B to 20 characters, and the width of column C to 26 characters. Autofit the height of row 1.
5. Enter the asset and liability values shown in Figure 1-34 into the corresponding cells in the Balance Sheet worksheet for each of the last three years.

Figure 1-34 **Halley Foods assets and liabilities**

		2013	2012	2011
Current Assets	Cash and equivalents	806	589	423
	Short-term investments	1,194	1,029	738
	Accounts receivable	1,283	1,151	847
	Net inventories	683	563	463
	Deferred taxes	510	366	332
	Other current assets	162	153	128
Other Assets	Investments	7,077	5,811	4,330
	Restricted investments	910	797	681
	Property and equipment	779	696	420
	Other assets	1,178	484	485
Current Liabilities	Accounts payable	350	293	192
	Income taxes payable	608	442	352
	Accrued payroll	661	564	389
	Other accrued liabilities	1,397	1,250	775
Minority Interest		44	43	36
Shareholders' Equity	Preferred and common stock	5,557	4837	3,515
	Retained earnings	5,666	4,007	3,401
	Other comprehensive income	299	203	187

6. Use AutoSum to calculate the total current assets, other assets, current liabilities, and shareholders' equity in the ranges D11:F11, D17:F17, D25:F25, and D33:F33, respectively, for each of the previous three years.
7. Insert a formula in the range D19:F19 to calculate the total assets (current assets plus other assets) for each year.
8. Insert a formula in the range D36:F36 to calculate the value of the total current liabilities plus the minority interest plus the total shareholders' equity for each year.
9. Use the spelling checker to correct any spelling mistakes in the Balance Sheet worksheet, and then proofread the worksheet.
10. Change the zoom level of the Balance Sheet worksheet to 70% in Normal view to view the entire contents of the sheet in the workbook window.
11. View the Balance Sheet worksheet in Page Layout view zoomed to 80%, and then scale the height and width of the worksheet to fit on one page.
12. Insert a new worksheet named **Documentation** at the beginning of the workbook.
13. In the Documentation worksheet, enter the following data:

    Cell A1: **Halley Foods**

    Cell A3: **Author** Cell B3: your name

    Cell A4: **Date** Cell B4: the current date

    Cell A5: **Purpose** Cell B5: **Balance Sheet for Halley Foods for 2011 through 2013**
14. Save, preview, and then print the entire Halley Foods workbook.
15. Print the formula view of the Balance Sheet worksheet on two pages in landscape orientation. Return the Balance Sheet worksheet to Page Layout view when you're finished.
16. Save and close the workbook, and then submit the finished workbook and printouts to your instructor.

Explore using AutoSum to calculate production statistics.

CHALLENGE

Case Problem 3

Data File needed for this Case Problem: Global.xlsx

Global Site GPS Kevin Hodge is a production assistant at Global Site GPS, a leading manufacturer of GPS devices located in Crestwood, Missouri. One of Kevin's jobs is to monitor output at the company's five regional plants. He wants to create an Excel workbook that reports the monthly production at the five sites, including the monthly average, minimum and maximum production, and total production for the previous year. You will create the workbook that reports these statistics. Complete the following:

1. Open the **Global** workbook located in the Excel1\Case3 folder, and then save the workbook as **Global Site** in the same folder.
2. Rename the Sheet1 worksheet as **Production History**, and then insert 12 new rows at the top of the worksheet.
3. Increase the width of column A to 23 characters and the width of columns B through F to 14 characters.
4. In the range B7:F7, enter the titles **Plant1**, **Plant2**, **Plant3**, **Plant4**, and **Plant5**, respectively.
5. In the range A8:A11, enter **Total Units Produced**, **Average per Month**, **Maximum**, and **Minimum**, respectively.
6. EXPLORE Select the range B26:F26, use AutoSum to calculate the sum of the production values for each of the five plants, and then drag and drop the selected cells to the range B8:F8.
7. EXPLORE Select the range B26:F26, use AutoSum to calculate the average of the production values for each of the five plants, and then drag and drop the selected cells to the range B9:F9.

EXPLORE 8. Repeat Step 7 to calculate the maximum values for each of the five plants and move those calculated values to the range B10:F10, and then repeat to calculate the minimum production values and drag and drop those calculated values to the range B11:F11.

9. In the Production History worksheet, enter the following data:
   Cell A1: **Global Site GPS**
   Cell A2: **Production Report**
   Cell A3: **Model** Cell B3: **MapTracker 201**
   Cell A4: **Year** Cell B4: **2013**
   Cell A5: **Total Units Produced**
10. In cell B5, use the SUM function to add the values in the range B8:F8.
11. Insert a new worksheet named **Plant Directory**, and then move it to be the first worksheet in the workbook.
12. In cells A1 and A2, enter **Global Site GPS** and **Plant Directory**, respectively, and then enter the text shown in Figure 1-35 in the range A4:D9, making sure that the address is entered on two lines within the cell.

Figure 1-35 **Plant directory data**

Plant	Plant Manager	Address	Phone
1	Karen Brookers	300 Commerce Avenue Crestwood, MO 63126	(314) 555-3881
2	Daniel Gomez	15 North Main Street Edison, NJ 08837	(732) 555-0012
3	Jody Hetrick	3572 Howard Lane Weston, FL 33326	(954) 555-4817
4	Yong Jo	900 South Street Kirkland, WA 98033	(425) 555-8775
5	Sandy Nisbett	3771 Water Street Helena, MT 59623	(406) 555-4114

13. Set the width of column B to 15 characters, the width of column C to 30 characters, and the width of column D to 16 characters. Autofit the height of each row to its content.
14. Insert a new worksheet named **Documentation**, move it to be the first worksheet in the workbook, and then enter the following data:
    Cell A1: **Global Site GPS**
    Cell A3: **Author** Cell B3: your name
    Cell A4: **Date** Cell B4: the current date
    Cell A5: **Purpose** Cell B5: **Production report for Global Site GPS**
15. Switch the Production History worksheet to Page Layout view, change the orientation to landscape, and then verify that the worksheet fits on a single page.
16. Save your workbook, preview and print the workbook, close the workbook, and then submit the finished workbook and printouts to your instructor.

Create an Excel workbook to record service calls for a lawn service agency.

CREATE

Case Problem 4

There are no Data Files needed for this Case Problem.

Green Lawns Green Lawns provides yard service and maintenance for homes in and around Mount Vernon, Ohio. Gary Taylor manages the accounts for Green Lawns and wants to use Excel to record weekly service calls made by the company. Gary provides you with the list of service calls made in the first week of August. You will use this data to create the workbook for Gary. Complete the following:

1. Open a blank workbook, and then save it as **Green Lawns** in the Excel1\Case4 folder included with your Data Files.
2. Rename the Sheet1 worksheet as **Documentation**, and then enter information documenting the workbook. Include the name of the company, your name, the current date, and a brief description of the purpose of the workbook. The layout and appearance of the worksheet are up to you.
3. In the Sheet2 worksheet, enter the service calls shown in Figure 1-36, and then enter appropriate formulas to calculate the service charge for each customer. Green Lawns charges each customer a base fee plus a working fee that is equal to the hourly rate multiplied by the number of hours worked. Also, enter a formula to calculate the total charges for all customer calls. The layout and appearance of the page are up to you.

Figure 1-36 **August service calls (week 1)**

Customer	Address	Phone	Last Service	Hours	Base Fee	Hourly Rate
David Lane	391 Country Drive Mount Vernon, OH 43050	(740) 555-4439	8/2/2013	3	$35	$17.50
Robert Gomez	151 Apple Lane Mount Vernon, OH 43051	(740) 555-0988	8/2/2013	3.5	$35	$17.50
Sandra Lee	112 Main Street Mount Vernon, OH 43050	(740) 555-3773	8/3/2013	1.5	$20	$14.50
Gregory Sands	305 Country Drive Mount Vernon, OH 43050	(740) 555-4189	8/3/2013	5	$35	$21.50
Betty Oaks	205 Second Street Mount Vernon, OH 43049	(740) 555-0088	8/3/2013	1.5	$20	$14.50

4. Rename the Sheet2 worksheet as **Service Calls**, and then delete any unused sheets from the workbook.
5. Check the spelling in the workbook, correcting any spelling errors, and then proofread the workbook.
6. Save the workbook, preview the worksheets to ensure that each fits onto a single page, and then print the entire workbook. Close the workbook, and then submit the finished workbook and printouts to your instructor.

ASSESS

SAM: Skills Assessment Manager

For current SAM information, including versions and content details, visit SAM Central (http://samcentral.course.com). If you have a SAM user profile, you may have access to hands-on instruction, practice, and assessment of the skills covered in this tutorial. Since various versions of SAM are supported throughout the life of this text, check with your instructor for the correct instructions and URL/Web site for accessing assignments.

ENDING FILES

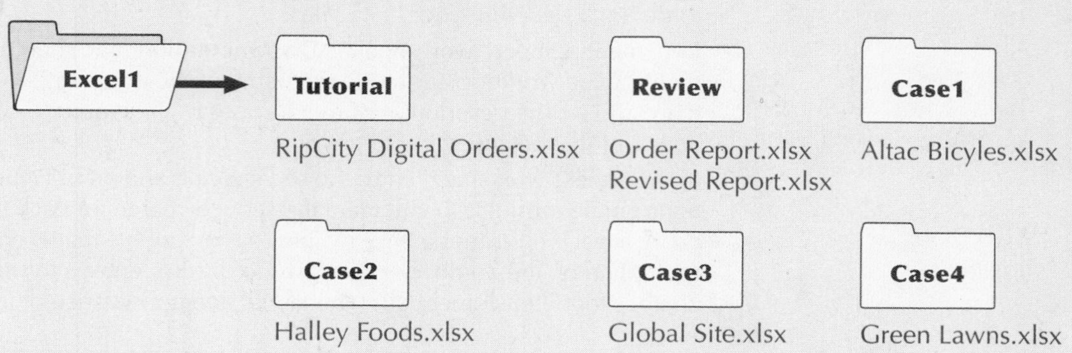

TUTORIAL 2

Formatting a Workbook

Designing a Financial Report

OBJECTIVES

Session 2.1
- Format text, numbers, and dates
- Change fonts and font colors
- Add fill colors and background images
- Create formulas to add, subtract, and divide values
- Apply number formats
- Align, indent, and rotate cell contents
- Merge a range into a single cell
- Copy and paste formats

Session 2.2
- Apply built-in cell styles
- Change the theme of a workbook
- Create formulas to add and subtract values
- Apply a built-in table style and select table style options
- Highlight cells with conditional formats
- Hide worksheet rows
- Define the print area, insert page breaks, and add print titles
- Create headers and footers
- Select page margins

Case | *ExerComp Exercise Equipment*

ExerComp, based in Mason, Ohio, manufactures electronic and computer components for fitness machines and sporting goods. At the upcoming annual sales meeting, sales managers will present reports that detail the sales history of different ExerComp products. Sales manager Tom Uhen will report on the recent sales history of the X310 heart rate monitor.

Tom has already created a workbook and entered the sales figures for the past two years. He wants you to enter formulas to calculate total sales and increases in sales. He also wants you to make the data more readable and informative. To do this, you will work with formatting tools to modify the appearance of the data in each cell, the cell itself, and the entire worksheet. Because much of Tom's data has been stored in tables, you will also use some special formatting tools designed for tables.

STARTING DATA FILES

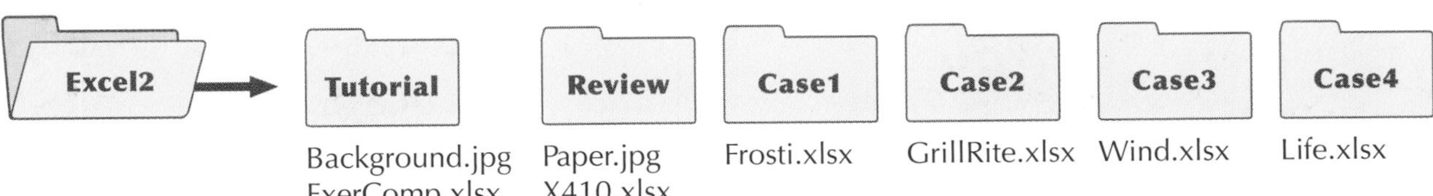

Tutorial: Background.jpg, ExerComp.xlsx
Review: Paper.jpg, X410.xlsx
Case1: Frosti.xlsx
Case2: GrillRite.xlsx
Case3: Wind.xlsx
Case4: Life.xlsx

SESSION 2.1 VISUAL OVERVIEW

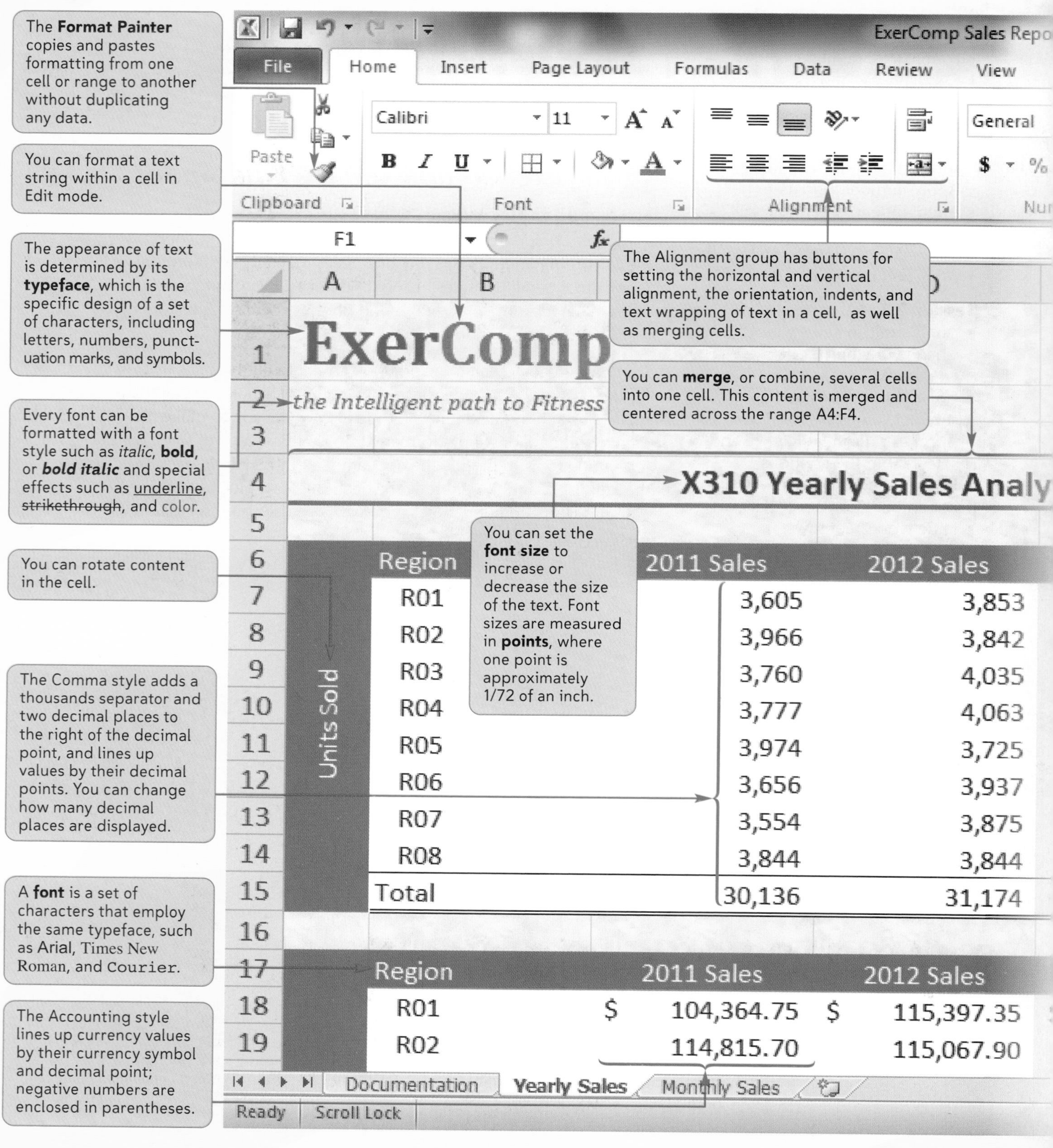

WORKSHEET FORMATTING

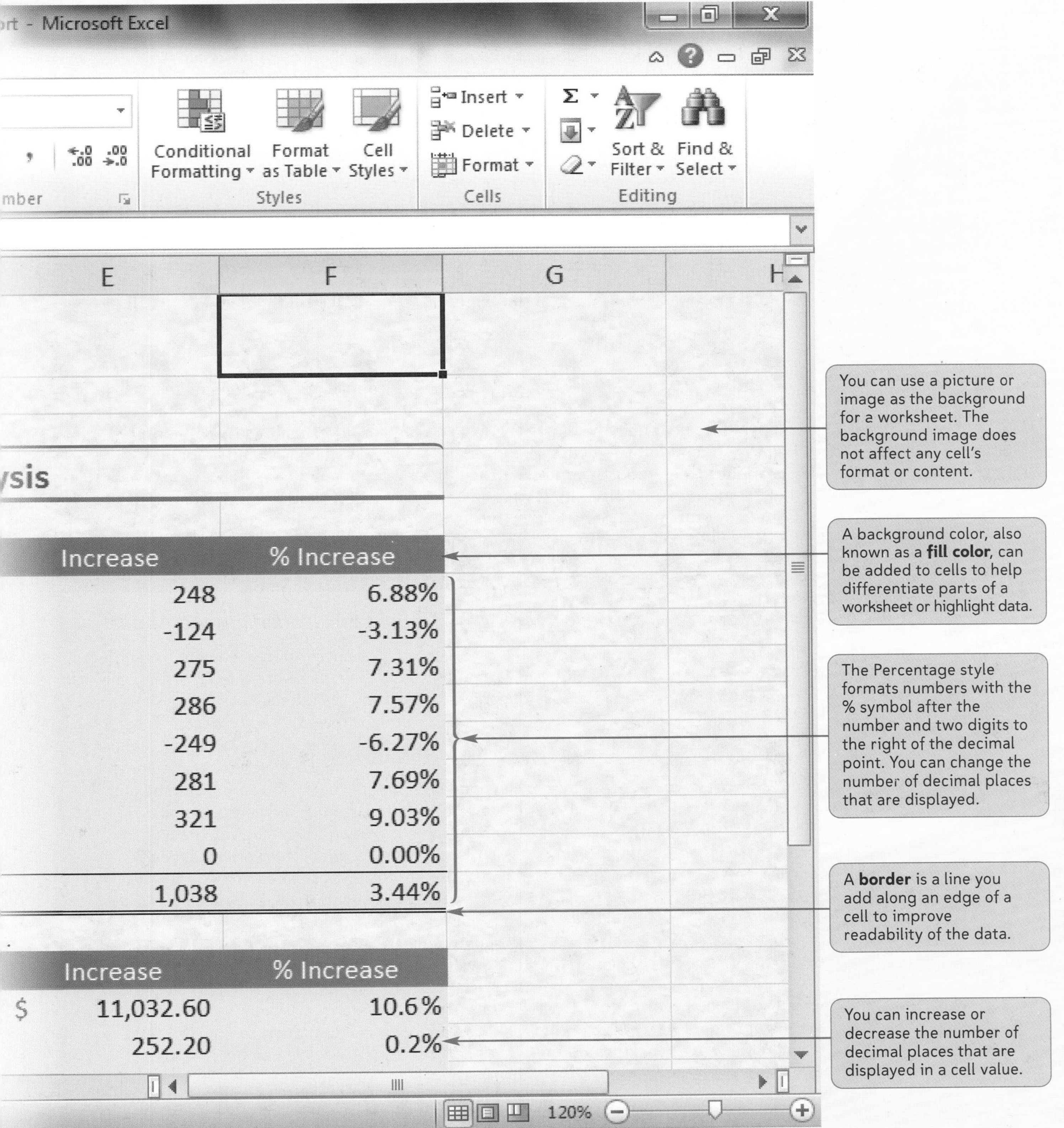

Formatting Cell Text

Tom has already entered the data and some formulas in a workbook, which is only a rough draft of what he wants to submit to the company. The Documentation sheet describes the workbook's purpose and content. The Yearly Sales sheet displays the sales history of the X310 heart rate monitor including the total number of units sold per sales region (labeled R01 through R08) and the total revenue generated by those sales in the past two years. The Monthly Sales sheet also reports the number of X310 units sold by region and month. In its current form, the data is difficult to read and interpret. Tom wants you to format the workbook contents to improve its readability and visual appeal. You'll open the workbook and review its content.

To open the workbook:

1. Open the **ExerComp** workbook located in the **Excel2\Tutorial** folder included with your Data Files, and then save the workbook as **ExerComp Sales Report**.
2. In the Documentation sheet, enter your name in cell B4 and the date in cell B5.
3. Review the contents of the three worksheets.

Formatting is the process of changing a workbook's appearance by defining the fonts, styles, colors, and decorative features. Formatting changes only the appearance of data—it does not affect the data itself. Excel organizes its formatting tools in terms of themes. A **theme** is a collection of formats for text, colors, images, and graphical effects applied throughout a workbook. Each theme has a name. The Office theme is the default, although you can apply other themes or create your own. You can also use fonts and colors that are not part of the current theme. As you format a workbook, Live Preview shows the effects of the formats on the workbook's appearance.

PROSKILLS

Written Communication: Formatting Workbooks for Readability and Appeal

Designing a workbook requires the same care as designing any written document or report. A well-formatted workbook is easier to read and establishes a sense of professionalism with readers. Do the following to improve the appearance of your workbooks:

- Clearly identify each worksheet's purpose with column or row titles and a descriptive sheet name.
- Don't crowd individual worksheets with too much information. Each worksheet should deal with only one or two topics. Place extra topics on separate sheets. Readers should be able to interpret each worksheet with a minimal amount of horizontal and vertical scrolling.
- Place worksheets containing the most important information first in the workbook. Position worksheets summarizing your findings near the front of the workbook. Position worksheets with detailed and involved analysis near the end as an appendix.
- Use consistent formatting throughout the workbook. If negative values appear in red on one worksheet, format them in the same way on all sheets. Also, be consistent in the use of thousands separators, decimal places, and percentages.
- Pay attention to the format of the printed workbook. Make sure your printouts are legible with informative headers and footers. Check that the content of the printout is scaled correctly to the page size and that page breaks divide the information into logical sections.

Excel provides many formatting tools. However, too much formatting can be intrusive, overwhelm data, and make the document difficult to read. Always remember, the goal of formatting is not simply to make a "pretty workbook," but also to accentuate important trends and relationships in the data. A well-formatted workbook should seamlessly convey your data to the reader. If the reader is thinking about how your workbook looks, it means he or she is not thinking about your data.

Applying Fonts and Font Styles

Excel organizes fonts into theme and non-theme fonts. A **theme font** is associated with a particular theme and used for headings and body text in the workbook. These fonts change automatically when you change the theme applied to the workbook. When you don't want to apply a font associated with a particular design, you use a **non-theme font**. Text formatted with a non-theme font retains its appearance no matter what theme is used with the workbook.

Fonts appear in different character styles. **Serif fonts**, such as Times New Roman, have extra decorative strokes at the end of each character. **Sans serif fonts**, such as Arial, do not include these decorative strokes. Other fonts are purely decorative such as a font used for specialized logos.

Every font can be further formatted with a font style such as *italic*, **bold**, or ***bold italic***, and special effects such as underline, ~~strikethrough~~, and color. Finally, you can set the font size to increase or decrease the size of the text.

You'll format the company name displayed at the top of each worksheet to appear in large, bold letters using the default heading font from the Office theme. Tom wants the slogan "The Intelligent Path to Fitness" displayed below the company name to appear in the heading font, but in smaller, italicized letters.

To format text in the Documentation worksheet:

1. Click the **Documentation** sheet tab to make it the active worksheet, and then click cell **A1** to make it the active cell.
2. In the Font group on the Home tab, click the **Font arrow** to display a list of fonts available on your computer. The first two fonts are the theme fonts for headings and body text—Cambria and Calibri. See Figure 2-1.

Figure 2-1 Theme and non-theme fonts in the font list

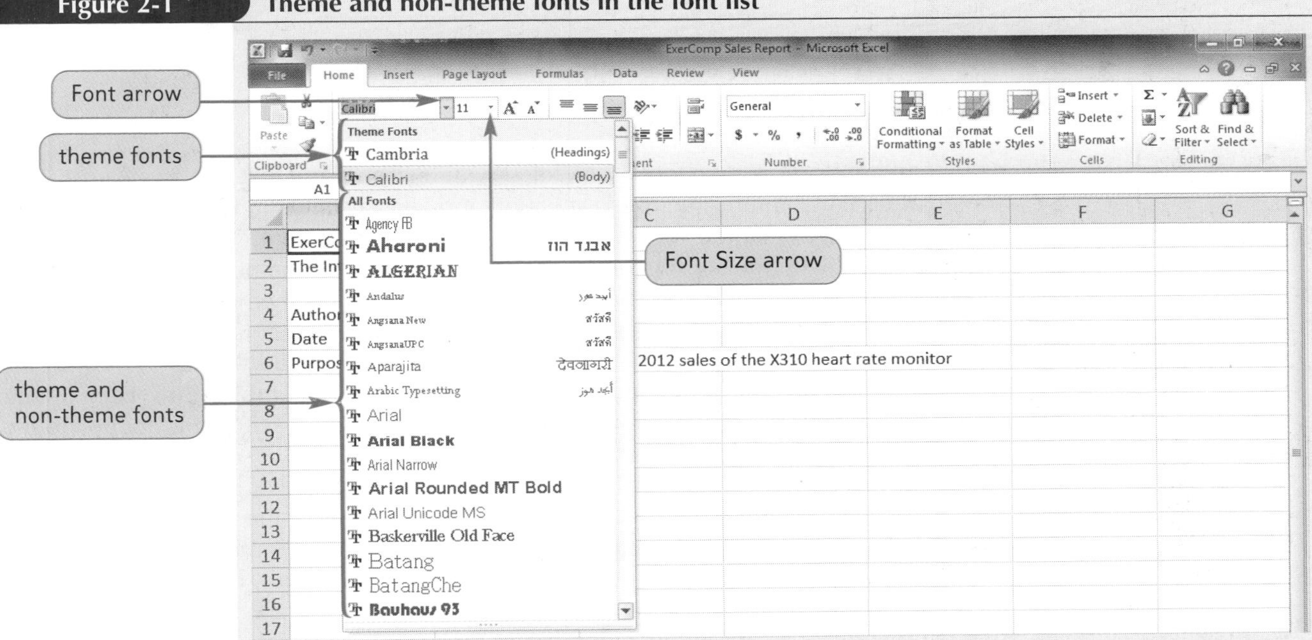

3. Click **Cambria**. The company name in cell A1 changes to the Cambria font, the default headings font in the current theme.

TIP

You can also change the font size incrementally by clicking the Increase Font Size or Decrease Font Size button in the Font group on the Home tab.

4. In the Font group, click the **Font Size arrow** to display a list of font sizes, and then click **26**. The company name changes to 26 points.
5. In the Font group, click the **Bold** button **B**. The company name is boldfaced. Next, you'll format the company slogan.
6. Click cell **A2** to make it active. The slogan text is selected.
7. In the Font group, click the **Font arrow**, and then click **Cambria**. The slogan text changes to the Cambria font.
8. In the Font group, click the **Font Size arrow**, and then click **10**. The slogan text changes to 10 points.
9. In the Font group, click the **Italic** button *I*. The slogan in cell A2 is italicized.
10. Select the range **A4:A6**, click the **Bold** button **B** in the Font group, and then click cell **A7**. The column labels are bolded. The formatted text is shown in Figure 2-2.

Figure 2-2 **Formatted cell text**

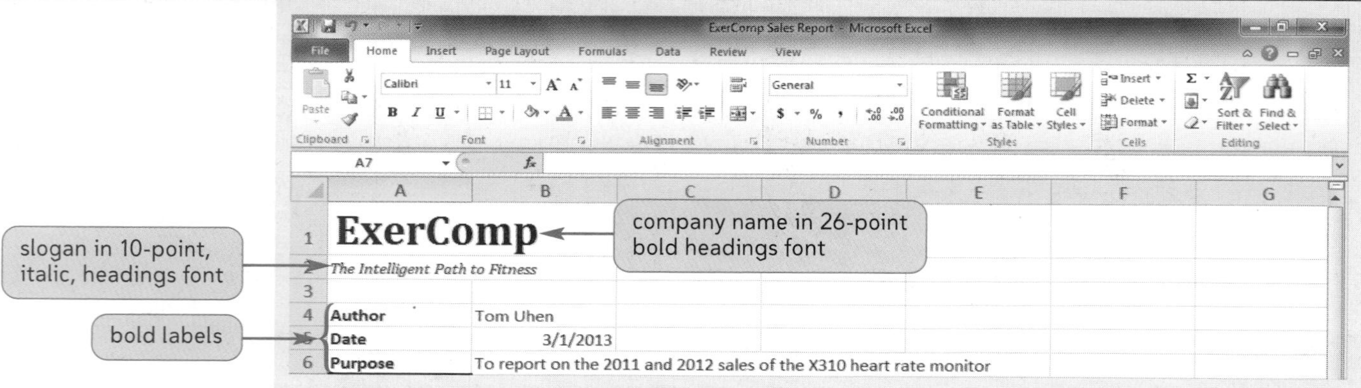

Applying a Font Color

Color can transform a plain workbook filled with numbers and text into a powerful presentation that captures the user's attention and adds visual emphasis to the points you want to make. By default, Excel displays text in a black color font.

Just as it did with fonts, Excel organizes colors into theme and non-theme colors. **Theme colors** are the 12 colors that belong to the workbook's theme. Four colors are designated for text and backgrounds, six colors are used for accents and highlights, and two colors are used for hyperlinks (followed and not followed links). These 12 colors are designed to work well together and to remain readable in all combinations. Each theme color has five variations, or **accents**, in which a different tint or shading is applied to the theme color.

Ten **standard colors**—dark red, red, orange, yellow, light green, green, light blue, blue, dark blue, and purple—are always available regardless of the workbook's theme. You can also open an extended palette of 134 standard colors. You can create a **custom color** by specifying a mixture of red, blue, and green color values, making available 16.7 million custom colors—more colors than the human eye can distinguish. Some dialog boxes have an **automatic color** option that uses your Windows default text and background colors, usually black text on a white background.

Tom wants the labels in the Documentation worksheet to stand out so you will change the ExerComp title and slogan to blue.

To change the title and slogan font color:

1. Select the range **A1:A2**.
2. In the Font group, click the **Font Color button arrow** to display the theme and standard colors. (The two colors for hyperlinked text are not shown.)
3. Point to the **Blue** color (the eighth color) in the Standard Colors section. The color name appears in a ScreenTip and you see a Live Preview of the text with the blue font color. See Figure 2-3.

Figure 2-3 Available font colors

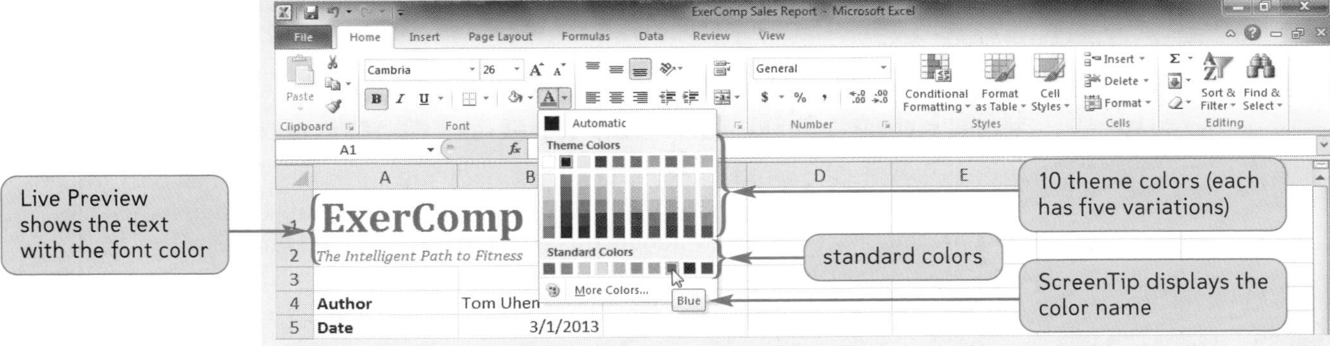

4. Click the **Blue** color. The company name and slogan change to blue.

Formatting Text Selections

In the ExerComp logo, "Exer" appears in blue text and "Comp" appears in red text. You'll need to format part of the contents in cell A1 one way and the rest a different way. When you select text in Edit mode, you can format the selection with a different font, size, style, and color. You'll format "Comp" in a red font.

TIP

You can also use the buttons on the Mini toolbar to change the font, size, style, and color of selected text within a cell.

To format the Comp text selection:

1. Double-click cell **A1** to select the cell and go into Edit mode, and then select **Comp**.
2. In the Font group on the Home tab, click the **Font Color button arrow**, and then click the **Red** color in the Standard Colors section. The text color changes. See Figure 2-4.

Figure 2-4 Text selection being formatted

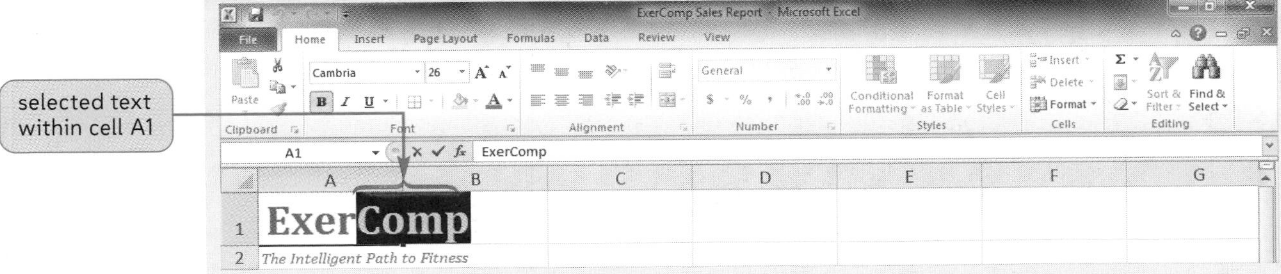

3. Click cell **A7** to deselect the cell. The text "ExerComp" in cell A1 is blue and red.

REFERENCE

Formatting Cell Content

- To change the font, select the cell or range. In the Font group on the Home tab, click the Font arrow, and then click a font.
- To change the font size, select the cell or range. In the Font group on the Home tab, click the Font Size arrow, and then click a font size.
- To change a font style, select the cell or range. In the Font group on the Home tab, click the Bold, Italic, or Underline button.
- To change a font color, select the cell or range. In the Font group on the Home tab, click the Font Color button arrow, and then click a color.
- To format a text selection, double-click the cell to enter Edit mode, select the text to format, change the font, size, style, or color, and then press the Enter key.

Working with Colors and Backgrounds

Another way to distinguish sections of a worksheet is by formatting the cell background. You can fill the cell background with color or an image. Tom wants you to format the Documentation worksheet by adding fill colors and background images.

Changing a Fill Color

TIP

You can add a fill color to a sheet tab. In the Cells group on the Home tab, click the Format button, point to Tab Color, and then click a color.

By default, Excel does not add any background color to worksheet cells; but background colors, also known as fill colors, can be added using the same color palette you use for font colors. The labels in the Documentation worksheet should be in a white font on a blue background. The author's name, current date, and purpose of the worksheet should be in a blue font on a white background. You will make both of these changes to the Documentation worksheet.

To change the background fill color:

1. Select the range **A4:A6**.
2. In the Font group on the Home tab, click the **Fill Color button arrow**, and then click the **Blue** color (the eighth color) in the Standard Colors section.
3. In the Font group, click the **Font Color button arrow**, and then click the **White** color in the Theme Colors section.
4. Select the range **B4:B6**, and then format the cells with a blue font on a white background.
5. Increase the width of column B to **55** characters.
6. Click cell **A7**. See Figure 2-5.

Figure 2-5 Formatted labels and text in the Documentation worksheet

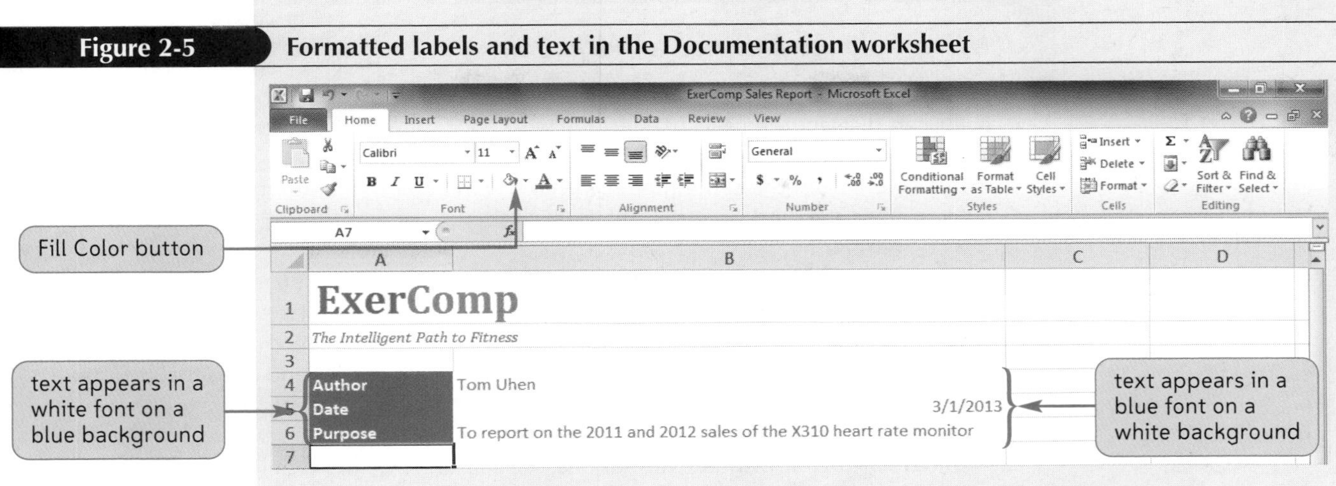

Adding a Background Image

You can use a picture or an image as the background for a worksheet. An image can give the worksheet a textured appearance, like that of granite, wood, or fibered paper. The image is repeated until it fills the entire worksheet. The background image does not affect any cell's format or content. Background colors applied to cells appear on top of the image, covering that portion of the image. Background images do not print.

Tom has provided an image for you to use as the background of the Documentation worksheet.

To add a background image to the Documentation worksheet:

1. Click the **Page Layout** tab on the Ribbon. The page layout options appear on the Ribbon.
2. In the Page Setup group, click the **Background** button. The Sheet Background dialog box opens.
3. Navigate to the **Excel2\Tutorial** folder included with your Data Files, click the **Background** JPEG image file, and then click the **Insert** button. The image is added to the background of the Documentation worksheet. See Figure 2-6.

Figure 2-6 Background image added to the worksheet

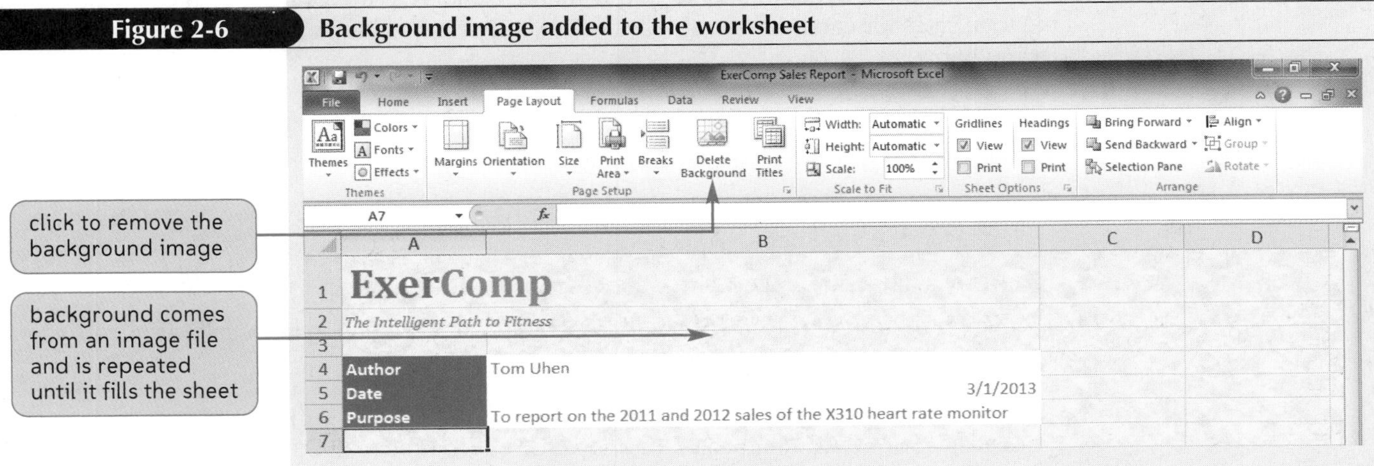

INSIGHT

Using Color to Enhance a Workbook

When used wisely, color can enhance any workbook. However, when used improperly, color can distract the user, making the workbook more difficult to read. As you format a workbook, keep in mind the following tips:

- Use colors from the same theme within a workbook to maintain a consistent look and feel across the worksheets. If the built-in themes do not fit your needs, you can create a custom theme.
- Use colors to differentiate types of cell content and to direct users where to enter data. For example, format a worksheet so that formula results appear in cells without a fill color and users enter data in cells with a light gray fill color.
- Avoid garish color combinations that can annoy the reader and be difficult to read.
- Print the workbook on both color and black-and-white printers to ensure that the printed copy is readable in both versions.
- Understand your printer's limitations and features. Colors that look good on your monitor might not look as good when printed.
- Be sensitive to your audience. About 8 percent of all men and 0.5 percent of all women have some type of color blindness and might not be able to see the text when certain color combinations are used. Red-green color blindness is the most common, so avoid using red text on a green background or green text on a red background.

Formatting Calculated Values

When you format numeric values, the goal is to make the workbook easier for the reader to interpret (which is same goal of any formatting you apply to a workbook). For example, adding a comma as a thousands separator, controlling the number of decimal places, and using percentage and currency symbols can make a large table of numbers easier to read and understand.

For Tom's report, you'll format the values in the worksheets that contain the sales figures for the past two years.

Creating Formulas to Add, Subtract, and Divide Values

The Yearly Sales worksheet contains the annual sales figures from 2011 and 2012 for the X310 heart rate monitor. The upper section of the worksheet displays the number of units sold in each sales region per year, and the lower section displays the revenue generated by sales region per year in dollars. You will add formulas to the worksheet to calculate the total sales for each year as well as the net and percent change in sales from one year to another.

To calculate the total yearly sales:

1. Click the **Yearly Sales** sheet tab. The Yearly Sales worksheet is now the active sheet in the workbook.
2. In cells B15 and B26, enter the label **Total**.
3. Select the range **C15:D15**. You'll insert the SUM function in both cells at once.
4. Click the **Home** tab on the Ribbon.
5. In the Editing group, click the **Sum** button Σ. The formulas inserted in these cells, =SUM(C7:C14) in cell C15 and =SUM(D7:D14) in cell D15, calculate the total units sold for 2011 and 2012, which are 30136 and 31174, respectively.

6. In the Clipboard group on the Home tab, click the **Copy** button. The formulas are copied to the Clipboard.
7. Scroll down and select the range **C26:D26**. These are the cells in which you want to paste the copied formulas.
8. In the Clipboard group, click the **Paste** button. The formulas to calculate the total annual revenues are pasted in the selected range, displaying totals of 872437.2 in 2011 and 933661.3 in 2012. See Figure 2-7.

Figure 2-7 **Formulas calculate the total units sold and total revenue**

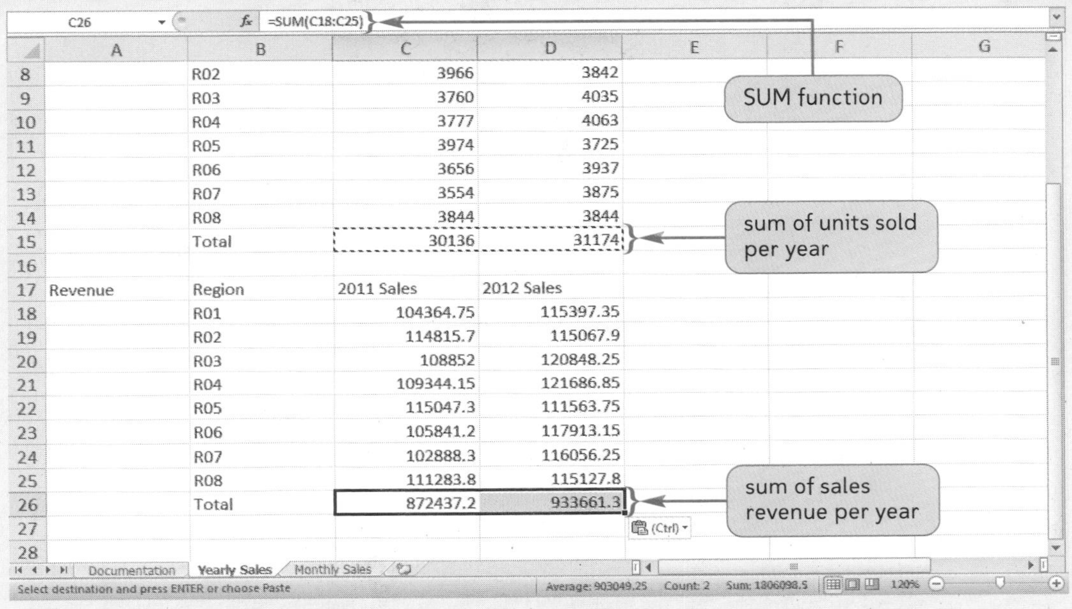

The formula results are difficult to read in their current form. You'll correct that problem shortly.

To calculate the net change in units sold and revenue from 2011 to 2012, you'll subtract the 2011 figures from the 2012 figures. To calculate the percent change, you'll divide the net change by the 2011 units sold and revenue figures for each sales region as well as across all sales regions.

To calculate the net and percent change from 2011 to 2012:

1. In cells E6 and E17, enter the label **Increase**, and then, in cells F6 and F17, enter the label **% Increase**.
2. In cell E7, enter the formula **=D7–C7** to calculate the increase in units sold from 2011 to 2012.
3. In cell F7, enter the formula **=E7/C7** to calculate the percent increase in units sold from 2011 to 2012. When calculating a percent increase, always divide the amount of increase by the starting value and not the ending value.
4. Select the range **E7:F7**. Rather than reenter the formulas in cells E7 and F7, you'll copy and paste them into the rest of the worksheet.

5. In the Clipboard group on the Home tab, click the **Copy** button. The range is copied to the Clipboard.
6. Select the nonadjacent range **E8:F15;E18:F26**. You want to paste the formulas in these cells.
7. In the Clipboard group, click the **Paste** button. The formulas are pasted in the selected ranges.
8. Click cell **A6** to deselect the range. The formulas calculate the values for the net and percent increase in units sold and revenue from 2011 to 2012. See Figure 2-8.

Figure 2-8 Net and percent increase in sales and revenue

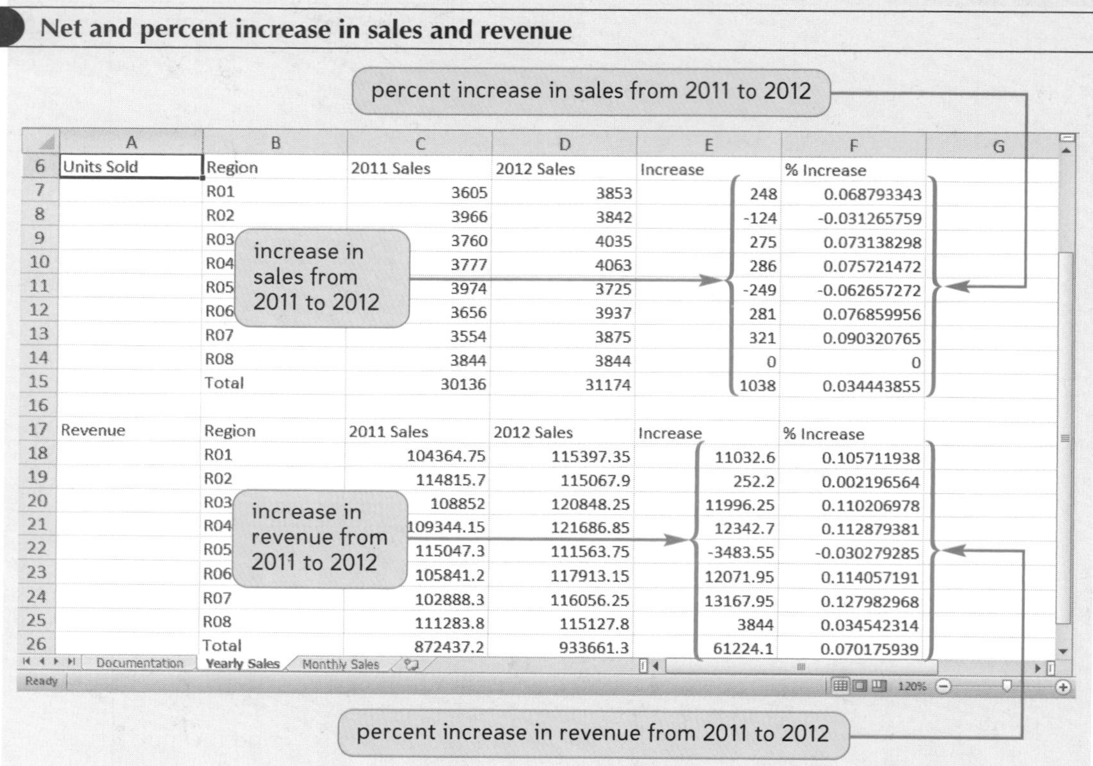

	A	B	C	D	E	F
6	Units Sold	Region	2011 Sales	2012 Sales	Increase	% Increase
7		R01	3605	3853	248	0.068793343
8		R02	3966	3842	-124	-0.031265759
9		R03	3760	4035	275	0.073138298
10		R04	3777	4063	286	0.075721472
11		R05	3974	3725	-249	-0.062657272
12		R06	3656	3937	281	0.076859956
13		R07	3554	3875	321	0.090320765
14		R08	3844	3844	0	0
15		Total	30136	31174	1038	0.034443855
16						
17	Revenue	Region	2011 Sales	2012 Sales	Increase	% Increase
18		R01	104364.75	115397.35	11032.6	0.105711938
19		R02	114815.7	115067.9	252.2	0.002196564
20		R03	108852	120848.25	11996.25	0.110206978
21		R04	109344.15	121686.85	12342.7	0.112879381
22		R05	115047.3	111563.75	-3483.55	-0.030279285
23		R06	105841.2	117913.15	12071.95	0.114057191
24		R07	102888.3	116056.25	13167.95	0.127982968
25		R08	111283.8	115127.8	3844	0.034542314
26		Total	872437.2	933661.3	61224.1	0.070175939

Applying Number Formats

You can format values using a **number format**, which displays the values in a way that makes it easy for the reader to quickly understand and interpret them. You can change the number format for the displayed value without affecting the underlying stored value. Excel formats numbers by default in the **General number format**, which, for the most part, displays values exactly as they are typed by the user. If the value is calculated from a formula or function, Excel shows as many digits after the decimal point as will fit in the cell with the last displayed digit rounded. Calculated values too large to fit into the cell are displayed in scientific notation.

The General number format is good for simple calculations, but some values require additional formatting to make the numbers easier to interpret. Using Excel, you can:

- Set the number of digits displayed to the right of the decimal point
- Add commas to act as a thousands separator for large values
- Apply currency or accounting symbols to numeric values to identify the monetary unit being used
- Display percentages using the % symbol

The values in the Yearly Sales worksheet are difficult to interpret. For example, it is unclear whether a particular value represents sales revenue or units sold, and it is hard to determine, without study, whether a revenue value is expressed in millions or hundreds of thousands of dollars. You will format these values to make them easier to read.

To apply a thousands separator to the units sold values:

1. Select the range **C7:E15**.
2. In the Number group on the Home tab, click the **Comma Style** button. Each value in the selected range now includes a thousands separator. Two digits were also added to the right of the decimal point. Because the units sold values are expressed in integers, you will remove the digits to the right of the decimal place.
3. In the Number group, click the **Decrease Decimal** button twice. The two extra digits are removed. See Figure 2-9.

Figure 2-9 **Units sold values formatted**

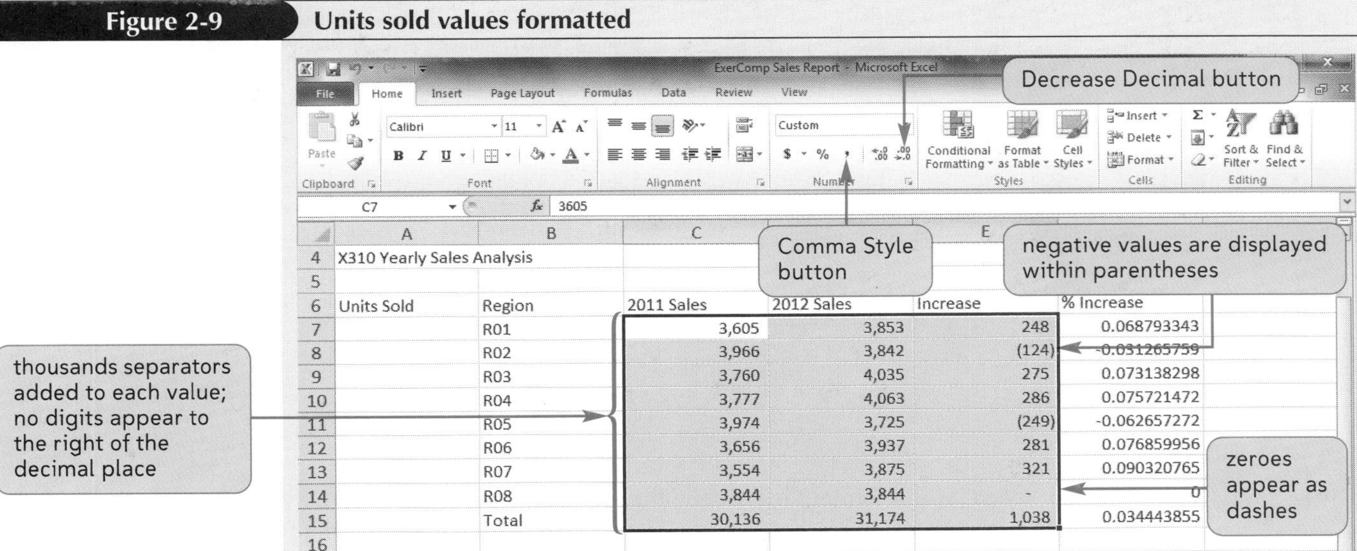

Though you used the Comma Style button to add the thousands separator, the button actually applies an accounting style used for currency values to the values in the columns. This accounting style lines up currency values within a column by the currency symbol and decimal point. When the values do not have a currency symbol, the values are aligned by the decimal point. The accounting style also encloses negative numbers, such as –124 in cell E8, within parentheses, such as (124). This is a standard format used in accounting documents. If you prefer to display negative numbers in a different way, you can modify this format. Another standard accounting practice is to add a currency symbol to only the first and last entries within a column of values.

You will display the revenue values in columns C through E using the same accounting style, but with two decimal places and with the currency symbol appearing only in rows 18 and 26.

TIP

For international documents, you can select other currency symbols: In the Number group on the Home tab, click the Accounting Number Format button arrow, and then click a currency symbol.

To format the revenue values:

1. Select the range **C18:E26**.
2. In the Number group on the Home tab, click the **Comma Style** button.
3. Select the nonadjacent range **C18:E18;C26:E26**.
4. In the Number group, click the **Accounting Number Format** button. As shown in Figure 2-10, $ symbols are added to the revenue values in the first and last row.

Figure 2-10 **Revenue values formatted**

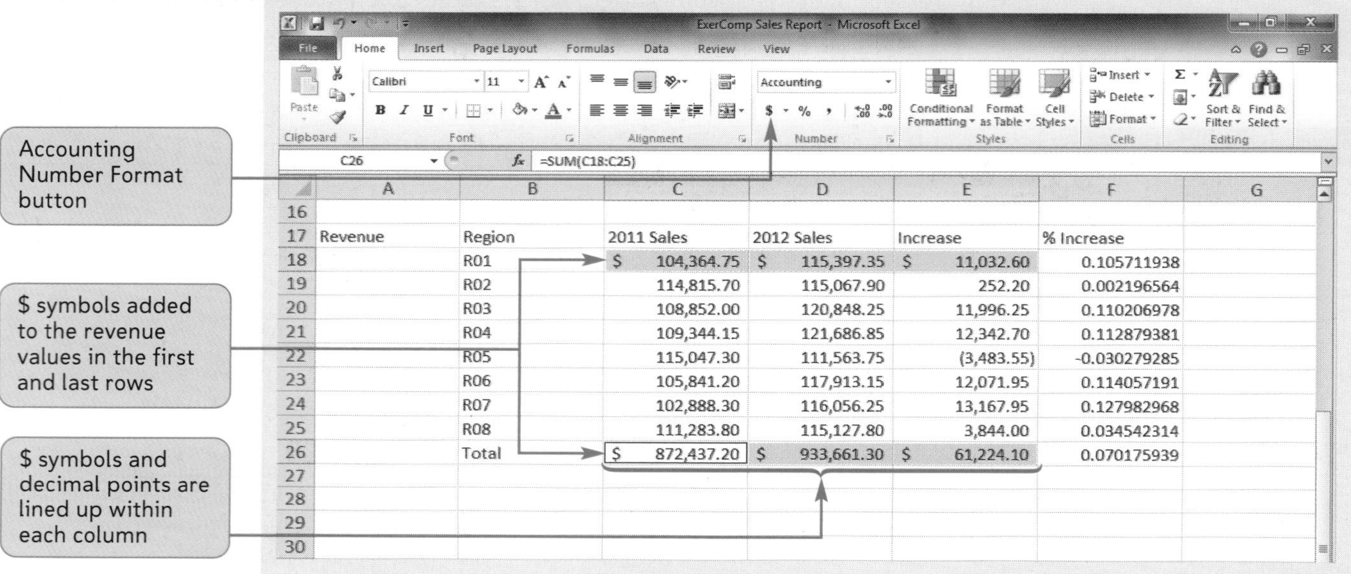

Next, you'll format the percent change values in column F. When you format values as percentages, the % symbol appears after the number and no digits appear to the right of the decimal point. You can change how many decimal places are displayed in the cell. Tom wants the percentages in column F to display the % symbol with two decimal places.

To format the percentages in column F:

1. Select the nonadjacent range **F7:F15;F18:F26**.
2. In the Number group on the Home tab, click the **Percent Style** button.
3. In the Number group, click the **Increase Decimal** button twice to display the percentages to two decimal places.
4. Scroll up and click cell **A6** to deselect the range. Figure 2-11 shows the formatted numbers in the worksheet.

Figure 2-11 Percent increase values formatted

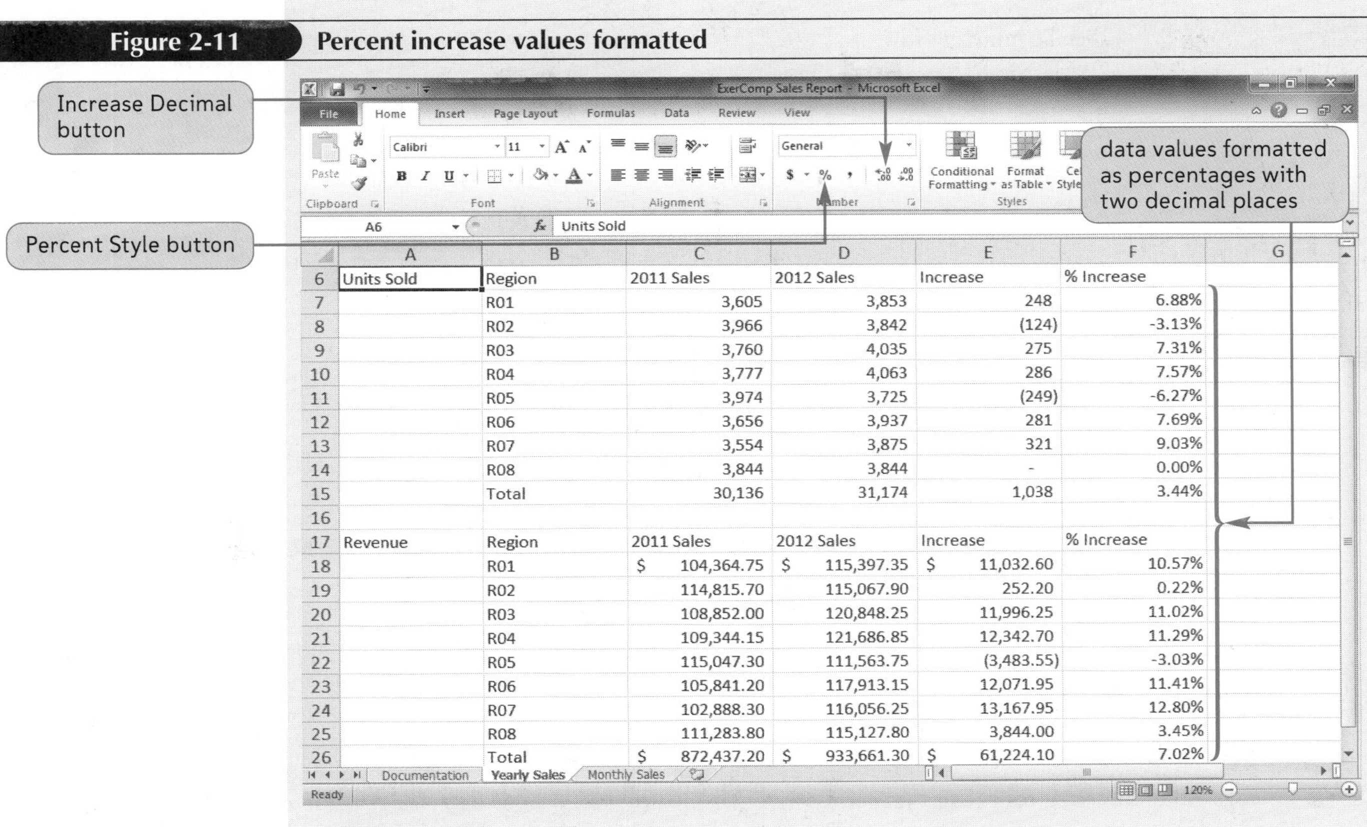

	A	B	C	D	E	F
6	Units Sold	Region	2011 Sales	2012 Sales	Increase	% Increase
7		R01	3,605	3,853	248	6.88%
8		R02	3,966	3,842	(124)	-3.13%
9		R03	3,760	4,035	275	7.31%
10		R04	3,777	4,063	286	7.57%
11		R05	3,974	3,725	(249)	-6.27%
12		R06	3,656	3,937	281	7.69%
13		R07	3,554	3,875	321	9.03%
14		R08	3,844	3,844	-	0.00%
15		Total	30,136	31,174	1,038	3.44%
16						
17	Revenue	Region	2011 Sales	2012 Sales	Increase	% Increase
18		R01	$ 104,364.75	$ 115,397.35	$ 11,032.60	10.57%
19		R02	114,815.70	115,067.90	252.20	0.22%
20		R03	108,852.00	120,848.25	11,996.25	11.02%
21		R04	109,344.15	121,686.85	12,342.70	11.29%
22		R05	115,047.30	111,563.75	(3,483.55)	-3.03%
23		R06	105,841.20	117,913.15	12,071.95	11.41%
24		R07	102,888.30	116,056.25	13,167.95	12.80%
25		R08	111,283.80	115,127.80	3,844.00	3.45%
26		Total	$ 872,437.20	$ 933,661.30	$ 61,224.10	7.02%

With the data reformatted, Tom can more easily see that the company sold 1038 more units in 2012 than in 2011—an increase of 3.44 percent, which increased revenue by $61,224.10, or 7.02 percent. This was not uniform across all sales regions. Total units sold and revenue for Region R05, for example, decreased between 2011 and 2012.

Formatting Dates and Times

The date in the Documentation sheet is displayed in an abbreviated format, *mm/dd/yyyy*. Tom wants you to use an extended format that includes the day of the week, the full month name, the day, and the year.

Because Excel stores dates and times as numbers and not as text, you can apply different formats without affecting the date and time value. The abbreviated format entered into the Documentation sheet is referred to as the Short Date format. You can also apply a Long Date format that displays the day of the week and the full month name in addition to the day of the month and the year. Other built-in Excel formats include formats for displaying time values in 12- or 24-hour time.

You will change the date in the Documentation sheet to the Long Date format.

To format the date in the Long Date format:

1. Click the **Documentation** sheet tab to make the Documentation worksheet active, and then select cell **B5**.
2. In the Number group on the Home tab, click the **Number Format** arrow, and then click **Long Date**. The date format changes to show the weekday name, month name, day, and year. See Figure 2-12.

Figure 2-12 **Formatted date**

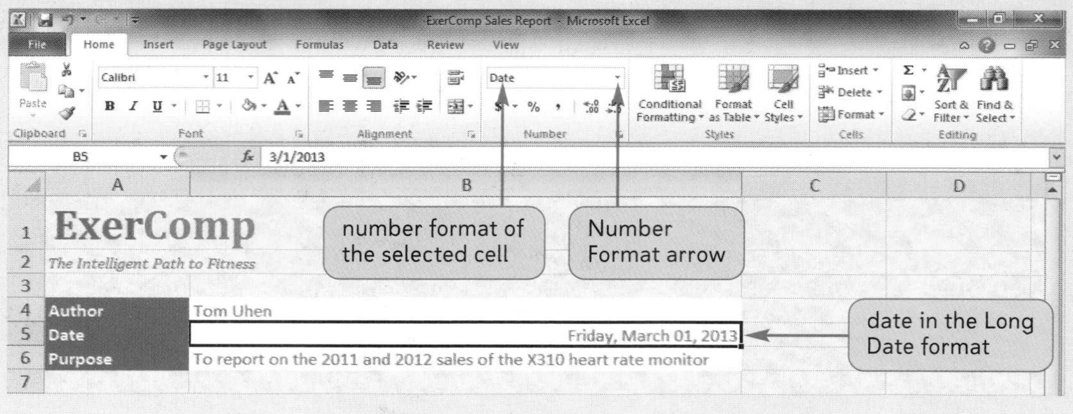

INSIGHT

Excel Dates and Times as Numeric Values

Although dates and times entered into a cell usually are displayed as text, they are actually stored by Excel as numbers measuring the interval between the specified date and time and January 1, 1900 at 12:00 a.m. For example, the date April 1, 2013 is stored as 41,365, which is the number of days between April 1, 2013 and January 1, 1900.

Times are stored as fractional parts of one day. A time of 6:00 a.m. is stored as 0.25 because that represents one-fourth of a 24-hour day (starting the day from 12:00 a.m.). Similarly, a cell containing the date and time of April 1, 2013 at 6:00 a.m. would be stored as 41,365.25.

Excel stores dates and times as numbers to make it easier to calculate time intervals. For example, to calculate the difference between one date and another, you just subtract the earlier date from the later date. If you subtract the date and time of March 30, 2013 at 12:00 p.m. from April 1, 2013 at 6:00 a.m., Excel displays 1.75—or one and three quarters of a day.

You can always view the actual date and time by selecting the cell that contains the date/time entry and applying the General number format, or by switching the workbook window to Formula view.

Formatting Worksheet Cells

You can format the appearance of individual cells by modifying the alignment of text within the cell, indenting cell text, or adding borders of different styles and colors to individual cells or ranges. You'll make these changes to the cells in Tom's workbook.

Aligning Cell Content

By default, cell text is aligned with the left and bottom borders of a cell and cell values are aligned with the right and bottom borders. In some cases, you might want to change the text alignment to make the text more readable or visually appealing. In general, you should center column titles, left-align other cell text, and align numbers to keep their decimal places lined up within a column. The buttons to set these alignment options are located in the Alignment group on the Home tab. Figure 2-13 describes the operations of these buttons.

Figure 2-13 **Alignment buttons**

Button	Description
	Aligns the cell content with the cell's top edge
	Vertically centers the cell content within the cell
	Aligns the cell content with the cell's bottom edge
	Aligns the cell content with the cell's left edge
	Horizontally centers the cell content within the cell
	Aligns the cell content with the cell's right edge
	Decreases the size of the indentation used in the cell
	Increases the size of the indentation used in the cell
	Rotates the cell content to any angle within the cell
	Forces the cell text to wrap within the cell borders
	Merges the selected cells into a single cell

Although the date in the Documentation worksheet is formatted to display as text, it is right-aligned in the cell (because Excel treats dates and times as numbers). You'll use the Alignment group buttons to left-align the date in the Documentation worksheet and center the column titles in the Yearly Sales worksheet.

To left-align the date and center the column titles:

1. If necessary, select cell **B5**.
2. In the Alignment group on the Home tab, click the **Align Text Left** button. The date shifts to the left edge of the cell.
3. Click the **Yearly Sales** sheet tab to make that worksheet active, and then select the nonadjacent range **C6:F6;C17:F17**.
4. In the Alignment group, click the **Center** button. The column titles in columns C, D, E, and F are centered.

Indenting Cell Content

Sometimes you want a cell's content moved a few spaces from the cell left edge. This is particularly useful for entries that are considered subsections of a worksheet. For example, Tom recorded sales for eight regions and then added the totals. Each region can be considered a subsection, and Tom thinks it would look better if the region labels were indented a few spaces. You increase the indentation by roughly one character space each time you click the Increase Indent button in the Alignment group on the Home tab. To decrease or remove an indentation, click the Decrease Indent button.

You'll increase the indent for the region labels.

To indent the region labels:

1. Select the nonadjacent range **B7:B14;B18:B25**.
2. In the Alignment group on the Home tab, click the **Increase Indent** button. Each region label indents one character space.
3. Click cell **A6** to deselect the range. See Figure 2-14.

Figure 2-14 Centered and indented text

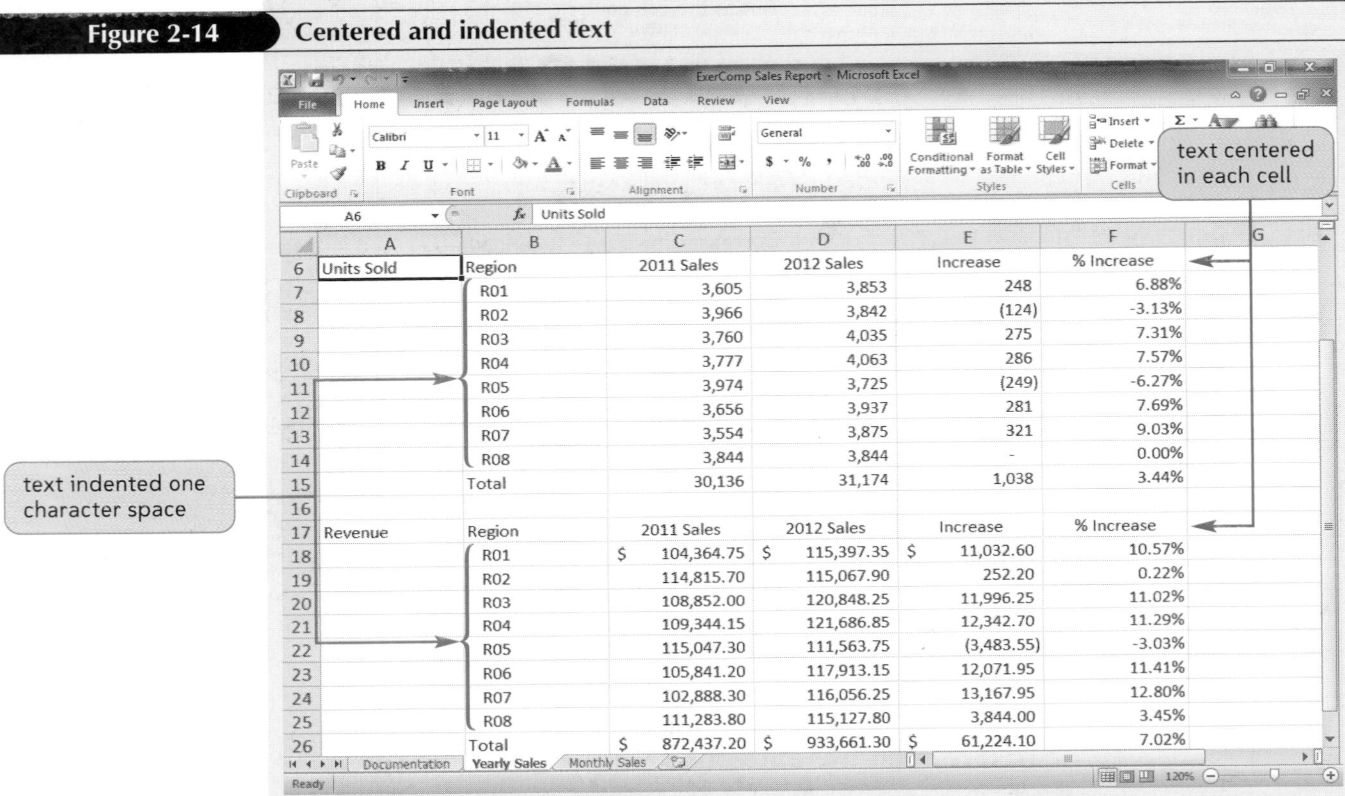

	A	B	C	D	E	F
6	Units Sold	Region	2011 Sales	2012 Sales	Increase	% Increase
7		R01	3,605	3,853	248	6.88%
8		R02	3,966	3,842	(124)	-3.13%
9		R03	3,760	4,035	275	7.31%
10		R04	3,777	4,063	286	7.57%
11		R05	3,974	3,725	(249)	-6.27%
12		R06	3,656	3,937	281	7.69%
13		R07	3,554	3,875	321	9.03%
14		R08	3,844	3,844	-	0.00%
15		Total	30,136	31,174	1,038	3.44%
16						
17	Revenue	Region	2011 Sales	2012 Sales	Increase	% Increase
18		R01	$ 104,364.75	$ 115,397.35	$ 11,032.60	10.57%
19		R02	114,815.70	115,067.90	252.20	0.22%
20		R03	108,852.00	120,848.25	11,996.25	11.02%
21		R04	109,344.15	121,686.85	12,342.70	11.29%
22		R05	115,047.30	111,563.75	(3,483.55)	-3.03%
23		R06	105,841.20	117,913.15	12,071.95	11.41%
24		R07	102,888.30	116,056.25	13,167.95	12.80%
25		R08	111,283.80	115,127.80	3,844.00	3.45%
26		Total	$ 872,437.20	$ 933,661.30	$ 61,224.10	7.02%

Merging Cells

In the Yearly Sales worksheet, Tom wants the title "X310 Yearly Sales Analysis" in cell A4 centered over columns A through F. One way to align text over several columns or rows is to merge several cells into one cell. When you merge cells, only the content from the upper-left cell in the range is retained. The cell reference for the merged cell is the upper-left cell reference. So, if you merge cells A1 and A2, the merged cell reference is cell A1.

After you merge a range into a single cell, you can realign its content. The Merge button in the Alignment group on the Home tab includes the following options:

- **Merge & Center** merges the range into one cell and horizontally centers the content.
- **Merge Across** merges each of the rows in the selected range across the columns in the range.
- **Merge Cells** merges the range into a single cell, but does not horizontally center the cell content.
- **Unmerge Cells** reverses a merge, returning the merged cell back into a range of individual cells.

You will merge and center the title in cell A4 across the range A4:F4.

To merge and center the title across a cell range:

1. Select the range **A4:F4** in the Yearly Sales worksheet.
2. In the Alignment group on the Home tab, click the **Merge & Center** button. The range A4:F4 merges into one cell with a cell reference of A4 and the text is centered within the cell.
3. Select the range **A6:A15**, and then click the **Merge & Center** button. The cells are merged vertically into a single cell, displaying the text "Units Sold" aligned with the bottom cell border.
4. Select the range **A17:A26**, and then click the **Merge & Center** button. The cells in the range are also merged vertically into a single cell.
5. Click cell **A3**. Figure 2-15 shows the merged cells in the Yearly Sales worksheet.

Figure 2-15 **Merged ranges with centered text**

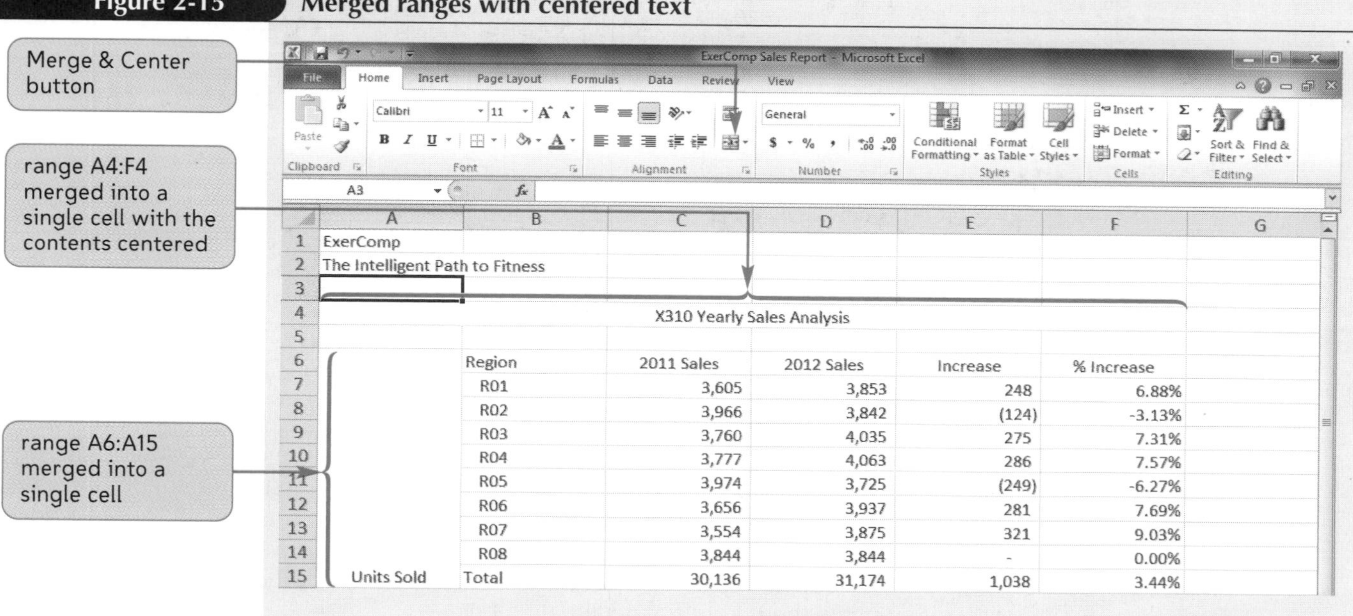

Rotating Cell Contents

Text and numbers are displayed within cells horizontally. However, you can rotate cell text to any angle to save space or to provide visual interest to a worksheet. The Units Sold and Revenue titles were placed at the bottom of their respective merged cells, which makes them difficult to read. The titles would look better and take up less room if they were rotated vertically within their cells. You will rotate the titles.

To rotate the titles:

1. Click the merged cell **A6** to select it.
2. In the Alignment group on the Home tab, click the **Orientation** button, and then click **Rotate Text Up**. The cell text rotates 90 degrees counterclockwise.
3. In the Alignment group, click the **Middle Align** button. The rotated text vertically aligns within the merged cell.

4. Click the merged cell **A17** to select it, and then repeat Steps 1 through 3 to rotate and align the text.
5. Reduce the width of column A to **5** characters. See Figure 2-16.

Figure 2-16 Rotated cell text

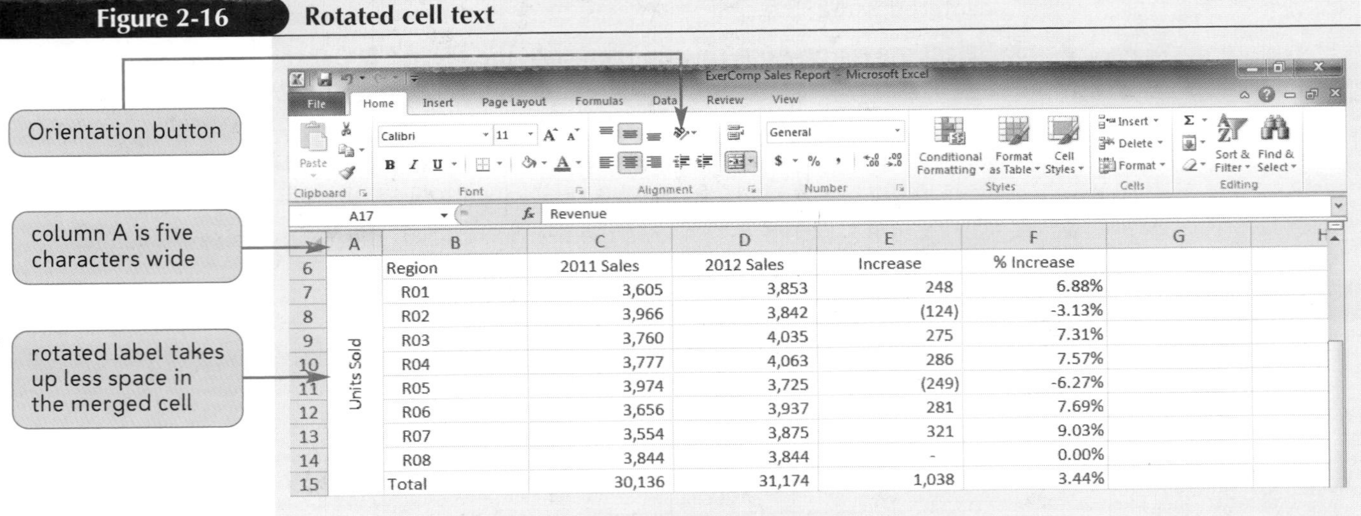

Adding Cell Borders

TIP

You set the gridlines or the row and column headings to print by clicking the appropriate Print check box in the Sheet Options group on the Page Layout tab.

When a worksheet is printed, the gridlines that surround the cells are not printed by default. They only appear on the worksheet as a guide. Sometimes you want to include lines along the edges of cells to enhance the readability of the rows and columns of data. One way to do this is by adding a border to a cell or range. You can add borders to the left, top, right, or bottom of a cell or range; around an entire cell; or around the outside edges of a range. You can also specify the thickness of and the number of lines in the border.

Tom wants you to add borders to the column titles and Total rows. Standard accounting practice is to add a single top border and a double bottom border to the Total rows to clearly differentiate them from financial data.

To add cell borders to the column labels and Total rows:

1. Select the nonadjacent range **B6:F6;B17:F17**. You'll add a bottom border to these column labels.
2. In the Font group on the Home tab, click the **Border button arrow**, and then click **Bottom Border**. A border is added to the bottom of the selected cells.
3. Select the nonadjacent range **B15:F15;B26:F26**. You'll add top and bottom borders to these Total rows.
4. In the Font group, click the **Border button arrow**, and then click **Top and Double Bottom Border**. The Total rows both have a single top border and a double bottom border, following standard accounting practice.
5. Click cell **A5** to deselect the range. See Figure 2-17.

Figure 2-17 Borders added to cells

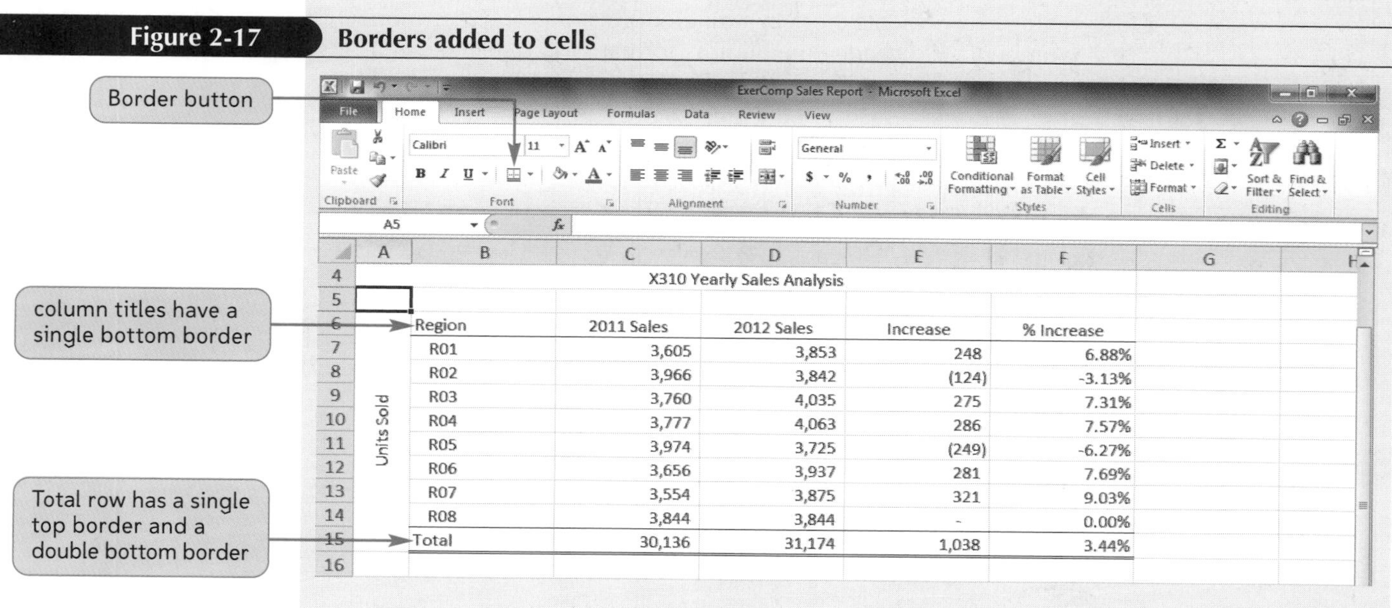

Exploring Options in the Format Cells Dialog Box

The buttons on the Home tab provide quick access to the most commonly used formatting choices. For more options, you can use the Format Cells dialog box. For example, the numbers in cells E8 and E11 are displayed in parentheses to indicate that they are negative. Although parentheses are common in accounting to indicate negative currency values, Tom wants you to reformat the units sold numbers to display negative numbers with a minus symbol. You can do this in the Format Cells dialog box.

TIP

You can also open the Format Cells dialog box by right-clicking a cell or selected range, and then clicking Format Cells on the shortcut menu.

To open the Format Cells dialog box:

1. Select the range **E7:E15**.
2. In the Number group on the Home tab, click the **Dialog Box Launcher**. The Format Cells dialog box opens with the Number tab active.

The Format Cells dialog box has six tabs, each focusing on a different set of formatting options, as described below. You can apply the formats in this dialog box to selected worksheet cells.

- **Number** provides options for formatting the appearance of numbers, including dates and numbers treated as text (for example, telephone or Social Security numbers).
- **Alignment** provides options for how data is aligned within a cell.
- **Font** provides options for selecting font types, sizes, styles, and other formatting attributes such as underlining and font colors.
- **Border** provides options for adding and removing cell borders as well as selecting a line style and color.
- **Fill** provides options for creating and applying background colors and patterns to cells.
- **Protection** provides options for locking or hiding cells to prevent other users from modifying their contents.

Although you've applied many of these formats from the Home tab, the Format Cells dialog box presents them in a different way and provides more choices. You'll use the Number tab to change the number format for the selected cells. Remember, modifying the number format does not affect the value stored in the workbook.

To set the format for negative values:

1. In the Category box on the left side of the Format Cells dialog box, click **Number**.
2. Verify that **0** (zero) appears in the Decimal places box.
3. Verify that the **Use 1000 Separator (,)** check box contains a check mark.
4. In the Negative numbers box, verify that **–1,234** (the first option) is selected. See Figure 2-18.

Figure 2-18 Number tab in the Format Cells dialog box

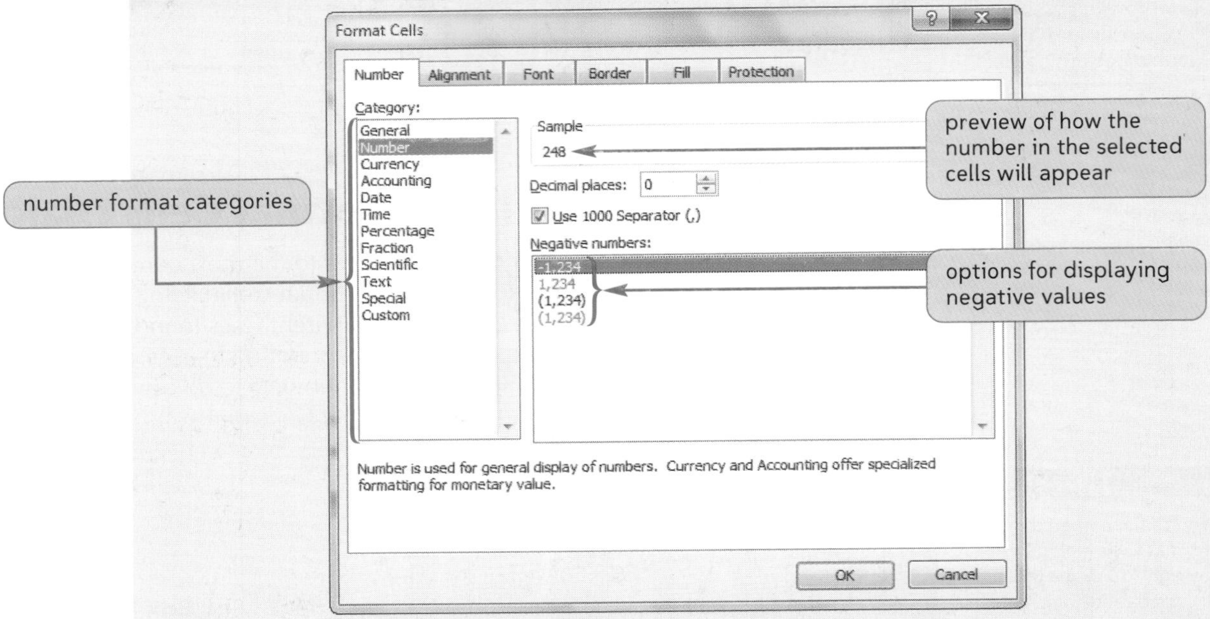

5. Click the **OK** button. The Format Cells dialog box closes and the negative numbers in the range E7:E15 appear with a minus symbol, a comma as the thousands separator, and no decimal places.

Tom wants the bottom border color used for the column titles changed from black to green. You'll use the Border tab in the Format Cells dialog box to set the border line color and make this change. On the Border tab, you can select a line style ranging from thick to thin, choose double to dotted lines, and place these lines anywhere around the cells in the selected range.

To set the border color for the column labels:

1. Select the nonadjacent range **B6:F6;B17:F17**.
2. In the Font group on the Home tab, click the **Borders button arrow**, and then click **More Borders**. The Format Cells dialog box opens with the Border tab active.

3. In the Line group, click the **Color arrow** to display the color palette, and then click **Green** (the sixth color) in the Standard Colors section.
4. Click the bottom border of the border preview. A green bottom border is shown in the preview. See Figure 2-19.

Figure 2-19 Border tab in the Format Cells dialog box

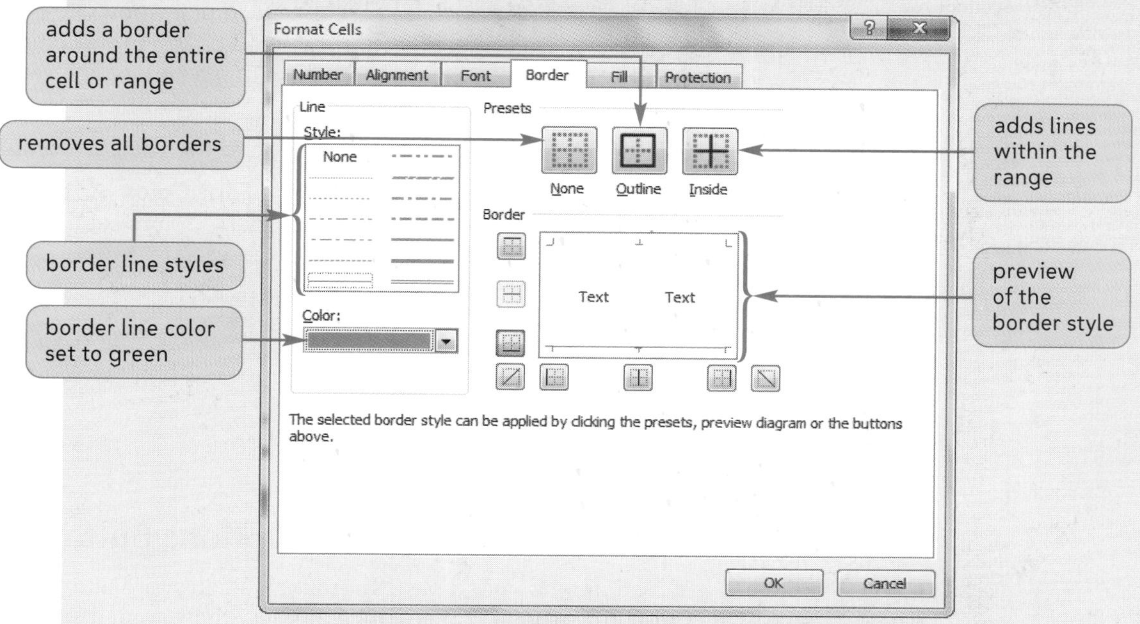

5. Click the **OK** button. The dialog box closes and the cells with column titles have a green bottom border.

Copying and Pasting Formats

You have not yet formatted the titles in cells A1 and A2 of the Yearly Sales worksheet to match the style you used for the Documentation worksheet. You could repeat the same steps to format these cells, but a quicker method is to copy those formats from the Documentation worksheet into the Yearly Sales worksheet.

Copying Formats with the Format Painter

Using the Format Painter is a fast and efficient way of maintaining a consistent look and feel throughout a workbook. So, after you set the formatting in one cell, you can copy that formatting to another cell or range without duplicating the data.

You'll use the Format Painter to copy the cell formats from the range A1:A2 in the Documentation worksheet into the same range in the Yearly Sales worksheet.

To copy and paste a format:

1. Click the **Documentation** sheet tab to make that worksheet active, and then select the range **A1:A2**.
2. In the Clipboard group on the Home tab, click the **Format Painter** button. The formats from the selected cells are copied to the Clipboard.
3. Click the **Yearly Sales** sheet tab to make that worksheet active, and then select the range **A1:A2**. The formatting from the Documentation worksheet is removed from the Clipboard and applied to the selected cells. Format Painter does not copy formatting applied to text selections within a cell, so the red color you applied to "Comp" was not included in the pasted formatting.
4. Double-click cell **A1** to switch to Edit mode, and then select **Comp** in the cell.
5. In the Font group on the Home tab, click the **Font Color button arrow** A, and then click **Red** (the second color) in the Standard Colors section. The selected text changes to red.
6. Press the **Enter** key to exit Edit mode.
7. Select the range **A1:A2** in the Yearly Sales worksheet, and then repeat Steps 2 through 6 to copy the formatting to the range A1:A2 in the Monthly Sales worksheet.

TIP

You can double-click the Format Painter button to paste the same format multiple times. Click the Format Painter button again to turn it off.

Copying Formats with the Paste Options Button

Sometimes you want to copy and paste more than a cell's formatting. When you want to paste the formatting from a copied range along with its contents, you can use the Paste Options button. As shown in Figure 2-20, each time you paste, the Paste Options button appears in the lower-right corner of the pasted cell or range. When you click the Paste Options button, you can choose from a list of pasting options, such as pasting only the values or only the formatting.

Figure 2-20 **Paste Options button**

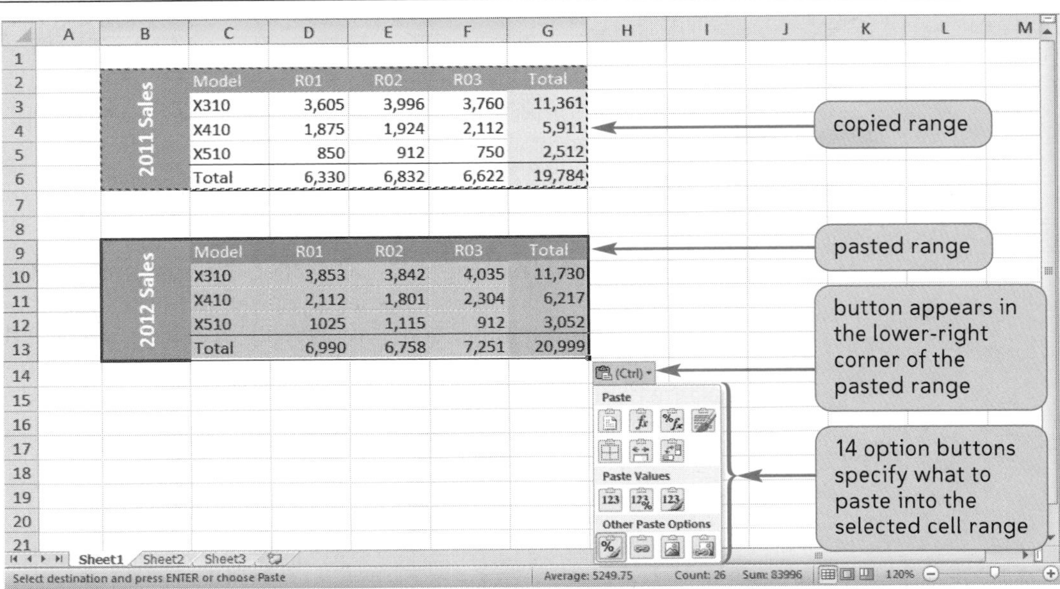

Copying Formats with Paste Special

The Paste Special command is another way to control what you paste from the Clipboard. To use Paste Special, select and copy a range, select the range where you want to paste the Clipboard contents, click the Paste button arrow in the Clipboard group on the Home tab, and then click Paste Special to open the dialog box shown in Figure 2-21. From the Paste Special dialog box, you can control exactly how to paste the copied range.

Figure 2-21 Paste Special dialog box

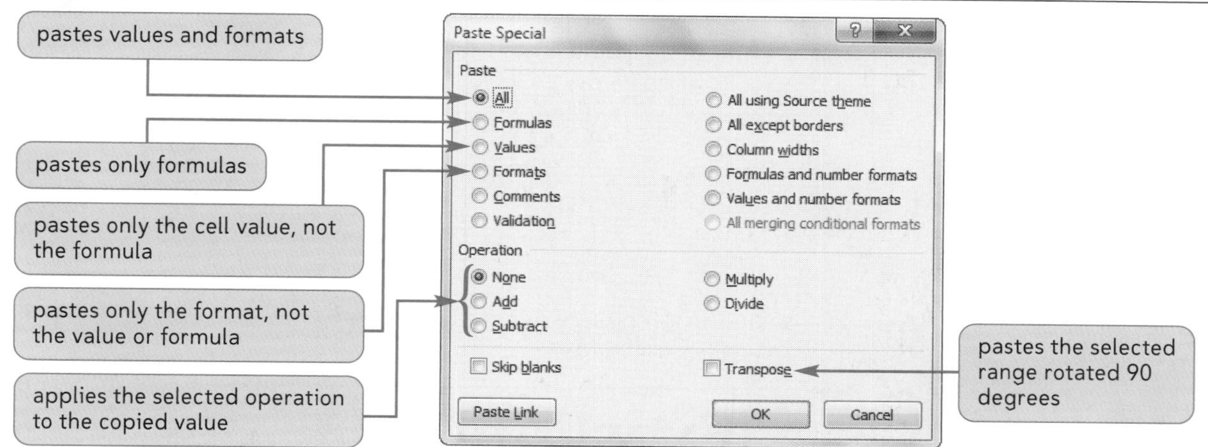

So far, you have formatted cells and ranges in Tom's workbook. In the next session, you'll work with built-in styles, themes, table styles, conditional formatting, and page layout tools.

REVIEW

Session 2.1 Quick Check

1. What is the difference between a serif font and a sans serif font?
2. What is the difference between a theme color and a standard color?
3. What is the General number format?
4. Why are dates right-aligned within a worksheet cell by default?
5. The range A1:C5 is merged into a single cell. What is the cell reference of this merged cell?
6. Where can you access all the formatting options for worksheet cells?
7. What are three tools you can use to copy and paste only the formatting of a cell?
8. Describe how you would use the Paste Special dialog box to multiply every value in a selected range by 2.

SESSION 2.2 VISUAL OVERVIEW

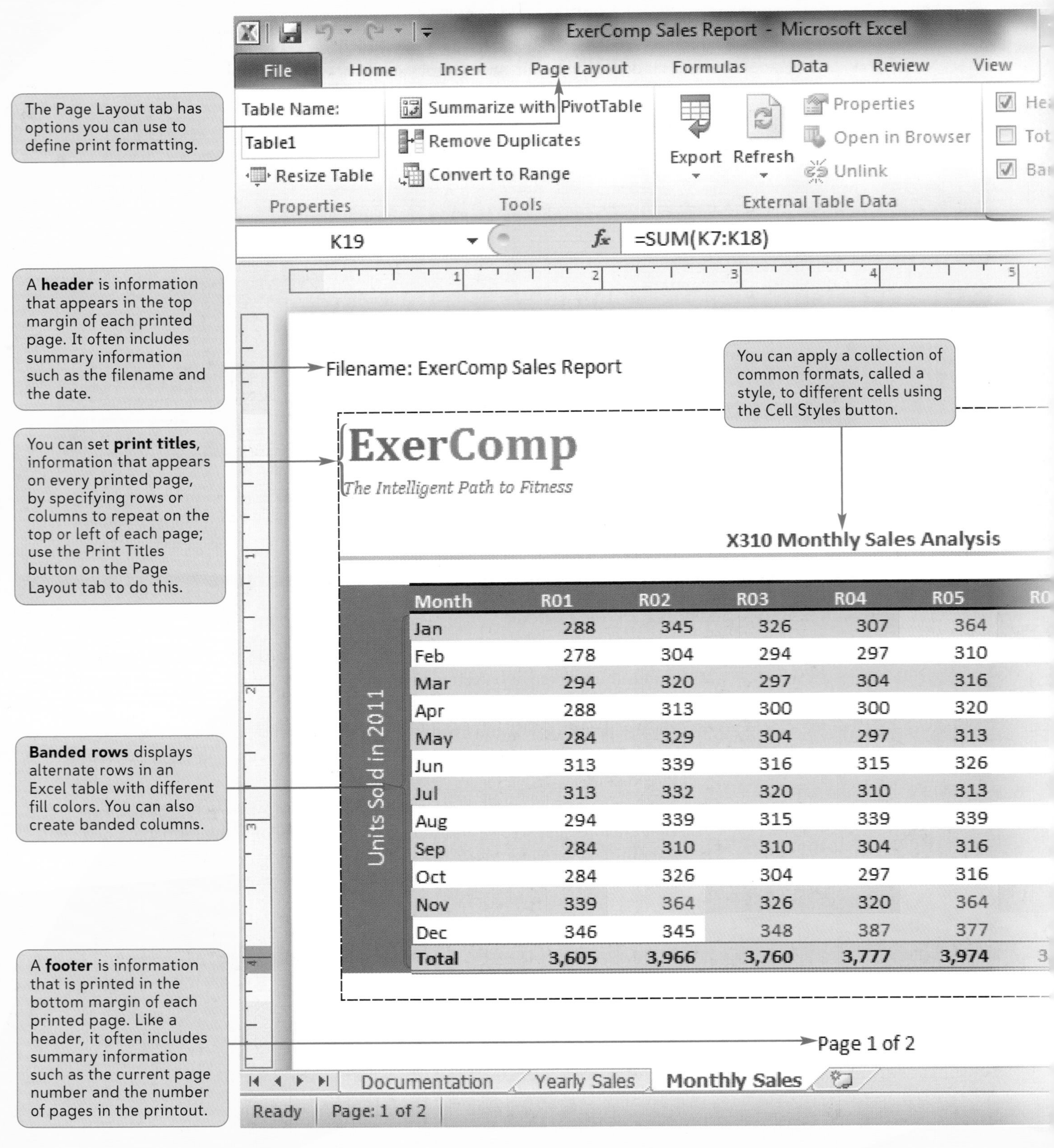

TABLE STYLES AND PAGE FORMATTING

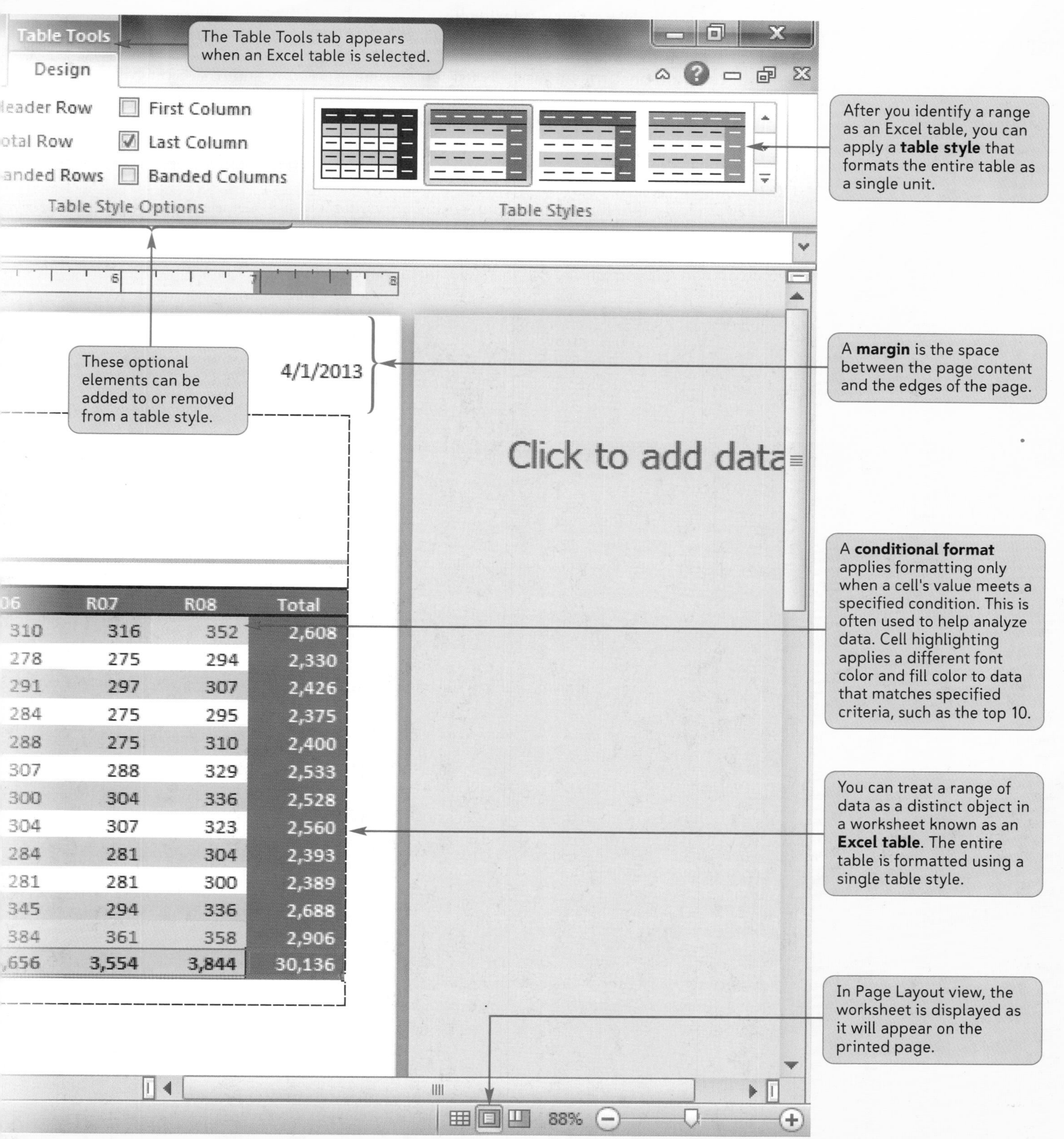

06	R07	R08	Total
310	316	352	2,608
278	275	294	2,330
291	297	307	2,426
284	275	295	2,375
288	275	310	2,400
307	288	329	2,533
300	304	336	2,528
304	307	323	2,560
284	281	304	2,393
281	281	300	2,389
345	294	336	2,688
384	361	358	2,906
,656	3,554	3,844	30,136

Applying Cell Styles

A workbook often contains several cells that store the same type of data. For example, each worksheet might have a cell displaying the sheet title, or a range of financial data might have several cells containing summary totals. It's good design practice to apply the same format to worksheet cells that contain the same type of data.

One way to ensure that you are using consistent formats is to copy and paste your formats using the Format Painter. The Format Painter is effective, but it can also be time consuming if you need to copy the same format to several cells scattered across the workbook. Moreover, if you decide to modify the format, you must copy and paste the revised format all over again. Another way to ensure that cells displaying the same type of data use the same format is with styles.

A style is a selection of formatting options using a specific font and color from the current theme. For example, you can create a style to display sheet titles in a bold, white, 20-point Calibri font on a blue background. You can then apply that style to any sheet title in a workbook. If you later revise the style, the appearance of any cell formatted with that style is updated automatically. This saves you the time and effort of reformatting each cell individually.

Excel has a variety of built-in styles to format worksheet titles, column and row totals, and cells with emphasis. You used the built-in Currency and Percent styles when you formatted data in the Yearly Sales worksheet as currency and percentages. Some styles are based on the workbook's current theme and may change if the theme is changed.

REFERENCE

Applying a Cell Style

- Select the cell or range to which you want to apply a style.
- In the Styles group on the Home tab, click the Cell Styles button.
- Point to each style in the Cell Styles gallery to see a Live Preview of that style on the selected cell or range.
- Click the style you want to apply to the selected cell or range.

You will use some of the built-in styles to add more color and visual interest to the Yearly Sales worksheet.

To apply built-in styles to the Yearly Sales worksheet:

1. If you took a break after the previous session, open the ExerComp Sales Report workbook located in the Excel2\Tutorial folder included with your Data Files.
2. Click the **Yearly Sales** sheet tab to make that worksheet active, and then select the merged cell **A4**.
3. In the Styles group on the Home tab, click the **Cell Styles** button. The Cell Styles gallery opens.
4. Point to the **Heading 1** style in the Titles and Headings section. Live Preview shows cell A4 in a 15-point, bold font with a solid blue bottom border. See Figure 2-22.

Figure 2-22 Cell Styles gallery

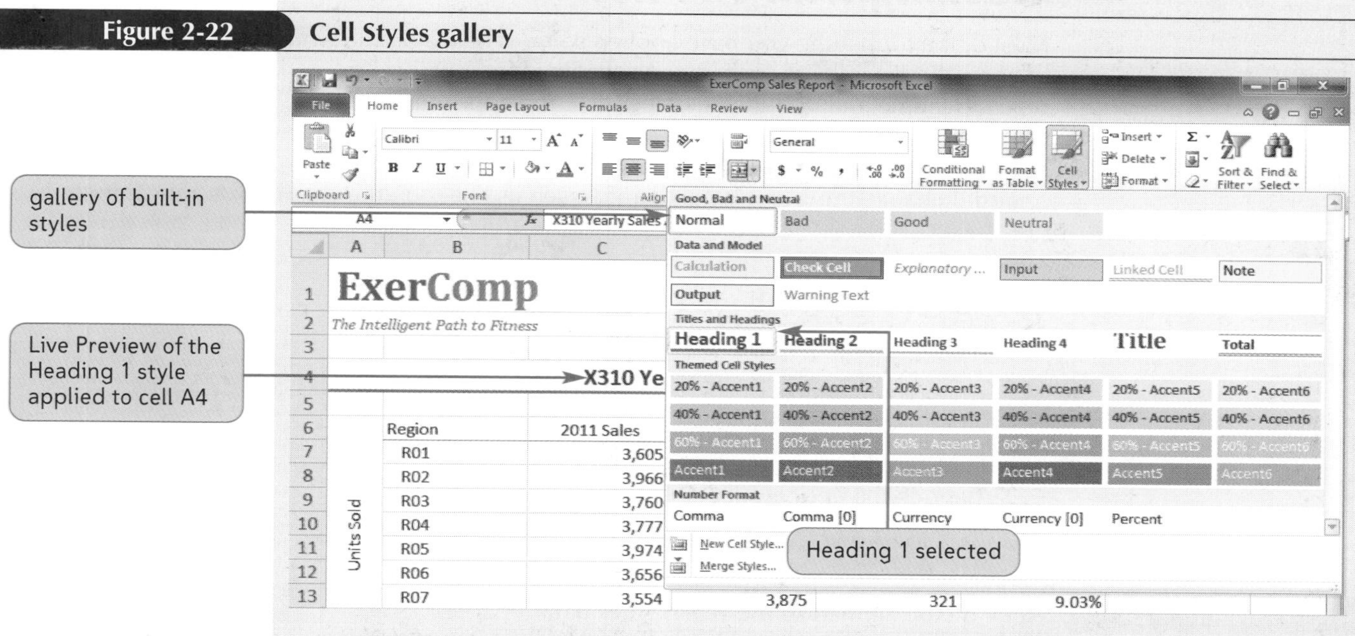

5. Move the pointer over different styles in the Cell Styles gallery to preview cell A4 with each style, and then click the **Heading 1** style. The style is applied to cell A4.
6. Select the nonadjacent range **B6:F6;B17:F17**, click the **Cell Styles** button, and then click the **Accent1** style in the Themed Cell Styles section. Each column heading is formatted.
7. Select the nonadjacent range **E7:F15;E18:F26**, click the **Cell Styles** button, and then click the **20% – Accent1** style in the Themed Cell Styles section. The calculated values are formatted differently from the data.
8. Click cell **F1** to deselect the range. See Figure 2-23.

Figure 2-23 Formatted yearly sales data

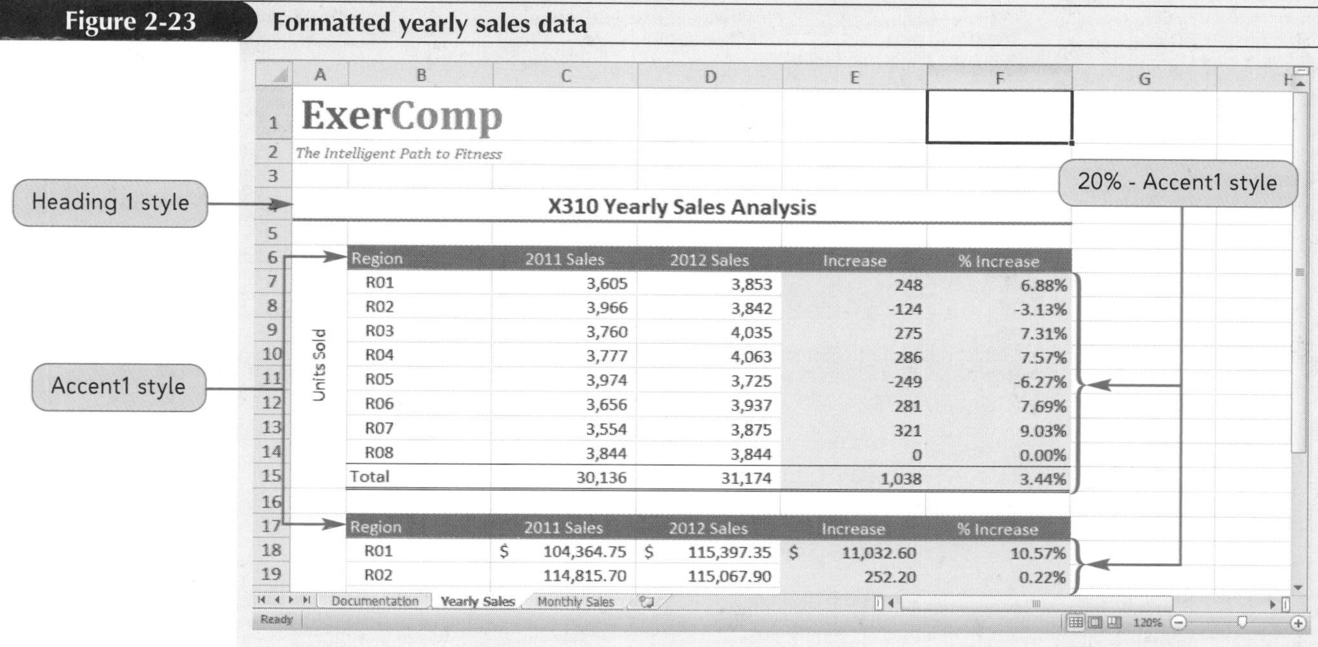

Working with Themes

Most of the formatting you have applied so far is based on the workbook's current theme—the default Office theme. As you've seen, fonts, colors, and cell styles are organized in theme and non-theme categories. The appearance of these fonts, colors, and cell styles depends on the workbook's current theme. If you change the theme, the formatting of these elements also changes throughout the entire workbook.

You'll change the workbook's theme to see its effect on the workbook's appearance.

To change the workbook's theme:

1. Click the **Page Layout** tab on the Ribbon.
2. In the Themes group, click the **Themes** button. The Themes gallery opens. Office—the current theme—is the default.
3. Point to each theme in the Themes gallery. Live Preview shows how each theme changes the appearance of the Yearly Sales worksheet.
4. Click the **Apex** theme to apply that theme to the workbook. See Figure 2-24.

Figure 2-24 Apex theme applied to the yearly sales data

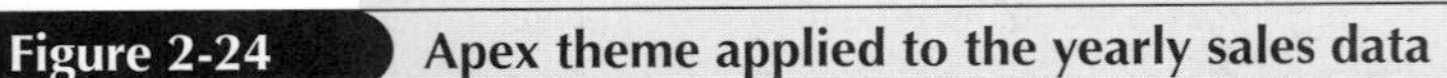

Region	2011 Sales	2012 Sales	Increase	% Increase
R01	3,605	3,853	248	6.88%
R02	3,966	3,842	-124	-3.13%
R03	3,760	4,035	275	7.31%
R04	3,777	4,063	286	7.57%
R05	3,974	3,725	-249	-6.27%
R06	3,656	3,937	281	7.69%
R07	3,554	3,875	321	9.03%
R08	3,844	3,844	0	0.00%
Total	30,136	31,174	1,038	3.44%

Region	2011 Sales	2012 Sales	Increase	% Increase
R01	$ 104,364.75	$ 115,397.35	$ 11,032.60	10.57%

Changing the theme made a significant difference in the worksheet's appearance. The most obvious changes are the fill colors and the fonts. Only elements directly tied to a theme change when you select a different theme. The cells you formatted with the Accent1 cell style changed because the Accent1 color is blue in the Office theme and orange in the Apex theme. The Heading 1 style you applied to the titles in cells A1 and A2 uses the Cambria typeface in the Office theme and the Lucida Sans typeface in the Apex theme. The Apex theme also uses a different font for body text, which is why the rest of the text changed size and appearance.

The logo colors in cell A1 did not change because you used two standard colors, blue and red, which are not part of a theme. Changing the theme does not affect these colors.

Tom prefers the default Office theme, so you'll reapply that theme.

To select the Office theme:

1. In the Themes group on the Page Layout tab, click the **Themes** button, and then click the **Office** theme from the gallery of themes.

PROSKILLS

Teamwork: Sharing Styles and Themes

Using a common style and design theme for all the files you create in Microsoft Office is a simple way to give your files a consistent look and feel and project a professional image. This consistency is especially important when a team of workers is collaborating on a set of documents. When all team members work from a common set of style and design themes, readers will not be distracted by inconsistent or clashing styles.

To quickly copy the styles from one workbook to another, open the workbook with the styles you want to copy, and then open the workbook in which you want to copy those styles. In the Styles group on the Home tab, click the Cell Styles button, and then click Merge Styles. The Merge Styles dialog box opens, listing the currently open workbooks. Select the workbook with the styles you want to copy, and then click the OK button to copy those styles into the current workbook. If you modify any styles, you must copy the styles to the other workbook; Excel does not update styles between workbooks.

Because other Office files, including those created with Word or PowerPoint, use the same file format for themes, you can create one theme to use with all the Office files you create. To save a theme, in the Themes group on the Page Layout tab, click the Themes button, and then click Save Current Theme. The Save Current Theme dialog box opens. Select a save location (in a default Theme folder on your computer or another folder), type a descriptive name in the File name box, and then click the Save button. If you saved the theme file in a default Theme folder, the theme appears in the Themes gallery, and any changes made to the theme are reflected in any Office file that uses that theme.

By creating a library of styles and themes, you can create a report containing pages generated from different Office programs and those pages will still share a consistent set of design elements. Employees with expertise in page design can design a theme for the rest of the team to use. If those styles and themes are changed or modified, the new design style can be quickly applied to new and existing documents without having to reformat each document. Through careful planning, a well-designed theme can save you and your colleagues a lot of effort later on.

Creating Formulas to Add and Subtract Values

Next, you'll work with the Monthly Sales worksheet, which contains the sales results by month for the eight sales regions over the past two years. Tom wants to use this data to identify trends. He's more interested in the "big picture" than in specific numbers. He wants to know which sales regions are performing well and which are underperforming. He also wants to explore the pattern of monthly sales throughout the year.

Creating Formulas to Calculate Totals

The top of the worksheet contains annual sales for the previous two years. The bottom of the worksheet displays the increase in annual sales for each region and month. Tom wants you to calculate the monthly totals broken down by region. You'll start with the 2011 sales values.

To calculate the monthly and regional totals for 2011:

1. Click the **Monthly Sales** sheet tab to make the worksheet active.
2. In cells K6 and B19, enter the label **Total**.
3. Select the nonadjacent range **K7:K18;C19:K19**. You'll add the formula to calculate the total in these cells.
4. In the Editing group on the Home tab, click the **Sum** button [Σ]. The 2011 monthly and regional sales totals are entered in the selected range. See Figure 2-25.

Figure 2-25 **Monthly and regional sales totals for 2011**

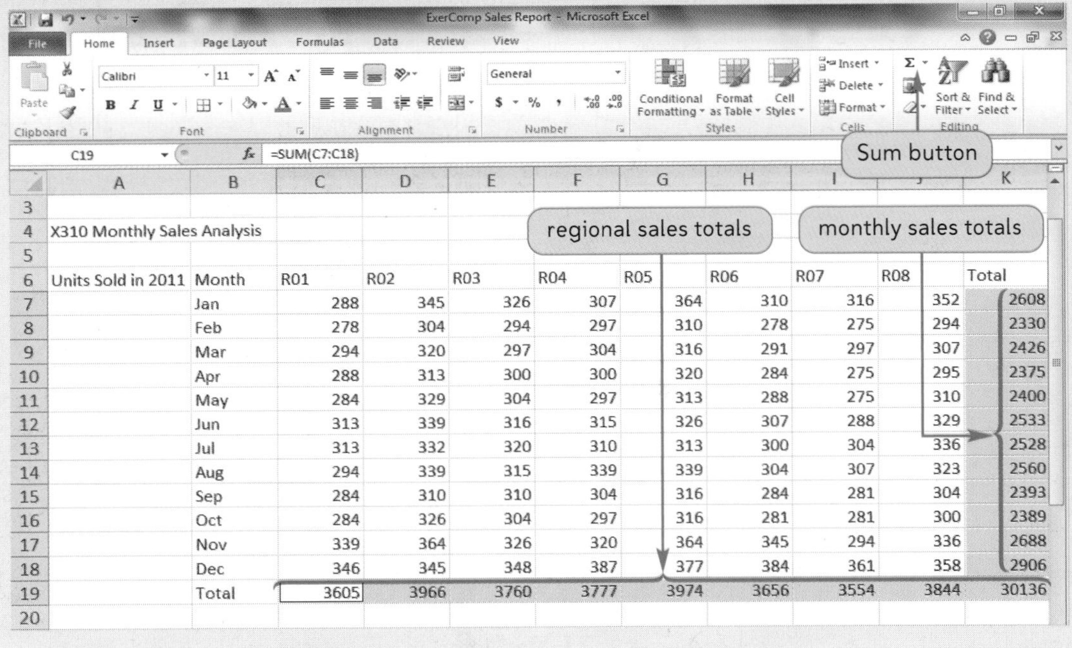

Units Sold in 2011	Month	R01	R02	R03	R04	R05	R06	R07	R08	Total
	Jan	288	345	326	307	364	310	316	352	2608
	Feb	278	304	294	297	310	278	275	294	2330
	Mar	294	320	297	304	316	291	297	307	2426
	Apr	288	313	300	300	320	284	275	295	2375
	May	284	329	304	297	313	288	275	310	2400
	Jun	313	339	316	315	326	307	288	329	2533
	Jul	313	332	320	310	313	300	304	336	2528
	Aug	294	339	315	339	339	304	307	323	2560
	Sep	284	310	310	304	316	284	281	304	2393
	Oct	284	326	304	297	316	281	281	300	2389
	Nov	339	364	326	320	364	345	294	336	2688
	Dec	346	345	348	387	377	384	361	358	2906
	Total	3605	3966	3760	3777	3974	3656	3554	3844	30136

Next, you will calculate the monthly and regional sales totals for 2012. Rather than retyping the text and formulas, you can copy and paste them from 2011.

To calculate the monthly and regional totals for 2012:

1. Select the range **K6:K19**, and then click the **Copy** button in the Clipboard group on the Home tab. The cell contents are copied to the Clipboard.
2. Click cell **K21**, and then click the **Paste** button. Excel inserts formulas to calculate the 2012 monthly sales totals into the range K21:K34.
3. Select the range **B19:J19**, and then click the **Copy** button.
4. Click cell **B34**, and then click the **Paste** button. Excel inserts formulas to calculate the 2012 regional sales totals into the range B34:J34. See Figure 2-26.

Figure 2-26 Monthly and regional sales totals for 2012

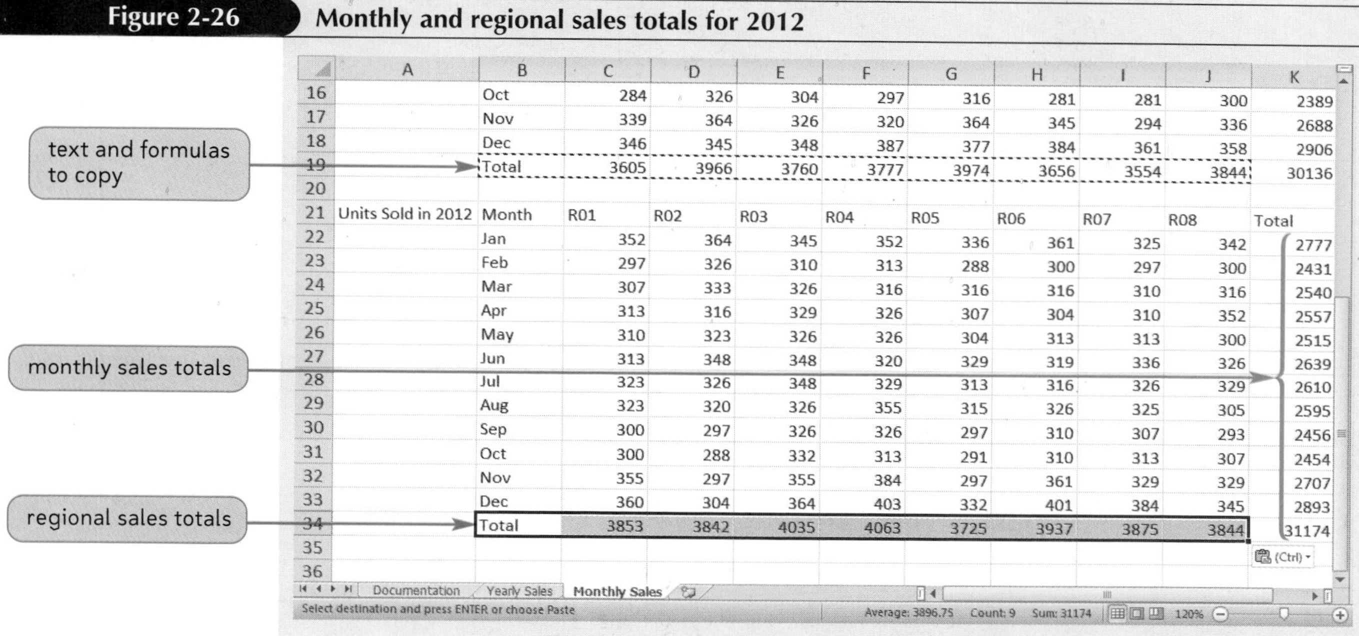

	A	B	C	D	E	F	G	H	I	J	K
16		Oct	284	326	304	297	316	281	281	300	2389
17		Nov	339	364	326	320	364	345	294	336	2688
18		Dec	346	345	348	387	377	384	361	358	2906
19		Total	3605	3966	3760	3777	3974	3656	3554	3844	30136
20											
21	Units Sold in 2012	Month	R01	R02	R03	R04	R05	R06	R07	R08	Total
22		Jan	352	364	345	352	336	361	325	342	2777
23		Feb	297	326	310	313	288	300	297	300	2431
24		Mar	307	333	326	316	316	316	310	316	2540
25		Apr	313	316	329	326	307	304	310	352	2557
26		May	310	323	326	326	304	313	313	300	2515
27		Jun	313	348	348	320	329	319	336	326	2639
28		Jul	323	326	348	329	313	316	326	329	2610
29		Aug	323	320	326	355	315	326	325	305	2595
30		Sep	300	297	326	326	297	310	307	293	2456
31		Oct	300	288	332	313	291	310	313	307	2454
32		Nov	355	297	355	384	297	361	329	329	2707
33		Dec	360	304	364	403	332	401	384	345	2893
34		Total	3853	3842	4035	4063	3725	3937	3875	3844	31174
35											
36											

Creating Formulas to Subtract Values

Tom also wants you to calculate the change in sales from one year to another, broken down by region and month. You'll use the copy and paste features to quickly add this third table to the Monthly Sales worksheet. Then you will add formulas to calculate the increase in units sold between 2011 and 2012.

To calculate the change in sales from one year to the next:

1. In cell A36, enter the label **Net Increase**.
2. Copy the range **B21:K21**, and then paste it into the range **B36:K36**.
3. Copy the range **B22:B34**, and then paste it into the range **B37:B49**.
4. In cell C37, enter the formula **=C22–C7**. After you press the Enter key, the value 64 appears in the cell; this is the increase in January sales for region R01.
5. Copy cell **C37**, and then paste it into the range **C37:K49**. The formula =C22–C7 is copied and pasted into the range of cells with the remaining months and regions.
6. Click cell **A36** to deselect the range. Figure 2-27 shows the completed table.

Figure 2-27 Net increase in sales by region and month

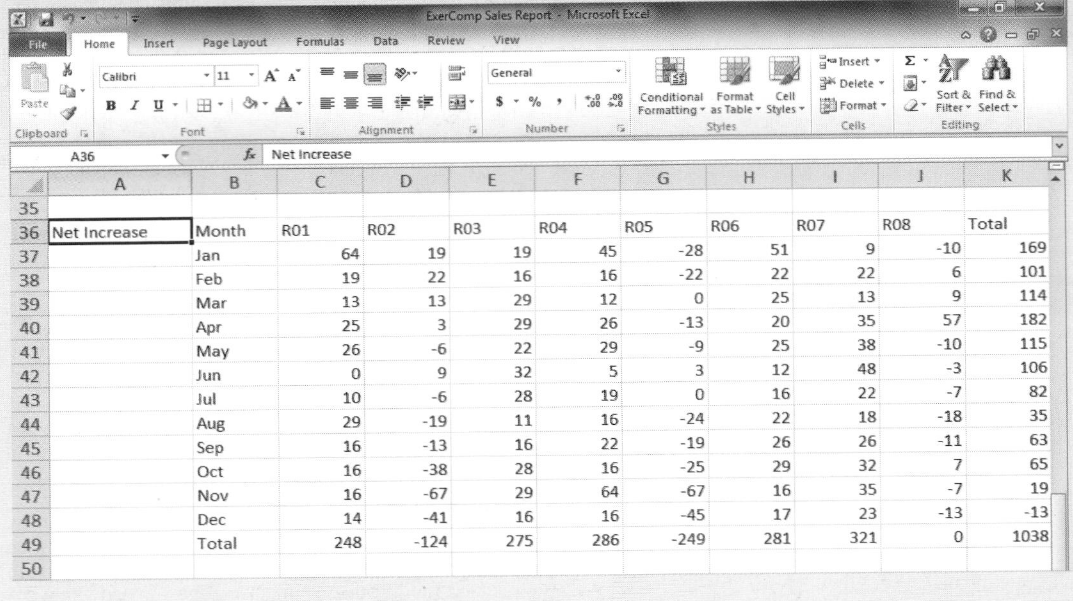

	A	B	C	D	E	F	G	H	I	J	K
35											
36	Net Increase	Month	R01	R02	R03	R04	R05	R06	R07	R08	Total
37		Jan	64	19	19	45	-28	51	9	-10	169
38		Feb	19	22	16	16	-22	22	22	6	101
39		Mar	13	13	29	12	0	25	13	9	114
40		Apr	25	3	29	26	-13	20	35	57	182
41		May	26	-6	22	29	-9	25	38	-10	115
42		Jun	0	9	32	5	3	12	48	-3	106
43		Jul	10	-6	28	19	0	16	22	-7	82
44		Aug	29	-19	11	16	-24	22	18	-18	35
45		Sep	16	-13	16	22	-19	26	26	-11	63
46		Oct	16	-38	28	16	-25	29	32	7	65
47		Nov	16	-67	29	64	-67	16	35	-7	19
48		Dec	14	-41	16	16	-45	17	23	-13	-13
49		Total	248	-124	275	286	-249	281	321	0	1038
50											

Next, you'll format the row and column titles for these tables. You'll use the formatting options on the Home tab and in the Format Cells dialog box to format the new table to match the other tables.

To format the titles:

1. Select the range **A4:K4**, and then click the **Merge & Center** button in the Alignment group on the Home tab. The title is centered in the merged cell.
2. In the Styles group, click the **Cell Styles** button, and then click the **Heading 1** style. The Heading 1 style is applied to the title.
3. Select the range **A6:A19**, and then click the **Merge & Center** button in the Alignment group. The label is centered in the merged cell.
4. In the Alignment group, click the **Orientation** button, and then click **Rotate Text Up**. The text in the cell rotates 90 degrees.
5. In the Alignment group, click the **Middle Align** button. The text is centered both horizontally and vertically in the cells.
6. Reduce the width of column A to **5** characters.
7. Select the range **C7:K19**, and then, in the Number group on the Home tab, click the **Dialog Box Launcher**. The Format Cells dialog box opens with the Number tab displayed.
8. Click **Number** in the Category box, type **0** (a zero) in the Decimal places box, click the **Use 1000 Separator (,)** check box to insert a check mark, verify that the **–1,234** option is selected, and then click the **OK** button. The numbers display a thousands separator and use a minus symbol for negatives.

   Next you'll copy this format to the two other tables on the worksheet.
9. Select the range **A6:K19**.

Be sure to double-click the Format Painter button so you can paste the copied format into multiple cells.

10. In the Clipboard group, double-click the **Format Painter** button.
11. Click cell **A21**. All of the formats in the range A6:K19 are applied to the cell.
12. Click cell **A36**. Once again, all of the formats are applied to the selected cell.
13. In the Clipboard group, click the **Format Painter** button to turn off the Format Painter.
14. Scroll up to the top of the worksheet and select cell **A1**. Figure 2-28 shows the formatted values for the first table.

Figure 2-28 Formatted table

	A	B	C	D	E	F	G	H	I	J	K
1	ExerComp										
2	*The Intelligent Path to Fitness*										
3											
4					X310 Monthly Sales Analysis						
5											
6		Month	R01	R02	R03	R04	R05	R06	R07	R08	Total
7	Units Sold in 2011	Jan	288	345	326	307	364	310	316	352	2,608
8		Feb	278	304	294	297	310	278	275	294	2,330
9		Mar	294	320	297	304	316	291	297	307	2,426
10		Apr	288	313	300	300	320	284	275	295	2,375
11		May	284	329	304	297	313	288	275	310	2,400
12		Jun	313	339	316	315	326	307	288	329	2,533
13		Jul	313	332	320	310	313	300	304	336	2,528
14		Aug	294	339	315	339	339	304	307	323	2,560
15		Sep	284	310	310	304	316	284	281	304	2,393
16		Oct	284	326	304	297	316	281	281	300	2,389
17		Nov	339	364	326	320	364	345	294	336	2,688
18		Dec	346	345	348	387	377	384	361	358	2,906
19		Total	3,605	3,966	3,760	3,777	3,974	3,656	3,554	3,844	30,136

Documentation | Yearly Sales | Monthly Sales

Ready 120%

Working with Table Styles

You can identify a range as an Excel table, which makes available tools designed for analyzing tabular data, such as the ability to sort data, transfer data to and from an external file, and filter the data to show only those rows that match specified criteria. Excel tables can include optional elements such as a header row that contains titles for the different columns in the table, and a total row that contains formulas summarizing the values in the table's data. You can also apply a table style, which specifies formats such as font color, fill color, and so on for each of these elements. Formatting an entire table with a table style is more efficient than formatting individual cells in the table. (This tutorial covers only the styles associated with Excel tables.

TIP

Applying a table style also marks the range as an Excel table.

In addition, using a table style ensures that the table's formatting reflects any changes made to the table, such as adding or deleting table rows or columns. For example, many tables display alternate rows with different fill colors. This banded rows effect makes the data easier to read, especially in large tables with many rows. You could create the banded rows effect by applying a cell style with a background fill to every other row in the table; but if you later add or delete a row from the table, the banded rows effect might be lost. A table style, on the other hand, applies alternating row colors to the entire Excel table and adjusts the banded rows effect as needed if you add or delete rows. This is because a table style treats the table as a single object rather than a collection of cells. Figure 2-29 shows the banded rows effect applied both manually and with a table style.

Figure 2-29 **Banded rows in a table**

	A	B	C	D
1	Region	Year 1 Sales	Year 2 Sales	Difference
2	R01	3,605	3,853	248
3	R02	3,966	3,842	-124
4	R03	3,760	4,035	275
5	R04	3,777	4,063	286
6	R05	3,974	3,725	-249
7	R06	3,656	3,937	281
8	R07	3,554	3,875	321
9	R08	3,844	3,844	0
10	Total	30,136	31,174	1,038
11				

original table with banded rows

	A	B	C	D
1	Region	Year 1 Sales	Year 2 Sales	Difference
2	R01	3,605	3,853	248
3	R02	3,966	3,842	-124
4	R03	3,760	4,035	275
5	R07	3,554	3,875	321
6	R08	3,844	3,844	0
7	Total	18,729	19,449	720
8				

after deleting a row from a table formatted manually, the banded effect is lost

	A	B	C	D
1	Region	Year 1 Sales	Year 2 Sales	Difference
2	R01	3,605	3,853	248
3	R02	3,966	3,842	-124
4	R03	3,760	4,035	275
5	R07	3,554	3,875	321
6	R08	3,844	3,844	0
7	Total	18,729	19,449	720
8				

after deleting a row from a table formatted with a table style, the table formatting adjusts to keep banded rows

Tom wants you to format the sales data in the Monthly Sales worksheet as Excel tables. First, you'll apply a table style to the units sold in 2011 data.

To apply a table style to the 2011 sales data:

1. Select the range **B6:K19**.
2. In the Styles group on the Home tab, click the **Format as Table** button, and then click **Table Style Medium 2** (the second style in the first row in the Medium section). The Format As Table dialog box opens, confirming the range you selected for the table and whether the table includes header rows.
3. Verify that the range is **=$B$6:$K$19** and then verify that the **My table has headers** check box contains a check mark to include the text labels in the table.
4. Click the **OK** button to apply the table style to the selected range, and then click cell **A5** to deselect the range. See Figure 2-30.

Figure 2-30 **Range formatted with a table style**

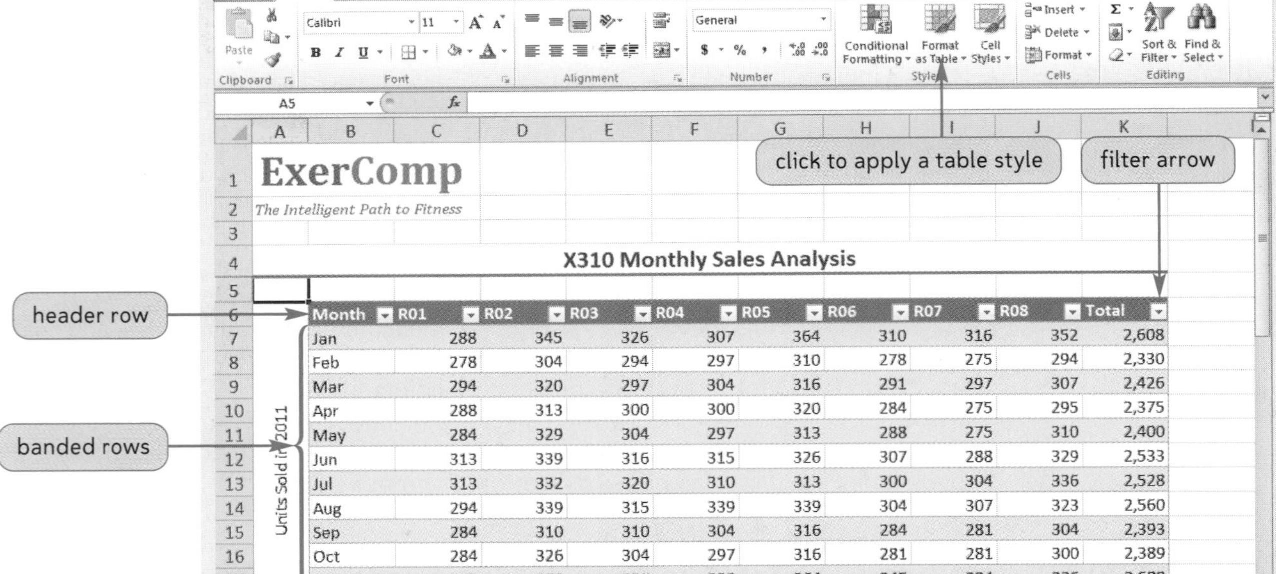

Month	R01	R02	R03	R04	R05	R06	R07	R08	Total
Jan	288	345	326	307	364	310	316	352	2,608
Feb	278	304	294	297	310	278	275	294	2,330
Mar	294	320	297	304	316	291	297	307	2,426
Apr	288	313	300	300	320	284	275	295	2,375
May	284	329	304	297	313	288	275	310	2,400
Jun	313	339	316	315	326	307	288	329	2,533
Jul	313	332	320	310	313	300	304	336	2,528
Aug	294	339	315	339	339	304	307	323	2,560
Sep	284	310	310	304	316	284	281	304	2,393
Oct	284	326	304	297	316	281	281	300	2,389
Nov	339	364	326	320	364	345	294	336	2,688

The table style treated the range as a single unit and modified its overall appearance. In this case, Table Style Medium 2 formatted the range so the header row appears in a white font on a blue fill and the remaining rows are formatted as banded rows. In addition, filter arrows appear next to the column titles in the header row. These filter arrows are applied when the user wants to hide or filter out different table rows that contain certain data.

Tom doesn't want to filter the data right now, so you will remove the arrows and work only with elements related to the table style.

To remove the filter arrows from the table:

1. Click cell **B6** to make the table active.
2. Click the **Data** tab on the Ribbon.
3. In the Sort & Filter group, click the **Filter** button. The filter arrows disappear from the header row.

Selecting Table Style Options

After you apply a table style, you can choose which table elements to include in the style. Table styles have the following six elements that can be turned on or off:

- **Header Row**, which formats the first row of the table
- **Total Row**, which inserts a new row at the bottom of the table that adds the column values
- **First Column**, which formats the first column of the table
- **Last Column**, which formats the last column of the table
- **Banded Rows**, which formats alternating rows in different colors
- **Banded Columns**, which formats alternating columns in different colors

For example, if you turn on the Header Row option, you can specify a format for the table's first row, which usually contains text that describes the contents of each table column. If you insert a new row at the top of the table, the new row becomes the header row and is formatted with the table style.

In the table style you just used, only the Header Row and Banded Rows options are on. Although the other elements are still part of the table structure, the current style does not format them. Tom wants you to format the table's last column and header row as well as remove the banded rows effect.

TIP

You can click any cell within a table to make the table active; you do not need to select all of the table cells.

To modify the table style:

1. If necessary, click cell **B6** to make the table active. The Table Tools contextual tab appears on the Ribbon.
2. Click the **Design** tab on the Ribbon. The table design options appear on the Ribbon.
3. In the Table Style Options group, click the **Last Column** check box to insert a check mark. The last column is formatted.
4. In the Table Style Options group, click the **Banded Rows** check box to remove the check mark. The banded rows are removed from the table.

   Only the Header Row and Last Column elements appear in the table. You'll use a built-in table style to format them.
5. In the Table Styles group, click the **More** button. The Table Styles gallery opens.

6. In the Medium section, click **Table Style Medium 20** (the third table style in the sixth column). The table styles in the gallery show the formatting applied to the current table elements. See Figure 2-31.

Figure 2-31 **Revised table style**

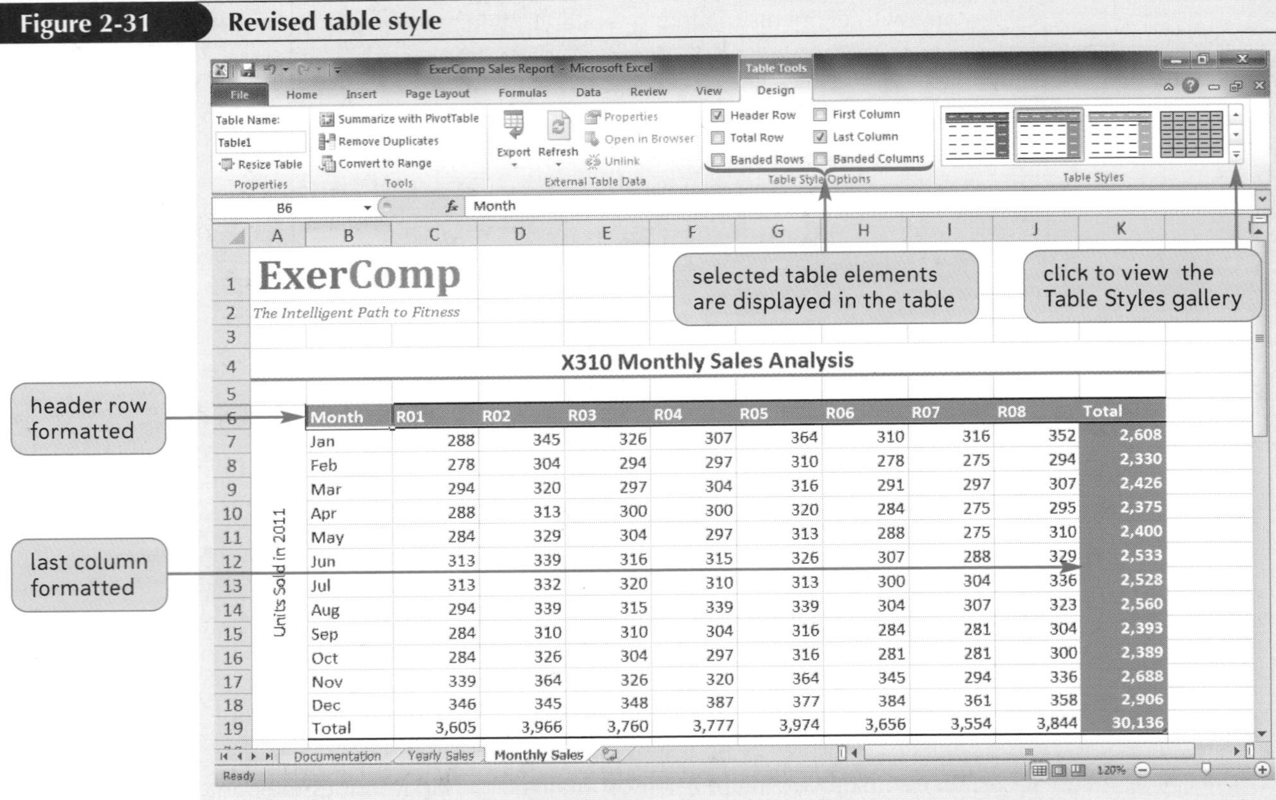

A table style might not format a table exactly the way you want. For example, Tom wants the column titles in the header row to be centered and the Total row to have a single top border and a double bottom border. Because the table style you used does not include either of these formats, you'll add these formats to the table cells. You can use cell styles and the formatting tools you've used with individual cells and ranges to format Excel tables.

To format the header row and the Total row:

1. Select the range **C6:K6**. You'll change the alignment of the header row.
2. Click the **Home** tab on the Ribbon, and then click the **Center** button in the Alignment group. The column titles are centered.
3. Select the range **B19:K19**. You'll apply a different cell style to the Total row.
4. In the Styles group, click the **Cell Styles** button, and then click **Total** (the sixth cell style) in the Titles and Headings section.
5. Click cell **A5** to deselect the range. The Total row is formatted in bold with a single top border and a double bottom border.

Tom likes the formatting of the first table, and wants you to format the other two tables similarly. You cannot use the Format Painter to copy table formats, and you must format each range as a table separately.

To format the other two tables:

1. Select the range **B21:K34**.
2. In the Styles group on the Home tab, click the **Format as Table** button, click **Table Style Medium 6** (the sixth table style in the first row of the Medium section), and then click the **OK** button in the Format As Table dialog box. The range is formatted as a table.
3. Click the **Data** tab on the Ribbon, and then click the **Filter** button in the Sort & Filter group to turn off the filter arrows.
4. Click the **Design** tab on the Ribbon, and then, in the Table Style Options group, click the **Banded Rows** check box to remove the check mark and click the **Last Column** check box to insert a check mark. The banded rows are removed and the last column is formatted.
5. In the Table Styles group, click the **More** button, and then click **Table Style Medium 20** (the sixth table style in the third row of the Medium section). The table is quickly reformatted with a new style.
6. Select the range **C21:K21**, click the **Home** tab on the Ribbon, and then click the **Center** button in the Alignment group. The column headings are centered.
7. Select the range **B34:K34**; in the Styles group, click the **Cell Styles** button, and then click **Total** (the sixth cell style in the Titles and Headings section). The Total row is formatted.
8. Select the range **B36:K49** and repeat Steps 2 through 5, select the range **C36:K36** and repeat Step 6, and then select the range **B49:K49** and repeat Step 7. The third table is formatted to match the first two tables.

Highlighting Cells with Conditional Formats

The formatting you have applied to the workbook has made the content more readable. However, Tom also wants this worksheet to highlight important trends and sales values of interest. For example, Tom is interested in knowing which regions and months have the highest sales or showed the highest increase between 2011 and 2012.

You can answer these kinds of questions using conditional formats, in which the format applied to a cell depends upon the value or content of the cell. For example, a conditional format can make negative numbers red and positive numbers black. Conditional formats are dynamic, so that if the cell's value changes, the cell's format also changes as needed. Each conditional format has a set of rules that define how the formatting should be applied and under what conditions the format will be changed.

REFERENCE

Highlighting a Cell Based on Its Value

- Select the range in which you want to highlight cells that match a specified rule.
- In the Styles group on the Home tab, click the Conditional Formatting button, point to Highlight Cells Rules or Top/Bottom Rules, and then click the appropriate rule.
- Select the appropriate options in the dialog box, and then click the OK button.

Excel has four conditional formats—data bars, highlighting, color scales, and icon sets. In this tutorial, you will apply cell highlighting, which changes the cell's font color or background color based on the cell's value. Figure 2-32 describes some of the ways that cells can be highlighted with conditional formats.

Figure 2-32 **Highlighting rules**

Rule	Highlights
Greater Than	Cells that are greater than a specified number
Less Than	Cells that are less than a specified number
Between	Cells that are between two specified numbers
Equal To	Cells that are equal to a specified number
Text That Contains	Cells that contain specified text
A Date Occurring	Cells that contain a specified date
Duplicate Values	Cells that contain duplicate or unique values

Tom wants to highlight sales regions that showed an increase in sales from 2011 to 2012. With all of the data on the Monthly Sales worksheet, this information can be difficult to locate. To make this data stand out, you will use a conditional format to display worksheet cells with a positive value using a different font or fill color than cells containing zero or a negative value.

To highlight the positive sales numbers:

1. Select the range **C37:J48**. This range shows the difference in sales by region and month for 2011 and 2012.
2. In the Styles group on the Home tab, click the **Conditional Formatting** button, point to **Highlight Cells Rules**, and then click **Greater Than**. The Greater Than dialog box opens. You want to highlight those regions and months in which sales increased, which means that they are greater than zero.
3. Type **0** (a zero) in the Format cells that are GREATER THAN box, click the **with** arrow, and then click **Green Fill with Dark Green Text**. This rule formats any cells that display a number greater than zero in a green font with a green background.
4. Click the **OK** button to apply the highlighting rule.
5. Click cell **A35** to deselect the range. Cells with positive numbers are highlighted in green. See Figure 2-33.

Figure 2-33 **Conditional format highlights positive cell values**

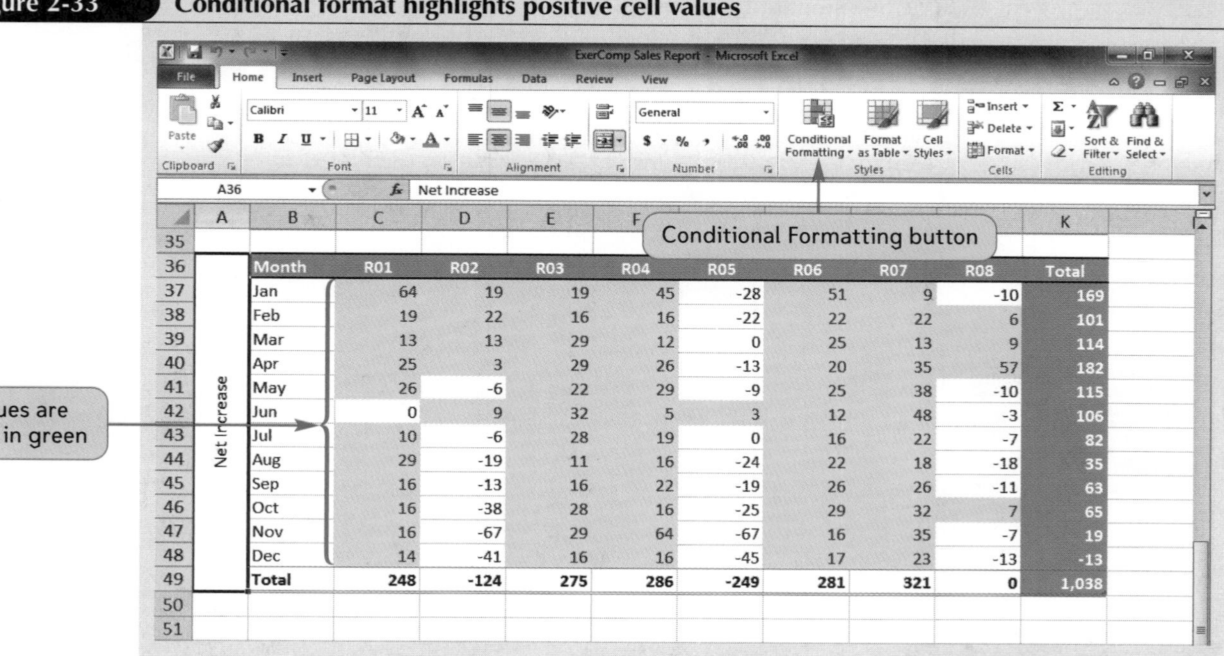

Month	R01	R02	R03	R04	R05	R06	R07	R08	Total
Jan	64	19	19	45	-28	51	9	-10	169
Feb	19	22	16	16	-22	22	22	6	101
Mar	13	13	29	12	0	25	13	9	114
Apr	25	3	29	26	-13	20	35	57	182
May	26	-6	22	29	-9	25	38	-10	115
Jun	0	9	32	5	3	12	48	-3	106
Jul	10	-6	28	19	0	16	22	-7	82
Aug	29	-19	11	16	-24	22	18	-18	35
Sep	16	-13	16	22	-19	26	26	-11	63
Oct	16	-38	28	16	-25	29	32	7	65
Nov	16	-67	29	64	-67	16	35	-7	19
Dec	14	-41	16	16	-45	17	23	-13	-13
Total	248	-124	275	286	-249	281	321	0	1,038

From the highlighting, you can tell that most regions and months had increased sales in 2012. Most of the declines occurred in regions R02, R05, and R08. Tom wonders if some months or regions had particularly strong sales increases. You'll first clear the current highlighting. Note that clearing a conditional format doesn't affect the contents of the cells.

To clear a conditional format:

1. Select the range **C37:J48**.
2. In the Styles group on the Home tab, click the **Conditional Formatting** button, point to **Clear Rules**, and then click **Clear Rules from Selected Cells**. The current highlighting is removed.

Now add a conditional format that highlights the regions and months that rank in the top 10 percent in terms of net sales increase from 2011 to 2012.

To highlight the top 10 percent in sales increase:

1. Make sure the range **C37:J48** is still selected.
2. In the Styles group, click the **Conditional Formatting** button, point to **Top/Bottom Rules**, and then click **Top 10 %**. The Top 10% dialog box opens.
3. Verify that **10** is entered in the % box, click the **with** arrow, and then click **Green Fill with Dark Green Text**.
4. Click the **OK** button. Cells whose sales increases for 2011 and 2012 were in the top 10 percent are highlighted in green.
5. Click cell **A35** to deselect the range. See Figure 2-34.

Figure 2-34 **Conditional formats highlight the top 10 percent sales increases**

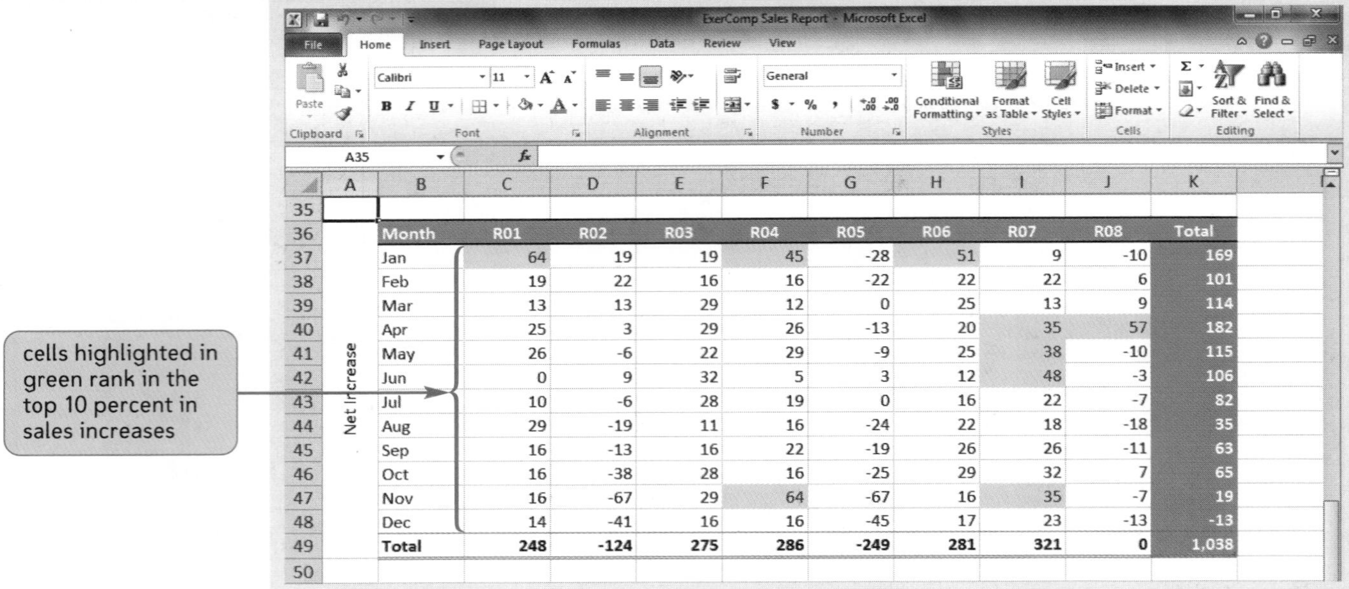

cells highlighted in green rank in the top 10 percent in sales increases

	Month	R01	R02	R03	R04	R05	R06	R07	R08	Total
Net Increase	Jan	64	19	19	45	-28	51	9	-10	169
	Feb	19	22	16	16	-22	22	22	6	101
	Mar	13	13	29	12	0	25	13	9	114
	Apr	25	3	29	26	-13	20	35	57	182
	May	26	-6	22	29	-9	25	38	-10	115
	Jun	0	9	32	5	3	12	48	-3	106
	Jul	10	-6	28	19	0	16	22	-7	82
	Aug	29	-19	11	16	-24	22	18	-18	35
	Sep	16	-13	16	22	-19	26	26	-11	63
	Oct	16	-38	28	16	-25	29	32	7	65
	Nov	16	-67	29	64	-67	16	35	-7	19
	Dec	14	-41	16	16	-45	17	23	-13	-13
	Total	**248**	**-124**	**275**	**286**	**-249**	**281**	**321**	**0**	**1,038**

The results provide Tom with some interesting information. For example, region R08, which underperformed for most of the year, had one of the largest sales increases during April (cell J40). In fact, the increase in sales during that one month compensated for the sales declines in other months; so that by the end of the year, region R08 showed no overall decline in sales. Also, region R01 had a large increase in sales during January 2012 but demonstrated the same level of increase for the rest of the year. Finally, four of the nine cells highlighted in the table are from region R07; three of those occurred during the spring months, which are traditionally slow times for the company.

Tom wonders what insights he could gain from highlighting the bottom 10 percent of the table—the regions and months that showed the lowest sales increases in 2012.

To highlight the bottom 10 percent in sales increases:

1. Select the range **C37:J48**.
2. In the Styles group on the Home tab, click the **Conditional Formatting** button, point to **Top/Bottom Rules**, and then click **Bottom 10 %**. The Bottom 10% dialog box opens.
3. Verify that **10** is entered in the % box and **Light Red Fill with Dark Red Text** is selected in the with box.
4. Click the **OK** button. Red cells highlight the regions and months that placed in the bottom 10 percent for sales increases from 2011 to 2012.
5. Click cell **A35** to deselect the range. See Figure 2-35.

Figure 2-35 Conditional formats highlight the bottom 10 percent of sales increases

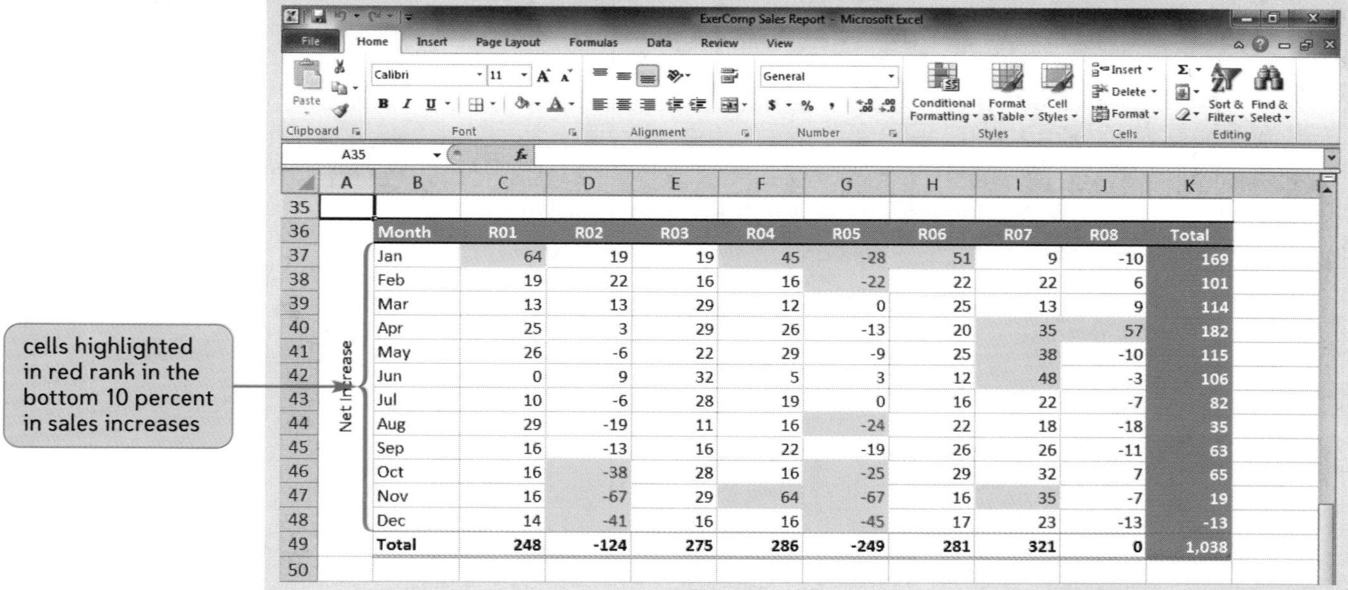

cells highlighted in red rank in the bottom 10 percent in sales increases

Net Increase

Month	R01	R02	R03	R04	R05	R06	R07	R08	Total
Jan	64	19	19	45	-28	51	9	-10	169
Feb	19	22	16	16	-22	22	22	6	101
Mar	13	13	29	12	0	25	13	9	114
Apr	25	3	29	26	-13	20	35	57	182
May	26	-6	22	29	-9	25	38	-10	115
Jun	0	9	32	5	3	12	48	-3	106
Jul	10	-6	28	19	0	16	22	-7	82
Aug	29	-19	11	16	-24	22	18	-18	35
Sep	16	-13	16	22	-19	26	26	-11	63
Oct	16	-38	28	16	-25	29	32	7	65
Nov	16	-67	29	64	-67	16	35	-7	19
Dec	14	-41	16	16	-45	17	23	-13	-13
Total	**248**	**-124**	**275**	**286**	**-249**	**281**	**321**	**0**	**1,038**

Tom immediately sees that the bottom 10 percent come from only regions R02 and R05, and that six of the nine cells highlighted occurred in the most recent months: October, November, and December. Conditional formatting helped Tom isolate and highlight potential problem areas, which he can investigate further.

When you use conditional formatting to highlight cells in a worksheet, you should always include a **legend**, which is a key that shows each color used in the worksheet and what it means, so others know why certain cells are highlighted. You will add a legend to the Monthly Sales worksheet.

To create a conditional formatting legend:

1. In cell D51, type **light red**, and then click cell D51 to make it the active cell. You will use a highlight rule to fill this cell with the light red color used for the bottom 10 percent sales increases.
2. In the Styles group on the Home tab, click the **Conditional Formatting** button, point to **Highlight Cells Rules**, and then click **Text that Contains**. The Text That Contains dialog box opens.
3. Verify that **light red** appears in the Format cells that contain the text box, select **Light Red Fill with Dark Red Text** in the with box, and then click the **OK** button. Cell D51 is filled with the same light red fill color used for the bottom 10 percent values.
4. In cell D52, type **light green**, and then click cell **D52** to make it the active cell. You will use a highlight rule to fill this cell with the green color used for the top 10 percent sales increases.
5. In the Styles group, click the **Conditional Formatting** button, point to **Highlight Cells Rules**, and then click **Text that Contains**. The Text That Contains dialog box opens.

6. Verify that **light green** appears in the Format cells that contain the text box, select **Green Fill with Dark Green Text** in the with box, and then click the **OK** button. Cell D52 is filled with the same light green fill color used for the top 10 percent values.
7. In cell E51, enter **Bottom 10% in terms of sales increase** and then, in cell E52, enter **Top 10% in terms of sales increase**.
8. Select the range **E51:E52**. You'll format these cells with a cell style to distinguish them from the rest of the text in the worksheet.
9. In the Styles group, click the **Cell Styles** button, and then, in the Data and Model section, click **Explanatory** (the third cell style in the first row).
10. Click cell **A35** to deselect the range. The legend is complete. See Figure 2-36.

Figure 2-36 Conditional formatting legend

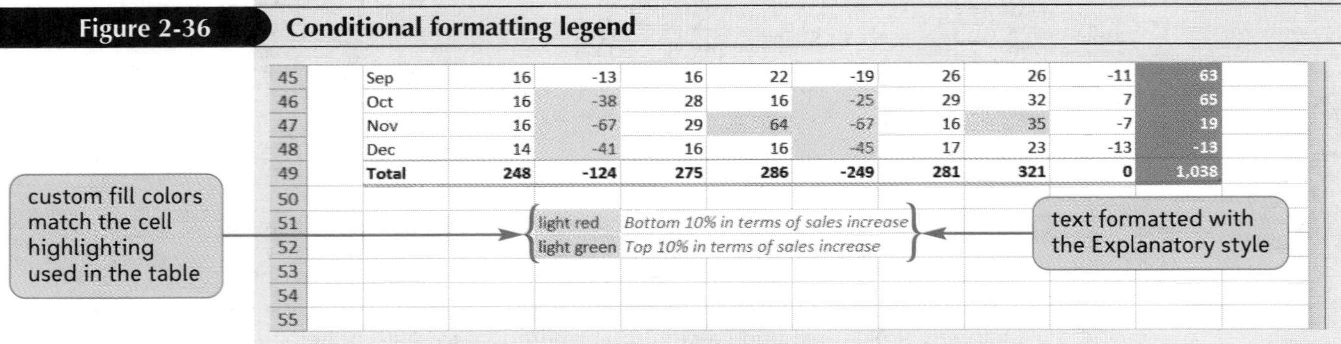

45	Sep	16	-13	16	22	-19	26	26	-11	63	
46	Oct	16	-38	28	16	-25	29	32	7	65	
47	Nov	16	-67	29	64	-67	16	35	-7	19	
48	Dec	14	-41	16	16	-45	17	23	-13	-13	
49	**Total**	**248**	**-124**	**275**	**286**	**-249**	**281**	**321**	**0**	**1,038**	
50											
51			light red	*Bottom 10% in terms of sales increase*							
52			light green	*Top 10% in terms of sales increase*							
53											
54											
55											

The conditional formatting in the Monthly Sales worksheet helps Tom understand how sales of the X310 heart rate monitor changed over the past two years and helps him focus on particular sales regions for additional analysis.

INSIGHT

Using Conditional Formatting Effectively

Conditional formatting is an excellent way to highlight important trends and data values to clients and colleagues. However, it should be used judiciously. An overuse of conditional formatting can sometimes obscure the very data values you want to emphasize. You'll need to make decisions about what to highlight and how it should be highlighted. Keep in mind the following tips as you consider the best ways to effectively communicate your findings to others:

- **Document the conditional formats you use.** If a bold, green font means that a sales number is in the top 10 percent of all sales, include that information in a legend in the worksheet.
- **Don't clutter data with too much highlighting.** Limit highlighting rules to one or two per data set. Highlights are designed to draw attention to points of interest. If you use too many, you'll end up highlighting everything—and, therefore, nothing.
- **Use color sparingly in worksheets with highlights.** It's difficult to tell a highlight color from a regular fill color, especially when fill colors are used in every cell.
- **Consider alternatives to conditional formats.** If you want to highlight the top 10 sales regions, it might be more effective to simply sort the data with the best-selling regions at the top of the list.

Remember that the goal of highlighting is to provide a strong visual clue of important data or results. Careful use of conditional formatting helps readers to focus on the important points you want to make rather than be distracted by secondary issues and facts.

Hiding Worksheet Data

The Monthly Sales worksheet contains too much data to fit into the worksheet window without drastically reducing the zoom level, which would make the contents too small to read easily. One way to manage the contents of a large worksheet is to selectively hide (and later unhide) those rows and columns containing extraneous information, allowing you to focus your attention on only a select few data points. Hiding rows, columns, and worksheets is a good way to manage a large volume of information; but it should never be used to hide data that is crucial to understanding a workbook. Note that hiding a row or column does not affect the other formulas in the workbook. Formulas still show the correct value even if they reference a cell in a hidden row or column.

Tom wants to view only the third table, which shows the difference in sales between 2011 and 2012, but not the other tables. You'll hide the rows that contain the first two tables and then unhide those rows after Tom has looked at the third table.

TIP

You can also hide or unhide a row or column by right-clicking the row or column header and clicking Hide or Unhide from the shortcut menu.

To hide and unhide worksheet rows:

1. Select row **6** through row **35** in the Monthly Sales worksheet.
2. In the Cells group on the Home tab, click the **Format** button, point to **Hide & Unhide**, and then click **Hide Rows**. Rows 6 to 35 are hidden, and the row numbers in the worksheet jump from row 5 to row 36. The data in the third table hasn't changed even though its formulas use data from the hidden tables.
3. Select row **5** and row **36**, which are the rows before and after the hidden rows.
4. In the Cells group, click the **Format** button, point to **Hide & Unhide**, and then click **Unhide Rows**. The hidden rows 6 through 35 reappear.

Formatting the Worksheet for Printing

Your final task is to prepare the workbook for the printer. Excel supports a wealth of print options, including the ability to set the page orientation as well as specify whether the page will include headers and footers. Print settings can be applied to an entire workbook or to individual sheets. Because it is likely that other people, such as clients and colleagues, will see the printed version of your spreadsheet, you should take as much care in formatting the printed output as you do in formatting the contents of the electronic file.

Tom wants you to print the analysis of the monthly sales figures. You'll look at the Monthly Sales worksheet in Page Layout view to see how it would currently print.

To view a worksheet in Page Layout view:

1. Click the **Page Layout** button on the status bar. The worksheet switches to Page Layout view.
2. Change the zoom level of the worksheet to **70%** to view more of the page layout. See Figure 2-37.

Figure 2-37 Page Layout view of the Monthly Sales worksheet

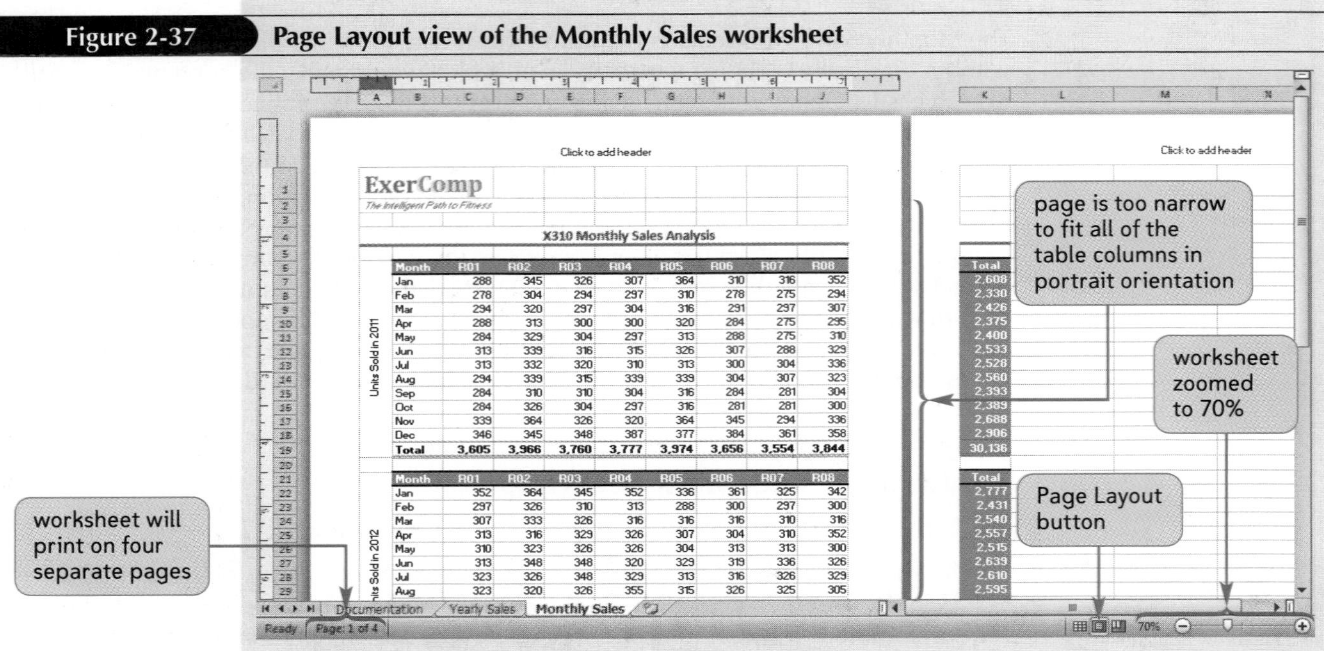

In the worksheet's current orientation, its contents do not fit on a single page and the tables break across pages. You'll change the orientation from portrait to landscape so that the page is wide enough to fit all the table columns on one page.

To change to landscape orientation:

1. Click the **Page Layout** tab on the Ribbon.
2. In the Page Setup group, click the **Orientation** button, and then click **Landscape**. The page orientation changes to landscape, making each page wide enough to display all of the columns of each table.

Defining the Print Area

By default, all cells in the active worksheet containing text, formulas, or values are printed. The region that is sent to the printer from the active sheet is known as the **print area**. To print part of a worksheet, you can define the print area, overriding the default setting. A print area can cover an adjacent or nonadjacent range in the current worksheet.

There are many different ways to define the print area, but it's generally easiest to set the print area in Page Break Preview. For example, if Tom wanted to print only the first table in the Monthly Sales worksheet, you could define the print area to cover that range while in Page Break Preview. You will go to Page Break Preview, and then set the print area.

To switch to Page Break preview and set the print area:

1. Click the **Page Break Preview** button on the status bar.

   Trouble? If the Welcome to Page Break Preview dialog box opens, click the OK button.
2. Change the zoom level of the worksheet to **70%**.
3. Select the range **A1:K19**, which is the range of the first table.

4. In the Page Setup group on the Page Layout tab, click the **Print Area** button, and then click **Set Print Area**. The print area changes to cover only the range A1:K19. The rest of the worksheet content is shaded to indicate that it will not be part of the printout.
5. In the Page Setup group, click the **Print Area** button, and then click **Clear Print Area**. The print area is reset to cover the entire contents of the worksheet.

Inserting Page Breaks

Often the contents of a worksheet do not fit onto a single page. By default, Excel prints as much of the content that fits on single page without resizing the content, and then inserts **automatic page breaks** to continue printing the remaining worksheet content on successive pages. This can result in page breaks that leave a single column or row on a separate page or split worksheet content in awkward places such as within a table.

One way to fix this problem is to scale the printout by reducing the font size to fit on a single sheet of paper. However, if you have more than one or two columns or rows to fit onto the page, the resulting text is often too small to read comfortably. The better fix is usually to split the worksheet into logical segments, which you can do by inserting **manual page breaks** that specify exactly where the page breaks occur. A page break is inserted directly above and to the left of a selected cell, directly above a selected row, or to the left of a selected column.

REFERENCE

Inserting and Removing Page Breaks

To insert a page break:
- Select the first cell below the row where you want to insert a page break.
- In the Page Setup group on the Page Layout tab, click the Breaks button, and then click Insert Page Break.

To remove a page break:
- Select any cell below or to the right of the page break you want to remove.
- In the Page Setup group on the Page Layout tab, click the Breaks button, and then click Remove Page Break (or click Reset All Page Breaks to remove all the page breaks from the worksheet).

Tom wants the three tables in the Monthly Sales worksheet to print on separate pages. You'll insert page breaks to accomplish this.

To insert page breaks between the tables:

1. Click cell **A20**. With this cell selected, a page break will be inserted between rows 19 and 20.
2. In the Page Setup group on the Page Layout tab, click the **Breaks** button, and then click **Insert Page Break**. A page break separates row 19 from row 20.
3. Click cell **A35**, and then repeat Step 2 to insert a page break that splits the second table from the third. The printout is now three pages. See Figure 2-38.

TIP

In Page Break Preview, a dashed blue line indicates an automatic page break and a solid blue line indicates a manual page break.

Figure 2-38 **Worksheet in Page Break Preview**

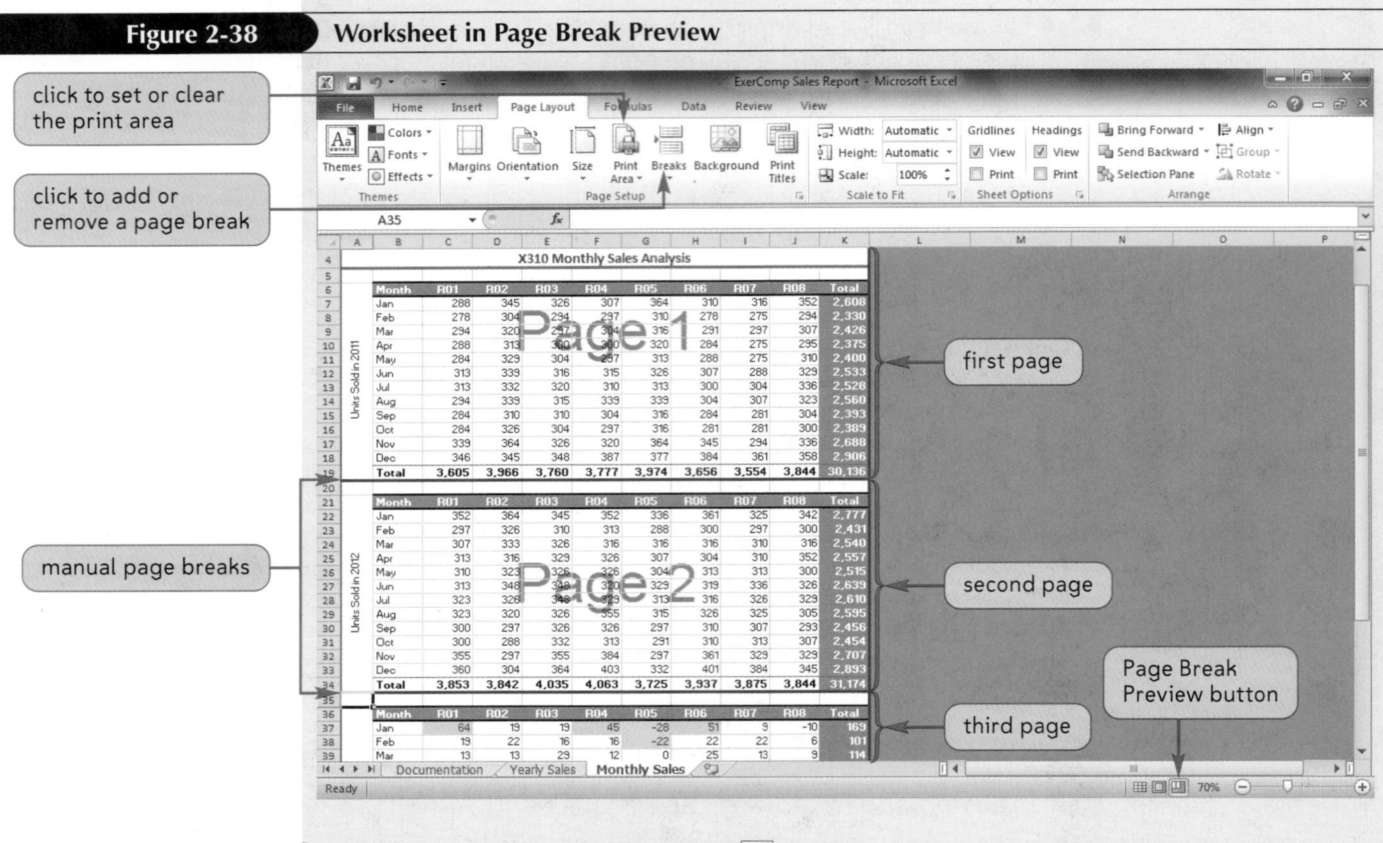

4. Click the **Page Layout** button on the status bar, and then verify that each table appears on a separate page.

Adding Print Titles

It is a good practice to include descriptive information, such as the company name, logo, and worksheet title on each page of a printout in case a page becomes separated from the other pages. You can repeat information, such as the company name, by specifying which rows or columns in the worksheet act as print titles. If a worksheet contains a large table, you can print the table's column headings and row headings on every page of your printout by designating those initial columns and rows as print titles.

In the Monthly Sales worksheet, the company name, the slogan, and the worksheet title all appear on the first page of the printout, but do not appear on the other two pages. You will define the range that includes this text as a print title. These four rows will then print on each page.

To define the print title for the pages:

1. In the Page Setup group on the Page Layout tab, click the **Print Titles** button. The Page Setup dialog box opens with the Sheet tab displayed.
2. Click the **Rows to repeat at top** box, move your pointer over the worksheet, and then select the range **A1:A4**. A flashing border appears around the first four rows of the worksheet as a visual indicator that the contents of the first four rows will be repeated on each page of the printout. The cell reference $1:$4 appears in the Rows to repeat at top box.

3. Click the **OK** button.
4. Scroll through the second and third pages of the printout in Page Layout view to verify that the company name, slogan, and worksheet title appear on each page. See Figure 2-39.

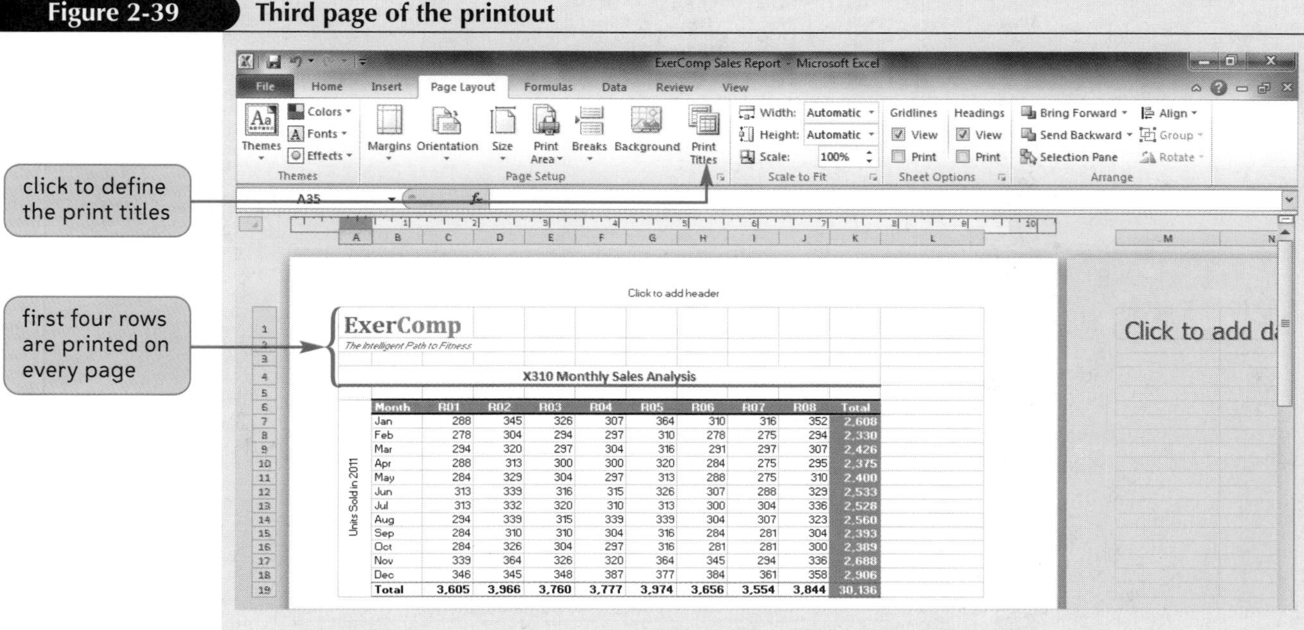

Month	R01	R02	R03	R04	R05	R06	R07	R08	Total
Jan	288	345	326	307	364	310	316	352	2,608
Feb	278	304	294	297	310	278	275	294	2,330
Mar	294	320	297	304	316	291	297	307	2,426
Apr	288	313	300	300	320	284	275	295	2,375
May	284	329	304	297	313	288	275	310	2,400
Jun	313	339	316	315	326	307	288	329	2,533
Jul	313	332	320	310	313	300	304	336	2,528
Aug	294	339	315	339	339	304	307	323	2,560
Sep	284	310	310	304	316	284	281	304	2,393
Oct	284	326	304	297	316	281	281	300	2,389
Nov	339	364	326	320	364	345	294	336	2,688
Dec	346	345	348	387	377	384	361	358	2,906
Total	**3,605**	**3,966**	**3,760**	**3,777**	**3,974**	**3,656**	**3,554**	**3,844**	**30,136**

Figure 2-39 **Third page of the printout**

The Sheet tab in the Page Setup dialog box provides other print options, such as printing the gridlines or row and column headings. You can also print the worksheet in black and white or in draft quality. For a multiple page printout, you can specify whether the pages are ordered by going down the worksheet and then across, or across first and then down.

Creating Page Headers and Footers

Another way to repeat information on each printed page is with headers and footers. Headers and footers contain helpful and descriptive text that is usually not found within the worksheet, such as the workbook's author, the current date, or the workbook filename. If the printout covers multiple pages, you can display the page number and the total number of pages in the printout to help ensure you and others have all the pages.

The header and footer each have three sections: a left section, a center section, and a right section. Within each section, you type the text you want to appear or insert elements such as the worksheet name or the current date and time. These header and footer elements are dynamic; if you rename the worksheet, for example, the name is automatically updated in the header or footer.

Tom wants his printouts to display the workbook's filename in the header's left section and the current date in the header's right section. He wants the center footer to display the page number and the total number of pages in the printout, and the right footer to display your name as the workbook's author.

To insert a header and footer:

1. In Page Layout view, change the zoom level of the worksheet to **90%**.

2. Scroll to the top of the worksheet, and then click the left section of the header directly above cell A1. The Header & Footer Tools contextual tab appears on the Ribbon.
3. Type **Filename:** in the left section of the header, press the **spacebar**, and then, in the Header & Footer Elements group on the Design tab, click the **File Name** button. The code &[File], which displays the filename of the current workbook, is added into the left section of the header.
4. Press the **Tab** key twice to move to the right section of the header, and then click the **Current Date** button in the Header & Footer Elements group. The code &[Date] is added into the right section of the header. See Figure 2-40.

Figure 2-40 **Page header with content**

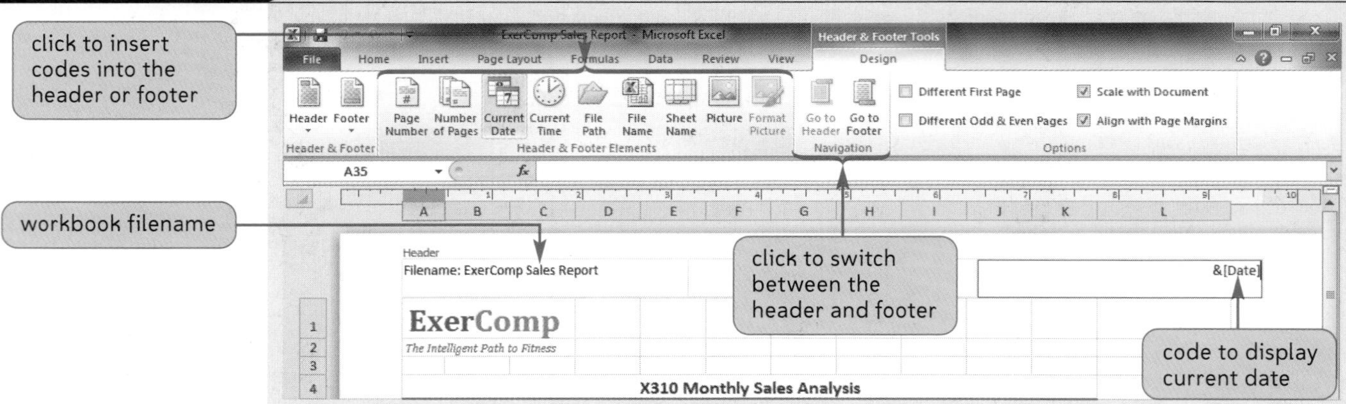

5. In the Navigation group on the Design tab, click the **Go to Footer** button. The right section of the footer is selected.
6. Click the center section of the footer, type **Page**, press the **spacebar**, and click the **Page Number** button in the Header & Footer Elements group.
7. Press the **spacebar**, type **of**, press the **spacebar**, and then click the **Number of Pages** button in the Header & Footer Elements group. The text Page &[Page] of &[Pages] appears in the center section of the footer.
8. Press the **Tab** key to move to the right section of the footer, type **Prepared by:**, press the **spacebar**, and then type your name. See Figure 2-41.

Figure 2-41 **Page footer**

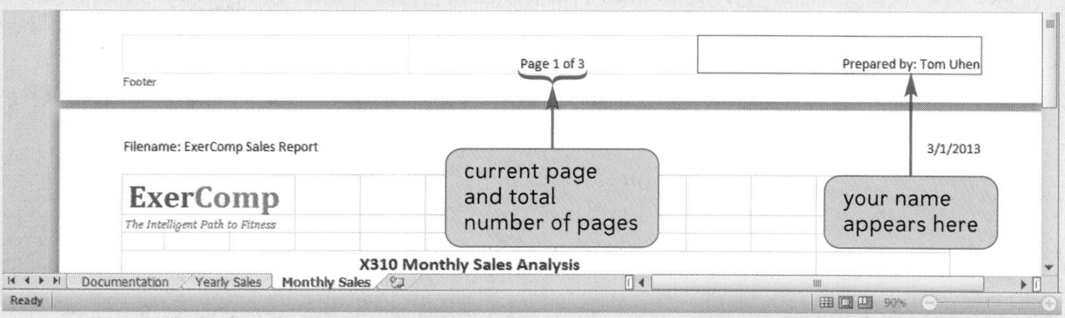

9. Click cell **A1**, and then scroll through the other two pages of the worksheet to verify that the same header appears for each page, and the center section of the footer displays the correct page number and total number of pages.

Defining the Page Margins

Another way to fit a large worksheet on a single page is to reduce the size of the page margins. By default, Excel sets the page margins to between 0.7 and 0.75 inches, and allows for 0.3-inch margins around the page header and footer. You can reduce or increase these margins as needed by selecting from a set of predefined margin sizes or defining your own.

Tom's reports need wide margins to accommodate the page binding. You will change the default margins for the printout.

To set the page margins:

1. Click the **Page Layout** tab on the Ribbon.
2. In the Page Setup group, click the **Margins** button. A menu opens with a list of predefined margins.
3. Click **Wide** to set 1-inch margins around the printed content with 0.5-inch margins around the header and footer. The size of the margins around the page increases, but does not affect the content. Each of the three tables and the print titles still fit on single sheets.

Tom is happy with the appearance of the worksheet and the layout of the printout. You will save the workbook, and then print the Monthly Sales worksheet.

To save the workbook and print the worksheet:

1. Click the **Normal** button on the status bar to return the Monthly Sales worksheet to Normal view.
2. Save the workbook.
3. Print the Monthly Sales worksheet, and then close the workbook. Each table is printed on a separate page, and the headers and footers display the filename, current date, page number and total number of pages, and your name.

Tom will distribute the finished report during the upcoming sales meeting.

REVIEW

Session 2.2 Quick Check

1. Discuss two methods of applying the same format to different ranges.
2. Describe the difference between a cell style and a table style.
3. What are the six table style options you can turn on and off?
4. What is a conditional format?
5. How would you highlight the top five values in the range A1:C20?
6. How do you insert a page break into a worksheet?
7. What are print titles?
8. Describe how to add the workbook filename in the center section of the footer on every page of your printout.

Practice the skills you learned in the tutorial using the same case scenario.

PRACTICE

Review Assignments

Data Files needed for the Review Assignments: X410.xlsx, Paper.jpg

ExerComp introduced another heart rate monitor, the X410, two years ago. Tom wants you to format a workbook that compares the sales of the X310 and X410 models during that time. The workbook already has a Documentation sheet, a Model Comparison sheet comparing the total units sold for each model in the eight sales regions, and a Monthly Sales sheet reporting the number of units sold per month.

In the Model Comparison sheet, you will highlight the sales regions that showed the greatest sales increases from 2011 to 2012. In the Monthly Sales sheet, you will calculate the monthly sales totals for both models during 2011 and 2012. Complete the following:

1. Open the **X410** workbook located in the Excel2\Review folder included with your Data Files, and then save the workbook as **X410 Sales Comparison**.
2. In the Documentation sheet, enter your name in cell B4 and the date in the format *mm/dd/yyyy* in cell B5.
3. In the Documentation sheet, set the font color of cells A1 and A2 to blue, format the text in cell A1 in a 26-point Times New Roman font, and then format the text in cell A2 in a 10-point italicized Times New Roman font. In cell A1, change the font color of the text "Comp" to red.
4. In the range A4:A6, set the font color to white and set the fill color to blue. In the range B4:B6, set the fill color to white. In the range A4:B6, add border lines around all of the cells.
5. In cell B5, display the date with the Long Date format and left-align it within the cell.
6. In the Documentation sheet, insert a background image using the **Paper.jpg** image file located in the Excel2\Review folder included with your Data Files.
7. Use the Format Painter to copy the format from the range A1:A2 in the Documentation sheet to the range A1:A2 in the other two sheets. In cell A1, change the font color of the text "Comp" to red.
8. Go to the Model Comparison sheet. In cells E6 and E17, enter **Increase**. In ranges E7:E14 and E18:E25, enter formulas to calculate the increase in sales for each region.
9. In cells F6 and F17, enter the text **% Increase**. In ranges F7:F14 and F18:F25, enter formulas to calculate the percent increase in sales for each region.
10. In cells B15 and B26, enter the text **Total**. In cells C15, D15, C26, and D26, enter formulas to calculate the total units sold per year for each model. In cells E15 and E26, enter formulas to calculate the total increase in sales. In cells F15 and F26, enter formulas to calculate the percent increase in total sales from 2011 to 2012.
11. Merge and center the range A6:A15, center the text vertically, and then change the orientation to vertical text. Center the text in the range C6:F6, and then indent the region labels in the range B7:B14 one character.
12. In the range C7:E15, format the numbers in a Number format using a thousands separator, no decimal places, and negative numbers displayed with a minus symbol. In the range F7:F15, format the numbers in a Percentage format with two decimal places.
13. Apply the Accent1 cell style to the range B6:F6 and the merged cell A6. Change the font of cell A6 to 18 points and bold. Apply the Total cell style to the range B15:F15.
14. In the range E7:E14, apply a conditional format that adds a Top/Bottom Rule to display the highest number in the range in dark green text with a green fill. In the range F7:F14, apply a conditional format that adds a Top/Bottom Rule to display the highest number in the range in dark red text with a light red fill.
15. Use the Format Painter to copy all of the formats from the range A6:F15 to the range A17:F26.

16. In cell D3, enter **highest**, and then apply a conditional format to cell D3 that adds a Highlight Cells Rule to format the cell that contains the text "highest" with Green Fill with Dark Green Text. In cell D4, enter **highest**, and then apply a conditional format to cell D4 that adds a Highlight Cells Rule to format the cell that contains the text "highest" with Light Red Fill with Dark Red Text.
17. In cell E3, enter **Highest increase in units sold**. In cell E4, enter **Highest % increase in units sold**. Format both cells with the Explanatory Text cell style.
18. Go to the Monthly Sales sheet. In cells D5 and I5, enter the text **All Models**. In cells A18 and F18, enter the text **Total**.
19. Enter formulas in the worksheet to calculate the total sales by month, by model, and then over all months and over both models.
20. Merge and center the range A4:D4, merge and center the range F4:I4, and then apply the Heading 1 style to both merged cells. In the range B5:D5;G5:I5, center the text.
21. In the nonadjacent range B6:D18;G6:I18, format the numbers to show a thousands separator (,) with no decimal places to the right of the decimal point.
22. Select the range A5:D18, and then apply Table Style Light 8 (the first table style in the second row of the Light section in the Table Styles gallery). Turn off the filter arrows, and then display only the header row, first column, and last column table style options. In the range A18:D18, apply the Total cell style.
23. Select the range F5:I18, and then repeat Step 22, applying the Total cell style to the range F18:I18.
24. For the Model Comparison and Monthly Sales worksheets, set the page orientation to landscape, display your name in the center section of the header, display the sheet name in the left section of the footer, display the workbook filename in the center section of the footer, and then display the current date in the right section of the footer.
25. Save and close your workbook. Submit the finished workbook to your instructor, either in printed or electronic form, as requested.

Case Problem 1

If you have a SAM 2010 user profile, your instructor may have assigned an autogradable version of this assignment. If so, log into the SAM 2010 Web site at www.cengage.com/sam2010 to download the instructions and start files.

APPLY

Data File needed for the Case Problem: Frosti.xlsx

FrostiWear Linda Young is a sales manager for FrostiWear, a successful new store based in Hillsboro, Oregon. She's tracking the sales figures for FrostiWear's line of gloves. She created a workbook that contains the sales figures from the past year for three glove models. She wants you to help format the sales report. Complete the following:

1. Open the **Frosti** workbook located in the Excel2\Case1 folder included with your Data Files, and then save the workbook as **FrostiWear Sales Report**.
2. In the Documentation sheet, enter your name in cell B3 and the date in cell B4. Set the background color for all the cells in the worksheet to standard blue, and then set the background color for the range B3:B5 to white. Add a border line around each cell in the range B3:B5.
3. Change the font of cell A1 to the Headings font of the current theme, change the font size to 36 points, change the font color to white, and then bold the text. Change the font size of the range A3:A5 to 16 points, change the font color to white, and then bold the text.
4. Go to the Glove Sales worksheet. Add formulas to calculate the total sales for each month and region over the three glove models.
5. Merge and center the range A1:H1, apply the Title cell style, and then increase the font size to 26 points. Merge and center the range A2:H2, apply the Heading 4 cell style, and then increase the font size to 16 points.

6. Merge and center the range A3:A16, set the alignment to Middle Align, rotate the text up, apply the Accent1 cell style, increase the font size to 18 points, and then bold the text.
7. Use the Format Painter to copy the format of merged cell A3 into the two ranges A18:A31 and A33:A46.
8. Center the text in the range C3:H3. Format the range C4:H16 to include thousands separators (,) and no decimal places. Use the Format Painter to copy the formats in the range C3:H16 to the two ranges C18:H31 and C33:H46.
9. In the range B3:H16, apply the Table Style Medium 2 table style. Turn off the filter arrows, and then display the header row, first column, last column, and banded rows. In the range B16:H16, change the fill color of the Total row to standard yellow.
10. Repeat Step 9 for the other two tables in the worksheet.
11. In the Glove Sales worksheet, set the page orientation to landscape, insert manual page breaks at cells A18 and A33, and then repeat the first two rows of the worksheet on every printed page.
12. Display your name in the center header, display the filename in the left footer, display **Page** *page number* **of** *number of pages* in the center footer, and then display the current date in the right footer.
13. Save and close your workbook. Submit the finished workbook to your instructor.

Add formulas and formatting to create a packing slip.

CREATE

Case Problem 2

Data File needed for the Case Problem: GrillRite.xlsx

GrillRite Grills Brian Simpko is a shipping manager at GrillRite Grills in Hammond, Indiana. He uses an Excel workbook to provide shipping and order information for customer orders and deliveries. You will create and format the worksheet that Brian can use to enter information for packing slips. Complete the following:

1. Open the **GrillRite** workbook located in the Excel2\Case2 folder included with your Data Files, and then save the workbook as **GrillRite Grills Packing Slip**. In the Documentation sheet, enter your name in cell B3 and the date in cell B4.
2. Insert a new worksheet at the end of the workbook, and then rename it **Packing Slip**.
3. In the Packing Slip worksheet, select all of the cells in the worksheet. (*Hint*: Click the Select All button at the intersection of the row and column headings.) Change the font to the Body font of the current theme. For the range A1:D3, set the fill color to black and the font color to white.
4. Set the width of columns A through D to 20 characters. Set the height of row 1 to 36 characters.
5. Merge the range A1:B3, and then left- and top-align the merged cell. Merge the range C1:D3, and then right- and top-align the merged cell.
6. In cell A1, enter the following three lines of text, and then format the first line in a 26-point bold font using the Headings font of the current theme:

   GrillRite Grills

   200 Commerce Lane

   Hammond, Indiana 46324

7. In cell C1, enter **Packing Slip**, and then format the text in a 26-point bold font using the Headings font of the current theme.
8. In the range A5:A7, enter the following three lines of text in a bold font, and then right-align the text and indent the text one character:
   Order Date
   Order Number
   Purchase Order
9. Format cell B5 in the Long Date format. Insert border lines around each of the cells in the range B5:B7.
10. In the range C5:C7, enter the following three lines of text, and then use the Format Painter to copy the formats from the range A5:B7 to the range C5:D7:
    Date
    Sales Rep
    Account Num
11. In cell B9, enter **Ship To**. In cell D9, enter **Bill To**. Format the text in both cells in a bold font.
12. In cell A10, enter **Address** in a bold font, right-align the text, and then indent it one character.
13. Merge the cells in the range B10:B15, left- and top-align the cell contents, and then insert a border around the merged cell. Click the Wrap Text button from the Alignment group on the Home tab to ensure that text within this cell wraps to a new line.
14. In cell C10, enter **Address**. Copy the format from the range A10:B15 into the range C10:D15.
15. Enter the following data into the worksheet:
    Cell A17: **Item**
    Cell B17: **Product No.**
    Cell C17: **Description**
    Cell D17: **Order Quantity**
    cells A18:A27: the numbers from **1** to **10**

EXPLORE

16. For the range A17:D27, apply Table Style Medium 1, turn off the filter arrows, and display the header row, Total row, and banded rows. In cell D28, select the SUM function from the list.
17. In cell A30, enter **Comments** in a bold font.
18. Merge the range A31:D39, left- and top-align the cell contents, and then add a thick box border around the merged cell.
19. In cell D40, enter **Thank you for your business!** in an italic, 16-point font, and then right-align the cell contents.
20. Enter the packing slip data shown in Figure 2-42.

Figure 2-42 GrillRite Grills packing slip

	A	B	C	D	E
1	**GrillRite Grills**			**Packing Slip**	
2	200 Commerce Lane				
3	Hammond, Indiana 46324				
4					
5	**Order Date**	Tuesday, April 30, 2013	**Date**	Friday, May 03, 2013	
6	**Order Number**	GR3985-11	**Sales Rep**	Linda Bingham	
7	**Purchase Order**	GR005-205-11	**Account Num**	188	
8					
9		**Ship To**		**Bill To**	
10	**Address**	Blake Stout	**Address**	Hilltop Hardware	
11		Hilltop Hardware		450 Drake Avenue	
12		450 Drake Avenue		Monroe, WI 53566	
13		Monroe, WI 53566			
14					
15					
16					
17	**Item**	**Product No.**	**Description**	**Order Quantity**	
18	1	MG304-29	Mini-Grill Set	7	
19	2	TTG044-22	Table Top Grill Box	4	
20	3	GC141-35	Grill Cleanser Box (35)	10	
21	4	GTK412-15	Grill Toolkit (Standard)	8	
22	5	GPK252-29	Grill Parts Kit (Standard)	10	
23	6				
24	7				
25	8				
26	9				
27	10				
28	**Total**			**39**	
29					
30	**Comments**				
31	Please contact shipping manager Brian Simpko (ext. 315) regarding discount shipping rates.				
32					
33					
34					
35					
36					
37					
38					
39					
40			*Thank you for your business!*		

21. Make sure the worksheet's page orientation is set to portrait, and then add a footer that displays your name in the left section, the filename in the center section, and the current date in the right section.
22. Save and close your workbook. Submit the finished workbook to your instructor, either in printed or electronic form, as requested.

Apply conditional formats to create a wind speed grid.

CHALLENGE

Case Problem 3

Data File needed for the Case Problem: Wind.xlsx

Arcadia Wind Farm Tara Young is a researcher at Arcadia Wind Farm, a government research center near Topeka, Kansas, involved in exploring how to create economical and efficient wind farms. One of Tara's jobs is to record wind speeds from different sectors of the wind farm. Tara has entered the wind speed data into a workbook as a table with wind speed measures laid out in a grid. Because the numbers are difficult to read and interpret, you will color code the wind speed values using a conditional format. Complete the following:

1. Open the **Wind** workbook located in the Excel2\Case3 folder included with your Data Files, and then save the workbook as **Wind Farm**. In the Documentation sheet, enter your name and the date.
2. Go to the Wind Speed Grid worksheet. Merge the range A1:V1, and then apply the Heading 1 style to the merged cell and set the font size to 20 points.
3. Select the range B3:V3, and then change the font style to white text on a black background. Copy this formatting to the grid coordinates in the range A4:A64.
4. Select the range B4:V64. The data in this range comprises the wind speed measures for different sensors in Sector 5.

EXPLORE

5. Create a conditional formatting that highlights cells whose value equals 18 with fill color equal to the RGB color value (99, 37, 35). (*Hint*: In the Equal To dialog box, select Custom Format in the with box to open the Format Cells dialog box. On the Fill tab, in the Background Color section, click the More Colors button, and then click the Custom tab to enter the RGB color value.)

EXPLORE

6. Repeat Step 5 to continue creating conditional formats that set highlight colors for the following wind speed values:

Wind Speed	RGB Color Value
16 m/s	(150, 54, 52)
14 m/s	(218, 150, 148)
12 m/s	(230, 184, 183)
10 m/s	(242, 220, 219)
8 m/s	(242, 242, 242)
6 m/s	(255, 255, 255)
4 m/s	(197, 217, 241)
2 m/s	(141, 180, 226)
0 m/s	(83, 141, 213)

7. In the range B4:V64, reduce the font size of the values to 1 point.
8. Enclose each of the cells in the range B4:V64 in a light gray border.
9. Apply the conditional highlight colors specified in Steps 5 and 6 to the legend values in the cell range X3:X12.
10. Merge the range Y3:Y12, and then center the contents of the merged cell and rotate the text down. Display the text in a bold 18-point font.
11. Set the print area of the page to the range A1:Y64.

EXPLORE

12. On the Page Layout tab, scale the page to fit on a single page. (*Hint*: Use the Width and Height boxes in the Scale to Fit group to force the worksheet to fit on one page.)
13. Add a header to the printed page with your name in the top-left header and the filename in the top-right header.
14. Save and close your workbook. Submit the finished workbook to your instructor, either in printed or electronic form, as requested.

Format a meal-planning worksheet that highlights high-calorie and high-fat foods.

CREATE

Case Problem 4

Data File needed for the Case Problem: Life.xlsx

Life Managers Kate Dee is a dietician at Life Managers, a company in Kleinville, Michigan, that specializes in personal improvement, particularly in areas of health and fitness. Kate wants to create a meal-planning workbook for her clients who want to lose weight and improve their health. One goal of meal planning is to decrease the percentage of fat in the diet. Kate thinks it would be helpful to highlight foods that have a high percentage of fat as well as list their total fat calories. She already created an Excel workbook that contains a few sample food items and lists the number of calories and grams of fat in each item. She wants you to format this workbook. Complete the following:

1. Open the **Life** workbook located in the Excel2\Case4 folder included with your Data Files, and then save the workbook as **Life Managers Nutrition Table**. In the Documentation sheet, enter your name in cell B3 and the date in cell B4.
2. In the Meal Planner worksheet, add a column that calculates the calories from fat for each food item. Fat contains nine calories per gram.
3. Add a column that calculates the percentage of fat for each food item. This value is calculated by dividing the calories from fat by the total number of calories.
4. Display all values for calories and grams of fat with one decimal place. Display the fat percentages as percentages with one decimal place.
5. Format the rest of the Meal Planner worksheet attractively, but be sure to include at least one example of each of the following design elements:
   - A range merged into a single cell
   - Text centered and rotated within a cell
   - Cell styles applied to one or more elements
   - Borders applied to one or more elements
6. For good health, the FDA recommends that the fat percentage should not exceed 30 percent of the total calories per day. Apply a rule to the fat percentages to highlight those food items that exceed the FDA recommendation. Include a legend to document the highlighting color you used.
7. Add descriptive headers and footers to the printed document. Also insert page breaks and print titles to ensure that the printout is easily read and interpreted.
8. Save and close your workbook. Submit the finished workbook to your instructor, either in printed or electronic form, as requested.

ASSESS

SAM: Skills Assessment Manager

For current SAM information, including versions and content details, visit SAM Central (http://samcentral.course.com). If you have a SAM user profile, you may have access to hands-on instruction, practice, and assessment of the skills covered in this tutorial. Because various versions of SAM are supported throughout the life of this text, check with your instructor for the correct instructions and URL/Web site for accessing assignments.

ENDING DATA FILES

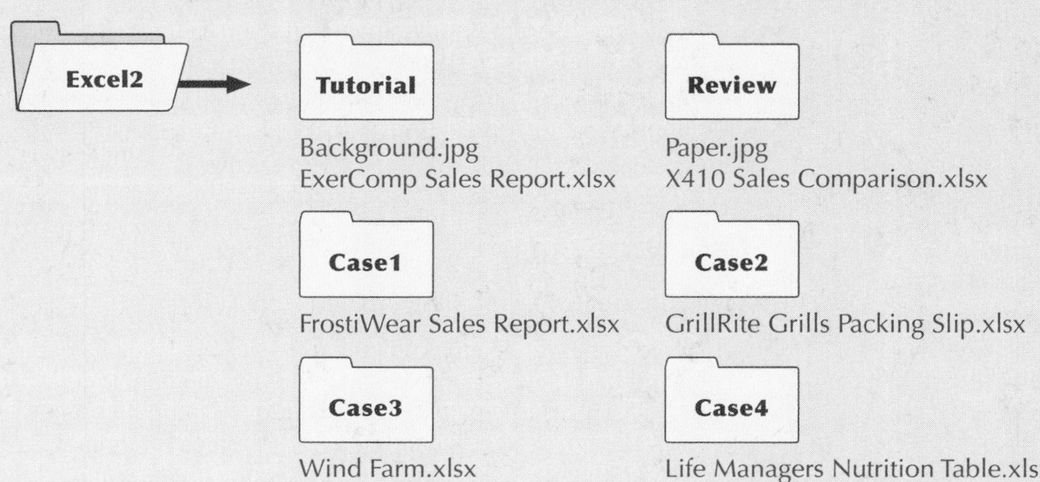

TUTORIAL 3

Working with Formulas and Functions

Developing a Family Budget

EXCEL

OBJECTIVES

Session 3.1
- Copy formulas
- Build formulas containing relative, absolute, and mixed references
- Review function syntax
- Insert a function with the Insert Function dialog box
- Search for a function
- Type a function directly in a cell

Session 3.2
- Use AutoFill to fill in a formula and complete a series
- Enter the IF logical function
- Insert the date with the TODAY function
- Use the PMT financial function to calculate monthly mortgage payments

Case | *Drake Family Budget*

Newlyweds Diane and Glenn Drake are trying to balance career, school, and family life. The couple's income and expenses vary throughout the year. Diane works full-time as a legal assistant, but earns less in the summer months when she cuts back her work hours to attend summer courses. Glenn is in a graduate program at a nearby university where he recently was hired as a lab assistant. In the summer, Glenn takes on other work to earn additional income. The couple just moved into a new apartment, but plan to purchase a house within the next several years. Although Glenn and Diane's salaries have grown in the past few years, the couple seems to have less cash on hand. This financial shortage has prompted them to take a closer look at their finances and figure out how to best manage them.

Diane has set up an Excel workbook and entered the monthly income from their two jobs. She has identified and entered expenses the family pays on a monthly basis, such as the rent and grocery bill, as well as other expenses that occur only a few times a year, such as Glenn's tuition and vacations. She wants to calculate how much money they are bringing in and how much money they are spending. She also wants to come up with a savings plan for the down payment on a house they hope to buy in a few years.

You'll help Diane complete the workbook. You will enter formulas to perform the calculations that will provide Diane with a better overall picture of the family's finances. Diane and Glenn will be able to use this information to manage their money more effectively.

STARTING DATA FILES

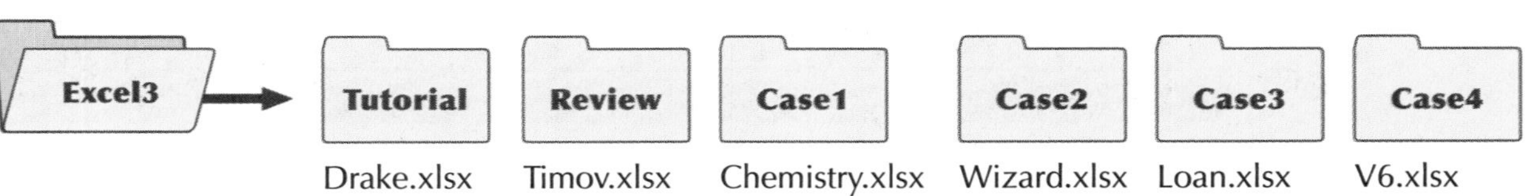

SESSION 3.1 VISUAL OVERVIEW

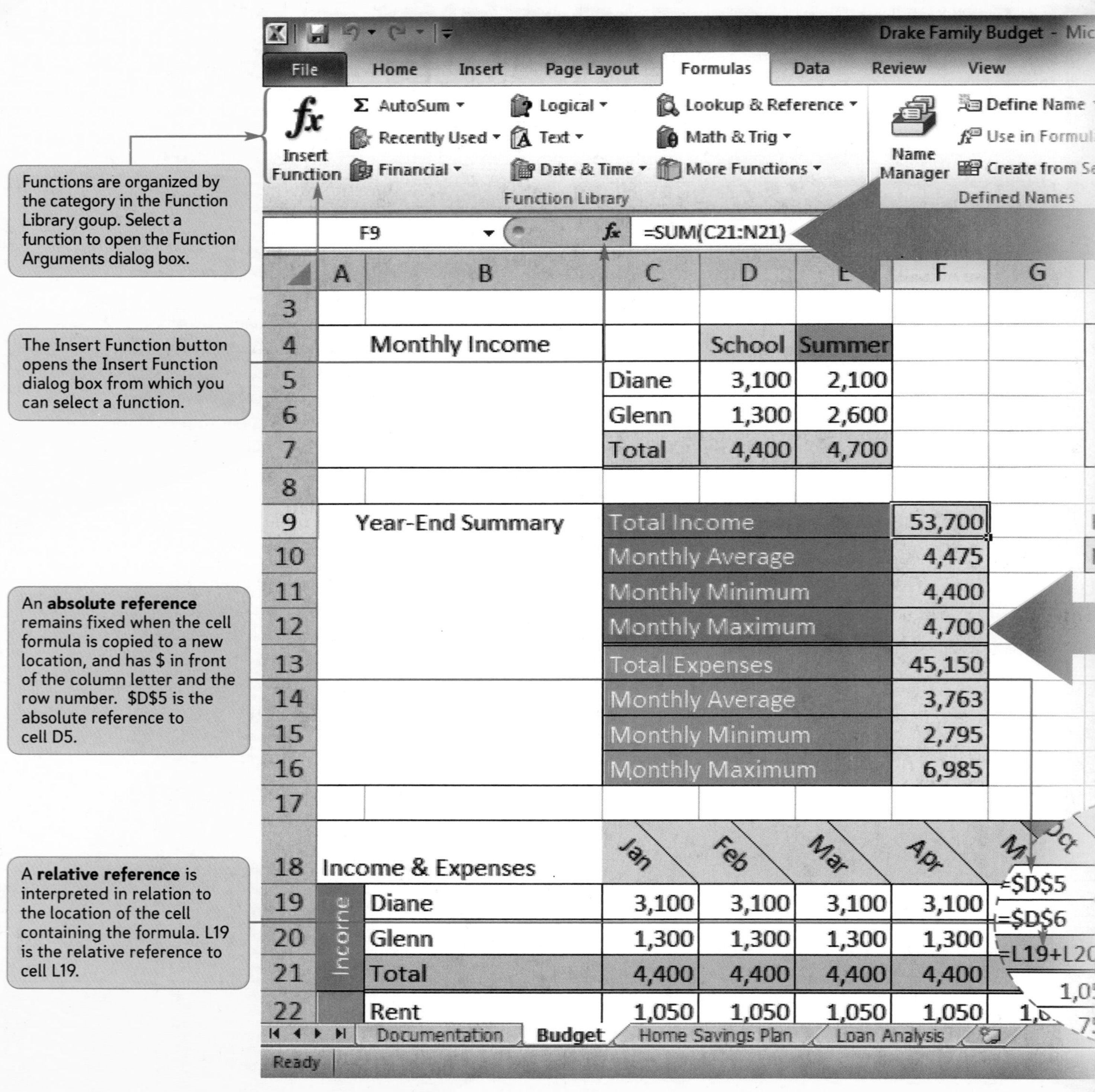

CELL REFERENCES AND EXCEL FUNCTIONS

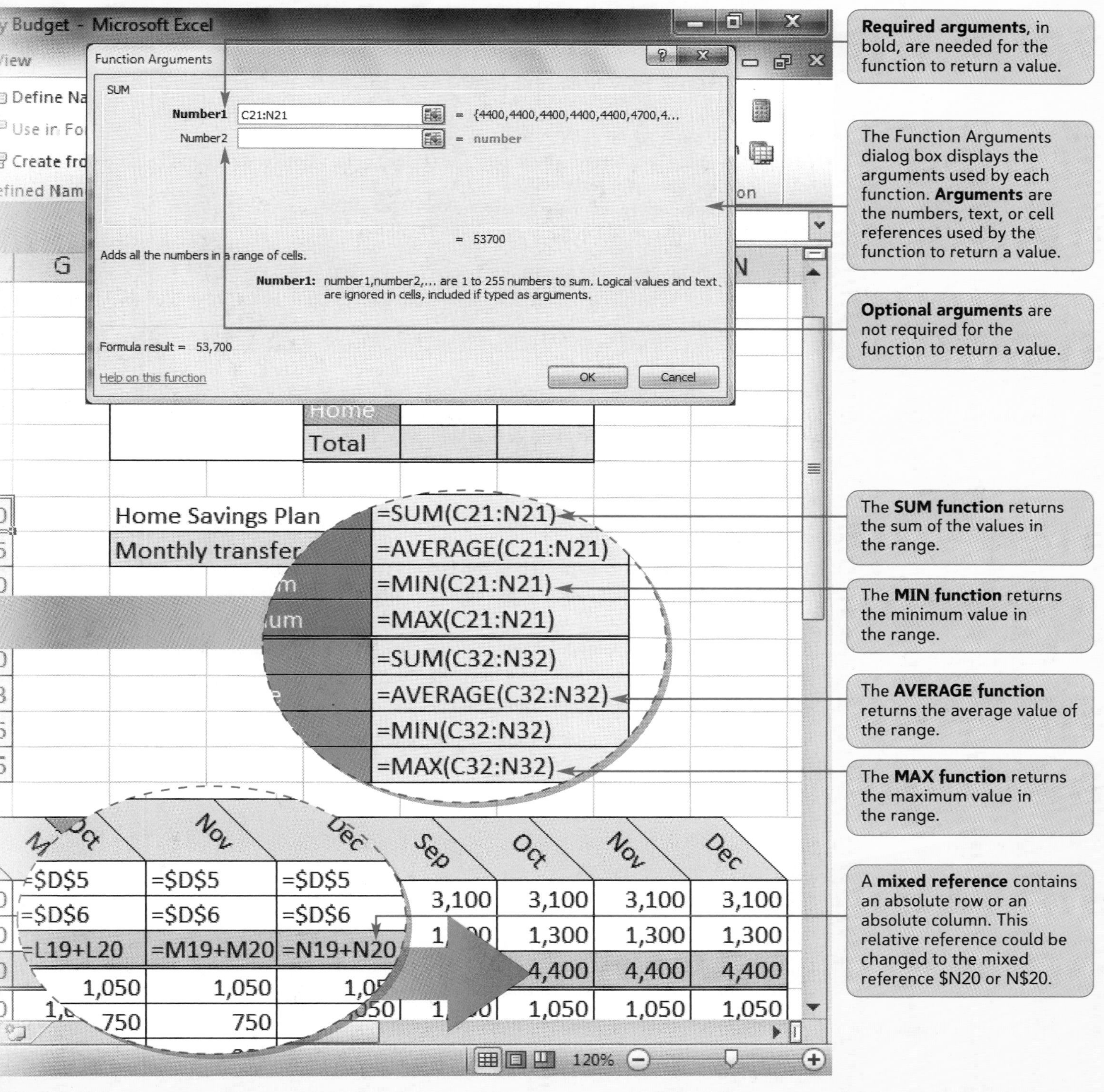

Required arguments, in bold, are needed for the function to return a value.

The Function Arguments dialog box displays the arguments used by each function. **Arguments** are the numbers, text, or cell references used by the function to return a value.

Optional arguments are not required for the function to return a value.

The **SUM function** returns the sum of the values in the range.

The **MIN function** returns the minimum value in the range.

The **AVERAGE function** returns the average value of the range.

The **MAX function** returns the maximum value in the range.

A **mixed reference** contains an absolute row or an absolute column. This relative reference could be changed to the mixed reference $N20 or N$20.

Understanding Cell References

Most Excel workbooks are created to record and analyze data. To do this effectively, you enter data in cells in a worksheet, and then reference the cells with data in formulas that perform calculations on that data, such as adding the total of a column of numbers as part of a budget.

REFERENCE

Entering Relative, Absolute, and Mixed References

- To enter a relative reference, type the cell reference as it appears in the worksheet. For example, enter B2 for cell B2.
- To enter an absolute reference, type $ (a dollar sign) before both the row and column references. For example, enter $B$2.
- To enter a mixed reference, type $ before either the row or column reference. For example, enter $B2 or B$2.

or

- Select the cell reference you want to change.
- Press the F4 key to cycle the reference from relative to absolute to mixed and then back to relative.

Diane has already done a lot of the work on her family budget. She used data from the past year to estimate the couple's monthly expenses for the upcoming year and entered this data into an Excel workbook. You will open this workbook and review her estimates of the family's monthly expenses.

To open Diane's workbook:

1. Open the **Drake** workbook located in the **Excel3\Tutorial** folder included with your Data Files, and then save the workbook as **Drake Family Budget** in the same folder.
2. In the Documentation worksheet, enter your name in cell B3 and the date in cell B4.
3. Switch to the Budget worksheet, and then review its contents.
4. Scroll down to view the range A18:N32. This range lists Diane's estimate of her family's monthly expenses by category for the upcoming year. See Figure 3-1.

Figure 3-1 Monthly expenses for the Drake family

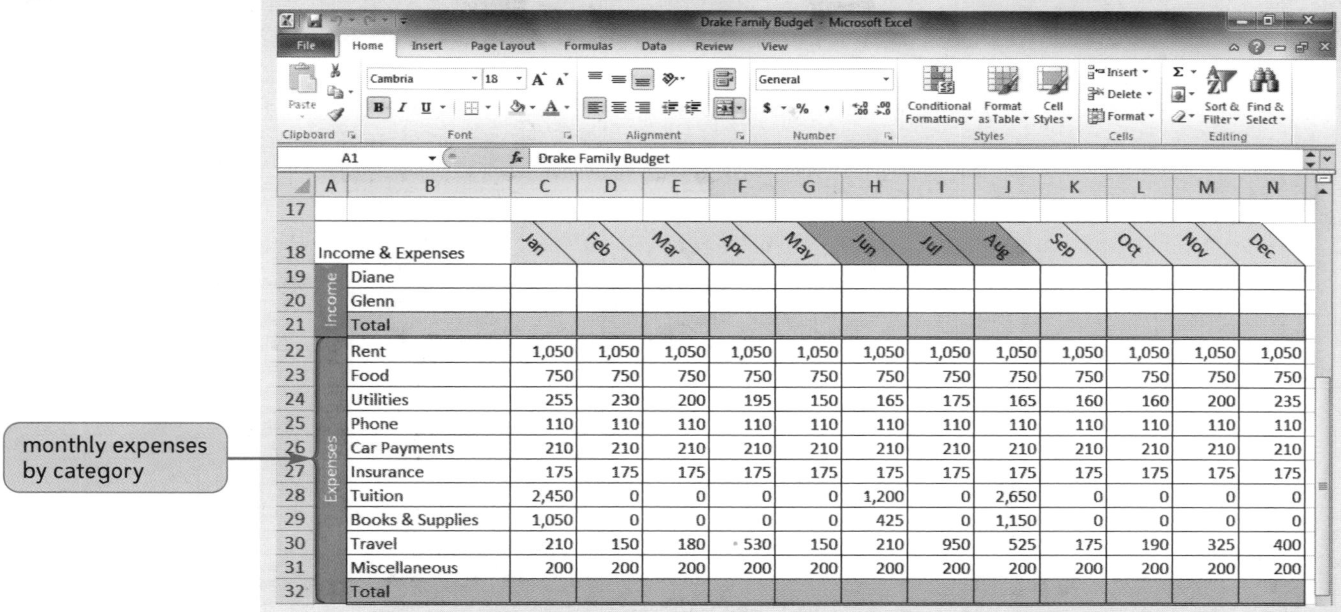

Drake Family Budget - Microsoft Excel

A1 Drake Family Budget

	A	B	C	D	E	F	G	H	I	J	K	L	M	N
17														
18	Income & Expenses		Jan	Feb	Mar	Apr	May	Jun	Jul	Aug	Sep	Oct	Nov	Dec
19	Income	Diane												
20		Glenn												
21		Total												
22	Expenses	Rent	1,050	1,050	1,050	1,050	1,050	1,050	1,050	1,050	1,050	1,050	1,050	1,050
23		Food	750	750	750	750	750	750	750	750	750	750	750	750
24		Utilities	255	230	200	195	150	165	175	165	160	160	200	235
25		Phone	110	110	110	110	110	110	110	110	110	110	110	110
26		Car Payments	210	210	210	210	210	210	210	210	210	210	210	210
27		Insurance	175	175	175	175	175	175	175	175	175	175	175	175
28		Tuition	2,450	0	0	0	0	1,200	0	2,650	0	0	0	0
29		Books & Supplies	1,050	0	0	0	0	425	0	1,150	0	0	0	0
30		Travel	210	150	180	530	150	210	950	525	175	190	325	400
31		Miscellaneous	200	200	200	200	200	200	200	200	200	200	200	200
32		Total												

monthly expenses by category

Diane wants you to calculate the total expenses for each month. You'll start by inserting the formula to calculate the January expenses and then paste that formula into the remaining months of the year.

To calculate the total monthly expenses:

1. In cell C32, enter the formula **=SUM(C22:C31)** to add the estimated expenses for the month of January. The value 6,460 is displayed in cell C32, indicating that Diane estimates the couple will spend $6,460 in January of the upcoming year.
2. Click cell **C32** to select it.
3. Click the **Home** tab on the Ribbon, if necessary, and then click the **Copy** button in the Clipboard group.
4. Select the range **D32:N32**, and then click the **Paste** button in the Clipboard group. The SUM function is pasted into the selected range, calculating the total expenses for the remaining months of the year. See Figure 3-2.

Figure 3-2 **Total monthly expenses**

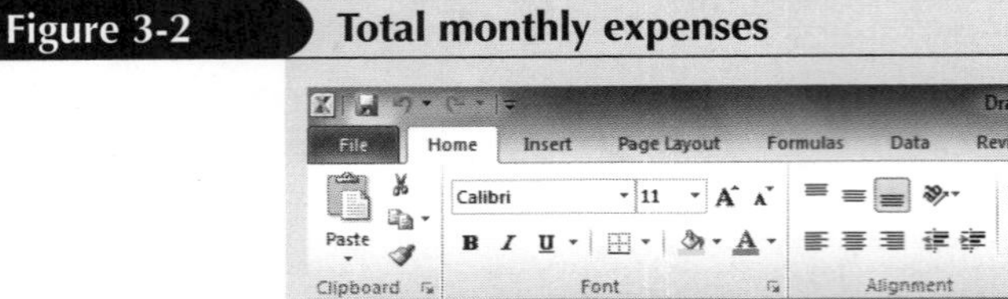

	A	B	C	D	E	F	G	H	I	J	K	L	M	N
17														
18	Income & Expenses		Jan	Feb	Mar	Apr	May	Jun	Jul	Aug	Sep	Oct	Nov	Dec
19	Income	Diane												
20		Glenn												
21		Total												
22	Expenses	Rent	1,050	1,050	1,050	1,050	1,050	1,050	1,050	1,050	1,050	1,050	1,050	1,050
23		Food	750	750	750	750	750	750	750	750	750	750	750	750
24		Utilities	255	230	200	195	150	165	175	165	160	160	200	235
25		Phone	110	110	110	110	110	110	110	110	110	110	110	110
26		Car Payments	210	210	210	210	210	210	210	210	210	210	210	210
27		Insurance	175	175	175	175	175	175	175	175	175	175	175	175
28		Tuition	2,450	0	0	0	0	1,200	0	2,650	0	0	0	0
29		Books & Supplies	1,050	0	0	0	0	425	0	1,150	0	0	0	0
30		Travel	210	150	180	530	150	210	950	525	175	190	325	400
31		Miscellaneous	200	200	200	200	200	200	200	200	200	200	200	200
32		Total	6,460	2,875	2,875	3,220	2,795	4,495	3,620	6,985	2,830	2,845	3,020	3,130
33														

5. Review the total expenses for each month. January and August are particularly expensive months because Glenn has to pay tuition and purchase books for the upcoming semester.
6. Click each cell in the range D32:N32, reviewing the formula entered in the cell. The formulas pasted into the range D32:N32 all calculate the sums of values in different cell references. For example, the formula =SUM(D22:D31) was inserted in cell D32, the formula =SUM(E22:E31) was inserted in cell E32, and so forth.

Using Relative References

When you entered the formula in cell C32 to sum the January expenses, Excel interprets the cell references in that formula relative to the location of cell C32. In other words, Excel interprets the formula =SUM(C22:C31) as adding the values entered in the 10 cells directly above cell C32.

Excel uses this interpretation of the cell references when the formula is pasted into other cells. For example, when you pasted the formula in cell D32, the formula changed to =SUM(D22:D31), which has a different cell reference but the same meaning: adding the values of the 10 cells directly above the active cell. The formulas in the remaining cells of the range D32:E32 were similarly adjusted so that each formula displays the total expenses for the selected month.

The cell references used in these formulas are called relative references because when Excel copies and pastes them, they are always interpreted in relation, or relative, to the location of the cell containing the formula. Figure 3-3 illustrates how a relative cell reference in a formula changes when the formula is copied to another group of cells.

Figure 3-3 **Formulas using a relative reference**

formula references a cell three rows up and three columns to the left of the active cell

	A	B	C	D	E	F
1	Referenced Cells					
2	10	20				
3	30	40				
4				Formulas with Relative References		
5				=A2		
6						
7						
8						

when copied to new cells, each formula still references a cell three rows up and two columns to the left

	A	B	C	D	E	F
1	Referenced Cells					
2	10	20				
3	30	40				
4				Formulas with Relative References		
5				=A2	=B2	
6				=A3	=B3	
7						(Ctrl)
8						

values returned by each formula

	A	B	C	D	E	F
1	Referenced Cells					
2	10	20				
3	30	40				
4				Formulas with Relative References		
5				10	20	
6				30	40	
7						(Ctrl)
8						

In this figure, the formula =A2 entered in cell D5 displays the value of 10, which is the value entered in cell A2. When pasted to a new location, each of the pasted formulas contains a reference to a cell that is three rows up and three rows to the left of the current cell's location. One of the great advantages of relative references is that you can quickly generate row and column totals without having to worry about revising the formulas as you copy them to new locations.

Using Absolute References

A good practice when designing a workbook is to enter values in their own cells in one location of the worksheet, and then reference the appropriate cells in formulas throughout the worksheets. This reduces the amount of data entry when you need to use the same data in more than one location. It also makes it faster and more accurate when you need to change a data value, as all the formulas based on that cell are updated to reflect the new value.

Next, you will enter the Drakes' monthly income. The couple's income changes in the summer as Diane works fewer hours and Glenn works more. Rather than inserting these same values each month, you'll enter them in cells at the top of the worksheet and then reference those values in the income/expenses table at the bottom of the worksheet. Later, if Diane modifies the monthly income estimates, you'll need to change them in only one location rather than in 12 different locations.

To enter the couple's estimated monthly income:

1. Scroll to the top of the worksheet, and then enter the following data in the specified cells:

   cell D5: **2800** cell E5: **2100**
   cell D6: **1300** cell E6: **2600**

2. Select the range **D7:E7**. You'll enter the monthly income totals in these cells.
3. In the Editing group on the Home tab, click the **Sum** button [Σ]. The total estimated income is calculated for the school and summer months. See Figure 3-4.

Figure 3-4 **Monthly income estimates**

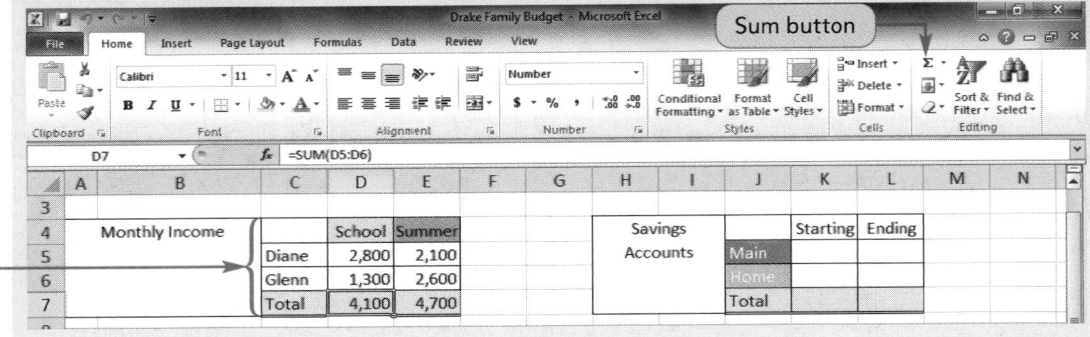

Next, you'll calculate the couple's projected income for January through May by referencing the values you just entered at the top of the worksheet. The couple will have the same income for the next four months as they did in January, so you can copy the formulas from January into February through May.

To insert the monthly income for January through May:

1. Click cell **C19**, type **=D5**, and then press the **Enter** key. The value 2,800, Diane's income for January, appears in cell C19.
2. In cell C20, enter the formula **=D6**. The value 1,300, Glenn's income for January, appears in cell C20.
3. In cell C21, enter the formula **=C19+C20**. This formula calculates the total income for the couple in the month of January, displaying the value 4,100.
4. Select the range **C19:C21**, and then click the **Copy** button in the Clipboard group on the Home tab. The three formulas are copied to the Clipboard.
5. Select the range **D19:G21**, and then click the **Paste** button in the Clipboard group. The formulas are pasted and calculate the couple's income for January through May. See Figure 3-5.

Figure 3-5 **Income values inserted for January through May**

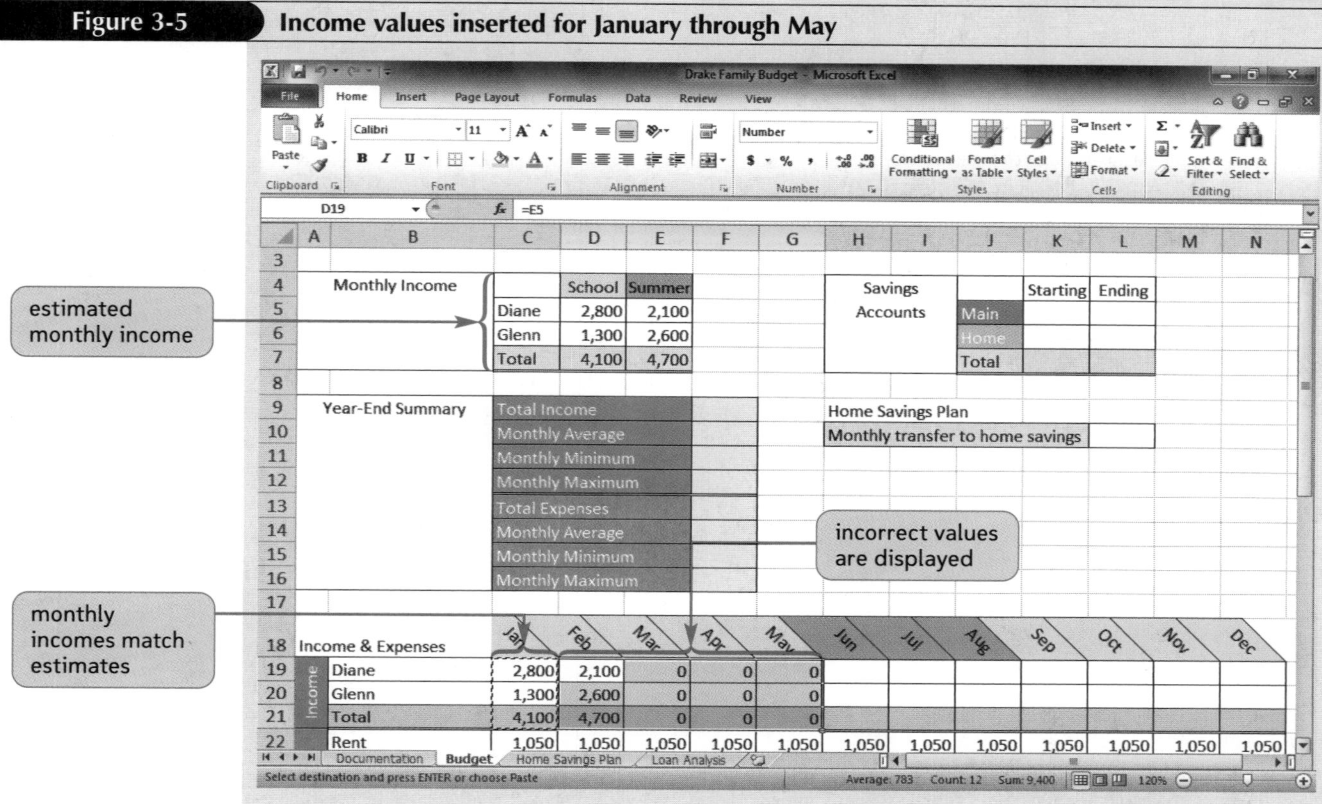

The formulas you copied and pasted from January resulted in incorrect values for February, March, April, and May. The February column show the couple's estimated monthly income for the summer, and the March, April, and May columns display the value 0. What went wrong?

The problem is that the formulas use relative references. For example, the formula in cell C19 is =D5, which references the cell located 14 rows up and 1 column to the right of the current cell. When you pasted that formula to cell G19, Excel inserted the formula =H5, which references the empty cell located 14 rows up and 1 column to the right of cell G19, so that the value displayed in the cell is 0.

Instead of using relative references, you need to use a cell reference that will remain fixed when the formula is copied to a new location. Cell references that remain fixed are called absolute references. In Excel, absolute references have a $ (dollar sign) before each column and row designation. For example, B8 is a relative reference to cell B8, whereas $B$8 is an absolute reference to cell B8. When you copy a formula that contains an absolute reference to a new location, the reference does not change. Figure 3-6 shows an example of how copying a formula with an absolute reference results in the same cell reference being pasted in different cells regardless of their location.

Figure 3-6 Formulas using an absolute reference

formula containing an absolute reference to the sales tax rate in cell A2

	A	B	C	D	E	F
1	Sales Tax Rate		Purchase	Sales Tax	Total	
2	0.05		$24.95	=C2*$A$2	=C2+D2	
3			$122.35			
4			$199.81			
5			$45.40			
6						
7						

absolute reference to cell A2

relative references to cells C2 and D2

when pasted into a new location, the absolute reference remains unchanged

	A	B	C	D	E	F
1	Sales Tax Rate		Purchase	Sales Tax	Total	
2	0.05		$24.95	=C2*$A$2	=C2+D2	
3			$122.35	=C3*$A$2	=C3+D3	
4			$199.81	=C4*$A$2	=C4+D4	
5			$45.40	=C5*$A$2	=C5+D5	
6						(Ctrl)
7						

$A$2 continues to be referenced in the formula

relative references change based on cell location

values returned by the cell formulas

	A	B	C	D	E	F
1	Sales Tax Rate		Purchase	Sales Tax	Total	
2	5%		$24.95	$1.25	$26.20	
3			$122.35	$6.12	$128.47	
4			$199.81	$9.99	$209.80	
5			$45.40	$2.27	$47.67	
6						(Ctrl)
7						

In this figure, the sales tax of different purchases is calculated and displayed. All items have the same 5 percent tax rate applied to the purchase, with the tax rate stored in cell A2. The sales tax and total cost of the first item are calculated in cells D2 and E2, respectively. When those formulas are copied and pasted to the remaining purchases, the relative references in the formulas are modified to point to the new location of the purchase cost; however, the sales tax rate continues to point to cell A2, regardless of the location of the selected cell.

You will modify the formulas in the Budget worksheet so that they reference Diane's income estimates using absolute rather than relative references.

To use absolute references to display the monthly income:

1. In cell C19, enter **=$D$5**. This formula contains an absolute reference to cell D5, which contains Diane's monthly income during the school months.
2. In cell C20, enter **=$D$6**. This formula contains an absolute reference to cell D6, which contains Glenn's monthly income during the school months.
3. Copy the corrected formulas in the range **C19:C20**, and then paste them in the range **D19:G20**. As shown in Figure 3-7, the months of February through May now correctly show the monthly income values for the school months.

Figure 3-7 **Results of formulas with absolute references**

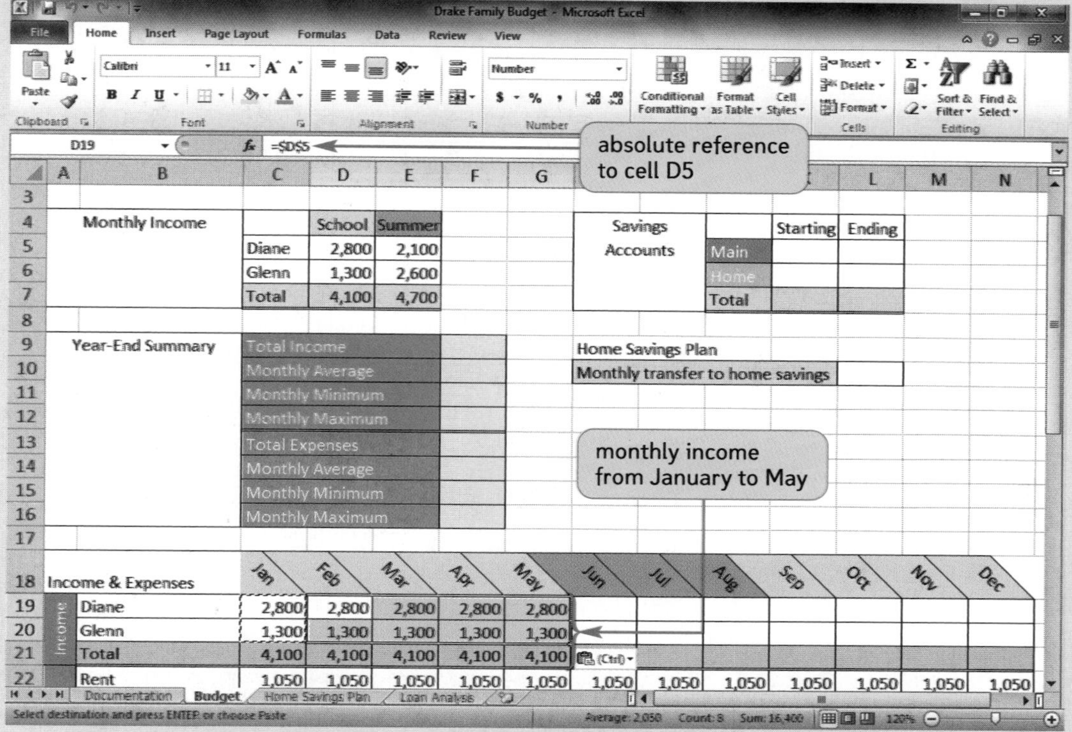

4. Click each cell in the range D19:G20 and verify that the formulas =$D$5 and =$D$6 were copied into the appropriate cells.

Using Mixed References

A formula can also include cell references that are mixed. A mixed reference contains both relative and absolute references. For example, a mixed reference for cell A2 can be either $A2 or A$2. In the mixed reference $A2, the column reference to column A is absolute and the reference to row 2 is relative. In the mixed reference A$2, the column reference is relative and the row reference is absolute. As you can see, a mixed reference "locks" one part of the cell reference while the other part can change. When you copy and paste a formula with a mixed reference to a new location, the absolute portion of the cell reference remains fixed and the relative portion shifts.

Figure 3-8 shows an example of using mixed references to complete a multiplication table. The first cell in the table, cell B3, contains the formula =$A3*B$2, which multiplies the first column entry (A3) by the first row entry (B2), returning the value 1. When this formula is copied to another cell, the absolute portions of the cell references remain unchanged and the relative portions of the references change. For example, if the formula is copied to cell E6, the first mixed cell reference changes to $A6 because the column reference is absolute and the row reference is relative, and the second cell reference changes to E$2 because the row reference is absolute and the column reference is relative. The result is that cell E6 contains the formula =$A6*E$2 and returns the value 16. Other cells in the multiplication table are similarly modified so that each entry returns the multiplication of the row and column headings.

Figure 3-8 A multiplication table using a mixed reference

original formula with a mixed cell reference that multiplies the first row by the first column

	A	B	C	D	E	F	G
1			Multiplication Table				
2		1	2	3	4	5	
3	1	=$A3*B$2					
4	2						
5	3						
6	4						
7	5						
8							
9							

formula copied to the B3:F7 range with mixed ranges to multiply the first row entries by the first column entries

	A	B	C	D	E	F	G
1			Multiplication Table				
2		1	2	3	4	5	
3	1	=$A3*B$2	=$A3*C$2	=$A3*D$2	=$A3*E$2	=$A3*F$2	
4	2	=$A4*B$2	=$A4*C$2	=$A4*D$2	=$A4*E$2	=$A4*F$2	
5	3	=$A5*B$2	=$A5*C$2	=$A5*D$2	=$A5*E$2	=$A5*F$2	
6	4	=$A6*B$2	=$A6*C$2	=$A6*D$2	=$A6*E$2	=$A6*F$2	
7	5	=$A7*B$2	=$A7*C$2	=$A7*D$2	=$A7*E$2	=$A7*F$2	
8							(Ctrl)
9							

values returned by each formula

	A	B	C	D	E	F	G
1			Multiplication Table				
2		1	2	3	4	5	
3	1	1	2	3	4	5	
4	2	2	4	6	8	10	
5	3	3	6	9	12	15	
6	4	4	8	12	16	20	
7	5	5	10	15	20	25	
8							(Ctrl)
9							

INSIGHT

Understanding When to Use Relative, Absolute, and Mixed References

Part of effective formula writing is knowing when to use relative, absolute, and mixed references. Use relative references when you want to repeat the same formula with cells in different locations on your worksheet. Relative references are commonly used when copying a formula that sums a column of numbers or that calculates the cost of several items by multiplying the item cost by the quantity being purchased.

Use absolute references when you want different formulas to refer to the same cell. This usually occurs when a cell contains a constant value, such as a tax rate, that will be used in formulas throughout the worksheet.

Mixed references are seldom used other than when creating tables of calculated values such as a multiplication table in which the values of the formula or function can be found in the initial rows and columns of the table.

As you develop formulas and worksheets, you might want to quickly switch a cell reference from relative to absolute or mixed. Rather than retyping the formula, you can switch the reference in editing mode by selecting the cell reference and pressing the F4 key. As you press the function key, Excel cycles through the different reference types, starting by changing a relative reference to an absolute reference, then to a mixed reference with the row absolute, then to a mixed reference with the column absolute, and then finally back to a relative reference.

You'll use the F4 key to cycle through the different types of references as you enter the remaining formulas with the income for the summer months.

To insert the remaining references to the couple's monthly income:

1. Click cell **H19**, type **=**, and then click cell **E5**. The formula =E5 appears in the cell, which remains in Edit mode. This formula enters Diane's income for the summer months.
2. Press the **F4** key. The formula changes to =$E$5, which is an absolute reference.

   Trouble? If the formula shows anything other than the absolute reference, you probably pressed the F4 key too many times. Continue to press the F4 key to loop through all of the cell reference types until the formula returns to =$E$5, which contains the absolute reference.
3. Press the **Enter** key. The formula is entered and 2,100 (Diane's monthly income in the summer) appears in cell H19.
4. In cell H20, enter the formula **=$E$6**. This formula uses an absolute reference to enter Glenn's monthly income in the summer.
5. In cell H21, enter the formula **=H19+H20**. This formula adds Diane and Glenn's income for June; their combined monthly income in the summer is 4,700.
6. Copy the range **H19:H21**, and then paste the copied formulas into the range **I19:J21**. The summer take-home pay values appear for the months of June through August.

   You'll complete the monthly income values for the remaining school months.
7. Copy the range **C19:C21**, and then paste it into the range **K19:N21**. The couple's monthly income is entered for all months of the year.

Working with Functions

Excel functions provide a quick way to calculate summary data such as the total, average, minimum, and maximum values in a collection of values. You'll use these functions to summarize Diane and Glenn's income and expense data at the top of the Budget worksheet.

Understanding Function Syntax

Every function has to follow a set of rules, or **syntax**, which specifies how the function should be written. The general syntax of all Excel functions is

FUNCTION(argument1, argument2, ...)

where *FUNCTION* is the name of the function, and *argument1*, *argument2*, and so forth are arguments, which are the numbers, text, or cell references used by the function to return a value. Arguments are always separated by a comma.

Not all functions have arguments. Some functions have optional arguments, which are not required for the function to return a value, but can be included to provide more control over how Excel calculates the returned value. If an optional argument is not included, Excel assumes a default value for it. These tutorials show optional arguments within square brackets along with the argument's default value, as follows:

```
FUNCTION(argument1, [argument2=value2, ...])
```

TIP

Optional arguments are always placed last in the argument list.

In this function, *argument1* is required, *argument2* is an optional argument, and *value2* is the default value used for this argument. As you learn more about individual functions, you will learn which arguments are required and which are optional, and the default values used for optional arguments.

The hundreds of available Excel functions are organized into 11 categories. Figure 3-9 describes these different categories.

Figure 3-9 **Excel function categories**

Category	Functions That
Cube	Retrieve data from multidimensional databases involving online analytical processing or OLAP
Database	Retrieve and analyze data stored in databases
Date & Time	Analyze or create date and time values and time intervals
Engineering	Analyze engineering problems
Financial	Have financial applications
Information	Return information about the format, location, or contents of worksheet cells
Logical	Return logical (true-false) values
Lookup & Reference	Look up and return data matching a set of specified conditions from a range
Math & Trig	Have math and trigonometry applications
Statistical	Provide statistical analyses of a set of data
Text	Return text values or evaluate text

You can learn about each function using the Help system. Figure 3-10 describes some of the more common Math, Trig, and Statistical functions used in workbooks.

Figure 3-10 **Common Math, Trig, and Statistical functions**

Function	Category	Description
AVERAGE(*number1* [, *number2*, *number3*, ...])	Statistical	Calculates the average of a collection of numbers, where *number1, number2,* and so forth are either numbers or cell references. Only *number1* is required. For more than one cell reference or to enter numbers directly into the function, use the optional arguments *number2, number3,* and so forth.
COUNT(*value1* [, *value2*, *value3*, ...])	Statistical	Counts how many cells in a range contain numbers, where *value1, value2,* and so forth are text, numbers, or cell references. Only *value1* is required. For more than one cell reference or to enter numbers directly into the function, use the optional arguments *value2, value3,* and so forth.
COUNTA(*value1* [, *value2*, *value3*, ...])	Statistical	Counts how many cells are not empty in ranges *value1, value2,* and so forth, or how many numbers are listed within *value1, value2*, and so forth.
INT(*number*)	Math & Trig	Displays the integer portion of a number, *number*.
MAX(*number1* [, *number2*, *number3*, ...])	Statistical	Calculates the maximum value of a collection of numbers, where *number1, number2,* and so forth are either numbers or cell references.
MEDIAN(*number1* [, *number2*, *number3*, ...])	Statistical	Calculates the median, or middle, value of a collection of numbers, where *number1, number2*, and so forth are either numbers or cell references.
MIN(*number1* [, *number2*, *number3*, ...])	Statistical	Calculates the minimum value of a collection of numbers, where *number1, number2,* and so forth are either numbers or cell references.
RAND()	Math & Trig	Returns a random number between 0 and 1.
ROUND(*number*, *num_digits*)	Math & Trig	Rounds a number to a specified *number* of digits, where number is the number you want to round and *num_digits* specifies how many digits to which you want to round the number.
SUM(*number1* [, *number2*, *number3*, ...])	Math & Trig	Adds a collection of numbers, where *number1*, *number2*, and so forth are either numbers or cell references.

For example, the AVERAGE function calculates the average value from a collection of numbers. The syntax of the AVERAGE function is

```
AVERAGE(number1 [, number2, number3, ...])
```

where *number1*, *number2*, *number3*, and so forth are either numbers or cell references to numbers. The following formula uses the AVERAGE function to calculate the average of 1, 2, 5, and 8, returning the value 4:

```
=AVERAGE(1, 2, 5, 8)
```

However, functions usually reference values entered in the worksheet. So, if the range A1:A4 contains the values 1, 2, 5, and 8, the following formula also returns a value of 4:

```
=AVERAGE(A1:A4)
```

The advantage of using cell references is that the values used in the function are visible to users and can be easily edited as needed. Functions can be included as part of larger formulas. For example, the following formula, which includes the MAX function, returns the maximum value from the range A1:A100, and then divides that value by 100:

```
=MAX(A1:A100)/100
```

Functions can also be placed inside another function, or **nested**. If a formula contains several functions, Excel starts with the innermost function and then moves outward. For example, the following formula first calculates the average of the values in the range A1:A100 using the AVERAGE function, and then extracts the integer portion of that value using the INT function:

```
=INT(AVERAGE(A1:A100))
```

One challenge of nesting functions is to make sure that you include all of the parentheses. You can check this by counting the number of left parentheses, and making sure that number matches the number of right parentheses. Excel will also display different levels of nested parentheses in different colors to make it easier to match the opening and closing parentheses in the formula. If the number of parentheses doesn't match, Excel will not accept the formula and will offer a suggestion for rewriting the formula so the number of left and right parentheses does match.

PROSKILLS

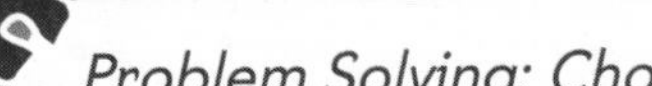

Problem Solving: Choosing the Right Summary Function

Problem solving involves determining how to best summarize a large sample of data into a few easy-to-use statistics. The field of statistics provides several summary measures, each with its own advantages and disadvantages.

One of the most common statistical approaches is to average the sample data. You can calculate the average in Excel with the AVERAGE function. However, determining an average is not always the best choice. Averages are susceptible to extremely large or small data values. Imagine calculating the average size of homes in a neighborhood that has one huge mansion and several small houses. In this case, the average value is heavily influenced by the size of that single mansion, and might not represent a typical neighborhood house.

When the data includes a few extremely large or extremely small values that have the potential to skew results, it's often better to use the **median**, or middle, value from the sample. For example, in a survey of nine homes, the median would be the size of the fifth largest—or middle-sized—home in the sample. You can calculate the median in Excel with the MEDIAN function.

Another approach is to calculate the most common value in the data, otherwise known as the **mode**. The mode is most often used with data that has only a few possible values, each of which might be repeated several times. Rather than using square feet, you might want to express the value in terms of the number of bedrooms each home contains. The mode would return the most common number of bedrooms in the homes included in the sample. You can calculate the mode in Excel using the MODE function.

By knowing which summary measure best fits your data, you can create useful and precise information that will aid you and others in interpreting the results.

Inserting a Function

Functions are organized in the Function Library group on the Formulas tab on the Ribbon. In the Function Library, you can select a function from a function category or you can open the Insert Function dialog box to search for a particular function. When you select a function, the Function Arguments dialog box opens, listing all the arguments associated with that function. Required arguments are in bold type; optional arguments are in normal type.

You'll use the SUM function to add the total income and expenses for the year in Diane's proposed budget.

To calculate annual income and expenses with the SUM function:

1. Click cell **F9** to select it.
2. Click the **Formulas** tab on the Ribbon.
3. In the Function Library group, click the **Math & Trig** button. An alphabetical listing of all the math and trigonometry functions opens.
4. Scroll down the list, and then click **SUM**. The Function Arguments dialog box opens, listing all of the arguments associated with the SUM function.
5. Click in the worksheet, and then select the range **C21:N21**. The dialog box reduces to its title bar as you select the range. The range reference, which includes all the monthly income amounts, appears as the value of the Number1 argument. See Figure 3-11.

TIP

You can click the Collapse Dialog Box button to shrink the Function Arguments dialog box to see more of the worksheet, select the range, and then click the Expand Dialog Box button to restore the dialog box.

Figure 3-11 Function Arguments dialog box

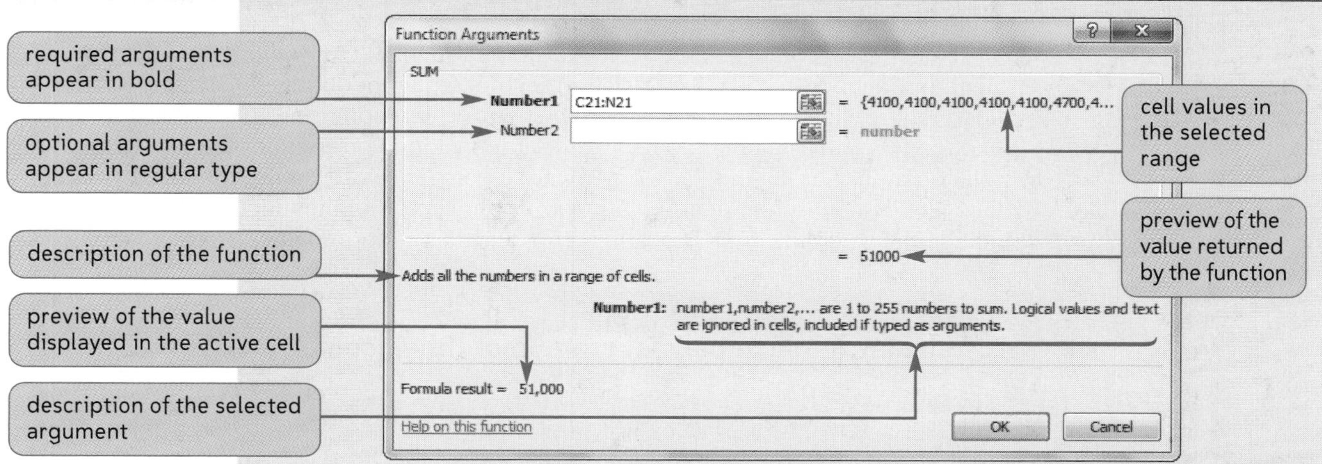

6. Click the **OK** button. The formula =SUM(C21:N21) is inserted into cell F9, which displays the value 51,000. This represents Diane and Glenn's total annual income.
7. Click cell **F13**. This is where you want the SUM function to add the monthly expenses for the year.
8. In the Function Library group on the Formulas tab, click the **Math & Trig** button, and then click **SUM**. The Function Arguments dialog box opens. You'll enter the monthly expenses stored in the range C32:N32 for the argument.

9. Click in the worksheet, and then select the range **C32:N32**.
10. In the Function Arguments dialog box, click the **OK** button. The formula =SUM(C32:N32) is inserted in cell F13, which displays the value 45,150. This represents the total projected expenses for the upcoming year. See Figure 3-12.

Figure 3-12 Total annual income and expenses

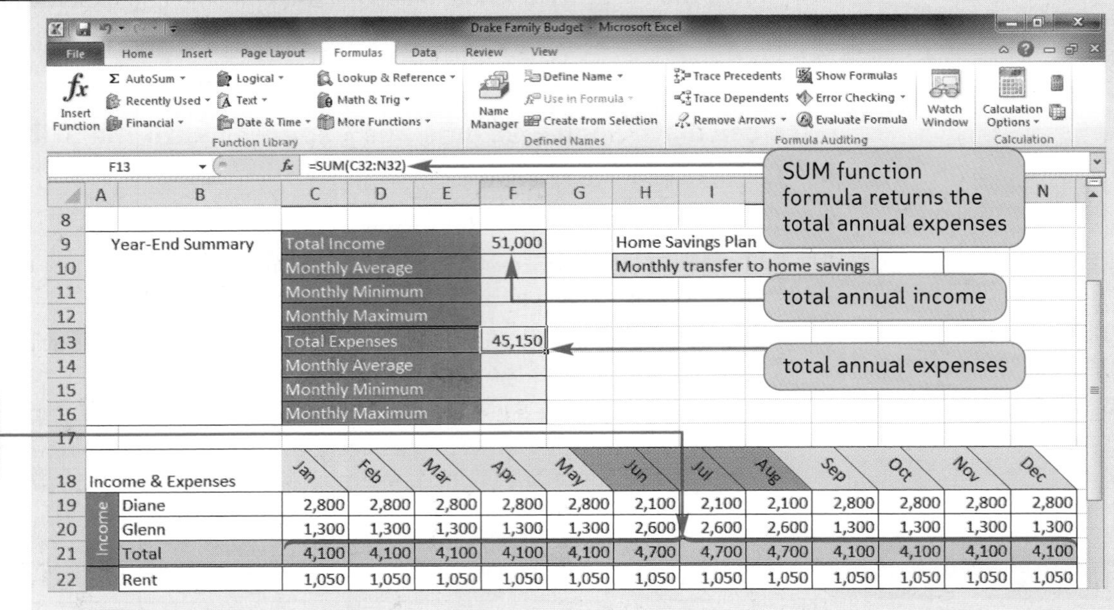

Diane projects that she and Glenn will earn roughly $6,000 more than they will spend throughout the year. It's easier for Diane to plan her budget if she knows how much, on average, the couple earns and spends each month. You can use the AVERAGE function to do this calculation using the same method you used for the SUM function.

If you aren't sure of the function's name or category, you can use the Insert Function dialog box. The Insert Function dialog box organizes all of the functions by category and includes a search feature for locating functions that perform particular calculations.

To calculate the couple's average monthly income:

1. Click cell **F10**. This is the cell in which you want to enter the AVERAGE function formula.
2. In the Function Library group on the Formulas tab, click the **Insert Function** button. The Insert Function dialog box opens.
3. In the Search for a function box, type **Calculate an average value**, and then click the **Go** button. Functions for calculating an average appear in the Select a function box. See Figure 3-13.

TIP

You can also click the Insert Function button on the formula bar to open the Insert Function dialog box.

Figure 3-13 Insert Function dialog box

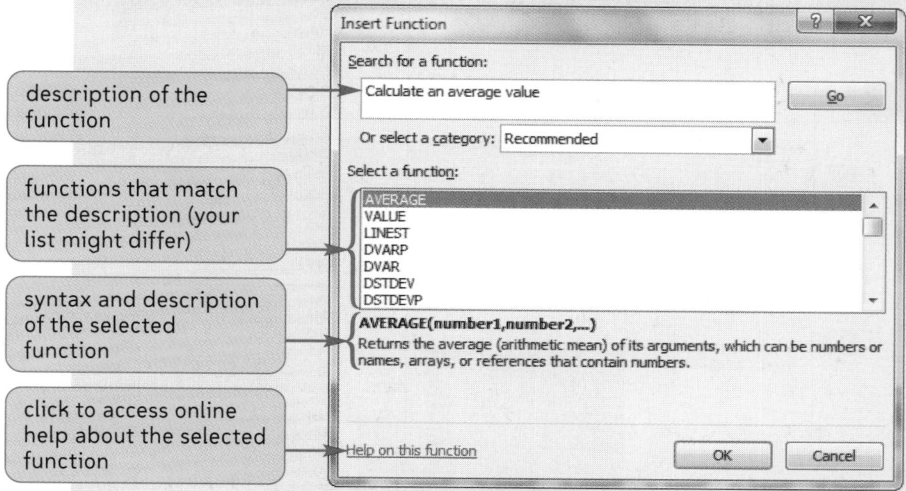

4. Verify that **AVERAGE** is selected in the Select a function box, and then click the **OK** button. The Function Arguments dialog box opens with the arguments for the AVERAGE function. A range reference for a cell directly above this cell already appears for the Number1 argument.
5. Select the range reference in the Number1 argument box, and then select the range **C21:N21** in the worksheet.
6. Click the **OK** button. The dialog box closes, and the formula =AVERAGE(C21:N21) is entered in cell F10, which displays the value 4,250—the couple's average monthly income.

How does the couple's average monthly income compare to their average monthly expenses? To find out, you'll use the AVERAGE function again. Because the function has already been used in your workbook, you can select it from a list of recently used functions.

To calculate the average monthly expenses:

1. Click cell **F14**. This is the cell where you want to calculate the average monthly expenses.
2. On the formula bar, click the **Insert Function** button fx. The Insert Function dialog box opens.
3. If necessary, click the **Or select a category** arrow, and then click **Most Recently Used**. The most recently used functions, sorted in order of recent use, appear in the Select a function box. The AVERAGE function is at the top followed by the SUM function.
4. Verify that **AVERAGE** is selected in the Select a function box, and then click the **OK** button.
5. Select the range **C32:N32** in the worksheet to insert the range reference C32:N32 in the Number1 box.

6. Click the **OK** button. The formula =AVERAGE(C32:N32) is entered in cell F14, displaying the value 3,763. This represents the average expenses per month under Diane's budget. See Figure 3-14.

Figure 3-14 Average family income and expenses

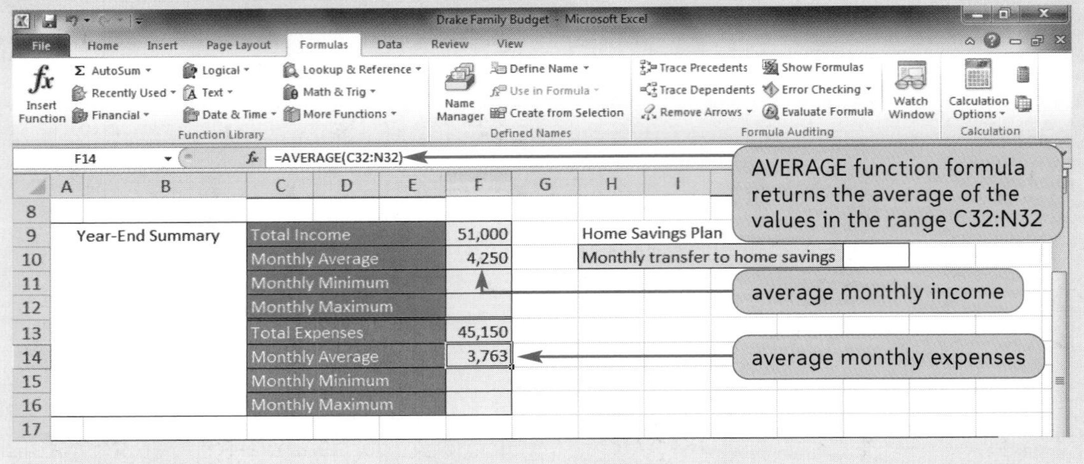

The average monthly expense, 3,763, is displayed to the nearest dollar amount. This is because Diane has formatted the workbook to not display decimal values. The actual value, 3,762.50, is stored in the cell although it is not displayed.

Typing a Function

After you become more familiar with functions, it is often faster to type the functions directly in cells rather than using the Insert Function dialog box or the Function Library. As you begin to type a function name within a formula, a list of functions that begin with the letters you typed appears. For example, when you type *S*, the list shows all of the functions starting with the letter *S*; when you type *SU*, the list shows only those functions starting with the letters *SU*, and so forth. This helps to ensure that you're entering a legitimate Excel function name.

The income and expenses averages show that the couple will bring in about $500 more than they spend each month. That does not leave much money to deal with an unexpected expense, so Diane wants to know how much variation is in the budget. What is the most money she could expect to take home during a single month in the upcoming year? What is the least? And what are the highest and lowest values for the monthly expenses? You'll use the MAX and MIN functions to calculate those values.

To calculate the minimum value for monthly income and expenses:

1. Click cell **F11**. This is the cell in which you want to enter the monthly income.
2. Type **=M**. As you type a formula, a list with function names starting with *M* opens.
3. Type **I**. The list shows only those functions starting with *MI*. See Figure 3-15. As soon as the function you want appears in the list, you can double-click its name to enter it in the cell without typing the rest of its name.

Figure 3-15 **Function being typed into a cell**

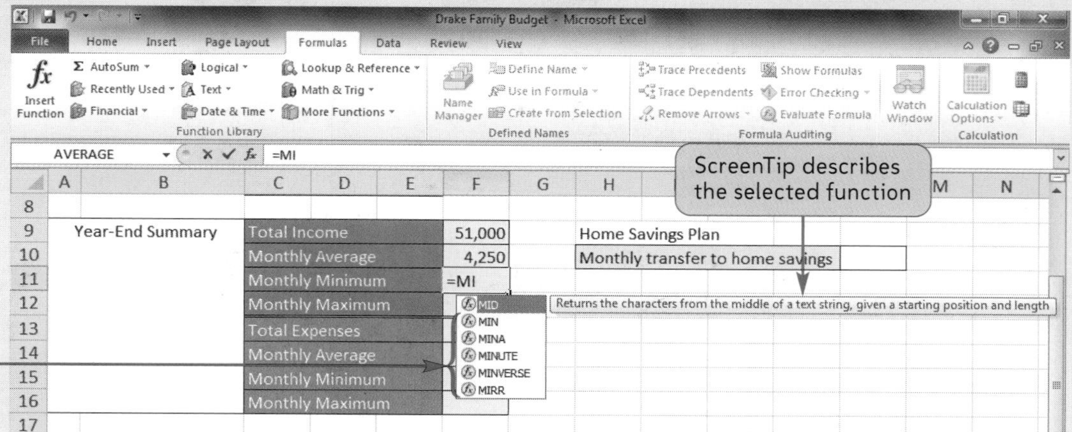

4. Double-click **MIN** in the list box. The MIN function with its opening parenthesis is inserted into cell F11 and a ScreenTip shows the syntax for the function. At this point, you can either type in the range reference or select the range with your mouse. To avoid typing errors, it's often better to use your mouse to enter range references.
5. Select the range **C21:N21**. The range reference is added to the formula.
6. Type **)** (the closing parenthesis), and then press the **Enter** key. The formula =MIN(C21:N21) is inserted in cell F11, displaying the value 4,100. This is the minimum amount that Diane expects the couple to bring home in a single month for the upcoming year.

   Next, you'll calculate the minimum monthly expense projected for the year.
7. Click cell **F15**, and then repeat Steps 2 through 6 to enter the formula **=MIN(C32:N32)** in cell F15. The cell displays the value 2,795, which is the lowest amount that Diane expects to spend in a single month in the upcoming year.

Be sure to end this and all functions with the closing parenthesis) to ensure that Excel interprets the formula correctly.

The final piece of the year-end summary is the maximum monthly value for both income and expenses. Maximum values are calculated using the MAX function.

To calculate the maximum value for monthly income and expenses:

1. Click cell **F12**, and then enter the formula **=MAX(C21:N21)**. The value 4,700 appears in cell F12, indicating that the maximum income the couple can expect in a single month is $4,700.

   Trouble? If #NAME? appears in the cell, you probably mistyped the function name. Edit the formula to correct the misspelling.
2. Click cell **F16**, and then enter the formula **=MAX(C32:N32)**. The value 6,985 appears in cell F16, indicating that the maximum expenses for a single month are projected to be $6,985. See Figure 3-16.

Figure 3-16 Year-end summary values

F16 =MAX(C32:N32)

MAX function formula returns the maximum value in the range C32:N32

Row	B	C–E	F
9	Year-End Summary	Total Income	51,000
10		Monthly Average	4,250
11		Monthly Minimum	4,100
12		Monthly Maximum	4,700
13		Total Expenses	45,150
14		Monthly Average	3,763
15		Monthly Minimum	2,795
16		Monthly Maximum	6,985

Home Savings Plan

Monthly transfer to home savings

minimum and maximum monthly income

minimum and maximum monthly expenses

Based on the year-end summary, Diane and Glenn's monthly income will range from a minimum of $4,100 to a maximum of $4,700 with an average of $4,250. Monthly expenses, on the other hand, range from a minimum of $2,795 to a maximum of $6,985 with an average of $3,763. This budget does not have a lot of wiggle room.

Diane has just been promoted at work. Her income will increase to $3,100 per month during the school year. She wants to know how this affects the year-end summary.

To modify Diane's estimated income:

1. In cell D5, enter the value **3100**.
2. Confirm that Diane's monthly income for January through May and September through December has been automatically updated.
3. Review how the year-end summary data has changed. See Figure 3-17.

Figure 3-17 Revised income projection

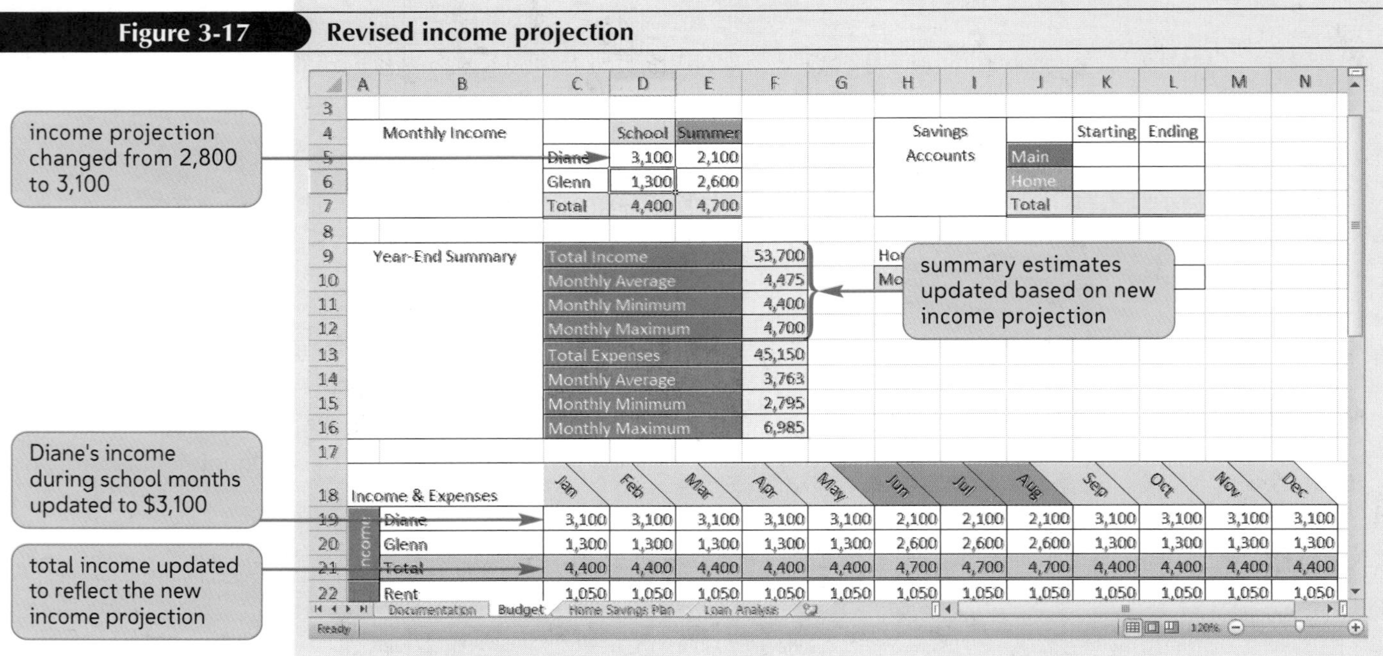

With Diane's promotion, the couple's annual income increases from $51,000 to $53,700 and the monthly average increases from $4,250 to $4,475. The couple's income should exceed their expenses by about $700 per month. The monthly income now ranges from a minimum of $4,400 up to a maximum of $4,700.

Diane now has a better picture of the family's finances for the upcoming year, and she is more confident about how to manage the couple's budget. She and Glenn hope to save enough for a down payment on a house in a few years. With the promotion, this seems like a real possibility. In the next session, you'll help Diane explore the couple's options in planning for the purchase of a house.

REVIEW

Session 3.1 Quick Check

1. You need to reference cell Q57 in a formula. What is the absolute cell reference? What are the two mixed references?
2. Assume that cell R10 contains the formula =R1+R2. What formula is entered if this formula is copied and pasted into cell S20?
3. Assume that cell T10 contains the formula =$T1+T$2. What formula is entered if this formula is copied and pasted into cell U20?
4. Assume that cell V10 contains the formula =AVERAGE($U1:$U5). What formula is entered if this formula is copied and pasted into cell W20?
5. What are optional arguments? What happens if you do not include an optional argument in a function?
6. What function formula can you use to add the numbers in the range X1:X10?
7. The range of a set of values is defined as the maximum value minus the minimum value. What formula with functions can you enter to calculate the range of the values in Y1:Y10?
8. What formula with functions can you enter to calculate the ratio of the maximum value in the range Z1:Z10 to the minimum value?

SESSION 3.2 VISUAL OVERVIEW

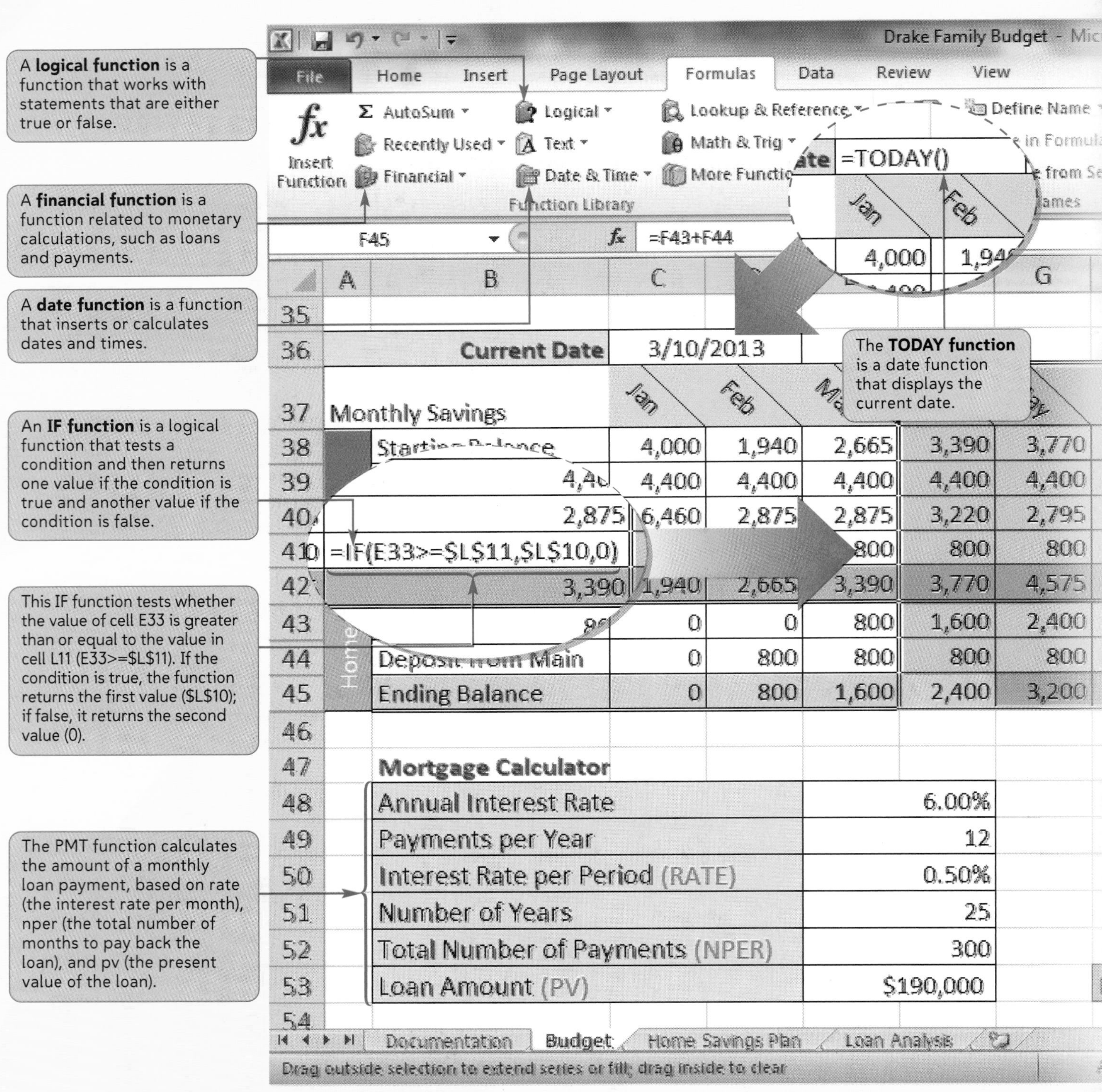

AUTOFILL AND MORE FUNCTIONS

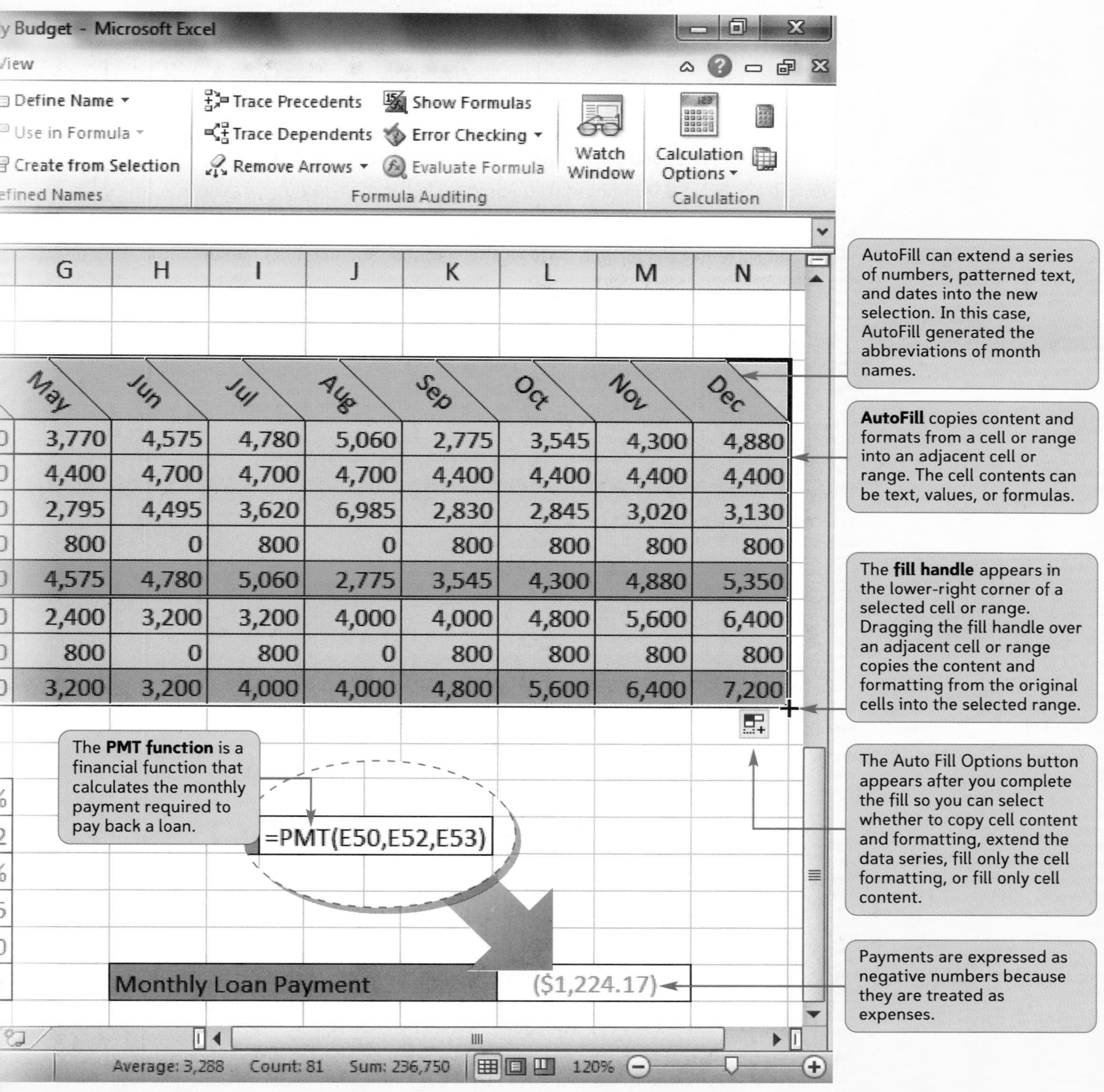

AutoFill can extend a series of numbers, patterned text, and dates into the new selection. In this case, AutoFill generated the abbreviations of month names.

AutoFill copies content and formats from a cell or range into an adjacent cell or range. The cell contents can be text, values, or formulas.

The **fill handle** appears in the lower-right corner of a selected cell or range. Dragging the fill handle over an adjacent cell or range copies the content and formatting from the original cells into the selected range.

The Auto Fill Options button appears after you complete the fill so you can select whether to copy cell content and formatting, extend the data series, fill only the cell formatting, or fill only cell content.

The **PMT function** is a financial function that calculates the monthly payment required to pay back a loan.

Payments are expressed as negative numbers because they are treated as expenses.

Entering Data and Formulas with AutoFill

Diane and Glenn hope to purchase a home in the next three years. Currently, they have $4,000 in their main savings account, and they plan to open a second account reserved for saving toward a down payment on a home. You will enter the initial balance for the main account and set up the home account with an initial balance of $0 into the Budget worksheet.

To enter the savings account information:

1. If you took a break after the previous session, make sure the Drake Family Budget workbook is open and the Budget worksheet is active.
2. In cell K5, enter **4,000** (the starting amount in the main savings account).
3. In cell K6, enter **0** (the starting amount in the home savings account).
4. In cell K7, enter the formula **=K5+K6** to sum the total initial amount in both accounts. See Figure 3-18.

Figure 3-18 **Savings account information**

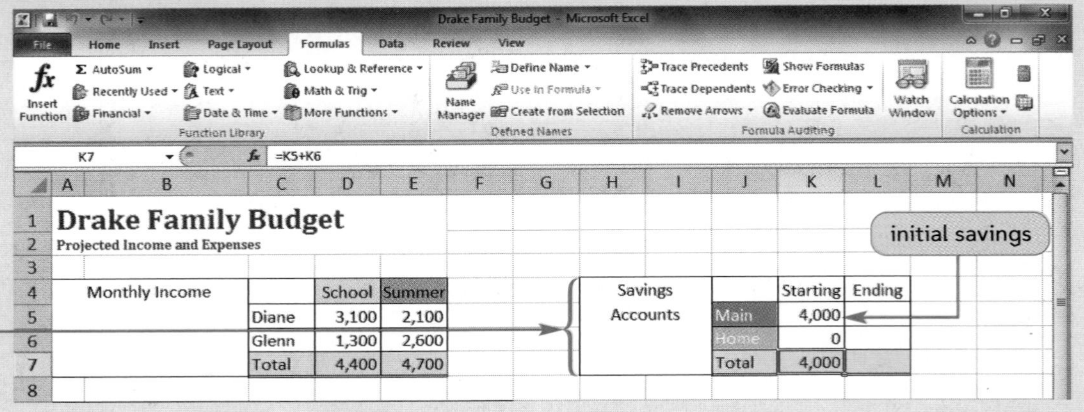

Diane wants to learn how much the couple could add to their savings accounts each month. To find out, you must first determine the couple's monthly net cash flow, which is equal to the amount of money they earn each month after paying all of their expenses. You will start by formatting the cells where you'll enter this data and calculating the net cash flow during the month of January.

To calculate the net cash flow for January:

1. Merge and center the range **A33:B33**, and then right-align the cell contents.
2. In the merged cell A33, enter **Net Cash Flow**.
3. In cell C33, enter the formula **=C21–C32**. This formula subtracts total expenses from total income for the month of January. The resulting –2,060 indicates a projected shortfall of $2,060 for the month of January.
4. Apply conditional formatting to cell C33 to highlight the cell with a red fill and red text if the value in the cell is less than 0. Months with negative cash flow will be highlighted on the worksheet. See Figure 3-19.

Figure 3-19 **January net cash flow**

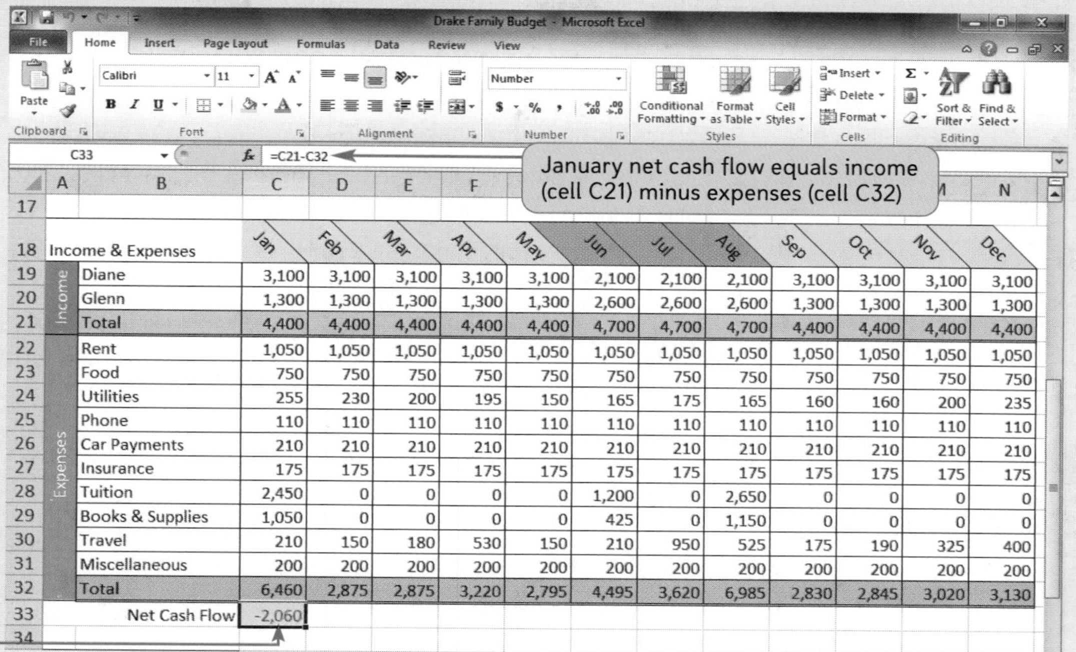

	Income & Expenses	Jan	Feb	Mar	Apr	May	Jun	Jul	Aug	Sep	Oct	Nov	Dec
Income	Diane	3,100	3,100	3,100	3,100	3,100	2,100	2,100	2,100	3,100	3,100	3,100	3,100
	Glenn	1,300	1,300	1,300	1,300	1,300	2,600	2,600	2,600	1,300	1,300	1,300	1,300
	Total	4,400	4,400	4,400	4,400	4,400	4,700	4,700	4,700	4,400	4,400	4,400	4,400
Expenses	Rent	1,050	1,050	1,050	1,050	1,050	1,050	1,050	1,050	1,050	1,050	1,050	1,050
	Food	750	750	750	750	750	750	750	750	750	750	750	750
	Utilities	255	230	200	195	150	165	175	165	160	160	200	235
	Phone	110	110	110	110	110	110	110	110	110	110	110	110
	Car Payments	210	210	210	210	210	210	210	210	210	210	210	210
	Insurance	175	175	175	175	175	175	175	175	175	175	175	175
	Tuition	2,450	0	0	0	0	1,200	0	2,650	0	0	0	0
	Books & Supplies	1,050	0	0	0	0	425	0	1,150	0	0	0	0
	Travel	210	150	180	530	150	210	950	525	175	190	325	400
	Miscellaneous	200	200	200	200	200	200	200	200	200	200	200	200
	Total	6,460	2,875	2,875	3,220	2,795	4,495	3,620	6,985	2,830	2,845	3,020	3,130
	Net Cash Flow	-2,060											

conditional formatting highlights the negative cash flow (less than 0) for January

Your calculations show that the couple's expenses will exceed their income by more than $2,000 in January. This is due to the cost of tuition that must be paid that month. You could copy and paste the formula and formatting from cell C33 into the rest of the row to calculate the net cash flow for the other months, as you've done before, but AutoFill is faster.

Using the Fill Handle

After you select a range, the fill handle appears in the lower-right corner of the selection. When you drag the fill handle over an adjacent range, Excel uses AutoFill to copy the content and formats from the original cell into the adjacent range. This process is often more efficient than the two-step process of copying and pasting.

REFERENCE

Copying Formulas and Formats with AutoFill

- Select the cell or range that contains the formula or formulas you want to copy.
- Drag the fill handle in the direction you want to copy the formula(s) and then release the mouse button.
- To copy only the formats or only the formulas, click the Auto Fill Options button and select the appropriate option.

or

- Select the cell or range that contains the formula or formulas you want to copy.
- In the Editing group on the Home tab, click the Fill button.
- Select the appropriate fill direction and fill type.

or

Click Series, enter the desired fill series options, and then click the OK button.

You will use the fill handle to copy the formula and conditional formatting you entered in cell C33 into the remaining cells in the Net Cash Flow row.

To copy the cash flow formula and formatting with the fill handle:

1. Click cell **C33** to select it, if necessary. The fill handle appears in the lower-right corner of the cell.
2. Position the pointer over the fill handle in the lower-right corner of the cell. The pointer changes to +.
3. Click and drag the fill handle over the range **D33:N33**. A dotted outline appears around the selected range as you move the pointer.
4. Release the mouse button. The selected range is filled in with the formula and formatting from cell C33, and the Auto Fill Options button appears in the lower-right corner of the selected cells. See Figure 3-20.

TIP

With AutoFill, formulas can easily be copied into the wrong range; if that happens, click the Undo button and try again.

Figure 3-20 Formulas and formatting pasted with AutoFill

C33 =C21-C32

formula to calculate the January net cash flow

	A	B	C	D	E	F	G	H	I	J	K	L	M	N
17														
18	Income & Expenses		Jan	Feb	Mar	Apr	May	Jun	Jul	Aug	Sep	Oct	Nov	Dec
19	Income	Diane	3,100	3,100	3,100	3,100	3,100	2,100	2,100	2,100	3,100	3,100	3,100	3,100
20		Glenn	1,300	1,300	1,300	1,300	1,300	2,600	2,600	2,600	1,300	1,300	1,300	1,300
21		Total	4,400	4,400	4,400	4,400	4,400	4,700	4,700	4,700	4,400	4,400	4,400	4,400
22	Expenses	Rent	1,050	1,050	1,050	1,050	1,050	1,050	1,050	1,050	1,050	1,050	1,050	1,050
23		Food	750	750	750	750	750	750	750	750	750	750	750	750
24		Utilities	255	230	200	195	150	165	175	165	160	160	200	235
25		Phone	110	110	110	110	110	110	110	110	110	110	110	110
26		Car Payments	210	210	210	210	210	210	210	210	210	210	210	210
27		Insurance	175	175	175	175	175	175	175	175	175	175	175	175
28		Tuition	2,450	0	0	0	0	1,200	0	2,650	0	0	0	0
29		Books & Supplies	1,050	0	0	0	0	425	0	1,150	0	0	0	0
30		Travel	210	150	180	530	150	210	950	525	175	190	325	400
31		Miscellaneous	200	200	200	200	200	200	200	200	200	200	200	200
32		Total	[illegible],460	2,875	2,875	3,220	2,795	4,495	3,620	[illegible],985	2,830	2,845	3,020	3,130
33		Net Cash Flow	-2,060	1,525	1,525	1,180	1,605	205	1,080	-2,285	1,570	1,555	1,380	1,270
34														
35	Monthly Savings													
36		Starting Balance												

Documentation | Budget | Home Savings Plan | Loan Analysis

Ready — Average: 713 Count: 12 Sum: 8,550 120%

conditional formatting highlights months of negative cash flow

the formulas and formats in cell C33 are filled into the selected range

Auto Fill Options button

fill handle

5. Review the monthly net cash flows to confirm that AutoFill correctly copied the formula and conditional formatting into the selected range.

These calculations provide Diane with a better picture of how the couple's net cash flow varies from month to month. Only in January and August, when Glenn's tuition payments are due, do the couple's expenses exceed their income. In most months, their income exceeds expenses by about $1,500. In June, however, the net cash flow, while positive, is projected to be only $205.

Using the Auto Fill Options Button

By default, AutoFill copies both the content and the formatting of the original range to the selected range. However, sometimes you might want to copy only the content or only the formatting. The Auto Fill Options button that appears after you release the mouse button lets you specify what is copied. As shown in Figure 3-21, clicking this button provides a list of Auto-Fill options. The Copy Cells option, which is the default, copies both the content and the formatting. The Fill Formatting Only option copies the formatting into the selected cells but not any content. The Fill Without Formatting option copies the content but not the formatting.

Figure 3-21 **Auto Fill Options button**

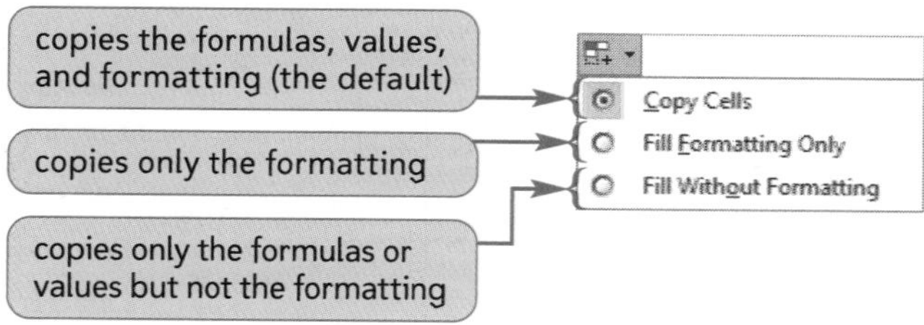

Filling a Series

AutoFill can also be used to create a series of numbers, dates, or text based on a pattern. To create a series of numbers, you enter the initial values in the series in a selected range and then use AutoFill to complete the series. Figure 3-22 shows how AutoFill can be used to insert the numbers from 1 to 10 in a selected range. You enter the first few numbers in the range A1:A3 to establish the pattern for AutoFill to use, consecutive positive integers in this example. Then, you select the range and drag the fill handle over the cells where you want the pattern continued. In Figure 3-22, the fill handle is dragged over the range A4:A10 and Excel fills in the rest of the series.

Figure 3-22 **AutoFill extends a numeric sequence**

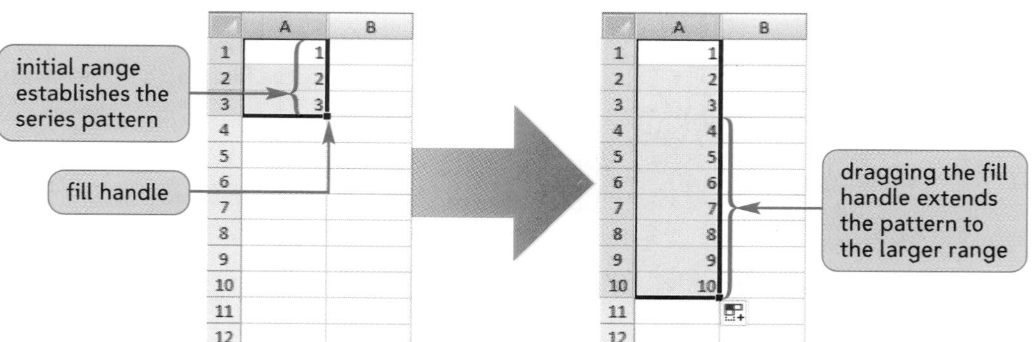

AutoFill can extend a wide variety of series, including dates and times and patterned text. Figure 3-23 shows examples of some series that AutoFill can generate. In each case, you must provide enough information for AutoFill to identify the pattern. AutoFill can recognize some patterns from only a single value, such as Jan or January, to create a series of month abbreviations or names, or Mon or Monday, to create a series of the days of the week. A text pattern that includes a text string and a number such as Region 1, Region 2, and so on can also be automatically extended using AutoFill.

Figure 3-23 **AutoFill applied to values, dates and times, and patterned text**

Type	Initial Pattern	Extended Series
Values	1, 2, 3	4, 5, 6, ...
	2, 4, 6	8, 10, 12, ...
Dates and Times	Jan	Feb, Mar, Apr, ...
	January	February, March, April, ...
	15-Jan, 15-Feb	15-Mar, 15-Apr, 15-May, ...
	12/30/2013	12/31/2013, 1/1/2014, 1/2/2014, ...
	12/31/2013, 1/31/2014	2/28/2014, 3/31/2014, 4/30/2014, ...
	Mon	Tue, Wed, Thu, ...
	Monday	Tuesday, Wednesday, Thursday, ...
	11:00AM	12:00PM, 1:00PM, 2:00PM, ...
Patterned Text	1st period	2nd period, 3rd period, 4th period, ...
	Region 1	Region 2, Region 3, Region 4, ...
	Quarter 3	Quarter 4, Quarter 1, Quarter 2, ...
	Qtr3	Qtr4, Qtr1, Qtr2, ...

For more complex patterns, you can use the Series dialog box. To do so, enter the first value of the series in a worksheet cell, select the entire range that will contain the series, click the Fill button in the Editing group on the Home tab, and then click Series. The Series dialog box opens. From the Series dialog box you can specify a linear or growth series for numeric values; a Date series for dates that increase by day, weekday, month, or year; or an AutoFill series for patterned text. With numeric values, you can also specify the step value (indicating how much each numeric value increases over the previous entry) and a stop value (to specify the endpoint for the entire series).

REFERENCE

Creating a Series with AutoFill

- Enter the first few values of the series into a range.
- Select the range, and then drag the fill handle of the selected range over the cells you want to fill.

or

- Enter the first few values of the series into a range.
- Select the entire range into which you want to extend the series.
- In the Editing group on the Home tab, click the Fill button, and then click Down, Right, Up, Left, Series, or Justify to set the direction in which you want to extend the series.

Diane wants to see how the monthly balances in the main savings account are affected by the couple's changing income and expenses. She wants to make sure that the balance doesn't drop too low after months with particularly high expenses—such as January and August. You'll add data to the worksheet to display the monthly savings balance, starting with the month labels.

To use AutoFill to enter a series of months:

1. In cell C35, enter **Jan**. This is the first value in the series. Because "Jan" is a common abbreviation for January, Excel recognizes it as a month and you don't need to type "Feb" for the next month in the series.
2. Select cell **C35**, if necessary.
3. Drag the fill handle over the range **D35:N35**. As you drag the fill handle, ScreenTips show the month abbreviations for the selected cell.
4. Release the mouse button. AutoFill enters the remaining three-letter abbreviations for each month of the year.
5. Select the range **C18:N18**, and then click the **Format Painter** button in the Clipboard group on the Home tab. You'll apply this formatting to the entries in the range C35:N35.
6. Click cell **C35** to apply the format to the range C35:N35, and then click cell **A35** to deselect the column titles. See Figure 3-24.

Figure 3-24 Month labels and formatting

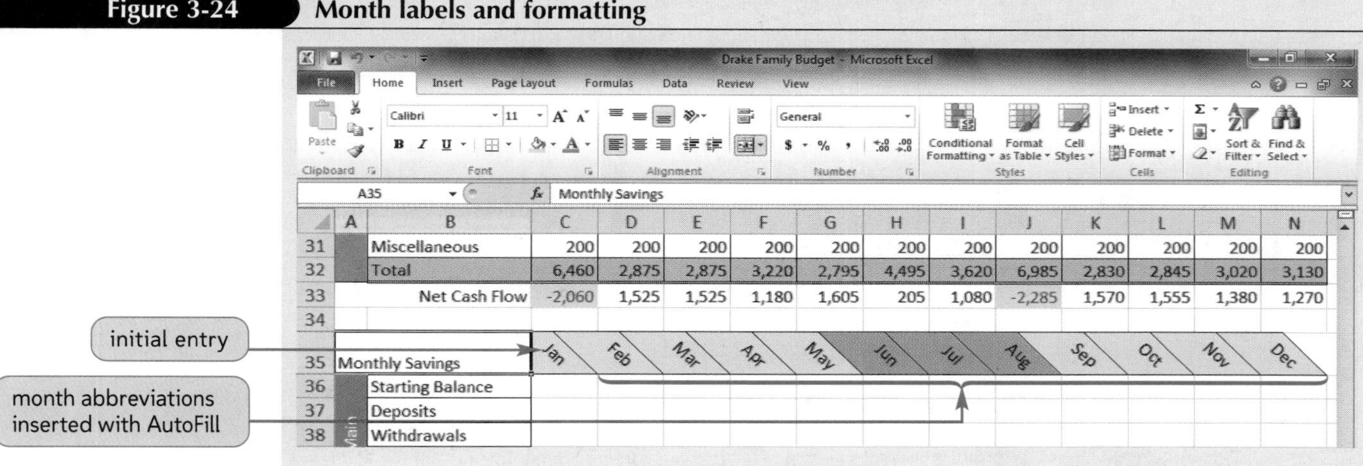

Next, you'll enter formulas to calculate the changing balance in the couple's main savings account. The main savings account balance at the end of each month is determined by four factors:

1. The balance at the beginning of the month
2. Money deposited from the couple's paychecks at the beginning of the month
3. Money withdrawn to pay for expenses
4. Money transferred into a home savings account reserved for a down payment on a mortgage. (Diane and Glenn have not yet decided how much they want to transfer into this account, so you'll leave that value blank for now.)

You'll start by calculating the balance in the couple's account at the end of January.

To calculate the January balance in the savings account:

1. In cell C36, enter the formula **=K5**. The formula references the balance in the main savings account at the beginning of the year, which is stored in cell K5.
2. In cell C37, enter **=C21** to retrieve the couple's January income. The relative reference will change when you copy the formula to other months.

3. In cell C38, enter **=C32** to retrieve the January expenses. The relative reference will change when you copy the formula to other months. You'll leave cell C39 blank because, at this point, you won't assume that any money will be transferred from the main savings account to the home savings account.
4. In cell C40, enter **=C36+C37–C38–C39**. This formula calculates the ending balance for the main savings account, which is equal to the starting balance plus any deposits minus the withdrawals and transfers. Cell C40 displays 1,940, which is the projected balance in the main savings account at the end of January.
5. Format the range C36:C39 to add borders around all of the cells.
6. Use the Format Painter to copy the formatting from cell C32 to cell **C40**, and then change the fill color to **Blue, Accent 1, Lighter 60%** (the fifth color in the third row of the Theme Colors section) to change the background color of the cell.
7. Click cell **A35**. Figure 3-25 shows the formatted January savings values.

Figure 3-25 **January savings**

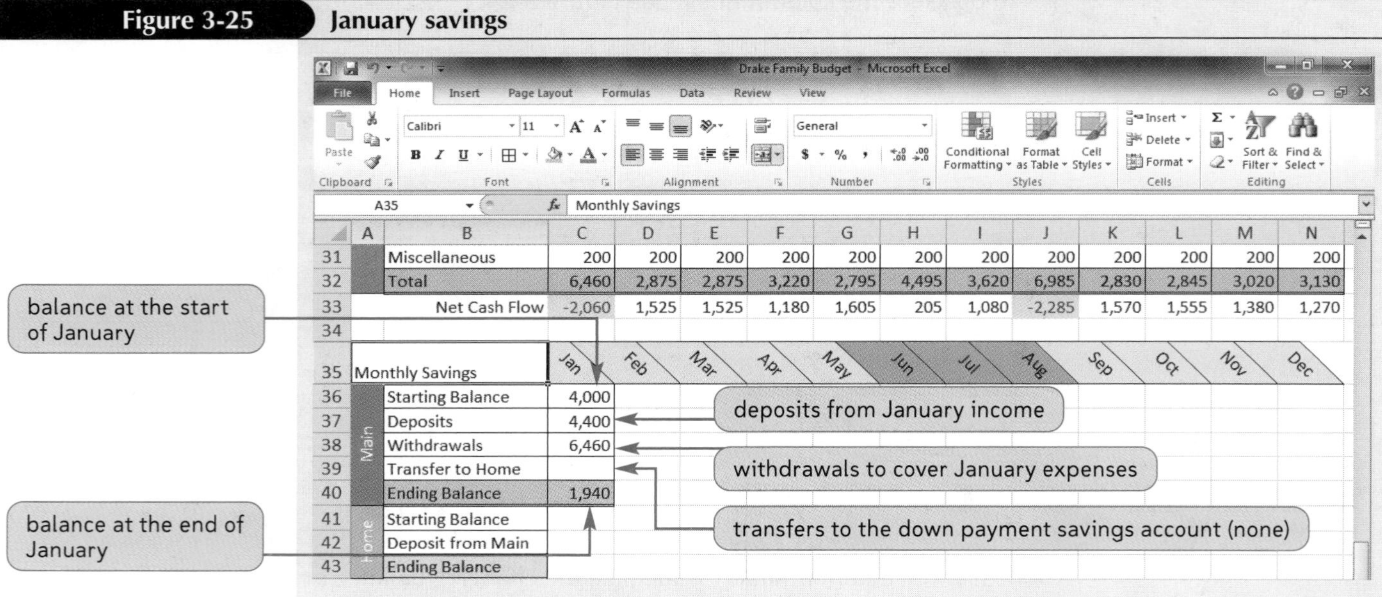

At this point, the couple's projected savings at the end of January will be $1,940, which is $2,060 less than their starting balance of $4,000 at the beginning of the year. The savings formulas for the remaining months are the same as for January except that their starting balances are based on the ending balance of the previous month. You will calculate the activity in the couple's main savings account for the remaining months of the year.

To calculate the remaining balances in the main savings account:

1. Select the range **C36:C40** and drag the fill handle over the February savings in the range **D36:D40**.
2. Change the formula in cell D36 to **=C40** so that the February starting balance for the main savings account is based on the January ending balance.
3. Select the range **D36:D40**, and then drag the fill handle over the range **E36:N40**. The formulas and formatting from February are copied into the remaining months of the year.

4. Click cell **A35** to deselect the main savings account data. See Figure 3-26.

Figure 3-26 **January through December savings**

	A	B	C	D	E	F	G	H	I	J	K	L	M	N
34														
35	Monthly Savings		Jan	Feb	Mar	Apr	May	Jun	Jul	Aug	Sep	Oct	Nov	Dec
36	Main	Starting Balance	4,000	1,940	3,465	4,990	6,170	7,775	7,980	9,060	6,775	8,345	9,900	11,280
37		Deposits	4,400	4,400	4,400	4,400	4,400	4,700	4,700	4,700	4,400	4,400	4,400	4,400
38		Withdrawals	6,460	2,875	2,875	3,220	2,795	4,495	3,620	6,985	2,830	2,845	3,020	3,130
39		Transfer to Home												
40		Ending Balance	1,940	3,465	4,990	6,170	7,775	7,980	9,060	6,775	8,345	9,900	11,280	12,550
41	Home	Starting Balance												
42		Deposit from Main												
43		Ending Balance												

5. In cell L5, enter the formula **=N40**. The ending balance of the main savings account in December—12,550—appears in cell L5. Diane can quickly see that the couple's savings in the main account will increase by $8,550 in the upcoming year.

Developing a Savings Plan

Under her current budget projections, Diane expects to have $12,550 in the main savings account at the end of the next year but nothing in the home savings account. She wants to transfer money into the home savings account each month. Because the home savings account is used for longer-term savings, Diane cannot withdraw money from it without penalty. So, she wants to make sure the main savings account always has enough money to meet monthly expenses and any unexpected bills without relying on money from the home savings account.

Diane needs to balance her desire to keep a reasonable amount in the main savings account and her desire to save enough for a down payment on a home mortgage. To achieve this balance, she needs to determine her overall savings goal and how soon she and Glenn want to meet that goal.

Diane wants to know how much money the couple can save if they transfer $500 to $1,000 into the home savings account each month for the next three years. You'll create a table that shows the total amount saved in one, two, and three years from deposits starting at $500 that increase in $100 increments through $1,000.

To create a table for different savings plans:

1. Go to the **Home Savings Plan** worksheet.
2. Merge and center the range **B3:G3**, enter **Savings Deposit per Month** in the merged cell, and then format the merged cell using the **Heading 2** cell style.
3. In cell A4, enter **Months**, and then format the cell in bold.
4. In cell B4, enter **500** and then, in cell C4, enter **600**. You entered the first two values in the series so that you could extend the numeric series.

5. Select the range **B4:C4**, and then drag the fill handle to cell **G4**. The values entered in the series—500, 600, 700, 800, 900, and 1000—are the different amounts the Drakes might transfer into their home savings account each month.

   Trouble? If the number 600 was entered in each cell instead of the series, you probably did not select both cells B4 and C4 before dragging the fill handle. Repeat Step 5, being sure to select both cells before filling.

6. In the range A5:A7, enter the values **12**, **24**, and **36**. These monthly values are equal to one year, two years, and three years, respectively. You entered the years in months because Diane and Glenn plan to deposit money into their home savings account each month. So, they would make 12 deposits in one year, they would make 24 deposits in two years, and they would make 36 deposits in three years.

7. Format the nonadjacent range B4:G4;A5:A7 with the **Input** cell style.

Next, you'll enter formulas to calculate the amount of money saved under each plan. The amount saved is equal to the number of months of savings multiplied by the deposit per month. You'll create this table using the same formulas with mixed cell references discussed earlier in Figure 3-8.

To enter formulas with mixed references to calculate the savings amounts:

1. In cell **B5**, enter **=$A5*B$4**. This formula uses mixed references to calculate the amount of savings generated by saving $500 per month for 12 months. The calculated value 6000 is displayed in the cell.

2. Select cell **B5** and drag the fill handle over the range **C5:G5** to calculate total savings over 12 months for deposits of $500 to $1,000 per month.

3. With B5:G5 still selected, drag the fill handle down to **G7** to apply the formula to the remaining cells in the multiplication table.

4. Format the values in the range B5:G7 using a thousands separator with no digits to the right of the decimal point, and add a border around each of the cells in the range.

5. Click cell **B5**. Figure 3-27 shows the completed and formatted values.

Figure 3-27 **Savings plan table**

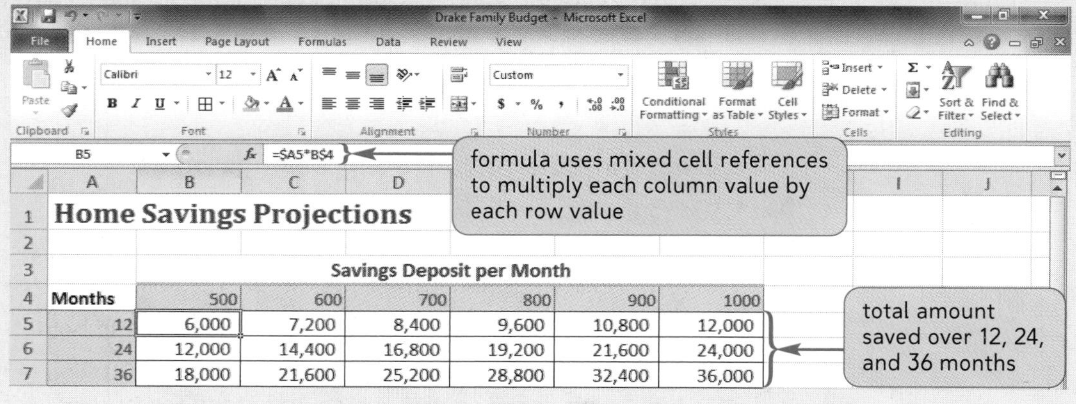

Months	500	600	700	800	900	1000
12	6,000	7,200	8,400	9,600	10,800	12,000
24	12,000	14,400	16,800	19,200	21,600	24,000
36	18,000	21,600	25,200	28,800	32,400	36,000

The data shows how increasing the monthly amount that Diane and Glenn save toward a down payment quickly adds up. For example, if they save $800 per month, at the end of three years (36 months), they would have saved $28,800. This is just a little less than the $30,000 they want to save for the down payment. You will add the transfer of $800 from the main savings account to the home savings account each month to the proposed budget. So that Diane can explore the impact of transferring different amounts of money per month, you'll enter the $800 value at the top of the Budget worksheet where it can be easily referenced and modified.

To specify the $800 transfer amount:

1. Return to the **Budget** worksheet.
2. In cell L10, enter **800**. See Figure 3-28.

Figure 3-28 **Home savings plan**

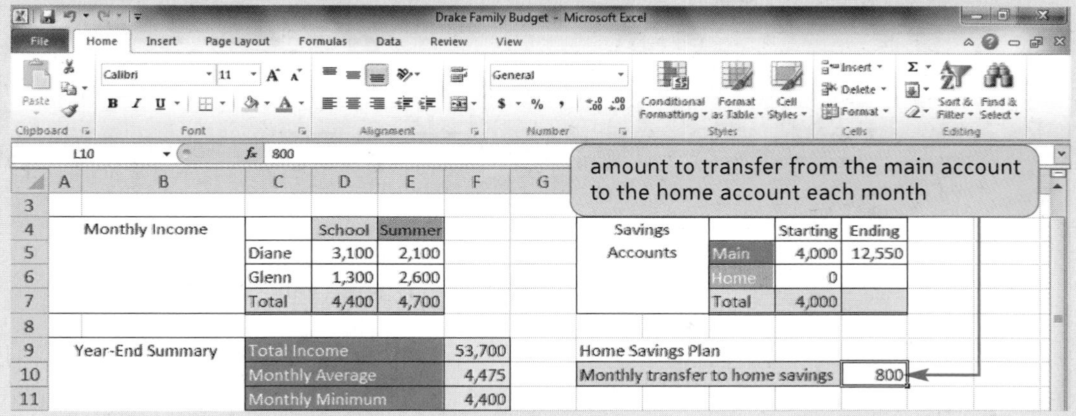

Next, you'll apply this monthly savings goal to Diane's proposed budget. You'll start by calculating the impact of transferring $800 on the January balances in the two savings accounts.

To modify the January balances:

1. In cell C39, enter the formula =**$L$10** to insert the amount of money withdrawn from the main savings account in January. The ending balance for the main account falls to $1,140. You used an absolute cell reference so that this formula continues to refer to cell L10 when you copy it into the remaining months of the year.
2. In cell C41, enter the formula **=K6** to insert the starting balance ($0) in the home account.
3. In cell C42, enter the formula **=C39** to insert the amount deposited from the main account into the home account.
4. In cell C43, enter the formula **=C41+C42** to calculate the ending balance in the home account.
5. Use the Format Painter to copy the formatting from the range **C38:C40** to the range **C41:C43**.

6. Change the fill color of cell C43 to **Orange, Accent 6, Lighter 60%** (the last color in the third row of the Theme Colors section).
7. Click cell **C43** to select it, if necessary. See Figure 3-29.

Figure 3-29 **Ending January balances in the Main and Home accounts**

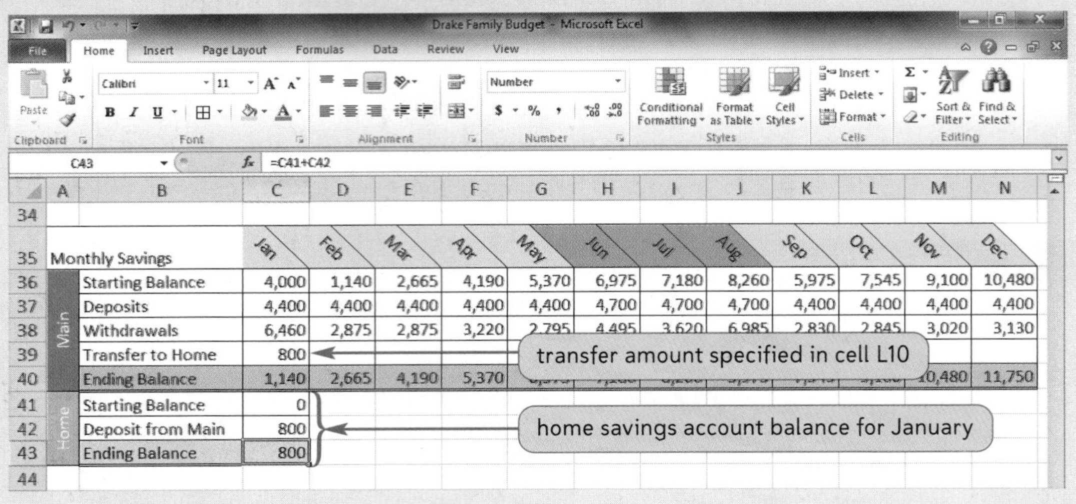

Now you'll insert the savings balances for the remaining months of the year, transferring $800 each month from the main savings account to the home savings account. As you did for the main savings account, you need to modify the formulas in row 41 so that the starting balance for February through December is taken from the ending balance of the previous month.

To complete the formulas for the home savings account:

1. Click cell **C39**, and then drag the fill handle over the range **D39:N39**. The formula =$L$10 is inserted in each cell in the range. The ending balance for December drops to $2,950, which is the final balance in the main account after transferring $800 per month.
2. Copy the range **C41:C43**, and then paste it into the range **D41:D43**. The formulas and formatting from January are entered for February. The starting balance for February shows the initial balance in the home savings account, $0, rather than the ending balance from January, $800.
3. Change the formula in cell D41 to **=C43** so that the February starting balance is taken from the January ending balance. Cell D41 correctly shows the February starting balance of 800, and cell D43 displays the value 1,600, the ending balance for February.
4. Select the range **D41:D43**, and then drag the fill handle over the range **E41:N43**. The formulas and formatting from February are copied to the remaining months of the year.
5. Click cell **N43** to deselect the range. Figure 3-30 shows the monthly balances for both accounts from January through December.

Figure 3-30 **Projected monthly savings balances for the year**

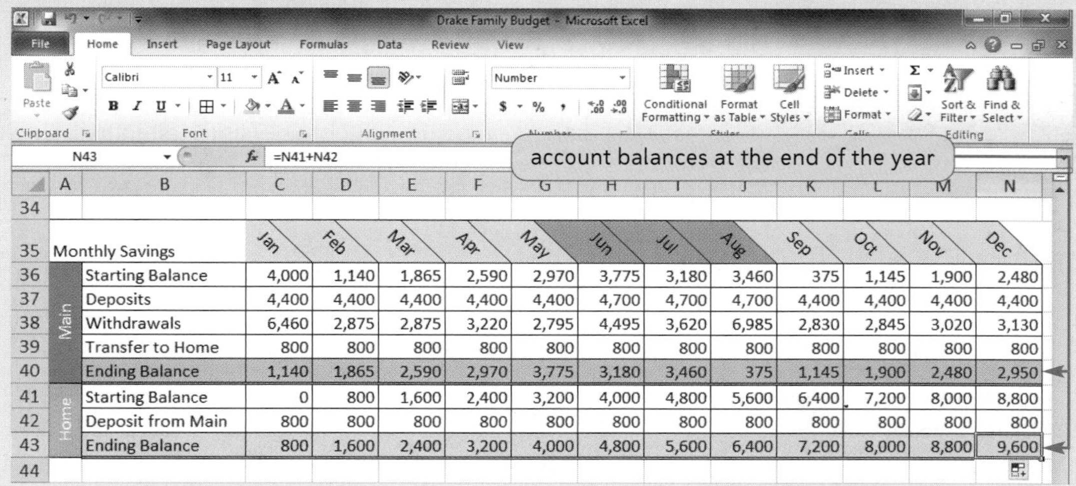

	A	B	C	D	E	F	G	H	I	J	K	L	M	N
34														
35	Monthly Savings		Jan	Feb	Mar	Apr	May	Jun	Jul	Aug	Sep	Oct	Nov	Dec
36	Main	Starting Balance	4,000	1,140	1,865	2,590	2,970	3,775	3,180	3,460	375	1,145	1,900	2,480
37		Deposits	4,400	4,400	4,400	4,400	4,400	4,700	4,700	4,700	4,400	4,400	4,400	4,400
38		Withdrawals	6,460	2,875	2,875	3,220	2,795	4,495	3,620	6,985	2,830	2,845	3,020	3,130
39		Transfer to Home	800	800	800	800	800	800	800	800	800	800	800	800
40		Ending Balance	1,140	1,865	2,590	2,970	3,775	3,180	3,460	375	1,145	1,900	2,480	2,950
41	Home	Starting Balance	0	800	1,600	2,400	3,200	4,000	4,800	5,600	6,400	7,200	8,000	8,800
42		Deposit from Main	800	800	800	800	800	800	800	800	800	800	800	800
43		Ending Balance	800	1,600	2,400	3,200	4,000	4,800	5,600	6,400	7,200	8,000	8,800	9,600
44														

6. In cell L6, enter the formula **=N43**. The savings plan table at the top of the worksheet displays 9,600, which is the year-end balance for the home account.

7. In cell L7, enter the formula **=L5+L6** to calculate the total savings amount from both accounts at the end of the year. Under Diane's current plan, the couple will have $2,950 in the main savings account and $9,600 in the home savings account at the end of the year.

Working with Logical Functions

Although Diane is pleased that $9,600 will be moved into the home savings account in the next year, she's concerned about the amount of money left in the main savings account. Even more troubling are the month-to-month balances in that account. For example, the balance in the main savings account will be only $375 at the end of August and will remain well below $2,000 for several months of the year. Diane is concerned that this savings plan will leave the couple with insufficient funds in the main savings account to handle unforeseen expenses.

Part of the problem is that the couple's net cash flow is negative during several months of the year. If they continue to transfer $800 into the home savings account during those months, the main savings account might fall below an acceptable level. Diane wants to modify her savings plan so that money is not transferred into the home savings account unless the net cash flow for that month is greater than or equal to $1,000. You need a formula that can "choose" whether to transfer the funds. You can build this kind of decision-making capability into a formula through the use of a logical function.

A logical function is a function that works with statements that are either true or false. Consider a statement such as "cell A5 = 3". If cell A5 is equal to 3, this statement has a value of true; if cell A5 is not equal to 3, this statement has a value of false. Excel supports many different logical functions, one of which is the IF function.

Using the IF Function

The IF function is a logical function that returns one value if a statement is true and returns a different value if that statement is false. The syntax of the IF function is

```
IF(logical_test, [value_if_true,] [value_if_false])
```

where *logical_test* is a statement that is either true or false, *value_if_true* is the value returned by the IF function if the statement is true, and *value_if_false* is the value returned by the function if the statement is false. For example, the following formula tests whether the value in cell A1 is equal to the value in cell B1. If it is, the formula returns a value of 100; otherwise it returns a value of 50.

```
=IF(A1=B1, 100, 50)
```

In many cases, however, you will not use values directly in the IF function. The following formula uses cell references, returning the value of cell C1 if A1 equals B1; otherwise, it returns the value of cell C2:

```
=IF(A1=B1, C1, C2)
```

The = symbol in these formulas is a comparison operator. A **comparison operator** is a symbol that indicates the relationship between two values. Figure 3-31 describes the comparison operators that can be used within a logical function.

Figure 3-31 **Comparison operators**

Operator	Statement	Description
=	A1 = B1	Tests whether the value in cell A1 *is equal to* the value in cell B1
>	A1 > B1	Tests whether the value in cell A1 *is greater than* the value in cell B1
<	A1 < B1	Tests whether the value in cell A1 *is less than* the value in cell B1
>=	A1 >= B1	Tests whether the value in cell A1 *is greater than or equal to* the value in cell B1
<=	A1 <= B1	Tests whether the value in cell A1 *is less than or equal to* the value in cell B1
<>	A1 <> B1	Tests whether the value in cell A1 *is not equal to* the value in cell B1

The IF function also works with text. For example, the following formula tests whether the value of cell A1 is equal to YES. If the value of cell A1 is equal to YES, the formula returns the text DONE; otherwise, it returns the text RESTART.

```
=IF(A1="YES", "DONE", "RESTART")
```

In addition, you can nest other functions inside an IF statement. The following formula first tests whether cell A5 is equal to the maximum of values within the range A1:A100. If it is, the formula returns the text "Maximum"; otherwise, it returns no text.

```
=IF(A5=MAX(A1:A100), "Maximum","")
```

In Diane and Glenn's budget, you will use an IF function for each month to test whether the net cash flow for that month is $1,000 or greater. If it is, Diane wants to transfer some of it into the home savings account. On the other hand, if the net cash flow is less than $1,000, she does not want to transfer any of it into the home account. You'll start creating this function by entering the minimum net cash flow into the worksheet.

To specify the minimum net cash flow:

1. In cell H11, enter the label **Minimum required net cash flow**.
2. In cell L11, enter **1000**. This is the minimum cash flow amount.
3. Use the Format Painter to copy the formatting from the range **H10:L10** to the range H11:L11.

Next, you'll enter a formula to determine how much to transfer each month. For the month of January, the formula to determine how much money is transferred is:

```
=IF(C33>=$L$11, $L$10, 0)
```

Cell C33 contains the net cash flow for the month of January, cell L11 contains the minimum net cash flow needed before Diane will transfer the money between accounts, and cell L10 contains the amount of money that Diane wants to transfer when the net cash flow meets or exceeds the minimum. For the current worksheet, this function tests whether the net cash flow for the month of January (cell C33) is greater than or equal to 1000 (cell L11). If it is, the formula returns 800 (cell L10) as the amount to transfer from the main savings account into the home savings account. Otherwise, it returns 0 and no money will be transferred that month.

This logical test uses both relative and absolute references. The C33 reference is relative because you will copy this formula into cells for the remaining months of the year. The $L$11 and $L$10 references are absolute so that the expression always references the minimum net cash flow specified in cell L11 and the amount to transfer specified in cell L10.

You'll replace the formula in cell C39 with this IF function.

To insert the IF function to determine the monthly transfer amount:

1. Clear the contents of cell **C39**.
2. Click the **Formulas** tab on the Ribbon, if necessary.
3. In the Function Library group, click the **Logical** button, and then click **IF** in the list of logical functions. The Function Arguments dialog box for the IF function opens.
4. In the Logical_test box, enter **C33>=$L$11**. This tests whether the net cash flow for January is greater than or equal to the value in cell L11 (1000).
5. In the Value_if_true box, enter **$L$10**. If the value in cell C33 is greater than or equal to the value in cell L11, the formula returns the value in cell L10 (800).
6. In the Value_if_false box, enter **0**. If the value in cell C33 is less than the value in cell L11, the formula returns 0 and no money will be transferred from the main savings account into the home savings account that month. See Figure 3-32.

TIP

When you type the IF function directly in the cell, remember that the *value_if_true* argument comes before the *value_if_false* argument.

Figure 3-32 **Function Arguments dialog box for the IF function**

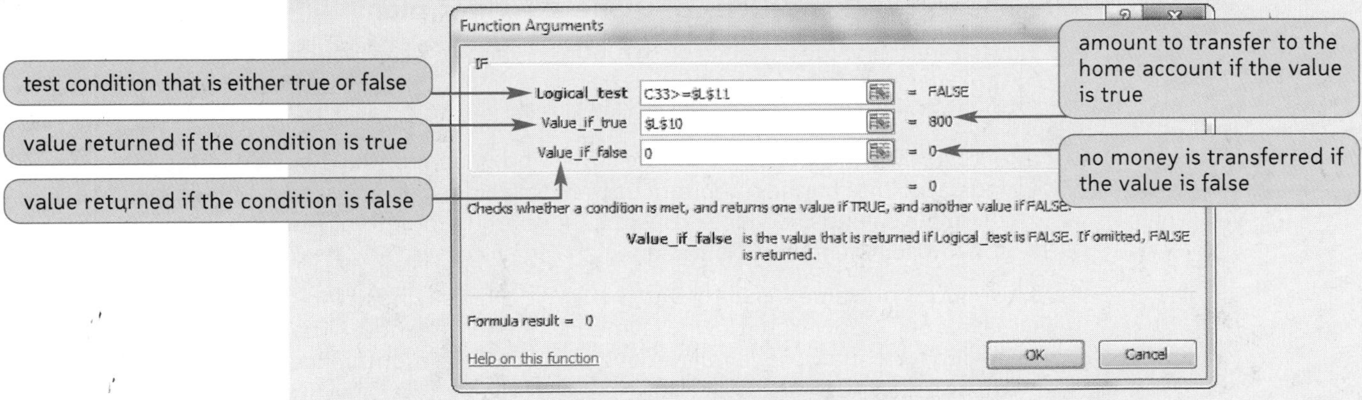

7. Click the **OK** button. A value of 0 is displayed in cell C39. Because the net cash flow for January is –2,060, no money will be transferred from the main savings account into the home savings account that month.
8. Drag the fill handle for cell C39 over the range **D39:N39** to copy this formula with the IF function into the remaining months of Diane's proposed budget.

9. Click cell **N40** to deselect the range. The new savings account balances are shown in Figure 3-33.

Figure 3-33 Monthly savings account balances

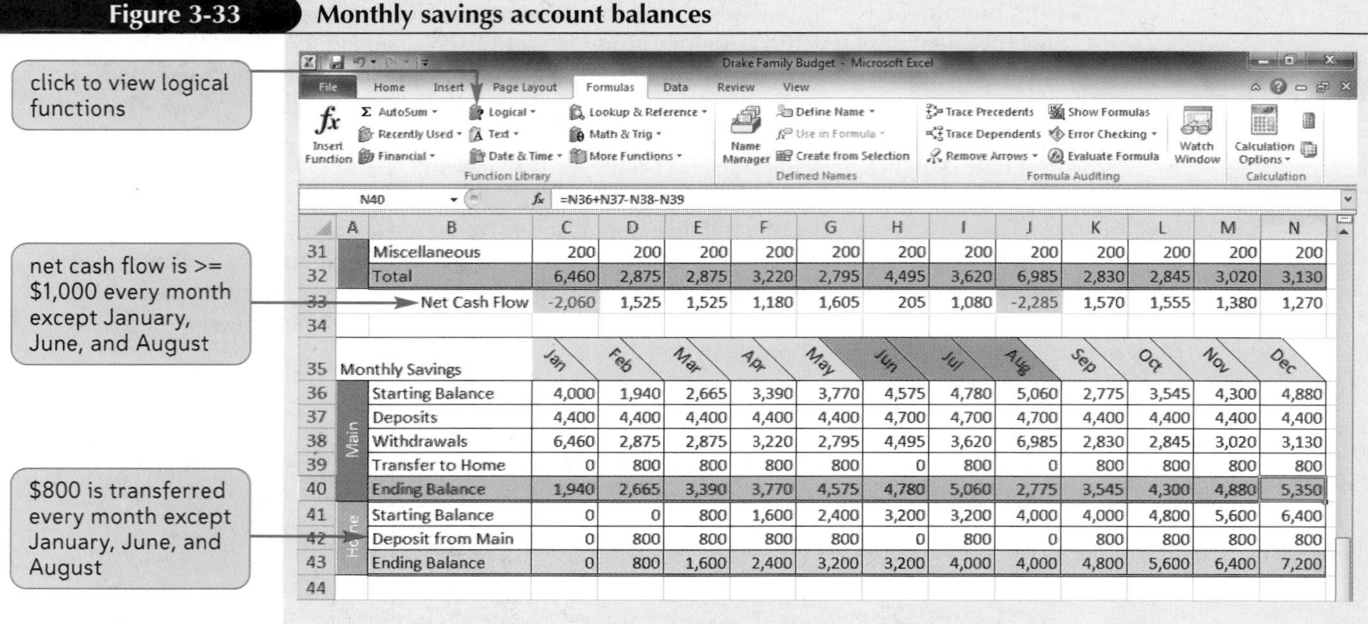

With this savings plan, the ending balance in the main savings account remains above $3,000 for most months of the year, and $800 is transferred from the main savings account into the home savings account in nine months of the year. Only in January, June, and August will Diane not transfer money into the home account. By the end of the year, the couple will have $5,350 in the main savings account and $7,200 in the home savings account.

Diane wants to explore what would happen if she increases the monthly transfer from $800 to $1,000. How would that affect the monthly balance of the main savings account?

To change the conditions of Diane's savings plan:

1. Change the value in cell L10 to **1000**. The end-of-year balance in the home savings account increases to $9,000 (cell L6) while the main savings account balance decreases to $3,550 (cell L5).
2. Scroll down the worksheet and examine how the monthly balance in the main savings account changes throughout the year. Under this revised plan, the balance in the main savings account drops to $1,775 in the month of August. This is a little too low for Diane.
3. Change the value in cell L10 to **900**. With this savings plan, the couple will save $8,100 toward a down payment on a home, and the balance in their main savings account will remain above $2,000 every month except January, when it dips to $1,940.

Diane feels that this revised savings plan is a good compromise between the need to save money for their future home while still maintaining a decent balance in their main savings account.

PROSKILLS

Decision Making: Using the IF Function to Explore Financial Options

Decision making is the process of choosing between possible courses of action. No decisions should be made until after the analysis of all potential alternatives is complete.

With financial decisions, you will often explore the impact of alternative scenarios on a projected outcome. Budget planning should not be limited to a single budget projection, but instead include several possible budgets. Your decision is then based on the evaluation of these different budgets. The budget you choose should prepare you to deal with shortages in future revenue or ways to take advantage of better-than-expected revenue.

Using Excel to manage your finances allows you to quickly explore these multiple scenarios. You can quickly examine how changing one or more values will affect such outcomes as income, expenses, and cash flow. You can use logical functions such as the IF function to help you explore these what-if scenarios because you can set the outcome of one value only if certain conditions are met. Different scenarios can be coded with names such as Option1, Option2, and Option 3. By using these scenario names as input values to an IF function, you can set up the worksheet to display the results specific to each scenario. In a well-designed workbook, you can quickly switch between scenarios simply by changing a few values in the worksheet.

By applying Excel's logical functions, you can more easily plan for different outcomes, and avoid the problems associated with unexpected occurences.

Working with Date Functions

To be effective, budgets need to be monitored and updated as conditions change. In the upcoming year, Diane plans to use this workbook to enter her and Glenn's actual salaries, expenses, and savings. This will enable Diane to track how well her projected values match the actual values. Because Diane will be updating the workbook throughout the year, she wants the worksheet to always display the current date so she can tell how far she is into her budget projections. You can accomplish this using a date function. Seven date functions supported by Excel are described in Figure 3-34. You can use these functions to help with scheduling or to determine on what days of the week certain dates occur.

Figure 3-34 **Date and time functions**

Function	Description
DATE(*year*, *month*, *day*)	Creates a date value for the date represented by the *year*, *month*, and *day* arguments
DAY(*date*)	Extracts the day of the month from the *date* value
MONTH(*date*)	Extracts the month number from the *date* value where 1=January, 2=February, and so forth
YEAR(*date*)	Extracts the year number from the *date* value
WEEKDAY(*date*, [*return_type*])	Calculates the day of the week from the *date* value, where 1=Sunday, 2=Monday, and so forth; to choose a different numbering scheme, set the optional *return_type* value to "1" (1=Sunday, 2=Monday, ...), "2" (1=Monday, 2=Tuesday, ...), or "3" (0=Monday, 1=Tuesday, ...)
NOW( )	Displays the current date and time
TODAY( )	Displays the current date

Perhaps the most commonly used date function is the TODAY function, which returns the current date. The syntax of the TODAY function is:

```
=TODAY()
```

TIP

If you don't want the date and time to change, you must enter the date and time value directly in the cell.

The TODAY function doesn't have any arguments. Neither does the NOW function, which returns both the current date and the current time. The values returned by the TODAY and NOW functions are updated automatically whenever you reopen the workbook or enter a new calculation.

Diane wants the Budget worksheet to display the current date.

To display the current date:

1. In cell I1, enter the label **Current Date**.
2. Merge cells **I1** and **J1**, left-align the merged cell, and change the cell's fill color to **Tan, Background 2** (the third color in the first row of the Theme Colors section).
3. Click cell **K1**. You'll enter the TODAY function in this cell.
4. Click the **Formulas** tab on the Ribbon.
5. In the Function Library group, click the **Date & Time** button, and then click **TODAY** in the date functions list. The Function Arguments dialog box opens, with a description of the function and a reminder that there are no arguments for the TODAY function.
6. Click the **OK** button. The Function Arguments dialog box closes, and the =TODAY() function is inserted into cell L1.
7. Merge and center the range **K1:L1**, and then add a border around each of the cells in the range I1:L1.
8. Click cell **K1** to deselect the range. See Figure 3-35.

Figure 3-35 TODAY function displays the current date

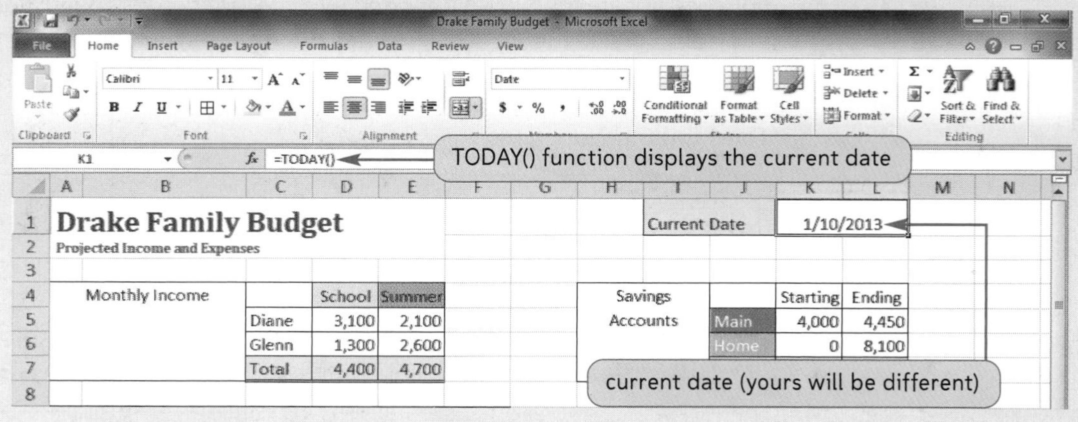

Working with Financial Functions

Excel provides a wide range of financial functions related to loans and interest payments. One of these is the PMT function, which can be used to calculate a payment schedule required to completely pay back a mortgage or loan. Figure 3-36 describes the PMT function and some of the other financial functions often used to develop budgets. These financial functions are the same as those widely used in business and accounting to perform various financial calculations, such as depreciation of an asset, the amount of interest paid on an investment, and the present value of an investment.

Figure 3-36 Financial functions for loans and investments

Function	Description
FV(*rate*, *nper*, *pmt*, [*pv*=0] [,*type*=0])	Calculates the future value of an investment, where *rate* is the interest rate per period, *nper* is the total number of periods, *pmt* is the payment in each period, *pv* is the present value of the investment, and *type* indicates whether payments should be made at the end of the period (0) or the beginning of the period (1)
PMT(*rate*, *nper*, *pv*, [*fv*=0] [,*type*=0])	Calculates the payments required each period on a loan or investment, where *fv* is the future value of the investment
IPMT(*rate*, *per*, *nper*, *pv*, [*fv*=0] [,*type*=0])	Calculates the amount of a loan payment devoted to paying the loan interest, where *per* is the number of the payment period
PPMT(*rate*, *per*, *nper*, *pv*, [*fv*=0] [,*type*=0])	Calculates the amount of a loan payment devoted to paying off the principal of a loan
PV(*rate*, *nper*, *pmt*, [*fv*=0] [,*type*=0])	Calculates the present value of a loan or investment based on periodic, constant payments
NPER(*rate*, *pmt*, *pv*, [*fv*=0] [,*type*=0])	Calculates the number of periods required to pay off a loan or investment
RATE(*nper*, *pmt*, *pv*, [*fv*=0] [,*type*=0])	Calculates the interest rate of a loan or investment based on periodic, constant payments

The cost of a loan to the borrower is largely based on three factors: the principal, the interest, and the time required to pay back the loan. **Principal** is the amount of money being loaned, and **interest** is the amount added to the principal by the lender. You can think of interest as a kind of "user fee" because the borrower is paying for the right to use the lender's money for a period of time. A few years ago, Diane and Glenn borrowed money to buy a second car and are still repaying the bank for the principal and interest on that loan. On the other hand, Diane and Glenn have also deposited money in their main savings account and receive interest payments from the bank in return.

Interest is calculated either as simple interest or as compound interest. In **simple interest**, the interest is equal to a percentage of principal for each period that the money has been lent. For example, if Diane and Glenn deposit $1,000 at a simple interest rate of 5 percent, they will receive $50 in interest payments each year. After one year their investment will be worth $1,050, after two years it will be worth $1,100, and so forth.

With **compound interest**, the interest is applied not only to the principal but also to any accrued interest. If Diane and Glenn deposit $1,000 in a bank at 5 percent annual interest compounded every year, they will earn $50 in the first year, raising the value of the account to $1,050. If they leave that money in the bank for another year, the interest payment in the second year rises to 5 percent of $1,050 or $52.50, resulting in a total value of $1,102.50. So they earn more money the second year because they are receiving interest on their interest.

Compound interest payments are divided into the period of time in which the interest is applied. For example, an 8 percent annual interest rate compounded monthly results in 12 interest payments per year with the interest each month equal to 1/12 of 8 percent, or about 0.67 percent per month.

Another factor in calculating the cost of a loan is the length of time required to pay it back. The longer it takes to pay back a loan, the more the loan costs because the borrower is paying interest over a longer period of time. To save money, loans should be paid back quickly and in full.

INSIGHT

Using Functions to Manage Personal Finances

Excel has many financial functions to manage personal finances. The following list can help you determine which function to use for the most common personal finance problems:

- To determine how much an investment will be worth after a series of monthly payments at some future time, use the FV (future value) function.
- To determine how much you have to spend each month to repay a loan or mortgage within a set period of time, use the PMT (payment) function.
- To determine how much of your monthly loan payment is used to pay the interest, use the IPMT (interest payment) function.
- To determine how much of your monthly loan payment is used for repaying the principal, use the PPMT (principal payment) function.
- To determine the largest loan or mortgage you can afford given a set monthly payment, use the PV (present value) function.
- To determine how long it will take to pay off a loan with constant monthly payments, use the NPER (number of periods) function.

For most loan and investment calculations, you need to enter the annual interest rate divided by the number of times the interest is compounded during the year. If interest is compounded monthly, divide the annual interest rate by 12; if interest is compounded quarterly, divide the annual rate by 4. You must also convert the length of the loan or investment to the number of interest payments per year. If you will make payments monthly, multiply the number of years of the loan or investment by 12.

Using the PMT Function

Diane and Glenn plan to purchase a house in the next several years. Diane wants to know how large of a mortgage she and Glenn could afford given their current income and expenses. To calculate the costs associated with a loan or mortgage, you need the following information:

- The amount being borrowed
- The annual interest rate
- The number of payment periods per year
- When loan payments are due
- The length of the loan in terms of the number of payment periods

In Diane and Glenn's neighborhood, starter homes are selling for about $240,000. If Diane and Glenn can keep to their savings plan, they will have saved $8,100 by the end of the year (as shown in cell L6 in the Budget worksheet). If they save this same amount for the next three years, they will have $24,300 in their home savings account to put toward the down payment. Based on this, Diane estimates that she and Glenn will need a home loan of almost $215,000.

Diane wants to know how much a mortgage of this size would cost in monthly payments. To determine this, you'll use the PMT function, which has the syntax

```
PMT(rate, nper, pv, [fv=0] [type=0])
```

where *rate* is the interest rate for each payment period, *nper* is the total number of payment periods required to pay off the loan, and *pv* is the present value of the loan or the amount that needs to be borrowed. For Diane and Glenn, the present value of the proposed loan is $215,000.

The PMT function has two optional arguments: *fv* and *type*. The *fv* argument is the future value of the loan. Because the intent with most loans is to pay them off completely, the future value is equal to 0 by default. The *type* argument specifies when the interest is charged on the loan, either at the end of the payment period (*type*=0), which is the default, or at the beginning of the payment period (*type*=1).

For most mortgages, the payment period is one month. This means that Diane and Glenn must make a payment on the loan every month, and interest on the loan is compounded every month. The annual interest rate on home loans in Diane and Glenn's area is 6.0 percent. To determine the interest rate per month, you divide the annual interest rate by 12. For Diane and Glenn, the interest rate each month is 6 percent divided by 12, or about 0.5 percent per month.

Diane and Glenn want to pay off their home loan in 20 years, or 240 months (20 years multiplied by 12 months per year). Putting all of this information together, you can calculate the monthly payment for the couple's home loan with the following formula:

```
=PMT(0.06/12, 20*12, 215000)
```

This formula returns a value of –$1,540.33. The value is negative because the payment is considered an expense, which Excel treats as a negative value. If you want to display this value as a positive number in a worksheet, enter a minus sign directly before the PMT function as follows:

```
=-PMT(0.06/12, 20*12, 215000)
```

Based on these calculations, Diane and Glenn would have to pay the bank $1,540.33 every month for 20 years before the loan and the interest are completely paid. Right now, the couple is spending about $1,050 per month on rent. So this home loan would be a significant increase over their current expenses.

Diane wants you to calculate the monthly payment for a home loan under other possible scenarios. You'll start by examining the costs associated with a $200,000 loan.

To create a loan payment worksheet:

1. Go to the **Loan Analysis** worksheet. You will do the loan calculations in this worksheet.
2. In cell B3, enter **6.00%**. This is the annual interest rate for the loan.
3. In cell B4, enter **12** for the number of payments per year.
4. In cell B5, enter the formula **=B3/B4** to calculate the interest per period, which is 0.50% per month.
5. In cell B6, enter **20** for the length of the mortgage in years.
6. In cell B7, enter the formula **=B4*B6** to calculate the total number of monthly payments, which is 240.
7. In cell B8, enter **$200,000** for the amount of the loan. All the values for the loan are entered.

The Loan Analysis worksheet includes all the data you need to calculate the monthly payment required to pay off the mortgage in 20 years at 6 percent interest compounded monthly. You will enter the PMT function to calculate this value.

To use the PMT function to calculate the monthly payment:

1. Click cell **B10** to select it.
2. In the Function Library group on the Formulas tab, click the **Financial** button, and then click **PMT** in the list of financial functions. The Function Arguments dialog box opens.
3. In the Rate box, enter the cell reference **B5**, which is the cell with the interest rate per month.
4. In the Nper box, enter the cell reference **B7**, which is the cell with the total number of monthly payments required to pay back the loan.
5. In the Pv box, enter the cell reference **B8**, which is the cell with the present value of the loan. See Figure 3-37.

TIP

Be sure to enter the interest rate per month for the Rate argument and not the annual interest rate for any loan or investment that has monthly payments.

Figure 3-37 **Function Arguments dialog box for the PMT function**

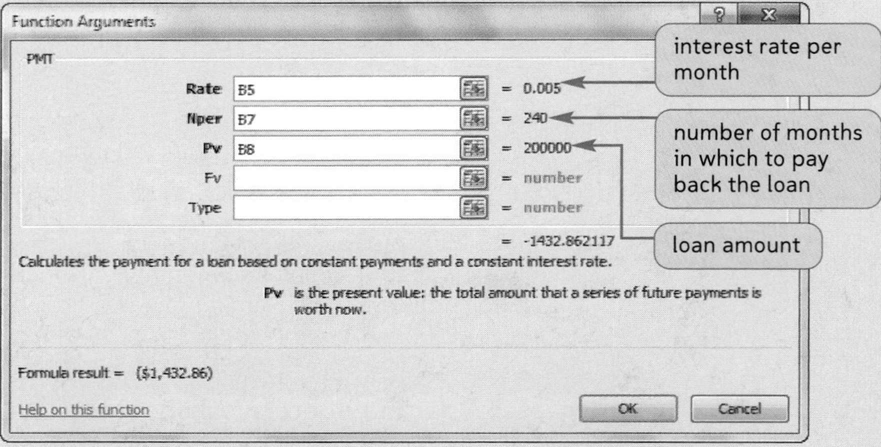

6. Click the **OK** button. The value $1,432.86 is displayed in parentheses in cell B10 to indicate a negative currency value. See Figure 3-38.

Figure 3-38 Money payments to pay back a $200,000 loan

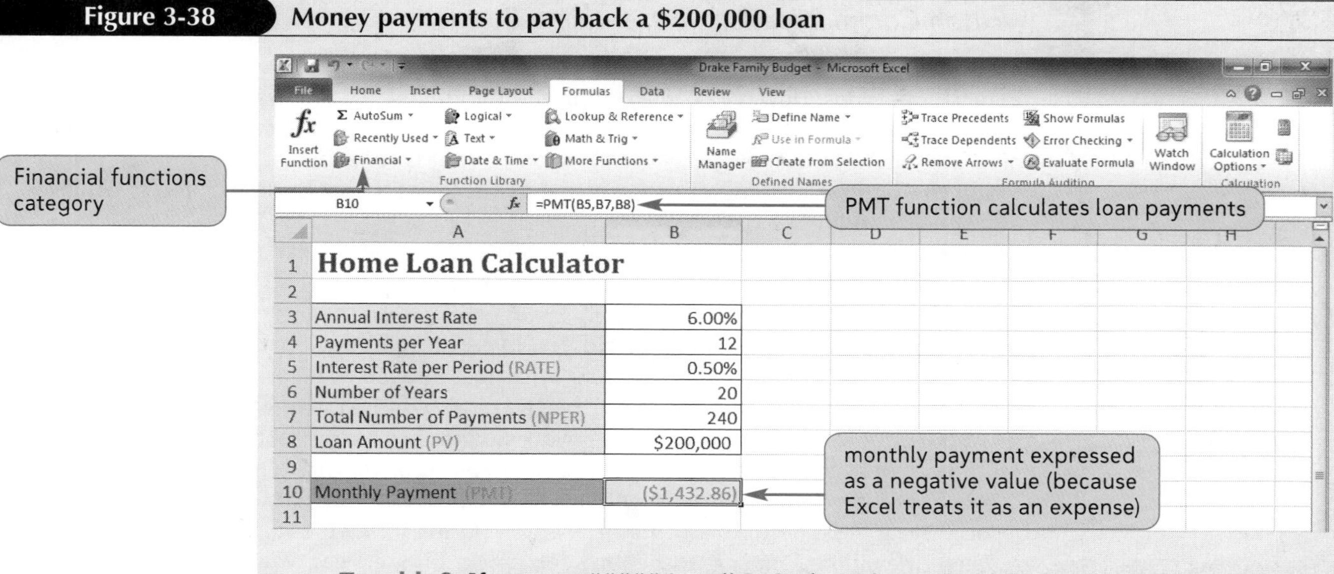

Trouble? If you see ##### in cell B10, the column width is too small to view the entire value. Increase the width of column B to display the monthly payment value.

Diane and Glenn would have to pay more than $1,400 per month for 20 years to repay a $200,000 loan at 6 percent interest. This is still too high. Diane is interested in other possibilities. Because you already set up the worksheet, you can quickly try other scenarios without having to reenter any formulas. Diane wonders whether extending the length of the loan would reduce the monthly payment by a sizeable margin. She asks you to calculate the monthly payment for different loan options.

To analyze other loan options:

1. Change the value in cell B6 to **30**. The amount of the monthly payment drops to $1,199.10, which is a decrease of $200 per month.
2. Change the value of cell B8 to **175,000**. For this smaller home loan, the monthly payment drops even further to $1,049.21 per month. This is almost exactly equal to what the couple is currently paying in rent.
3. Save the workbook, and then close it.

You've completed your work on Diane and Glenn's budget. Your analysis has shown Diane several important things. Her projected budget allows the couple to transfer enough money to the home savings account to make a down payment on a home in about three years. This savings plan leaves enough funds in the main savings account to cover their monthly expenses. Finally, the possible monthly mortgage payments for a loan will not be substantially more than what Diane and Glenn are currently paying in rent. So, not only will Diane and Glenn be able to save enough to make the initial down payment, their monthly income should also cover the monthly payments. Of course, all budgets must be revised periodically to meet changing expenses and income, and many different options exist in the home mortgage market. For example, Diane and Glenn could receive a mortgage with a lower interest rate or one that requires a smaller down payment. Your work has given Diane and Glenn enough information to make informed choices about their immediate financial future.

PROSKILLS

Written Communication: Presenting a Budget

In business, government, and personal lives, budgets play a key role in making sound financial decisions. However, a well-organized budget is only the first step. The budget must also convey information that is easily grasped by your audience or clients. Keep in mind the following guidelines as you work on budget spreadsheets:

- **Plan the budget around a few essential goals.** What is your budget trying to achieve? Be specific and focused.
- **Pick out a few important measures or "bottom lines" that can convey whether the proposed budget will meet your goals.** Are you trying to pay off a debt, raise money, or achieve a specific level of savings?
- **Look at your financial history to aid you in creating budget projections.** Search for important trends and take into account other factors such as inflation in your projections.
- **When explaining the budget, describe the results in terms of everyday examples.** Avoid the temptation of overwhelming your audience with raw facts and figures; rather, interpret what those facts and figures mean in terms of your bottom line measures.

You want your budget spreadsheet to remain current as new data and projections become available. This means continually updating the budget. But, do not just overwrite or delete the old budget spreadsheets. Keep earlier budgets easily accessible so you can access the original assumptions and goals when preparing the next budget. By keeping an audit trail of your past work, you can make your future budgets more accurate and reliable.

REVIEW

Session 3.2 Quick Check

1. How do you use AutoFill to copy a set of cell values, but not the formatting?
2. If the first three selected values in a series are 3, 6, and 9, what are the next three values that will be inserted using AutoFill?
3. If cell P5 contains the text "Mon," and then you select the cell and drag the fill handle over the range P6:P8, what text will be entered into those cells?
4. If cell Q3 is greater than cell Q4, you want to display "OK"; otherwise, you want to display "RETRY". Write the formula that accomplishes this.
5. Write the formula to display the current date.
6. Write the formula to display the current date and time.
7. You want to take out a loan for $130,000. The interest on the loan is 5 percent compounded monthly. You intend to pay back the loan in 20 years. Write the formula to calculate the monthly payment required to pay off the loan under those conditions.
8. What financial function do you use to determine how many payment periods are required to pay off a loan?

Practice the skills you learned in the tutorial using the same case scenario.

PRACTICE

Review Assignments

Data File needed for the Review Assignments: Timov.xlsx

Sergei and Ava Timov, friends of Diane and Glenn, ask you to create a similar workbook for their family budget. The Timovs want to purchase a new home. They are considering two houses with different mortgages. They want the budget worksheet you create to display the impact of monthly mortgage payments on the couple's cash flow. They also want to be able to quickly switch between one mortgage plan and another to observe the impact of each plan on their budget. The couple has already designed the workbook and entered estimates of their income and expenses for the upcoming year. You need to set up the formulas. Complete the following:

1. Open the **Timov** workbook located in the Excel3\Review folder included with your Data Files, and then save the workbook as **Timov Family Budget**.
2. In the Documentation sheet, enter your name in cell B3. Use the TODAY function to display the current date in cell B4.
3. In the Family Budget worksheet, in the range C18:N18, use AutoFill to replace the month numbers with the abbreviations **Jan** through **Dec**.
4. In the range C21:N21, calculate the couple's total income. In the range C27:N27, calculate the couple's total monthly expenses. In the range C28:N28, calculate the monthly net cash flow (equal to the total income minus the total expenses).
5. In cell C7, enter a formula to calculate the sum of Sergei's monthly income for the entire year. In cell D7, calculate Sergei's average monthly income. In cell E7, calculate Sergei's maximum monthly income. In cell F7, calculate Sergei's minimum monthly income.
6. Complete the Year-End Summary table by first selecting the range C7:F7. Use AutoFill to copy the formula in the range C7:F7 into the range C7:F16. Use the Auto Fill Options button to copy only the formulas into the selected range and not both the formulas and the formats. (*Hint*: Because you haven't yet entered any mortgage payment values, cell D14 will show the value #DIV/0!, indicating that Excel cannot calculate the average mortgage payment. You'll correct that problem shortly.)
7. In the range K2:K7, enter the following loan and loan conditions of the first mortgage:
   a. In cell K2, enter **6.7%** as the annual interest rate.
   b. In cell K3, enter **12** as the number of payments per year.
   c. In cell K4, calculate the monthly interest rate.
   d. In cell K5, enter **30** as the number of years in the mortgage.
   e. In cell K6, calculate the total number of months to repay the loan.
   f. In cell K7, enter **395,000** as the loan amount.
8. In cell K8, use the PMT function to calculate the monthly payment required to repay this loan.
9. Edit the formula in cell K8, adding a minus sign directly before the PMT function to make the value returned by the formula positive rather than negative.
10. In the range K10:K15, enter the following conditions of the second mortgage plan, and calculate the monthly interest rate and the total number of months to repay the loan:
    - The annual interest rate is **6.7%**.
    - The interest rate is compounded **12** times a year (or monthly).
    - The mortgage will last **20** years.
    - The loan amount (or value of the principal) is **$300,000**.

11. In cell K16, enter the PMT function to calculate the monthly payment needed to pay off this loan, and then edit the formula to make the value displayed in the cell positive by placing a negative sign in front of the PMT function.
12. Sergei and Ava want to be able to view their monthly cash flow under both mortgage plans. The mortgage being applied to the budget will be determined by whether 1 or 2 is entered into cell E3. To switch from one mortgage to another, do the following:
    a. In cell C26, enter an IF function that tests whether cell E3 equals 1. If it does, return the value of cell K8; otherwise, return the value of cell K16. Use absolute cell references for all references in the formula.
    b. Use AutoFill to copy the formula in cell C26 into the range D26:N26.
    c. Verify that the values in the range C26:N26 match the monthly payment for the first mortgage condition. (Note that the worksheet will display the monthly payment amount to the nearest dollar.)
13. In cell E3, change the value from 1 to **2**. Verify that the monthly payment for the second mortgage appears in the range C26:N26.
14. Sergei and Ava want to maintain an average net cash flow of at least $1,000 per month. Is this achieved on either mortgage plan?
15. Save and close the workbook, and then submit the finished workbook to your instructor, either in printed or electronic form, as requested.

APPLY

Case Problem 1

If you have a SAM 2010 user profile, your instructor may have assigned an autogradable version of this assignment. If so, log into the SAM 2010 Web site at www.cengage.com/sam2010 to download the instructions and start files.

Data File needed for this Case Problem: Chemistry.xlsx

Chemistry 303 Karen Raul is a professor of chemistry at a community college in Shawnee, Kansas. She has started using Excel to calculate the final grade for students in her Chemistry 303 course. The final score is a weighted average of the scores given for three exams and the final exam. One way to calculate a weighted average is by multiplying each student's exam score by the weight given to the exam, and then totaling the results. For example, consider the following four exam scores:

Exam 1 = 84 Exam 2 = 80 Exam 3 = 83 Final Exam = 72

If the first three exams are each given a weight of 20 percent and the final exam is given a weight of 40 percent, the weighted average of the four scores is:

84*0.2 + 80*0.2 + 83*0.2 + 72*0.4 = 78.2

Karen has already entered the scores for her students and formatted much of the workbook. You will enter the formulas and highlight the top 10 overall scores in her class. Complete the following:

1. Open the **Chemistry** workbook located in the Excel3\Case1 folder included with your Data Files, and then save the workbook as **Chemistry 303 Final Scores**.
2. In the Documentation sheet, enter your name in cell B3 and the date in cell B4.
3. In the First Semester Scores worksheet, in cell F17, enter a formula to calculate the weighted average of the first student's four exams. Use the weights found in the range C8:C11, matching each weight with the corresponding exam score. Use absolute cell references for the four weights.
4. Use AutoFill to copy the formula in cell F17 into the range F18:F52.
5. In cell B5, use the COUNT function to calculate the total number of students in the class.
6. In cell D8, calculate the median score for the first exam.
7. In cell E8, calculate the maximum score for the first exam.
8. In cell F8, calculate the minimum score for the first exam.

9. In cell G8, calculate the range of scores for the first exam, which is equal to the difference between the maximum and minimum score.
10. Repeat Steps 6 through 9 for each of the other two exams, the final exam, and the overall weighted score.
11. Use conditional formatting to highlight the top 10 scores in the range F17:F52 in a light red fill with dark red text.
12. Insert a page break at cell A14, repeat the first three rows of the worksheet in any printout, and verify that the worksheet is in portrait orientation.
13. Save and close the workbook, and then submit the finished workbook to your instructor, either in printed or electronic form, as requested.

Use formulas and functions to create an order form for a fireworks company.

APPLY

Case Problem 2

Data File needed for this Case Problem: Wizard.xlsx

WizardWorks Andrew Howe owns and operates WizardWorks, an online seller of fireworks based in Franklin, Tennessee. Andrew wants you to help him develop an order form for his business. The form needs to contain formulas to calculate the charge for each order. The total charge is based on the quantity and type of items ordered plus the shipping charge and the 5 percent sales tax. Orders can be shipped using standard 3- to 5-day shipping for $3.99 or overnight for $10.99. Andrew is also offering a 4 percent discount for orders that exceed $200. Both the shipping option and the discount need to be calculated using formulas based on values entered into the worksheet. Complete the following:

1. Open the **Wizard** workbook located in the Excel3\Case2 folder included with your Data Files, and then save the workbook as **WizardWorks Order Form**.
2. In the Documentation sheet, enter your name in cell B3 and enter the date in cell B4.
3. In the Order Form worksheet, in cell C4, enter the customer name, **Kevin Kemper**. In cell C6, enter the order number, **28314**. In the range C9:C13, enter the following address:

Address 1:	**315 Avalon Street**
City:	**Greenfield**
State:	**IN**
Zip:	**46140**

4. In cell C5, enter a function that displays the current date.
5. In the range B20:E22, enter the following orders:

Item	Name	Price	Qty
BF001	**Bucket of Fireworks**	**$45.75**	**1**
NAF	**Nightair Fountain**	**$12.95**	**4**
MR20B	**Mountain Rockets (Box 20)**	**$55.25**	**2**

6. In cell C15, enter **overnight** to ship this order overnight.

EXPLORE

7. In cell F20, enter an IF function that tests whether the order quantity in cell E20 is greater than 0 (zero). If it is, return the value of cell E20 multiplied by cell D20; otherwise, return no text by entering "". AutoFill this formula into the range F21:F25.
8. In cell F27, calculate the sum of the values in the range F20:F25.
9. In cell F28, enter an IF function that tests whether cell F27 is greater than 200. If it is, return the value of cell F27 multiplied by the discount percentage in cell F12; otherwise, return the value 0 (zero).
10. In cell F29, subtract the discount value in cell F28 from the subtotal value in cell F27.
11. In cell F31, calculate the sales tax by multiplying the after discount value in cell F29 by the sales tax percentage, 0.05.

EXPLORE 12. In cell F32, determine the shipping charge by entering an IF function that tests whether cell C15 equals "standard". If it does, return the value in cell F9; otherwise, return the value in cell F10.

13. In cell G32, display the value of cell C15.
14. In cell F34, calculate the total of the after discount value, the sales tax, and the shipping fee.
15. Reduce the quantity of Mountain Rockets boxes from 2 to **1**, and then verify that the discount is changed to 0 for the order.
16. Change the shipping option from overnight to **standard**, and then verify that the shipping fee is changed to the fee for standard shipping.
17. Save and close the workbook, and then submit the finished workbook to your instructor, either in printed or electronic form, as requested.

Explore how to use relative and absolute references and the PMT function to create a loan table.

CHALLENGE

Case Problem 3

Data File needed for this Case Problem: Loan.xlsx

Eason Financial Services Jesse Buchmann is a finance officer at Eason Financial Services in Meridian, Idaho. She works with people who are looking for home mortgages. Most clients want mortgages they can afford, and affordability is determined by the size of the monthly payment. The monthly payment is determined by the interest rate, the total number of payments, and the size of the home loan. Jesse can't change the interest rate, but homebuyers can reduce their monthly payments by increasing the number of years to repay the loan. Jesse wants to give her clients a grid that displays combinations of loan amounts and payment periods so that they can select a loan that best meets their needs and budget. Jesse already entered much of the layout and formatting for the worksheet containing the loan payment grid. You will enter the PMT function. Complete the following:

1. Open the **Loan** workbook located in the Excel3\Case3 folder included with your Data Files, and then save the workbook as **Loan Grid**.
2. In the Documentation sheet, enter your name and the date.
3. In the Loan Calculation worksheet, in cell E3, enter a monthly payment of **$1,750**.
4. In cell E5, enter the annual interest rate of **5.75%**. In cell E6, enter **12** to indicate that the interest payment is compounded 12 times a year, or monthly.
5. In the range C10:C20, use AutoFill to enter the currency values **$250,000** through **$350,000** in increments of $10,000. In the range D9:H9, use AutoFill to enter the year values **15** through **35** in increments of 5 years.

EXPLORE 6. In cell D10, use the PMT function to calculate the monthly payment required to repay a **$250,000** loan in **15** years at **5.75%** interest compounded monthly. Use absolute references to cells E5 and E6 to enter the annual interest rate and number of payments per year. Use the mixed references D$9 and $C10 to cells D9 and C10, respectively, to reference the number of years to repay the loan and the loan amount. Place a minus sign before the PMT function so that the value returned by the function is positive rather than negative.

EXPLORE 7. Using AutoFill, copy the formula in cell D10 into the range E10:H10, and then copy that range of formulas into the range D11:H20.

EXPLORE 8. Conditionally format the range D10:H20 to highlight all of the values in the range that are less than the value in cell E3 in a dark green font on a green fill.

9. Add a second conditional format to the range D10:H20 to highlight all of the values in the range that are greater than the value in cell E3 in a dark red font on a red fill.

EXPLORE 10. Change the value in cell E3 from $1,750 to **$1,800**. If this represents the maximum affordable monthly payment, use the values in the grid to determine the largest mortgage for payment schedules lasting 15 through 35 years. Can any of the home loan values displayed in the grid be repaid in 20 years at $1,800 per month?

11. Save and close the workbook, and then submit the finished workbook to your instructor, either in printed or electronic form, as requested.

Create a workbook that automatically grades a driving exam.

CREATE

Case Problem 4

Data File needed for this Case Problem: V6.xlsx

V-6 Driving Academy Sebastian Villanueva owns and operates the V-6 Driving Academy, a driving school located in Pine Hills, Florida. In addition to driving, students must take multiple-choice tests offered by the Florida Department of Motor Vehicles. Students must answer at least 80 percent of the questions correctly to pass each test. Sebastian has to grade these tests himself. Sebastian could save a lot of time if the test questions were in a workbook and Excel totaled the test results. Sebastian has already entered a 20-question test into a workbook. You will format this workbook and insert the necessary functions and formulas to grade a student's answers. Complete the following:

1. Open the **V6** workbook located in the Excel3\Case4 folder included with your Data Files, and then save the workbook as **V6 Driving Test**.
2. In the Documentation sheet, enter your name in cell B3 and enter the date in cell B4.
3. In the Exam1 worksheet, format the questions and possible answers so that the worksheet is easy to read. The format is up to you. At the top of the worksheet, enter a title that describes the exam, and then enter a function that returns the current date.
4. Add a section somewhere on the Exam1 worksheet where Sebastian can enter each student's name and answers to each question. Design the workbook so that Sebastian can always go back and review any student's completed exam.
5. The answers for the 20 questions are listed below. Use this information to write functions that will grade each answer, giving 1 point for a correct answer and 0 otherwise. Assume that all answers are in lowercase letters; therefore, the function that tests the answer to the first question should check for a "c" rather than a "C".

Question	Answer	Question	Answer	Question	Answer
1	c	8	a	15	b
2	a	9	c	16	b
3	b	10	b	17	b
4	a	11	c	18	b
5	c	12	b	19	b
6	b	13	b	20	c
7	c	14	a		

6. At the top of the worksheet, insert a formula to calculate the total number of correct answers for each student.
7. Insert another formula that divides the total number of correct answers by the total number of exam questions on the worksheet. Display this value as a percentage.
8. Enter a logical function that displays the message "PASS" on the exam if the percentage of correct answers is greater than or equal to 80 percent; otherwise, the logical function displays the message "FAIL".
9. Test your worksheet with the following student exams. Which students passed and which failed? What score did each student receive on the exam?

Juan Marquez

Question	Answer	Question	Answer	Question	Answer
1	a	8	a	15	b
2	b	9	c	16	b

3	b	10	b	17	a
4	a	11	c	18	b
5	c	12	b	19	b
6	b	13	a	20	c
7	c	14	a		

Kurt Bessette

Question	Answer	Question	Answer	Question	Answer
1	a	8	a	15	c
2	a	9	b	16	b
3	b	10	c	17	a
4	a	11	c	18	b
5	c	12	a	19	a
6	b	13	b	20	c
7	c	14	a		

Rebecca Pena

Question	Answer	Question	Answer	Question	Answer
1	c	8	a	15	c
2	a	9	c	16	b
3	b	10	a	17	b
4	a	11	c	18	b
5	c	12	b	19	b
6	b	13	b	20	b
7	c	14	a		

10. Format the worksheet so that it prints nicely with no questions crossing over a page break, and the names of the students and the name of the driving academy at the top of each page.
11. Save and close the workbook, and then submit the finished workbook to your instructor, either in printed or electronic form, as requested.

ASSESS

SAM: Skills Assessment Manager

For current SAM information, including versions and content details, visit SAM Central (http://samcentral.course.com). If you have a SAM user profile, you may have access to hands-on instruction, practice, and assessment of the skills covered in this tutorial. Since various versions of SAM are supported throughout the life of this text, check with your instructor for the correct instructions and URL/Web site for accessing assignments.

ENDING DATA FILES

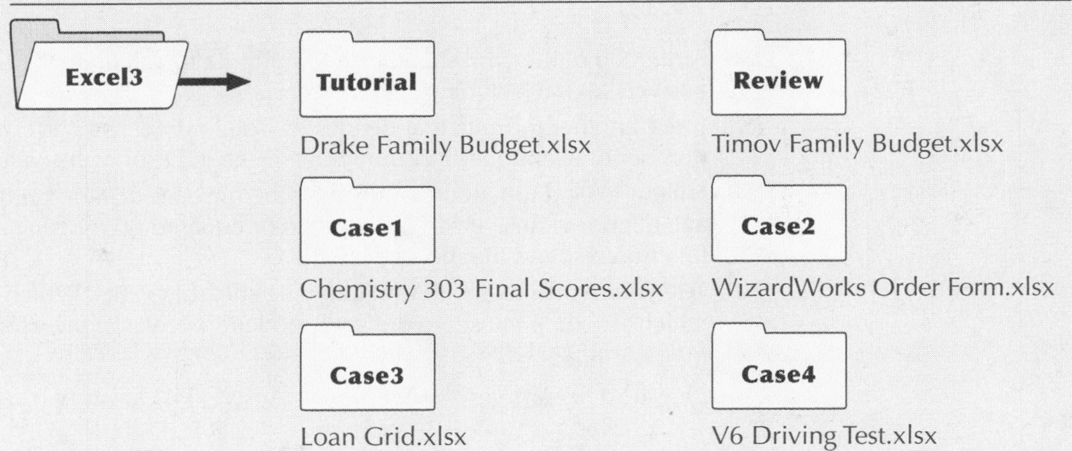

TUTORIAL 4

Enhancing a Workbook with Charts and Graphs

Charting Financial Data

OBJECTIVES

Session 4.1
- Create an embedded chart
- Create and format a pie chart
- Work with chart titles and legends
- Create and format a column chart

Session 4.2
- Create and format a line chart
- Modify a chart data source
- Create and format a combined chart
- Create a 3-D chart
- Create and format sparklines and data bars
- Create a chart sheet

Case | *Seaborg Group*

Ajita Gupte is a financial assistant for the Seaborg Group, a financial consulting agency located in Providence, Rhode Island. One of her duties is to prepare financial reports on the investments the Seaborg Group makes for its clients. These reports go into a binder containing the financial status of each client's different investments. The client receives the binder at annual meetings with his or her financial advisor, and receives updates on the status of the investments periodically throughout the year.

Many of the company's clients invest in the New Century Fund, a large growth/large risk mutual fund that has been operating for the past 10 years. Ajita needs to create a report that summarizes the fund's financial holdings as well as its 10-year performance record. She already entered the financial data into an Excel workbook, but needs help finishing the report. Because many clients are overwhelmed by tables of numbers, Ajita wants to include charts and graphs in the report that display the current and past performance of the New Century Fund. You will help Ajita to create these charts.

STARTING DATA FILES

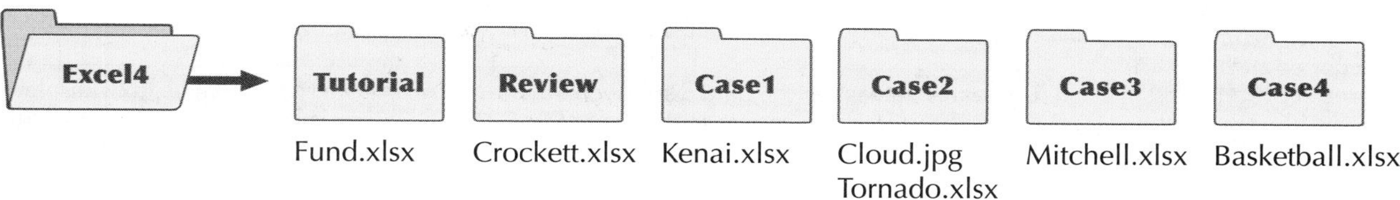

SESSION 4.1 VISUAL OVERVIEW

Chart layouts provide different options for organizing chart elements.

A **chart**, or **graph**, is a visual representation of a set of data values. Charts show trends or relationships that may not be readily apparent from numbers alone.

An **embedded chart** is an object in a worksheet.

Each chart has a **data source**, which is the range that contains the data to display in the chart. The data source for the Fund Assets pie chart is the range A2:B6.

The **series name**, the first row of the data range, identifies the data series. In this case, the series name is row 9.

A data source is a collection of one or more **data series**, which is a range of values that is plotted as a single unit on the chart.

The first column of the data range is the **category values**, which are the groups or categories that the series values belong to. These categories each include three subcategories in the range A10:B21.

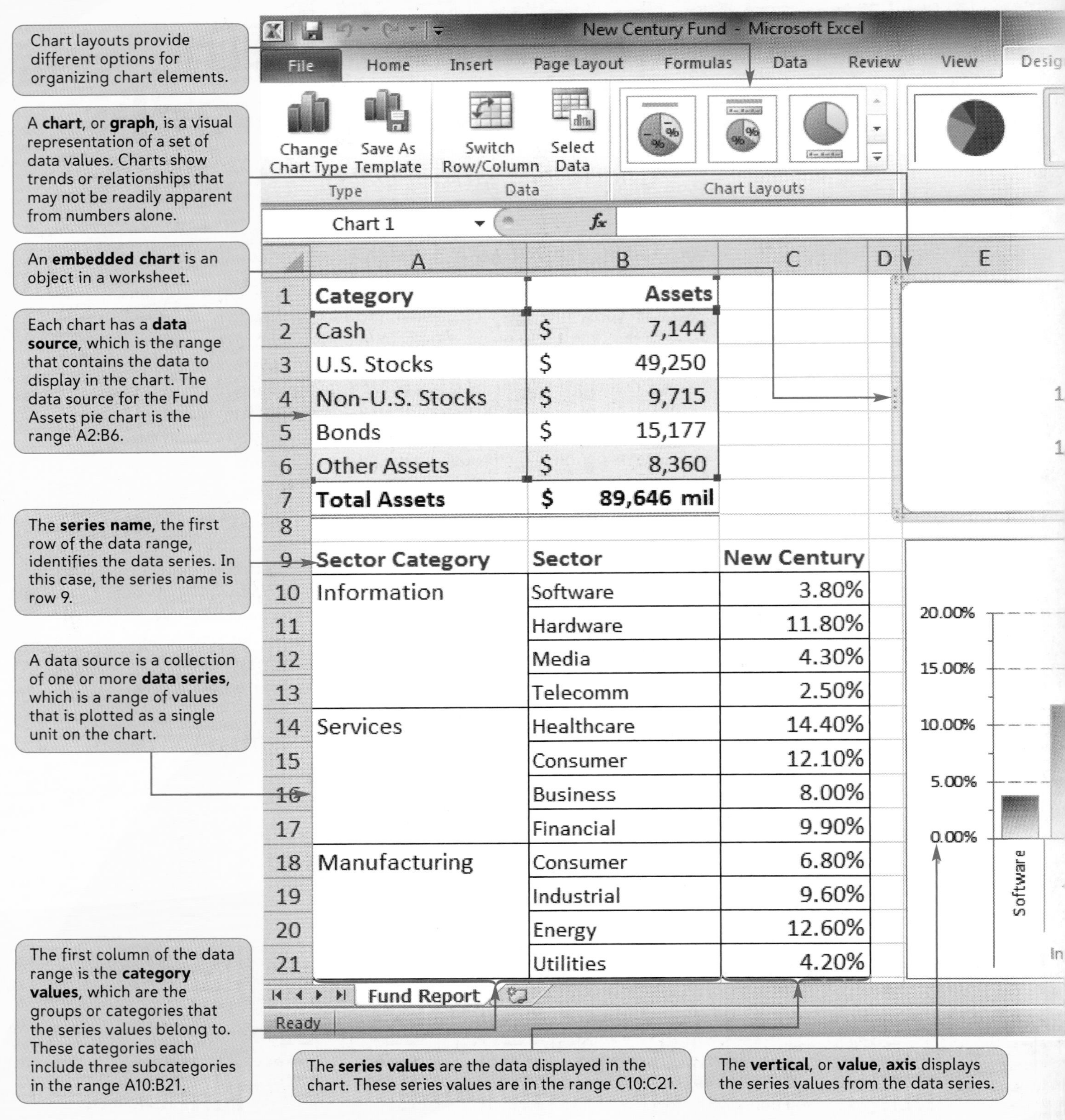

The **series values** are the data displayed in the chart. These series values are in the range C10:C21.

The **vertical**, or **value**, **axis** displays the series values from the data series.

CHART ELEMENTS

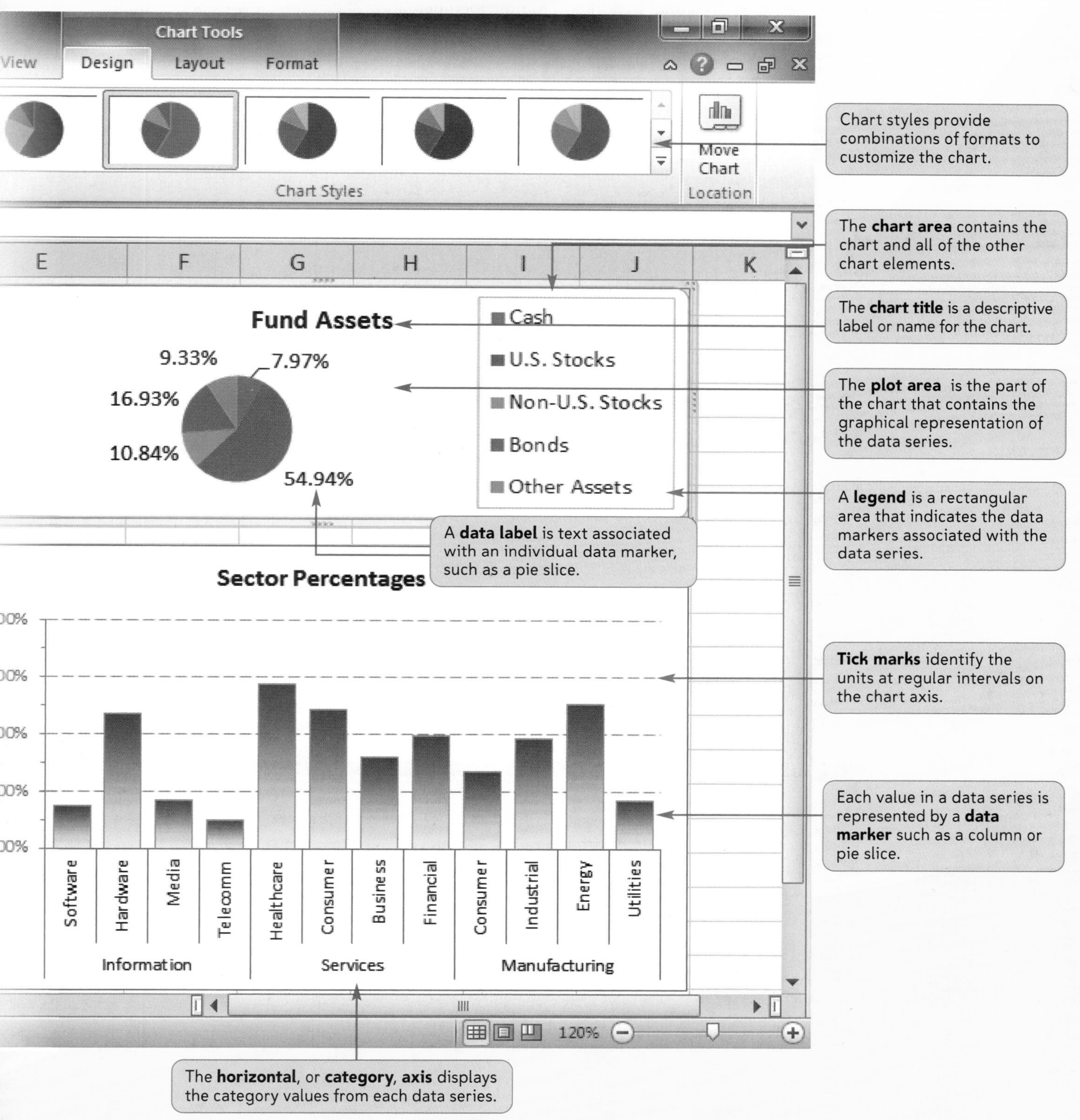

Creating an Excel Chart

Ajita already created a workbook in which she entered and formatted data that describes the New Century Fund. In addition to the Documentation sheet, the New Century Fund workbook contains the following five worksheets:

- The Summary Report worksheet includes summary data and facts about the New Century Fund.
- The Fund History worksheet provides a table that shows how well the New Century Fund performed over the past 10 years compared to a similar fund and the S&P 500 index.
- The Assets worksheet lists the assets of the New Century Fund grouped by investment categories.
- The Sectors worksheet shows the economic sectors in which the New Century Fund invests.
- The Sector History worksheet provides a table showing how each of the economic sectors in the New Century Fund has performed in the last 10 years.

You'll begin by opening this workbook and reviewing its contents.

To open and review Ajita's workbook:

1. Open the **Fund** workbook located in the **Excel4\Tutorial** folder included with your Data Files, and then save the workbook as **New Century Fund** in the same folder.
2. In the Documentation sheet, enter your name in cell B3 and the date in cell B4.
3. Take some time to review the contents of the workbook.

Charts show trends or relationships in data that are more difficult to see by simply looking at numbers, such as the range of months in which the New Century Fund performed exceptionally well. Ajita wants financial data from the Fund History, Assets, and Sectors worksheets displayed in the Summary Report worksheet as charts, or graphs. In the summary report, she wants one chart that shows the performance of the New Century Fund compared to two similar funds, and she wants two charts that show how money in the New Century Fund is currently invested. The final Summary Report worksheet will be a single page that includes all of the information Ajita wants her clients to see.

REFERENCE

Inserting a Chart

- Select the data source with the range of data you want to chart.
- In the Charts group on the Insert tab, click a chart type, and then click a chart subtype in the Chart gallery.
- In the Location group on the Chart Tools Design tab, click the Move Chart button to place the chart in a chart sheet or embed it into a worksheet.

Selecting a Data Source

Each chart has a data source. After you select a range to use as the chart's data source, Excel uses the first row of the selected range as the series name, the first column as the category values, and the remaining columns as the series values. If the data source is organized in rows rather than in columns, the first row contains the category values, the remaining rows contain the data values for each data series, and the first column of each series row contains the series names.

The first chart you will create is based on data in the Assets worksheet that indicates how the New Century Fund's holdings are divided among different investment categories. The data source you will select has only one data series that shows the assets for five investment categories.

To select the data source for the assets chart:

1. Click the **Assets** sheet tab to make the Assets worksheet active.
2. Select the range **A3:B8**. The data source in this range has one data series, named Assets. Its category values in the range A4:A8 list the different asset categories, and its series values in the range B4:B8 contain the data to be charted. See Figure 4-1.

Figure 4-1 **Data source selected for the assets chart**

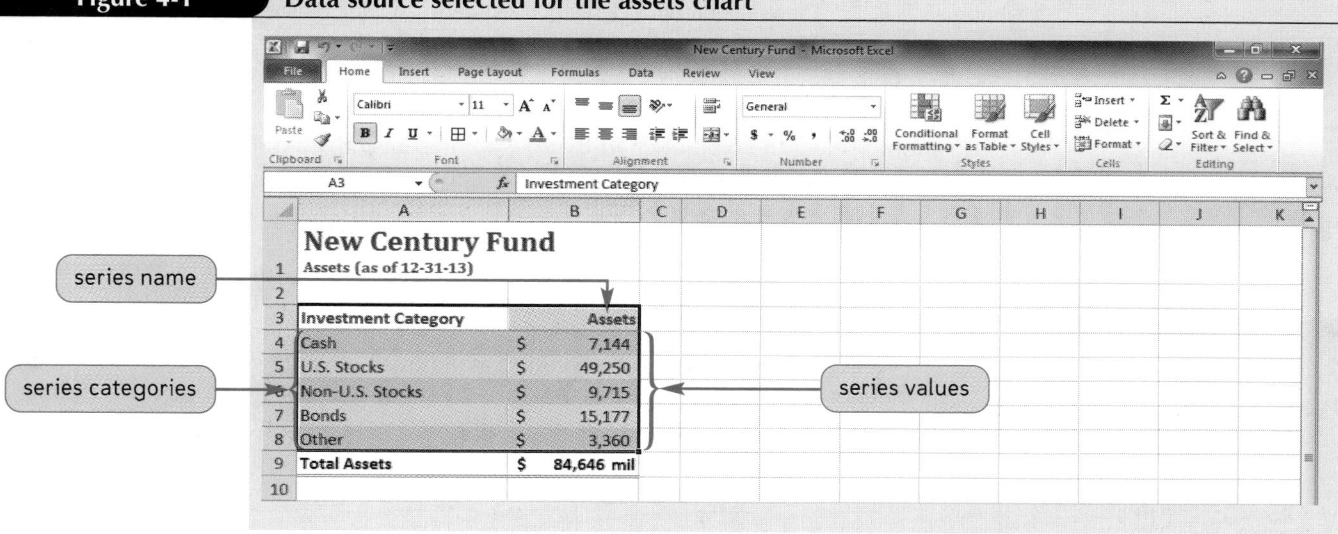

Selecting a Chart Type

You can apply a wide variety of chart types to the selected data source. Excel supports 73 built-in charts organized into 11 categories, which are described in Figure 4-2. You can also create custom chart types based on the built-in charts.

Figure 4-2 **Excel chart types**

Chart Type	Description
Column	Compares values from different categories. Values are indicated by the height of the columns.
Line	Compares values from different categories. Values are indicated by the height of the line. Often used to show trends and changes over time.
Pie	Compares relative values of different categories to the whole. Values are indicated by the areas of the pie slices.
Bar	Compares values from different categories. Values are indicated by the length of the bars.
Area	Compares values from different categories. Similar to the line chart except that areas under the lines contain a fill color.
Scatter	Shows the patterns or relationship between two or more sets of values. Often used in scientific studies and statistical analyses.
Stock	Displays stock market data, including the high, low, opening, and closing prices of a stock.
Surface	Compares three sets of values in a three-dimensional chart.
Doughnut	Compares relative values of different categories to the whole. Similar to the pie chart except that it can display multiple sets of data.
Bubble	Shows the patterns or relationship between two or more sets of values. Similar to the XY (Scatter) chart except the size of the data marker is determined by a third value.
Radar	Compares a collection of values from several different data sets.

You should select the type of chart that best represents the data. For example, a pie chart provides the best way to show the breakout of the asset data you selected. A **pie chart** is a chart in the shape of a circle (like a pie) that shows data values as a percentage of the whole. Each value in the data series represents a slice of the pie. The larger the value, the larger the pie slice. For the asset data, each slice will represent the percentage of the total assets from each investment category in the New Century Fund.

TIP

The data source for a pie chart should include only the category labels and data values and not row or column totals because Excel will treat those totals as another category to be graphed.

Pie charts are most effective with six or fewer slices, and when each slice is large enough to view. The pie chart of the asset data will have five large slices, representing the five asset categories—Cash, U.S. Stocks, Non-U.S. Stocks, Bonds, and Other. The Total Assets row, which you did not select as part of the data source, is not an asset category and should not be included in a pie chart.

To insert a pie chart:

1. Click the **Insert** tab on the Ribbon. The Ribbon displays the insert options.
2. In the Charts group, click the **Pie** button. The Pie Charts gallery opens.
3. In the 2-D Pie section, click **Pie** (the first pie chart in the first row). The pie chart is inserted in the Assets sheet, and three new tabs appear on the Ribbon with a label identifying them as Chart Tools contextual tabs. See Figure 4-3.

Figure 4-3 Pie chart inserted into the Assets sheet

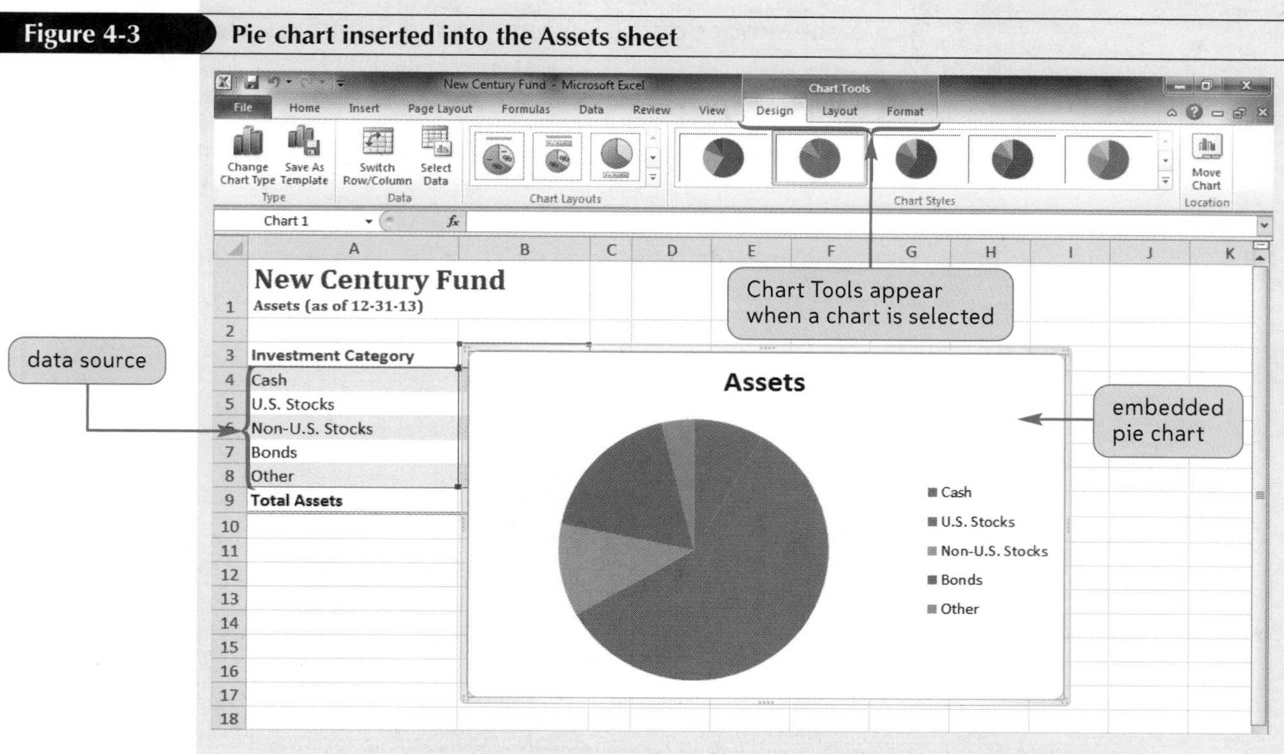

Each slice in the pie chart you just created is a different size based on its value in the data series. The biggest slice of the pie represents U.S. Stocks, which is the category that has the largest value in the data series. The smallest slice of the pie represents the Other category, which has the smallest value in the data series.

When you create or select a chart, three Chart Tools contextual tabs appear on the Ribbon. The Design, Layout, and Format tabs provide additional commands for working with the chart's content and appearance. On the Design tab, you set the chart's overall design. On the Layout tab, you work with individual elements of the chart, such as the chart's title. On the Format tab, you format graphic shapes found in the chart, such as the chart's border or markers placed in the chart. When you select a worksheet cell or another object that is not a chart, the Chart Tools contextual tabs disappear until you reselect the chart.

Moving a Chart to a Different Worksheet

By default, a chart is inserted as an embedded chart. The advantage of an embedded chart is that you can display the chart alongside any text or graphics that can explain the chart's meaning and purpose. However, an embedded chart covers worksheet cells, which might contain data and formulas. You'll learn how to move and resize an embedded chart in this section.

You can move an embedded chart to a different worksheet in the workbook or you can move it into a chart sheet (a sheet that contains only the chart and no worksheet cells). Likewise, you can move a chart from a chart sheet and embed it in any worksheet you select. The Move Chart dialog box provides options for moving charts between worksheets and chart sheets. You can also cut and paste a chart to a new location in the workbook.

The assets pie chart was embedded in the Assets worksheet by default. Ajita wants the chart embedded in the Summary Report worksheet. You will move the chart.

To move the embedded pie chart to the Summary Report worksheet:

1. In the Location group on the Chart Tools Design tab, click the **Move Chart** button. The Move Chart dialog box opens.

   Trouble? If you don't see the Chart Tools contextual tabs on the Ribbon, the chart is probably not selected. Click the chart in the Assets sheet to select it, and then repeat Step 1.

2. Click the **Object in** arrow to display a list of worksheets in the active workbook, and then click **Summary Report**. See Figure 4-4.

Figure 4-4 Move Chart dialog box

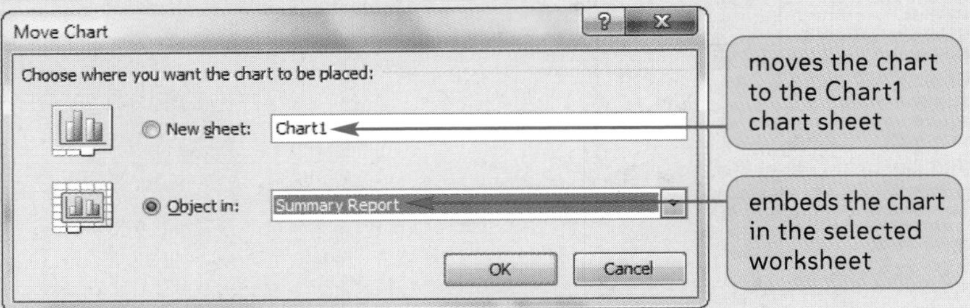

3. Click the **OK** button. The embedded pie chart moves from the Assets worksheet to the Summary Report worksheet, and remains selected.

Moving and Resizing Charts

An embedded chart might cover other data in the worksheet or be placed in an awkward location. You can fix this by moving or resizing the embedded chart. To do so, first select the chart, which displays a **selection box**, which is a box surrounding the chart object that is used to move or resize the object. To move the chart, drag the selection box to a new location in the worksheet. To resize the chart, drag a **sizing handle**, which is a square or dot on the selection box that is used to change the object's width and height.

You will move and resize the assets pie chart so that it does not cover the data on the Summary Report worksheet.

To move and resize the assets pie chart:

Be sure to click the chart area; otherwise, elements in the chart might move.

1. Move the pointer over an empty area of the selected chart until the pointer changes to the move pointer and the "Chart Area" ScreenTip appears.

2. Drag the chart down and to the left until its upper-left corner is in cell **A13**, and then release the mouse button. The chart moves to a new location, but it still covers some data.

   Trouble? If the pie chart resizes or does not move to the new location, you probably didn't drag the chart from the chart area. Press the Ctrl+Z keys to undo your last action, and then repeat Steps 1 and 2, being sure to drag the pie chart from the chart area.

TIP

To retain the chart's proportions, hold down the Shift key as you drag the sizing handle.

3. Move the pointer over the sizing handle in the lower-right corner of the chart until the pointer changes to the resize pointer, and then drag the sizing handle up to cell **E21**. The chart resizes to cover the range A13:E21 and remains selected. See Figure 4-5.

Figure 4-5 **Moved and resized pie chart**

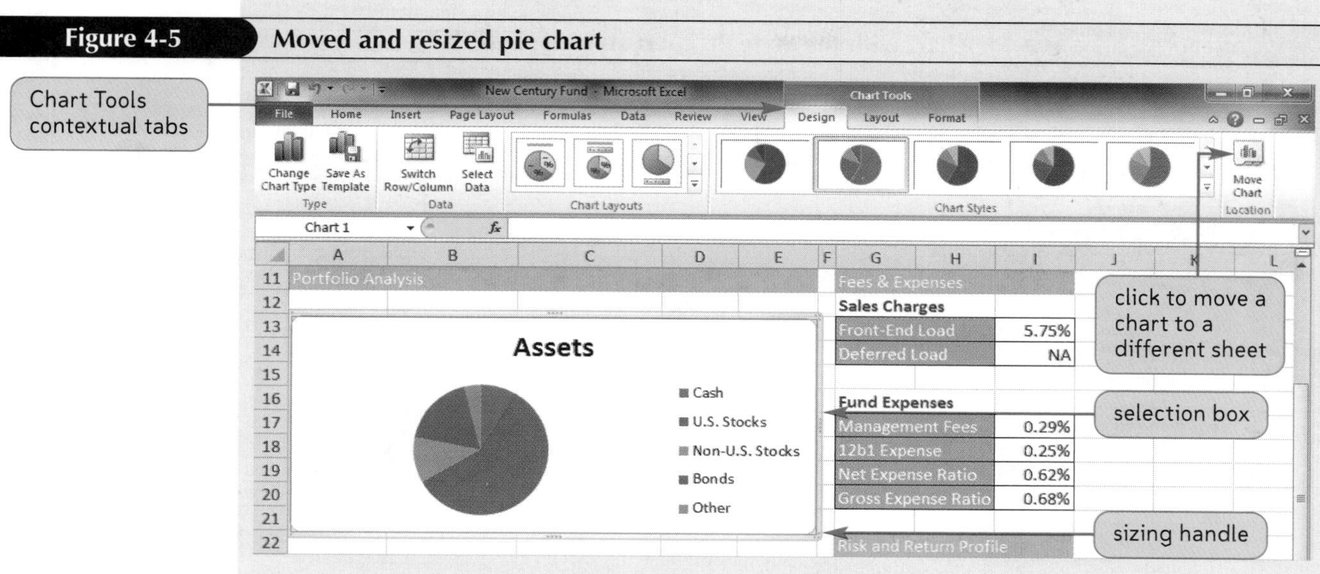

Designing a Pie Chart

Charts include individual elements that can be formatted, including the chart area, the chart title, the plot area, data markers, and a legend. You can choose which of these elements to include in the chart as well as how each element looks. You can make these changes using a built-in style that formats the entire chart or by selecting and formatting an individual element.

To apply formatting to an individual chart element, you can double-click that chart element to open a dialog box with format options specific to the selected element. You can also open the dialog box by clicking the appropriate element button on the Layout tab.

Choosing a Chart Style

A chart style is similar to a cell style or a table style in that it applies several formats to the chart at one time. When you create a chart, Excel applies the default chart style for that chart type. For example, the default pie chart style applies a solid color to each slice. You can quickly change the appearance of the entire chart by selecting a different chart style in the Chart Styles gallery.

Ajita wants you to use a style that gives each pie slice a rounded, three-dimensional look.

To apply a different chart style to the assets pie chart:

1. Click the **Chart Tools Design** tab on the Ribbon, if necessary. The design options for charts appear on the Ribbon.
2. In the Chart Styles group, click the **More** button to open the Chart Styles gallery, and then click **Style 26** (the second style in the fourth row). Each pie slice now has a rounded, raised look. See Figure 4-6.

Figure 4-6 Pie chart with the Style 26 chart style applied

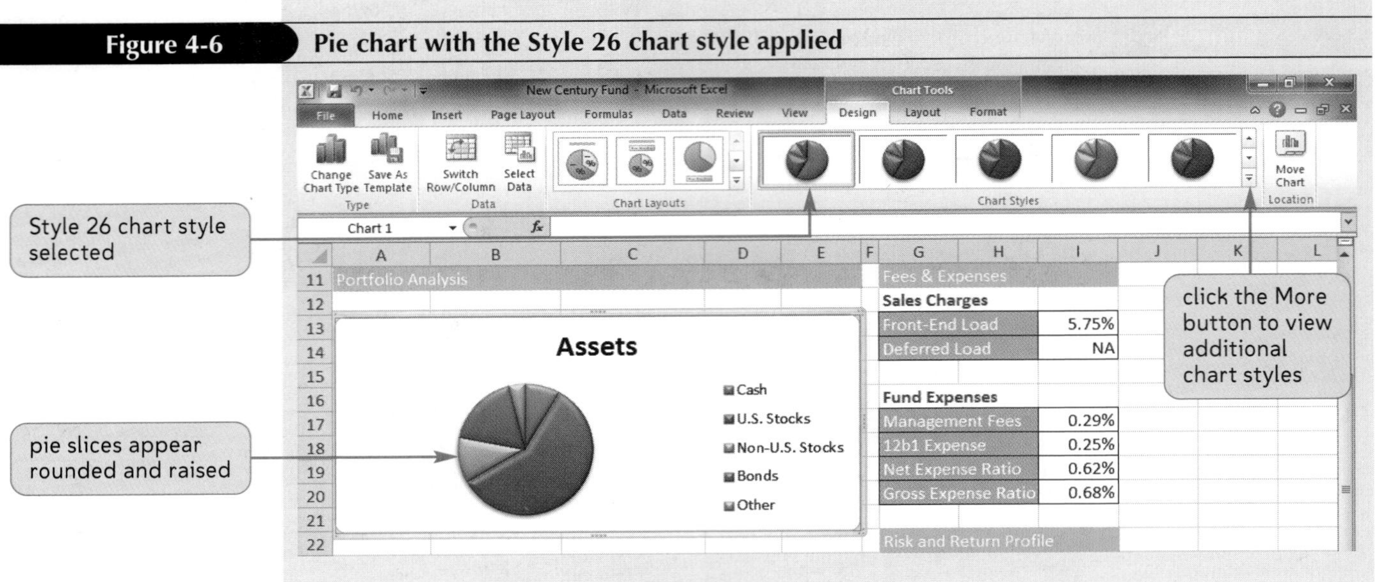

Choosing a Chart Layout

The built-in chart layouts specify which chart elements are displayed and how they are formatted. The chart layouts include some of the most common ways of displaying different charts. Each chart type has its own collection of layouts. Depending on the pie chart layout you choose, you can hide or display the chart title, display a chart legend or place legend labels in the pie slices, and add percentages to the pie slices.

To clarify the relationship between the pie slices in the assets pie chart, Ajita wants each slice to display its percentage of the whole. You'll do this by changing the chart layout.

To apply the Layout 6 chart layout to the assets pie chart:

1. In the Chart Layouts group on the Chart Tools Design tab, click the **More** button to open the Chart Layouts gallery.
2. Click **Layout 6** (the third layout in the second row). Percentages appear on or next to the slices in the pie chart, and the chart title and legend remain in their original locations. See Figure 4-7.

TIP

Percentages appear on pie slices large enough to fit the number; otherwise, percentages appear next to the slices in the chart area.

Figure 4-7 Pie chart with the Layout 6 chart layout

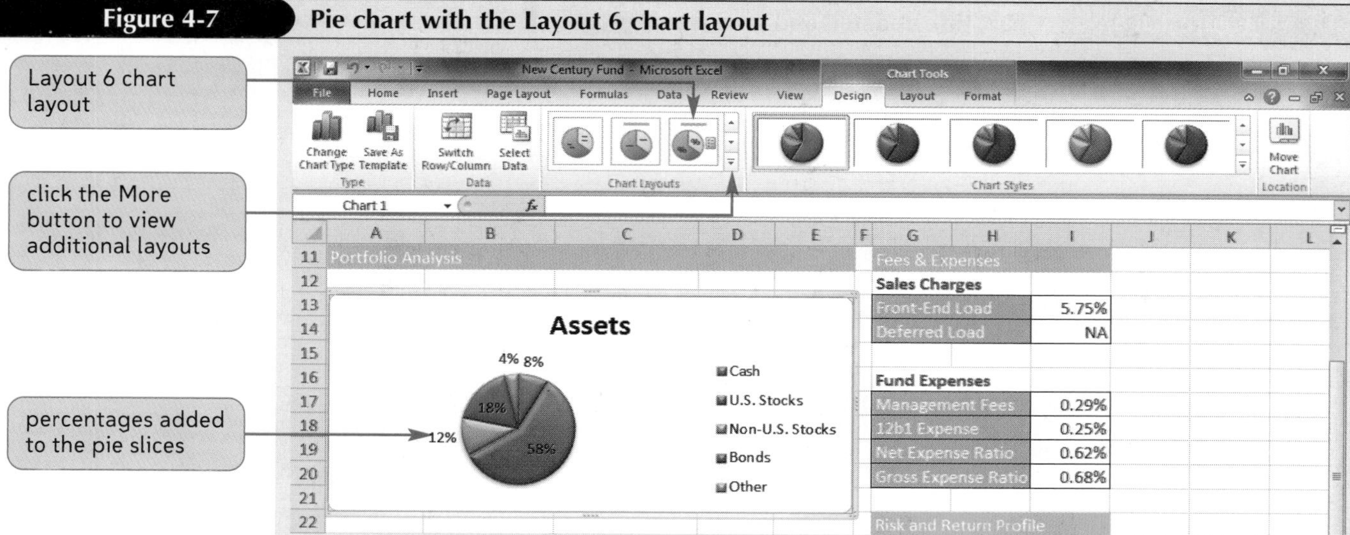

Trouble? Depending on your monitor size and resolution, your chart might look different from that shown in Figure 4-7. This does not affect your work with the pie chart.

With the percentages displayed on the pie chart, clients can quickly see how the assets of the New Century Fund are allocated. For example, 58 percent of the New Century Fund is invested in U.S. stocks and 12 percent in non-U.S. stocks. To fit the percentages, Excel reduced the size of the pie chart in the plot area. You'll format some of the other chart elements smaller to make more space for the pie.

Formatting the Chart Title

The chart title provides a description of the chart. By default, Excel uses the series name for the chart title. You can edit or replace the default chart title. You can also format the text of the chart title just like you can any other text in the workbook.

Ajita wants a more descriptive chart title. You'll also reduce the title's font size to make more room for the pie chart.

TIP

You can revise the title text rather than replacing it by double-clicking the chart title to place the insertion point in the text, and then editing the text.

To change and resize the chart title:

1. Click the **chart title** to select it. A selection box appears around the chart title.
2. Type **Allocation of Assets**. The new chart title appears in the formula bar, but no changes are made to the title in the chart itself.
3. Press the **Enter** key. The chart title is updated with the entry and remains selected.
4. Click the **Home** tab on the Ribbon.
5. In the Font group, click the **Font Size arrow**, and then click **12**. The chart title shrinks from 18 points to 12 points, and the pie chart increases in size to fill the extra space. See Figure 4-8.

Figure 4-8 Chart title updated and formatted

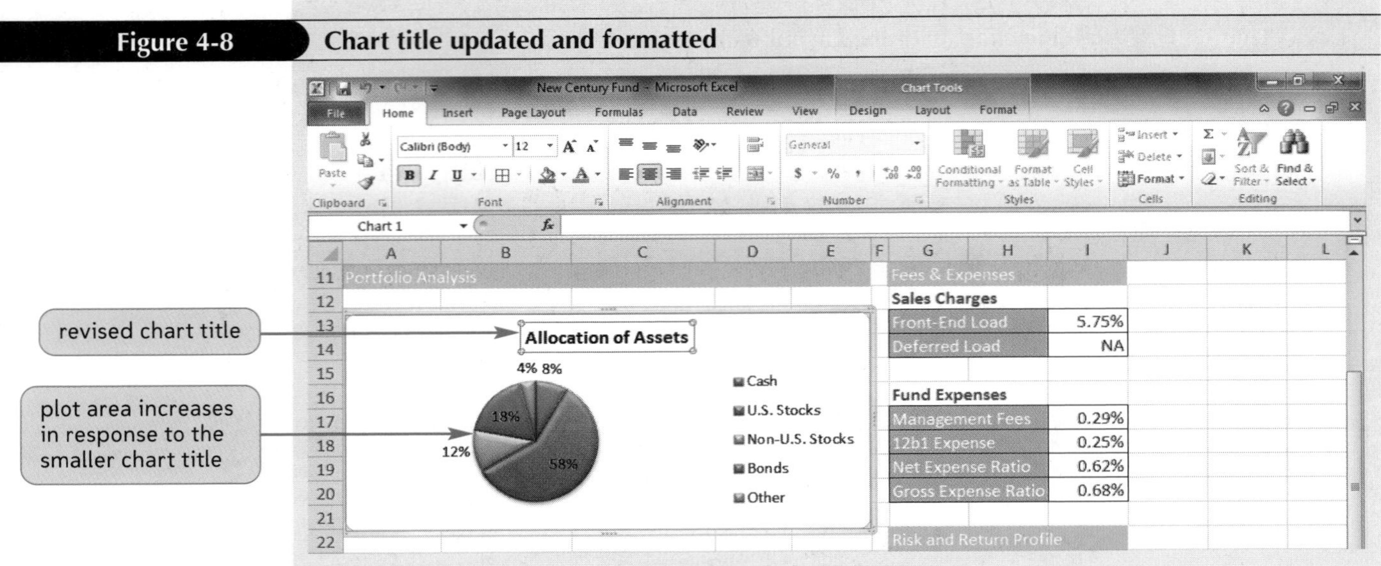

Formatting the Chart Legend

The chart legend identifies each of the data series in the chart. With a pie chart, the legend shows the colors used for each slice and the corresponding category values. In this case, the category values are the different asset groups. As with the other elements, you can choose the location of the legend and format it using tools on the Chart Tools Layout tab.

Ajita wants you to move the legend to the left side of the chart and add an orange border around the legend text to distinguish it from the rest of the chart.

To format the chart legend:

1. Click the **Chart Tools Layout** tab on the Ribbon.
2. In the Labels group, click the **Legend** button, and then click **Show Legend at Left**. The legend moves to the left side of the chart.
3. In the Labels group, click the **Legend** button, and then click **More Legend Options**. The Format Legend dialog box opens, providing more advanced options to format the element's appearance.
4. Click **Border Color** in the list on the left side of the dialog box. The Border Color options appear on the right side of the dialog box.
5. Click the **Solid line** option button. Two options related to border colors appear in the dialog box.
6. Click the **Color** button to open the color palette, and then click **Orange, Accent 6, Lighter 40%** (the last color in the fourth row) in the Theme Colors section. See Figure 4-9.

Figure 4-9 **Border Color options in the Format Legend dialog box**

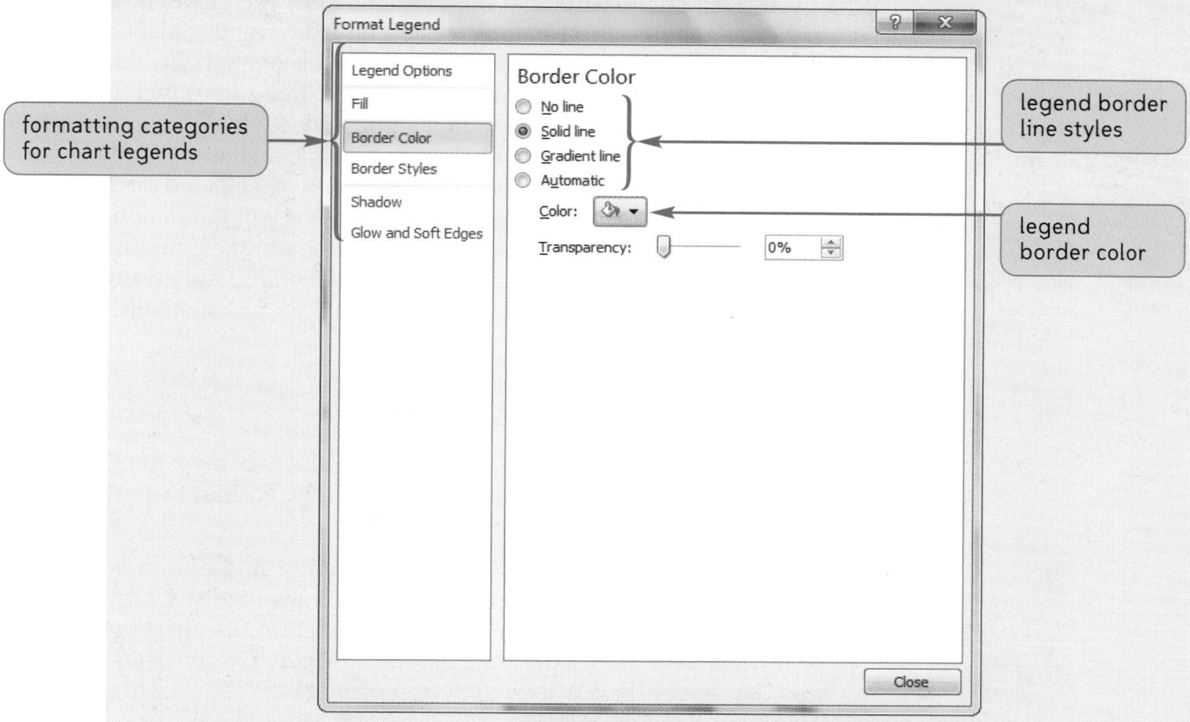

Format Legend

Legend Options
Fill
Border Color
Border Styles
Shadow
Glow and Soft Edges

Border Color
No line
Solid line
Gradient line
Automatic
Color:
Transparency: 0%

Close

formatting categories for chart legends

legend border line styles

legend border color

7. Click the **Close** button. The legend now has a light orange border.
8. Click the **chart area** to deselect the legend. See Figure 4-10.

Figure 4-10 **Chart legend moved and formatted**

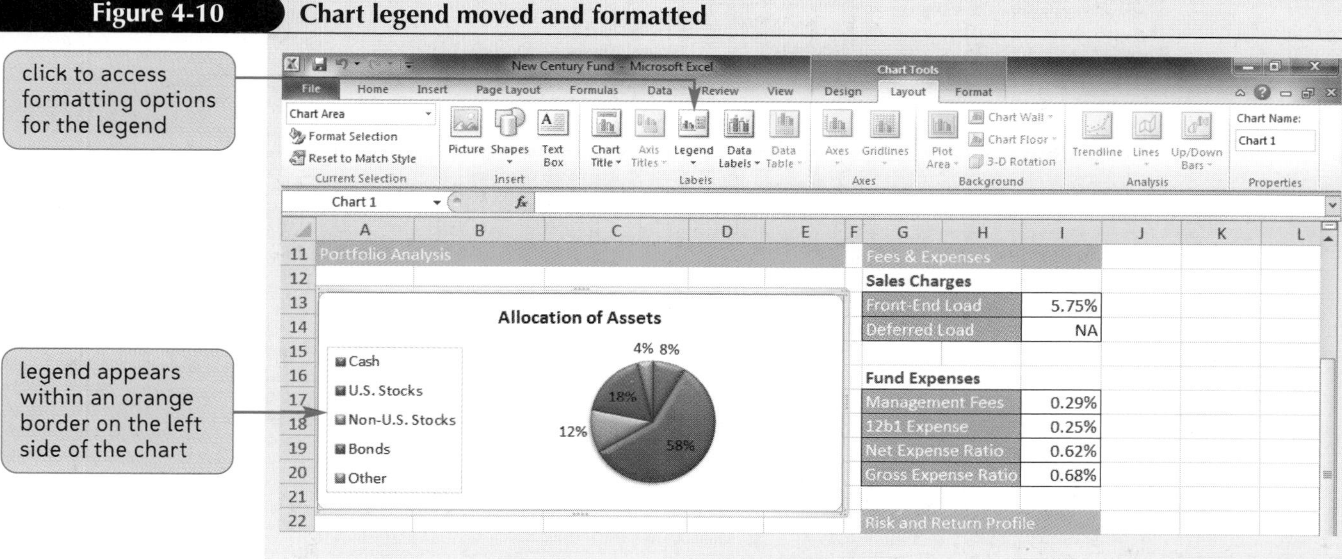

Formatting Data Labels

Data labels provide descriptive text for the individual data markers, such as pie slices. When you use a chart layout that shows data labels, each label is placed where it best fits—either on the pie slice or along its side. You can use this placement to specify that all data labels appear next to their pie slices. Labels placed outside of the pie might appear far from their slices. In those cases, **leader lines**, lines that connect each data label to its corresponding data marker, can be added. Note that a leader line disappears when enough space exists in the chart area to place a label next to its slice.

You added data labels to the assets chart when you selected the Layout 6 chart layout. These percentage values were placed where they best fit in relation to the pie slices. For some asset categories, the label appears within the pie slice; for others, the label appears next to the slice. For consistency and for ease of reading, Ajita wants all the data labels to appear outside the pie chart. You'll show leader lines for the labels.

To format the pie chart's data labels:

1. In the Labels group on the Chart Tools Layout tab, click the **Data Labels** button, and then click **More Data Label Options**. The Format Data Labels dialog box opens with the Label Options displayed.
2. In the Label Position section, click the **Outside End** option button. In the Label Contains section, the Percentage and the Show Leader Lines check boxes are already checked because these were included in the chart layout you applied earlier. These options set the data labels to display percentages outside the pie chart and use leader lines when needed to connect the labels with their corresponding pie slices. See Figure 4-11.

Figure 4-11 Label Options in the Format Data Labels dialog box

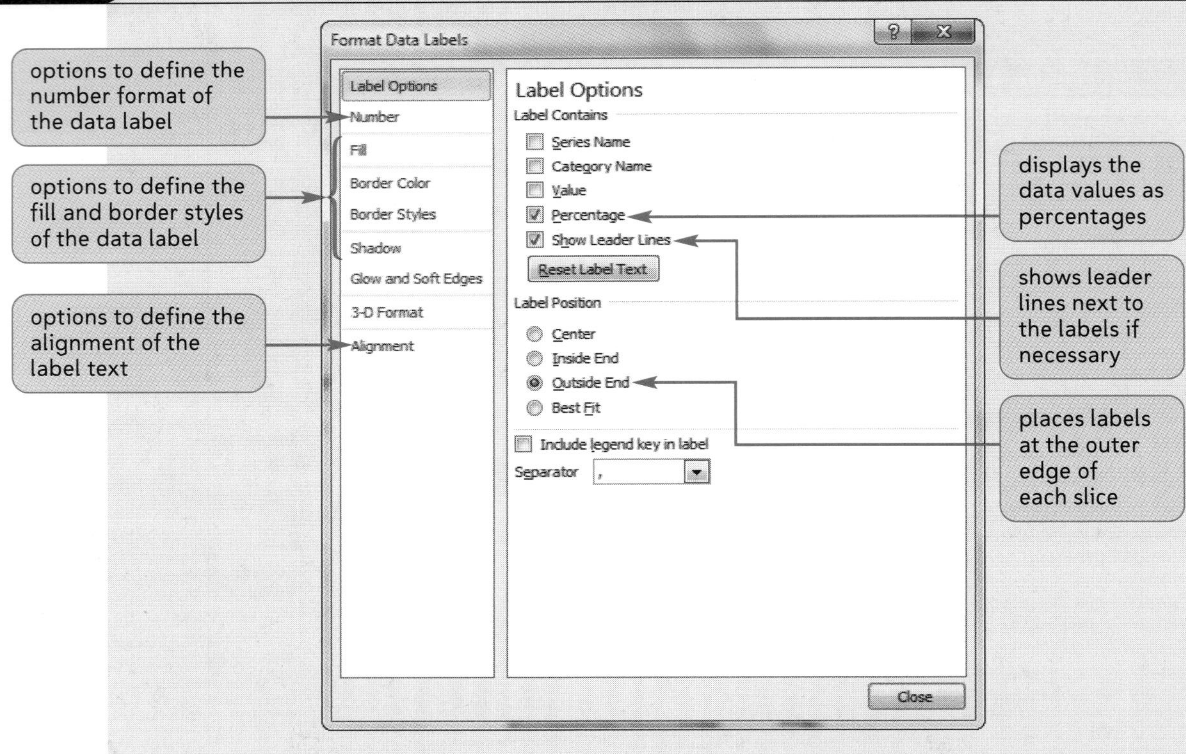

3. Click **Number** in the list on the left side of the dialog box. The options related to number formats appear in the dialog box.
4. Click **Percentage** in the Category box, and then verify that **2** appears in the Decimal places box. The percentage values for each slice show two decimal places for more accuracy.
5. Click the **Close** button. The data labels appear as percentages on the outer edges of the slices. Note that leader lines don't appear in the pie chart because the chart area has enough space to place the labels close to their slices. See Figure 4-12.

Figure 4-12 Formatted data labels

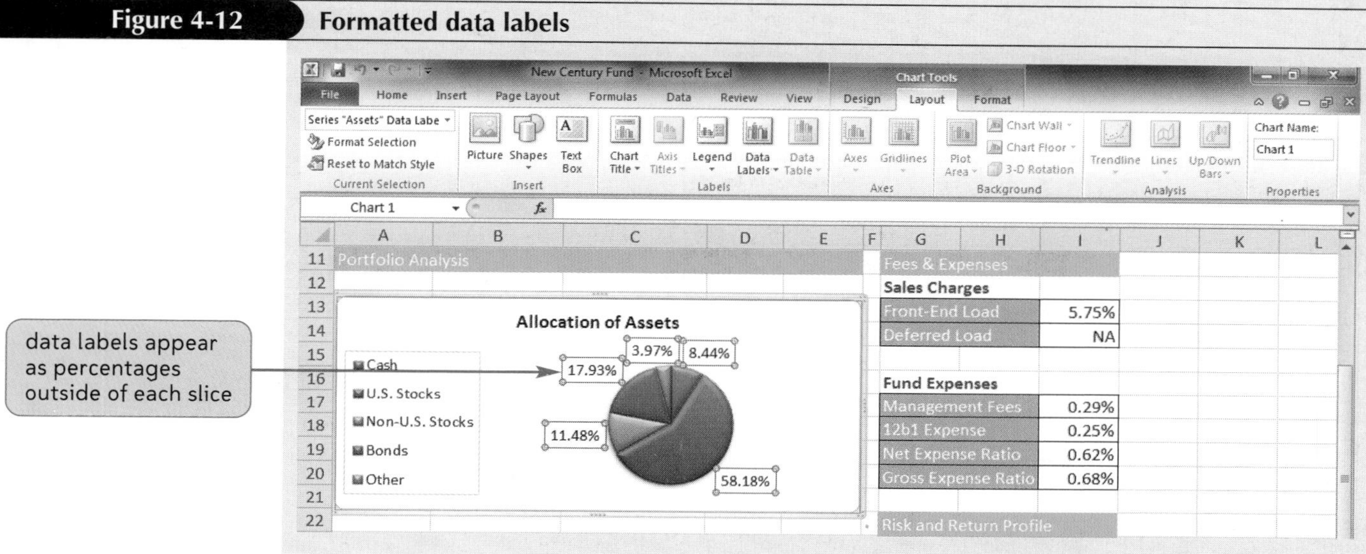

Changing Pie Slice Colors

Pie slice colors should be as distinct as possible to avoid confusion. Using distinct colors is especially important for adjacent slices. Depending on the printer quality or the monitor resolution, similarly colored slices might be difficult to distinguish in the final report. You can change the colors used for each slice. Because each slice in a pie chart represents a different value in the series, you must format each slice rather than the entire data series.

In the assets pie chart, the slices for Cash, Bonds, and Other have similar colors. You'll change the fill color of the Other and Cash slices.

To select and format pie slices in the assets pie chart:

1. Click the pie to select the entire data series.
2. Click the light blue **Other** slice, which represents 3.97 percent of the pie. Only that value, or slice, is selected.
3. Click the **Home** tab on the Ribbon.
4. In the Font group, click the **Fill Color button arrow**, and then click **Yellow** (the fourth color in the Standard Colors section). The Other slice and legend marker change to yellow.
5. Click the dark blue **Cash** slice, which covers 8.44 percent of the pie.

6. In the Font group, click the **Fill Color button arrow**, and then click **Light Blue** (the seventh color in the Standard Colors section). The Cash slice and legend marker change to light blue. Each slice of the pie now has a distinct color. See Figure 4-13.

Figure 4-13 **Pie slices with new colors**

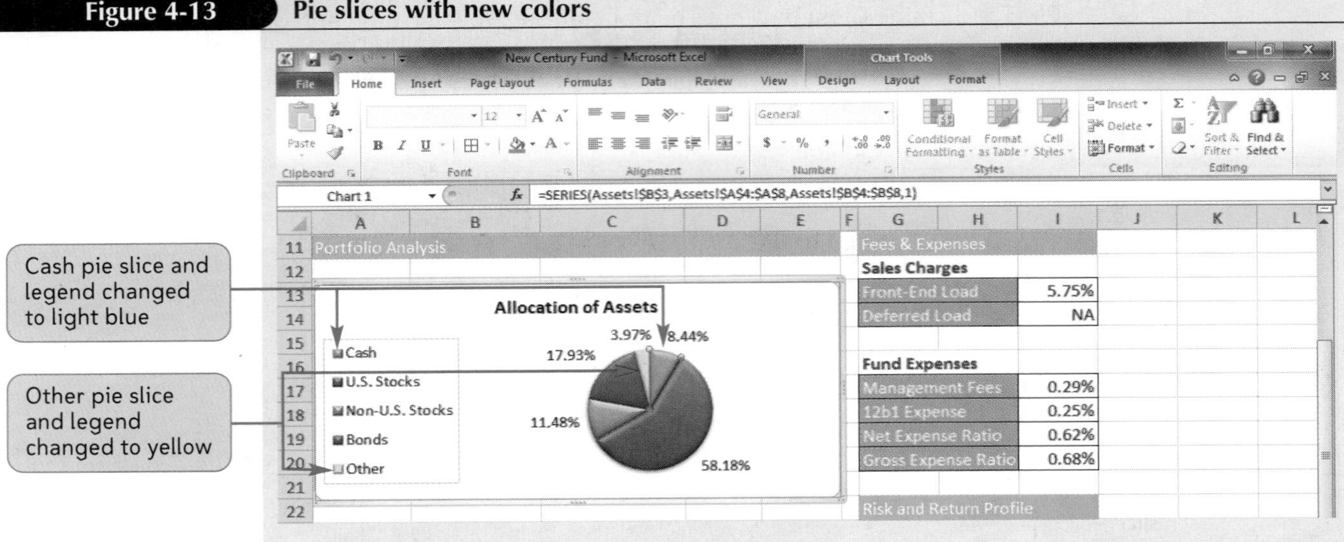

The pie chart in the summary report clearly shows that most assets of the New Century Fund are allocated toward U.S. stocks.

INSIGHT

Exploding a Pie Chart

Pie slices do not need to be fixed within the pie. An **exploded pie chart** moves one slice away from the others as if someone were taking the piece away from the pie. Exploded pie charts are useful for emphasizing one category above all of the others. For example, to emphasize how much of the New Century Fund is allocated toward U.S. stocks, you could explode that single slice, moving it away from the other slices in the pie.

To explode a pie slice, select that slice from the pie chart and then drag the slice away from the pie. You can also explode multiple slices by selecting each slice and dragging them away. To explode all of the slices, select the entire pie and drag the pointer away from the pie's center. Each slice will be exploded and separated from the others. Although you can explode more than one slice, the resulting pie chart is rarely effective as a visual aid to the reader.

Creating a Column Chart

A **column chart** displays values in different categories as columns; the height of each column is based on its value. Related to the column chart is the **bar chart**, which is a column chart turned on its side so that the length of each bar is based on its value.

Column and bar charts are superior to pie charts when the number of categories is large or the categories are close in value. It is easier to compare height or length than area. Figure 4-14 displays the same data as a pie chart and a column chart. As you can see, it's more difficult to determine which pie slice has the largest area and by how much. This is much simpler to determine with the column chart.

Figure 4-14 **Comparing pie charts and column charts**

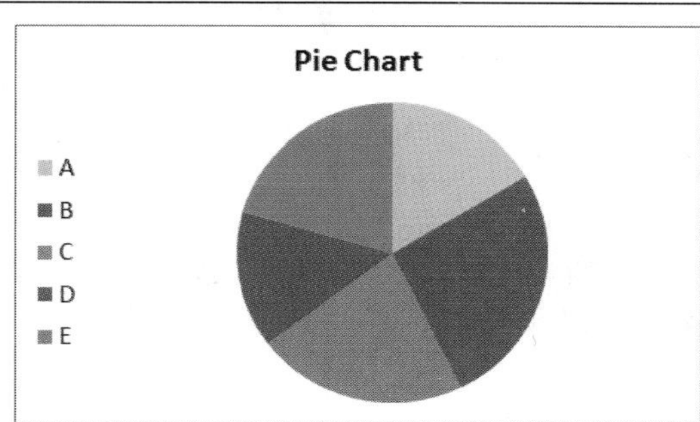

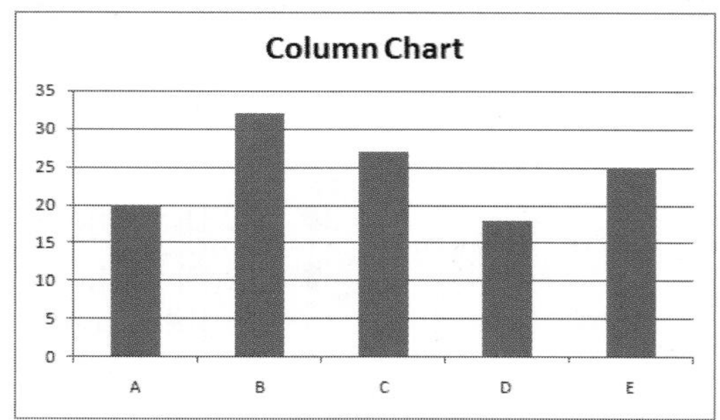

Column and bar charts can also be applied to a wider range of data than pie charts. For example, you can demonstrate how a set of values changes over time, such as the value of the New Century Fund over several years. You can also include several data series in a column or bar chart, such as the value of three funds over several years. The values from different data series are displayed in columns side by side. Pie charts usually show only one data series.

Inserting a Column Chart

The process for creating a column chart is the same as for creating a pie chart. First, you select the data source. Then, you select the type of chart you want to create. After the chart is embedded in the worksheet, you can move and resize the chart as well as change the chart's design, layout, and format.

The next part of the summary report lists the type of stocks being purchased by the fund. Each mutual fund invests in different kinds of stocks. Some funds are heavily invested in information technology, others in the service industry, and still others in manufacturing. Diversification (the distribution of investments among a variety of companies or sectors to limit losses in the event one company or sector has an economic downturn) is important, so all funds are invested to some degree in multiple economic sectors. The New Century Fund is invested in 12 different economic sectors, organized into the categories of information, services, and manufacturing.

Ajita wants you to create a chart that shows how the New Century Fund is distributed among the 12 sectors in which it is invested. A pie chart cannot display 12 categories effectively, so you will create a column chart to display this economic sector data. The columns will represent only one data series, so you'll use the 2-D Clustered Column chart type. A clustered column chart uses vertical rectangles to compare values across categories.

To create a column chart from the sector data:

1. Go to the **Sectors** worksheet, and then select the range **A3:C15**. This range covers the New Century Fund data that you want to include on the column chart.
2. Click the **Insert** tab on the Ribbon.
3. In the Charts group, click the **Column** button, and then click the **Clustered Column** chart (the first chart in the 2-D Column section). The column chart is inserted in the Sectors worksheet, and the Chart Tools Design tab on the Ribbon is selected.
4. In the Location group on the Chart Tools Design tab, click the **Move Chart** button. The Move Chart dialog box opens. You'll move the chart to the Summary Report worksheet.

5. Click the **Object in** arrow, click **Summary Report**, and then click the **OK** button. The column chart moves to the Summary Report worksheet.
6. In the Summary Report worksheet, click a blank spot in the chart area of the column chart to make sure the chart is selected.
7. Drag the selected column chart down so its upper-left corner is in cell **A23**.
8. Drag the sizing handle in the lower-right corner of the chart until the chart covers the range **A23:E37**. The chart is resized smaller. See Figure 4-15.

Figure 4-15 Column chart of investment sectors in the New Century Fund

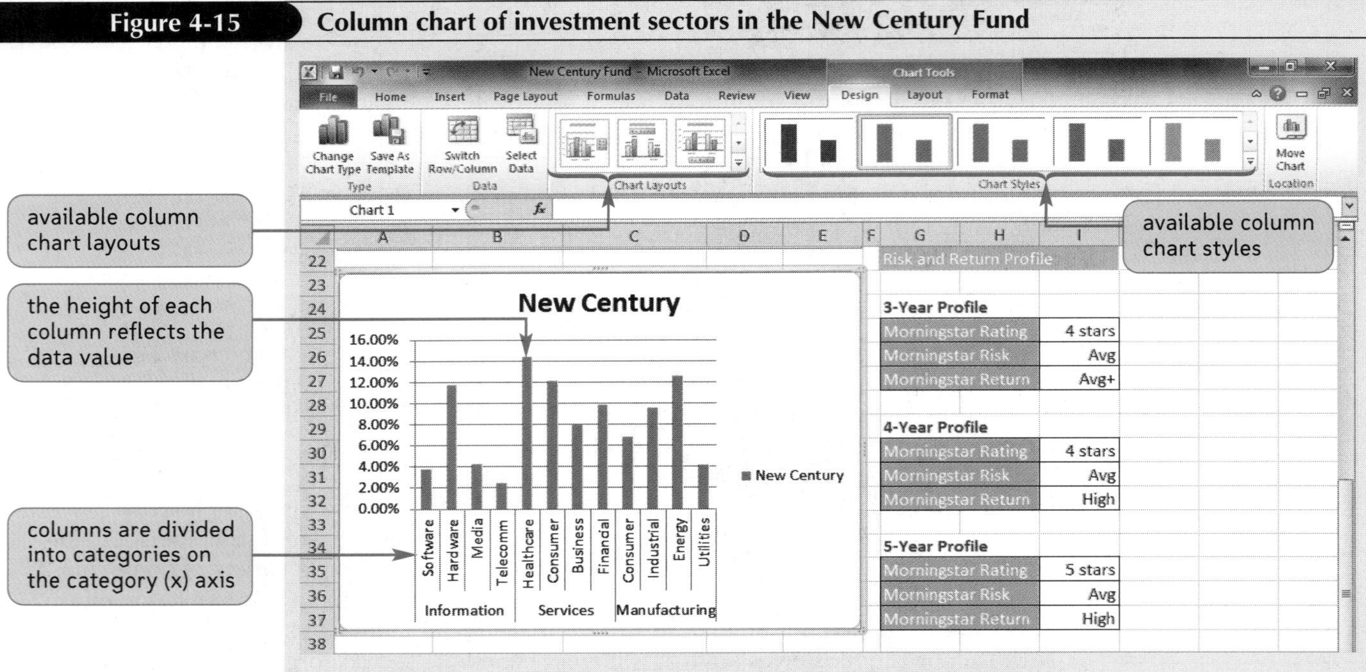

The column chart shows that the New Century Fund is most heavily invested in hardware information technology, healthcare and consumer services, and energy manufacturing. On the other hand, the fund does not invest much in software, media, and telecommunications.

Formatting a Column Chart Title and Legend

The Design tab provides a gallery of column chart layouts and a gallery of column chart styles. As with the pie chart you created, you can design the appearance of a column chart by selecting one of the chart styles or formatting individual chart elements. The default column chart layout includes a title and legend. When a chart has only one data series—such as the column chart you just created—the chart title and legend are redundant.

You will remove the legend, and then edit and format the chart title to provide a more descriptive title.

To remove the legend and format the chart title of the column chart:

1. Click the **Chart Tools Layout** tab on the Ribbon.
2. In the Labels group, click the **Legend** button, and then click **None**. The chart legend is removed from the chart, and the column chart resizes to fill the available space.
3. Click the chart title to select it, and then click the **Home** tab on the Ribbon.
4. In the Font group, click the **Font Size arrow**, and then click **12**. The chart title is reduced to 12 points, and remains selected.
5. Type **Sector Percentages** as the new chart title, and then press the **Enter** key.

Editing the Axis Scale and Text

The vertical or value axis shows the range of series values, and the horizontal or category axis shows the category values. The range of values, or **scale**, of an axis is based on the values in the data source. The default scale usually ranges from 0 (if the data source has no negative values) up through the maximum value. If the scale includes negative values, it ranges from the minimum value up through the maximum value. Excel divides the scale into regular intervals, which are marked on the axis with tick marks and labels. For example, the scale of the vertical axis for the Sector Percentages chart ranged from 0.00 percent up to 16.00 percent in increments of 2.00 percent. Having more tick marks at smaller intervals could make the chart more difficult to read because the tick mark labels might start to overlap. Likewise, having fewer tick marks at larger intervals could make the chart less informative. Major tick marks identify the main units on the chart axis. You can also add minor tick marks to identify smaller intervals between the major tick marks. Gridlines extend the tick marks across the plot area.

Some charts involve multiple data series that have vastly different values. In those instances, you can plot one data series against a **primary axis**, which usually appears along the left side of the chart, and the other against a **secondary axis**, which is usually placed on the right side of the chart. The two axes can use different scales and labels.

By default, no titles appear next to the value and category axes. This is fine when the axis labels are self-explanatory; otherwise, you can add descriptive axis titles. In general, you should avoid adding extra chart elements such as axis titles when that information is easily understood from other parts of the chart.

Ajita thinks that the value axis scale is too crowded and wants tick marks placed at 5 percent intervals, ranging from 0 percent to 25 percent. You will modify the scale of the value axis.

To change the scale of the vertical axis:

1. Click the **Chart Tools Layout** tab on the Ribbon.
2. In the Axes group, click the **Axes** button, point to **Primary Vertical Axis**, and then click **More Primary Vertical Axis Options**. The Format Axis dialog box opens with the Axis Options displayed. The value axis options are set to Auto, which causes Excel to set the values.
3. Next to Maximum, click the **Fixed** option button, and then type **0.25** in the box. The maximum value will be 25 percent.
4. Next to Major Unit, click the **Fixed** option button, and then enter **0.05** in the box. The major tick marks will appear at 5 percent intervals. See Figure 4-16.

Figure 4-16 Axis options in the Format Axis dialog box

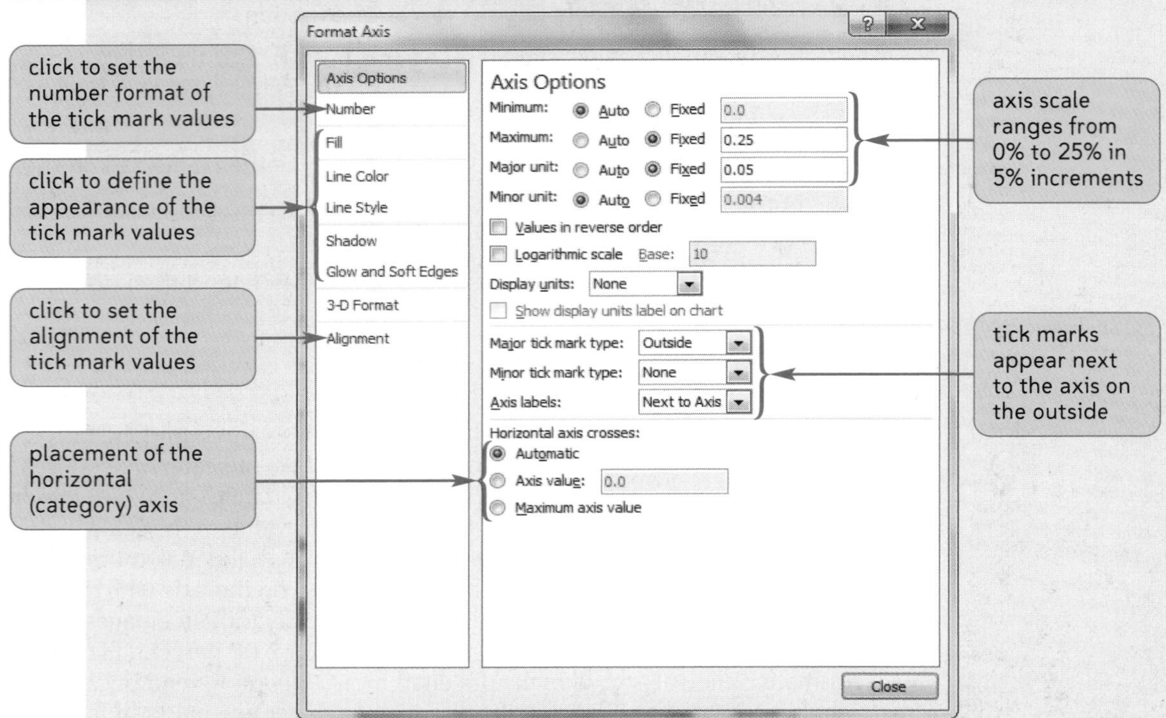

5. Click **Number** on the left side of the dialog box, make sure **Percentage** is selected in the Category box, and then type **0** in the Decimal places box. The percentage values in the vertical axis will show no decimal places.
6. Click the **Close** button. The percentages on the value axis range from 0 percent to 25 percent in 5 percent intervals with no decimal places.

These changes make the value axis easier to read. Ajita also thinks that the font size of both the value axis and the category axis is too large, dominating the rest of the graph. You will reduce the font size of the axes so that more of the chart area is available for the column chart itself.

To modify the font size of the axis titles and labels:

1. Make sure that the vertical axis is still selected, and then click the **Home** tab on the Ribbon.
2. In the Font group, click the **Font Size arrow**, and then click **8**. The values displayed in the vertical axis are smaller, leaving more room for the data series.
3. Click anywhere within the **category axis** to select it, and then change the axis font size to **8** points. The revised column chart is easier to read. See Figure 4-17.

Figure 4-17 **Formatted chart axes**

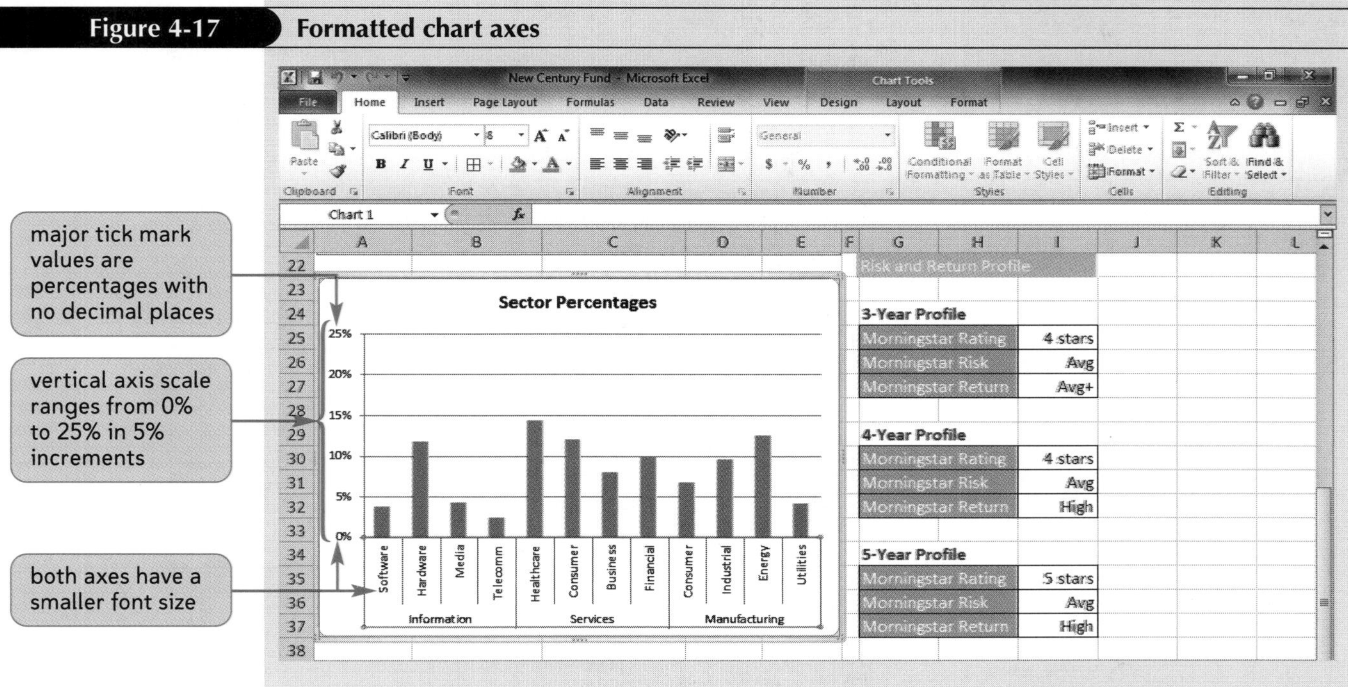

Formatting the Chart Columns

In a pie chart, each slice or data marker has a different format. In a column chart, all of the columns usually have a common format because the columns are distinguished by height, not color. (However, you can format individual columns in a data series to highlight a particular column value.) You can modify the appearance of the data markers in a column chart using a variety of formatting options.

Ajita thinks that the columns are spaced too widely and could be formatted more attractively. You will reduce the gap between the columns, and change their fill color and appearance to make the columns stand out.

TIP

You can also select a data series by clicking any of its columns in the column chart.

To format the chart columns:

1. Click the **Chart Tools Layout** tab on the Ribbon, and then click the **Chart Elements arrow** in the Current Selection group. The list includes each element you can select in the column chart.
2. Click **Series "New Century"**. All the columns for the data series in the chart are selected.
3. In the Current Selection group, click the **Format Selection** button. The Format Data Series dialog box opens with the Series Options displayed.
4. Drag the Gap width slider to **50%** to reduce the gap between adjacent columns. The columns become wider to fill the space.

   Trouble? If you cannot drag the Gap width slider to exactly 50%, type 50 in the Gap width box below the slider.
5. Click **Fill** on the left side of the dialog box, and then click the **Gradient fill** option button to fill the columns with a gradually changing mix of colors.

6. Click the **Direction** button to open a gallery of fill directions, and then click **Linear Right** (the fourth fill direction in the first row). The columns will have a gradient fill that blends to the right. See Figure 4-18.

Figure 4-18 **Fill options in the Format Data Series dialog box**

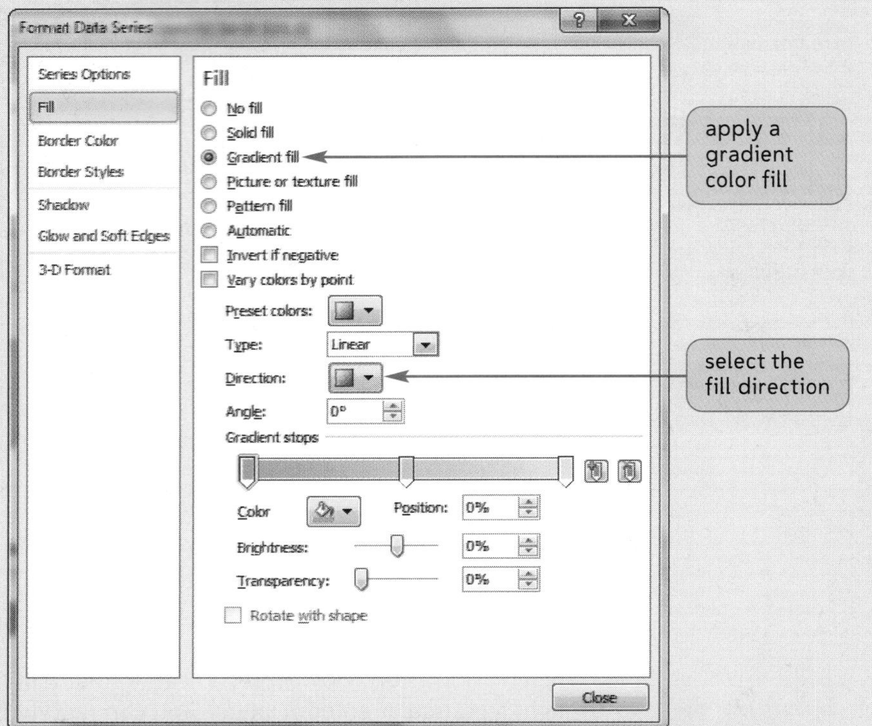

7. Click the **Close** button, and then click cell **A38** to deselect the chart. See Figure 4-19.

Figure 4-19 **Formatted chart columns**

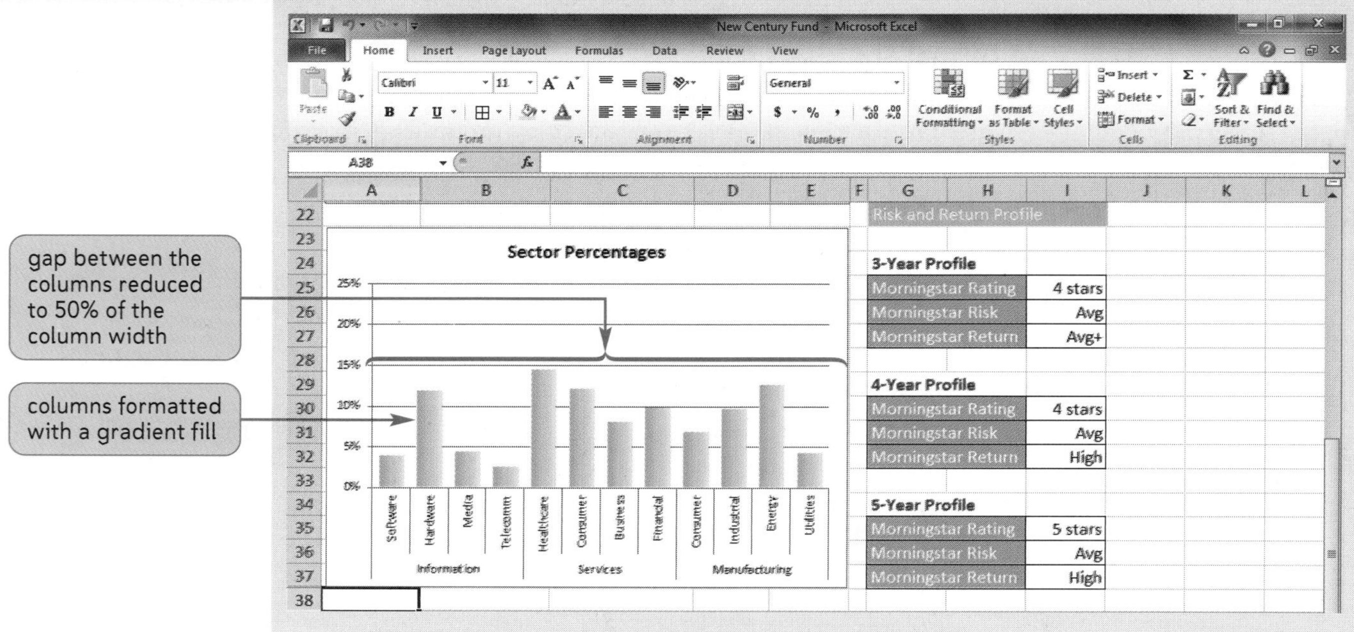

PROSKILLS

Written Communication: Communicating Effectively with Charts

Studies show that people interpret information easier in a graphic form than in a tabular format. As a result, charts can help communicate the real story underlying the facts and figures you present to colleagues and clients. A well-designed chart can illuminate the bigger picture that might be hidden by viewing only the numbers. However, poorly designed charts can mislead readers and make it more difficult to interpret data.

To create effective and useful charts, keep in mind the following tips as you design charts:

- **Keep it simple.** Do not clutter a chart with too many graphic elements. Focus attention on the data rather than on decorative elements that do not inform.
- **Focus on the message.** Design the chart to highlight the points you want to convey to readers.
- **Limit the number of data series used in the chart.** Line charts and column charts should display no more than three or four data series. Pie charts should have no more than six slices.
- **Use gridlines in moderation.** Gridlines should be used to provide only approximate values for the data markers. Having too many gridlines can obscure the data being graphed.
- **Choose colors carefully.** Display different data series in contrasting colors to make it easier to distinguish one series from another. Modify the default colors as needed to make them distinct on the screen and in the printed copy.
- **Limit your chart to a few text styles.** Use a maximum of two or three different text styles in the same chart. Having too many text styles in one chart can distract attention from the data.

The goal of written communication is always to inform the reader in the simplest, most accurate, and most direct way possible. When creating worksheets and charts, everything in the workbook should be directed toward that end.

Ajita is pleased with the two charts you've created and formatted. In the next session, you'll create a line chart and you'll explore options for creating 3-D charts, chart sheets, and sparklines.

REVIEW

Session 4.1 Quick Check

1. What are the three components of a data series?
2. In what two locations can a chart be placed?
3. What is the difference between the chart area and the plot area?
4. A data series contains values divided into 10 categories. Would this data be better displayed as a pie chart or a column chart? Why?
5. What are major tick marks, minor tick marks, and gridlines?
6. What is a bar chart?
7. How do you change the scale of a chart axis?

SESSION 4.2 VISUAL OVERVIEW

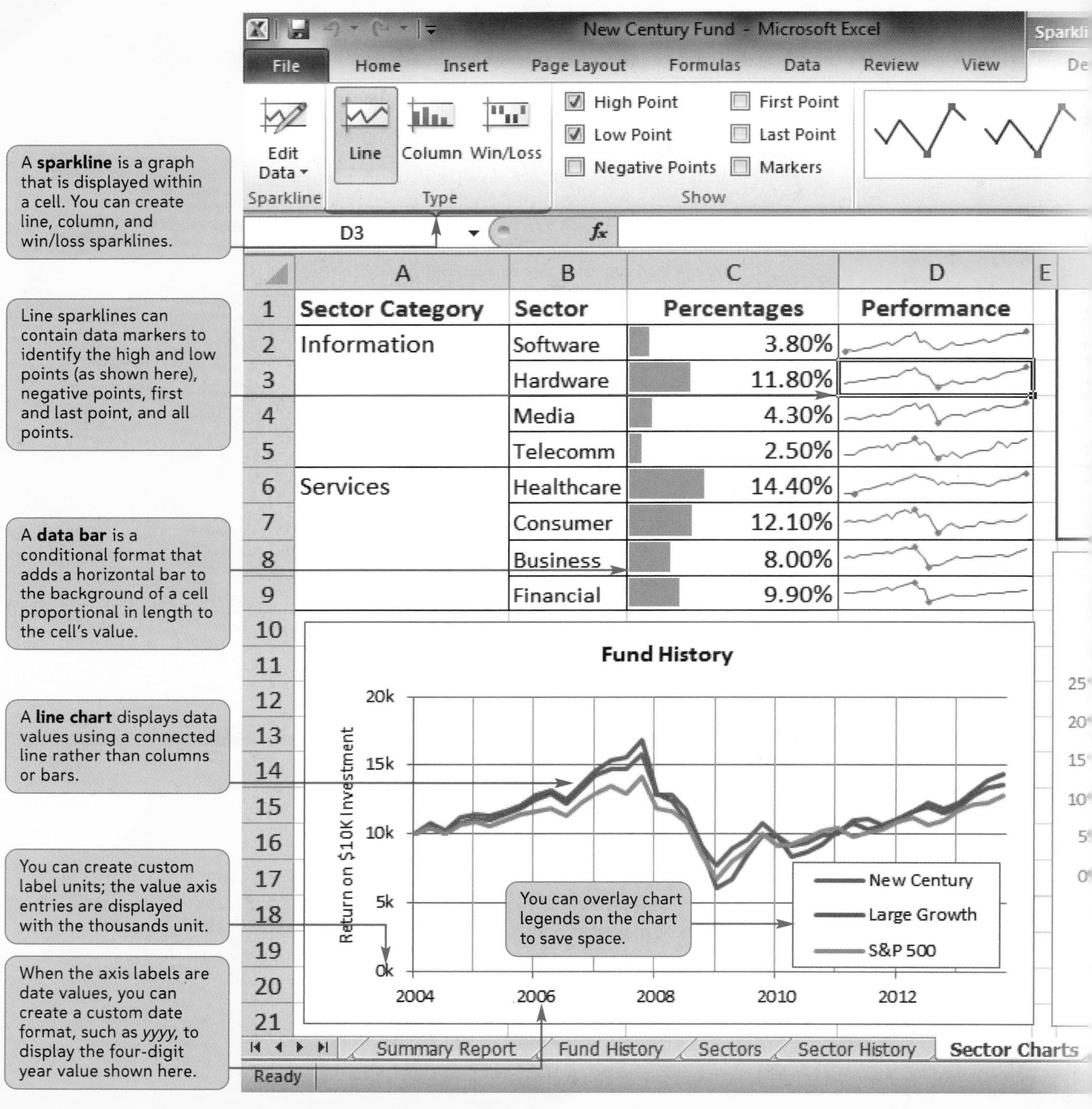

CHARTS, SPARKLINES, AND DATA BARS

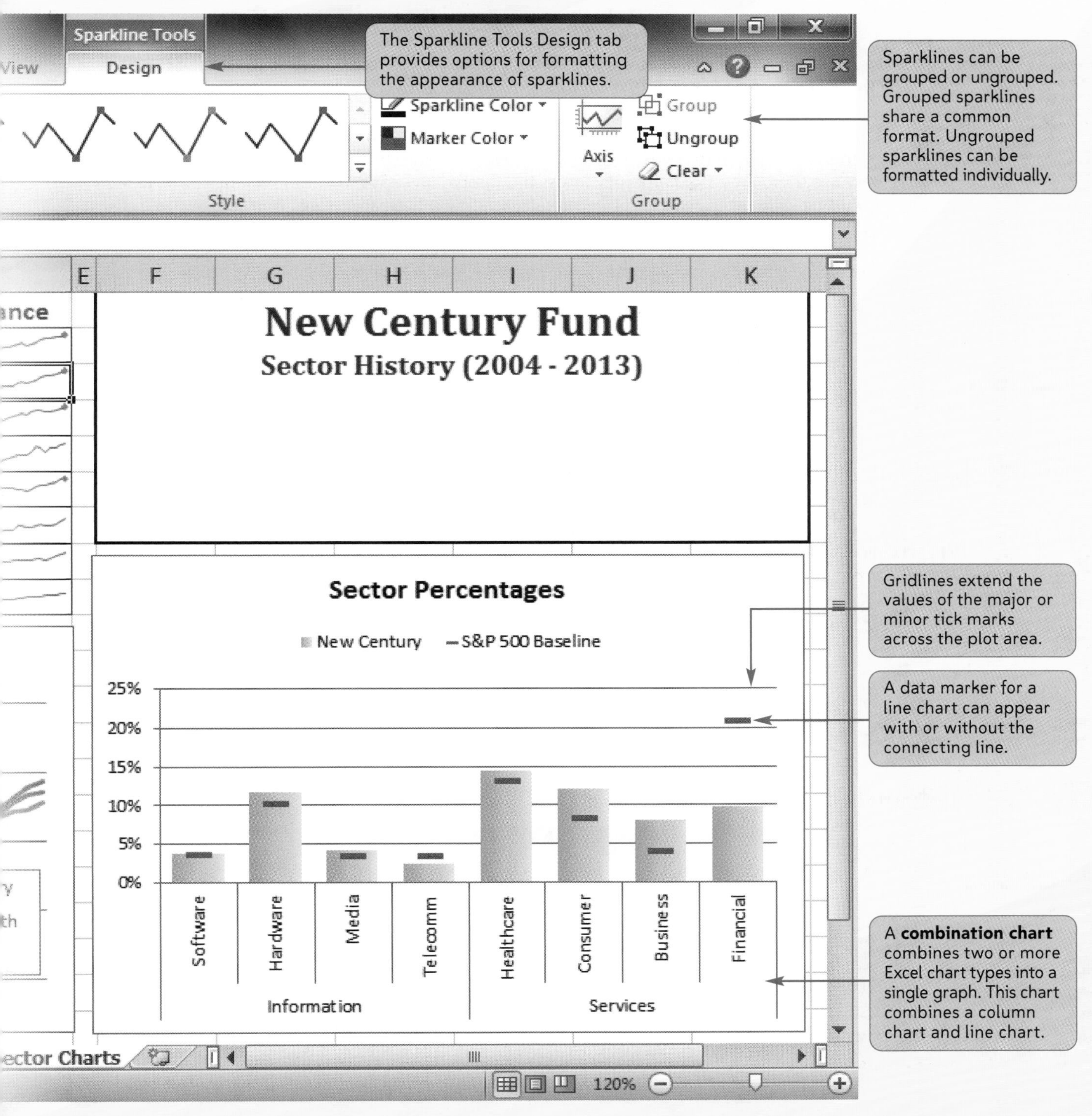

Sparklines can be grouped or ungrouped. Grouped sparklines share a common format. Ungrouped sparklines can be formatted individually.

Gridlines extend the values of the major or minor tick marks across the plot area.

A data marker for a line chart can appear with or without the connecting line.

A **combination chart** combines two or more Excel chart types into a single graph. This chart combines a column chart and line chart.

Creating a Line Chart

Line charts are typically used when the data consists of values drawn from categories that follow a sequential order at evenly spaced intervals, as with historical data in which the data values are recorded periodically such as monthly, quarterly, or yearly.

Ajita wants the summary report to include a chart of the performance history of the New Century Fund against two other investments: a large growth fund and the S&P 500. (The Standard and Poor's 500 is an index of 500 blue chip stocks that is commonly used to measure the performance of stocks and funds.)

Ajita has already entered this data in the Fund History worksheet. She calculated the quarterly value over the past 10 years of a $10,000 investment in each of the three funds. Because there are 40 data points across the three data series, a column chart of this data would be difficult to read and interpret. Instead, you'll create a line chart for the New Century Fund performance, plotting the value of the three investments against time.

To create the fund history line chart:

1. If you took a break at the end of the previous session, make sure that the New Century Fund workbook is open.
2. Go to the **Fund History** worksheet, and then select the range **A4:D44**. This range contains the data for the value of the New Century Fund, the average value of large growth funds, and the value of the S&P 500 for each quarter of 2004 through 2013.
3. Click the **Insert** tab on the Ribbon.
4. In the Charts group, click the **Line** button, and then click the **Line** chart (the first chart in the 2-D Line section). A line chart is embedded in the Fund History worksheet.
5. In the Location group on the Chart Tools Design tab, click the **Move Chart** button. The Move Chart dialog box opens.
6. Click the **Object in** arrow, and then click **Summary Report**.
7. Click the **OK** button. The line chart moves to the Summary Report worksheet.
8. Move and resize the chart to cover the range **D1:I9**. See Figure 4-20.

Figure 4-20 Line chart moved and resized

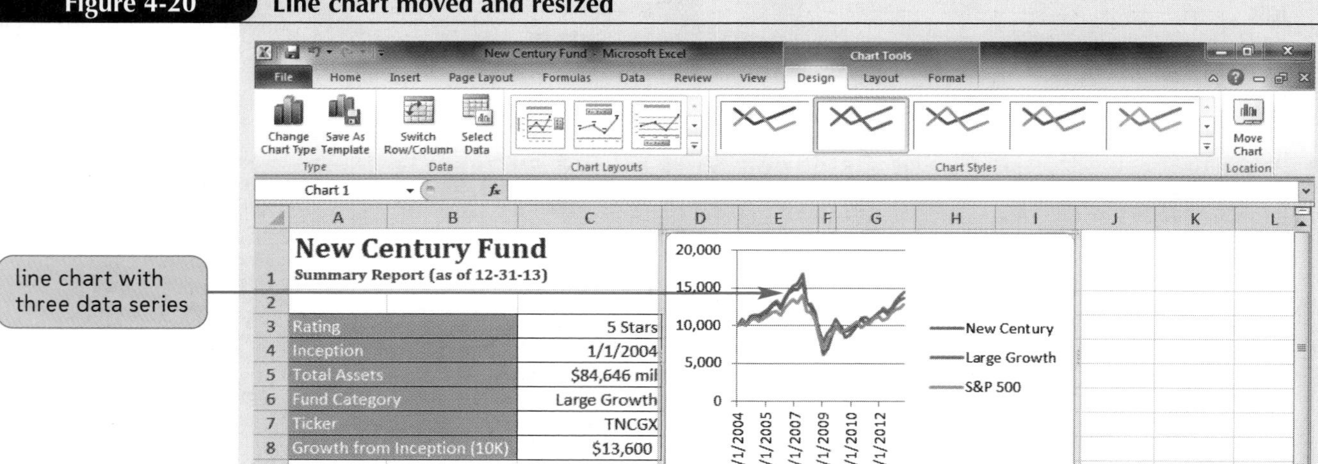

The line chart includes three data series—the New Century Fund, a competing large growth fund, and the S&P 500. Each series has a different line color. The line chart is crowded by the default size of the legend and axis labels. You'll reduce the font size of the axis and legend, and then add a chart title that describes the chart's content.

To edit the fund history line chart:

1. Click the **Chart Tools Layout** tab on the Ribbon.
2. In the Labels group, click the **Chart Title** button, and then click **Above Chart**. A chart title appears above the line chart surrounded by a selection box.
3. Type **Fund History**, and then press the **Enter** key. The new, descriptive title appears above the chart.
4. Click the **Home** tab on the Ribbon.
5. In the Font group, click the **Font Size arrow**, and then click **10**. The chart title is reduced to 10 points.
6. Click the **value axis** to select it, and then set its font size to **8** points.
7. Click the **category axis** to select it, and then set its font size to **8** points.
8. Click the **chart legend** to select it, and then set its font size to **8** points. The line chart resizes to fill the space left by the smaller chart titles, axes, and chart legend.

Next, you will change the scale used in the value axis so that the values range from $0 to $20,000 in $5,000 increments.

To modify the value axis scale:

1. Double-click the **value axis** to open the Format Axis dialog box.
2. Next to Maximum, click the **Fixed** option button, and then type **20000** in the box.
3. Next to Major Unit, click the **Fixed** option button, and then type **5000** in the box.
4. Click the **Close** button. The scale of the vertical axis ranges from $0 to $20,000 in $5,000 increments.

Formatting Date Labels

In addition to numbers, a scale can be based on dates, as the category axis in the Fund History line chart is. As with numerical scales, you can set the minimum and maximum dates to use in the scale's range. You can also set the major and minor units as days, months, or years to use for the scale's interval.

Ajita is more interested in the general trend from year to year than the exact dates on which the fund values were calculated. Because of this, she wants the scale of the category axis to show only years. You can save space by showing the labels every other year. To do this, you'll set the major tick marks to appear at two-year intervals, and then set the minor tick marks to appear at one-year intervals, even though you won't display the minor tick marks on the chart until later.

To format the category axis labels:

1. Double-click the **category axis** to open the Format Axis dialog box with the Axis Options displayed.
2. Next to Major unit, click the **Fixed** option button, type **2** in the box, and then select **Years** in the list. The major tick marks are set to every two years.
3. Next to Minor unit, click the **Fixed** option button, type **1** in the box, if necessary, and then select **Years** in the list. The minor tick marks are set to every year. See Figure 4-21.

Figure 4-21 **Date intervals for tick marks**

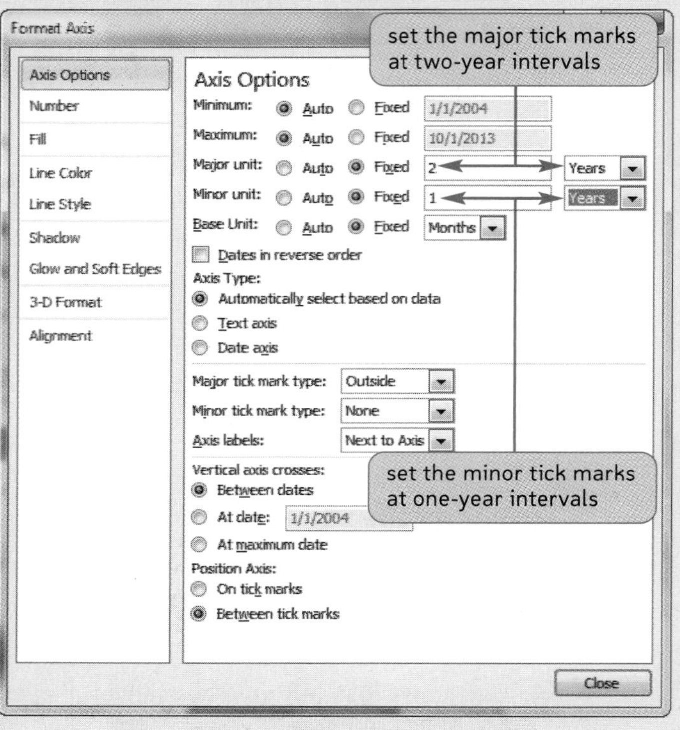

Next, you'll format the category labels to show the four-digit year value rather than the complete date. Excel does not have a built-in format to display only four-digit year values, but you can create a custom format to accomplish this.

Custom date formats use combinations of the letters "m", "d", and "y" for months, days, and years, respectively. The number of letters controls how Excel displays the date, as follows:

- With months, *m* or *mm* displays the one- or two-digit month number, *mmm* displays the month's three-letter abbreviation, and *mmmm* displays the month's full name.
- With days, *d* or *dd* displays the one- or two-digit day value and *dddd* displays the day's full name.
- With years, *yyyy* displays the four-digit year value.

For example, a custom format of *mmm-dd* displays a three-letter month abbreviation followed by a hyphen and a two-digit day number (such as Apr-05). The current date format used in the category axis is *m/d/yyyy*, which—for example—displays March 14, 2013 as 3/14/2013.

You'll create a custom format for the category axis that displays only the four-digit year.

To create a custom format for the four-digit year:

1. Click **Number** on the left side of the Format Axis dialog box.
2. Type **yyyy** in the Format Code box, which is the code for displaying only years. See Figure 4-22.

Figure 4-22 Custom date format

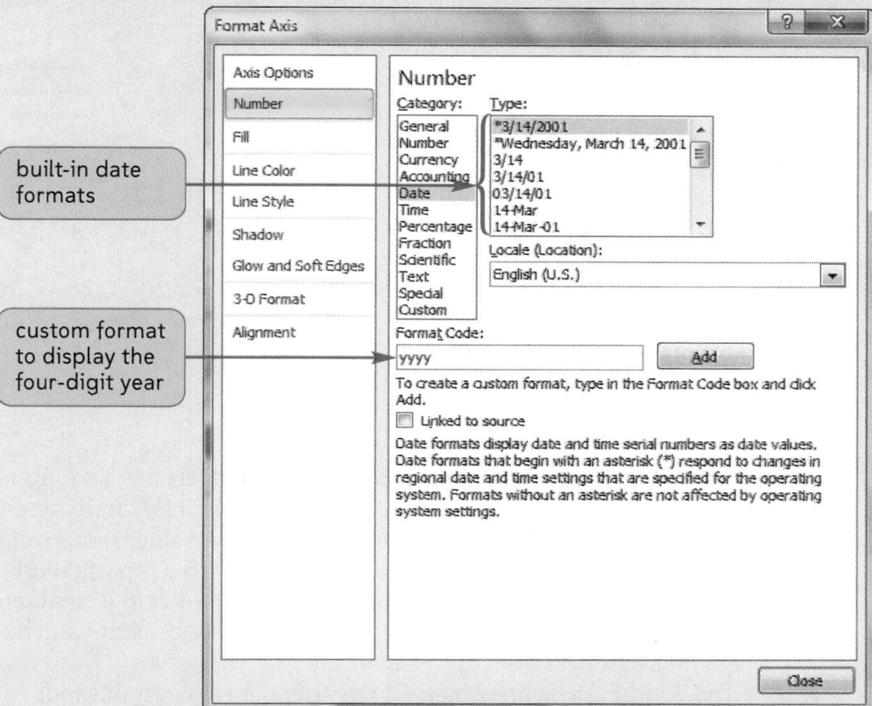

3. Click the **Add** button. The four-digit year format code is added to the list of custom formats and is selected.
4. Click the **Close** button. The Format Axis dialog box closes, and the category axis labels show values for every other year on the major tick marks. See Figure 4-23.

Figure 4-23 **Rescaled vertical and horizontal axes**

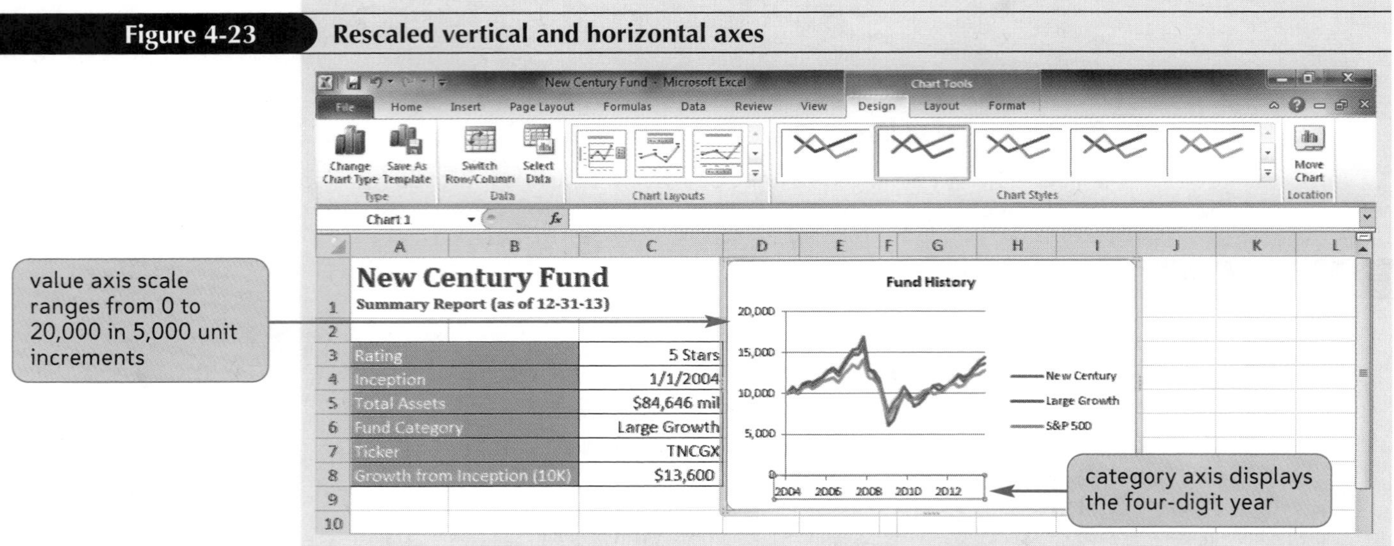

The category axis shows four-digit year values for 2004, 2006, 2008, 2010, and 2012. Because fewer years are included on the axis, there is enough room to display the labels horizontally instead of vertically.

Setting Label Units

When a chart involves large numbers, the axis labels can take up a lot of the available chart area and be difficult to read. You can simplify the chart's appearance by displaying units of measure more appropriate to the data values. For example, you can display the value 20 to represent 20,000 or 20,000,000. This is particularly useful when space is at a premium, such as in an embedded chart confined to a small area of the worksheet. When you select the display units, such as Thousands, you can choose to show the display unit in the axis title.

The Fund History line chart displays data in tens of thousands of dollars. Rather than displaying a large value such as 20,000, Ajita wants to save space by displaying numbers in units of thousands. You will change the display units for the value axis but not show the units in the axis title.

To set the display unit for the value axis:

1. Double-click the **value axis** to open the Format Axis dialog box with the Axis Options displayed.
2. Click the **Display units** arrow, and then click **Thousands**.
3. Move the dialog box so you can see the line chart's value axis. The scale of the value axis changed from 0 to 20,000 in intervals of 5,000 to 0 through 20 in intervals of 5. The axis title "Thousands" indicates that the values are expressed in units of 1000. To save space, you'll remove this title from the chart.
4. Click the **Show display units label on chart** check box to remove the check mark. The axis title is removed from the chart.

You can apply custom formats to numbers just as you did earlier with dates. One application of custom formats is to add text to a number. This is often used to include the units of measure alongside the value, such as 10k to indicate 10,000. To add text to a value, you use the custom format *value"text"*, where *value* is the number format applied to the value and *text* is the text to include next to the value. The text must be placed within quotation marks.

TIP

Use Excel Help to learn more about custom format codes.

Without the Thousands title, the Fund History line chart provides no indication of what the value axis numbers mean. Ajita suggests you add the letter "k" to each number, displaying the values as 10k, 20k, and so forth. To do this, you'll create a custom format. Excel uses the format #,##0 to display integers, so you'll change this format to #,##0"k" to display the letter "k" at the end of the value.

To create a custom format showing the thousands unit:

1. Click **Number** on the left side of the Format Axis dialog box.
2. Click in the Format Code box after the number format, and then type **"k"** to make the format code #,##0"k".
3. Click the **Add** button. This format code is added to the list of custom formats in the Type box.
4. Click the **Close** button. The Format Axis dialog box closes, and the value axis labels are revised, with the letter "k" added after each value. See Figure 4-24.

Figure 4-24 **Custom value axis label units**

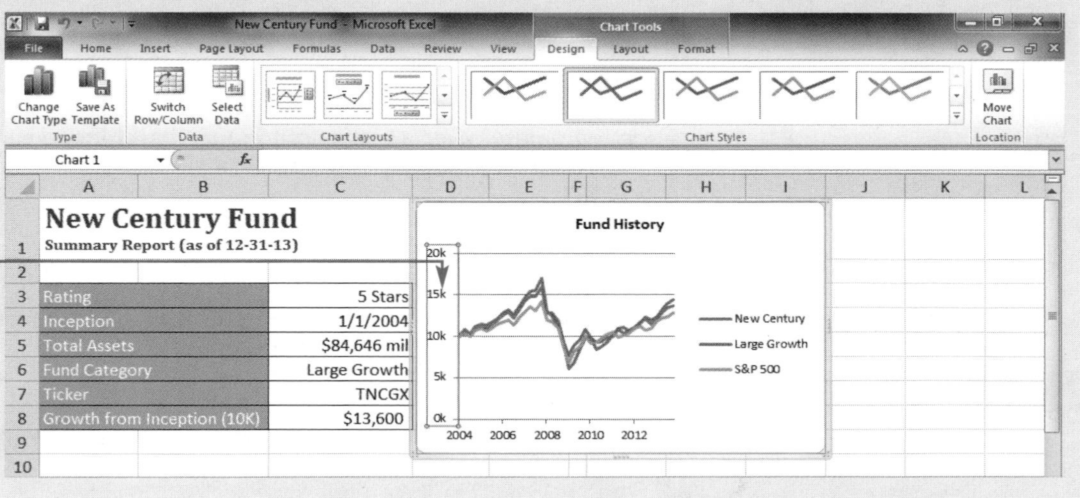

Overlaying a Chart Legend

Chart elements, such as titles and legends, overlay the chart area, which means they are placed on top of the chart. Overlaying chart elements is a way to make more space for the plot area because the chart does not resize to make room for that element. After you overlay an element, you might want to format it to make it easier to read.

Ajita thinks the legend takes up too much space on the right side of the chart. You will overlay the legend, leaving more room in the chart area for the chart itself, and then format it.

To overlay and format the chart legend:

1. Double-click the **legend** to open the Format Legend dialog box.
2. Click the **Show the legend without overlapping the chart** check box to remove the check mark. The size of the chart increases, and the legend is now overlaying the chart. The plot and the legend intersect, and the plot area shows through the legend.
3. Click **Fill** on the left side of the Format Legend dialog box, and then click the **Solid fill** option button.
4. Click the **Color** button, and then click **white** (the first color in the Theme Colors section). The legend now has a solid white background, making it easier to read.
5. Click **Border Color** on the left side of the Format Legend dialog box, and then click the **Solid line** option button.
6. Click the **Color** button, and then click **Blue** (the eighth color in the Standard Colors section).
7. Click the **Close** button. The Format Legend dialog box closes, and the reformatted legend overlays the chart.

An overlaid chart element floats in the chart area and is not fixed to a particular position. This means that you can drag the chart element to a new location. This is helpful because when you overlay a chart element, it might overlap some of the chart contents, as the legend does. You'll drag the overlaid legend down a bit so that it doesn't obscure any of the data in the line chart.

To move the chart legend:

1. Position the pointer over a blank spot in the chart legend so the pointer changes to and "Legend" appears in a ScreenTip.
2. Drag the legend to the lower-right corner of the plot area so the bottom of the legend is on the horizontal axis.
3. Click and drag the upper-left sizing handle of the legend down a few pixels until the legend no longer overlaps the lines on the chart. See Figure 4-25.

Figure 4-25 **Legend overlaid, moved, and resized**

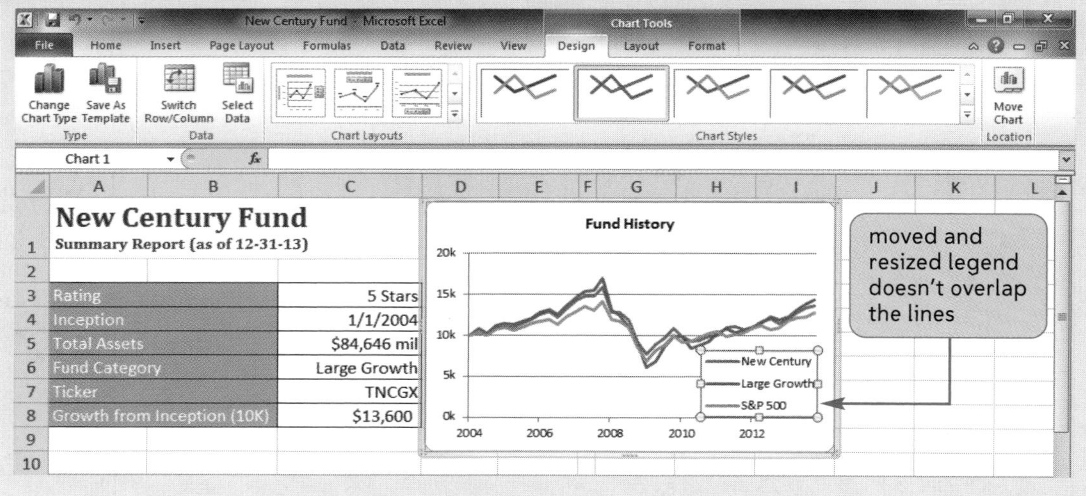

Adding Gridlines

TIP

Gridlines are similar to borders in that you can change their color and design style as well as add drop shadows or glowing color effects.

By default, Excel places horizontal gridlines on line charts and column charts. Each gridline is aligned with a major tick mark on the value axis. You can change the gridlines so that they appear for only the minor units, appear for both the major and minor units, or do not appear at all. The category axis has these same gridline options.

Ajita wants you to add vertical gridlines at the minor tick marks on the category axis.

To add vertical gridlines to the chart:

1. Click the **Chart Tools Layout** tab on the Ribbon.
2. In the Axes group, click the **Gridlines** button.
3. Point to **Primary Vertical Gridlines**, and then click **Minor Gridlines**. Vertical gridlines appear on the chart at each minor tick mark (in this case, every year).

Adding an Axis Title

An axis title is descriptive text that appears next to the axis values. An axis title can provide additional information that is not covered in the chart title. It can include information about the source of the data and the units in which the data is measured.

The values in the chart represent the return that the investor would have enjoyed from a $10,000 investment starting in 2004. Because this fact is not obvious from the chart, Ajita wants you to add the title "Return on $10K Investment" to the vertical axis.

To add a title to the vertical axis:

1. In the Labels group on the Chart Tools Layout tab, click **Axis Titles**, point to **Primary Vertical Axis Title**, and then click **Rotated Title**. A title rotated 90 degrees is added to the axis.
2. Type **Return on $10K Investment**, and then press the **Enter** key. The descriptive title is entered, but doesn't fit well in the chart area.
3. Click the **Home** tab on the Ribbon.
4. In the Font group, click the **Font Size button arrow**, and then click **8**. The font size is reduced to 8 points.
5. In the Font group, click the **Bold** button **B** to remove the boldface from the axis title.
6. Click cell **A9** to deselect the chart. The final version of the line chart is easier to read than the unformatted version, and highlights how the New Century Fund has performed over the past 10 years compared to the two benchmarks. See Figure 4-26.

Figure 4-26 **Final line chart**

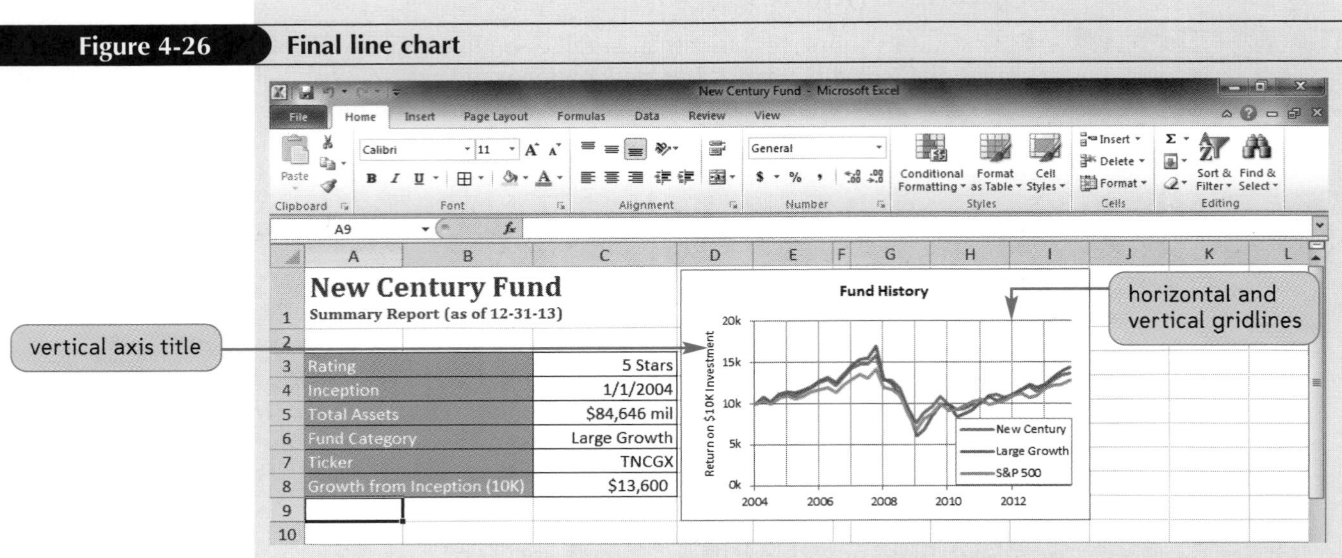

Editing and Revising Chart Data

Chart data can be edited and revised at any time. You do this by modifying the data range that the chart is based on, not by directly modifying the data in the chart. The change can be as simple as updating a specific value within the data source. Or it can be as involved as adding another data series to the chart.

Changing a Data Value

Charts remain linked or connected to their data sources, even if they appear in different worksheets. If you change any values or labels in the data source, the chart is automatically updated to show the new content. One advantage of Excel charts is that you can quickly see how changing one or more values affects a graph.

Ajita found a data entry error in the Assets worksheet—the amount of assets in the Other category entered in cell B8 should be $8,360, not $3,360. She also wants the label "Other" to be changed to "Other Assets." This change also needs to be reflected in the Allocation of Assets pie chart you created based on this data. Because both the asset values and the asset labels are linked to the pie chart, when you make these changes in the Assets worksheet, they will automatically be reflected in the pie chart.

To edit the data source for the assets pie chart:

1. Go to the **Assets** worksheet.
2. In cell A8, edit the text to **Other Assets**.
3. In cell B8, change the value to **8360**.
4. Go to the **Summary Report** worksheet, and then verify that the pie chart was updated with the new data value and category name. Note that the percentage values for each category were recalculated based on the new data. As a result, the Other Assets slice increased in size to reflect its larger percentage of the whole, and the remaining slices decreased in size. See Figure 4-27.

Figure 4-27 Revised pie chart

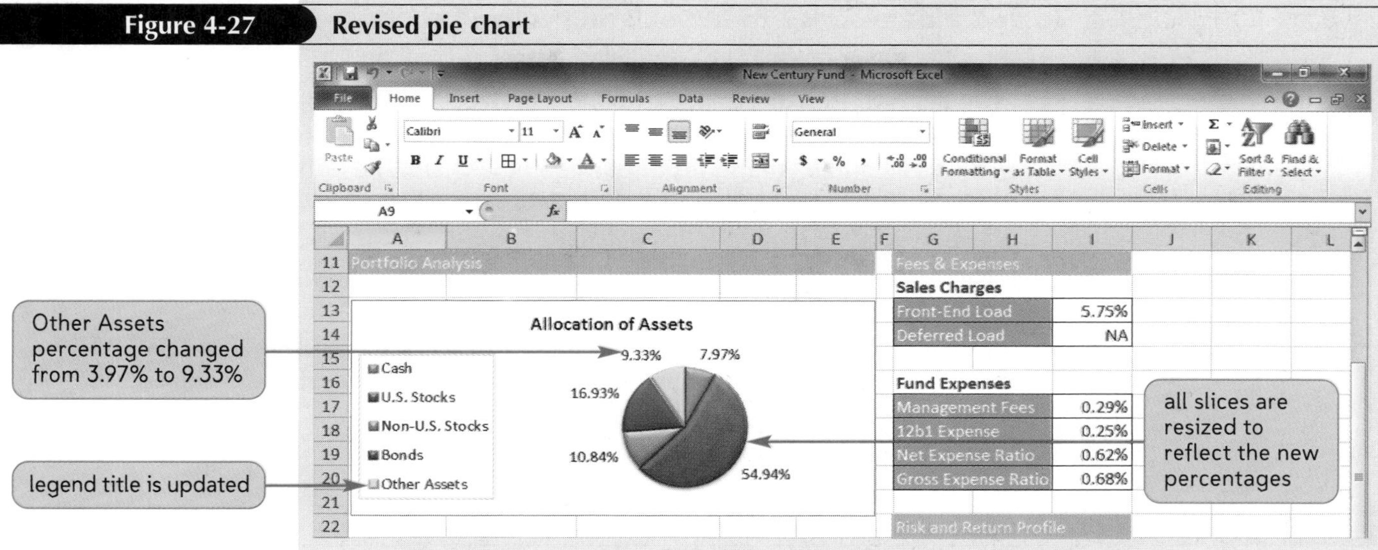

Occasionally, you will want a chart to show a "snapshot" of the data at a certain time. Before updating the values in the data source, copy and paste the chart as a picture. Select the chart, copy it as usual, click the Paste button arrow, and then click Picture. The chart is pasted as a picture without any connection to its data source.

Adding a Data Series to an Existing Chart

You can also modify a chart by adding a new data series. The new data series appears in the chart with a different set of data markers in the same way that the line chart you created had different data markers for each of the three different series.

REFERENCE

Adding a Data Series to a Chart

- Select the chart to which you want to add a data series.
- In the Data group on the Chart Tools Design tab, click the Select Data button.
- Click the Add button in the Select Data Source dialog box.
- Select the range with the series name and series values you want for the new data series.
- Click the OK button in each dialog box.

The column chart you created shows the distribution of stocks in the New Century Fund. Ajita wonders how this distribution compares to the distribution in the S&P 500 index. For example, does the New Century Fund invest more in the information sector, and is that why it outperformed the S&P 500 for the past 10 years? Ajita included the sector percentages for the S&P 500 in the Sectors worksheet. You will add this information to the column chart you've already created.

To add a data series to the existing column chart:

1. Click the **Sector Percentages** column chart to select it.
2. Click the **Chart Tools Design** tab on the Ribbon, and then, in the Data group, click the **Select Data** button. The Select Data Source dialog box opens. The left side lists all of the data series displayed in the chart. The right side lists the category axis labels associated with each data series. You can add, edit, or remove any of these data series from the chart.
3. Click the **Add** button. The Edit Series dialog box opens. In this dialog box, you specify the name of the new data series and its range of data values.
4. With the insertion point in the Series name box, click the **Sectors** sheet tab, click cell **D3**, and then press the **Tab** key. The cell with the series name is entered and the insertion point moves to the Series values box.
5. Select the range **D4:D15**. See Figure 4-28.

Figure 4-28 Edit Series dialog box

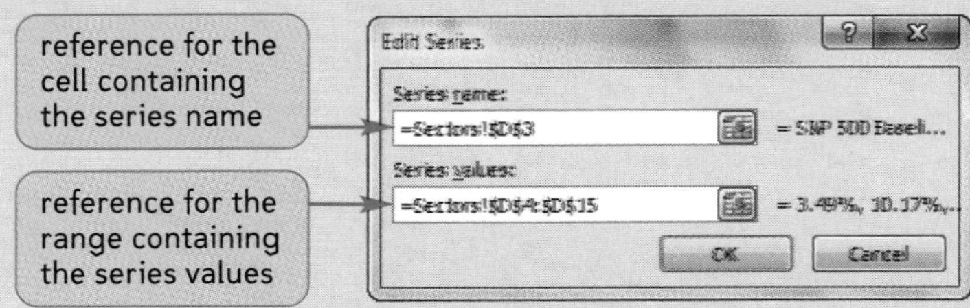

6. Click the **OK** button. The Select Data Source dialog box reappears with the S&P 500 data added to the list of data series in the chart. See Figure 4-29.

Figure 4-29 Select Data Source dialog box

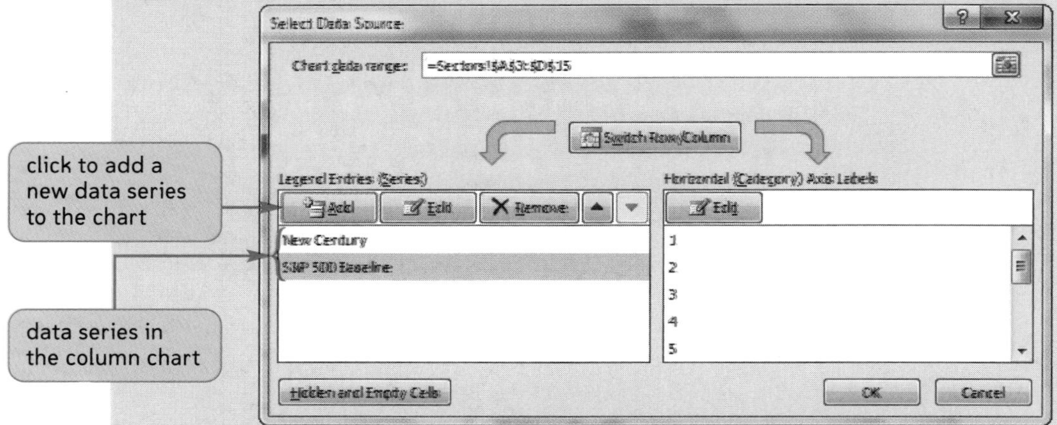

7. Click the **OK** button. The S&P 500 sector values appear as red columns in the chart. See Figure 4-30.

Figure 4-30 **Column chart with added data series**

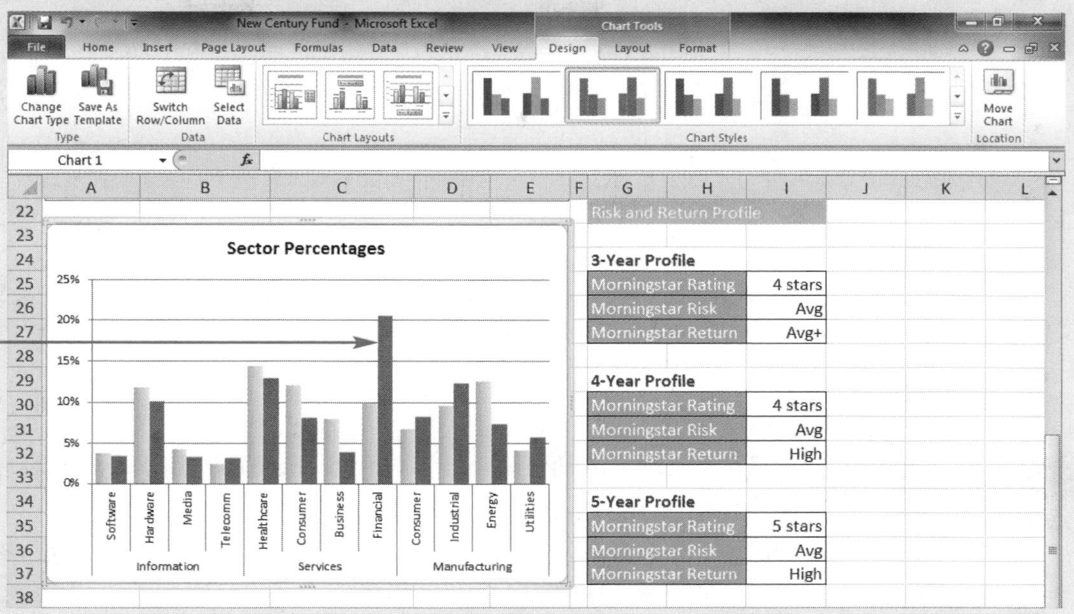

S&P 500 values are shown in red columns

INSIGHT

Understanding the Series Function

If you select a chart's series and look at the formula bar, the formula being displayed uses the SERIES function. The SERIES function describes the content of a chart data series and has the syntax

```
=SERIES(name, categories, values, order)
```

where *name* is the name that appears in the chart, *categories* are the labels that appear on the category axis of the chart, *values* are the values that Excel plots for the data series, and *order* is the order in which the series appears in the chart. For example, a data series might be represented by the following SERIES function:

```
=SERIES(Sheet1!$D$1,Sheet1!$A$2:$A$9,Sheet1!$D$2:$D$9,3)
```

In this function, the name of the series is in cell D1 of the Sheet1 worksheet, the labels are in the range A2:A9 in the Sheet1 worksheet, the data values are in the range D2:D9 in the Sheet1 worksheet, and the series is the third data series in the chart.

Note that although you can edit the SERIES function within the formula bar to make quick changes to your chart, the function is tied to an existing chart. It cannot be used within a worksheet cell or referenced from another Excel formula.

Creating a Combination Chart

A combination chart is a chart that combines two or more chart types in a single graph, such as a column chart and a line chart. To create a combination chart, you select a data series in an existing chart, and then apply a new chart type to that series, leaving the other data series in its original format.

REFERENCE

Creating a Combination Chart

- Select a data series in an existing chart that you want to appear as another chart type.
- In the Type group on the Chart Tools Design tab, click the Change Chart Type button, and then click the chart type you want.
- Click the OK button.

With so many columns in the Sector Percentages column chart, the data is difficult to read and interpret. Ajita suggests you separate the S&P 500 values from the New Century Fund values by plotting them as lines rather than columns. To do that, you'll create a chart that is a combination of a column and a line chart.

To apply the line chart type to the S&P 500 data series:

1. Click the **Chart Tools Layout** tab on the Ribbon.
2. In the Current Selection group, click the **Chart Elements arrow**, and then click **Series "S&P 500 Baseline"** to select the data series.
3. Click the **Chart Tools Design** tab on the Ribbon, and then click the **Change Chart Type** button in the Type group. The Change Chart Type dialog box opens.
4. In the Line section, click **Line with Markers** (the fourth Line chart type).
5. Click the **OK** button. The S&P 500 values change to a line chart with markers. See Figure 4-31.

Figure 4-31 Combination chart

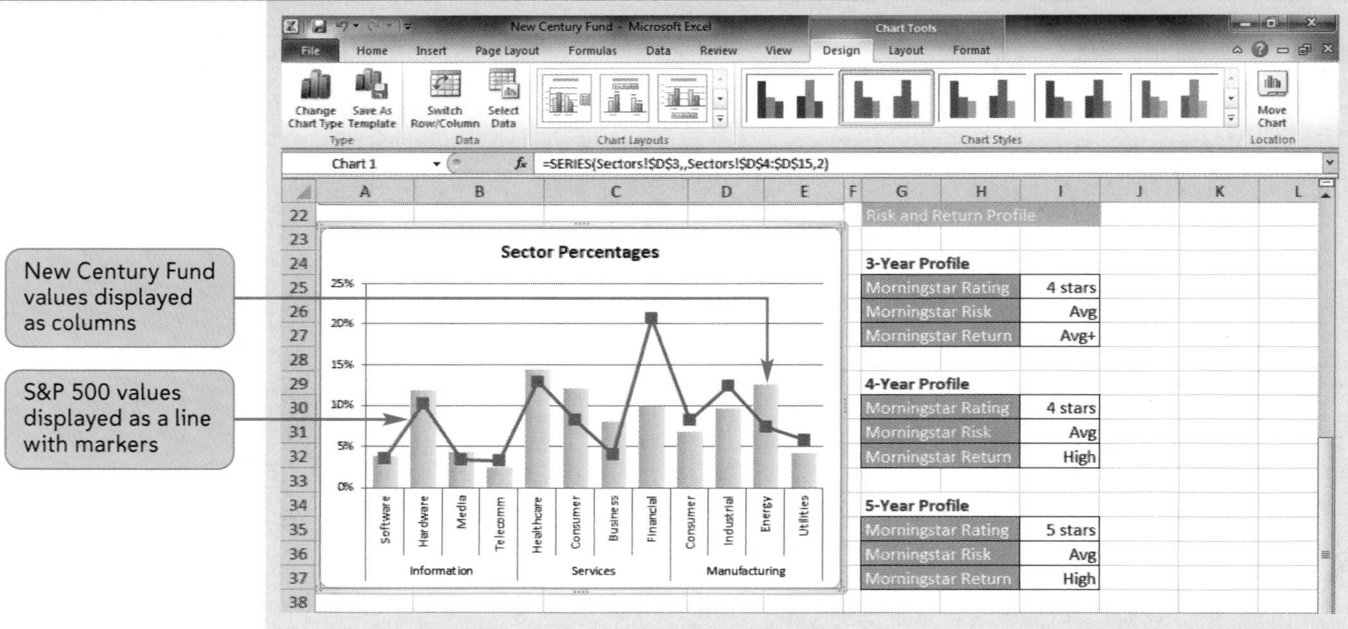

As noted earlier, line charts are appropriate when the categories can be ordered sequentially such as the Fund History line chart in which the categories represented dates. In Figure 4-31, the sector categories do not have a sequential order and the lines connecting the different categories have no meaning. You'll remove these lines from the chart to avoid confusing Ajita's clients. Also, you'll change the square markers to horizontal line markers at each data point.

To remove the lines and edit the markers in the line chart:

1. Click the line for the S&P 500 data series to select it, if necessary.
2. Click the **Chart Tools Layout** tab on the Ribbon, and then click **Format Selection** in the Current Selection group. The Format Data Series dialog box opens.
3. Click **Line Color** on the left side of the dialog box, and then click the **No line** option button to remove the line from the line chart.
4. Click **Marker Options** on the left side of the dialog box, and then click the **Built-in** option button. You can now select the type and size of the marker.
5. Click the **Type arrow**, and then click the horizontal line marker (the seventh marker in the list).
6. Click the **Size** up arrow until 10 appears in the box. See Figure 4-32.

Figure 4-32 **Marker Options in the Format Data Series dialog box**

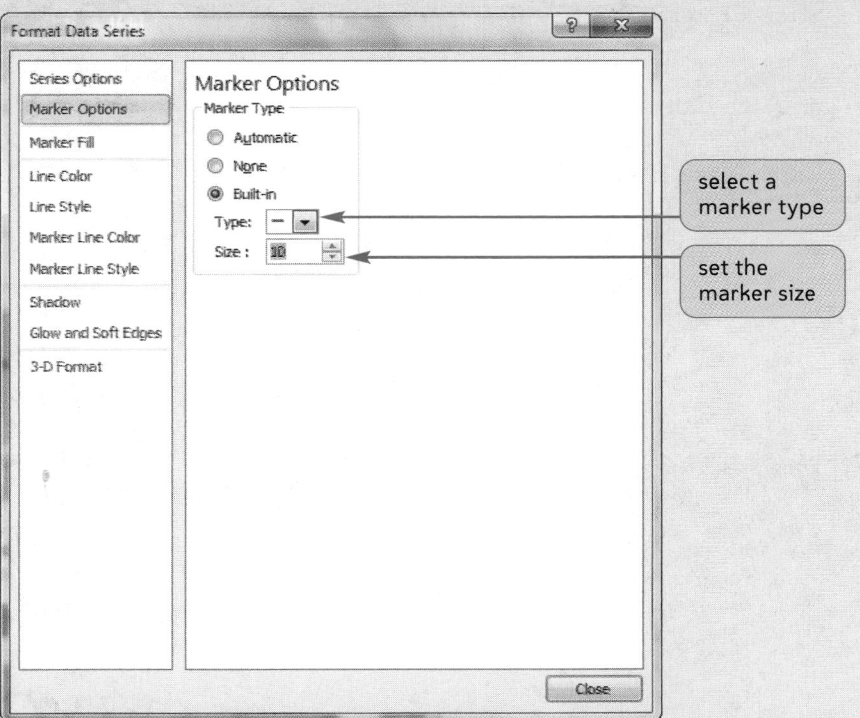

7. Click the **Close** button. The S&P 500 values appear only as data markers.

Because the chart now has two data series, you'll add a legend to the top of the chart to identify them.

To add a legend to the combination chart:

1. In the Labels group on the Chart Tools Layout tab, click the **Legend** button, and then click **Show Legend at Top**. The legend appears above the chart.
2. Click the **legend** to select it.
3. Click the **Home** tab on the Ribbon, and then reduce the font size of the legend to **8** points.
4. Click cell **A38** to deselect the chart. See Figure 4-33.

Figure 4-33 **Completed combination chart**

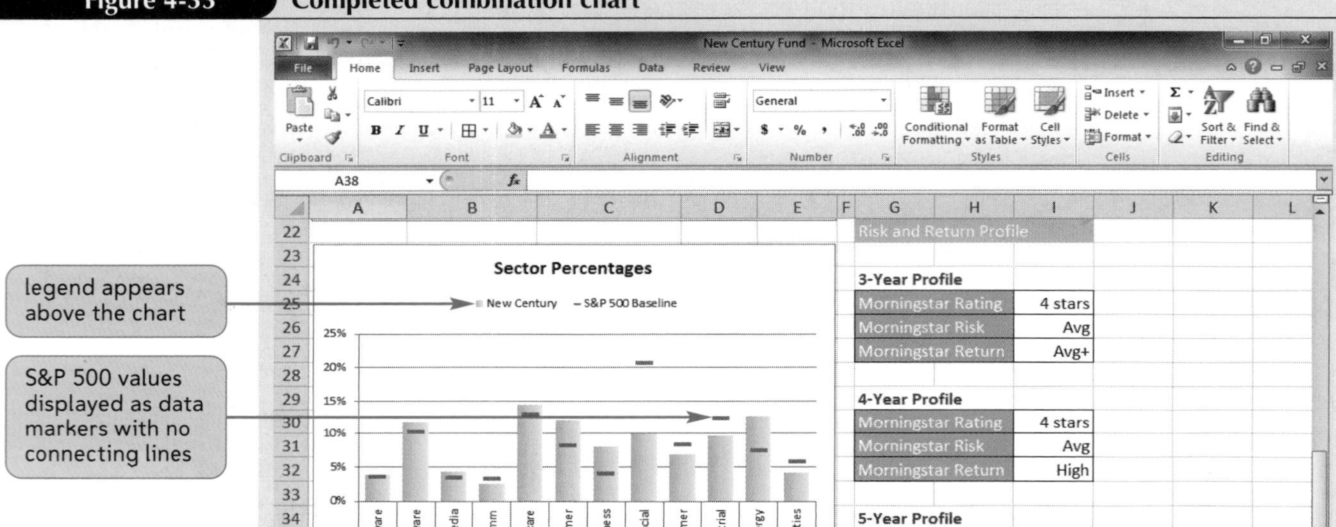

The combination chart effectively shows that the New Century Fund invests less than the S&P 500 in sectors from the financial service industry, and invests more in other sectors such as energy, consumer services, and hardware. This might account for the higher performance of the New Century Fund.

PROSKILLS

Decision Making: Choosing the Right Chart

Excel supports a wide variety of charts and chart styles. Deciding which type of chart to use requires evaluating your data and determining the ultimate purpose or goal of the chart. Consider how your data will appear with each type of chart before making a final decision.

In general, pie charts should be used only when the number of categories is small and the relative sizes of the different slices can be easily distinguished. If you have several categories, use a column or bar chart.

Line charts are best for categories that follow a sequential order. Be aware, however, that the time intervals must be a constant length if used in a line chart. Line charts will distort data that occurs in irregular time intervals, making it appear that the data values occurred at regular intervals when they did not.

Pie, column, bar, and line charts assume that numbers are plotted against categories. In science and engineering applications, you will often want to plot two numeric values against one another. For that data, use **XY scatter charts**, which show the patterns or relationship between two or more sets of values. XY scatter charts are also useful for data recorded at irregular time intervals.

If you still can't find the right chart to meet your needs, you can create a custom chart based on the built-in chart types. Third-party vendors also sell software to allow Excel to create charts not built into the software.

Choosing the right chart and chart style can make your presentation more effective and informative.

Creating a 3-D Chart

You can add visual interest to charts by using 3-D (three dimensional) effects. The 3-D effects provide the illusion of depth and distance, which makes the charts appear to stand out on the page. You'll change the format of the Allocation of Assets pie chart to a 3-D style.

To change the assets pie chart to 3-D:

1. Click the **Allocation of Assets pie chart**, and then click the **Chart Tools Design** tab on the Ribbon.
2. In the Type group, click the **Change Chart Type** button. The Change Chart Type dialog box opens.
3. In the Pie section, click **Pie in 3-D** (the second Pie chart type).
4. Click the **OK** button. The pie chart is now a 3-D chart, and has a slight shadow along its lower edge.

To create a 3-D effect, Excel adds three spatial dimensions to the chart, which it labels the x-, y-, and z-axes. The **x-axis** represents the length of the object. The **y-axis** represents the height of the object. The **z-axis** represents the object's depth. These Excel definitions of the x-, y-, and z-axes might not match what you have learned in math classes about 3-D charting.

Currently, the 3-D pie chart does not look very different from the 2-D version because you are looking straight down on the chart from "above," directly along the y-axis. To increase the 3-D effect, you need to rotate the chart. You can only rotate the chart horizontally or vertically. Increasing the rotation horizontally spins the chart clockwise (as seen from above); increasing the rotation vertically raises the user's viewpoint higher above the chart. Often you'll need to experiment to find the right angles for a 3-D chart by rotating the chart in different directions until it looks good without distorting the data.

Excel charts cannot be rotated around the z- or depth axis, but you can specify the chart's depth. Depth values can range from 0 to 2000 units. The larger the value, the thicker or deeper the chart appears to extend away from the viewer. You can also change the chart's **perspective**, which controls how fast the chart appears to recede from the viewer's eye. Perspective values range from 0 degrees to 90 degrees. A 90 degree perspective value exaggerates the 3-D effect, making distant objects appear very small, whereas perspective values near 0 degrees minimize this effect. Excel immediately applies your choices for depth and perspective, so you can try different depth and perspective values to determine which work best for your chart.

You'll rotate the Allocation of Assets pie chart along the horizontal axis so that the largest slice is on the left side of the pie. You'll also orient the chart so that the viewer's eye level is slightly above the chart. You will not change the chart's perspective or depth.

To rotate and reorient the 3-D pie chart:

1. Click the **Chart Tools Layout** tab on the Ribbon.
2. In the Background group, click the **3-D Rotation** button. The Format Chart Area dialog box opens with the 3-D Rotation options displayed.
3. In the Rotation section, type **90** in the X box, and then type **20** in the Y box. See Figure 4-34.

Figure 4-34 Format Chart Area dialog box with 3-D Rotation options

TIP

You can use the 3-D Format options to add drop shadows, raised or beveled corners, and textured surfaces that give the illusion of light reflecting off the chart elements.

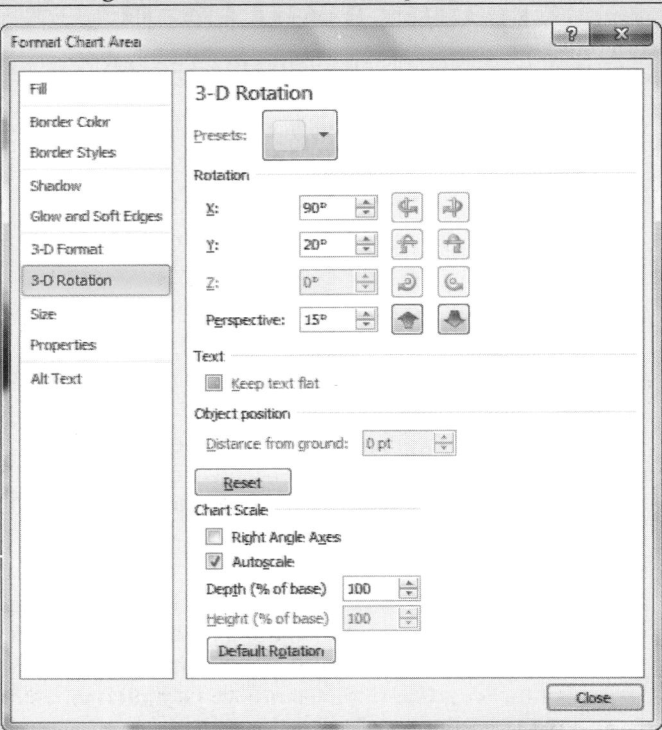

4. Click the **Close** button. The pie chart rotates based on the new x-axis and y-axis values. See Figure 4-35.

Figure 4-35 **Rotated 3-D pie chart**

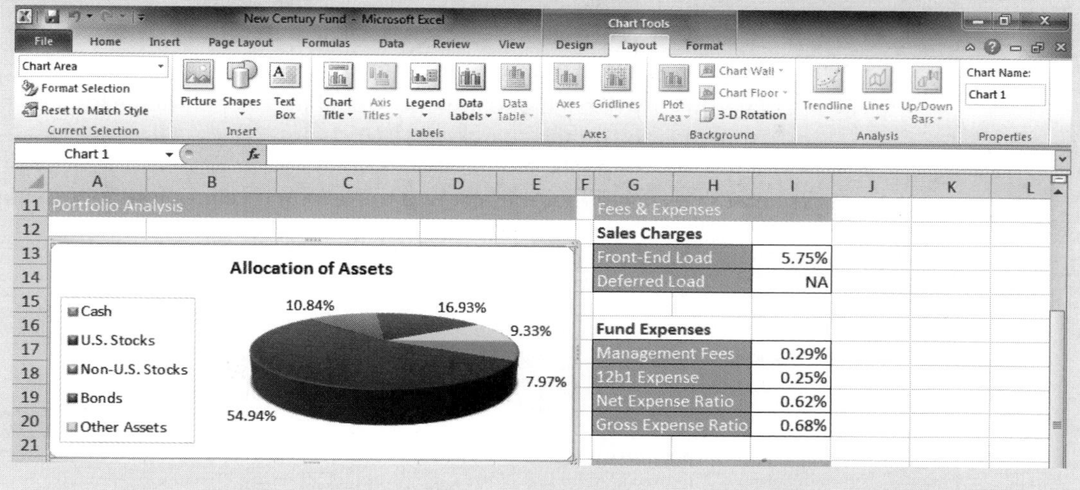

The horizontal and vertical rotation has a significant impact on the way the chart looks. The pie chart was rotated clockwise one-quarter of the way around the circle so that the largest slice, the red U.S Stocks slice, is in the front. The vertical rotation turned the pie chart so that the viewer is looking down on the chart at a lower angle above the horizontal axis. Ajita is pleased with the 3-D effect you added.

INSIGHT

Creating Effective 3-D Charts

Although 3-D charts are visually attractive, they can obscure the relationship between the values in the chart. This is especially true when an exaggerated perspective obscures the relative sizes of different chart elements, such as pie slices.

Because of the visual distortion that can result with 3-D representations, you should include data labels with all 3-D charts. Also, try to avoid extreme viewing angles that elongate chart elements and might cause the viewer to misread the data. Although 3-D charts can be eye-catching, do not use this effect if it overrides the main purpose of a chart, which is data interpretation.

Adding Sparklines and Data Bars

For more compact graphing, you can insert charts within worksheet cells. Excel provides two tools to do this—sparklines and data bars. Both convey graphical information about worksheet data without occupying a lot of space.

Creating Sparklines

A sparkline is a mini chart that is displayed within a worksheet cell. Because sparklines are compact in size, they don't include chart elements such as legends, titles, gridlines, or axes. The goal of a sparkline is to convey the maximum amount of graphical information within a very small space. As a result, sparklines are useful when you don't want charts to overwhelm the rest of your worksheet or take up valuable page space.

Excel supports the following three types of sparklines:

- A line sparkline for highlighting trends
- A column sparkline used for column charts
- A win/loss sparkline for highlighting positive and negative values

Figure 4-36 shows examples of each type of sparkline. The line sparklines show the sales history of each department and all four departments for a computer manufacturer. From glancing at the sparklines, you can quickly see the recent sales history within and across departments. Notice that although total sales rose steadily during the year, peripheral sales lagged for the first two-thirds of the year before increasing in the final third.

Figure 4-36 **Types of sparklines**

line sparklines

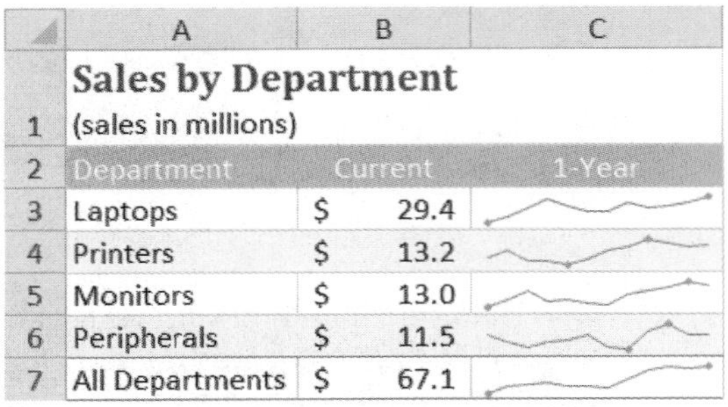

	A	B	C
1	Sales by Department (sales in millions)		
2	Department	Current	1-Year
3	Laptops	$ 29.4	
4	Printers	$ 13.2	
5	Monitors	$ 13.0	
6	Peripherals	$ 11.5	
7	All Departments	$ 67.1	

column sparklines

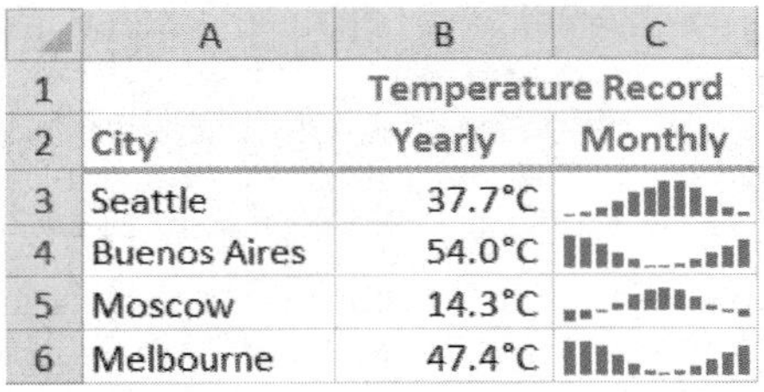

	A	B	C
1		Temperature Record	
2	City	Yearly	Monthly
3	Seattle	37.7°C	
4	Buenos Aires	54.0°C	
5	Moscow	14.3°C	
6	Melbourne	47.4°C	

win/loss sparklines

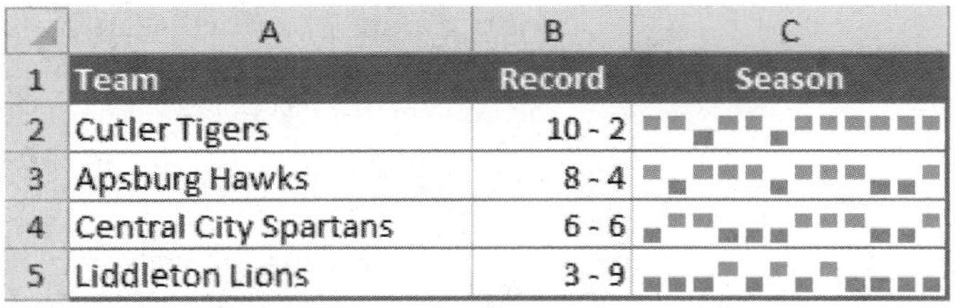

	A	B	C
1	Team	Record	Season
2	Cutler Tigers	10 - 2	
3	Apsburg Hawks	8 - 4	
4	Central City Spartans	6 - 6	
5	Liddleton Lions	3 - 9	

The column sparklines present a record of monthly temperature averages for four cities. Temperatures above 0°C are presented in blue columns; temperatures below 0°C are presented in red columns that extend downward.

Finally, the win/loss sparklines reveal a snapshot of the season results for four sports teams. Wins are displayed in blue; losses are in red. From the sparklines, you can quickly see that the Cutler Tigers finished their 10-2 season with six straight wins and the Liddleton Lions finished their 3-9 season with four straight losses.

To create a set of sparklines, you first select a data range containing the data you want to graph, and then you select a location range where you want the sparklines to appear. Note that the cells in which you insert the sparklines need not be blank. Sparklines are added as part of the cell background and do not replace any cell content.

REFERENCE

Creating and Editing Sparklines

- In the Sparklines group on the Insert tab, click the Line, Column, or Win/Loss button.
- In the Data Range box, enter the range for the data source of the sparkline.
- In the Location Range box, enter the range into which to place the sparkline.
- Click the OK button.
- To edit a sparkline's appearance, click the Sparkline Tools Design tab.
- In the Show group, click the appropriate check boxes to specify which markers to display on the sparkline.
- In the Group group, click the Axis button, and then click Show Axis to add an axis to the sparkline.

Ajita wants to add graphs to the Sectors worksheet to indicate how each of the 12 investment sectors performed during the last 10 years. Rather than create a separate chart for each sector, you'll conserve space in the worksheet by creating sparklines.

To insert sparklines in the Sectors worksheet:

1. Go to the **Sectors** worksheet.
2. In cell E3, enter **10-Year History**, and then apply the **Heading 4** cell style to the cell and center the text within the cell.
3. Select the range **E4:E15**. This is the location range, the cells in which you want to insert the sparklines.
4. Click the **Insert** tab on the Ribbon, and then click the **Line** button in the Sparklines group. The Create Sparklines dialog box opens. The location range is already entered because you selected it before opening the dialog box.
5. With the insertion point in the Data Range box, click the **Sector History** sheet tab, and then select the data in the range **B6:M45**. This is the range that contains the data you want to chart in the sparklines. See Figure 4-37.

Figure 4-37 **Create Sparklines dialog box**

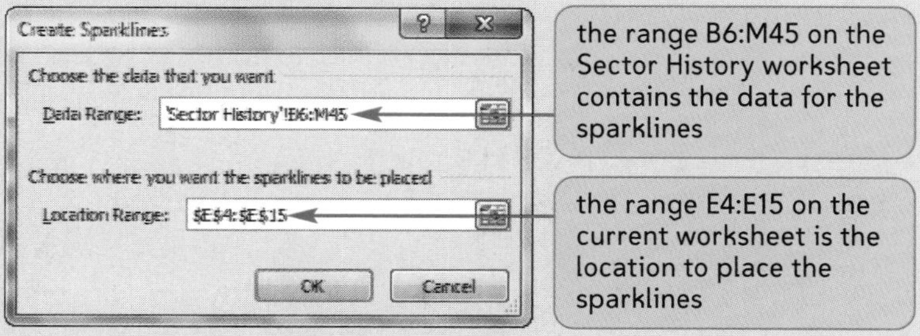

6. Click the **OK** button. Sparklines are inserted into each cell in the selected range. See Figure 4-38.

Figure 4-38 **Line sparklines created for each sector**

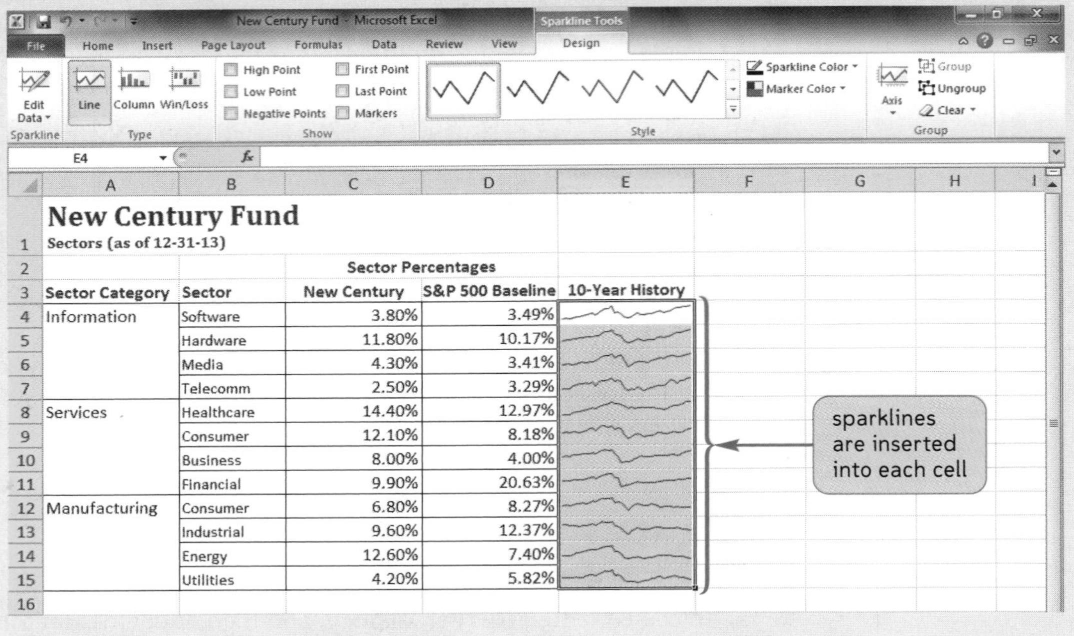

Sector Category	Sector	New Century	S&P 500 Baseline	10-Year History
Information	Software	3.80%	3.49%	
	Hardware	11.80%	10.17%	
	Media	4.30%	3.41%	
	Telecomm	2.50%	3.29%	
Services	Healthcare	14.40%	12.97%	
	Consumer	12.10%	8.18%	
	Business	8.00%	4.00%	
	Financial	9.90%	20.63%	
Manufacturing	Consumer	6.80%	8.27%	
	Industrial	9.60%	12.37%	
	Energy	12.60%	7.40%	
	Utilities	4.20%	5.82%	

Ajita quickly notices from the sparklines that all of the investment sectors experienced a sharp decline mid-way through the previous decade. The stocks in the information sector category recovered from that loss to post gains during the second half of the decade. However, the manufacturing stocks showed little or no increase after that mid-decade decline. The stocks in the service category showed a moderate increase in the second half of the decade.

Adding and Formatting Sparkline Markers

As with other charts, Excel provides built-in styles for sparklines. Because of the compactness of sparklines, you can specify only the line color and the marker color. For line sparklines, you can create markers for the following points: the highest value, the lowest value, all the negative values, the first value, and the last value. You can also create markers for all data points regardless of their value or position in the data source.

Ajita wants you to add data markers for the high and low points within each sparkline so that she can more easily track the progress each sector made during the decade and locate the decade's maximum and minimum values.

TIP

You can change the sparkline color by clicking the Sparkline Color button in the Style group on the Sparkline Tools Design tab. You can change the marker color by clicking the Marker Color button.

To add high and low markers to the sparklines:

1. Click the **Sparkline Tools Design** tab on the Ribbon, if necessary. The tab contains options associated with the selected sparklines—in this case, line sparklines.
2. In the Show group, click the **High Point** and **Low Point** check boxes to display markers for the high and low points within each sparkline.
3. In the Style group, click the **More** button to open the Style gallery, and then click **Sparkline Style Colorful #2** (the second style in the last row). The color of the high and low point markers changes to reflect the selection. See Figure 4-39.

Figure 4-39 Data markers added to sparklines

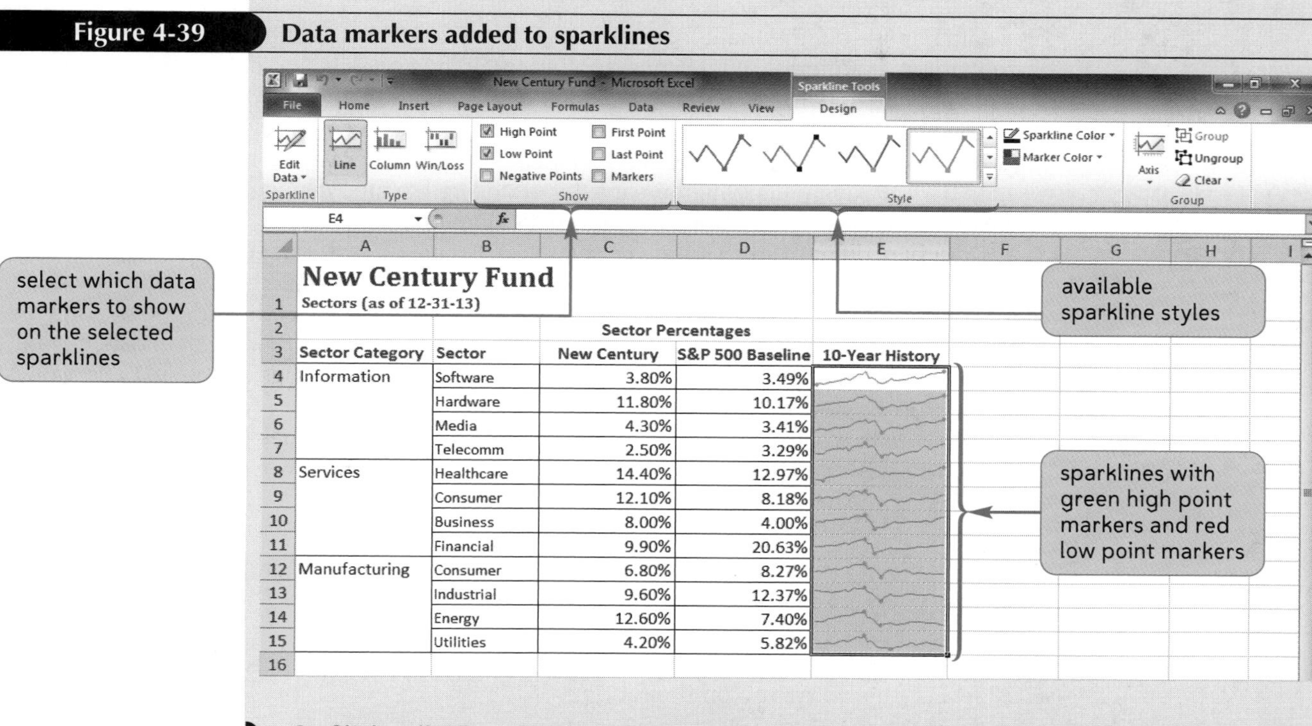

4. Click cell **A2** to deselect the location range containing the sparklines. You can more clearly see that the formatted sparklines use a green marker for the high points and a red marker for the low points.

The only other feature you can add to a sparkline is an axis. The sparkline axis is simply a horizontal line that separates positive values from negative values. To add an axis to a sparkline, click the Axis button in the Group group on the Sparkline Tools Design tab, and then click Show Axis. You won't add an axis to the 10-Year History sparklines because all of the fund values are positive and an axis would not add any information to the charts.

INSIGHT

Sparkline Groups

When you create sparklines, all the sparklines in the location range are part of a single group. Clicking any cell in the location range selects all of the sparklines in the group. Similarly, any formatting you apply affects all the sparklines in the group. This ensures that all the sparklines for related data are formatted consistently.

In some instances, you might want to differentiate one sparkline from others in its group. You can do this by applying a different format to that sparkline. To format an individual sparkline, select the sparkline you want to format, and then click the Ungroup button in the Group group on the Sparkline Tools Design tab. The selected sparkline is split from the rest of the sparklines in the group. You can then apply a unique format to the selected sparkline. To regroup the sparklines, select all of the cells in the location range containing sparklines, and then click the Group button in the Group group.

One advantage of breaking up a sparkline group is that Excel can display each sparkline based on the maximum and minimum values associated with the individual sparkline's data series. This becomes an important consideration if your data source contains multiple data series covering vastly different ranges.

Creating Data Bars

A data bar is a conditional format that adds a horizontal bar to the background of a cell containing a numeric value. When applied to a range of cells, the data bars have the same appearance as a bar chart with each cell containing one bar.

The lengths of data bars are based on the value of each cell in the selected range. Cells with larger values have longer bars; cells with smaller values have shorter bars. Data bars are dynamic, which means that if one cell's value changes, the lengths of the data bars in the selected range are automatically updated.

Data bars differ from sparklines in that the bars are always placed in the cells containing the value they represent and each cell represents only a single bar from the bar chart. By contrast, a column sparkline can be inserted anywhere within the workbook and can represent data from several rows or columns. However, like sparklines, data bars can be used to create compact graphs that can be easily integrated alongside the text and values stored in your worksheet cells.

Ajita wants you to add data bars to the sector percentage values in the Sectors worksheet. The data bars will provide a visual picture of how the New Century Fund and the S&P 500 compare in their investments in different sectors.

To add data bars to the sector percentages:

1. In the Sectors worksheet, select the range **C4:D15**.
2. Click the **Home** tab on the Ribbon.
3. In the Styles group, click the **Conditional Formatting** button, and then point to **Data Bars** to display the Data Bars gallery.
4. In the Solid Fill group, click **Blue Data Bar** (the first data bar style). The data bars are added to the selected cells.
5. Click cell **A2** to deselect the sector percentages range. See Figure 4-40.

Figure 4-40 **Data bars added to the Sectors worksheet**

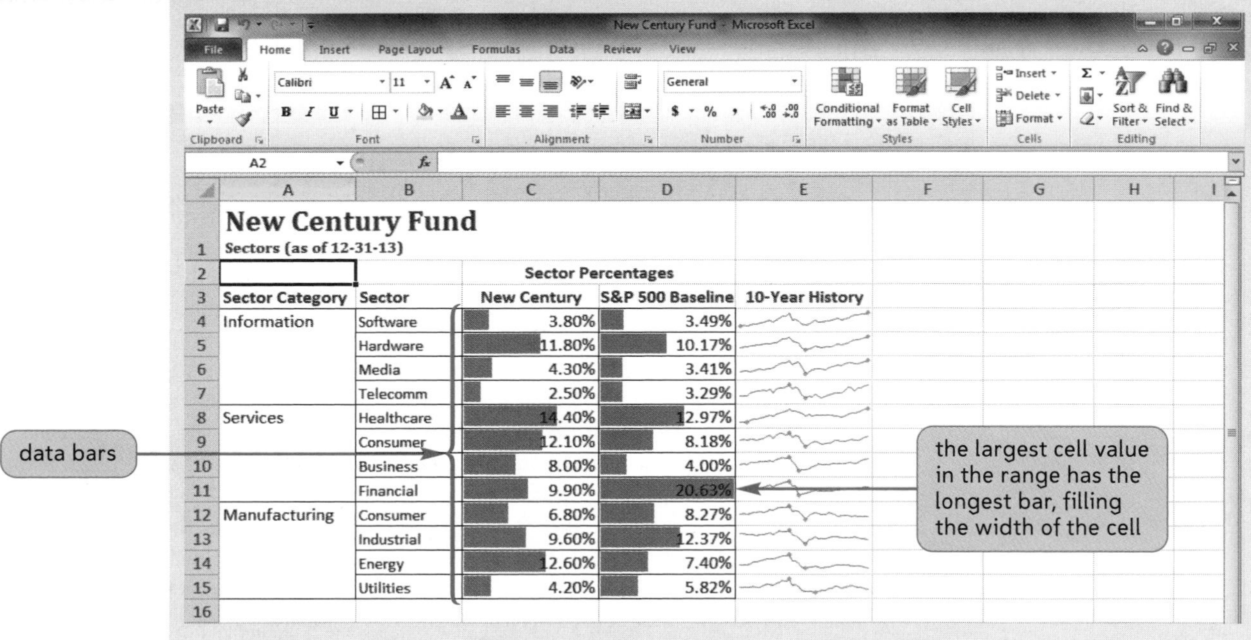

The data bars shown in Figure 4-40 present essentially the same information as the combination column and line chart you created earlier. However, the data bars have the advantage of being compact in size and integrated with the values in the Sector Percentages table.

Modifying a Data Bar Rule

The lengths of the data bars are determined based on the values in the selected range. The cell with the largest value contains a data bar that extends across the entire width of the cell, and the lengths of the other bars in the selected range are determined relative to that bar. In some cases, this means that the longest data overlaps the cell's data value, making it difficult to read. You can modify the length of the data bars by altering the rules of the conditional format.

In the Sector Percentages data, cell D11 contains the largest value (20.63 percent) in the range C4:D15 and has the longest data bar. The data bar in cell D5, representing 10.17 percent, fills only half the cell width by comparison. Ajita does not want data bars to overlap the cell values. You will modify the data bar rule to proportionally reduce the lengths of the data bars so that the longest of them only fills less than half of a cell rather than an entire cell.

TIP

When data bars are used with negative values, the data bars originate from the center of the cell with negative bars extending to the left and positive bars extending to the right.

To modify the data bar rule:

1. Select the range **C4:D15**, which contains the data bars.
2. In the Styles group on the Home tab, click the **Conditional Formatting** button, and then click **Manage Rules**. The Conditional Formatting Rules Manager dialog box opens, displaying all the rules applied to any conditional format in the workbook.
3. Make sure **Current Selection** appears in the Show formatting rules for box. You'll edit the rule applied to the current selection, the data bars in the Sectors worksheet.
4. Click the **Edit Rule** button. The Edit Formatting Rule dialog box opens. You want to modify this rule so that the maximum value for the data bar is set to 0.40, or 40 percent. All data bar lengths will then be defined relative to this value.
5. In the Type row, click the **Maximum** arrow, and then click **Number**.
6. In the Value row, type **0.40** in the Maximum box. See Figure 4-41.

Figure 4-41 **Edit Formatting Rule dialog box**

Edit Formatting Rule

Select a Rule Type:

- ► Format all cells based on their values
- ► Format only cells that contain
- ► Format only top or bottom ranked values
- ► Format only values that are above or below average
- ► Format only unique or duplicate values
- ► Use a formula to determine which cells to format

Edit the Rule Description:

Format all cells based on their values:

Format Style: Data Bar | Show Bar Only

	Minimum	Maximum
Type:	Automatic	Number
Value:	(Automatic)	0.4

Bar Appearance:

Fill	Color	Border	Color
Solid Fill		No Border	

Negative Value and Axis... Bar Direction: Context

Preview:

OK Cancel

hides the cell value, showing only the data bar

defines the value used for the shortest data bar

defines the value used for the longest data bar

sets the fill and border colors of the data bars

click to define how negative values will be presented in the data bars

7. Click the **OK** button in each dialog box, and then click cell **A2**. The lengths of the data bars are reduced so that the longest bar covers less than half the cell width. See Figure 4-42.

Figure 4-42 **Revised data bars**

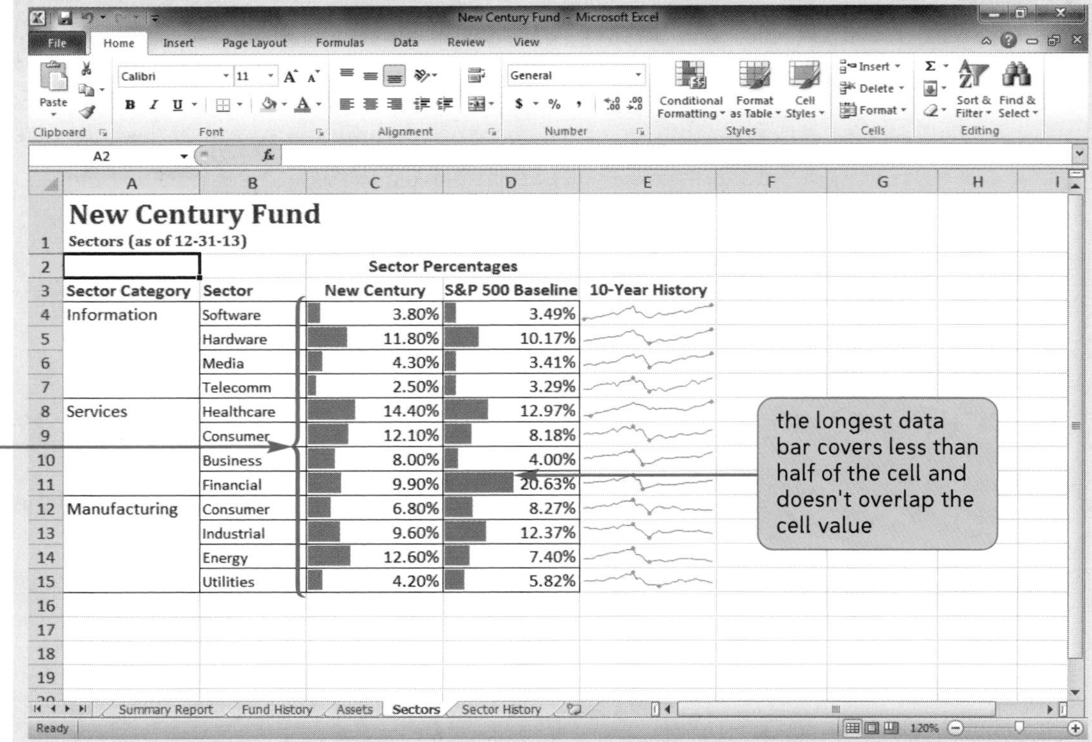

INSIGHT

Edward Tufte and Chart Design Theory

Any serious study of chart design will include the works of Edward Tufte, who pioneered the field of information design. One of Tufte's most important works is *The Visual Display of Quantitative Information* in which he laid out several principles for the design of charts and graphics.

Tufte was concerned with what he termed as "chart junk," in which a proliferation of chart elements—chosen because they look "nice"—confuse and distract the reader. One measure of chart junk is Tufte's data-ink ratio, which is the amount of "ink" used to display quantitative information compared to the total ink required by the chart. Tufte advocated limiting the use of non-data ink. Non-data ink is any part of the chart that does not convey information about the data. One way of measuring the data-ink ratio is to determine how much of the chart you can erase without affecting the user's ability to interpret the chart. Tufte would argue for high data-ink ratios with a minimum of extraneous elements and graphics.

To this end, Tufte helped developed sparklines, which convey information with a high data-ink ratio within a compact space. Tufte believed that charts that can be viewed and comprehended at a glance have a greater impact on the reader than large and cluttered graphs, no matter how attractive they might be.

Creating a Chart Sheet

TIP

You can also embed charts in a chart sheet, enabling you to display several charts in a single chart sheet.

Chart sheets are helpful for detailed charts that need more space to be seen clearly or when you want to show a chart without any worksheet text or data. Some reports require large expansive charts rather than compact graphs to provide more detail and make them easier to view and share. In those situations, you may want to devote an entire sheet to a graph rather than embed it within a worksheet. To create a larger version of a chart that covers an entire sheet, you move the chart to a chart sheet. Chart sheets are used for graphic elements like charts and images, and do not contain worksheet cells for calculating numeric values.

Ajita asks you to create a chart sheet for the workbook that shows a 3-D image of the performance of the New Century Fund over the past 10 years. In this case, the chart sheet is purely decorative; Ajita plans to use it as a cover page for the New Century Fund report.

To create the chart sheet for the New Century Fund report:

1. Go to the **Fund History** worksheet, and then select the range **A4:B44**. This range contains the data you want to use in the chart.
2. Click the **Insert** tab on the Ribbon.
3. In the Charts group, click the **Line** button, and then click the **3-D Line** chart type. The 3-D line chart is embedded in the Fund History worksheet. You'll move this chart to a chart sheet.
4. In the Location group on the Chart Tools Design tab, click the **Move Chart** button. The Move Chart dialog box opens.
5. Click the **New sheet** option button, and then type **Cover Sheet** in the box as the name for the new chart sheet.
6. Click the **OK** button. A chart sheet named "Cover Sheet" that contains the 3-D line chart is inserted in the workbook.

7. Drag the **Cover Sheet** sheet tab to the right of the Documentation sheet tab. The Cover Sheet appears before the Summary Report worksheet and the worksheets that contain the detailed data used to create the summary report. See Figure 4-43.

Figure 4-43 3-D chart in a chart sheet

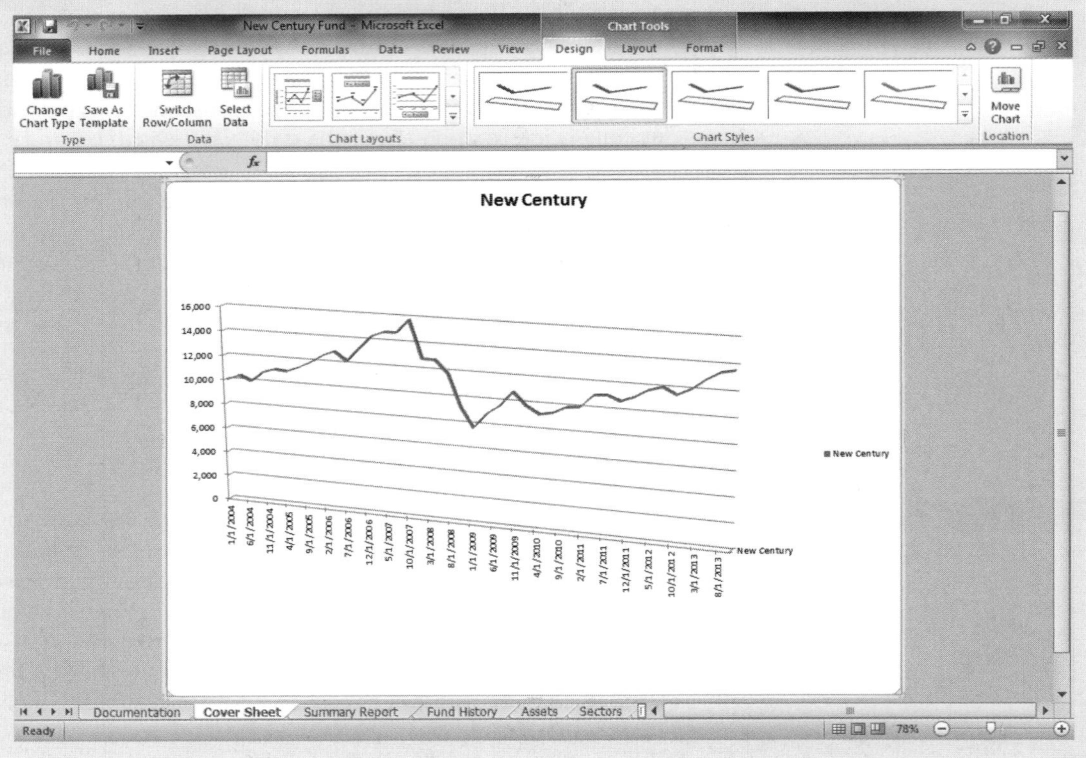

You can format a chart in a chart sheet using all the same options and tools as you do to format a chart embedded in a worksheet. You'll remove the axis labels and legend from the chart and rotate the chart in three dimensions. To increase the 3-D effect, you'll widen the chart's base from 100 to 1000 points.

To format the chart in the chart sheet:

1. In the Chart Styles group on the Chart Tools Design tab, click the **More** button, and then click **Style 40** (the last style in the fifth row in the Chart Styles gallery).
2. Click the **Chart Tools Layout** tab on the Ribbon.
3. In the Labels group, click the **Legend** button, and then click **None** to turn off the legend.
4. In the Axes group, click the **Axes** button, point to **Primary Horizontal Axis**, and then click **None** to remove the horizontal axis.
5. In the Axes group, click the **Axes** button, point to **Primary Vertical Axis**, and then click **None** to remove the vertical axis from the chart.
6. In the Axes group, click the **Axes** button, point to **Depth Axis**, and then click **None** to remove the depth axis.

7. In the Background section, click the **3-D Rotation** button. The Format Chart Area dialog box opens, displaying the 3-D Rotation options.
8. In the Rotation section, change the X value to **60°**, change the Y value to **20°**, and then change the Perspective value to **80°**. These settings rotate the chart.
9. In the Chart Scale section, change the Depth (% of base) value to **1000**. This setting exaggerates the 3-D effect, making the chart appear thicker.
10. Click **Fill** on the left side of the dialog box, and then click the **Gradient fill** option button. The background color of the chart area is set to a gradient fill.
11. Click the **Preset colors** button, and then click **Daybreak** (the fourth color in the first row).
12. Click the **Direction** button, and then click **Linear Down** (the second direction in the first row).
13. Click the **Close** button to return to the chart sheet. See Figure 4-44.

Figure 4-44 Rotated 3-D chart with exaggerated perspective

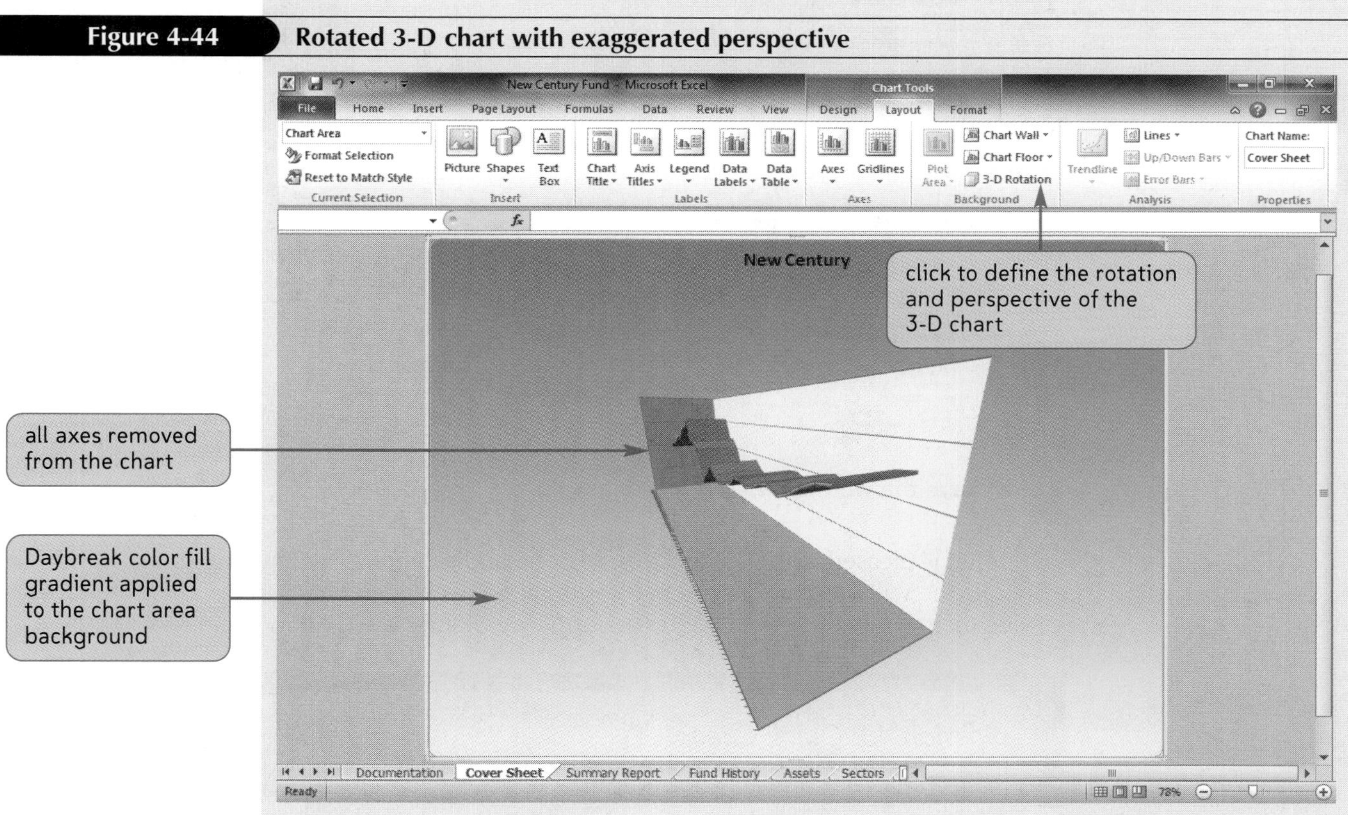

To complete the chart sheet, you'll overlay the chart title "The New Century Fund" over the chart and format it in a 48-point white font.

To overlay and format the chart title:

1. In the Labels group on the Chart Tools Layout tab, click the **Chart Title** button, and then click **Centered Overlay Title**. The chart title is overlaid above the chart. The chart expands to fill the extra space in the chart area.
2. Type **The New Century Fund**, and then press the **Enter** key. The new title is entered.

3. Click the **Home** tab on the Ribbon, and then change the font size to **36** points and the font color to **white**.
4. Click outside of the chart to deselect it. The cover sheet is final. See Figure 4-45.

Figure 4-45 Final cover sheet

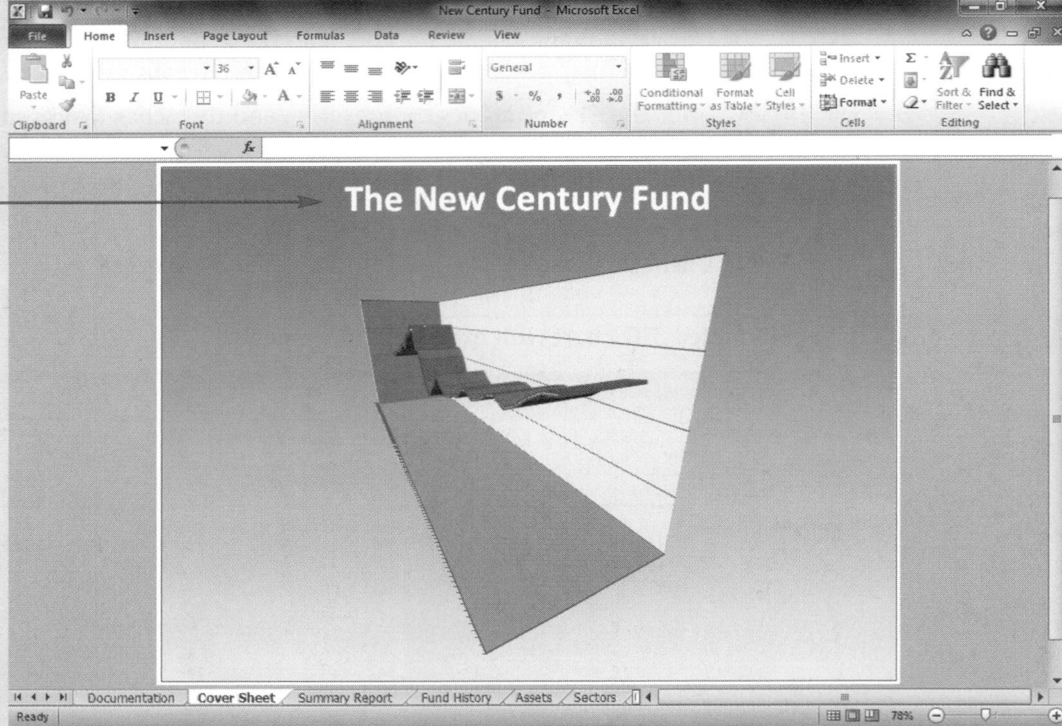

5. Save the workbook, and then close it.

Ajita is pleased with the work you've done adding charts and graphics to the workbook. She will present the workbook with all of its different charts to her clients to provide them a concise report on the performance of the New Century Fund.

REVIEW

Session 4.2 Quick Check

1. When should you use a line chart in place of a column chart?
2. How do you overlay a chart legend?
3. How do you add a data series to an already existing chart?
4. What is a combination chart? Describe how to create a combination chart.
5. Explain how 3-D charts can lead to a false interpretation of the data. What can you do to correct this problem?
6. What are sparklines? Describe the three types of sparklines.
7. What are data bars? Describe how data bars differ from sparklines.
8. How do you create a chart sheet?

Practice the skills you learned in the tutorial using the same case scenario.

PRACTICE

Review Assignments

Data File needed for the Review Assignments: Crockett.xlsx

Ajita has to create a report on the investment portfolio for Brian and Tammy Crockett. She wants to add charts that display where the couple's money is currently being invested and how their portfolio has performed in recent years. She's already entered the data. You will complete the report by adding the charts and a decorative cover sheet. Complete the following:

1. Open the **Crockett** workbook located in the Excel4\Review folder included with your Data Files, and then save the workbook as **Crockett Portfolio**. In the Documentation sheet, enter your name in cell B3 and the date in cell B4.
2. In the Composition worksheet, select the range A3:B8, and then insert the first 2-D pie chart. Move and resize the embedded pie chart to cover the range D1:G9 in the Portfolio Report worksheet.
3. Move the legend to the left side of the chart area. Change the chart title to **Investment Categories** and set its font size to 11 points. Change the fill color of the Cash slice to yellow. Add data labels that show the percentage of each pie slice to two decimal places outside of the pie chart, and then set the font size of the labels to 8 points.
4. Change the pie chart to a 3-D pie chart and set the 3-D rotation of the x-axis to 230° and the y-axis to 40°.
5. In the Sectors worksheet, select the range A3:D15, and then insert a 2-D clustered column chart. Move and resize the embedded chart to cover the range A12:D25 in the Portfolio Report worksheet.
6. Change the font size of the axis labels and legend to 8 points. Insert the chart title **Sector Percentages** above the plot and set its font size to 11 points. Change the format of the percentages in the vertical axis to display no decimal places. Overlay the legend at the top of the chart, and then change its fill color to white and insert a solid border around the legend.
7. Change the chart type of the S&P 500 series to a line chart, remove the line connecting the markers in the chart, and then change the marker type to a solid horizontal line of size 10.
8. Change the fill color of the columns for the Portfolio data series to the theme color Purple, Accent 4, Lighter 60%. Set the gap width of the columns in the Portfolio data series to 30%.
9. In the Portfolio History worksheet, select the range A3:B127, and then insert a line chart. Move and resize the chart to cover the range D29:G37 in the Portfolio Report worksheet. (*Hint*: Scroll down the Portfolio Report worksheet to locate the embedded chart.)
10. Remove the chart legend. Set the font size of the chart title to 11 points, and then set the font size of the axis labels to 8 points.
11. Set the major tick mark interval for the category axis at two years and the minor tick mark interval at one year. Use a custom format that displays the category axis date values as four-digit year values. Insert vertical gridlines for the minor tick marks.
12. Change the scale of the value axis to range from $200,000 to $350,000. Add major tick marks every $50,000. Add minor tick marks every $25,000. Insert horizontal gridlines for every minor tick mark.
13. In cell B32, insert a line sparkline for the data range C4:C127 of the Portfolio History worksheet to describe the growth of the portfolio over consecutive three-month periods. Mark the high point and the low point with green and red markers, respectively.
14. In cell B37, insert a line sparkline for the data range D4:D127 of the Portfolio worksheet to show the growth of the portfolio over consecutive one-year periods. Add high/low data markers and an axis to this sparkline to match the first sparkline.

15. In cell B42, insert a line sparkline showing the growth of the portfolio over consecutive three-year periods using the data range E4:E127 of the Portfolio worksheet. Format the sparkline to match the other two sparklines.
16. Add solid blue data bars to the values in the range G13:G20. Modify the data bar rule so that the maximum length of the data bar corresponds to a number value of 1.8. Repeat to create data bars for the area values in the range G23:G25.
17. Select the range A3:B127 in the Portfolio History worksheet, and insert a line chart. Move the embedded chart to a new chart sheet named **Cover Sheet**. Move the Cover Sheet worksheet directly after the Documentation sheet.
18. Change the chart style to Style 34 (the second style in the fifth row of the Chart Styles gallery). Remove the display of the horizontal, vertical, and depth axes. Remove the chart legend.
19. For the 3-D rotation, set the x-axis to 60°, the y-axis to 10°, the perspective to 15°, and the depth of the base to 2000.
20. Change the chart title to **Crockett Family Portfolio**. Set the font size of the chart title to 40 points.
21. Save and close your workbook, and then submit the finished workbook to your instructor, either in printed or electronic form, as requested.

APPLY

Case Problem 1

If you have a SAM 2010 user profile, your instructor may have assigned an autogradable version of this assignment. If so, log into the SAM 2010 Web site at www.cengage.com/sam2010 to download the instructions and start files.

Data File needed for this Case Problem: Kenai.xlsx

Kenai Fjords National Park Maria Sanford is the chief of interpretation at Kenai Fjords National Park. Part of her job is to report on park usage at the visitor centers. She wants to create a chart sheet that displays the park usage data. She has recorded last year's usage data in an Excel workbook. She asks you to present this data in a 3-D column chart for an upcoming meeting with her supervisor. She wants the chart to show the monthly usage totals organized by visitor center. She also wants a 3-D pie chart superimposed on the column chart and a table of park usage data. Complete the following:

1. Open the **Kenai** workbook located in the Excel4\Case1 folder included with your Data Files, and then save the workbook as **Kenai Fjords Park**. In the Documentation sheet, enter your name in cell B3 and the date in cell B4.
2. In the Park Usage Data worksheet, select the range A3:D15, and then insert the 3-D Column chart (the last chart in the 3-D Column section in the Charts gallery).
3. Move the chart to a chart sheet named **Monthly Visits**. Place the Monthly Visits chart sheet directly after the Documentation sheet.
4. Change the style of the chart to Style 42 (the second style in the sixth row in the Chart Styles gallery).
5. Insert a chart title using the centered overlay title format, change the title to **Kenai Fjords National Park 2013 Census**, and then set its font size to 24 points. Remove the legend from the chart.
6. Add the title **Monthly Visitors** to the vertical axis. Rotate the title 90° and set the font size to 14 points.
7. Rotate the 3-D chart using the following parameters: x-axis rotation 30°, y-axis rotation 20°, perspective 25°, and depth 130. (*Hint*: Uncheck the Right Angle Axes check box in the Chart Scale section to make the Perspective box active.)

EXPLORE

8. Modify the depth axis so that the values are displayed in reverse order. (*Hint*: Use the Axes button in the Axes group on the Chart Tools Layout tab to modify the depth axis.)

EXPLORE

9. Insert a data table without legend keys below the 3-D chart to provide the data values for the different columns. (*Hint*: Use the Data Table button in the Labels group on the Chart Tools Layout tab.)

10. Change the fill color of the Visitor Center series to orange.
11. In the Park Usage Data worksheet, select the range B3:D3;B16:D16, and then insert a 3-D pie chart.
12. Move the embedded chart to the Monthly Visits chart sheet.
13. Insert the chart title **Total Visits** above the pie chart, and set its font size to 16 points and its color to white.
14. Change the color of the Visitor Center slice to orange.
15. Remove the chart legend from the pie chart.
16. Add data labels to the inside of each slice, displaying the slice's value.
17. Change the fill color of the chart area to none (removing the fill color) and change the border color to no line (removing the border). Resize the embedded pie chart and move it to the lower-left of the column chart.
18. Go to the Park Usage Data worksheet, and then add data bars to the range B4:D15. Modify the rule for the data bars so that the maximum data bar length matches a value of 100,000.
19. Save and close your workbook, and then submit the finished workbook to your instructor, either in printed or electronic form, as requested.

Create a combination chart describing tornado events.

APPLY

Case Problem 2

Data Files needed for this Case Problem: Tornado.xlsx, Cloud.jpg

Midwest Tornado Institute Joyce Bishop is a meteorologist at the Midwest Tornado Institute located in Decatur, Illinois. Joyce is preparing for a talk she is giving to a local civic group on the possible effects of global warming on tornados. She has collected data on minor, moderate, and major tornado sightings in five-year periods during the second half of the twentieth century and wants you to create a graph for her talk showing her data. She's already entered this data into an Excel workbook. Complete the following:

1. Open the **Tornado** workbook located in the Excel4\Case2 folder included with your Data Files, and then save the workbook as **Tornado Sightings**. In the Documentation sheet, enter your name in cell B3 and the date in cell B4.
2. In the Sightings History worksheet, select the range A3:E13, and then insert a 2-D clustered column chart. Move the embedded chart to a chart sheet named **Sightings Chart**.
3. Change the chart style to Style 32 (the last chart style in the fourth row of the Chart Styles gallery).
4. Insert the chart title **Tornado Sightings: 1950–1999** at the top of the chart, and then change the font size to 24 points.
5. Add the vertical axis title **Sightings** in a 14-point font with horizontal orientation. Add the horizontal axis title **Years** in a 14-point font.
6. Move the legend to the bottom of the chart, and then set its font size to 14 points.
7. EXPLORE — Change the line style of the horizontal gridline from a solid line to a dashed line. (*Hint*: Use the Dash type button in the Line Style options in the Format Major Gridlines dialog box.)
8. Add vertical gridlines to the major tick marks in the chart. Display the gridlines as dashed lines.
9. Change the chart type of the All data series from a column chart to a 2-D line chart. Change the color of the line to standard blue.
10. EXPLORE — Select the plot area and change the fill to a picture fill, using the **Cloud.jpg** file located in the Excel4\Case2 folder included with your Data Files. (*Hint*: Open the Format Plot Area dialog box. In the Fill options, click the Picture or texture fill option button, click the File button, and then locate and select the picture file.)

11. Go to the Sightings History worksheet, and then insert orange data bars in the range B4:D13. Insert blue data bars in the range E4:E13. Note that the meaning of the lengths of the two sets of data bars is different because they are applied to different ranges.
12. In cell B2, insert a sparkline for the data in the range B4:B13 (do *not* include the total in cell B14). Repeat to insert a sparkline in each cell in the range C2:E2.
13. Save and close your workbook, and then submit the finished workbook to your instructor, either in printed or electronic form, as requested.

Explore how to use Excel to chart stock market data.

CHALLENGE

Case Problem 3

Data File needed for this Case Problem: Mitchell.xlsx

Hardin Financial Kurt Lee is a financial analyst for Hardin Financial, a consulting firm in Owatonna, Minnesota. As part of his job, he records stock market activity in Excel workbooks. One workbook contains the recent stock market activity of Mitchell Oil. He wants your help in creating a chart displaying the stock values. The chart should display the stock's opening, high, low, and closing values, and the number of shares traded for each day of the past few weeks. The volume of shares traded should be expressed in terms of millions of shares. Complete the following:

1. Open the **Mitchell** workbook located in the Excel4\Case3 folder included with your Data Files, and then save the workbook as **Mitchell Oil**. In the Documentation sheet, enter your name in cell B3 and the date in cell B4.
2. EXPLORE In the Stock Values worksheet, select the range A3:F33, and then insert a Volume-Open-High-Low-Close stock chart. (*Hint*: Click the Other Charts button in the Charts group on the Insert tab to locate the stock charts.) Move the embedded chart to the chart sheet named **Stock History**.
3. Insert the chart title **Mitchell Oil** above the chart area, and then set the font size of the chart title to 18 points. Remove the chart legend.
4. Add the title **Date** to the primary horizontal axis, and then set its font size to 14 points. Add the title **Shares Traded** to the primary vertical axis, set its font size to 14 points, and then rotate the title 270°.
5. EXPLORE Add the title **Stock Value** to the secondary vertical axis, set its font size to 14 points, and rotate the title 90°. (*Hint*: Open the Format Axis Title dialog box for the secondary vertical axis and use the Text direction button found in the Alignment category.)
6. Set the font size of all axis values to 12 points.
7. Display the horizontal and vertical gridlines using a dashed line style. Set the interval between major tick marks on the primary horizontal axis to 7 days.
8. For the primary vertical axis, display the values in units of one million, change the number format to two decimal place accuracy, and then set the maximum value of the axis scale to 2,000,000.
9. For the secondary vertical axis, set the minimum value of the scale to 10.
10. Decrease the gap width between the columns in the plot to 30% and change the fill color to light blue.
11. Change the fill color of the plot area to light yellow.
12. EXPLORE In a stock market chart, the daily chart values will show either an increase or a decrease from the previous day. Increases are shown with an up bar displayed in white and decreases are shown with a down bar displayed in black. Select the data series for the up bars and change their fill colors to light green. Select the data series for the down bars and change their fill colors to red.

EXPLORE

13. Go to the Stock Values worksheet. Add a column sparkline to cell B2 to display the Shares Traded values in the range B4:B33.
14. Add a line sparkline to cell F2 to display the closing values of the stock over the range F4:F33.
15. In the range G3:G33, create a new column of values named **Difference** that is equal to the difference between the stock's closing value and its opening value on each day. Display the difference values using the same format as in column F.

EXPLORE

16. Add a win/loss sparkline to cell G2 that indicates the days that the stock gained value and the days that the stock lost value.
17. Save and close your workbook, and then submit the finished workbook to your instructor, either in printed or electronic form, as requested.

Create an Excel workbook to provide a report on a sporting event.

CREATE

Case Problem 4

Data File needed for this Case Problem: Basketball.xlsx

Blowout Sports Steve Eagan is the owner and operator of Blowout Sports, a sports information and scouting company located in Lexington, Kentucky. One of Steve's jobs is to provide detailed graphical reports and analysis of college basketball games for the media, coaches, and interested fans. Steve has been placing box score data and game logs into an Excel workbook. He wants to summarize this data in one worksheet using charts and graphs. He's asked you to help develop the workbook. Steve has a sample workbook containing the results of a recent basketball game for you to work on. Complete the following:

1. Open the **Basketball** workbook located in the Excel4\Case4 folder included with your Data Files, and then save the workbook as **Basketball Report**. In the Documentation sheet, enter your name in cell B3 and the date in cell B4.
2. The Game Log worksheet contains the minute-by-minute score of the game. Use the data in this worksheet to create a line chart describing the ebb and flow of the game that is embedded in the Game Report worksheet. The format of the chart is up to you, but it should include titles for the chart and the axes, a chart legend overlay, vertical gridlines spaced at 4-minute intervals, and horizontal gridlines at 5-point intervals. (*Hint*: To display vertical gridlines at 4-minute intervals, you must turn off the multi-level category labels.)
3. The Box Score worksheet contains statistical summaries of the game. Use the data in this worksheet to create two column charts describing the points scored by each player on the two teams. Embed the charts in the Game Report worksheet. The format of the charts is up to you, but it should include titles for the chart and axes, and gradient fill colors for the columns.
4. The Box Score worksheet also contains team statistics. Use this data to create several pie charts that compare the two teams. Embed the pie charts in the Game Report worksheet. The final pie charts should include data labels for the pie slices and slice colors that match the team's colors (red for Wisconsin, gold for Iowa).
5. The Season Record worksheet contains a record of each team's season including wins and losses. Use this data to create a win/loss sparkline displayed on the Game Report worksheet alongside each team's season record.

6. Create a chart sheet for the report that will be a cover sheet. The cover sheet should include a 3-D chart of some of the data in the workbook. The format of the chart and chart sheet is up to you.
7. Save and close your workbook, and then submit the finished workbook to your instructor, either in printed or electronic form, as requested.

ASSESS

SAM: Skills Assessment Manager

For current SAM information, including versions and content details, visit SAM Central (http://samcentral.course.com). If you have a SAM user profile, you may have access to hands-on instruction, practice, and assessment of the skills covered in this tutorial. Since various versions of SAM are supported throughout the life of this text, check with your instructor for the correct instructions and URL/Web site for accessing assignments.

ENDING DATA FILES

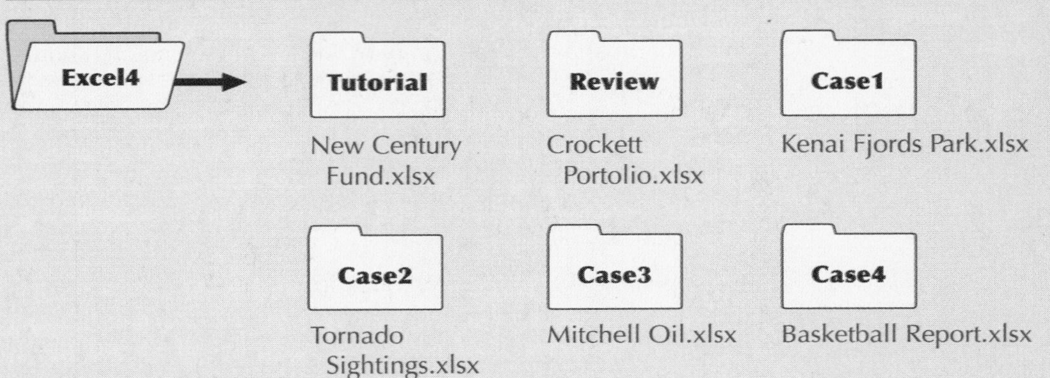

ProSkills

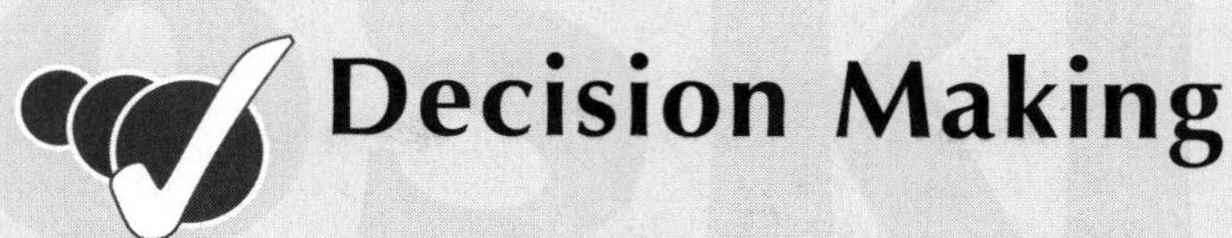

Decision Making

Creating a Budget Worksheet to Make Financial Decisions

Decision making is the process of choosing between alternative courses of action, usually in response to a problem that needs to be solved. Having an understanding of decision-making processes will lead to better decisions and greater confidence in carrying out those decisions. This is especially important when making financial decisions.

Gather Relevant Information

Begin by collecting data and information related to the decision you need to make. This information can include data expressed as currency or numbers, as well as data that cannot be measured numerically. For example, when creating a budget, numerical data includes your income and expenses, current savings, future savings and purchases, and so on. Other data might include the amount of savings you need to feel comfortable before making a large purchase, such as buying a car or paying tuition.

Evaluate the Gathered Information and Develop Alternatives

Evaluate the data you collected and determine potential alternatives. Excel workbooks are well suited to evaluating numerical data. You can also use workbooks to evaluate potential outcomes based on other data by assigning numerical weights to them. For example, you can enter your monthly income and fixed expenses into a worksheet along with variable expenses to determine your cash flow. You can then consider this information along with your current savings to determine how much money to contribute to savings or earmark for a purchase. Based on these results, you can develop alternatives for how to distribute your available money among variable expenses (such as entertainment), savings, and a large purchase.

Select the Best Alternative

Carefully evaluate the alternatives you developed based on your analysis. Before making a decision, be sure to take into account all factors. Consider such questions as:

- Does this alternative make sense for the long term? For example, does this budget allow you to achieve all your financial goals?
- Can you realistically carry out this alternative? For example, does this budget provide enough for necessities such as food and housing as well as for luxuries such as entertainment?
- Will this alternative be acceptable even if its outcome is not perfect or some unconsidered factors emerge? For example, will this budget cover unforeseen expenses such as car repair or an unexpected trip?
- How comfortable are you with this decision? For example, does this budget relieve or add stress about managing your finances?

After analyzing all the factors, one alternative should begin to emerge as the best alternative. If it doesn't, you might need to develop additional alternatives.

ProSkills

Prepare an Action Plan

After making a decision, you need to plan how to implement that decision. Consider what steps you need to take to achieve the final outcome. For example, do you need to open a bank account or change services to reduce expenses (such as switching to a less expensive cell phone plan)? Determine a reasonable time table. When do you want start? How long will each task take? What tasks must be completed before others start? Can tasks be performed at the same time? Develop milestones to track the success of your plan. For example, one milestone might be to see your savings increase by 10 percent in three months. Finally, identify what resources you need to be successful. For example, do you need to talk to a financial advisor at your bank?

Take Action and Monitor the Results

After you develop the action plan, the actual plan begins. For example, you can open bank accounts, change telephone services, and so forth as outlined in your action plan. Be sure to check off completed tasks and assess how well those actions produce the desired outcome. For example, is the budget achieving the financial goals you set? If so, then continue to follow the established plan. If not, you may need to modify the action plan or reevaluate your decision.

PROSKILLS

Develop a Budget Worksheet

Excel is valuable to a wide audience of users: from accountants of *Fortune 500* companies to homeowners managing their budgets. An Excel workbook can be a complex document, recording data from thousands of financial transactions, or it can track a few monthly household expenses. Anyone who has to balance a budget, track expenses, or project future income can use the financial tools in Excel to help them make good financial decisions about their financing and future expenditures.

In this exercise, you will use Excel to create a sample budget workbook that will contain information of your choice, using Excel skills and features presented in Tutorials 1 through 4. Use the following steps as a guide to completing your workbook.

Note: Please be sure *not* to include any personal information of a sensitive nature in any workbooks you create to be submitted to your instructor for this exercise. Later, you can update the workbooks with such information for your personal use.

1. Gather the data related to your monthly cash inflows and outflows. For example, how much do you take home in your paychecks each month? What other sources of income do you have? What expenses do you have—rent, utilities, gas, insurance, groceries, entertainment, car payments, and so on?
2. Create a new workbook for the sample financial data. Use the first worksheet as a documentation sheet that includes your name, the date on which you start creating the workbook, and a brief description of the workbook's purpose.
3. Plan the structure of the second worksheet, which will contain the budget. Include a section to enter values that remain consistent from month to month, such as monthly income and expenses. As you develop the budget worksheet, reference these cells in formulas that require those values. Later, you can update any of these values and see the changes immediately reflected throughout the budget.

ProSkills

4. In the budget worksheet, enter realistic monthly earnings for each month of the year. Use formulas to calculate the total earnings each month, the average monthly earnings, and the total earnings for the entire year.
5. In the budget worksheet, enter realistic personal expenses for each month. Divide the expenses into at least three categories, providing subtotals for each category and a grand total of all the monthly expenses. Calculate the average monthly expenses and total expenses for the year.
6. Calculate the monthly net cash flow (the value of total income minus total expenses).
7. Use the cash flow values to track the savings throughout the year. Use a realistic amount for savings at the beginning of the year. Use the monthly net cash flow values to add or subtract from this value. Project the end-of-year balance in the savings account under your proposed budget.
8. Format the worksheet's contents using appropriate text and number formats. Add colors and line borders to make the content easier to read and interpret. Use cell styles and themes to provide your worksheet with a uniform appearance.
9. Use conditional formatting to automatically highlight negative net cash flow months.
10. Insert a pie chart that compares the monthly expenses for the categories.
11. Insert a column chart that charts all of the monthly expenses regardless of the category.
12. Insert a line chart or sparkline that shows the change in the savings balance throughout the 12 months of the year.
13. Insert new rows at the top of the worksheet and enter titles that describe the worksheet's contents.
14. Examine your assumptions. How likely are certain events to occur? Perform several what-if analyses on your budget, providing the impact of (a) reducing income with expenses remaining constant, (b) increasing expenses with income remaining constant, (c) reducing income and expenses, and (d) increasing income and expenses. Discuss the different scenarios you explored. How much cushion does your projected income give you if expenses increase? What are some things you can do in your budget to accommodate this scenario?
15. Think of a major purchase you might want to make—for example, a car or a computer. Determine the amount of the purchase and the current annual interest rate charged by your local bank. Provide a reasonable length of time to repay the loan, such as five years for a car loan or 20 to 30 years for a home loan. Use the PMT function to determine how much you would have to spend each month on the payments for your purchase. You can do these calculations in a separate worksheet
16. Add the loan information to your monthly budget and evaluate the purchase of this item on your budget. Is it affordable? Examine other possible loans you might pursue and evaluate their impact on your budget. Come up with the most realistic way of paying off the loan while still maintaining a reasonable monthly cash flow and a cushion against unexpected expenses. If the payment exceeds your budget, reduce the estimated price of the item you're thinking of purchasing until you determine the monthly payment you can afford under the conditions of the loan.

ProSkills

17. After settling on a budget and the terms of a loan that you can afford, develop an action plan for putting your budget into place. What are some potential pitfalls that will prohibit you from following through on your proposed budget? How can you increase the likelihood that you will follow the budget? Be specific, and write down a list of goals and benchmarks that you'll use to monitor your progress in following your financial plan.
18. With the worksheet set up and your budget in place, you can take action and monitor your results. You will want to update your worksheet each month as income or expense items change to be sure you remain on track to meet your goals. You will also want to confirm that you made a good decision. If not, evaluate your budget and determine what new action you need to take to get yourself back on track.
19. Format the worksheets for your printer. Include headers and footers that display the workbook filename, the workbook's author, and the date on which the report is printed. If the report extends across several pages, repeat appropriate print titles on all of the pages and include page numbers and the total number of pages on every printed page.
20. Save and close your workbook, and then submit the completed workbook to your instructor, in printed or electronic form, as requested.

TUTORIAL 5

Working with Excel Tables, PivotTables, and PivotCharts

Tracking Museum Art Objects

EXCEL

OBJECTIVES

Session 5.1
- Explore a structured range of data
- Freeze rows and columns
- Plan and create an Excel table
- Rename and format an Excel table
- Add, edit, and delete records in an Excel table
- Sort data

Session 5.2
- Filter data
- Insert a Total row to summarize an Excel table
- Split a worksheet into two panes
- Insert subtotals into a range of data
- Use the Outline buttons to show or hide details

Session 5.3
- Create and modify a PivotTable
- Apply PivotTable styles and formatting
- Filter and sort a PivotTable
- Insert a slicer to filter a PivotTable
- Group PivotTable items
- Create a PivotChart

Case | *LaFouch Museum*

Henry LaFouch, a rancher in Missoula, Montana, amassed a huge collection of North American art, particularly art of the West. Henry was a well-respected, active member of the community, and he often donated art to the town. Similarly, he loaned the town artwork to place in public locations and community centers. Upon his death, Henry donated his art collection to the town of Missoula and its people. They established an art museum in his name.

Mary Littlefield was recently hired as the curator and director of the LaFouch Museum. She is responsible for assessing the current holdings and using the endowment set aside by Henry to purchase additional art in keeping with his vision for the collection. One of Mary's first tasks was to establish an accurate inventory of the museum's holdings. For each piece of artwork, she identified the title, the artist, the date acquired, the type of art, and other pertinent facts such as its location in the museum, its condition, and its appraised value. Then, she entered all this data in an Excel worksheet.

You will help Mary maintain this data so she can provide current and accurate information to the administration and board of directors about the art objects. You'll work with the data using Excel table features. You will sort the data and add, modify, and delete the data to ensure it is current. You'll also filter the information to display only data that meets certain criteria. Finally, you'll summarize the data using a PivotTable and a PivotChart.

STARTING DATA FILES

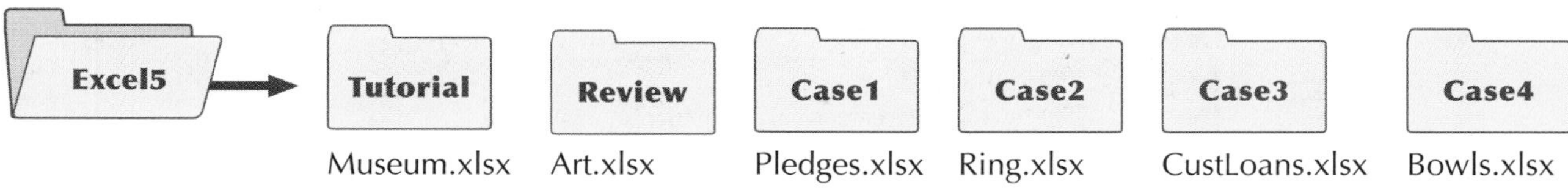

SESSION 5.1 VISUAL OVERVIEW

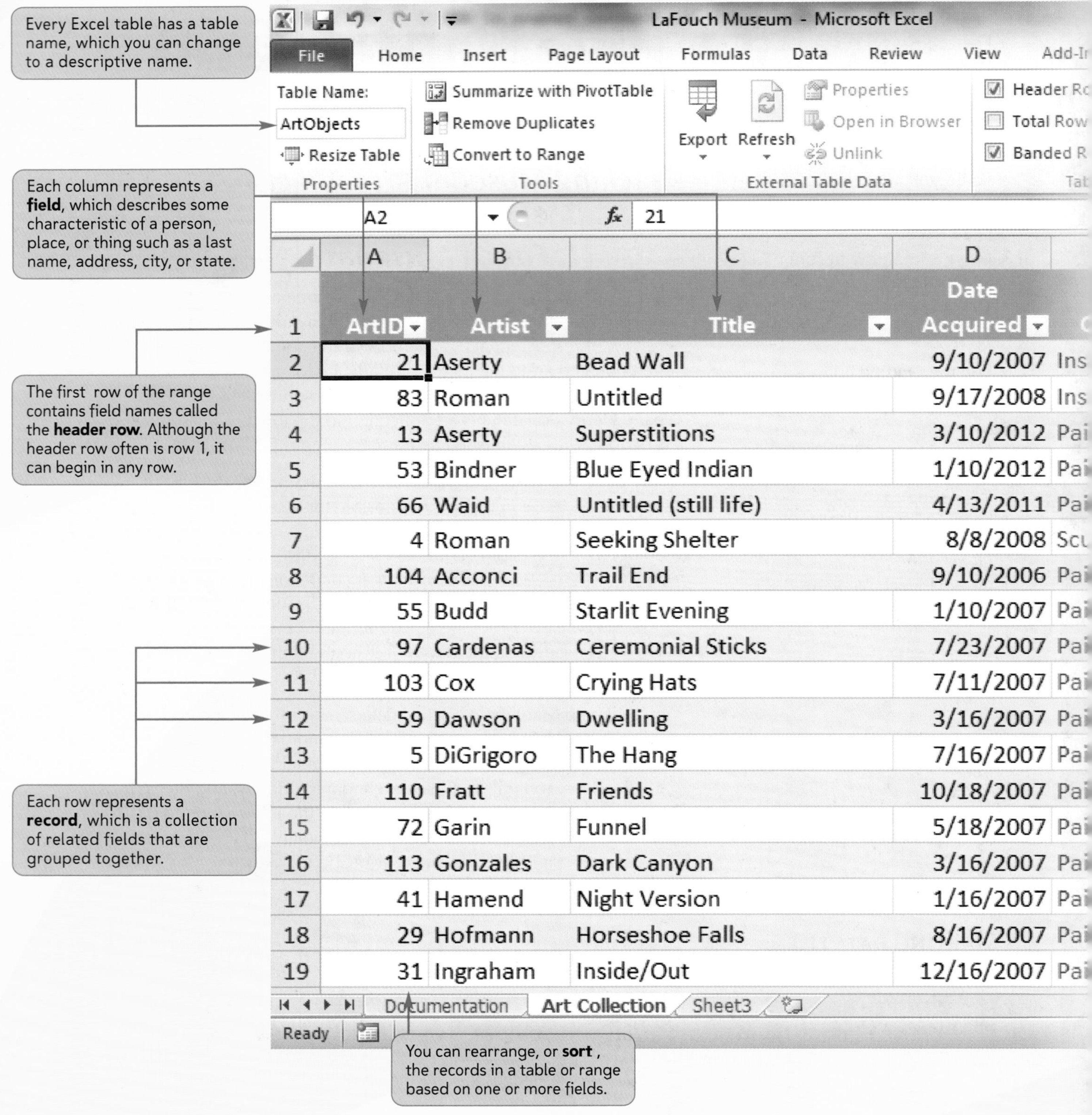

AN EXCEL TABLE

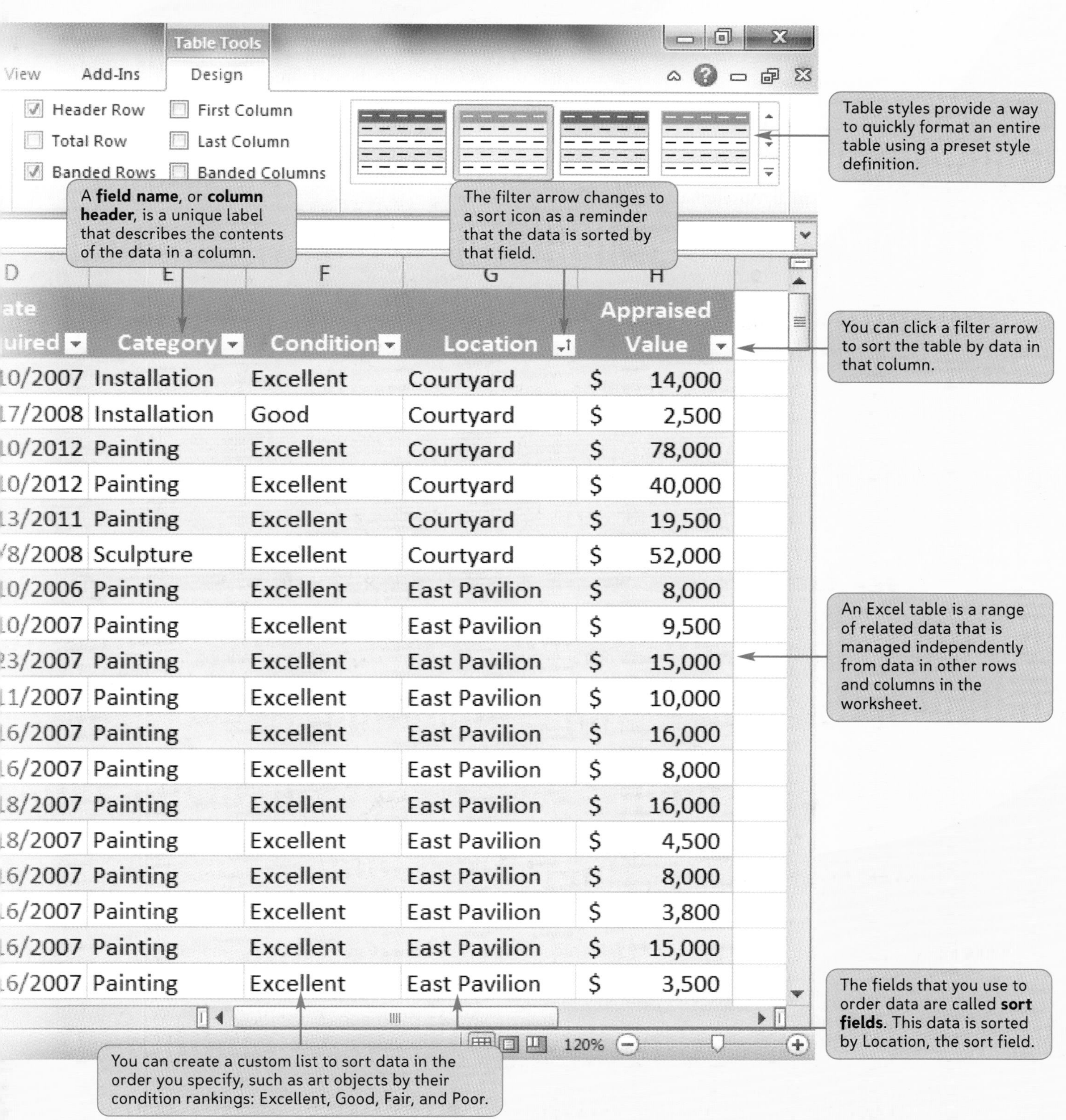

Planning a Structured Range of Data

One of the more common uses of a worksheet is to manage data, such as lists of clients, products, and transactions. Using Excel, you can store and update data, sort data, search for and retrieve subsets of data, summarize data, and create reports. In Excel, a collection of similar data can be structured in a range of columns and rows, representing fields and records, respectively.

Figure 5-1 shows a portion of the data Mary compiled for the LaFouch Museum's art objects. In this data, the ArtID, Artist, and Title columns are the first three fields. Each row is a record that stores the data for each art object—art ID, artist name, title, date acquired, category, condition, location, and appraised value. All the art object records make up the *structured range of data*. A structured range of data is commonly referred to as a list or table.

Figure 5-1 **LaFouch Museum art objects data**

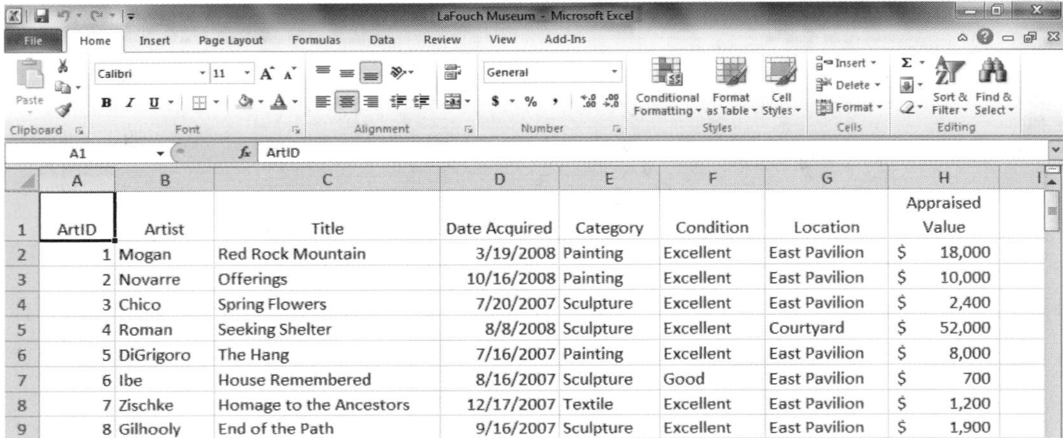

ArtID	Artist	Title	Date Acquired	Category	Condition	Location	Appraised Value
1	Mogan	Red Rock Mountain	3/19/2008	Painting	Excellent	East Pavilion	$ 18,000
2	Novarre	Offerings	10/16/2008	Painting	Excellent	East Pavilion	$ 10,000
3	Chico	Spring Flowers	7/20/2007	Sculpture	Excellent	East Pavilion	$ 2,400
4	Roman	Seeking Shelter	8/8/2008	Sculpture	Excellent	Courtyard	$ 52,000
5	DiGrigoro	The Hang	7/16/2007	Painting	Excellent	East Pavilion	$ 8,000
6	Ibe	House Remembered	8/16/2007	Sculpture	Good	East Pavilion	$ 700
7	Zischke	Homage to the Ancestors	12/17/2007	Textile	Excellent	East Pavilion	$ 1,200
8	Gilhooly	End of the Path	9/16/2007	Sculpture	Excellent	East Pavilion	$ 1,900

PROSKILLS

Decision Making: The Importance of Planning

Before you create a structured range of data, be sure to create a plan. Planning involves gathering relevant information about the data and deciding your goals. The end results you want to achieve will help you determine the kind of data to include in each record and how to divide that data into fields. Specifically, do the following to create an effective plan:

- Spend time thinking about how you will use the data.
- Consider what reports you want to create for different audiences (supervisors, customers, directors, and so forth) and the fields needed to produce those reports.
- Think about the various questions, or *queries*, you want answered and the fields needed to create these results.

Careful and thorough planning will help you avoid having to redesign a structured range of data later.

Before creating the list of art objects, Mary carefully planned what information she needs and how she wants to use it. Mary plans to use the data to track where each art object is located in the museum, its condition, the date it was acquired, its art category, and its appraised value. She wants to be able to create reports that show specific lists of art objects, such as all the objects by a specific artist or all the objects that are paintings. Based on her needs, Mary developed a **data definition table**, which is documentation that lists the fields to be maintained for each record (in this case, each art object) and a description of the information each field will include. Figure 5-2 shows Mary's completed data definition table.

Figure 5-2 **Data definition table for the art objects**

Field	Description
ArtID	Unique number
Artist	Name of artist
Title	Title of art object
Date Acquired	Date of purchase or donation of art object
Category	Painting, Sculpture, Installation, Textile
Condition	Excellent, Good, Fair, Poor
Location	Location of art object
Appraised Value	Current value of art object

After you determine the fields and records you need, you can enter the data in a blank worksheet or use a range of data that is already entered in a worksheet. You can then work with the data in many ways, including the following common operations:

- Add, edit, and delete data in the range.
- Sort the data range.
- Filter to display only rows that meet specified criteria.
- Insert formulas to calculate subtotals.
- Create summary tables based on the data in the range (usually with PivotTables).

You'll perform many of these operations on the art objects data.

INSIGHT

Creating an Effective Structured Range of Data

For a range of data to be used effectively, it must have the same structure throughout. Keep in mind the following guidelines:

- Enter field names in the top row of the range.
- Use short, descriptive field names. Shorter field names are easier to remember and enable more fields to appear in the workbook window at once.
- Format field names to distinguish the header row from the data. For example, apply bold, color, and a different font size.
- Enter the same kind of data for a State field in each record. For example, enter CA, AZ, or IL for State, but not cities such as Los Angeles, Tucson, or Chicago.
- Separate the data (including the header row) from other information in the worksheet by *at least* one blank row and one blank column. The blank row and column enable Excel to accurately determine the range of the data.

You'll open the workbook in which Mary entered the art objects data according to the data definition table.

To open and review the Museum workbook:

1. Open the **Museum** workbook located in the Excel5\Tutorial folder included with your Data Files, and then save the workbook as **LaFouch Museum**.
2. In the Documentation sheet, enter your name in cell B3 and the date in cell B4.

3. Switch to the **Art Collection** worksheet. This worksheet (which was shown in Figure 5-1) contains data about the museum's art objects. Currently, the worksheet lists 115 art objects. Each art object record is a separate row (rows 2 through 116) and contains eight fields (columns A through H). The top row, the header row, contains labels that describe the data in each column.
4. Scroll the worksheet to row **116**, the last record. The column headers, in the top row, are no longer visible.
5. Press the **Ctrl+Home** keys to return to cell A1.

Freezing Rows and Columns

You want to see the column headers as you scroll the art objects data. Without the column headers visible, it is difficult to know what the data entered in each column represents. You can select rows and columns to remain visible in the workbook window as you scroll around the worksheet. **Freezing** a row or column lets you keep headings visible as you work with the data in a large worksheet. As you scroll the data, the first row remains on the screen so the column headers are visible, making it easier to identify the data in each record.

You'll freeze the first row, which contains the column headers.

To freeze the top row in the worksheet:

1. Click the **View** tab on the Ribbon. The Ribbon displays the View options.
2. In the Window group, click the **Freeze Panes** button, and then click **Freeze Top Row**. A dark, horizontal line appears below the column headers to indicate which row is frozen.
3. Scroll the worksheet to row **99**. This time, the column headers remain visible as you scroll. See Figure 5-3.

Figure 5-3 Top row of the worksheet is frozen

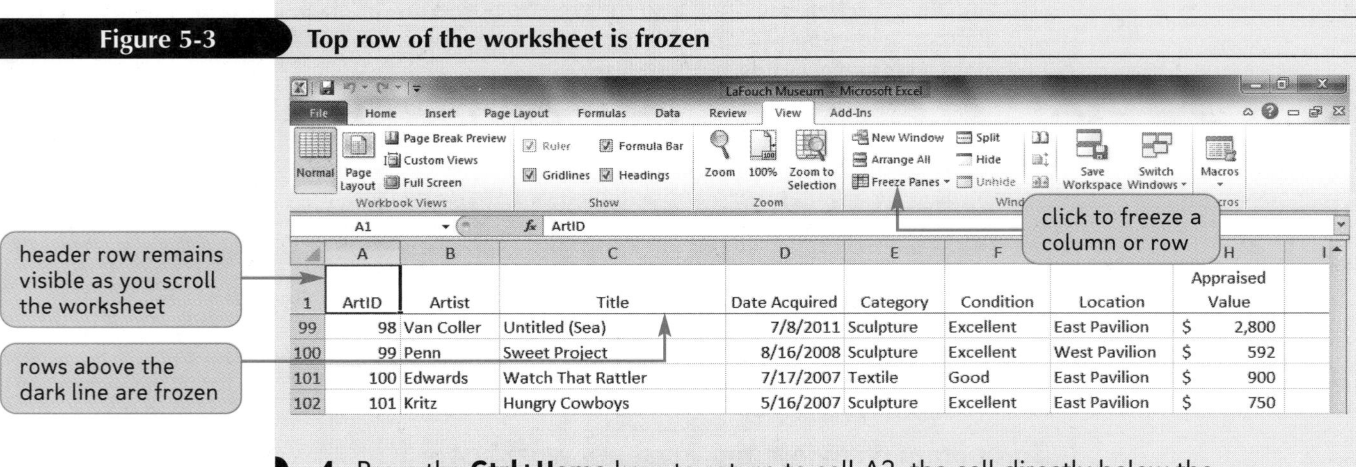

4. Press the **Ctrl+Home** keys to return to cell A2, the cell directly below the frozen row.

After you freeze panes, the first option on the Freeze Panes menu changes to Unfreeze Panes. This option releases the frozen headers, which means that all the columns and rows in worksheet shift when you scroll the worksheet. You will use a different method to keep the column headers visible, so you will unfreeze the top row of the worksheet.

To unfreeze the top row of the worksheet:

1. In the Window group on the View tab, click the **Freeze Panes** button. The first Freeze Panes option is now Unfreeze Panes.
2. Click **Unfreeze Panes**. The headers are no longer frozen and the dark, horizontal line below the column headers is removed. You can now scroll all the rows and columns in the worksheet.

Creating an Excel Table

You can convert a structured range of data, such as the art objects data in the range A1:H116, to an Excel table. An Excel table makes it easier to identify, manage, and analyze the groups of related data. You can create more than one Excel table in a worksheet. Although you can perform all of the tasks in this section without creating an Excel table, there are many advantages to creating a table rather than leaving the art collection data as a range of data.

INSIGHT

Saving Time with Excel Table Features

Excel tables provide many advantages to structured ranges of data. When you create an Excel table, you can perform the same operations as you can for a structured range of data. In addition, you can use Excel tables to do the following to be more productive and reduce the chance of error:

- Format the Excel table quickly using a table style.
- Add new rows and columns to the Excel table that automatically expand the range.
- Add a Total row to calculate the summary function you select, such as SUM, AVERAGE, COUNT, MIN, and MAX.
- Enter a formula in one table cell that is automatically copied to all other cells in that table column.
- Create formulas that reference cells in a table by using table and column names instead of cell addresses.

These Excel table features let you focus on analyzing and understanding the data, leaving the more time-consuming tasks for the program to perform.

Next, you'll create an Excel table from the art objects data in the Art Collection worksheet. By doing so, you'll be able to take advantage of the many features and tools for working with Excel tables to analyze data effectively.

TIP

If the first row of data does not contain column headers, uncheck the My table has headers check box. Excel adds headers with the default names Column1 and so on.

To create an Excel table from the art objects data:

1. Verify that the active cell is cell **A2**, which is in the range of art objects data.
2. Click the **Insert** tab on the Ribbon. The Ribbon displays the Insert options.
3. In the Tables group, click the **Table** button. The Create Table dialog box opens. The range of data for the table is entered in the dialog box.

4. Click the **OK** button. The dialog box closes, and the range of data is converted to an Excel table. Filter arrows appear in the header row, the table is formatted with a predefined table style, and the Table Tools Design contextual tab appears on the Ribbon. See Figure 5-4.

Figure 5-4 Excel table created for the art objects data

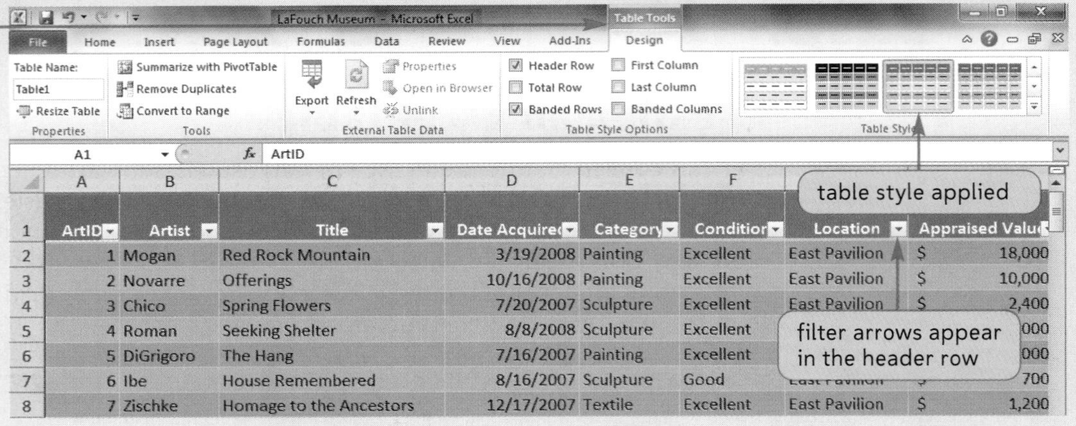

5. Scroll the table down. The text of the header row replaces the standard lettered column headings (A, B, C, and so on) as you scroll so that you don't need to freeze panes to keep the header row visible. See Figure 5-5.

Figure 5-5 Art objects table scrolled

header row replaces the letters in the column headers

	ArtID	Artist	Title	Date Acquired	Category	Condition	Location	Appraised Value
73	72	Garin	Funnel	5/18/2007	Painting	Excellent	East Pavilion	$ 4,500
74	73	Cridler	Dancing in the Light	1/15/2007	Sculpture	Fair	East Pavilion	$ 1,000
75	74	Parker	Storm on the Rise	8/23/2008	Painting	Good	East Pavilion	$ 8,000
76	75	Bindner	Western Boots and Spurs	1/10/2007	Painting	Fair	East Pavilion	$ 6,000
77	76	Wright	Ride the Bronco	10/15/2012	Sculpture	Poor	East Pavilion	$ 1,500
78	77	Bindner	Bull Riding	9/10/2007	Painting	Poor	East Pavilion	$ 5,200
79	78	Guys	Chuckwagon	7/11/2006	Sculpture	Excellent	East Pavilion	$ 32,000

6. Press the **Ctrl+Home** keys to make cell A1 active. The column headings return to the standard display, and the header row scrolls back into view as row 1.

Renaming an Excel Table

TIP

You can use the underscore character instead of spaces to separate words in a table name.

Excel assigns the name Table1 to the first Excel table created in a workbook. Any additional Excel tables you create in the workbook are named consecutively, Table2, Table3, and so forth. You can assign a more descriptive name to a table, making it easier to identify a particular table by its content. Descriptive names are especially useful when you create more than one Excel table in the same workbook. Table names must start with a letter or an underscore and can use any combination of letters, numbers, and underscores for the rest of the name. Table names cannot include spaces.

You will change the name of the Excel table you just created from the art objects data.

To rename the Table1 table:

1. In the Properties group on the Design tab, select **Table1** in the Table Name box. See Figure 5-6.

Figure 5-6 Table Name box

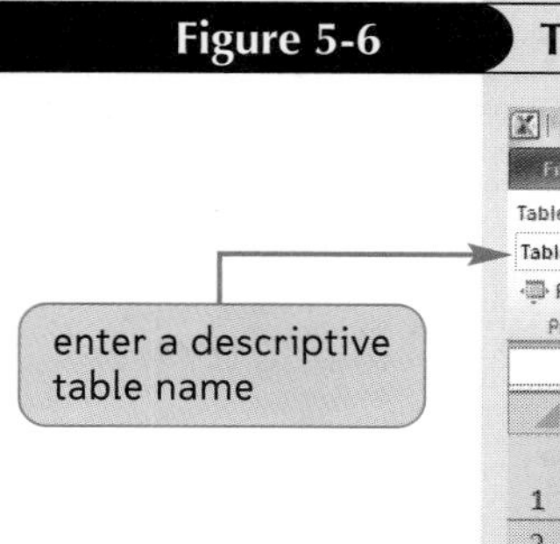

	A	B	C	D	E	F	G	H
1	ArtID	Artist	Title	Date Acquired	Category	Condition	Location	Appraised Value
2	1	Mogan	Red Rock Mountain	3/19/2008	Painting	Excellent	East Pavilion	$ 18,000
3	2	Novarre	Offerings	10/16/2008	Painting	Excellent	East Pavilion	$ 10,000
4	3	Chico	Spring Flowers	7/20/2007	Sculpture	Excellent	East Pavilion	$ 2,400

2. Type **ArtObjects**, and then press the **Enter** key. The Excel table is renamed as "ArtObjects."

Formatting an Excel Table

The check boxes in the Table Style Options group on the Design tab enable you to quickly and easily add or remove table elements or change the table's formatting. For example, you can display or hide the header row and select whether to format the table with banded rows, banded columns, or neither. You can also apply a table style.

You will format the table by selecting which table style options are applied to the Excel table.

To format the ArtObjects table:

1. In the Table Style group on the Table Tools Design tab, click the **More** button.
A gallery of table styles opens.
2. In the Table Styles gallery, click **Table Style Medium 4**. The table now has a green theme.
3. Change the width of column D to **12** characters. The width of the Date Acquired column better fits the dates.
4. Change the width of columns E, F, and H to **12** characters.
5. If cell A1 is not already the active cell, click cell **A1**.

Maintaining Data in an Excel Table

Mary has several changes you need to make to the data in the ArtObjects table. First, the museum acquired a new painting and received a sculpture from an anonymous donor; both art objects need to be added to the table. Second, the condition of the Moonlight painting has deteriorated and requires repairs; its condition needs to be changed from "Fair" to "Poor." Finally, one of the paintings has been sold to raise money for new acquisitions; the record for this art object needs to be deleted from the table. You will update the ArtObjects table to reflect these changes.

Adding Records

As you maintain data in an Excel table, you often need to add new records. You add a record to an Excel table in a blank row. The simplest and most convenient way to add a record to an Excel table is to enter the data in the first blank row below the last record. You can then sort the data to arrange the table in the order you want. If you want the record in a specific location, you can also insert a row within the table for the new record.

REFERENCE

Adding a Record to an Excel Table

- Click in the row below the last row of the Excel table.
- Type the values for the new record, pressing the Tab key to move from field to field.
- Press the Tab key to create another new record.

or

Press the Enter key if this is the last record.

Next, you'll add records for the new painting and sculpture to the ArtObjects table.

To add two records to the ArtObjects table:

1. Press the **End+↓** keys to make cell A116 the active cell. This cell is in the last row of the table.
2. Press the ↓ key to move the active cell to cell A117. This is the first blank row below the table.
3. In cell A117, type **116**, and then press the **Tab** key. Cell B117 in the Artist column becomes the active cell. The table expands to include a new row in the table structure with the same formatting as the rest of the table. The AutoCorrect Options button appears so you can undo the table formatting if you hadn't intended the new data to be part of the existing table. The sizing handle in the lower-right corner of the table indicates the last row and column in the table. You can use the sizing handle to add columns or rows to the Excel table to expand it, or remove them to make the table smaller. See Figure 5-7.

Figure 5-7 New row added to the ArtObjects table

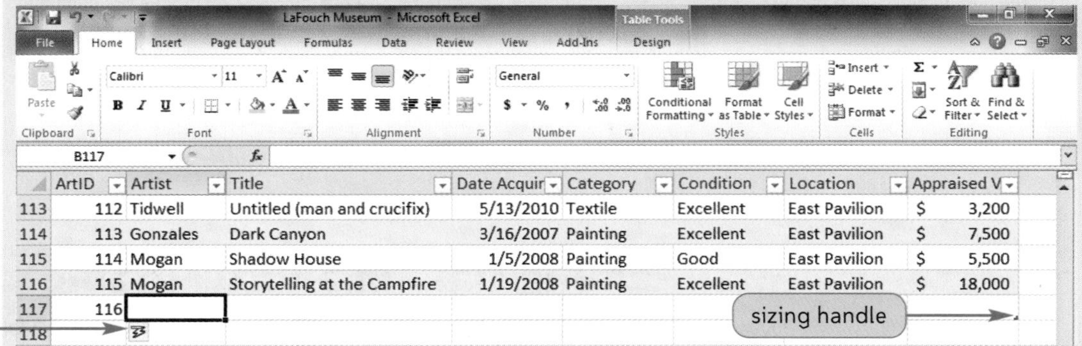

Trouble? If cell A118 is the active cell, you probably pressed the Enter key instead of the Tab key. Click cell B117 and then continue entering the data in Step 4.

TIP

As you type in a cell, AutoComplete displays any existing entry in the column that matches the characters you typed. Press the Tab key to accept the entry; continue typing to replace it.

4. In the range B117:H117, enter **Giama** for the artist, **Starry Night** for the title, **4/3/2013** for the date acquired, **Painting** for the category, **Excellent** for the condition, **South Pavilion** for the location, and **8500** for the appraised value, pressing the **Tab** key after each entry. Cell A118 becomes the active cell and the table expands to incorporate row 118.
5. In the range A118:H118, enter **117** for the art ID, **Higgins** for the artist, **Apache Warrior** for the title, **4/5/2013** for the date acquired, **Sculpture** for the category, **Excellent** for the condition, **Garden** for the location, and **23000** for the appraised value, press the **Enter** key, and then click cell **A119** after the last entry. The record for the sculpture is added to the table. See Figure 5-8.

Figure 5-8 **Records added to the ArtObjects table**

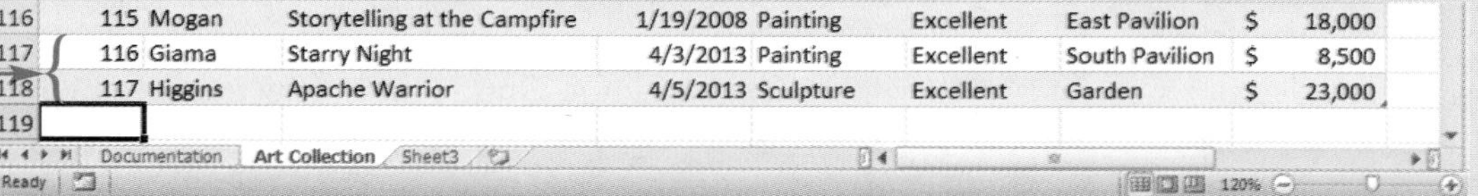

Trouble? If a new row is added to the table, you probably pressed the Tab key instead of the Enter key after the last entry in the record. On the Quick Access Toolbar, click the Undo button to remove the extra row.

Finding and Editing Records

You need to update the condition for the art object with the title "Moonlight." Although you can manually scroll through the table to find a specific record, a quicker and more accurate way to locate a record is to use the Find command. You edit the data in a field the same way as you edit data in a worksheet cell. You'll use the Find command to locate the record for the Moonlight painting, which has deteriorated to poor condition. Then, you'll edit the record in the table to change the condition to "Poor."

To find and edit the record for the Moonlight painting:

1. Press the **Ctrl+Home** keys to move to the top of the worksheet, and then click cell **C2** to make it the active cell.
2. In the Editing group on the Home tab, click the **Find & Select** button, and then click **Find**. The Find and Replace dialog box opens.
3. Type **Moonlight** in the Find what box, and then click the **Find Next** button. Cell C69, which contains the title "Moonlight," is selected. This is the record you want. If it wasn't, you would click the Find Next button again to display the next record that meets the search criteria.
4. Click the **Close** button. The Find and Replace dialog box closes.
5. Press the **Tab** key three times to move the active cell to the Condition column, and then type **P**. AutoComplete displays "Poor" in the cell, which is the condition text you want to enter.
6. Press the **Tab** key to enter the AutoComplete entry. The painting's condition is changed in the table.
7. Press the **Ctrl+Home** keys to make cell A1 active.

Deleting a Record

The final update you need to make to the ArtObjects table is to delete the record for the Trappers painting (ArtID 90), which was sold. You'll use the Find command to locate the painting's record. Then, you'll delete the record from the table.

TIP

You can find fields whose contents match a value (such as 90) exactly by clicking the Options button in the Find and Replace dialog box, and checking the Match entire cell contents check box.

Be sure to verify that you selected the correct record before you delete; a dialog box does *not* open to confirm the delete operation.

To find and delete the Trappers painting record:

1. In the Editing group on the Home tab, click the **Find & Select** button, and then click **Find**. The Find and Replace dialog box opens.
2. Type **90** in the Find what box, and then click the **Find Next** button. Because Excel searches the entire worksheet (not just the current column), and because it finds the search value even if it is part of another value, the appraised value $1,900 is selected. This is not the record you want to delete.
3. Click the **Find Next** button to highlight the appraised value $1,900 for a different record, and then click the **Find Next** button again to highlight the value 90 in the ArtID column. This is the record you need to delete.
4. Click the **Close** button. The Find and Replace dialog box closes.
5. In the Cells group on the Home tab, click the **Delete button arrow**, and then click **Delete Table Rows**. The record for the Trappers painting is deleted from the table.

   Trouble? If a different record was deleted, the active cell was not in the record for the Trappers painting. On the Quick Access Toolbar, click the Undo button to restore the record, and then repeat Steps 1 through 5.
6. Press the **Ctrl+Home** keys to make cell A1 active.

Sorting Data

The records in the ArtObjects table appear in the order that Mary entered them. As you work, however, you'll want to view the same records in a different order, such as by the artist name or by the art object's location in the museum. For example, if you want to arrange the art objects by artist name, you can sort the data using the Artist column as the sort field.

You can sort data in ascending or descending order. **Ascending order** arranges text alphabetically from A to Z, numbers from smallest to largest, and dates from oldest to newest. **Descending order** arranges text in reverse alphabetical order from Z to A, numbers from largest to smallest, and dates from newest to oldest. In both ascending and descending order, blank fields are placed at the end of the table.

Sorting One Column Using the Sort Buttons

You can quickly sort data with one sort field using the Sort A to Z button or the Sort Z to A button. Mary wants you to sort the art objects in ascending order by the artist. This will rearrange the table data so that the records appear in alphabetical order by the artist name.

TIP

You can also click the Sort & Filter button in the Editing group on the Home tab, and then click a sort option.

To sort the ArtObjects table in ascending order by the artist name:

1. Click any cell in the Artist column. You do not need to select the entire ArtObjects table, which consists of the range A1:H117. Excel determines the table's range when you click any cell in the table.
2. Click the **Data** tab on the Ribbon. The Data options appear on the Ribbon.

3. In the Sort & Filter group, click the **Sort A to Z** button. The data is sorted in ascending order by Artist. The Artist filter arrow indicates the data is sorted by that column. See Figure 5-9.

Figure 5-9 ArtObjects table sorted by Artist

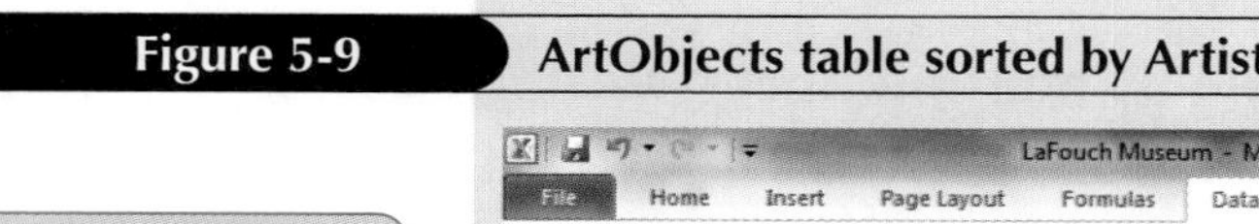

arrow changes to a sort icon

art objects appear in alphabetical order by the artists' names

	A	B	C	D	E	F	G	H
1	ArtID	Artist	Title	Date Acquired	Category	Condition	Location	Appraised Value
2	38	Acconci	Spring Flowers	9/10/2006	Sculpture	Good	East Pavilion	$ 800
3	50	Acconci	Cattle Ranch	5/19/2007	Textile	Good	East Pavilion	$ 10,000
4	104	Acconci	Trail End	9/10/2006	Painting	Excellent	East Pavilion	$ 8,000
5	42	Ames	Coffee on the Trail	8/9/2006	Painting	Good	East Pavilion	$ 7,544
6	13	Aserty	Superstitions	3/10/2012	Painting	Excellent	Courtyard	$ 78,000
7	21	Aserty	Bead Wall	9/10/2007	Installation	Excellent	Courtyard	$ 14,000
8	34	Aserty	Beaver Pole Jumble	1/10/2010	Installation	Excellent	South Pavilion	$ 28,000
9	63	Aserty	Asleep in the Garden	8/10/2012	Installation	Excellent	Garden	$ 110,000
10	70	Baron	Beginnings	7/10/2013	Textile	Fair	East Pavilion	$ 27,500
11	36	Battenberg	Blackhawk	5/10/2007	Sculpture	Excellent	East Pavilion	$ 25,500

Trouble? If the data is sorted in the wrong order, you might have clicked in a different column than the Artist column. Repeat Steps 1 through 3.

Sorting Multiple Columns Using the Sort Dialog Box

Sometimes, sorting by one sort field is not adequate for your needs. For example, Mary wants you to arrange the ArtObjects table so that all the art objects in each location are together, and then all the objects for each artist within each location are together, and then each artist's work is arranged by the date acquired. You must sort on more than one column to accomplish this. The first sort field is called the **primary sort field**, the second sort field is called the **secondary sort field**, and so forth. You can use up to 64 sort fields in a single sort, although you most typically will use one to three sort fields. In this case, the Location field is the primary sort field, the Artist field is the secondary sort field, and the Date Acquired field is the tertiary sort field. When you have more than one sort field, you should use the Sort dialog box to specify the sort criteria.

REFERENCE

Sorting Data Using Multiple Sort Fields

- Click any cell in a table or range.
- In the Sort & Filter group on the Data tab, click the Sort button.
- If necessary, click the Add Level button to insert the Sort by row.
- Click the Sort by arrow, select the column heading for the primary sort field, click the Sort On arrow to select the type of data, and then click the Order arrow to select the sort order.
- To sort by a second column, click the Add Level button. Click the Then by arrow, select the column heading for the secondary sort field, click the Sort On arrow to select the type of data, and then click the Order arrow to select the sort order.
- To sort by additional columns, click the Add Level button and select appropriate Then by, Sort On, and Order values.
- Click the OK button.

You will sort the art objects by location, and then within location by artist, and then within artist by date acquired, with the most recently acquired objects for the artist appearing before the older ones. This will make it faster for Mary to find information about the location and the creator of the art objects in each location.

To sort the ArtObjects table by multiple sort fields:

1. Click cell **A1** in the ArtObjects table. Cell A1 is the active cell, although you can click any cell in the table to sort the table data.
2. In the Sort & Filter group on the Data tab, click the **Sort** button. The Sort dialog box opens. Any sort specifications (sort field, type of data sorted on, and sort order) from the last sort appear in the dialog box.
3. Click the **Sort by** arrow to display the list of the column headers in the ArtObjects table, and then click **Location**. The primary sort field is set to Location.
4. If necessary, click the **Sort On** arrow to display the type of sort, and then click **Values**. Typically, you want to sort by the numbers, text, or dates stored in the cells, which are all values. You can also sort by formats such as cell color, font color, and cell icon (a graphic that appears in a cell due to a conditional format).
5. If necessary, click the **Order** arrow to display sort order options, and then click **A to Z**. The sort order is set to ascending.
6. Click the **Add Level** button. A Then by row is added below the primary sort field.
7. Click the **Then by** arrow and click **Artist**, and then verify that **Values** appears in the Sort On box and **A to Z** appears in the Order box.
8. Click the **Add Level** button to add a second Then by row.
9. Click the second **Then by** arrow, click **Date Acquired**, verify that **Values** appears in the Sort On box, click the **Order** arrow, and then click **Newest to Oldest** to specify a descending sort order for the Date Acquired values. See Figure 5-10.

Figure 5-10 Sort dialog box with complete sort specifications

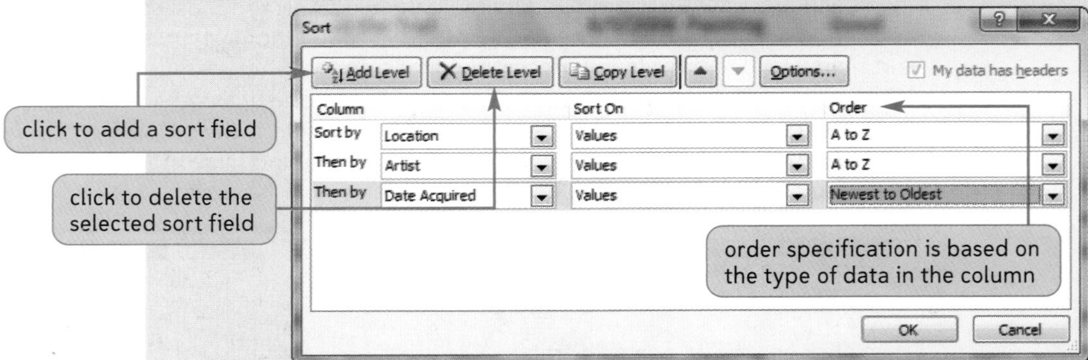

10. Click the **OK** button. Excel sorts the table records first in ascending order by the Location field, then within each location by the Artist field (again, in ascending order), and then within each artist by the Date Acquired field. For example, notice the three works by Acconci located in the East Pavilion; the works are arranged in descending order by the value in the Date Acquired column, so that the newer works appear before the older works. See Figure 5-11.

Figure 5-11 Art objects sorted by Location, then by Artist, and then by Date Acquired

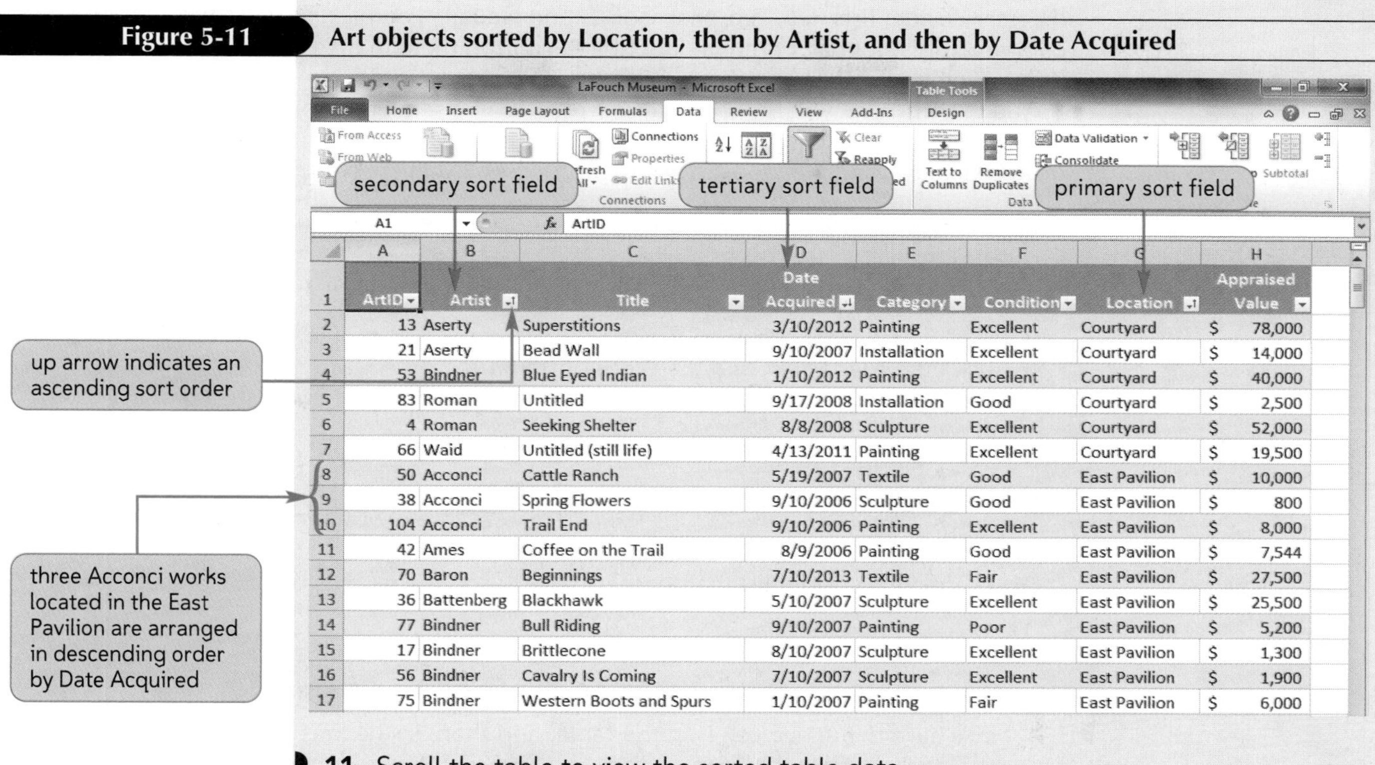

	ArtID	Artist	Title	Date Acquired	Category	Condition	Location	Appraised Value
2	13	Aserty	Superstitions	3/10/2012	Painting	Excellent	Courtyard	$ 78,000
3	21	Aserty	Bead Wall	9/10/2007	Installation	Excellent	Courtyard	$ 14,000
4	53	Bindner	Blue Eyed Indian	1/10/2012	Painting	Excellent	Courtyard	$ 40,000
5	83	Roman	Untitled	9/17/2008	Installation	Good	Courtyard	$ 2,500
6	4	Roman	Seeking Shelter	8/8/2008	Sculpture	Excellent	Courtyard	$ 52,000
7	66	Waid	Untitled (still life)	4/13/2011	Painting	Excellent	Courtyard	$ 19,500
8	50	Acconci	Cattle Ranch	5/19/2007	Textile	Good	East Pavilion	$ 10,000
9	38	Acconci	Spring Flowers	9/10/2006	Sculpture	Good	East Pavilion	$ 800
10	104	Acconci	Trail End	9/10/2006	Painting	Excellent	East Pavilion	$ 8,000
11	42	Ames	Coffee on the Trail	8/9/2006	Painting	Good	East Pavilion	$ 7,544
12	70	Baron	Beginnings	7/10/2013	Textile	Fair	East Pavilion	$ 27,500
13	36	Battenberg	Blackhawk	5/10/2007	Sculpture	Excellent	East Pavilion	$ 25,500
14	77	Bindner	Bull Riding	9/10/2007	Painting	Poor	East Pavilion	$ 5,200
15	17	Bindner	Brittlecone	8/10/2007	Sculpture	Excellent	East Pavilion	$ 1,300
16	56	Bindner	Cavalry Is Coming	7/10/2007	Sculpture	Excellent	East Pavilion	$ 1,900
17	75	Bindner	Western Boots and Spurs	1/10/2007	Painting	Fair	East Pavilion	$ 6,000

11. Scroll the table to view the sorted table data.

Mary wants to review the condition of each art object to determine how many objects need repairs. It is easier to do this with the objects sorted by their condition. Because you need to sort by only one field, you'll use the Sort A to Z button.

To sort the art objects by condition:

1. Click any cell in the **Condition** column.
2. In the Sort & Filter group on the Data tab, click the **Sort A to Z** button. The previous sort is removed and the art objects are now sorted in ascending order by condition.
3. Scroll the table to see the reordered art objects.

The table data is sorted in alphabetical order by the condition of the art objects: Excellent, Fair, Good, and Poor. This default sort order for fields with text values is not appropriate for the condition ratings. Instead, Mary wants you to base the sort on quality ranking rather than alphabetical order. You'll use a custom sort list to set up the sort order Mary wants.

Sorting Using a Custom List

Text is sorted in ascending or descending alphabetical order unless you specify a different order using a custom list. A **custom list** indicates the sequence in which you want data ordered. Excel provides four predefined custom sort lists. Two days-of-the-week custom lists (Sun, Mon, Tues, ... and Sunday, Monday, Tuesday, ...) and two months-of-the-year custom lists (Jan, Feb, Mar, Apr, ... and January, February, March, April, ...). If a column consists of day or month labels, you can sort them in their correct chronological order using one of these predefined custom lists.

You can also create custom lists to sort records in a sequence you define. In this case, you want to create a custom list to arrange the art objects based on their condition, with the top quality condition appearing first, as follows: Excellent, Good, Fair, Poor.

REFERENCE

Creating a Custom List

- In the Sort & Filter group on the Data tab, click the Sort button.
- Click the Order arrow, and then click Custom List.
- In the List entries box, type each entry for the custom list, pressing the Enter key after each entry.
- Click the Add button.
- Click the OK button.

You'll create a custom list that Mary can use to sort the records by the Condition field.

To create the custom list based on the Condition field:

1. Make sure the active cell is in the table, and then, in the Sort & Filter group on the Data tab, click the **Sort** button. The Sort dialog box opens, showing the sort specifications from the previous sort.
2. If necessary, click the **Sort by** arrow, click **Condition** to select the sort field (if necessary), and then verify that **Values** appears in the Sort On box.
3. Click the **Order** arrow to display the sort order options, and then click **Custom List**. The Custom Lists dialog box opens.
4. In the Custom lists box, click **NEW LIST** to place the insertion point in the List entries box.

   Next, you'll enter the condition values in the order you want them sorted. You must press the Enter key after each entry.

TIP

You can also use commas to separate entries in a custom list.

5. Type **Excellent**, press the **Enter** key to move the insertion point to the next line, type **Good**, press the **Enter** key, type **Fair**, press the **Enter** key, type **Poor**, and then press the **Enter** key. The four items appear in the List entries box.
6. Click the **Add** button. The custom list entries are added to the Custom lists box. See Figure 5-12.

Figure 5-12 Custom Lists dialog box with custom list defined

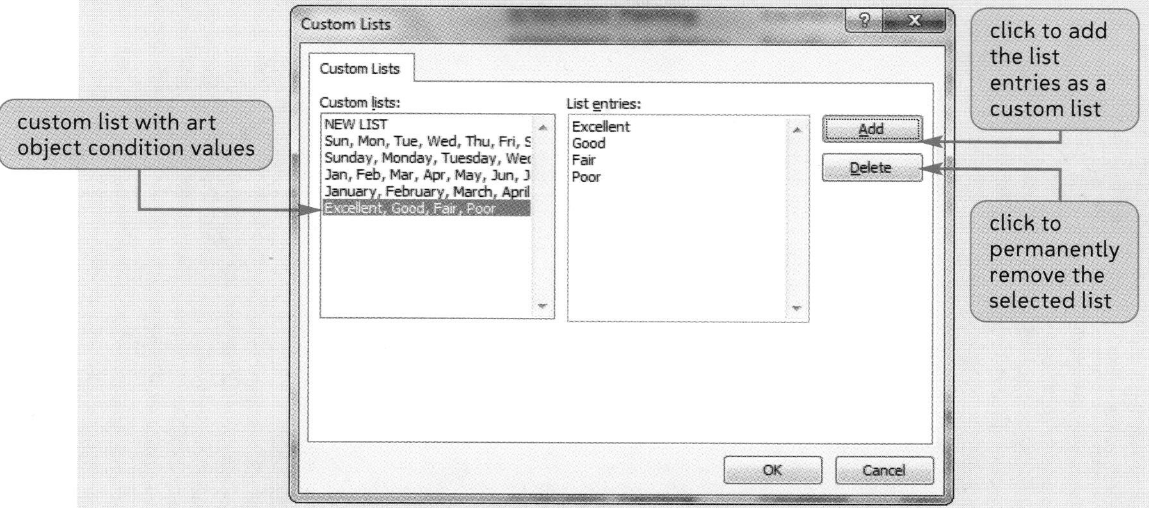

7. Click the **OK** button to return to the Sort dialog box. The custom sort list—Excellent, Good, Fair, Poor—appears in the Order box.
8. Click the **OK** button. The table is sorted based on the custom list.
9. Scroll the sorted table to verify that the art objects are sorted by their condition rankings: Excellent, Good, Fair, and Poor. Six art objects are in poor condition.

So far, you created an Excel table for the art objects, and then named and formatted the table. You updated the table by adding, editing, and deleting records. You also sorted the records and created a custom list to sort the Condition field by its quality ratings. In the next session, you will filter the ArtObjects table to retrieve specific information on some of the art objects.

REVIEW

Session 5.1 Quick Check

1. What is the purpose of the Freeze Panes button in the Window group on the View tab? Why is this feature helpful?
2. What three elements indicate an Excel table is created in the worksheet?
3. A field that you use to order data is referred to as a(n) ______________ field.
4. An Excel table of college students tracks each student's first name, last name, major, and year of graduation. How can you order the table so that students graduating in the same year appear together in alphabetical order by the student's last name?
5. How do you enter a new record in an Excel table?
6. An Excel table of faculty data includes the Rank field with the values Full, Associate, Assistant, and Instructor. How can you sort the data by rank in the following order: Full, Associate, Assistant, and Instructor?
7. If you sort table data from the most recent purchase date to the oldest purchase date, in what order have you sorted the data?

SESSION 5.2 VISUAL OVERVIEW

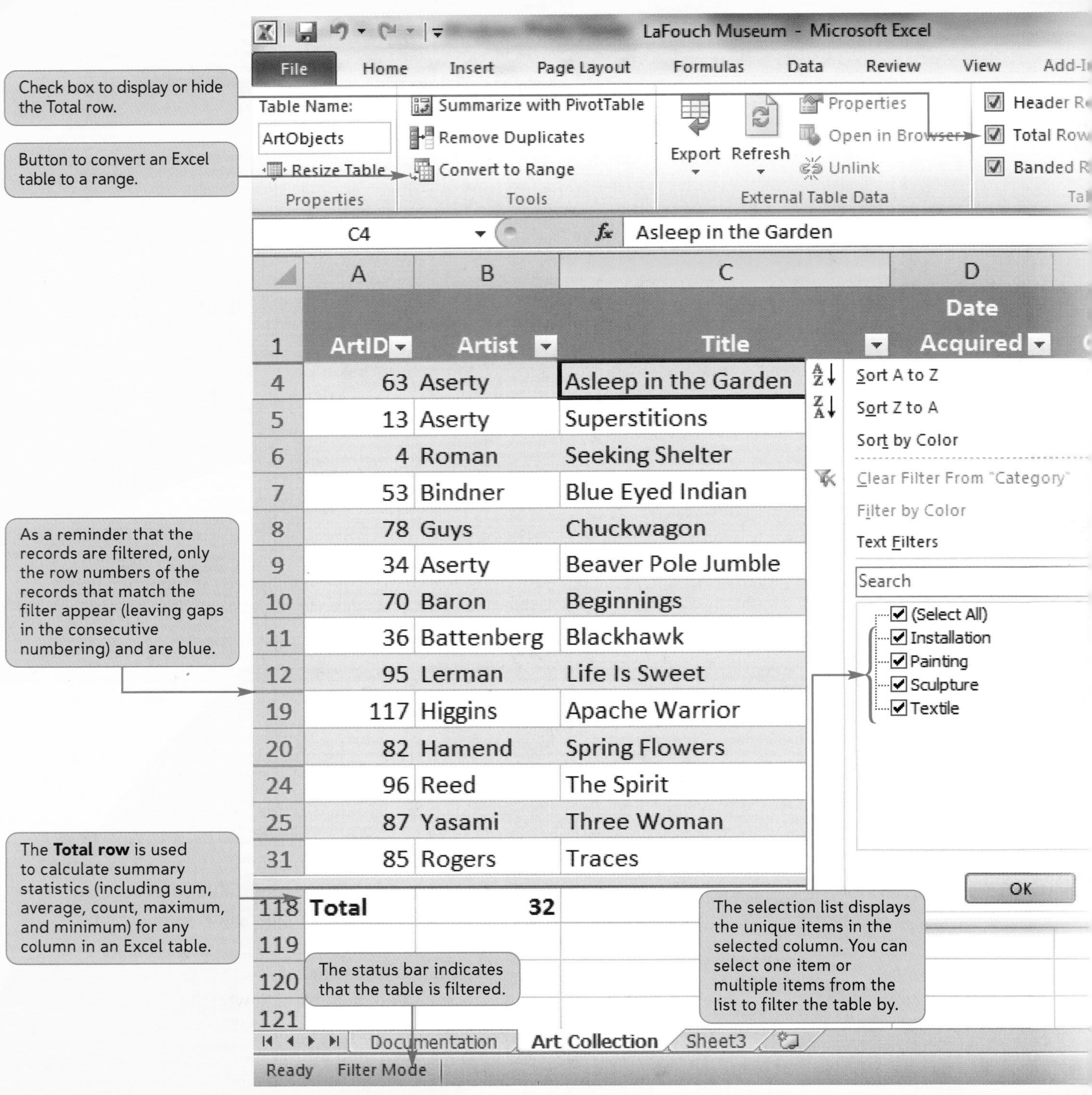

FILTERING TABLE DATA

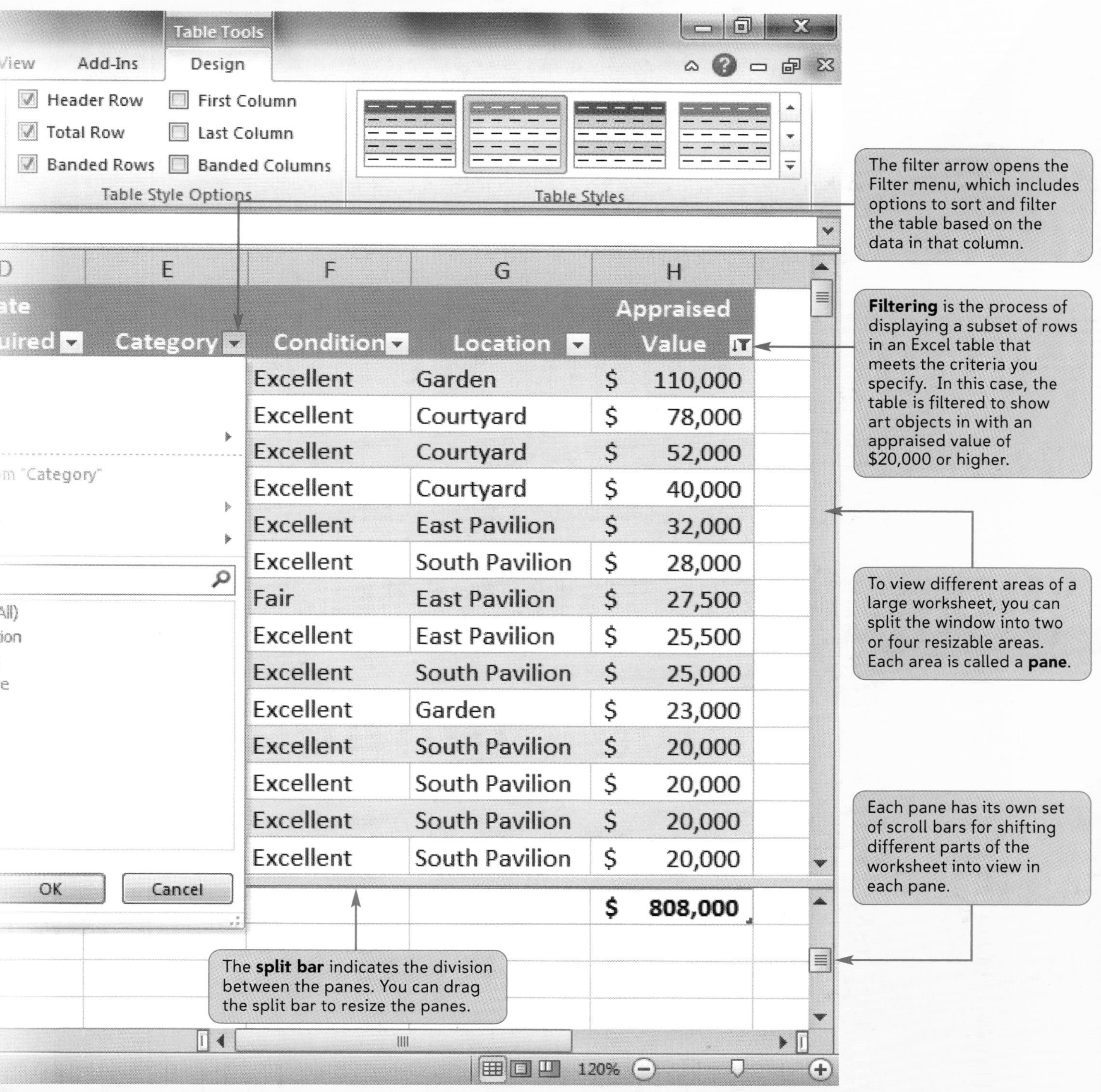

Filtering Data

Mary needs to determine which art objects the museum can afford to repair this year. She asks you to prepare a list of all paintings in poor condition. Although you could sort the list of paintings by condition to group those in poor condition, you are still working with the entire table. A better solution is to display only the specific records you want. Filtering the data temporarily hides any records that do not meet the specified criteria. After data is filtered, you can sort, copy, format, chart, and print it.

Filtering Using One Column

TIP

You can display or hide filter arrows for an Excel table or a range of data by using the Filter button in the Sort & Filter group on the Data tab.

When you create an Excel table, a filter arrow appears in each column header. You click a filter arrow to open the AutoFilter menu for that field. You can use options on the AutoFilter menu to create three types of filters. You can filter a column of data by its cell colors or font colors; by a specific text, number, or date filter, although the choices depend on the type of data in the column; or by selecting the exact values by which you want to filter in the column. After you filter a column, the Clear Filter command becomes available so you can remove the filter and redisplay all the records.

Mary wants to see only paintings in poor condition. First, you'll filter the ArtObjects table to show only those records with the value "Paintings" in the Category column.

To filter the ArtObjects table to show only paintings:

1. If you took a break after the previous session, make sure the LaFouch Museum workbook is open, the Art Collection worksheet is active, and the ArtObjects table is active.
2. Click the **Category filter arrow**. The AutoFilter menu opens, as shown in Figure 5-13, listing the unique entries in the Category column: Installation, Painting, Sculpture, and Textile. All the items are selected initially, but you can set which items to use to filter the data. In this case, you want to select the Painting item.

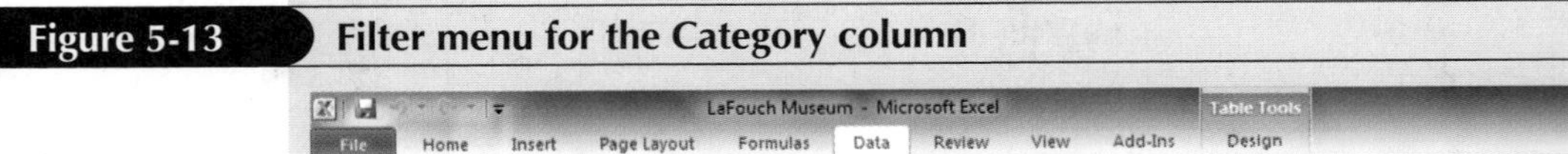

Figure 5-13 Filter menu for the Category column

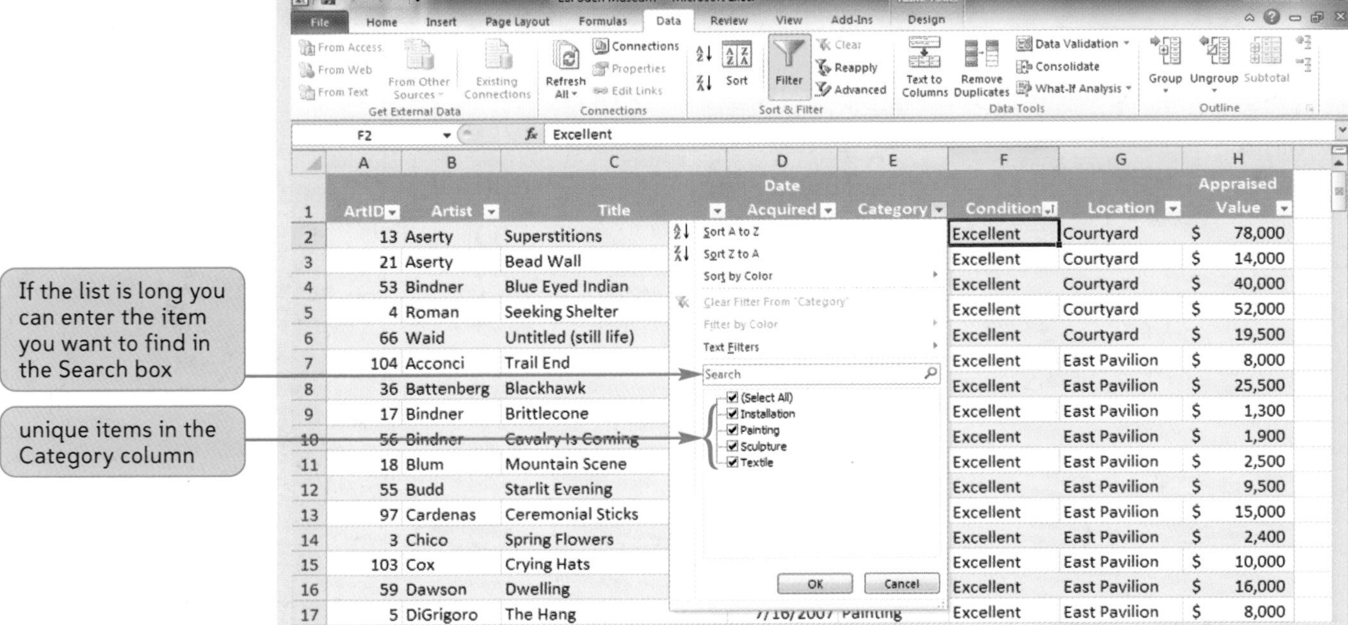

3. Click the (**Select All**) check box to remove the check marks from all the Category items, and then click the **Painting** check box to insert a check mark. The filter will show only those records that match the checked item and hide records that contain the unchecked items.
4. Click the **OK** button. The filter is applied. The status bar lists the number of paintings found in the entire table. Fifty-seven of the 116 records in the table are displayed. See Figure 5-14.

Figure 5-14 **ArtObjects table filtered to show only paintings**

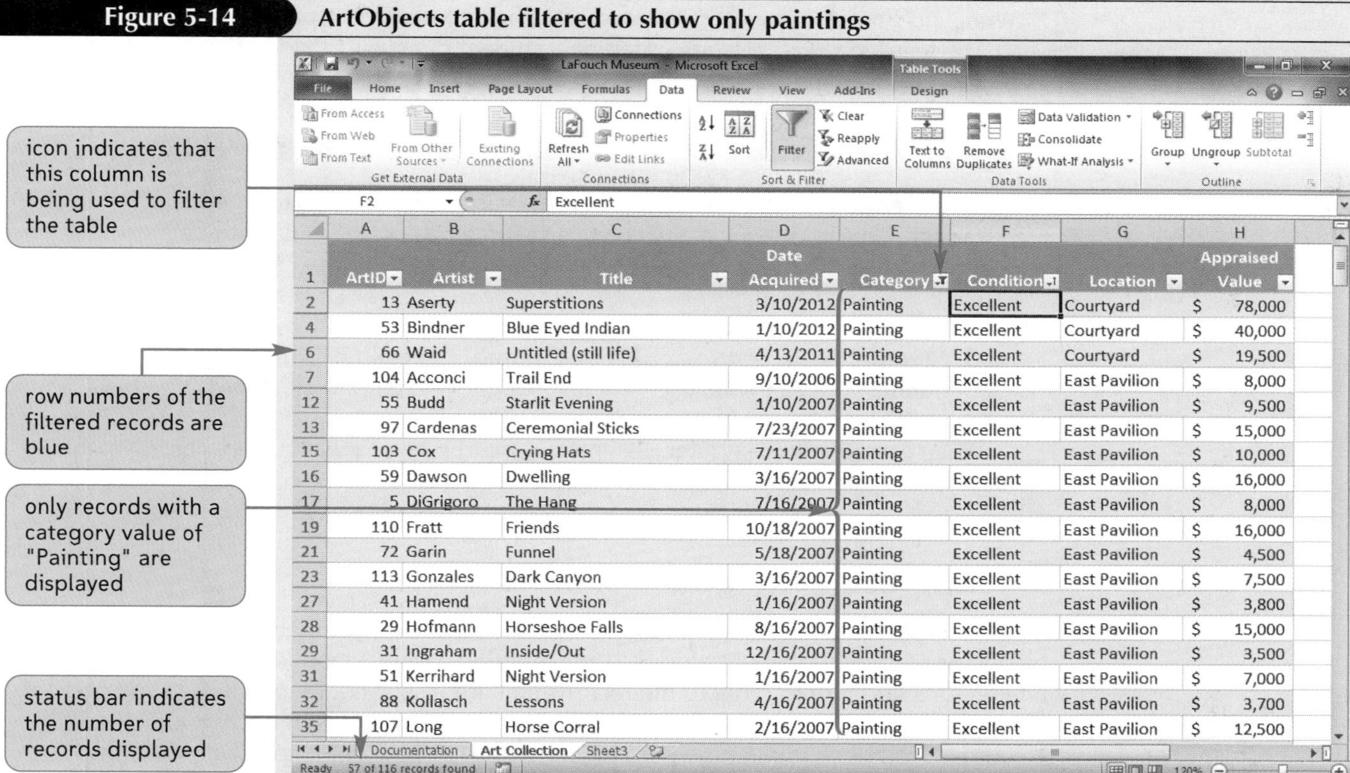

	ArtID	Artist	Title	Date Acquired	Category	Condition	Location	Appraised Value
2	13	Aserty	Superstitions	3/10/2012	Painting	Excellent	Courtyard	$ 78,000
4	53	Bindner	Blue Eyed Indian	1/10/2012	Painting	Excellent	Courtyard	$ 40,000
6	66	Waid	Untitled (still life)	4/13/2011	Painting	Excellent	Courtyard	$ 19,500
7	104	Acconci	Trail End	9/10/2006	Painting	Excellent	East Pavilion	$ 8,000
12	55	Budd	Starlit Evening	1/10/2007	Painting	Excellent	East Pavilion	$ 9,500
13	97	Cardenas	Ceremonial Sticks	7/23/2007	Painting	Excellent	East Pavilion	$ 15,000
15	103	Cox	Crying Hats	7/11/2007	Painting	Excellent	East Pavilion	$ 10,000
16	59	Dawson	Dwelling	3/16/2007	Painting	Excellent	East Pavilion	$ 16,000
17	5	DiGrigoro	The Hang	7/16/2007	Painting	Excellent	East Pavilion	$ 8,000
19	110	Fratt	Friends	10/18/2007	Painting	Excellent	East Pavilion	$ 16,000
21	72	Garin	Funnel	5/18/2007	Painting	Excellent	East Pavilion	$ 4,500
23	113	Gonzales	Dark Canyon	3/16/2007	Painting	Excellent	East Pavilion	$ 7,500
27	41	Hamend	Night Version	1/16/2007	Painting	Excellent	East Pavilion	$ 3,800
28	29	Hofmann	Horseshoe Falls	8/16/2007	Painting	Excellent	East Pavilion	$ 15,000
29	31	Ingraham	Inside/Out	12/16/2007	Painting	Excellent	East Pavilion	$ 3,500
31	51	Kerrihard	Night Version	1/16/2007	Painting	Excellent	East Pavilion	$ 7,000
32	88	Kollasch	Lessons	4/16/2007	Painting	Excellent	East Pavilion	$ 3,700
35	107	Long	Horse Corral	2/16/2007	Painting	Excellent	East Pavilion	$ 12,500

5. Review the records to verify that only records with a value equal to "Painting" in the Category column are visible. All records that do not have the value "Painting" in this column are hidden, leaving gaps in the row numbers.
6. Point to the **Category filter arrow**. A ScreenTip—Category: Equals "Painting"—describes the filter applied to the column.

The AutoFilter menu includes options to Sort by Color and Filter by Color. These options enable you to filter and sort data using color, one of many cell attributes. Suppose that Mary used specific cell background colors for certain works of art in the ArtObjects table. For example, she might want to highlight the works given to the museum by its two most generous donors, using yellow for one and red for the other. So the cells in the Title column for the two donors would be formatted with these colors. You could then click the Sort by Color option in the AutoFilter menu to display a list of available colors by which to sort, and then click the specific color so that all the records for the first donor (formatted with yellow) would appear together, and all the records for the second donor (formatted with red) would appear together. Similarly, you could click the Filter by Color option to display a submenu with the available colors by which to filter, and then click a color. In this example, if you selected yellow, only the records for the first donor would be displayed in the table, allowing you to focus on just those records.

INSIGHT

Exploring Text Filters

You can use different text filters to display the records you want. If you know only part of a text value or if you want to match a certain pattern, you can use the Begins With, Ends With, and Contains operators to filter a text field to match the pattern you specify.

The following examples are based on a student directory table that includes First Name, Last Name, Address, City, State, and Zip fields:

- To find a student named Smith, Smithe, or Smythe, create a text filter using the Begins With operator. In this example, use "Begins With Sm" to display all records that have "Sm" at the beginning of the text value.
- To Find anyone whose Last Name ends in "son" (such as Robertson, Anderson, Dawson, Gibson, and so forth), create a text filter using the Ends With operator. In this example, use "Ends With son" to display all records that have "son" as the last characters in the text value.
- To find anyone whose street address includes "Central" (such as 101 Central Ave., 1024 Central Road, or 457 Avenue De Central), create a text filter using the Contains operator. In this example, use "Contains Central" to display all records that have "Central" anywhere in the text value.

When you create a text filter, think about the results you want. Then, consider what text filter you can use to best achieve those results.

Filtering Using Multiple Columns

If you need to further restrict the records that appear in a filtered table, you can filter by one or more of the other columns. Each additional filter is applied to the currently filtered data and further reduces the records that are displayed. Mary wants to see only paintings that are in poor condition, rather than all the paintings in the ArtObjects table. To do this, you need to filter the painting records to display only those with the value "Poor" in the Condition column. You'll use the filter arrow in the Condition column to add this second filter criterion to the filtered data.

To filter the painting records to show only those in poor condition:

1. Click the **Condition filter arrow**. The AutoFilter menu opens.
2. Click the **Excellent**, **Fair**, and **Good** check boxes to remove the check marks. The Poor check box remains checked, so only paintings in poor condition will be displayed.
3. Click the **OK** button. The ArtObjects table is further filtered and shows the three paintings that are in poor condition. See Figure 5-15.

Figure 5-15 ArtObjects table filtered to show only paintings in poor condition

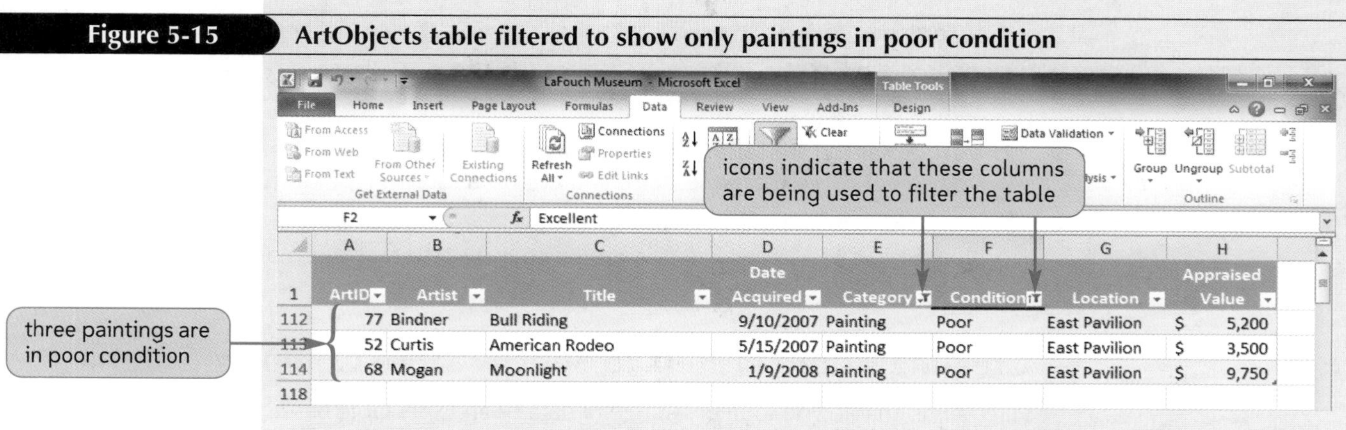

Clearing Filters

When you want to redisplay all of the data in a filtered table, you need to **clear** (or remove) the filters. When you clear a filter from a column, any other filters are still applied. For example, in the ArtObjects table, you would see all the paintings in the table if you cleared the filter from the Condition field, or you would see all the art objects in poor condition if you cleared the filter from the Category field. To redisplay all the art objects in the table, you need to clear both the Condition filter and the Category filter. You will do this now to redisplay the entire table of art objects.

To clear the filters to show all the records in the ArtObjects table:

1. Click the **Condition filter arrow**, and then click **Clear Filter From "Condition"**. The Condition filter is removed from the table. The table shows only paintings because the Category filter is still in effect.
2. Click the **Category filter arrow**, and then click **Clear Filter From "Category"**. The Category condition is removed, and all the records in the ArtObjects table are displayed again.

Selecting Multiple Filter Items

You can often find the information you need by selecting a single filter item from a list of filter items. Sometimes, however, you need to specify a more complex set of criteria to find the records you want. Earlier, you selected one filter item for the Category column and one filter item for the Condition column to display the records whose Category field value equals Painting AND whose Condition field value equals Poor. The records had to contain both values to be displayed. The AND condition requires that all of the selected criteria be true for the record to be displayed.

Now you want to select two filter items for the Category column to display records whose Category field value equals Installation OR whose Category field value equals Sculpture. The records must have at least one of these values to be displayed. A filter that selects more than one item from the list of items in a single column uses the OR condition, which requires that only one of the selected criteria be true for a record to be displayed. For example, if you check the Installation and Sculpture check boxes in the Category filter items, you create the filter condition "Category equals Installation" OR "Category equals Sculpture."

The museum's board of directors wants a list of all installations or sculptures valued at more than $20,000. You will create a list of these holdings.

To select multiple filter items:

1. Click the **Category filter arrow**, and then click the **Painting** and **Textile** check boxes to remove the check marks.
2. Verify that the **Installation** and **Sculpture** check boxes remain checked. When you select more than one item, you create a multiselect filter.
3. Click the **OK** button. The ArtObjects table is filtered, and the status bar indicates that 51 out of 116 records are either an installation or a sculpture.

Creating Criteria Filters to Specify More Complex Criteria

Filter items enable you to filter a range of data or an Excel table based on exact values in a column. However, many times you need broader criteria. **Criteria filters** enable you to specify various conditions in addition to those that are based on an "equals" criterion. For example, you might want to find all art objects with an appraised value greater than $20,000 or those that were acquired after 7/1/2011. You use criteria filters to create these conditions.

The type of criteria filters available change depending on whether the data in a column contains text, numbers, or dates. Figure 5-16 shows some of the options for text, number, and date criteria filters.

Figure 5-16 **Options for text, number, and date criteria filters**

Filter	Criteria	Records Displayed
Text	Equals	Exactly match the specified text string
	Does Not Equal	Do not exactly match the specified text string
	Begins With	Begin with the specified text string
	Ends With	End with the specified text string
	Contains	Have the specified text string anywhere
	Does Not Contain	Do not have the specified text string anywhere
Number	Equals	Exactly match the specified number
	Greater Than or Equal to	Are greater than or equal to the specified number
	Less Than	Are less than the specified number
	Between	Are greater than or equal to *and* less than or equal to the specified numbers
	Top 10	Are the top or bottom 10 (or the specified number)
	Above Average	Are greater than the average
Date	Today	Have the current date
	Last Week	Are in the prior week
	Next Month	Are in the month following the current month
	Last Quarter	Are in the previous quarter of the year (quarters defined Jan, Feb, Mar; Apr, May, June; and so on)
	Year to Date	Are since January 1 of the current year to the current date
	Last Year	Are in the previous year (based on the current date)

PROSKILLS

Problem Solving: Using Filters to Find Appropriate Data

Problem solving often requires finding information from a set of data to answer specific questions. When you're working with a range of data or an Excel table that contains hundreds or thousands of records, filters help you find that information without having to review each record in the table. For example, a human resources manager can use a filter to narrow the search for a specific employee of the 2,500 working at the company knowing only that the employee's first name is Elliot.

Filtering limits the data to display only the specific records that meet the criteria you set, enabling you to more effectively analyze the data. The following examples further illustrate how filtering can help people to quickly locate the data they need to answer a particular question:

- A customer representative can use a filter to search a list of 10,000 products to find all products priced between $500 and $1,000.
- A donations coordinator can use a filter to prepare a report that shows the donations received during the first quarter of the current year.
- A professor who has 300 students in a psychology class can use a filter to develop a list of potential student assistants for next semester from the names the professor has high-lighted in blue because their work was impressive. Filtering by the blue color generates a list of students to interview.
- The author of a guide to celebrity autographs can use a filter to determine whether an entry for a specific celebrity already exists in an Excel table and, if it does, determine whether the entry needs to be updated. If the entry does not exist, the author will know to add the autograph data to the autograph price table.

As these example show, filtering is a useful tool for locating the answers to a wide variety of questions. You then can use this information to help you resolve problems.

You will modify the filtered ArtObjects table to add a criteria filter that includes only objects that have values greater than $20,000.

To create a number filter:

1. Click the **Appraised Value filter arrow**, and then point to **Number Filters**. A menu opens, displaying the comparison operators available for columns of numbers.
2. Click **Greater Than**. The Custom AutoFilter dialog box opens. The upper-left box lists *is greater than*, the comparison operator you want to use to filter the Appraised Value column. You enter the value you want to use for the filter criteria in the upper-right box, which, in this case, is $20,000.
3. Type **20000** in the upper-right box. See Figure 5-17. You use the lower set of boxes if you want the filter to meet a second condition. You click the And option button to display rows that meet both criteria. You click the Or option button to display rows that meet either of the two criteria. You only want to set one criterion for this filter, so you'll leave the lower boxes empty.

Figure 5-17 Custom AutoFilter dialog box

Custom AutoFilter

Show rows where:

Appraised Value

is greater than | 20000

And | Or

Use ? to represent any single character

Use * to represent any series of characters

OK | Cancel

operator for the first condition

criterion for the first condition

boxes to specify a second condition for the list

4. Click the **OK** button. The status bar indicates that 7 of 116 records were found. The seven records that appear in the ArtObjects table are either installations or sculptures and have an appraised value greater than $20,000.

Before Mary sends this list to the board of directors, you'll sort the filtered data to show the largest appraised value first. Although you can sort the data using Sort buttons, as you did earlier, these sort options are also available on the AutoFilter menu for your convenience. If you want to perform a more complex sort, you still need to use the Sort dialog box.

To sort the filtered table data:

1. Click the **Appraised Value filter arrow**. The AutoFilter menu opens. The sort options are at the top of the menu.
2. Click **Sort Largest to Smallest**. The filtered table now displays installations and sculptures with an appraised valued greater than $20,000 sorted in descending order. See Figure 5-18.

Figure 5-18 Filtered ArtObjects table

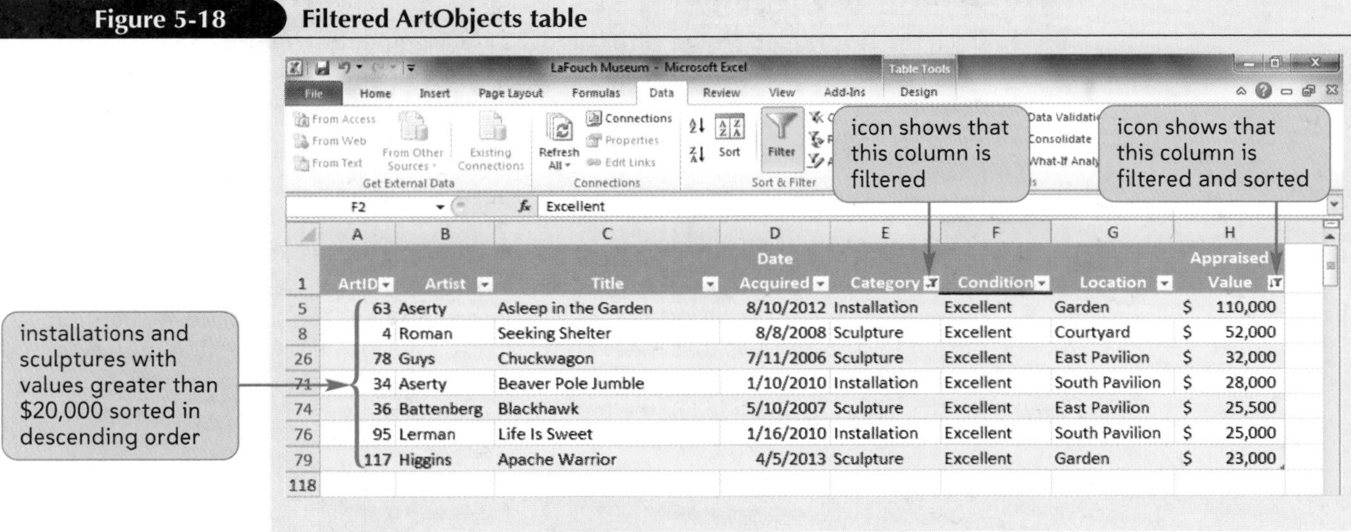

Mary will send this list to the board of directors. You need to restore the entire table of art objects, which you can do by clearing all the filters at one time.

To clear all the filters from the ArtObjects table:

1. Click the **Data** tab on the Ribbon, if necessary.
2. In the Sort & Filter group, click the **Clear** button. All the records appear in the table.

Using the Total Row to Calculate Summary Statistics

You can calculate summary statistics (including sum, average, count, maximum, and minimum) on all the columns in an Excel table or on a filtered table in a Total row, which you can display at the end of the table. When you click in each cell in the Total row, an arrow appears that you can click to open a list of the most commonly used functions.

Mary is creating a brochure for an upcoming fund-raising event, and wants to know the number and value of the items in the current museum collection, excluding art objects in poor condition. You will filter the table to display art objects that are in excellent, good, and fair condition (art objects in poor condition will not be displayed). Then, you will display the Total row for the ArtObjects table to count the number of art objects in excellent, good, and fair condition, and add their total appraised value.

To add a Total row and select summary statistics:

1. Click the **Condition filter arrow**, click the **Poor** check box to remove the check mark, and then click the **OK** button. The ArtObjects table displays objects that are in excellent, good, or fair condition. The status bar indicates that 110 of 116 records remain in the filtered table.
2. Click the **Table Tools Design** tab on the Ribbon, and then click the **Total Row** check box in the Table Style Options group to insert a check mark.
3. Scroll to the end of the table. The Total row is the last row of the table, the word "Total" appears in the far-left cell, and the total appraised value $1,118,723 appears in the far-right cell. By default, the Total row adds the numbers in the last column of the Excel table or counts the number of records if the data in the last column contains text. See Figure 5-19.

Figure 5-19 Total row added to the ArtObjects table

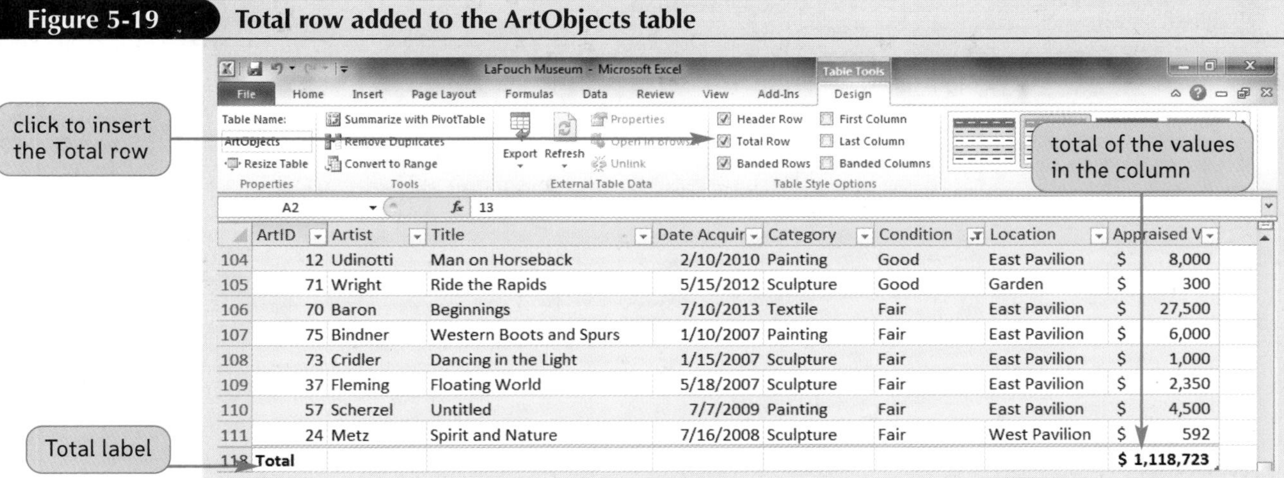

	ArtID	Artist	Title	Date Acquir	Category	Condition	Location	Appraised V
104	12	Udinotti	Man on Horseback	2/10/2010	Painting	Good	East Pavilion	$ 8,000
105	71	Wright	Ride the Rapids	5/15/2012	Sculpture	Good	Garden	$ 300
106	70	Baron	Beginnings	7/10/2013	Textile	Fair	East Pavilion	$ 27,500
107	75	Bindner	Western Boots and Spurs	1/10/2007	Painting	Fair	East Pavilion	$ 6,000
108	73	Cridler	Dancing in the Light	1/15/2007	Sculpture	Fair	East Pavilion	$ 1,000
109	37	Fleming	Floating World	5/18/2007	Sculpture	Fair	East Pavilion	$ 2,350
110	57	Scherzel	Untitled	7/7/2009	Painting	Fair	East Pavilion	$ 4,500
111	24	Metz	Spirit and Nature	7/16/2008	Sculpture	Fair	West Pavilion	$ 592
118	Total							$ 1,118,723

In the Artist cell of the Total row, you want to count the number of records whose appraised values were added in the last column.

4. Click cell **B118** (the Artist cell in the Total row), and then click the **arrow button** to display a list of functions. "None" is the default function in all columns except the last column. See Figure 5-20.

Figure 5-20 Total row functions

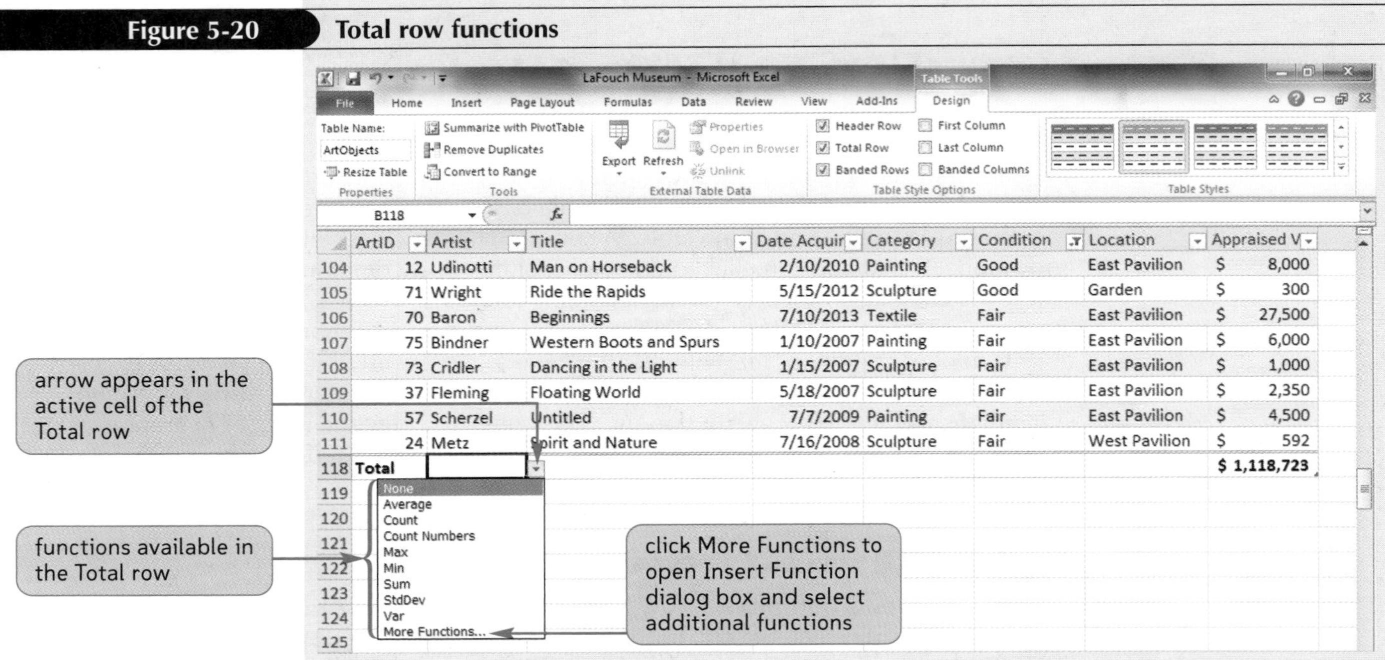

5. Click **Count**. The number 110, which is the number of records in the filtered ArtObjects table, appears in the cell. See Figure 5-21.

Figure 5-21 Count of records in the filtered table

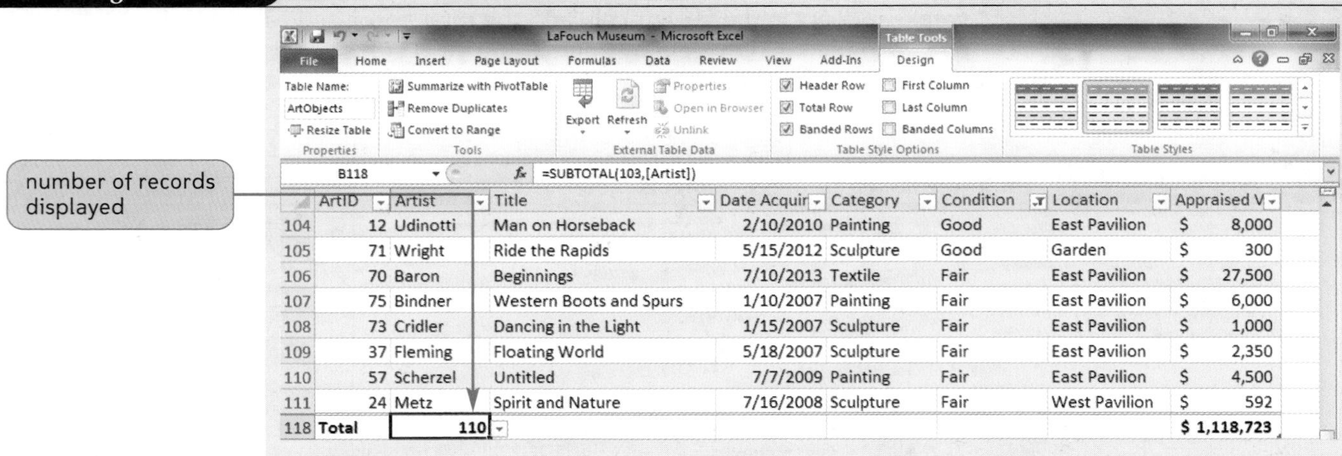

Splitting the Worksheet Window into Panes

You can split the worksheet window into two or four separate panes. This allows you to easily view data from several areas of the worksheet at the same time. Each pane has its own scroll bars so you can navigate easily within one pane or display different parts of the worksheet. You can move between panes using the mouse. To create two panes, select a cell in row 1 or column A; to create four panes, select any other cell.

Mary wants to view the art collection summary totals at the same time she views the data on individual art objects. You will divide the worksheet into two horizontal panes to view the art object records in the top pane and the totals in the bottom pane.

To split the Art Collection worksheet window into panes:

1. Press the **Ctrl+Home** keys to jump to the top of the table, and then click cell **A17**.
2. Click the **View** tab on the Ribbon, and then click the **Split** button in the Window group. The worksheet window splits into two panes. Each pane has its own set of scroll bars. See Figure 5-22.

Figure 5-22 Worksheet split into two panes

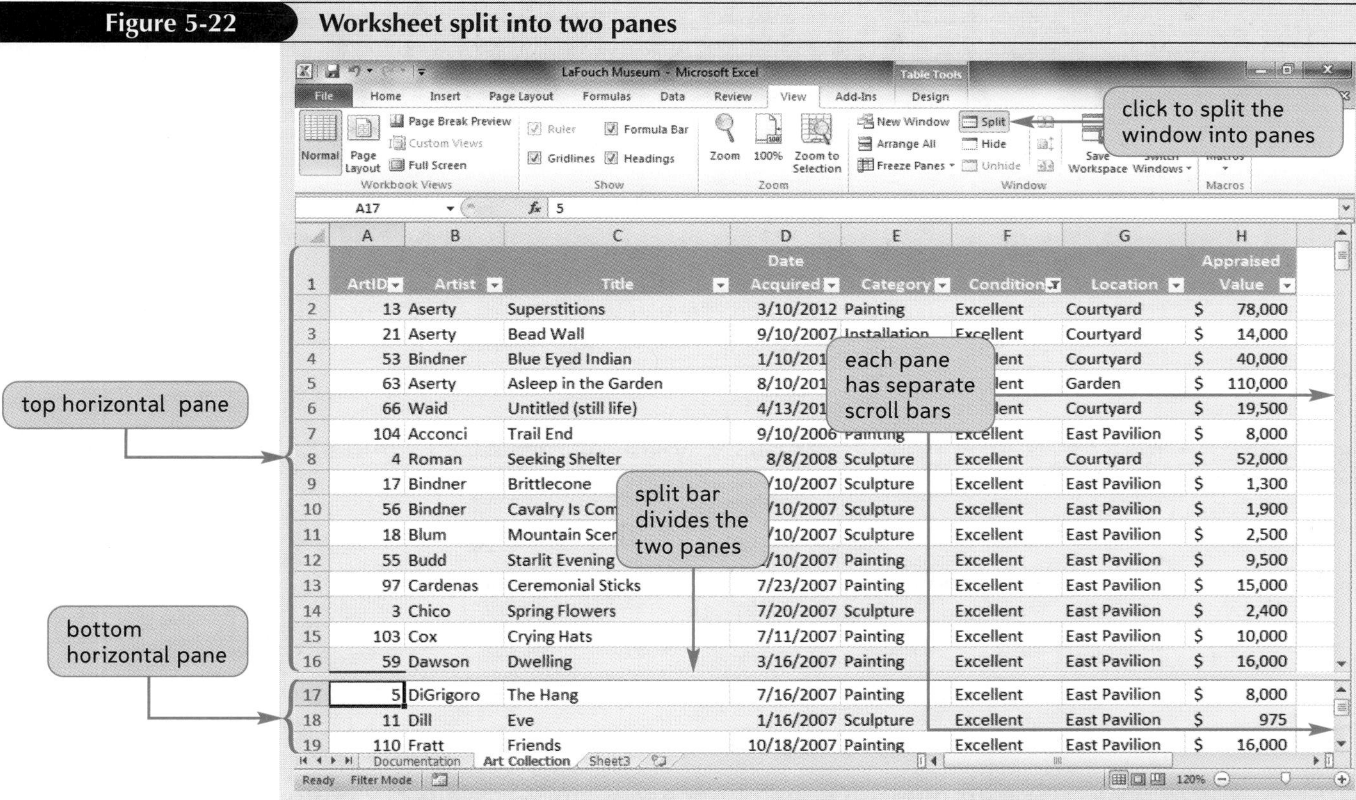

3. If necessary, click cell **A17** to activate the bottom pane.
4. Using the lower scroll bar, scroll down until row 118, the Total row, appears immediately below the split bar. See Figure 5-23.

Figure 5-23 Total row displayed in the bottom pane

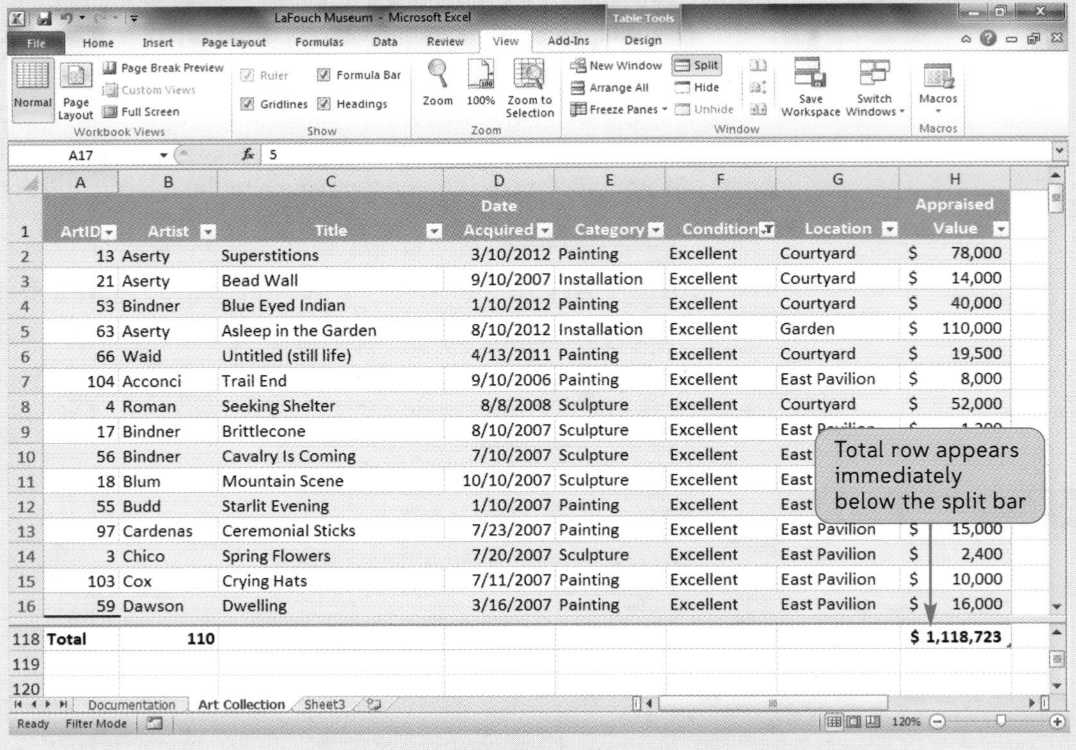

	ArtID	Artist	Title	Date Acquired	Category	Condition	Location	Appraised Value
2	13	Aserty	Superstitions	3/10/2012	Painting	Excellent	Courtyard	$ 78,000
3	21	Aserty	Bead Wall	9/10/2007	Installation	Excellent	Courtyard	$ 14,000
4	53	Bindner	Blue Eyed Indian	1/10/2012	Painting	Excellent	Courtyard	$ 40,000
5	63	Aserty	Asleep in the Garden	8/10/2012	Installation	Excellent	Garden	$ 110,000
6	66	Waid	Untitled (still life)	4/13/2011	Painting	Excellent	Courtyard	$ 19,500
7	104	Acconci	Trail End	9/10/2006	Painting	Excellent	East Pavilion	$ 8,000
8	4	Roman	Seeking Shelter	8/8/2008	Sculpture	Excellent	Courtyard	$ 52,000
9	17	Bindner	Brittlecone	8/10/2007	Sculpture	Excellent	East	
10	56	Bindner	Cavalry Is Coming	7/10/2007	Sculpture	Excellent	East	
11	18	Blum	Mountain Scene	10/10/2007	Sculpture	Excellent	East	
12	55	Budd	Starlit Evening	1/10/2007	Painting	Excellent	East	
13	97	Cardenas	Ceremonial Sticks	7/23/2007	Painting	Excellent	East Pavilion	$ 15,000
14	3	Chico	Spring Flowers	7/20/2007	Sculpture	Excellent	East Pavilion	$ 2,400
15	103	Cox	Crying Hats	7/11/2007	Painting	Excellent	East Pavilion	$ 10,000
16	59	Dawson	Dwelling	3/16/2007	Painting	Excellent	East Pavilion	$ 16,000
118	Total	110						$ 1,118,723

A popular painting named "Dark Canyon" had a new appraisal. Its value is now $8,000. You will change the appraised value of this painting.

To update the appraised value of the Dark Canyon painting:

1. Click any cell in the top pane.
2. Use the Find command to locate the art object with ArtID **113**.
3. In the Appraised Value cell, enter **8000**. The total appraised value in the bottom pane changed from $1,118,723 to $1,119,223.

Next, you will remove the split panes from the worksheet window.

To remove the split panes from the Art Collection worksheet window:

1. If necessary, click the **View** tab on the Ribbon.
2. In the Window group, click the **Split** button. The split bar is removed, and the worksheet is again a single window.

TIP

You can also double-click the split bar to remove the panes.

Now, you will remove the Total row and clear the filter.

To remove the Total row and clear the filter from the ArtObjects table:

1. Click the **Table Tools Design** tab on the Ribbon.
2. In the Table Style Options group, click the **Total Row** check box to remove the check mark. The Total row is no longer visible.
3. Click the **Condition filter arrow**, and then click **Clear Filter From "Condition"**. The ArtObjects table displays all the art objects.
4. Press the **Ctrl+Home** keys to return to cell A1.

TIP

If you redisplay the Total row, the functions you last used will appear even after you save, close, and then reopen the file.

The board of directors asked Mary to create a report that shows all the museum's art objects sorted by Category with the total appraised value of the art objects in each category. The board also wants to see the total appraised value for each category after the last item of that category. Although you could use the Total row in the Excel table to calculate the results, you would need to filter, total, and print the data for each category separately. A faster way to provide the information Mary needs is to use the Subtotal command.

Inserting Subtotals

You can summarize data in a range by inserting subtotals. The Subtotal command offers many kinds of summary information, including counts, sums, averages, minimums, and maximums. The Subtotal command inserts a subtotal row into the range for each group of data and adds a grand total row below the last row of data. Because Excel inserts subtotals whenever the value in a specified field changes, you need to sort the data so that records with the same value in a specified field are grouped together *before* you use the Subtotal command. The Subtotal command cannot be used in an Excel table, so you must first convert the Excel table to a range.

REFERENCE

Calculating Subtotals for a Range of Data

- Sort the data by the column for which you want a subtotal.
- If the data is in an Excel table, in the Tools group on the Table Tools Design tab, click the Convert to Range button, and then click the Yes button to convert the Excel table to a range.
- In the Outline group on the Data tab, click the Subtotal button.
- Click the At each change in arrow, and then click the column that contains the group you want to subtotal.
- Click the Use function arrow, and then click the function you want to use to summarize the data.
- In the Add subtotal to box, click the check box for each column that contains the values you want to summarize.
- To calculate another category of subtotals, click the Replace current subtotals check box to remove the check mark, and then repeat the previous three steps.
- Click the OK button.

To produce the results Mary needs, you will sort the art objects by category and calculate subtotals in the Appraised Value column for each category grouping. You will also convert the Excel table to a normal range.

To sort the art objects and convert the table to a range:

TIP

Be sure to sort the table and then convert the table to a range before calculating subtotals.

1. Click the **Category filter arrow**, and then click **Sort A to Z** on the AutoFilter menu. The ArtObjects table is sorted in ascending order by the Category field. This ensures one subtotal is created for each category.
2. In the Tools group on the Table Tools Design tab, click the **Convert to Range** button. A dialog box opens, asking if you want to convert the table to a normal range.
3. Click the **Yes** button. The Excel table is converted to a range. You can tell this because the filter arrows and the Table Tools Design tab disappear, and the Home tab on the Ribbon is selected.

Next, you'll calculate the subtotals.

To calculate appraised values subtotals for each category of art object:

1. Click the **Data** tab on the Ribbon, and then, in the Outline group, click the **Subtotal** button. The Subtotal dialog box opens. See Figure 5-24.

Figure 5-24 Subtotal dialog box

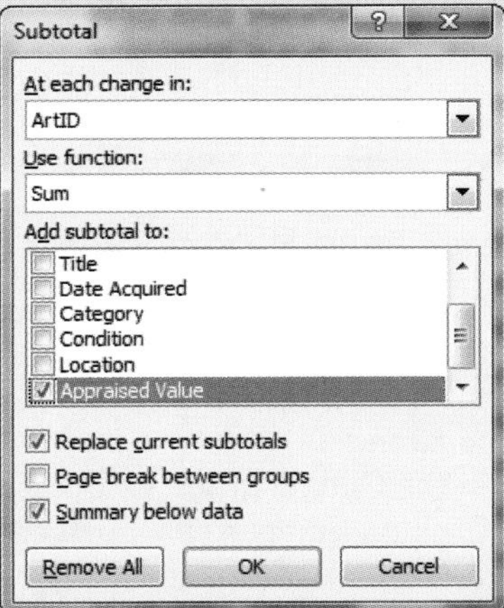

2. Click the **At each change in** arrow, and then click **Category**. This is the column you want Excel to use to determine where to insert the subtotals; it's the column you sorted. A subtotal will be calculated at every change in the Category value.
3. If necessary, click the **Use function** arrow, and then click **Sum**. The Use function list provides several options for subtotaling data, including counts, averages, minimums, maximums, and products.

4. In the Add subtotal to list box, make sure only the **Appraised Value** check box is checked. This specifies the Appraised Value field as the field to be subtotaled. If the data already included subtotals, you would check the Replace current subtotals check box to replace the existing subtotals or uncheck the option to display the new subtotals on separate rows above the existing subtotals. Because the data has no subtotals, it makes no difference whether you select this option.
5. Make sure the **Summary below data** check box is checked. This option places the subtotals below each group of data, instead of above the first entry in each group, and places the grand total at the end of the data, instead of at the top of the column just below the row of column headings.
6. Click the **OK** button. Excel inserts rows below each category group and displays the subtotals for the appraised value of each art category. A series of Outline buttons appears to the left of the worksheet so you can display or hide the detail rows within each subtotal.

   Trouble? If each item has a subtotal following it, you probably forgot to sort the data by Category. Click the Undo button on the Quick Access Toolbar, sort the data by Category, and then repeat Steps 1 through 6.
7. Scroll through the data to see the subtotals below each category and the grand total at the end of the data. See Figure 5-25.

Figure 5-25 Subtotals and grand total added to the art objects data

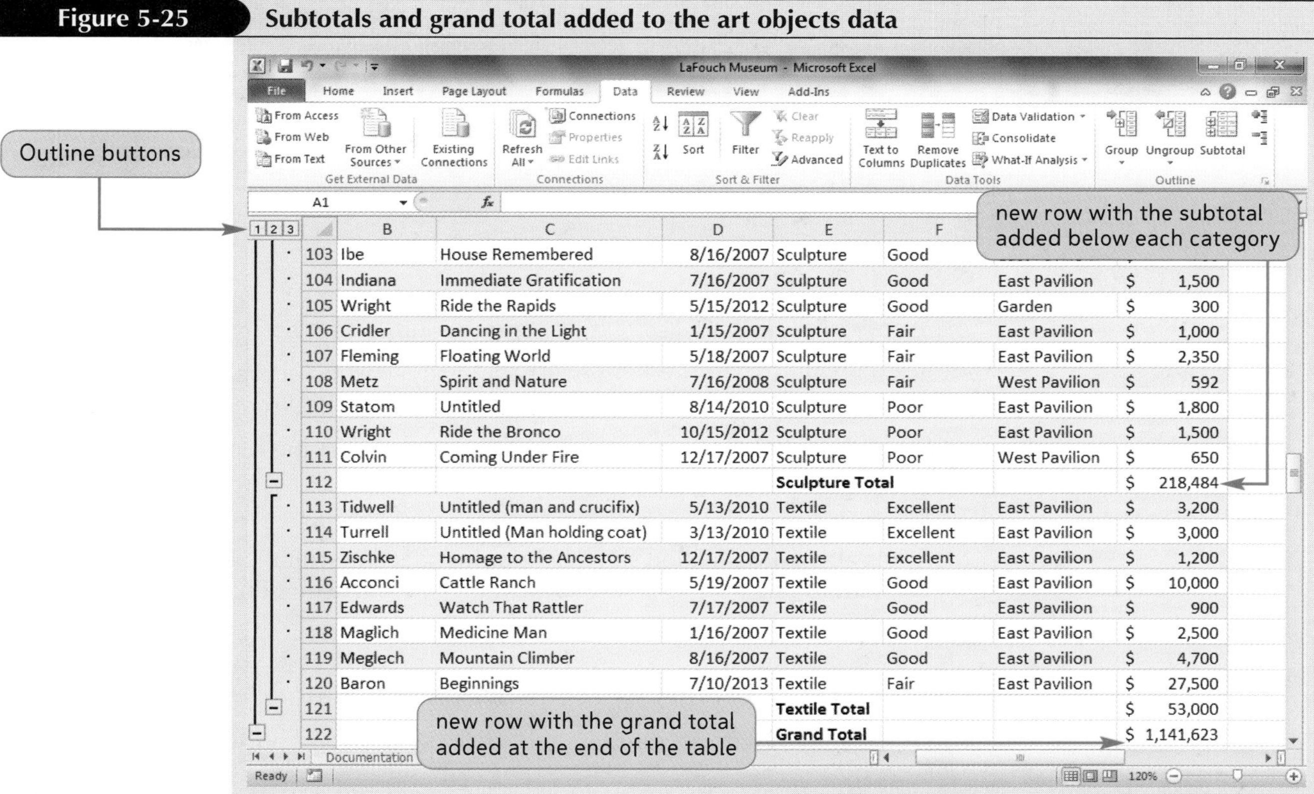

	B	C	D	E	F	G	H
103	Ibe	House Remembered	8/16/2007	Sculpture	Good		
104	Indiana	Immediate Gratification	7/16/2007	Sculpture	Good	East Pavilion	$ 1,500
105	Wright	Ride the Rapids	5/15/2012	Sculpture	Good	Garden	$ 300
106	Cridler	Dancing in the Light	1/15/2007	Sculpture	Fair	East Pavilion	$ 1,000
107	Fleming	Floating World	5/18/2007	Sculpture	Fair	East Pavilion	$ 2,350
108	Metz	Spirit and Nature	7/16/2008	Sculpture	Fair	West Pavilion	$ 592
109	Statom	Untitled	8/14/2010	Sculpture	Poor	East Pavilion	$ 1,800
110	Wright	Ride the Bronco	10/15/2012	Sculpture	Poor	East Pavilion	$ 1,500
111	Colvin	Coming Under Fire	12/17/2007	Sculpture	Poor	West Pavilion	$ 650
112				**Sculpture Total**			$ 218,484
113	Tidwell	Untitled (man and crucifix)	5/13/2010	Textile	Excellent	East Pavilion	$ 3,200
114	Turrell	Untitled (Man holding coat)	3/13/2010	Textile	Excellent	East Pavilion	$ 3,000
115	Zischke	Homage to the Ancestors	12/17/2007	Textile	Excellent	East Pavilion	$ 1,200
116	Acconci	Cattle Ranch	5/19/2007	Textile	Good	East Pavilion	$ 10,000
117	Edwards	Watch That Rattler	7/17/2007	Textile	Good	East Pavilion	$ 900
118	Maglich	Medicine Man	1/16/2007	Textile	Good	East Pavilion	$ 2,500
119	Meglech	Mountain Climber	8/16/2007	Textile	Good	East Pavilion	$ 4,700
120	Baron	Beginnings	7/10/2013	Textile	Fair	East Pavilion	$ 27,500
121				**Textile Total**			$ 53,000
122				**Grand Total**			$ 1,141,623

Using the Subtotal Outline View

In addition to displaying subtotals, the Subtotal feature "outlines" your worksheet so you can control the level of detail that is displayed. The three Outline buttons at the top of the outline area, as shown in Figure 5-25, allow you to show or hide different levels of detail in the worksheet. By default, the highest level is active; in this case, Level 3. Level 3 displays the most detail—the individual art object records, the subtotals, and the grand total. Level 2 displays the subtotals and the grand total, but not the individual records. Level 1 displays only the grand total.

The subtotals are useful, but Mary wants you to isolate the different subtotal sections so that she can focus on them individually. You will use the Outline buttons to prepare a report for Mary that includes only subtotals and the grand total.

To use the Outline buttons to hide records:

1. Click the **Level 2 Outline** button, and then scroll up to view all the category subtotals, if necessary. The individual art object records are hidden, and you see only the subtotals for each category and the grand total. See Figure 5-26.

Figure 5-26 Table displaying only subtotals and grand total

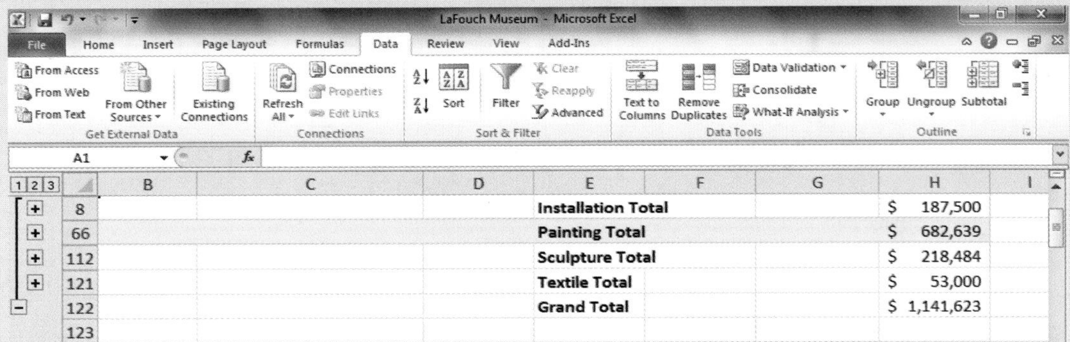

Trouble? If necessary, scroll the worksheet up to see the complete Level 2 list.

2. Click the **Level 1 Outline** button. The individual art object records and the subtotals for each category are hidden. Only the grand total remains visible.
3. Click the **Level 3 Outline** button. Scroll to the top. All the records along with the subtotals and the grand total are visible.

Mary has all the information she needs for her meeting with the board to review financial plans for the next fiscal cycle. So you can remove the subtotals from the data.

To remove the subtotals from the art objects data:

1. In the Outline group on the Data tab, click the **Subtotal** button. The Subtotal dialog box opens.
2. Click the **Remove All** button. The subtotals are removed from the data, and only the records appear in the worksheet.

   You'll reset the art objects data as an Excel table.
3. Make sure the active cell is a cell within the structured range of data.

4. Click the **Insert** tab on the Ribbon, and then click the **Table** button in the Tables group. The Create Table dialog box opens.
5. Click the **OK** button to create the Excel table, and then click any cell in the table. The table structure is active.
6. In the Properties group on the Table Tools Design tab, type **ArtObjects** in the Table Name box, and then press the **Enter** key. The Excel table is again named "ArtObjects."

In this session, you filtered the table data and determined totals and subtotals for the data. Mary needs to generate information for a board meeting about the appraised values of the museum's art objects. You will work with PivotTables and PivotCharts in the next session to gather the information that Mary needs.

REVIEW

Session 5.2 Quick Check

1. Explain the relationship between the Sort and Subtotal commands.
2. An Excel table includes records for 500 employees. What can you use to calculate the average salary of employees in the finance department?
3. How can you display a list of marketing majors with a GPA of 3.0 or greater from an Excel table with records for 300 students?
4. After you display subtotals, how can you change the amount of detail displayed?
5. True or False. The COUNT function is a valid subtotal function when using the Subtotal command.
6. An Excel table of Major League Baseball players includes the column Position (pitchers, catchers, infielders, outfielders, and so forth). What feature can you use to display only pitchers and catchers in the table?
7. If you have a list of employees that includes fields for gender and salary, among others, how can you determine the average salary for females using the Total row feature?

SESSION 5.3 VISUAL OVERVIEW

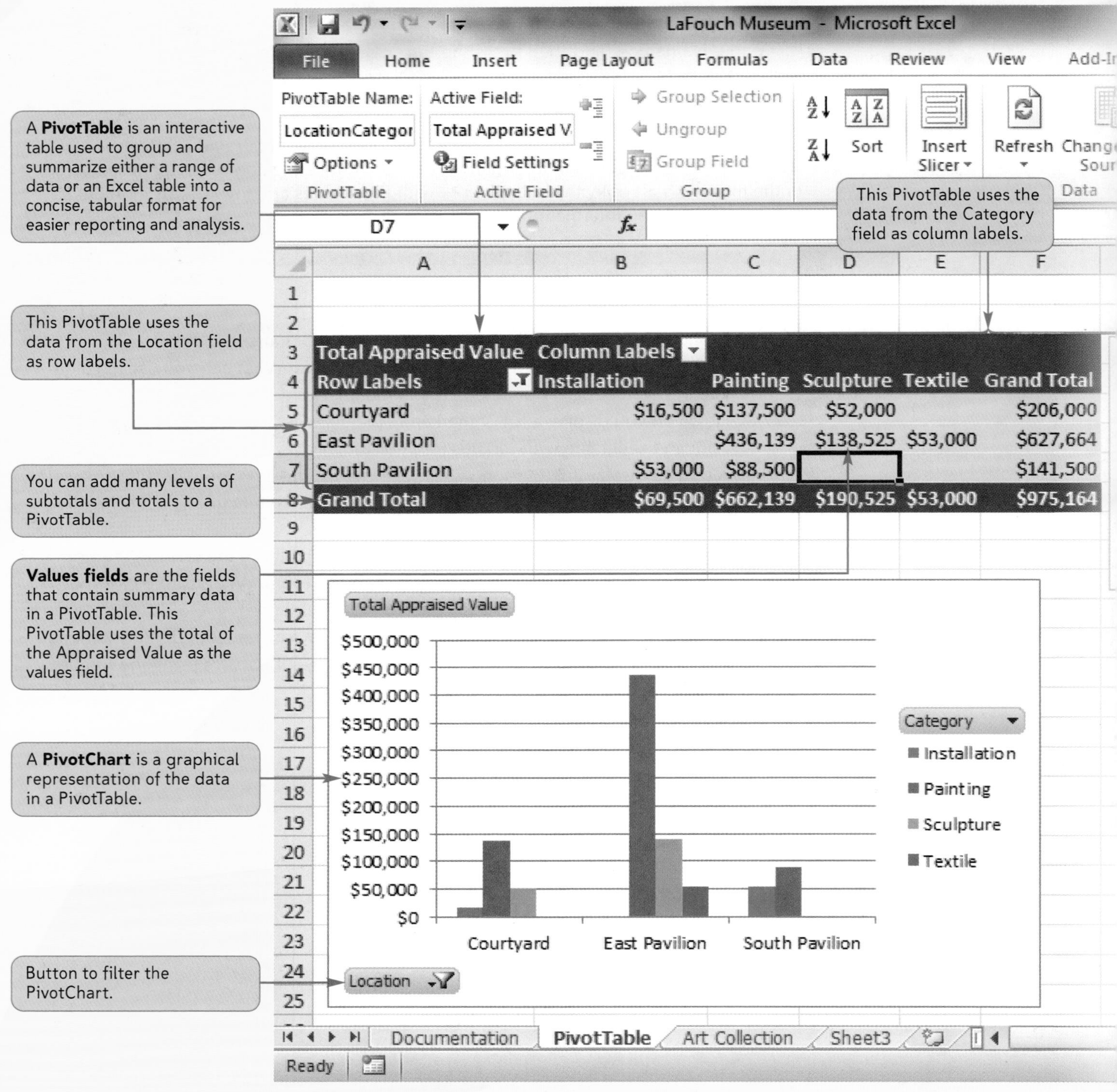

PIVOTTABLE AND PIVOTCHART

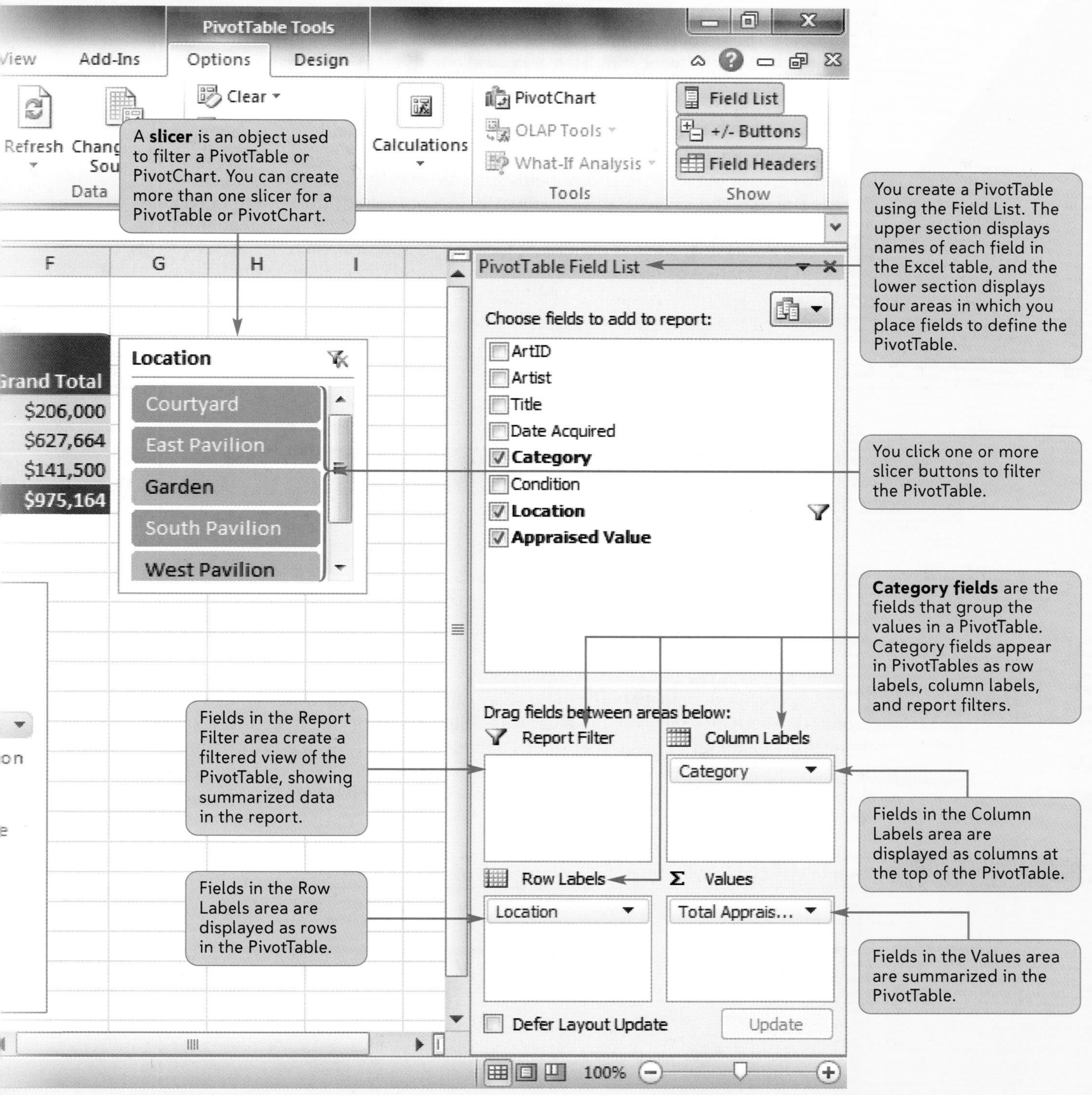

A **slicer** is an object used to filter a PivotTable or PivotChart. You can create more than one slicer for a PivotTable or PivotChart.

You create a PivotTable using the Field List. The upper section displays names of each field in the Excel table, and the lower section displays four areas in which you place fields to define the PivotTable.

You click one or more slicer buttons to filter the PivotTable.

Category fields are the fields that group the values in a PivotTable. Category fields appear in PivotTables as row labels, column labels, and report filters.

Fields in the Report Filter area create a filtered view of the PivotTable, showing summarized data in the report.

Fields in the Column Labels area are displayed as columns at the top of the PivotTable.

Fields in the Row Labels area are displayed as rows in the PivotTable.

Fields in the Values area are summarized in the PivotTable.

Analyzing Data with PivotTables

An Excel table can contain a wealth of information. However, the large amounts of detailed data it contains often make it difficult to form a clear, overall view of that information. You can use a PivotTable to help organize the data into a meaningful summary. A PivotTable summarizes data into categories using functions such as COUNT, SUM, AVERAGE, MAX, and MIN. For example, Mary is preparing a presentation for the museum's board of directors that will include a report of the appraised value of the museum's art objects by location, category, and condition. Although there are several ways to generate the information Mary needs, a PivotTable can generate this information quickly and concisely.

To create a PivotTable report, you need to specify which fields in the data source to summarize. In the ArtObjects table, the Appraised Value field is the most likely field to summarize. In other applications, fields such as salaries, sales, and costs are frequently summarized in PivotTables. In PivotTable terminology, the fields that contain summary data are known as values fields. Category fields are the fields that group the values in a PivotTable, such as condition, location, and year acquired. Category fields appear in PivotTables as row labels, column labels, and report filters, which allows you to focus on a subset of the PivotTable by displaying one, several, or all items. Figure 5-27 shows the PivotTable you will create.

Figure 5-27 **Sample PivotTable**

	A	B	C	D	E	F
2						
3	Total Appraised Value					
4		Installation	Painting	Sculpture	Textile	Grand Total
5	East Pavilion		$436,639	$141,525	$53,000	$631,164
6	Courtyard	$16,500	$137,500	$52,000		$206,000
7	Garden	$118,000		$24,100		$142,100
8	South Pavilion	$53,000	$88,500			$141,500
9	West Pavilion		$20,000	$3,859		$23,859
10	Grand Total	$187,500	$682,639	$221,484	$53,000	$1,144,623

You can easily rearrange, hide, and display different category fields in the PivotTable to provide alternative views of the data. This ability to "pivot" the table—for example, change row headings to column positions and vice versa—gives the PivotTable its name and makes it a powerful analytical tool. In Figure 5-28, the PivotTable is rearranged so that the Category items appear as row labels and the Location items appear as column labels.

Figure 5-28 **Sample PivotTable with rows and columns pivoted**

	A	B	C	D	E	F	G
1							
2	Total Appraised Value						
3		Courtyard	East Pavilion	Garden	South Pavilion	West Pavilion	Grand Total
4	Installation	$ 16,500		$ 118,000	$ 53,000		$ 187,500
5	Painting	$ 137,500	$ 436,639		$ 88,500	$ 20,000	$ 682,639
6	Sculpture	$ 52,000	$ 141,525	$ 24,100		$ 3,859	$ 221,484
7	Textile		$ 53,000				$ 53,000
8	Grand Total	$ 206,000	$ 631,164	$142,100	$ 141,500	$ 23,859	$1,144,623

To conceptualize the layout of a PivotTable and convey your ideas to others who might implement them, a useful first step in creating a PivotTable is to sketch its layout. Mary's sketch, shown in Figure 5-29, illustrates the PivotTable you will create to show the appraised value of the art objects organized by location, category, and condition.

Figure 5-29 **PivotTable sketch**

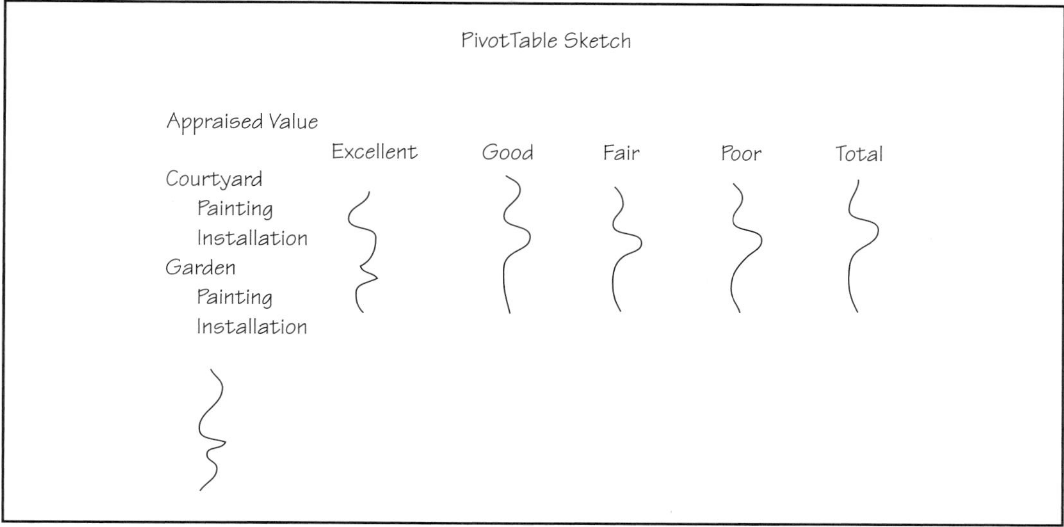

You are ready to create a PivotTable summarizing the total appraised value of art objects by location, category, and condition.

PROSKILLS

Written Communication: Summarizing Data with a PivotTable

PivotTables are a great way to summarize data from selected fields of an Excel table or range, which can help you back up or support specific points in written documents. The PivotTable omits all the detailed data, enabling readers to focus on the bigger picture. This makes it easier for readers to understand the results and gain insights about the topic.

You can show summaries in written documents based on function results in PivotTables. The SUM function is probably the most frequently used function. For example, you might show the total sales for a region. However, you can use many other functions to summarize the data, including COUNT, AVERAGE, MIN, MAX, PRODUCT, COUNT NUMBERS, STDEV, STDEVP, VAR, and VARP. For example, you might show the average sales for a region, the minimum price of a product, or a count of the number of products sold.

When you write a report, you want supporting data to be presented in the way that best communicates your points. With PivotTables, you display the values in different views. For example, to compare one item to another item in the PivotTable, you can show the values as a percentage of a total. You can display the data in each row as a percentage of the total for the row. You can also display the data in each column as a percentage of the total for the column or display the data as a percentage of the grand total of all the data in the PivotTable. Viewing data as a percentage of the total is useful for analyses such as comparing product sales with total sales within a region or comparing expense categories to total expenses for the year

As you can see, PivotTables provide great flexibility in how you analyze and display data. This makes it easier to present data in a way that highlights and supports the points you are communicating, making your written documents much more effective.

Creating a PivotTable

To create the PivotTable that will provide the information Mary needs, you will use the PivotTable dialog box to select the data to analyze and the location of the PivotTable report. Often when creating a PivotTable, you begin with data stored in a worksheet, although a PivotTable can also be created using data stored in an external database file such as one in Access. In this case, you will use the ArtObjects table to create the PivotTable and place the PivotTable in a new worksheet.

REFERENCE

Creating a PivotTable

- Click in the Excel table or select the range of data for the PivotTable.
- In the Tables group on the Insert tab, click the PivotTable button.
- Click the Select a table or range option button and verify the reference in the Table/Range box.
- Click the New Worksheet option button or click the Existing Worksheet option button and specify a cell.
- Click the OK button.
- Click the check boxes for the fields you want to add to the PivotTable (or drag fields to the appropriate box in the layout section).
- If needed, drag fields to different boxes in the layout section.

When you create a PivotTable, you need to specify where to find the data for the PivotTable. The data can be in an Excel table or range in the current workbook or an external data source such as an Access database file. You also specify whether to place the PivotTable in a new or an existing worksheet. If you place the PivotTable in an existing worksheet, you must also specify the cell in which you want the upper-left corner of the PivotTable to appear. For the appraised value PivotTable report, you will use the ArtObjects table and place the PivotTable in a new worksheet.

TIP

You can also create a PivotTable by clicking the Summarize with PivotTable button in the Tools group on the Table Tools Design tab.

To create a PivotTable using the ArtObjects table:

1. If you took a break after the previous session, make sure the LaFouch Museum workbook is open, the Art Collection worksheet is active, and the Excel table is active.
2. Click the **Insert** tab on the Ribbon, and then, in the Tables group, click the **PivotTable** button. The Create PivotTable dialog box opens. See Figure 5-30.

Figure 5-30 **Create PivotTable dialog box**

Create PivotTable
Choose the data that you want to analyze
Select a table or range
Table/Range: ArtObjects
Use an external data source
Choose Connection...
Connection name:
Choose where you want the PivotTable report to be placed
New Worksheet
Existing Worksheet
Location:
OK Cancel

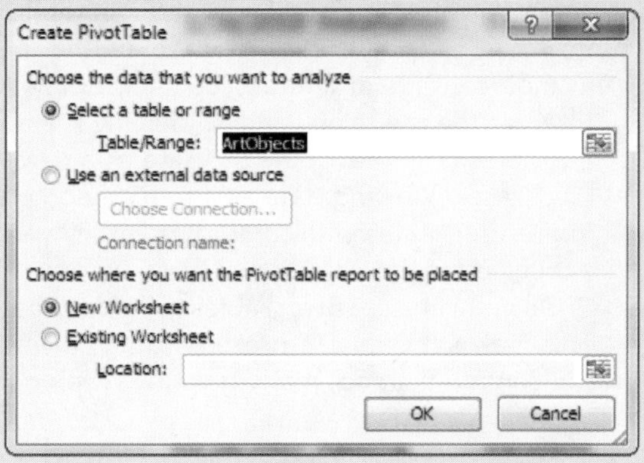

3. Make sure the **Select a table or range** option button is selected and **ArtObjects** appears in the Table/Range box.
4. Click the **New Worksheet** option button, if necessary. This sets the PivotTable report to be placed in a new worksheet.
5. Click the **OK** button. A new worksheet, Sheet1, is inserted to the left of the Art Collection worksheet. The empty PivotTable report area is where the finished PivotTable will be placed. You use the PivotTable Field List to build the PivotTable by adding, removing, and arranging fields, or columns. The PivotTable Tools contextual tabs appear on the Ribbon. See Figure 5-31.

Figure 5-31 **PivotTable report area and PivotTable Field List**

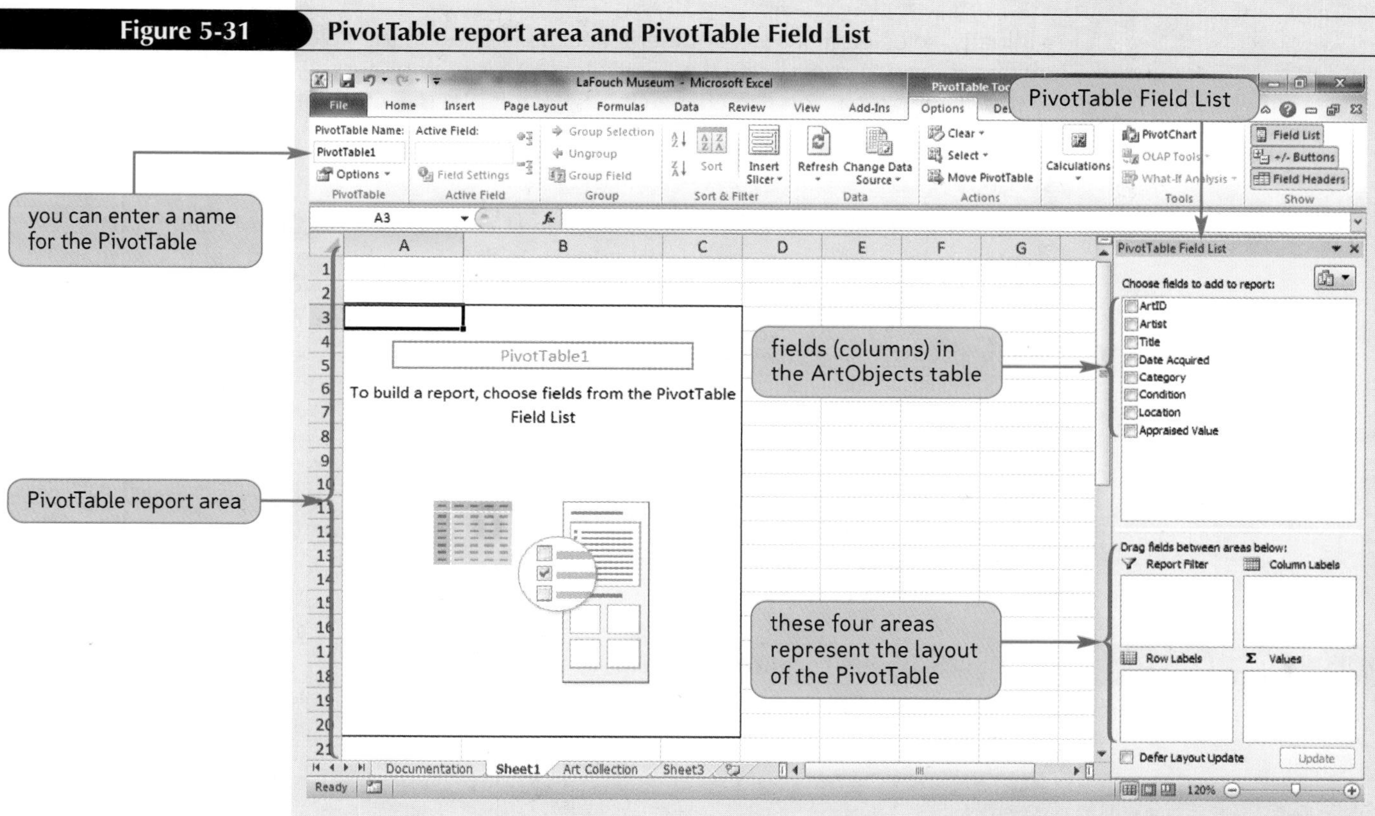

The PivotTable Field List is divided into two sections. The upper field list section displays the names of each field in the ArtObjects table. You check a field check box to add that field to the PivotTable. The lower layout section includes boxes for the four areas in which you can place fields: Report Filter, Row Labels, Column Labels, and Values. Figure 5-32 describes the function of each area.

Figure 5-32 Layout areas for a PivotTable

Layout Area	Description
Row Labels	The fields you want to display as the rows in the PivotTable. One row is displayed for each unique item in this area. You can have nested row fields.
Column Labels	The fields you want to display as columns at the top of the PivotTable. One column is displayed for each unique item in this area. You can have nested column fields.
Report Filter	A field used to filter the report by selecting one or more items, enabling you to display a subset of data in a PivotTable report.
Values	The fields you want to summarize.

Initially, selected fields with numeric data are placed in the Values area and the SUM function is used to summarize the PivotTable. Fields with nonnumeric data are placed in the Row Labels area. You can change these default placements of fields.

Adding Fields to a PivotTable

You need to calculate the total appraised value of art objects by location, within location by category, and within category by condition. In the PivotTable, you'll begin by adding the Location, Category, and Condition fields to appear as row labels, and the data in the Appraised Value field to be summarized. First, you will create a PivotTable summarizing the appraised value by location.

To add fields to the PivotTable:

1. In the PivotTable Field List, click the **Location** check box. The Location field is added to the Row Labels box and the unique values in the Location field—Courtyard, East Pavilion, Garden, South Pavilion, and West Pavilion—appear in the PivotTable report area. See Figure 5-33.

Figure 5-33 PivotTable with the Location field items as row labels

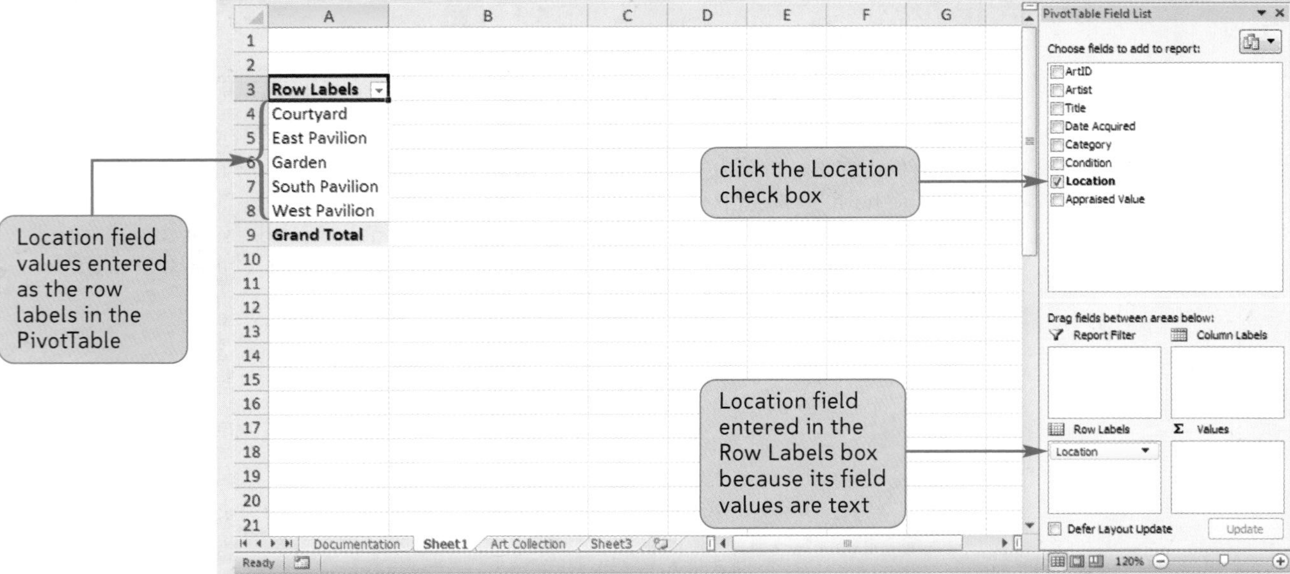

2. In the PivotTable Field List, click the **Appraised Value** check box. The Sum of Appraised Value button appears in the Values box. The PivotTable groups the items from the ArtObjects table by location, and calculates the total appraised value for each location. The grand total appears at the bottom of the PivotTable. See Figure 5-34.

Figure 5-34 PivotTable of the appraised value of art objects by location

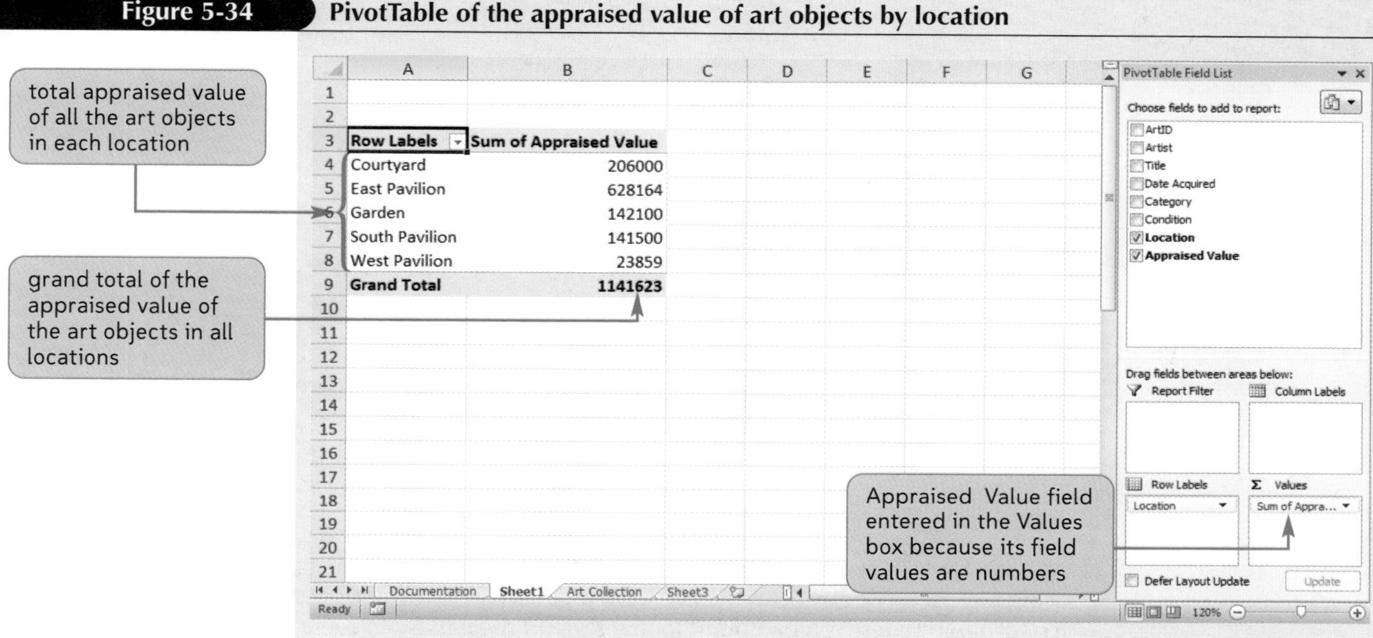

3. Rename the worksheet as **Appraised Value Summary**.

By default, the PivotTable report uses the SUM function for numbers in the Values area and the COUNT function for text and other nonnumeric values. If you want a different summary function, such as AVERAGE, MAX, or MIN, click the appropriate button in the Values box (in this case, the button is called "Sum of Appraised Value") in the PivotTable Field List, and then click Value Field Settings. The Value Field Settings dialog box opens. You can then select the type of calculation you want from the list of available functions, and then click the OK button.

Next, you'll add the Category and Condition fields to the PivotTable.

To add the Category and Condition fields to the PivotTable:

1. In the PivotTable Field List, click the **Category** check box. The Category field appears in the Row Labels box below the Location field, and the unique items in the Category field are indented below each location field item in the PivotTable.

   Trouble? If the PivotTable Field List is not visible, the active cell is probably not in the PivotTable. Click any cell within the PivotTable to redisplay the PivotTable Field List.

2. In the PivotTable Field List, click the **Condition** check box. The Condition field appears in the Row Labels box below the Category field, and its unique items are indented below the Location and Category fields already in the PivotTable. See Figure 5-35.

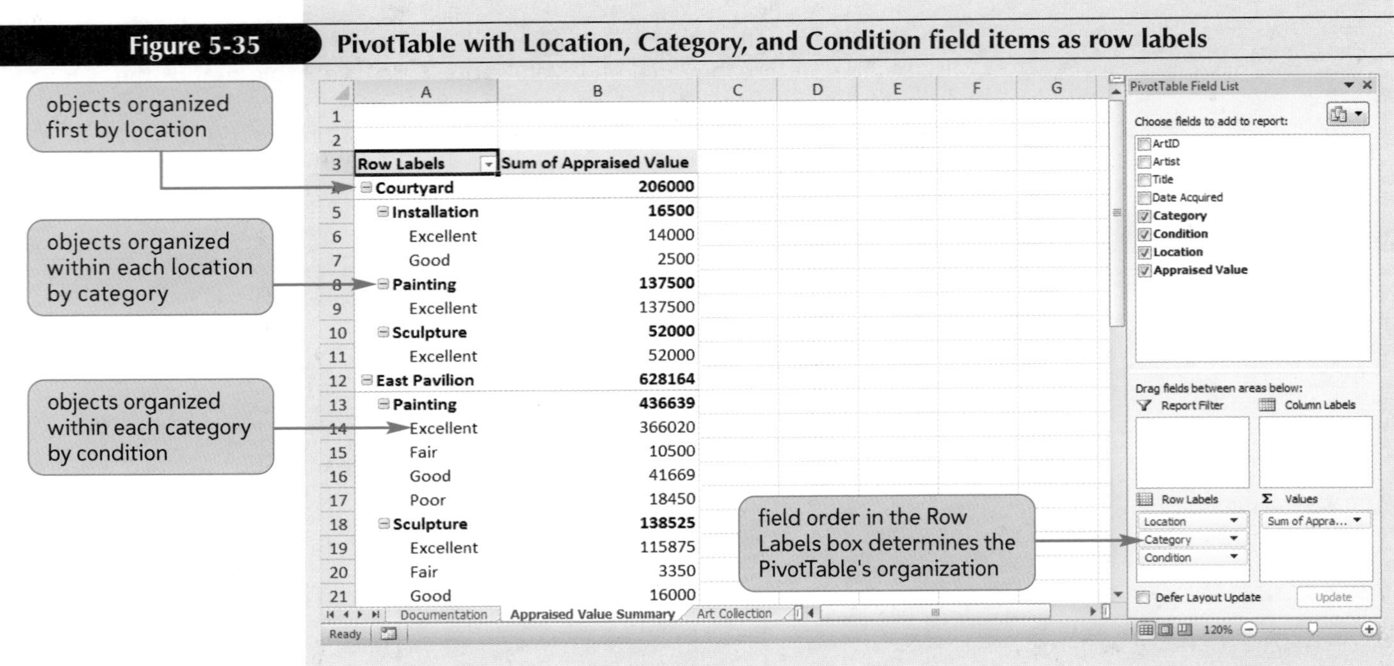

Figure 5-35 PivotTable with Location, Category, and Condition field items as row labels

Applying PivotTable Styles

As with worksheet cells and Excel tables, you can quickly format a PivotTable report using a preset style. You can choose from a gallery of PivotTable styles similar to the gallery of Table styles. You can point to any style in the gallery to see a Live Preview of the PivotTable with that style applied. You also can modify the appearance of PivotTables by adding or removing banded rows, banded columns, row headers, and column headers.

You will apply the Dark 4 style, which makes each group in the PivotTable stand out and subtotals in the report easier to find.

To apply a PivotTable style to the PivotTable report:

1. Make sure the active cell is in the PivotTable, and then click the **PivotTable Tools Design** tab on the Ribbon.
2. In the PivotTable Styles group, click the **More** button to open the PivotTable Styles gallery.
3. Move the pointer over each style to see the Live Preview of the PivotTable report with that style.
4. Click the **Pivot Style Dark 4** style (the fourth style in the Dark section). The style is applied to the PivotTable.

Formatting PivotTable Values Fields

Applying PivotTable styles does not change the numeric formatting in the PivotTable. Mary wants the numbers in the PivotTable to be quickly recognized as currency. You can format cells in a PivotTable the same way as you do cells in the worksheet. You'll change the total appraised values in the PivotTable to Currency style.

To format the appraised value numbers in the PivotTable:

1. Click any cell in the **Sum of Appraised Value** column of the PivotTable report.
2. Click the **PivotTable Tools Options** tab on the Ribbon, and then click the **Field Settings** button in the Active Field group. The Value Field Settings dialog box opens. See Figure 5-36.

Figure 5-36 Value Field Settings dialog box

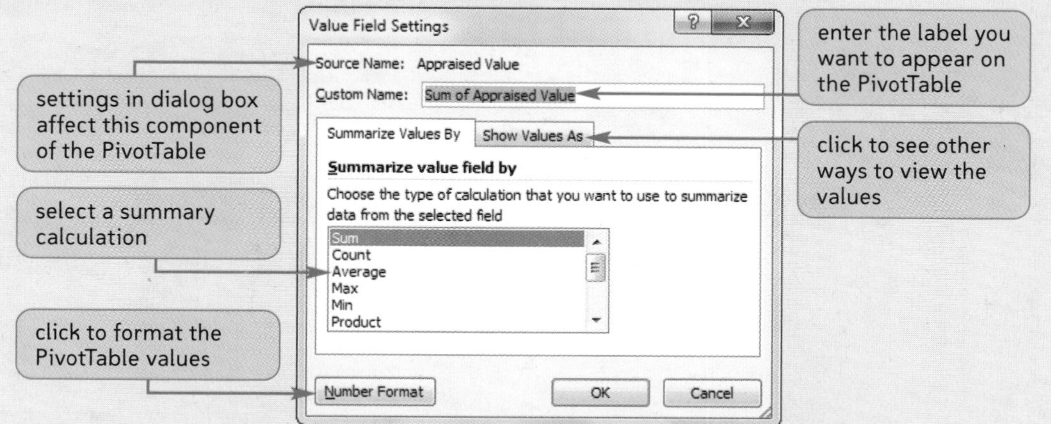

TIP

You can use the Summarize Values By tab to change the SUM function to a different summary function, such as AVERAGE. The name is updated to reflect your selection.

3. Click the **Number Format** button. The Format Cells dialog box opens. This is the same dialog box you've used before to format numbers in worksheet cells.
4. Click **Currency** in the Category box, and then type 0 in the Decimal places box.
5. Click the **OK** button. The numbers in the PivotTable will be formatted as currency with no decimal places.
6. In the **Custom Name** box, replace "Sum Of Appraised Value" with **Total Appraised Value**.
7. Click the **OK** button. The Value Field Settings dialog box closes, and the name used to describe the calculations in the PivotTable report is changed to the custom name you entered.

Rearranging a PivotTable

You can add, remove, and rearrange fields to change the PivotTable's layout. Recall that the benefit of a PivotTable is that it summarizes large amounts of data into a readable format. After you create a PivotTable, you can view the same data in different ways. The PivotTable Field List enables you to change, or pivot, the view of the data in the PivotTable by dragging the field buttons to different areas in the layout section.

Refer back to Mary's PivotTable sketch in Figure 5-29. As illustrated in the sketch, the Condition field items should be positioned as column labels instead of row labels in the PivotTable. You'll move the Condition field now to produce the format Mary wants.

To move the Condition field:

1. In the layout section of the PivotTable Field List, locate the Condition field button in the Row Labels box.

2. Drag the **Condition** field button from the Row Labels box to the Column Labels box. The PivotTable is rearranged so that the Condition field is a column label instead of a row label. See Figure 5-37. Each time you make a change in the PivotTable Field List, the PivotTable layout is rearranged.

Figure 5-37 **PivotTable rearranged with Condition as a column label**

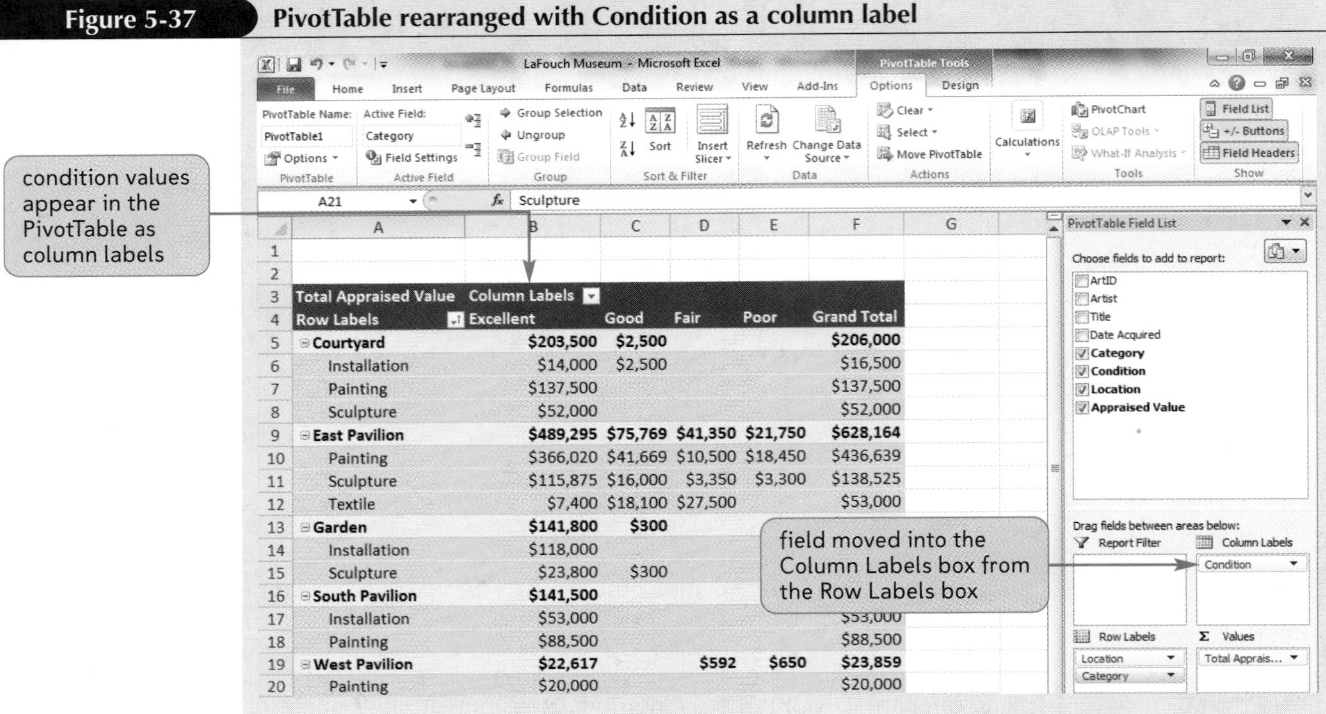

Changing the PivotTable Report Layout Options

The Compact report layout, shown in Figure 5-37, places all fields from the row area in a single column and indents the items from each field below the outer fields. This is the default layout for PivotTable reports. You can choose two other layouts. In the Outline report layout, each field in the row area takes a column in the PivotTable. By default, the outline form shows the subtotals for each group at the top of every group. The Tabular report layout displays one column for each field and leaves space for column headers. A total for each group appears at the bottom of each group. You can find these report layout options on the PivotTable Tools Design tab in the Layout group.

You will see how the PivotTable looks in these alternative layouts.

To display the PivotTable in Outline and Tabular layouts:

1. Click the **PivotTable Tools Design** tab on the Ribbon.
2. In the Layout group, click the **Report Layout** button, and then click **Show in Outline Form**. The PivotTable layout changes to the Outline report layout. See Figure 5-38.

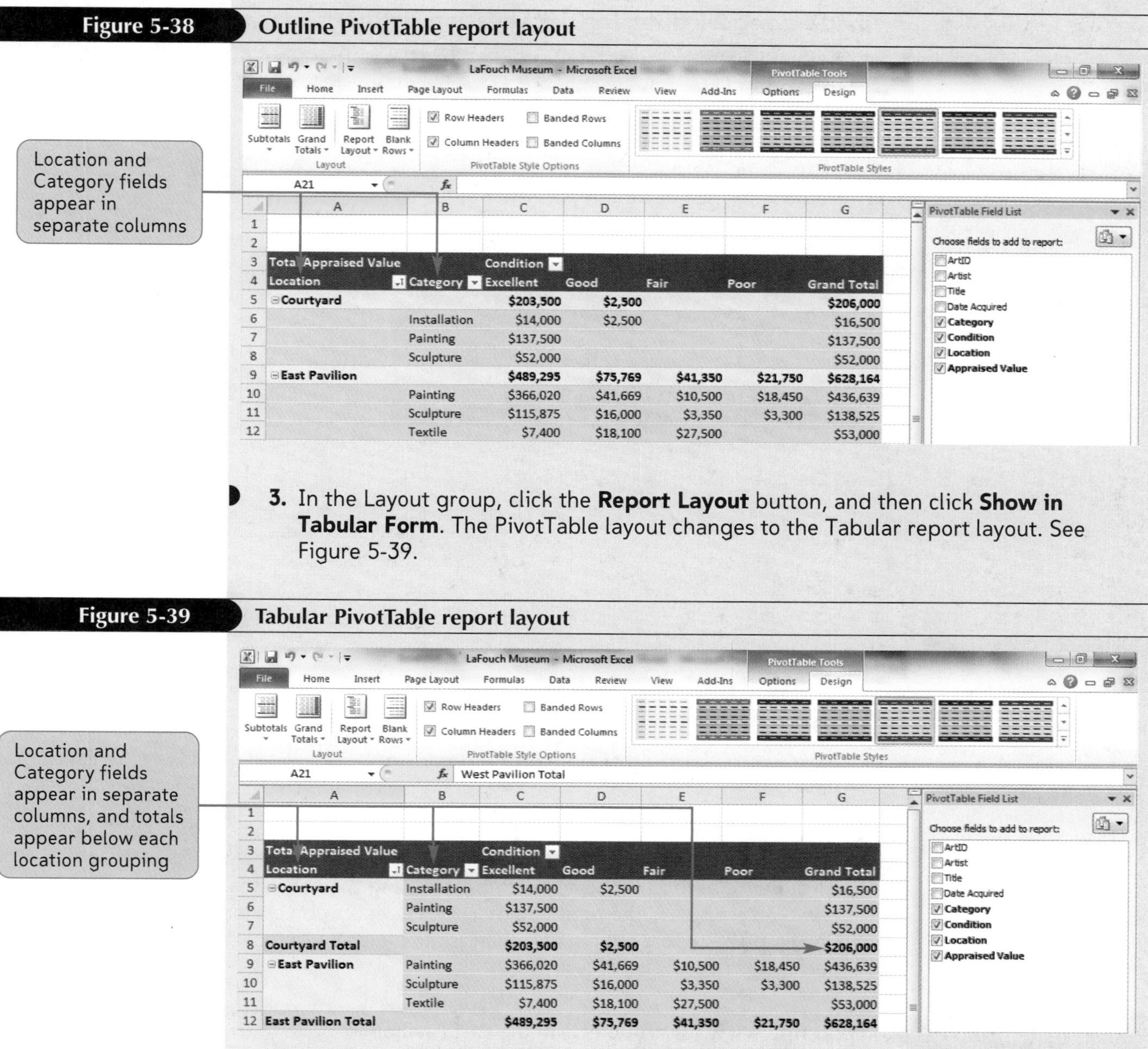

Figure 5-38 Outline PivotTable report layout

3. In the Layout group, click the **Report Layout** button, and then click **Show in Tabular Form**. The PivotTable layout changes to the Tabular report layout. See Figure 5-39.

Figure 5-39 Tabular PivotTable report layout

4. In the Layout group, click the **Report Layout** button, and then click **Show in Compact Form**. The PivotTable returns to the original layout, the Compact form.

Adding a Report Filter to a PivotTable

You can drag a field to the Report Filter area to create a filtered view of the PivotTable report. A report filter is used to filter the PivotTable to display summarized data for one or more field items or all field items in the Report Filter area. For example, creating a report filter for the Location field allows you to view or print the total appraised value for all locations or for specific locations such as the Courtyard.

You will add a report filter for the Location field to see if displaying the information in this way adds value to the report.

To add a report filter for the Location field:

1. In the PivotTable Field List, drag the **Location** button from the Row Labels box to the Report Filter box. The Report Filter field item shows "All" to indicate that the PivotTable report displays all the summarized data associated with the Location field. See Figure 5-40.

Figure 5-40 PivotTable with the Location report filter applied

PivotTable shows all the values in the Location field

	A	B	C	D	E	F
1	Location	(All)				
2						
3	Total Appraised Value	Column Labels				
4	Row Labels	Excellent	Good	Fair	Poor	Grand Total
5	Installation	$185,000	$2,500			$187,500
6	Painting	$612,020	$41,669	$10,500	$18,450	$682,639
7	Sculpture	$194,292	$16,300	$3,942	$3,950	$218,484
8	Textile	$7,400	$18,100	$27,500		$53,000
9	Grand Total	$998,712	$78,569	$41,942	$22,400	$1,141,623

PivotTable Field List
Choose fields to add to report:
ArtID
Artist
Title
Date Acquired
Category
Condition
Location
Appraised Value
Drag fields between areas below:
Report Filter: Location
Column Labels: Condition
Row Labels: Category
Values: Total Apprais...
Defer Layout Update
Update
Documentation | Appraised Value Summary | Art Collection

field moved into the Report Filter box

TIP

To filter more than one location at a time, click the Select Multiple Items check box in the AutoFilter menu to add a check mark next to each item, and then uncheck items you don't want to include.

Next, you'll change the summarized report to show only art objects in the East Pavilion.

2. Click the **report filter arrow** in cell B1. The AutoFilter menu opens, showing the field items displayed.
3. Click **East Pavilion** in the AutoFilter menu, and then click the **OK** button. The PivotTable displays the total appraised value of art objects located only in the East Pavilion. The report filter arrow changes to an icon to indicate the PivotTable is currently filtered. See Figure 5-41.

Figure 5-41 Report filter view for art objects in the East Pavilion

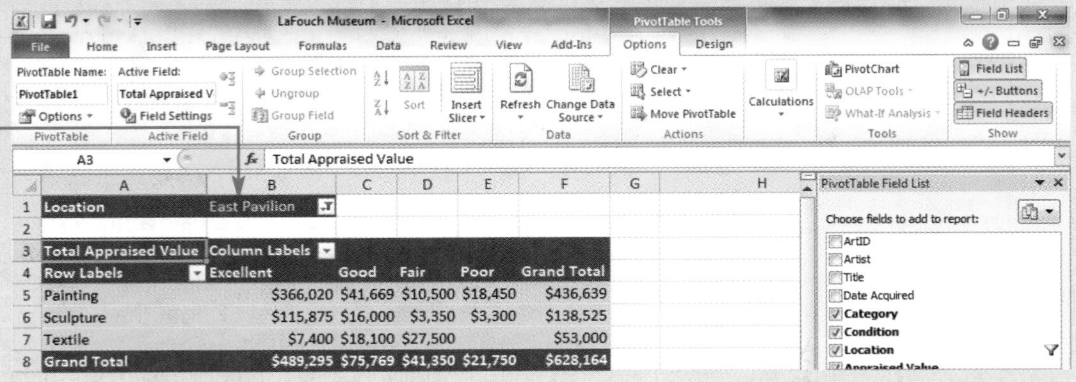

filtered PivotTable shows the appraised values of art objects located in the East Pavilion

4. In the PivotTable Field List, drag the **Location** button from the Report Filter box to the top of the Row Labels box. The Location field is positioned above the Category field, and the PivotTable returns to its previous layout.

   Trouble? If the PivotTable report is arranged differently, the Location field is not the top field in the Row Labels box. Drag the Location button in the Row Labels box above the Category button.

Filtering PivotTable Fields

Filtering a field lets you focus on a subset of items in that field. You can filter field items in the PivotTable by clicking the field arrow button in the PivotTable that represents the data you want to hide, and then uncheck the check box for each item you want to hide. To show hidden items, you click the field arrow button and check the check box for the item you want to show.

Mary wants to focus her analysis on art objects in excellent, good, and fair condition. She asks you to remove art objects in poor condition from the PivotTable. You will hide the art objects in poor condition from the PivotTable report.

To filter the Condition field items from the PivotTable:

1. In the PivotTable, click the **Column Labels filter arrow**. The AutoFilter menu displays the list of items in the Condition field.
2. Click the **Poor** check box to remove the check mark. The Select All check box is deselected as well.
3. Click the **OK** button. The Poor column is removed from the PivotTable. The PivotTable includes only art objects in excellent, good, and fair condition. See Figure 5-42. You can show the hidden objects by clicking the Column Labels arrow and checking the Poor check box.

Figure 5-42 PivotTable report filtered by condition

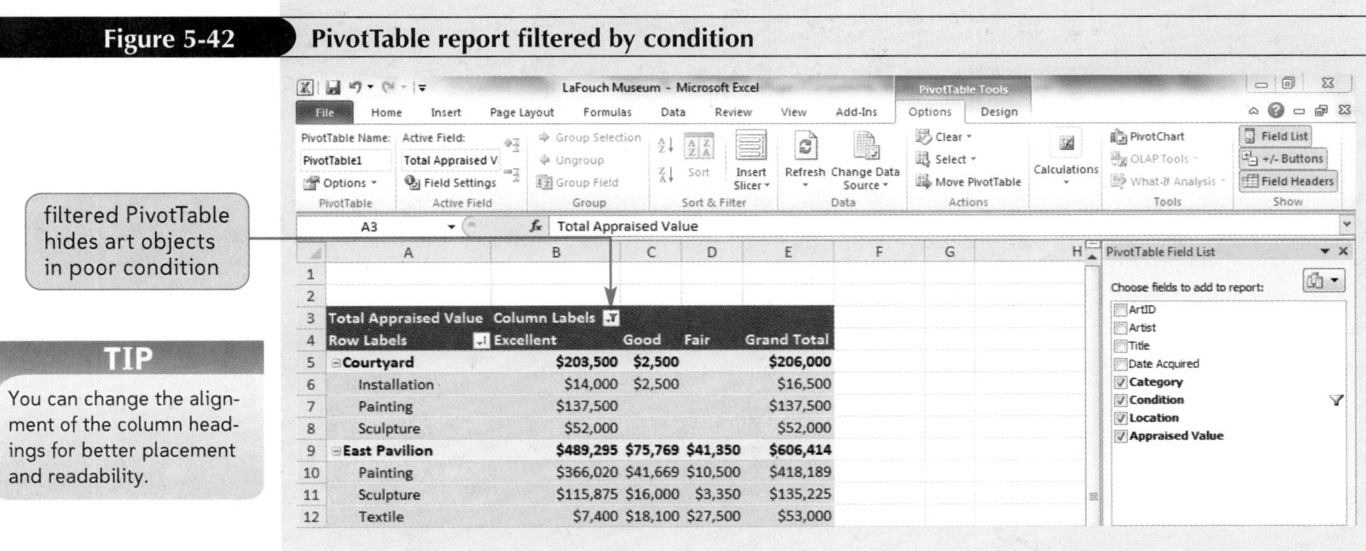

TIP

You can change the alignment of the column headings for better placement and readability.

Collapsing and Expanding Items

You can expand and collapse items in the row labels of the PivotTable to view fields at different levels of detail. The Expand and Collapse buttons identify where more details exist. The Expand button [+] indicates you can show more details for that item, and the Collapse button [–] indicates you can hide details for that item. The lowest level of the hierarchy does not have Expand and Collapse buttons because there is no data to expand or collapse. These buttons are helpful when you have complex PivotTables where you want to switch quickly between a detailed view and an overview.

Mary wants to see the total appraised value for each location without the Category items in the PivotTable. You will collapse the level of detail so that only the Location items are showing. Currently, all items are expanded.

To collapse the Courtyard items in the PivotTable:

1. Point to the **Collapse** button [–] next to Courtyard until the pointer changes to ↖.
2. Click the **Collapse** button [–] next to Courtyard. The detail items below Courtyard are hidden, and the Collapse button changes to an Expand button.
3. Click the **Collapse** button [–] next to East Pavilion, Garden, South Pavilion, and West Pavilion. The details for these four locations are hidden, and only the Location items are displayed. The PivotTable provides a higher level summary without displaying the Category details. See Figure 5-43.

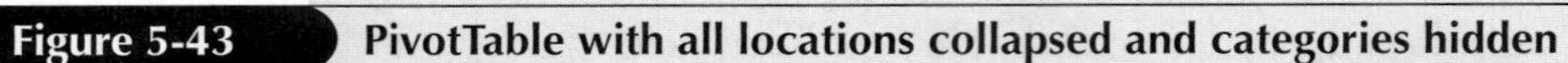

Figure 5-43 PivotTable with all locations collapsed and categories hidden

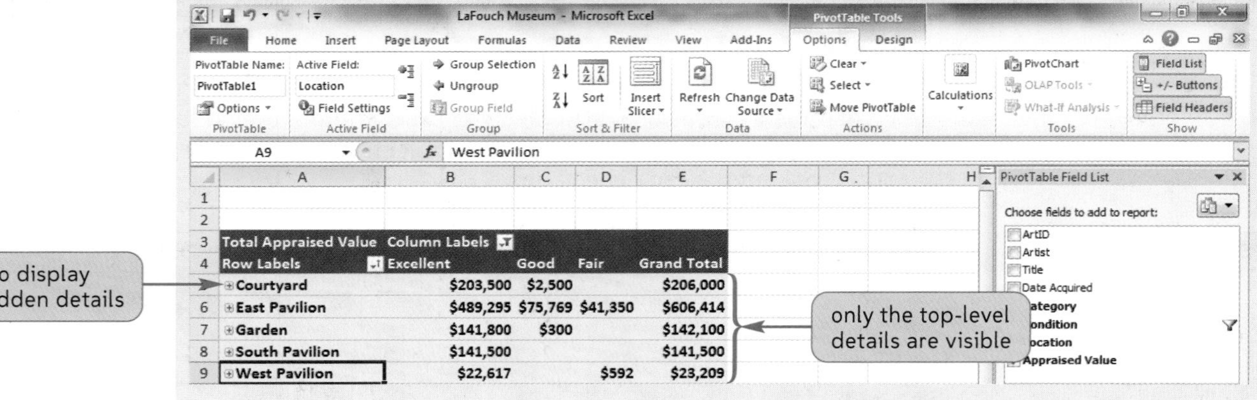

You can collapse or expand all level of detail in a PivotTable at one time. You'll do this to return to the original level of detail.

To expand all items in the PivotTable:

1. Click the **PivotTable Tools Options** tab on the Ribbon.
2. In the Active Field group, click the **Expand Entire Field** button. The detail items for all levels reappear. The lowest level of the hierarchy does not have Expand and Collapse buttons.

Sorting PivotTable Fields

You can sort a PivotTable field either by its own items—for example, alphabetizing fields such as Location and Category—or by the values in the body of the PivotTable. To sort a PivotTable field, you can use any of the Sort buttons on the Options tab to sort the information in a PivotTable report. These options are similar to the sort options you used earlier in the tutorial.

The PivotTable might be more informative if the appraised values in each location were sorted in descending order. You will sort the PivotTable so that the location with the highest total appraised value is displayed first.

To sort the PivotTable:

1. Click cell **E5**, which contains the Grand Total for Courtyard. This is the field total you want to sort.
2. In the Sort & Filter group on the PivotTable Tools Options tab, click the **Sort Largest to Smallest** button. The Location field is sorted based on the total appraised value for each location. For example, the East Pavilion location appears first in the PivotTable because it has the highest total appraised value, $606,414. The Courtyard location appears next because it has the second highest total appraised value, $206,000, and so on. See Figure 5-44.

Figure 5-44 PivotTable results sorted by location

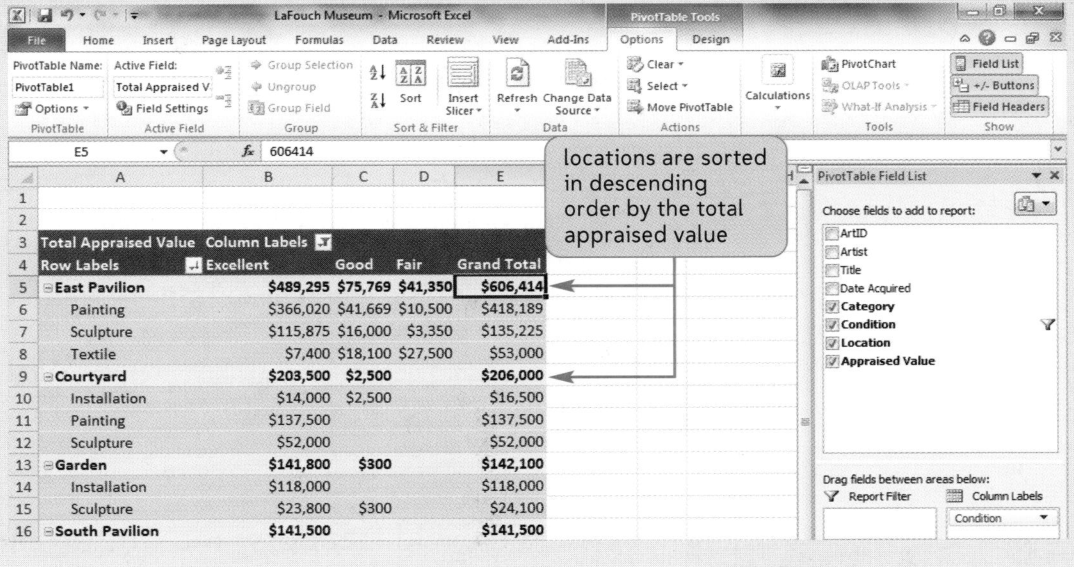

Adding a Second Values Field to a PivotTable

You can expand a PivotTable to create a more informative table by adding fields to the Values layout area. For example, Mary believes that a more accurate presentation of the art objects would include the number of objects corresponding to the total value in each cell of the PivotTable. Adding the Title field to the Values box would count the number of art objects in each location-category-condition combination (because the title is a non-numeric field). You will add the Title field to the PivotTable.

To add the Title field to the Values box:

1. In the PivotTable Field List, drag **Title** from the field area to immediately below the Total Appraised Value button in the Values box. The PivotTable displays the number of art objects as well as the total appraised value. The Values box in the layout area includes a second button, Count of Title, and fields from the Values box are added to the Column Labels box. See Figure 5-45.

Figure 5-45 Count of art objects added to the PivotTable

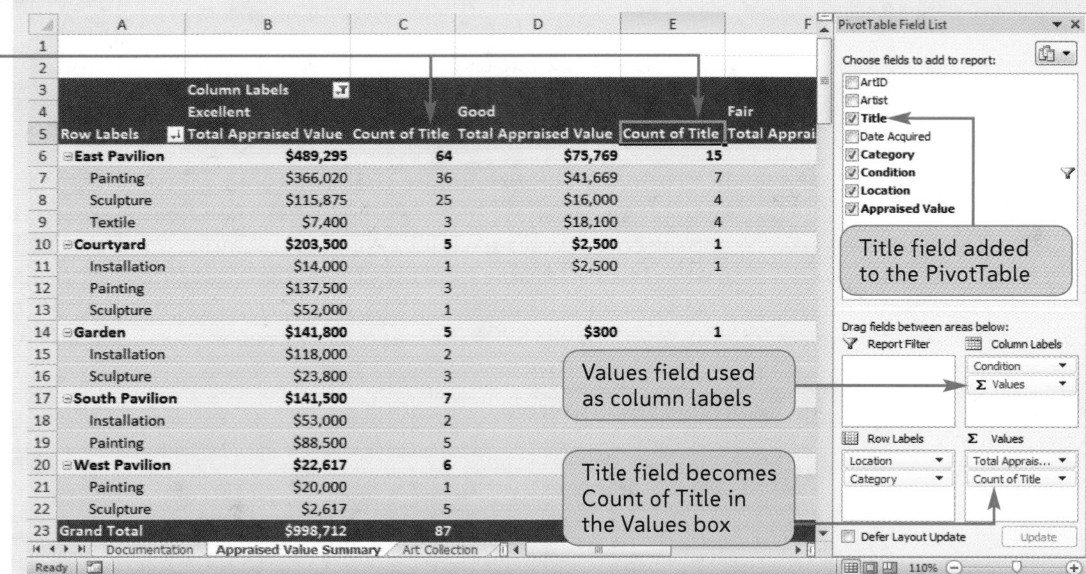

2. In the Show group on the PivotTable Tools Options tab, click the **Field List** button. The PivotTable Field List closes, so a section of the PivotTable is no longer hidden. More of the PivotTable is now visible.
3. In the PivotTable, click any of the **Count of Title** labels. You want to change the "Count of Title" label to "Count."
4. On the PivotTable Tools Options tab, click the **Active Field** box in the Active Field group, type **Count**, and then press the **Enter** key. The Count label replaces the Count of Title label.

Removing a Field, Field Headers, and Buttons from a PivotTable

The PivotTable report with the Count column looks cluttered and is difficult to read. You will remove the Title field from the PivotTable. Removing a field from the PivotTable has no effect on the underlying Excel table.

To remove the Title field from the PivotTable:

1. In the Show group on the PivotTable Tools Options tab, click the **Field List** button to display the PivotTable Field List.
2. In the PivotTable Field List, click the **Title** check box in the field area. The Count column is removed from the PivotTable, which returns to its previous layout. The Title field is still in the ArtObjects table.

The PivotTable is almost complete. Mary wants you to improve the appearance of the PivotTable by removing the field headers (Row Labels and Column Labels) and hiding the Expand/Collapse buttons.

To remove the field headers and hide the Expand/Collapse buttons:

1. In the Show group on the PivotTable Tools Options tab, click the **+/- Buttons** button. The Expand/Collapse buttons disappear from the PivotTable.
2. In the Show group, click the **Field Headers** button. The Column Labels and Row Labels headers are hidden. See Figure 5-46.

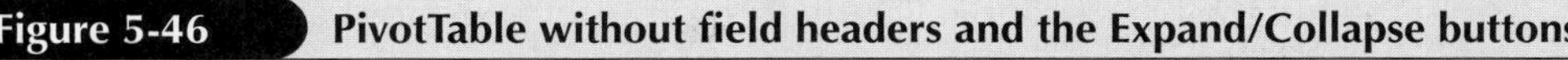

Figure 5-46 PivotTable without field headers and the Expand/Collapse buttons

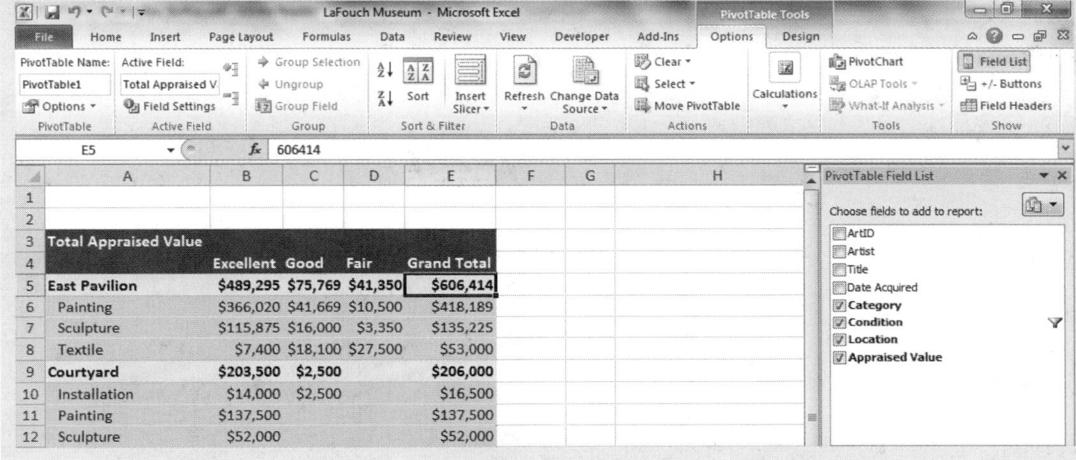

Using a Slicer to Filter a PivotTable

Although you can filter a PivotTable using the report filter arrow, column label arrows, and row label arrows, a slicer provides a quicker and easier way to filter a PivotTable or PivotChart. You can create a slicer for any field in a range or an Excel table. Every slicer consists of an object that contains a button for each unique value in that field. You can format the slicer and its buttons, changing its style, height, and width. You also can create more than one slicer at a time. For example, you can have a slicer for Category that has a button for each unique category value and a second slicer for Condition. This allows you to filter a PivotTable report so that it displays the results for all paintings in Excellent or Good condition by clicking the corresponding slicer buttons.

You will add a Location slicer to the current PivotTable so that Mary can have more flexibility in making changes to the PivotTable.

To add the Location slicer to the PivotTable:

1. Set the width of column F to **8**.
2. In the Sort & Filter group on the PivotTable Tools Options tab, click the **Insert Slicer** button. The Insert Slicers dialog box opens, displaying a list of available PivotTable fields. You can select any or all of the fields.

3. Click the **Location** check box to insert a check mark, and then click the **OK** button. The Location slicer control appears on the worksheet.
4. Drag the **Location slicer control** to the right of the PivotTable, placing its upper-left corner in cell G3.
5. If necessary, click the **Location** slicer to select the slicer object. The Slicer Tools Options tab appears on the Ribbon.
6. In the Size group on the Slicer Tools Options tab, change the height to **1.9"** and change the width to **1.3"**. The slicer object is resized, eliminating the extra space below the buttons and to the right of the labels.
7. In the Slicer Styles group, click the **More** button, and then click **Slicer Style Dark 3**. The slicer colors now match the PivotTable. See Figure 5-47.

Figure 5-47 Location slicer control

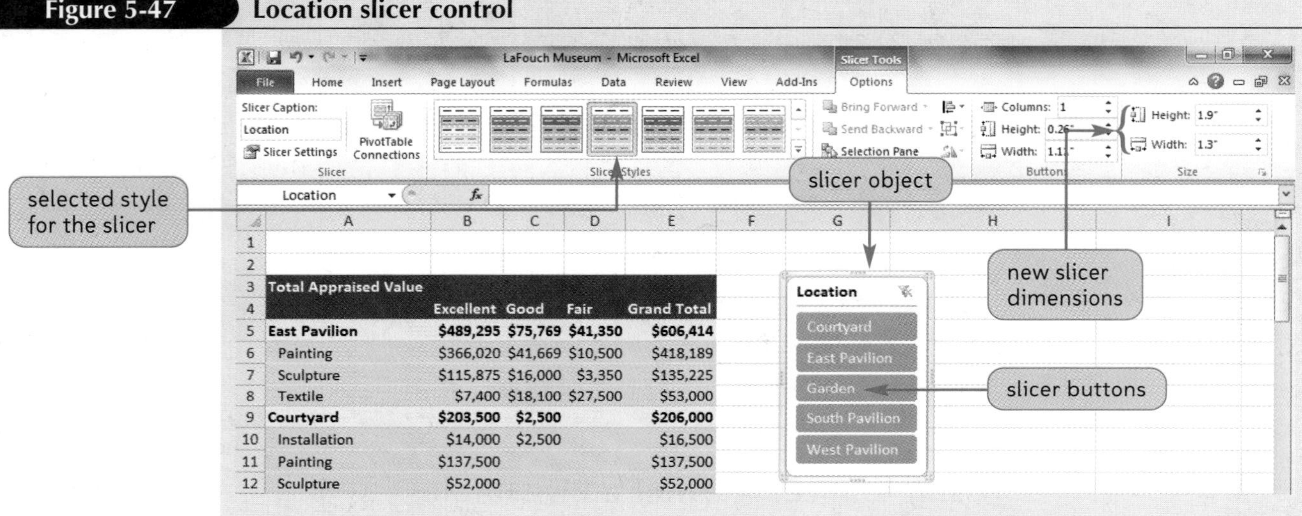

Mary wants you to display the results of the PivotTable for all the pavilion rooms—East, South, and West. You can do this quickly using the Location slicer.

To filter the PivotTable using the Location slicer:

1. In the Location slicer control, click the **East Pavilion** button. The PivotTable is filtered to display only the results for the East Pavilion. The other slicer buttons are gray because those locations have been filtered and are not part of the report.
2. Press and hold the **Ctrl** key, click the **South Pavilion** button, and then release the Ctrl key. The South Pavilion data also appears in the PivotTable.
3. Press and hold the **Ctrl** key, click the **West Pavilion** button, and then release the Ctrl key. The West Pavilion data is added to the PivotTable. See Figure 5-48.

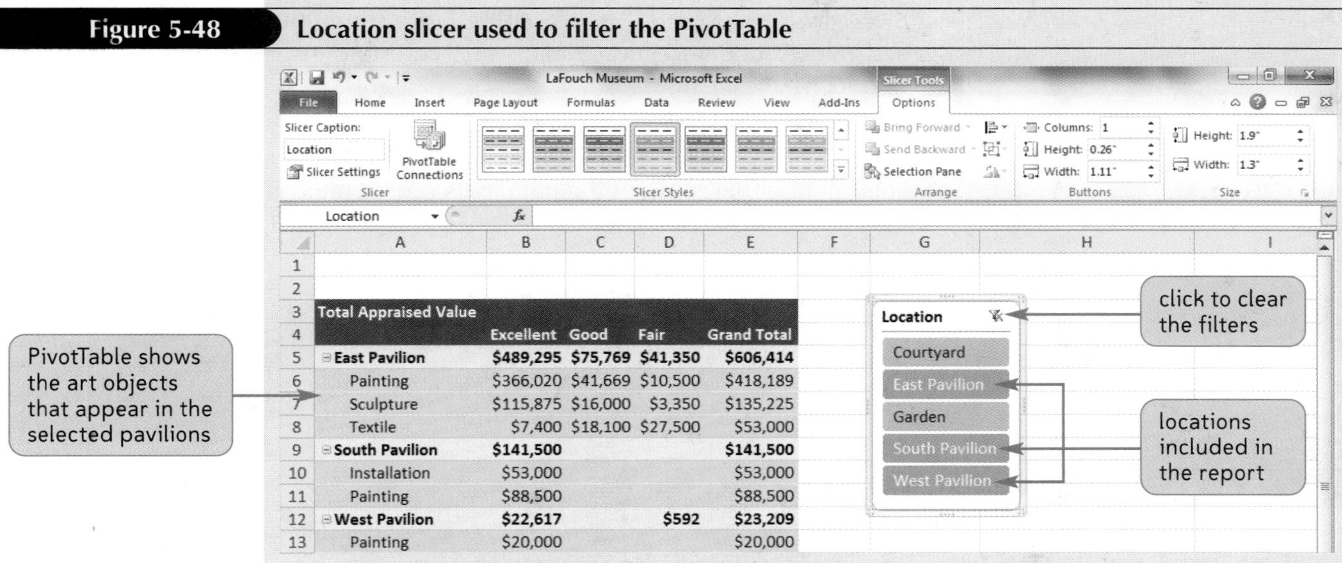

Figure 5-48 Location slicer used to filter the PivotTable

Next, you will remove all the filters so that Mary can view the PivotTable with all locations.

To remove the filters from the PivotTable:

1. In the Location slicer, click the **Clear Filter** button. The filters are removed and all locations appear in the PivotTable.
2. In the Location slicer, notice that all the buttons are deselected, indicating that no filters are being used.

Refreshing a PivotTable

The art object titled "Dancing in the Light" by Cridler has been reappraised and is now valued at $4,000 (not $1,000 as indicated in its current listing). You cannot change data directly in the PivotTable. Instead, you must edit the Excel table, and then **refresh**, or update, the PivotTable to reflect the updated data—in this case, the current state of the art objects list.

You'll edit the record for Dancing in the Light in the ArtObjects table. This sculpture is located in the East Pavilion and is in fair condition. This one change will affect the PivotTable in several locations. For example, currently the Total value of objects in the East Pavilion is $606,414; the sculptures in the East Pavilion are valued at $135,225; and sculptures in the East Pavilion in fair condition are valued at $3,350. After you update the appraised value of this art object in the Excel table, all these values in the PivotTable will increase by $3,000.

To update the ArtObjects table:

1. Switch to the **Art Collection** worksheet, and then find **Cridler, Dancing in the Light** (ArtID 73).

2. Click the record's Appraised Value cell, and then enter **4000**. The sculpture's appraised value is updated in the table. You'll return to the PivotTable report to see the effect of this change.
3. Switch to the **Appraised Value Summary** worksheet. The appraised value totals for the East Pavilion are still $606,414, $135,225, and $3,350, respectively. The PivotTable is not updated when the data in its source table is updated, so you need to refresh the PivotTable manually.
4. Click any cell in the PivotTable.
5. Click the **PivotTable Tools Options** tab on the Ribbon, and then click the **Refresh** button in the Data group. The PivotTable report is updated. The appraised value totals are now $609,414, $138,225, and $6,350.
6. In the Show group, click the **Field List** button. See Figure 5-49.

Figure 5-49 Refreshed PivotTable

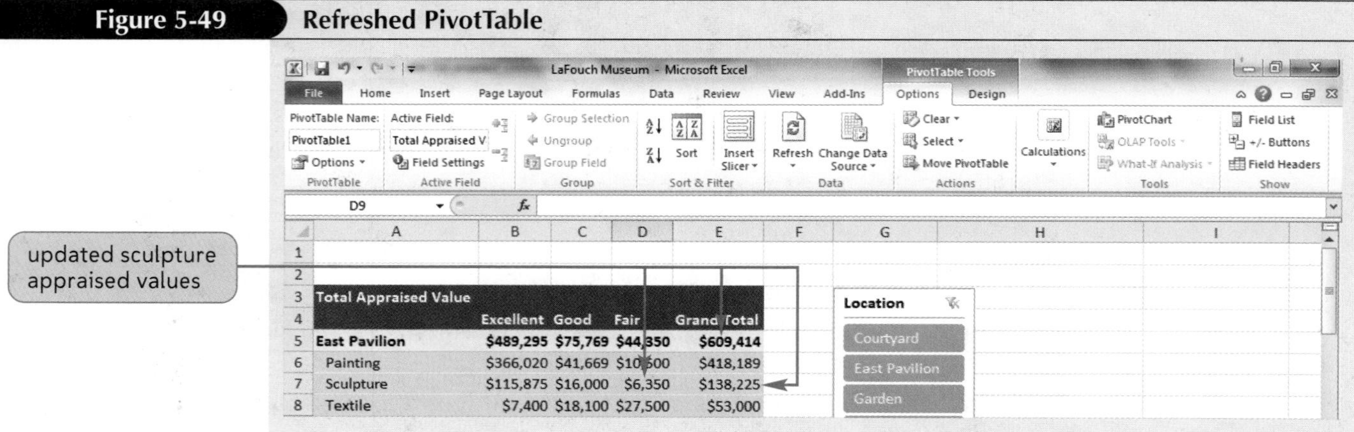

Grouping PivotTable Items

When a field contains numbers, dates, or times, you can combine items in the rows of a PivotTable and combine them into groups automatically. Mary thinks a PivotTable that displays the number of objects acquired each year would be of interest to the board of directors. This report involves using the Date Acquired field as a row label and ArtID as the values field, although you could use any field as the values field. When using a date field as a row label in a PivotTable, each date initially appears as a separate item.

Typically, you want to analyze date data by month, quarter, or year. To do that, you need to group the data in the Date Acquired field. Grouping items combines dates into larger groups such as months, quarters, or years so that the PivotTable can include the desired level of summarization. You can also group numeric items, typically into equal ranges. For example, you can calculate the number of art objects in appraised value groups based on increments of any amount you specify (for example, 1–25,000, 25,001–50,000, and so on).

You'll add a second PivotTable in a new worksheet.

To create a PivotTable based on the Date Acquired field:

1. Switch to the **Art Collection** worksheet, and then click any cell in the Excel table. The table is active.

2. Click the **Insert** tab on the Ribbon, and then click the **PivotTable** button in the Tables group. The Create PivotTable dialog box opens.
3. Verify that the Table/Range box shows **ArtObjects** and the **New Worksheet** option button is selected, and then click the **OK** button. The PivotTable report area and PivotTable Field List appear in a new worksheet.
4. In the PivotTable Field List, click the **Date Acquired** check box. The Date Acquired field appears in the Row Labels box. Each unique date appears in the PivotTable report area. Mary wants each year to appear as a row label. You will correct that shortly.
5. Click the **ArtID** check box in the PivotTable Field List. "Sum of ArtID" appears in the Values box in the layout area because the ArtID field contains numeric data. See Figure 5-50.

Figure 5-50 PivotTable with Sum of ArtID for each date

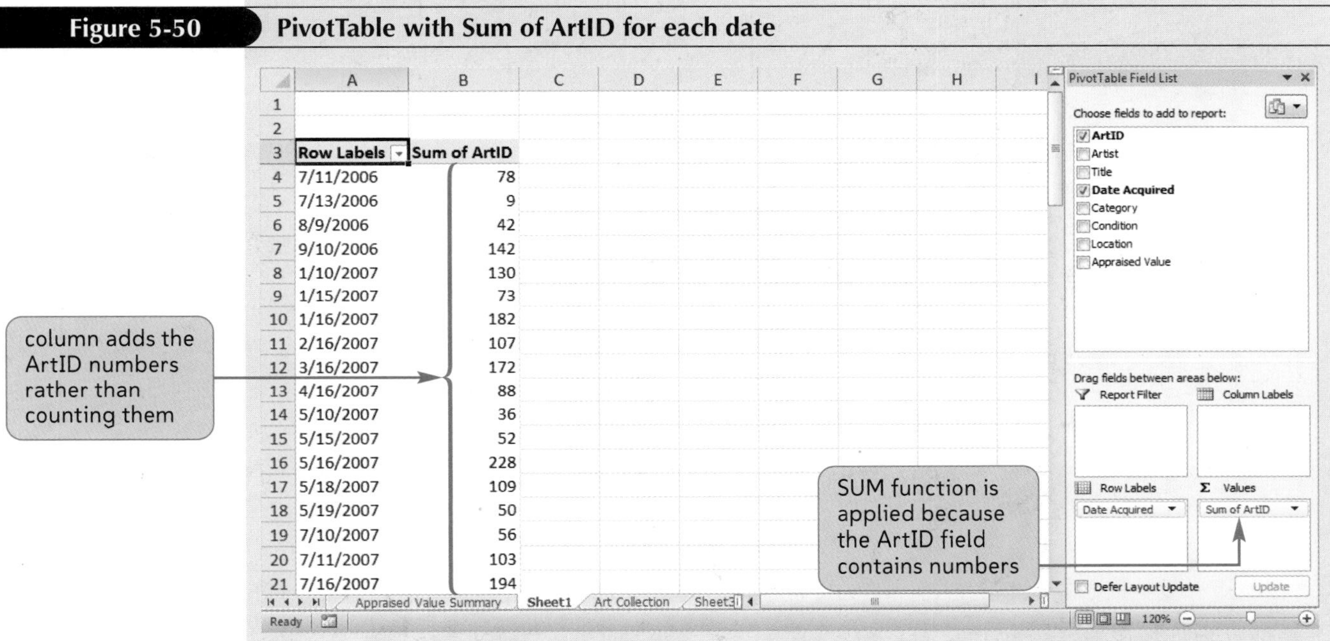

The PivotTable includes the sum of ArtIDs instead of a count of art objects, as Mary requested. This occurs because fields that contain numbers placed in the Values area are summed. Adding all the ArtIDs together to get a total is meaningless; you need to count the number of ArtIDs in each year. To do this, you need to change the SUM function to the COUNT function so Excel will *count* the number of objects in each group.

To count the number of objects in each group:

1. Click any value in the **Sum of ArtID** column, and then click the **PivotTable Tools Options** tab on the Ribbon.
2. Click the **Calculations button arrow**, click the **Summarize Values By** button, and then click **Count**. The label indicating the type of summary in the PivotTable changes to Count of ArtID, and the PivotTable report displays the number of art objects acquired by date. See Figure 5-51.

Figure 5-51 PivotTable report with count

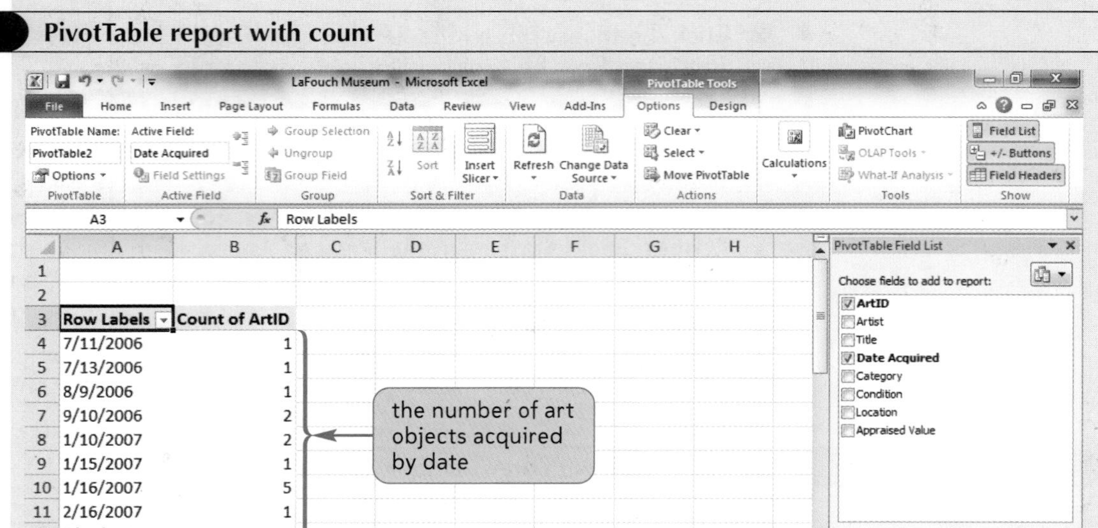

Grouping Date Fields

Mary wants the PivotTable layout to show a count of acquisitions by year, not by date. You can group a range of dates into periods such as months, quarters, or years using the Group Field command. You will group the Date Acquired dates by year.

To group acquisitions by year:

1. Click any date value in the Row Labels column of the PivotTable.
2. In the Group group on the PivotTable Tools Options tab, click the **Group Field** button. The Grouping dialog box opens.
3. Click **Months** to deselect it, and then click **Years** to select it.
4. Click the **OK** button. The PivotTable report is grouped by year, displaying the number of art acquisitions in each year. See Figure 5-52.

Figure 5-52 PivotTable report of annual acquisitions

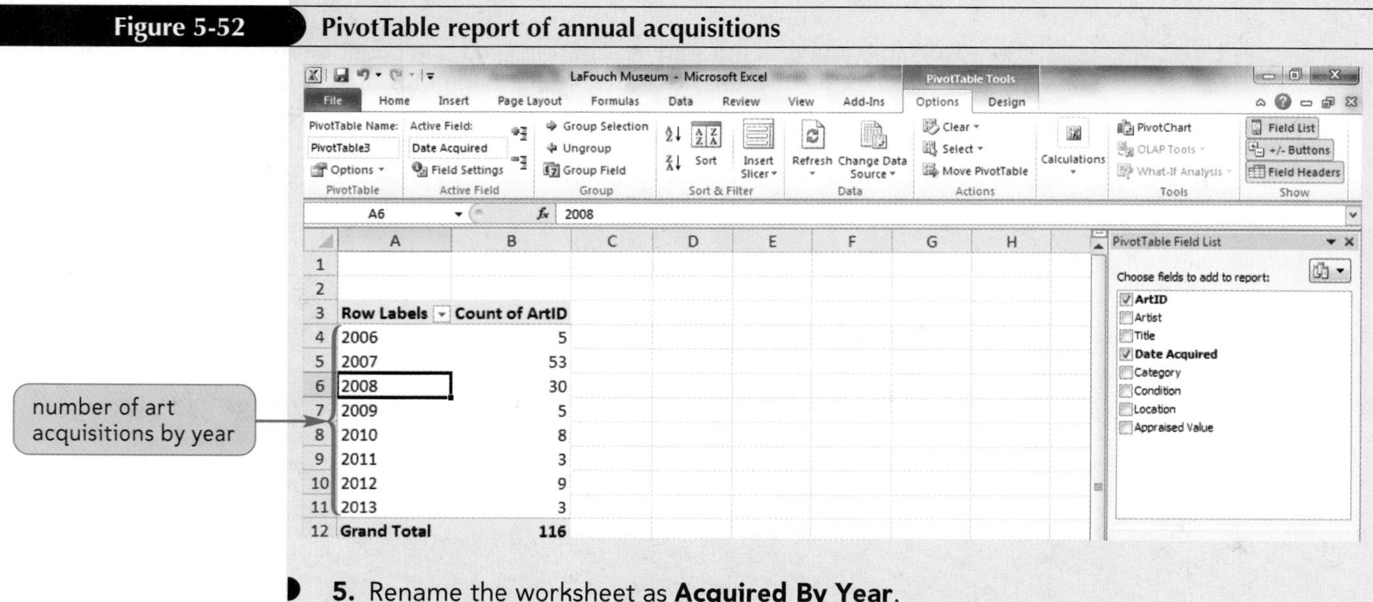

5. Rename the worksheet as **Acquired By Year**.

INSIGHT

Creating Different Types of PivotTable Reports

This tutorial only scratched the surface of the variety of PivotTable reports you can create. Here are a few more examples:

- Most PivotTable summaries are based on numeric data, but PivotTables can also contain only nonnumeric data. You cannot add nonnumeric data, so you must use the COUNT function to produce summaries. For example, you could count the number of art objects by Location and Category.
- You can use PivotTables to combine items into groups. Items that appear as row labels or column labels can be grouped. If items are numbers or dates, they can be grouped automatically using the Grouping dialog box, or they can be grouped manually using the Ctrl key to select items in a group and choosing Group from the shortcut menu. For example, you can manually combine the Courtyard and Garden locations into an Outdoor group, combine the three pavilion locations into an Indoor group, and then provide counts or total appraised values by these groups within the PivotTable. Being able to combine categories that aren't part of your original data using the grouping feature gives you flexibility to summarize your PivotTables in a way that meets your analysis requirements.
- You can develop PivotTables using the value filter, which allows you to filter one of your row or column fields in the PivotTable based on numbers that appear in the Values area of the PivotTable. For example, a PivotTable can show the total value of art objects for each artist and be filtered to display only artists whose total is greater than $25,000. Filtering provides you with a more precise way to view the PivotTable results by enabling you to include or remove data from the report.

Creating a PivotChart

Mary wants you to add a PivotChart next to the PivotTable. A PivotChart allows you to interactively add, remove, filter, and refresh data fields in the PivotChart similar to working with a PivotTable. PivotCharts can have all the same formatting as other charts, including layouts and styles. You can move and resize chart elements, or change formatting of individual data points.

You will prepare a clustered column chart next to the new PivotTable report. You can create a PivotChart from the PivotTable.

To create the PivotChart:

1. Click any cell in the PivotTable.
2. In the Tools group on the PivotTable Tools Options tab, click the **PivotChart** button. The Insert Chart dialog box opens.
3. Click the **Clustered Column** chart (the first chart in the first row of the Column section), if necessary, and then click the **OK** button. A PivotChart appears next to the PivotTable along with the PivotTable Field List.
4. Click the **PivotChart Tools Layout** tab, click the **Legend button arrow** in the Labels group, and then click **None**. The legend is removed from the PivotChart. You do not need a legend because the PivotChart has only one series.
5. In the PivotChart, right-click the **chart title**, and then click **Edit Text**. The insertion point appears in the title so you can edit it.
6. Select the title, type **Number Acquired By Year** as the new title, and then click the chart area to deselect the title.

TIP

You can also create a PivotChart based directly on an Excel table, in which case both a PivotTable and a PivotChart are created.

7. Drag the **PivotChart** so its upper-left corner is in cell C3. The PivotChart is aligned with the PivotTable. See Figure 5-53.

Figure 5-53 **PivotChart added to the PivotTable report**

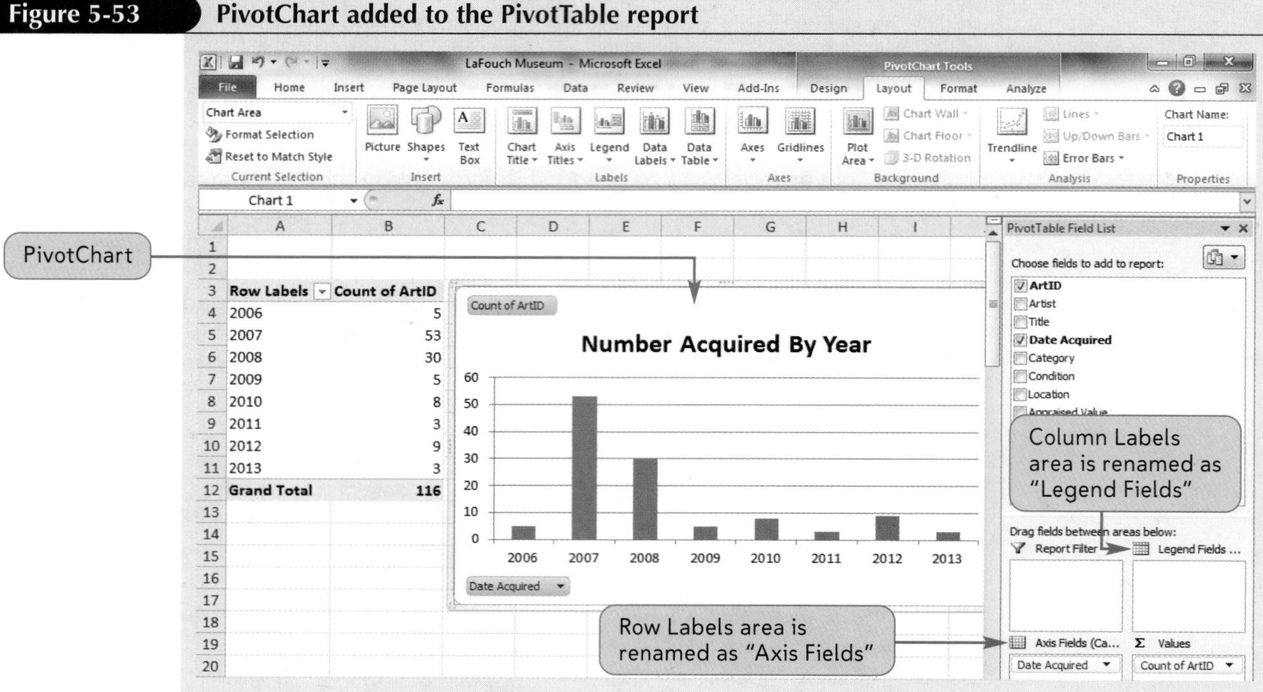

The PivotChart Tools contextual tabs enable you to manipulate and format the selected PivotChart the same way as an ordinary chart. A PivotChart and its associated PivotTable are linked. When you modify one, the other also changes.

You can quickly display different chart views of the PivotChart using the chart filter button on the PivotChart to filter the data. Mary wants you to display only art acquisitions after 2009.

To filter items in the PivotChart:

1. Make sure the PivotChart is selected, and then click the **Date Acquired** axis field button in the PivotChart. The AutoFilter menu opens.
2. Click the **Select All** check box. All the check boxes are deselected.
3. Click the **2010**, **2011**, **2012**, and **2013** check boxes. The years after 2009 are selected.
4. Click the **OK** button. The PivotChart displays only art objects acquired after 2009. The PivotTable is also filtered to display the same results.
5. Click cell **A1**. See Figure 5-54.

Figure 5-54 **Filtered PivotChart**

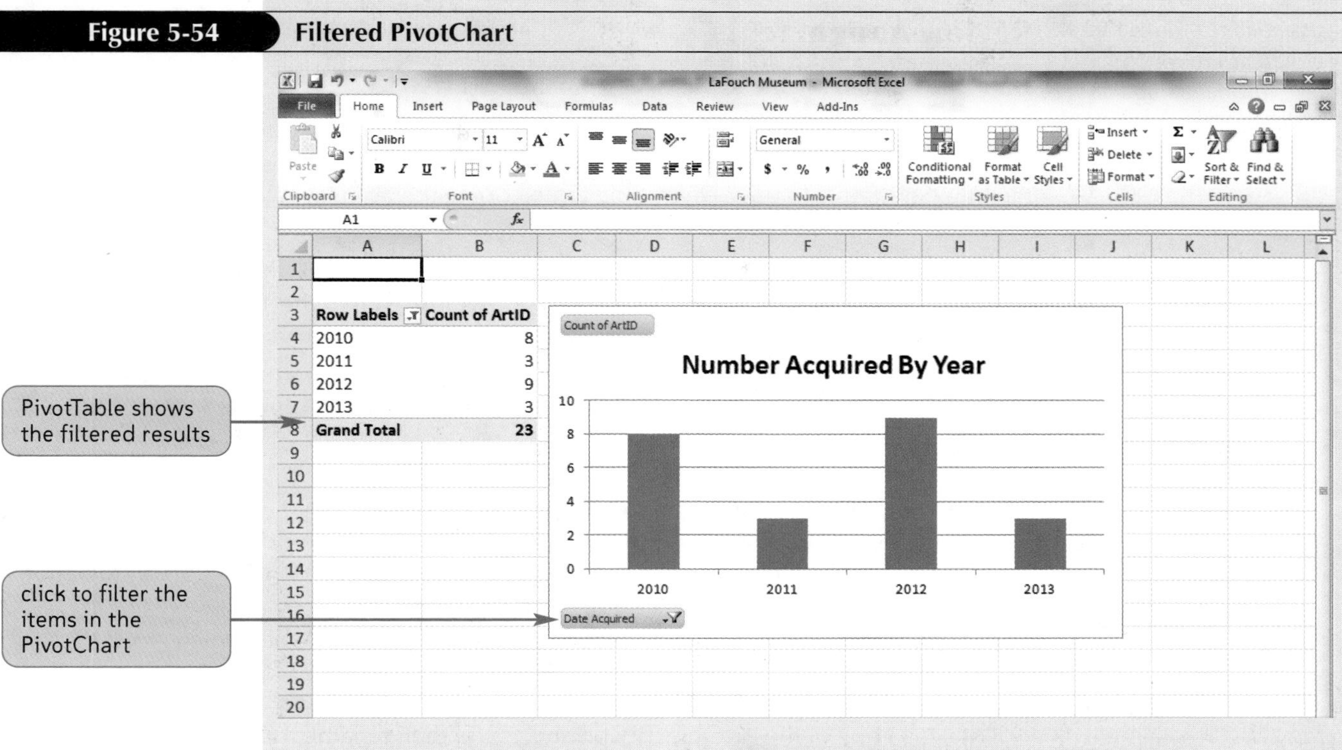

6. Save the LaFouch Museum workbook, and then close it.

Mary is pleased with the PivotTable and PivotChart. Both show the number of art objects acquired by year, which will be important information for her upcoming board meeting.

REVIEW

Session 5.3 Quick Check

1. What is the default summary function for numeric data in a PivotTable?
2. When creating a PivotTable, what do you use to lay out the fields in the PivotTable report?
3. After you update data in an Excel table, what must you do to a PivotTable based on that Excel table?
4. How are fields such as region, state, and country most likely to appear in a PivotTable?
5. How are fields such as revenue, costs, and profits most likely to appear in a PivotTable?
6. A list of college students includes a code to indicate the student's gender (male or female) and a field to identify the student's major. Which tool—Filter or PivotTable—would you use to (a) create a list of all females majoring in history, and (b) count the number of males and females in each major?
7. When the Date Acquired field is displayed in a row of a PivotTable by month or year, you have ____________ the Date Acquired field.
8. A PivotChart displays the number of art objects in each Location. How would you exclude the art objects in the Courtyard from the PivotTable?

Practice the skills you learned in the tutorial using the same case scenario.

PRACTICE

Review Assignments

Data File needed for the Review Assignments: Art.xlsx

Mary has another art object to enter in the art objects list. She wants to sort the data by the date acquired. She wants to filter data to retrieve all art with the word "cowboy" in the title. She wants to use a PivotTable to determine the average value of the artwork for each artist. Complete the following:

1. Open the **Art** workbook located in the Excel5\Review folder included with your Data Files, and then save the workbook as **Art Museum** in the same folder.
2. In the Documentation sheet, enter your name and the date.
3. Switch to the ArtObjects worksheet. Create an Excel table for the art objects data, and then change the table style to Medium 25. Format the Appraised Value field using the Accounting number format with no decimal places.
4. Rename the Excel table as **Collection**.
5. Make a copy of the ArtObjects worksheet, and then rename the copied worksheet as **Q5** (for "Question 5"). (*Hint*: To make a copy of the worksheet, press and hold the Ctrl key and drag the sheet tab to the right of the ArtObjects sheet tab.) Sort the art objects by date acquired to display the newest objects first.
6. Make a copy of the ArtObjects worksheet, and then rename the copied worksheet as **Q6**. Sort art objects by category (Z to A), location (A to Z), artist (A to Z), and date acquired (showing the oldest first).
7. Make a copy of the ArtObjects worksheet, and then rename the copied worksheet as **Q7**. Filter the Collection table to produce a list of art objects with the word "cowboy" in the title.
8. Make a copy of the ArtObjects worksheet, and then rename the copied worksheet as **Q8**. Use the Total row to calculate the average value of objects acquired between 2009 and 2013. Change the label in the Total row from Total to **Average**. Sort the filtered data by date acquired (newest first).
9. Make a copy of the ArtObjects worksheet, and then rename the copied worksheet as **Q9**. Use the Subtotal command to count how many art objects there are in each location, displaying the count in the ArtID column.
10. Create a PivotTable to show the average value of art objects by artist. Format the Value column appropriately. Rename the worksheet with the PivotTable as **Q10-11**.
11. Sort the PivotTable showing the artist with the highest average value first.
12. Create a PivotTable to show the number of art objects and the total value by category. Include location as a Report Filter field, and then filter the report so the number and total value by category is based on the Courtyard location. Rename the worksheet with the PivotTable as **Q12**.
13. Save and close the workbook. Submit the finished workbook to your instructor, either in printed or electronic form, as requested.

Use the skills you learned to analyze and summarize donation data.

APPLY

Case Problem 1

Data File needed for this Case Problem: Pledges.xlsx

Hewart Zoo Marvis Chennard is the director of fund-raising for the Hewart Zoo. The zoo relies on donations to fund operations, temporary exhibits, and special programs. Marvis created an Excel table to track information about donors and their pledges. You will analyze the data in the list. Complete the following:

1. Open the **Pledges** workbook located in the Excel5\Case1 folder included with your Data Files, and then save the workbook as **Zoo Pledges** in the same folder.

2. In the Documentation worksheet, enter your name and the date, and then switch to the Pledges worksheet.
3. Create an Excel table, apply the Medium 7 table style, and then rename the table as **PledgeData**.
4. Make a copy of the Pledges worksheet, and then rename the copied worksheet as **Q4-6** (for "Question 4-6"). (*Hint*: Press the Ctrl key and drag the sheet tab to the right of the Pledges sheet tab to make a copy of the worksheet.) Sort the data in ascending order by donor type and fund name, and in descending order by amt pledged (largest first).
5. In the Q4-6 worksheet, insert a Total row. Display the number of pledges in the Donor Name column, the average pledge in the Amt Pledged column, the total received in the Amt Received column, and the total owed in the Amt Owed column.
6. In the Q4-6 worksheet, split the worksheet into two horizontal panes at row 23. In the top pane, display the pledge transactions. In the bottom pane, display the Total row.
7. Make a copy of the Pledges worksheet, and then rename the copied worksheet as **Q7**. Filter the data to display individual donors whose amt owed is greater than zero. Sort the filtered data by pledge date, with the oldest date displayed first.
8. Make a copy of the Pledges worksheet, and then rename the copied worksheet as **Q8**. Filter the data to display records that have a pledge date in October through December. Sort the filtered data by amt pledged (largest first).
9. Make a copy of the Pledges worksheet, and then rename the copied worksheet as **Q9**. Filter the data to display only records with an amt received greater than zero. Then use the Subtotal command (SUM) to display the total amt received by fund name.
10. Create a PivotTable that displays the total and average amt owed by each donor type and fund name. Place the PivotTable in a new worksheet, and then rename the worksheet as **Q10**. Select an appropriate report layout and format. Insert a Donor Type slicer and filter using the Organization donor type.
11. Using Figure 5-55 as a guide, create a PivotTable in a new worksheet that shows the amt pledged by month and fund name. Format the PivotTable appropriately, and then rename the worksheet as **Q11**.

Figure 5-55 **PivotTable for the amount pledged**

	A	B	C	D	E	F
1						
2						
3	Total Pledged					
4		Bird Sanctuary	Children's Zoo	General Support	ZooMobile	Grand Total
5	Jan		$ 100.00	$ 1,000.00		$ 1,100.00
6	Feb		$ 1,100.00		$ 150.00	$ 1,250.00
7	Mar		$ 100.00		$ 1,000.00	$ 1,100.00
8	Apr	$ 75.00	$ 425.00	$ 500.00		$ 1,000.00
9	Jun		$ 1,000.00		$ 50.00	$ 1,050.00
10	Jul	$ 1,000.00		$ 1,000.00		$ 2,000.00
11	Sep	$ 100.00	$ 250.00	$ 25.00	$ 150.00	$ 525.00
12	Oct	$ 200.00		$ 200.00		$ 400.00
13	Nov			$ 250.00		$ 250.00
14	Dec		$ 150.00		$ 750.00	$ 900.00
15	**Grand Total**	**$ 1,375.00**	**$ 3,125.00**	**$ 2,975.00**	**$ 2,100.00**	**$ 9,575.00**

12. Save and close the workbook. Submit the finished workbook to your instructor, either in printed or electronic form, as requested.

Use the skills you learned to analyze and summarize expenditure data.

APPLY

Case Problem 2

Data File needed for this Case Problem: Ring.xlsx

Ring Family Farm Fred and Alesia Ring own a small family farm outside Abita Springs, Louisiana. The couple wants to better organize their financial records. They created an Excel workbook to record their expenses. Typical expenses include those associated with hay production (seed, fertilizer, and irrigation), animal husbandry, fence maintenance, veterinary services, vehicles and maintenance, and so forth. The workbook includes categories associated with these expenses as well as an area to record how much is spent, the purpose of the expenditure, the check number, and the date paid. Complete the following:

1. Open the **Ring** workbook located in the Excel5\Case2 folder included with your Data Files, and then save the workbook as **Ring Farm** in the same folder.
2. Insert a new worksheet. Enter the company name, your name, the date, and a purpose statement, and then rename the worksheet as **Documentation**.
3. Create an Excel table in the Expenditures worksheet. Rename the table as **Checkbook**.
4. Replace the category code "Farm" in each record with **Payroll**.
5. Make a copy of the Expenditures worksheet, and then rename the copied worksheet as **Q5**. (*Hint*: Press the Ctrl key and drag the Expenditures sheet tab to the right of the Expenditures sheet tab to make a copy of the worksheet.) Sort the Checkbook table in ascending order by category, then by payee, and then by date paid (newest first).
6. Make a copy of the Expenditures worksheet, and then rename the copied worksheet as **Q6**. Filter the Checkbook table to display all expenditures for equipment and repairs in December, and then sort by amount (smallest first).
7. Make a copy of the Expenditures worksheet, and then rename the copied worksheet as **Q7**. Filter the Checkbook table to display all checks that include the word "vet" in the payee's name. Include the total amount at the bottom of the table.
8. Make a copy of the Expenditures worksheet, and then rename the copied worksheet as **Q8**. Use conditional formatting to apply a yellow fill with dark yellow text to all outstanding checks. (*Hint*: "Yes" appears in the Outstanding column.)
9. Make a copy of the Expenditures worksheet, and then rename the copied worksheet as **Q9**. Use the Subtotal command to display the total amount for each category, displaying the subtotal in the Amount column.
10. Create a PivotTable that summarizes expenditures by category and month. Place the PivotTable in a new worksheet, and then rename the worksheet as **Q10-11**. Format the PivotTable appropriately and choose a layout.
11. Insert a PivotChart with the Clustered Column chart type on the Q10-11 worksheet.
12. Create the PivotTable shown in Figure 5-56 in a new worksheet, rename the worksheet as **Q12**, and then sort the Total Amount column in descending order. (*Hint*: Click the Show Values As button in the Calculations group on the PivotTable Tools Options tab on the Ribbon to calculate the Pct Of Total column.)

Figure 5-56 PivotTable for the amount by category

	A	B	C
1	**Category**	**Total Amount**	**Pct Of Total**
2	Equipment	$6,575.00	37.05%
3	Payroll	$2,638.27	14.87%
4	Vet	$2,320.57	13.08%
5	Repairs	$2,003.44	11.29%
6	Feed	$2,002.24	11.28%
7	Medicine	$1,249.32	7.04%
8	Administration	$958.09	5.40%
9	**Grand Total**	**$17,746.93**	**100.00%**

13. Save and close the workbook. Submit the finished workbook to your instructor, either in printed or electronic form, as requested.

Use the skills you learned to analyze and summarize loan data for a bank.

APPLY

Case Problem 3

Data File needed for this Case Problem: CustLoans.xlsx

High Desert Bank Eleanor Chimayo, loan manager for High Desert Bank, is getting ready for the bank's quarterly meeting. Eleanor is expected to present data on the status of different types of loans within three New Mexican cities. Eleanor asks you to summarize and analyze the data for her presentation. Complete the following:

1. Open the **CustLoans** workbook located in the Excel5\Case3 folder included with your Data Files, and then save the workbook as **High Desert Bank** in the same folder.
2. In the Documentation sheet, enter your name and the date.
3. In the Loans worksheet, create an Excel table, and then rename the table as **LoanData**.
4. Format the Amount and Interest Rate fields so that it is clear that these fields contain dollars and percentages, respectively.
5. Format the table using the table style of your choice.
6. To the right of the Type column, insert a new column named **Monthly Payment**. Use the PMT function to calculate the monthly payment for each loan. Adjust the formula so that each loan is displayed as a positive amount, and then improve the formatting.
7. Make a copy of the Loans worksheet, and then rename the copied worksheet as **Q7-8**. (*Hint*: Press the Ctrl key and drag the sheet tab to the right of the current sheet tab to make a copy of the worksheet.) Sort the loan data in ascending order by type, within type by city, and within city by last name.
8. Use conditional formatting to display all loans in Taos using a format of your choice to highlight these loans.
9. Make a copy of the Loans worksheet, and then rename the copied worksheet as **Q9-10**. Filter the LoanData table to display loans made during April and May of 2013.
10. Insert a Total row in the Q9-10 worksheet. Display the average amount of loans and the total monthly payment for the filtered data in Question 9.
11. Make a copy of the Loans worksheet, and then rename the copied worksheet as **Q11**. Sort the loans in ascending order by city, then by type of loan, and then by amount of loan (largest loan first). Insert subtotals (Average) for the loan amount and monthly payment by city and type of loan. Prepare the worksheet for printing. Include the worksheet name in the center of the custom header. Include your name in the left section of the custom footer and page numbers in the right section of the custom footer. Fit all columns on one page.
12. Create a PivotTable that displays the number (Count) and average loan by type and city. Place the PivotTable in a new worksheet, and then rename the PivotTable worksheet as **Q12 Loans-Type And City**. Remove the Other loan type from the PivotTable. Format the PivotTable appropriately.
13. Create a second PivotTable, as shown in Figure 5-57, in a new worksheet, and then rename the PivotTable worksheet as **Q13 Loans-Type and Date**. The PivotTable shows three calculations: number of loans, total loan amount, and average monthly payment categorized by type of loan. Insert a report filter based on the loan date, grouped so you can filter by month. Insert a Loan Date slicer and filter the PivotTable report for March and April.

Figure 5-57 PivotTable for loans by type and date

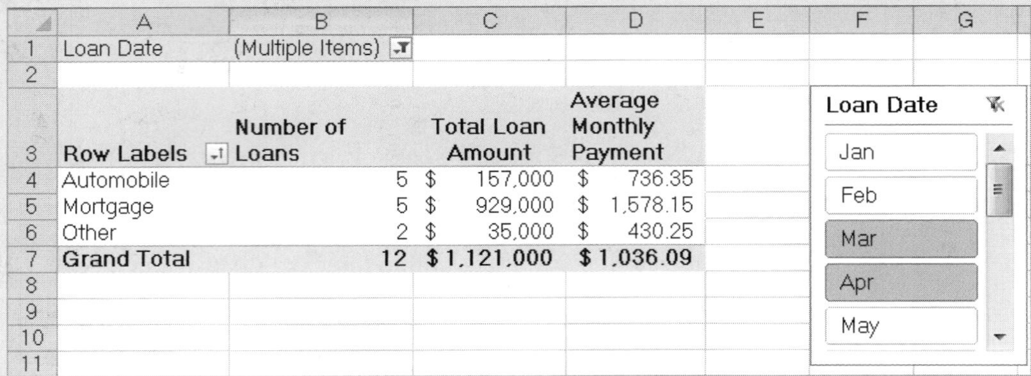

14. Save and close the workbook. Submit the finished workbook to your instructor, either in printed or electronic form, as requested.

Explore how to summarize data by creating subtotals, PivotTables, and PivotCharts.

CHALLENGE

Case Problem 4

Data File needed for this Case Problem: Bowls.xlsx

Bowls Department Stores Bowls Department Stores, with corporate headquarters in Portland, Oregon, operates department stores in midsize towns in selected areas of the Northwest. Although the organization maintains a large computer system for its accounting operations, the sales department often downloads data to complete additional analysis of its operations. Daniel Partner, analyst for the corporate sales department, regularly downloads data by territories and product areas including automotive, electronics, garden centers, and sporting goods. He often presents reports based on his analysis of sales by product areas and territory, best- and worst-performing product group periods, and total sales for certain regions and product groups. You will help Daniel compile and summarize the data. Complete the following:

1. Open the **Bowls** workbook located in the Excel5\Case4 folder included with your Data Files, and then save the workbook as **Bowls Stores** in the same folder.
2. In the Documentation sheet, enter your name, the date, and an appropriate purpose statement.
3. In the SalesData worksheet, create an Excel table. Rename the table as **ProductSales**. Format the Sales column in the Currency number format with no decimal places.
4. Make a copy of the SalesData worksheet, and then rename the copied worksheet as **Q4**. (*Hint*: Press the Ctrl key and drag the sheet tab to the right of the SalesData sheet tab to make a copy of the worksheet.) Sort the table in ascending order by territories, then by product group, then by year, and then by month. Month should be sorted in chronological order (Jan, Feb, Mar, ...), not in alphabetical order.
5. Make a copy of the SalesData worksheet, and then rename the copied worksheet as **Q5**. Display records for Automotive and Electronics products in 2013, excluding sales in Vancouver. Sort this data by sales in descending order. Add a Total row and calculate the average sales for the filtered data. Change the label in the Total row to **Average**. Split the worksheet into two panes. In the top pane, display all the rows except the last row on your screen. In the bottom pane, display the Total row.

EXPLORE

6. Make a copy of the SalesData worksheet, and then rename the copied worksheet as **Q6**. Display subtotals for sales (Sum) by year, month (Jan, Feb, Mar, ...), and territory.

7. Make a copy of the SalesData worksheet, and then rename the copied worksheet as **Q7**. Display the five lowest periods based on sales. Assume each row represents a period. Sort the sales so lowest sales appears first.

EXPLORE

8. Create a PivotTable similar to the one shown in Figure 5-58, displaying percentage of sales by product group, territories, and year. Omit the columnar grand totals. Use a tabular layout, inserting subtotals at the bottom of each product group and excluding the Toy product group. Rename the worksheet as **Q8**.

Figure 5-58 **Sample PivotTable showing percentage of sales**

	A	B	C	D
1				
2				
3	**Pct of Sales**		**Year**	
4	**Product Group**	**Territories**	**2012**	**2013**
5	⊟ **Automotive**	Oregon	10.05%	8.85%
6		Vancouver	7.32%	9.71%
7		Washington	6.88%	9.94%
8	**Automotive Total**		**24.25%**	**28.50%**
9	⊟ **Electronics**	Oregon	7.53%	8.67%
10		Vancouver	7.61%	6.88%
11		Washington	8.05%	9.22%
12	**Electronics Total**		**23.20%**	**24.78%**
13	⊟ **Gardening**	Oregon	8.19%	6.85%
14		Vancouver	8.46%	5.89%
15		Washington	9.77%	9.91%
16	**Gardening Total**		**26.42%**	**22.66%**
17	⊟ **Houseware**	Oregon	6.86%	5.01%
18		Vancouver	8.20%	7.67%
19		Washington	11.07%	11.39%
20	**Houseware Total**		**26.14%**	**24.07%**
21	**Grand Total**		**100.00%**	**100.00%**

EXPLORE

9. Using Figure 5-59 as a guide, create a PivotChart of total sales by product group. Create a second PivotChart of total sales by territory in the same worksheet. Rename the worksheet as **Q9**.

Figure 5-59 **Sample PivotChart of total sales by product group**

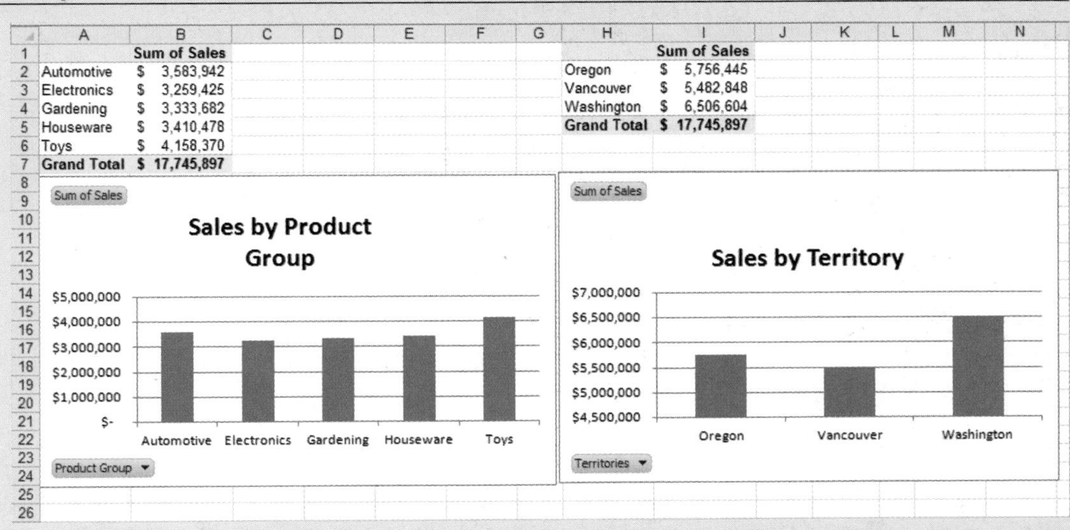

EXPLORE 10. Using Figure 5-60 as a guide, create a PivotTable to show four calculations: average, total, minimum, and maximum sales, categorized by territories and product group, and filtered by year and territories using two slicer filters. Display the results for 2013 and the Vancouver and Washington territories. Rename the worksheet as **Q10**.

Figure 5-60 **Sample PivotTable showing calculations**

	A	B	C	D	E	F	G	H	I
1	Year	2013							
2									
3	**Territories**	**Product Group**	**Average**	**Sum**	**Minimum**	**Maximum**			
4	**Vancouver**	Automotive	$ 55,074	$ 660,886	$ 865	$ 99,526			
5		Electronics	$ 39,033	$ 468,391	$ 2,141	$ 98,044			
6		Gardening	$ 33,419	$ 401,027	$ 467	$ 97,793			
7		Houseware	$ 43,473	$ 521,678	$ 4,046	$ 80,035			
8		Toys	$ 60,199	$ 722,385	$ 29,824	$ 94,129			
9	**Vancouver Total**		**$ 46,239**	**$ 2,774,367**	**$ 467**	**$ 99,526**			
10	**Washington**	Automotive	$ 56,359	$ 676,304	$ 3,893	$ 99,258			
11		Electronics	$ 52,307	$ 627,680	$ 15,485	$ 84,624			
12		Gardening	$ 56,206	$ 674,471	$ 5,507	$ 94,166			
13		Houseware	$ 64,579	$ 774,942	$ 27,164	$ 94,725			
14		Toys	$ 63,189	$ 758,272	$ 17,919	$ 90,879			
15	**Washington Total**		**$ 58,528**	**$ 3,511,669**	**$ 3,893**	**$ 99,258**			
16	**Grand Total**		**$ 52,384**	**$ 6,286,036**	**$ 467**	**$ 99,526**			

Year slicer: 2012, 2013

Territories slicer: Oregon, Vancouver, Washington

11. Save and close the workbook. Submit the finished workbook to your instructor, either in printed or electronic form, as requested.

ASSESS

SAM: Skills Assessment Manager

For current SAM information, including versions and content details, visit SAM Central (http://samcentral.course.com). If you have a SAM user profile, you may have access to hands-on instruction, practice, and assessment of the skills covered in this tutorial. Because various versions of SAM are supported throughout the life of this text, check with your instructor for the correct instructions and URL/Web site for accessing assignments.

ENDING DATA FILES

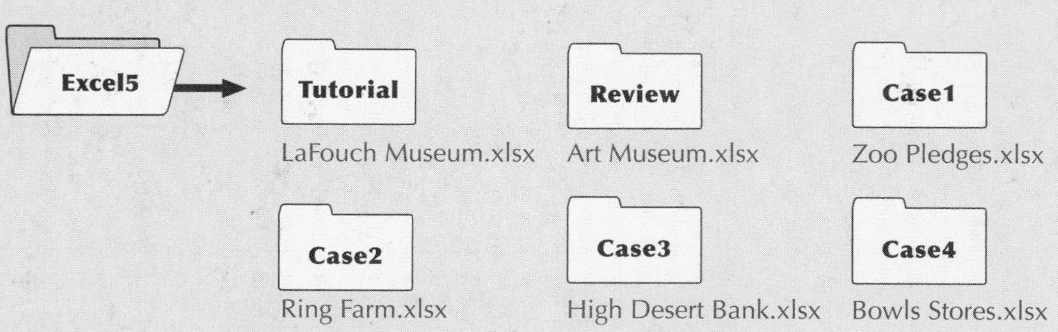

TUTORIAL 6

Managing Multiple Worksheets and Workbooks

Summarizing Ticket Sales

OBJECTIVES

Session 6.1
- Create a worksheet group
- Format and edit multiple worksheets at once
- Create cell references to other worksheets
- Consolidate information from multiple worksheets using 3-D references
- Create and print a worksheet group

Session 6.2
- Create a link to data in another workbook
- Create a workbook reference
- Learn how to edit links
- Create and use an Excel workspace

Session 6.3
- Insert a hyperlink in a cell
- Create a custom template
- Save a workbook to SkyDrive and use the Excel Web App

Case | *Global Travel*

Global Travel, a member-owned organization, provides a variety of services ranging from travel assistance to insurance programs to discounted vacation packages. The company also offers special services and discounts to one-time entertainment events. Global Travel purchases tickets to selected theme and amusement parks to resell to its members. Each local office of Global Travel markets and sells these tickets to its members. Theme and amusement park sales account for more than 10 percent of Global Travel's sales.

Rhohit Gupta, accountant for Global Travel in New Mexico, is responsible for tracking ticket sales within the state and preparing an analysis for Alvin Alton, the corporate controller. Rhohit asks you to create a summary report that shows the quarterly sales in New Mexico for the past year. He already entered each quarter's values in separate worksheets, but wants you to summarize all the quarterly information in one worksheet.

Alvin has already received workbooks with the quarterly sales for Colorado and Utah. After Alvin receives the New Mexico workbook, you will create a workbook that summarizes the annual totals from each state workbook in the Southwest region.

STARTING DATA FILES

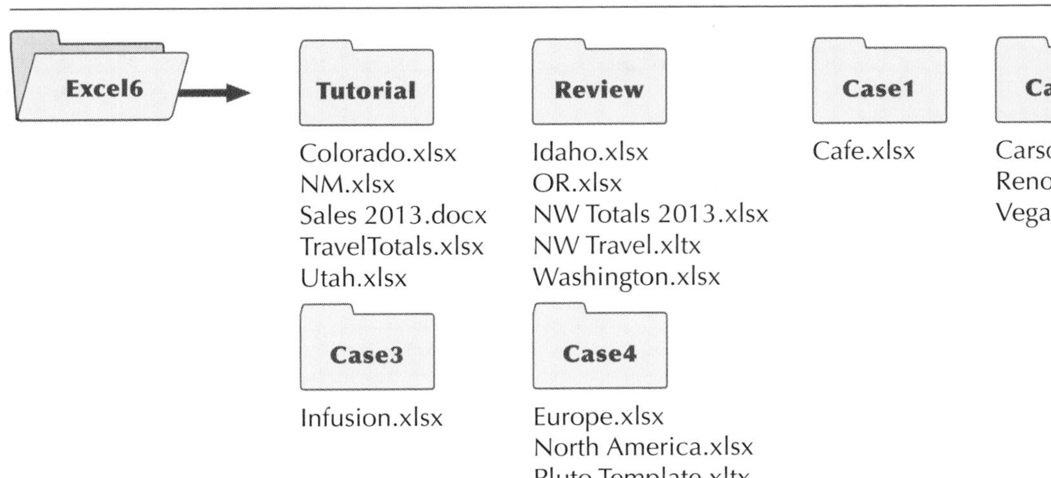

SESSION 6.1 VISUAL OVERVIEW

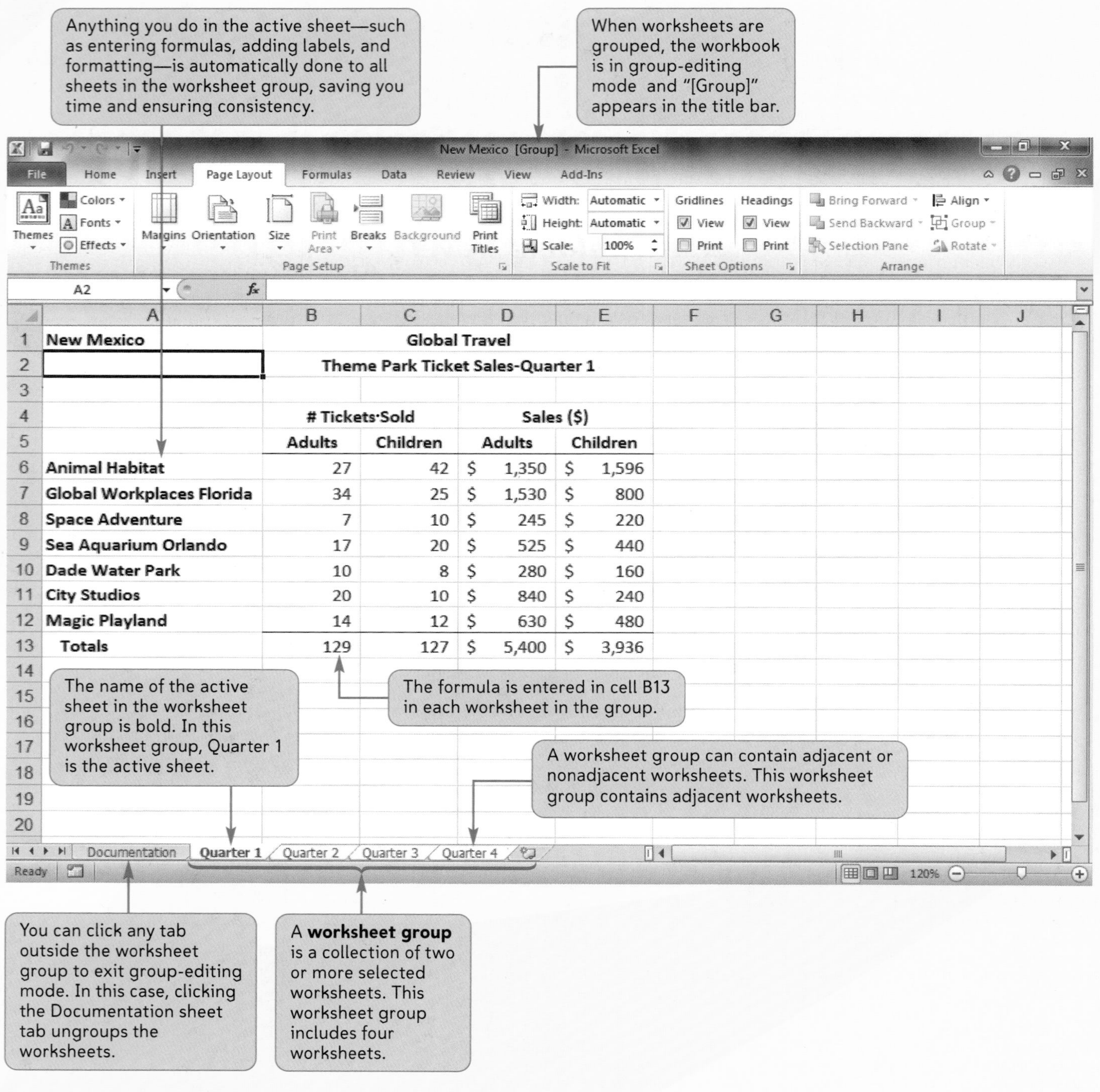

WORKSHEET GROUPS AND 3-D REFERENCES

A **3-D reference** is a reference to the same cell or range in multiple worksheets in the same workbook. This 3-D reference refers to cell B6 in the Quarter 1, Quarter 2, Quarter 3, and Quarter 4 worksheets.

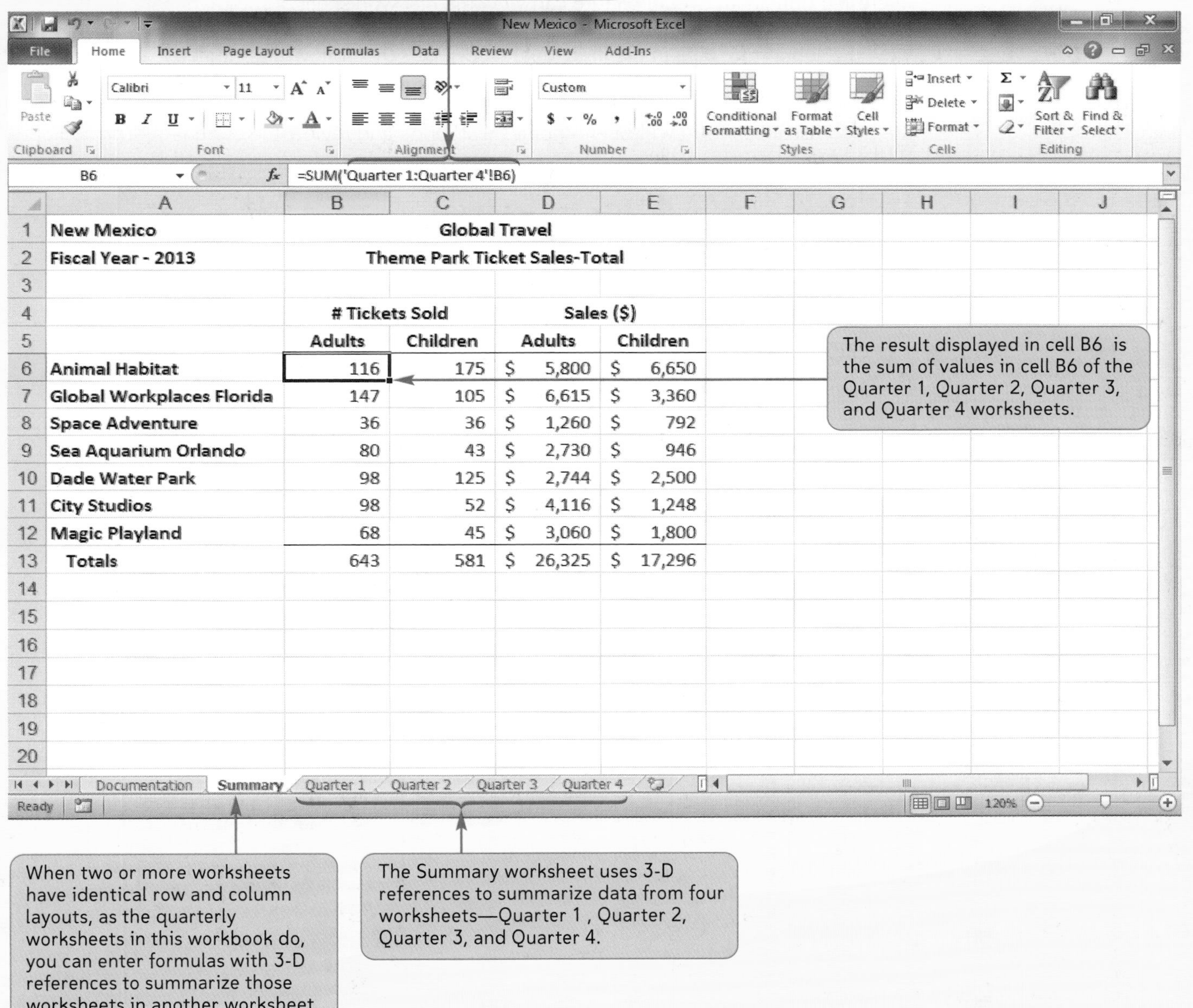

The result displayed in cell B6 is the sum of values in cell B6 of the Quarter 1, Quarter 2, Quarter 3, and Quarter 4 worksheets.

When two or more worksheets have identical row and column layouts, as the quarterly worksheets in this workbook do, you can enter formulas with 3-D references to summarize those worksheets in another worksheet.

The Summary worksheet uses 3-D references to summarize data from four worksheets—Quarter 1 , Quarter 2, Quarter 3, and Quarter 4.

Grouping Worksheets

Workbook data is often placed in several worksheets. Using multiple worksheets makes it easier to group and summarize data. For example, a company such as Global Travel with branches in different geographic regions can place sales information for each region in separate worksheets. Rather than scrolling through one large and complex worksheet that contains data for all regions, users can access sales information for a specific region simply by clicking a sheet tab in the workbook.

TIP

If a worksheet group includes all the worksheets in a workbook, you can edit only the active worksheet; any changes will be made to all the worksheets in the group. Clicking another sheet tab ungroups the worksheets.

Using multiple worksheets enables you to place summarized data first. Managers interested only in an overall picture can view the first worksheet of summary data without looking at the details available in the other worksheets. Others, of course, might want to view the supporting data in the individual worksheets that follow the summary worksheet. In the case of Global Travel, Rhohit used separate worksheets to summarize the number of tickets sold and sales in dollars for the New Mexico branch offices for each quarter of the 2013 fiscal year. You will open Rhohit's workbook and review the current information.

To open and review the Global Travel workbook:

1. Open the **NM** workbook located in the Excel6\Tutorial folder included with your Data Files, and then save the workbook as **New Mexico** in the same folder.
2. In the **Documentation** worksheet, enter your name and the date.
3. Switch to the **Quarter 1** worksheet, and then view the number of tickets sold and sales for the first quarter of the year. See Figure 6-1.

Figure 6-1 Quarter 1 worksheet for Global Travel – New Mexico

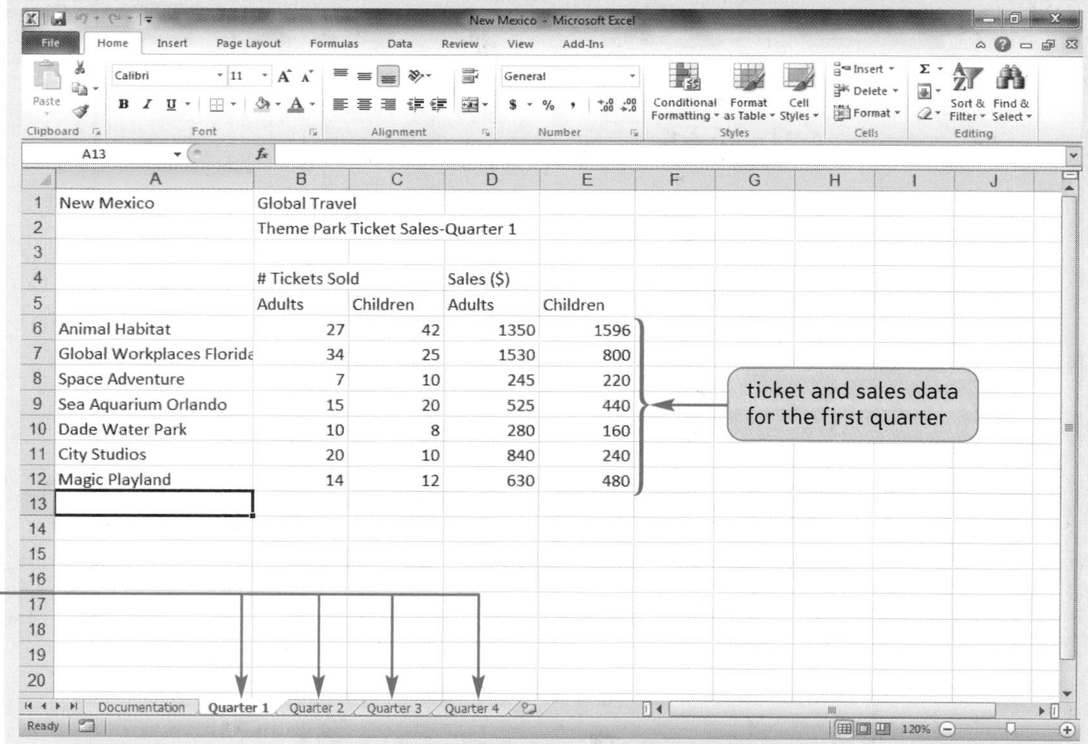

4. Review the **Quarter 2**, **Quarter 3**, and **Quarter 4** worksheets. The layout for all four worksheets is identical.

Rhohit didn't enter any formulas in the workbook. You need to enter formulas to calculate the total number of tickets and sales for each column (B through E) in all four worksheets. Rather than retyping the formulas in each worksheet, you can enter them all at once by creating a worksheet group. A worksheet group, like a range, can contain adjacent or nonadjacent worksheets. In group-editing mode, most editing tasks that you do to the active worksheet also affect the other worksheets in the group. By forming a worksheet group, you can:

- Enter or edit data and formulas in the active worksheet to enter or edit the data and formulas in the same cells in all the worksheets in the group. Find and replace can also be used with a worksheet group.
- Apply formatting to the active worksheet to format all the worksheets in the group, including changing row heights or column widths and applying conditional formatting.
- Insert or delete rows and columns of the active worksheet to make the same changes to all the worksheets in the group.
- Set the page layout options in one worksheet to apply the settings to all worksheets in the group, such as changing the orientation, scaling to fit, and inserting headers and footers.
- Apply view options such as zooming, showing and hiding worksheets, and so forth to all worksheets in the group.
- Print all the worksheets in the worksheet group at the same time.

Worksheet groups save you time and help improve consistency among the worksheets because you can perform an action once, yet affect multiple worksheets.

REFERENCE

Grouping and Ungrouping Worksheets

- To select an adjacent group, click the sheet tab of the first worksheet in the group, press and hold the Shift key, click the sheet tab of the last worksheet in the group, and then release the Shift key.
- To select a nonadjacent group, click the sheet tab of one worksheet in the group, press and hold the Ctrl key, click the sheet tabs of the remaining worksheets in the group, and then release the Ctrl key.
- To ungroup the worksheets, click the sheet tab of a worksheet not in the group.

  or
- Right-click the sheet tab of one worksheet in the group, and then click Ungroup Sheets on the shortcut menu.

In the New Mexico workbook, you'll group an adjacent range of worksheets: the Quarter 1 worksheet through the Quarter 4 worksheet.

TIP

If you cannot see the sheet tab of a worksheet you want to include in a group, use the sheet navigation controls to display it.

To group the quarterly worksheets:

1. Click the **Quarter 1** sheet tab to make the worksheet active. This is the first worksheet you want to include in the group.
2. Press and hold the **Shift** key, and then click the **Quarter 4** sheet tab. This is the last worksheet you want to include in the group.
3. Release the **Shift** key. The sheet tabs for Quarter 1 through Quarter 4 are white, indicating they are all selected. The text "[Group]" appears in the title bar to remind you that a worksheet group is selected in the workbook. See Figure 6-2.

Figure 6-2 **Grouped worksheets**

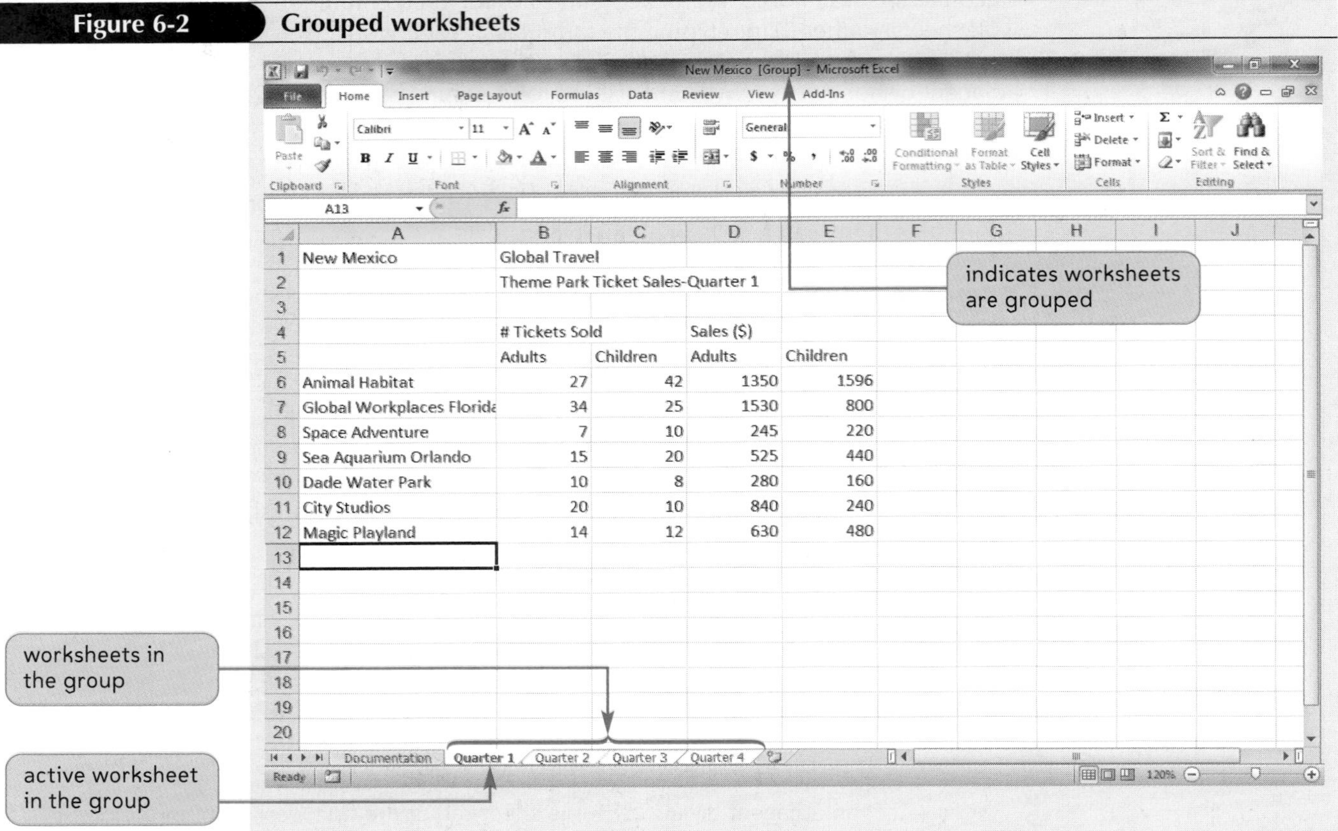

Entering Formulas in a Worksheet Group

When you enter a formula in the active worksheet (in this case, the Quarter 1 worksheet), the formula is entered in the same cells in all the worksheets in the group. The grouped worksheets must have the exact same organization and layout (rows and columns) for this to work. Otherwise, any formulas you enter in the active sheet will be incorrect in the other worksheets in the group and could overwrite existing data. With the quarterly sheets grouped, you will enter the formulas to calculate the total number of tickets sold and total sales.

To enter formulas in the worksheet group:

1. Click cell **B13**. You want to enter the formula in cell B13 in each of the four worksheets in the group.
2. In the Editing group on the Home tab, click the **Sum** button Σ, and then press the **Enter** key. The formula =SUM(B6:B12) is entered in the cell, adding the total number of adult tickets sold in the quarter, which is 127.
3. Copy the formula in cell B13 to the range **C13:E13**. The formula calculates the total number of children's tickets sold (127), the total adult ticket sales ($5400), as well as the total children's ticket sales ($3936).
4. In cell A13, enter **Totals**, and then click the **Increase Indent** button in the Alignment group on the Home tab. The label shifts to the right.

   The formulas and label you entered in the Quarter 1 worksheet were entered in the Quarter 2, 3, and 4 worksheets at the same time.

5. Click the **Quarter 2** sheet tab, and then click cell **B13**. The value 174 appears in the cell and the formula =SUM(B6:B12), which adds the number of adult tickets sold in Quarter 2, appears in the formula bar.

6. Click the **Quarter 4** sheet tab, and then make sure that cell **B13** is the active cell. The value 177 appears in the cell, and the same formula used in cell B13 in the Quarter 1 and Quarter 2 worksheets appears in the formula bar. See Figure 6-3.

Figure 6-3 **Formulas entered in all worksheets in the group**

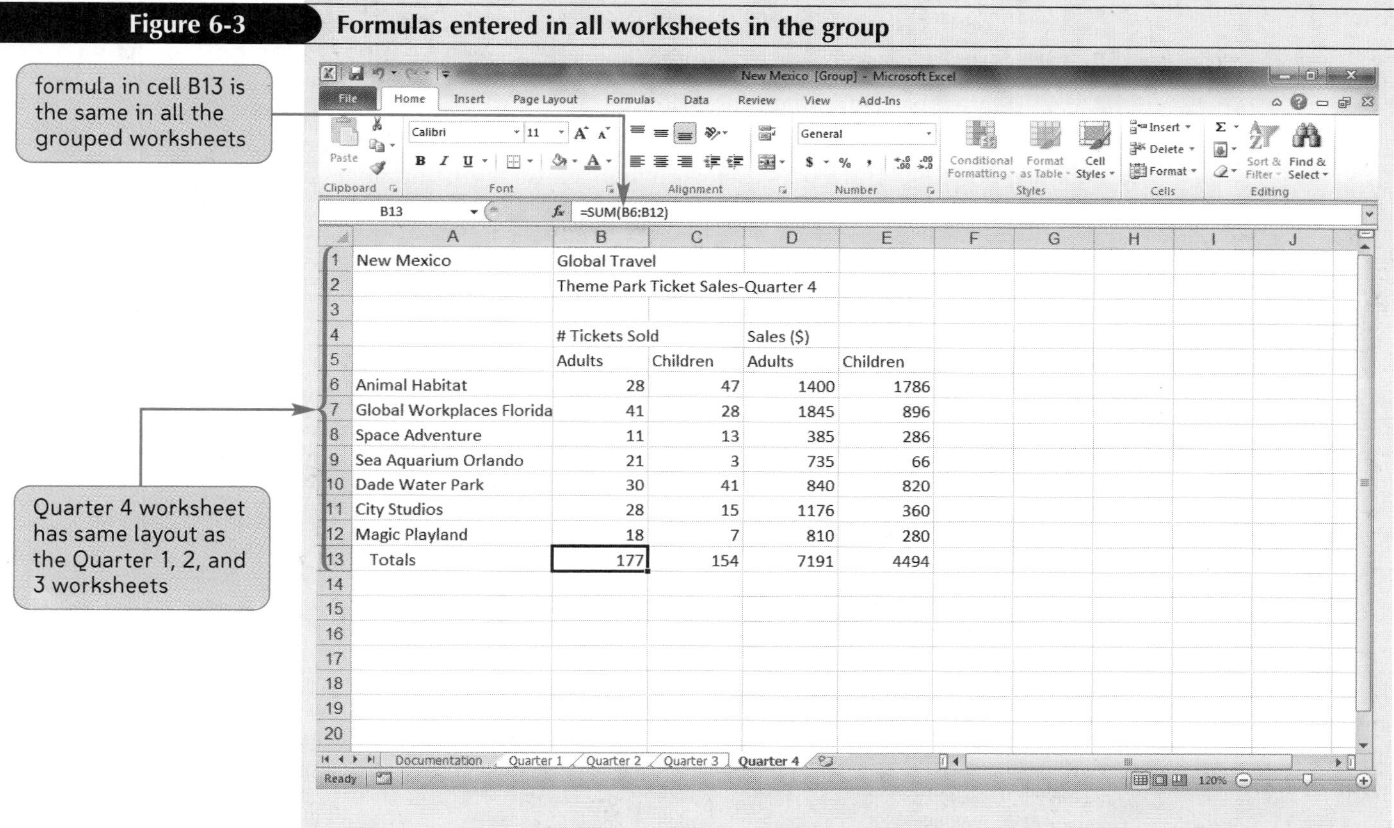

7. Click the **Quarter 1** sheet tab to redisplay the Quarter 1 results.

INSIGHT

Editing Grouped Worksheets

When you enter, edit, or format cells in a worksheet group, the changes you make to one worksheet are automatically applied to the other worksheets in the group. For example, if you delete a value from one cell, the content is also deleted from the same cell in all the worksheets in the group. Be cautious when editing a worksheet that is part of a group. If the layout and structure of the other grouped worksheets are not exactly the same, you may inadvertently overwrite data in some of the worksheets. Also, remember to ungroup the worksheet group after you finish entering data, formulas, and formatting. Otherwise, changes you intend to make in one worksheet will be made to all the worksheets in the group, potentially producing incorrect results.

Formatting a Worksheet Group

As with inserting formulas and text, any formatting changes you make to the active sheet are applied to all sheets in the group. You will format the quarterly worksheets.

To apply formatting to the worksheet group:

1. Bold the text in the nonadjacent range **A1:B2;A6:A13;B4:E5**.
2. Increase the width of column A to **24**.
3. Merge and center each of the following ranges: **B1:E1**, **B2:E2**, **B4:C4**, and **D4:E4**.
4. Center the text in the range **B5:E5**.
5. Apply the **Comma Style** number format with no decimal places to the range B6:C13. No change is visible because all the numbers are less than 1000.
6. Apply the **Accounting** number format with no decimal places to the range D6:E13 so the values appear with a dollar sign and no decimal places.
7. Add a **bottom border** to the ranges B5:E5 and B12:E12.
8. Click cell **A1**. All the worksheets in the group are formatted. See Figure 6-4.

Figure 6-4 **Formatting applied to the worksheet group**

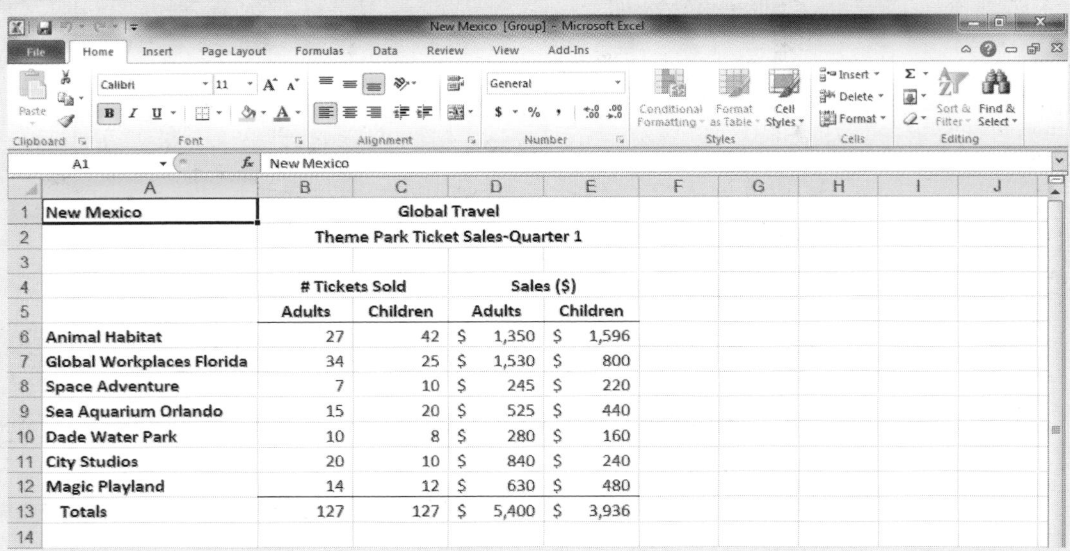

	A	B	C	D	E
1	New Mexico	Global Travel			
2		Theme Park Ticket Sales-Quarter 1			
3					
4		# Tickets Sold		Sales ($)	
5		Adults	Children	Adults	Children
6	Animal Habitat	27	42	$ 1,350	$ 1,596
7	Global Workplaces Florida	34	25	$ 1,530	$ 800
8	Space Adventure	7	10	$ 245	$ 220
9	Sea Aquarium Orlando	15	20	$ 525	$ 440
10	Dade Water Park	10	8	$ 280	$ 160
11	City Studios	20	10	$ 840	$ 240
12	Magic Playland	14	12	$ 630	$ 480
13	Totals	127	127	$ 5,400	$ 3,936
14					

9. Click each sheet tab in the worksheet group and review the formatting changes, and then click the **Quarter 1** sheet tab.

Ungrouping Worksheets

When you ungroup the worksheets, each worksheet functions independently again. If you forget to ungroup the worksheets, any changes you make in one worksheet will be applied to all the worksheets in the group. So be sure to ungroup worksheets when you are finished with changes that apply to multiple worksheets.

You will ungroup the quarterly worksheets so you can work in each worksheet separately.

To ungroup the quarterly worksheets:

Be sure to ungroup the worksheets; otherwise, any changes you make will affect all worksheets in the group.

1. Click the **Documentation** sheet tab. The worksheets are ungrouped because the Documentation worksheet was not part of the worksheet group. The text "[Group]" no longer appears in the Excel title bar.
2. Verify that the worksheets are ungrouped and the word "[Group]" no longer appears in the title bar.

PROSKILLS

Written Communication: Using Multiple Worksheets with Identical Layouts

Using multiple worksheets to organize complex data can help make it simpler to understand and analyze as well as to navigate to specific data. For example, a workbook that contains data about a variety of products, stores, or regions could use a different worksheet for each product, store, or region. This organization provides a way to view discrete units of data that can be combined and summarized in another worksheet.

When you use multiple worksheets to organize similar types of data, the worksheets should have identical layouts. You can quickly group the worksheets with the identical layouts, and then enter the formulas, formatting, and labels in all of the grouped worksheets at once. This helps to ensure consistency and accuracy among the worksheets as well as make it faster to create the different worksheets needed.

Using multiple worksheets with identical layouts enables you to use 3-D references to quickly summarize the data in another worksheet. The summary worksheet provides an overall picture of the data that is detailed in the other worksheets. Often, managers are more interested in this big picture view. However, the supporting data is still available in the individual worksheets when a deeper analysis is needed.

So, when you are working with a large and complex worksheet filled with data, consider the different ways to organize it in multiple worksheets. Not only will you save time when entering and finding data, but also the data becomes more understandable, and connections and results become clearer.

Working with Multiple Worksheets

Rhohit wants the workbook to include a Summary worksheet that adds the annual totals of tickets and sales from the quarterly worksheets. Rather than starting from scratch, you will copy one of the quarterly worksheets as a starting point. The formulas you create in the Summary worksheet will reference cells in each quarterly worksheet using 3-D references. You can then group the completed worksheets to develop a consistent page setup in all worksheets and then print them all at once.

Copying Worksheets

Often, after spending a lot of time developing a worksheet, you can use the existing worksheet as a starting point for creating another, saving you time and energy compared to building a new worksheet from scratch. Copying a worksheet duplicates all the values, formulas, and formats into the new worksheet, leaving the original worksheet intact. You can then edit, reformat, and enter new content as needed to create the exact worksheet you need.

Next, you'll create the Summary worksheet to provide an overall picture of the data included in the detailed quarterly worksheets. The Summary worksheet needs the same formatting and structure as the quarterly worksheets. To ensure consistency among worksheets, you will copy the Quarter 1 worksheet, and then modify its contents.

REFERENCE

Copying Worksheets

- Select the sheet tabs of the worksheets you want to copy.
- Right-click the sheet tabs, and then click Move or Copy on the shortcut menu.
- Click the To book arrow, and then click the name of an existing workbook or click (new book) to create a new workbook for the worksheets.
- In the Before sheet box, click the worksheet you want to insert the new worksheet before.
- Click the Create a copy check box to insert a check mark to copy the worksheets.
- Click the OK button.

or

- Select the sheet tabs of the worksheets you want to copy.
- Press and hold the Ctrl key as you drag the selected sheet tabs to a new location in the sheet tabs, and then release the Ctrl key.

You'll copy the Quarter 1 worksheet to the beginning of the workbook, and then modify the new copy to create the Summary worksheet.

To copy the Quarter 1 worksheet and create the Summary worksheet:

1. Click the **Quarter 1** sheet tab, and then press and hold the **Ctrl** key as you drag the worksheet to the left of the Documentation sheet. The pointer changes to and a triangle indicates the drop location.
2. Release the mouse button, and then release the **Ctrl** key. An identical copy of the Quarter 1 worksheet appears in the new location. The sheet tab shows "Quarter 1 (2)" to indicate that this is the copied sheet.
3. Rename the Quarter 1 (2) worksheet as **Summary**.
4. Move the **Summary** worksheet between the Documentation worksheet and the Quarter 1 worksheet.
5. Make sure the **Summary** worksheet is the active sheet. You will modify the Summary worksheet.
6. In cell A2, enter **2013**. This is the year to which the summary refers.
7. In cell B2, enter **Theme Park Ticket Sales-Total**. The new title reflects this worksheet's content.
8. Select the range **B6:E12**, and then press the **Delete** key. The Quarter 1 sales data is removed, but the formatting remains intact and will apply to the combined sales data for all four quarters that you will enter shortly.

TIP

To move a worksheet or worksheet group to another location in the same workbook, select the worksheets and then drag and drop them by the selected sheet tabs.

Referencing Cells and Ranges in Other Worksheets

When you use multiple worksheets to organize related data, you can reference a cell or range in another worksheet in the same workbook. For example, the Summary worksheet references cells in the four quarterly worksheets to calculate the total sales for the entire year. The syntax to reference a cell or range in a different worksheet is as follows:

```
=SheetName!CellRange
```

In this formula, *SheetName* is the worksheet's name as listed on the sheet tab and *CellRange* is the reference for the cell or range in that worksheet. An exclamation mark (!) separates the worksheet reference from the cell or range reference. For example, you could enter the following formula in the Summary worksheet to reference cell D10 in the Quarter1 worksheet:

```
=Quarter1!D10
```

If the worksheet name contains spaces, you must enclose the sheet name in single quotation marks. For example, the following formula references cell D10 in the Quarter 1 worksheet:

```
='Quarter 1'!D10
```

You can use these references to create formulas that reference cells in different locations in different worksheets. For example, to add sales from two worksheets—cell E12 in the Quarter 1 worksheet and cell D12 in the Quarter 2 worksheet—you would enter the following formula:

```
='Quarter 1'!E12+'Quarter 2'!D12
```

You could type the formula directly in the cell, but it is faster and more accurate to use the point-and-click method to enter references to other worksheets.

REFERENCE

Entering a Formula with References to Another Worksheet

- Click the cell where you want to enter the formula.
- Type = and begin entering the formula.
- To insert a reference from another worksheet, click the sheet tab for the worksheet, and then click the cell or select the range you want to reference.
- When the formula is complete, press the Enter key.

Rhohit wants you to enter a formula in cell A2 in each quarterly worksheet that displays the fiscal year from cell A2 in the Summary worksheet. All four quarterly worksheets will use the formula =Summary!A2 to reference the fiscal year in cell A2 of the Summary sheet.

To enter the formula that references the Summary worksheet:

1. Click the **Quarter 1** sheet tab, press and hold the **Shift** key, and then click the **Quarter 4** worksheet. The Quarter 1 through Quarter 4 worksheets are grouped.
2. Click cell **A2**. This is the cell in which you want to enter the formula to display the fiscal year.
3. Type **=** to begin the formula, click the **Summary** sheet tab, and then click cell **A2**. The reference to cell A2 in the Summary worksheet is added to the formula in cell A2 in the grouped worksheets.
4. On the formula bar, click the **Enter** button ✓. The formula =Summary!A2 is entered in cell A2 in all the worksheets in the group. The formula appears in the formula bar and 2013 appears in cell A2. See Figure 6-5.

Figure 6-5 Formula with a worksheet reference

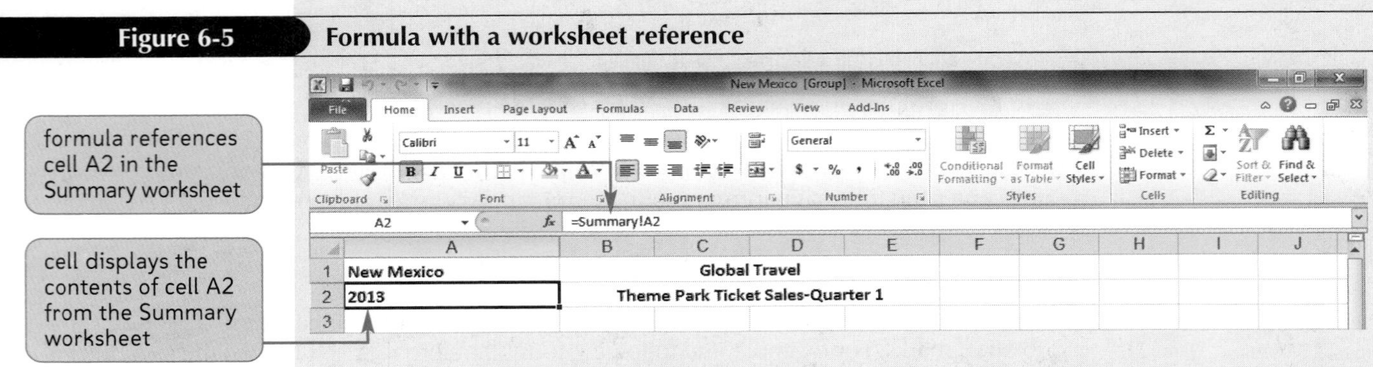

5. In each worksheet in the group, verify that the formula =Summary!A2 appears in the formula bar and 2013 appears in cell A2.
6. Switch to the **Summary** worksheet. The quarterly worksheets are ungrouped.
7. In cell A2, enter **Fiscal Year - 2013**. The descriptive label in cell A2 is entered in the Summary worksheet, and is also displayed in the quarterly worksheets because of the formula you entered.
8. Verify that the label "Fiscal Year - 2013" appears in cell A2 in the Quarter 1 through Quarter 4 worksheets.

Using 3-D References to Add Values Across Worksheets

You need to calculate the number of tickets sold and the total sales for each theme park for the year, and display the totals for the fiscal year in the Summary worksheet. To calculate the totals for the year, you can add the results from each quarterly worksheet and place the sum in the Summary worksheet. For example, in cell B6 of the Summary worksheet, you can enter the formula:

```
='Quarter 1'!B6+'Quarter 2'!B6+'Quarter 3'!B6+'Quarter 4'!B6
```

This formula calculates the number of Adult tickets sold to Animal Habitat by adding the values in cell B6 in each of the quarterly worksheets. Continuing this approach for the entire worksheet is time consuming and error prone.

Instead, when two or more worksheets have *identical* row and column layouts, as do the quarterly worksheets in the New Mexico workbook, you can enter formulas with 3-D references to summarize those worksheets in another worksheet. The 3-D reference specifies not only the range of rows and columns, but also the range of worksheet names in which the cells appear. The general syntax of a 3-D cell reference is:

```
WorksheetRange!CellRange
```

In this syntax, *WorksheetRange* is the range of worksheets you want to reference and is entered as *FirstSheetName:LastSheetName* with a colon separating the first and last worksheets in the worksheet range. *CellRange* is the same cell or range in each of those worksheets that you want to reference. An exclamation mark (!) separates the worksheet range from the cell or range. For example, the following formula adds the values in cell E13 in the worksheets between Quarter1 and Quarter4, including Quarter1 and Quarter4:

```
=SUM(Quarter1:Quarter4!E13)
```

If worksheets named Quarter1, Quarter2, Quarter3, and Quarter4 are included in the workbook, the worksheet range Quarter1:Quarter4 references all four worksheets. Although the Quarter2 and Quarter3 worksheets aren't specifically mentioned in this 3-D reference, all worksheets positioned within the starting and ending names are included in the calculation.

INSIGHT

Managing 3-D References

The results of a formula using a 3-D reference reflect the current worksheets in the worksheet range. If you move a worksheet outside the referenced worksheet range or remove a worksheet from the workbook, the formula results will change. For example, consider a workbook with four worksheets named Quarter1, Quarter2, Quarter3, and Quarter4. If you move the Quarter3 worksheet after the Quarter4 worksheet, the worksheet range Quarter1:Quarter4 includes only the Quarter1, Quarter2, and Quarter4 worksheets. Similarly, if you insert a new worksheet or move an existing worksheet within the worksheet range, the formula results reflect the change. To continue the example, if you insert a Quarter5 worksheet before the Quarter4 worksheet, the 3-D reference Quarter1:Quarter4 includes the Quarter5 worksheet.

When you create a formula, make sure that the 3-D cell reference reflects the appropriate worksheets. Also, if you later insert or delete a worksheet within the 3-D reference, be aware of how doing so will affect the formula results.

3-D references are often used in formulas that contain Excel functions, including SUM, AVERAGE, COUNT, MAX, MIN, STD, and VAR.

REFERENCE

Entering a Function That Contains a 3-D Reference

- Click the cell where you want to enter the formula.
- Type = to begin the formula, type the name of the function, and then type (to indicate the beginning of the argument.
- Click the sheet tab for the first worksheet in the worksheet range, press and hold the Shift key, and then click the tab for the last worksheet in the worksheet range.
- Select the cell or range to reference, and then press the Enter key.

In the New Mexico workbook, you'll use 3-D references in the Summary worksheet to add the total number of tickets sold and sales for the year. You will begin by entering a formula to add the number of tickets sold to adults for the Animal Habitat theme park in all four quarters of the year. Then, you'll copy this formula to calculate the tickets sold to adults and children for each theme park as well as the sales generated.

To enter a formula with a 3-D reference to the quarterly worksheets:

1. In the Summary worksheet, click cell **B6**, and then type **=SUM(** to begin the formula. A ScreenTip shows the SUM function syntax. See Figure 6-6. You'll enter a 3-D reference to cell B6 in the four quarterly worksheets.

Figure 6-6 Formula for the 3-D reference

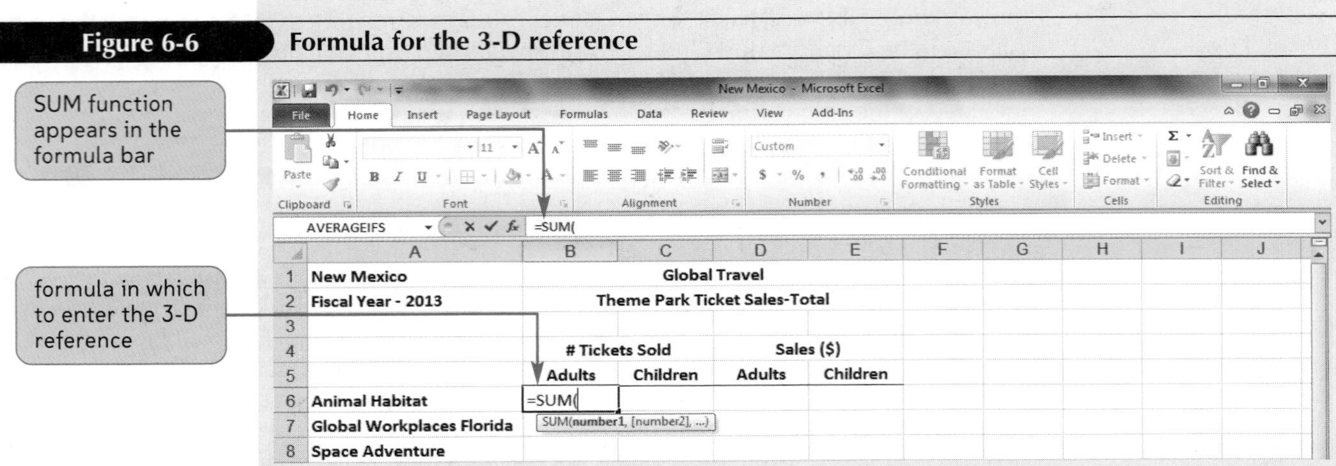

2. Click the **Quarter 1** sheet tab, press and hold the **Shift** key, click the **Quarter 4** sheet tab, and then release the **Shift** key. The worksheet range is selected and added to the SUM function as 'Quarter 1:Quarter 4'. Single quotation marks appear around the worksheet range because the worksheet names include spaces.

3. In the Quarter 1 worksheet, click cell **B6**. The cell is selected and added to the function. See Figure 6-7.

Figure 6-7 SUM function with a 3-D reference

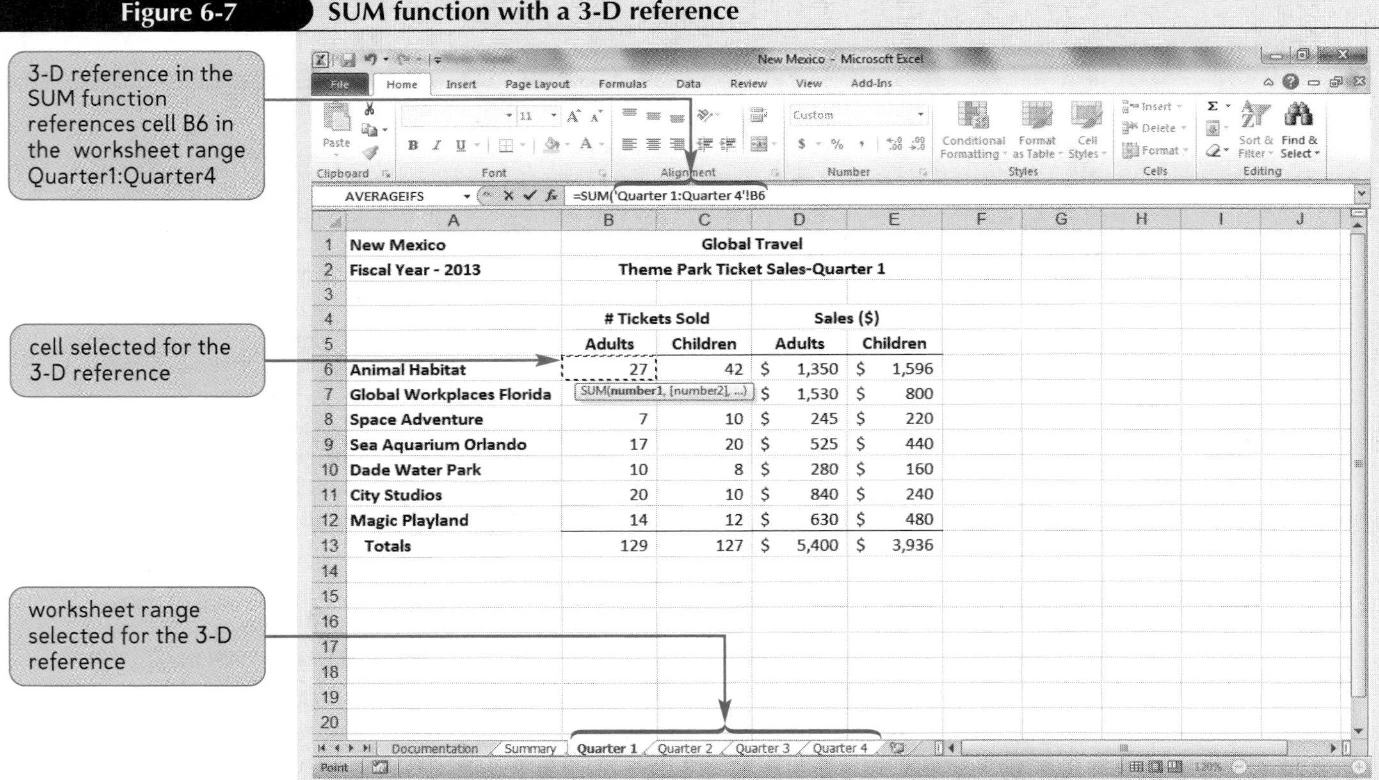

4. Press the **Enter** key to complete the formula. The closing right parenthesis is automatically inserted at the end of the formula.

5. In the Summary worksheet, click cell **B6**. The completed formula =SUM('Quarter 1:Quarter 4'!B6) appears in the formula bar. The total number of tickets for Animal Habitat sold to adults in 2013—116—appears in cell B6.

You'll repeat the process to enter a 3-D reference in cell C6 that adds the total number of tickets sold to children for Animal Habitat in 2013.

To enter another formula with a 3-D reference:

TIP

You could also copy the formula in cell B6 to cells C6 to E6.

1. In the Summary worksheet, click cell **C6**, and then type **=SUM(** to begin the formula.
2. Click the **Quarter 1** sheet tab, press and hold the **Shift** key, click the **Quarter 4** sheet tab, and then release the **Shift** key. The quarterly worksheets are grouped.
3. In the Quarter 1 worksheet, click cell **C6** to select the cell, and then press the **Enter** key to complete the formula and return to the Summary worksheet.
4. In the Summary worksheet, click cell **C6**. The formula =SUM('Quarter 1:Quarter 4'!C6) appears in the formula bar. Also, the value 175—the total number of tickets sold to children for Animal Habitat in 2013—appears in cell C6.

In cells D6 and E6, you'll enter the SUM function with a 3-D reference to calculate the total revenue from tickets sales for Animal Habitat.

To calculate total sales revenue for Animal Habitat:

1. In the Summary worksheet, click cell **D6**, and then type **=SUM(** to begin the formula.
2. Group the **Quarter 1** through **Quarter 4** worksheets, and then click cell **D6**.
3. Press the **Enter** key. The SUM function with a 3-D reference to cell D6 in the quarterly worksheets is entered. The completed formula is =SUM('Quarter 1:Quarter 4'!D6) and the total revenue from ticket sales to adults for Animal Habitat in 2013 is $5,800.
4. In the Summary worksheet, click cell **E6**, and then enter the SUM function formula with a 3-D reference to cell **E6** in the quarterly worksheets. The completed formula is =SUM('Quarter 1:Quarter 4'!E6) and the total revenue from ticket sales to children for Animal Habitat in 2013 is $6,650.

Instead of entering the SUM function to create the totals for the remaining theme parks, you can copy the formulas to the rest of the range. You copy formulas with 3-D references the same way you copy other formulas—using copy and paste or AutoFill. You'll copy the formulas in the range B6:E6 to the range B7:E12 so you can calculate the total ticket sales and revenue in 2013 for the remaining theme parks.

To copy the formulas with 3-D cell references:

1. Select the range **B6:E6**. This range contains the SUM functions with the 3-D references you already entered.

2. Drag the fill handle over the range B7:E12. The formulas are copied for the rest of the theme park rows. The Auto Fill Options button appears below the copied range.

3. Click the **Auto Fill Options** button, and then click the **Fill Without Formatting** option button. You don't want to copy the formatting in this case because you want to keep the bottom border formatting in the range B12:E12. The total values for the year appear in the range.

4. Click cell **B6** to deselect the range. The Summary worksheet now shows the totals for 2013 in New Mexico for each theme park as well as statewide totals. See Figure 6-8.

Figure 6-8 Summary worksheet with all the 3-D reference formulas

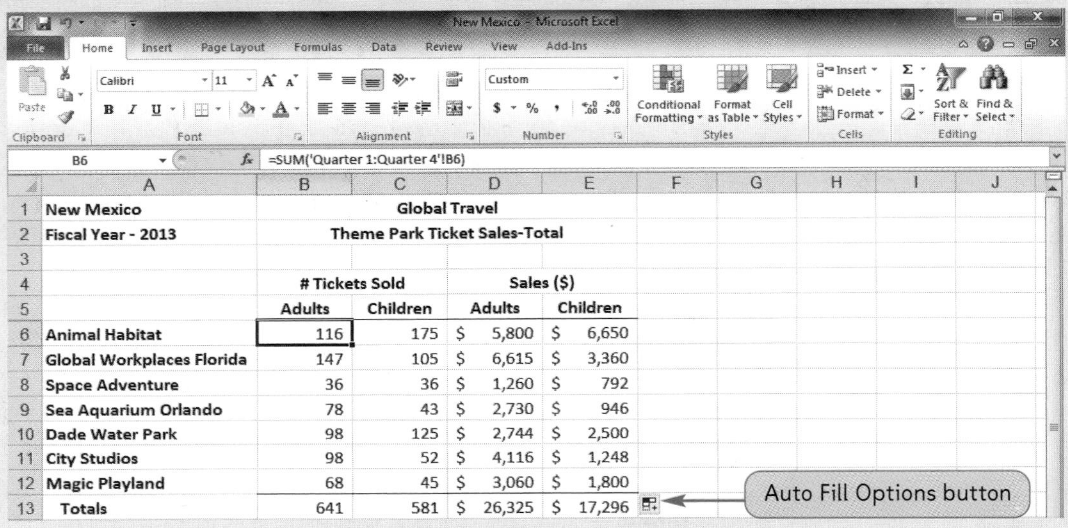

	A	B	C	D	E
1	New Mexico	Global Travel			
2	Fiscal Year - 2013	Theme Park Ticket Sales-Total			
3					
4		# Tickets Sold		Sales ($)	
5		Adults	Children	Adults	Children
6	Animal Habitat	116	175	$ 5,800	$ 6,650
7	Global Workplaces Florida	147	105	$ 6,615	$ 3,360
8	Space Adventure	36	36	$ 1,260	$ 792
9	Sea Aquarium Orlando	78	43	$ 2,730	$ 946
10	Dade Water Park	98	125	$ 2,744	$ 2,500
11	City Studios	98	52	$ 4,116	$ 1,248
12	Magic Playland	68	45	$ 3,060	$ 1,800
13	Totals	641	581	$ 26,325	$ 17,296

One benefit of summarizing data using 3-D reference formulas, like any other formula, is that if you change the value in one worksheet, the results of formulas that reference that cell reflect the change. Rhohit has discovered an error in the ticket sales data. Sea Aquarium Orlando sold 17 adult tickets in Quarter 1, not 15. You will correct the number of tickets sold for Sea Aquarium Orlando in Quarter 1.

To change the ticket value in the Quarter 1 worksheet:

1. In the Summary worksheet, note that 78 adult tickets were sold for Sea Aquarium Orlando in 2013 and 641 total adult tickets were sold.

2. Switch to the **Quarter 1** worksheet, and then, in cell B9, enter **17**. The total adult tickets sold in Quarter 1 is now 129.

   The results in the Summary worksheet are also updated because of the 3-D references in the formulas.

3. Switch to the **Summary** worksheet. The total number of tickets sold to adults for Sea Aquarium Orlando in 2013 is now 80, and the total number of tickets sold to adults for all theme parks in 2013 is now 643. See Figure 6-9.

Figure 6-9 Summary worksheet with the updated ticket data

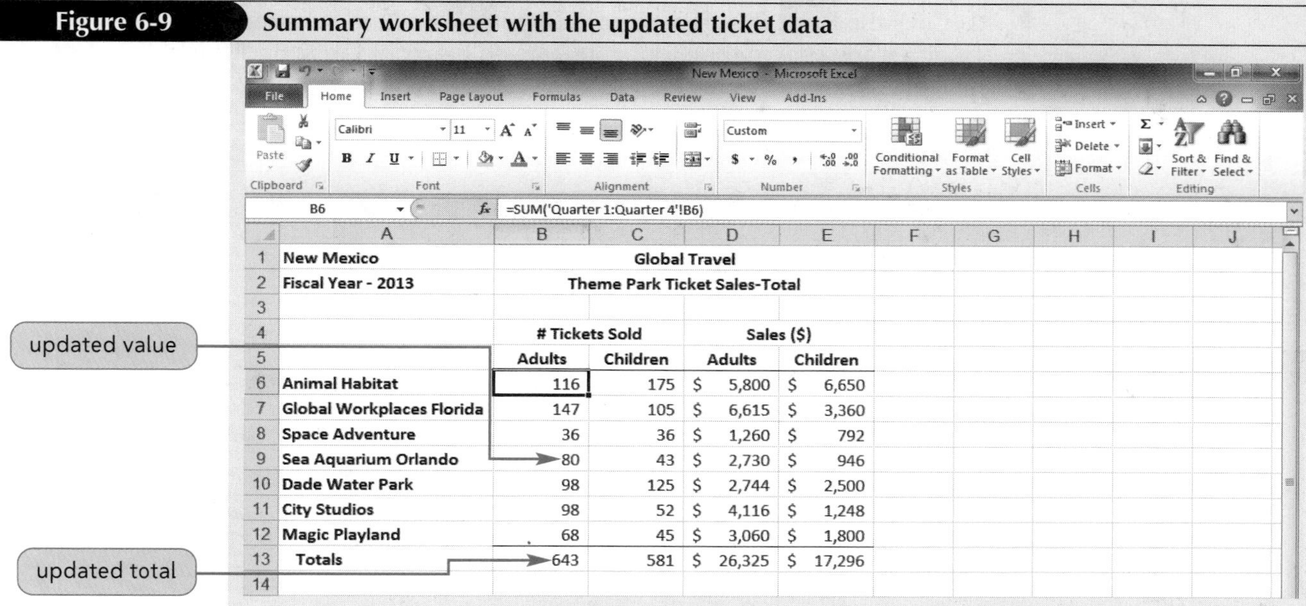

Printing a Worksheet Group

By creating a worksheet group, you apply the same page layout settings to all the worksheets in the group at the same time. You can also print all the worksheets in the group at once.

Rhohit wants a printed copy of the five ticket sales worksheets to include in his report. Each page should have the same setup. Because the layout will be the same for all the quarterly worksheets in the New Mexico workbook, you can speed the page layout setup by creating a worksheet group before selecting settings.

To print the Summary and quarterly worksheets with a custom header and footer:

Be sure to include all five worksheets in the group so that you can apply page layout settings and print the worksheets at once.

1. Group the **Summary**, **Quarter 1**, **Quarter 2**, **Quarter 3**, and **Quarter 4** worksheets. The five worksheets are grouped.
2. Click the **Page Layout** tab on the Ribbon, and then, in the Page Setup group, click the **Dialog Box Launcher**. The Page Setup dialog box opens with the Page tab active.
3. Click the **Margins** tab, and then, in the Center on page section, click the **Horizontally** check box to insert a check mark. The printed content will be centered horizontally on the page.
4. Click the **Header/Footer** tab, click the **Custom Header** button to open the Header dialog box, click in the **Center section** box, click the **Insert Sheet Name** button to add the &[Tab] code in the section box to insert the sheet tab name in the center section of the header, and then click the **OK** button. A preview of the header appears in the upper portion of the dialog box.
5. Click the **Custom Footer** button to open the Footer dialog box, type your name in the Left section box, click in the Right section box, click the **Insert Date** button to add the &[Date] code in the section box to insert the current date in the right section of the footer, and then click the **OK** button.

6. Click the **Print Preview** button. The preview of the Summary worksheet, the first worksheet in the group, appears on the Print tab in Backstage view. See Figure 6-10.

Figure 6-10 Preview of the worksheet group

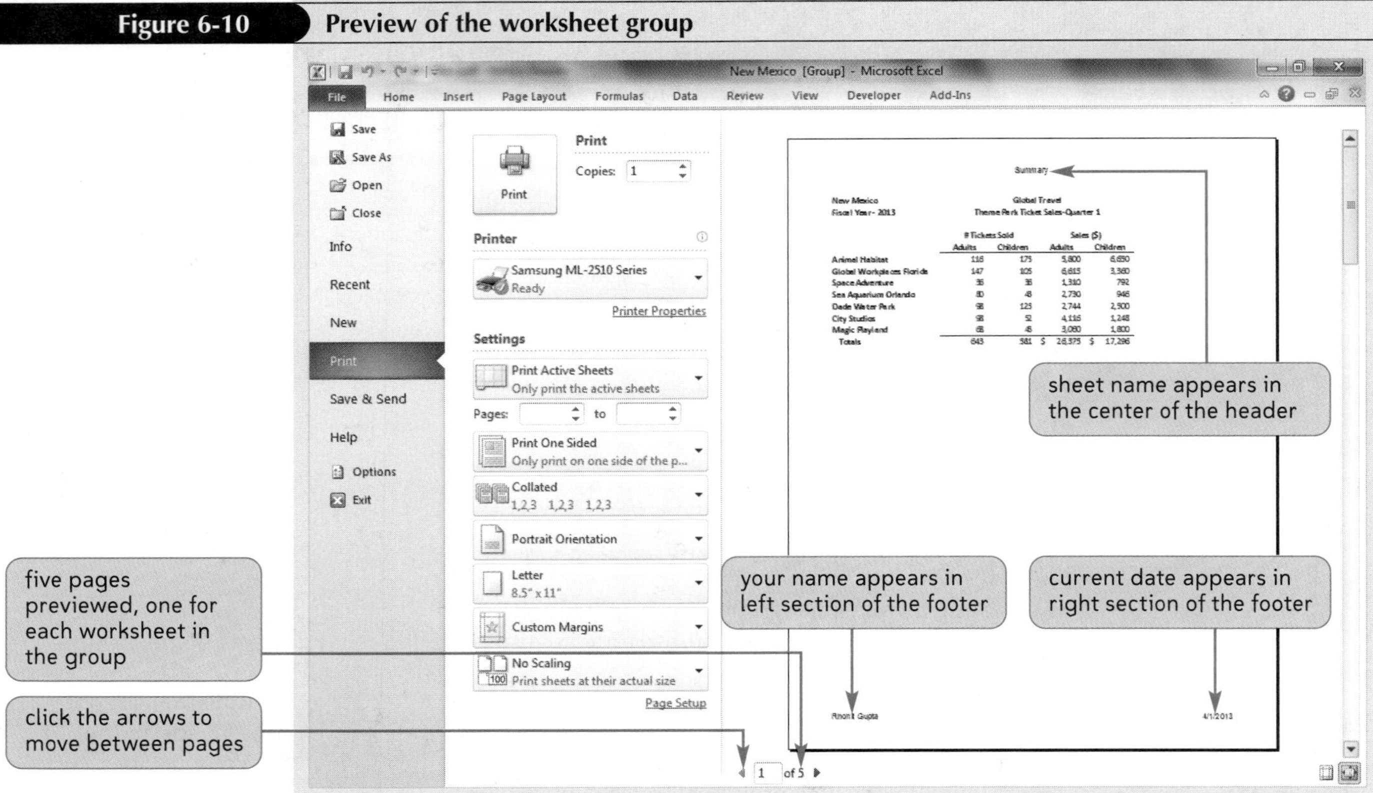

7. Below the preview, click the **Next Page** button four times to view the other worksheets in the group. Each page has the same page layout but the header shows the sheet tab names.

   Trouble? If only one page appears in the preview, the worksheets are not grouped. Click the File tab to exit Backstage view, and then repeat Steps 1 through 7.

8. Unless you are instructed to print, click the **Home** tab to exit Backstage view without printing the worksheet group. Otherwise, click the **Print** button.

9. Switch to the **Documentation** sheet to ungroup the worksheets, and then switch to the **Summary** worksheet.

In this session, you consolidated the data in Global Travel's New Mexico workbook in a Summary sheet, so that Rhohit and Alvin can quickly see the totals for the theme park sales. In the next session, you will help Alvin determine the annual totals for all of Global Travel's Southwest locations—New Mexico, Utah, and Colorado.

REVIEW

Session 6.1 Quick Check

1. What is a worksheet group?
2. How do you select an adjacent worksheet group? How do you select a non-adjacent worksheet group? How do you deselect a worksheet group?
3. What formula would you enter in the Summary worksheet to reference cell A10 in the Quarter 2 worksheet?
4. What is the 3-D cell reference to cell A10 in the adjacent Summary 1, Summary 2, and Summary 3 worksheets?
5. Explain what the formula =MAX(Sheet1:Sheet4!B1) calculates.
6. If you insert a new worksheet named Sheet5 after Sheet4, how would you change the formula =MAX(Sheet1:Sheet4!B1) to include Sheet5 in the calculation?
7. If you insert a new worksheet named Sheet5 before Sheet4, how would you change the formula =MAX(Sheet1:Sheet4!B1) to include Sheet5 in the calculation?
8. How do you apply the same page layout to all of the worksheets in a workbook at one time?

SESSION 6.2 VISUAL OVERVIEW

An **external reference** is a reference to cells or ranges in a worksheet from another workbook. For example, *'[New Mexico.xlsx]Summary''!$B6* references cell B6 in the Summary worksheet in the New Mexico workbook.

When two workbooks are linked, the **destination file** (sometimes referred to as the dependent file) is the workbook that receives data from another workbook. In this case, the Totals 2013 workbook is the destination file.

The total value shown in the destination file is calculated from values in the three source files.

Whenever a value in a source file changes, the destination is also updated to reflect the most recent information. For example, if Animal Habitat sales in New Mexico increase by four tickets, the changes are also reflected in the Totals 2013 workbook.

	A	B	C	D
1	All States		Global Travel	
2			Theme Park Ticket Sale	
3				
4		# Tickets Sold		
5		Adults	Children	Adul
6	Animal Habitat	346	499	$ 17,
7	Global Workplaces Florida	451	376	$ 20,
8	Space Adventure	115	97	$ 4,

	A	B	C	D
1	New Mexico		Global Travel	
2	Fiscal Year - 2013		Theme Park Ticket Sales-	
3				
4		# Tickets Sold		Sa
5		Adults	Children	Adults
6	Animal Habitat	116	175	$ 5,80
7	Global Workplaces Florida	147	105	$ 6,61
8	Space Adventure	36	36	$ 1,31

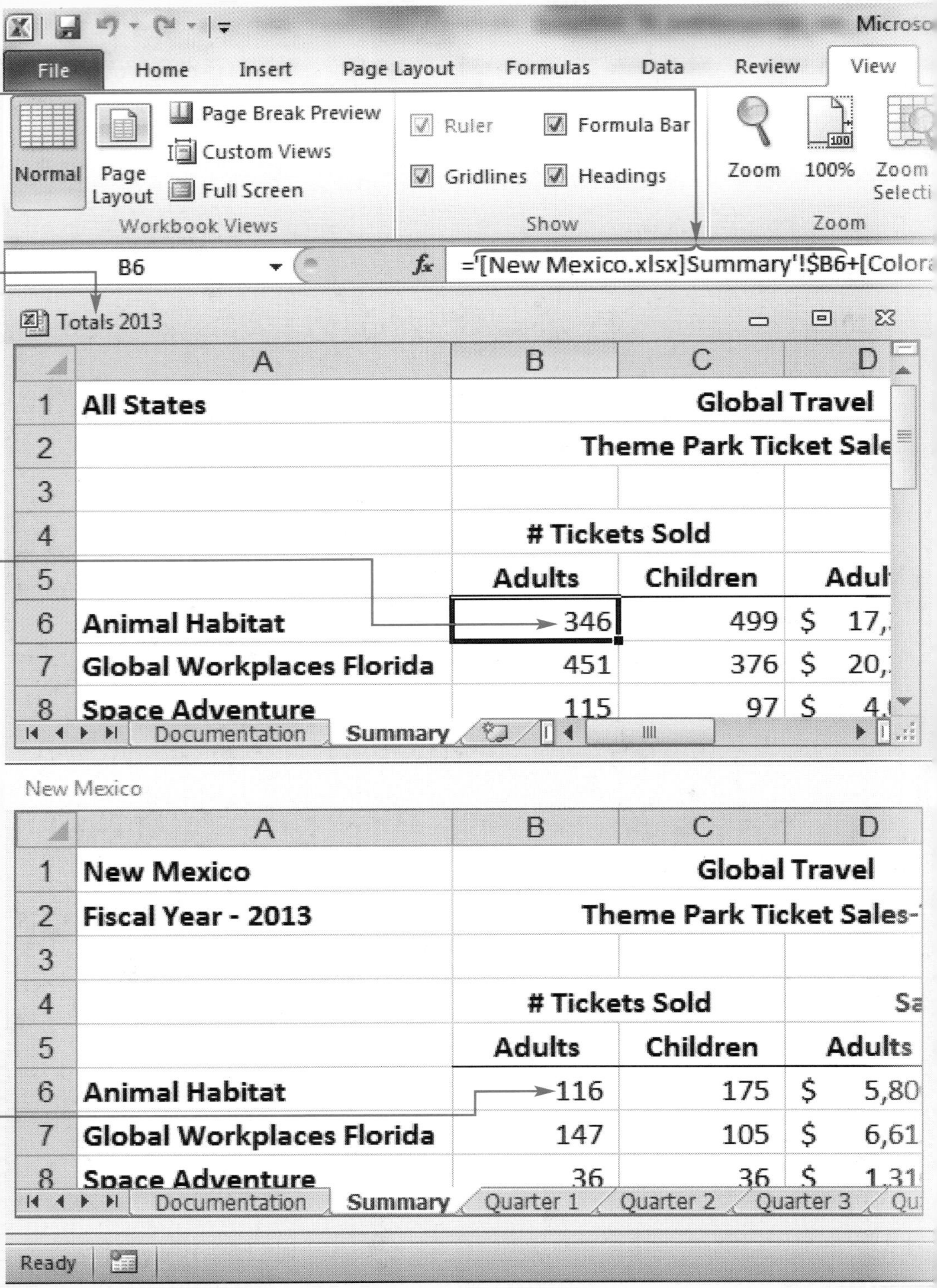

LINKS AND EXTERNAL REFERENCES

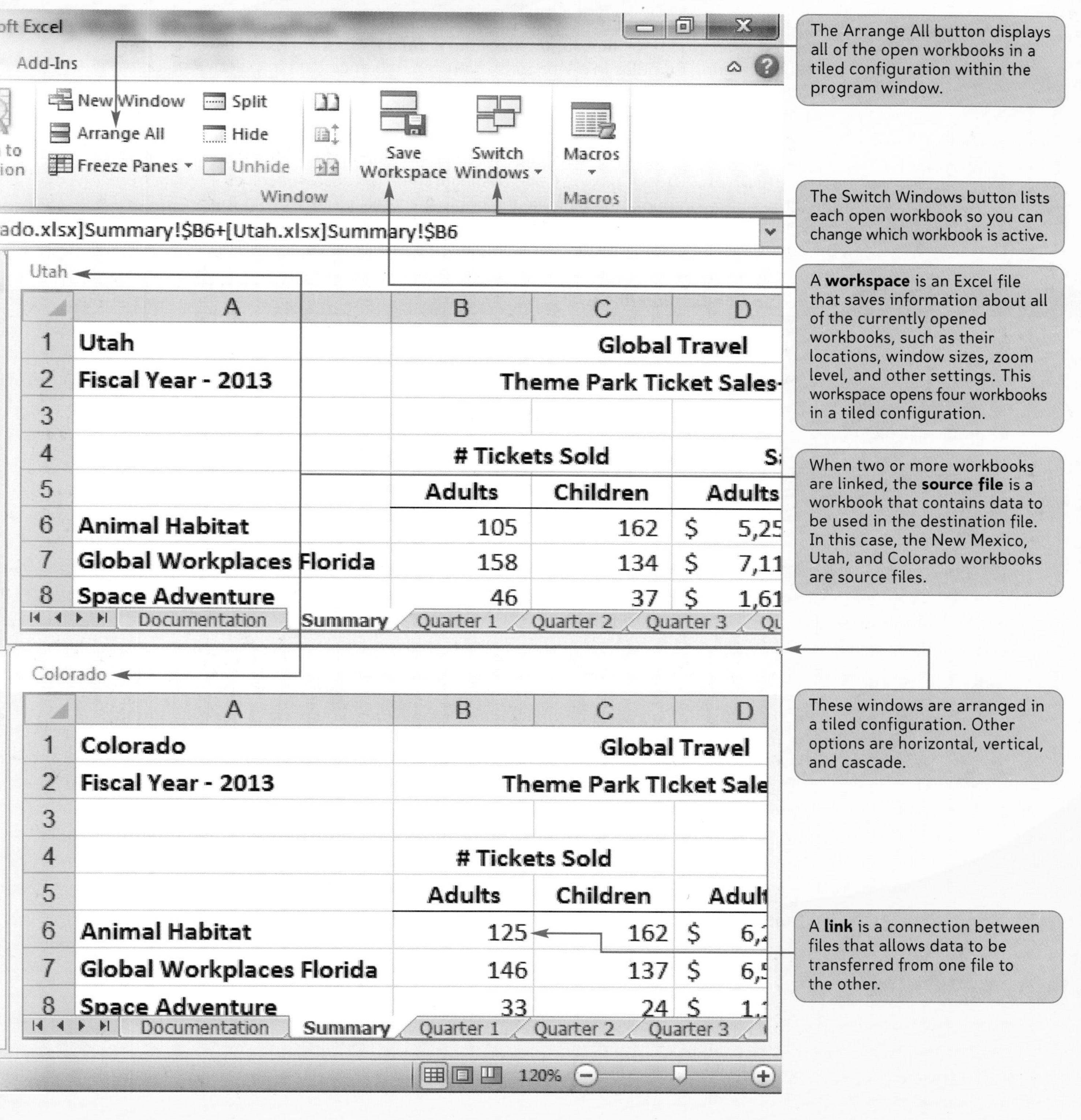

The Arrange All button displays all of the open workbooks in a tiled configuration within the program window.

The Switch Windows button lists each open workbook so you can change which workbook is active.

A **workspace** is an Excel file that saves information about all of the currently opened workbooks, such as their locations, window sizes, zoom level, and other settings. This workspace opens four workbooks in a tiled configuration.

When two or more workbooks are linked, the **source file** is a workbook that contains data to be used in the destination file. In this case, the New Mexico, Utah, and Colorado workbooks are source files.

These windows are arranged in a tiled configuration. Other options are horizontal, vertical, and cascade.

A **link** is a connection between files that allows data to be transferred from one file to the other.

Linking Workbooks

Alvin has workbooks from the Colorado and Utah accountants similar to the one you helped Rhohit prepare. These three travel workbooks (named New Mexico, Colorado, and Utah) contain the number of tickets sold and sales for 2013. Alvin wants to create a company-wide workbook that summarizes the annual totals from each state workbook.

When creating formulas in a workbook, you can reference data in other workbooks. To do so, you must create a link between the workbooks. When two files are linked, the source file contains the data, and the destination file (sometimes called the *dependent* file) receives the data. In this case, as illustrated in Figure 6-11, the New Mexico, Utah, and Colorado workbooks are the source files because they contain the data from the three states. The Totals 2013 workbook is the destination file because it receives the data from the three state workbooks to calculate the company totals for 2013. The Totals 2013 workbook will always have access to the most recent information in the state workbooks because it can be updated whenever any of the linked values change.

Figure 6-11 Source and destination files

destination file

Totals 2013

	A	B	C	D	E
1	All States		Global Travel		
2			Theme Park Ticket Sales-Total		
3					
4		# Tickets Sold		Sales ($)	
5		Adults	Children	Adults	Children
6	Animal Habitat	='[New Mexico.xlsx]Summary'!$B$6+[Colorado.xlsx]Summary!$B$6+[Utah.xlsx]Summary!$B$6			
7	Global Workplaces Florida				
8	Space Adventure				

source file

New Mexico | Colorado | Utah

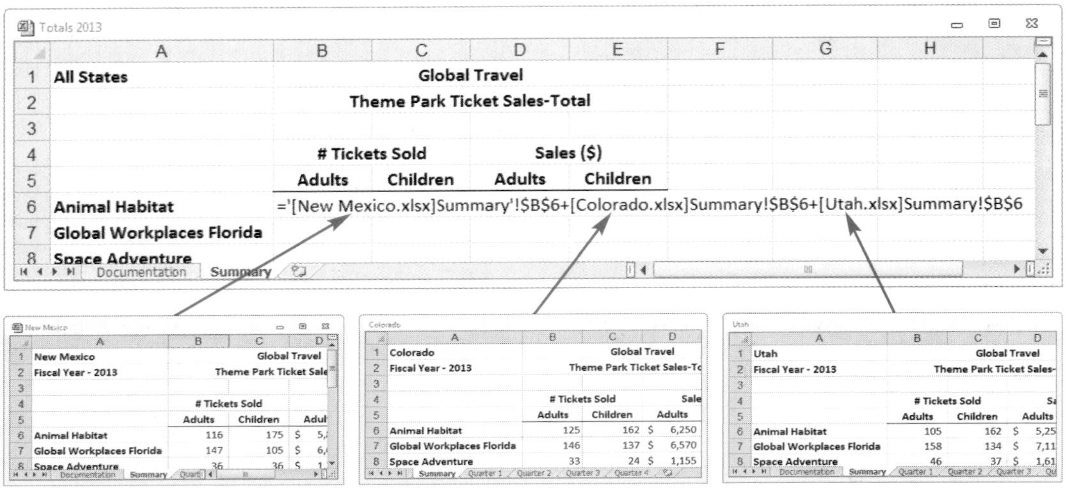

To create the link between destination and source files, you need to insert a formula in the Totals 2013 workbook that references a specific cell or range in the three state workbooks. That reference, called an external reference, has the syntax

```
[WorkbookName]WorksheetName!CellRange
```

where *WorkbookName* is the filename of the workbook (including the file extension) enclosed in square brackets; *WorksheetName* is the name of the worksheet that contains the data followed by an exclamation mark; and *CellRange* is the cell or range that contains the data. For example, the following formula references cell B6 in the Summary worksheet of the Colorado.xlsx workbook:

```
=[Colorado.xlsx]Summary!B6
```

TIP

When you use the point-and-click method to build formulas with external references, Excel enters all of the required punctuation, including quotation marks.

If the workbook name or the worksheet name contains one or more spaces, you must enclose the entire workbook name and worksheet name in single quotation marks. For example, the following formula references cell B6 in the Summary worksheet of the New Mexico.xlsx workbook:

```
='[New Mexico.xlsx]Summary'!B6
```

When the source and destination workbooks are stored in the same folder, you need to include only the workbook name in the external reference. However, when the source and destination workbooks are located in different folders, the workbook reference must include the file's complete location (also called the path). For example, if the destination file is stored in C:\TicketSales and the source file is stored in C:\TicketSales\Domestic Sales, the complete reference in the destination file would be:

```
='C:\TicketSales\Domestic Sales\[New Mexico.xlsx]Summary'!B6
```

The single quotation marks start at the beginning of the path and end immediately before the exclamation mark.

PROSKILLS

Decision Making: Understanding When to Link Workbooks

More than one person is usually involved in developing information that will be used in an organization's decision-making process. If each person has access to only part of the data, everyone's ability to see the whole picture and make good decisions is limited. Linking workbooks provides one way to pull together all of the data being compiled by different people or departments to support the decision-making process.

When deciding whether to link workbooks, consider the following questions:

- **Can separate workbooks have the same purpose and structure?** With linked workbooks, each workbook can focus on a different store, branch office, or department with the same products or expenditure types and reporting periods (such as weekly, monthly, and quarterly).
- **Is a large workbook too unwieldy to use?** A large workbook can be divided into smaller workbooks for each quarter, division, or product and then linked to provide the summary information.
- **Can information from different workbooks be summarized?** Linked workbooks provide a way to quickly and accurately consolidate information from multiple source workbooks, and the summary worksheet will always contain the most current information even when information is later updated.
- **Are source workbooks received from another person or group continually updated?** With linked workbooks, an outdated source workbook can be replaced and the destination workbook will then reflect the latest information.

If you can answer yes to these questions, then linked workbooks are the way to go. Creating linked workbooks can help you analyze data better, leading to better decision making. It also provides greater flexibility as data becomes more expansive and complex.

Navigating Multiple Workbooks

You'll combine the three state worksheets into one regional summary. You'll open all the workbooks you need to reference. Then, you'll switch between them to make each Summary worksheet the active sheet in preparation for creating the external references.

To open the workbooks needed to create the regional summary:

1. If you took a break after the previous session, make sure the New Mexico workbook is open and the Summary worksheet is active.
2. Open the **TravelTotals** workbook located in the Excel6\Tutorial folder included with your Data Files, and then save the workbook as **Totals 2013**.
3. In the Documentation sheet, enter your name and the date, and then make the **Summary** worksheet active.
4. Open the **Utah** and **Colorado** workbooks located in the Excel6\Tutorial folder included with your Data Files.

You'll need to move between open workbooks when you create the external reference formulas in the Totals 2013 workbook. The Switch Windows button in the Window group on the View tab lists each open workbook so you can change which workbook is active. Another method is to click the Excel program button on the taskbar and then click the thumbnail of the workbook you want to make active.

To switch between the open workbooks:

1. Click the **View** tab on the Ribbon, and then, in the Window group, click the **Switch Windows** button to display a list of all the workbooks that are currently open.
2. Click **Utah** to make it the active workbook, and then make the **Summary** sheet active.
3. In the Window group, click the **Switch Windows** button, click **Colorado** to switch to the Colorado workbook, and then make the **Summary** worksheet active.
4. Make the **Totals 2013** workbook the active workbook.

Arranging Multiple Workbooks

You might also want to display all the open workbooks on your screen at the same time. This way, you can easily click among the open workbooks to create links without having to continually change the active workbook, as well as quickly compare the contents of worksheets in different workbooks. You can arrange workbooks in the following layouts:

- **Tiled**, which divides the open workbooks evenly on the screen.
- **Horizontal**, which divides the open workbooks into horizontal bands.
- **Vertical**, which divides the open workbooks into vertical bands.
- **Cascade**, which layers the open workbooks on the screen.

The layout you select will depend on the contents being displayed and your purpose.

REFERENCE

Arranging Workbooks

- On the View tab, in the Window group, click the Arrange All button.
- Select the layout in which you want to arrange the open workbooks.
- When arranging multiple workbooks, uncheck the Windows of active workbook option. When arranging multiple worksheets within one workbook, check the option.
- Click the OK button.

Currently, four workbooks are open but only one is visible. You'll arrange the workbooks using the tiled arrangement.

To tile the open workbooks:

1. In the Window group on the View tab, click the **Arrange All** button. The Arrange Windows dialog box opens so you can select the layout arrangement you want.
2. Click the **Tiled** option button, if necessary. The Tiled option arranges the four Global Travel workbooks evenly on the screen.
3. Click the **OK** button. The four open workbooks appear in a tiled layout.

4. Click in the **Totals 2013** workbook to make it the active workbook, if necessary. In the tiled layout, the active workbook has darker text in the title bar, a gray background, scroll bars, and the active cell. See Figure 6-12.

Figure 6-12 **Four workbooks arranged in a tiled layout**

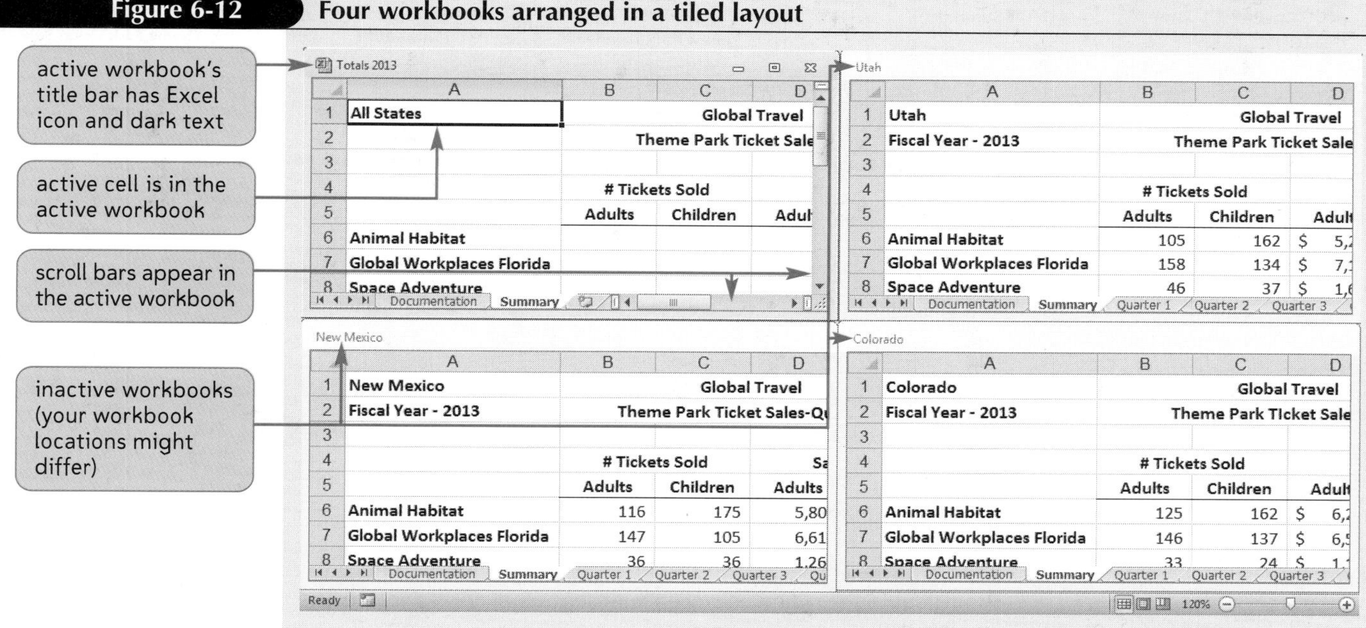

Creating Formulas with External References

A formula can include a reference to another workbook (called an external reference), which creates a set of linked workbooks. The process for entering a formula with an external reference is the same as entering any other formula using references within the same worksheet or workbook. You can enter the formulas by typing them or using the point-and-click method. In most situations, you will use the point-and-click method to switch between the source files and destination files so that Excel enters the references to the workbook, worksheet, and cell using the correct syntax.

You need to enter the external reference formulas in the Totals 2013 workbook to summarize the states' totals into one workbook for Alvin. You'll start by creating the formula that adds the total number of adult tickets to Animal Habitat sold in New Mexico, Utah, and Colorado. You cannot use the SUM function with 3-D references here because you are referencing multiple workbooks and 3-D references can only be used to reference multiple worksheets in the same workbook.

To create the external reference formula to total adult tickets for Animal Habitat:

1. In the Summary worksheet in the Totals 2013 workbook, click cell **B6**, and then type = to begin the formula.

As you create the formula, be sure to verify each external reference before going to the next step.

2. Click anywhere in the **New Mexico** workbook, and then, in the Summary worksheet, click cell **B6**. The external reference to cell B6 in the Summary worksheet of the New Mexico workbook—'[New Mexico.xlsx]Summary'!$B$6—is added to the formula in the Totals 2013 workbook. See Figure 6-13.

Figure 6-13 External reference entered in the formula

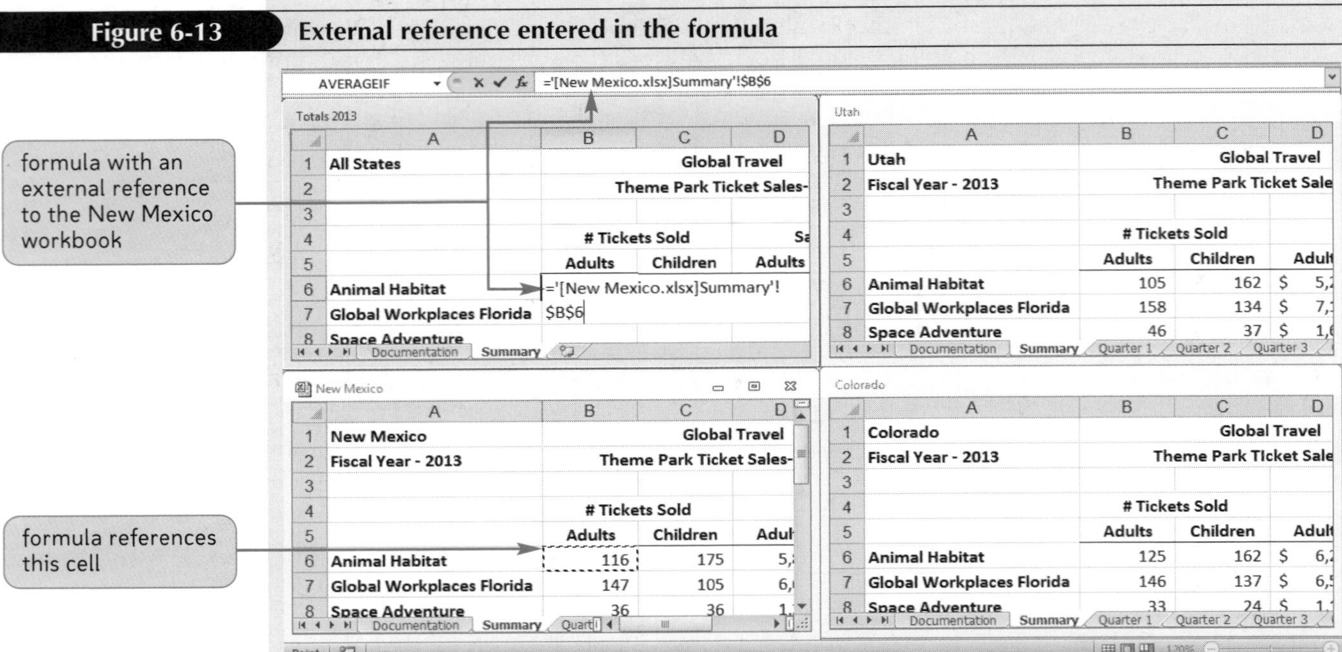

3. Type **+**. The Totals 2013 workbook becomes active and you can continue entering the formula. You need to create an external reference to the Colorado workbook.

4. Click anywhere in the **Colorado** workbook, click cell **B6** in the Summary worksheet, and then type **+**. The formula in the Totals 2013 workbook includes the external reference to the cell that has the total number of adult tickets to Animal Habitat sold in Colorado.

5. Click anywhere in the **Utah** workbook, click cell **B6** in the Summary worksheet, and then press the **Enter** key. The formula with three external references is entered in the Summary sheet in the Totals 2013 workbook.

6. In the Totals 2013 workbook, in the Summary sheet, click cell **B6**. The complete formula appears in the formula bar and the formula results appear in cell B6, showing that 346 adult tickets to Animal Habitat were sold in the three states: 116 in New Mexico, 105 in Utah, and 125 in Colorado. See Figure 6-14.

Figure 6-14 Complete formula with external references

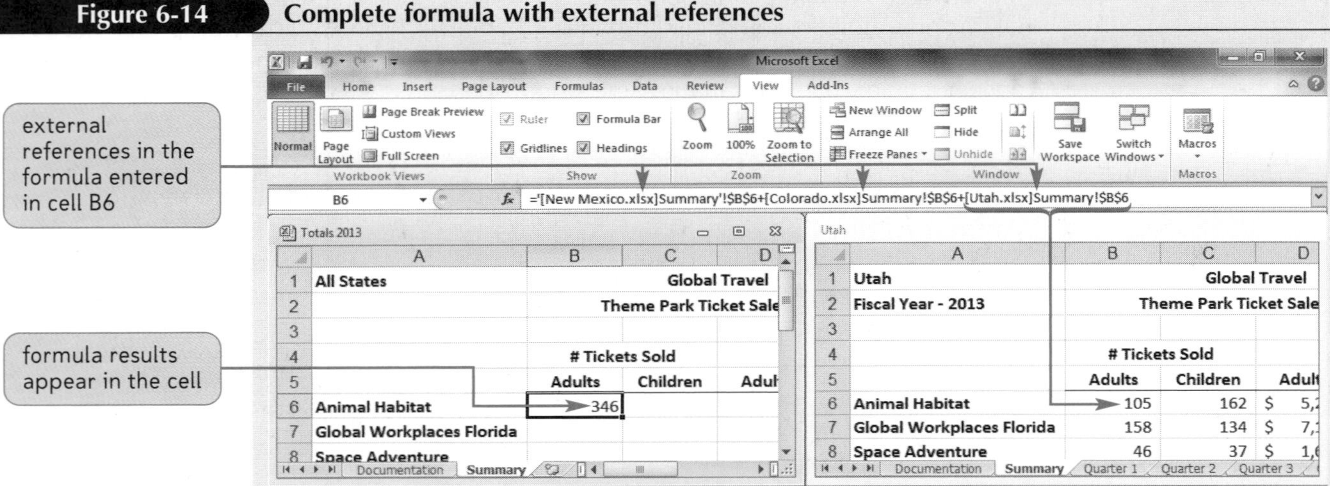

Trouble? If 346 doesn't appear in cell B6 in the Summary sheet in the Totals 2013 workbook, you might have clicked an incorrect cell for an external reference in the formula. Repeat Steps 1 through 6 to correct the formula.

You'll use the same process to enter the external reference formula for cell C6, which is the number of children's tickets to Animal Habitat sold in the three states. Then you'll do the same to create the formulas to calculate the total sales from all three states.

To create the remaining external reference formulas:

1. In the Totals 2013 workbook, in the Summary worksheet, click cell **C6**, and then type = to begin the formula.
2. Click the **New Mexico** workbook, click cell **C6** in the Summary worksheet, and then type **+**. The formula in the Totals 2013 workbook includes the external reference to cell C6 in the Summary worksheet in the New Mexico workbook.
3. Click the **Colorado** workbook, click cell **C6** in the Summary worksheet, and then type **+**. The formula includes an external reference to cell C6 in the Summary worksheet in the Colorado workbook.
4. Click the **Utah** workbook, click cell **C6** in the Summary worksheet, and then press the **Enter** key. The external reference formula is complete.
5. In the Totals 2013 workbook, click cell **C6** in the Summary sheet. Cell C6 displays 499, the total children's tickets sold to Animal Habitat, and the following formula appears in the formula bar: ='[New Mexico.xlsx]Summary'!$C$6+[Colorado.xlsx]Summary!$C$6+[Utah.xlsx]Summary!$C$6.

   Next, you'll enter the external reference formulas in cells D6 and E6 to add the total sales from adult and children's tickets to Animal Habitat.
6. Use the same procedure in Steps 1 through 4 to enter the formula in cell **D6** in the Summary worksheet in the Totals 2013 workbook. The formula results displayed in cell D6 are 17300—the total sales from adult tickets to Animal Habitat in New Mexico, Colorado, and Utah.
7. Use the same procedure in Steps 1 through 4 to enter the formula in cell **E6** in the Summary worksheet in the Totals 2013 workbook. You may need to scroll each worksheet to see cell E6. The formula results displayed in cell E6 are 18962—the total sales from children's tickets to Animal Habitat in New Mexico, Colorado, and Utah.

You need to enter the remaining formulas for the other six theme parks. Rather than creating the rest of the external reference formulas manually, you can copy the formulas in row 6 to rows 7 through 12. The formulas created using the point-and-click method contain absolute references. Before you copy them to other cells, you need to change them to use mixed references because the rows in the formula need to change.

To edit the external reference formulas to use mixed references:

1. Maximize the Totals 2013 workbook. The Totals 2013 workbook fills the program window. The other workbooks are still open but are not visible.
2. In the Summary worksheet, double-click cell **B6** to enter Edit mode and display the formula in the cell.

TIP

You can also create the mixed reference by deleting the $ symbol from the row references in the formula.

3. Click in the first absolute reference in the formula, and then press the **F4** key twice to change the absolute reference $B$6 to the mixed reference $B6.
4. Edit the other two absolute references in the formula to be mixed references with absolute column references and relative row references.
5. Press the **Enter** key. The formula is updated to include mixed references, but the formula results aren't affected. Cell B6 still displays 346, which is correct.
6. Edit the formulas in cells C6, D6, and E6 to change the absolute references to the mixed references $C6, $D6, and $E6, respectively. The formulas are updated, but the cells in the range C6:E6 still correctly display 499, 17300, and 18962, respectively.

With the formulas corrected to include mixed references, you can now copy the external reference formulas in cells B6:E6 to the other rows. Then, you'll enter the SUM function to total the values in each column.

To copy and paste the external reference formulas:

1. Select the range **B6:E6**, and then drag the fill handle to select the range **B7:E12**. The formulas are copied to the range B7:E12 and the formula results appear in the cells. The Auto Fill Options button appears in the lower-right corner of the selected range, but you do not need to use it.
2. In cell B13, enter the SUM function to add the range **B6:B12**. A total of 2035 adult tickets were sold for all theme parks.
3. Copy the formula in cell B13 to the range **C13:E13**. The totals are 1855, 81889, and 55704, respectively.
4. Format the range B6:C13 with the **Comma** style and no decimal places, and then format the range D6:E13 with the **Accounting** number format and no decimal place.
5. Format the range B12:E12 with a **bottom border**, and then click cell **A1** to deselect the range. See Figure 6-15.

Figure 6-15 **Completed formulas in the Summary worksheet in the Totals 2013 workbook**

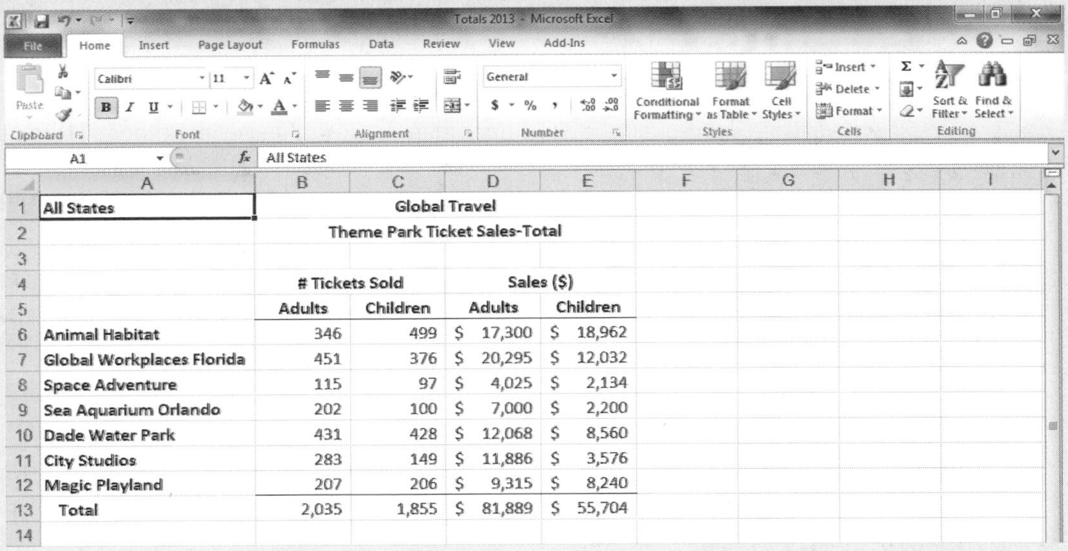

Totals 2013 - Microsoft Excel

File | Home | Insert | Page Layout | Formulas | Data | Review | View | Add-Ins

A1 | fx | All States

	A	B	C	D	E
1	All States	Global Travel			
2		Theme Park Ticket Sales-Total			
3					
4		# Tickets Sold		Sales ($)	
5		Adults	Children	Adults	Children
6	Animal Habitat	346	499	$ 17,300	$ 18,962
7	Global Workplaces Florida	451	376	$ 20,295	$ 12,032
8	Space Adventure	115	97	$ 4,025	$ 2,134
9	Sea Aquarium Orlando	202	100	$ 7,000	$ 2,200
10	Dade Water Park	431	428	$ 12,068	$ 8,560
11	City Studios	283	149	$ 11,886	$ 3,576
12	Magic Playland	207	206	$ 9,315	$ 8,240
13	Total	2,035	1,855	$ 81,889	$ 55,704
14					

Alvin is pleased; the regional summary results match the executive team's expectations.

INSIGHT

Managing Linked Workbooks

As you work with a linked workbook, you might need to replace a source file or change where you stored the source and destination files. However, replacing or moving a file can affect the linked workbook. Keep in mind the following guidelines to manage your linked workbooks:

- If you rename a source file, the destination workbook won't be able to find it. A dialog box opens, indicating "This workbook contains one or more links that cannot be updated." Click the Continue button to open the workbook with the most recent values, or click the Change Source button in the Edit Links dialog box to specify the new name of that linked source file.
- If you move a source file to a different folder, the link breaks between the destination and source files. Click the Change Source button in the Edit Links dialog box to specify the new location of the linked workbook.
- If you receive a replacement source file, you can swap the original source file with the replacement file. No additional changes are needed.
- If you receive a destination workbook but the source files are not included, Excel will not be able to find the source files, and a dialog box opens with the message "This workbook contains one or more links that cannot be updated." Click the Continue button to open the workbook with the most recent values, or click the Break Link button in the Edit Links dialog box to replace the external references with the existing values.
- If you change the name of a destination file, you can open that renamed version destination file without affecting the source files or the original destination file.

Updating Linked Workbooks

When workbooks are linked, it is important that the data in the destination file accurately reflects the contents of the source file. When data in a source file changes, you want the destination file to reflect those changes. If both the source and destination files are open when you make a change, the destination file is updated automatically. If the destination file is closed when you make a change in a source file, you choose whether to update the link to display the current values, or continue to display the older values from the destination file when you open the destination file.

Updating a Destination Workbook with Source Workbooks Open

When both the destination and source workbooks are open, any changes you make in a source workbook appear in the destination workbook. Rhohit tells Alvin that the total New Mexico children's sales for Animal Habitat in Quarter 4 is actually $1,000 more than recorded. After you correct the value in the Quarter 4 worksheet, the amount in the Summary worksheet of the New Mexico workbook and the regional total in the Totals 2013 workbook also change if both the source and destination files are open.

To update the source workbook with the destination file open:

1. Switch to the **New Mexico** workbook, and then make the **Quarter 4** worksheet active. You'll update the value of the Animal Habitat children's dollar amount in this worksheet.

2. In cell E6, enter **2786**. The Animal Habitat children's sales are updated.
3. Switch to the **Summary** worksheet in the New Mexico workbook, and then verify that the total Animal Habitat children's sales is now $7,650.
4. Switch to the **Totals 2013** workbook, and then, in the Summary worksheet, verify that the value in cell E6 is $19,962 and the total dollar amount from sales of children's tickets is $56,704, reflecting the new value you entered in the New Mexico workbook. Because both the destination and source files are open, Excel updated the destination file automatically.
5. Save the New Mexico and Totals 2013 workbooks, and then close the Utah, Colorado, and Totals 2013 workbooks. The New Mexico workbook remains open.

Updating a Destination Workbook with Source Workbooks Closed

When you save a workbook that contains external reference formulas, such as Totals 2013, Excel stores the most recent results of those formulas in the destination file. Source files, such as the New Mexico, Colorado, and Utah workbooks, are often updated while the destination file is closed. In that case, the values in the destination file are not updated at the same time the source files are updated. The next time you open the destination file, the cells containing external reference formulas still display the old values. Therefore, some of the values in the edited source workbooks are different from the values in the destination workbook.

To update the destination workbook with the current data, you must specify that you want the update to occur. As part of the Excel security system that attempts to protect against malicious software, links to other workbooks are not updated without your permission. When you open a workbook with external reference formulas (the destination file), a Security Warning appears in the Information Bar, notifying you that the automatic update of links has been disabled. If you "trust" the provider of the source file(s), you can enable the content, which allows the external reference formulas to function and updates the links in the destination workbook. If you do not "trust" the provider of the source files or do not want the destination file updated at that time, do not enable the content. The old values in the destination workbook are displayed and the links to the source files remain disabled.

Rhohit informs Alvin that the New Mexico workbook needs a second correction. Space Adventure adult sales in Quarter 4 are $435, not $385, which is the current value in the New Mexico workbook. You will increase the amount of the Space Adventure adult sales in Quarter 4 by $50. As a result, sales in the Summary sheet of the New Mexico workbook and the regional total in the Totals 2013 workbook will both increase by $50. You'll edit the source file, the New Mexico workbook, while the destination file is closed.

To update the source workbook with the destination file closed:

1. In the New Mexico workbook, make the **Quarter 4** worksheet active.
2. In cell D8, enter **435**. The sales total for adults in Quarter 4 increases to $7,241.
3. Switch to the **Summary** worksheet. The sales total for 2013 in cell D8 is $1,310 and the adult sales total is $26,375. See Figure 6-16.

Figure 6-16 **Summary worksheet with revised Quarter 4 sales for Space Adventure**

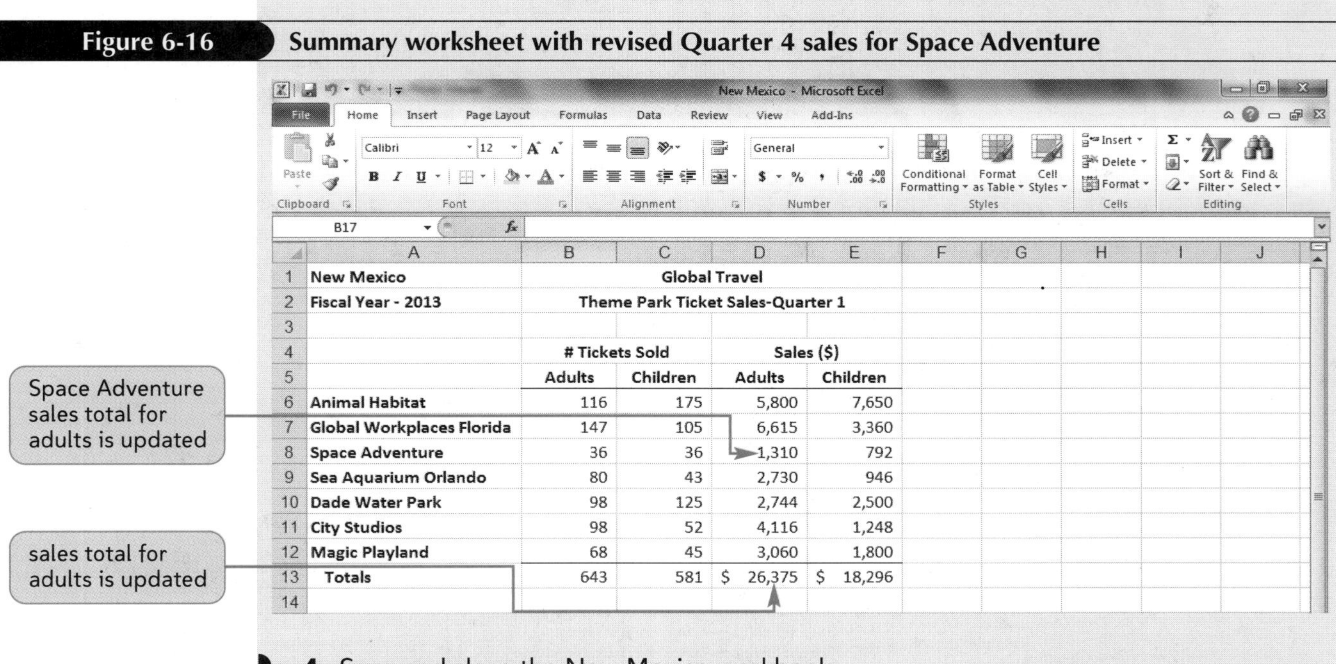

	A	B	C	D	E
1	New Mexico	Global Travel			
2	Fiscal Year - 2013	Theme Park Ticket Sales-Quarter 1			
3					
4		# Tickets Sold		Sales ($)	
5		Adults	Children	Adults	Children
6	Animal Habitat	116	175	5,800	7,650
7	Global Workplaces Florida	147	105	6,615	3,360
8	Space Adventure	36	36	1,310	792
9	Sea Aquarium Orlando	80	43	2,730	946
10	Dade Water Park	98	125	2,744	2,500
11	City Studios	98	52	4,116	1,248
12	Magic Playland	68	45	3,060	1,800
13	Totals	643	581	$ 26,375	$ 18,296

4. Save and close the New Mexico workbook.

Now you'll open the destination file (the Totals 2013 workbook). The total adult sales calculated from the source workbooks won't be updated until you specify that they should. When the destination file is open and the source files are closed, the complete file path is included as part of the external reference formula that appears in the formula bar.

To open and update the destination workbook:

1. Open the **Totals 2013** workbook, and then switch to the **Summary** worksheet, if necessary. The value in cell D8 has *not* changed; it still is $4,025. A Security Warning message appears in the Information Bar, indicating that automatic update of links has been disabled. See Figure 6-17.

Figure 6-17 **Security Warning in the Information Bar**

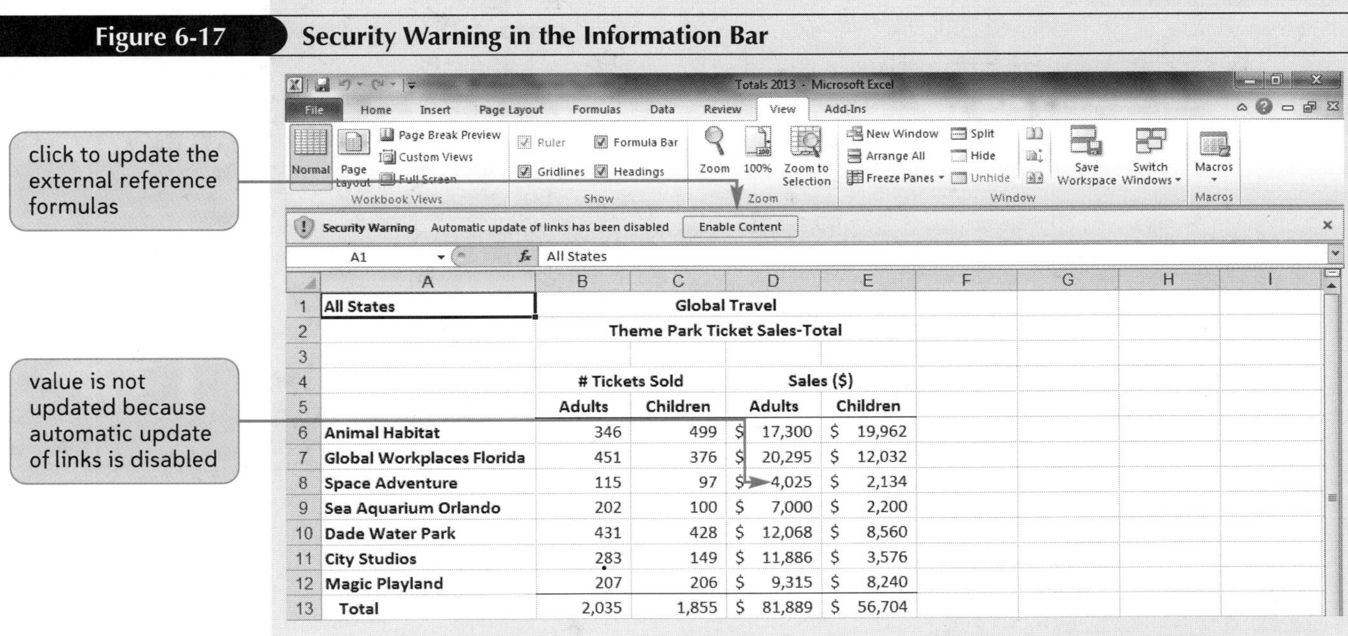

	A	B	C	D	E
1	All States	Global Travel			
2		Theme Park Ticket Sales-Total			
3					
4		# Tickets Sold		Sales ($)	
5		Adults	Children	Adults	Children
6	Animal Habitat	346	499	$ 17,300	$ 19,962
7	Global Workplaces Florida	451	376	$ 20,295	$ 12,032
8	Space Adventure	115	97	$ 4,025	$ 2,134
9	Sea Aquarium Orlando	202	100	$ 7,000	$ 2,200
10	Dade Water Park	431	428	$ 12,068	$ 8,560
11	City Studios	283	149	$ 11,886	$ 3,576
12	Magic Playland	207	206	$ 9,315	$ 8,240
13	Total	2,035	1,855	$ 81,889	$ 56,704

You want the current values in the source files to appear in the destination workbook.

2. In the Information Bar, click the **Enable Content** button. The values in the destination file are updated. The sales total in cell D8 of the Totals 2013 workbook increases to $4,075 and the total in cell D13 increases to $81,939.
3. Click cell **D8**, and then look at the complete file path for each external reference in the formula. The full path appears because the source workbooks are closed.
4. Save the workbook.

Managing Links

When workbooks are linked, the Edit Links dialog box provides ways to manage the links. You can review the status of the links, update the data in the files, repair broken links, open the source file, and break the links, which converts all external reference formulas to their most recent values.

After the fiscal year audit is completed and the source workbooks are final, Alvin will archive the summary workbook and move the files to an off-site storage location as part of his year-end backup process. You will save a copy of the Totals 2013 workbook and then break the links to the source files in the copy.

To save a copy of the Totals 2013 workbook and open the Edit Links dialog box:

1. Save the Totals 2013 workbook as **Audited 2013** in the Excel6\Tutorial folder included with your Data Files. The Totals 2013 workbook closes and the Audited 2013 workbook remains open.
2. Click the **Data** tab on the Ribbon.
3. In the Connections group, click the **Edit Links** button. The Edit Links dialog box opens. See Figure 6-18.

Figure 6-18 **Edit Links dialog box**

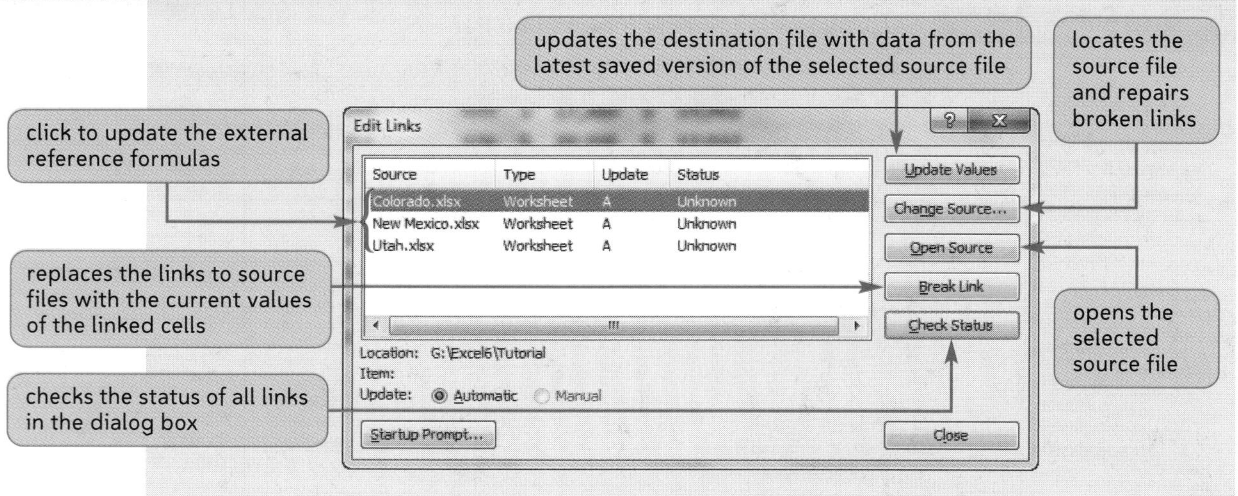

The Edit Links dialog box lists all of the files that the destination workbook is linked to so that you can update, change, open, or remove the links. You can see that the destination workbook, Audited 2013, has links to the Colorado, New Mexico, and Utah workbooks. The dialog box shows the following information about each link:

- **Source** indicates the file to which the link points. The Audited 2013 workbook contains three links pointing to the New Mexico.xlsx, Colorado.xlsx, and Utah.xlsx workbooks.
- **Type** identifies the type of each source file. In this case, the type is an Excel worksheet but it could also be a Word document, a PowerPoint presentation, or some other type of file.
- **Update** specifies the way values are updated from the source file. The letter *A* indicates the link is updated automatically when you open the workbook or when both the source and destination files are open simultaneously. The letter *M* indicates the link must be updated manually by the user, which is useful when you want to see the older data values before updating to the new data. To manually update the link and see the new data values, click the Update Values button.
- **Status** shows whether Excel successfully accessed the link and updated the values from the source document (status is OK), or Excel has not attempted to update the links in this session (status is Unknown). The status of the three links in the Audited 2013 workbook is Unknown.

You'll break the links so that the Audited 2013 workbook contains only the updated values (and is no longer affected by changes in the source files). Then you'll save the Audited 2013 workbook for Alvin to archive. This allows Alvin to store a "snapshot" of the data at the end of the fiscal year.

To convert all external reference formulas to their current values:

TIP

You cannot undo the break link action. To restore the links, you must reenter the external reference formulas.

1. Click the **Break Link** button. A dialog box opens, alerting you that breaking links in the workbook permanently converts formulas and external references to their existing values.
2. Click the **Break Links** button. No links appear in the Edit Links dialog box.
3. Click the **Close** button. The Audited 2013 workbook now contains values instead of formulas with external references.
4. Click cell **B6**. The value 346 appears in the cell and the formula bar; the link (the external reference formula) was replaced with the data value. All cells in the range B6:E12 contain values rather than external reference formulas.
5. Save and close the Audited 2013 workbook. The Totals 2013 workbook has external reference formulas, and the Audited 2013 workbook has current values.

Creating an Excel Workspace

When working with multiple related workbooks, such as Alvin's four workbooks that contain the ticket sales data, you may want to access all of the workbooks at one time. Rather than having to open each workbook individually, you can create a workspace to open multiple workbooks at one time, saving time and avoiding having to remember all the filenames and folder locations.

A workspace is an Excel file that saves information about all of the currently opened workbooks, such as their locations, window sizes, zoom magnifications, and other settings. The workspace file has the file extension .xlw. The workspace does not contain the workbooks themselves—only information about them. To use that set of workbooks, you open the workspace file. Excel then opens the workbooks and settings in the same configuration they were in when you saved the workspace file. Even if a workbook is included in a workspace file, you can still open that workbook separately.

You will create a workspace file for Alvin that includes the four workbooks in a cascade layout, which arranges the open workbooks so that they overlap each other with all the title bars visible. Alvin prefers this layout because he can see more of the active workbook.

TIP

The workspace file contains only the location and name of each file, not the actual workbooks and worksheets. To use the workspace on another computer, you must copy the workspace file *and* the workbook files.

To create the Theme Parks workspace file:

1. Open the **Colorado**, **New Mexico**, **Utah**, and **Totals 2013** workbooks located in the Excel6\Tutorial folder included with your Data Files, clicking the **Don't Update** button in the dialog that opens indicating that the workbook contains links. Four workbooks are open.
2. Make sure the **Summary** worksheet is the active worksheet in each workbook.
3. Switch to the **Totals 2013** workbook.
4. Click the **View** tab on the Ribbon, and then click the **Arrange All** button in the Window group. The Arrange Windows dialog box opens.
5. Click the **Cascade** option button, and then click the **OK** button. The four workbooks overlap each other, with the title bars visible. See Figure 6-19.

Figure 6-19 Workbooks arranged in cascade layout

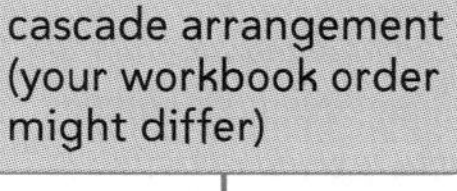

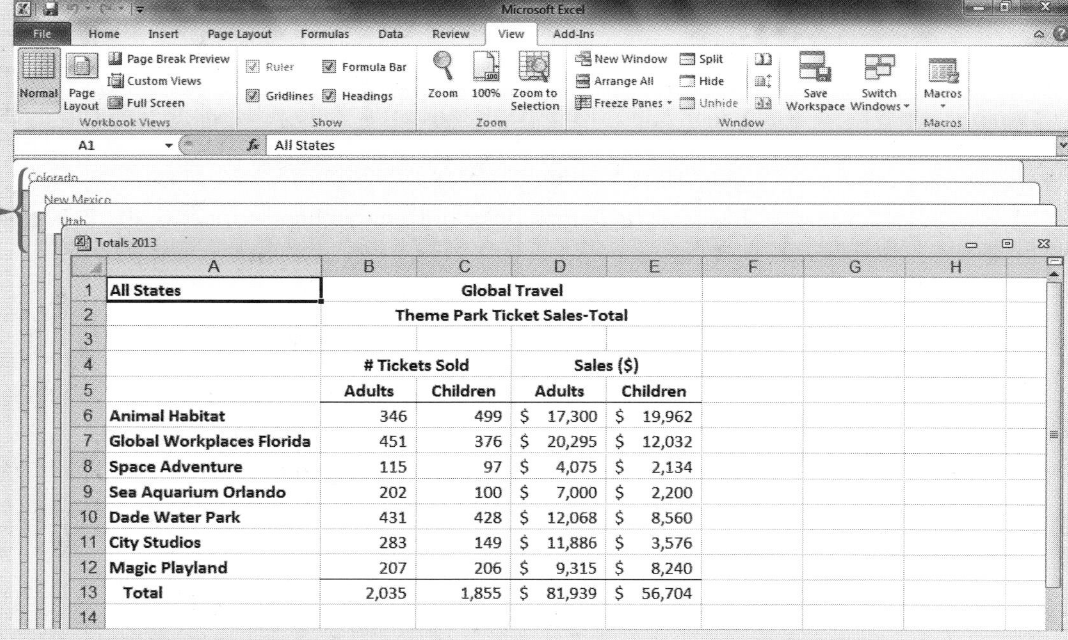

6. In the Window group, click the **Save Workspace** button. The Save Workspace dialog box opens and functions similarly to the Save As dialog box.
7. Type **Theme Parks** in the File name box, verify that **Workspaces** is selected in the Save as type box, verify that the save location is the Excel6\Tutorial folder, and then click the **Save** button. A dialog box might open, prompting you to save your changes to the open workbook files, if you haven't already done so.
8. If prompted to save changes, click the **Save** button. The Theme Parks workspace file is saved. The workspace file has the file extension .xlw.

You will test the workspace file you created to make sure it opens all four Global Travel workbooks.

To open the Theme Parks workspace:

1. Close all four workbooks.
2. Click the **File** tab on the Ribbon, and then click the **Open** command in the navigation bar. The Open dialog box opens, displaying the Excel6\Tutorial folder. The icon for the Theme Parks workspace file is different from the Excel workbook file icon.
3. Click the **Theme Parks** workspace file, and then click the **Open** button. A dialog box opens, indicating that the workbook contains links.
4. Click the **Don't Update** button. The four travel workbooks open and are arranged in a cascade layout, the same layout in which you saved them. You can work with the workbooks as usual.
5. Click the **Colorado** workbook title bar to bring it to the front of the cascaded workbooks. Colorado is now the active workbook.

   The workspace file provides a quick way to open a series of workbooks in a specific display. Because it doesn't actually contain the workbooks, you must close each workbook separately, saving as needed.
6. Close the New Mexico, Utah, Colorado, and Totals 2013 workbooks without saving any changes.

In this session, you worked with multiple worksheets and workbooks, summarizing data and linking workbooks. This ensures that the data in the summary workbook is accurate and remains updated with the latest data in the source files. In the next session, you will create templates, hyperlinks, and a Web page.

REVIEW

Session 6.2 Quick Check

1. What is the external reference to the range A1:A10 in the Sales Info worksheet in the Product Report workbook located in the Reports folder on drive D?
2. What is a source file?
3. What is a destination file?
4. How are linked workbooks updated when both the destination and source files are open?
5. How are linked workbooks updated when the source file is changed and the destination file is closed?
6. How would you determine to what workbooks a destination file is linked?
7. What is a workspace?
8. Explain how creating a workspace file can help you organize your work.

SESSION 6.3 VISUAL OVERVIEW

This Travel expense report workbook was created from one of the templates available from Office.com. Microsoft provides many other templates that you can download.

From Backstage view, you can save the open workbook to your SkyDrive and then use the Exel Web App to work on that file from any computer with an Internet connection.

A **template** is a workbook with labels, formats, and formulas already built into it with data removed. In other words, a template includes everything but the variable data.

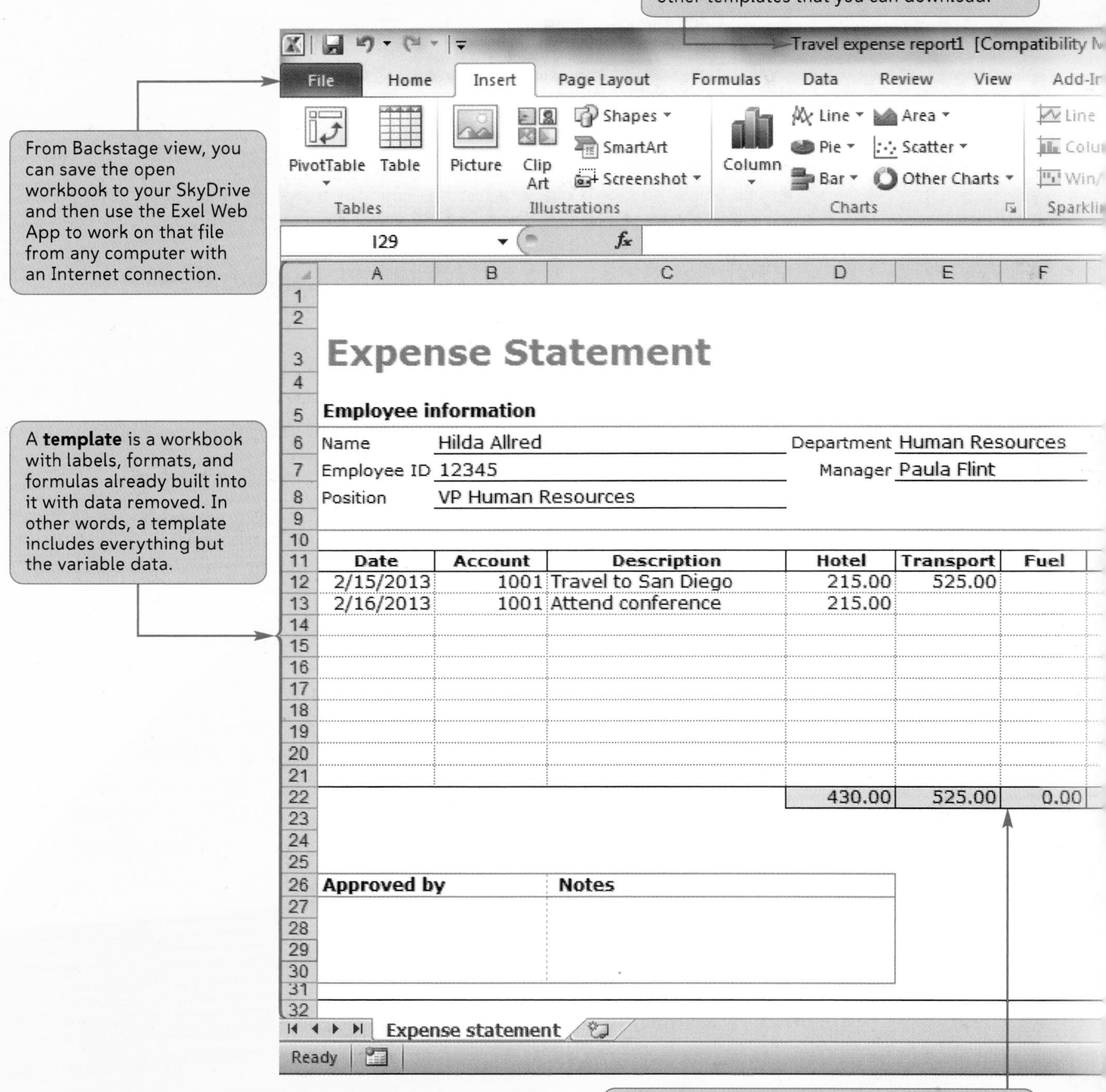

A template can use any Excel feature, including formatting, formulas, charts, data validation, cell protection, and macros. The template used to create this workbook includes labels, formatting, and formulas.

TEMPLATES AND HYPERLINKS

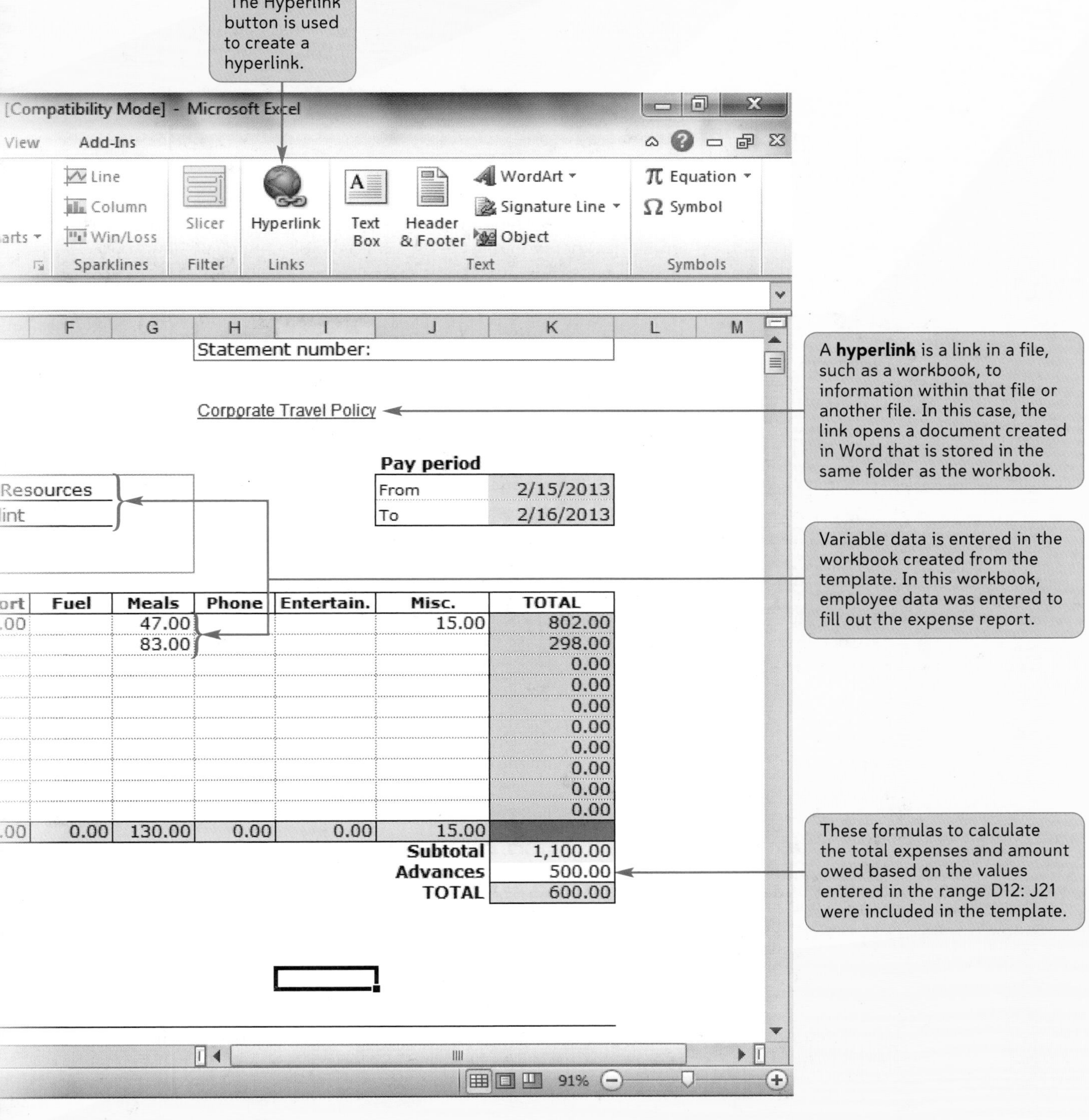

Creating a Hyperlink

A hyperlink is a link in a file, such as a workbook, to information within that file or another file. Although hyperlinks are most often found on Web pages, they can also be placed in a worksheet and used to quickly jump to a specific cell or range within the active worksheet, another worksheet, or another workbook. Hyperlinks can also be used to jump to other files, such as a Word document or a PowerPoint presentation, or sites on the Web.

Inserting a Hyperlink

You can insert a hyperlink directly in a workbook file to link to information in that workbook, another workbook, or a file associated with another application on your computer, a shared file on a network, or a Web site. Hyperlinks are usually represented by colored words with underlines or images. When you click a hyperlink, the computer switches to the file or portion of the file referenced by the hyperlink.

REFERENCE

Inserting a Hyperlink

- Select the text, graphic, or cell in which you want to insert the hyperlink.
- In the Links group on the Insert tab, click the Hyperlink button.
- To link to a file or Web page, click Existing File or Web Page in the Link to list, and then select the file or Web page from the Look in box.
- To link to a location in the current workbook, click Place in This Document in the Link to list, and then select the worksheet, cell, or range in the current workbook.
- To link to a new document, click Create New Document in the Link to list, and then specify the filename and path of the new document.
- To link to an email address, click E-mail Address in the Link to list, and then enter the email address of the recipient and a subject line for the message.
- Click the OK button.

Alvin wrote a memo summarizing the sales results for New Mexico, Utah, and Colorado in 2013. He wants the Totals 2013 workbook to include a link to this memo that points to the Sales 2013 Word document.

To insert a hyperlink into the Totals 2013 workbook:

1. Open the **Totals 2013** workbook located in the Excel6\Tutorial folder included with your Data Files, but don't update the links.
2. Maximize the Totals 2013 worksheet window.
3. Switch to the **Documentation** worksheet, and then click cell **A8**. You want to create the hyperlink in this cell.
4. Click the **Insert** tab on the Ribbon, and then click the **Hyperlink** button in the Links group. The Insert Hyperlink dialog box opens. You use this dialog box to define the hyperlink.

5. If necessary, click the **Existing File or Web Page** button in the Link to bar and click the **Current Folder** button in the Look in area. All the existing files and folders in the Tutorial folder, which is the folder where the Totals 2013 workbook is stored, are displayed. See Figure 6-20.

Figure 6-20 Insert Hyperlink dialog box

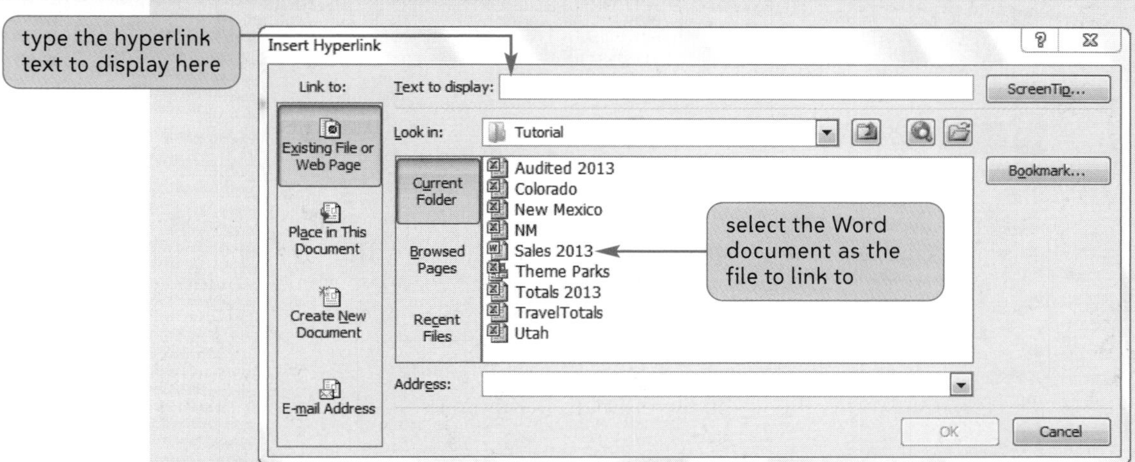

6. Click the **Text to display** box, and then type **Click here to read Executive Memo**. This is the hyperlink text that will appear in cell A8 in the Documentation worksheet.
7. Click the **Sales 2013** Word document in the list of files. This is the file you want to open when the hyperlink is clicked.
8. Click the **OK** button. As shown in Figure 6-21, the hyperlink text entered in cell A8 is underlined and in a blue font, indicating that the text within the cell is a hyperlink.

Figure 6-21 Hyperlink to the Sales 2013 document

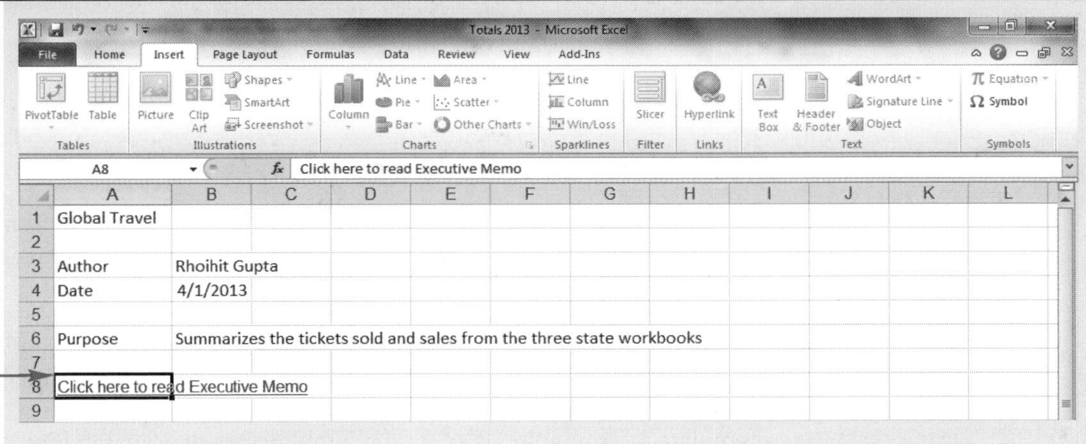

You will test the hyperlink that you just created to ensure it works correctly. To use a hyperlink in a worksheet, you must click the text inside the cell that contains the link. If you click white space in the cell or any text that flows into an adjacent cell, the hyperlink does not work.

To test the hyperlink:

1. Point to the text in cell **A8** until the pointer changes to the pointer icon, and then click the hyperlink. The Sales 2013 document opens in Word.

   Trouble? If the hyperlink doesn't work, you might have clicked the text that overflows cell A8. Point to the text within cell A8, and then click the hyperlink.

2. Close the Word document and exit Word. The Documentation worksheet in the Totals 2013 workbook is active. The hyperlink in cell A8 changed color to indicate that you used the link.

TIP

To delete a hyperlink, right-click the hyperlink cell and then click Clear Contents. To delete the hyperlink but keep the text, right-click the hyper-link cell, and then click Remove Hyperlink.

Editing a Hyperlink

You can modify an existing hyperlink by changing its target file or Web page, modifying the text that is displayed, or changing the ScreenTip for the hyperlink. ScreenTips, which appear whenever you place the pointer over a hyperlink, provide additional information about the target of the link. The default ScreenTip is the folder location and filename of the file you will link to, which isn't very helpful. You can insert a more descriptive ScreenTip when you create a hyperlink or edit an existing hyperlink.

You will edit the hyperlink to the memo so that it has a more descriptive ScreenTip.

To edit the hyperlink:

1. In the Documentation worksheet, right-click cell **A8**, and then click **Edit Hyperlink** on the shortcut menu. The Edit Hyperlink dialog box opens; it has the same layout and information as the Insert Hyperlink dialog box.
2. Click the **ScreenTip** button. The Set Hyperlink ScreenTip dialog box opens.
3. Type **Click to view sales analysis for 2013** in the ScreenTip text box, and then click the **OK** button.
4. Click the **OK** button to close the Edit Hyperlink dialog box.
5. Point to the text in cell **A8**, and then confirm that the ScreenTip "Click to view sales analysis for 2013" appears just below the cell.
6. Save and close the Totals 2013 workbook.

Creating Templates

If you want to create a new workbook that has the same format as an existing workbook, you could save the existing workbook with a new name and replace the values with new data or blank cells. The potential drawback to this method is that you might forget to rename the original file and overwrite data you intended to keep. A better method is to create a template workbook that includes all the text (row and column labels), formatting, and formulas but does not contain any data. The template workbook is a model from which you create new workbooks. When you create a new workbook from a template, an unnamed copy of the template opens. You can then enter data as well as modify the existing content or structure as needed. Any changes or additions you make to the new workbook do not affect the template file; the next time you create a workbook based on the template, the original text, formatting, and formulas will be present.

The three state workbooks for 2013 have the same format. Alvin wants to use this workbook format for data collection and analysis for next year. You will create a template from one of the state workbooks.

PROSKILLS

Teamwork: Using Excel Templates

A team working together will often need to create the same types of workbooks. Rather than each person or group designing a different workbook, each team member should create a workbook from the same template. The completed workbooks will then all have the same structure with identical formatting and formulas. Not only does this ensure consistency and accuracy, it also makes it easier to compile and summarize the results. Templates help teams work better together and avoid misunderstandings.

For example, a large organization may need to collect the same information from several regions. By creating and distributing a workbook template, each region knows what data to track and where to enter it. The template already includes the formulas, so the results are calculated consistently.

The following are just some of the advantages of building and using templates to create multiple workbooks with the same features:

- Templates save time and ensure consistency in the design and content of workbooks because all labels, formatting, and formulas are entered once.
- Templates ensure accuracy because formulas can be entered and verified once, and then be used with confidence in all workbooks.
- Templates standardize the appearance and content of workbooks.
- Templates prevent data from being overwritten when an existing workbook is inadvertently saved with new data rather than saved as a new workbook.

If you are part of a team that needs to create the same type of workbook repeatedly, it's a good idea to use a template to both save time and ensure consistency in the design and content of the workbooks.

Creating a Workbook Based on an Existing Template

The blank Book1 workbook that opens when you start Excel is based on the **default template**. The default template contains no text or formulas, but it includes all the formatting available in every new workbook: General number format applied to numbers, Calibri 11-point font, labels aligned to the left side of a cell, values and the formula results aligned to the right side of a cell, column width set to 8.43 characters, three worksheets inserted in the workbook, and so forth.

Excel has many other templates available. Some are automatically installed on your hard drive when you install Excel. Other templates are available to download from the Office.com site. These templates provide commonly used worksheet formats, saving you from "reinventing the wheel." Some of the task-specific templates available from the Office.com site include:

- **Monthly Family Budget.** This template builds projections and actual expenditures for items such as housing, transportation, and insurance.
- **Inventory List.** This template tracks the cost and quantity reorder levels of inventory.
- **Team Roster.** This template organizes a list with each player's name, phone number, email address, and so forth.
- **Time sheets.** This template creates an online time card to track employees' work hours.

You will create a new workbook based on one of the Excel templates provided by Microsoft.

REFERENCE

Creating a Workbook Based on a Template

- Click the File tab on the Ribbon, and then click the New tab in the navigation bar.
- In the center pane, click a template category for the type of workbook you want to create, and then click a template.
- In the right pane, check the preview, and then click the Download button.
- Save the workbook with a new filename.

You'll download the Employee Timecard template. Note that you need an Internet connection to complete the following set of steps. If you don't have an Internet connection, you should read but not complete the steps involving creating and using the online template.

To create a workbook based on the Employee Timecard template:

1. Click the **File** tab on the Ribbon, and then click the **New** tab in the navigation bar. The center pane shows the available templates on your computer and template categories on Office.com.
2. Click the **Time sheets** folder. All the available templates in this category appear in the center pane. There are several time sheet templates.

   Trouble? If you cannot find the Time sheets folder, you can search for the folder. In the search box to the ri ght of the Office.com Templates header, type **Employee timecard**, and then click the Start searching arrow.
3. Click the **Employee timecard (daily, weekly, monthly, and yearly)** template. A preview of a worksheet based on the selected template appears in the right pane. See Figure 6-22.

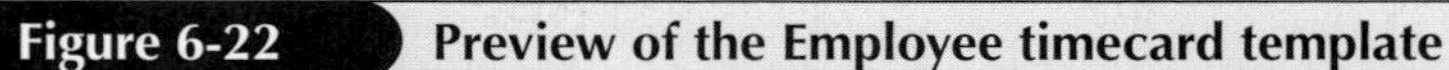

Figure 6-22 Preview of the Employee timecard template

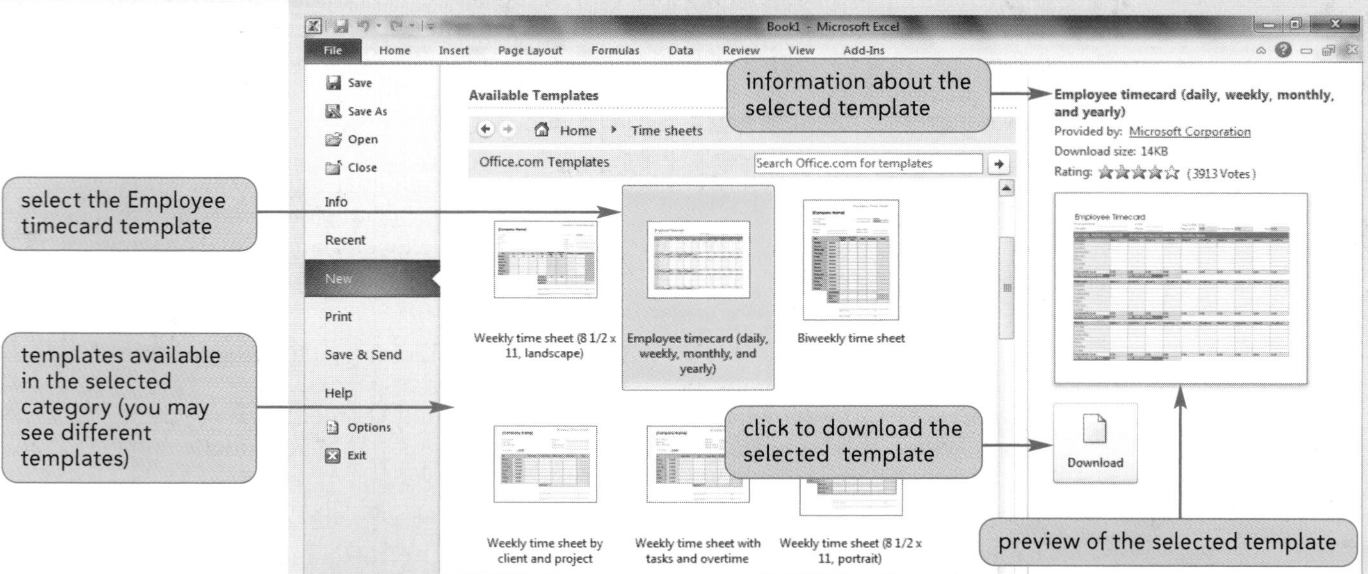

4. Click the **Download** button in the right pane. A new workbook based on the selected template opens. See Figure 6-23.

Figure 6-23 Workbook created from the Employee timecard template

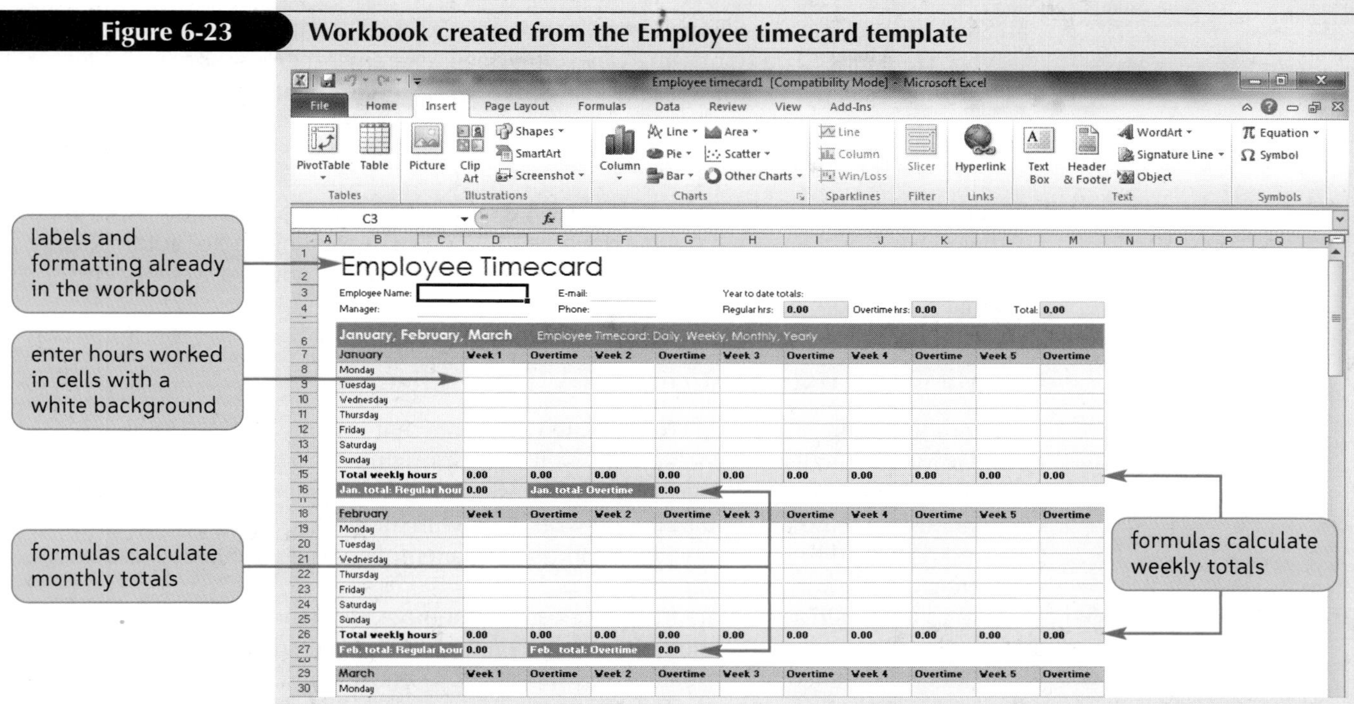

A workbook based on a specific template always displays the name of the template followed by a sequential number. Just as a blank workbook that you open is named Book1, Book2, and so forth, the workbook based on the Employee timecard template is named "Employee timecard1" in the title bar, not "Employee timecard." Any changes or additions to data, formatting, or formulas that you make affect only this workbook and not the template (in this case, the Employee timecard template). If you want to save your changes, you must save the workbook with a new name, the same way you save any new workbook.

Look at the labels and formatting already included in the Employee timecard workbook. Some cells have descriptive labels, others are blank so you can enter data in them, and still other cells contain formulas where calculations for total hours worked each day and pay category will be automatically displayed as data is entered.

You'll enter data for Ed Hoot, the student assisting Alvin, in the worksheet based on the Employee timecard template.

To enter data in the Employee timecard1 workbook:

1. In cell C3, enter **Ed Hoot**.
2. In cell D8, enter **8**. This is the total regular hours Ed worked on Monday. Totals appear in cells D15, D16, I4, and M4 because formulas are already entered into these cells. Cell D15 shows 8 hours worked that week, cell D16 shows the number of hours worked in January, cell I4 shows the number of regular hours worked that year, and cell M4 shows the number of total hours worked that year.
3. In cell D9, enter **8** as the regular hours Ed worked on Tuesday, and then, in cell E9, enter **2** as the overtime hours Ed worked on Tuesday. The totals are updated to 16 regular hours worked that week, 2 overtime hours worked that week, and 18 total hours worked that year.

4. Save the workbook as **Hoot Time Card** in the Excel6\Tutorial folder included with your Data Files. The Hoot Time Card workbook, like any other workbook, is saved with the .xlsx file extension. It does not overwrite the template file.
5. Close the workbook.

Each day Ed Hoot works at Global Travel, he or his supervisor can open the Hoot Time Card workbook and enter the hours Ed worked that day. The total hours are automatically updated. You can see how useful templates with formulas can produce a weekly time card that is fully formatted.

Creating a Custom Workbook Template

A **custom template** is a workbook template you create that is ready to run with the formulas for all calculations included as well as all formatting. A template can use any Excel feature, including formulas, charts, data validation, cell protection, and macros. To create a custom template, you build the workbook with all the necessary labels, formatting, and data, and then you save the workbook as a template. The template includes everything but the variable data.

Before you create a template from an existing workbook, you should make sure that all the formulas work as intended, the numbers and text are entered correctly, and the worksheet is formatted appropriately. You should also remove any values and text that will change in each workbook created from the custom template. Be careful not to delete the formulas. When you are sure the workbook is complete and accurate, you save it as an Excel template file. You can store template files in any folder, but keep in mind that custom template files stored in the Templates folder are available on the New tab in Backstage view.

TIP

It may be helpful to replace variable data values with spaces and apply a background color to cells in which users enter data to differentiate them from other cells in the worksheet.

REFERENCE

Creating a Custom Template

- Prepare the workbook: enter values, text, and formulas as needed; apply formatting; and replace data values with zeros or blank cells.
- Click the File tab on the Ribbon, and then click the Save As command in the navigation bar.
- In the File name box, enter the template name.
- Click the Save as type button, and then click Excel Template.
- Save the file in the Templates folder or select an alternative folder location.
- Click the Save button.

Alvin wants you to use the New Mexico workbook as the basis for creating a custom template. Then, Alvin can create new workbooks based on that template and distribute them to the accountants preparing the state workbooks. You'll reopen the workbook and clear the data values in the worksheets, leaving all of the formulas intact. After completing these modifications, you will save the workbook as a template.

To replace the data values in the New Mexico workbook:

1. Open the **New Mexico** workbook located in the Excel6\Tutorial folder included with your Data Files.
2. Group the **Quarter 1** through **Quarter 4** worksheets. The worksheet group includes the four quarterly worksheets but not the Summary and Documentation worksheets.

3. Select the range **B6:E12**. This range includes the specific ticket and sales data for each theme park. You want to delete these values.
4. Right-click the selected range, and then click **Clear Contents** on the shortcut menu. The data values are cleared from the selected range in each of the quarterly worksheets, but the formulas and formatting remain intact. The cleared cells are blank. The range B13:E13 displays dashes, representing zeros, where there are formulas.

TIP

To delete the data values, you can also click the Clear button in the Editing group on the Home tab, and then click Clear Contents.

5. Apply an orange fill color (the third color in the Standard Colors section of the Fill Color gallery) to the selected range. The range B6:E12 has an orange fill to indicate where users should enter data for the number of tickets sold and the sales amount in the quarterly worksheets.
6. In cell A1, enter **=Summary!A1**. This formula inserts the contents of cell A1 in the Summary worksheet into cell A1 in the quarterly worksheets. The text "New Mexico" is still displayed because that text is currently in cell A1 in the Summary worksheet.
7. Switch to the **Summary** worksheet. The quarterly worksheets are ungrouped, and dashes, representing zeros, appear in the cells in the range B6:E13, which contain formulas.
8. In cell A1, enter **Enter state name here** and then, in cell A2, enter **Enter Fiscal Year – yyyy**. This text will remind users to enter the correct state name and year. See Figure 6-24.

Figure 6-24 Worksheet with formatting and formulas but no data

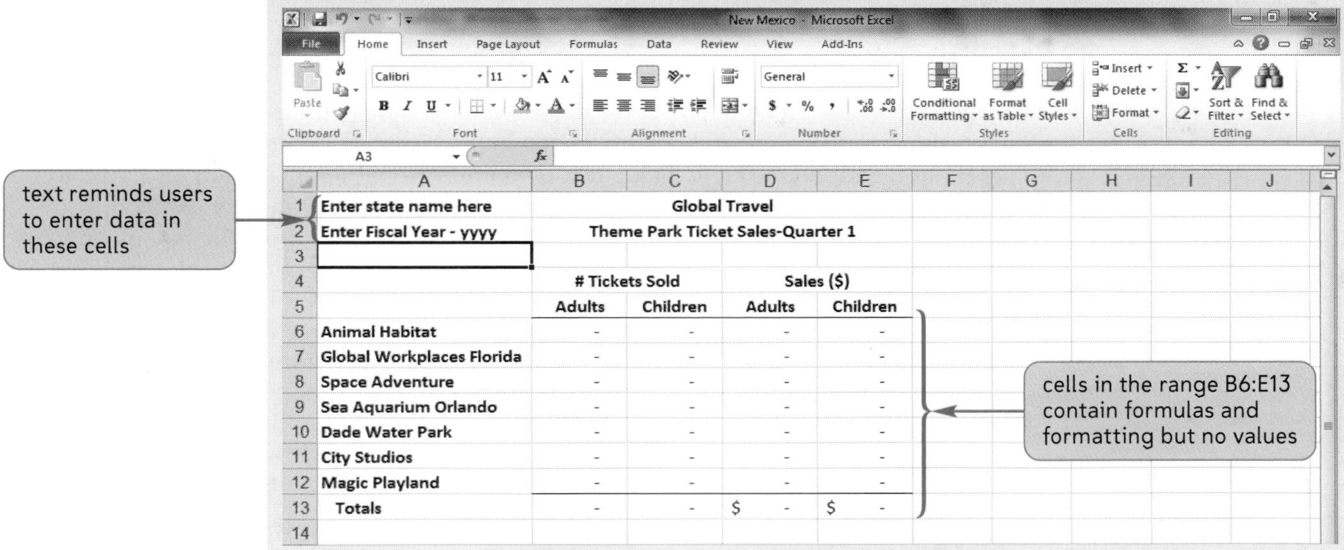

	A	B	C	D	E
1	Enter state name here		Global Travel		
2	Enter Fiscal Year - yyyy		Theme Park Ticket Sales-Quarter 1		
3					
4		# Tickets Sold		Sales ($)	
5		Adults	Children	Adults	Children
6	Animal Habitat	-	-	-	-
7	Global Workplaces Florida	-	-	-	-
8	Space Adventure	-	-	-	-
9	Sea Aquarium Orlando	-	-	-	-
10	Dade Water Park	-	-	-	-
11	City Studios	-	-	-	-
12	Magic Playland	-	-	-	-
13	Totals	-	-	$ -	$ -
14					

9. Switch to the **Documentation** worksheet, delete your name and the date from the range B3:B4, enter **Theme park ticket sales** in cell B6, and then click cell **A1**. The Documentation sheet is updated to reflect the purpose of the workbook.

When you save the workbook as a template, the save location opens to the Templates folder, which is where custom template files are often stored. Excel, by default, looks for template files in this folder. However, you can store templates in other folders as well. Because you might not have access to the Templates folder, you will save the template file with the other Data Files. All template files have the .xltx file extension. This extension differentiates template files from workbook files, which have the .xlsx file extension.

After you have saved a workbook in a template format, you can make the template accessible to other users.

The New Mexico workbook no longer contains any specific data, but the formulas and formatting will still be in effect when new data is entered. It is ready to save in template format.

To save the New Mexico workbook as a template:

1. Click the **File** tab on the Ribbon to open Backstage view, and then click the **Save As** command in the navigation bar. The Save As dialog box opens.
2. Type **Travel Template** in the File name box.
3. Click the **Save as type** button, and then click **Excel Template**. The Address bar displays the Templates folder on your computer. You will change this location.
4. Navigate to the **Excel6\Tutorial** folder included with your Data Files.
5. Click the **Save** button. The Travel Template is saved in the same folder as your Data Files.
6. Close the Travel Template workbook template.

Make sure the save location and save as type are accurate so that you can locate and use the template file later in this session.

Alvin will use the Travel Template file to create the workbooks to track next year's sales for each state and then distribute the workbooks via email to each accountant. By basing these new workbooks on the template file, Alvin has a standard workbook with identical formatting and formulas for each accountant to use. He also avoids the risk of accidentally changing the workbook containing the 2013 data when preparing for 2014.

Creating a New Workbook from a Template

After you have saved a template, you can access the template from the New tab in Backstage view. If you saved the template file in the Templates folder, click the My templates button to open the New dialog box with the Personal Templates tab displayed to select the template you want to use. If you saved the template to another location, you can use the New from existing button to create a new workbook from the file, much like creating a workbook based on a template found in the Templates folder. The New from existing button opens a copy of the selected file, not the selected file. Also, the copy of the workbook that opens has a number at the end of the filename, and is considered an unnamed file, which prevents anyone from inadvertently overwriting the original file.

You will use the New from existing button to create a workbook from the Travel Template file because you saved the template in your Excel6\Tutorial folder.

To create a new workbook based on the Travel Template file:

1. Click the **File** tab on the Ribbon to open Backstage view, and then click the **New** tab in the navigation bar. The New tab appears in Backstage view.
2. Click the **New from existing** button. The New from Existing Workbook dialog box opens, with All Excel Files displayed.

> **TIP**
> The active worksheet in the new workbook is the same worksheet that was active when you saved the template file.

3. Click **Travel Template** located in the Excel6\Tutorial folder included with your Data Files, and then click the **Create New** button. A copy of the Travel Template workbook opens named "Travel Template1" to indicate this is the first copy of the Travel Template workbook created during the current Excel session.
4. Click the **Summary** sheet tab, enter **New Mexico** in cell A1, and then enter **Fiscal Year - 2014** in cell A2.
5. Switch to the **Quarter 1** worksheet. The text "New Mexico" appears in cell A1, and the text "Fiscal Year - 2014" appears in cell A2.
6. Enter the following test data in the data area (range B6:E6, which has the orange background fill color), and then review the column totals in the range B13:E13 (the cells that contain formulas to sum each column):

   cell B6: **120**
   cell C6: **150**
   cell D6: **3000**
   cell E6: **2850**

7. Enter the following test data in the range B7:E7, and then notice that the formulas in the range B13:E13 are updated. See Figure 6-25.

   cell B7: **180**
   cell C7: **200**
   cell D7: **3500**
   cell E7: **3150**

Figure 6-25 New workbook based on the Travel Template

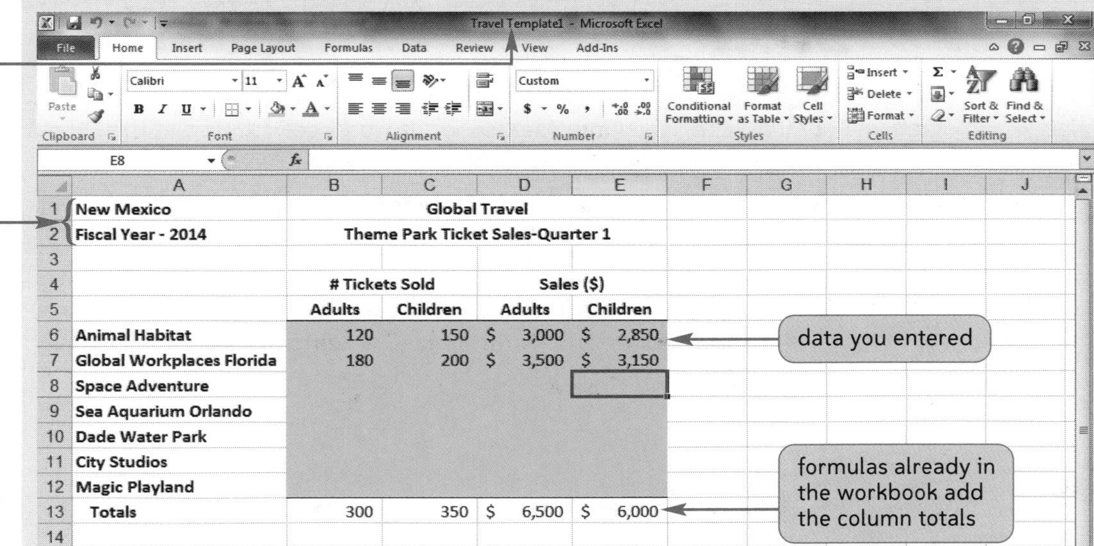

8. Switch to the **Summary** worksheet. Totals appear in the ranges B6:E7 and B13:E13 as a result of the formulas in this worksheet. See Figure 6-26.

Figure 6-26 Summary worksheet after data is entered

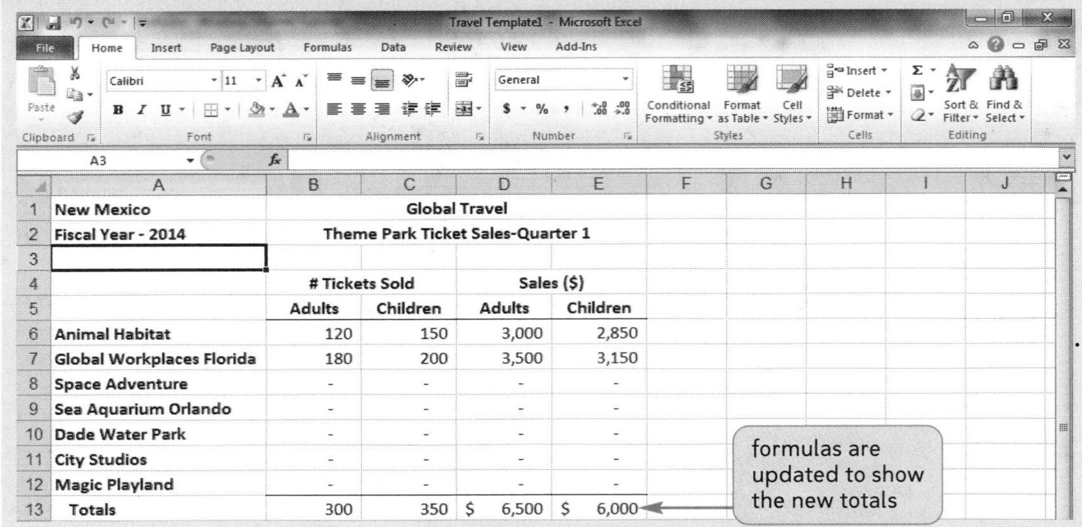

9. Save the workbook as **New Mexico 2014** in the Excel6\Tutorial folder included with your Data Files, and then close the workbook. The copy of the template is saved as a workbook with the .xlsx file extension. The original template file is not changed.

You'll add data to the Quarter 2, Quarter 3, and Quarter 4 worksheets to verify that the Summary worksheet is correctly adding numbers from the four worksheets.

To test the New Mexico 2014 workbook:

1. Open the **New Mexico 2014** workbook located in the Excel6\Tutorial folder included with your Data Files.
2. Group the **Quarter 2**, **Quarter 3**, and **Quarter 4** worksheets, enter **120** in cell B6, and then, enter **150** in cell C6.
3. Switch to the **Summary** worksheet. The total in cell B6 is 480 and the total in cell C6 is 600. The formulas in the Summary worksheet correctly add values from all the quarterly worksheets. The template workbook is functioning as intended.
4. Save and close the workbook.

Using the Excel Web App and SkyDrive

Office Web Apps are Web-based versions of Microsoft Excel, Word, PowerPoint, and OneNote. These Web apps allow you to create, view, and edit Office files directly from a Web browser as well as share files and collaborate with other users online. Office Web Apps are a part of **Windows Live**, which is a collection of services and Web applications that you can use to be more productive. For example, you can use Windows Live to upload Office files to an online storage and file sharing service called SkyDrive. The service requires a Windows Live ID, allowing you to keep your files private, share them with individuals you specify, or make the files public. You can save your files directly from Microsoft Office 2010 onto SkyDrive from Backstage view.

TIP

Cloud computing refers to data, applications, and even resources that are stored on servers that you access over the Internet rather than on your own computer.

Note: SkyDrive and Office Web Apps are dynamic Web pages, and might change over time, including the way they are organized and how commands are performed. The steps and figures in this tutorial were accurate at the time this book was published.

Obtaining a Windows Live ID

To save files to SkyDrive or use the Office Web Apps, you need a Windows Live ID. You obtain a Windows Live ID by going to the Windows Live Web site and creating a new account. Once you have a Windows Live ID, you can access your SkyDrive and use it to store files, create new files, and share your files with others.

Note: If you already have a Windows Live ID, you can skip this set of steps.

To obtain a Windows Live ID:

1. Start your Web browser, and then go to **www.windowslive.com**. The page where you can sign into Windows Live opens.

   Trouble? If the URL doesn't bring you to the page where you can sign into Windows Live, use a search engine to search for "Windows Live."

2. Click the **Sign up** button. The Create your Windows Live ID page opens.
3. Follow the instructions on the screen to create a Windows Live ID.
4. Sign out of Windows Live, exit your browser, and return to Excel.

Saving a Workbook to SkyDrive

After you have a Windows Live ID, you can access your SkyDrive and the Office Web Apps. You can access your SkyDrive from the Windows Live page in your browser after you signed in with your Windows Live ID, or from Backstage view in Excel. You can save a file to a private or public folder on your SkyDrive.

REFERENCE

Saving a Workbook to SkyDrive

- Open the workbook you want to save to SkyDrive.
- Click the File tab, click Save & Send in the navigation pane, and then click the Save to Web command in the center pane.
- In the right pane, click the Sign In button, and then complete the sign-in process.
- Click the folder in which to save the workbook, and then click the Save As button.
- Enter a filename in the File name box, and then click the Save button.

You'll save the New Mexico 2014 workbook to the My Documents folder on your SkyDrive. This is a private folder that only you can access.

To save the workbook from Excel to the My Documents folder on your SkyDrive:

1. In Excel, open the **New Mexico 2014** workbook located in the Excel6/Tutorial folder.
2. Click the **File** tab, and then click **Save & Send** in the navigation bar. The Save & Send options appear in Backstage view.
3. Under Save & Send, click the **Save to Web** button. A Sign in button appears that you use to sign in to your Windows Live account. See Figure 6-27.

Figure 6-27 Save to Web options on the Save & Send tab in Backstage view

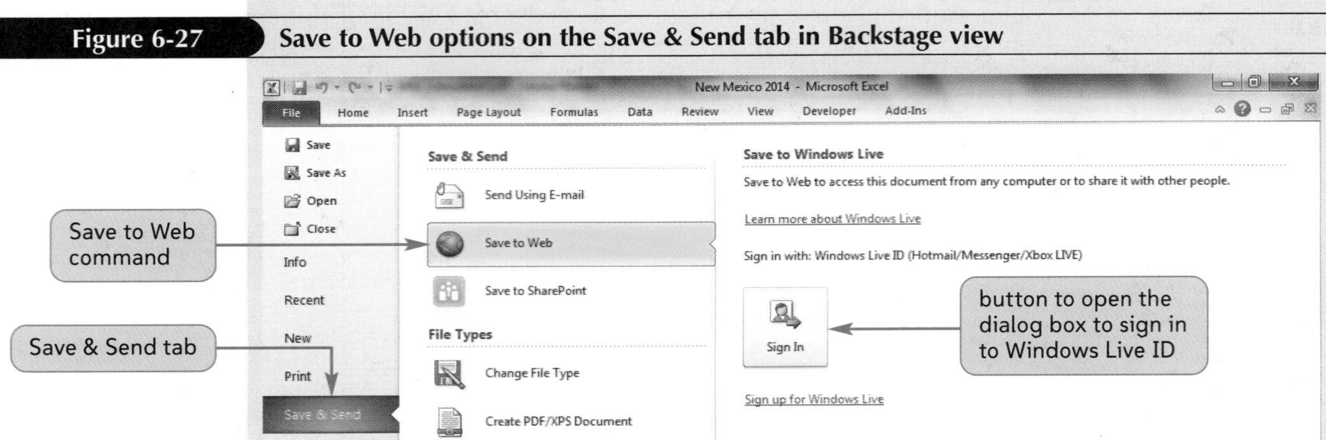

Trouble? If you're already signed into Windows Live, you'll see the folders in your SkyDrive account and the Save As button (see Figure 6-28). Continue with Step 8.

4. Click the **Sign In** button. The Connecting to docs.live.net dialog box opens.
5. In the E-mail address box, type the email address associated with your Windows Live ID, and then press the **Tab** key.
6. In the Password box, type the password associated with your Windows Live ID.
7. Click the **OK** button. The dialog box closes, and another dialog box appears while you connect to the Windows Live server. After you connect to Windows Live, the right pane in Backstage view lists the folders on your SkyDrive and a Save As button appears. See Figure 6-28.

Figure 6-28 Save & Send tab after connecting to Windows Live

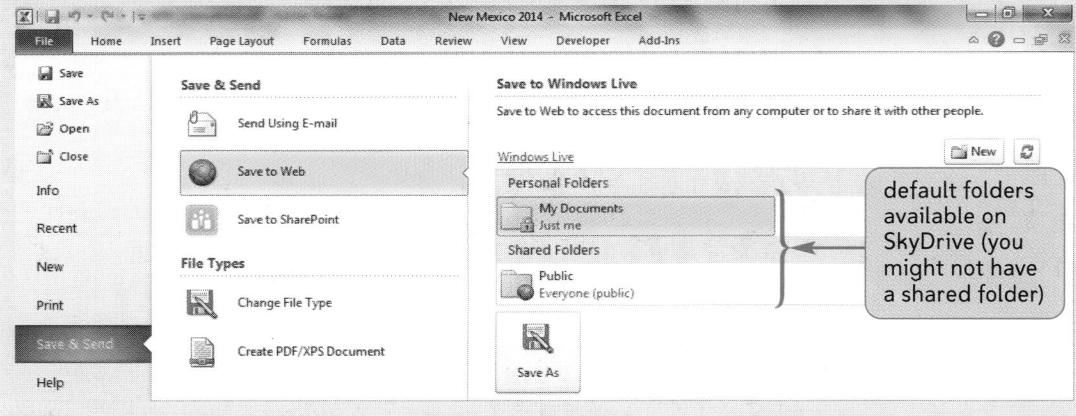

8. In the right pane, click the **My Documents** folder, if necessary, and then click the Save As button. Backstage view closes, and the **Save As** dialog box opens.
9. Click the **Save** button. The workbook is saved in the My Documents folder on your SkyDrive. In Excel, close the workbook.

Editing a Workbook with the Excel Web App

You can view and edit workbooks in the Excel Web App. The interface for the Excel Web App is similar to the interface of the full-featured program on your computer; however, only a limited number of commands are available.

You'll sign in to your Windows Live account and use the Excel Web App to update the New Mexico 2014 workbook on your SkyDrive.

To edit the workbook using the Excel Web App:

1. Start your browser, and then go to **www.windowslive.com** and sign in to your SkyDrive using your Windows Live ID.
2. If your SkyDrive account is not open, click the **Office** link at the top of the Windows Live page, and then click **Your documents**.
3. Click **My Documents**, and then point to **New Mexico 2014**. See Figure 6-29.

Figure 6-29

New Mexico 2014 Information page on SkyDrive

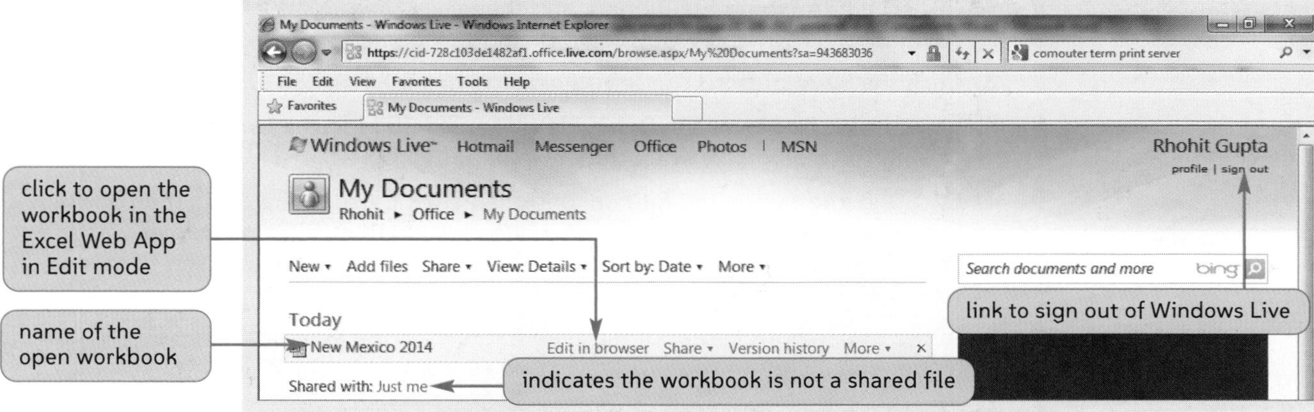

4. Click the **Edit in browser** link. The New Mexico 2014 workbook opens in the Excel Web App in Edit mode so you can make changes to the file.

   Trouble? If this is the first time you have opened a file in SkyDrive file, you might be asked to read and accept the user agreement in order to continue. Accept the user agreement, and then continue with Step 5.

5. Click the **Quarter 1** sheet tab, and then enter **200** in cell B8, **1500** in cell C8, **1500** in cell D8, and **4000** in cell E8. See Figure 6-30.

Figure 6-30
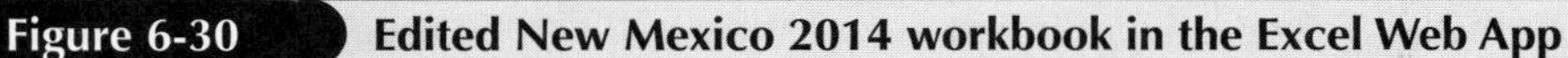
Edited New Mexico 2014 workbook in the Excel Web App

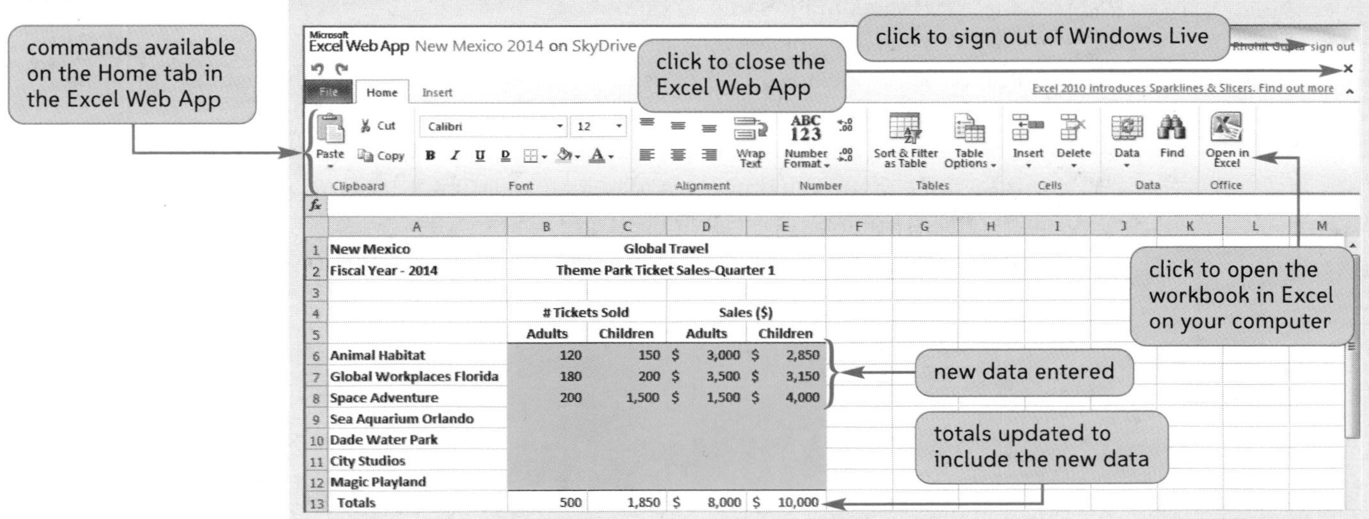

6. Switch to the **Summary** worksheet and verify that the data on the Summary worksheet was also updated.

TIP

To open the file in Excel on your computer, click the Open in Excel button in the Office group on the Home tab of the Excel Web App (refer to Figure 6-30).

The Excel Web App in Edit mode does not have all of the features of the program installed on your computer available. To use the other features, you need to open the workbook in the full-featured program on your computer. You can save a workbook from SkyDrive to your computer and then continue working in the full version of Excel. You'll save the updated version of the New Mexico 2014 workbook to your computer.

To save the workbook from SkyDrive to your computer:

1. Click the **File** tab on the Ribbon, and then click **Download a Copy** in the navigation bar. The File Download dialog box opens.
2. Click the **Save** button. The Save As dialog box opens.
3. Save the workbook as **SkyDrive New Mexico 2014** in the Excel6/Tutorial folder, closing the dialog box when the download is complete.
4. Click the **File** tab on the Ribbon, and then **click** Close in the navigation bar. The New Mexico 2014 workbook closes. Files are automatically updated as you enter data in the workbook on your SkyDrive. As a result, you do not need to save your workbook in SkyDrive.
5. In the upper-right corner of the Web page, click the **sign out** link. You are no longer connected to your Windows Live account.
6. Close your Web browser.

With the ability to edit a workbook from any computer, Rhohit can be sure that his workbooks are always updated. The templates you created will ensure that all regions enter data consistently, making it simpler for Alvin to track ticket sales for Global Travel.

REVIEW

Session 6.3 Quick Check

1. How do you insert a hyperlink into a worksheet cell?
2. True or False. A hyperlink in a worksheet cell can be used to jump to another worksheet in the same workbook.
3. What is a template?
4. What is one advantage of using a custom template rather than simply using the original workbook file to create a new workbook?
5. How do you save a file as a template?
6. You can use Windows Live to upload your Office files to an online storage and file sharing service called ______________.
7. True or False. You need a Windows Live ID to save files to your SkyDrive and use the Office Web Apps.

Practice the skills you learned in the tutorial using the same case scenario.

PRACTICE

Review Assignments

Data Files needed for the Review Assignments: OR.xlsx, Idaho.xlsx, Washington.xlsx, NW Totals 2013.xlsx, and NW Travel.xltx

Elaine Dennerson, accountant for Global Travel in Oregon, needs your help. Global Travel has added Oregon to its Northwest territory, which already includes Washington and Idaho. You will complete the Summary worksheet in the Oregon workbook, and then enter the formulas in the NW Totals 2013 workbook to summarize the regional totals in one workbook. Complete the following:

1. Open the **OR** workbook located in the Excel6\Review folder included with your Data Files, and then save the workbook as **Oregon** in the same folder.
2. In the Documentation sheet, enter your name and the date, and then review the worksheets in the workbook.
3. Create a worksheet group that contains the Qtr 1 through Qtr 4 worksheets.
4. In the worksheet group, insert formulas in the range B13:E13 to total each column.
5. Format the quarterly worksheets as specified below, and then ungroup the worksheets:
   a. Bold the range A1:B2;A6:A13; and B4:E5.
   b. Merge and center the ranges B1:E1, B2:E2, B4:C4, and D4:E4.
   c. Format the range A6:A12 in italic.
   d. Add a top and double bottom border to the range B13:E13.
   e. Add a fill color to the range B1:E2 using the Orange color in the Standard Colors section.
   f. Apply the Accounting number format with no decimal places to the range D6:E13.
6. Make a copy of the Qtr 1 worksheet, rename it as **Summary**, and place it after the Documentation worksheet.
7. In the Summary worksheet, remove the data from the range B6:E12, change the heading in cell B2 to **Theme Park Ticket Sales – Total** and then enter the label **Fiscal Year – 2013** in cell A2.
8. In worksheets Qtr 1 through Qtr 4, enter formulas to reference the labels in cells A1 and A2 of the Summary worksheet.
9. In the Summary worksheet, create 3-D reference formulas to calculate annual totals for theme park tickets sold and sales.
10. Prepare all worksheets except the Documentation sheet for printing. Display the name of the workbook and the name of the worksheet on separate lines in the right section of the header. Display your name and the date on separate lines in the right section of the footer. Preview the five worksheets.
11. Ungroup the worksheets and save the workbook.
12. Open the regional **NW Totals 2013** workbook located in the Excel6\Review folder included with your Data Files, and then save the workbook as **Northwest Totals 2013**. In the Documentation worksheet, enter your name and the date.
13. In the Summary worksheet, enter external reference formulas to create a set of linked workbooks to summarize the totals for Oregon, Washington, and Idaho in the Northwest Totals 2013 workbook.
14. In the Northwest Totals 2013 workbook, switch to the Documentation sheet. In the range A10:A12, enter the name of each state (**Idaho**, **Oregon**, and **Washington**). Create hyperlinks from each state label to its corresponding workbook. Add appropriate text for the ScreenTip to each hyperlink. Test each hyperlink.

15. Create a workspace with the following four workbooks in a tiled layout: Idaho, Oregon, Washington, and Northwest Totals 2013. Make the Summary worksheet in each workbook the active worksheet, and make the Northwest Totals 2013 workbook the active workbook. Save the workspace as **NW Workspace**.
16. Create a new workbook based on the **NW Travel** template located in the Excel6\Review folder included with your Data Files. Save the workbook as **Oregon 2014** in the same folder. In the Documentation worksheet, enter your name and the date.
17. In the Summary worksheet, enter **Oregon** in cell A1 and **Fiscal Year – 2014** in cell A2. In the Qtr 1 worksheet, enter **2000** in each cell of the range B6:C12. In the Qtr 2 worksheet, enter **3000** in each cell of the range B6:C12. Confirm that the values entered in this step were correctly totaled in the Summary worksheet. Save the Oregon 2014 workbook.
18. Save the Oregon 2014 workbook to the My Documents folder on your SkyDrive using the same name. In the Qtr 3 worksheet, enter **4000** in each cell in the range B6:C12. Download the file to your computer using the name **SkyDrive Oregon 2014**.
19. Close all the workbooks. Submit the finished files to your instructor, either in printed or electronic form, as requested.

Use the skills you learned to summarize sales data.

APPLY

Case Problem 1

Data File needed for this Case Problem: Cafe.xlsx

Java Café Java Café currently has three stores in the Southwest: Tucson, Arizona; Las Cruces, New Mexico; and Dallas, Texas. Jayne Mitchell manages the three stores and uses Excel to summarize sales data from these stores. She asks you to total the sales by product group and store for each quarter and then format each worksheet. Jayne also needs you to add another worksheet to calculate Summary sales for the stores and product groups. Complete the following:

1. Open the **Cafe** workbook located in the Excel6\Case1 folder included with your Data Files, and then save the workbook as **Java Cafe** in the same folder.
2. In the Documentation worksheet, enter your name and the date, and then switch to the Quarter 1 worksheet.
3. Group the four quarterly worksheets. For each quarter, calculate the product totals in the range B8:F8 and the store locations in the range F5:F7. Improve the look of the quarterly worksheets using the formatting of your choice. Ungroup the worksheets.
4. Place a copy of one of the quarterly worksheets between the Documentation and Quarter 1 worksheets, rename the new worksheet as **Summary Sales**, and then delete the values in the range B5:E7. The Summary Sales worksheet is identical in appearance to the quarterly worksheets.
5. In the Summary Sales worksheet, in the range B5:E7, insert the formulas that add the sales in the corresponding cells of the four quarterly worksheets. Use 3-D references to calculate the totals for each product group and store.
6. Set up the Summary Sales and four quarterly worksheets for printing. Each worksheet should be centered horizontally, fit on one page, display the name of the worksheet centered in the header, and display your name and the date on separate lines in the right section of the footer.
7. Save the Java Cafe workbook, and then remove the sales data, but not the formulas, from each of the quarterly worksheets.
8. Return to the Documentation worksheet, and then save the workbook as an Excel template with the name **Java Template** in the Excel6\Case1 folder included with your Data Files.

9. Use the Java Template file to create a new workbook. Save the workbook as **Java Cafe 2014** in the Excel6\Case1 folder. In the range B5:E7 of all four quarterly worksheets, enter **1**. Verify that the formulas in each worksheet summarize the data accurately.
10. Save the Java Cafe 2014 workbook to the My Documents folder on your SkyDrive using the same name. In the Quarter 1 worksheet, change coffee sales in Tucson to **$30,000**. Download the file to your computer using the name **SkyDrive Java Cafe 2014**.
11. Save and close the workbook. Submit the finished files to your instructor, either in printed or electronic form, as requested.

Link workbooks to summarize sales data for a car dealership.

APPLY

Case Problem 2

Data Files needed for this Case Problem: Carson.xlsx, Reno.xlsx, and Vegas.xlsx

UTE Auto Sales & Services Hardy Ute is founder and operator of UTE Auto Sales & Services, which has dealerships in Las Vegas, Reno, and Carson City, Nevada. His dealerships sell new and used cars, hybrids, SUVs, and trucks, as well as service customers' vehicles. To analyze sales and service at each of his three dealerships, Hardy wants his staff to prepare a report that shows the unit and dollar sales of new and used vehicles by type as well as service by vehicle type. Complete the following:

1. Open the **Carson** workbook located in the Excel6\Case2 folder included with your Data Files, and then save the workbook as **UTE Carson City** in the same folder.
2. In the Documentation worksheet, enter your name, the date, and an appropriate purpose statement, and then switch to the Quarter 1 worksheet.
3. Group the four quarterly worksheets. For each quarter, calculate the totals in the range B10:G10, and then improve the formatting of the quarterly worksheets by merging and centering cells B4:C4, cells D4:E4, and cells F4:G4, and then center aligning the range B5:G5. Ungroup the worksheets.
4. Insert a new worksheet between the Documentation and Quarter 1 worksheets, and then rename this worksheet as **Summary**. Format the worksheet identically to the quarterly worksheets except leave the range B6:G9 blank. (*Hint*: Copy one of the quarterly worksheets, and then modify it as needed.)
5. In the Summary worksheet, in the range B6:G9, insert formulas that add the sales in the corresponding cells of the four quarterly worksheets.
6. Prepare the Summary and four quarterly sales worksheets for printing. Center the worksheets horizontally, center the worksheet name in the header, and place your name and the current date on separate lines in the right section of the footer.
7. Save and close the workbook.
8. Open the **Reno** workbook located in the Excel6\Case2 folder included with your Data Files, and then save the workbook as **UTE Reno**. Repeat Steps 2 through 7 for this workbook.
9. Open the **Vegas** workbook located in the Excel6\Case2 folder, and then save the workbook as **UTE Vegas**. Repeat Steps 2 through 7 for this workbook.
10. Create a new workbook, and then use Figure 6-31 as a guide to create a summary of the three dealerships' workbooks. Save the workbook as **UTE Summary**.

Figure 6-31 UTE sales for all dealers

	A	B	C	D	E	F	G
1	UTE Auto Sales & Service						
2	Sales - All Dealers						
3							
4		New		Pre-owned		Service	
5		Units	Sales ($)	Units	Sales ($)	Units	Sales ($)
6	Cars	733	$ 14,940,828	203	$ 1,476,397	5405	$ 1,058,958
7	Hybrids	288	$ 7,979,268	76	$ 478,632	1798	$ 492,525
8	SUVs	166	$ 3,928,990	87	$ 750,758	1007	$ 328,662
9	Trucks	113	$ 1,639,386	64	$ 341,907	691	$ 117,874
10	Totals	1300	$ 28,488,472	430	$ 3,047,694	8901	$ 1,998,019

11. Use the UTE Carson City workbook to create an Excel template with the name **UTE Template** in the Excel6\Case2 folder included with your Data Files. Add appropriate formatting of your choice and remove the date in cell B4 from the Documentation worksheet.
12. Create a new workbook using the UTE Template. Add appropriate test data for Quarter 1. Save the workbook as **Carson City 2014** in the Excel6\Case2 folder included with your Data Files. In the Documentation sheet, enter the date in cell B4.
13. Save the Carson City 2014 workbook to the My Documents folder on your SkyDrive using the same name. In the Quarter 2 worksheet, enter **75** new cars at a value of **$825,000**. Download the file to your computer using the name **SkyDrive Carson City 2014**.
14. Close any open workbooks. Submit the finished files to your instructor, either in printed or electronic form, as requested.

Create a worksheet to summarize sales data.

CREATE

Case Problem 3

Data File needed for this Case Problem: Infusion.xlsx

Infusion Blend Micki Goldstein is a sales representative for Infusion Blend, a specialty soft drink producer. Micki is based in Tampa, and she travels around Florida to meet and make product presentations to managers of stores ranging from major supermarket chains to small corner markets. Although Micki does not personally make the deliveries, she often works closely with the delivery staff to assure quality service to her customers.

Micki must report her sales progress to her regional manager in Atlanta, Georgia. These reports include the overall sales volume, the types of products sold, locations, and stores where the products were delivered. For the larger markets, she must prepare a separate workbook for each chain store. Complete the following:

1. Open the **Infusion** workbook located in the Excel6\Case3 folder included with your Data Files, and then save the workbook as **Infusion 2013** in the same folder.
2. In the Documentation worksheet, enter your name and the date, and then switch to the January worksheet.
3. Group the 12 monthly worksheets. For each month (January through December), enter formulas to calculate the total sales for each product and store, and then improve the formatting of the monthly worksheets using the formatting of your choice. Ungroup the worksheets.

4. Insert a new worksheet between the Documentation and January worksheets that has the same content as the monthly worksheets except the range B6:G12 is blank, rename the worksheet as **YTD Summary**, and then format this worksheet identically to the monthly worksheets.
5. Use 3-D reference formulas to calculate the total number of cases sold for each product by store from January through December. For example, in cell B6, the formula results in 1335 cases of the Popgo product sold in the Elteron store.
6. Insert formulas that calculate total cases sold by product for all stores in column G, and total cases of all products sold by store in row 12. Calculate the Summary total for all products sold in all stores.

EXPLORE

7. Insert a new worksheet following the Documentation worksheet, and then rename this worksheet as **Annual Recap**. Using Figure 6-32 as a guide, create three summaries on this worksheet by product, store, and month, using the following formulas:
   a. Insert formulas that add the total cases sold of each product in the range C7:C12 (column G in the monthly worksheets). Calculate the total for all products.
   b. Insert formulas that add the total cases sold at each store in the range G7:G11 (row 12 in the monthly worksheets). Calculate the total for all stores.
   c. Insert formulas that add the total cases sold each month in the range K7:K18 (cell G12 in each monthly worksheet). Calculate the total for all months.
   d. Insert formulas in column D to calculate the percentage of cases sold for each product to the total cases sold for all products. Calculate the percentage of each product's total to the total cases sold for all products.
   e. Insert formulas in column H to calculate the percentage of cases sold by each store total to the total cases sold by all stores. Calculate the percentage of each store's total to the total for all stores.
   f. Insert formulas in column L to calculate the percentage of cases sold each month to the total cases sold for the year. Calculate the percentage of each month's total to the total for the year.

Figure 6-32 **Infusion Blend's sales by product, store, and month**

	A	B	C	D	E	F	G	H	I	J	K	L
1		Infusion Blend Sales by Product, Store and Month										
2		Cases Sold										
3												
4												
5		Breakdown by Product				Breakdown by Store				Breakdown by Month		
6		Products	Cases Sold	Percent		Store	Cases Sold	Percent		Month	Cases Sold	Percent
7		Popgo	7,065	30.7%		Elteron	4,700	20.5%		January	8,975	39.1%
8		Diet Popgo	4,760	20.7%		Everett	4,600	20.0%		February	7,120	31.0%
9		Mt. Spring	3,360	14.6%		Franklin	4,700	20.5%		March	3,905	17.0%
10		Red Burst	1,675	7.3%		Grant	4,625	20.1%		April	2,980	13.0%
11		Dr Selsa	3,135	13.6%		Grover	4,355	19.0%		May	-	0.0%
12		L & L	2,985	13.0%		Totals	22,980	100.0%		June	-	0.0%
13		Totals	22,980	100%						July	-	0.0%
14										August	-	0.0%
15										September	-	0.0%
16										October	-	0.0%
17										November	-	0.0%
18										December	-	0.0%
19										Totals	22,980	100.0%

8. Save the Infusion 2013 workbook, and then use the Save As command to save a copy of the Infusion 2013 workbook with the name **Infusion with May 2013**.
9. In the Infusion with May 2013 workbook, insert the May results, shown in Figure 6-33, into the May worksheet.

Figure 6-33 **Infusion Blend's May sales**

	A	B	C	D	E	F	G
1	Infusion Blend Sales by Store and Product						
2	Cases Sold						
3							
4		Stores					
5	Products	Elteron	Everett	Franklin	Grant	Grover	Totals
6	Popgo	515	545	560	670	510	2,800
7	Diet Popgo	435	445	435	430	410	2,155
8	Mt. Spring	235	275	240	240	205	1,195
9	Red Burst	125	125	150	150	325	875
10	Dr Selsa	160	145	150	160	125	740
11	L & L	325	240	175	245	225	1,210
12	Totals	1,795	1,775	1,710	1,895	1,800	8,975

10. In the Documentation worksheet, in the range A8:A19, type the months **January** through **December**. Create hyperlinks from each cell to its corresponding worksheet. Test the hyperlinks.
11. Save and close the workbook. Submit the finished workbooks to your instructor, either in printed or electronic form, as requested.

Explore using worksheet groups, 3-D and external references, workspaces, and templates.

CHALLENGE

Case Problem 4

Data Files needed for this Case Problem: Europe.xlsx, North America.xlsx, South America.xlsx, and PlutoTemplate.xltx

Pluto Pharmaceuticals Pluto Pharmaceuticals is a multinational manufacturer of healthcare products. The chief financial analyst, Kevin Cross, asks you to prepare the first quarter revenue summary based on workbooks from the regions of North America, South America, and Europe. Each workbook has monthly worksheets displaying forecasted and actual revenues of the major product groups for the first quarter. Kevin wants you to calculate the difference between forecasted and actual sales (Difference) and the percent change between forecasted and actual sales (% Change). He also wants you to summarize each workbook, reporting the quarterly forecasted and actual totals for revenues in a new worksheet. After you have added this information to each workbook, Kevin wants you to consolidate the information from the three regional workbooks, reporting in a single workbook the summarized information for each region. Complete the following:

1. Open the **Europe**, **North America**, and **South America** workbooks located in the Excel6\Case4 folder included with your Data Files. Save the Europe workbook as **PlutoEU**, save the North America workbook as **PlutoNA**, and save the South America workbook as **PlutoSA**. In the Documentation worksheet in each regional revenue workbook, enter your name and the date.
2. Each regional workbook contains a Documentation worksheet, a first quarter summary worksheet, and three monthly worksheets. Complete the monthly worksheets in each region's workbook by doing the following:
   a. Calculate the difference for each product group: Actual–Forecast.
   b. Calculate the % change for each product group: Difference/Forecast.
   c. Calculate the total revenue for the Forecast, Actual, and Difference columns, and then calculate the total % change.
   d. Format the numbers to improve the appearance of the worksheets.

3. In each workbook, complete the Quarter 1 worksheet by first summarizing the forecasted and actual totals for product groups for the first three months of the year, then calculating the difference and the % change, and, finally, summarizing the forecasted, actual, difference, and % change values for the quarter. (*Hint*: The Total Revenue % change in cell E10 is not the sum of the column; it is the percent change between the forecasted and actual totals.) Use Figure 6-34 as a guide as you complete the worksheet.

Figure 6-34 **First quarter North America revenue**

	A	B	C	D	E
1	Pluto Pharmaceuticals-North America				
2	Revenue - Quarter 1				
3					
4	Product Group	Forecast	Actual	Difference	% Change
5	Personal Care	$ 2,295,600	$ 2,363,891	$ 68,291	3.0%
6	Beauty	$ 340,500	$ 363,536	$ 23,036	6.8%
7	Animal Healthcare	$ 2,079,100	$ 2,101,693	$ 22,593	1.1%
8	Prescription Medicine	$ 522,300	$ 526,672	$ 4,372	0.8%
9	Photo	$ 1,006,200	$ 976,096	$ (30,104)	-3.0%
10	**Total Revenue**	$ 6,243,700	$ 6,331,888	$ 88,188	1.4%

4. Format the Quarter 1 worksheet for each regional workbook with the same formatting used for the monthly worksheets, and then save the workbooks.
5. Create a new workbook, and save it as **PlutoSummary** in the Excel6\Case4 folder included with your Data Files. Rename the Sheet1 worksheet as **Documentation**, and in column A enter the same labels used in the Documentation worksheets in the other workbooks. In column B, enter **Corporate** as the region, your name as the author, the current date as the date created, and **To report on revenue for all regions** as the purpose. Format the Documentation worksheet to match the Documentation worksheet formatting in the PlutoNA, PlutoSA, and PlutoEU workbooks.
6. Switch to the Sheet2 worksheet, and then enter the text shown in Figure 6-35. Enter formulas to total the Forecasted and Actual revenue for each product group. Compute the difference and % change for each product group. Include the totals for the Forecast, Actual, and Difference columns, and calculate the % change for the total revenue for the quarter. Rename the worksheet as **Quarter 1**.

Figure 6-35 **First quarter corporate revenue**

	A	B	C	D	E
1	Pluto Pharmaceuticals-Corporate				
2	Revenue - Quarter 1				
3					
4	Product Group	Forecast	Actual	Difference	% Change
5	Personal Care	$ 5,670,800	$ 5,913,673	$ 242,873	4.3%
6	Beauty	$ 1,210,500	$ 1,250,000	$ 39,500	3.3%
7	Animal Healthcare	$ 4,632,300	$ 4,662,070	$ 29,770	0.6%
8	Prescription Medicine	$ 1,432,900	$ 1,507,357	$ 74,457	5.2%
9	Photo	$ 2,707,600	$ 2,657,288	$ (50,312)	-1.9%
10	**Total Revenue**	$ 15,654,100	$ 15,990,388	$ 336,288	2.1%

EXPLORE

7. Insert a bar chart similar to Figure 6-36 that compares the actual and forecast sales by product group. Place the chart beneath the data you entered in the Quarter 1 worksheet. Change the axis so the sales (Displayed Units) are displayed in millions of dollars.

Figure 6-36 **Chart of first quarter corporate revenue**

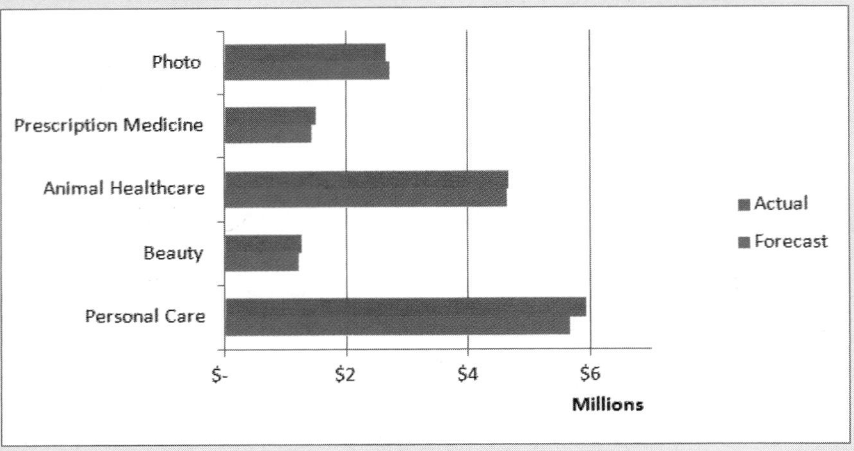

8. Prepare the three regional and corporate workbooks for printing. On each page, include the worksheet name in the center section of the header and your name in the left section of the footer.
9. Create a workspace that opens with the Quarter 1 worksheet active in each of the four workbooks using a horizontal layout for the four workbooks, and then save it as **Quarter1 Files** in the Excel6\Case4 folder included with your Data Files.
10. Save a copy of the **PlutoSummary** workbook located in the Excel6\Case4 folder as **Pluto Yearend** in the same folder. For year-end backup, break the links in the Pluto Yearend workbook.

EXPLORE

11. You receive a new source file to substitute for the original source file. The new source file has a different name.
    a. Open the **PlutoSummary** workbook, save the workbook as **PlutoSummaryTest** in the Excel6\Case4 folder, and then close the workbook.
    b. Open the **PlutoNA** workbook, and then save the workbook as **PlutoNorth**. In the PlutoNorth workbook in the March worksheet, change the actual personal care revenue in cell C5 to **$863,298**. Save and close the PlutoNorth workbook.
    c. Open the **PlutoSummaryTest** workbook, and change the link to the source workbook from PlutoNA to **PlutoNorth**. (*Hint*: Use the Edit Links dialog box.) Save and close the PlutoSummaryTest workbook.

EXPLORE

12. Update the source file but not the destination file.
    a. Open the **PlutoEU** workbook, and then save the workbook as **PlutoEurope**.
    b. Open the **PlutoSummaryTest** workbook, and change the link to the source workbook from PlutoEU to **PlutoEurope**. Note the actual total revenue in the Quarter 1 worksheet (cell C10). Close the PlutoSummaryTest workbook.
    c. In the PlutoEurope workbook, switch to the March worksheet and change the actual animal healthcare revenue in cell C7 to **$275,569**. Save and close the PlutoEurope workbook.
    d. Open the **PlutoSummaryTest** workbook and click the Don't Update button. How does this affect the Quarter 1 total actual revenue (cell C10) in the PlutoSummaryTest workbook (compare the current value to the value you noted in Step b)?
    e. Use the Edit Links dialog box to update the PlutoSummaryTest workbook. How does this affect the Quarter 1 total actual revenue (cell C10) in the PlutoSummaryTest workbook (compare the current value to the value you noted in Step d)?

EXPLORE

13. Modify the template named **PlutoTemplate** located in the Excel6\Case4 folder. Make the following two changes to the template, and then save the modified template as **PlutoTemplateRevised**:
    a. In the quarterly and monthly worksheets, change the formula in column E to display 0.0% when no values are entered in column B (Forecast) instead of #DIV/0!.
    b. In the monthly worksheets, apply a fill color of your choice to the range B5:C9 to identify where to enter data.
14. Create a new workbook from the PlutoTemplateRevised template. In the Documentation worksheet, enter your name and the date. In each monthly worksheet, enter **$500,000** in the range B5:B9 and enter **$550,000** in the range C5:C9. Save the workbook as **Pluto2014**.
15. Save and close all workbooks. Submit the finished workbooks to your instructor, either in printed or electronic form, as requested.

ASSESS

SAM: Skills Assessment Manager

For current SAM information, including versions and content details, visit SAM Central (http://samcentral.course.com). If you have a SAM user profile, you may have access to hands-on instruction, practice, and assessment of the skills covered in this tutorial. Since various versions of SAM are supported throughout the life of this text, check with your instructor for the correct instructions and URL/Web site for accessing assignments.

ENDING DATA FILES

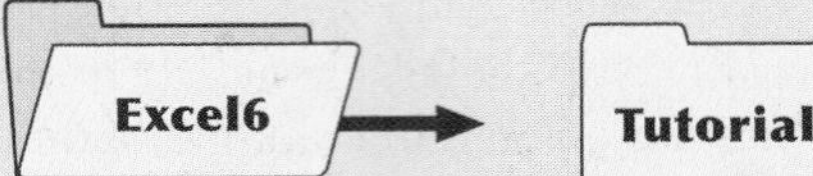

Tutorial

Audited 2013.xlsx
Colorado.xlsx
Hoot Time Card.xlsx
New Mexico.xlsx
New Mexico 2014.xlsx
Sales 2013.docx
SkyDrive New Mexico 2014.xlsx
Theme Parks.xlw
Totals 2013.xlsx
Travel Template.xltx
Utah.xlsx

Review

Idaho.xlsx
Northwest Totals 2013.xlsx
NW Workspace.xlw
Oregon.xlsx
Oregon 2014.xlsx
SkyDrive Oregon 2014.xlsx
Washington.xlsx

Case1

Java Cafe.xlsx
Java Cafe 2014.xlsx
Java Template.xltx
SkyDrive Java Cafe 2014.xlsx

Case2

Carson City 2014.xlsx
SkyDrive Carson City 2014.xlsx
UTE Carson City.xlsx
UTE Reno.xlsx
UTE Summary.xlsx
UTE Template.xltx
UTE Vegas.xlsx

Case3

Infusion 2013.xlsx
Infusion with May 2013.xlsx

Case4

Pluto2014.xlsx
PlutoEU.xlsx
PlutoEurope.xlsx
PlutoNA.xlsx
PlutoNorth.xlsx
PlutoSA.xlsx
PlutoSummary.xlsx
PlutoSummaryTest.xlsx
PlutoTemplateRevised.xltx
PlutoYearend.xlsx
Quarter1 Files.xlw

TUTORIAL 7

Using Advanced Functions and Conditional Formatting

Calculating Employee Benefits

EXCEL

OBJECTIVES

Session 7.1
- Use the IF function
- Use the AND function
- Use the OR function
- Use structured references in formulas

Session 7.2
- Nest the IF function
- Use the VLOOKUP function
- Review the HLOOKUP function
- Use the IFERROR function

Session 7.3
- Use conditional formatting to highlight duplicate values
- Summarize data using the COUNTIF, SUMIF, and AVERAGEIF functions

Case | *Talent Tracs*

Rita Corvales started Talent Tracs, a software development company for the music and entertainment business that is located in Austin, Texas. Talent Tracs sells EasyTracs, a software program that matches venues with artists, and then schedules the performances. As the company's reputation grew, the business expanded rapidly. Today, Talent Tracs has nearly 100 employees, ranging from software developers to online customer relations staff. Rita uses Excel to track basic employee information such as each employee's name, gender, birth date, hire date, health plan, job status, pay type (hourly or salaried), pay grade, and annual salary.

Rita needs to track employee enrollment in and costs related to the benefit programs offered by the company. She wants to calculate each employee's life insurance premium and how much the company contributes to each employee's 401(k) retirement account and health plan. Rita also needs to calculate the amount Talent Tracs spends on bonuses, which are based on employee pay grades and performance. To provide Rita with all this information, you'll use a variety of logical functions, filters, and conditional formatting. After you calculate those values, Rita wants you to summarize information in the Employee Summary worksheet so she can quickly see the impact of the compensation and benefits package on the company. You will use functions to calculate counts, sums, and averages based on search criteria.

STARTING DATA FILES

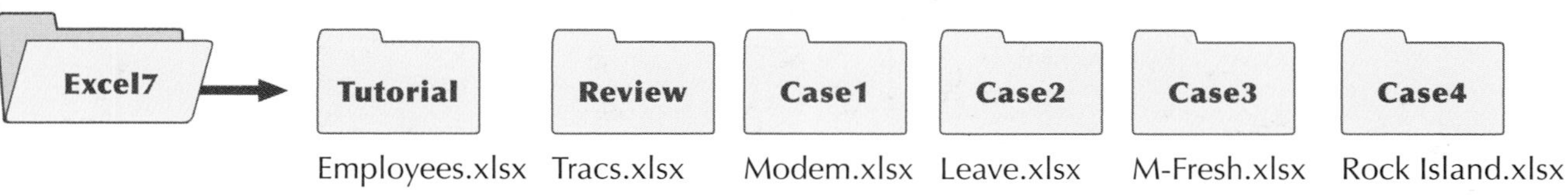

SESSION 7.1 VISUAL OVERVIEW

When you create a formula that references all or parts of an Excel table, you can replace a specific cell or range address with a **structured reference**, which is the actual table name or column header.

The **AND function** is a logical function that returns a TRUE value if all of the logical conditions are true, and a FALSE value if any or all of the logical conditions are false.

The Function Arguments dialog box makes it simpler to build an IF function with a nested AND function (shown here) or a nested OR function for the logical test.

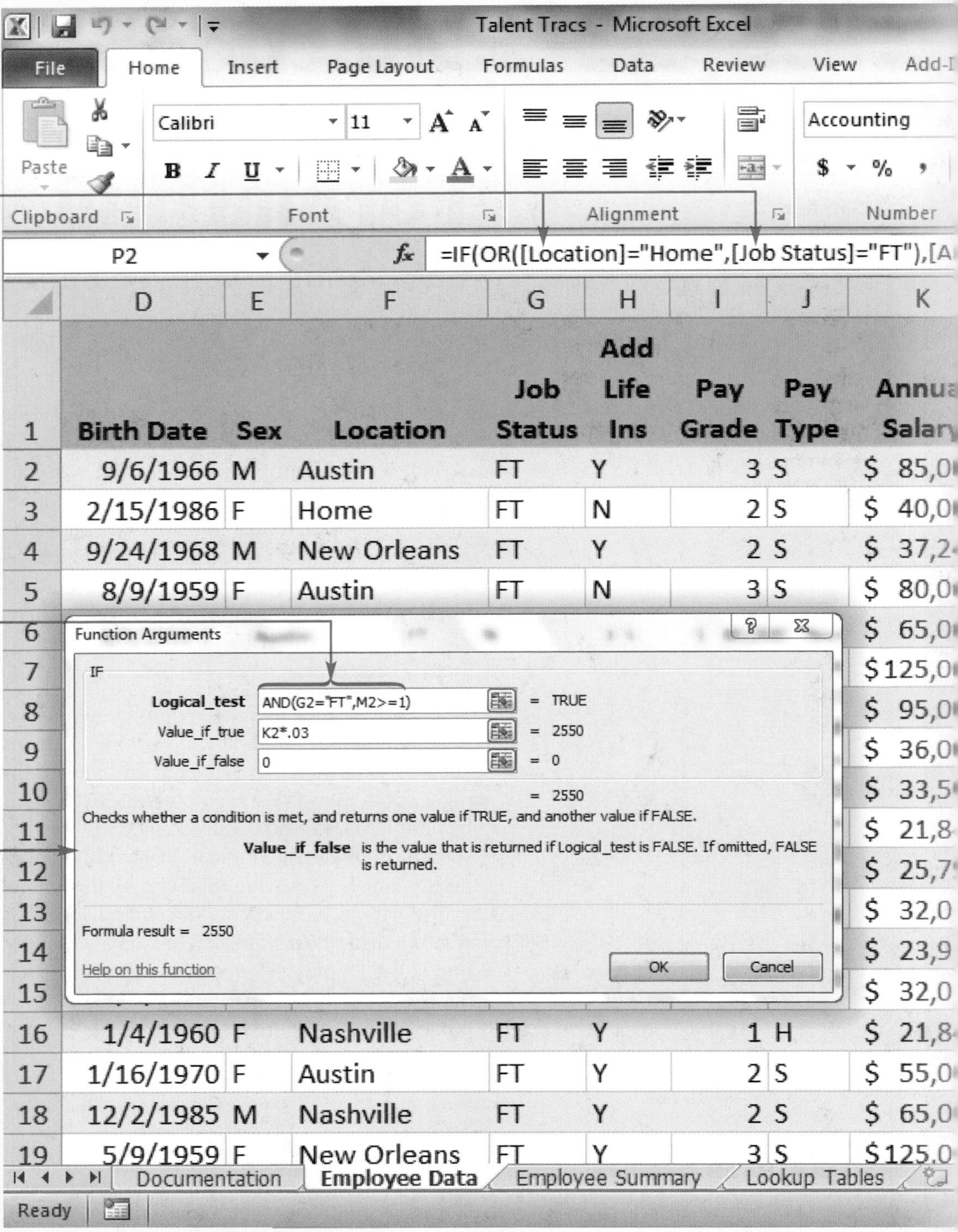

Talent Tracs - Microsoft Excel

=IF(OR([Location]="Home",[Job Status]="FT"),[A

	D	E	F	G	H	I	J	K
1	Birth Date	Sex	Location	Job Status	Add Life Ins	Pay Grade	Pay Type	Annual Salary
2	9/6/1966	M	Austin	FT	Y	3	S	$ 85,0
3	2/15/1986	F	Home	FT	N	2	S	$ 40,0
4	9/24/1968	M	New Orleans	FT	Y	2	S	$ 37,2
5	8/9/1959	F	Austin	FT	N	3	S	$ 80,0
16	1/4/1960	F	Nashville	FT	Y	1	H	$ 21,8
17	1/16/1970	F	Austin	FT	Y	2	S	$ 55,0
18	12/2/1985	M	Nashville	FT	Y	2	S	$ 65,0
19	5/9/1959	F	New Orleans	FT	Y	3	S	$125,0

Function Arguments

IF

Logical_test AND(G2="FT",M2>=1) = TRUE

Value_if_true K2*.03 = 2550

Value_if_false 0 = 0

= 2550

Checks whether a condition is met, and returns one value if TRUE, and another value if FALSE.

Value_if_false is the value that is returned if Logical_test is FALSE. If omitted, FALSE is returned.

Formula result = 2550

Help on this function OK Cancel

Documentation | Employee Data | Employee Summary | Lookup Tables

Ready

LOGICAL FUNCTIONS

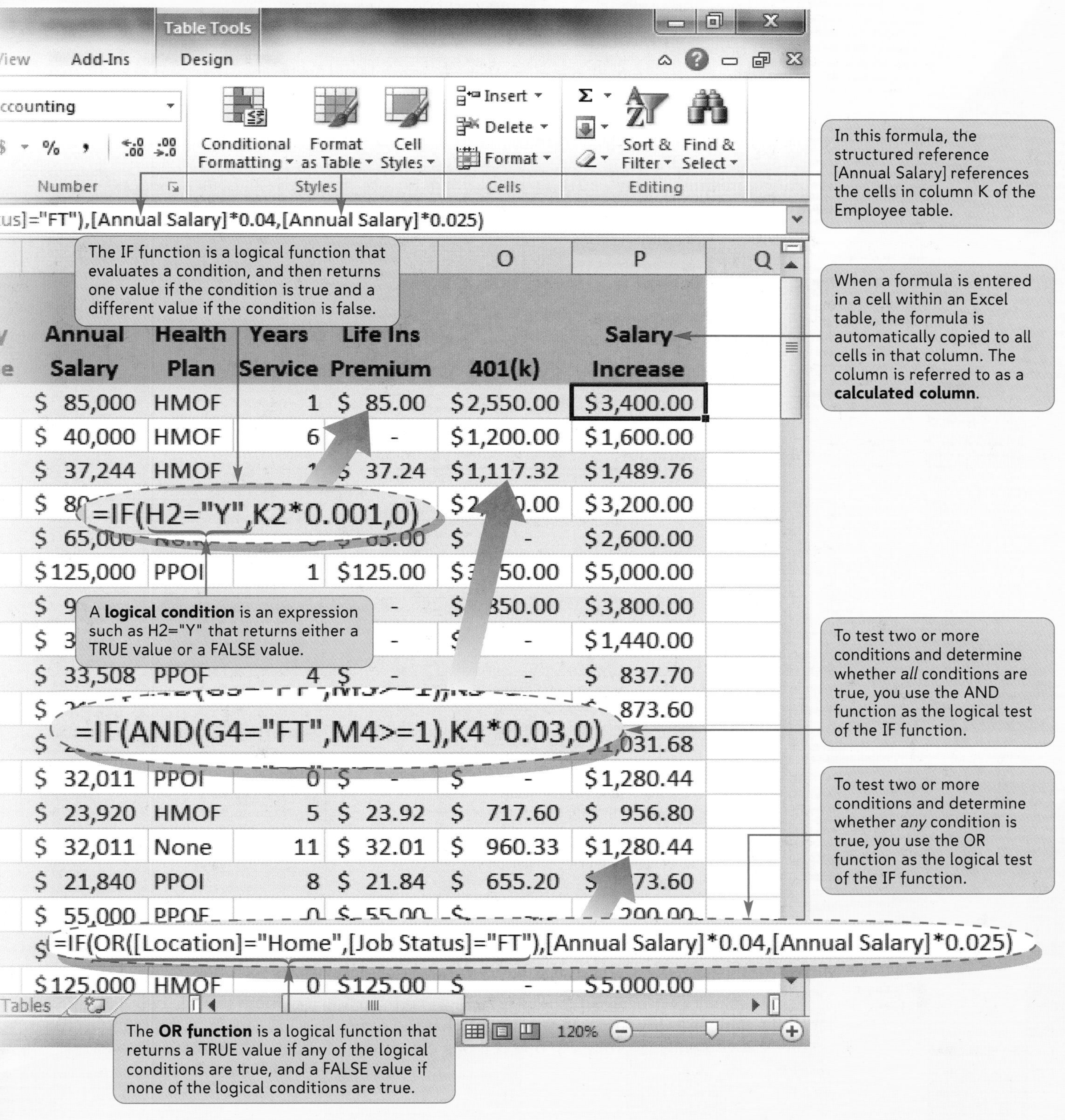

Working with Logical Functions

Logical functions such as IF, AND, and OR determine whether a condition is true or false. The condition uses one of the comparison operators <, <=, =, <>, >, or >= to compare two values. You can combine two or more functions in one formula, creating more complex conditions.

Rita created a workbook that contains data for each Talent Tracs employee. She stored this information in an Excel table. The table includes each employee's ID, last name, hire date, birth date, gender, location, job status, additional life insurance coverage, pay grade, pay type, annual salary, health plan, and years of service at Talent Tracs. You will use IF, AND, and OR functions to calculate each Talent Tracs employee's additional life insurance premium (if any), 401(k) cost, health plan cost, proposed salary increase, and bonus amount. You will open Rita's workbook and review the employee data.

To open the Talent Tracs workbook:

1. Open the **Employees** workbook located in the Excel7\Tutorial folder included with your Data Files, and then save the workbook as **Talent Tracs**.
2. In the Documentation worksheet, enter your name and the date.
3. Switch to the **Employee Data** worksheet. See Figure 7-1.

Figure 7-1 Employee Data worksheet

	A	B	C	D	E	F	G	H	I	J	K	L	M	N
1	Emp ID	Last Name	Hire Date	Birth Date	Sex	Location	Job Status	Add Life Ins	Pay Grade	Pay Type	Annual Salary	Health Plan	Years Service	
2	1024	Hovey	8/28/2011	9/6/1966	M	Austin	FT	Y	3	S	$ 85,000	HMOF	1	
3	1025	Overton	5/24/2007	2/15/1986	F	Home	FT	N	2	S	$ 40,000	HMOF	6	
4	1026	Fetherston	4/24/2012	9/24/1968	M	New Orleans	FT	Y	2	S	$ 37,244	HMOF	1	
5	1027	Lebrun	7/18/2011	8/9/1959	F	Austin	FT	N	3	S	$ 80,000	None	1	
6	1028	Hanson	8/21/2012	7/15/1950	M	Austin	FT	Y	3	S	$ 65,000	None	0	
7	1029	Philo	3/5/2012	5/2/1958	M	New Orleans	FT	Y	3	S	$125,000	PPOI	1	
8	1030	Stolt	3/1/2010	12/7/1977	M	New Orleans	FT	N	3	S	$ 95,000	HMOI	3	
9	1031	Akhalaghi	12/8/2012	12/4/1961	M	Austin	FT	N	2	S	$ 36,000	None	0	
10	1032	Vankeuren	8/11/2008	1/10/1959	F	Austin	PT	N	1	H	$ 33,508	PPOF	4	
11	1033	Mccorkle	6/12/2006	1/30/1942	F	Nashville	FT	N	1	H	$ 21,840	None	7	
12	1034	Nightingale	5/4/2009	8/27/1989	M	Nashville	FT	N	1	H	$ 25,792	PPOF	4	
13	1035	Croasdale	12/18/2012	1/6/1968	F	Austin	FT	N	1	H	$ 32,011	PPOI	0	
14	1036	Lambrechts	5/4/2008	4/28/1958	F	Nashville	FT	Y	1	H	$ 23,920	HMOF	5	
15	1037	Palmer	11/26/2001	10/4/1971	F	Austin	FT	Y	1	H	$ 32,011	None	11	
16	1038	Tetreault	2/22/2005	1/4/1960	F	Nashville	FT	Y	1	H	$ 21,840	PPOI	8	
17	1039	Cugini	12/4/2012	1/16/1970	F	Austin	FT	Y	2	S	$ 55,000	PPOF	0	
18	1040	Dash	10/12/2012	12/2/1985	M	Nashville	FT	Y	2	S	$ 65,000	HMOF	0	
19	1041	Donnelly	12/4/2012	5/9/1959	F	New Orleans	FT	Y	3	S	$125,000	HMOF	0	

Documentation | Employee Data | Employee Summary | Lookup Tables

Ready 120%

Inserting Calculated Columns in an Excel Table

TIP

Calculated columns work only in Excel tables. To achieve the same results in a range of data, you must copy and paste the formula or use the AutoFill feature.

An Excel table does not have a fixed structure. When you add a column to an Excel table, the table expands and the new column has the same table formatting as the other columns. If you enter a formula in one cell of a column, the formula is automatically copied to all cells in that column. These calculated columns are helpful as you add formulas to an Excel table.

If you need to modify the formula in a calculated column, you edit the formula in any cell in the column and the formulas in all the cells in that table column are also modified. If you want to edit only one cell in a calculated column, you need to enter a value or a formula that is different from all the others in that column. A green triangle appears in the upper-left corner of the cell with the custom formula in the calculated column, making the inconsistency easy to find. After a calculated column contains one inconsistent formula or value, any other edits you make to that column are no longer automatically copied to the rest of the cells in that column. Excel does not overwrite custom values.

PROSKILLS

Written Communication: Creating Excel Table Fields

Excel tables should be easy to use as well as understand. This requires labeling and entering data in a way that effectively communicates a table's content or purpose. If a field is entered in a way that is difficult to use and understand, it becomes more difficult to find and present data in a meaningful way.

To effectively communicate a table's function, keep the following guidelines in mind when creating fields in an Excel table:

- **Create fields that require the least maintenance.** For example, hire date and birth date require no maintenance after entered, unlike age and years of service, whose values change each year. If you need to know the specific age or years of service, use calculations to determine them based on values in the Hire Date and Birth Date columns.
- **Store the smallest unit of data possible in a field.** For example, use three separate fields for City, State, and Zip code rather than one field. Using separate fields for each unit of data enables you to sort or filter each field. If you want to display data from two or more fields in one column, you can use a formula to reference the City, State, and Zip code columns. For example, you can use the & operator to combine the city, state, and zip code in one cell as follows: `=C2&D2&E2`.
- **Apply a text format to fields with numerical text data.** For example, formatting fields such as zip codes and Social Security numbers as text ensures that leading zeros are stored as part of the data. Otherwise, the zip code 02892 is stored as a number and displayed as 2892.

Using these guidelines means that you and others will spend less time interpreting data and more time analyzing results. This lets you more effectively communicate the data in an Excel table.

Using the IF Function

In many situations, the value you store in a cell depends on certain conditions. Consider the following examples:

- An employee's gross pay depends on whether that employee worked overtime.
- An income tax rate depends on the taxpayer's adjusted taxable income.
- A shipping charge depends on the size of an order.

To evaluate these types of conditions, you use the IF function. Recall that the IF function is a logical function that evaluates a condition, and then returns one value if the condition is true and another value if the condition is false. The IF function has the syntax

```
IF(logical_test, [value_if_true,] [value_if_false])
```

where *logical_test* is a condition that is either true or false, *value_if_true* is the value returned by the function if the condition is true, and *value_if_false* is the value returned by the function if the condition is false. The IF function results in only one value—either the *value_if_true* or the *value_if_false*.

For example, the following IF function tests whether the value in cell A5 is equal to "Yes." If it is, the *value_if_true* argument, C5+B5, is calculated and its value is displayed in the cell. Otherwise, the *value_if_false* argument, B5–C5, is calculated and its value is displayed in the cell.

```
=IF(A5="Yes",C5+B5,B5-C5)
```

You will use the IF function to calculate the additional life insurance premiums in the Employee table. Talent Tracs employees can elect to purchase additional life insurance coverage. This is indicated in the Add Life Ins column with Y for yes and N for no. The premium amount is equal to the employee's annual salary multiplied by the premium rate (.001). Rita sketched the flowchart shown in Figure 7-2 to illustrate the logic for calculating an employee's additional life insurance premium. The flowchart shows that if the employee elected additional life insurance (Add Life Ins = "Y" is True), the premium is calculated using the formula Salary*.001. If the employee did not elect additional life insurance (Add Life Ins = "Y" is False), the premium is 0.

Figure 7-2 **Flowchart with logic for the additional life insurance premium**

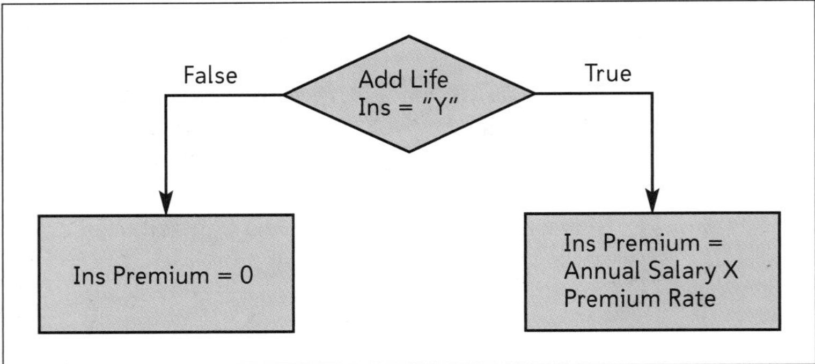

You'll add a column to the Employee table to display the results of the IF function that calculates the premium employees will pay if they elect additional life insurance coverage.

To calculate the life insurance premium using an IF function:

1. In cell N1, enter **Life Ins Premium**. The Excel table expands to include this column and applies the table formatting to all the rows in the new column.
2. Make sure cell **N2** is the active cell, and then click the **Insert Function** button *fx* in the formula bar. The Insert Function dialog box opens.
3. Click **Logical** in the Or select a category list, click **IF** in the Select a function box, and then click the **OK** button. The Function Arguments dialog box for the IF function opens.
4. In the Logical_test box, type **H2="Y"** and then press the **Tab** key. This sets the logical test to evaluate whether the employee wants additional life insurance, indicated by "Y" for Yes or "N" for No in cell H2. TRUE appears to the right of the Logical_test argument box, indicating the result for the employee in row 2 is true. That is, the employee wants additional life insurance.
5. In the Value_if_true box, type **K2*0.001**. This argument specifies that if the condition is true (the employee wants additional life insurance), the result of the employee's current salary (listed in cell K2) is multiplied by 0.1% and displayed in cell N2. The value to the right of the Value_if_true argument box is 85, which is the premium the employee will pay for additional life insurance if the condition is true.
6. In the Value_if_false box, type **0**. This argument specifies that if the condition is false (the employee does not want additional life insurance), 0 is displayed in cell N2. The value to the right of the Value_if_false argument box is 0, which is the value that will appear in cell N2 if the condition is false. See Figure 7-3.

Figure 7-3 **Function Arguments dialog box for the IF Function**

function arguments applied to the employee in the current row of the table

Function Arguments

IF

Logical_test H2="Y" = TRUE

Value_if_true K2*0.001 = 85

Value_if_false 0 = 0

= 85

Checks whether a condition is met, and returns one value if TRUE, and another value if FALSE.

Value_if_false is the value that is returned if Logical_test is FALSE. If omitted, FALSE is returned.

Formula result = 85

Help on this function — OK — Cancel

7. Click the **OK** button. The formula =IF(H2="Y",K2*0.001,0) appears in the formula bar, and 85 appears in cell N2 because the condition is true. The formula is automatically copied to all the cells in column N of the table.
8. Position the pointer just above cell **N1** until the pointer changes to ⬇, and then click to select the range N2:N101. The data in the Life Ins Premium column is selected, but not the column header.
9. Format the selected range N2:N101 with the **Accounting** number format, which includes the dollar sign and two decimal places. The Life Ins Premium column shows the additional life insurance premiums employees will pay formatted as currency.
10. Click cell **N2** to deselect the column. See Figure 7-4.

> **TIP**
>
> Click just above a cell in the header row of an Excel table (not the worksheet column heading) to select the column data but not the header; double-click to select the entire column including the column header.

Figure 7-4 **Life Ins Premium column added to the Employee table**

formula to calculate the life insurance premium

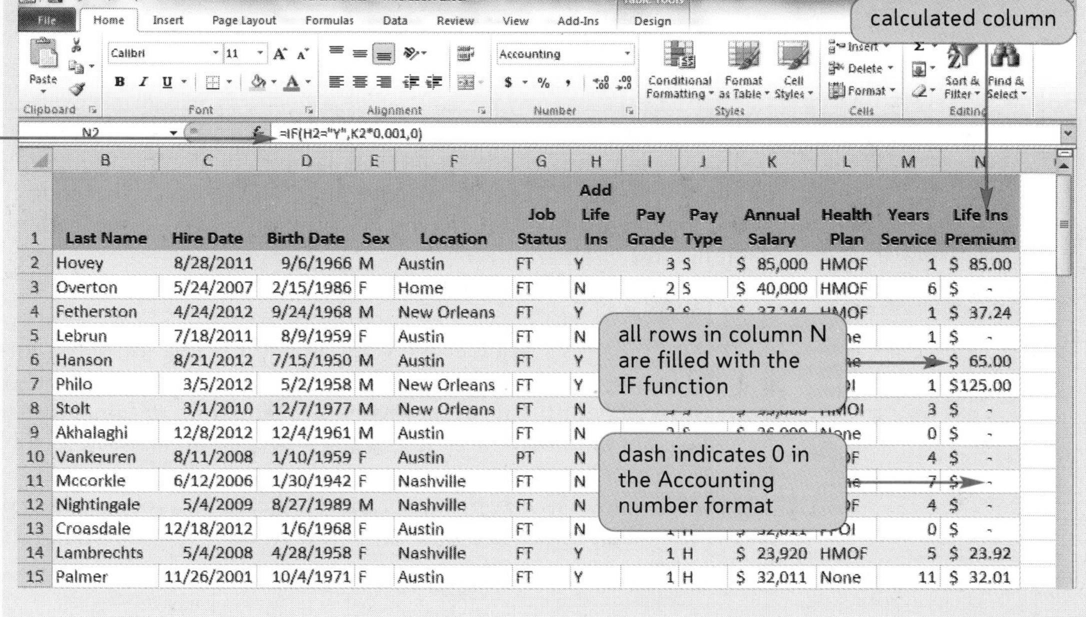

Using the AND Function

The IF function evaluates a single condition. However, you often need to test two or more conditions and determine whether *all* conditions are true. You can do this with the AND function. The AND function is a logical function that returns the value TRUE if all the logical conditions are true and the value FALSE if any or all of the logical conditions are false. The syntax of the AND function is

```
AND(logical1 [,logical2,]...)
```

where *logical1* and *logical2* are conditions that can be either true or false. If all of the logical conditions are true, the AND function returns the logical value TRUE; otherwise, the function returns the logical value FALSE. You can include up to 255 logical conditions in an AND function. However, keep in mind that *all* the logical conditions listed in the AND function must be true for the AND function to return a TRUE value.

Talent Tracs employees are eligible for the 401(k) benefit if they are full-time employees (FT in Job Status) *and* have worked for the company for one or more years (1 or greater in Years Service). As long as *both* conditions are true, the company contributes an amount equal to 3 percent of the employee's salary to the employee's 401(k). If neither condition is true or if only one condition is true, the employee is not eligible for the 401(k) benefit and the company's contribution is 0. Rita outlined these eligibility conditions in the flowchart shown in Figure 7-5.

Figure 7-5 **Flowchart illustrating AND logic for the 401(k) benefit**

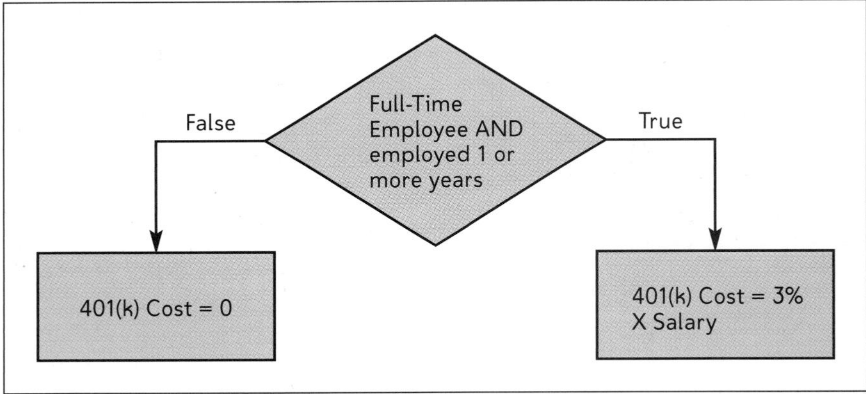

To calculate the cost of the 401(k) plan for each employee, you need to use the AND function with the IF function. You use the AND function shown in the following formula as the logical test to evaluate whether each employee in the Employee table fulfills the eligibility requirements:

```
=AND(G2="FT",M2>=1)
```

This formula tests whether the value in cell G2 (the job status for the first employee) is equal to FT (an abbreviation for full time) and whether the value in cell M2 (the years of service for the first employee) is greater than or equal to one (indicating one or more years of employment at Talent Tracs). When an employee is a full-time employee (G2="FT") *and* has worked one or more years at Talent Tracs (M2>=1), the AND function returns the value TRUE; otherwise, the AND function returns the value FALSE. Figure 7-6 shows the result returned by the AND function for four different sets of employee values for job status and years of service.

Figure 7-6 **Example of AND function results**

Purpose: To determine employee eligibility for the company's 401(k) plan

Logic Scenario: An employee is eligible for the 401(k) plan if the employee's status is full time (FT) AND the employee's years of service total one or more years.

Formula: AND function with two conditions
`=AND(G2="FT",M2>=1)`

Data: cell G2 stores Employee Status
cell M2 stores Years Service

Example:

Data		Condition1	Condition2	Results
Cell G2	Cell M2	G2="FT"	M2>=1	(Eligible?)
FT	1	True	True	True
FT	0	True	False	False
PT	5	False	True	False
PT	0	False	False	False

The AND function shows only whether an employee is eligible for the 401(k) plan. It does not calculate how much Talent Tracs will contribute to that employee's 401(k) plan if the employee is eligible. To determine whether an employee is eligible *and* to calculate the amount of the 401(k) contribution, you use this AND function within an IF function. When the results of one function are used as the argument of another function, the functions are nested. In the following formula, the AND function (shown in red) is nested within the IF function and is used as the logical test that determines whether the employee is eligible for a 401(k) contribution. If the employee is eligible, the AND function returns the logical value TRUE and the IF function multiplies the employee's annual salary by 3 percent. If the AND function returns the logical value FALSE, the IF function displays the value 0.

```
=IF(AND(G2="FT",M2>=1),K2*0.03,0)
```

Figure 7-7 illustrates how the AND function is used to determine student eligibility for the dean's list. In this scenario, when students have 12 or more credits (stored in cell B1) *and* their GPA is greater than 3.25 (stored in cell B2), they are placed on the dean's list. Both conditions must be true for the AND function to return the logical value TRUE.

Figure 7-7 Additional AND function example

Purpose: To determine dean's list requirements

Logic Scenario: 12 or more semester credits and GPA above 3.25

Formula: AND function with two conditions
`=AND(B1>=12,B2>3.25)`

Data: cell B1 stores number of credits
cell B2 stores student's GPA

Example:

Data		Condition1	Condition2	Results
Cell B1	Cell B2	B1>=12	B2>3.25	(Dean's List?)
15	3.5	True	True	True
12	3.25	True	False	False
6	3.4	False	True	False
10	3.0	False	False	False

You'll insert a new column in the Employee table, and then enter the formula to calculate the 401(k) contribution.

To use the IF and AND functions to calculate the 401(k) contribution:

1. In cell O1, enter **401(k)** as the column header. The Excel table expands to include the new column, and cell O2 is the active cell.
2. Make sure cell O2 is the active cell, and then click the **Insert Function** button *fx* in the formula bar. The Insert Function dialog box opens.
3. Click **IF** in the Select a function box, and then click the **OK** button. The Function Arguments dialog box opens.
4. In the Logical_test box, type **AND(G2="FT",M2>=1)** and then press the **Tab** key. This logical test evaluates whether the employee is full time, indicated by "FT" in cell G2, and has worked at Talent Tracs for one year or more. TRUE appears to the right of the Logical_test box, indicating the result for the employee in row 2 is true. This employee is eligible for the 401(k) plan.
5. In the Value_if_true box, type **K2*0.03** and then press the **Tab** key. This argument specifies that if the condition is true (the employee is eligible for the 401(k) plan as determined by the AND function), the amount in the employee's salary cell is multiplied by 3 percent. The amount of this employee's 401(k) contribution, 2550, appears to the right of the Value_if_true box.
6. In the Value_if_false box, type **0**. This argument specifies that if the condition is false (the employee is not eligible for the 401(k) as determined by the AND function), the amount displayed in cell O2 is 0, which appears to the right of the Value_if_false box. See Figure 7-8.

Figure 7-8 **Function Arguments dialog box for the IF function with the AND function**

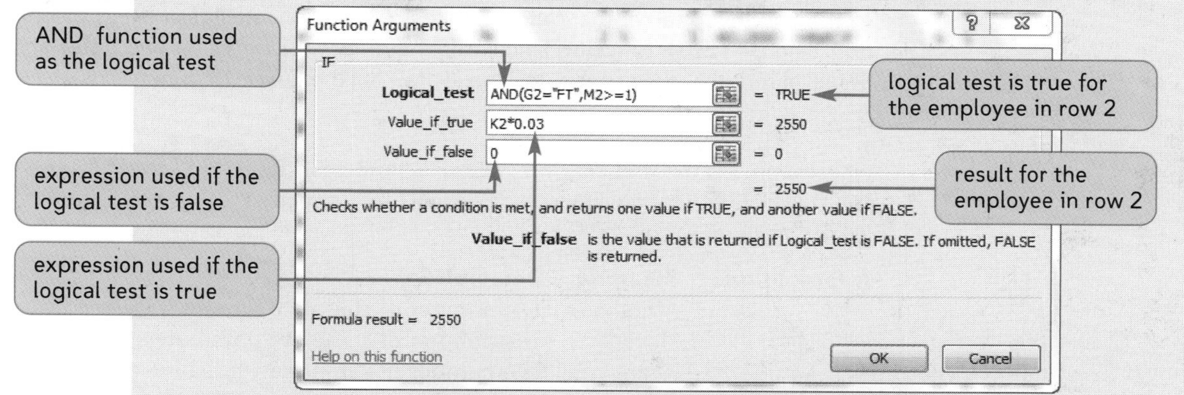

7. Click the **OK** button. The formula with the IF function that you just created is entered in cell O2 and copied to all rows in column O of the table.
8. Position the pointer at the top of cell **O1** until the pointer changes to ⬇, click to select the 401(k) data values, and then format the range using the **Accounting** number format.
9. Click cell **O2** to make it the active cell. The formula =IF(AND(G2="FT",M2>=1),K2*0.03,0) appears in the formula bar and $2,550.00 appears in cell O2 because the condition is true. See Figure 7-9.

Figure 7-9 **IF function with the AND function to calculate 401(k)**

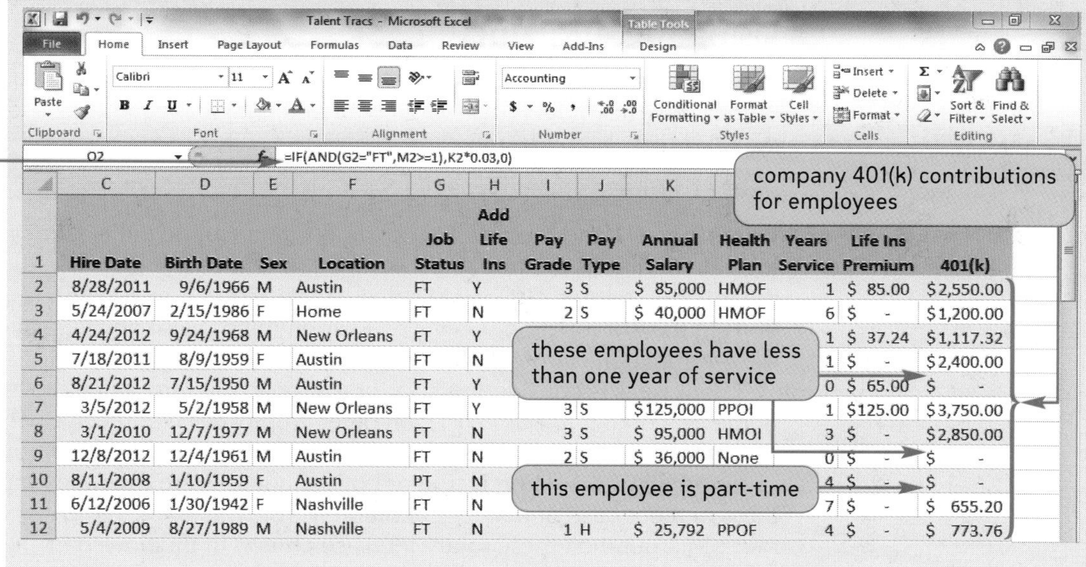

	Hire Date	Birth Date	Sex	Location	Job Status	Add Life Ins	Pay Grade	Pay Type	Annual Salary	Health Plan	Years Service	Life Ins Premium	401(k)
2	8/28/2011	9/6/1966	M	Austin	FT	Y	3	S	$ 85,000	HMOF	1	$ 85.00	$2,550.00
3	5/24/2007	2/15/1986	F	Home	FT	N	2	S	$ 40,000	HMOF	6	$ -	$1,200.00
4	4/24/2012	9/24/1968	M	New Orleans	FT	Y					1	$ 37.24	$1,117.32
5	7/18/2011	8/9/1959	F	Austin	FT	N					1	$ -	$2,400.00
6	8/21/2012	7/15/1950	M	Austin	FT	Y					0	$ 65.00	$ -
7	3/5/2012	5/2/1958	M	New Orleans	FT	Y	3	S	$125,000	PPOI	1	$125.00	$3,750.00
8	3/1/2010	12/7/1977	M	New Orleans	FT	N	3	S	$ 95,000	HMOI	3	$ -	$2,850.00
9	12/8/2012	12/4/1961	M	Austin	FT	N	2	S	$ 36,000	None	0	$ -	$ -
10	8/11/2008	1/10/1959	F	Austin	PT	N					4	$ -	$ -
11	6/12/2006	1/30/1942	F	Nashville	FT	N					7	$ -	$ 655.20
12	5/4/2009	8/27/1989	M	Nashville	FT	N	1	H	$ 25,792	PPOF	4	$ -	$ 773.76

INSIGHT

Using the DATEDIF Function to Calculate Years of Service

In the Employee table, the Years Service column was calculated using the DATEDIF function. The **DATEDIF function** calculates the difference between two dates and shows the result in months, days, or years. The syntax for the DATEDIF function is

```
DATEDIF(Date1,Date2,Interval)
```

where *Date1* is the earliest date, *Date2* is the latest date, and *Interval* is the unit of time the DATEDIF function will use in the result. You specify the *Interval* with one of the following interval codes:

Interval Code	Meaning	Description
"m"	Months	The number of complete months between Date1 and Date2
"d"	Days	The number of complete days between Date1 and Date2
"y"	Years	The number of complete years between Date1 and Date2

For example, the following formula calculates years of service at Talent Tracs in complete years:

```
=DATEDIF(C2,$AB$1,"y")
```

The earliest date is located in cell C2, the hire date. The latest date is in cell $AB$1, which shows the date used to compare against the hire date—years of service as of a cut-off date. The Interval "y" indicates that you want to display the number of complete years between these two dates.

The DATEDIF function is undocumented in Excel, but it has been available since Excel 97. To learn more about this function, search the Web using "DATEDIF function in Excel" as the search text in your favorite search engine.

Using the OR Function

The OR function is a logical function that returns a TRUE value if any of the logical conditions are true and a FALSE value if all of the logical conditions are false. The syntax of the OR function is

```
OR(logical1 [,logical2,]...)
```

where *logical1* and *logical2* are conditions that can be either true or false. If any of the logical conditions are true, the OR function returns the logical value TRUE; otherwise, the function returns the logical value FALSE. You can include up to 255 logical conditions in the OR function. However, keep in mind that if *any* logical condition listed in the OR function is true, the OR function returns a TRUE value.

Talent Tracs is considering awarding a 4 percent raise to employees working from home *or* working full-time (FT); all other employees will receive a 2.5 percent increase. The criteria for awarding a salary increase is based on two conditions—location and job status. If either condition is true or both conditions are true, the employee will receive the 4 percent raise. If neither condition is true, the employee will receive the 2.5 percent raise. Rita outlined these salary increase criteria in the flowchart shown in Figure 7-10.

Figure 7-10 **Flowchart of the OR function**

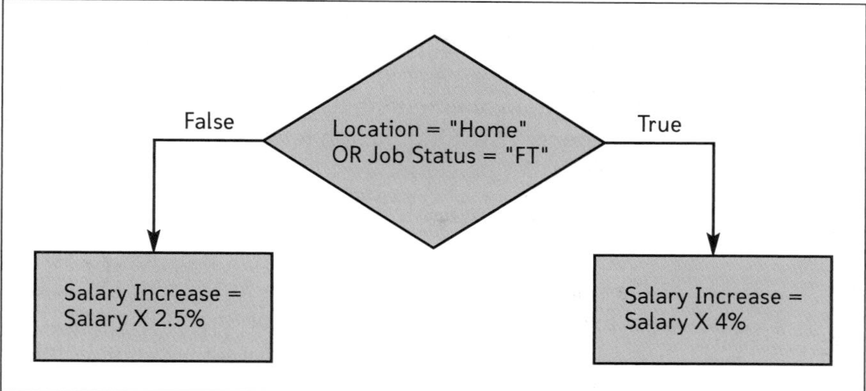

You need to use the OR function to test whether an employee meets the criteria for the 4 percent or 2.5 percent salary increase. The following formula uses the OR function to test whether the value in cell F2 (the work location for the first employee) is equal to "Home" or whether the value in cell G2 (the job status for the first employee) is equal to "FT." If the employee works from home *or* the employee works full time *or* the employee both works from home and works full time, the OR function returns the value TRUE; otherwise, the OR function returns the value FALSE.

```
=OR(F2="Home", G2="FT")
```

Figure 7-11 shows the results returned using the OR function for four different sets of values for employee work location and job status.

Figure 7-11 **Examples of OR function results**

Purpose: To determine an employee's salary increase percentage

Logic Scenario: Proposed 4 percent salary increase to full-time (FT) employees or employees working from home

Formula: OR function with two conditions
`=OR(F2="Home",G2="FT")`

Data: cell F2 stores Location
cell G2 stores Job Status

Example:

Data		Condition1	Condition2	Results
Cell F2	Cell G2	F2="Home"	G2="FT"	(4% increase)
Home	FT	True	True	True
Austin	FT	False	True	True
Home	PT	True	False	True
Nashville	PT	False	False	False

The OR function only determines which raise an employee is eligible for. It does not calculate the amount of the salary increase. To determine the amount of the salary increase, the OR function must be nested within an IF function. In the following formula, the logical test of the IF function uses the OR function (shown in red) to determine whether an employee is either working from home or working full-time or both. If the OR function returns a TRUE value, the IF function multiplies the annual salary by 4 percent. If the OR function returns a FALSE value, the IF function multiplies the annual salary by 2.5 percent.

```
=IF(OR(F2="Home",G2="FT"),K2*0.04,K2*0.025)
```

Figure 7-12 illustrates how the OR function is used to determine eligibility for a 10 percent discount. In this scenario, anyone who is 65 years or older (stored in cell B1) *or* anyone who is a college student (stored in cell B2) receives a 10 percent discount. At least one condition must be true for the OR function to return the logical value TRUE.

Figure 7-12 **Additional example of the OR function**

Purpose: To determine who is eligible for a discount

Logic Scenario: Discount is 10 percent for seniors (65 or older) or college students (Status = STU)

Formula: OR function with two conditions
`=OR(B1>=65,B2="STU")`

Data: cell B1 stores Age
cell B2 stores Status (STU, FAC, STF)

Example:

Data		Condition1	Condition2	Results
Cell B1	Cell B2	B1>=65	B2="STU"	(Discount?)
22	STU	False	True	True
65	FAC	True	False	True
67	STU	True	True	True
45	STF	False	False	False

Using Structured References to Create Formulas in Excel Tables

When you create a formula that references all or parts of an Excel table, you can replace the specific cell or range address with a structured reference, the actual table name or column header. This makes the formula easier to create and understand. The default Excel table name is Table1, Table2, and so forth unless you entered a more descriptive table name, as you did for the Employee table. Column headers provide a description of the data entered in each column. Structured references make it easier to create formulas that use portions or all of an Excel table because the names or headers are usually simpler to identify than cell addresses. For example, in the Employee table, the table name

TIP

If you are not sure of a table's name, click in the table, click the Table Tools Design tab on the Ribbon, and then check the Table Name box in the Properties group.

"Employee" refers to the range A2:N101, which is the range of data in the table excluding the header row and the Total row. When you want to reference an entire column of data in a table, you create a column qualifier, which has the syntax

```
Tablename[qualifier]
```

where *Tablename* is the name entered in the Table Name box in the Properties group on the Table Tools Design tab, and *qualifier* is the column header enclosed in square brackets. For example, the structured reference Employee[Annual Salary] references the annual salary data in the range K2:K101 of the Employee table.

You use structured references in formulas. The following formula adds the annual salary data in the range K2:K101 of the Employee table; in this case, [Annual Salary] is the column qualifier:

```
=SUM(Employee[Annual Salary])
```

When you create a calculated column, as you did to calculate life insurance premiums and 401(k) contributions in the Employee table, you can use structured references to create the formula. A formula that includes a structured reference can be fully qualified or unqualified. In a fully qualified structured reference, the table name precedes the column qualifier. In an unqualified structured reference, only the column qualifier appears in the reference. For example, you could have used either of the following formulas with structured references to calculate Life Ins Premium in the calculated column you added to the Employee table:

Fully qualified

```
=IF(Employee[Add Life Ins]="Y",Employee[Annual Salary]*.001,0)
```

Unqualified

```
=IF([Add Life Ins]="Y",[Annual Salary]*.001,0)
```

If you are creating a calculated column or formula within an Excel table, you can use either the fully qualified structured reference or the unqualified structured reference in the formula. If you use a structured reference outside the table or in another worksheet to reference an Excel table or portion of the table, you must use a fully qualified reference.

You'll use structured references to calculate the salary increases for Talent Tracs employees.

To calculate the salary increase:

1. In cell P1, enter **Salary Increase** as the column header. The Excel table expands to include the new column, and cell P2 is the active cell.
2. Make sure cell P2 is the active cell, and then click the **Insert Function** button in the formula bar. The Insert Function dialog box opens.
3. Click **IF** in the Select a function box, and then click the **OK** button. The Function Arguments dialog box opens.
4. Next to the Logical_test box, click the **Collapse Dialog Box** button. The Function Arguments dialog box reduces to show only the Logical_test box.
5. In the Logical_test box, type **OR([Location]="Home",[Job Status]="FT")** to enter the OR function with structured references. This logical test evaluates whether the employee works from home or works full-time or both. See Figure 7-13.

Be sure to type square brackets around the structured references and use the exact spelling and location shown. Otherwise, the formula will return an error.

Figure 7-13 **Logical_test argument for the OR function**

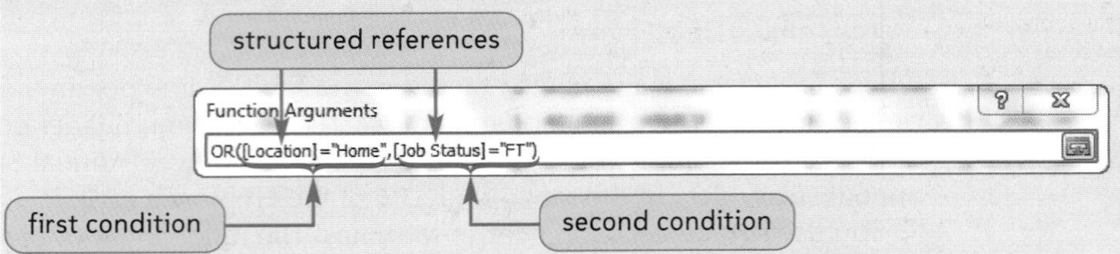

6. Click the **Expand Dialog Box** button to show the full Function Arguments dialog box, and then press the **Tab** key. TRUE appears to the right of the Logical_test box, indicating the result for the employee in the active row, row 2, is true. This employee is eligible for the 4 percent salary increase.

   Trouble? If "Invalid" appears instead of "TRUE" as the logical test results, you probably mistyped the logical test. Compare the function in your Logical_test box to the one shown in Figure 7-13, confirming that you used square brackets around the structured references [Location] and [Job Status] and typed all the text correctly.

7. In the Value_if_true box, type **[Annual Salary]*0.04** and then press the **Tab** key. This argument specifies that if the logical test is true (the employee is eligible for the 4 percent increase), the amount in the employee's salary cell is multiplied by 4 percent. The salary increases for all employees, beginning in row 2, whose logical test is true appear to the right of the Value_if_true box.

8. In the Value_if_false box, type **[Annual Salary]*0.025**. This argument specifies that if the logical test is false (the employee is not eligible for the 4 percent increase), the amount in the employee's salary cell is multiplied by 2.5 percent. The salary increases for all employees, beginning in row 2, whose logical test is false appear to the right of the Value_if_false box. See Figure 7-14.

Figure 7-14 **Function Arguments dialog box for the IF function with an OR function**

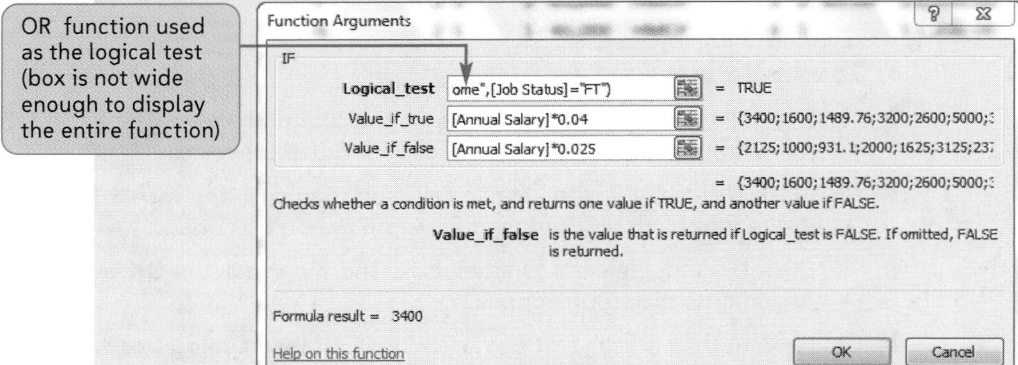

9. Click the **OK** button. The formula =IF(OR([Location]="Home",[Job Status]="FT"), [Annual Salary]*0.04,[Annual Salary]*0.025) appears in the formula bar and the value 3400 appears in cell P2 because the condition is true. The results are automatically copied to all rows in column P of the table.

10. Position the pointer at the top of cell **P1** until the pointer changes to ⬇, click to select the Salary Increase data values, and then format the range using the **Accounting** number format.

11. Click cell **P2** to deselect the column. See Figure 7-15.

Figure 7-15 **IF function with the OR function calculates salary increase**

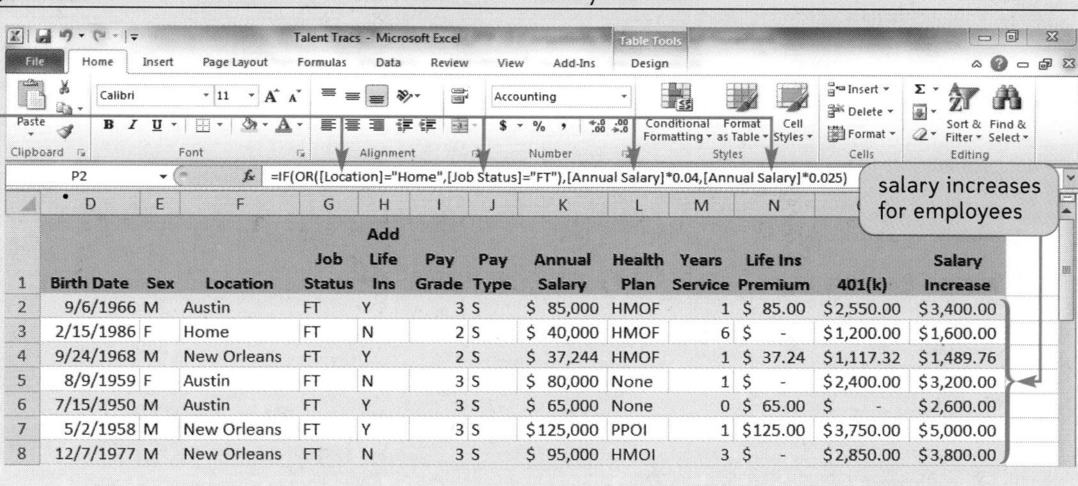

	D	E	F	G	H	I	J	K	L	M	N	O	P
1	Birth Date	Sex	Location	Job Status	Add Life Ins	Pay Grade	Pay Type	Annual Salary	Health Plan	Years Service	Life Ins Premium	401(k)	Salary Increase
2	9/6/1966	M	Austin	FT	Y	3	S	$ 85,000	HMOF	1	$ 85.00	$2,550.00	$3,400.00
3	2/15/1986	F	Home	FT	N	2	S	$ 40,000	HMOF	6	$ -	$1,200.00	$1,600.00
4	9/24/1968	M	New Orleans	FT	Y	2	S	$ 37,244	HMOF	1	$ 37.24	$1,117.32	$1,489.76
5	8/9/1959	F	Austin	FT	N	3	S	$ 80,000	None	1	$ -	$2,400.00	$3,200.00
6	7/15/1950	M	Austin	FT	Y	3	S	$ 65,000	None	0	$ 65.00	$ -	$2,600.00
7	5/2/1958	M	New Orleans	FT	Y	3	S	$125,000	PPOI	1	$125.00	$3,750.00	$5,000.00
8	12/7/1977	M	New Orleans	FT	N	3	S	$ 95,000	HMOI	3	$ -	$2,850.00	$3,800.00

In this session, you used the IF, AND, and OR functions to calculate the additional life insurance premiums, 401(k) benefits, and next year's salary increases for Talent Tracs employees. Rita still needs to calculate the employee bonuses, health plan costs, and the employee recognition award for each employee. In the next session, you will create formulas with functions to perform these calculations.

REVIEW

Section 7.1 Quick Check

1. What changes occur in the appearance and size of an Excel table after you enter a new column header named "Phone"?
2. Whenever you enter a formula in an empty column of an Excel table, Excel automatically fills the column with the same formula. What is this called?
3. If an Excel worksheet stores the cost per meal in cell Q5, the number of attendees in cell Q6, and the total cost of meals in cell Q7, what IF function would you enter in cell Q7 to calculate the total cost of meals (cost per meal times the number of attendees) with a minimum cost of $10,000?
4. True or False. The AND function is a logical function that returns a TRUE value if any of the logical conditions are true and a FALSE value if all of the logical conditions are false.
5. Write the formula that displays the label "Outstanding" if the amount owed (cell X5) is greater than 0 and the transaction date (cell R5) is before 3/15/2013, but otherwise leaves the cell blank.
6. When you create a formula that references all or parts of an Excel table, you can use ______________ to replace the specific cell or range addresses with the actual table or column header names.
7. If the formula `=IF(OR(B25="NY",B25="CA",B25="TX"),"Select","Ignore")` is entered in cell B26, and "PA" is entered in cell B25, what is displayed in cell B26?
8. What OR function represents the rule, "A potential enlistee in the Army is not eligible to enlist if younger than 17 or older than 42." The age is stored in cell B25.

SESSION 7.2 VISUAL OVERVIEW

A **nested IF function** is when one IF function is placed inside another IF function to test an additional condition, such as calculating employee bonuses based on pay grade.

The **lookup value** is the value you are trying to find. In this case, the lookup value is the code in the Health Plan column.

The invalid code in the Health Plan column causes the IFERROR message to appear in the Health Cost column.

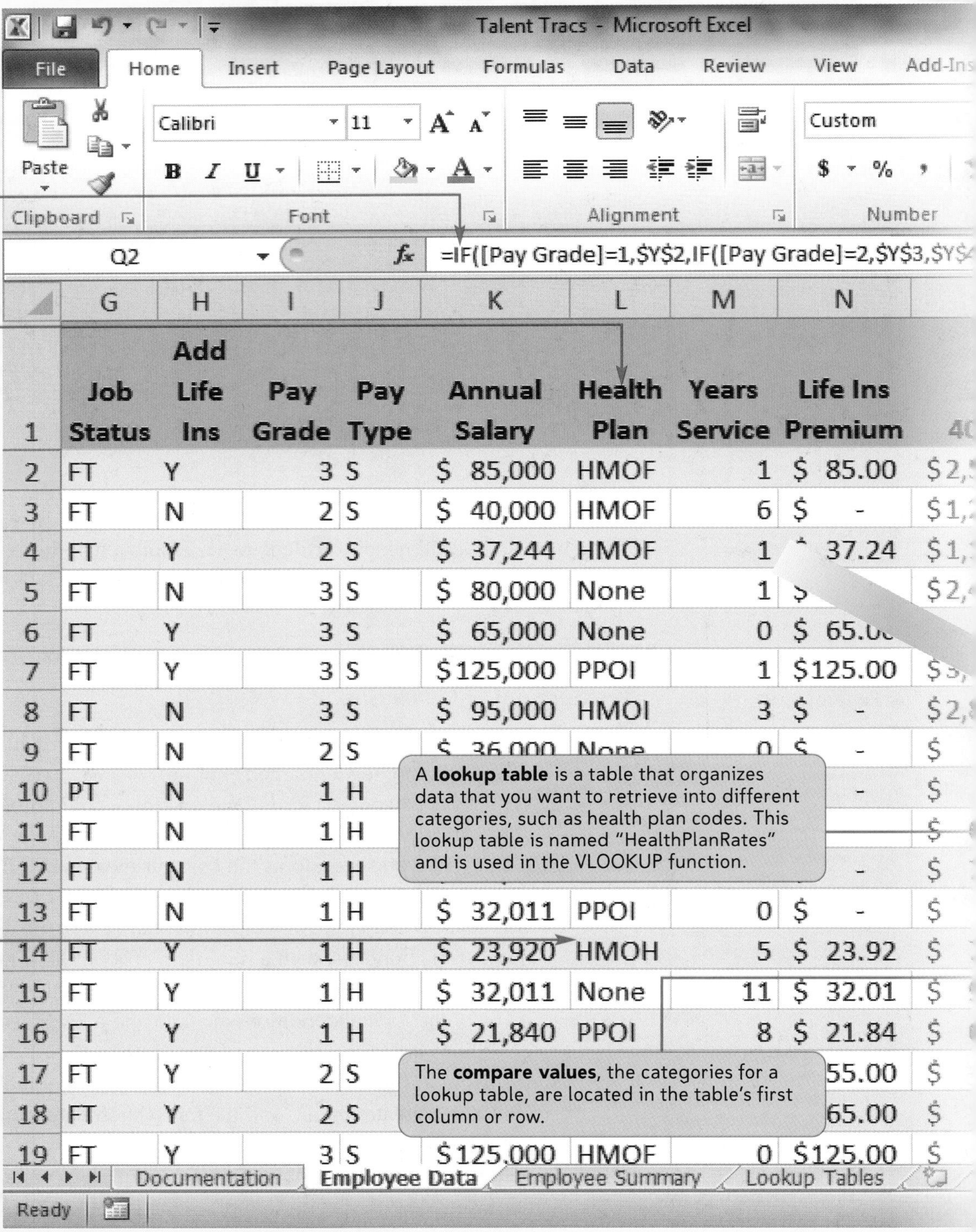

Talent Tracs - Microsoft Excel

File | Home | Insert | Page Layout | Formulas | Data | Review | View | Add-Ins

Paste | Calibri | 11 | Custom | $ - % ,

Clipboard | Font | Alignment | Number

Q2 | =IF([Pay Grade]=1,$Y$2,IF([Pay Grade]=2,$Y$3,Y

	G	H	I	J	K	L	M	N	
1	Job Status	Add Life Ins	Pay Grade	Pay Type	Annual Salary	Health Plan	Years Service	Life Ins Premium	4(
2	FT	Y	3	S	$ 85,000	HMOF	1	$ 85.00	$2,
3	FT	N	2	S	$ 40,000	HMOF	6	$ -	$1,
4	FT	Y	2	S	$ 37,244	HMOF	1	37.24	$1,
5	FT	N	3	S	$ 80,000	None	1	$	$2,
6	FT	Y	3	S	$ 65,000	None	0	$ 65.0	
7	FT	Y	3	S	$125,000	PPOI	1	$125.00	$3,
8	FT	N	3	S	$ 95,000	HMOI	3	$ -	$2,
9	FT	N	2	S	$ 36,000	None	0	$ -	$
10	PT	N	1	H				-	$
11	FT	N	1	H					$
12	FT	N	1	H				-	$
13	FT	N	1	H	$ 32,011	PPOI	0	$ -	$
14	FT	Y	1	H	$ 23,920	HMOH	5	$ 23.92	$
15	FT	Y	1	H	$ 32,011	None	11	$ 32.01	$
16	FT	Y	1	H	$ 21,840	PPOI	8	$ 21.84	$
17	FT	Y	2	S				55.00	$
18	FT	Y	2	S				65.00	$
19	FT	Y	3	S	$125,000	HMOF	0	$125.00	$

Documentation | Employee Data | Employee Summary | Lookup Tables

Ready

A **lookup table** is a table that organizes data that you want to retrieve into different categories, such as health plan codes. This lookup table is named "HealthPlanRates" and is used in the VLOOKUP function.

The **compare values**, the categories for a lookup table, are located in the table's first column or row.

NESTED IFS AND LOOKUP TABLES

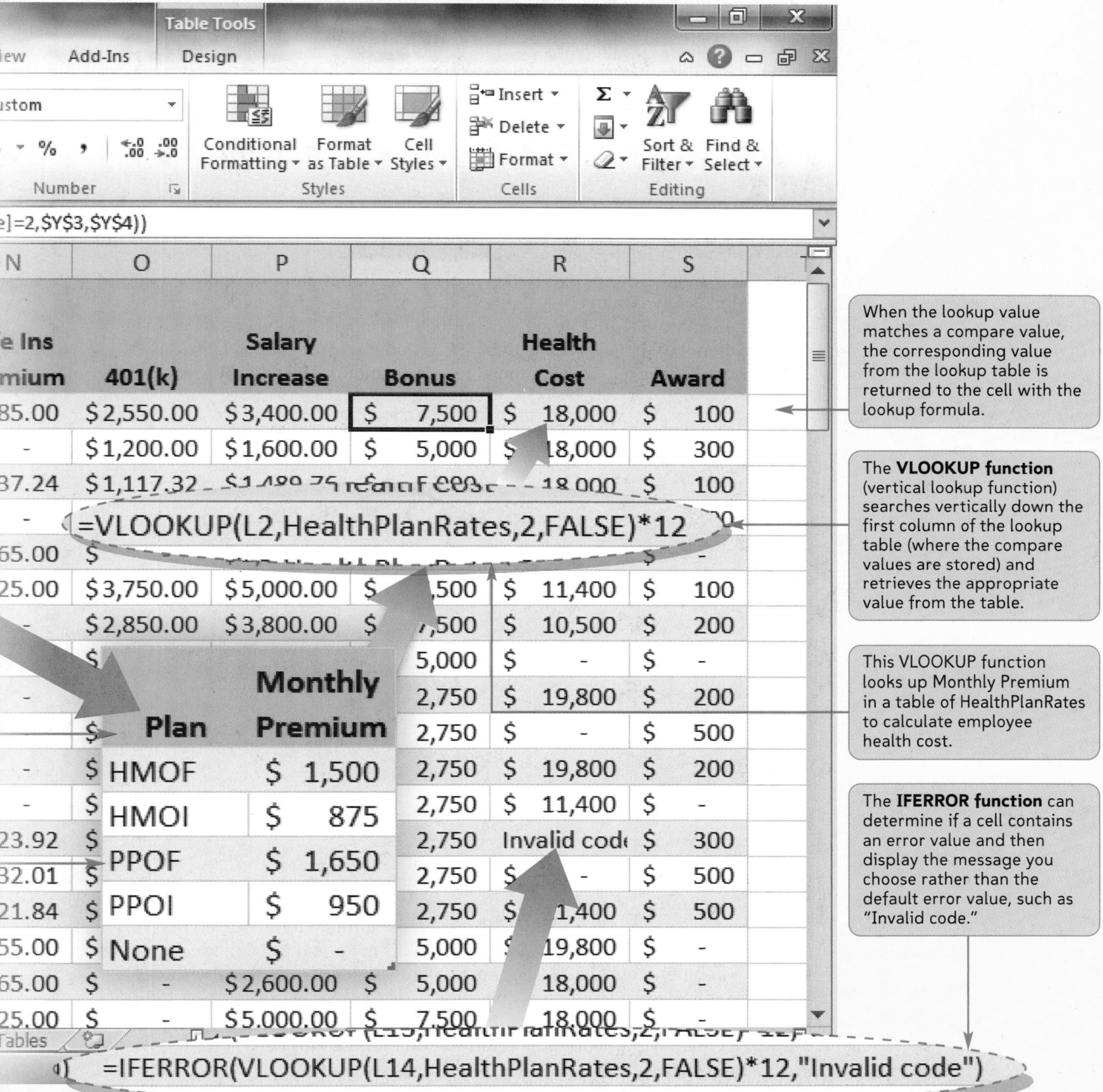

Creating Nested IFs

The IF function can choose between only two outcomes; it cannot choose from among three or more outcomes. However, you can nest IF functions to allow for three or more outcomes. A nested IF function is when one IF function is placed inside another IF function to test an additional condition. You can nest more than one IF function.

Talent Tracs pays three levels of employee bonuses. Each bonus is based on the employee's pay grade, which is a system Talent Tracs uses to group jobs based on difficulty and responsibility. Talent Tracs has three pay grade codes (1, 2, and 3). Pay grade 1 has a starting bonus of $2,500, pay grade 2 has a starting bonus of $5,000, and pay grade 3 has a starting bonus of $7,500. Supervisors can increase or decrease these amounts based on the employee's performance. In this case, you need to nest two IF functions to calculate the different series of outcomes for the employee bonuses.

Rita created the flowchart shown in Figure 7-16 to illustrate the logic for determining bonus awards. She used different colors to identify each nested IF function. The flowchart shows that if an employee's pay grade equals 1, the bonus amount equals 2500 and the IF function (shown in green) is finished. If the employee's pay grade does not equal 1, then the second IF function (shown in blue) is evaluated. If the employee's pay grade equals 2, then the bonus amount equals 5000 and the IF function is finished. If the employee's pay grade does not equal 2, then the bonus amount equals 7500.

Figure 7-16 Flowchart illustrating nested IF functions to determine the bonus amount

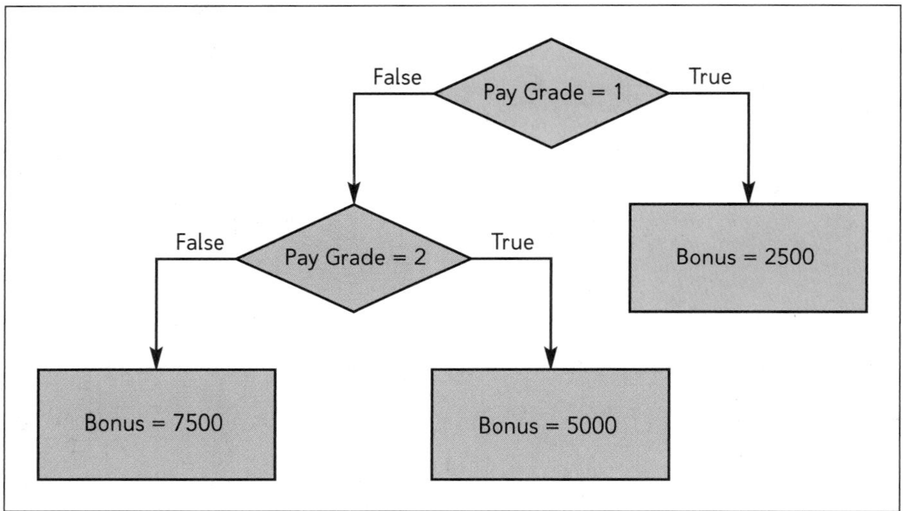

The following formula converts Rita's flowchart into a formula with nested IF functions. The first IF function (shown in green) tests whether the value in the Pay Grade cell is equal to 1. If this condition ([Pay Grade]=1) is true, the formula returns 2500 in the Bonus cell. If this condition is false (the Pay Grade cell is not equal to 1), the second IF function (shown in blue) is evaluated. The second IF function tests whether the value in the Pay Grade cell is equal to 2. If this condition ([Pay Grade]=2) is true, the formula returns 5000 in the Bonus cell. If this condition is false (the value in the current Pay Grade cell is not equal to 2), the formula returns 7500 in the Bonus cell.

```
=IF([Pay Grade]=1,2500,IF([Pay Grade]=2,5000,7500))
```

Figure 7-17 illustrates how one nested IF function is used to determine among three outcomes—whether the home football team won, lost, or tied a game. The first IF function evaluates whether the home team score (stored in cell B1) is greater than the visiting team score (stored in cell B2). If the home team score is higher, "Won" appears in the cell. If not, the nested IF function evaluates whether the visiting team score is greater than the home team score. If the visiting team score is higher, "Lost" appears in the cell. Otherwise, "Tie" appears in the cell.

Figure 7-17 **Additional example of nested IF functions**

Purpose: To determine the outcome of football games for the home team

Logic Scenario: Display Won, Lost, or Tie based on home team and visitor team scores

Formula: Nested IF functions

```
=IF(B1>B2,"Won",IF(B2>B1,"Lost","Tie"))
```

Data: cell B1 stores the home team score
cell B2 stores the visitor team score

Example:

Data		Condition1	Condition2	Results
Cell B1	Cell B2	B1>B2	B2>B1	(Outcome)
21	18	True	Not evaluated	Won
17	24	False	True	Lost
9	9	False	False	Tie

Figure 7-18 illustrates how two nested IFs are used to determine among four possible outcomes for a driver's license based on the applicant's age (stored in cell B1). The first IF function evaluates whether the applicant is less than 16 years old. If the applicant is younger than 16, "Too Young" appears in the cell. If not, the first nested IF function evaluates whether the applicant is 45 years old or younger. If so, 30 appears in the cell as the fee. If not, the second nested IF function evaluates whether the applicant is 60 years old or younger. If so, 25 appears in the cell as the fee. Otherwise, 20 appears in the cell as the fee.

Figure 7-18 **Additional example of nested IF functions**

Purpose: To determine the fee for a driver's license

Logic Scenario: Driver's license fee varies by age

Below 16	"Too Young"
16–45	$30
46–60	$25
61 and older	$20

Formula: Nested IF functions

```
=IF(B1<16,"Too Young",IF(B1<=45,30,IF(B1<=60,25,20)))
```

Data: cell B1 stores the driver's age

Example:

Data	Condition1	Condition2	Condition3	Results
Cell B1	B1<16	B1<=45	B1<=60	(Fee)
15	True	Not evaluated	Not evaluated	Too Young
25	False	True	Not evaluated	30
55	False	False	True	25
65	False	False	False	20

PROSKILLS

Problem Solving: Finding and Fixing Errors in Formulas

Errors occur in spreadsheets as illustrated in the following real-life incident: "City officials miscalculated the amount of sales taxes generated from a local sporting goods store. The mistake inflated the tax figures by tens of thousands of dollars, which, in turn, meant the total sales estimate was overblown by millions of dollars. The city believed the mistake was a result of an error in a spreadsheet formula...."

If formulas in a worksheet are returning errors or not working as expected, you need to find and fix the problems. Two common categories of formula errors in Excel are syntax errors and logic errors. A syntax error is an error in a statement that violates the rules of Excel. A syntax error might occur due to unmatched parentheses or a required argument that is omitted in a function. Logic errors occur in formulas that work but return an incorrect result. A logic error could occur because the formula uses the wrong calculation, the formula references the wrong cell, or the formula uses faulty reasoning, leading to incorrect results.

Some problem-solving approaches can help resolve these types of errors. First, examine the formulas in worksheet cells instead of the results by pressing the Ctrl+~ keys to show the formulas in each cell. Next, troubleshoot problem areas in the worksheet by pressing the F9 key to highlight part of a formula and temporarily display the actual value in the cell so you can check intermediate results. Press the Esc key to return the cell references. Finally, you can use the Formula Auditing tools on the Formulas tab to visually identify and trace cells used in a formula. This can help you locate and fix inaccurate cell references and faulty logic.

Carefully evaluating formulas and fixing any problems help to ensure that a worksheet is error-free and returns accurate results.

Next, you'll add a Bonus column to the Employee table and enter the formula to calculate the bonus amount. The bonus amounts for each pay grade are not yet final. To make the bonus calculation more flexible, Rita stored the three bonus amounts (2500, 5000, and 7500) in the Employee worksheet. You will reference these cells in the formula to calculate the employee bonus. This approach enables you to quickly update the calculated bonus amounts in the Employee worksheet without having to edit the bonus formula.

To enter nested IFs to calculate employee bonuses:

1. If you took a break at the end of the previous session, make sure the Talent Tracs workbook is open and the Employee Data worksheet is active.
2. In cell Q1, enter **Bonus** as the column header. The Excel table expands to include the new column, and cell Q2 is the active cell.
3. Make sure cell Q2 is the active cell, and then click the **Insert Function** button *fx* in the formula bar. The Insert Function dialog box opens.
4. Click **IF** in the Select a function box, and then click the **OK** button. The Function Arguments dialog box opens.
5. In the Logical_test box, type **[Pay Grade]=1** and then press the **Tab** key to enter the logical test using a structured reference. This logical test evaluates whether the employee has a pay grade equal to 1. The values to the right of the Logical_test box are {False;False;..., indicating that the pay grades for the first few employees are not equal to 1.

   Trouble? If the value to the right of the Logical_test box is "Invalid," you probably mistyped the logical test. Select the text in the Logical_test box, and then repeat Step 5, typing the logical test exactly as shown, being sure to use square brackets around the structured reference.
6. In the Value_if_true box, type **$Y$2** and then press the **Tab** key. The value to the right of the Value_if_true argument box is 2500, which is the value in cell Y2. This argument specifies that if the logical test is true (the Pay Grade cell is equal to 1), the value stored in cell Y2 (the 2500 bonus amount) is displayed.
7. In the Value_if_false box, type **IF([Pay Grade]=2,$Y$3,$Y$4)**. This argument is a nested IF function that specifies if the logical condition is true (the Pay Grade cell is equal to 2), the value stored in cell Y3 (the 5000 bonus amount) is displayed; otherwise, the value stored in cell Y4 (the 7500 bonus amount) is displayed. The values to the right of the Value_if_false box are {7500;5000;5000;... indicating the bonus amounts for the employees in the first few rows. See Figure 7-19.

TIP

If you type a formula directly in a cell, the available structured references appear when you type the opening bracket. Double-click the structured reference to add it to the formula, and then type the closing bracket.

Figure 7-19 Function Arguments dialog box with a nested IF

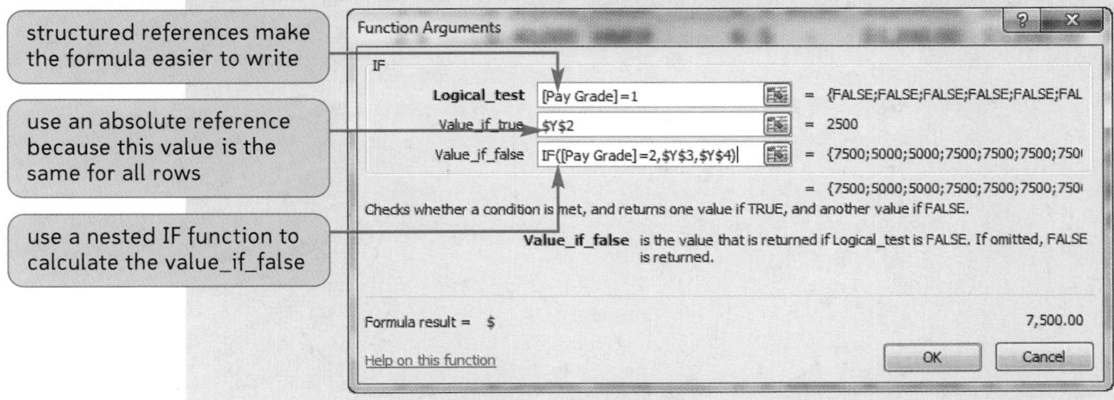

8. Click the **OK** button. The formula =IF([Pay Grade]=1,$Y$2,IF([Pay Grade]=2,$Y$3, $Y$4)) appears in the formula bar, and the value 7500 appears in cell Q2 because this employee has a pay grade of 3. The bonus formula is automatically copied to all other rows in the Bonus column. The references to cells Y2, Y3, and Y4 are absolute references and do not change from cell to cell in the Bonus column.
9. Select the Bonus values, and then format the selected range using the **Accounting** number format with no decimal places.
10. Click cell **Q2** to deselect the column. See Figure 7-20.

Figure 7-20 **Nested IF function calculating the employee bonus amounts**

formula uses a nested IF function and structured references to calculate the bonus amount

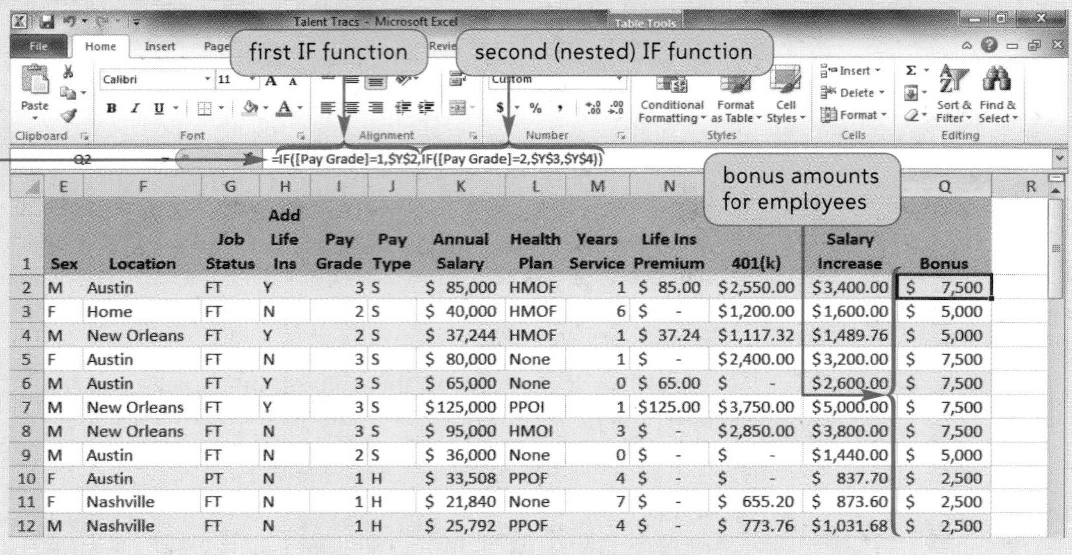

	Sex	Location	Job Status	Add Life Ins	Pay Grade	Pay Type	Annual Salary	Health Plan	Years Service	Life Ins Premium	401(k)	Salary Increase	Bonus
2	M	Austin	FT	Y	3	S	$ 85,000	HMOF	1	$ 85.00	$2,550.00	$3,400.00	$ 7,500
3	F	Home	FT	N	2	S	$ 40,000	HMOF	6	$ -	$1,200.00	$1,600.00	$ 5,000
4	M	New Orleans	FT	Y	2	S	$ 37,244	HMOF	1	$ 37.24	$1,117.32	$1,489.76	$ 5,000
5	F	Austin	FT	N	3	S	$ 80,000	None	1	$ -	$2,400.00	$3,200.00	$ 7,500
6	M	Austin	FT	Y	3	S	$ 65,000	None	0	$ 65.00	$ -	$2,600.00	$ 7,500
7	M	New Orleans	FT	Y	3	S	$125,000	PPOI	1	$125.00	$3,750.00	$5,000.00	$ 7,500
8	M	New Orleans	FT	N	3	S	$ 95,000	HMOI	3	$ -	$2,850.00	$3,800.00	$ 7,500
9	M	Austin	FT	N	2	S	$ 36,000	None	0	$ -	$ -	$1,440.00	$ 5,000
10	F	Austin	PT	N	1	H	$ 33,508	PPOF	4	$ -	$ -	$ 837.70	$ 2,500
11	F	Nashville	FT	N	1	H	$ 21,840	None	7	$ -	$ 655.20	$ 873.60	$ 2,500
12	M	Nashville	FT	N	1	H	$ 25,792	PPOF	4	$ -	$ 773.76	$1,031.68	$ 2,500

INSIGHT

Checking Formulas for Matching Parentheses

A common problem when creating formulas is mismatched parentheses. As you write a formula, you should verify that you enclosed the correct argument, function, or term within the parentheses of the formula you are creating. This is especially important when you develop a complex formula that includes many parentheses, such as a nested IF function. Excel color-codes the parentheses as you build a formula so you can quickly determine whether you have complete pairs of them. You can also verify that the formula includes matching pairs of parentheses by selecting the cell with the formula and then clicking in the formula bar. Press the → key to move the insertion point through the formula one character at a time. When the insertion point moves across one parenthesis, its matching parenthesis is also highlighted briefly. This color coding helps you ensure that all parentheses in a formula are paired (opening and closing parentheses).

The executive team has increased the bonus for employees in pay grade 1 from $2,500 to $2,750. Rita asks you to update this bonus amount so the employee bonuses will be current.

TIP

Placing cell references to input values rather than constants in formulas makes a worksheet more flexible and easier to update.

To update the bonus amount for Pay Grade 1:

1. In cell Y2, enter **2750**.
2. Scroll to the **Bonus** column and observe that all employees with a pay grade equal to 1 show a bonus amount of $2,750.

Using Lookup Tables and Functions

Lookup functions allow you to use tables of data to "look up" values and insert them in another worksheet location. For example, you might enter a product table in a worksheet that includes the product ID, product name, and price of all products a company sells. You could then use this product table to build an invoice in another worksheet by entering a product ID and having Excel look up the product name and price, and insert these values in the invoice.

The table that stores the data you want to retrieve is called a lookup table, and it organizes the data you want to retrieve into different categories, such as by product ID. The categories for the lookup table, called compare values, are located in the table's first column or row. To retrieve a particular value from the table, a lookup value (the value you are trying to find) needs to match one of the compare values. When a match is found, the corresponding value in the lookup table is displayed in the cell where the lookup formula is entered. Lookup values can also be used as part of a formula.

At Talent Tracs, all employees are eligible for the company's health plan. Employees can choose one of four health plans: an HMO for individuals (HMOI), an HMO for families (HMOF), a PPO for individuals (PPOI), or a PPO for families (PPOF). Each plan has a different cost, and Talent Tracs pays the entire health plan cost. If an employee shows evidence of coverage elsewhere, there is no health plan cost. You could calculate the health plan costs for each employee using several nested IF functions. However, a simpler approach is to use a lookup function.

You can use the HealthPlanRates table shown in Figure 7-21 as a lookup table. The lookup table shows the available plans and the corresponding monthly premiums. The health plan cost for each eligible employee is based on the plan the employee selected. The lookup value is the employee's health plan code, which is entered in column L of the Employee table. The compare values come from the first column of the HealthPlanRates table, which is in the range B3:C8 in the Lookup Tables worksheet. To retrieve the monthly cost for an employee, Excel moves down the first column in the HealthPlanRates lookup table until it finds the health plan code that matches the lookup value. Then it moves to the second column in the lookup table to locate the monthly cost, which is displayed in the cell where the lookup formula is entered or used as part of a calculation.

Figure 7-21 **HealthPlanRates table used for an exact match lookup**

	A	B	C
1			
2			
3		**Plan**	**Monthly Premium**
4		HMOF	$ 1,500
5		HMOI	$ 875
6		PPOF	$ 1,650
7		PPOI	$ 950
8		None	$ -
9			

Lookup tables can be constructed as either exact match or approximate match lookups. An **exact match lookup** occurs when the value entered must match one of the values in the first column of the lookup table. The HealthPlanRates table in Figure 7-21 is an example of an exact match lookup because the health plan code must match one of the values in the HealthPlanRates table or a value is not returned. An **approximate match lookup** occurs when the value entered falls within a range of values in the first column of the lookup table. A discount based on the quantity of items purchased where each discount covers a range of units purchased is an example of an approximate match lookup. Figure 7-22 shows the approximate match lookup table for these quantity discounts. In this example, purchases of fewer than 25 units receive no discount, purchases of between 25 and 99 units receive a 2 percent discount, purchases of between 100 and 499 units receive a 3 percent discount, and purchases of 500 or more units receive a 4 percent discount.

Figure 7-22 **Approximate match lookup table**

Quantity	Discount Rate
0	0%
25	2%
100	3%
500	4%

Using the VLOOKUP Function to Find an Exact Match

To retrieve the correct value from the lookup table, you use the VLOOKUP function. This function searches a lookup table and, based on what you entered, retrieves the appropriate value from that table. The VLOOKUP function searches vertically down the first column of the lookup table. The VLOOKUP function has the syntax

```
VLOOKUP(lookup_value, table_array, col_index_num, [range_lookup])
```

where *lookup_value* is the value you want to use to search the first column of the lookup table, *table_array* is the range reference of the lookup table or its table name, *col_index_num* is the number of the column in the lookup table that contains the value you want to return, and *range_lookup* indicates whether the compare values are a range of values (for an approximate match) or an exact match. When you use a range of values (such as in a tax rate table), you set the *range_lookup* value to TRUE; when you want the *lookup_value* to exactly match a value in the first column of the *table_array* (such as in the HealthPlanRates table), you set the *range_lookup* value to FALSE. The *range_lookup* argument is optional; if you don't include a *range_lookup* value, the value is considered TRUE (an approximate match).

You'll use the VLOOKUP function to calculate the annual health plan cost for Talent Tracs because you want to search the values in the first column of the lookup table. You can use range references or structured references when you create the formula for the annual health plan cost for an employee from the HealthPlanRates table, as follows:

Range references `=VLOOKUP(L2,'Lookup Tables'!$B$4:$C$8,2,FALSE)*12`

Structured references `=VLOOKUP([HealthPlan],HealthPlanRates,2,FALSE)*12`

Both of these formulas use the VLOOKUP function to search for the code in the Health Plan column (column L) of the Employee table, in the first column of the lookup table (the HealthPlanRates table in the range B4:C8 in the Lookup Tables worksheet), and then return the value in the second column of the HealthPlanRates lookup table, which shows the monthly cost. The formulas use FALSE as the *range_lookup* argument because you want the lookup value to exactly match a value in the first column of the HealthPlanRates table.

To find an exact match in the HealthPlanRates table:

1. In cell R1, enter **Health Cost**. The table expands to include the new column.
2. Make sure cell R2 is the active cell, and then click the **Insert Function** button *fx* in the formula bar. The Insert Function dialog box opens.
3. Click the **Or select a category** arrow, click **Lookup & Reference**, and then double-click **VLOOKUP** in the Select a function box. The Function Arguments dialog box opens.
4. Drag the Function Arguments dialog box below row 2 so you can see the column headers.
5. In the Lookup_value box, enter **L2** and then press the **Tab** key. The lookup value is the employee's health plan code, which is located in column L.
6. In the Table_array box, type **HealthPlanRates** and then press the **Tab** key. HealthPlanRates is the table name assigned to the range B4:C8 in the Lookup Tables worksheet. If the HealthPlanRates data was entered in a range of cells, the table_array argument would be entered as 'Lookup Tables'!B4:C8, and you would need to change the range to absolute references ('Lookup Tables'!$B$4:$C$8) so the formula would copy correctly to other cells.
7. In the Col_index_num box, type **2** and then press the **Tab** key. The number 2 indicates the monthly cost is stored in the second column of the HealthPlanRates lookup table.
8. In the Range_lookup box, type **FALSE**. This sets the function to find an exact match in the lookup table. See Figure 7-23.

TIP

For the col_index_num value, be sure to enter the number that corresponds to the column's position rather than its column letter; otherwise, the VLOOKUP formula may return #NAME? or #VALUE! as the result.

Figure 7-23 **Function Arguments dialog box for the VLOOKUP function**

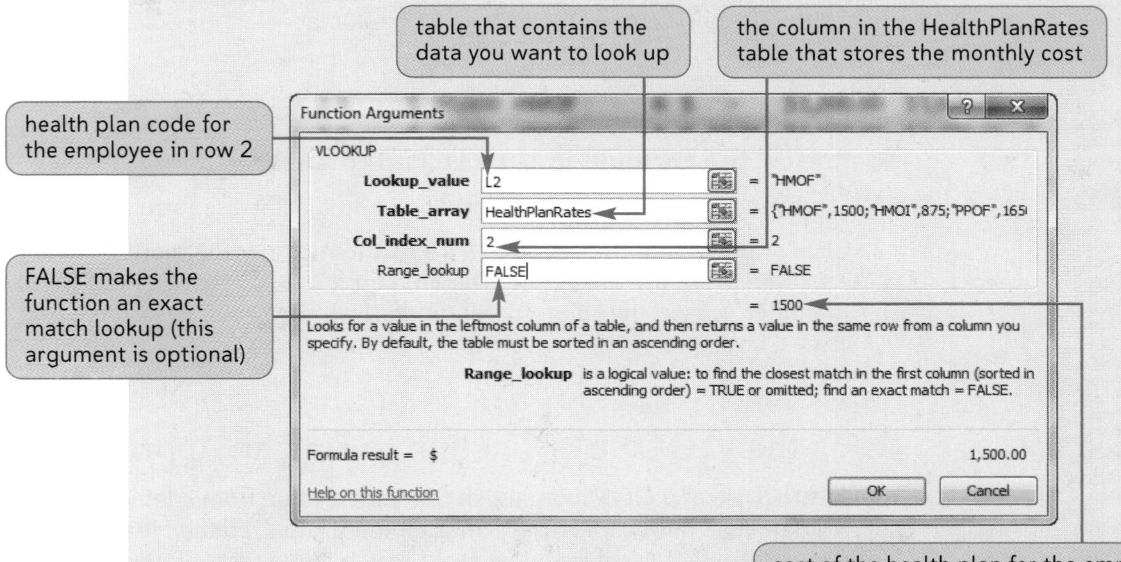

9. Click the **OK** button. The dialog box closes, 1500 appears in cell R2, and the formula VLOOKUP(L2,HealthPlanRates,2,FALSE) appears in the formula bar. The remaining rows in the Health Cost column are filled with the VLOOKUP function. If the value in column L does not match a value in the first column of the HealthPlanRates table, an exact match does not exist and the function returns #N/A in the cell.

10. Select the Health Cost values, and then format the range using the **Accounting** number format with no decimal places.
11. Click cell **R2** to deselect the column. See Figure 7-24.

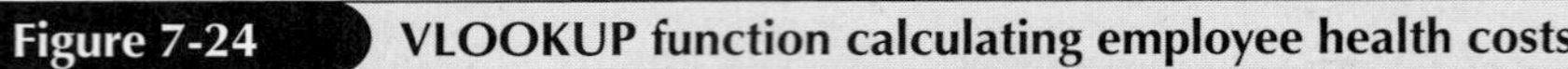

Figure 7-24 VLOOKUP function calculating employee health costs

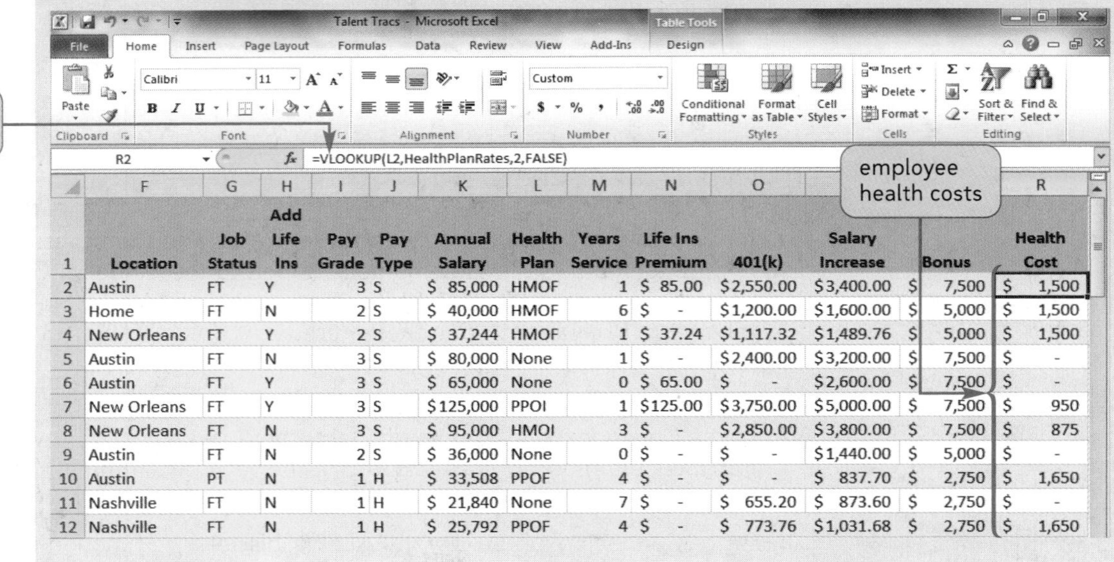

	Location	Job Status	Add Life Ins	Pay Grade	Pay Type	Annual Salary	Health Plan	Years Service	Life Ins Premium	401(k)	Salary Increase	Bonus	Health Cost
2	Austin	FT	Y	3	S	$ 85,000	HMOF	1	$ 85.00	$2,550.00	$3,400.00	$ 7,500	$ 1,500
3	Home	FT	N	2	S	$ 40,000	HMOF	6	$ -	$1,200.00	$1,600.00	$ 5,000	$ 1,500
4	New Orleans	FT	Y	2	S	$ 37,244	HMOF	1	$ 37.24	$1,117.32	$1,489.76	$ 5,000	$ 1,500
5	Austin	FT	N	3	S	$ 80,000	None	1	$ -	$2,400.00	$3,200.00	$ 7,500	$ -
6	Austin	FT	Y	3	S	$ 65,000	None	0	$ 65.00	$ -	$2,600.00	$ 7,500	$ -
7	New Orleans	FT	Y	3	S	$125,000	PPOI	1	$125.00	$3,750.00	$5,000.00	$ 7,500	$ 950
8	New Orleans	FT	N	3	S	$ 95,000	HMOI	3	$ -	$2,850.00	$3,800.00	$ 7,500	$ 875
9	Austin	FT	N	2	S	$ 36,000	None	0	$ -	$ -	$1,440.00	$ 5,000	$ -
10	Austin	PT	N	1	H	$ 33,508	PPOF	4	$ -	$ -	$ 837.70	$ 2,750	$ 1,650
11	Nashville	FT	N	1	H	$ 21,840	None	7	$ -	$ 655.20	$ 873.60	$ 2,750	$ -
12	Nashville	FT	N	1	H	$ 25,792	PPOF	4	$ -	$ 773.76	$1,031.68	$ 2,750	$ 1,650

The health plan costs in the Employee table are monthly amounts rather than annual amounts. You need to modify the formula in the Health Cost column to reflect the annual amounts. Because the formula is in a calculated table column, you need to make the change in only one cell and the change will automatically be copied to all the cells in the column.

To modify the formula in the calculated column:

1. Double-click cell **R2** to enter Edit mode and display the formula in the cell.
2. Click at the end of the formula, type ***12** to multiply the monthly amount by 12, and then press the **Enter** key. The amount in cell R2 changes to $18,000 and all the other cells in the column are updated with the revised formula and display the annual cost.

Using the VLOOKUP Function to Find an Approximate Match

You can also use a VLOOKUP function to return a value from a table that is based on an approximate match lookup. The previous table lookup used the HealthPlanRates table to return a value only if Excel found an exact match in the first column of the lookup table. The categories in the first column or row of a lookup table can also represent a range of values. Quantity discounts, shipping charges, and income tax rates are a few examples of approximate match lookups.

As part of Talent Tracs' 10-year anniversary, management plans to give employee-recognition awards based on the number of years individuals have worked for Talent Tracs. Rita developed the criteria shown in Figure 7-25 to summarize how the company plans to distribute the recognition awards.

Figure 7-25 **Recognition Awards table**

Years of Service	Award
>=0 years and <1 year	0
>=1 year and <3 years	100
>=3 years and <5 years	200
>=5 years and <7 years	300
7 years or more	500

In the Recognition Awards table, you are not looking for an exact match for the lookup value. Instead, you need to use an approximate match lookup, which determines whether the lookup value falls within a range of values. You want to use the table lookup to determine what service range an employee falls into, and then return the recognition award based on the appropriate row. To accomplish this, you must rearrange the first column of the lookup table so that each compare value (row) in the table represents the low end of the category range, as shown in Figure 7-26.

Figure 7-26 **Recognition Awards table**

	F	G	H
1			
2			
3		Years of Service	Recognition Award
4		0	$ -
5		1	$ 100
6		3	$ 200
7		5	$ 300
8		7	$ 500

To determine whether a lookup value falls within a range of values in the revised lookup table, Excel searches the first column of the table until it locates the largest value that is less than the lookup value. Then Excel moves across the row in the table to retrieve the corresponding value. For an employee working at Talent Tracs for six years, Excel would search the lookup table until the compare value is 5 (the largest value less than the lookup value) and retrieve 300 from column 2 of the corresponding row.

When a lookup table is used with a range of values, the compare values must be sorted in alphabetical order if they are text and in low-to-high order if they are numbers. When the compare values are arranged in a different order, Excel may not retrieve the correct value, leading to incorrect results. Even though the VLOOKUP function is accurate, the data in the lookup table is not organized the right way. The setup of the lookup table in an approximate match is critical for a VLOOKUP formula to work.

INSIGHT

Setting Up an Approximate Match Lookup Table

Approximate lookup tables are commonly used to find a taxpayer's tax rate in a tax table, find a shipping charge based on the weight of a package in a shipping charges table, or determine a student's letter grade from a table of grading criteria. Setting up the lookup tables for an approximate match lookup can be tricky. Consider the following example, in which an instructor uses Excel to calculate grades. The instructor assigns final grades based on the following grading policy table:

Score	**Grade**
90–100	A
80–89	B
70–79	C
60–69	D
0–59	F

To set up the lookup table so it works in Excel, the leftmost column in the lookup table must represent the lower end of the range for each category, and the lookup table must be sorted in ascending order based on the value in the first column. Otherwise, Excel cannot retrieve the correct result. Following this structure, the lookup table for the instructor's grading policy would be arranged as follows:

Score	**Grade**
0	F
60	D
70	C
80	B
90	A

You'll create a formula in the Employee table to determine the recognition award for each employee. You will use an approximate match VLOOKUP formula because the years of service in the lookup table have a range of values.

To insert an approximate match VLOOKUP formula:

1. In cell S1, enter **Award**. A new column is added to the table, and cell S2 is the active cell.
2. Click the **Insert Function** button *fx* in the formula bar. The Insert Function dialog box opens with the Lookup & Reference category active.
3. In the Select a function box, double-click **VLOOKUP**. The Function Arguments dialog box opens.
4. In the Lookup_value box, type **[Years Service]** and then press the **Tab** key. The lookup value is entered using the column header (structured reference) for the employee's years of service, which is located in column M. You can also enter the lookup value as M2. The number 1 appears as the lookup value for the current row.
5. In the Table_array box, type **Recognition** and then press the **Tab** key. Recognition is the table name assigned to the range G4:H8 in the Lookup Tables worksheet. If the Recognition data was entered in a range of cells, the table_array argument would be entered as 'Lookup Tables'!G4:H8, and you would need to change the range to absolute references ('Lookup Tables'!$G$4:$H$8) so that the formula would copy correctly to other cells.

6. In the Col_index_num box, type **2**. The number 2 indicates the column where the amount of the award is stored—in the second column of the Recognition table. See Figure 7-27. You do not need to enter the optional fourth argument in the VLOOKUP formula because Excel assumes the value to be TRUE and will use an approximate match table lookup.

Figure 7-27 **Function Arguments dialog box for the VLOOKUP function**

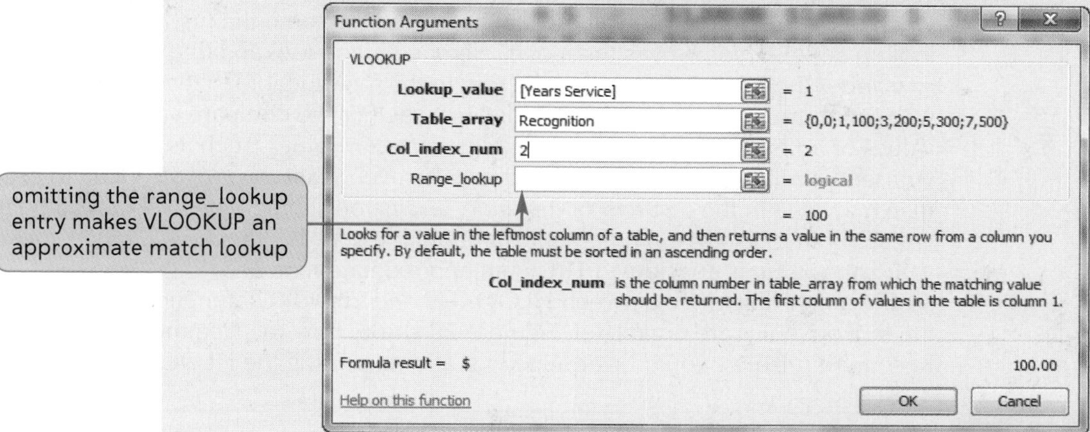

7. Click the **OK** button. All the cells in the Award calculated column are filled with the VLOOKUP formula and display the award amounts. The employee in row 2 has 1 year of service and will receive a recognition award of $100. The employee in row 3 has 6 years of service and will receive an award of $300. This second employee is a good illustration of the approximate match lookup, because 6 does not equal a value in the first column of the lookup table. Instead, it falls within two values in the table.
8. Make sure that the values in the Award column are formatted with the Accounting number format and no decimal places.
9. Click cell **S2** to deselect the column. See Figure 7-28.

Figure 7-28 **Award column**

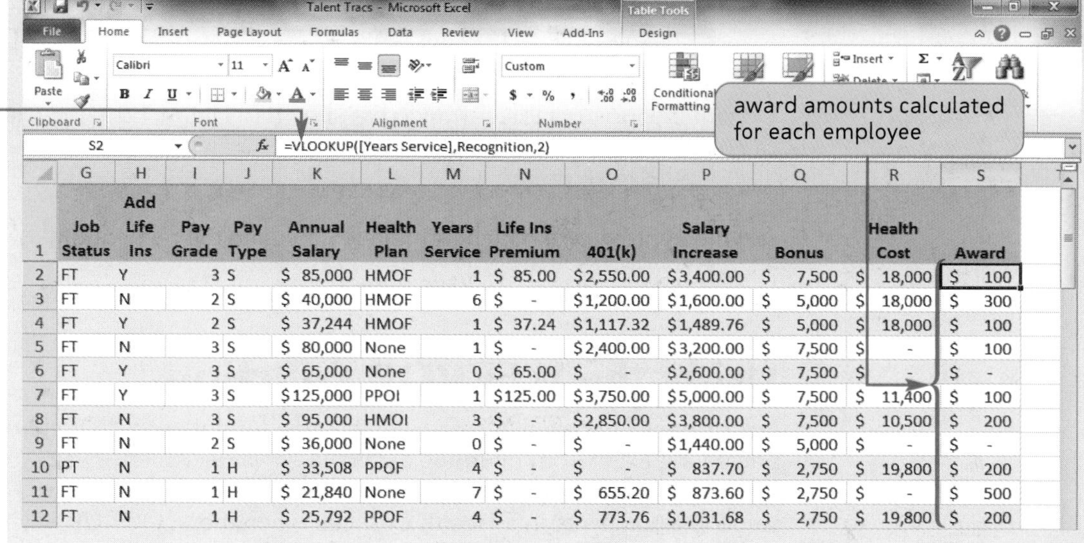

	G	H	I	J	K	L	M	N	O	P	Q	R	S
1	Job Status	Add Life Ins	Pay Grade	Pay Type	Annual Salary	Health Plan	Years Service	Life Ins Premium	401(k)	Salary Increase	Bonus	Health Cost	Award
2	FT	Y	3	S	$ 85,000	HMOF	1	$ 85.00	$2,550.00	$3,400.00	$ 7,500	$ 18,000	$ 100
3	FT	N	2	S	$ 40,000	HMOF	6	$ -	$1,200.00	$1,600.00	$ 5,000	$ 18,000	$ 300
4	FT	Y	2	S	$ 37,244	HMOF	1	$ 37.24	$1,117.32	$1,489.76	$ 5,000	$ 18,000	$ 100
5	FT	N	3	S	$ 80,000	None	1	$ -	$2,400.00	$3,200.00	$ 7,500	$ -	$ 100
6	FT	Y	3	S	$ 65,000	None	0	$ 65.00	$ -	$2,600.00	$ 7,500	$ -	$ -
7	FT	Y	3	S	$125,000	PPOI	1	$125.00	$3,750.00	$5,000.00	$ 7,500	$ 11,400	$ 100
8	FT	N	3	S	$ 95,000	HMOI	3	$ -	$2,850.00	$3,800.00	$ 7,500	$ 10,500	$ 200
9	FT	N	2	S	$ 36,000	None	0	$ -	$ -	$1,440.00	$ 5,000	$ -	$ -
10	PT	N	1	H	$ 33,508	PPOF	4	$ -	$ -	$ 837.70	$ 2,750	$ 19,800	$ 200
11	FT	N	1	H	$ 21,840	None	7	$ -	$ 655.20	$ 873.60	$ 2,750	$ -	$ 500
12	FT	N	1	H	$ 25,792	PPOF	4	$ -	$ 773.76	$1,031.68	$ 2,750	$ 19,800	$ 200

Looking Up Values Using the HLOOKUP Function

The HLOOKUP function is very similar to the VLOOKUP function. The **HLOOKUP function** (horizontal lookup function) searches horizontally across the top row of the lookup table and retrieves the value in the column you specify. You use the HLOOKUP function when the comparison values are located in the first row of the lookup table and you want to look down a specified number of rows to find the data to enter in another cell.

The HLOOKUP function has the syntax

```
HLOOKUP(lookup_value, table_array, row_index_num, [range_lookup])
```

where *lookup_value* is the value you want to use to search the first row of the lookup table, *table_array* is the range reference of the lookup table or its table name, *row_index_num* is the number of the row in the lookup table that contains the value you want to return, and *range_lookup* indicates whether the compare values are a range of values or an exact match. When you use a range of values (such as in a tax rate table), you set the *range_lookup* value to TRUE; when you want the *lookup_value* to exactly match a value in the first row of the *table_array*, you set the *range_lookup* value to FALSE. The *range_lookup* argument is optional; if you don't include a *range_lookup* value, the value is considered TRUE (an approximate match).

The major difference between HLOOKUP and VLOOKUP functions is the way the lookup tables are organized. Figure 7-28 shows how the HealthPlanRates and Recognition tables would be arranged for a lookup using the HLOOKUP function.

Figure 7-29 Lookup tables for the HLOOKUP function

	A	B	C	D	E	F	G
1		Health Rate Plans					
2							
3		Plan	HMOF	HMOI	PPOF	PPOI	None
4		Monthly Premium	$ 1,500	$ 875	$ 1,650	$ 950	$ -
5							
6							
7		Recognition Award					
8							
9		Years of Service	0	1	3	5	7
10		Recognition Award	$ -	$ 100	$ 200	$ 300	$ 500
11							

With the lookup tables arranged as shown in Figure 7-29, the exact match formula to calculate the annual health plan cost is

```
=HLOOKUP([HealthPlan],HealthPlanRates,2,FALSE)*12
```

and the approximate match formula to calculate the recognition award is

```
=HLOOKUP([Years Service],Recognition,2)
```

Using the IFERROR Function

Error values indicate that some element in a formula or a cell referenced in a formula is preventing Excel from returning a calculated value. An error value begins with a number sign (#) followed by an error name that indicates the type of error. For instance, the error value #N/A appears in a Health Cost cell when the VLOOKUP function cannot find the health plan code in the HealthPlanRates lookup table because it was entered incorrectly. Figure 7-30 describes common error values you might see in workbooks.

Figure 7-30 **Excel error values**

Error Value	Description of Error
#DIV/0!	The formula or function contains a number divided by 0.
#NAME?	Excel doesn't recognize text in the formula or function, such as when the function name is misspelled.
#N/A	A value is not available to a function or formula, which can occur when an invalid value is specified in the LOOKUP function.
#NULL!	A formula or function requires two cell ranges to intersect, but they don't.
#NUM!	Invalid numbers are used in a formula or function, such as text entered in a function that requires a number.
#REF!	A cell reference used in a formula or function is no longer valid, which can occur when the cell used by the function was deleted from the worksheet.
#VALUE!	The wrong type of argument is used in a function or formula. This can occur when you supply a range of values to a function that requires a single value.

These error value messages are not particularly descriptive or helpful. To display a more descriptive message that helps users fix the problem, you can use the IFERROR function. The IFERROR function can determine if a cell contains an error value and then display the message you choose rather than the default error value. The IFERROR function has the syntax

```
IFERROR(expression, valueIfError)
```

where *expression* is the formula you want to check for an error, and *valueIfError* is the message you want displayed if Excel detects an error in the formula you are checking. If Excel does not detect an error, the result of the *expression* is displayed.

The IFERROR function enables you to easily find and handle formula errors. For example, you can enter the following formula to determine whether an invalid code was entered in the Health Plan column of the Employee table and then display a more descriptive message if Excel detects an error:

```
=IFERROR(VLOOKUP(L2,HealthPlanRates,2,False)*12,"Invalid code")
```

Based on this formula, if the value in cell L2 is HMOF, the result of the VLOOKUP formula is $1,500 (the corresponding value from the HealthPlanRates table), the first argument in the IFERROR function (shown in purple) is executed, and the health cost is displayed. On the other hand, if cell L2 has an invalid health plan code, such as HMOG, the VLOOKUP function returns the error value #N/A, the second argument in the IFERROR function (shown in red) is executed, and "Invalid code" is displayed.

You will scroll the Health Cost column to verify that all employees have an amount assigned to Health Cost.

To check for an error value in the Health Cost column:

1. Scroll to row **54** of the Health Plan column to see the error value #N/A in cell R54.
2. Click cell **R54**. See Figure 7-31.

Figure 7-31 **Error value in the Health Cost column**

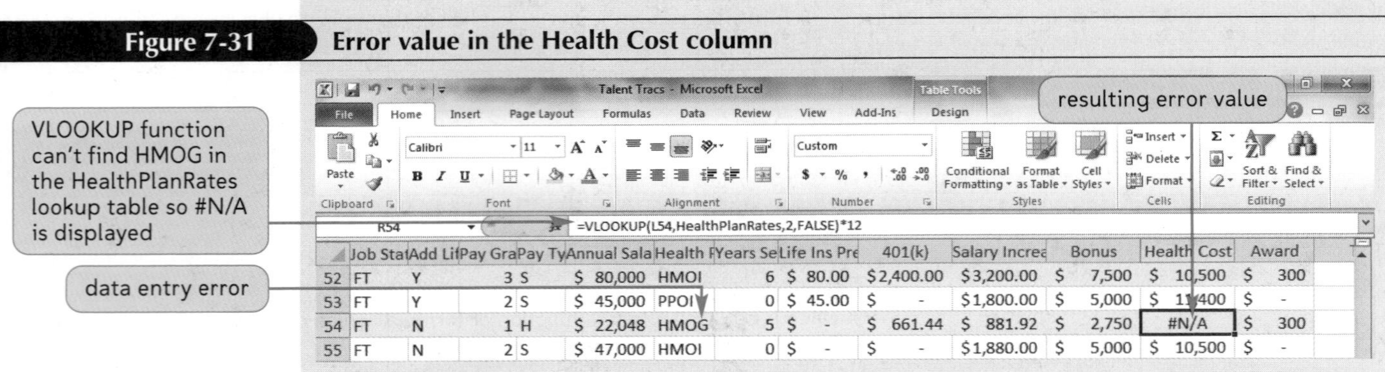

3. In row 54 in the Health Plan column, observe that the health plan code is HMOG, which is an invalid code.

Rita asks you to modify the formulas in the Health Cost column so that the descriptive error message "Invalid code" appears rather than the error value. The IFERROR function will check for errors in the formula, and display the error message you create rather than the error value if it finds an error.

You'll nest the VLOOKUP function within the IFERROR function to display the message "Invalid code" in the Health Cost column if Excel detects an error value.

To nest the VLOOKUP function within the IFERROR function:

1. Double-click cell **R54** (the cell in row 54 of the Health Cost column) to enter Edit mode. The formula =VLOOKUP(L54,HealthPlanRates,2,False)*12 appears in the cell and the formula bar. You'll nest this formula within the IFERROR function.
2. Click to the right of = (the equal sign), and then type **IFERROR(** to begin entering the IFERROR function. The first argument in the IFERROR function is the formula you want to use if no error value is found; this is the VLOOKUP function already entered in the cell.
3. Move the insertion point to the right of the VLOOKUP formula, and then type **,"Invalid code")** to add the text you want to display if an error is found.
4. Press the **Enter** key. The error message "Invalid code" appears in cell R54, and the revised formula is automatically copied to all cells in the column. See Figure 7-32.

Figure 7-32 **Invalid code message in the Health Cost column**

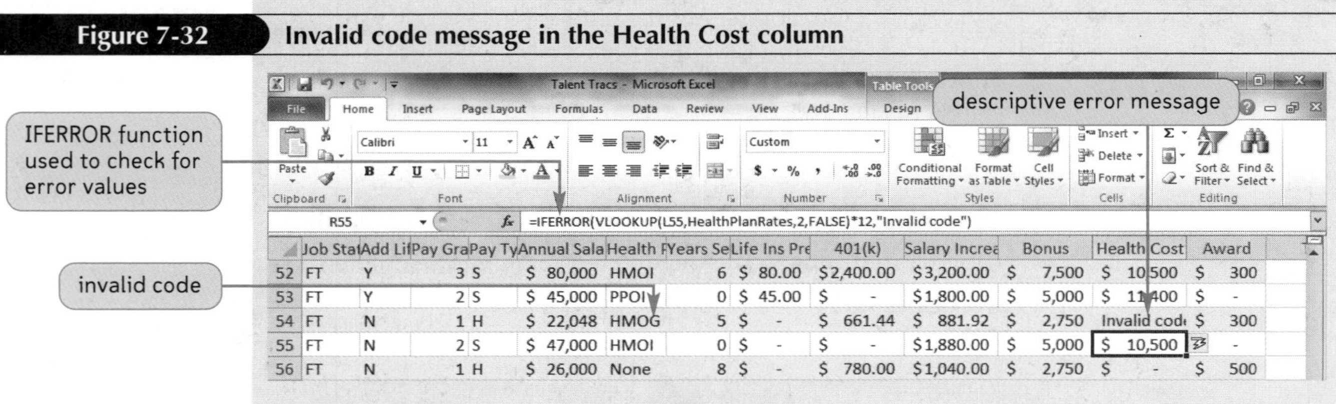

Trouble? If the error #NAME? appears in cell R54, you may have omitted quotation marks around the descriptive error message, "Invalid code." Correct the formula, and then continue with Step 5.

5. In cell L54 (the cell in row 54 of the Health Plan column), enter **HMOF**. The health plan code you entered is valid, so the health cost value $18,000 appears in cell R54.
6. Scroll to the top of the table, click cell **R2**, and observe in the formula bar that the IFERROR formula was copied to this cell.

In this session, you used nested IF functions to determine employee bonuses, the VLOOKUP function to calculate health cost and recognition award amounts, and the IFERROR function to display a descriptive message if invalid health plan codes are entered in the Employee table. In the next session, you will use conditional formatting and the COUNTIF, SUMIF, and AVERAGEIF functions to report on employee salaries.

REVIEW

Session 7.2 Quick Check

1. When you include one IF function inside another IF function, you have created a(n) ______________.
2. If cell Y5 displays the value 24, cell Y6 displays the value 27, and cell Y7 contains the following formula, what is displayed in cell Y7?
   `=IF(Y5>Y6,"Older",IF(Y5<Y6,"Younger","Same Age"))`
3. Explain the difference between an exact match and an approximate match table lookup.
4. A customer table includes columns for name, street address, city, state abbreviation, and zip. A second table includes state abbreviations and state names from all 50 states (one state per row). You need to add a new column to the customer table with the state name. What is the most appropriate function to use to display the state name in this new column?
5. Convert the following table that shows the criteria used to determine a student's level to a table that can be used in a VLOOKUP function to display the level of each student:

Earned Credits	Level
0 but < 30	Freshman
30 but < 60	Sophomore
60 but < 90	Junior
90 or more	Senior

6. In cell X5, the error value #DIV/0! appears when you divide by 0. Use the IFERROR function with the formula =W5/W25 so that instead of the error value #DIV/0! being displayed, the message "Dividing by zero" appears in the cell.
7. The following Sales Tax Rate table and the ______________ function could be used to display the sales tax rate for a customer in one of these four states.

State	AZ	NM	OK	TX
Sales Tax Rate	8.5%	7%	9%	9.25%

SESSION 7.3 VISUAL OVERVIEW

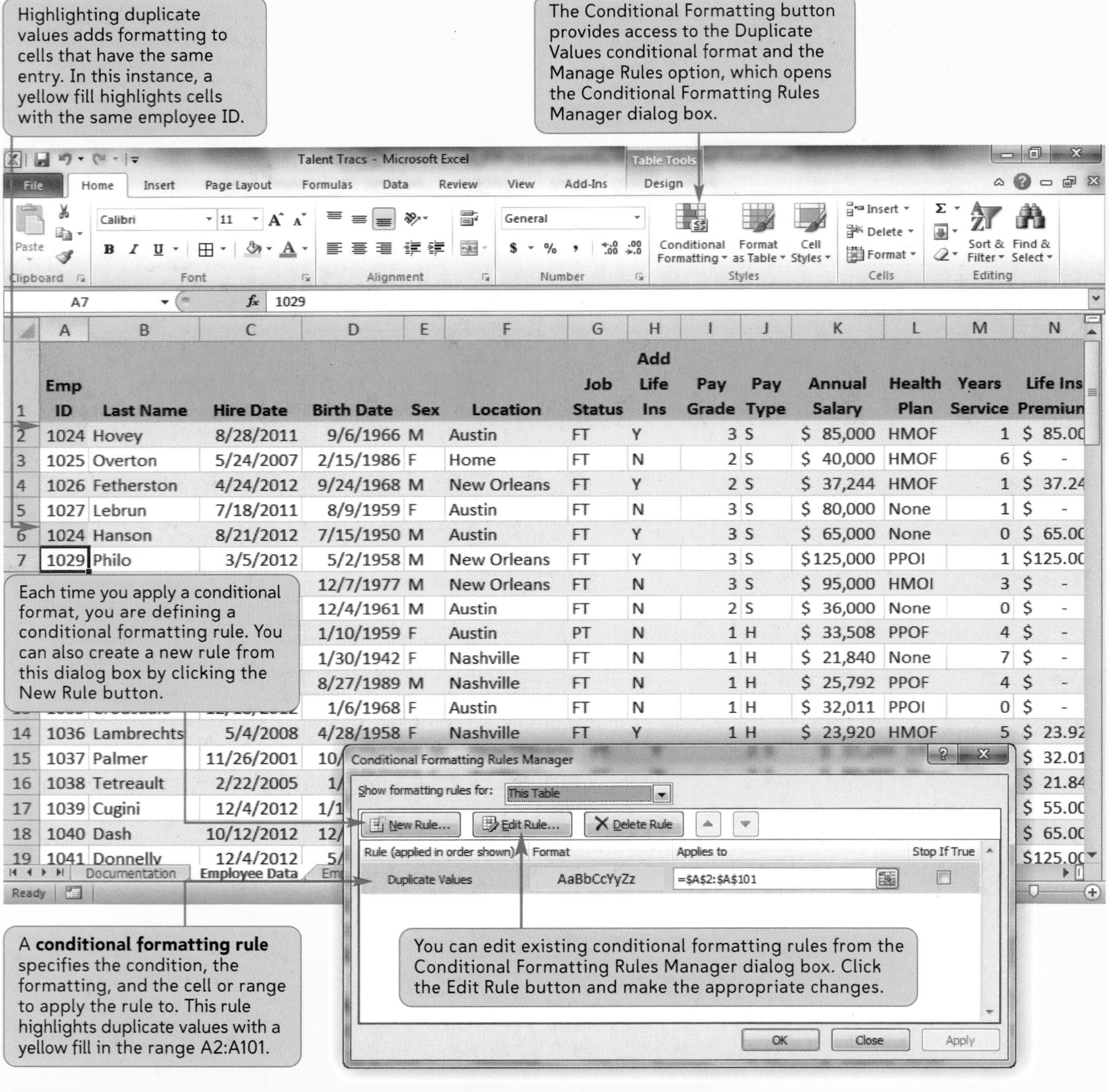

CONDITIONAL FORMATTING

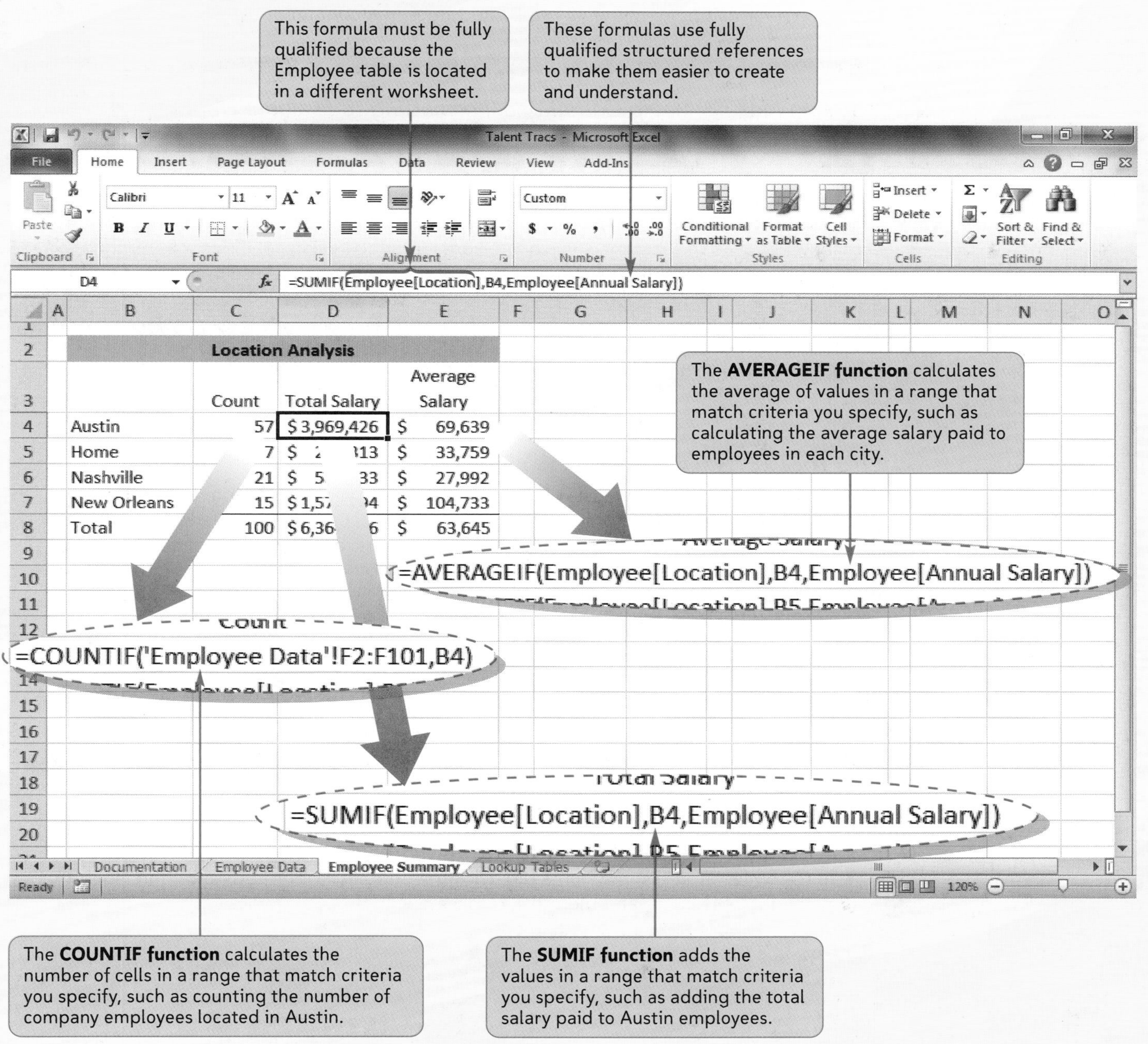

The **COUNTIF function** calculates the number of cells in a range that match criteria you specify, such as counting the number of company employees located in Austin.

The **SUMIF function** adds the values in a range that match criteria you specify, such as adding the total salary paid to Austin employees.

Conditional Formatting

Conditional formatting changes a cell's formatting when its contents match a specified condition. You've already used conditional formatting to highlight cells based on their values and to add data bars that graph the relative values in a range. You can also use conditional formatting to highlight duplicate values in a column of data.

PROSKILLS

Decision Making: Using Conditional Formatting to Evaluate Data

Decisions are made by evaluating data. However, this becomes complex when large quantities of data or dynamic data are involved. In these instances, conditional formatting can be a useful tool to help with your decision making. Conditional formatting is designed to make searching a data range both simple and efficient. For instance, you can quickly find the latest market prices in a real-time stock quote spreadsheet by using conditional formatting to highlight them. You can use conditional formatting to find stocks whose price drops below the target buy price by highlighting the row of any stock that meets the buy criteria. You can use conditional formatting to quickly identify bank accounts with a bank balance that is overdrawn by highlighting accounts with a negative balance. Mastering the art of conditional formatting will help you make better decisions.

Highlighting Duplicate Values

Excel is often used to manage lists of data, such as employee information, inventory, or phone numbers. These types of lists often include data that repeats in different records, such as the employee's state in his or her mailing address, a warehouse location for inventory, or an area code for phone numbers. On the other hand, some of the data is usually unique for each record, such as an employee ID or a product number. As the list of data becomes more extensive, duplicate entries may inadvertently occur. One way to identify unintended duplicate entries is to use conditional formatting to highlight duplicate values in a range with a font and/or fill color. This color coding makes it easier to identify the duplicates so you can then determine whether an entry needs to be corrected. In addition to the colors provided, you can create a custom format for the highlighting.

REFERENCE

Highlighting Duplicate Values

- Select the range in which to highlight duplicate values.
- In the Styles group on the Home tab, click the Conditional Formatting button, point to Highlight Cells Rules, and then click Duplicate Values.
- Select the appropriate formatting option.
- Click the OK button.

You will use duplicate value highlighting to verify that each cell in the employee ID column has a unique entry. Rita believes the current employee ID data in the Employee table is accurate, but wants you to use conditional formatting to ensure that there are no duplicate entries.

To highlight duplicate employee IDs:

1. If you took a break at the end of the previous session, make sure the Talent Tracs workbook is open and the Employee Data worksheet is active.

2. Scroll to column **A**, and then select the data in the Emp ID column. Rows 2 through 101 in the Emp ID column are selected.
3. Click the **Home** tab on the Ribbon, if necessary, and then click the **Conditional Formatting** button in the Styles group.
4. Point to **Highlight Cells Rules**, and then click **Duplicate Values**. The Duplicate Values dialog box opens.
5. Click the **values with** arrow to display a list of formatting options, and then click **Custom Format** to create a format that is not in the list. The Format Cells dialog box opens. You'll change the background fill color to red.
6. Click the **Fill** tab, and then, in the Background Color palette, click **red** (the second color in the last row).
7. Click the **OK** button in the Format Cells dialog box, and then click the **OK** button in the Duplicate Values dialog box. Any duplicate values in the ID column appear in a red cell.
8. Scroll the table to ensure that no duplicate values are found.

After you enter a formula, you should test all situations to verify how the formula performs in each case. In this case, you should test the column both with duplicate values and without duplicate values. No duplicate records appear in the Employee table, so you'll change the ID of the last record from 1123 to 1024, which is the ID of the first employee. The backgrounds of the cells with the duplicate IDs should turn red, which will confirm that the conditional formatting is working as intended. Then, you will return the ID to its original value and confirm that the duplicate value highlighting disappears.

To test the duplicate value conditional formatting:

1. Click in the **Name** box, and then enter **A101**. The active cell moves to the last record in the Employee table.
2. In cell A101, enter **1024**. The ID changes from 1123 to 1024 and cell A101 is filled with a red background because it contains a duplicate ID. See Figure 7-33.

Figure 7-33 Duplicate record highlighted

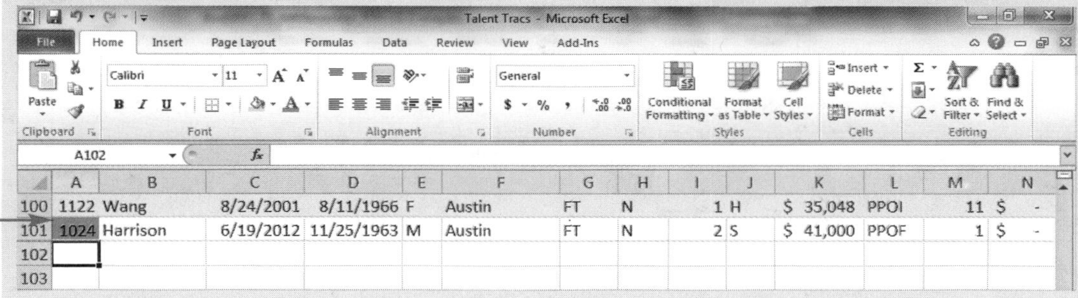

3. Press the **Ctrl+Home** keys. Cell A1 becomes the active cell. Cell A2 has a red background fill because it has the same ID that you entered in cell A101. The conditional formatting correctly identified the duplicate values.

Using the Conditional Formatting Rules Manager

Each time you apply a conditional format, you are defining a conditional formatting rule. A rule specifies the type of condition (such as formatting cells greater than a specified value), the type of formatting when that condition occurs (such as light red fill with dark red text), and the cell or range the formatting is applied to. You can edit existing conditional formatting rules from the Conditional Formatting Rules Manager dialog box.

REFERENCE

Editing a Conditional Formatting Rule

- Select the range with the conditional formatting you want to edit.
- In the Styles group on the Home tab, click the Conditional Formatting button, and then click Manage Rules.
- Select the rule you want to edit, and then click the Edit Rule button.
- In the Select a Rule Type box, click a rule type, and then make the appropriate changes in the Edit the Rule Description section.
- Click the OK button in each dialog box.

The red background fill makes the cell content difficult to read. Rita asks you to use a yellow fill color to better contrast with the black text. You'll use the Conditional Formatting Rules Manager dialog box to edit the rule that specifies the formatting applied to duplicate values in the ID column.

To change the duplicate values background fill color:

1. In the Styles group on the Home tab, click the **Conditional Formatting** button, and then click **Manage Rules**. The Conditional Formatting Rules Manager dialog box opens, listing all the formatting rules for the current selection, which, in this case, is the Employee table.
2. Verify that the Show formatting rules for box shows **This Table**. All the rules currently in effect in the Employee table are displayed. You can add new rules and edit or delete existing rules. You also can control which formatting rules are displayed in the dialog box, such as all rules in a specific worksheet or table. See Figure 7-34.

Figure 7-34 **Conditional Formatting Rules Manager dialog box**

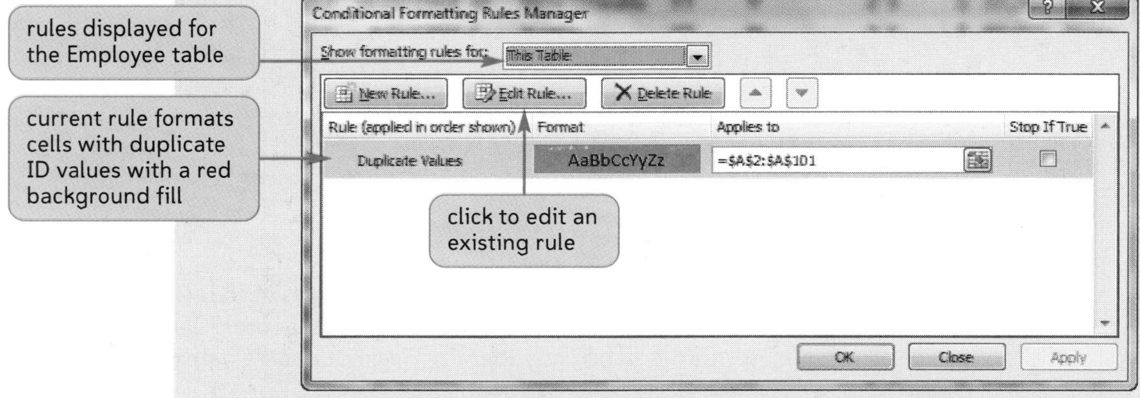

3. Click **Duplicate Values** in the Rule list to select the rule, and then click the **Edit Rule** button. The Edit Formatting Rule dialog box opens. See Figure 7-35.

Figure 7-35 Edit Formatting Rule dialog box

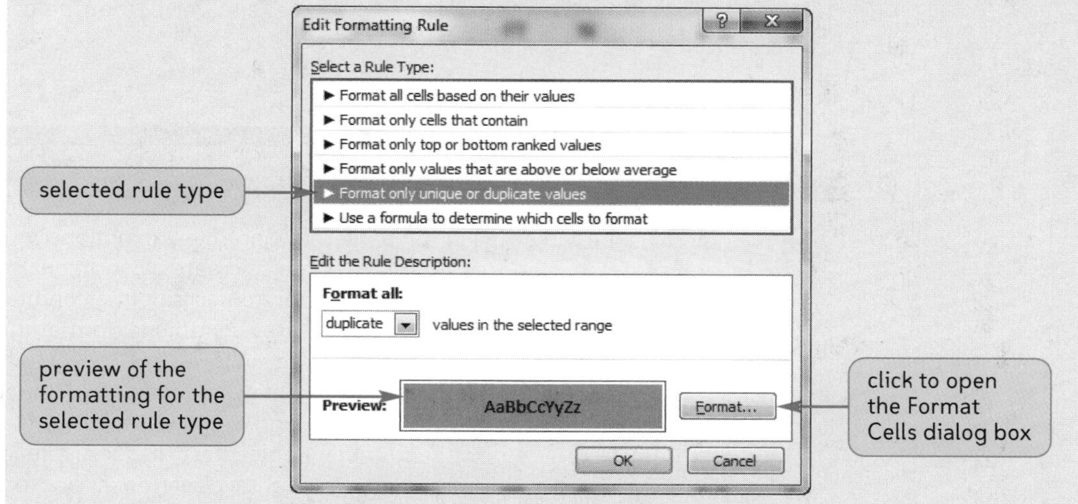

TIP

You can filter a table by color. Display the filter arrows, click a filter arrow, point to Filter by Color, and then click a color to display only cells with that fill or click No Fill to display only cells without a fill.

4. Click the **Format** button. The Format Cells dialog box opens.
5. Click the **Fill** tab, if necessary, and then, in the Background Color palette, click **yellow** (the fourth color in the last row).
6. Click the **OK** button in each dialog box. The duplicate records in the table are formatted with a yellow background color. See Figure 7-36.

Figure 7-36 Revised conditional formatting for duplicate records

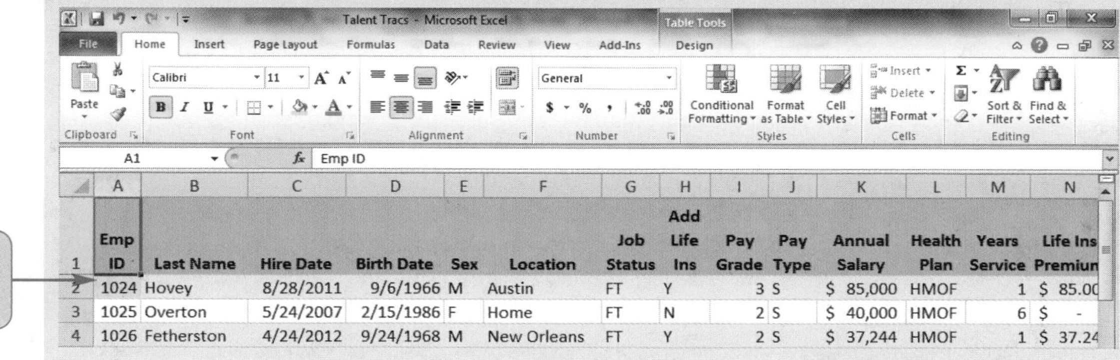

Emp ID	Last Name	Hire Date	Birth Date	Sex	Location	Job Status	Add Life Ins	Pay Grade	Pay Type	Annual Salary	Health Plan	Years Service	Life Ins Premiun
1024	Hovey	8/28/2011	9/6/1966	M	Austin	FT	Y	3	S	$ 85,000	HMOF	1	$ 85.0
1025	Overton	5/24/2007	2/15/1986	F	Home	FT	N	2	S	$ 40,000	HMOF	6	$ -
1026	Fetherston	4/24/2012	9/24/1968	M	New Orleans	FT	Y	2	S	$ 37,244	HMOF	1	$ 37.24

The cell text is easier to read on the yellow background. You'll correct the duplicate ID in cell A101 by entering the employee's actual ID number. The conditional format will remain active, and apply to any new records that Rita adds to the Employee table. Keep in mind that the Duplicate Values rule enables you to verify that each entry in the ID column is unique, but it does not ensure that each unique value is accurate.

To correct the duplicate ID:

1. Make cell **A101** the active cell, and then enter **1123**. The employee's ID is updated and the conditional formatting disappears because the value in the ID column is no longer a duplicate.
2. Scroll to the top of the Employee table, and verify that the conditional formatting no longer appears in cell A2.

INSIGHT

Creating a Formula to Conditionally Format Cells

Sometimes the built-in conditional formatting rules do not apply the formatting you need. In these instances, you may be able to create a conditional formatting rule based on a formula that uses a logical expression to describe the condition you want. For example, you can create a formula that uses conditional formatting to compare cells in different columns or to highlight an entire row.

When you create the formula, keep in mind the following guidelines:

- The formula must start with an equal sign.
- The formula must be in the form of a logical test that results in a True or False value.
- In most cases, the formula should use relative references and point to the first row of data in the table. If the formula references a cell or range outside the table, use an absolute reference.
- After you create the formula, enter test values to ensure the conditional formatting works in all situations that you intended.

For example, to use conditional formatting to highlight whether the hire date entered in column C is less than the birth date entered in column D, you need to enter a formula that applies conditional formatting that compares cells in different columns of a table. The following steps describe how to create this formula:

1. Select the range you want to format (in this case, the Hire Date column).
2. Click the Conditional Formatting button in the Styles group on the Home tab, and then click New Rule.
3. In the Select a Rule Type box, click the "Use a formula to determine which cells to format" rule.
4. In the Format values where this formula is true box, enter the appropriate formula (in this case, =C2<D2).
5. Click the Format button to open the Format Cells dialog box, and select the formatting you want to apply.
6. Click the OK button in each dialog box.

Another example is to highlight the entire row if an employee has 10 or more years of service. In this case, you would select the range of data, such as A2:S101, and enter =M$2>=10 in the Format values where this formula is true box. The other steps remain the same.

Summarizing Data Conditionally

The COUNT function tallies the number of data values in a range, the SUM function adds the values in a range, and the AVERAGE function calculates the average of the values in a range. However, sometimes you need to calculate a conditional count, sum, or average using only those cells that meet a particular condition. In those cases, you need to use the COUNTIF, SUMIF, and AVERAGEIF functions. Rita wants you to create a report that shows the number, total, and average salaries for employees in Austin, New Orleans, and Nashville as well as for those employees who work from home.

Using the COUNTIF Function

You can calculate the number of cells in a range that match criteria you specify using the COUNTIF function, which is sometimes referred to as a **conditional count**. The COUNTIF function has the syntax

```
COUNTIF(range, criteria)
```

where *range* is the range of cells you want to count, and *criteria* is an expression that defines which cells to count.

Rita wants to know how many employees are located in Austin. You can use the COUNTIF function to find this answer because you want a conditional count (a count of employees who meet a specified criterion; in this case, employees located in Austin). The location information is stored in column F of the Employee table. To count the number of employees in Austin, you can use either one of the following formulas:

TIP

You can use structured references or cell and range addresses to reference cells within an Excel table. If an Excel table has not been created for a range of data, you must use cell and range addresses.

Cell references `=COUNTIF('Employee Data'!F2:F101,"Austin")`

Fully qualified structured references `=COUNTIF(Employee[Location],"Austin")`

With either formula, Excel counts all the cells in the Location column of the Employee table that contain the text "Austin". Because Austin is text, you must enclose it within quotation marks. Numbers are not enclosed in quotation marks.

You will enter this formula using the COUNTIF function in the Employee Summary worksheet. You will use the Insert Function dialog box to help you build the formula using worksheet and range references to calculate the number of employees who work in Austin.

To count employees located in Austin:

1. Switch to the **Employee Summary** worksheet.
2. Click cell **C4**, and then click the **Insert Function** button *fx* in the formula bar. The Insert Function dialog box opens.
3. Click the **Or select a category** arrow, and then click **Statistical**.
4. In the Select a function box, double-click **COUNTIF**. The Function Arguments dialog box opens.
5. In the Range box, type **'Employee Data'!F2:F101** to enter the range to search, and then press the **Tab** key. The range 'Employee Data'!F2:F101 refers to all data values in the range F2:F101 (Location column) in the Employee Data worksheet.
6. In the Criteria box, type **B4**. Cell B4 contains "Austin," which is the criterion you want Excel to use to determine which employee records to count. See Figure 7-37.

Figure 7-37 Function Arguments dialog box for the COUNTIF function

beginning values in the Location column

number of cells in the range that contain the criterion "Austin"

criterion to determine which employee records to count

Function Arguments

COUNTIF

Range 'Employee Data'!F2:F101 = {"Austin";"Home";"New Orleans";"Austin

Criteria B4 = "Austin"

= 57

Counts the number of cells within a range that meet the given condition.

Criteria is the condition in the form of a number, expression, or text that defines which cells will be counted.

Formula result = 57

Help on this function

OK Cancel

7. Click the **OK** button. Cell C4 remains active. The formula =COUNTIF('Employee Data'!F2:F101,B4) appears in the formula bar and 57 appears in cell C4, indicating that the company employs 57 workers in Austin. See Figure 7-38.

Figure 7-38 Location Analysis with Austin workers

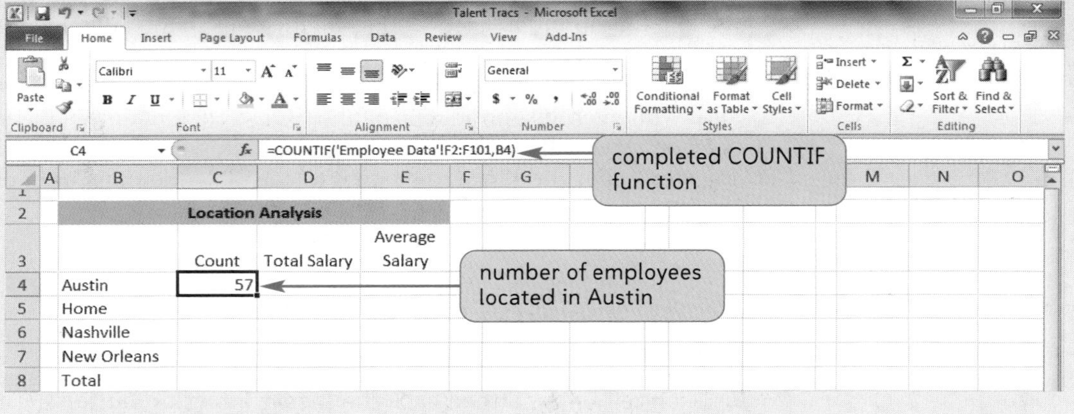

You will enter a similar formula to calculate the number of employees who work from home. This time, however, you will use structured references to specify the range to search.

To count the number of employees who work from home:

1. Click cell **C5**, and then click the **Insert Function** button in the formula bar. The Insert Function dialog box opens with the Statistical category still selected.
2. In the Select a function box, double-click **COUNTIF**. The Function Arguments dialog box opens.
3. In the Range box, type **Employee[Location]** to enter the range to search, and then press the **Tab** key. The range Employee[Location] is a structured reference that refers to all data values in the Location column in the Employee table (range F2:F101). The beginning values in the Location column appear to the right of the Range box.

4. In the Criteria box, type **B5**. Cell B5 contains "Home" (the value shown to the right of the Criteria box), which is the criterion Excel will use to determine which employee records to count.
5. Click the **OK** button. Cell C5 remains active. The formula =COUNTIF(Employee[Location],B5) appears in the formula bar and 7 appears in cell C5, indicating 7 employees work from home.

You need to count employees at two other locations—Nashville and New Orleans. Rather than enter the COUNTIF formula, you'll copy the formula in cell C5 to cells C6 and C7.

To copy the COUNTIF formula:

1. Copy the formula in cell **C5** to cell **C6** and cell **C7** to calculate the number of employees for Nashville (cell B6) and New Orleans (cell B7). Talent Tracs has 21 employees working in Nashville and 15 employees working in New Orleans.
2. In cell C8, enter the **SUM** function to calculate the total number of employees working at Talent Tracs. Talent Tracs has a total of 100 employees.

Using the SUMIF Function

The SUMIF function adds the values in a range that meet criteria you specify. The SUMIF function is also called a **conditional sum**. The syntax of the SUMIF function is

```
SUMIF(range, criteria [, sum_range])
```

where *range* is the range of cells you want to filter before calculating a sum, *criteria* is the condition used to filter the range, and *sum_range* is the range of cells to total. The *sum_range* is optional; if you omit it, Excel will total the values specified in the *range* argument. For example, if you want to total the salaries for all employees with salaries greater than $50,000, you do not use the optional third argument.

Rita wants to know the total salaries paid to employees at each location. She can use the SUMIF function to do this, because she wants to conditionally add salaries of employees at a specified location. Location is recorded in column F of the Employee Data worksheet, and the salary data is stored in column K. You can use either of the following formulas to calculate this value:

Cell references

```
=SUMIF('Employee Data'!F2:F101,"Austin", 'Employee Data'!K2:K101)
```

Fully qualified structured references

```
=SUMIF(Employee[Location],"Austin",Employee[Annual Salary])
```

Both of these formulas state that the salary of any employee whose location is Austin will be added to the total. Using the SUMIF function, you will insert the formula with structured references into the Employee Summary worksheet.

To sum employee salaries in different locations:

1. Click cell **D4**, and then click the **Insert Function** button *fx* in the formula bar. The Insert Function dialog box opens.
2. Click the **Or select a category** arrow, and then click **Math & Trig**.

3. In the Select a function box, double-click **SUMIF**. The Function Arguments dialog box opens.
4. In the Range box, type **Employee[Location]** to specify the range of data to filter, and then press the **Tab** key. The range Employee[Location] is a structured reference that refers to all data values in the Location column in the Employee table (range F2:F101).
5. In the Criteria box, type **B4** and then press the **Tab** key. Cell B4 contains "Austin" (shown to the right of the Criteria box), which is the criterion Excel will use to determine which employee records to sum.
6. In the Sum_range box, type the structured reference **Employee[Annual Salary]** to indicate that the Annual Salary column in the Employee table contains the data to sum in the filtered rows. The values to the right of the Sum_range box are the amounts in the filtered Annual Salary column. See Figure 7-39.

Figure 7-39 **Function Arguments dialog box for the SUMIF function**

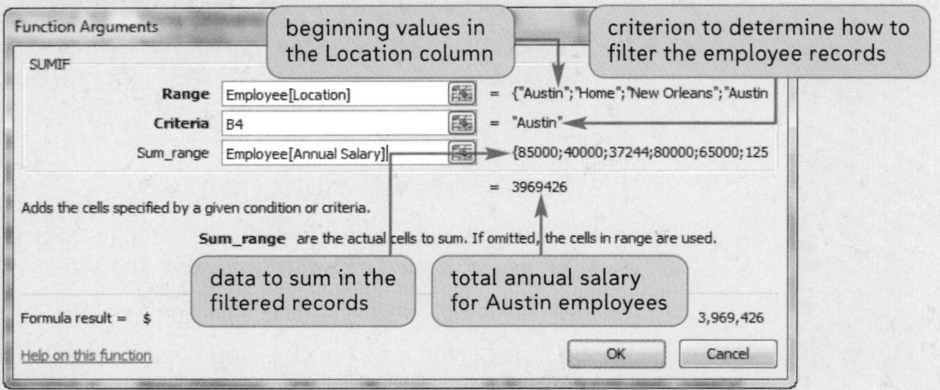

7. Click the **OK** button. Cell D4 is active. The formula =SUMIF(Employee[Location], B4,Employee[Annual Salary]) appears in the formula bar and $3,969,426 appears in cell D4, indicating the total annual salaries paid to Austin employees.
8. Copy the SUMIF formula in cell D4 to the range **D5:D7**. The total annual salary for employees working from home is $236,313. The total annual salary for Nashville employees is $587,833. The total annual salary for New Orleans employees is $1,570,994.
9. In cell D8, enter a SUM function to calculate the total salaries of all employees. The total salary of all Talent Tracs employees is $6,364,566.

Using the AVERAGEIF Function

The AVERAGEIF function is similar to the SUMIF function. You use the AVERAGEIF function to calculate the average of values in a range that meet criteria you specify. The syntax of the AVERAGEIF function is

```
AVERAGEIF(range, criteria [, average_range])
```

where *range* is the range of cells you want to filter before calculating the average, *criteria* is the condition used to filter the range, and *average_range* is the range of cells to average. The *average_range* is optional; if you omit it, Excel will average the values specified in the *range* argument.

Rita wants to know the average salaries paid to employees at each location. Location is recorded in column F of the Employee Data worksheet, and the annual salary data is stored in column K. The formula to calculate this value is:

Cell references

```
=AVERAGEIF('Employee Data'!F2:F101,"Austin", 'Employee Data'!K2:K101)
```

Fully qualified structured references

```
=AVERAGEIF(Employee[Location],"Austin",Employee[Annual Salary])
```

Both of these formulas state that the annual salary of any employee whose location is Austin will be included in the average. You will enter the formula using the AVERAGEIF function with structured references into the Employee Summary worksheet.

To average employee salaries in different locations:

1. Click cell **E4**, and then click the **Insert Function** button in the formula bar. The Insert Function dialog box opens.
2. Click the **Or select a category** arrow, and then click **Statistical**.
3. In the Select a function box, double-click **AVERAGEIF**. The Function Arguments dialog box opens.
4. In the Range box, type the structured reference **Employee[Location]** to specify the range of data to filter, and then press the **Tab** key. The range Employee[Location] is a structured reference that refers to all data values in the Location column in the Employee table (range F2:F101).
5. In the Criteria box, type **B4** and then press the **Tab** key. Cell B4 contains "Austin" (shown to the right of the Criteria box), which is the criterion Excel will use to determine which employee records to average.
6. In the Average_range box, type **Employee[Annual Salary]** to indicate that the Annual Salary column in the Employee table contains the data to average in the filtered rows. See Figure 7-40.

Figure 7-40 **Function Arguments dialog box for the AVERAGEIF function**

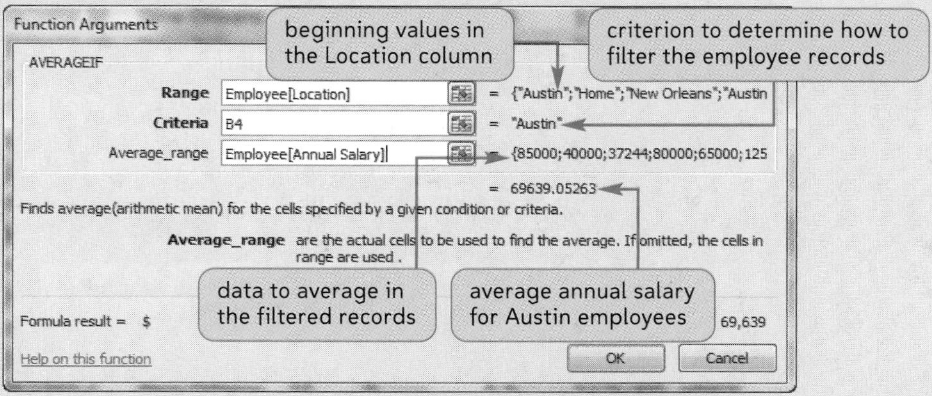

7. Click the **OK** button. Cell E4 remains active. The formula =AVERAGEIF(Employee [Location],B4,Employee[Annual Salary]) appears in the formula bar and $69,639 appears in cell E4, indicating the average salary paid to Austin employees.
8. Copy the formula in cell E4 to the range **E5:E7**. Talent Tracs pays an average of $33,759 to employees working at home, $27,992 to employees working in Nashville, and $104,733 to employees working in New Orleans.

9. In cell E8, enter **=D8/C8** to calculate the average salary at Talent Tracs by dividing the total salaries at Talent Tracs by the number of employees at the company. The average salary for all Talent Tracs employees is $63,646.
10. If necessary, format the range E4:E8 in the **Accounting** number format with no decimal places.
11. Add a bottom border to the range C7:E7, and then click cell **E4** to deselect the range. See Figure 7-41.

Figure 7-41 **Completed Location Analysis report**

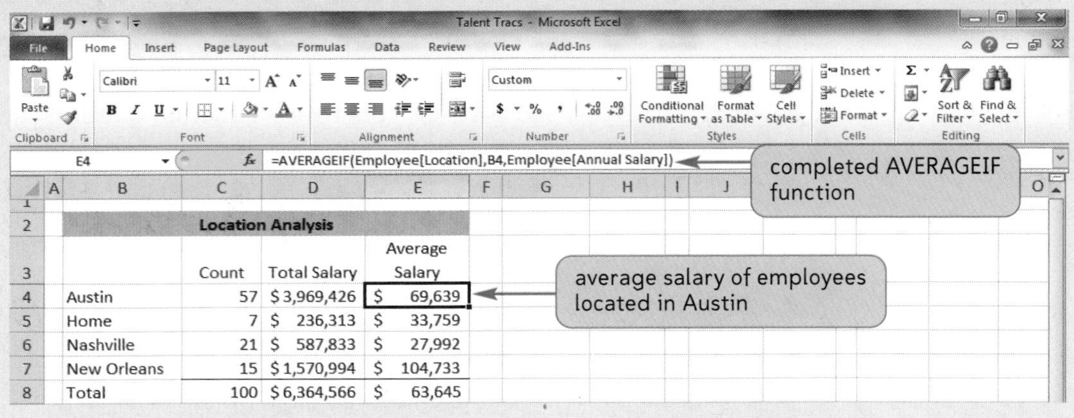

As Rita enters new employees or edits the location or annual salary values of current employees, the values in the Employee Summary worksheet will be automatically updated because the formulas reference the Employee table.

Rita has recently hired a new employee and asks you to add the new record to the Excel table.

To add a record to the Employee table:

1. Switch to the **Employee Data** worksheet, and then click cell **A102**. You will enter the new employee record in this row.
2. In the range A102:L102 enter **1124** for Emp ID, **Joplin** for last name, **4/1/2013** for hire date, **11/15/1970** for birth date, **M** for sex, **Home** for location, **PT** for job status, **N** for Add Life Ins, **1** for pay grade, **H** for pay type, **23000** for annual salary, and **None** for health plan, and then click cell **A103**. The new employee record is added to the Employee table.
3. Switch to the **Employee Summary** worksheet. The Location Analysis report has been updated to reflect the new employee. See Figure 7-42.

Figure 7-42 **Updated Location Analysis report**

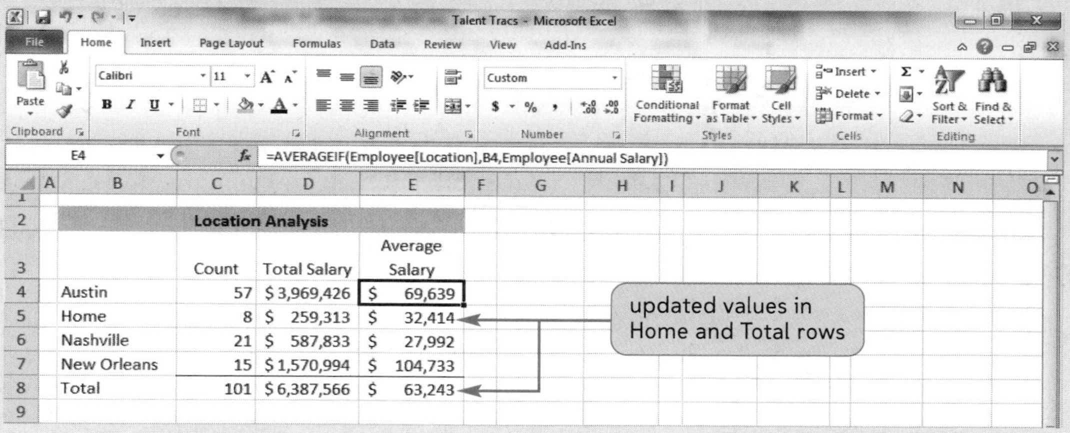

	Location Analysis		
	Count	Total Salary	Average Salary
Austin	57	$ 3,969,426	$ 69,639
Home	8	$ 259,313	$ 32,414
Nashville	21	$ 587,833	$ 27,992
New Orleans	15	$ 1,570,994	$ 104,733
Total	101	$ 6,387,566	$ 63,243

If the employee data had been stored as a range of data instead of an Excel table, the Location Analysis report would not have been automatically updated. Instead, you would have had to modify all the formulas in the report to reflect the expanded range of employee data. Rita is pleased with the formulas you added to the Employee Data and Employee Summary worksheets.

REVIEW

Session 7.3 Quick Check

1. Would you apply the duplicate value conditional formatting rule to a table column of last names? Why or why not?
2. If you receive a worksheet that includes conditional formatting, which dialog box would you use to find out what criteria were used for the formatting?
3. Explain what the formula =COUNTIF(Employee[Sex],"F") calculates.
4. Explain what the formula =AVERAGEIF(Employee[Pay Type],"H",Employee [Annual Salary]) calculates.
5. Explain what the formula =SUMIF(Employee[Job Status],"FT",Employee[Annual Salary]) calculates.
6. Explain what the formula =COUNTIF(Employee[Annual Salary],">100000") calculates.
7. True or False. To display the number of females working from home, you could use the COUNTIF function.
8. True or False. Applying the duplicate value conditional formatting rule deletes the duplicate record.

Practice the skills you learned in the tutorial using the same case scenario.

PRACTICE

Review Assignments

Data File needed for the Review Assignments: Tracs.xlsx

Rita wants you to try some alternative calculations for bonuses and benefits for the Talent Tracs employees. Complete the following:

1. Open the **Tracs** workbook located in the Excel7\Review folder included with your Data Files, save the workbook as **Tracs Employees** in the same folder, and then, in the Documentation worksheet, enter your name and the date.
2. Go to the Employee Data worksheet, and then rename the Excel table as **EmpData**.
3. Employees who elect additional life insurance coverage (Add Life Ins) pay 0.1 percent times their annual salary. The life insurance premium rate of 0.1 percent is entered in cell Y5. Employees who do not elect additional coverage pay nothing. In the Life Ins Premium column, enter an IF function to calculate the life insurance premiums; use a reference to cell **Y5** to obtain the life insurance rate and enter **0** for employees who do not elect coverage.
4. All full-time (Job Status) employees over the age of 30 (Age) are eligible for the 401(k) benefit. In the 401(k) column, enter the IF and AND functions to calculate the 401(k) benefit as 3 percent of annual salary; use a reference to cell **Y6** to obtain the 401(k) matching percent rate (3 percent). If the employee is not eligible, enter **0**.
5. All employees with one or more years of service (Years Service) are eligible for a bonus. Pay Grade 1 employees receive $3,000 (cell Y2), Pay Grade 2 employees receive $6,000 (cell Y3), and Pay Grade 3 employees receive $8,000 (cell Y4). In the Bonus column, enter nested IF functions to calculate the bonus. For employees not eligible for a bonus, display the label **NE**.
6. In the Salary Increase column, enter IF and OR functions to insert the text **Not Eligible** if the individual's job status is a consultant (CN) or the pay grade is 4. Leave the cell blank if the individual is eligible for a salary increase.
7. In the Health Cost column, enter the HLOOKUP function to do an exact match lookup to calculate the health plan cost. The layout of HealthPlanRates data ($B$2:$F$3) in the Lookup Tables worksheet has been revised to work with the HLOOKUP function. Use the range address reference in the HLOOKUP function to reference HealthPlanRates data.
8. In the Award column, modify the VLOOKUP function to incorporate the IFERROR function and display the message **Invalid hire date**. Test the modified formula by changing the date in cell C2 from 3/13/2008 to **13/13/2008**. Increase the column width to view the entire message.
9. In the Emp ID column, change the format color of the duplicate value conditional formatting rule to Green (the sixth color in the last row of the Background Color palette) using the Conditional Formatting Rules Manager dialog box.
10. Go to the Reports worksheet, and then enter the COUNTIF function in cells C4 and C5 to count the number of female and male employees.
11. In cells D4 and D5, enter the AVERAGEIF function to calculate the average salary of female employees and the average salary of male employees.
12. Save and close the workbook. Submit the finished workbook to your instructor, either in printed or electronic form, as requested.

Apply the skills you learned to analyze and summarize sales data.

APPLY

Case Problem 1

Data File needed for this Case Problem: Modem.xlsx

PC-Market Distribution Linda Klaussen works for PC-Market Distribution, a computer supply store. She needs your help with designing an Excel workbook to enter purchase order information. She has already entered the product information on PC-Market's line of modems. She wants you to insert a lookup function to look up data from the product table. The company also offers three shipping options—Standard, Express, and Overnight—that vary in price. She wants the purchase order worksheet to be able to calculate the total cost of the order, including the type of shipping the customer requests. Complete the following:

1. Open the **Modem** workbook located in the Excel7\Case1 folder included with your Data Files, save the workbook as **PC Modem** in the same folder, and then, in the Documentation worksheet, enter your name and the date.
2. Go to the Purchase Order worksheet. In cell B5, enter the Product ID **1050**. In cell C7, create a lookup function to display the product type. In cell C8, create a lookup function to display the model name. In cell C9, create a lookup function to display the price. Product information is displayed in the Product List worksheet.
3. If an incorrect Product ID is entered in cell B5, cells C7, C8, and C9 will display the #N/A error value. Modify the formula in these cells so that **Product ID not found** is displayed in the cell if the ID entered is not found.
4. In the range D40:E42, enter labels and shipping costs based on the following information: **Standard**, **$9.50**; **Express**, **$14.50**; and **Overnight**, **$18.50**. In cell B15, enter **Express**.
5. In cell C17, use nested IF functions to display the shipping costs for the option entered in cell B15. If the shipping option in cell B15 is blank, then cell C17 should be blank. (*Hint*: The IF functions should reference the cells in the range D40:E42.)
6. In cell C19, enter a formula to display the total cost of the product (price times quantity) plus shipping. In cell B12, enter **4**.
7. In cell C19, modify the formula so that if the cell equals an error value (#Value!), the message **Check Product ID, Quantity, or Shipping option** is displayed.
8. Go to the Product List worksheet, and then use conditional formatting to highlight all duplicate values in the ID column with the formatting you choose. To test that conditional formatting is working, temporarily change the Product ID in cell A119 to **1121**. When the test is completed, return the value in cell A119 to **1122**.
9. In the Product List worksheet, use conditional formatting to highlight all prices above $300 with the formatting you choose.
10. Go to the Summary worksheet, and then enter appropriate functions in the range B5:C7 to determine the average modem price and count for each modem type.
11. Save and close the workbook. Submit the finished workbook to your instructor, either in printed or electronic form, as requested.

Apply the skills you learned to track employee vacation and family leave.

APPLY

Case Problem 2

Data File needed for this Case Problem: Leave.xlsx

Town of Baltic Administrative Office Alan Welton, HR Generalist at the Town of Baltic Administrative Office in Baltic, Indiana, wants to create a workbook that tracks the amount of vacation time and family leave used by each employee of the town. The workbook needs to calculate how much vacation and family leave each employee is eligible for. Then it should subtract the time already used from that amount. It should also calculate the total number of vacation and family leave days used by all employees, as well as the total number of days remaining. The eligibility requirements for the different vacation and family leave plans are as follows:

For vacation:

- 15 days for full-time employees
- 10 days for part-time employees
- 0 days for everyone else

For family leave:

- 5 days for full-time employees who have worked 1 or more years
- 0 days for everyone else

Use these eligibility requirements to calculate the available vacation and family leave time for each employee. Complete the following:

1. Open the **Leave** workbook located in the Excel7\Case2 folder included with your Data Files, save the workbook as **Baltic Leave** in the same folder, and then, in the Documentation worksheet, enter your name and the date.
2. Go to the LeaveData worksheet. Create an Excel table in the range A5:J107, name the Excel table **Leave**, and then remove the filter arrows. Set the column width for columns B through J to **10**.
3. In column D, enter a formula to calculate Years Employed. Use the Date Hired cell and the current date (assume 7/1/2013, which is stored in cell Z6), and express the length of time employed in years. (*Hint*: Use the formula **(current date–Date Hired)/365**.)
4. In column E, enter a formula using a nested IF function to determine the number of vacation days (based on the vacation rules above) each employee is eligible for based on the employee's job status in column B.
5. In column G, enter a formula to subtract the amount of vacation used from the available vacation time, which displays the remaining vacation time for each employee.
6. In column H, enter a formula to determine each employee's total family leave time (based on the Family leave rules above).
7. In column J, enter a formula to subtract used family leave from the total family leave to determine the remaining family leave available for each employee.
8. In column J, apply conditional formatting that highlights the remaining family leave of any employee who has not used any family leave days. You decide the formatting.
9. Go to the Leave Summary worksheet. In the range C4:C6, use a function to count the total number of employees eligible for each vacation plan. (*Hint*: Any employee who is eligible for 15 vacation days will have the value 15 in column E of the LeaveData worksheet.)
10. In the range D4:D6, use functions to calculate the total number of vacation days for each vacation plan.
11. In the range E4:E6, use functions to calculate the total vacation days remaining for each vacation plan.
12. In the range C7:E7, calculate totals for Number Eligible, Total Days, and Days Remaining.
13. Save and close the workbook. Submit the finished workbook to your instructor, either in printed or electronic form, as requested.

Create reports for a water company that determine different billing plans.

CHALLENGE

Case Problem 3

Data File needed for this Case Problem: M-Fresh.xlsx

M-Fresh Water Company M-Fresh Water Company is a small independent water company in Miami, Oklahoma, that provides water to commercial customers throughout the region, delivering the water supply through pipelines, on-demand storage tanks, and bottles. Customers of M-Fresh Water range from government offices to nonprofit organizations to commercial retail shops and markets. Town regulations tax the latter group of commercial customers based on their usage, whereas nonprofit and government offices are not taxed. Furthermore, M-Fresh Water will occasionally waive a water bill based on its charitable-giving policy. Dawes Cado is in charge of the billing system that must take into account these business rules and assure accurate and on-time billing, which occurs quarterly. Complete the following:

1. Open the **M-Fresh** workbook located in the Excel7\Case3 folder included with your Data Files, save the workbook as **Water Bill** in the same folder, and then, in the Documentation worksheet, enter your name and the date.
2. In the Quarterly Data worksheet, create an Excel table for the range A1:F73, and name the table **WaterData**. Remove the filter arrows. Format the data in the Gal Used column with the Comma Style number format and no decimal places.
3. Add a column named **Gal Billed** to the table, and then enter a formula to calculate the number of gallons billed based on the following rules: If a customer's bill is waived (Bill Waived column) or the number of gallons used is less than 25,000 (Gal Used column), display **0** in Gal Billed column; otherwise, display the value from the Gal Used column in the Gal Billed column.
4. Add a column named **Water Bill** to the table, and then enter a formula to calculate the water bill based on the following rules: The billing rate varies based on the type of customer (Cust Type column). The billing rate is \$3, \$2, or \$1.50 per *thousand* gallons billed, depending on the customer type (see the lookup table in cells B2:C5 of the Billing Rate worksheet). For example, a commercial customer using 75,000 gallons has a water bill of \$225 (75 X \$3), whereas a government customer using 100,000 gallons pays \$150 (100 X \$1.50). A commercial customer using 15,000 gallons has a water bill of \$0 (see Gal Used rule in question 3).
5. Add a column named **Tax** to the table, and then enter a formula to calculate the tax based on the following rule: If a customer pays tax (Taxable column), then multiply the Water Bill by 3.5 percent; otherwise, the tax is 0. The tax rate is stored in cell T1.
6. Add a column named **Total Bill** to the table, and then enter a formula to calculate the bill amount by adding the Water Bill column and the Tax column.
7. Improve the formatting of the number fields in the WaterData table.
8. Make a copy of the Quarterly Data worksheet, rename the copied worksheet as **Q2-Q8**, and then add a Totals row to the Excel table displaying totals for the Gal Used, Gal Billed, Tax, and Total Bill columns.

EXPLORE

9. Make another copy of the Quarterly Data worksheet, rename the copied worksheet as **Q9**, and then use conditional formatting to highlight the top 15 percent of the Total Bill amounts with a yellow background color. Filter the table so that only the top 15 percent are displayed. Sort the filtered table by largest to smallest.
10. Insert a new worksheet, rename the worksheet as **Billing Summary**, and then create the report shown in Figure 7-43, using COUNTIF, AVERAGEIF, and SUMIF functions to prepare the report.

Figure 7-43 **Water usage and billing by customer type**

	A	B	C	D	E
1					
2					
3					
4					
5		Customer Type	Nbr Customers	Avg Gallons Used	Total Billed
6		Commercial	37	322,437	$37,043.12
7		Nonprofit	11	87,661	$ 224.18
8		Government	24	774,532	$27,901.44
9		Total	72	437,267	$65,168.74

EXPLORE 11. Make another copy of the Quarterly Data worksheet, and then rename the copied worksheet as **Q11**. Add a custom filter to the table to display only those organizations that have "church" or "center" as part of the customer name.

EXPLORE 12. Make another copy of the Quarterly Data worksheet, and then rename the copied worksheet as **Q12**. Use the lookup table in cells E2:H3 of the Billing Rate worksheet and the HLOOKUP function to modify the formula to calculate the Water Bill column (column H).

13. Save and close the workbook. Submit the finished workbook to your instructor, either in printed or electronic form, as requested.

Create a worksheet that compiles and summarizes reports for a newspaper.

CREATE

Case Problem 4

Data File needed for this Case Problem: Rock Island.xlsx

Rock Island Home Sales Tim Derkson is a reporter for *Rock Island Times*, a newspaper in Rock Island, Illinois. He is compiling a quarterly real estate sales analysis for his newspaper. He obtained data on home sales from the local real estate association and county records. He wants to create a worksheet that will display summary information on the home sales in Rock Island. Tim has already set up and formatted the workbook, but he wants you to insert the correct formulas. Tim stored the housing data in the Home Sales Data worksheet. He wants to use the Home Summary worksheet to search for information about the homes. Complete the following:

1. Open the **Rock Island** workbook located in the Excel7\Case4 folder included with your Data Files, save the workbook as **Home Sales** in the same folder, and then, in the Documentation worksheet, enter your name and the date.
2. In the Home Sales Data worksheet, create an Excel table in the range A1:K118. Remove the filter arrows. Rename the Excel table as **SalesData**.
3. In column L, add a calculated column named **Days on Market**, and then enter a formula to verify that the date sold occurs after the date listed. If it does not, display the message **Check Dates**; otherwise, calculate the number of days on the market. (*Hint*: You might need to format this column in the General number format.)
4. An incentive bonus of $1,000 is awarded if the sales price is above the asking price or the number of days on the market is less than 25 days. In column M, add a calculated column named **Incentive**, and then enter a formula to calculate the bonus amount.
5. Use conditional formatting to highlight records in the Days on Market column where the house was on the market for 300 or more days.
6. Display the Total row in the SalesData table. In this row, display a count of homes sold (place in Listing ID), average asking price, average taxes, average sales price, and average days on the market.

7. Split the Home Sales Data worksheet so that the top pane shows rows in the SalesData table and the bottom pane displays the Total row.
8. Insert a new worksheet, and then rename it as **Sales Summary**. Create a report on home sales based on the style sold and the average sales price, as shown in Figure 7-44.

Figure 7-44 **Home sales by type of home**

	A	B	C	D
1		Rock Island Home Sales		
2		Overall Data		
3				
4		By Style of Home		
5				
6		Style	Number Sold	Average Sales Price
7		Condo	23	$ 90,347.83
8		Ranch	46	$ 91,842.39
9		Victorian	48	$ 113,567.71
10		Total	117	$ 100,461.54
11				

EXPLORE 9. Create a PivotTable report with the information shown in Figure 7-45. Rename the worksheet as **DaysOnMarket**.

Figure 7-45 **Days on Market PivotTable report**

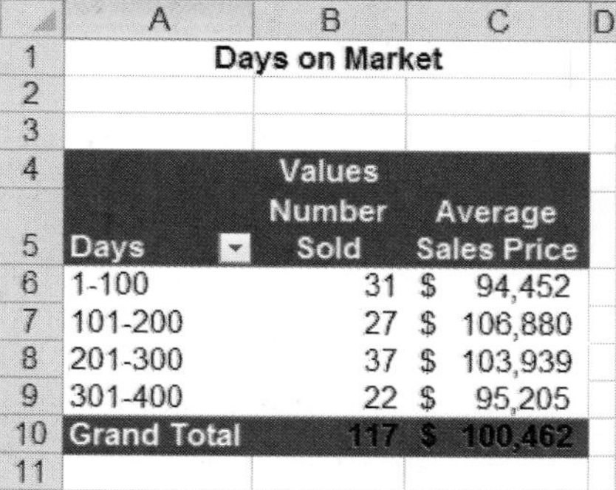

	A	B	C	D
1	Days on Market			
2				
3				
4		Values		
5	Days	Number Sold	Average Sales Price	
6	1-100	31	$ 94,452	
7	101-200	27	$ 106,880	
8	201-300	37	$ 103,939	
9	301-400	22	$ 95,205	
10	Grand Total	117	$ 100,462	
11				

EXPLORE 10. Make a copy of the Home Sales Data worksheet, and then rename the worksheet as **Q10**. Remove the current conditional formatting, and then add conditional formatting to highlight records in the Sales Price column where the sales price was above the asking price. Use appropriate formatting. (*Hint*: Create a new rule by selecting the Use formula to determine which cells to format rule type, and then editing the rule description to enter a formula with a conditional statement that compares the first data row between the two columns of interest.)

11. Save and close the workbook. Submit the finished workbook to your instructor, either in printed or electronic form, as requested.

SAM

ASSESS

SAM: Skills Assessment Manager

For current SAM information, including versions and content details, visit SAM Central (http://samcentral.course.com). If you have a SAM user profile, you may have access to hands-on instruction, practice, and assessment of the skills covered in this tutorial. Since various versions of SAM are supported throughout the life of this text, check with your instructor for the correct instructions and URL/Web site for accessing assignments.

ENDING DATA FILES

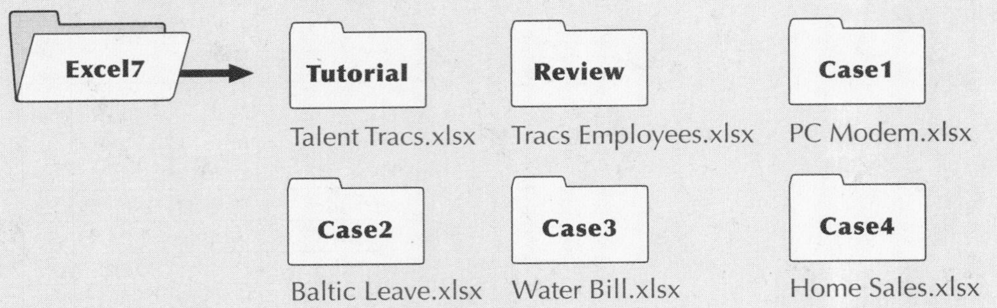

TUTORIAL 8

Developing an Excel Application

Creating an Invoice

OBJECTIVES

Session 8.1
- Create an application
- Create, edit, and delete defined names for cells and ranges
- Paste a list of defined names as documentation
- Use defined names in formulas
- Add defined names to existing formulas

Session 8.2
- Create validation rules for data entry
- Protect the contents of worksheets and workbooks
- Add, edit, and delete comments

Session 8.3
- Learn about macro viruses and Excel security features
- Add the Developer tab to the Ribbon
- Create and run a macro
- Edit a macro using the Visual Basic Editor
- Assign a macro to a keyboard shortcut and a button
- Save and open a workbook in macro-enabled format
- Minimize the Ribbon

Case | *Eugene Community Theatre*

Ellen Jefferson, business manager for the Eugene Community Theatre in Eugene, Oregon, is automating several processes for the theatre's business office. Each year, the theatre mails a brochure to patrons and other interested individuals showcasing the upcoming season's offerings. Then, theatre-goers make their selections and mail in the order form. Ellen wants to automate the process of invoicing, capturing the order, calculating the charges, and printing an invoice. She also wants the invoice system to reflect specific requests for tickets (number, series, and location in theatre).

Many of these tasks can be accomplished in Excel. But without validating data entry, protecting cells with formulas from accidental deletion, and reducing repetitious keystrokes and mouse clicks, Ellen realizes too many opportunities for errors exist. In addition, as a nonprofit organization, the theatre relies on numerous volunteers who have varying degrees of computer experience and skill. To accommodate these varying skill levels and reduce potential errors, Ellen wants to create a custom interface for this project that does not rely exclusively on the Ribbon, galleries, and so forth. You will help Ellen create a unique Excel application that can resolve these issues and help ensure accurate data entry.

STARTING DATA FILES

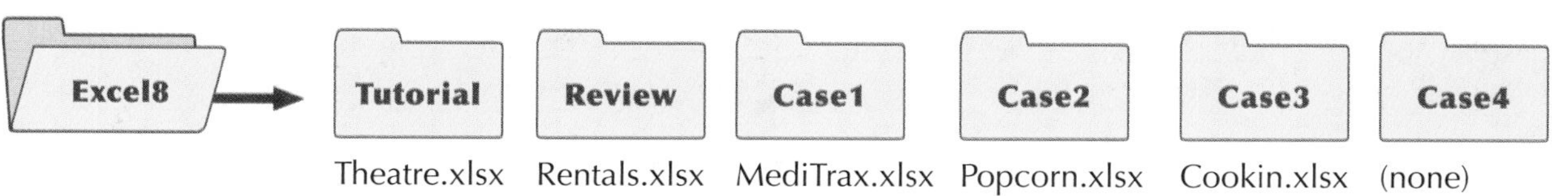

Theatre.xlsx Rentals.xlsx MediTrax.xlsx Popcorn.xlsx Cookin.xlsx (none)

SESSION 8.1 VISUAL OVERVIEW

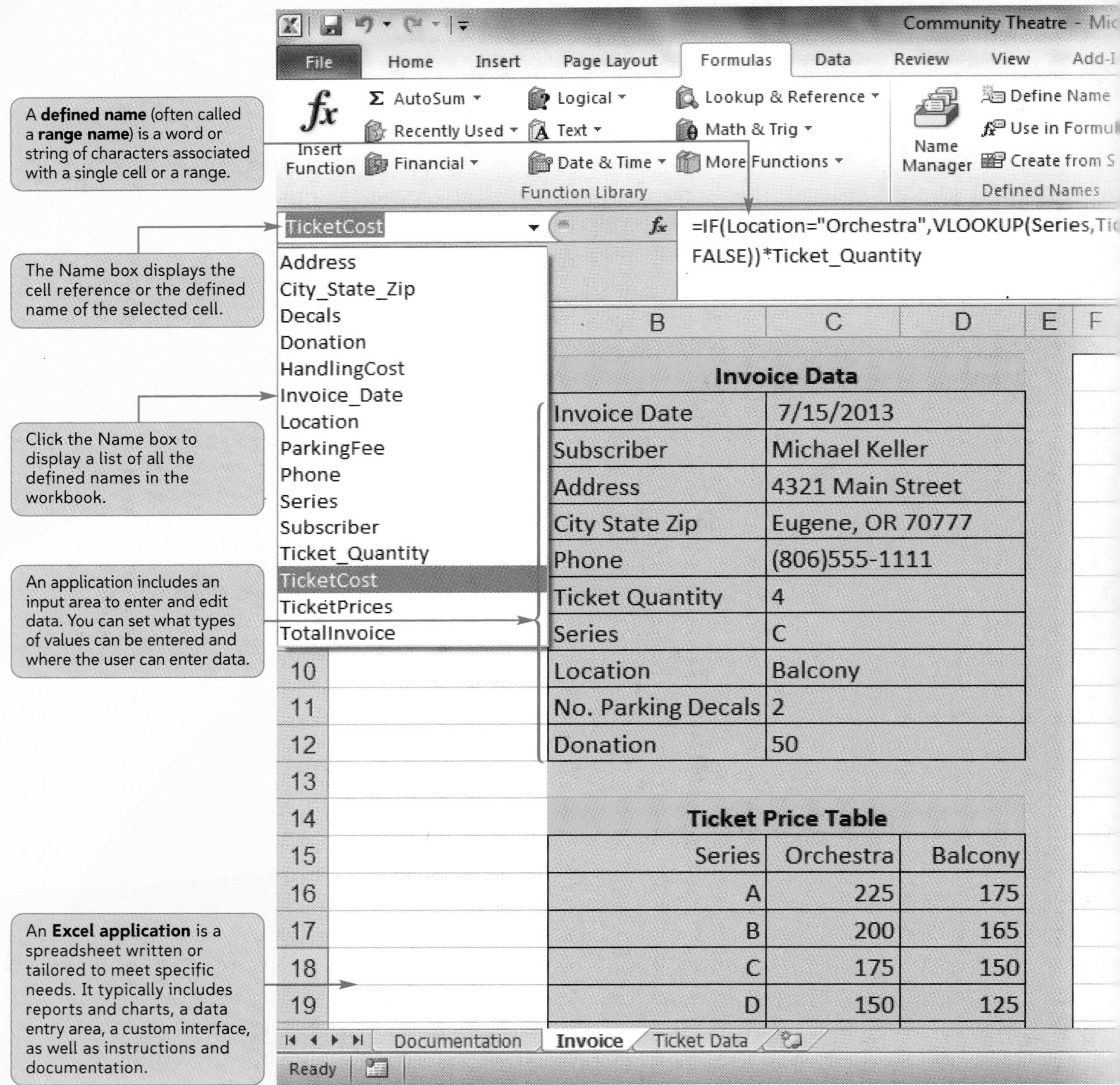

EXCEL APPLICATION AND DEFINED NAMES

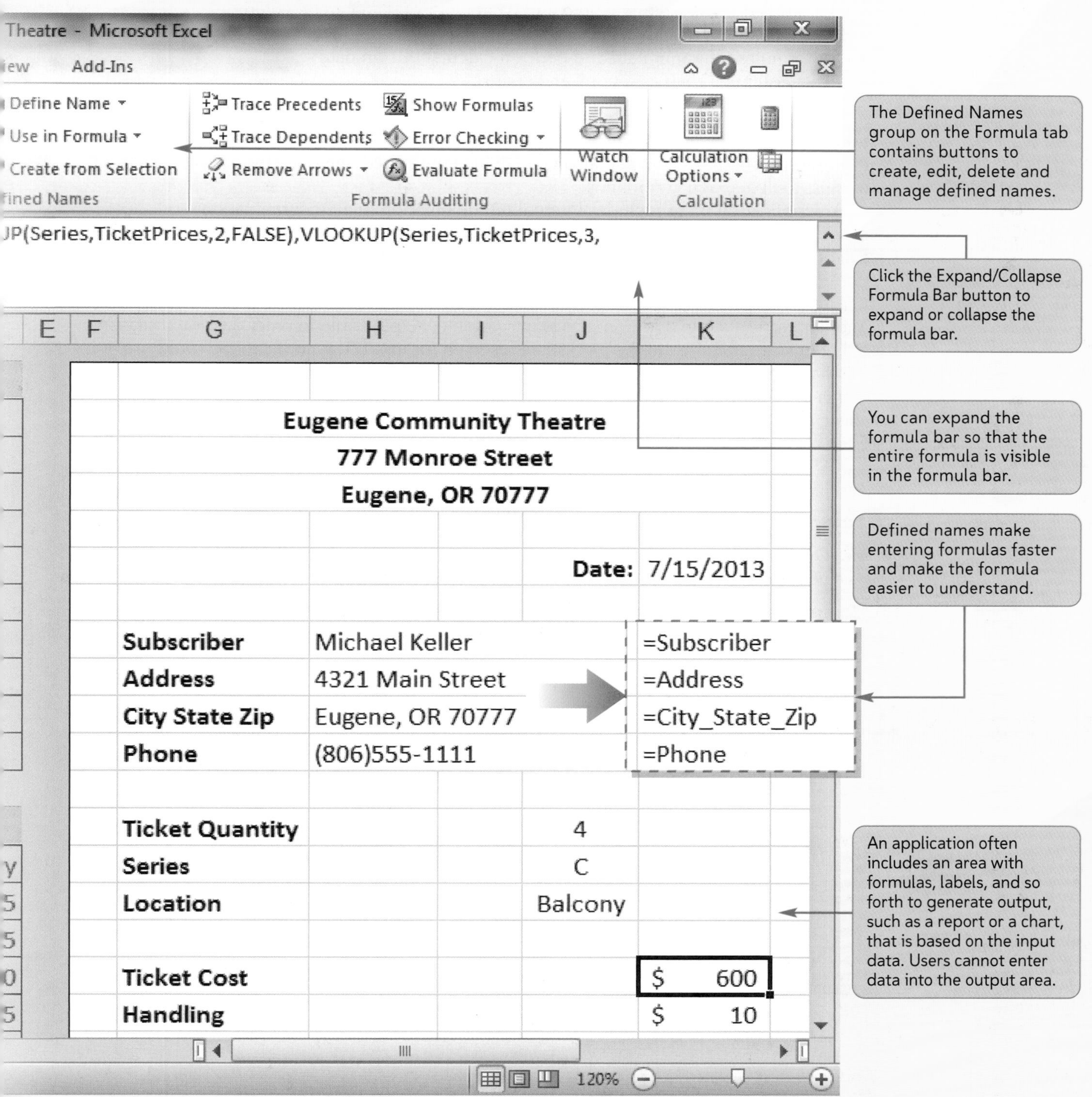

Planning an Excel Application

Planning an Excel application includes designing how the worksheet(s) will be organized. You can include different sections for each function, depending on the complexity of the project. For example, an application often includes separate sections to:

- Enter and edit data (setting where and what types of data can be entered)
- Store data after it has been entered
- Use formulas to manipulate and perform calculations on data
- Display outputs, such as reports and charts

An application's interface helps others use it. For example, you can have separate sections for inputting data and displaying outputs. You can create special buttons for performing specific tasks. You can also change the entire Excel interface by adding custom menus, toolbars, and commands.

An application often includes internal documentation in a Documentation worksheet as well as comments to explain cell contents and provide instructions. It can also include a set of clearly written instructions. All of these help you and others use the workbook correctly and accurately.

Ellen wants to be able to easily print the invoice and transfer the invoice items to another worksheet. In addition, she wants volunteers to be able to enter data for a season ticket in a specific area of the worksheet reserved for input. The application would use this data to automatically generate and print the invoice. To keep the process simple, she wants users to be able to click buttons to print a single invoice, print the entire worksheet, and transfer the data from one worksheet to another. You'll open the workbook Ellen created.

To open and review the Theatre workbook:

1. Open the **Theatre** workbook located in the Excel8\Tutorial folder included with your Data Files, and then save the workbook as **Community Theatre**.
2. In the Documentation worksheet, enter your name and the date.
3. Review the contents of the workbook, and then switch to the **Invoice** worksheet. See Figure 8-1.

Figure 8-1 Initial Invoice worksheet

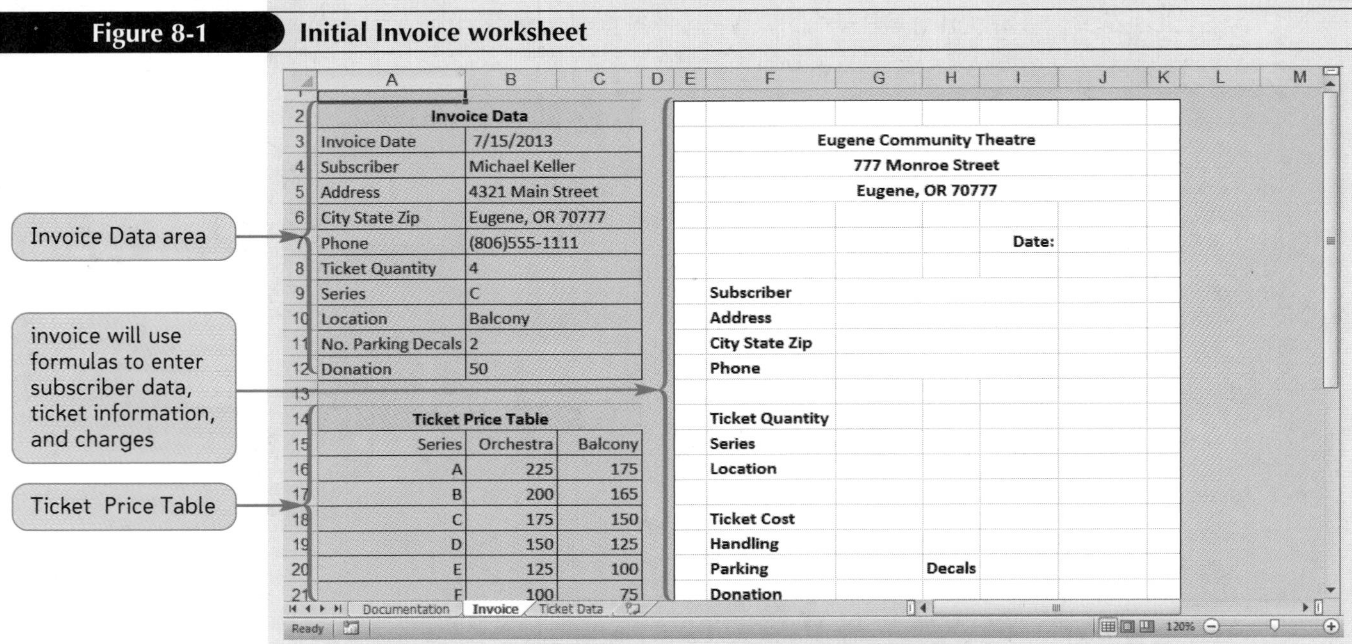

TIP

Larger and more complex applications often place the input and output sections in separate worksheets.

In addition to the Documentation worksheet, the Community Theatre workbook includes two other worksheets: Invoice and Ticket Data. The Invoice worksheet contains input, output, and transfer sections. The input section is divided into the following three areas:

- Invoice Data contains items that change for each subscriber transaction such as the subscriber name, address, phone number, ticket quantity, series, and location of seats.
- Ticket Price Table contains the table with ticket prices for the upcoming season.
- Invoice Constants contains charges for items that will not change during the upcoming season, such as the cost for parking ($15/decal) and the handling charge ($10/invoice).

The output section contains formulas and labels used to generate the invoice based on data in the input section. The invoice in the output section will be printed. The transfer section gathers selected data from the invoice in one area before the data is transferred to the Ticket Data worksheet for storage. The transfer section makes it simpler to move the data to the Ticket Data worksheet.

Naming Cells and Ranges

So far, you have referred to a cell or range by its address except when you entered formulas within an Excel table. Cell and range references do not indicate what data is stored in those cells. Instead, you can use a defined name to assign a meaningful, descriptive name to a cell or range. For example, if the range D1:D100 contains sales data for 100 transactions, you can define the name "Sales" to refer to the range of sales data.

A defined name enables you to quickly navigate within a workbook to the cell with the defined name. You can also use defined names to create more descriptive formulas.

In the Invoice worksheet, the range B3:B12 contains the data values for each request for season tickets. As you can see, this range includes many variables. It will be simpler to remember where different data is stored by assigning a descriptive name to each cell or range rather than using its cell address. For example, the name Subscriber better identifies what is stored in the cell than cell B4.

PROSKILLS

Written Communication: Saving Time with Defined Names

Words can be more descriptive than numbers. This is especially true in cell references. Instead of using the letter and number references for cells, you can create defined names to provide more intuitive references. Defined names have several advantages over cell references, especially as a worksheet becomes longer and more complex. Some advantages include:

- Names, such as TaxRate and TotalSales, are more descriptive than cell references, making it easier to remember what a cell or range contains.
- Names can be used in formulas, making it easier for users to understand the calculations being performed. For example, =GrossPay–Deductions is more understandable than =C15–C16.
- When you move a named cell or range within a worksheet, its name moves with it. Any formulas that contain the name automatically reference the new location.
- In a formula, referencing a named cell or range is the same as referencing the cell or range's absolute reference. So, if you move a formula that includes a defined name, the reference remains pointed to the correct cell or range.

By using defined names, you'll often save time and everyone reviewing the worksheet will have a clearer understanding of what a formula is calculating.

Creating Defined Names

Creating defined names for cells or ranges makes building an application more intuitive and easier to document. When you define a name for a cell or range, keep in mind the following rules:

- The name must begin with a letter or _ (an underscore).
- The name can include letters and numbers as well as periods and underscores, but not other symbols or spaces. To distinguish multiword names, use an underscore between the words or capitalize the first letter of each word. For example, the names *Net_Income* and *NetIncome* are valid, but *Net Income* and *Net-Income* are not.
- The name cannot be a valid cell address (such as FY2013), function name, or reserved word (such as *Print_Area*).
- The name can include as many as 255 characters, although short, meaningful names of 5 to 15 characters are more practical.
- The name is not case sensitive. For example, both *Sales* and *SALES* refer to the same cell or range.

REFERENCE

Creating a Defined Name for a Cell or Range

- Select the cell or range to which you want to assign a name.
- Click in the Name box on the formula bar, type the name, and then press the Enter key.
  or
  In the Defined Names group on the Formulas tab, click the Define Name button, type a name in the Name box, and then click the OK button.

or

- Select the range with labels to which you want to assign a name.
- In the Defined Names group on the Formulas tab, click the Create from Selection button.
- Specify whether to create the ranges based on the top row, bottom row, left column, or right column in the list.
- Click the OK button.

The fastest way to create a defined name is to use the Name box. You'll use the Name box to define names for the cells and ranges in the worksheet.

To create defined names using the Name box:

1. Click cell **B24** to make it active, and then click the **Name box** on the formula bar. The cell reference for the active cell, B24, is selected in the Name box.
2. Type **HandlingCost** and then press the **Enter** key. Cell B24 remains active, and "HandlingCost" appears in the Name box instead of the cell reference. See Figure 8-2.

Figure 8-2 **Defined name for cell B24**

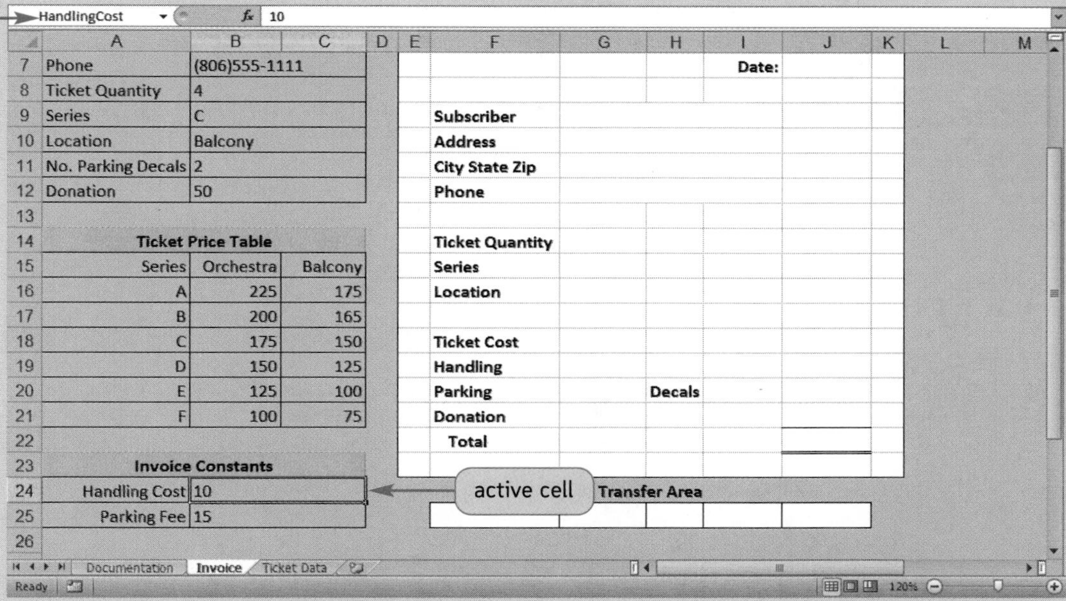

Trouble? If "HandlingCost" appears in cell B24, you probably did not click the Name box before typing the name. On the Quick Access Toolbar, click the Undo button, and then repeat Steps 1 and 2.

Trouble? If "cell B24" appears in the Name box instead of "HandlingCost," you probably didn't press the Enter key. Repeat Steps 1 and 2 being sure to press the Enter key to assign the defined name to cell B24.

3. Click cell **B25** to make it active, click the **Name box** to select the cell reference, type **ParkingFee** and then press the **Enter** key. Cell B25 remains active, and ParkingFee appears in the Name box instead of the cell reference.
4. Select the range **A16:C21**. The cell reference for the active cell in the range appears in the Name box.
5. Click the **Name box**, type **TicketPrices** and then press the **Enter** key. The name TicketPrices is assigned to the range A16:C21.
6. Select the range **F25:J25**, click the **Name box**, type **TransferArea** and then press the **Enter** key. The name TransferArea is assigned to the range F25:J25.
7. Click cell **J18** to make it active, click the **Name box** to select the cell reference, type **TicketCost** and then press the **Enter** key. Cell J18 remains active, and TicketCost appears in the Name box instead of the cell reference.
8. Click cell **J22** to make it active, click the **Name box** to select the cell reference, type **TotalInvoice** and then press the **Enter** key. Cell J22 remains active, and TotalInvoice appears in the Name box instead of the cell reference.

The Name box displays all of the names in a workbook. You can select a name in the Name box to quickly select the cell or range referenced by the name. You'll view the defined names you added to the workbook.

To select cells and ranges with the Name box:

1. Click the **Name box arrow** to open a list of defined names in the workbook. Six names appear in the list. See Figure 8-3.

Figure 8-3 Name box with the defined names in the workbook

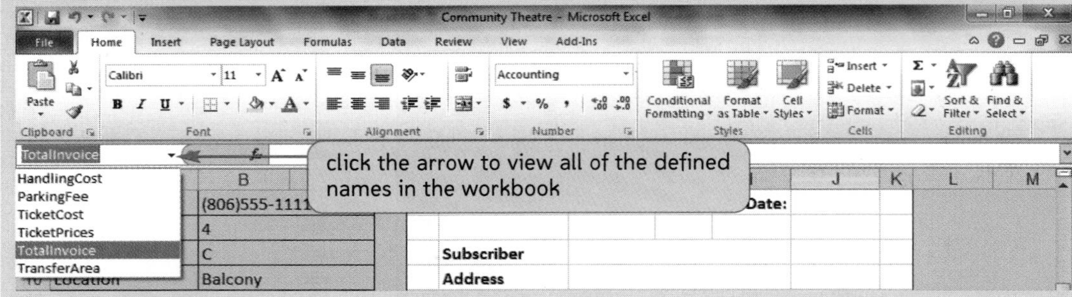

2. Click **ParkingFee**. The active cell moves to cell B25.
3. Click the **Name box arrow**, and then click **TicketPrices**. The range A16:C21 is selected in the worksheet, and cell A16 is the active cell.

You can quickly define names without typing them if the data is organized in a table format with labels in the first or last column or top or bottom row. The names are based on the row or column labels. Any blank or parenthesis in the labels are changed to an underscore (_) in the defined name.You will create names for each cell in the Invoice Data area, using the labels in the range A3:A11.

To create defined names by selection for the Invoice Data area:

Select only the range A3:B12 though text extends into column C; otherwise, formulas you create later in this tutorial will not work.

1. Select the range **A3:B12**. In this range, column A contains the labels you want to use as the defined names, and column B contains the cells you want to name.
2. Click the **Formulas** tab on the Ribbon, and then click the **Create from Selection** button in the Defined Names group. The Create Names from Selection dialog box opens. See Figure 8-4.

Figure 8-4 Create Names from Selection dialog box

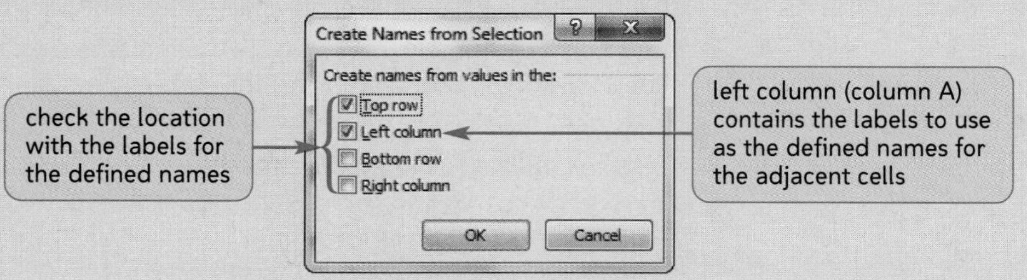

3. Click the **Top row** check box to remove the check mark because this range doesn't include labels at the top, and then verify that the **Left column** check box contains a check mark. The labels in the left column will be used to create the defined names.
4. Click the **OK** button. Each cell in the range B3:B12 is named based on its label in column A.

5. Click the **Name box arrow** to see the 16 defined names in the list.
6. Press the **Esc** key to close the list of defined names.

Although you can use the Name box to verify the names were created, the Name Manager dialog box lists all of the names currently defined in the workbook, including Excel table names. You can also use the Name Manager dialog box to create a new name, edit or delete existing names, and filter the list of names.

The name No._Parking_Decals is too long, so you'll change it to Decals. You will also delete the TransferData defined name, which Ellen decides is not needed.

TIP

The Name Manager dialog box also lists Excel table names.

To edit and delete defined names with the Name Manager dialog box:

1. In the Defined Names group on the Formulas tab, click the **Name Manager** button. The Name Manager dialog box opens, listing the 16 defined names based on the labels in the range A3:A12 in the Invoice Data area, as well as the six names you defined with the Name box. See Figure 8-5.

Figure 8-5 Name Manager dialog box

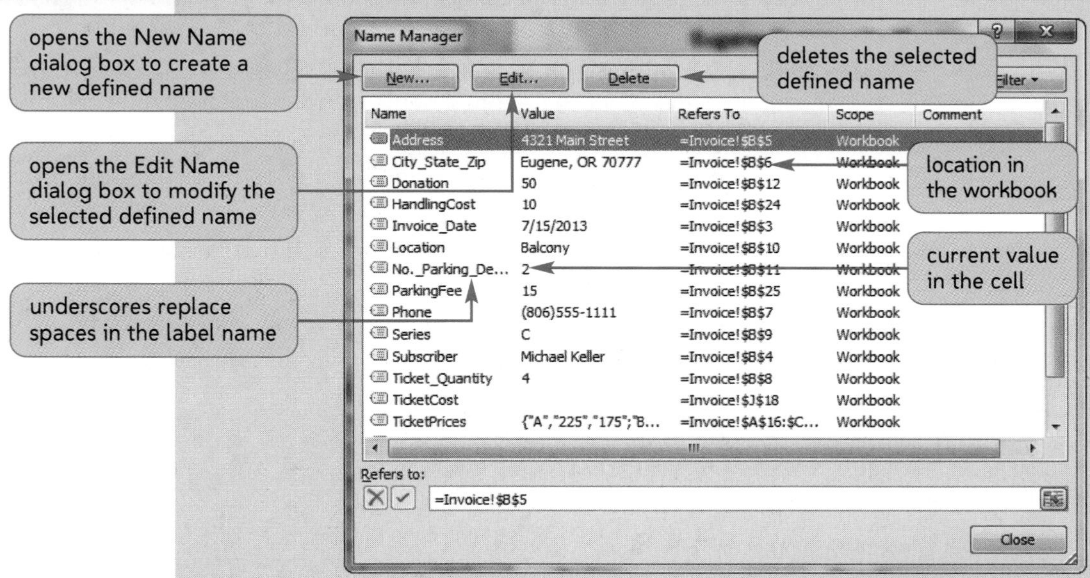

2. Click **No._Parking_Decals** in the Name list, and then click the **Edit** button. The Edit Name dialog box opens. See Figure 8-6.

Figure 8-6 Edit Name dialog box

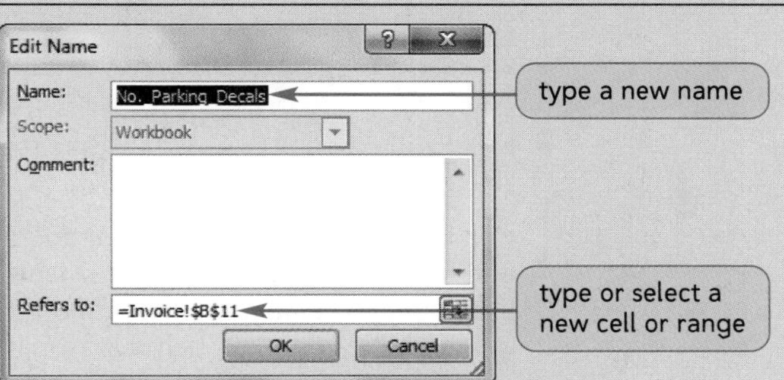

3. In the Name box, type **Decals** and then click the **OK** button. The edited name appears in the list in the Name Manager dialog box.
4. Scroll to find the TransferArea name, click **TransferArea**, and then click the **Delete** button. A dialog box opens to confirm that you want to delete the selected name.
5. Click the **OK** button. The name is removed from the list.
6. Click the **Close** button. The Name Manager dialog box closes.

Using the Paste Names Command

When a workbook contains many defined names, it can be helpful to list all of the defined names and their corresponding cell addresses in the workbook's documentation. You can generate a list of names using the Paste Names command.

To create a list of defined names in the Documentation worksheet:

1. Switch to the **Documentation** worksheet.
2. Click in cell **A10**, type **Defined Names** and then press the **Enter** key. The label for the list of defined names appears in cell A10, and cell A11 is the active cell.
3. In the Defined Names group on the Formulas tab, click the **Use in Formula** button. The list includes all of the defined names in the workbook followed by the Paste Names command.
4. Click **Paste Names**. The Paste Name dialog box opens. You can paste any selected name, or you can paste the entire list of names.
5. Click the **Paste List** button. The defined names and their associated cell references are pasted into the range A11:B25.
6. Deselect the range. See Figure 8-7.

Figure 8-7 **Defined names in the Community Theatre workbook**

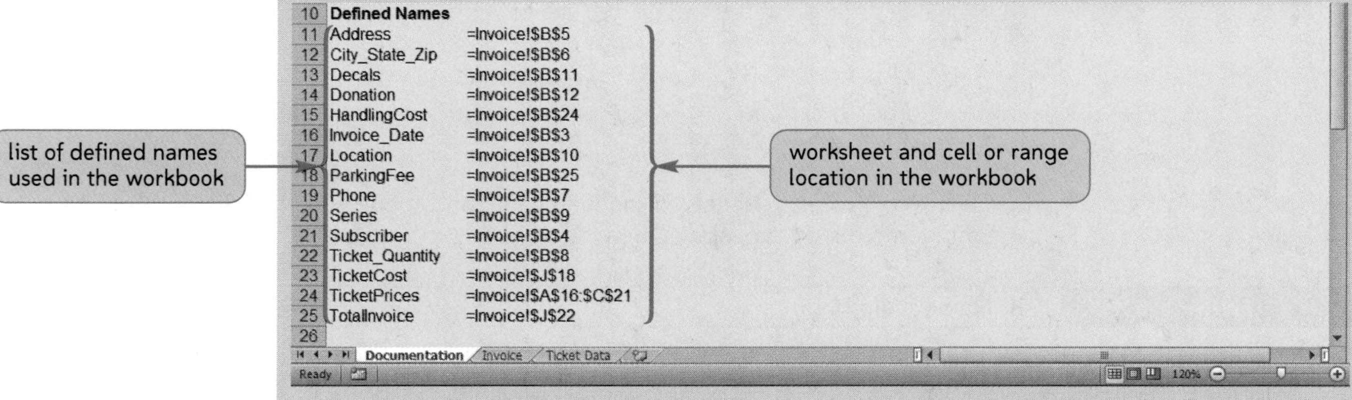

7. Switch to the **Invoice** worksheet.

If you edit a defined name or add a new defined name, the list of defined names and their addresses in the Documentation worksheet is not updated. You must paste the list again to update the names and locations. Usually, it is a good idea to wait until the workbook is complete before pasting defined names in the Documentation worksheet.

Using Defined Names in Formulas

You can create more descriptive formulas by using defined names instead of cell or range references in formulas. For example, in the following formulas, the defined name Sales replaces the range reference D1:D100 in a formula to calculate average sales:

Range reference	`=AVERAGE(D1:D100)`
Defined name	`=AVERAGE(Sales)`

Keep in mind that if you enter a formula using a range reference rather than a defined name, the defined names do *not* automatically replace the range reference in the formula.

You need to enter the formulas required to generate the invoice. You'll start by entering formulas to display the invoice date, the subscriber's name, and the subscriber's address entered in the Invoice Data area in the invoice.

To enter formulas to display the subscriber's name and address:

1. In cell J7, enter **=B3**. The invoice date recorded in the Invoice Data area, 7/15/2013, appears in the cell.
2. In cell G9, enter **=B4**. Michael Keller, the subscriber's name, appears in the cell.
3. In cell G10, enter **=B5**. The subscriber's address, 4321 Main Street, appears in the cell.
4. Click cell **G10**. The formula =B5 appears in the formula bar.

You entered these formulas using cell addresses rather than defined names. Although you defined names for cells B3, B4, and B5, the names do not automatically replace the cell addresses in the formula. Because defined names make formulas simpler to enter and understand, you will use named cells and ranges in the remaining formulas.

As you type a defined name in a formula, the Formula AutoComplete box lists functions and defined names that begin with the letters you typed. As you type additional letters, the list narrows. You can double-click the name you want in the Formula AutoComplete box or press the Tab key to enter the selected name. You can also just continue to type the rest of the name.

To type defined names in formulas:

1. In cell G11, type **=C** to display a list of functions and defined names that begin with the letter "C."
2. Type **i** to narrow the list to the defined name =City_State_Zip.
3. Press the **Tab** key to enter the defined name in the formula, and then press the **Enter** key. The subscriber's city, state, and zip code appear in the cell.
4. Click cell **G11**. The data from cell B6 appears in the cell, and the formula with the defined name, =City_State_Zip, appears in the formula bar.
5. In cell G12, enter **=Phone** and then click cell **G12**. The sample data from cell B7 appears in the cell, and the formula with the defined name, =Phone, appears in the formula bar.

You can also use the point-and-click method to create a formula with defined names. When you click a cell or select a range, Excel substitutes the defined name for the cell reference in the formula. You'll use this method to enter formulas that display the ticket quantity, series, and theatre location from the input area in the invoice.

To enter formulas with defined names using the point-and-click method:

1. Click cell **I14**, type = and then click cell **B8**. The formula uses the defined name Ticket_Quantity rather than the cell reference B8.
2. Click the **Enter** button ✓ on the formula bar. The number 4, which is the number of tickets the subscriber ordered, appears in cell I14. See Figure 8-8.

Figure 8-8 **Formula with a defined name**

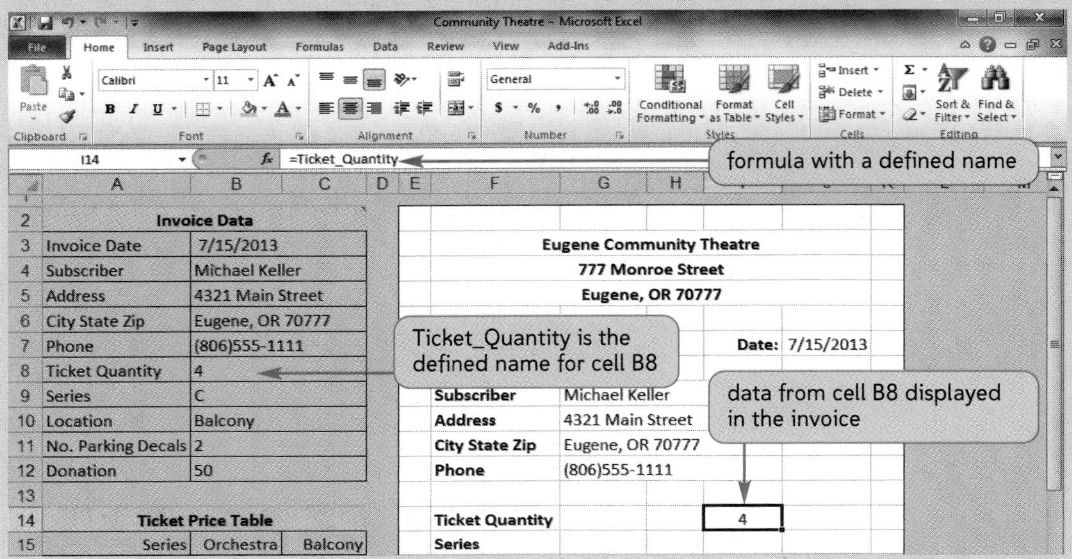

3. In cell I15, type = and then click cell **B9**. The formula uses the defined name Series rather than the cell reference B9.
4. Press the **Enter** key. The letter "C," indicating the series the subscriber selected, appears in cell I15.
5. In cell I16, type =, click **B10**, and then click the **Enter** button ✓ on the formula bar. The subscriber's preferred seat location, Balcony, appears in cell I16, and the formula with the defined name, =Location, appears in the formula bar.

Next, you will enter the formula to calculate the ticket cost to the subscriber. You need to combine two VLOOKUP functions within an IF function to create the formula to calculate ticket costs. The VLOOKUP functions will find the ticket price. The lookup value is the Series the subscriber selects (A, B, C, D, E, or F). Recall that the lookup value searches the first column of the lookup table to find the appropriate row. In this case, the lookup table is the Ticket Price Table (the range you earlier named TicketPrices), which contains two columns of ticket prices. Column 2 of the table lists the prices for the Orchestra, and column 3 of the table lists the prices for the Balcony. The column used to return the ticket prices depends on the Location the subscriber selected. You need to use an IF function to determine whether to search the second or third column for the ticket price.

To enter the formula to determine ticket cost:

1. Click cell **J18** to make it the active cell. The defined name, TicketCost, appears in the Name box.
2. In the Function Library group on the Formulas tab, click the **Logical** button, and then click **IF**. The Function Arguments dialog box opens.
3. In the Logical_test box, type **Location="Orchestra"**. This logical test evaluates whether the subscriber wants to sit in the Orchestra. If the value in cell B10 equals Orchestra, then the condition is true. False appears to the right of the Logical_test box, indicating the subscriber wants to sit in the Balcony.
4. In the Value_if_true box, type **VLOOKUP(Series,TicketPrices,2,FALSE)**. This argument specifies that if the logical_test is true (the customer wants to sit in the Orchestra), the ticket price is determined using a VLOOKUP function, returning a value from column 2 (Orchestra prices) in the TicketPrices range. The first argument of the VLOOKUP function, Series, is the defined name that stores the Series code (A, B, C, and so on) used to look up a value in the second argument, TicketPrices (range A16:C21). The third argument, 2, returns a ticket price from the second column (Orchestra) of the TicketPrices table. The fourth argument, FALSE, indicates an exact match lookup.
5. In the Value_if_false box, type **VLOOKUP(Series,TicketPrices,3,FALSE)**. This argument specifies that if the logical_test is false (the customer wants to sit in the Balcony), the ticket price is determined using a VLOOKUP function, returning a value from column 3 (Balcony prices) in the TicketPrices range.
6. Click the **OK** button. The following formula appears in the formula bar, and 150 appears in cell J18 because the condition is false: =IF(Location="Orchestra", VLOOKUP(Series,TicketPrices,2,FALSE),VLOOKUP(Series,TicketPrices,3,FALSE)).

   Trouble? If #Name?, #Value?, or VLOOKUP appears in cell J18, you probably mistyped the formula. Click cell J18, compare the formula you entered with the complete formula in Step 6, and then edit the formula in the formula bar as needed. Also, make sure the references in your defined names are correct (refer to Figure 8-7 for the list of defined names used in the workbook).

   Next, you will complete the formula by multiplying the cost for one ticket by the number of tickets purchased.
7. Double-click cell **J18** to enter Edit mode and display the formula in the cell.
8. Click at the end of the formula, type ***Ticket_Quantity** and then press the **Enter** key. The amount in cell J18 changes to $600.
9. Click cell **J18**, and then click the **Expand Formula Bar** button on the right side of the formula bar. The entire formula is visible in the expanded formula bar. The IF function determines which column in the TicketPrices range to use to return the ticket price. If Location in the Invoice Data area is Orchestra, then the condition Location="Orchestra" is TRUE and the VLOOKUP function returns a ticket price from column 2. If the Location in the Invoice Data area is Balcony, then the VLOOKUP function searches column 3 for the ticket price. The price for one ticket, as determined by the IF and VLOOKUP functions, is then multiplied by the ticket quantity to calculate the total ticket cost for this transaction. See Figure 8-9.

Figure 8-9 **Formula to calculate the ticket cost**

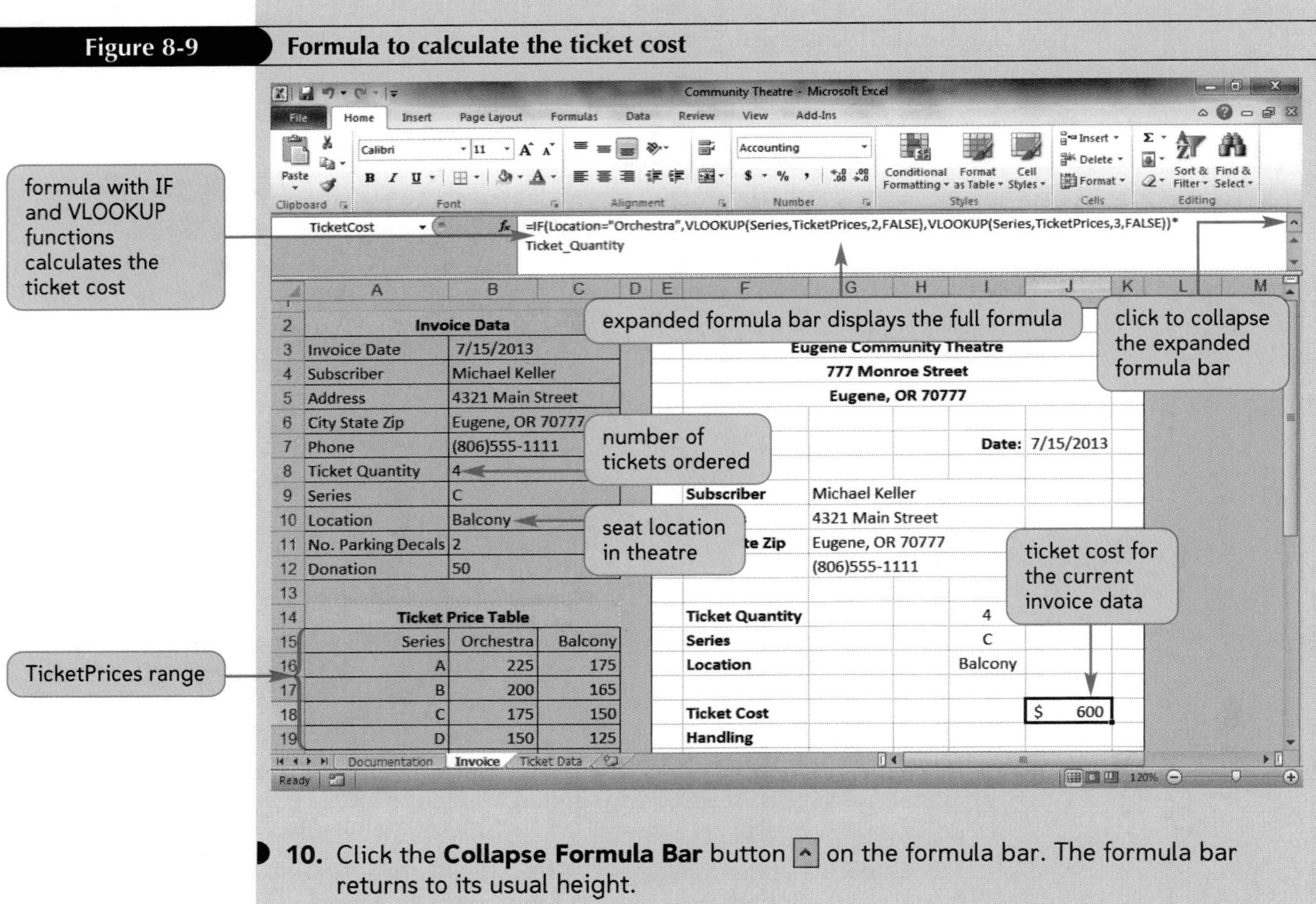

10. Click the **Collapse Formula Bar** button on the formula bar. The formula bar returns to its usual height.

You'll enter the remaining formulas needed to complete the invoice.

TIP

If a formula uses a defined name that doesn't exist, #NAME? appears in the cell. Verify the defined name spelling and that the name wasn't deleted from the worksheet.

To enter the remaining formulas in the invoice:

1. In cell J19, enter **=HandlingCost**. The handling cost is $10, which is the amount in cell B24 in the Invoice Constants area.
2. In cell I20, enter **=Decals**. The number of parking decals ordered is 2, which is the number listed in cell B11 in the Invoice Data area.
3. In cell J20, enter **=Decals*ParkingFee**. The parking cost is $30, which is the number of parking decals listed in cell B11 multiplied by the parking fee in cell B25. The defined names make entering this calculation faster and the formula easier to understand.
4. In cell J21, enter **=Donation**. The donation amount is $50, which is listed in cell B12.
5. In cell J22, enter **=SUM(J18:J21)**. The SUM function adds all of the costs to determine the total invoice amount of $690. See Figure 8-10.

Figure 8-10 **Invoice with all formulas entered**

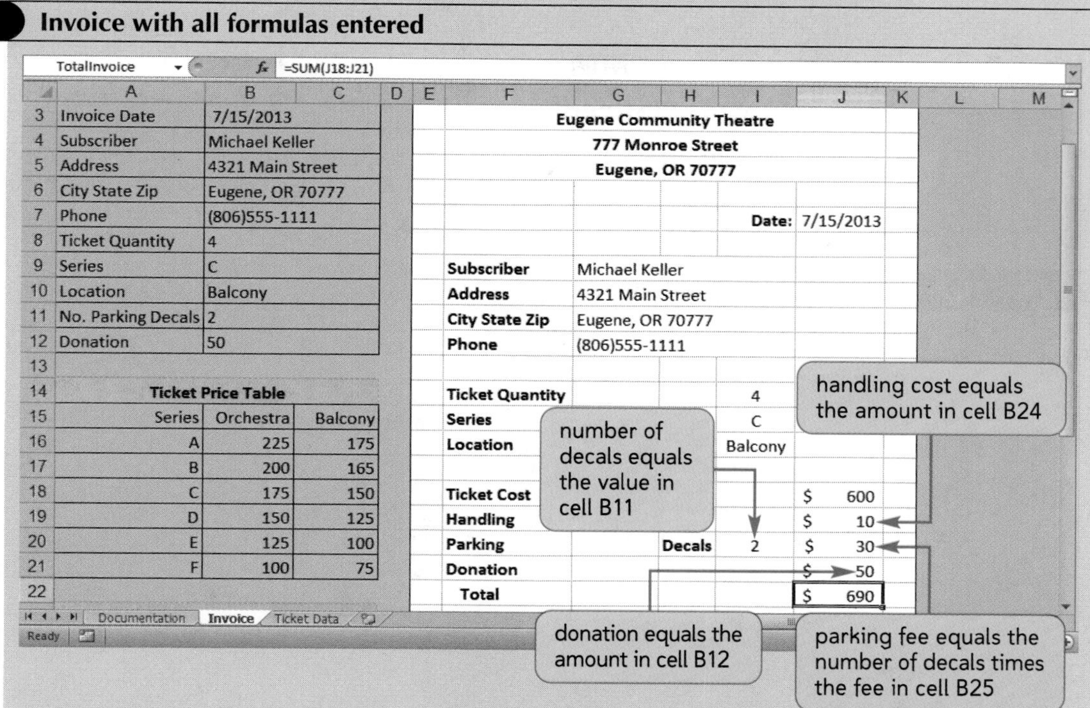

Adding Defined Names to Existing Formulas

Sometimes, you might name cells after creating formulas in the worksheet. Other times, you might not use the defined names when you create formulas (as with the first three formulas you created in the invoice for the invoice date, subscriber name, and address). Because defined names are not automatically substituted for the cell addresses in a formula, you can replace cell addresses in existing formulas in the worksheet with their defined names to make the formulas more understandable.

REFERENCE

Adding Defined Names to Existing Formulas

- In the Defined Names group on the Formulas tab, click the Define Name button arrow, and then click Apply Names (if the cell reference and defined name are in the same worksheet).
- In the Apply Names dialog box, select the names you want to apply.
- Click the OK button.

or

- Edit the formula by selecting the cell reference and typing the defined name or clicking the appropriate cell.

You'll change the two formulas you created to display the subscriber name and address in the invoice to use defined names instead of cell references.

To add defined names to existing formulas in the invoice:

1. In the Defined Names group on the Formulas tab, click the **Define Name button arrow**, and then click **Apply Names**. The Apply Names dialog box opens. See Figure 8-11.

Figure 8-11 Apply Names dialog box

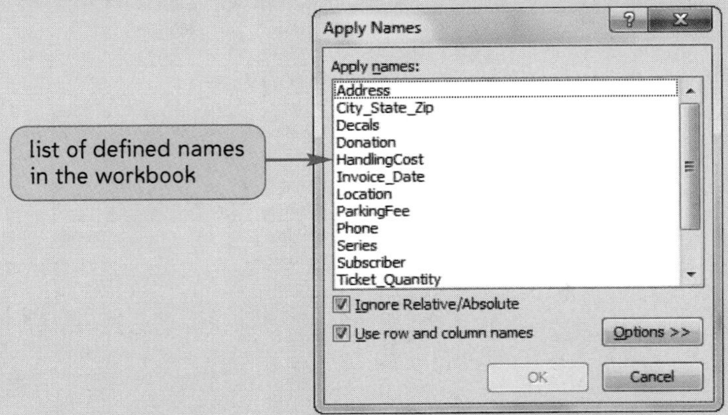

You want to select only the names you need for the existing formulas with cell references.

2. If any name is selected in the Apply names list, click that name to deselect it.
3. In the Apply names list, click **Address**, **Invoice_Date**, and **Subscriber**. The three names you want to apply to the formulas are selected.
4. Click the **OK** button. The three selected names are applied to the formulas.
5. Click cell **J7** and verify that the formula changed to =Invoice_Date.
6. Click cell **G9** and verify that the formula changed to =Subscriber.
7. Click cell **G10** and verify that the formula changed to =Address.

Ellen wants to store the following items in the Ticket Data worksheet: subscriber name, transaction date, ticket quantity, ticket cost, and total amount owed from the invoice. Displaying these data items in the Transfer Area enables you to copy and paste all of the items to the Ticket Data worksheet at once. You'll enter formulas to display the appropriate items in this section of the worksheet.

To enter formulas to display data in the Transfer Area:

1. In cell F25, enter **=Subscriber**. The formula displays the subscriber name in this cell.
2. In cell G25, enter **=Invoice_Date**. The formula displays the current date.
3. In cell H25, enter **=Ticket_Quantity**. The formula displays the number of tickets.
4. In cell I25, enter **=TicketCost**. The formula displays the ticket cost.
5. In cell J25, enter **=TotalInvoice**. The formula displays the total cost.

The worksheet contains all of the formulas required to create the invoice based on the subscriber information. Because Ellen relies on volunteers to enter season ticket requests into the worksheet and print invoices, she wants to be sure the values entered are correct. You will continue to work on Ellen's application by creating validation checks, which are designed to prevent users from inserting incorrect data values. You will also protect cells so that volunteers cannot accidentally overwrite or delete the formulas. You'll do both of these tasks in the next session.

REVIEW

Session 8.1 Quick Check

1. What is a defined name?
2. What are two advantages of using names in workbooks?
3. Describe three ways to create a name.
4. Which of the following is a valid defined name?
   a. Annual_Total
   b. 3rdQtr
   c. Annual total
5. How can you quickly select a cell or range using its name?
6. In the Report workbook, the defined name "Expenses" refers to a list of expenses stored in the range D2:D100. Currently, the total expenses are calculated by the formula =SUM(D2:D100). Change this formula to use the defined name.
7. True or False. If you create a defined name for a range referenced in an existing formula, you cannot change the formula to use the new name.

SESSION 8.2 VISUAL OVERVIEW

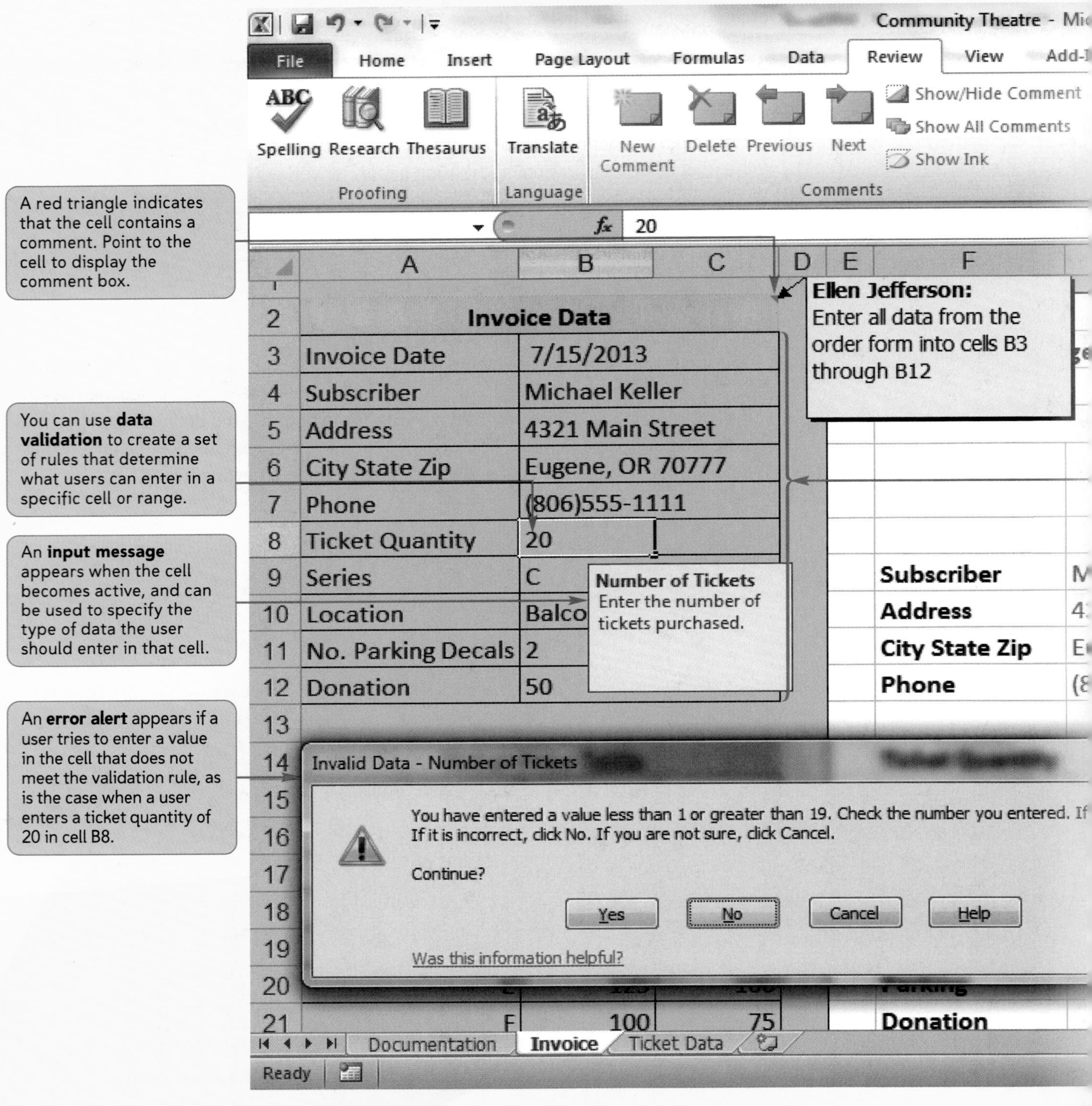

DATA VALIDATION AND PROTECTION

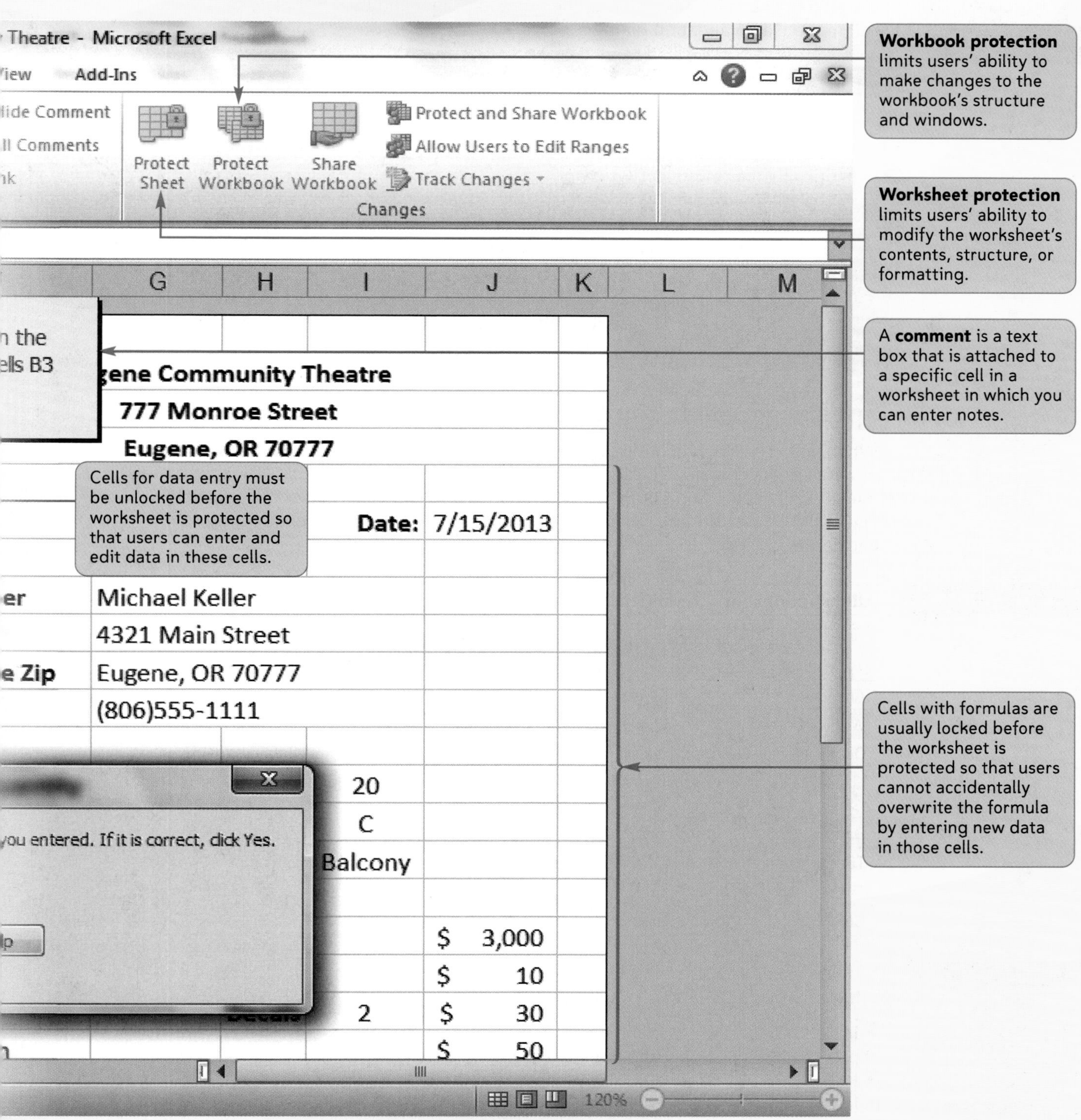

Workbook protection limits users' ability to make changes to the workbook's structure and windows.

Worksheet protection limits users' ability to modify the worksheet's contents, structure, or formatting.

A **comment** is a text box that is attached to a specific cell in a worksheet in which you can enter notes.

Cells with formulas are usually locked before the worksheet is protected so that users cannot accidentally overwrite the formula by entering new data in those cells.

Validating Data Entry

TIP

Each cell can have only one validation rule. Creating a second validation rule for a cell replaces the existing rule.

To ensure that correct data is entered and stored in a worksheet, you can use data validation. Each **validation rule** defines criteria for the data that can be stored in a cell or range. You can also add input and error alert messages for the user to that cell or range. You specify the validation criteria, the input message, and the error alert for the active cell in the Data Validation dialog box.

REFERENCE

Validating Data

- In the Data Tools group on the Data tab, click the Data Validation button.
- Click the Settings tab.
- Click the Allow arrow, click the type of data allowed in the cell, and then enter the validation criteria for that data.
- Click the Input Message tab, and then enter a title and text for the input message.
- Click the Error Alert tab, and then, if necessary, click the Show error alert after invalid data is entered check box to insert a check mark.
- Select an alert style, and then enter the title and text for the error alert message.
- Click the OK button.

Specifying Validation Criteria

When you create a validation rule, you specify the type of data allowed as well as a list or range of acceptable values (called validation criteria). For example, you might specify integers between 1 and 100, or a list of codes such as Excellent, Good, Fair, and Poor. Figure 8-12 describes the types of data you can allow and the acceptable values for each type.

Figure 8-12 **Allow options for the validation**

Type	Acceptable Values
Any value	Any number, text, or date; removes any existing data validation
Whole number	Integers only; you can specify the range of acceptable integers
Decimal	Any type of number; you can specify the range of acceptable numbers
List	Any value in a range or entered in the Data Validation dialog box separated by commas
Date	Dates only; you can specify the range of acceptable dates
Time	Times only; you can specify the range of acceptable times
Text length	Text limited to a specified number of characters
Custom	Values based on the results of a logical formula

TIP

To apply a validation rule to all of the cells in an Excel table column, select the column of data to which the validation rule will be applied, and then create the validation rule.

Ellen wants you to add the following three validation rules to the workbook to help ensure that volunteers enter valid data in the Invoice worksheet:

- In cell B8, the Ticket Quantity value should be a whole number between 1 and 19. In previous years, 19 was the maximum number of tickets purchased.
- In cell B9, the Series value should be one of the following list: A, B, C, D, E, or F.
- In cell B10, the Location value should be one of the following list: Orchestra or Balcony.

You will define the validation rule for the number of season tickets. Cell B8, which records the ticket quantity, requires an integer that is greater than 0 and less than 20.

To create the validation rule for the Ticket Quantity cell:

1. If you took a break after the previous session, make sure the Community Theatre workbook is open and the Invoice worksheet is active.
2. Click cell **B8**. You will enter a whole number validation rule for this cell.
3. Click the **Data** tab on the Ribbon, and then click the **Data Validation** button in the Data Tools group. The Data Validation dialog box opens. You use the Settings tab to enter the validation rule for the active cell.
4. On the Settings tab, click the **Allow** arrow, and then click **Whole number**. The Data Validation dialog box expands to display the options specific to whole numbers. The Ignore blank check box is checked, which means the validation rule is not applied when the cell is empty. If you uncheck the option, users are required to make an entry in the cell.
5. If necessary, click the **Data** arrow, and then click **between**. The dialog box reflects the selected criteria.
6. Click the **Minimum** box, and then type **1** to specify the smallest value a user can enter.
7. Press the **Tab** key to move to the Maximum box, and then type **19** to specify the largest value a user can enter. See Figure 8-13.

Figure 8-13 Settings tab in the Data Validation dialog box

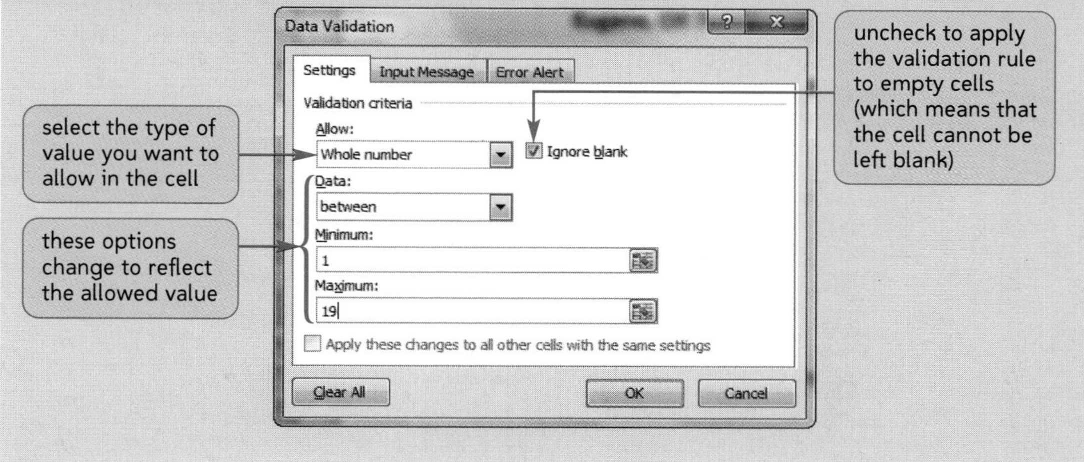

INSIGHT

Validating Existing Data

Validation rules come into play only during data entry. If you add validation rules to a workbook that already contains data with erroneous values, Excel does not determine if any existing data is invalid. Instead, you can use the Circle Invalid Data command to help identify invalid data that is already in the workbook. (You'll learn about the Circle Invalid Data command later in this tutorial.)

Creating an Input Message

One way to reduce the chance of a data-entry error is to display an input message when a user makes the cell active. An input message provides additional information about the type of data allowed for that cell. Input messages appear as ScreenTips next to the cell when the cell is selected. You can add an input message to a cell even if you don't set up a rule to validate the data in that cell.

Before volunteers enter a value for the ticket quantity, Ellen wants them to see the acceptable values that can be entered in the cell. The input message will help minimize the chance of a volunteer entering an invalid value. You will create an input message for cell B8.

To create an input message for the Ticket Quantity cell:

1. In the Data Validation dialog box, click the **Input Message** tab. You enter the input message title and text on this tab.
2. Verify that the **Show input message when cell is selected** check box contains a check mark. If you uncheck this option, you cannot enter a new input message and any existing input message will not be displayed when the selected cell becomes active.
3. Click in the **Title** box, and then type **Number of Tickets**. This title will appear in bold at the top of the ScreenTip above the text of the input message.
4. Press the **Tab** key to move the insertion point to the Input message box, and then type **Enter the number of tickets purchased.** This text will appear in the ScreenTip when the cell becomes active. See Figure 8-14.

TIP

The maximum number of characters allowed in the Title box is 32.

Figure 8-14 Input Message tab in the Data Validation dialog box

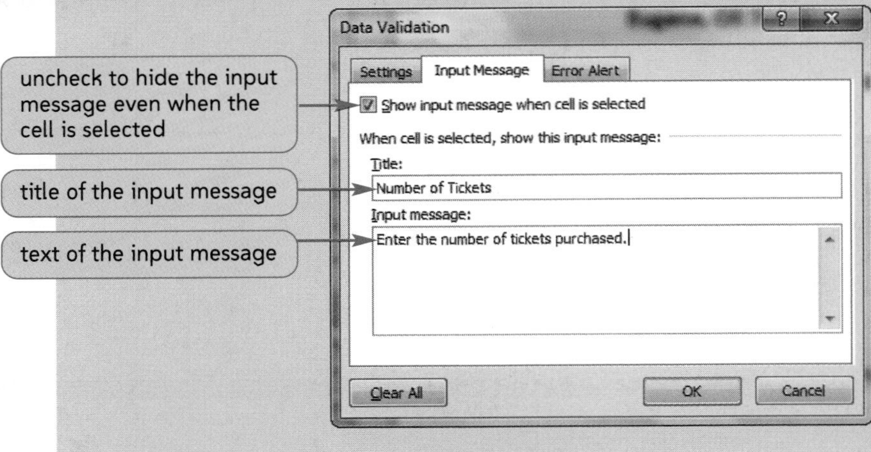

Creating an Error Alert Style and Message

An error alert determines what happens after a user attempts to make an invalid entry in a cell that has a validation rule defined. The three error alert styles are Stop, Warning, and Information. The Stop alert prevents the entry from being stored in the cell. The Warning alert prevents the entry from being stored in the cell unless the user overrides the rejection and decides to continue using the data. The Information alert accepts the data value entered, but allows the user to choose to cancel the data entry.

Ellen wants to display an error alert if a volunteer enters data that violates the validation rule. Although ticket quantities between 1 and 19 are the norm for the theatre, occasionally a subscriber may want to purchase 20 or more tickets, and those entries should be allowed. To account for this possibility, you will create a Warning error alert that appears when a user enters a ticket quantity value greater than 20 or less than 1. The user can then verify the number entered. If the entry is correct, the user can accept the entry. If the entry is incorrect, the user can reenter the correct number.

You'll create the Warning error alert for the Ticket Quantity cell.

To create the Warning error alert for the Ticket Quantity cell:

1. In the Data Validation dialog box, click the **Error Alert** tab. You use this tab to select the type of error alert and enter the message you want to appear.
2. Make sure that the **Show error alert after invalid data is entered** check box is checked. If unchecked, the error alert won't appear when an invalid value is entered in the cell.
3. Click the **Style** arrow, and then click **Warning**. This style allows the user to accept the invalid value, return to the cell and reenter a valid value, or cancel the data entry and restore the previous value to the cell.
4. Click in the **Title** box, and then type **Invalid Data - Number of Tickets**. This text will appear as the title of the error alert box.
5. Press the **Tab** key to move the insertion point to the Error message box, and then type **You have entered a value less than 1 or greater than 19. Check the number you entered. If it is correct, click Yes. If it is incorrect, click No. If you are not sure, click Cancel.** See Figure 8-15.

TIP

You might hide the input and error alert messages when only experienced users will enter data in the workbook by unchecking the Show check box. You can show them again if a new user will enter data.

Figure 8-15 Error Alert tab in the Data Validation dialog box

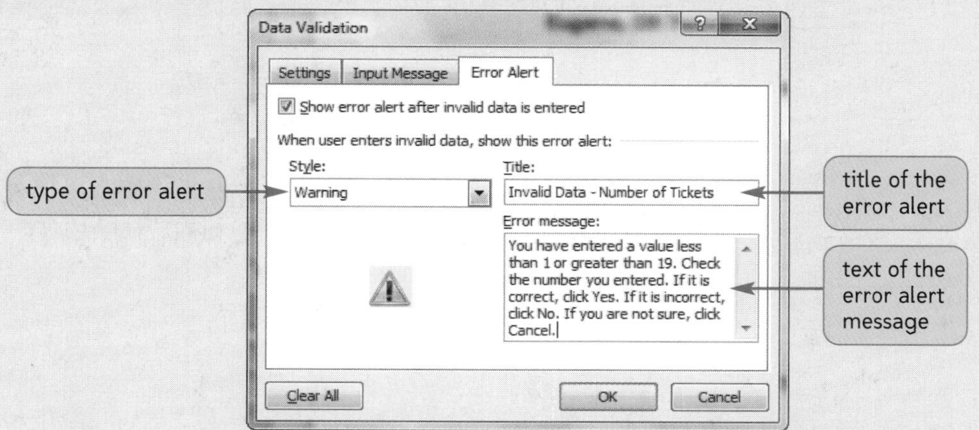

6. Click the **OK** button. The input message appears below cell B8 because the cell is active. See Figure 8-16.

Figure 8-16 **Input message for cell B8**

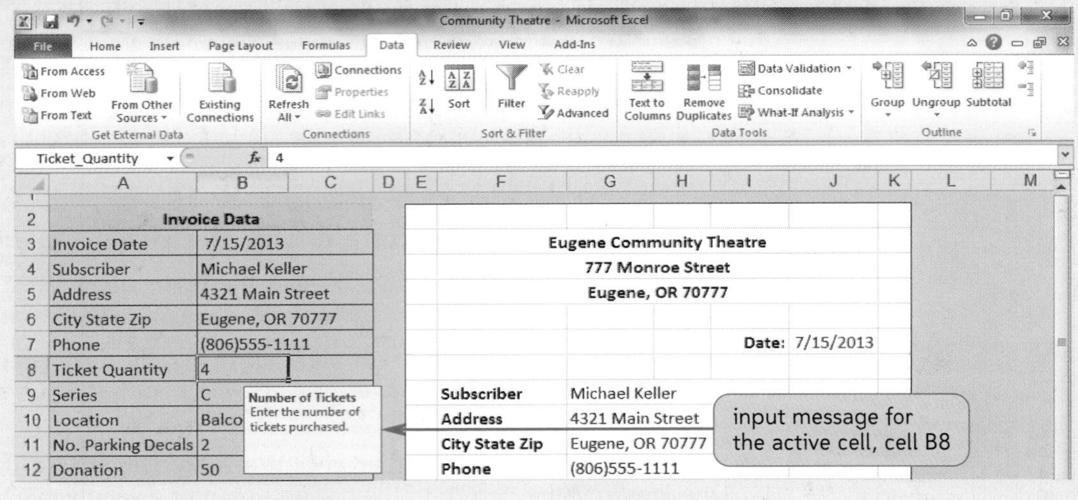

INSIGHT

Using Formulas to Define Complex Validation Criteria

The built-in data validation rules are adequate for most simple needs. Sometimes, however, those rules just don't fit your specific worksheet. In those cases, you need to create a custom validation rule that includes a formula. To create a custom validation rule, open the Data Validation dialog box. On the Settings tab, click the Allow arrow, and then click Custom. You can then create the data validation formula.

The formula you specify must be in the form of a condition that returns either True or False. If True is returned, the data entered is considered valid and accepted. If False is returned, the entry is considered invalid and an error alert message is displayed. Consider two data validation examples.

The first example uses data validation to prevent the entry of dates that fall on Saturday or Sunday. The WEEKDAY function returns a number (1 to 7) for the date entered in the cell, and then you create a formula to display an error alert if values of 1 (Sunday) or 7 (Saturday) are detected. Assuming the date is entered in cell B2, the following formula returns False if either Saturday or Sunday is entered in cell B2:

```
=AND(WEEKDAY(B2)<>1,WEEKDAY(B2)<>7)
```

The second example uses data validation to ensure all product codes begin with the letter "C." To prevent any letter except a "C" from being entered as the first character in cell A2, you would use the LEFT function to extract the first character in the cell. The following formula returns True if the first character entered in cell A2 begins with a "C"; otherwise, an error alert message is displayed:

```
=LEFT(A2,1) = "C"
```

Creating a List Validation Rule

You can use the data validation feature to restrict a cell to accept only entries that are on a list you create. You can create the list of valid entries in the Data Validation dialog box, or you can use a list of valid entries in a single column or row.

You will enter the validation rule for the Series being requested, which is one of the following six values: A, B, C, D, E, and F.

To restrict the Series values to a list of entries:

1. Click cell **B9**. You will create a list validation rule for this cell.
2. In the Data Tools group on the Data tab, click the **Data Validation** button to open the Data Validation dialog box, and then click the **Settings** tab.
3. Click the **Allow** arrow, and then click **List**. The dialog box expands to display the Source box. You can enter values separated by commas directly in the Source box, or you can select a range of valid entries in the worksheet.
4. Click the **Collapse** button next to the Source box so you can see the entire worksheet.
5. Select the range **A16:A21**, which lists the valid six entry values, and then click the **Expand** button. The Data Validation dialog box returns to its full size and displays =$A$16:$A$21. Next, you'll enter an input message.
6. Click the **Input Message** tab, click in the **Title** box, and then type **Series** to enter the title of the input message.
7. Click in the Input message box, and then type **Click the arrow and select one of the choices listed.** to enter the text of the input message.
8. Click the **Error Alert** tab, and then verify that **Stop** appears in the Style box. You want to prevent a user from entering a value that is not included in the list of values you specified.
9. In the Title text box, type **Invalid Series** to enter the title of the error alert.
10. In the Error message box, type **An invalid series has been entered. Click Retry. Press the Esc key, and click the arrow to the right of cell B9. Select A, B, C, D, E, or F.** to enter the text of the error message.
11. Click the **OK** button. An arrow appears to the right of cell B9 and the input message appears in a ScreenTip.

You need to enter a data validation rule for cell B10, which indicates the subscriber's choice of seat location. This list validation rule will allow a user to select either Orchestra or Balcony and will include an error alert.

To create a list validation rule for the Location cell:

1. Click cell **B10**. You will create a list validation rule for this cell.
2. In the Data Tools group on the Data tab, click the **Data Validation** button. The Data Validation dialog box opens.
3. Click the **Settings** tab, select **List** in the Allow box, click the **Source** box, and then select the range **B15:C15**. This range contains the two values you want to allow users to select for the seat location.
4. Click the **Input Message** tab, type **Location** in the Title box, and then type **Click the arrow and select Orchestra or Balcony.** in the Input message box.
5. Click the **Error Alert** tab, verify that **Stop** appears in the Style box, type **Invalid Location** in the Title box, and then type **An invalid location has been entered. Click Retry, press Esc, and click the arrow to the right of cell B10. Select Orchestra or Balcony.** in the Error message box.
6. Click the **OK** button. An arrow appears to the right of cell B10 and the input message appears in a ScreenTip.

After you create validation rules, you should test them. You do this by entering incorrect values that violate the validation rules. Keep in mind that the only way an error occurs in cells that have a list validation is if an incorrect entry is *typed* in the cell. Entering invalid data will ensure that validation rules work as expected. You will test the validation rules you've just created.

To test the data validation rules:

1. Click cell **B8**. The input message appears in a ScreenTip, indicating the type of data allowed in the cell. You will enter an invalid value to test the validation rule for the Ticket Quantity field.
2. Type **30** and then press the **Tab** key. The Invalid Data - Number of Tickets message box opens, informing you that the value you entered might be incorrect. The entry 30 is incorrect; you'll enter a valid number.
3. Click the **No** button, type **4** in cell B8, and then press the **Enter** key. The data is entered in cell B8. Cell B9 is the active cell and the input message for Series appears.
4. Click the **arrow** to the right of cell B9, and then click **B**. The value is accepted. The only way an error occurs in cells that have a list validation is if an incorrect entry is *typed* in the cell. You'll try that method.
5. In cell B9, enter **G**. The Invalid Series message box opens.
6. Click the **Retry** button to close the message box, and then press the **Esc** key to return the original value from the cell.
7. Click the **arrow** to the right of cell B9, and then click **C**.
8. In cell B10, enter **Mezzanine**. The Invalid Location message box opens, indicating that the location must be Orchestra or Balcony.
9. Click the **Retry** button, and then press the **Esc** key to return the original value entered. The three validation rules you entered work as you intended.

TIP

After the error alert appears, you must press the Esc key to return the original value to the cell; otherwise, the error alert will reappear when you click the arrow to make another selection.

INSIGHT

Using the Circle Invalid Data Command

Validation rules come into play only during data entry. If you add validation rules to a workbook that already contains data with erroneous values, Excel does not determine if any existing data is invalid.

To ensure the entire workbook contains valid data, you need to also verify any data previously entered in the workbook. You can use the Circle Invalid Data command to find and mark cells that contain invalid data. Red circles appear around any data that does not meet the validation criteria, making it simple to scan a worksheet for errors. After you correct the data in a cell, the circle disappears.

To display circles around invalid data, perform the following steps:

1. Apply validation rules to existing range.
2. In the Data Tools group on the Data tab, click the Data Validation button arrow, and then click Circle Invalid Data. Red circles appear around cells that contain invalid data.
3. To remove the circle from a single cell, enter valid data in the cell.
4. To hide all circles, in the Data Tools group on the Data tab, click the Data Validation button arrow, and then click Clear Validation Circles.

To ensure an error-free workbook, you should use the Circle Invalid Data command to verify data entered before you set up the validation criteria or to verify data in a workbook you inherited from someone else, such as a coworker.

Protecting a Worksheet and a Workbook

Another way to reduce data-entry errors is to limit access to certain parts of the workbook. Worksheet protection prevents users from changing cell contents, such as editing formulas in a worksheet. Workbook protection prevents users from changing the workbook's organization, such as inserting or deleting worksheets in the workbook. You can even keep users from viewing the formulas used in the workbook.

Ellen wants to protect the contents of the Invoice and Ticket Data worksheets. She wants volunteers to have access only to the range B3:B12 in the Invoice worksheet, where new invoice data is entered. She wants to prevent volunteers from editing the contents of any cells in the Ticket Data worksheet.

Locking and Unlocking Cells

Every cell in a workbook has a **locked property** that determines whether changes can be made to that cell. The locked property has no impact as long as the worksheet is unprotected. However, after you protect a worksheet, the locked property controls whether the cell can be edited. You unlock a cell by turning off the locked property. By default, the locked property is turned on for each cell, and worksheet protection is turned off.

So, unless you unlock cells in a worksheet *before* protecting the worksheet, all of the cells in the worksheet will be locked, and you won't be able to make any changes in the worksheet. Usually, you will want to protect the worksheet, but leave some cells unlocked. For example, you might want to lock cells that contain formulas and formatting so they cannot be changed, but unlock cells in which you want to enter data.

To protect some—but not all—cells in a worksheet, you first turn off the locked property of cells in which data can be entered. Then, you protect the worksheet to activate the locked property for the remaining cells.

In the Invoice worksheet, users should be able to enter data in the range B3:B12 but not any other cell. To do this, you must unlock the cells in the range B3:B12.

To unlock the cells in the range B3:B12:

1. In the Invoice worksheet, select the range **B3:B12**. You want to unlock the cells in this range before you protect the worksheet.
2. Click the **Home** tab on the Ribbon, and then click the **Dialog Box Launcher** in the Font group. The Format Cells dialog box opens with the Font tab active.
3. Click the **Protection** tab, and then click the **Locked** check box to remove the check mark.
4. Click the **OK** button. The cells in the range B3:B12 are unlocked.
5. Click cell **A1** to deselect the range.

Protecting a Worksheet

When you set up worksheet protection, you specify which actions are still available to users in the protected worksheet. For example, you can choose to allow users to insert new rows or columns, or to delete rows and columns. You can limit the user to selecting only unlocked cells, or allow the user to select any cell in the worksheet. These choices remain active as long as the worksheet is protected.

A protected worksheet can always be unprotected. You can also add a password to the protected worksheet that users must enter in order to turn off the protection. If you are concerned that users will turn off protection and make changes to formulas, you should use a password; otherwise, it's probably best to not specify a password.

REFERENCE

Protecting a Worksheet

- Select the cells and ranges to unlock so that users can enter data in them.
- In the Font group on the Home tab, click the Dialog Box Launcher.
- In the Format Cells dialog box, click the Protection tab, click the Locked check box to remove the check mark, and then click the OK button.
- In the Changes group on the Review tab, click the Protect Sheet button.
- Enter a password (optional).
- Select all of the actions you want to allow users to take when the worksheet is protected.
- Click the OK button.

Ellen wants to protect the Invoice and Ticket Data worksheets, but she doesn't want a password specified. You will enable worksheet protection that will allow users to select any cell in those worksheets, but enter data only in the unlocked cells.

To protect the Invoice worksheet:

1. Click the **Review** tab on the Ribbon, and then click the **Protect Sheet** button in the Changes group. The Protect Sheet dialog box opens. See Figure 8-17.

Figure 8-17 **Protect Sheet dialog box**

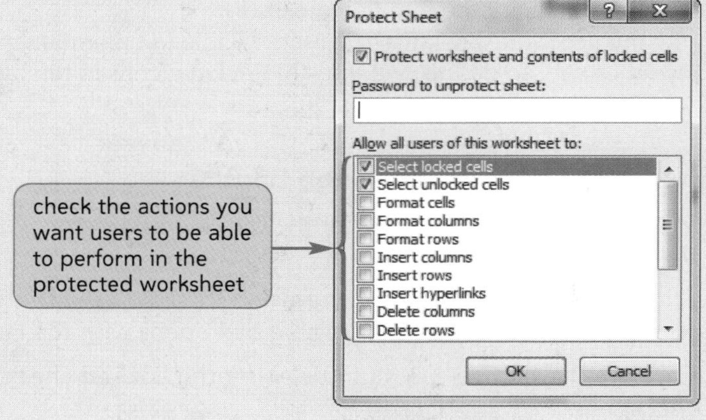

TIP

Keep passwords in a safe place. Remember, passwords are case sensitive. If you forget the password, it is very difficult to remove the worksheet protection.

You will leave the Password to unprotect sheet box blank because you do not want to use a password. By default, users can select locked and unlocked cells, which are all of the cells in the worksheet, but they can enter or edit values only in unlocked cells.

2. Click the **OK** button. The Protect Sheet dialog box closes.

Any time you modify a worksheet, you should test the worksheet to ensure that changes work as intended. You'll test the protection you added to the Invoice worksheet by trying to edit a locked cell and then trying to edit an unlocked cell in the Invoice worksheet.

To test the Invoice worksheet protection:

1. Click cell **I14**, and then type **8**. As soon as you press any key, a dialog box opens, indicating that the cell is protected and cannot be modified. See Figure 8-18.

Figure 8-18 **Message displayed after trying to change a protected cell**

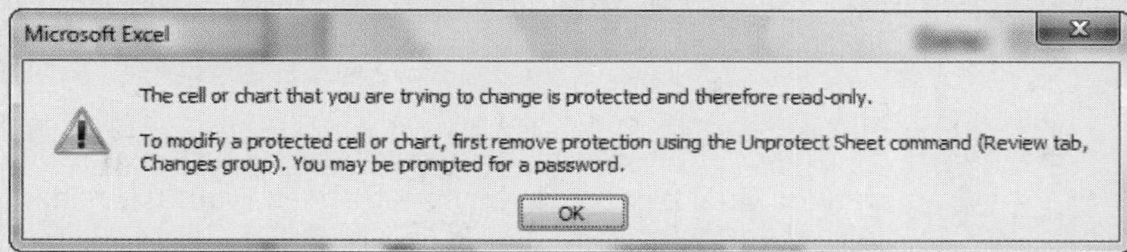

2. Click the **OK** button.
3. Click cell **B8**, type **8** and then press the **Enter** key. The ticket quantity is updated because you allowed editing in the range B3:B12. A user can enter and edit values in these cells. Although users can select any cell in the worksheet, they cannot make an entry in any other cell.
4. On the Quick Access Toolbar, click the **Undo** button to return the ticket quantity to 4.

You will repeat this process to protect all of the cells in the Ticket Data worksheet. Then you will test to see what would happen if someone tried to edit one of the cells in the Ticket Data worksheet.

To protect and test the Ticket Data worksheet:

1. Switch to the **Ticket Data** worksheet.
2. In the Changes group on the Review tab, click the **Protect Sheet** button. The Protect Sheet dialog box opens.
3. Click the **OK** button to accept the default set of user actions.
4. Click cell **A2**, and then type **B**. A dialog box opens, indicating that the cell is protected and cannot be modified. All of the cells in this worksheet are protected because no cells have been unlocked.
5. Click the **OK** button to close the dialog box.

Protecting a Workbook

Worksheet protection applies only to the contents of a worksheet, not to the worksheet itself. To keep a worksheet from being modified, you need to protect the workbook. You can protect both the structure and the windows of a workbook. Protecting the structure prohibits users from renaming, deleting, hiding, or inserting worksheets. Protecting the windows prohibits users from moving, resizing, closing, or hiding parts of the Excel window. The default is to protect only the structure of the workbook, not the windows used to display it.

You can also add a password to the workbook protection. However, the same guideline applies here as for protecting worksheets. Add a password only if you are concerned that others might unprotect the workbook and modify it. If you add a password, keep in mind that it is case sensitive and you cannot unprotect the workbook without it.

REFERENCE

Protecting a Workbook

- In the Changes group on the Review tab, click the Protect Workbook button.
- Click the check boxes to indicate whether you want to protect the workbook's structure, windows, or both.
- Enter a password (optional).
- Click the OK button.

The contents of the Invoice and Ticket Data worksheets, with the exception of the range B3:B12 in the Invoice worksheet, cannot be changed. However, a theatre volunteer could inadvertently rename or delete the protected worksheet. To keep the worksheets themselves from being modified, you will protect the workbook. Ellen doesn't want users to be able to change the structure of the workbook, so you will set workbook protection for the structure, but not the window.

To protect the Community Theatre workbook:

1. In the Changes group on the Review tab, click the **Protect Workbook** button. The Protect Structure and Windows dialog box opens. You can choose to protect the structure, protect the windows, or both. See Figure 8-19.

Figure 8-19 **Protect Structure and Windows dialog box**

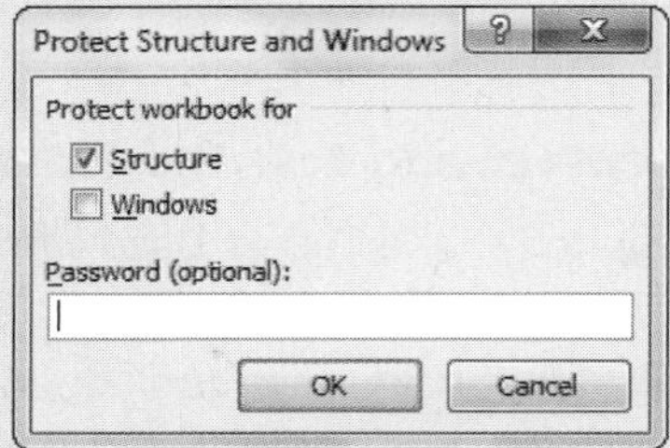

2. Make sure the **Structure** check box is checked, the **Windows** check box is unchecked, and the **Password** box is blank.
3. Click the **OK** button to protect the workbook without specifying a password.
4. Right-click the **Ticket Data** sheet tab. On the shortcut menu, notice that the Insert, Delete, Rename, Move or Copy, Tab Color, Hide, and Unhide commands are gray, indicating that the options that modify the worksheets are no longer available for the Ticket Data worksheet.
5. Press the **Esc** key to close the shortcut menu.

Unprotecting a Worksheet and a Workbook

You can turn off worksheet protection at any time. This is often referred to as unprotecting the worksheet. You need to unprotect a worksheet to edit its contents. If you assigned a password when you protected the worksheet, you would need to enter the password to remove worksheet protection. Likewise, you can unprotect the workbook. If you need to insert a new worksheet or rename an existing worksheet, you can unprotect the protected workbook, make the changes to the structure, and apply workbook protection again.

At this point, you still have a lot of editing to do in the Invoice worksheet, so you'll turn off worksheet protection in that worksheet. Later, when you've completed your modifications, Ellen can turn worksheet protection back on.

TIP

To remove workbook protection, click the Protect Workbook button in the Changes group on the Review tab.

To turn off worksheet protection for the Invoice worksheet:

1. Switch to the **Invoice** worksheet.
2. In the Changes group on the Review tab, click the **Unprotect Sheet** button. Worksheet protection is removed from the Invoice worksheet. The button changes back to the Protect Sheet button.

Inserting Comments

Comments are often used in workbooks to: (a) explain the contents of a particular cell, such as a complex formula; (b) provide instructions to users; and (c) share ideas and notes from several users collaborating on a project. The username for your installation of Excel appears in bold at the top of the comments box. If you collaborate on a workbook, the top of the comments boxes would show the name of each user who created that comment. A small red triangle appears in the upper-right corner of a cell with a comment. The comment box appears when you point to a cell with a comment.

REFERENCE

Inserting a Comment

- Click the cell to which you want to attach a comment.
- Right-click the cell, and then click Insert Comment on the shortcut menu.
  or
  In the Comments group on the Review tab, click the New Comment button.
- Type the comment into the box.

Ellen wants you to insert a note in cell A2 about entering data from the order form into the input section, and a note in cell J18 explaining how the IF and VLOOKUP functions are used to determine the cost of theatre tickets.

TIP

You can also add a comment by right-clicking the cell, and then clicking Insert Comment on the shortcut menu.

To insert comments in cells A2 and J18:

1. In the Invoice worksheet, click cell **A2**.
2. In the Comments group on the Review tab, click the **New Comment** button. A box opens to the right of cell A2. The username for your installation of Excel appears in bold at the top of the box. A small red triangle appears in the upper-right corner of the cell.
3. Type **Enter all data from the order form into cells B3 through B11** in the box. An arrow points from the box to cell A2, which contains the comment. A selection box with sizing handles appears around the box. See Figure 8-20.

Figure 8-20 Comment added to cell A2

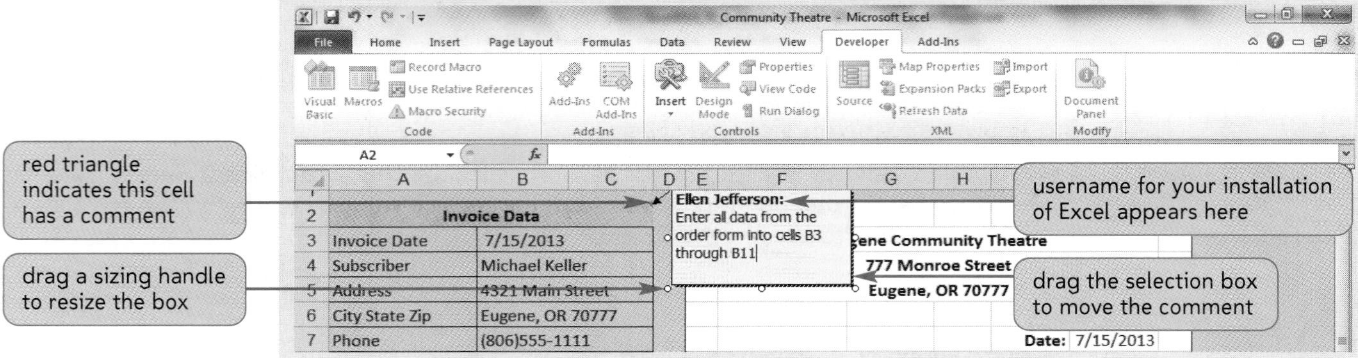

4. Click cell **B12** to hide the comment. The comment disappears. A small red triangle remains in the upper-right corner of cell A2 to indicate this cell contains a comment.
5. Move the pointer over cell **A2**. The comment appears.
6. Click cell **A2**.
7. In the Comments group on the Review tab, click the **Edit Comment** button. The comment appears with the insertion point at the end of the comment text, so you can edit the incorrect cell reference.
8. Select **B11** in the comment box, and then type **B12**. The comment in cell A2 now correctly references the range B3:B12.
9. Click any cell to hide the comment, and then point to cell **A2** to view the edited comment.
10. Click cell **J18**, and then click the **New Comment** button in the Comments group on the Review tab. A comment box opens to the right of cell J18.
11. Type **This IF function determines whether to use a VLOOKUP function referencing column 2 or 3 of the Ticket Price Table** in the box.
12. Drag the lower-right sizing handle down to increase the size of the box to fit the comment.
13. Click cell **I17** to hide the comment. A small red triangle remains in the upper-right corner of cell J18 to indicate it contains a comment.
14. Point to cell **J18** to see the comment. Ellen decides that the volunteers don't need to know how the ticket cost is calculated. You'll delete the comment in cell J18.
15. Click cell **J18**, and then click the **Delete** button in the Comments group on the Review tab. The comment is deleted, and the red triangle in the upper-right corner of cell J18 is removed.

TIP

To keep an active cell's comment on-screen, click the Show/Hide Comment button in the Comments group on the Review tab. Click the button again to hide the active cell's comment.

PROSKILLS

Written Communication: Documenting a Spreadsheet

Providing documentation for a spreasheet is important because it provides instructions on the spreadsheet's use, defines technical terms, explains complex formulas, and identifies assumptions. By documenting a spreadsheet, you help users work more effectively. In addition, documentation helps you recall months or years from now what is in the spreadsheet that might otherwise be forgotten. Furthermore, when someone else becomes responsible for modifying the spreadsheet in the future, the documentation will help that person get up to speed quickly.

It is helpful for you to create a Documentation worksheet to provide an overview, definitions, assumptions, and instructions on how to use various parts of a workbook. Excel also offers many tools to help you document spreadsheets, including:

- Defined names and structured references to make formulas easier to create and understand
- Data validation including input messages specifying what to enter in a cell, and error messages providing instructions on what to do if the data entered is incorrect
- Cell comments to explain complex formulas, give reminders, and so on
- Formula mode to view all formulas in a worksheet at one time

Providing documentation will help users get a better understanding of the application, saving time and frustration.

In this session, you used data validation to help ensure that all values entered in the Invoice worksheet are valid. You created validation rules that included input messages and error alert messages. You learned how to protect and unprotect both the worksheet and the workbook. In addition, you used comments to add notes to specific cells. In the next session, you'll automate some of the steps in the application by recording macros.

REVIEW

Session 8.2 Quick Check

1. Why do you want to validate data?
2. What is the purpose of the input message in the Data Validation command?
3. Describe the three types of error alert messages Excel can display when a user violates a validation rule.
4. What is a locked cell?
5. What is the difference between worksheet protection and workbook protection?
6. Can you rename a protected worksheet? Explain why or why not.
7. Give two reasons for adding a comment to a worksheet cell.

SESSION 8.3 VISUAL OVERVIEW

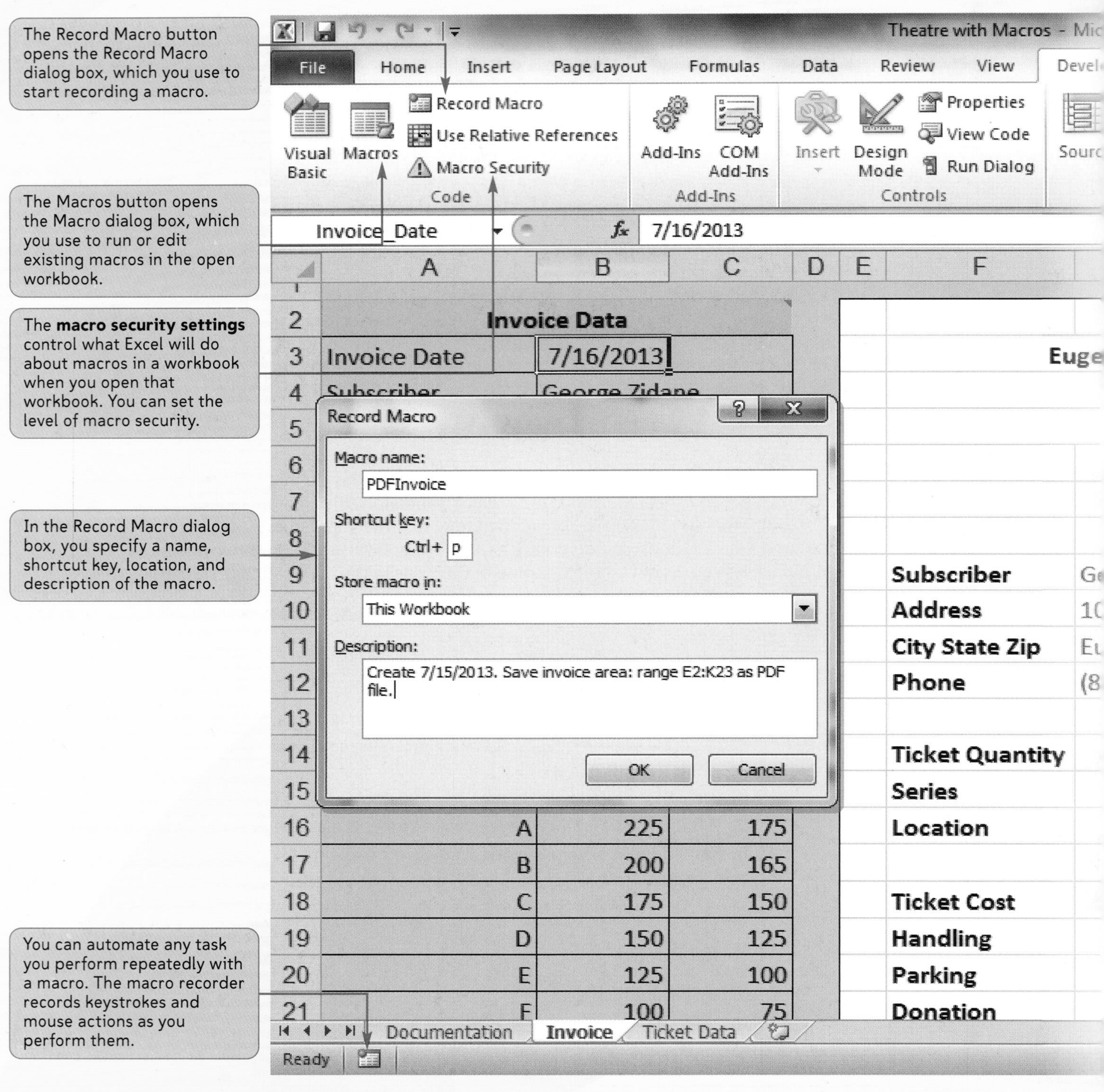

WORKING WITH MACROS

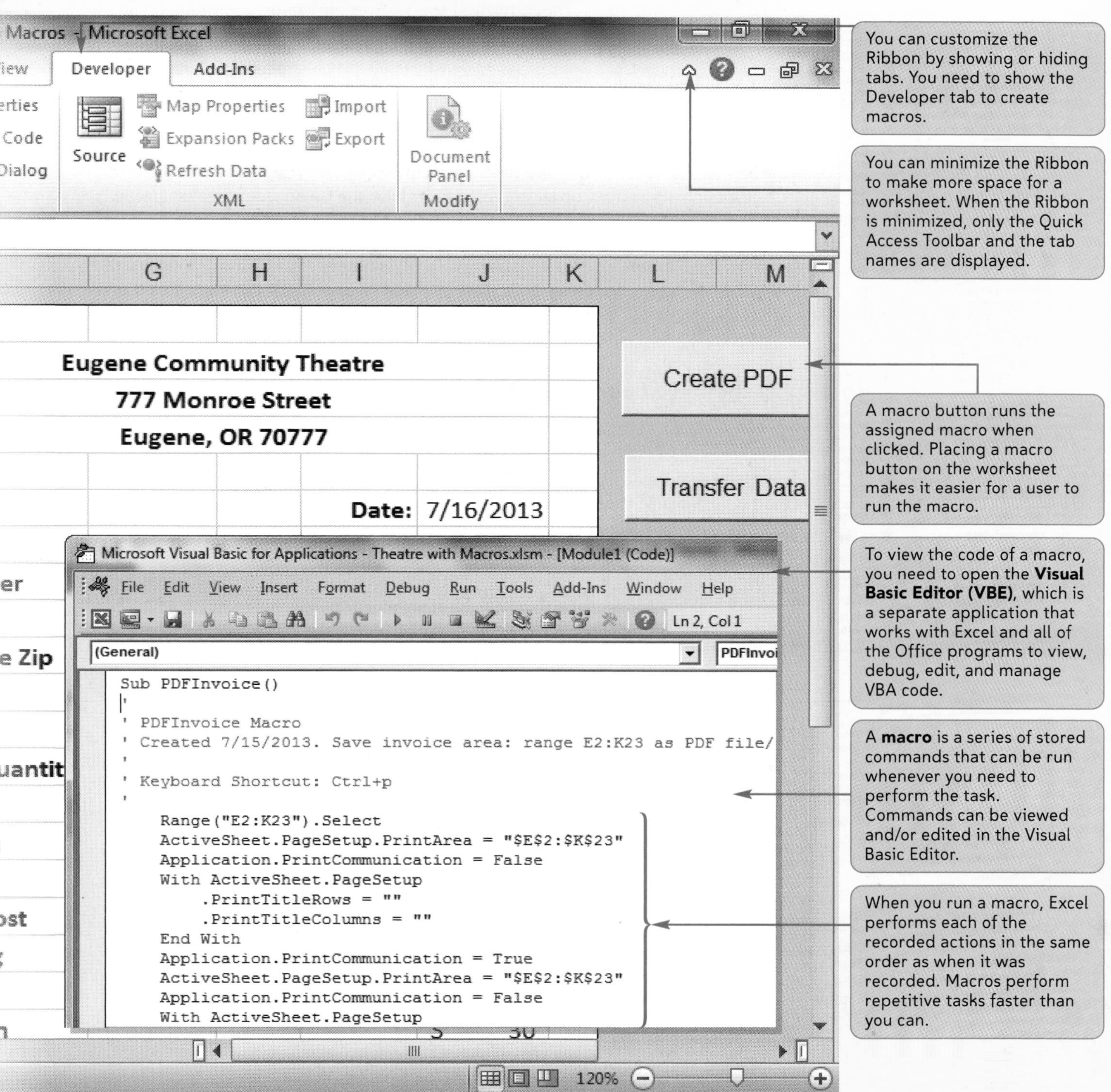

You can customize the Ribbon by showing or hiding tabs. You need to show the Developer tab to create macros.

You can minimize the Ribbon to make more space for a worksheet. When the Ribbon is minimized, only the Quick Access Toolbar and the tab names are displayed.

A macro button runs the assigned macro when clicked. Placing a macro button on the worksheet makes it easier for a user to run the macro.

To view the code of a macro, you need to open the **Visual Basic Editor (VBE)**, which is a separate application that works with Excel and all of the Office programs to view, debug, edit, and manage VBA code.

A **macro** is a series of stored commands that can be run whenever you need to perform the task. Commands can be viewed and/or edited in the Visual Basic Editor.

When you run a macro, Excel performs each of the recorded actions in the same order as when it was recorded. Macros perform repetitive tasks faster than you can.

Automating Tasks with Macros

Using a macro, you can automate any task you perform repeatedly. For example, you can create a macro to print a worksheet, insert a set of dates and values, or import data from a text file and store it in Excel. Macros perform repetitive tasks consistently and faster than you can. And, after the macro is created and tested, you can be assured the tasks are done exactly the same way each time.

Ellen needs to save only the invoice as a PDF file so she can later send it as an attachment to the season subscriber along with an email confirming the ticket purchase transaction. In addition, data from the invoice needs to be transferred to the Ticket Data worksheet. Ellen wants to simplify these tasks so volunteers don't need to repeat the same actions for each subscriber order and also to reduce the possibility of errors being introduced during the repetitive process. You will create a macro for each action.

To create and run macros, you need to use the Developer tab. By default, this tab is not displayed on the Ribbon, so you'll display it. The Developer tab has four groups: one for code, one for controls, one for XML, and one to modify document controls. You'll use the Code group when working with macros. You'll add the Developer tab to the Ribbon.

To display the Developer tab on the Ribbon:

1. If you took a break after the previous session, make sure the Community Theatre workbook is open and the Invoice worksheet is active.
2. Look for the **Developer** tab on the Ribbon. If you do not see the Developer tab, continue with Step 3. If you see the Developer tab, continue with Step 7.
3. Click the **File** tab on the Ribbon to open Backstage view, and then click the **Options** button in the navigation bar. The Excel Options dialog box opens.
4. In the left pane, click **Customize Ribbon**. See Figure 8-21.

Figure 8-21 Customize Ribbon options in the Excel Options dialog box

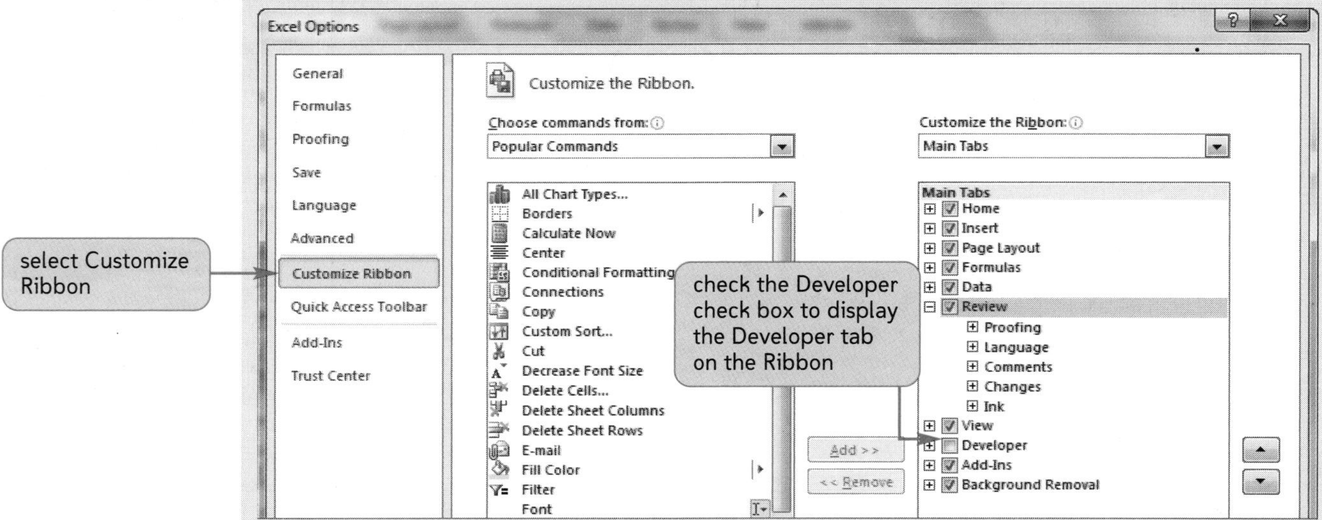

5. In the right pane, click the **Developer** check box to insert a check mark.
6. Click the **OK** button. The Developer tab appears on the Ribbon.

7. Click the **Developer** tab. See Figure 8-22.

Figure 8-22 Developer tab on the Ribbon

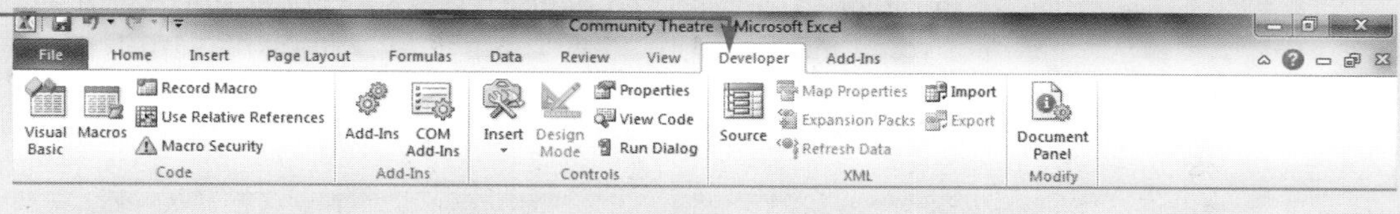

Protecting Against Macro Viruses

In recent years, viruses have been attached as macros to files created in Excel and other Office programs. A **virus** is a computer program designed to copy itself into other programs with the intention of causing mischief or harm. When unsuspecting users opened these infected workbooks, Excel automatically ran the attached virus-infected macro. **Macro viruses** are a type of virus that uses a program's own macro programming language to distribute the virus. Most macro viruses are not harmful and do not affect data in any way. For example, one macro virus changed the title bar text from *Microsoft Excel* to *Microsofa Excel*. Occasionally, macro viruses are destructive and can modify or delete files that may not be recoverable. Because it is possible for a macro to contain a virus, Microsoft Office 2010 provides several options from which you can choose to set a security level you feel comfortable with.

Macro Security Settings

The macro security settings control what Excel will do about macros in a workbook when you open that workbook. For example, one user may choose to run macros only if they are "digitally signed" by a developer who is on a list of trusted sources. Another user might want to disable all macros in workbooks and see a notification when a workbook contains macros. The user can then elect to enable the macros. Excel has four macro security settings, which are described in Figure 8-23.

Figure 8-23 Macro security settings

Setting	Description
Disable all macros without notification	All macros in all workbooks are disabled and no security alerts about macros are displayed. Use this setting if you don't want macros to run.
Disable all macros with notification	All macros in all workbooks are disabled, but security alerts appear when the workbook contains a macro. Use this default setting to choose on a case-by-case basis whether to run a macro.
Disable all macros except digitally signed macros	The same as the Disable all macros with notification setting except any macro signed by a trusted publisher runs if you have already trusted the publisher. Otherwise, security alerts appear when a workbook contains a macro.
Enable all macros	All macros in all workbooks run. Use this setting temporarily in such cases as when developing an application that contains macros. This setting is not recommended for regular use.

You set macro security in the Trust Center. The **Trust Center** is a central location for all of the security settings in Office 2010. By default, all potentially dangerous content, such as macros and workbooks with external links, is blocked without warning. If content is blocked, the Message Bar (also called the trust bar) located under the Ribbon appears, notifying you that some content was disabled. You can click the Message Bar to enable that content.

In Office 2010, you can define a set of locations (file paths) where you can place files you consider trustworthy. This feature is known as Trusted Locations. Any workbook opened from a trusted location is considered safe, and content such as macros will work without having to respond to additional security questions to use the workbook.

REFERENCE

Setting Macro Security in Excel

- In the Code group on the Developer tab, click the Macro Security button.
- Click the option button for the macro setting you want.
- Click the OK button.

or

- Click the File tab, and then click the Options button in the navigation bar.
- Click the Trust Center category, and then click the Trust Center Settings button.
- Click the Macro Settings category, and then click the option button for a macro setting.
- Click the OK button.

Ellen wants some protection against macro viruses, so she suggests you set the security level to "Disable all macros with notification." When you open a file with macros, this macro security level disables the macros and displays a security alert, allowing you to enable the macros if you believe the workbook comes from a trusted source. After the macros are enabled, you can run them.

To set the macro security level:

1. In the Code group on the Developer tab, click the **Macro Security** button. The Trust Center dialog box opens with the Macro Settings category displayed.
2. In the Macro Settings section, click the **Disable all macros with notification** option button if it is not selected. See Figure 8-24.

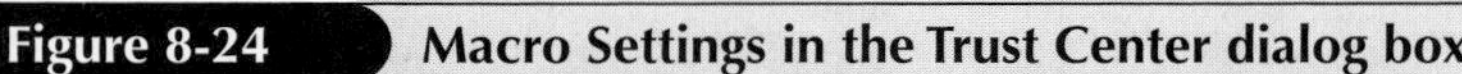

Figure 8-24 **Macro Settings in the Trust Center dialog box**

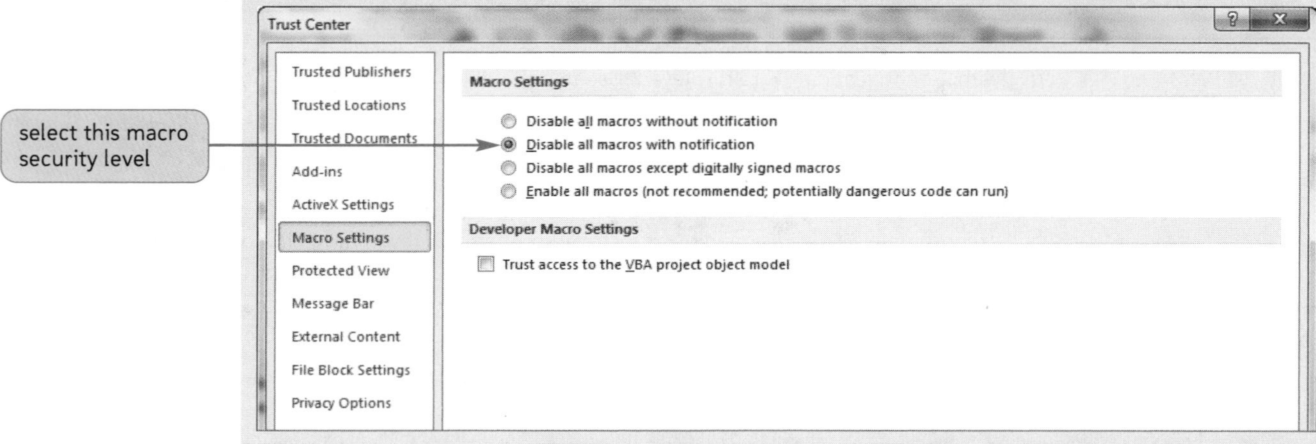

3. Click the **OK** button.

Each time you open a workbook that contains a macro detected by the Trust Center, the macro is disabled and a Message Bar containing the Security Warning that macros have been disabled appears below the Ribbon. If you developed the workbook or trust the person who sent you the workbook, click the Enable Content button to run the macros in the workbook. If you do not click the Enable Content button, you cannot run the macros in the workbook, but you can use the rest of the workbook.

INSIGHT

Using Digital Signatures with Macros

A **digital signature** is like a seal of approval. It's often used to identify the author of a workbook that contains macros. You add a digital signature as the last step before you distribute a file. Before you can add a digital signature to a workbook, you need to obtain a digital ID (also called a digital certificate) that proves your identity. Digital certificates are typically issued by a certificate authority. After you have a digital certificate, do the following to digitally sign a workbook:

1. Click the File tab on the Ribbon, and then, in the navigation bar, click Info.
2. On the Info tab, click the Protect Workbook button, and then click the Add a Digital Signature button.
3. If a message dialog box opens, click the OK button. The Sign dialog box opens.
4. In the Purpose for signing this document box, enter a reason why you are adding a digital signature to this workbook.
5. Click the Sign button, and then click the OK button. The invisible digital signature does not appear within the workbook, but users will see the Signatures button on the status bar.

By digitally signing a workbook that contains a macro you intend to publicly distribute, you assure others of two things: (1) the identity of the creator of the macro, and (2) the macro has not been altered since the digital signature was created.

When you open a digitally signed file, you can see who the author is and decide whether the information in the file is authentic and whether you trust that the macros in the workbook are safe to run.

The digital signature is removed any time a file is saved after the signature has been added to the file. Therefore, no one (including the original workbook author) can open a digitally signed file, make changes to the workbook, save the workbook, and then send the file to another user with the digital signature intact. The original author must digitally sign the modified workbook.

Recording a Macro

You can create an Excel macro in one of two ways: You can use the macro recorder to record keystrokes and mouse actions as you perform them, or you can enter a series of commands in the **Visual Basic for Applications (VBA)** programming language. The macro recorder can record only those actions you perform with the keyboard or mouse. The macro recorder is a good choice for creating simple macros. For more sophisticated macros, you might need to write VBA code directly in the Visual Basic Editor.

For Ellen's application, the tasks you need to perform can all be done with the keyboard and the mouse, so you will use the macro recorder to record the two macros. One macro will save the invoice as a PDF file, which is a file format created by Adobe Systems for document exchange. The second macro will transfer data from the Invoice worksheet to the Ticket Data worksheet.

PROSKILLS

Decision Making: Planning and Recording a Macro

Advance planning and practice help to ensure you create an error-free macro. First, decide what you want to accomplish. Then, consider the best way to achieve those results. Next, practice the keystrokes and mouse actions before you actually record the macro. This may seem like extra work, but it reduces the chance of error when you actually record the macro. As you set up the macro, consider the following:

- Choose a descriptive name that helps you recognize the macro's purpose.
- Weigh the benefits of selecting a shortcut key against its drawbacks. Although a shortcut key is an easy way to run a macro, you are limited to one-letter shortcuts, which can make it difficult to remember the purpose of each shortcut key. In addition, the macro shortcut keys will override the standard Office shortcuts for the workbook.
- Store the macro with the current workbook unless the macro can be used with other workbooks.
- Include a description that provides an overview of the macro and perhaps your name and contact information.

Good decision making includes thinking about what to do and what *not* to do as you progress to your goals. This is true when developing a macro as well.

Each macro must have a unique name that begins with a letter. The macro name can contain up to 255 characters, including letters, numbers, and the underscore symbol. The macro name cannot include spaces or special characters. It is helpful to use a descriptive name that describes the macro's purpose.

TIP

You can also use Ctrl+Shift+*letter* as the shortcut by entering the uppercase letter for the key.

You can assign a shortcut key to run the macro directly from the keyboard. Macro shortcut keys are used to run a macro. Assigning a shortcut key overrides the equivalent default Excel shortcut for the open workbook. For example, using the Ctrl+p keys to run a macro overrides the default Excel 2010 shortcut for printing a selected area while the workbook containing the macro is open. Some people find macro shortcut keys a quick way to run a macro; others dislike them because they override the original function of the shortcut key. It's a personal preference.

A macro needs to be stored somewhere. By default, the macro is stored in the current workbook, making the macro available in only that workbook when it is open. Another option is to store the macro in the **Personal Macro workbook**, a hidden workbook named Personal.xlsb that opens whenever you start Excel, making the macro available any time you use Excel. The Personal Macro workbook stores commonly used macros that apply to many workbooks. It is most convenient for users on stand-alone computers. Finally, you can store the macro in a new workbook. Keep in mind that the new workbook must be open to use the macro. For example, an accountant might store a set of macros that help with end-of-the-month tasks in a separate workbook.

You can also add a description of the macro to briefly explain what it does. You can also include the name of the person to contact and the date it was created.

REFERENCE

Recording a Macro

- In the Code group on the Developer tab, click the Record Macro button.
- Enter a name for the macro, and then specify the location to store the macro.
- Specify a shortcut key (optional).
- Enter a description of the macro (optional).
- Click the OK button to start the macro recorder.
- Perform the tasks you want to automate.
- Click the Stop Recording button.

Ellen provides you with the following outline of the actions needed for the macro to save the invoice as a PDF file:

1. Set the range E2:K23 as the print area.
2. Define the Page Layout setting with the custom heading "Customer Invoice."
3. Create the PDF file and name the PDF file "Invoice."
4. Make cell A1 the active cell.

You'll record the steps for this macro using a macro named "PDFInvoice" that is assigned a keyboard shortcut, has a description, and is stored in the Community Theatre workbook. You'll start the macro recorder.

If you make a mistake when recording the macro, you can close the workbook without saving, reopen the workbook, and then record the macro again.

To start the macro recorder:

1. Save your workbook.
2. In the Code group on the Developer tab, click the **Record Macro** button. The Record Macro dialog box opens. The Macro name box displays a default name for the macro that consists of the word "Macro" followed by a number that is one greater than the number of macros already recorded in the workbook during the current Excel session. See Figure 8-25.

Figure 8-25 Record Macro dialog box

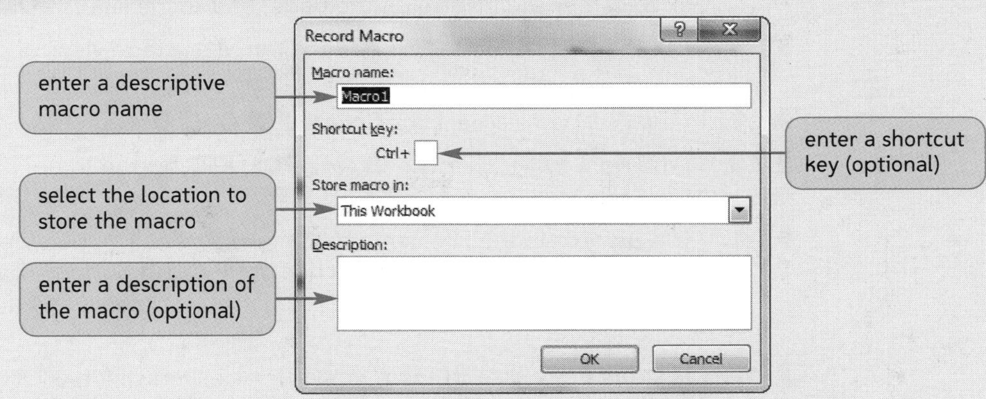

3. In the Macro name box, type **PDFInvoice** to change the default name to a more descriptive one, and then press the **Tab** key.
4. In the Shortcut key box, type **p** to set Ctrl+p as the shortcut to run the macro from the keyboard, and then press the **Tab** key.
5. Verify that the Store macro in box is set to **This Workbook** to store the macro in the Community Theatre workbook, and then press the **Tab** key.
6. In the Description box, type **Created 7/15/2013. Save invoice area: range E2:K23 as PDF file.** to enter notes about the macro.
7. Click the **OK** button. The workbook enters macro record mode. The Record Macro button in the Code group on the Developer tab changes to the Stop Recording button, which also appears on the status bar.

From this point on, *every* mouse click and keystroke you perform will be recorded and stored as part of the PDFInvoice macro. For that reason, it's very important to follow the instructions in the next steps precisely. Take your time as you perform each step, reading the entire step carefully first. After you finish recording the keystrokes, click the Stop Recording button to turn off the macro recorder.

To record the PDFInvoice macro:

1. Click the **Page Layout** tab on the Ribbon.
2. Select the range **E2:K23**. This range contains the invoice area.
3. In the Page Setup group, click the **Print Area** button, and then click **Set Print Area**. The invoice area is set as the print area. Next, you'll insert a custom header.
4. In the Page Setup group, click the **Dialog Box Launcher** to open the Page Setup dialog box.
5. Click the **Header/Footer** tab, and then click the **Custom Header** button to open the Header dialog box.
6. Click in the **Center section** box, type **Customer Invoice** and then click the **OK** button to close the Header dialog box.
7. In the Page Setup dialog box, click the **Margins** tab, click the **Horizontally** check box to center the invoice on the page, and then click the **OK** button.
8. Click the **File** tab on the Ribbon to open Backstage view, and then click **Save & Send** in the navigation bar.
9. In the File Types area, click **Create PDF/XPS Document**.
10. In the right pane, click the **Create PDF/XPS** button to open the Publish as PDF or XPS dialog box.
11. Type **Invoice** in the File name box, make sure the "Open file after publishing" check box is checked, and then click the **Publish** button. The invoice is saved as a PDF file in the same location as the Excel workbook, and automatically opens in Adobe Reader.
12. Close the PDF file, and then, in the Invoice worksheet, click cell **A1**.

    You've completed all of the steps in the PDFInvoice macro. You'll turn off the macro recorder.

13. Click the **Stop Recording** button on the status bar. The macro recorder turns off, and the button changes to the Record Macro button.

    Trouble? If you made a mistake while recording the macro, close the Community Theatre workbook without saving your changes. Reopen the workbook, and then repeat all of the steps beginning with the "To start the macro recorder" steps.

Be sure to turn off the macro recorder; otherwise, you'll continue to record your keystrokes and mouse clicks, leading to unintended consequences.

Be aware that the process for saving a workbook with a macro is different from saving one that does not contain a macro. If you need to save the workbook before you complete this session, refer to the section "Saving Workbooks with Macros" later in this session.

Running a Macro

After you record a macro, you should run it to test whether it works as intended. Running a macro means Excel performs each of the steps in the same order as when it was recorded. To run the macro you created, you can either use the shortcut key you specified or select the macro in the Macro dialog box. The Macro dialog box lists all of the macros in the open workbooks. From this dialog box, you can select and run a macro, edit the macro with VBA, run the macro one step at a time so you can determine in which step an error occurs, or delete it.

REFERENCE

Running a Macro

- Press the shortcut key assigned to the macro.

or

- In the Code group on the Developer tab, click the Macros button.
- Select the macro from the list of macros.
- Click the Run button.

You will test the PDFInvoice macro.

To run the PDFInvoice macro:

1. Click the **Developer** tab on the Ribbon, and then click the **Macros** button in the Code group. The Macro dialog box opens, listing all of the macros in the open workbooks. See Figure 8-26.

Figure 8-26 **Macro dialog box**

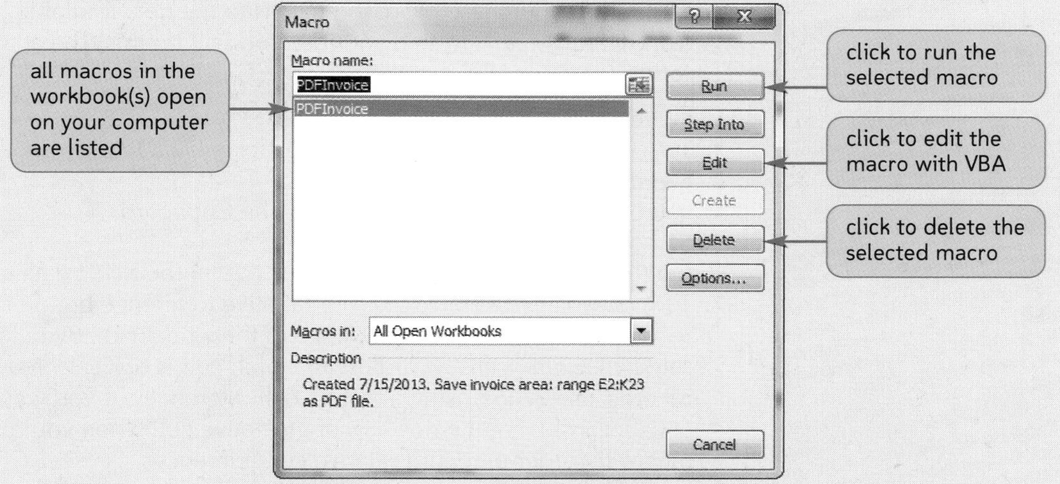

2. Verify that **PDFInvoice** is selected in the Macro name box, and then click the **Run** button. The PDFInvoice macro runs. The invoice is saved as a PDF file and the file is opened in Adobe Reader.
3. Close Adobe Reader. Cell A1 is the active cell in the Invoice worksheet.

   Trouble? If the PDFInvoice macro did not run properly, you might have made a mistake in the steps while recording the macro. Click the Developer tab, and then click the Macros button in the Code group. Select the PDFInvoice macro, and then click the Delete button. Click the OK button to confirm the deletion, and then repeat all of the steps beginning with the "To start the macro recorder" steps.

   Next, you will test the shortcut keys you used for the PDFInvoice macro.

4. Press the **Ctrl+p** keys. The PDFInvoice macro runs. The invoice is saved as a PDF file, and cell A1 in the Invoice worksheet is the active cell.

5. Close Adobe Reader.

Trouble? If your macro doesn't end on its own, you need to end it. Press the Ctrl+Break keys to stop the macro from running.

INSIGHT

How Edits Can Affect Macros

Be careful when making seemingly small changes to a workbook, as these can have a great impact on macros. If a run-time error (an error that occurs while running a macro) appears when you run a macro that has worked in the past, some part of the macro code no longer makes sense to Excel. For example, simply adding a space to a worksheet name can affect a macro that references the worksheet. If you recorded a macro that referenced a worksheet named "TicketData" (no spaces in the name) that you later changed to "Ticket Data" (space added to the name), the macro no longer works because the TicketData worksheet no longer exists. You could record the macro again, or you could edit the macro in VBA by changing "TicketData" to "Ticket Data."

Creating the TransferData Macro

You need to record one more macro. The data you entered earlier in the input section of the Invoice worksheet was never added to the Ticket Data worksheet. Ellen wants to add this data from the purchase of season tickets to the next available blank row in the Ticket Data worksheet. The macro that you'll record will do this. The actions of this macro will be as follows:

1. Switch to the Ticket Data worksheet.
2. Turn off worksheet protection in the Ticket Data worksheet.
3. Switch to the Invoice worksheet.
4. Select and copy the Transfer Area to the Clipboard.
5. Switch to the Ticket Data worksheet.
6. Go to cell A1, and then go to the last row in the ticket data table.
7. Turn on Relative References. The Relative Reference button controls how Excel records the act of selecting a range in the worksheet. By default, the macro will select the same cells regardless of which cell is first selected because the macro records a selection using absolute cell references. If you want a macro to select cells regardless of the position of the active cell when you run the macro, set the macro recorder to record relative cell references.
8. Move down one row.
9. Turn off Relative References.
10. Paste values to the Ticket Data worksheet.
11. Go to cell A1.
12. Turn on worksheet protection.
13. Switch to the Invoice worksheet, and then make cell B3 the active cell.

Ellen wants you to name this new macro "TransferData" and assign the Ctrl+t keys as the shortcut.

To record the TransferData macro:

1. Click the **Record Macro** button on the status bar to open the Record Macro dialog box, type **TransferData** in the Macro name box, type **t** in the Shortcut key box, type **Created 7/15/2013. Copy values in the transfer area in the Invoice worksheet to the Ticket Data worksheet.** in the Description box, and then click the **OK** button. The macro recorder is on.
2. Click the **Ticket Data** sheet tab, click the **Review** tab on the Ribbon, and then click the **Unprotect Sheet** button in the Changes group to turn off protection.
3. Click the **Invoice** sheet tab, and then select the range **F25:J25** in the Transfer Area.
4. Click the **Home** tab on the Ribbon, and then click the **Copy** button in the Clipboard group.
5. Click the **Ticket Data** sheet tab, click cell **A1**, and then press the **End+↓** keys to go to the last row with values.
6. Click the **Developer** tab on the Ribbon, and then click the **Use Relative References** button in the Code group. Relative references ensure that the invoice data being transferred is inserted in the next blank row (in this case, row 6) and not always in row 5 in the Ticket Data worksheet.
7. Click the **↓** key to move to the first blank cell in the worksheet.
8. In the Code group on the Developer tab, click the **Use Relative References** button. The Use Relative References button is toggled off.
9. Click the **Home** tab on the Ribbon.
10. In the Clipboard group, click the **Paste button arrow**, and then click the **Values** button in the Paste Values section. This option pastes the values rather than the formulas from the Transfer Area.

    Trouble? If #REF! appears in row 6 of the Ticket Data worksheet, you clicked the Paste button instead of the Paste Values button. Stop recording the macro. Delete the macro and begin recording the macro again.
11. Click cell **A1**, click the **Review** tab on the Ribbon, click the **Protect Sheet** button in the Changes group, and then click the **OK** button in the Protect Sheet dialog box.
12. Click the **Invoice** sheet tab, and then click cell **B3**.
13. Click the **Stop Recording** button on the status bar. The macro recorder turns off, and the button changes to the Record Macro button.

TIP

You can also turn off the macro recorder by clicking the Stop Recording button in the Code group on the Developer tab.

You've completed recording the TransferData macro. Next, you'll test whether it works. Ellen has a new season ticket subscription to add to the worksheet. You'll enter this data as you test the TransferData macro.

To test the TransferData macro:

1. Enter the following data into the range B3:B12, pressing the **Enter** key after each entry:

   7/15/2013
   Kate Holland
   186 Pinetop Drive
   Eugene, OR 70777
   (888) 555–1234
   2 tickets, D series, Balcony
   1 decal, 40 donation

2. Press the **Ctrl+t** keys. The TransferData macro runs and the data transfers to the Ticket Data worksheet.
3. Switch to the **Ticket Data** worksheet, verify that the data for Kate Holland appears in row 7, and then return to the **Invoice** worksheet.

Fixing Macro Errors

If a macro does not work correctly, you can fix it. Sometimes, you'll find a mistake when you test a macro you just created. Other times, you might not discover that error until later. No matter when you find an error in a macro, you have the following options:

- Rerecord the macro using the same macro name.
- Delete the recorded macro, and then record the macro again.
- Run the macro one step at a time to locate the problem, and then use one of the previous methods to correct the problem.

You can delete or edit a macro by opening the Macro dialog box (shown earlier in Figure 8-26), selecting the macro from the list, and then clicking the appropriate button. To rerecord the macro, simply restart the macro recorder and enter the same macro name you used earlier. Excel overwrites the previous version of the macro.

Working with the Visual Basic Editor

To view the code of a macro, you need to open the Visual Basic Editor (VBE), which is a separate application that works with Excel and all of the Office programs to view, debug, edit, and manage VBA code. The VBE consists of several components, including the Code window that contains the VBA code, the Project Explorer window that displays a treelike diagram consisting of every open workbook, and a menu bar with menus of commands you use to edit, debug, and run VBA statements. You can access the Visual Basic Editor through the Macro dialog box or the Visual Basic button in the Code group on the Developer tab.

REFERENCE

Editing a Macro

- In the Code group on the Developer tab, click the Macros button, select the macro in the Macro name list, and then click the Edit button.
  or
  In the Code group on the Developer tab, click the Visual Basic button.
- Use the Visual Basic Editor to edit the macro code.
- Click File on the menu bar, and then click Close and Return to Microsoft Excel.

Ellen wants the PDFInvoice macro to stop in cell B3 of the Invoice worksheet. Right now, the macro stops with cell A1 selected. Although you can delete the PDFInvoice macro and record it again, it is simpler to edit the existing macro. You will edit the VBA command in the macro.

To view the code for the PDFInvoice macro:

1. Click the **Developer** tab on the Ribbon, and then click the **Macros** button in the Code group. The Macro dialog box opens.
2. Click **PDFInvoice** in the Macro name list, and then click the **Edit** button. The Visual Basic Editor opens as a separate program, consisting of two windows—the Project Explorer and the Code window.
3. If the Code window is not maximized, click the **Maximize** button on the Code window title bar. The Code window contains the VBA code generated by the macro recorder. See Figure 8-27 (your window may differ).

Figure 8-27 Code window in the Visual Basic Editor

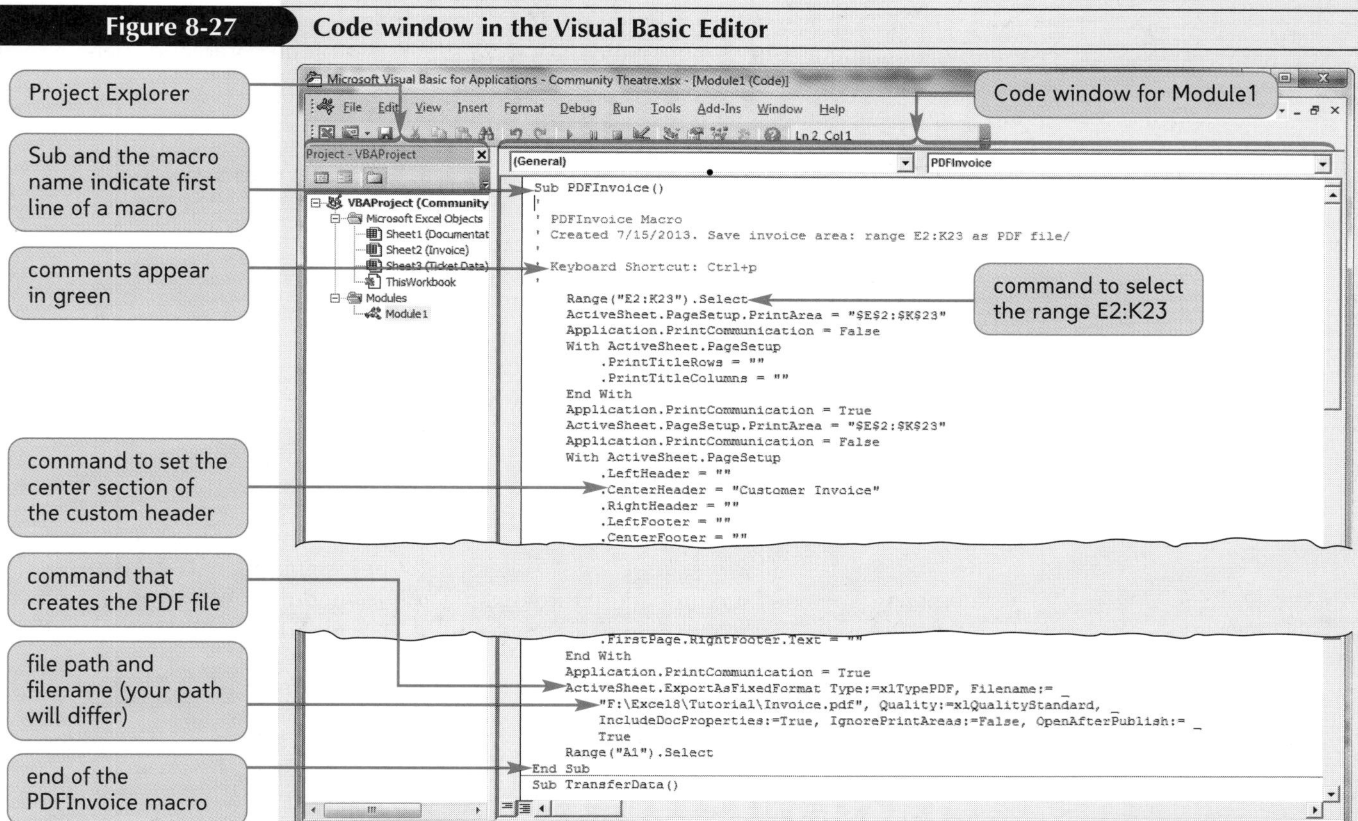

Trouble? If you see a different number of windows in the Visual Basic Editor, your computer is configured differently. You will be working with the Code window, so you can ignore any other windows.

Understanding the Structure of Macros

The VBA code in the Code window lists all of the actions you performed when recording the PDFInvoice macro. In VBA, macros are called **sub procedures**. Each sub procedure begins with the keyword *Sub* followed by the name of the sub procedure and a set of parentheses. In this example, the code begins with

```
Sub PDFInvoice()
```

which provides the name of this sub procedure, PDFInvoice—the name you gave the macro. The parentheses are used to include any arguments in the procedure. These arguments pass information to the sub procedure and have roughly the same purpose as the arguments in an Excel function. If you write your own VBA code, sub procedure arguments are an important part of the programming process. However, they are not used when you create macros with the macro recorder.

Following the Sub PDFInvoice() statement are comments about the macro, taken from the macro name, shortcut key, and description you entered in the Record New Macro dialog box. Each line appears in green and is preceded by an apostrophe ('). The apostrophe indicates that the line is a comment and does not include any actions Excel needs to perform.

After the comments is the body of the macro, a listing of all of the commands performed by the PDFInvoice macro as written in the language of VBA. Your list of commands might look slightly different, depending on the exact actions you performed when recording the macro. Even though you might not know VBA, some of the commands are easy to interpret. For example, near the top of the PDFInvoice macro you should see the following command, which tells Excel to select the range E2:K23:

```
Range("E2:K23").Select
```

Several lines below this command you see the following command, which sets the words "Customer Invoice" at the top of the print page in the center of the custom header:

```
.CenterHeader = "Customer Invoice"
```

At the bottom of the macro is the following statement, which indicates the end of the PDFInvoice sub procedure:

```
End Sub
```

A Code window can contain several sub procedures, with each procedure separated from the others by the Sub*ProcedureName*() statement at the beginning, and the End Sub statement at the end. Sub procedures are organized into **modules**. As shown in Figure 8-27, all of the macros that have been recorded are stored in the Module1 module (your window may differ).

Editing a Macro Using the Visual Basic Editor

The Visual Basic Editor provides tools to assist you in writing error-free code. As you type a command, the editor will provide pop-up windows and text to help you insert the correct code.

Ellen wants you to edit the following command in the PDFInvoice sub procedure, which sets the active cell to cell A1:

```
Range("A1").Select
```

You'll edit the command to the following to change the active cell from cell A1 to cell B3:

```
Range("B3").Select
```

To edit a command in the macro:

1. Scroll down the Code window to the line immediately before End Sub in the PDFInvoice macro.
2. In the line with the command `Range("A1")`, select **A1**, and then type **B3**. The command in the macro is edited to select a different cell. See Figure 8-28.

Figure 8-28 Edited line in the PDFInvoice macro

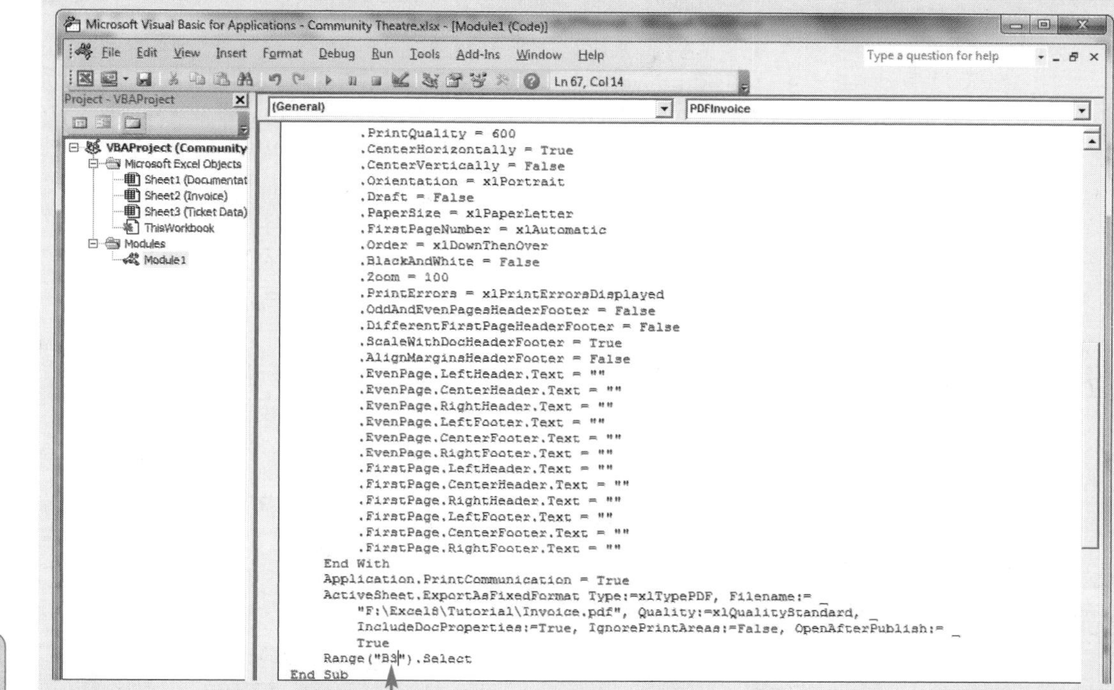

3. On the menu bar, click **File**, and then click **Close and Return to Microsoft Excel**. The Visual Basic Editor closes, and the Community Theatre workbook is displayed.

Ellen wants you to test the macro. You'll check to see whether cell B3 is the active cell once the macro has run.

To test the edited PDFInvoice macro:

1. Press the **Ctrl+p** keys. The PDFInvoice macro runs.

   Trouble? If a Microsoft Visual Basic message box appears with a run-time error, click the End button, click the Macros button, click PDFInvoice in the Macro name box, and then click the Edit button. In the Code window, find the line you edited (one line above End Sub), and then correct it to **Range("B3").Select**. On the menu bar, click File, and then click Close and Return to Microsoft Excel.
2. Close Adobe Reader. Cell B3 is the active cell.

Creating Macro Buttons

Another way to run a macro is to assign it to a button placed directly in the worksheet. Macro buttons are often a better way to run macros than shortcut keys. Clicking a button (with a descriptive label) is often more intuitive and simpler for users than trying to remember different combinations of keystrokes.

REFERENCE

Creating a Macro Button

- In the Controls group on the Developer tab, click the Insert button.
- In the Form Controls section, click the Button (Form Control) button.
- Click the worksheet where you want the macro button to be located, drag the pointer until the button is the size and shape you want, and then release the mouse button.
- In the Assign Macro dialog box, select the macro you want to assign to the button.
- With the button still selected, type a new label.

Ellen wants you to add two macro buttons to the Invoice worksheet, one for each of the macros you've created.

To insert a macro button in the worksheet:

1. Scroll to the right so that columns L and M are completely visible.
2. In the Controls group on the Developer tab, click the **Insert** button. The Form Controls appear, with a variety of objects that can be placed in the worksheet. You'll insert the Button form control. See Figure 8-29.

Figure 8-29 **Form Controls**

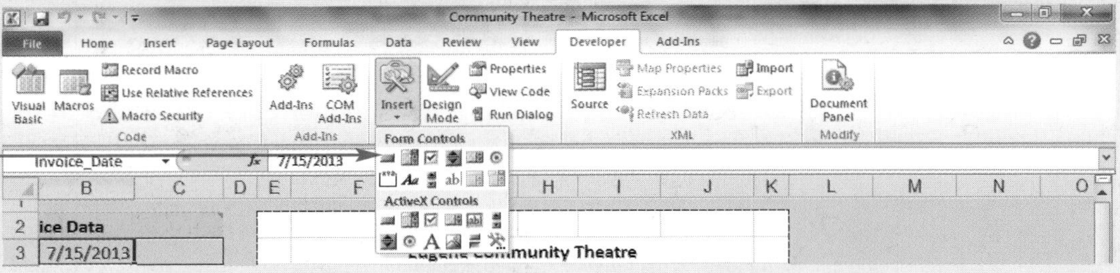

Trouble? If the Insert button is unavailable, the worksheet is protected. Click the Review tab on the Ribbon, click the Unprotect Sheet button in the Changes group to unprotect the Invoice worksheet, and then repeat Step 2.

3. In the Form Controls section, click the **Button (Form Control)** button, and then point to cell **L3**. The pointer changes to +.
4. Click and drag the pointer over the range **L3:M4**, and then release the mouse button. A button appears on the worksheet, and the Assign Macro dialog box opens with the button's default name in the Macro name box. See Figure 8-30.

Figure 8-30 **Assign Macro dialog box**

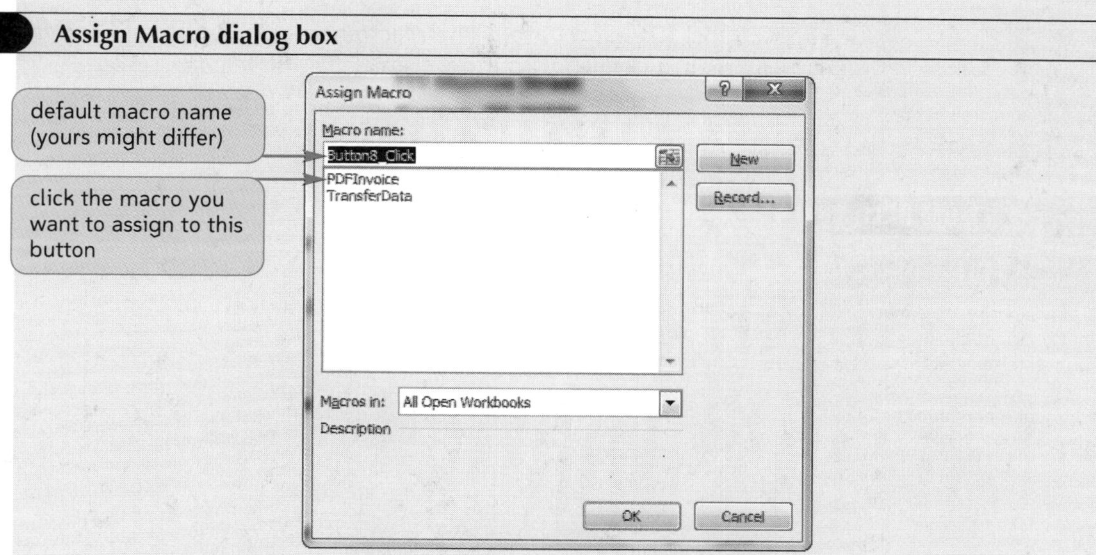

From the Assign Macro dialog box, you can assign a macro to the button. After you assign a macro to the button, the button appears with a default label. You can change the default label to a descriptive one that will indicate which macro will run when the button is clicked.

Ellen wants you to assign the PDFInvoice macro to this new button, and then rename the button with a label that reflects the PDFInvoice macro.

To assign the PDFInvoice macro to the new button:

1. Click **PDFInvoice** in the Macro name box, and then click the **OK** button. The PDFInvoice macro is assigned to the selected button.
2. With the sizing handles still displayed around the button, type **Create PDF** (do not press the Enter key). The new label replaces the default label.

   Trouble? If no sizing handles appear around the button, the button is not selected. Right-click the button, click Edit Text to place the insertion point within the button, and then repeat Step 2.

   Trouble? If you pressed the Enter key after entering the label on the button, you created a new line in the button. Press the Backspace key to delete the line, and then continue with Step 3.
3. Click any cell in the worksheet to deselect the macro button.

At this point, if you click the Create PDF button, the PDFInvoice macro will run. Before you test the PDFInvoice button, you will add the other button.

To add another macro button to the Invoice worksheet:

1. In the Controls group on the Developer tab, click the **Insert** button, click the **Button (Form Control)** button, and then drag the pointer over the range **L6:M7**.

2. Click **TransferData** in the Macro name box in the Assign Macro dialog box, and then click the **OK** button.
3. Type **Transfer Data** as the button label, and then click any cell in the worksheet to deselect the button. See Figure 8-31.

Figure 8-31 **Macro buttons in the Invoice worksheet**

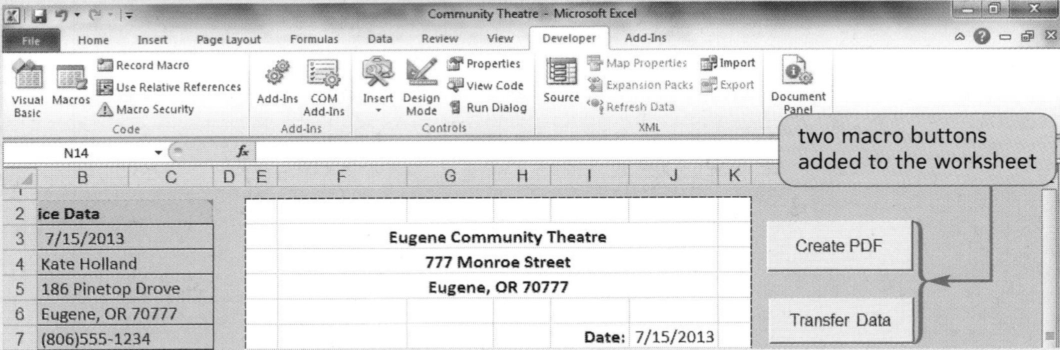

TIP

To move or resize a macro button, right-click the button to select it, press the Esc key to close the shortcut menu, and then drag a sizing handle or the selection box.

Trouble? If the macro buttons on your screen do not match the size and location of the buttons shown in the figure, right-click a button to select it, press the Esc key to close the shortcut menu, and then resize or reposition the button on the worksheet.

You have completed the application so you will reset worksheet protection.

4. Click the **Review** tab on the Ribbon, and then click the **Protect Sheet** button in the Changes group. The Protect Sheet dialog box opens.
5. Click the **OK** button to turn on worksheet protection.

Next, you will test the macro buttons to verify that they run the macros. Ellen received another subscriber order. You will use the new macro buttons as you enter this data.

To test the macro buttons:

1. In the range B3:B12, enter the following subscriber order:

   7/16/2013
   George Zidane
   105 Central Ave.
   Eugene, OR 70777
   (808) 555-5555
   3 tickets, E series, Balcony
   2 parking decals, 30 donation
2. Click the **Create PDF** button to save the current invoice as a PDF file.
3. Close Adobe Reader to return to the Invoice worksheet.
4. Click the **Transfer Data** button to transfer data to the Ticket Data worksheet. Excel inserts the new transaction in the table.

5. Switch to the **Ticket Data** worksheet, and then verify the data was transferred. See Figure 8-32.

Figure 8-32 **Ticket Data worksheet with the new transaction record**

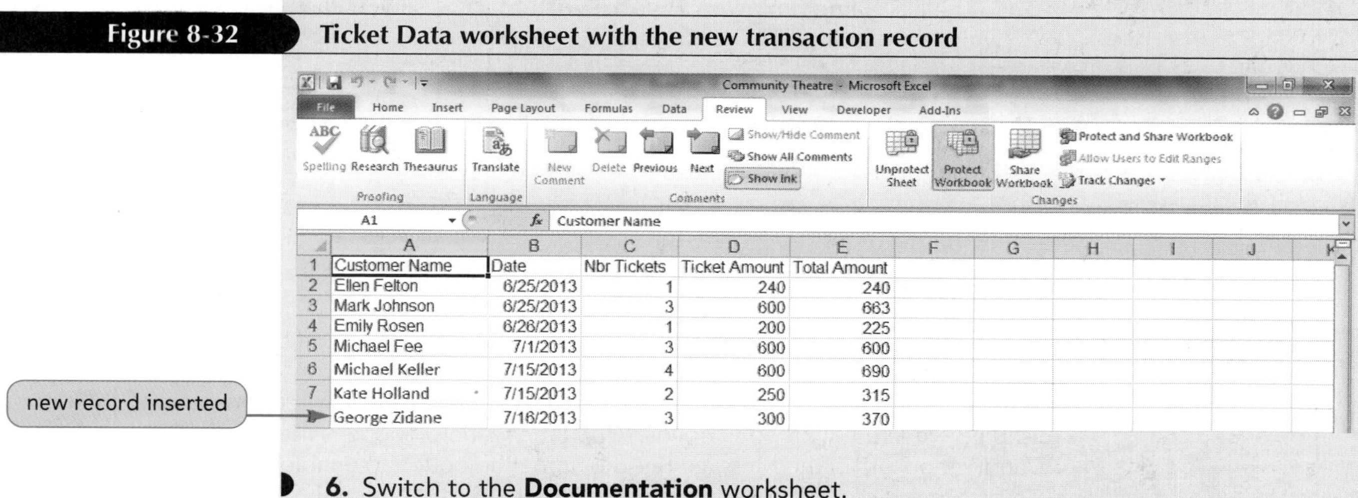

	A	B	C	D	E
1	Customer Name	Date	Nbr Tickets	Ticket Amount	Total Amount
2	Ellen Felton	6/25/2013	1	240	240
3	Mark Johnson	6/25/2013	3	600	663
4	Emily Rosen	6/26/2013	1	200	225
5	Michael Fee	7/1/2013	3	600	600
6	Michael Keller	7/15/2013	4	600	690
7	Kate Holland	7/15/2013	2	250	315
	George Zidane	7/16/2013	3	300	370

6. Switch to the **Documentation** worksheet.

Saving Workbooks with Macros

When you save a workbook that contains macros, a dialog box opens indicating that the workbook you are trying to save contains features that cannot be saved in a macro-free workbook. The default Excel workbook does not allow macros to be stored as part of the file. If you want to save the workbook without the macros, click the Yes button. The workbook will be saved as a macro-free workbook, which means the macros you created will be lost. If you want to save the workbook with the macros, click the No button, and then save the workbook as a new file—one that allows macros to be saved as part of the file. The default Excel Workbook format, which is a macro-free workbook, has the .xlsx file extension. You need to change this to a macro-enabled workbook, which has the .xlsm file extension.

You've completed your work on the Excel application, so you will save and close the workbook and then exit Excel.

To save the workbook with macros:

1. On the Quick Access Toolbar, click the **Save** button. A dialog box opens, indicating that the workbook you are trying to save contains features that cannot be saved in a macro-free workbook. See Figure 8-33.

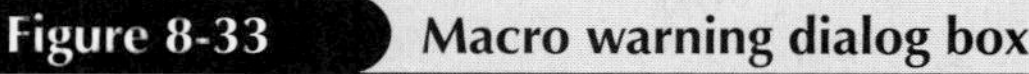

Figure 8-33 **Macro warning dialog box**

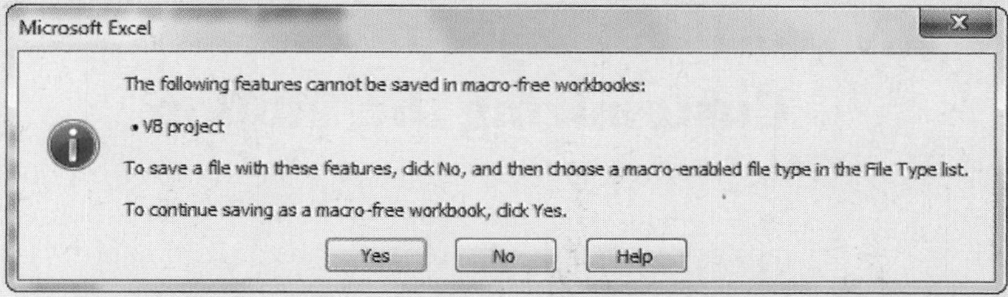

2. Click the **No** button. The Save As dialog box opens so you can save the workbook as a macro-enabled workbook.
3. In the File name box, type **Theatre with Macros** so you can easily determine which workbook contains macros.
4. Click the **Save as type** button, and then click **Excel Macro-Enabled Workbook**.
5. Click the **Save** button. The workbook is saved with the macros.
6. Close the workbook.

Opening a Workbook with Macros

TIP

After you enable the content, the filename is added to a list of trusted files and the Security Warning will not reappear as long as the workbook name or location is not changed.

When you open a file with macros, Excel checks the opening workbook to see if it contains any macros. The response you see is based on the security level set on the computer. Earlier, you disabled all macros with notification. So, all of the macros will be disabled when the workbook opens. When the workbook opens the first time, a Security Warning appears in the Message Bar providing the option to enable the macros so they can be run, or to open the workbook with the macros disabled. If you know a workbook contains macros that you or a coworker created, you can enable them, which adds the filename to a list of trusted files so that you won't see the Security Warning when you open this file again. If you do not click the Enable Content button, the macros remain disabled and unavailable during the current session, but the other features of the workbook are still available.

You'll open the Theatre with Macros workbook and enable the macros.

To open the Theatre with Macros workbook:

1. Open the **Theatre with Macros** workbook. The workbook opens, and "Security Warning: Macros have been disabled" appears in the Message Bar below the Ribbon. See Figure 8-34.

Figure 8-34 Security Warning appears when opening a workbook with macros

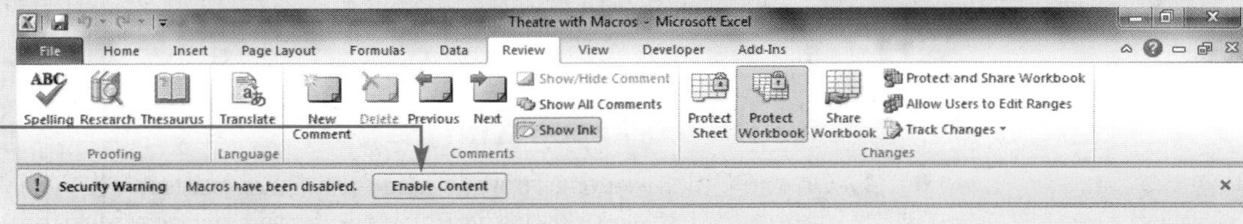

2. In the Message Bar, click the **Enable Content** button. The macros in the workbook are available for use.
3. Switch to the **Invoice** worksheet.

Customizing the Ribbon

Excel 2010 enables you to change the Ribbon to fit your work style. Among many other customization features, you can minimize the Ribbon, create new tabs and groups, hide tabs or commands, and rename tabs or commands.

Minimize the Ribbon

You can minimize the Ribbon to make more space for a worksheet. When the Ribbon is minimized, only the Quick Access Toolbar and the tab names are displayed. To access a command from the Ribbon, click the appropriate tab. The Ribbon expands to show all of the groups and buttons on that tab. After you click a button on the Ribbon or a cell in the worksheet, the Ribbon returns to its minimized state.

Now that the application is complete, Ellen wants to provide more screen space for the input and output sections of the worksheet.

TIP

You can also minimize the Ribbon by double-clicking any tab on the Ribbon. Repeat to maximize the Ribbon.

To minimize the Ribbon:

1. Near the upper-right corner of the Excel window, click the **Minimize the Ribbon** button. The Ribbon is minimized, leaving more room for the Invoice worksheet. See Figure 8-35.

Figure 8-35 **Minimized Ribbon**

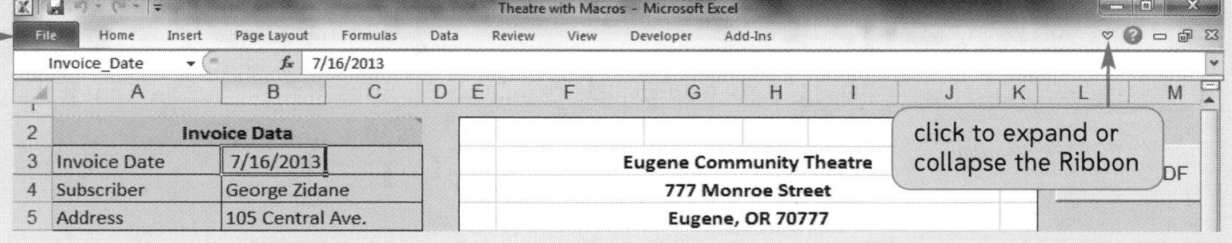

2. Click the **Home** tab. All of the buttons for this tab appear on the Ribbon.
3. Click cell **B3**. The Ribbon returns to its minimized state.

Removing a Tab from the Ribbon

If you decide you don't want a tab displayed on the Ribbon, you can remove it. Now that the macros are completed, Ellen doesn't need the Developer tab to appear on the Ribbon. You will remove the Developer tab from the Ribbon.

To remove the Developer tab from the Ribbon:

1. Click the **File** tab on the Ribbon, and then click the **Options** button in the navigation bar. The Excel Options dialog box opens.
2. Click **Customize Ribbon** in the left pane, and then click the **Developer** check box in the Customize the Ribbon box to remove the check mark.
3. Click the **OK** button. The Developer tab is removed from the Ribbon.

Expanding the Ribbon

If worksheet space is not an issue and you prefer to view the maximized Ribbon, you can expand the Ribbon to show the tabs with all of the options displayed. You will expand the Ribbon so that all tab contents are visible.

To expand the Ribbon:

1. Near the upper-right corner of the Excel window, click the **Expand the Ribbon** button. The Ribbon is maximized.
2. Save and close the workbook.

Ellen is pleased with the Community Theatre workbook. The workbook protection and macros will streamline the data entry process for theatre volunteers.

REVIEW

Session 8.3 Quick Check

1. The ______________ tab on the Ribbon is necessary to record a macro.
2. Discuss two ways of creating a macro.
3. What are the three places in which you can store a macro?
4. Identify two ways to run a macro.
5. What are the steps you follow to edit a macro?
6. How do you insert a macro button into your worksheet?
7. True or False. A workbook that contains a macro can be saved using the Excel Workbook format with the .xlsx extension.
8. How do you minimize the Ribbon?

Practice the skills you learned in the tutorial using the same case scenario.

PRACTICE

Review Assignments

Data File needed for the Review Assignments: Rentals.xlsx

You did such a good job helping Ellen with the Community Theatre application that she recommended you to a friend who has a similar project. Ellen's friend wants to create an invoice system for his new car rental company, Eugene Discount Car Rental. Complete the following:

1. Open the **Rentals** workbook located in the Excel8\Review folder included with your Data Files, and then save the workbook as **Discount Rentals**.
2. In the Documentation worksheet, enter your name and the date.
3. In the Customer worksheet, define names for cells as follows:

Cell	Defined Name	Cell	Defined Name
B4	**Customer**	H9	**ChargePerDay**
B5	**TypeCar**	H10	**ChargePerMile**
B6	**DaysRented**	A12:C16	**RentalRates**
B7	**MilesDriven**	B19	**SalesTaxRate**

4. Create the validation rules for cells B5, B6, and B7 shown in Figure 8-36.

Figure 8-36 **Validation rules for cells B5, B6, and B7**

Cell	Settings	Input Message	Error Alert
B5	List Source (A12:A16)	Title: Type of Car Message: Click arrow to select the type of car.	Style: Stop Title: Invalid Type Message: Invalid Type. Use arrow to select Type.
B6	Whole number between 1 and 29	Title: Number of Days Rented Message: Enter a whole number between 1 and 29.	Style: Warning Title: Warning Days Rented Message: Invalid entry. Enter whole number between 1 and 29.
B7	Whole number between 1 and 5000	Title: Number of Miles Driven Message: Enter a whole number between 1 and 5000.	Style: Warning Title: Warning Miles Message: Invalid entry. Enter a value between 1 and 5000.

5. Enter formulas based on the following using the defined names you created in Step 3 to calculate the Rental Bill:
   - Cell F6 is equal to the value in cell B4.
   - Cell F7 is equal to the value in cell B5.
   - Cell F9 is equal to the value in cell B6.
   - Cell F10 is equal to the value in cell B7.
   - Cell H9 is equal to the charge per day, which depends on the type of car entered in cell B5 and the rate table. (*Hint*: Use the VLOOKUP function.)
   - Cell H10 is equal to the charge per mile, which depends on the type of car entered in cell B5 and the rate table. (*Hint*: Use the VLOOKUP function.)

- Cell F12 is equal to the rental amount, which equals the number of days rented multiplied by the charge per day plus the miles driven multiplied by the charge per mile.
- Cell F13 is equal to the sales tax rate multiplied by the rental amount.
- Cell F14 is equal to the rental amount plus the sales tax.
- Use the IFERROR function in cells H9, H10, F12, F13, and F14 to test for an error value. If an error value is found, display a blank cell; otherwise, use the appropriate formula.

6. Test the worksheet using the following data: **Myles Fast**, **Intermediate**, **4**, **450**.
7. Protect the worksheet so a user can enter data only in the range B4:B7. Do not use a password to enable protection. Save the workbook.

   Note: In the following steps, you'll create one macro. Save your workbook before recording the macro. That way, if you make a mistake when recording the macro, you can close the workbook without saving the changes, and then reopen the workbook and try again. Be sure to read the list of tasks before you begin recording them.
8. Remove worksheet protection from the Customer worksheet.
9. Add the Developer tab to the Ribbon.
10. Save the workbook, then create a macro named **PDFBill** with the shortcut key **Ctrl+p** and the description **Created 7/15/2013. Macro saves the customer bill as a PDF file.**
11. Record the following macro steps to create a PDF file that displays only the bill portion of the worksheet:
    a. Select the range E3:H15, and set the range as the print area.
    b. Open the Page Layout dialog box, and then center the output horizontally on the page and insert your name in the right section of the custom footer.
    c. Create a PDF file using the Save & Send tab in Backstage view with **CustomerBill** as the filename.
    d. Close Adobe Reader.
    e. Stop the Macro Recorder.
12. Edit the PDFBill macro to set cell A1 in the Customer worksheet as the active cell when the macro stops running. Insert the following command immediately before the End Sub command:

    ```
    Range("A1").Select
    ```
13. Create a macro button, assign the PDFBill macro to the button, and then change the default label to **Create PDF**. Place the macro button in the range J3:K4.
14. Enter the following data for a new customer: **Ed Elders**, **Full**, **3** days, **2000** miles.
15. Test the PDFBill macro button using the customer bill for Ed Elders.
16. In the Documentation worksheet, use the Paste List command to document the defined names and their locations.
17. Turn on worksheet protection for the Customer worksheet. Do not assign a password.
18. Turn on workbook protection. Do not assign a password.
19. Remove the Developer tab from the Ribbon.
20. Save the workbook as **Rentals with Macros** in the macro-enabled workbook format, and then close it.
21. Submit the finished workbook to your instructor, either in printed or electronic form, as requested.

Apply the macro skills you learned to produce monthly reports.

APPLY

Case Problem 1

Data File needed for this Case Problem: MediTrax.xlsx

MediTrax Controls MediTrax Controls, a U.S. subsidiary of a European multinational corporation, is testing an HVAC system designed to eliminate large temperature variances in its medical storage rooms. Lisa Goodman is a product tester for MediTrax. Each week, she records 25 temperature readings, five samples each day, in an Excel workbook. At the end of the month, Lisa sends the results to the parent company's Quality Department. Because many repetitive steps occur in developing the output requested by the parent company, Lisa asks you to create a macro to speed the creation of the report and reduce chances for error. Complete the following:

1. Open the **MediTrax** workbook located in the Excel8\Case1 folder included with your Data Files, and then save the workbook as **MediTrax Controls**.
2. In the Documentation sheet, enter your name and the date, and then review all of the worksheets in the workbook. Make Week 1 the active worksheet.
3. Create a macro to convert the worksheet to the one shown in Figure 8-37. Name the macro **ConvertData**, assign the shortcut key **Ctrl+d** to run the macro, and insert the macro description **Automate the weekly temperature reading report**. The macro performs the following steps:
   a. Formats the dates in the Date column using the date format type (3/14/2013).
   b. Formats the times in the Time column so they are displayed in 24-hour notation (format type 13:30).
   c. Types the title **Celsius** in cell D1.
   d. Converts the Fahrenheit temperatures to Celsius by entering the following formula in cell D2, and then copying the formula down the column: **=5/9*(C2–32)**.
   e. Formats the cells in column D using the Number format to 1 decimal place.
   f. Bolds the column heading and resizes the column to fully display Fahrenheit.
   g. Places the label **Average** in cell A27, computes the average Celsius temperature for the week in cell D27, and then bolds the row.
   h. Makes cell F1 the active cell.
   i. Stops recording the macro.
4. Switch to the Week 2 worksheet and test the macro using the shortcut key.
5. Edit the macro so that you end at cell A1 instead of ending at cell F1.
6. Switch to the Week 3 worksheet and test the revised macro using the shortcut key.
7. In the Week 1 worksheet, add the following comment to cell A1: **Use macro shortcut Ctrl+d to prepare a formatted report.**
8. Save the workbook as **MTC with Macros** as an Excel Macro-Enabled workbook, and then close it.
9. Submit the finished workbook to your instructor, either in printed or electronic form, as requested.

Figure 8-37 Worksheet formatted by a macro

	A	B	C	D
1	**Date**	**Time**	**Fahrenheit**	**Celsius**
2	4/1/2013	1:05	60.5	15.8
3	4/1/2013	2:02	64.5	18.1
4	4/1/2013	6:42	63.8	17.7
5	4/1/2013	14:45	61.1	16.2
6	4/1/2013	21:12	60.2	15.7
7	4/2/2013	1:33	61.2	16.2
8	4/2/2013	2:25	62.9	17.2
9	4/2/2013	6:12	64.4	18.0
10	4/2/2013	15:35	62.3	16.8
11	4/2/2013	20:32	61.9	16.6
12	4/3/2013	1:56	63.9	17.7
13	4/3/2013	2:51	60.6	15.9
14	4/3/2013	6:55	62.6	17.0
15	4/3/2013	14:30	64.5	18.1
16	4/3/2013	22:18	63.2	17.3
17	4/4/2013	1:32	62.6	17.0
18	4/4/2013	2:58	62.7	17.1
19	4/4/2013	7:05	62.4	16.9
20	4/4/2013	14:12	63.5	17.5
21	4/4/2013	21:45	62.6	17.0
22	4/5/2013	1:22	64.8	18.2
23	4/5/2013	2:18	62.4	16.9
24	4/5/2013	6:50	61.9	16.6
25	4/5/2013	13:59	63.4	17.4
26	4/5/2013	22:03	64.2	17.9
27	**Average**			**17.1**

Apply the skills you've learned to create a profit analysis workbook.

APPLY

Case Problem 2

Data File needed for this Case Problem: Popcorn.xlsx

Seattle Popcorn Seattle Popcorn is a small company located in Tacoma, Washington, that produces gourmet popcorn distributed in the Northwest. Steve Wilkes has developed a workbook that will allow him to perform a profit analysis for the company. Using this workbook, he wants to create formulas to determine the break-even point for the company—the sales volume needed so that revenues will match the anticipated monthly expenses. Three factors determine the break-even point: the sales price of each unit of Seattle Popcorn, the variable manufacturing cost to the company for each unit, and the fixed expenses (salaries, rent, insurance, and so on) that the company must pay each month. Steve wants to be able to explore a range of possible values for each of these factors, as follows:

- The sales price of each unit of Seattle Popcorn can vary from $5 to $15 (in whole numbers).
- The variable manufacturing cost of each unit can vary from $5 to $15 (in whole numbers).
- The fixed monthly expense for the company can vary from $15,000 to $30,000 (in whole numbers).

Complete the following:

1. Open the **Popcorn** workbook located in the Excel8\Case2 folder included with your Data Files, and then save the workbook as **Seattle Popcorn**. In the Documentation sheet, enter your name and the date.
2. Switch to the Profit Analysis worksheet, and then define names for cells, as follows:
   cell C15: **PricePerUnit**
   cell C16: **CostPerUnit**
   cell C17: **MonthlyExpenses**
3. In the range H3:H43, enter a formula using defined names to calculate the revenue, which is determined by the units sold multiplied by the price per unit.
4. In the range I3:I43, enter a formula using defined names to calculate the expenses, which are determined by the units sold multiplied by the cost per unit plus the fixed monthly expense.
5. In cell C18, enter a formula to calculate the break-even point, which is determined by the fixed monthly expense divided by the difference between the price per unit and the number of units. Use the IFERROR function to display a blank cell instead of an error value.
6. In cell C19, enter a formula to calculate the revenue at the break-even point, which is determined by the break-even point multiplied by the sales price per unit. Use the IFERROR function to display a blank cell instead of an error value.
7. Create the validation rules for cells C15, C16, and C17, as shown in Figure 8-38.

Figure 8-38 **Validation rules for cells C15, C16, and C17**

Cell	Settings	Input Message	Error Alert
C15	Whole numbers between 5 and 15	Title: Price per Unit Message: *Enter an appropriate message.*	Style: Warning Title: Invalid Price per Unit Message: *Enter an appropriate message.*
C16	Whole numbers between 5 and 15	Title: Cost per Unit Message: *Enter an appropriate message.*	Style: Warning Title: Invalid Cost per Unit Message: *Enter an appropriate message.*
C17	Whole numbers between 15000 and 30000	Title: Monthly Expenses Message: *Enter an appropriate message.*	Style: Warning Title: Invalid Monthly Expense Message: *Enter an appropriate message.*

8. Protect the worksheet so the user can enter data only in cells C15, C16, and C17. Everything else in the worksheet should remain locked.
9. Enter the following values in the worksheet to determine how many units Seattle Popcorn must sell each month in order to break even:
   - Sales Price per Unit = **$13**
   - Manufacturing Cost per Unit = **$10**
   - Fixed Monthly Expense = **$30,000**
10. In cell C16, add the following comment: **Call Joe Heller in Cost Accounting for unit cost data.**

    Note: In the following steps, you'll create a macro. Save your workbook before recording the macro. That way, if you make a mistake while recording the macro, you can close the workbook without saving the changes, and then reopen the workbook and try again. Also, read the list of tasks before you begin recording them.
11. Save the workbook.
12. Create a macro named **PrintChart** with the shortcut key **Ctrl+a** and an appropriate macro description that performs the following tasks:
    a. Set the print area to include the chart and input/output area (range A1:E20).
    b. Set the page layout to landscape orientation, centered horizontally on the page, with the text **Break-even Analysis** in the center section of the header, and your name in the right section of the footer.
    c. Print the chart and input area.
    d. Make cell A1 the active cell.
    e. Stop recording the macro.
13. Test the PrintChart macro by pressing the Ctrl+a keys. If the macro doesn't work, close the workbook without saving your changes, reopen the workbook, and record the macro again.
14. Edit the PrintChart macro, replacing the line `ActiveWindow.SelectedSheets.PrintOut Copies:=1, Collate:=True, IgnorePrintAreas:=False` with **`ActiveSheet.PrintPreview`**. (*Hint*: The line to edit is four lines above the end of the macro.)
15. Create a button in the range A22:B23, assign the PrintChart macro to the button, and change the default label to a more descriptive one.
16. Run the PrintChart macro to test the button and the revised macro.
17. Save the workbook as a macro-enabled workbook using the name **SP with Macros**, and then close it.
18. Submit the finished workbook to your instructor, either in printed or electronic form, as requested.

Go beyond what you learned to design an Excel workbook to use as a data entry form.

CHALLENGE

Case Problem 3

Data File needed for this Case Problem: Cookin.xlsx

Cookin Good Cookin Good sells specialized home cooking products. The company employs individuals to organize "Cookin Good Parties" at which the company's products are sold. Cleo Benard is responsible for entering sales data from various Cookin Good Parties. She wants to design an Excel workbook to act as a data entry form. She has already created the workbook, but she needs your help with setting up data validation rules, creating a table lookup, and writing the macros to enter the data. Complete the following:

1. Open the **Cookin** workbook located in the Excel8\Case3 folder included with your Data Files, and then save the workbook as **Cookin Good**. In the Documentation sheet, enter your name and the date.
2. Go to the Sales Form worksheet. Create appropriate defined names for each cell in the range C3:C8. Assign the name **ProductInfo** to the range E4:G15.
3. In the Sales Form worksheet, create the following validation rules:
   a. The criteria allows only one of five regions (represented by the numbers 1, 2, 3, 4, and 5) to be entered in cell C3. Enter an appropriate input message and error alert.
   b. The criteria provides the list of 12 products (found in range E4:E15) in cell C4. Enter an appropriate input message and error alert.
   c. The criteria allows only whole numbers greater than 0 to be entered as the number of units sold in cell C7. Enter an appropriate input message and error alert.
4. In cells C5 and C6, enter a VLOOKUP function that automatically enters the product name and price into the sales form when the ProductID is entered. (*Hint*: Cells should be blank if an error value appears in a cell.)
5. In cell C8, enter a formula that automatically calculates the total sale for the order, which is determined by the number of units sold multiplied by the price of the product. Use the IFERROR function to display a blank cell if an error value occurs during the calculation of Total Sale.
6. Prevent users from entering data into any cell in the Sales Form worksheet other than cells C3, C4, and C7, and then protect the Sales Form worksheet.
7. Test the data entry form by entering the following new record: Region = **1**, Product ID = **CW**, Units Sold = **8**.
8. Save the workbook, and then create a macro named **AddData** with the shortcut key **Ctrl+d** that performs the following tasks:
   a. In the Sales Form worksheet, copy the values in the range C3:C8. (*Hint*: You'll paste later in the macro.)
   b. Switch from the Sales Form worksheet to the Sales Record worksheet. Click cell A1.
   c. Turn on Relative References.
   d. Use the End+↓ keys to locate the last used row in the first column. Then, press the ↓ key to move to the next row in the first column.
   e. Turn off Relative References.

   EXPLORE

   f. Paste the copied values from Step a into the blank row. (*Hint*: Use the Paste button arrow, and then click Paste Transpose button.)
   g. Switch to the Sales Table worksheet.
   h. Click inside the PivotTable and refresh the contents of the PivotTable to include the new data.
   i. Switch to the Sales Form worksheet and clear the values in cells C3, C4, and C7.

j. Make C3 the active cell.
k. Stop recording the macro.

9. Create a button in the range C11:C12 on the Sales Form worksheet and assign the AddData macro to the button. Change the button label to **Transfer Sales Data**.
10. Test the data entry form and AddData macro by entering the following new records:

Region	Product ID	Units Sold
3	**HR**	**4**
4	**OEG**	**2**

11. Create a macro named **ViewTable** with the **Ctrl+t** shortcut key that displays the contents of the Sales Table worksheet.
12. Create a macro named **ViewChart** with the **Ctrl+c** shortcut key that displays the Sales Chart worksheet.
13. Create a macro named **ViewForm** with the **Ctrl+f** shortcut key that displays the Sales Form worksheet. Test each macro using its shortcut keys.
14. In the Documentation worksheet, create three macro buttons below row 13 to view the Sales Table worksheet (Step 11), the Sales Chart worksheet (Step 12), and the Sales Form worksheet (Step 13). Assign the appropriate macro to each button, and change the labels on the buttons to be more descriptive.

EXPLORE

15. The Sales Table worksheet displays the total product sales in each region. Change the PivotTable to show the values in the cells as percentages of the Column Total. (*Hint*: On the Options tab, in the Calculations group, click the Show Values As button, and then click % of Column Total. You can return the original value by clicking No calculation.)

EXPLORE

16. Create two macros. The first displays the PivotTable as percentages of column totals (Step 15). Name this macro **ShowAsPercent**. The second macro displays the PivotTable as numbers (values shown as No Calculation). Name this macro **ShowAsNumber**.
17. Edit the ShowAsPercent macro to display the results with a percent style by adding the following three commands immediately before the End Sub statement:

```
Range("C5:H17").Select
Selection.Style = "Percent"
Range("A1").Select
```

18. Create two macro buttons below the PivotTable in the Sales Table worksheet to run each macro. Assign a macro to each button, and then change the button labels to be more descriptive.
19. Save the workbook as **CG with Macros**, and then close it. Submit the finished workbook to your instructor, either in printed or electronic form, as requested.

Define names, apply worksheet protection, and create macros to prepare an invoice.

CREATE

Case Problem 4

There are no Data Files needed for this Case Problem.

Alia's Senior Living Supplies Alia Moh left her job at a Chicago hospital to establish Alia's Senior Living Supplies, which provides products and services designed for seniors. Products offered by Alia on her Web site range from safety step ladders, doorknob grippers, and skid resistant surfaces to wheelchair ponchos. Alia has built up a large, steady client base—mainly seniors who find these uniquely designed products a great help in their daily lives. To ensure timely receipt of payments, Alia wants a billing/invoicing system to expedite that work. Figure 8-39 shows the finished application she has asked you to create.

Figure 8-39 Completed Invoice worksheet

	A	B	C	D	E	F	G	H	I	J	K	L
1												
2			Alia's Senior Living Supplies									
3			2256 Central Avenue								Print Invoice	
4			Arlington, Illinois 60005									
5			(555) 555-1212								Clear Inputs	
6												
7							February 15, 2013					
8												
9			Sold to:									
10			Mark Kipper									
11			123 Central Road									
12			Arlington	IL	60005							
13												
14												
15			Item			Qty	Per Unit	Total				
16			Economy Patient Gowns			4	$ 6.95	$ 27.80				
17			Doorknob Gripper			5	$ 4.95	$ 24.75				
18			Giant TV Remote			3	$ 34.95	$ 104.85				
19												
20												
36												
37							Subtotal	$ 157.40				
38							Sales Tax	$ 11.81				
39							Shipping	$ 16.00				
40							**Total Due**	**$ 185.21**				
41												

Complete the following:

1. Open a new workbook, and then save it as **AliaSupplies** in the Excel8\Case4 folder included with your Data Files.
2. Rename the first sheet as **Documentation**, and then enter the company name, your name, the date, and a purpose statement. Rename the second sheet as **Invoice**. Rename the third sheet as **Product Pricing and Shipping**.
3. In the Product Pricing and Shipping worksheet, enter the data for product pricing and shipping costs shown in Figure 8-40.

Figure 8-40 Product pricing and shipping costs

	A	B	C	D	E	F
1	**Product Pricing**					
2				**Subtotal**	**Shipping Cost**	
3	Adjustable Home Bed Rail	89.95		0	6.00	
4	Bed Cane	81.95		55	9.50	
5	Doorknob Gripper	4.95		100	12.50	
6	Easy Grip Utensils	32.95		150	16.00	
7	Economy Patient Gowns	6.95				
8	Full-Page Magnifier	4.99				
9	Giant TV Remote	34.95				
10	Inflatable Shampoo Basin	39.95				
11	Jar Opener	5.95				
12	Lamp Switch Enlarger	4.95				
13	Medication Dispenser	135.95				
14	No Rinse Shampoo	34.95				
15	Tilting Overbed Table	114.95				
16	Trolley Walker	139.95				
17	Wheelchair Poncho	51.95				

4. Complete the following to build the invoice shown in Figure 8-39 on the Invoice worksheet. Use defined names and structured referencing to assist in creating formulas. (*Hint*: Review the steps below before you begin to enter the tables, labels, and formulas to build the invoice.)
   a. Adjust the column widths so column A is 2.57; column B is 6.14; column C is 20.86; column D is 6.14; column E is 13.57; column F is 8.71; column G is 12.71; column H is 13.71; column I is 3.43; and column J is 2.29.
   b. Insert labels with the company's name and contact information in rows 2 through 5, and then merge and center the ranges C2:H2, C3:H3, C4:H4, and C5:H5.
   c. Enter the current date in cell G7, merge and center G7:H7, and then format the cell with bold.
   d. Insert comments as a reminder as to what data should be entered in cells C10, C11, C12, D12, and E12.
   e. Enter the column headers in row 15.
   f. Create an Excel table in the range C15:H35. Remove the filter arrows.
   g. Enter the appropriate labels in the range G37:G40, and then format the range G40:H40 as bold.
   h. Use defined names for Product Pricing and Shipping Cost data.
   i. In the Item column (the range C16:C35), create a list of the different items, which are listed in the Product Pricing table in the Product Pricing and Shipping worksheet, that users might order. (*Hint*: Use the data validation list feature.)
   j. In the Qty column, create an error alert warning message that appears if the quantity entered is more than 50.
   k. In the Per Unit column, enter a formula that uses a table lookup in the Product Pricing table based on the value selected in the Item column. Use the IFERROR function to display a blank cell instead of the error value.
   l. In the Total column, enter a formula to calculate the total charge for that row: Qty × Per Unit. Use the IFERROR function to display a blank cell instead of the error value. Format the column appropriately.
   m. In the Subtotal cell (cell H37), enter a formula to sum the Total column. Format this cell appropriately.
   n. In the Sales Tax cell, enter a formula to calculate 7.5% of the subtotal in cell H37 if the customer's state is IL (cell D12); otherwise, enter 0 for the sales tax. Format this cell appropriately.
   o. In the Shipping cell, enter a formula that does the following: If the subtotal is $200 or more, the shipping cost is 0; otherwise, look up the shipping cost (from the Shipping Cost table in the Product Pricing and Shipping worksheet) based on the subtotal in cell H37. Format this cell appropriately.
   p. In the Total Due cell, calculate the invoice total by entering a formula that adds the values in the Subtotal, Sales Tax, and Shipping cells. Format this cell appropriately.
5. Protect the worksheet so a user can enter data in cells C10, C11, C12, D12, and E12; items in the range C16:C35; and quantities in the range F16:F35 but not in any other cells. Do not use a password.
6. Save the workbook.
7. Create a macro named **PrintInvoice** that prints the invoice. Assign the **Ctrl+p** shortcut key and type a macro description as you begin recording this macro. Center the worksheet horizontally and scale it to fit on one printed page. The heading has the label **I N V O I C E** in the center of the page. Create a macro button on the Invoice worksheet in column K, assign the PrintInvoice macro to the button, and then enter a descriptive label for the button.

8. Create a macro named **ClearInputs** that deletes the values from cells C10, C11, C12, D12, and E12; items in the range C16:C35; and quantities in the range F16:F35. Assign the **Ctrl+c** shortcut key and type a macro description as you begin recording this macro. Create a macro button on the Invoice worksheet in column K, assign the ClearInputs macro to the button, and then enter a descriptive label for the button. (*Hint*: Use the Delete key to clear a value from a cell.)
9. In the Documentation worksheet, paste a list of the defined names with their locations, and below this entry type a list of the macro names and their shortcut keys.
10. Test the worksheet using the data in Figure 8-39.
11. Use the PrintInvoice macro button to print the bill for the data you entered in Step 10, and then use the ClearInputs macro button to remove the input data.
12. Save the workbook as **Alia with Macros**, and then close it. Submit the finished workbook to your instructor, either in printed or electronic form, as requested.

ASSESS

SAM: Skills Assessment Manager

For current SAM information, including versions and content details, visit SAM Central (http://samcentral.course.com). If you have a SAM user profile, you may have access to hands-on instruction, practice, and assessment of the skills covered in this tutorial. Since various versions of SAM are supported throughout the life of this text, check with your instructor for the correct instructions and URL/Web site for accessing assignments.

ENDING DATA FILES

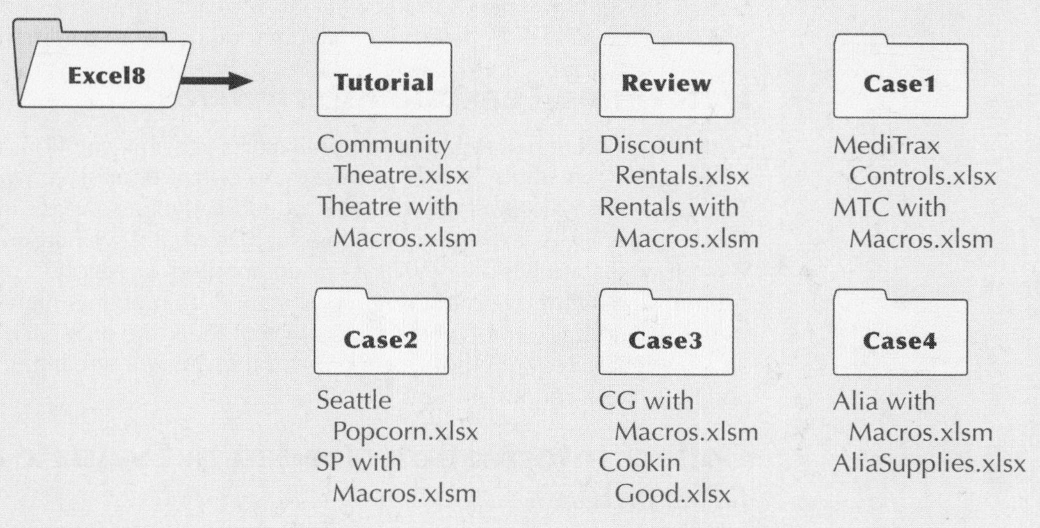

ProSkills

Problem Solving

Solving a Problem Using an Excel Table

Problem solving is the ability to identify a gap between an existing state and a desired state of being. A problem can be a one-time issue such as which car to purchase or a process-oriented dilemma such as how to track orders. The process of solving a problem follows a logical progression that consists of (1) recognizing and defining the problem, (2) determining feasible courses of action, (3) collecting information about those actions, and (4) evaluating the merits and drawbacks of each one in order to make a choice. Problem solving leads to decision making, and enables you to evaluate different courses of action and make an informed decision or select a good solution.

Recognize and Define the Problem

A problem is the gap between a desired state and reality. In order to recognize and define a problem, ask questions to determine the real issue and identify your ultimate goal. For example, ask such questions as: Why do I think there is a problem? Where is it occurring? When and how frequently is it occurring? What is causing the problem? Who is involved? Why is it occurring? The answers to these questions help you define the problem and determine what information you need to solve the problem. For instance, a company might want to make sure that employee benefits and overtime payments don't exceed a certain amount, and needs to track the cost of each employee's benefit package, salary, and overtime as well as determine that the total costs fall within the intended levels.

Determine Feasible Alternatives

With the problem defined, you can brainstorm possible solutions by collecting as many ideas as possible about how to correct the problem or achieve your goal. Write them all down. Don't discount any ideas as too radical, expensive, or impossible to achieve. Think creatively. Ask what-if questions, such as what if we had unlimited resources? What if we had new skills? What if our competitors or suppliers or customers acted in a certain way? What if I do nothing? For instance, a company might want to create a consistent way to track employee data, collecting the same data each time, categorizing the data by department or employee type, and then ensuring that paid benefits and overtime don't exceed a certain amount.

Collect Information Needed to Evaluate the Alternatives

Data is crucial to problem solving. Collect data and information related to each possible solution or alternative. This information can include data expressed as currency or numbers, as well as data that cannot be measured numerically. All collected data should be organized in a way that provides information for effective decision-making and follow-up. For example, a business needs to collect data that enables it to write checks to employees, prepare reports about overtime, report payroll taxes to government agencies, provide premiums to health insurance companies, track Social Security payments, and so on. This requires an organized system to capture the appropriate data such as employee IDs, employee names, hours worked each day, salary or hourly rate, and insurance premium. You'll likely start to see relationships between the collected information that can provide insights into the feasibility of the possible solutions.

ProSkills

Evaluate and Choose an Alternative

Document both the benefits and costs of all alternatives, whether numerical (cost savings) or other (employee morale). Spreadsheet software often helps problem solvers track and quantify merits and drawbacks. Consider the resources required—financial, human, equipment, and so on. Are they affordable? Is there enough time to implement the different solutions? What risks are associated with an alternative? What consequences would result if the solution didn't work? The best choice is to go with the solution that offers the greatest reward for the least amount of risk. In some cases, the solution may require developing a "Plan B" to fall back on in case the chosen solution fails to solve the problem. For instance, when collecting payroll data, it may become apparent that insurance premiums are higher percentage of payroll than previously thought, which requires further investigation and an alternative solution.

Don't try to select a solution that addresses every aspect of a problem, especially if it is complex. Solutions are rarely perfect. Instead, consider the overall effect each alternative may have. Will the resulting change generate positive results while solving the problem? Will the chosen alternative resolve the problem long-term? What is realistic, given the merits and drawbacks identified?

PROSKILLS

Develop an Excel Table

In daily life, you solve all sorts of problems, such as which car purchase makes the most economic sense when comparing purchase price, mileage, and maintenance, or which software package will help your biking club manage its funds, plan road trips, and keep memberships up-to-date. To solve these and other problems, you need to collect data that tracks the current situation, determine your ultimate goal, and then follow a logical progression to the best solution. Developing an Excel table can help you to track the data you need to solve such problems.

In this exercise, you need to select an activity you participate in or an organization you belong to and identify a one-time or process-oriented problem that needs to be solved. Then, create a worksheet and develop an Excel table to track relevant data and create a solution to the problem, using the Excel skills and features presented in Tutorials 5 through 8.

Note: Please be sure *not* to include any personal information of a sensitive nature in any worksheets you create to submit to your instructor. Later, you can update the worksheets with such information for your own personal use.

1. Identify a problem to solve. This can be a one-time problem, such as a car purchase, or a process-oriented problem, such as tracking membership data for a club you belong to. Determine feasible alternatives to solve the problem, and then collect the data you need to evaluate these alternatives.
2. Plan the organization of your workbook and the Excel table you will develop based on how you will use the data. Consider the outputs you want to create, and the fields needed to produce those outputs. Decide what each record represents (such as data on a participant) and then identify the fields and field names (such as last name, first name, birth date, as so on) within each record. What calculations will you need to perform? How do you want to format the information?

3. Create a Documentation worksheet that includes your name, the date, and the purpose of your workbook. Format it appropriately.
4. Create an Excel table to track the data needed to solve the problem you identified. Enter an appropriate table name and column headers to track the data needed to create a solution to the problem. Add one or more calculated columns to the table to perform calculations on the data that you will use to solve the problem.
5. Improve the appearance of the table using appropriate formatting.
6. Apply validity checks to improve the accuracy of data entry.
7. Add records to the table.
8. Apply conditional formatting to at least one column in the table to highlight some aspect of the data that will help you evaluate and solve the problem.
9. Add a comment to the column with the conditional formatting to explain what the conditional formatting shows and how it will help you to evaluate and solve the problem.
10. Insert a Total row in the table and make appropriate summary calculations that you can use to evaluate and solve the problem.
11. Divide the table into two horizontal panes—one for the data and the second for the Total row.
12. Sort the data in a logical way.
13. Use a filter to answer a question about the data that you can use to evaluate and solve the problem.
14. Create a PivotTable and a PivotChart to analyze the data. Format, filter, and sort the PivotTable appropriately.
15. In a Word document, explain the problem you solved, identify the alternatives you considered, document the data you collected to evaluate the alternatives, and then describe the results of your analysis. Include the PivotChart in the Word document.
16. In an appropriate worksheet, insert a hyperlink that links to the Word document you created.
17. If you have a Windows Live ID, save the workbook to the My Documents folder on your SkyDrive. Modify the workbook by editing cell content. Save the workbook to your computer using a new filename.
18. Create at least one macro to automate a repetitive task you need to perform in the workbook, such as printing or saving a worksheet as a PDF file.
19. Prepare your workbook for printing. Include headers and footers that indicate the filename of your workbook, the workbook's author, and the date on which the report is printed. If a printed worksheet will extend across several pages, repeat appropriate print titles across all of the pages and include page numbers and the total number of pages on each printed page.
20. Save the workbook. Submit the completed files to your instructor in printed or electronic form, as requested.

TUTORIAL 9

Working with Financial Tools and Functions

Developing a Financial Analysis

OBJECTIVES

Session 9.1
- Work with financial functions to analyze loans and investments
- Create an amortization schedule
- Calculate a conditional sum

Session 9.2
- Interpolate and extrapolate a series of values
- Calculate a depreciation schedule

Session 9.3
- Determine a payback period
- Calculate a net present value
- Calculate an internal rate of return
- Trace a formula error to its source

Case | *Bent Cycling*

Diane Cross is the owner of Bent Cycling, a small company in Longmont, Colorado, that designs and manufactures custom-made recumbent bicycles. Recumbents or "bents" are bicycles on which the rider sits in a reclined position with the pedals placed forward rather than below the feet. Interest in recumbents has increased in the past few years as more cyclists discover that recumbent bikes put less strain on the lower back than traditional bikes. This interest has carried over to Diane's company. By properly marketing Bent Cycling's products, market analysts believe her company could double its annual revenue in five years. However, that would entail completely rebuilding the company's workshop and design facility, which requires a major investment of time and money and poses some financial risk. Diane wants to use Excel to explore the different financing options available to her and to determine the profitability of such a venture. Excel supports a wealth of financial functions for just this kind of task.

STARTING DATA FILES

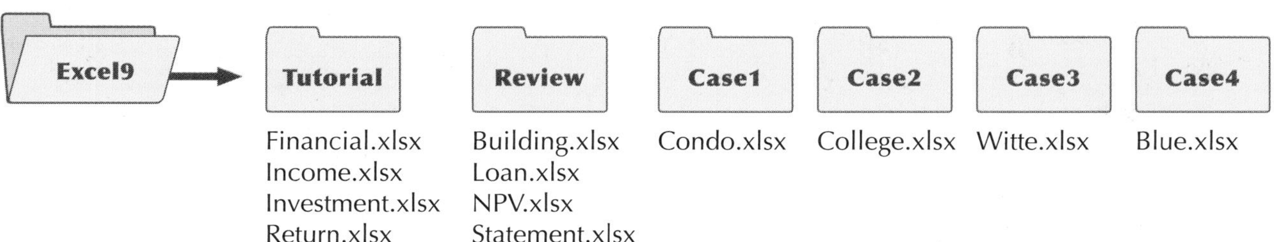

SESSION 9.1 VISUAL OVERVIEW

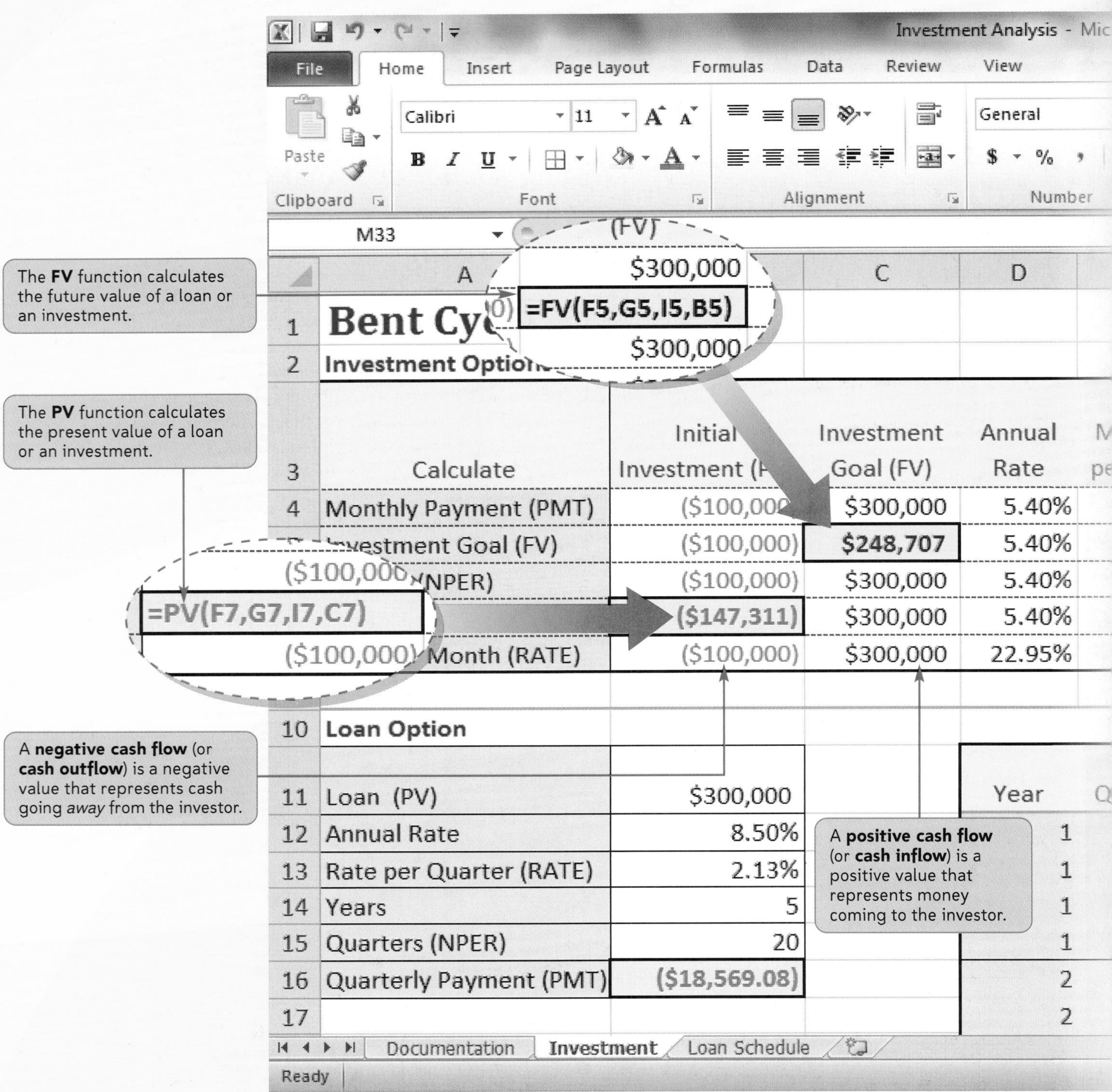

LOAN AND INVESTMENT FUNCTIONS

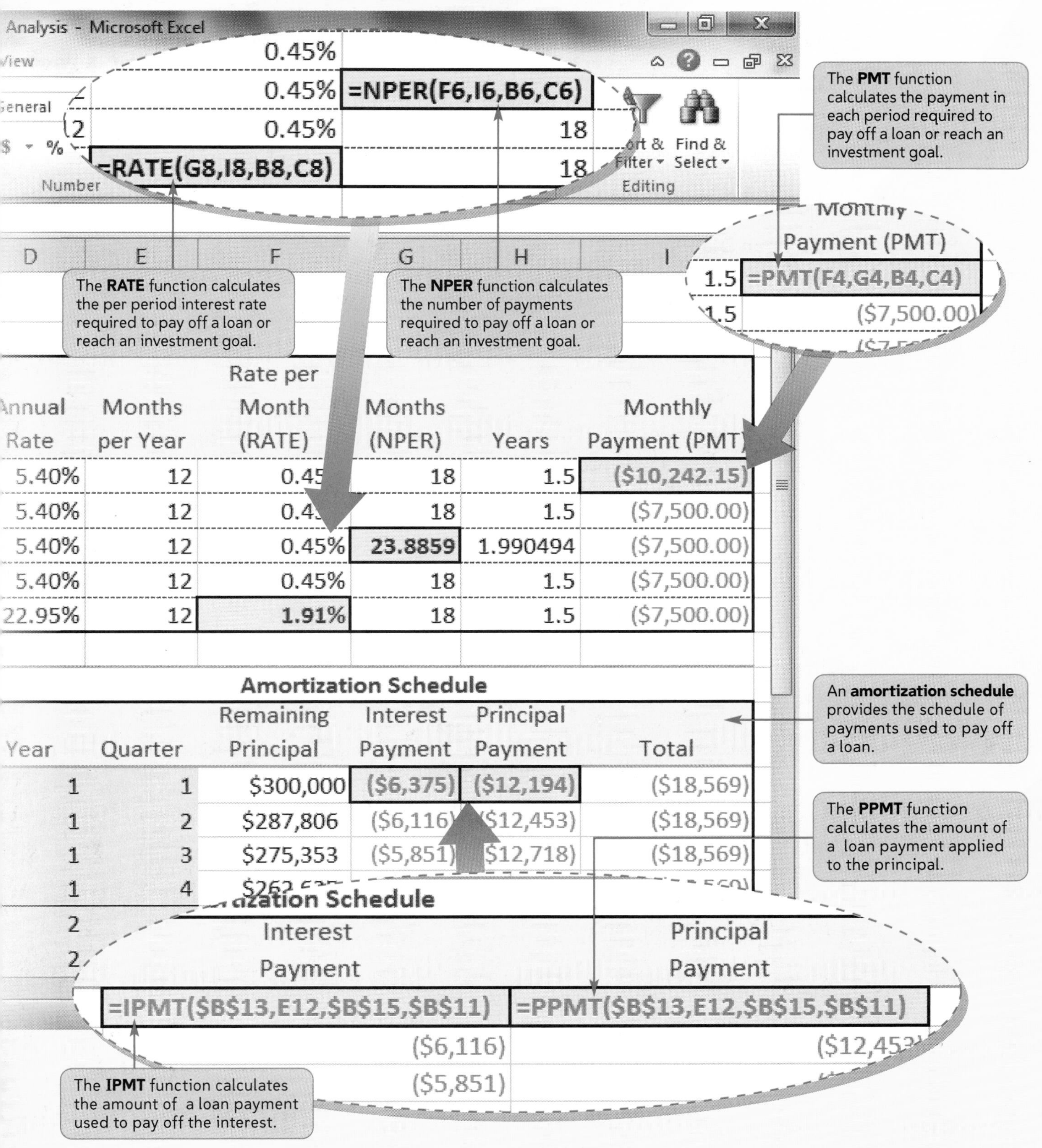

Evaluating Investment Options

Diane has been meeting with an industrial architect for the past few months to design Bent Cycling's new workshop and design facility. She wants the workshop to accommodate the increased demand for the company's cycles and incorporate the latest manufacturing techniques to deliver a quality product for the consumer. The new workshop will cost $300,000. Her business does not have that much available in ready capital, so Diane will have to look for other sources to finance the company's expansion.

Diane asks you to create a financial analysis of the situation. She wants to know what options are available to finance the expansion and how much each option will cost. Diane has already created Excel workbooks containing many of the worksheets you'll need to do the analysis.

To open Diane's workbook:

1. Open the **Investment** workbook located in the Excel9\Tutorial folder included with your Data Files, and then save the workbook as **Investment Analysis** in the same folder.
2. In the Documentation worksheet, enter your name in cell B3 and the date in cell B4.
3. Switch to the **Investment** worksheet.

Bent Cycling has $100,000 in cash reserves. Because this amount is not large enough to finance the proposed expansion, Diane can (1) continue to save money until her company can afford to build the new workshop and design facility, or (2) borrow the money and start building immediately. Diane has always financed her company without going deeply into debt. So, she first wants to examine whether the company can save enough money from its cash receipts to finance the proposed expansion in the near future. To answer that question, you'll use the FV, PV, RATE, NPER, and PMT functions to calculate the impact of investing money into interest-bearing accounts. In each case, the financial function returns the value of one financial variable based upon the values of the other four.

REFERENCE

Working with Loans and Investments

- To calculate the present value of a loan or an investment, use the PV function.
- To calculate the future value of a loan or an investment, use the FV function.
- To calculate the size of the monthly or quarterly payments required to pay off a loan or meet an investment goal, use the PMT function.
- To calculate the number of monthly or quarterly payments required to pay off a loan or meet an investment goal, use the NPER function.
- To calculate the interest on a loan or an investment, use the RATE function.

Calculating a Periodic Payment with the PMT Function

Currently, the $100,000 is invested in a money market fund that pays 5.4% annual interest, compounded monthly. Diane wants to know how much the company would have to add to this fund each month so that the value of the fund will reach $300,000 18 months from now. In other words, Diane wants to know the periodic payment, or PMT value, needed to reach her goal. To perform this calculation, you use the PMT function

```
=PMT(rate, nper, pv [, fv=0] [, type=0])
```

where *rate* is the interest rate per period, *nper* is the number of payment periods, *pv* is the present value of the investment or loan, and *fv* is the future value of the loan or investment. The *fv* argument is optional. If you don't include an *fv* value, Excel assumes a future value of 0. The PMT function, like the other Excel financial functions dealing with loans and investments, also includes an optional type argument. The type argument specifies whether payments are made at the end of each period (type=0) or at the beginning (*type*=1). The default is *type*=0, which is what you'll use with the calculations involving Diane's investments in the money market fund.

The interest rate and the payment period must use the same time unit. For example, if the interest rate is compounded monthly, the payment period must also be in months. Because the money market fund Diane uses has an annual interest rate of 5.4%, compounded monthly, you need to convert the annual interest rate to a monthly rate, which is 1/12 of 5.4%, or 0.45%. Diane plans to invest the money for 18 months, so the value of the *nper* argument is 18 because each month represents a payment period.

The PMT function, like the other four Excel financial functions, can be used with either investments or loans. The difference between a loan and an investment is based on the direction of the cash flow. When using the PMT function, the loan amount is treated as a positive cash value because it represents a payment to the company and the periodic payments used to pay off the loan are negative cash values. It's just the opposite with investments. The initial investment is treated as a negative cash value, and the periodic returns from the investment are positive cash values.

For example, consider Diane's plan to invest in a money market fund. Bent Cycling starts out with $100,000, which Diane takes *out of* the company and places into an investment fund. This represents a negative cash flow because money is leaving the company. After 18 months supplemented by additional monthly payments, Diane takes money out of the fund and moves it back *into* the company to pay for the expansion. This represents a positive cash flow because now the money is flowing back into Bent Cycling.

Cash flow, whether positive or negative, has nothing to do with who owns the money. Bent Cycling still owns the $100,000 it invests even if the money is transferred into an investment account. Cash flow is solely concerned with the direction of the money as it moves into and out of the company.

When applied to the PMT function, the value of the *pv* (present value) argument for Diane's investment is –$100,000 to indicate a negative cash flow as the money leaves the company to go into the money market fund. At the end of 18 months, Diane wants to retrieve $300,000 from the fund and put it back into the company, so the value of the *fv* (future value) argument is $300,000 to indicate a positive cash flow.

TIP

The financial functions automatically format calculated values as currency; negative cash flows appear in a red font within parentheses.

Based on this information, the PMT function to calculate the monthly payment Bent Cycling must make to increase the value of the money market fund from $100,000 to $300,000 in 18 months is:

```
=PMT(5.4%/12, 18, -100000, 300000)
```

This formula returns the currency value –$10,242.15, indicating that the company must invest a little more than $10,000 each month to meet its savings goal of $300,000 after 18 months. The value returned by the PMT function is negative in this case because it represents the amount of money flowing out of the company into the fund each month.

It is good practice to reference worksheet cells in which the values you will use in the function are entered so that the values are easily visible. You'll enter the PMT function to calculate the monthly payment the company must make to reach its savings goal. Diane has already formatted the worksheet.

To calculate the monthly payment to the investment fund:

1. In cell A5, enter **Monthly Payment (PMT)**.
2. In cell B5, enter **–100,000**, which is the amount of the initial investment. You enter a negative value to indicate a cash outflow from the company into the money market fund. The value appears as ($100,000) in a red font, representing a negative cash flow, because Diane already formatted the worksheet.

3. In cell C5, enter **300,000** for the investment goal, which is what you want the future value of the investment to be. The value appears as $300,000 to indicate a positive cash flow.
4. In cell D5, enter **5.4%** for the annual interest rate.
5. In cell E5, enter **12** for the number of months needed to convert the annual interest rate into a monthly interest rate.
6. In cell F5, enter the formula **=D5/E5** to calculate the interest rate per month, and then format the value as a percentage to two decimal places.
7. In cell G5, enter **18**, which is the number of months that Diane will transfer money into the fund.
8. In cell H5, enter the formula **=G5/E5** to calculate the number of years that the money will be invested.
9. In cell I5, enter the formula **=PMT(F5,G5,B5,C5)** to calculate the monthly payment (PMT). The formula returns the negative currency value ($10,242.15).
10. Select cell **I5**, and then apply the **Output** cell style. See Figure 9-1.

TIP

You can insert the PMT function and view its arguments and meanings using the Insert Function and Function Arguments dialog boxes by clicking the Insert Function button on the formula bar.

Figure 9-1 Monthly payment to reach the investment goal

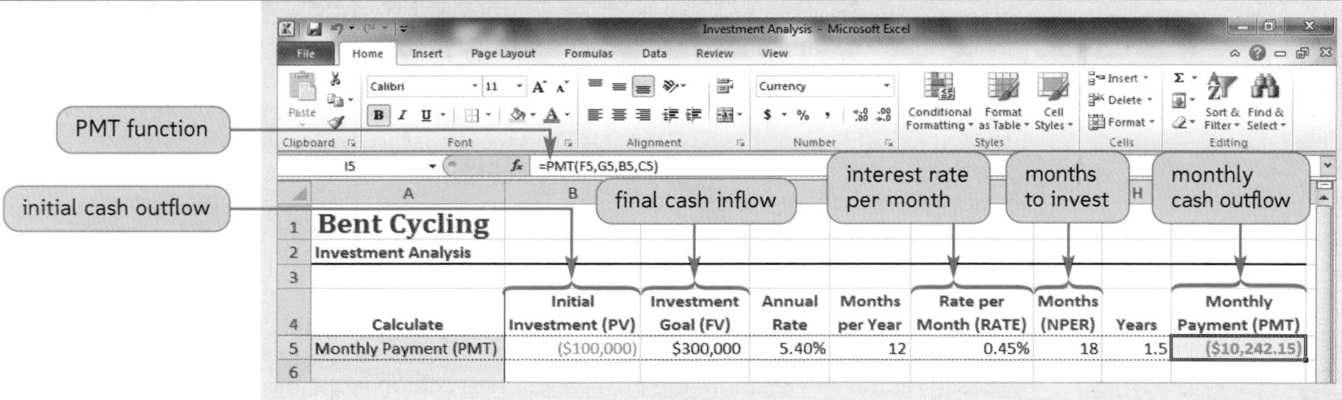

Calculating a Future Value with the FV Function

Bent Cycling needs to divert a little more than $10,000 per month from cash receipts into the investment fund to reach a savings goal of $300,000 in the next year and a half. However, Bent Cycling can afford to invest at most $7,500 each month. Diane wants to know how much the fund would be worth in 18 months if the company puts $7,500 a month into the fund. To calculate the fund's future value, you use the FV function

```
=FV(rate, nper, pmt [, pv=0] [, type=0])
```

where the *rate*, *nper*, *pmt*, and *type* arguments still represent the interest rate per period, the number of payments, the payment each period, and when the payment is due (beginning or end of the period). The pv argument is optional and represents the present value of the investment, which is assumed to be zero if no value is specified. The type argument is also optional and, as with the PMT function, indicates when payments are made into the loan or investment. For the Bent Cycling investment, these function argument values are:

```
=FV(5.4%/12, 18, -7500, -100000)
```

As with the PMT function, the interest rate is 5.4% divided by 12, the total number of payments is 18, the amount invested each month is –7,500 (a negative cash flow), and the present value is –100,000, also a negative cash flow because it represents money that has already been invested by the company.

You'll use the FV function to calculate the future value of the money market fund under this investment strategy.

To calculate the future value of the investment:

1. In cell A6, enter **Investment Goal (FV)**.
2. Copy the initial investment value in cell **B5** to cell **B6**.
3. Copy the rate and payment period formulas and values in the range **D5:H5** to the range **D6:H6**.
4. In cell I6, enter **–7,500** as the present value, which is the monthly payment Bent Cycling can afford.
5. In cell C6, enter the formula **=FV(F6,G6,I6,B6)**. The formula returns the value $248,707, which is the value of the fund after 18 months (cell G6) of depositing $7,500 each month (cell I6) at a 0.45% monthly interest rate (cell F6). The value is positive, indicating a positive cash flow from the fund back to the company.
6. Format cell C6 using the **Output** cell style. See Figure 9-2.

Figure 9-2 **Future value of the investment**

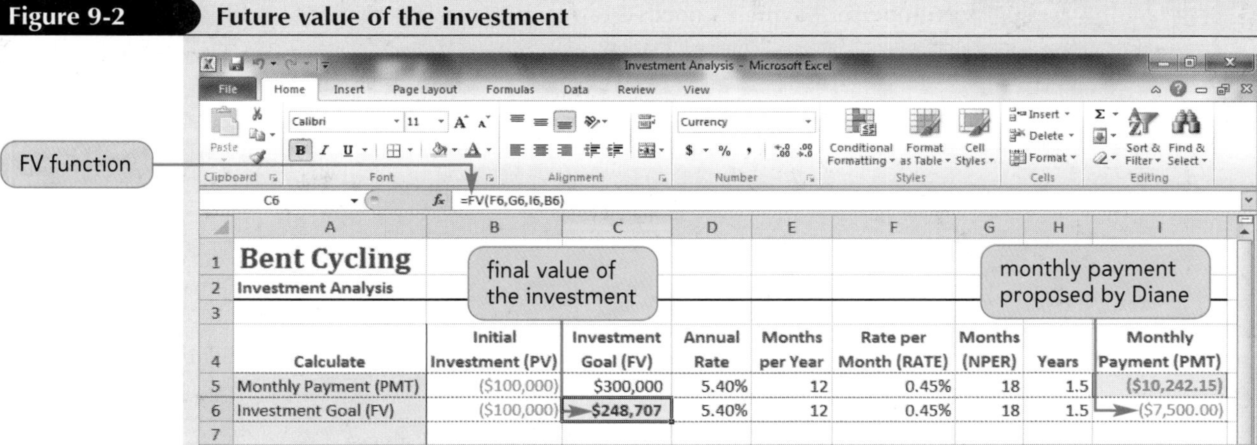

Calculating an Investment's Length with the NPER Function

By limiting the monthly deposit to $7,500, Bent Cycling could grow its savings to about $250,000 in the next year and a half. However, the expansion cannot be done for less than $300,000. Diane wants to know how long it would take to save $300,000 with a monthly deposit of $7,500. To calculate this, you must determine the number of payments that must be made into the fund. This is done with the NPER function

```
=NPER(rate, pmt, pv [, fv=0] [, type=0])
```

whose arguments have the same meaning as the other financial functions: the *rate* argument is the interest rate per period, the *pmt* argument is the payment amount per period, and the *pv* argument is the present value of the loan or investment. The *fv* argument storing the future value of the loan or investment is optional, and has a default value of 0. For the Bent Cycling investment, you use the following formula:

```
=NPER(5.4%/12, -7500, -100000, 300000)
```

Again, the interest rate per month is 5.4%/12 or 0.45%, the monthly cash outflow is –7,500, the initial value invested is also a cash outflow of –100,000, and the future value, or savings goal, is a cash inflow of 300,000.

The important point to remember about the NPER function is that it returns the number of payment periods, not necessarily the number of years. Recall that the financial functions are based on the time interval in which interest is compounded. So, if you are making periodic monthly payments and the interest is compounded monthly, the number of periods is also in months, not years.

TIP

If the NPER function returns #NUM!, the loan cannot be repaid in any length of time. This occurs when the monthly payments are less than the monthly interest charges, making it impossible to repay the loan.

To calculate the number of payments required to reach an investment goal:

1. In cell A7, enter **Months (NPER)**.
2. Copy the values and formulas in the range **B5:F5** to the range **B7:F7**.
3. Copy the values and formulas in the range **H6:I6** to the range **H7:I7**.
4. In cell G7, enter the formula **=NPER(F7,I7,B7,C7)**. The formula returns the value 23.886, which indicates that at the current interest rate (cell F7) with a monthly payment of $7,500 (cell I7), the number of months required to meet the investment goal (cell C7) would be almost 24 months, or 2 years.
5. Format cell G7 with the **Output** cell style. See Figure 9-3.

Figure 9-3 Number of payments needed to reach the investment goal

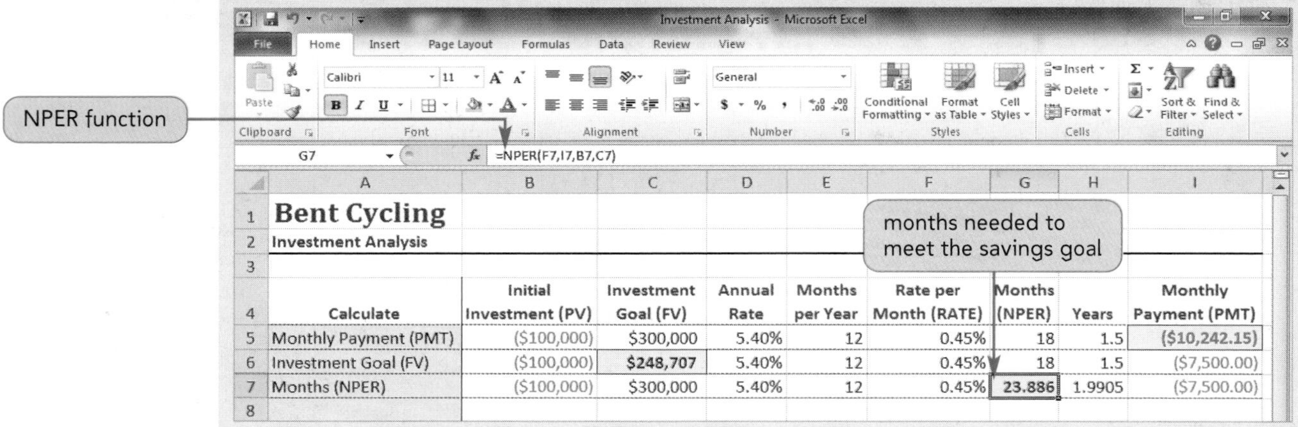

NPER function

G7 =NPER(F7,I7,B7,C7)

months needed to meet the savings goal

	A	B	C	D	E	F	G	H	I
1	Bent Cycling								
2	Investment Analysis								
3									
4	Calculate	Initial Investment (PV)	Investment Goal (FV)	Annual Rate	Months per Year	Rate per Month (RATE)	Months (NPER)	Years	Monthly Payment (PMT)
5	Monthly Payment (PMT)	($100,000)	$300,000	5.40%	12	0.45%	18	1.5	($10,242.15)
6	Investment Goal (FV)	($100,000)	$248,707	5.40%	12	0.45%	18	1.5	($7,500.00)
7	Months (NPER)	($100,000)	$300,000	5.40%	12	0.45%	23.886	1.9905	($7,500.00)
8									

Calculating an Investment's Present Value with the PV Function

It will take about two years for Bent Cycling to save $300,000 by making monthly payments of $7,500. With consumers' increasing interest in recumbents, Diane does not want to wait that long to upgrade the company's production facilities. Diane wonders whether Bent Cycling could reach its savings goal within the required 18 months by increasing the amount of the initial $100,000 investment. To determine how much the company must place into the account to reach its savings goal of $300,000 in 18 months, you must find the investment's present value by using the PV function

```
=PV(rate, nper, pmt [, fv=0] [, type=0])
```

where *rate* is the interest per period, *nper* is the number of payments, *pmt* is the payment made each period, *fv* is the future value, and *type* is when the payments are made within each period. For the Bent Cycling project, the following formula returns the present value of an investment needed to reach a future value of $300,000, assuming 18 additional payments of $7,500 at an annual interest rate of 5.4% interest compounded monthly:

```
=PV(5.4%/12, 18, -7500, 300000)
```

You'll find out how much the initial investment must be for Diane to reach her investment goal.

To calculate the present value of an investment needed to reach the investment goal:

1. In cell A8, enter **Initial Investment (PV)**.
2. Copy the value in cell **C7**, and then paste it into cell **C8**.
3. Copy the values in the range **D6:I6** and paste them into the range **D8:I8**.
4. In cell B8, enter the formula **=PV(F8,G8,I8,C8)**. The formula returns the value ($147,311), which is how much Diane needs in the account today to reach $300,000 in savings after 18 months of investing $7,500 per month at 5.4% annual interest.
5. Format cell **B8** using the **Output** cell style. See Figure 9-4.

Figure 9-4 **Present value of the investment**

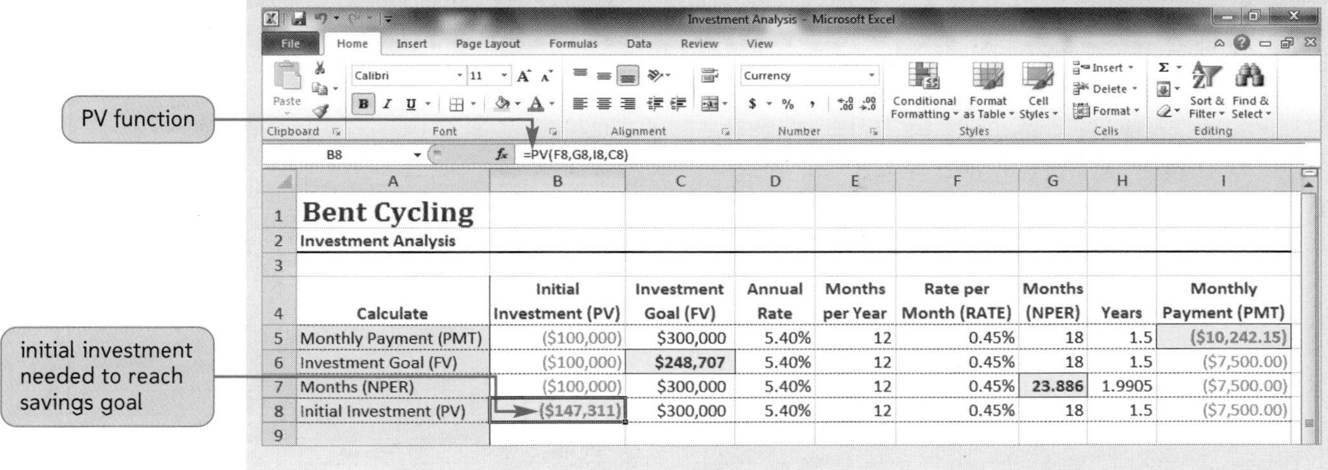

	A	B	C	D	E	F	G	H	I
1	Bent Cycling								
2	Investment Analysis								
3									
4	Calculate	Initial Investment (PV)	Investment Goal (FV)	Annual Rate	Months per Year	Rate per Month (RATE)	Months (NPER)	Years	Monthly Payment (PMT)
5	Monthly Payment (PMT)	($100,000)	$300,000	5.40%	12	0.45%	18	1.5	($10,242.15)
6	Investment Goal (FV)	($100,000)	$248,707	5.40%	12	0.45%	18	1.5	($7,500.00)
7	Months (NPER)	($100,000)	$300,000	5.40%	12	0.45%	23.886	1.9905	($7,500.00)
8	Initial Investment (PV)	($147,311)	$300,000	5.40%	12	0.45%	18	1.5	($7,500.00)
9									

Diane would have to increase the amount currently invested in the fund from $100,000 to almost $150,000 to reach her savings goal. The company doesn't have another $50,000 in ready cash assets to invest, so this is not a reasonable option for Diane.

Calculating an Investment's Interest Rate with the RATE Function

TIP

To calculate an annual rate, multiply the value returned by the RATE function by the number of payments per year. For monthly payments, multiply the rate value by 12.

With the 5.4% interest rate offered by the fund, Bent Cycling cannot save enough money in the next 18 months to finance the expansion. Diane wants to know what interest rate would be needed to reach her savings goal. To answer that question, you'll use the RATE function

```
=RATE(nper, pmt, pv [, fv=0] [, type=0])
```

where *nper* is the number of payments, *pmt* is the amount of each payment, *pv* is the investment's present value, *fv* is the investment's future value, and *type* defines when the payments are made. To calculate the interest rate for the Bent Cycling investment, you use the following formula with the RATE function:

```
=RATE(18, -7500, -100000, 300000)
```

The value returned by the rate function is based on 18 payments of $7,500 each with an initial investment of $100,000 that results in a future value of $300,000. The value returned by the RATE function is the interest rate per period, *not* the interest rate per year.

To calculate the interest rate required to reach the investment goal:

1. In cell A9, enter the text **Rate per Month (RATE)**.
2. Copy the values and formulas in the range **B7:C7** to the range **B9:C9**.
3. In cell E9, enter the value **12** and then copy the values and formulas in the range **G8:I8** to the range **G9:I9**.
4. In cell F9, enter the formula **=RATE(G9,I9,B9,C9)** to calculate the interest rate, which uses the worksheet cells for the number of payments (cell G9), the monthly payments (cell I9), the present value (cell B9), and the future value (cell C9). The function returns the value 1.91%, which represents the monthly interest rate.
5. In cell D9, enter the formula **=F9*E9** which multiplies the monthly interest rate by 12 months to calculate the annual interest rate of 22.95%.
6. Format cell F9 with the **Output** cell style. See Figure 9-5.

Figure 9-5 Interest rate for the investment

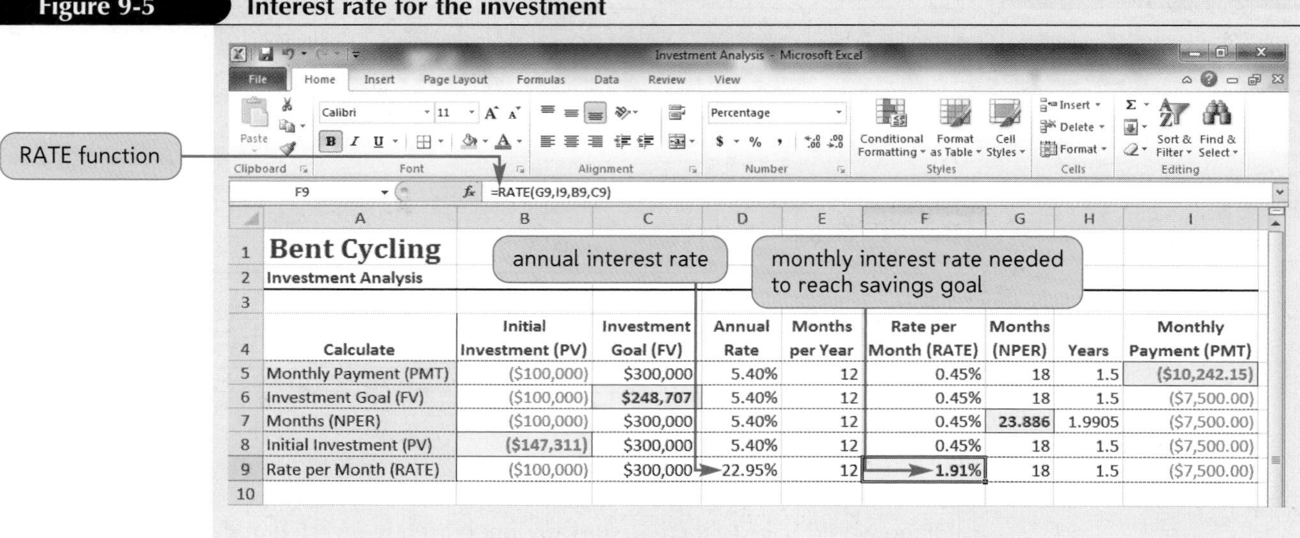

	A	B	C	D	E	F	G	H	I
1	Bent Cycling								
2	Investment Analysis								
3									
4	Calculate	Initial Investment (PV)	Investment Goal (FV)	Annual Rate	Months per Year	Rate per Month (RATE)	Months (NPER)	Years	Monthly Payment (PMT)
5	Monthly Payment (PMT)	($100,000)	$300,000	5.40%	12	0.45%	18	1.5	($10,242.15)
6	Investment Goal (FV)	($100,000)	$248,707	5.40%	12	0.45%	18	1.5	($7,500.00)
7	Months (NPER)	($100,000)	$300,000	5.40%	12	0.45%	23.886	1.9905	($7,500.00)
8	Initial Investment (PV)	($147,311)	$300,000	5.40%	12	0.45%	18	1.5	($7,500.00)
9	Rate per Month (RATE)	($100,000)	$300,000	22.95%	12	1.91%	18	1.5	($7,500.00)

Diane needs an investment with an annual interest rate of 22.95% compounded monthly. Because no such investment opportunity is available, Diane decides that the company will have to borrow the money to fund the expansion.

Working with Loans and Mortgages

Diane asks you to determine how much it will cost Bent Cycling to borrow the entire $300,000 rather than dipping into its cash reserves. A local bank will lend the entire amount at 8.5% annual interest compounded quarterly. Diane wants to repay the loan in five years. She needs you to calculate the quarterly payments to repay the loan within the specified time.

Calculating a Loan Payment

Loans and investments are calculated with the same Excel functions. The only difference is the direction of the cash flow. When you borrow money, the money you receive represents a positive cash flow because the money flows *to* you. As you repay the loan, each payment represents a negative cash flow because you are sending money *back* to the lending institution.

To calculate the quarterly payment for the loan, you use the PMT function. Because the interest is compounded quarterly, the value of the *rate* argument is 8.5% divided by 4, or 2.125%. The value of the *nper* argument is 20, which is the number of quarterly payments for the five-year period. The value of the *pv* argument is $300,000, the present value of the loan. The value is positive because cash is flowing into the company. The value of the *fv* argument is 0 because the company will repay the loan in full, making the future value of the loan 0 (that is, the company will not owe the bank anything after repaying the loan). Using these values, the complete PMT function is:

```
=PMT(8.5%/4, 20, 300000)
```

This formula doesn't include the optional *fv* argument. When omitted, Excel assumes a future value of 0, which is what you want. You'll enter this function into the Loan Schedule worksheet.

To calculate the monthly payment for the loan:

1. Switch to the **Loan Schedule** worksheet.
2. In cell A5, enter **$300,000**. The loan amount is entered as a positive cash flow because the money is going from the bank to Bent Cycling.
3. In cell B5, enter **8.5%** which is the annual interest rate.
4. In cell C5, enter **4** which is the number of quarters in the year.
5. In cell D5, enter the formula **=B5/C5**. The formula returns the value 2.13%, which is a quarterly interest rate of 2.125% displayed to two decimal places.
6. In cell E5, enter **5** which is the number of years needed to repay the loan.
7. In cell F5, enter the formula **=C5*E5** to calculate the total number of quarters to repay the loan.
8. In cell G5, enter the formula **=PMT(D5,F5,A5)**. The formula returns the value ($18,569), which is a negative cash flow displayed to the nearest dollar amount. See Figure 9-6.

Figure 9-6 Quarterly loan payment

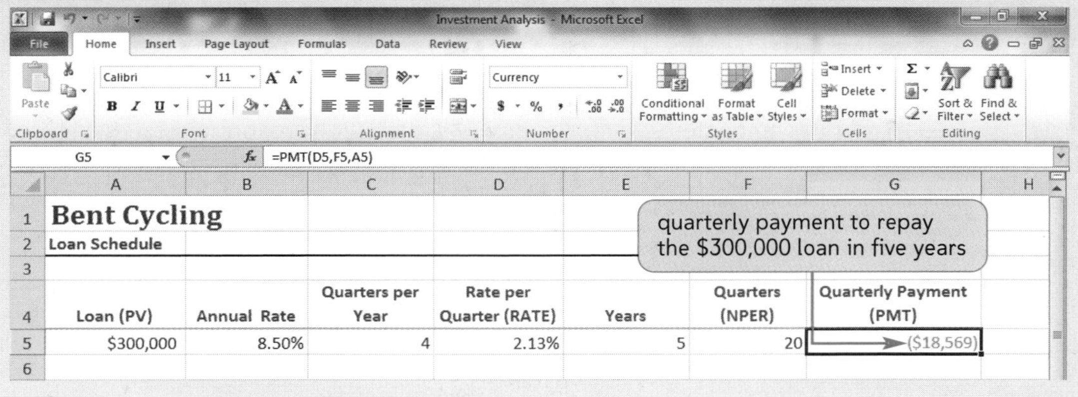

Bent Cycling could repay the loan in full with quarterly payments of $18,569 over the next five years. This is about $6,200 per month, which the company can afford.

Creating an Amortization Schedule

An **amortization schedule** is a table that specifies how much of each loan payment is devoted toward interest and toward repaying the principal. The **principal** is the amount of the loan that is still unpaid. When repaying loans, the initial payments mostly pay off the interest. As more of the loan is repaid, the percentage of each payment used for interest decreases (because less of the loan is left to charge interest upon) until the last few payments are used almost entirely for paying off the principal. Figure 9-7 shows a typical relationship between the amount paid toward interest and the amount paid toward the principal plotted against the number of payments.

Figure 9-7 Interest and principal payments

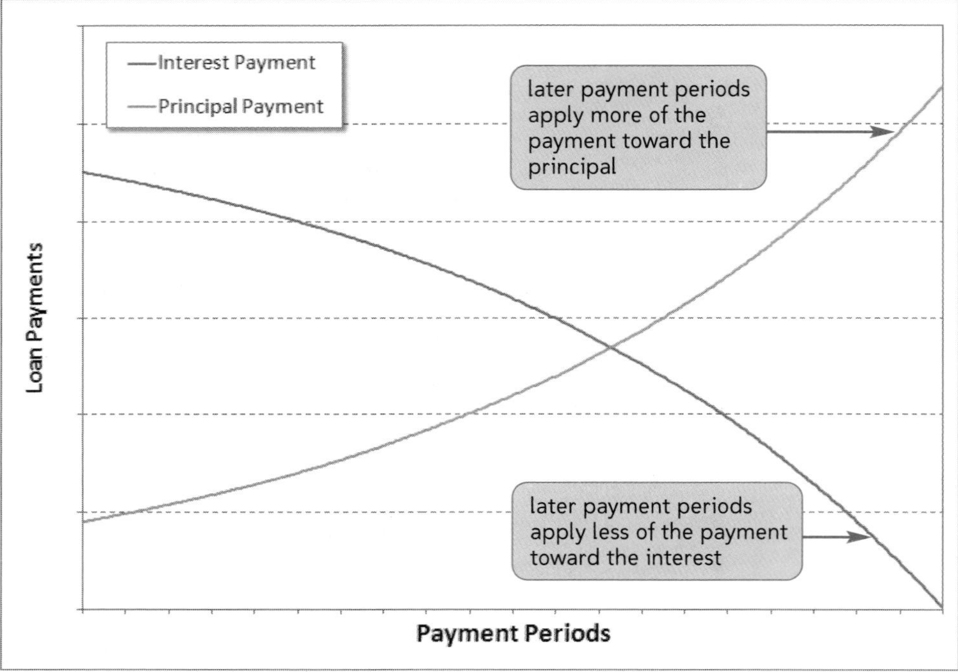

To calculate the amount of a loan payment devoted to interest and to principal, you can use the IPMT and PPMT functions. The IPMT function returns the amount of a particular payment that is used to pay the interest on the loan and has the syntax

```
=IPMT(rate, per, nper, pv [, fv=0] [, type=0])
```

where the *rate*, *nper*, *pv*, *fv*, and type arguments have the same meaning as they do for the PMT function. The per argument contains the period for which you want to calculate the interest due. For example, the following formula calculates how much interest is due in the fifth payment of the $300,000 loan that Diane is contemplating:

```
=IPMT(8.5%/4, 5, 20, 300000)
```

The formula returns the value –$5,304.99, which means that about $5,300 in interest is paid to the bank in the fifth payment. The *fv* argument was omitted because the loan will be paid off in full.

The PPMT function, which calculates the amount used to repay the principal, is similar. It has the following syntax:

```
=PPMT(rate, per, nper, pv [, fv=0] [, type=0])
```

The following formula calculates the amount of the principal that is repaid with the fifth payment:

```
=PPMT(8.5%/4, 5, 20, 300000)
```

The formula returns the value –$13,264.08, which means that the amount owed to the bank is reduced by about $13,200 after the fifth payment on the loan. Note that the sum of the interest payment and the principal payment is –$18,569.08, which is the same value returned by the PMT function earlier. The total amount paid to the bank each month doesn't change, only how that amount is allocated between paying the interest and paying off the principal.

Diane wants to know how much of the $18,569 is being used to pay interest on the loan and how much is being used to repay the principal. You will create an amortization schedule for the proposed loan. Diane has already created the schedule's structure. You'll enter the formulas to calculate the monthly payments on the loan's interest and principal.

To create the amortization schedule for the loan:

1. Click cell **C9**, type **$300,000** and then press the **Tab** key. Column C lists the amount of the principal remaining on the loan, so the initial value in cell C9 is the amount of the loan.
2. In cell D9, enter the formula **=IPMT($D$5,B9,$F$5,$A$5)** and then press the **Tab** key. The formula returns the value ($6,375), a negative cash flow in which $6,375 is spent on interest during the first quarter of the loan.
3. In cell E9, enter the formula **=PPMT($D$5,B9,$F$5,$A$5)** and then press the **Tab** key. The formula returns the value ($12,194), indicating a negative cash flow in which $12,194 is spent to reduce the principal during the first quarter of the loan.
4. In cell F9, enter the formula **=D9+E9** to calculate the total payment for the first period of the loan. The formula returns ($18,569), which matches the quarterly payment value shown in cell G5. See Figure 9-8.

TIP

In an amortization schedule, use absolute references to refer to the original loan conditions and use relative references to refer to information about specific payment periods.

Figure 9-8 Initial payment in the amortization schedule

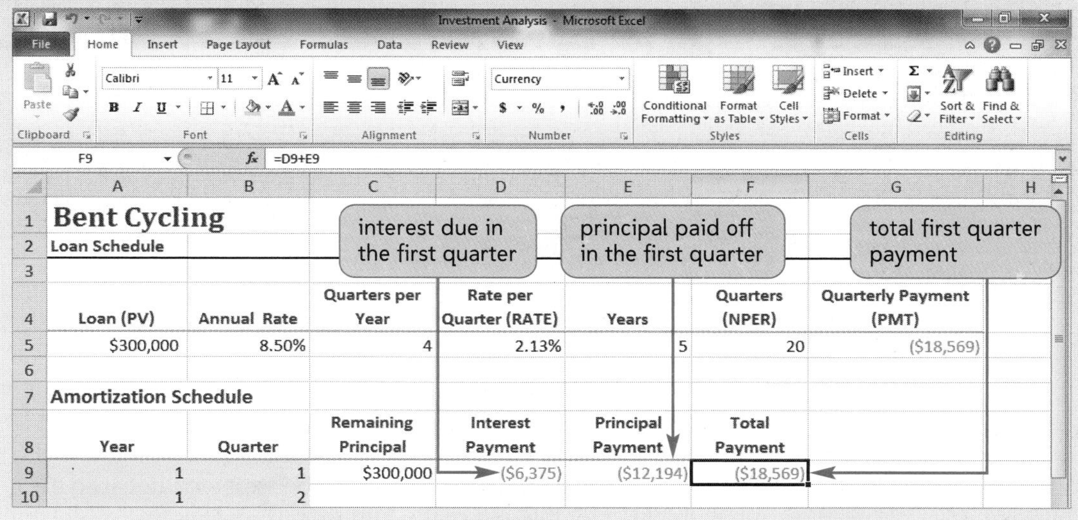

The formulas for the rest of the amortization schedule are similar to that for the first quarter except that the remaining principal in column C must be reduced by the amount paid toward the principal in the previous quarter.

To complete the amortization schedule:

1. In cell C10, enter the formula **=C9+E9** and then press the **Tab** key. The formula returns $287,806, which is the amount of the principal remaining at the start of the second quarter of the loan.
2. Copy the range **D9:F9**, and then paste the formulas into the range **D10:F10** to calculate the interest, principal, and total payment for the second quarter. The interest payment is ($6,116), the principal payment is ($12,453), and the total payment is ($18,569). The interest due for the second quarter is less than for the first quarter because the remaining principal is lower. As a result, more of the total payment for this quarter can be used to reduce the remaining principal.
3. Select the range **C10:F10**, and then drag the fill handle down to select the range **C10:F28**. The formulas are copied into the rest of the rows of the amortization schedule to calculate the remaining principal, interest payment, principal payment, and total payment for each of the remaining 18 quarters of the loan.
4. Click the **Auto Fill Options** button, and then click the **Fill Without Formatting** option button. The formulas are entered without overwriting the existing formatting in the worksheet.
5. In cell C29, enter the formula **=C28+E28** to calculate the final balance of the loan after the final payment. See Figure 9-9.

Figure 9-9 Completed amortization schedule

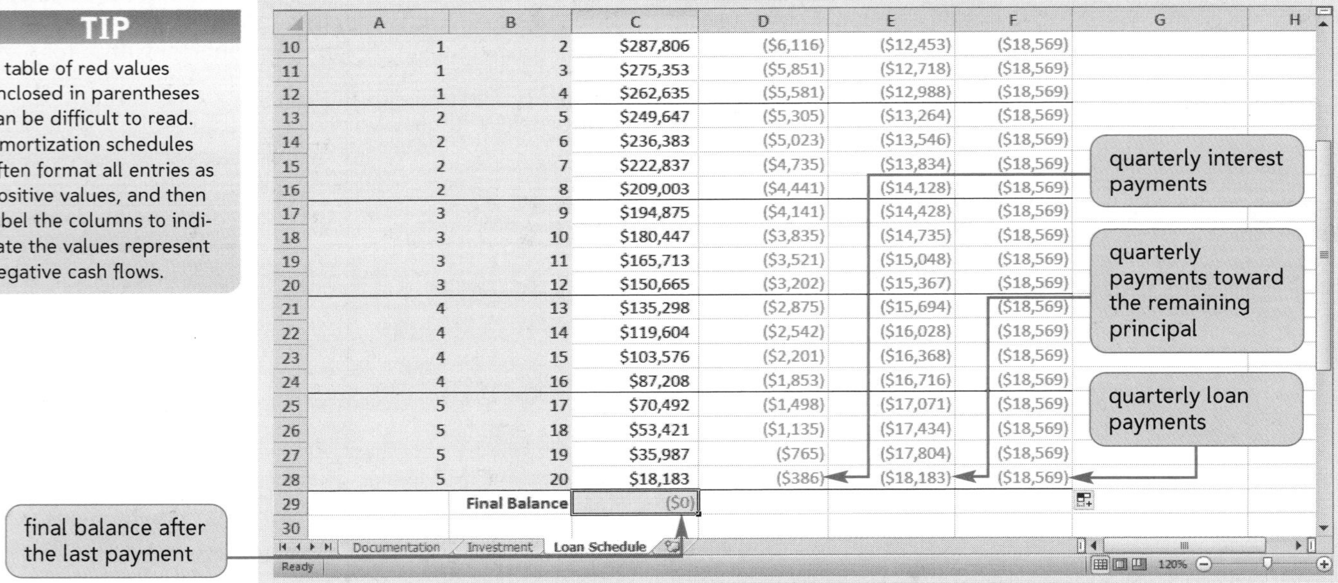

	A	B	C	D	E	F	G	H
10	1	2	$287,806	($6,116)	($12,453)	($18,569)		
11	1	3	$275,353	($5,851)	($12,718)	($18,569)		
12	1	4	$262,635	($5,581)	($12,988)	($18,569)		
13	2	5	$249,647	($5,305)	($13,264)	($18,569)		
14	2	6	$236,383	($5,023)	($13,546)	($18,569)		
15	2	7	$222,837	($4,735)	($13,834)	($18,569)		
16	2	8	$209,003	($4,441)	($14,128)	($18,569)		
17	3	9	$194,875	($4,141)	($14,428)	($18,569)		
18	3	10	$180,447	($3,835)	($14,735)	($18,569)		
19	3	11	$165,713	($3,521)	($15,048)	($18,569)		
20	3	12	$150,665	($3,202)	($15,367)	($18,569)		
21	4	13	$135,298	($2,875)	($15,694)	($18,569)		
22	4	14	$119,604	($2,542)	($16,028)	($18,569)		
23	4	15	$103,576	($2,201)	($16,368)	($18,569)		
24	4	16	$87,208	($1,853)	($16,716)	($18,569)		
25	5	17	$70,492	($1,498)	($17,071)	($18,569)		
26	5	18	$53,421	($1,135)	($17,434)	($18,569)		
27	5	19	$35,987	($765)	($17,804)	($18,569)		
28	5	20	$18,183	($386)	($18,183)	($18,569)		
29		Final Balance	($0)					
30								

TIP

A table of red values enclosed in parentheses can be difficult to read. Amortization schedules often format all entries as positive values, and then label the columns to indicate the values represent negative cash flows.

In the last quarterly payment at the end of the fifth year, only $386 of the $18,569 payment is used to pay the interest on the loan. The remaining $18,183 is used to pay the principal. The last principal payment is equal to the amount of the remaining principal, creating a final balance of $0. This is to be expected because the goal is to completely repay the loan by the end of the fifth year.

Calculating Cumulative Interest and Principal Payments

The breakdown of the quarterly payments in the amortization table is helpful. However, companies usually create annual budgets, not quarterly budgets. So companies want to know the total interest payments and principal payments during each year of the loan. You can calculate these cumulative payments on interest and principal using the CUMIPMT and CUMPRINC functions. The CUMIPMT function calculates the sum of several interest payments and has the syntax

```
=CUMIPMT(rate, nper, pv, start, end, type)
```

where *rate* is the interest rate per period, *nper* is the total number of payment periods, *pv* is the present value of the loan, *start* is the starting payment period for the interval you want to sum, *end* is the ending payment period, and type defines whether the payments are made at the beginning (0) or end (1) of each period. This function has no fv argument; the assumption is that loans are always completely paid off. Also, note that the type argument is *not* optional.

To calculate the cumulative total of payments made toward the principal, you use the CUMPRINC function, which has the syntax

```
=CUMPRINC(rate, nper, pv, start, end, type)
```

where the *rate, nper, pv, start, end,* and *type* arguments have the same meaning as they do for the CUMIPMT function.

For example, to calculate the total interest payments of the loan in the second year of the amortization schedule, you would enter the following formula:

```
=CUMIPMT(8.5%/4, 20, 300000, 5, 8, 0)
```

The starting and ending periods have values of 5 and 8, which represent the fifth through eighth quarters of the payment schedule. The formula returns ($19,505), indicating a negative cash flow in which about $19,500 is spent on interest payments in the second year of the loan. The value of the *type* parameter is 0 to indicate that the loan payments are due at the start of each quarter.

To calculate how much is spent when paying back the principal in that same time period, you would enter the following formula, which returns ($54,772), indicating that almost $55,000 will be spent in the second year repaying the principal on the $300,000 loan:

```
=CUMPRINC(8.5%/4, 20, 300000, 5, 8, 0)
```

You'll use both the CUMIPMT and CUMPRINC functions to calculate the total interest and principal payments for this proposed loan in each of the five years of the amortization schedule. The terms of the loan are already entered at the top of the worksheet in cell D5 (*rate* argument), cell F5 (*nper* argument), and cell A5 (*pv* argument). The table at the bottom of the Loan Schedule worksheet already has the starting and ending quarters for each of the five years of loan. You'll enter formulas with the CUMIPMT and CUMPRINC functions to calculate the yearly payments for the interest and the principal.

To calculate the yearly interest and principal payments:

1. In cell B36, enter the formula **=CUMIPMT($D$5,$F$5,$A$5,B34,B35,0)** to calculate the interest for the first year. The formula returns ($23,923), indicating that nearly $24,000 is paid toward interest in the first four quarters or the first year of the loan.
2. Copy the formula in cell **B36** to the range **C36:F36**. The absolute references for the *rate*, *nper*, and *pv* arguments always reference the loan conditions from the top of the worksheet ($D$5, $F$5, and $A$5, respectively) and the relative references for the *starting* and *end* parameters are updated in each table row. The yearly interest paid is calculated for the remaining four years of the loan, concluding with ($3,784), the amount paid in the fifth and final year.
3. In cell B37, enter the formula **=CUMPRINC($D$5,$F$5,$A$5,B34,B35,0)** to calculate the principal payment in the first year. The formula returns ($50,353), indicating that more than $50,000 will be spent in the first year toward reducing the size of the principal.
4. Copy the formula in cell **B37** to the range **C37:F37**. In the final year of the loan, $70,492 will be used to pay off the principal.

5. In cell G36, enter the formula **=SUM(B36:F36)** to calculate the total payment for interest.
6. In cell G37, enter the formula **=SUM(B37:F37)** to calculate the total payment for principal. See Figure 9-10.

Figure 9-10 **Interest and principal payments**

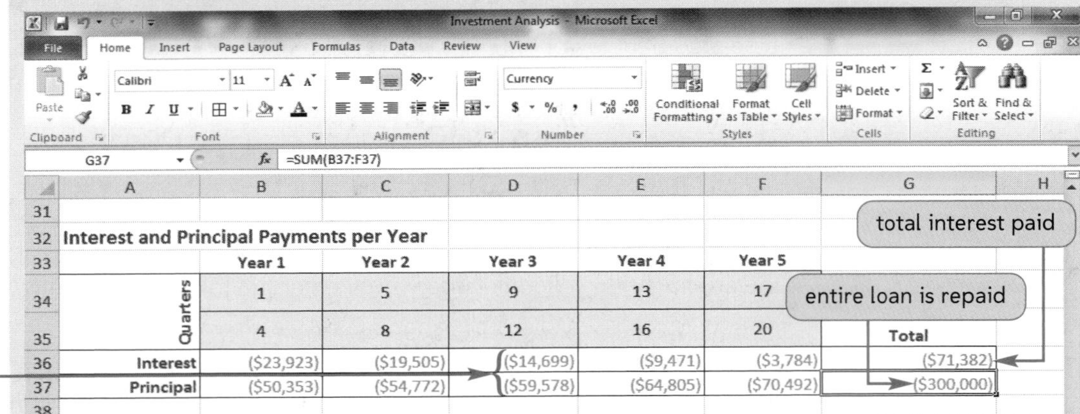

7. Save the workbook, and then close it.

At the end of five years, Bent Cycling will have spent more than $370,000 ($300,000 for the principal repayment plus $71,382 for interest) to receive $300,000 today.

PROSKILLS

Written Communication: Writing a Financial Workbook

The goal of all writing, whether a report or a worksheet, is communication. A properly written financial workbook should be simple for others to read and understand. It should also be easily edited to explore what-if scenarios, allowing your company or group to analyze the impact of different financial conditions on the bottom line.

To help ensure that any financial workbook you create meets these goals, keep in mind the following principles:

- Place all important financial variables at or near the top of a worksheet so that they can be easily read by others. For example, place the interest rate you use in calculations in a well-labeled worksheet cell.
- Use defined names with the financial variables to make it easier to apply them in formulas and functions.
- Clearly identify the direction of the cash flow in all of your financial calculations. Most Excel financial functions require a particular direction to the cash flow to return the correct value. Using the wrong sign will turn the calculation of a loan payment into an investment deposit or vice versa.
- Place argument values in worksheet cells where they can be viewed and easily changed. Never place these values directly into a financial formula.
- Use the same unit of time for all the arguments in a financial function. For example, when using the PMT function to calculate monthly loan payments, the interest rate and the number of payments should be based on the interest rate per month and the total months to pay off the loan.

A financial workbook that is easy to read and understand is more useful to yourself and others as you explore the financial aspects of business decisions.

So far, you have analyzed different investment and loan options for Bent Cycling, which will help Diane decide how to finance the potential expansion. In the next session, you'll make projections about the company's future earnings assuming Diane decides to finance the expansion.

REVIEW

Session 9.1 Quick Check

1. Explain the difference between positive and negative cash flow. If you borrow $10,000 from a bank, is that a positive or negative cash flow? Justify your answer.
2. Use Excel to calculate how much a savings account would be worth if the initial balance is $500 and you deposit $50 per month for 10 years at 5.8% annual interest compounded monthly.
3. You want a savings account to grow from $1,000 to $3,000 within two years. Assume the bank provides a 5.2% annual interest rate compounded monthly. Calculate how much you must deposit each month to meet your savings goal.
4. You want to take out a loan for $200,000 at 7% interest compounded monthly. If you can afford to make monthly payments of only $1,500 on the loan, how many months will it take you to pay off the loan completely?
5. Rerun your calculations from the previous question assuming that you can afford only a $1,000 monthly payment. What value does Excel return? How do you explain the result?
6. You take out a loan for $200,000. The loan must be repaid in 10 years with quarterly payments of $7,200. Under those terms, what is the annual interest rate of the loan?
7. You take out a 10-year loan for $150,000 at 6.3% interest compounded monthly. What is the monthly payment? How much of the first payment is used for interest and how much is used to pay off the principal?
8. For the loan conditions specified in Question 7, calculate how much interest you will pay in the first year and how much will you pay toward the principal.

SESSION 9.2 VISUAL OVERVIEW

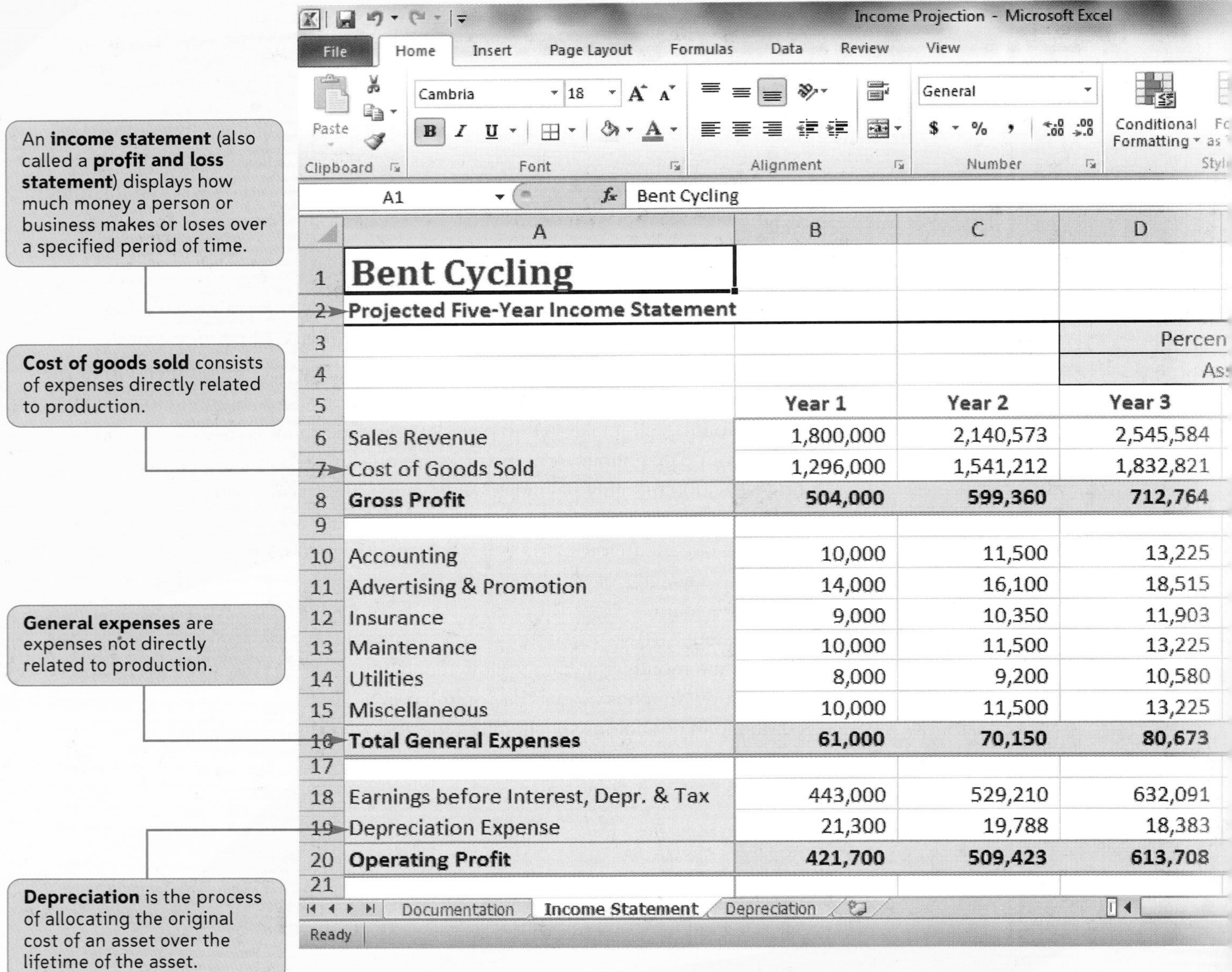

INCOME STATEMENT AND DEPRECIATION

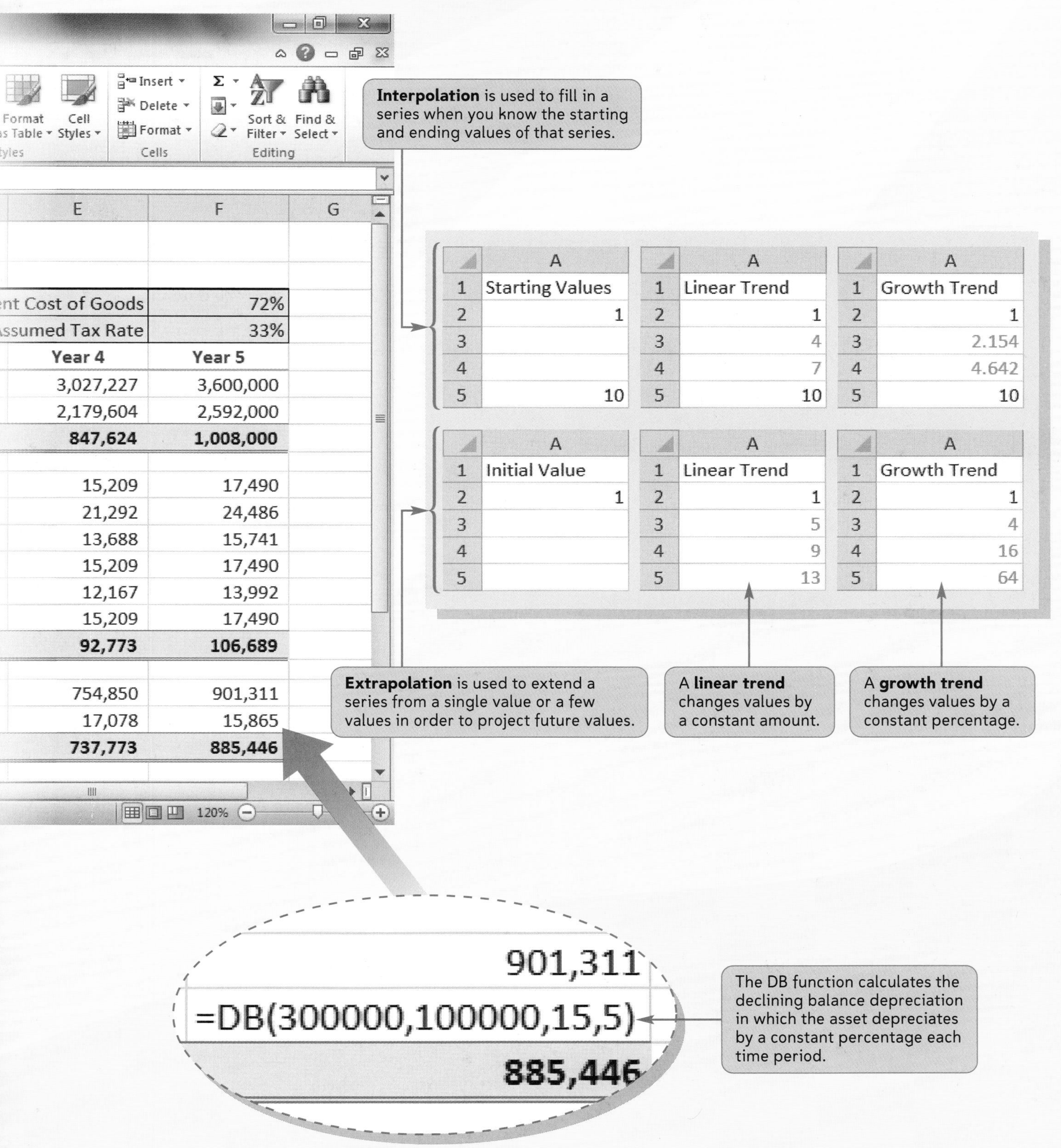

Projecting Future Income and Expenses

An income statement shows how much money a business makes or loses over a specified period of time. Income statements are often created monthly, semiannually, or annually. Bent Cycling will pay more than $70,000 in interest payments by the time the proposed loan is repaid. Diane wants to know how this additional expense will affect the company's income over the next five years. She is interested only in annual projections. To provide Diane with an answer, you'll complete an income statement. Diane already created the layout you'll use.

To open the income statement workbook:

1. Open the **Income** workbook located in the Excel9\Tutorial folder included with your Data Files, and then save the workbook as **Income Projection** in the same folder.
2. In the Documentation worksheet, enter your name in cell B3 and the date in cell B4.
3. Switch to the **Income Statement** worksheet. The Income Statement worksheet contains columns for income and expense projections over the next five years and is divided into the five sections shown in Figure 9-11.

Figure 9-11 **Income Statement worksheet**

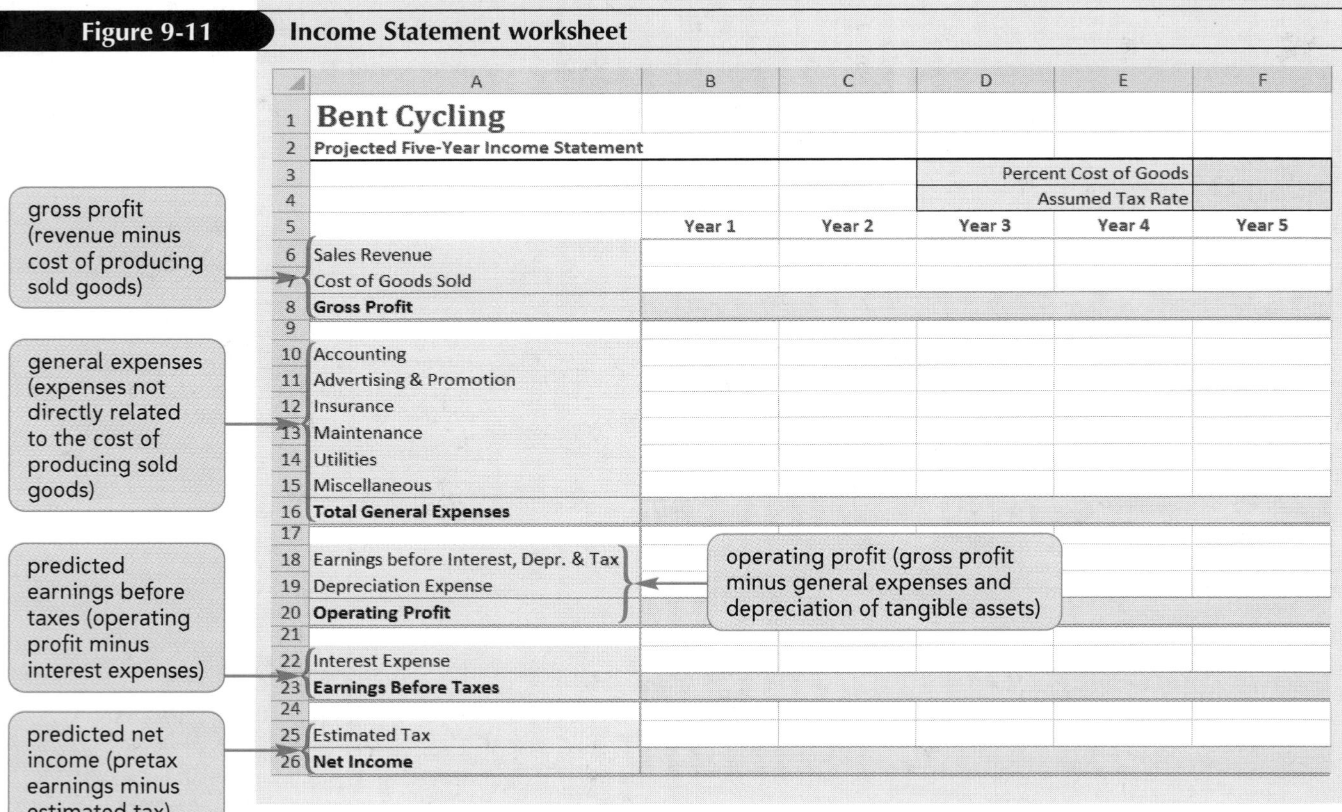

Exploring Linear and Growth Trends

Diane wants to project the company's future revenue. She sees two possibilities: (1) revenue will grow by a constant amount from year to year, or (2) revenue will grow by a constant percentage each year.

Diane's first possibility, in which the values change by a constant amount, is an example of a linear trend. When plotted, a linear trend appears as a straight line. The second possibility, in which the values change not by a constant amount but by a constant percentage, is an example of a growth trend. For example, each value in a growth trend might be 15% higher than the previous year's value. When plotted, a growth trend appears as a curve with the greatest increases occurring near the end of the series. Figure 9-12 shows a linear trend and a growth trend for revenue that starts at $1.8 million in Year 1 and doubles to $3.6 million by Year 5. The growth trend lags behind the linear trend in the early stages but reaches the same stopping value at the end of the time period.

TIP

Growth trend calculations are also called *exponential growth trends* or *exponential trends* in the fields of economics and statistics.

Figure 9-12 **Comparison of linear and growth trends**

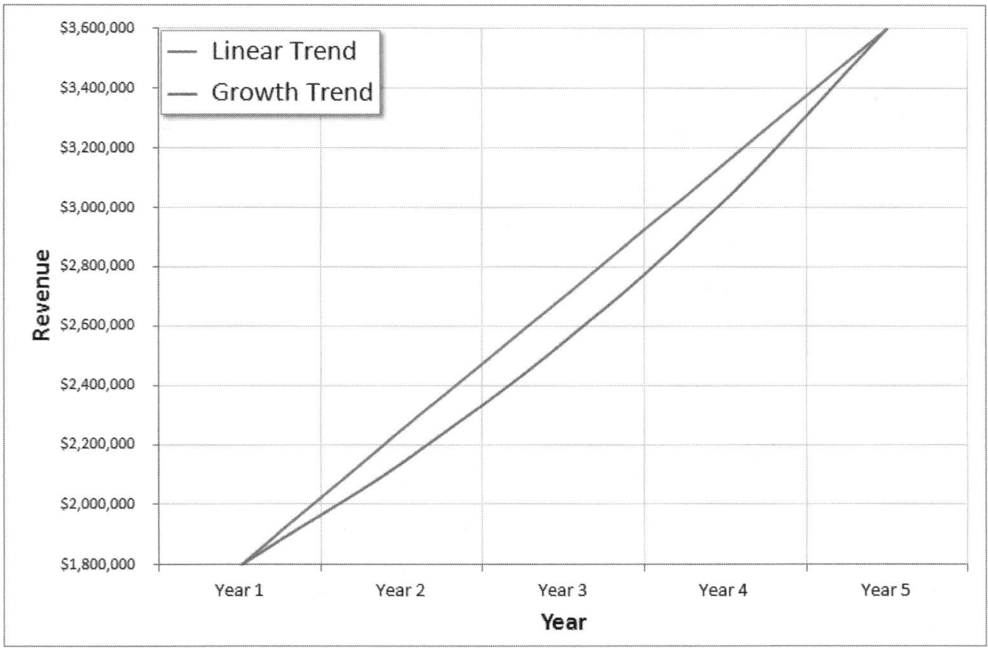

Interpolating within a Series of Values

If you know the beginning and ending values in a series of values and whether the values constitute a linear or growth trend, you can use AutoFill to fill in the missing values. You will use AutoFill to interpolate Bent Cycling's future revenue using a linear trend between Year 1 and Year 5.

To project the company's future revenue based on a linear trend:

1. In cell B6, enter **1,800,000** which is the projected revenue for the first of the next five years.
2. In cell F6, enter **3,600,000** which represents a doubling of the company's projected revenue by the end of the five-year period.

3. Select the range **B6:F6**. The projected sales revenue for each year will appear in this range.
4. In the Editing group on the Home tab, click the **Fill** button, and then click **Series**. The Series dialog box opens.
5. Verify that the **Rows** option button and the **Linear** option button are selected, and then click the **Trend** check box to insert a check mark. See Figure 9-13.

Figure 9-13 Series dialog box

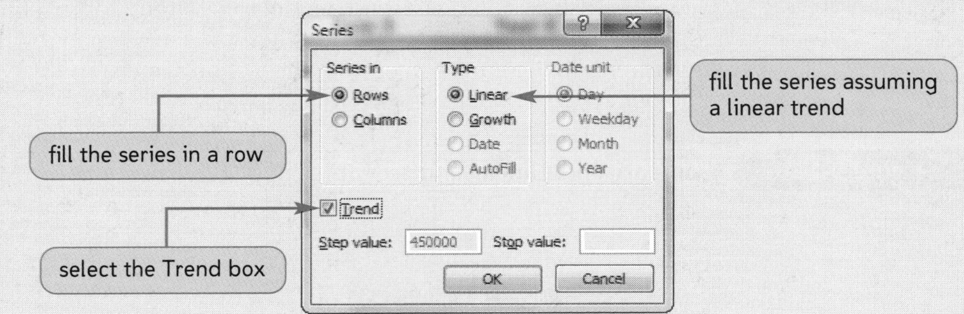

TIP

To interpolate a series, the cells between the first and last cells in the series must be blank.

6. Click the **OK** button. The values inserted into the range B6:F6 show the company's projected revenue based on a linear trend. In this case, the revenue increases $450,000 per year from Year 1 through Year 5.

Next, you'll interpolate the projected revenue using a growth trend. To interpolate the growth trend correctly, you first must remove the Year 2 through Year 4 values, leaving those cells blank.

To project the company's future revenue based on a growth trend:

1. Delete the values in the range **C6:E6**.
2. Select the range **B6:F6**. The projected sales revenue for each year will appear in this range.
3. In the Editing group on the Home tab, click the **Fill** button, and then click **Series**. The Series dialog box opens.
4. In the Type section, click the **Growth** option button, click the **Trend** check box to insert a check mark, and then click the **OK** button. The Year 1 through Year 5 revenue projections are now based on a growth trend. See Figure 9-14.

Figure 9-14 **Projected revenue based on a growth trend**

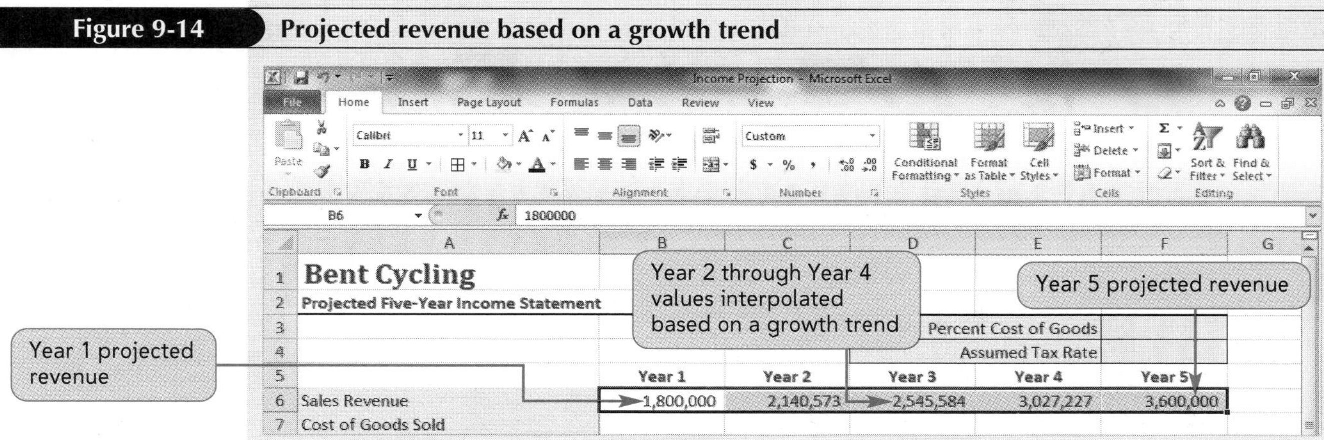

Under the growth trend projections, the largest revenue increases occur near the end of the five-year period. For example, the revenue grows by about $340,000 from Year 1 to Year 2, but by about $570,000 from Year 4 to Year 5. Calculating the percentage change in revenue from year to year under the growth trend projection rather than the absolute change in dollars shows that the projected revenue increase is about 19% each year. Diane is expecting the fastest growth a few years from now and asks you to base the income projections on a growth trend.

Projecting Future Expenses

The next part of the income statement displays the cost of goods sold. Bent Cycling needs to purchase basic parts and raw materials to manufacture recumbents. The more recumbents the company builds, the more parts and materials it must purchase, increasing the cost to the company. For every dollar of sales revenue earned, the company must spend 72 cents to cover the production costs. In other words, the cost of goods sold is about 72% of the revenue generated. The difference between the company's sales revenue and the cost of goods sold is the company's **gross profit**. You'll enter formulas to calculate the cost of goods sold and the gross profit.

To project the cost of goods sold and the gross profit:

1. In cell F3, enter **72%**.
2. In cell B7, enter the formula **=B6*$F$3**. This formula multiplies projected sales revenue by 72% to project the cost of goods sold, which is $1,296,000 for Year 1.
3. In cell B8, enter the formula **=B6–B7**. This formula subtracts the cost of goods sold from the sales revenue to project a gross profit of 504,000 for Year 1.
4. Copy the range **B7:B8** to the range **C7:F8** to project the cost of goods sold and gross profit for each of the next five years. See Figure 9-15.

Figure 9-15 **Projected gross profit**

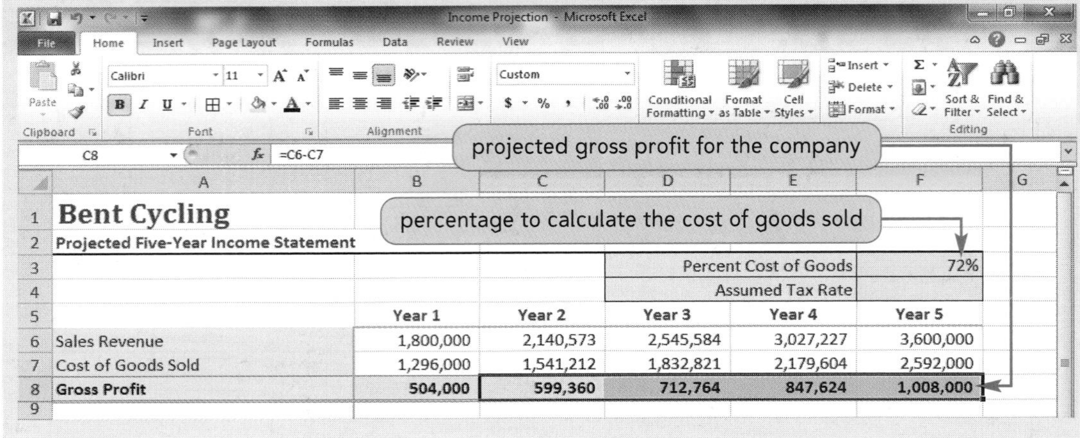

REFERENCE

Interpolating and Extrapolating a Series

To interpolate a series of values between starting and ending values:

- Select the range with the first cell containing the starting value, blank cells for middle values, and the last cell containing the ending value.
- In the Editing group on the Home tab, click the Fill button, and then click Series.
- Select whether the series is organized in rows or columns, select the type of series to interpolate, and then check the Trend check box.
- Click the OK button.

To extrapolate a series from a starting value:

- Select a range with the first cell containing the starting value followed by blank cells to store the extrapolated values.
- In the Editing group on the Home tab, click the Fill button, and then click Series.
- Select whether the series is organized in rows or columns, select the type of series to extrapolate, and then enter the step value in the Step value box.
- Click the OK button.

Extrapolating from a Series of Values

The next section of the income statement contains the projected general expenses for the company. These are expenses not directly related to production. For example, Bent Cycling must purchase insurance, provide for general maintenance and utilities, and pay for advertising regardless of the number of bikes it actually sells. Diane has projected values for Year 1 that she wants you to enter into the worksheet.

TIP

When you extrapolate a series, the Step value represents the amount that each value is increased or multiplied as the series is extended. You do not have to specify a stopping value.

To enter the Year 1 general expenses:

1. Enter the following expenses in the range B10:B15:
   cell B10: **10,000** cell B13: **10,000**
   cell B11: **14,000** cell B14: **8,000**
   cell B12: **9,000** cell B15: **10,000**
2. In cell B16, enter **=SUM(B10:B15)** to calculate the total general expenses for Year 1, which is 61,000.

Diane does not have projected expenses past the first year, but she expects that the proposed expansion will increase expenses by about 15% per year. To extend a series from one or more beginning values, you use extrapolation. You'll extrapolate the company's expenses over the next five years, assuming a growth trend in which the expenses increase by 15% each year. This is equivalent to multiplying each year's expenses by 1.15 to project the next year's expenses.

To extrapolate the Year 1 expenses through the next four years:

1. Select the range **B10:F15**.
2. In the Editing group on the Home tab, click the **Fill** button, and then click **Series**. The Series dialog box opens.
3. Click the **Rows** option button because you want to create a series of values in the rows of the selected range.
4. Click the **Growth** option button, enter **1.15** in the Step value box, and then click the **OK** button. The expense values from Year 1 are extrapolated into the Year 2 through Year 5 columns.
5. Copy the formula in cell **B16** to the range **C16:F16** to project the total general expenses for the company for each year.

Be sure to select the Rows option button so that the series values fill the row, not the column.

TIP

To extrapolate a trend that decreases rather than increases, use a step value of less than 0 for a linear trend, and between 0 and 1 for a growth trend.

These calculations show that the projected general expenses will rise to $106,689 by the end of Year 5. Next, you want to calculate the company's earnings during each of the next five years. The initial earnings estimate is equal to the company's gross profit minus the total general expenses.

To calculate the company's initial earnings:

1. In cell B18, enter the formula **=B8–B16** to calculate an initial estimate of the yearly earnings, which is equal to the gross profit minus the total general expenses. This value is $443,000 for Year 1.
2. Copy the formula in cell **B18** to the range **C18:F18** to project yearly earnings through Year 5. See Figure 9-16.

Figure 9-16 Projected general expenses and earnings

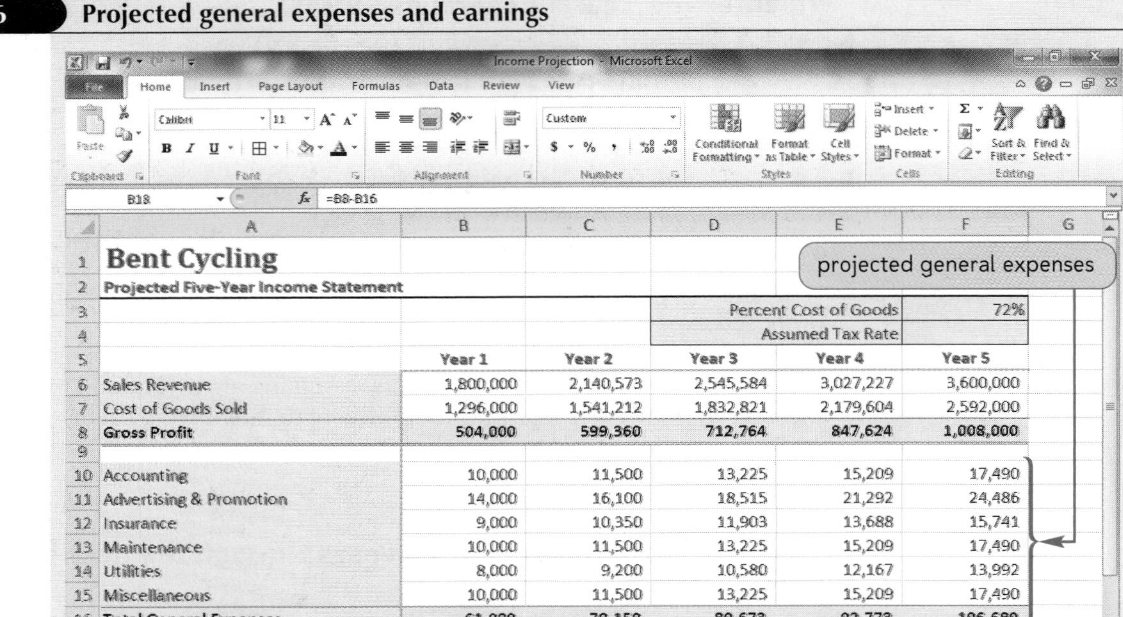

	A	B	C	D	E	F
1	Bent Cycling					
2	Projected Five-Year Income Statement					
3				Percent Cost of Goods		72%
4				Assumed Tax Rate		
5		Year 1	Year 2	Year 3	Year 4	Year 5
6	Sales Revenue	1,800,000	2,140,573	2,545,584	3,027,227	3,600,000
7	Cost of Goods Sold	1,296,000	1,541,212	1,832,821	2,179,604	2,592,000
8	Gross Profit	504,000	599,360	712,764	847,624	1,008,000
9						
10	Accounting	10,000	11,500	13,225	15,209	17,490
11	Advertising & Promotion	14,000	16,100	18,515	21,292	24,486
12	Insurance	9,000	10,350	11,903	13,688	15,741
13	Maintenance	10,000	11,500	13,225	15,209	17,490
14	Utilities	8,000	9,200	10,580	12,167	13,992
15	Miscellaneous	10,000	11,500	13,225	15,209	17,490
16	Total General Expenses	61,000	70,150	80,673	92,773	106,689
17						
18	Earnings before Interest, Depr. & Tax	443,000	529,210	632,091	754,850	901,311
19	Depreciation Expense					
20	Operating Profit					

Calculating Depreciation of Assets

The financial status of a company includes information about the company's tangible possessions such as equipment, land, buildings, and vehicles. These combined assets are known as **tangible assets** because they are long-lasting material assets not intended for sale but only for use by the company. Not all material assets are tangible assets. For example, assets such as the raw materials Bent Cycling uses to manufacture bikes are not considered tangible assets because they are used in the production process and are sold indirectly to the consumer in the form of a finished bicycle.

To calculate Bent Cycling's tax liability, you subtract any expenses the company incurs from the revenue it generates. However, the cost of building Diane's proposed workshop is neither income nor an expense. It's an investment in a tangible asset that will be used for many years to generate revenue for the company. Tax rules allow the original cost of the investment to be subtracted from the company's reported income, reducing the company's tax liability.

In many cases, however, the entire cost of such a building project is not reported in a single tax statement. Instead, the original cost is allocated over the years in which the asset is used. For example, instead of deducting the entire $300,000 from the company reported income in Year 1, the company might only be able to deduct $60,000 per year for the next five years from its reported income.

This process of allocating the original cost of the investment over the years of use is known as depreciation. Different types of tangible assets have different rules for depreciation. However, in general, to calculate the depreciation of an asset, you need to know the following about the asset:

- The asset's original cost
- The asset's useful life
- The asset's **salvage value**, which is the asset's value at the end of its useful life
- The rate at which the asset is depreciated over time

You already know the cost of the new workshop and design facility is $300,000. Given how quickly technology changes in bicycle design and manufacturing, Diane estimates the useful life of the new facility and its equipment is 15 years. After 15 years, she assumes the company will require another substantial upgrade of its facilities. At that point, Diane estimates that the salvage value of the old workshop will be one-third of its current value, or $100,000. You'll enter this information in the Depreciation worksheet.

To insert the depreciation parameters:

1. Switch to the **Depreciation** worksheet.
2. In cell B4, enter **$300,000**. This is the asset's initial value.
3. In cell B5, enter **$100,000**. This is the asset's estimated salvage value.
4. In cell B6, enter **15**. This is the projected useful life of the asset in years.

The only thing remaining is to determine how quickly the new facility depreciates from its original cost of $300,000 to $100,000. Excel has five financial functions to calculate depreciation under different assumptions. Figure 9-17 summarizes these depreciation functions.

Figure 9-17 Depreciation functions

Function	Description
`SLN(cost, salvage, life)`	Returns the straight-line depreciation in which the asset declines by a constant amount each year, where *cost* is the initial cost of the asset, *salvage* is the salvage value, and *life* is the useful lifetime of the asset.
`DB(cost, salvage, life, period[, month])`	Returns the declining balance depreciation in which the asset declines by a constant percentage each year, where *period* is the year of the depreciation and *month* is an optional argument that defines the number of months that assets were owned during Year 1.
`SYD(cost, salvage, life, period)`	Returns the sum-of-years' digit depreciation that results in a more accelerated depreciation than straight-line depreciation, but less than declining balance depreciation.
`DDB(cost, salvage, life, period[, factor=2])`	Returns the double-declining balance depreciation that doubles the depreciation under the straight-line method and applies that accelerated rate to the original asset value minus the cumulative depreciation. The *factor* argument specifies the factor by which the straight-line depreciation is multiplied. If no *factor* is specified, a factor of 2 (for doubling) is assumed.
`VDB(cost, salvage, life, start, end[, factor=2][, no_switch=FALSE])`	Returns a variable declining depreciation for any specified period using any specified depreciation method, where *start* is the starting period of the depreciation, *end* is the ending period, *factor* is the rate at which the depreciation declines, and *no_switch* specifies whether to switch to the straight-line method when the depreciation falls below the estimate given by the declining balance method.

REFERENCE

Calculating Depreciation

- To calculate a straight-line depreciation, use the SLN function.
- To calculate a declining balance depreciation, use the DB function.
- To calculate a sum-of-years' digit depreciation, use the SYD function.
- To calculate a double-declining balance depreciation, use the DDB function.
- To calculate a variable depreciation, use the VBD function.

Straight-Line Depreciation

TIP

You can estimate straight-line depreciation by using AutoFill to interpolate the linear trend using the initial value of the asset as the starting value and the salvage value as the stopping value.

With **straight-line depreciation**, the asset depreciates by equal amounts each year of its lifetime until it reaches the salvage value. You can calculate this annual depreciation by dividing the total depreciation of the asset by the number of years the asset is used. Based on Diane's numbers, the new workshop will depreciate $200,000 in value over 15 years, which is a straight-line depreciation of $13,333.33 per year. If you don't want to do this calculation manually, you can use the SLN function to calculate the yearly straight-line depreciation. The SLN function has the syntax

```
=SLN(cost, salvage, life)
```

where *cost* is the initial cost or value of the asset, *salvage* is the salvage value of the asset at the end of its useful life, and *life* is the number of years the asset will be used. To calculate the annual straight-line depreciation for Bent Cycling's new workshop, you enter the following formula, which returns $13,333.33:

```
=SLN(300000, 100000, 15)
```

You'll enter this function to calculate the annual depreciation of the new workshop. You'll also calculate the cumulative depreciation that will take place over the next five years, and the depreciated value of the workshop for each of the next five years.

To calculate the straight-line, cumulative, and value depreciation of the workshop:

1. In cell B10, enter the formula **=SLN($B$4,$B$5,$B$6)** to calculate the straight-line depreciation for Year 1. You use absolute references so the cells won't change when you copy the formula. The formula returns $13,333, which is the annual depreciation of this asset to the nearest dollar.
2. Copy the formula in cell **B10** to the range **C10:F10**. Because this is a straight-line depreciation, the asset depreciates the same amount each year.
3. In cell B11, enter the formula **=B10**, which displays the depreciation for the first year.
4. In cell C11, enter the formula **=C10+B11** to calculate the cumulative depreciation of the asset through the first two years.

5. Copy the formula in cell **C11** to the range **D11:F11** to calculate the cumulative depreciation of the asset over all five of the years. At the end of Year 5, the asset will have depreciated by $66,667.
6. In cell B12, enter the formula **=$B$4–B11** and then copy the formula in cell **B12** to the range **C12:F12** to calculate the depreciated value of the asset at the end of each of the five years by subtracting the value of the cumulative depreciation from the asset's original cost.
7. Click cell **B10** to deselect the range. Based on a straight-line depreciation, the new workshop's depreciated value will be $233,333 at the end of Year 5 or about 78% of its original value. See Figure 9-18.

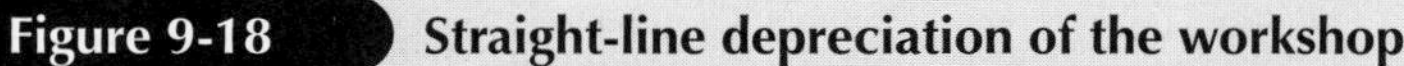

Straight-line depreciation of the workshop

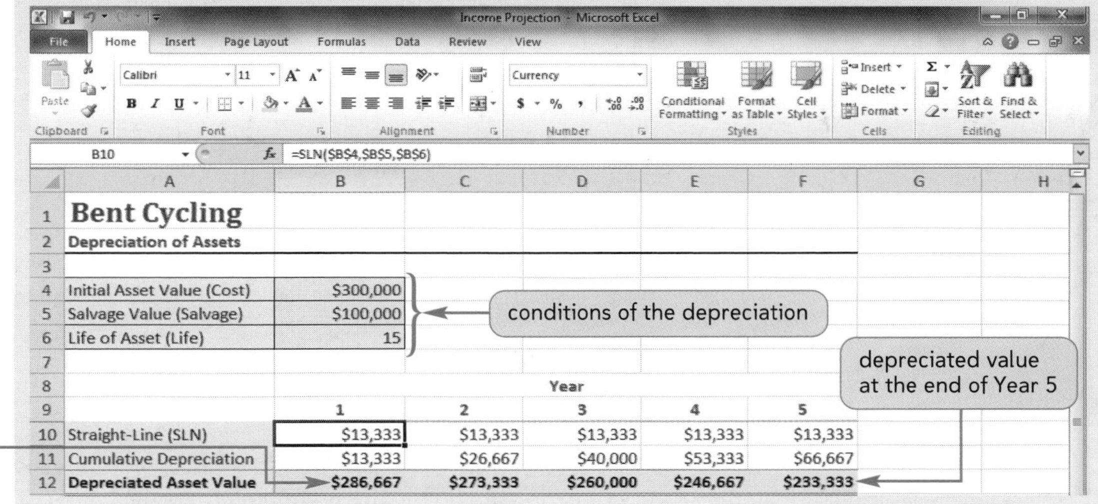

Declining Balance Depreciation

Another way to calculate depreciation is to use **declining balance depreciation**, in which the asset depreciates by a constant percentage each year rather than a constant amount. The depreciation value is highest early in its lifetime, so that is also when the highest declines occur. As the asset loses value, the depreciation amounts steadily decrease, though the percentage decrease remains the same. Figure 9-19 compares the straight-line and declining balance depreciation for an asset over a 15-year lifetime.

Figure 9-19 **Straight-line versus declining balance depreciation**

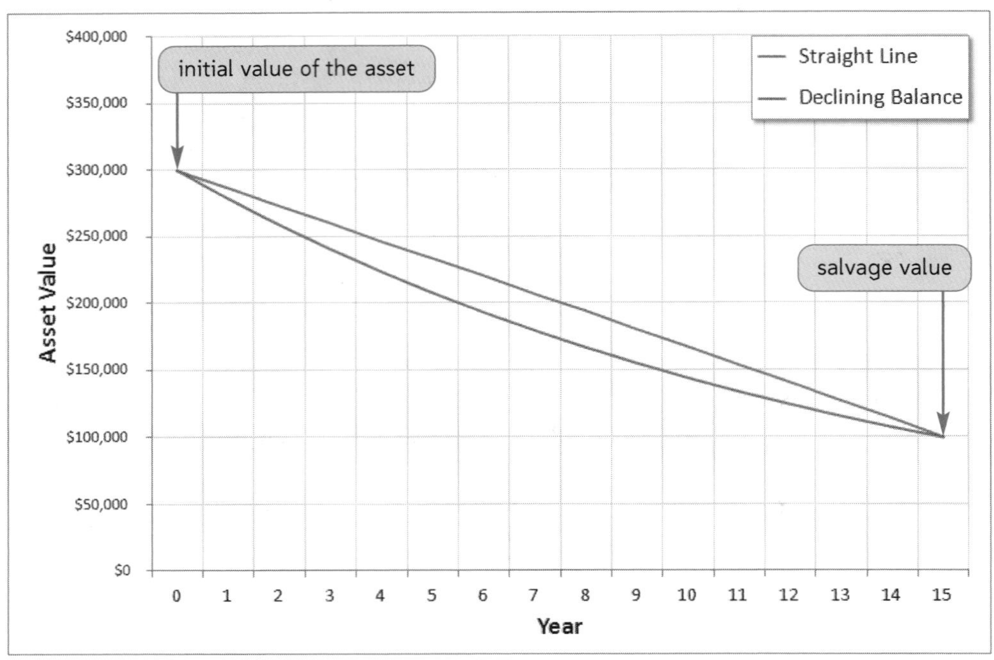

An asset depreciates more quickly initially under the declining balance model than under the straight-line model. The declining balance model is an example of a negative growth trend in which the asset depreciates in value by a constant percentage rather than by a constant amount as is the case with the straight-line model. The DB function calculates the declining balance depreciation. It has the syntax

```
=DB(cost, salvage, life, period [month])
```

where *cost*, *salvage*, and *life* are again the initial cost, salvage cost, and lifetime of the asset, and *period* is the period for which you want to calculate the depreciation. If you are calculating depreciation on a yearly basis, then the period argument would contain the year value of the depreciation. For example, to calculate the depreciation of the new workshop during the third year of its use, you could enter the following formula, which returns the value $18,383, indicating that the asset will depreciate by that amount during the third year of its use:

```
=DB(300000, 100000, 15, 3)
```

The DB function also supports an optional *month* argument, which is needed when the asset is used for only part of the first year. For example, if you are depreciating an asset for only two months of the first year, you would set the value of the *month* parameter to 2.

Diane wants you to calculate a depreciation schedule based on the declining balance assumption. You'll use the DB function to calculate the depreciation for each of the next five years.

To calculate the declining balance depreciation:

1. In cell B14, enter the formula **=DB($B$4,$B$5,$B$6,B9)** to calculate the declining balance depreciation for Year 1. The formula returns $21,300, the value that the new workshop will depreciate within its first year of operation. Note that you used the cell reference B9 to reference the value of the *period* argument.

2. Copy the formula in cell **B14** to the range **C14:F14** to calculate the depreciation for each of the remaining four years. The amount of depreciation decreases each year under the declining balance schedule.
3. Copy the range **B11:F12** to the range **B15:F16** to calculate the cumulative depreciation and depreciated value of the asset. Based on a declining balance depreciation, the depreciated value of the new workshop declines to a little more than $207,000 in value in five years.
4. Click cell **A14** to deselect the range. Figure 9-20 shows the depreciation, cumulative depreciation, and depreciated value for Years 1 through 5.

Figure 9-20 **Declining balance depreciation**

B14 fx =DB($B$4,$B$5,$B$6,B9)

	A	B	C	D	E	F
1	**Bent Cycling**					
2	**Depreciation of Assets**					
3						
4	Initial Asset Value (Cost)	$300,000				
5	Salvage Value (Salvage)	$100,000				
6	Life of Asset (Life)	15				
7						
8				Year		
9		1	2	3	4	5
10	Straight-Line (SLN)	$13,333	$13,333	$13,333	$13,333	$13,333
11	Cumulative Depreciation	$13,333	$26,667	$40,000	$53,333	$66,667
12	**Depreciated Asset Value**	**$286,667**	**$273,333**	**$260,000**	**$246,667**	**$233,333**
13						
14	Declining Balance (DB)	$21,300	$19,788	$18,383	$17,078	$15,865
15	Cumulative Depreciation	$21,300	$41,088	$59,470	$76,548	$92,413
16	**Depreciated Asset Value**	**$278,700**	**$258,912**	**$240,530**	**$223,452**	**$207,587**
17						

depreciated value at the end of Year 5

PROSKILLS

Decision Making: Choosing a Depreciation Schedule

How do you decide which method of depreciation is the most appropriate? The answer depends on the type of asset being depreciated. Tax laws allow different depreciation methods for different kinds of assets and different situations. In general, you want to choose the depreciation method that most accurately describes the financial status of the company. In tax statements, depreciation appears as an expense that is subtracted from the company's earnings. So, if you accelerate the depreciation of an asset in the early years of its use, you might be underestimating the company's profits, making it appear that the company is less profitable than it actually is. On the other hand, depreciating an asset slowly could make it appear that the company is more profitable than it really is. For this reason, the choice of a depreciation method is best made in consultation with a tax accountant, who is fully aware of the financial issues and the tax laws involved in depreciating an asset.

Now that you have an estimate of the depreciation of the proposed building project, you can add this information to the income statement. Diane wants a general picture of the depreciation of the proposed expansion and its impact on the company's income over the next five years. You'll enter the depreciation values in the income statement, and then calculate the operating profit for the company.

To include depreciation and operating profit in the income statement:

1. Return to the **Income Statement** worksheet.
2. Click cell **B19**, and then type **=** to begin the formula. You want to reference the value in cell B14 of the Depreciation worksheet, which contains the first year of depreciation that Diane would want to claim on the company's tax report.
3. Click the **Depreciation** sheet tab, click cell **B14**, and then press the **Enter** key to enter the formula =Depreciation!B14. A depreciation expense of 21,300 is entered for Year 1.
4. Copy cell **B19**, and then paste the formula into the range **C19:F19**. The depreciation expense for each of the five years is entered in the income statement.
5. In cell B20, enter the formula **=B18–B19** to calculate the operating profit for the company, which is the company's initial earnings estimate reduced by the amount of the depreciation of its assets during the year.
6. Copy the formula in cell **B20** to the range **C20:F20** to calculate the operating profit for each of the next five years. The projected operating profit of the company is $421,700 in Year 1 of the proposed expansion, rising to $885,446 at the end of the fifth year. See Figure 9-21.

Figure 9-21 Depreciation and operating profit for Year 1 through Year 5

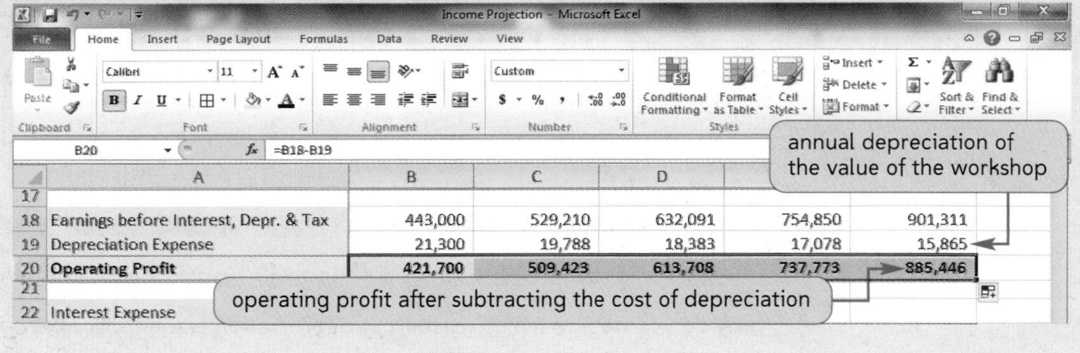

	A	B	C	D	E	F
17						
18	Earnings before Interest, Depr. & Tax	443,000	529,210	632,091	754,850	901,311
19	Depreciation Expense	21,300	19,788	18,383	17,078	15,865
20	Operating Profit	421,700	509,423	613,708	737,773	885,446
21						
22	Interest Expense					

Completing the Income Statement

The next part of the income statement records the company's expense from the interest payments on the $300,000 loan. You calculated these values at the end of the previous session in the Loan Schedule worksheet in the Investment Analysis workbook (shown earlier in Figure 9-10). Rather than reenter these values, you will reference the calculated values from that worksheet in the income statement. Because those values were entered as negative numbers, you'll change the sign to match the format of the Income Statement worksheet.

To reference the yearly interest payments on the proposed loan:

1. In cell B22, enter the formula **=–'[Investment Analysis.xlsx]Loan Schedule'!B36** and then press the **Enter** key. The value 23,923 appears in the cell.

   Trouble? If an error value or a different value appears in the cell, you probably mistyped the formula. Check the formula you entered in cell B22 and correct any mistakes in spelling or the use of quotation marks.

2. Copy the formula in cell **B22** to the range **C22:F22**. The values 19,505, 14,699, 9,471, and 3,784 for the interest expenses in Year 2 through Year 4 appear in the cells.

The income statement needs to include the company's taxable income, which is equal to the operating profit minus the interest payments that Diane expects to make on the proposed loan. You will estimate the pretax earnings in row 23 of the Income Statement worksheet.

To calculate the pretax earnings:

1. In cell B23, enter the formula **=B20–B22** to calculate the taxable income, which is the operating profit minus the interest payments. The formula returns $397,777, which is the taxable income for the company at the end of Year 1.
2. Copy the formula in cell **B23** to the range **C23:F23**. The taxable income by the end of Year 5 increases to $881,662.

Approximately one-third of the company's taxable income is paid toward taxes. So, for this projected income statement, you'll use a 33% tax rate for each of the five years.

The final row of the income statement displays the company's **net income**, which is the company's income after all expenses and taxes have been paid. Diane is most interested in this value because it provides a measure of the company's profitability.

To calculate the taxes and net income:

1. In cell F4, enter **33%**. This is the tax rate you'll use to calculate the taxes.
2. In cell B25, enter the formula **=B23*$F$4** to multiply the earnings before taxes in Year 1 by the tax rate. The estimated tax is 131,266, indicating that the company can expect to pay more than $130,000 in taxes in Year 1.
3. Copy the formula in cell **B25** to the range **C25:F25**. At the end of the fifth year, the company's tax burden is estimated to be $290,948.
4. In cell B26, enter the formula **=B23–B25** to calculate the net income by subtracting the estimated tax from the earnings before taxes. The net income for Year 1 is $266,511.
5. Copy the formula from cell **B26** to the range **C26:F26**. At the end of Year 5, the company's net income is projected to rise to $590,713. See Figure 9-22.

Figure 9-22 **Final income statement projections**

	A	B	C	D	E	F
1	**Bent Cycling**					
2	**Projected Five-Year Income Statement**					
3				Percent Cost of Goods		72%
4				Assumed Tax Rate		33%
5		**Year 1**	**Year 2**	**Year 3**	**Year 4**	**Year 5**
6	Sales Revenue	1,800,000	2,140,573	2,545,584	3,027,227	3,600,000
7	Cost of Goods Sold	1,296,000	1,541,212	1,832,821	2,179,604	2,592,000
8	**Gross Profit**	**504,000**	**599,360**	**712,764**	**847,624**	**1,008,000**
9						
10	Accounting	10,000	11,500	13,225	15,209	17,490
11	Advertising & Promotion	14,000	16,100	18,515	21,292	24,486
12	Insurance	9,000	10,350	11,903	13,688	15,741
13	Maintenance	10,000	11,500	13,225	15,209	17,490
14	Utilities	8,000	9,200	10,580	12,167	13,992
15	Miscellaneous	10,000	11,500	13,225	15,209	17,490
16	**Total General Expenses**	**61,000**	**70,150**	**80,673**	**92,773**	**106,689**
17						
18	Earnings before Interest, Depr. & Tax	443,000	529,210	632,091	754,850	901,311
19	Depreciation Expense	21,300	19,788	18,383	17,078	15,865
20	**Operating Profit**	**421,700**	**509,423**	**613,708**	**737,773**	**885,446**
21						
22	Interest Expense	23,923	19,505	14,699	9,471	3,784
23	**Earnings Before Taxes**	**397,777**	**489,918**	**599,009**	**728,302**	**881,662**
24						
25	Estimated Tax	131,266	161,673	197,673	240,340	290,948
26	**Net Income**	**266,511**	**328,245**	**401,336**	**487,962**	**590,713**

tax rate
projected taxes due each year
projected net income

6. Save and close the workbook.

If the company's revenue grow at the rate Diane projected, and if Diane's estimate of expenses is accurate, the company's net income will increase from about $266,000 in Year 1 to more than $590,000 by the end of Year 5. Although this is good news, Diane still wonders whether the new workshop is a good financial investment and how it compares to other investments. You'll use another set of financial functions to explore this question in the next session.

REVIEW

Session 9.2 Quick Check

1. The first value in a linear trend is 1000. The fifth value is 4000. What are the values of the second, third, and fourth items?
2. If the first value in a growth trend is 1000 and the fifth value is 4000, what are the values of the second, third, and fourth items?
3. The first value in a series is 1000. Extrapolate the next four values assuming a linear trend of 500.
4. If the value in a series is 1000, extrapolate the next four values assuming a growth trend of 15%.
5. A new business buys $25,000 worth of computer equipment. If the useful life of the equipment is 5 years with a salvage value of $2,000, how much will the equipment depreciate per year, assuming a straight-line depreciation?
6. Calculate how much the computer equipment described in Question 5 would depreciate in the first year assuming declining balance depreciation.
7. Calculate how much the computer equipment described in Question 5 would depreciate in the first year assuming double-declining balance depreciation with a factor of 2.

SESSION 9.3 VISUAL OVERVIEW

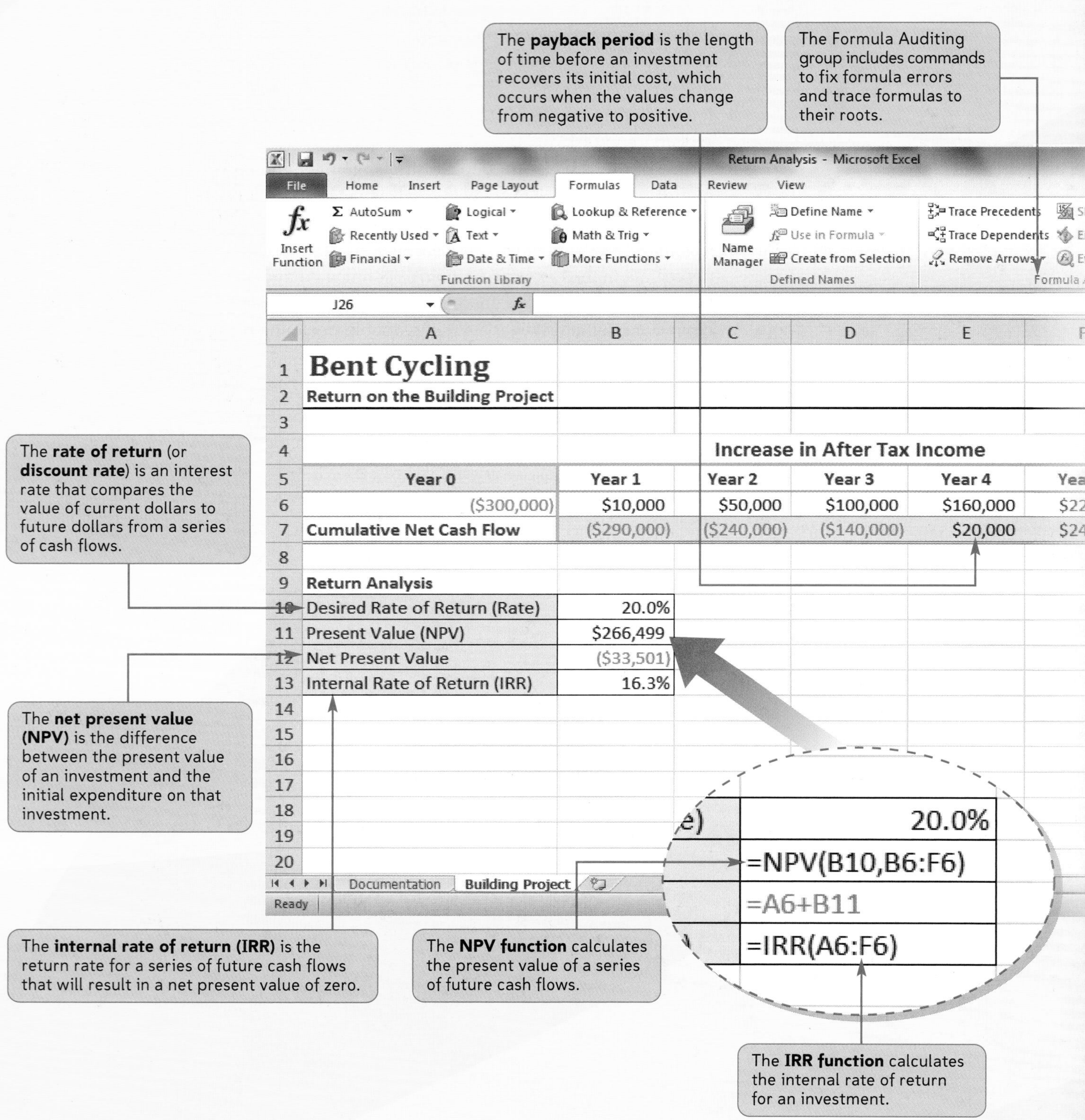

NPV, IRR, AND AUDITING

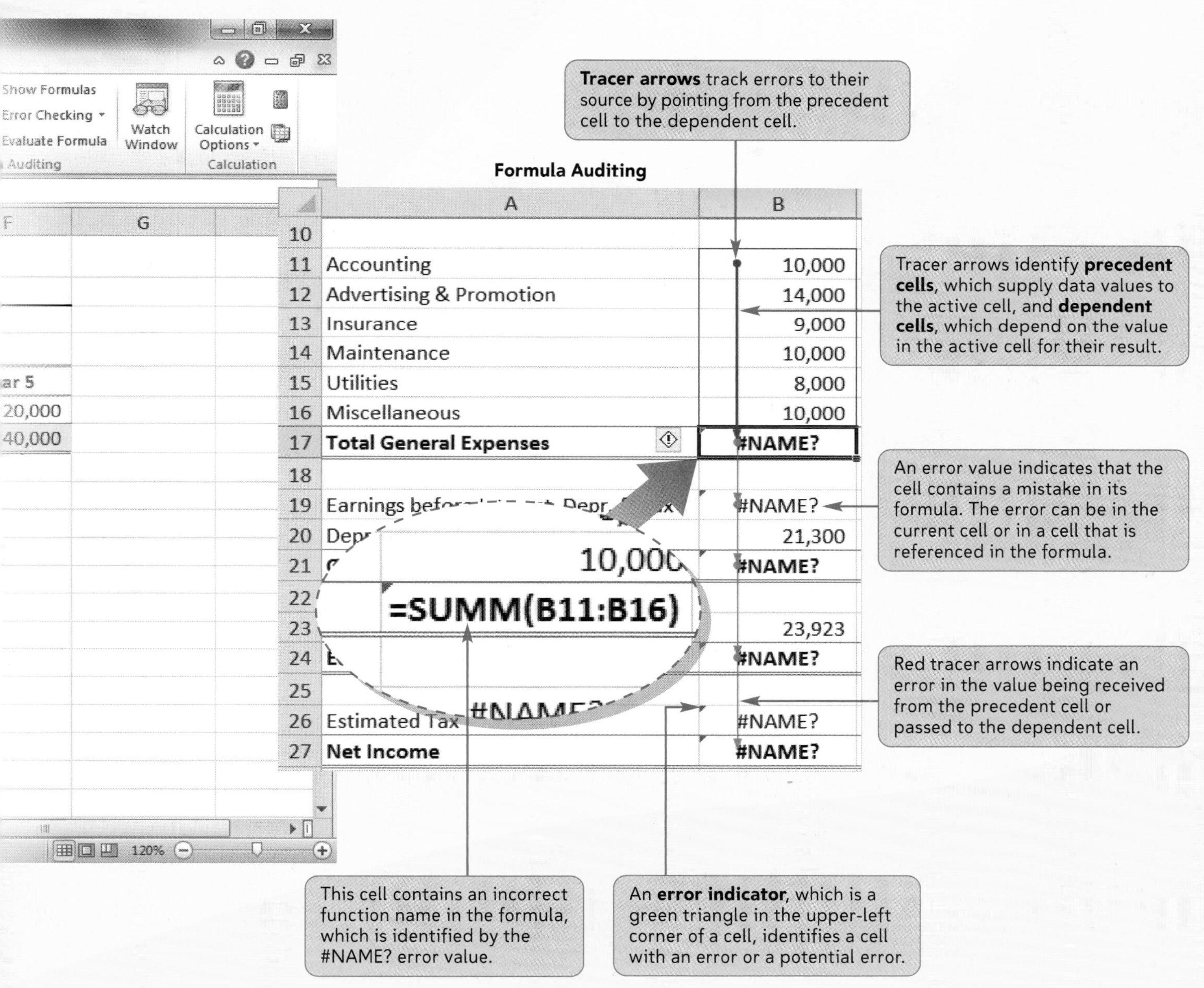

Calculating the Payback Period of an Investment

Diane has met with her colleagues and calculated how much additional net income will be generated by the building project compared to what the company could expect in the next five years without the new workshop. She's placed this information in an Excel workbook.

To open and review the Building Project worksheet:

1. Open the **Return** workbook located in the Excel9\Tutorial folder included with your Data Files, and then save the workbook as **Return Analysis** in the same folder.
2. In the Documentation worksheet, enter your name in cell B3 and the date in cell B4.
3. Switch to the **Building Project** worksheet, and then review the predicted yearly increases in net income that will be generated by the expansion. See Figure 9-23.

Figure 9-23 **Initial Building Project worksheet**

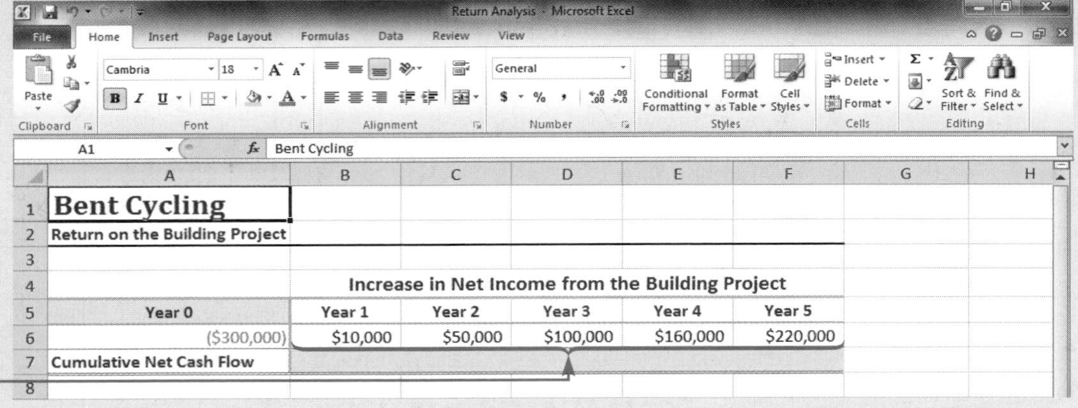

The predicted income increases don't tell Diane whether the initial investment is worth the total return. What if she used the $300,000 in a different way? How does the return on the company's investment from building the new workshop compare to the return it would get from investing the money elsewhere?

One simple measure of the return from an investment is the payback period, which is the length of time required for an investment to recover its initial cost. For example, if the $300,000 building project brought in an extra $50,000 per year in cash, it would take six years to pay back the cost of the initial investment. Diane expects the building project will increase the company's net income by $540,000 over the next five years compared to what it would have generated had she not funded the building project. You can use the cumulative cash flow values Diane entered in the Building Project worksheet to determine when the $300,000 investment will pay for itself.

To determine the payback period for the investment:

1. In cell B7, enter the formula **=B6+A6** which returns ($290,000). After the first year, about $290,000 still needs be recouped in extra revenue from the investment.
2. In cell C7, enter the formula **=C6+B7** which returns ($240,000). At the end of the second year, $240,000 of the initial investment remains to be paid.
3. Copy the formula in cell **C7** to the range **D7:F7** to calculate the remaining cumulative net cash flow values. See Figure 9-24.

Figure 9-24 Payback period for the building project

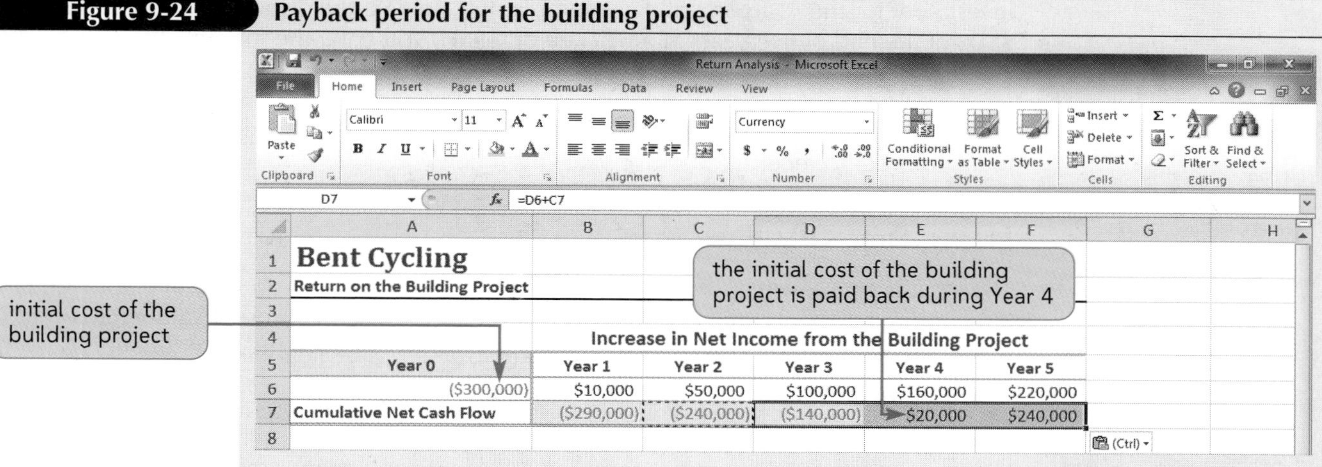

Based on these calculations, the additional revenue from building the workshop will pay back the $300,000 investment sometime during the fourth year (when the value of the cumulative net cash flow changes from negative to positive). By the end of the fifth year, the company will have shown a total profit of $240,000 from the $300,000 initial investment.

Calculating Net Present Value

The payback period is a quick method of projecting the value of an investment. The major drawback to the payback period is that it does not take into account the time value of money. To understand why, you must explore how time affects financial decisions.

The Time Value of Money

The **time value of money** is based on the observation that money received today is worth more than the same amount received later. One reason for this is that you can invest the money you receive today and earn interest on the investment. The time value of money can be expressed in terms of what represents a fair exchange between current dollars and future dollars.

For example, is it better to get $100 today or $105 one year from now? The answer depends on what you could do with that $100 over that year. If you could invest it in an account that pays 6% interest, the $100 would turn into $106 in one year, making it better to receive the $100 now. But, if you could only earn 4% interest on the $100, it is better to receive $105 after a year.

The interest rate you apply to your present funds is known as the rate of return or discount rate, and defines the time value of money by providing a way to measure future dollars in terms of current dollars. You can use the PV (present value) function to calculate the time value of money under different rates of return.

For example, to determine the present value of receiving $100 per year for the next five years at an annual rate of return of 6%, you would enter the formula

```
=PV(6%, 5, 100)
```

which returns -$421.24, indicating that it would be a fair exchange to spend $421.24 today in order to receive $100 per year for each of the next five years. In other words, $421.24 today is worth the same as $500 given in $100 annual payments over the next five years.

For investments that pay off at the end of the investment period without any intermediate payments, you enter 0 for the *pmt* argument and enter the amount returned by the investment for the *fv* argument. For example, to calculate the present value of receiving $500 at the end of five years at a 6% rate of return, you enter the formula

```
=PV(6%, 5, 0, 500)
```

which returns –$373.63, indicating that it would be a fair exchange to spend $373.63 today in order to receive $500 five years from now.

TIP

You can also use the FV (future value) function to estimate how much a dollar amount today is worth in future dollars. The formula =FV(5%, 2, 0, −100) returns $110.25, a positive cash flow indicating that spending $100 today with a discount rate of 5% is a fair exchange for receiving $110.25 two years from now.

Using the NPV Function

The PV function assumes that all future payments received from an investment are equal. If the future payments are not equal, you can use the NPV (net present value) function to determine what would constitute a fair exchange. The syntax of the NPV function is

```
=NPV(rate, value1 [, value2, value3, ...])
```

where *rate* is the rate of return, and *value1*, *value2*, *value3*, and so on are the values of future payments from the investment. The NPV function assumes that payments are paid at the end of each payment period and that the payment periods are equally spaced in time.

For example, to calculate the present value of a three-year investment that pays $100 at the end of the first year, $200 at the end of the second, and $500 at the end of the third with a 6% annual rate of return, you would enter the following formula, which returns $692.15, indicating that the value of such an investment is equal to receiving $692.15 today:

```
=NPV(6%, 100, 200, 500)
```

Unlike the PV function, which returns a negative value for the present value of the investment, the NPV function returns a positive value. This occurs because the PV function returns a cash flow value that indicates how much you need to invest now (a negative cash flow) in order to receive money later (a positive cash flow); whereas the NPV function calculates the value of those payments in today's dollars based on your chosen rate of return.

The future values of an investment do need to be positive. Consider an investment that has a 6% rate of return with the following transactions:

- Year 1: Investor receives $250
- Year 2: Investor receives $150
- Year 3: Investor receives $100
- Year 4: Investor pays $150
- Year 5: Investor pays $400

At first glance, this seems to be a bad investment: the investor receives a total of $500 but repays $550. However, this doesn't take into account the time value of money. When the present value of this transaction is calculated using the NPV function

```
=NPV(6%, 250, 150, 100, -150, -400)
```

the formula returns $35.59, indicating that the investment is actually worth more than $35 in current dollars to the investor. This is because the returns from the investment come early, but the payments are due later, paid in dollars of lesser value.

Choosing a Rate of Return

Choosing an appropriate rate of return is related to the concept of **risk**—the possibility that the entire transaction will fail, resulting in a loss of the initial investment. Investments with higher risks generally should have higher rates of return. If Diane takes $300,000 and invests the money in a simple bank account (a low-risk venture), she would not expect a high rate of return. On the other hand, using the $300,000 to fund an expansion of the company's facilities with the expectation that it will result in increased income merits a higher rate of return.

After discussing the issue with financial analysts, Diane has decided on a 12% rate of return. This means that Diane wants the expansion to return at least as much revenue over the next five years as she would get if she had invested $300,000 in an account that paid 12% annual interest. You'll use that rate of return in the NPV function as you calculate the net present value of the proposed expansion project.

To calculate the net present value of the building project:

1. In cell B10, enter **12%** for the desired rate of return.
2. In cell B11, enter the formula **=NPV(B10,B6:F6)** to calculate the net present value using 12% as the rate of return (cell B10) and the anticipated returns from the project (range B6:F6). The formula returns $346,483, indicating that the present value of the project is worth $346,483 in current dollars.
3. In cell B12, enter the formula **=A6+B11** to combine the present value with the initial $300,000 cash expenditure in Year 0 that pays for the project, which calculates the return from the initial investment. See Figure 9-25.

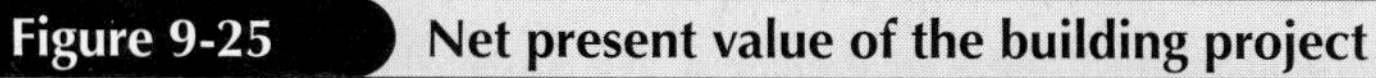

Figure 9-25 Net present value of the building project

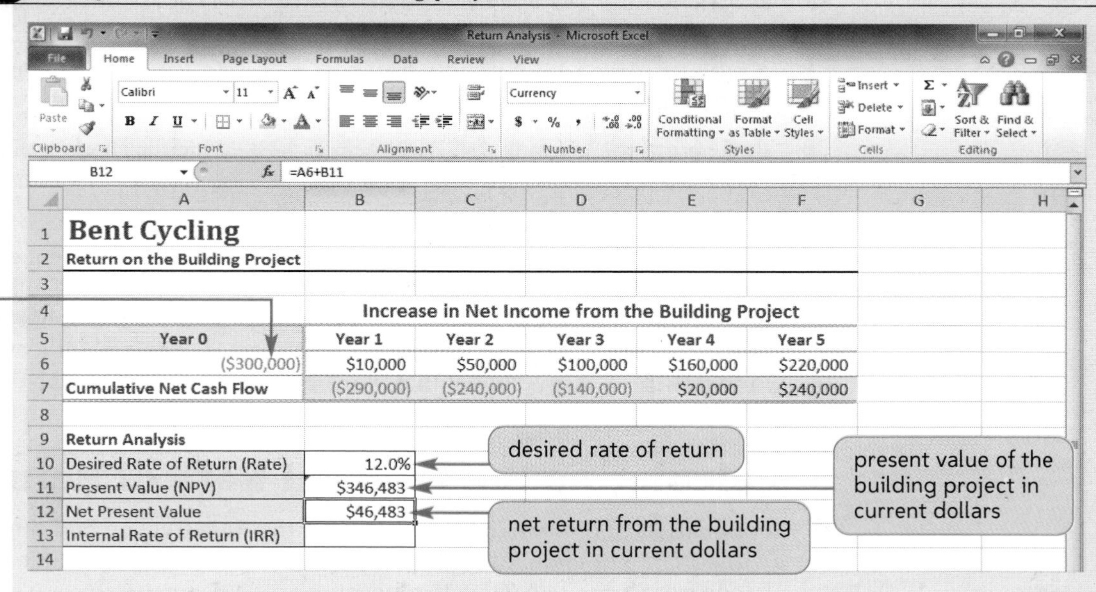

With a 12% rate of return, the net present value of the $300,000 building project is more than $46,000 in current dollars. In other words, if all of Diane's assumptions are correct, investing $300,000 in the project is worth about $46,000 more than investing the same amount in an account paying 12% annual interest. The proposed expansion appears to be profitable under those terms.

INSIGHT

Understanding Net Present Value and the NPV Function

The financial definition of net present value is the difference between the present value of future cash flows and the current cost of the initial investment. One source of confusion for Excel users is that despite its name, the NPV function does *not* return the net present value of an investment. Instead it returns the investment's present value.

To calculate the net present value in Excel, the cost of the initial investment must be subtracted from the value returned by the NPV function using the formula

```
NPV value - initial investment
```

where *NPV value* is the value returned by the NPV function, and *initial investment* is the initial cost of the investment. This formula assumes that the initial investment is made immediately, and not in the future using discounted dollars.

In any financial analysis, it is a good idea to test other values to see how they impact your conclusions. You will rerun your calculations using other possible rates of return.

To view the impact of different rates of return:

1. Change the value in cell B10 to **9%** to decrease the desired rate of return. The net present value in cell B12 increases to $84,810. The increase is due to the fact that the high returns in Year 4 and Year 5 are not discounted as much as they were at a 12% rate of return.
2. Change the value in cell B10 to **15%** to increase the desired rate of return. The net present value drops to $13,144.
3. Change the value in cell B10 to **20%** to further increase the desired rate of return. The net present value drops to –$33,501.
4. Change the value in cell B10 back to **12%**, which is Diane's desired rate of return for the expansion project.

At higher rates of return, the net present value of the investment goes down. That's not surprising when you realize the expansion is being compared with investments that offer higher and higher return values. Compared with an investment that offers a 20% interest rate, the net present value of the building project is negative, indicating that the project is worth less than an investment that offers 20% annual interest.

Calculating the Internal Rate of Return

Your analysis of different rates of return for the Bent Cycling building project illustrates an important principle: At some rate of return, the net present value of an investment will change from a positive value to a negative value. Figure 9-26 shows the change in net present value for a sample investment using different rates of return.

Figure 9-26 Net present values for different rates of return

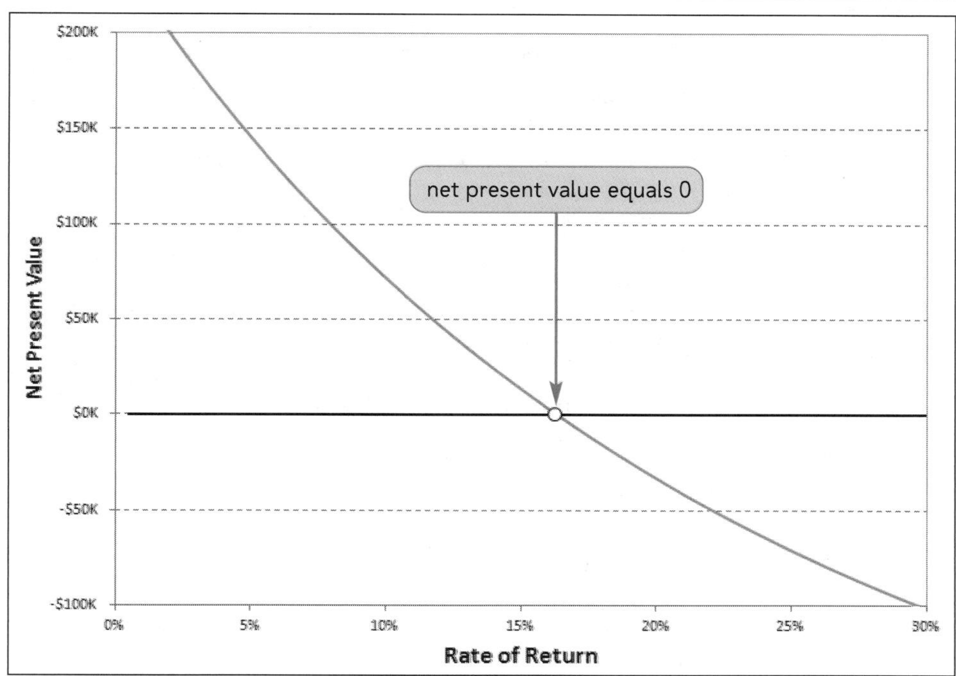

The point at which the net present value of an investment equals 0 is the internal rate of return (IRR) of the investment. The internal rate of return is another popular measure of the value of an investment because it forms a basis of comparison between one investment and another. Investments with higher internal rates of return are usually preferred to those with lower IRRs.

Using the IRR Function

The IRR function calculates the internal rate of return for an investment. The syntax of the IRR function is

```
=IRR(values [, guess=0.1])
```

where *values* are the cash flow values from the investment, and *guess* is an optional argument in which you guess the IRR value. A guess is needed for financial transactions that have several possible internal rates of return, such as investments that require the investor to make multiple future payments, rather than a single initial payment. For those types of transactions, an initial guess assists Excel in locating the final value for the IRR. Without the guess, Excel might not be able to calculate the IRR. If you don't include a guess, Excel will use an initial guess of 10% for the IRR and proceed from there to derive the answer. (Case Problem 2 explores how to use the guess argument in the IRR function and shows why it is sometimes necessary.)

The list of *values* in the IRR function must include at least one positive cash flow and one negative cash flow, and the order of the values must reflect the order in which the payments are made and the payoffs are received. Like the NPV function, the IRR function assumes that the payments and payoffs occur at evenly spaced intervals. Unlike the NPV function, you include the initial cost of the investment in the *values* list.

REFERENCE

Calculating the Value of an Investment

- To calculate the net present value when the initial investment is made immediately, use the NPV function with the discount rate and the series of cash returns from the investment. Subtract the cost of the initial investment from the value returned by the NPV function.
- To calculate the net present value when the initial investment is made at the end of the first payment period, use the NPV function with the discount rate and the series of cash returns from the investment. Include the initial cost of the investment as the first value in the series.
- To calculate the internal rate of return, use the IRR function with the cost of the initial investment as the first cash flow value in the series. For investments that have several positive and negative cash flow values, include a guess to aid Excel in finding a reasonable internal rate of return value.

You'll use the IRR function to calculate the internal rate of return for the building project.

To calculate the IRR for the proposed workshop:

1. In cell B13, enter the formula **=IRR(A6:F6)**, selecting all of the cash flow values including the initial expenditure of $300 in cell A6. The formula returns the IRR of 16.3%. See Figure 9-27.

Figure 9-27 **Internal rate of return for the investment**

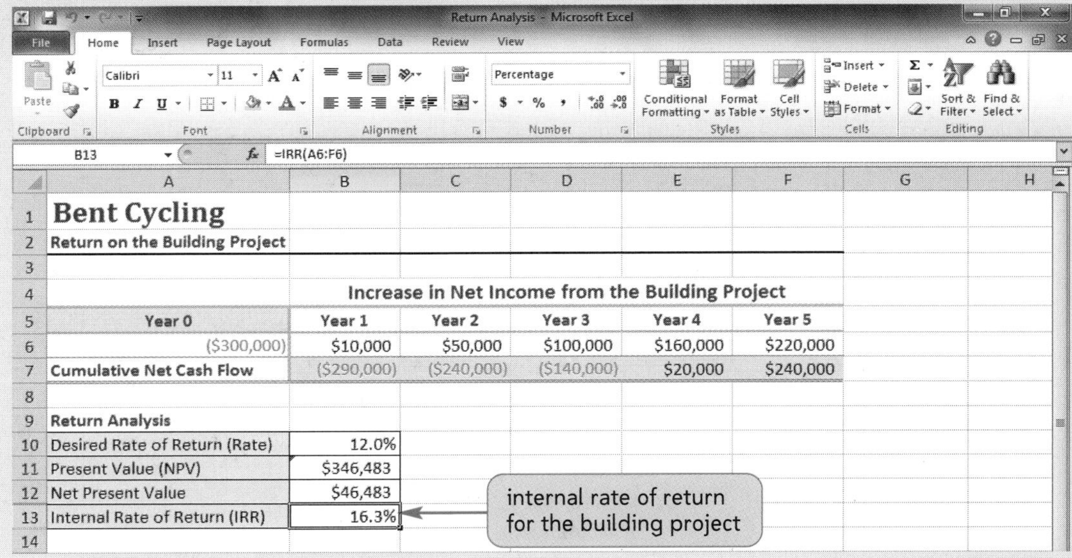

2. Save and close the workbook.

PROSKILLS

Decision Making: Using Net Present Value and Internal Rate of Return to Compare Investments

Companies or businesses often must decide between several possible investment options. In general, they want only investments that have positive net present values or internal rates of return higher than a specified rate. In comparing two investments, companies usually want to select the investment with the higher net present value or the higher internal rate of return.

If they rely on the net present value, they can receive contradictory results depending on what value is specified for the desired rate of return. For example, consider the following two returns from an initial investment of $1,000. Option 1 has a higher net present value for a desired rate of return greater than 9%, but Option 2 has a higher net present value when the rate of return is assumed to be 9% or less.

Investment	Year 1	Year 2	Year 3	Year 4
Option 1	$350	$350	$350	$350
Option 2	0	0	0	$1600

Using the internal rate of return instead of the net present value can also lead to contradictory results. This often occurs when an investment includes several positive and negative cash flows throughout the course of its history.

So, to choose between two or more investments, it's a good idea to graph the net present value for each investment against different possible rates of return. By comparing the graphs, you can reach a decision about which investment is the most profitable and under what conditions. This helps you make the best decision about which investment to select.

Exploring the XNPV and XIRR Functions

Both the NPV and IRR functions assume that the cash flows occur at evenly spaced intervals such as annual payments in which the cash receipts from an investment are returned at the end of the financial year. For cash flows that appear at unevenly spaced intervals, you use the XNPV and XIRR functions. The XNPV function syntax is

```
=XNPV(rate, values, dates)
```

where *rate* is the desired rate of return, *values* is the list of cash flows, and *dates* are the dates associated with each cash flow. The series of values must contain at least one positive and one negative value. The cash flow values are discounted starting after the first date in the list, with the first value not discounted at all. Figure 9-28 shows an investment in which the initial payment on September 1 of $300,000 is repaid in eight deposits spaced at irregular intervals over the next two years. The net present value of this investment is $25,694 based on a 5% rate of return.

Figure 9-28 **Net present value calculated over irregular time intervals**

	A	B
1	Rate of Return	5%
2		
3	Date	Cash Flow
4	September 01, 2013	($300,000)
5	December 03, 2013	$10,000
6	February 24, 2014	$15,000
7	June 01, 2014	$25,000
8	September 05, 2014	$35,000
9	December 10, 2014	$45,000
10	March 04, 2015	$60,000
11	June 15, 2015	$75,000
12	September 14, 2015	$85,000
13		
14	Net Present Value (XNPV)	$25,694

=XNPV(B1,B4:B12,A4:A12)

Likewise, the XIRR function calculates the internal rate of return for a series of unevenly spaced payments. The syntax of the XIRR function is

```
=XIRR(values, dates [, guess = 0.1])
```

where *values* is the list of cash flow values, *dates* are the dates of each cash flow, and *guess* is an optional argument used to help Excel arrive at an answer. Figure 9-29 shows the internal rate of return for the transaction shown in Figure 9-28. The IRR of this investment is 11.07%.

Figure 9-29 **Internal rate of return calculated over irregular time intervals**

	A	B
1	Date	Cash Flow
2	September 01, 2013	($300,000)
3	December 03, 2013	$10,000
4	February 24, 2014	$15,000
5	June 01, 2014	$25,000
6	September 05, 2014	$35,000
7	December 10, 2014	$45,000
8	March 04, 2015	$60,000
9	June 15, 2015	$75,000
10	September 14, 2015	$85,000
11		
12	Internal Rate of Return (XIRR)	11.07%

=XIRR(B2:B10,A2:A10)

For Diane's proposed building project, all of the cash flow values are projected at regular intervals, at the end of the upcoming fiscal years, so you do not need to use either the XNPV or the XIRR function.

Auditing a Workbook

Diane prepared a workbook summarizing the financial implications of the proposed building project. Unfortunately, the formulas contain several errors. The workbook has several worksheets, and formulas on one worksheet are often based on values found on several other worksheets. This makes it difficult to locate the source of the errors. You can use the Excel auditing tools to locate and correct the source of the errors.

You'll open and review Diane's workbook.

To open and review the Financial Report workbook:

1. Open the **Financial** workbook located in the Excel9\Tutorial folder included with your Data Files, and then save the workbook as **Financial Report** in the same folder.
2. In the Documentation worksheet, enter your name and the date.
3. Review the Income Statement, Cash Flow Schedule, Balance Sheet, and Summary worksheets.

The Financial Report workbook contains several worksheets projecting the financial future of the company under the proposed expansion. You have already worked with the Income Statement, Loan Schedule, and Depreciation worksheets in the first two sessions of this tutorial. The Cash Flow Schedule worksheet projects the company's annual cash flow. The Balance Sheet worksheet projects the company's expected assets, liabilities, and equity. The Summary worksheet summarizes the results shown in the other worksheets. As you scroll through the workbook, you will see that many of the worksheets contain cells displaying error codes.

Tracing an Error

When Excel cannot calculate a formula's value, it displays an error code in the cell. An error code begins with the number sign (#) followed by an error name. The error name indicates the type of error. For example, the #NAME? error code indicates an unrecognized formula name or range name, possibly due to a spelling error.

The error code does not specify where the mistake is located within the workbook. The error could be located in the cell displaying the error code. Or it could be in a precedent cell, which is a cell that is referenced by a formula. For example, if cell C15 contains the formula =C13+C14, then cells C13 and C14 are precedent cells for cell C15. Any errors in cell C13 or cell C14 would also be reported in cell C15. A cell can also be a dependent cell if other cells depend upon its value. In the preceding example, cell C15 is a dependent cell, depending on the values in cells C13 and C14. A cell can be both a precedent cell and a dependent cell.

TIP

After you select a cell with an error indicator, you can click the Error Alert button to display additional information about the possible error and determine if further action is needed.

An error indicator (a green triangle in the upper-left corner of a cell) flags cells with an error or a potential error. For example, an error indicator might highlight a cell that contains a formula that is markedly different from adjacent cells to notify you that you might have entered an incorrect formula.

Because errors will spread throughout a workbook from the precedent cells down through all of its descendents, you can use the auditing tools to trace an error back to its source. To identify the source of an error, select any cell containing an error value and locate its precedents. If any of those precedents display an error value, locate that cell's precedents, and so on. Eventually, you'll reach an error that has no precedents. That cell is the source of the error values in the dependent cells. After correcting the error, if other errors still exist, select another cell containing an error and repeat the process until you have removed all of the errors from the workbook.

REFERENCE

Tracing Error Values

- Select the cell containing an error value.
- In the Formula Auditing group on the Formulas tab, click the Error Checking button arrow, and then click Trace Error.
- Follow the tracer arrows to a precedent cell containing an error value.
- If the tracer arrow is connected to a worksheet icon, double-click the tracer arrow and open the cell references in the worksheet.
- Continue to trace the error value to its precedent cells until you locate a cell containing an error value that has no precedent cells with errors.

Cells throughout the Financial Report workbook display the #NAME? error code. You'll trace and correct the source of this error.

To trace an error value in the Financial Report workbook:

1. Switch to the **Summary** worksheet, and then click cell **F18**. You'll start tracing the error with cell F18.
2. Click the **Formulas** tab on the Ribbon.
3. In the Formula Auditing group, click the **Error Checking button arrow**, and then click **Trace Arrow**. A tracer arrow is attached to cell F18. See Figure 9-30.

Figure 9-30 **Error value being traced**

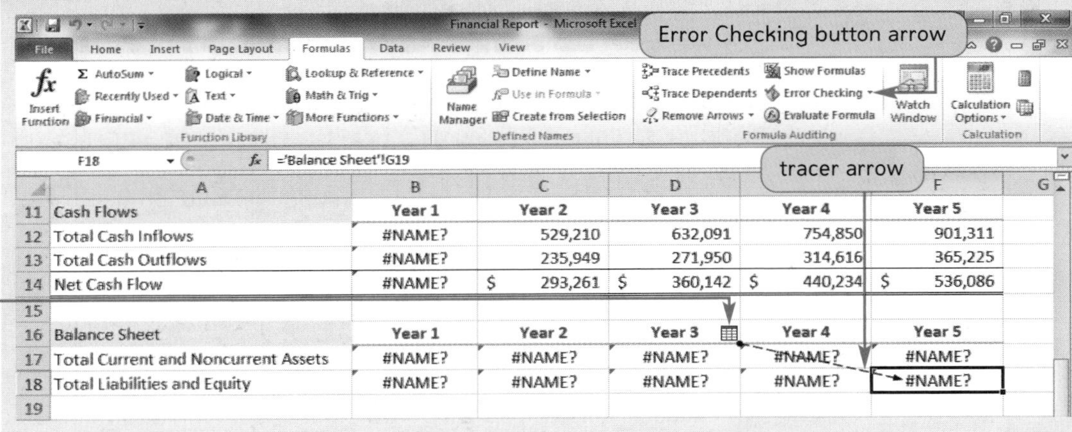

The tracer arrow provides a visual clue to the relationship between two cells by pointing from the precedent cell to the dependent cell. In this case, the tracer arrow points from a worksheet icon to cell F18. The worksheet icon indicates that the precedent for the active cell is in another worksheet. You'll jump to that cell.

To continue tracing the error to its source:

1. Double-click the **tracer arrow** that connects the worksheet icon to cell F18. The Go To dialog box opens, listing the reference to cell G19 in the Balance Sheet worksheet.

2. In the Go to box, click the cell reference, and then click the **OK** button. Cell G19 in the Balance Sheet worksheet is now the active cell. Notice that the #NAME? errors appear throughout this worksheet, too.
3. In the Formula Auditing group on the Formulas tab, click the **Error Checking button arrow**, and then click **Trace Error**. The tracer arrows go through several cells, once again stopping at a worksheet icon. See Figure 9-31.

Figure 9-31 **Error values traced across the worksheet**

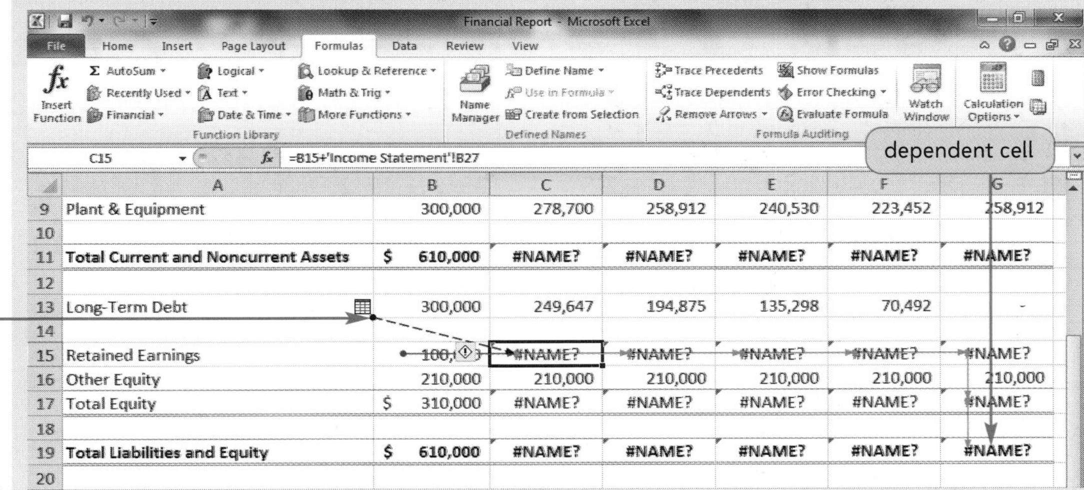

The tracer arrows provide a visual picture of how the formulas in the Balance Sheet worksheet are interconnected. The arrows show that cell G19 is dependent on the value in cell G17; cell G17 depends on the value in cell G15, which is dependent on cell F15 and then cells E15, D15, and C15. The value in cell C15 is dependent on the values in cell B15 and a cell in another worksheet. Red tracer arrows indicate that an error has been received from the precedent cell or passed to the dependent cell. A blue tracer arrow indicates that no error has been received or passed.

To locate the source of the error:

1. Double-click the **tracer arrow** that connects the worksheet icon to cell C15. The Go To dialog box opens.
2. Click the reference to cell **B27** in the Income Statement worksheet, and then click the **OK** button. Cell B27 in the Income Statement worksheet becomes active.
3. In the Formula Auditing group on the Formulas tab, click the **Error Checking button arrow**, and then click **Trace Error** to trace the source of the error in cell B17. As shown in Figure 9-32, the source of this error ends at cell B17.
4. Click cell **B17** if necessary, and then review the formula in the formula bar. The function name in the formula was entered incorrectly as *SUMM*, which is why the #NAME? error code is displayed in the cell.

Figure 9-32 Source of the error value

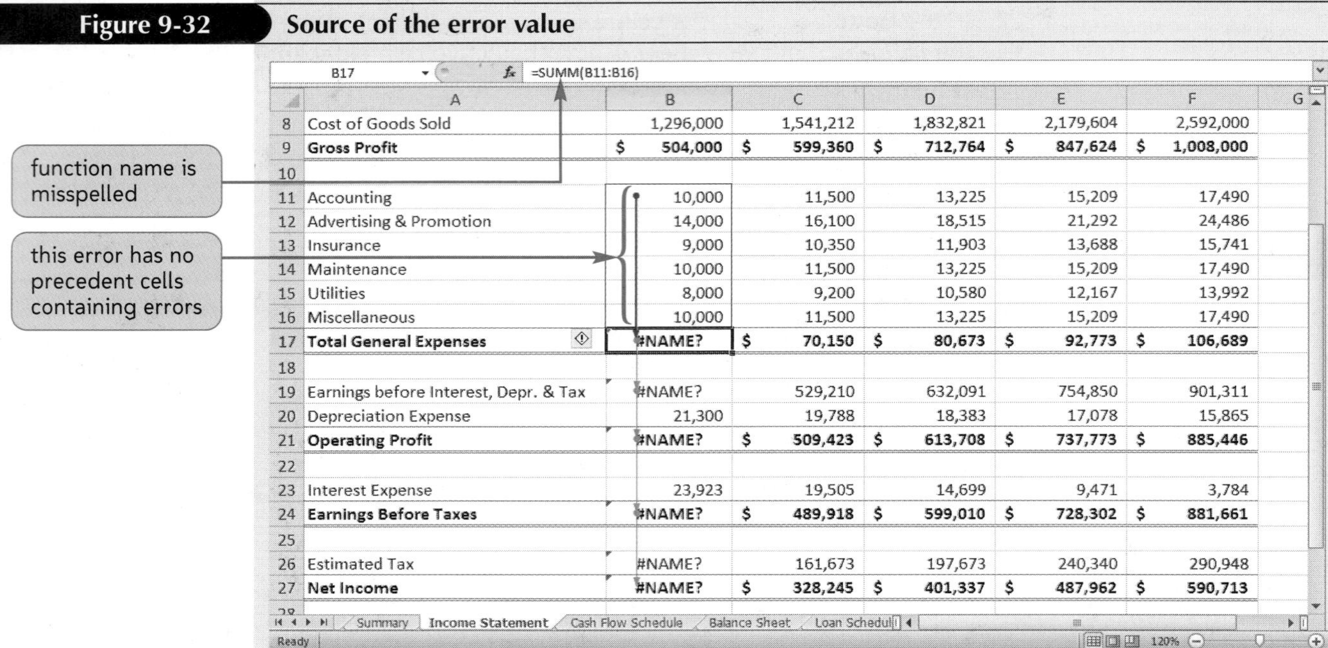

TIP

Tracer arrows disappear when you correct the error source, insert or delete columns and rows, and delete or move cells. To restore the tracer arrows, retrace the formulas in the workbook.

5. Change the value in cell B17 to **=SUM(B11:B16)** and then press the **Enter** key. When you change the formula, the #NAME? error codes disappear from the worksheet. Also, the color of the tracer arrows changes from red to blue because they no longer connect to cells containing errors.
6. In the Formula Auditing group on the Formulas tab, click the **Remove Arrows** button to remove all of the tracer arrows from the worksheet.

   Trouble? If the tracer arrows disappeared from your workbook, Excel removed them automatically. Continue with Step 7.
7. Verify that the #NAME? error values disappeared from all of the cells in the workbook, and then switch to the **Summary** worksheet.

You have located the source of the #NAME? error. Note that you can use the auditing tools to track any cell formula whether it contains an error or not. To trace the precedents of the active cell, click the Trace Precedents button in the Formula Auditing group on the Formulas tab. If you want to locate the cells that are dependent upon the active cell, click the Trace Dependents button.

Evaluating a Formula

One drawback to using tracer arrows is that they can clutter a worksheet. Sometimes, you want to trace only a single formula to its roots. Another way to explore the relationship between cells in the workbook is by evaluating formulas. From the Evaluate Formula dialog box, you can display the value of different parts of the formula or "drill down" through the cell references in the formula to discover the source of the formula's value.

In the Summary worksheet, cells F17 and F18 show Bent Cycling's total assets and total liabilities and equity in Year 5, which were calculated in the Balance Sheet worksheet. On a balance sheet, the total assets value should equal the total liabilities and equity value. Checking that these totals match is a basic step in auditing any financial report. In this case, the total assets value in cell F17 is $2,460,883, but the total liabilities and equity in cell F18 is $2,409,557. Because the values differ, an error must occur somewhere in the workbook. Although you could use the tracer arrows to trace the precedents of cells F17 and F18, you'll instead evaluate the formula in cell F17 of the Summary worksheet to locate the error.

To evaluate the formula in cell F17 of the Summary worksheet:

1. Click cell **F17**. You'll evaluate the formula in this cell, which returns the total assets on the balance sheet.
2. In the Formula Auditing group on the Formulas tab, click the **Evaluate Formula** button. The Evaluate Formula dialog box opens. The formula in cell F17 is displayed with any cell references underlined—cell G11 of the Balance Sheet worksheet, in this case. See Figure 9-33.

Figure 9-33 Evaluate Formula dialog box

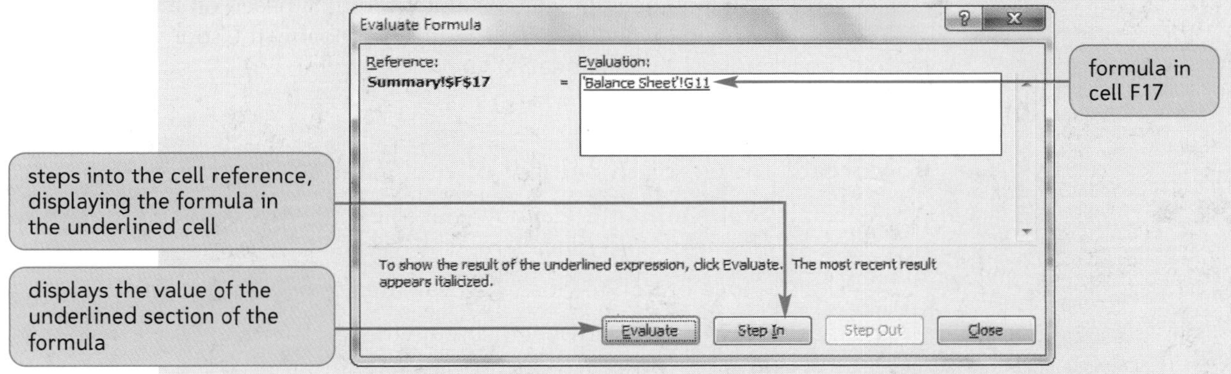

3. Click the **Step In** button to display the formula contained in the cell reference. Cell G11 in the Balance Sheet worksheet becomes the active cell and worksheet. The dialog box displays the formula in cell G11: =G7+G9. Cell G7, which contains the total current assets for the company in Year 5, is underlined.
4. Click the **Evaluate** button to display the value stored in cell G7. The Evaluate Formula dialog box displays 2201970.4929975+G9. Cell G9, which contains the depreciated value of the company's plant and equipment for Year 5, is underlined.
5. Click the **Step In** button. The dialog box displays the formula =Depreciation!C12, indicating that the depreciated value of the company's plant and equipment in Year 5 comes from cell C12 in the Depreciation worksheet.
6. Click the **Step In** button. Cell C12 in the Depreciation worksheet becomes active. See Figure 9-34.

Figure 9-34 **Drilling down through a formula**

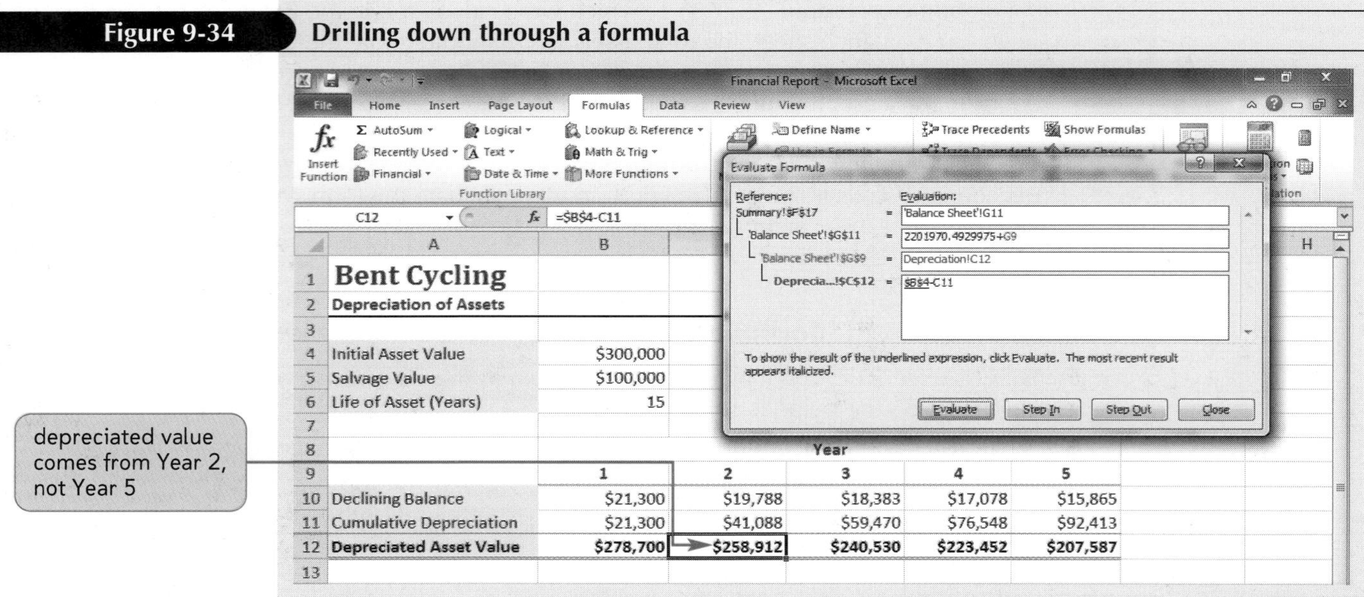

Diane tells you that the depreciated value should be based on the Year 5 value in cell F12, not the Year 2 value in cell C12. This is probably the source of the error. You'll correct the formula in the Balance Sheet worksheet.

To correct the error in cell G9 of the Balance Sheet worksheet:

1. Click the **Step Out** button to move back up in the hierarchy of formulas, returning to cell G9 in the Balance Sheet worksheet.
2. Click the **Close** button to close the Evaluate Formula dialog box.
3. In the Balance Sheet worksheet, change the formula in cell G9 to **=Depreciation!F12**.
4. Switch to the **Summary** worksheet, and then confirm that the values in cells F17 and F18 match. The Year 5 values for assets, liabilities, and equity are in balance.

Using the Watch Window

In a workbook that involves dozens of worksheets with interconnected formulas, you may often want to be able to view the impact of changing a value in one worksheet on cell values in other worksheets. Moving back and forth between worksheets can be time consuming and clumsy if the workbook contains many worksheets and the values you want to follow are spread across several of them. Rather than jumping between different worksheets, you can create a **Watch Window**, a dialog box that displays values of cells located throughout the workbook, allowing the user to view the impact of changing a cell's value on widely scattered dependent cells.

Diane wants to look at some of the underlying assumptions in the building project. When you worked on the income statement, you assumed a 33% income tax rate. Diane wants to know what would happen to the building proposal if the government increased taxes in the next five years. You'll create a Watch Window that displays the net present value and internal rate of return as you edit the income tax rate value.

To use the Watch Window to display cell values on the Summary worksheet:

1. Switch to the **Income Statement** worksheet.
2. In the Formula Auditing group on the Formulas tab, click the **Watch Window** button. The Watch Window dialog box opens.
3. Click the **Add Watch** button to open the Add Watch dialog box, click the **Summary** sheet tab, click cell **F9** in the Summary worksheet, and then click the **Add** button. The information in cell F9 is added to the Watch Window.
4. Click the **Add Watch** button, click the **Summary** sheet tab, click cell **F14** in the Summary worksheet, and then click the **Add** button. The information in cell F14 is added to the Watch Window.
5. Click the **Add Watch** button, click the **Summary** sheet tab, click cell **F17** in the Summary worksheet, and then click the **Add** button. The Watch Window displays the net income, net cash flow, and total asset values for Year 5, which are stored in the Summary worksheet. As you change values in the workbook, you can view the impact of those changes in the Watch Window.
6. In cell F5 of the Income Statement worksheet, change the assumed tax rate from 33% to **39%**. In the Watch Window, you instantly see that increasing the tax rate to 39% decreases the net income at the end of Year 5 to $537,813, drops the net cash flow for that year to $483,186, and reduces the total assets of the company to $2,221,537. See Figure 9-35.

Figure 9-35 Watch Window

7. Change the assumed tax rate value in cell F5 back to **33%**, and then close the Watch Window dialog box.
8. Save the workbook, and then close it.

You report to Diane that if income taxes increase six percentage points to 39%, the net income for the company at the end of Year 5 will drop by more than $50,000. A similar drop will be seen in the company's net cash flow. Diane will continue to use the Excel financial tools to project the company's financial future and evaluate different building plans and proposals.

REVIEW

Session 9.3 Quick Check

1. Why is the payback period not always appropriate for determining the value of an investment?
2. Suppose the rate of return is 5%. Is $95 today worth more, less, or the same as $100 a year from now?
3. Suppose you receive the following payments: $50 a year beginning now, $75 in two years, and $100 in three years. What is the present value of this investment? Assume a 6% rate of return.
4. Suppose you spend $350 on an investment that pays $75 a year for the next six years. If you make the payment immediately, what is the net present value of the investment? Assume a 6% rate of return.
5. Suppose that instead of spending $350 immediately on an investment, you spend $350 a year from now and then receive $75 a year for the next six years after that. What is the net present value assuming a 6% rate of return?
6. Calculate the internal rate of return for the investment in Question 4. If another investment is available that pays a 7.3% rate of return, should you take it?
7. What do red tracer arrows suggest?
8. A cell displays the #REF! error code. Suggest a possible source of this error.

Practice the skills you learned in the tutorial using the same case scenario.

PRACTICE

Review Assignments

Data Files needed for the Review Assignments: Building.xlsx, Loan.xlsx, NVP.xlsx, and Statement.xlsx

Diane is considering a different building proposal for Bent Cycling. Rather than building a new workshop and design facility, the company will substantially upgrade its existing facilities. The cost for remodeling is estimated to be $200,000. Diane wants you to analyze the financial aspects of the proposed remodeling, taking into account the cost of the loan and the yearly depreciation of the new equipment. You'll add the appropriate financial functions and formulas to the workbooks Diane created, correcting any errors you find. Complete the following:

1. Open the **Building**, **Loan**, **NPV**, and **Statement** workbooks located in the Excel9\Review folder, and then save them in the same folder as **Building Project**, **Loan Schedule**, **NPV and IRR**, and **Income Statement**, respectively. In the Documentation worksheet of each workbook, enter your name and the date.
2. Go to the Loan Schedule workbook, and then switch to the Loan Analysis worksheet. To pay for the remodeling, the company will take out a five-year loan for $200,000 at 7.5% interest, compounded monthly.
   a. In the range A5:F5, enter the conditions of the loan. Use formulas to calculate the rate per month and the number of payment periods in the loan.
   b. In cell G5, use the PMT function to calculate the total monthly payment on the loan based on the loan conditions already entered into the worksheet. Assume the loan will be completely paid off at the end of the last period.
3. In the range C17:F76, complete the amortization schedule. Use the IPMT function in column D to calculate the interest payment due per month. Use the PPMT function in column E to calculate how much of each monthly payment is used to pay off the principal. Display the total monthly payment in column F. Column C displays the remaining principal at the start of each month. The initial principal remaining is $200,000. The subsequent remaining principal values should be reduced by the principal payment made in the previous month.
4. In the range B11:G13, complete the yearly payment calculations on both the interest and principal, displaying how much the company will pay in interest each year and overall, and how much of the yearly payments will be used to reduce the principal. In row 11 use the CUMIPMT function to calculate the cumulative interest payments per year, and in row 12 use the CUMPRINC function to calculate the total payments made toward the principal. Save the Loan Schedule workbook.
5. Go to the Income Statement workbook. The Income Statement worksheet contains a five-year projection of the income statements for the company. Project the revenue and extrapolate the expense values for the company.
   a. In the range B8: F8, project the revenue in Years 2 through 4 by interpolating the increase in revenue between Year 1 ($1,800,000) and Year 5 ($3,600,000) assuming a growth trend.
   b. Extrapolate the expense values in the range B12:B17 through the range C12:F17 assuming a growth trend in which expenses rise by 12% per year.
6. Go to the Depreciation worksheet and complete the depreciation schedule.
   a. In the range B4:B6, enter the conditions of the depreciation based on Diane's estimates that the new equipment and features of the remodeled workshop will depreciate from $200,000 to $50,000 in 10 years.
   b. In the range B10:F10, calculate the yearly depreciation of the asset assuming a straight-line depreciation using the SLN function.
   c. In the range B14:F14, calculate the cumulative depreciation using the DB function.

d. In the range B12:F12, calculate the asset's depreciated value each year.
e. In the range B14:F16, calculate the yearly depreciation of the asset assuming a declining balance depreciation, the cumulative depreciation, and the asset's depreciated value each year.

7. In the Income Statement worksheet, apply the yearly depreciation you calculated in the Depreciation worksheet under the declining balance schedule to the range B21:F21.
8. In the range B24:F24, reference the interest expense values you calculated for each year from the Loan Schedule workbook in the Loan Analysis worksheet in the B11:F11 range. Save and close the Income Statement workbook and close the Loan Schedule workbook.
9. Go to the NPV and IRR workbook. In the Return on Investment worksheet, analyze the return on the remodeling project.
   a. The range B6:F6 contains the additional cash receipts predicted to be generated from the building project. In the range B7:F7, calculate the cumulative net cash flow from these receipts. In what year would the building project pay for itself?
   b. Compare this investment to what Diane would receive from an investment returning 10% annual interest. In cell B10, enter **10%**. In cell B11, calculate the net present value of the remodeling investment. How does it compare in current dollars to what Diane could have received by investing the $200,000 in an account paying 10% annual interest?
   c. In cell B12, calculate the internal rate of return for this investment. Save and close the NPV and IRR workbook.
10. Go to the Building Project workbook. Several cells display the #DIV/0! error value. Starting with cell E5 in the Balance Sheet worksheet, trace the error to its source and then correct it. Save and close the Building Project workbook.
11. Submit the finished workbooks to your instructor, either in printed or electronic form, as requested.

Use the skills you learned to calculate the return from investing in real estate.

APPLY

Case Problem 1

Data File needed for this Case Problem: Condo.xlsx

E-Park Real Estate Greg Baer is the owner of E-Park Real Estate, a small real-estate company in Estes Park, Colorado. Greg is examining the finances involved with purchasing a large condo outside of the village. E-Park Real Estate will hold on to the condominium for the next 10 years, receiving yearly income from rentals that will cover the expenses and will eventually pay back the cost of the initial investment. Greg wants you to calculate the return from this investment. He already created a worksheet containing the relevant financial data. You need to complete the worksheet by adding the formulas to project the value of the investment over the next 10 years. Complete the following:

1. Open the **Condo** workbook located in the Excel9\Case1 folder, and then save the workbook as **Condo Investment** in the same folder. In the Documentation sheet, enter your name in cell B3 and the date in cell B4.

   The Investment Analysis worksheet contains a projected income statement and a cash flow statement. Greg entered the initial conditions of the investment. The cost of the condo is $325,000. For tax purposes, Greg plans to depreciate the condo completely over the 10-year period of the investment. At the end of the 10-year period, he plans to sell the condo for $425,000. Greg assumes a 34% tax rate on rental income and also on the income resulting from the sale of the condo in Year 10. You need to complete the worksheet by adding the formulas to project the value of the investment over the next 10 years.

2. In the range C11:L11, enter the yearly rental income for the condo, assuming that the income grows at a linear trend from $42,000 in Year 1 to $56,000 in Year 10. In cell L12, enter a reference to the sales value of the condo already entered in cell B7. In the range C13:L13, calculate the total revenue generated by the rental and sale of the condo from Year 1 through Year 10.
3. In the range C17:L17, insert the annual property tax paid on the condo, assuming that $3,000 is paid in Year 1 and the tax increases following a linear trend to a value of $5,500 in Year 10. In the range C18:L18, insert the annual miscellaneous expenses, starting from a Year 1 value of $4,500 and assuming that expenses increase following a linear trend to a Year 10 value of $9,000. In the range C19:L19, calculate the total expenses for each year.
4. In the range C21:L21, calculate the initial earnings estimate by subtracting the total yearly expenses from the total yearly revenue.
5. In the range C22:L22, calculate the annual depreciation of the condo from Year 1 to Year 10. Assume a straight-line depreciation and use the initial cost, useful life, and salvage values entered at the top of the worksheet.
6. In the range C23:L23, calculate the taxable income by subtracting the yearly depreciation from the yearly initial earnings estimate.
7. In the range C25:L25, calculate the tax due on the taxable income for each of the next 10 years by multiplying the taxable income by the tax rate in cell B8.
8. In the range C27:L27, calculate the net income for each of the 10 years of the investment. The net income is equal to the taxable income minus the total tax due.
9. The cash flow schedule at the bottom of the worksheet calculates the yearly cash receipts that Greg expects to receive from owning the condo. Greg already entered all of the formulas to generate the cash flow schedule. The range B35:L35 contains the cumulative cash flow from the condo through the 10 years that Greg will own it. Based on his financial projections, how long will Greg have to wait until the yearly cash receipts generated from the condo cover the original purchase price?
10. In cell F4, enter **8%** because Greg wants his investment to have at least an 8% rate of return.
11. In cell F5, calculate the net present value of the investment using the cash flow values in the cell range C33:L33 as the yearly returns from the condo investment, and using the value in cell B4 as the initial cost of the investment. Assume that the initial expenditure on the condo occurs immediately.
12. In cell F6, calculate the internal rate of return on the investment using the net cash flow values from the range B33:L33. Based on your analysis, will purchasing the condo provide a greater return than a different investment offer with 8% annual interest? If the tax rate increases from 34% to 39%, will this still be the case?
13. Save and close the workbook. Submit the finished workbook to your instructor, either in printed or electronic form, as requested.

Calculate the net present value of a proposed college savings plan.

APPLY

Case Problem 2

Data File needed for this Case Problem: College.xlsx

Eason Financial Services Jesse Buchmann is a finance officer at Eason Financial Service. She's working with Andrew and Beth Ferris in developing a savings plan for their daughter Tyler, who is 11. The couple's goal is to save enough money over the next eight years to fund Tyler's four years of college. They plan to make annual deposits into their savings account starting immediately and through Tyler's four years of college. When Tyler begins school in eight years, they'll withdraw money at the beginning of each term to cover much of the cost of tuition, room, and board. They have several different options for the amount to deposit. Jesse has asked you to help her set up an Excel workbook to determine whether different savings plans will cover the cost of Tyler's college education. Complete the following:

1. Open the **College** workbook located in the Excel9\Case2 folder and save the workbook as **College Savings Plan** in the same folder. In the Documentation worksheet, enter your name in cell B3 and the date in cell B4.
2. Go to the Calculator worksheet. The couple is thinking about depositing their funds in an account that pays 6% annual interest. They would like to deposit $6,500 at the beginning of each year. Also, Tyler's grandmother wants to help by giving Tyler an extra $100 for her birthday on March 15, and Christmas each year up until she starts college. Enter these values as positive cash flows in the range B4:B6 on the worksheet.
3. Tyler starts college in eight years. The current cost to attend the local university is $15,000 per year. Andrew and Beth believe that college costs will increase at an annual rate of 4% per year. Enter these assumptions into the range B9:B11 of the worksheet.
4. You can specify the dates on which the couple will make deposits in the savings plan. They will make the $6,500 deposit at the beginning of each year on January 10. Tyler's birthday is March 15 and Christmas is December 25. Using the values you specified in the savings plan, enter the amount of the deposits into the savings account for each of the 12 years into the range G4:G33.

EXPLORE

5. Assuming that the term begins on August 15 each year, calculate the future value of the amount of money the couple will withdraw in each of the four years to pay for Tyler's education. Place your estimates into cells G28, G30, G32, and G34 as negative cash flows. (*Hint*: Use the FV function along with the current cost of education and the estimated inflation rate to determine the future annual cost of education for the couple.)
6. Calculate the projected cost of four years of Tyler's education in cell B12.

EXPLORE

7. Because the deposits and withdrawals do not occur at evenly spaced intervals, use the XNPV function to calculate the net present value of the savings plan, displaying your results in cell B15.
8. If the net present value of the savings plan is positive or zero, it will cover the cost of Tyler's education. If the net present value is negative, the plan is underfunded and will not cover the cost. Insert an IF function into B16 that displays Yes if the plan will cover the projected costs and No if it will not.
9. Apply conditional formatting to cell B16 that displays the text in a green font on a light green background if the cell's value is Yes, and red text on a light red background if the cell's value is No.
10. Based on estimates, does the proposed plan cover the projected cost of Tyler's education? Redo your analysis under the following assumptions:

College Inflation	Current College Cost	Annual Deposit
6%	$15,000	$6,500
6%	$15,000	$7,500
6%	$15,000	$8,000
7%	$12,000	$8,000
7%	$13,000	$8,000

11. Save and close the workbook. Submit the finished workbook and your answers to your instructor, either in printed or electronic form, as requested.

Explore the problem of multiple IRR values in investigating the profitability of a proposed limestone quarry.

CHALLENGE

Case Problem 3

Data File needed for the Case Problem: Witte.xlsx

Witte Limestone Sheila Dawson is a manager at Witte Limestone, a firm specializing in the excavation and processing of limestone. Sheila is currently working on a proposal for excavating a new limestone quarry outside of the town of New Berlin, Wisconsin. According to the most recent estimates, the area has enough limestone to support a quarry for the next 20 years. There will be a substantial startup cost as well as substantial costs at the end of the quarry's useful lifetime. The quarry will be most profitable in its early and middle stages of development, but will lose profitability in its later stages as it becomes more difficult to extract the remaining limestone deposits. Also, current environmental regulations require the company to restore the area to its original condition when the quarry work is finished. Sheila asks you to determine the profitability of the investment in the New Berlin quarry. Complete the following:

1. Open the **Witte** workbook located in the Excel9\Case3 folder, and then save the workbook as **Witte Limestone** in the same folder. In the Documentation worksheet, enter your name and the date.
2. The initial cost to set up the quarry is $3,800,000. Enter this value as a negative cash flow in cell B5 of the Investment Analysis worksheet.
3. Sheila estimates the quarry will generate $170,000 in cash during its first year of operation, with the yearly cash flow increasing to $980,000 by the end of Year 5. Interpolate the Year 1 through Year 5 cash flow values, assuming that the increase in cash follows a growth trend.
4. From Year 5 to Year 10, Sheila estimates the yearly cash flow will increase from $980,000 to $1,100,000. Interpolate the cash flow figures, assuming a linear trend in the increase in cash. From Year 10 to Year 15, Sheila estimates the yearly cash flow will decrease from $1,100,000 to $850,000. Interpolate the yearly cash flow figures once again assuming a linear trend in the decline.
5. From Year 15 to Year 20, the yearly cash flow from the quarry will decline from $850,000 to $50,000. Interpolate the yearly cash flow figures assuming a growth trend in the decline in net cash.
6. In Year 21, the quarry will close and the company will spend an estimated $12,000,000 to restore the area to its original pristine condition. Enter this value in cell B26 as a negative cash flow.
7. Calculate the total cash flow of the project by entering **Total** in cell A27 and the sum of the values in the range B5:B26 in cell B27. Format the range A27:B27 with the Total cell style. Based on this estimate, will the quarry pay back the cost of the initial investment and the environmental cleanup?
8. Create a chart of the net cash flow values from the range A6:B25 using the Scatter with Straight Lines chart type. Place the new chart on a chart sheet named **Cash Flow Chart**. Remove the legend from the chart. Add the chart title **Yearly Cash Returns from the New Berlin Quarry** above the chart. Add the title **Year** to the horizontal axis and the title **Net Cash Flow per Year** to the vertical axis.

EXPLORE

9. The company wants at least an 11% rate of return on this investment. In the Investment Analysis worksheet, estimate the internal rate of return for the entire investment from Year 0 through Year 21 by first inserting guesses on the IRR in cells D5 and D6. Enter the value **1%** in cell D5 and the value **10%** in cell D6. In cell E5, calculate the IRR of the investment, using the guess from cell D5. In cell E6, calculate the IRR of the investment using the guess from cell D6. Format the calculated IRRs to show two decimal places. Are the two IRR values consistent? Based on their results, can you confirm that the investment will have a return rate high enough for the company to proceed?

10. Calculate the net present value of the quarry project for different discount rates. Enter the values **1%** through **20%** in 1% increments into the range D9:D28. In the range E9:E28, calculate the net present value of the investment assuming the discount rates in column D and assuming that the initial investment in the quarry will occur immediately. For what discount rates is the NPV positive? For what discount rates is the NPV negative? Based on your calculations, can you determine whether the investment will be worthwhile if the desired rate of return is 11%? Compare your answer with your answer in Step 9. What accounts for the apparent discrepancy between the two answers?

EXPLORE

11. Create a chart of the net present values from the range D9:E28 using the Scatter with Smooth Lines chart type. Place the new chart on a chart sheet named **NPV Chart**. Remove the legend from the chart. Add the chart title **Net Present Values** above the chart. Add the title **Rate of Return** to the horizontal axis and the title **Net Present Value** to the vertical axis. Recall that the IRR value is the rate of return in which the net present value is equal to 0. Does your chart explain your results in Step 9?
12. The startup date for the quarry might be delayed because of local community action regarding environmental concerns about the quarry. Recalculate the net present values for each of the discount rates in D9:D28 by inserting new net present value calculations into the range F9:F28, assuming that the initial investment occurs not immediately but after a year's delay. Assuming a discount rate of 11%, how much will the delay cost the company in current dollars?
13. Save and close the workbook. Submit the finished workbook to your instructor, either in printed or electronic form, as requested.

Create a workbook to analyze the profitability of a new car wash.

CREATE

Case Problem 4

Data File needed for this Case Problem: Blue.xlsx

Blue Marlin Gas Yasmin Arizmendi is the business manager for Blue Marlin Gas, a gas station and convenience store in Hartford, Michigan. Yasmin is thinking about making some capital improvements, including adding a drive-through car wash to the station. He wants to perform an investment analysis to determine whether the capital improvement will pay off for the company. He has asked for your help in creating the workbook to determine what kind of return he can expect on his investment. Complete the following:

1. Open the **Blue** workbook located in the Excel9\Case4 folder, and then save the workbook as **Blue Marlin** in the same folder. In the Documentation worksheet, enter your name and the date.
2. Create a worksheet named **Investment Analysis** to analyze Yasmin's investment in the new car wash.
3. The initial cost to build a drive-through car wash is $350,000. Yasmin determines that the useful life of the equipment is 15 years with a salvage value of $50,000. Enter this information into the Investment Analysis worksheet.
4. Create an annual income statement table to project the income from the car wash from Year 0 (the current year) through Year 15. For each year, calculate the income from the car wash, the expense of building and operating the car wash, the taxable income from the car wash, the taxes due on the car wash income, and the net after tax income from the car wash.
5. Yasmin expects the car wash to generate $0 of cash in Year 0, $70,000 in Year 1, and $110,000 in Year 15. Calculate the income values in Year 2 through Year 14 assuming a linear trend.

6. The expenses should be broken down into two subcategories: the cost of building the car wash and the cost of operating the car wash. Set the Year 0 cost of building the car wash to $350,000, and set this cost to $0 for Year 1 through Year 15. Set the expense of operating the car wash to $0 in Year 0, $25,000 in Year 1, and $50,000 in Year 15. Calculate the Year 2 through Year 14 values assuming a linear trend in the expense of running the car wash. All expense values should be entered as negative cash flows. Calculate the total expenses incurred by the car wash in each year.
7. Calculate the initial earnings from the car wash for Year 0 through Year 15, equal to the revenue generated from the car wash minus the expense.
8. The depreciation of the car wash equipment is $0 in Year 0. In Year 1 through Year 15, calculate the amount that the equipment depreciates in value each year under a declining balance depreciation model.
9. Calculate the taxable income from the car wash for Year 0 to Year 15, equal to the initial earnings reduced by the depreciation of the equipment.
10. Assuming a 37% tax rate on the taxable income, calculate the amount of taxes owed for each year from the car wash operation, except for Year 0 in which no taxes are due.
11. Calculate the net income from the car wash for Year 0 through Year 15, equal to the taxable income reduced by the amount of taxes owed.

    Below the annual income statement table, insert another table to calculate the annual cash flow from running the car wash. The table should include the net cash inflow from operating the car wash in Year 0 through Year 15, and the net cash outflow from operating the car wash in Year 0 through Year 15.
12. Calculate the Year 0 through Year 15 cash flow from the new car wash. The cash inflow is equal to the taxable income added back to the depreciation value you calculated earlier. The Year 0 through Year 15 cash outflow will only consist of the taxes that you calculated in Step 10.
13. Calculate the net cash flow for Year 0 through Year 15 by reducing the net cash inflow by the net cash outflow.
14. Using the yearly net cash flow figures you calculated in Step 14, calculate the net present value of the investment in the new car wash over its projected 15 years of operation. Yasmin wants the investment to show at least a 7% rate of return. Assume that the initial investment of $350,000 in building the car wash is made immediately. Under those conditions, is the proposed car wash profitable in terms of its net present value?
15. Calculate the internal rate of return for the investment.
16. Summarize your findings, indicating whether the investment in the car wash will generate the return Yasmin is looking for.
17. Save and close the workbook. Submit the finished workbook to your instructor, either in printed or electronic form, as requested.

ASSESS

SAM: Skills Assessment Manager

For current SAM information, including versions and content details, visit SAM Central (http://samcentral.course.com). If you have a SAM user profile, you may have access to hands-on instruction, practice, and assessment of the skills covered in this tutorial. Because various versions of SAM are supported throughout the life of this text, check with your instructor for the correct instructions and URL/Web site for accessing assignments.

ENDING DATA FILES

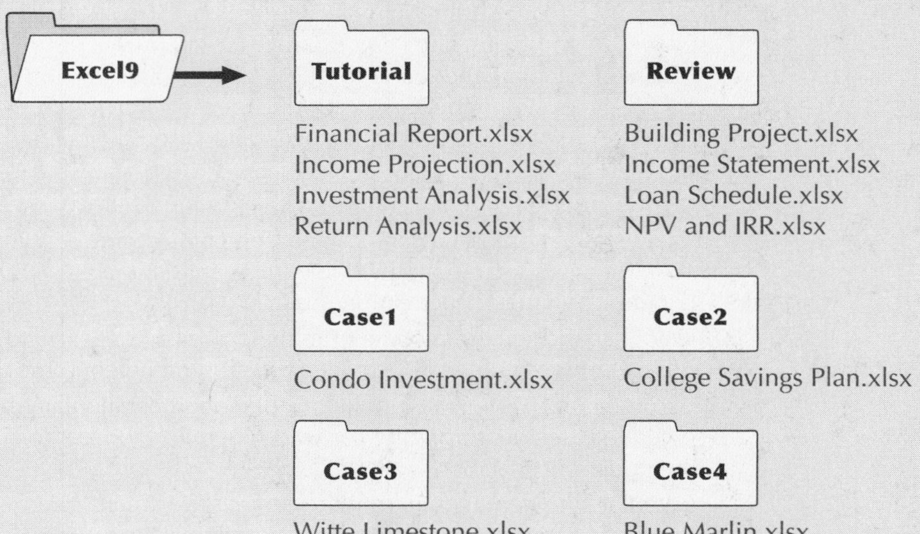

TUTORIAL 10

Performing What-If Analyses

Analyzing the Cost-Volume-Profit Relationship

EXCEL

OBJECTIVES

Session 10.1
- Explore the principles of cost-volume-profit relationships
- Perform a basic what-if analysis
- Use Goal Seek to calculate a solution
- Create a one-variable data table
- Create a two-variable data table

Session 10.2
- Create and apply different Excel scenarios
- Generate a scenario summary report
- Generate a scenario PivotTable report

Session 10.3
- Explore the principles of price elasticity
- Run Solver to calculate optimal solutions
- Create and apply constraints to a Solver model
- Save and load a Solver model

Case | *Creative Ventures*

Creative Ventures is a toy company in Fernwood, Illinois, founded by Todd and Brent Kendall. A few years ago, they created the HoverDisk, a toy that has attracted much attention and enthusiasm. Todd and Brent want to expand their market and need to do a what-if analysis to determine how much they can charge for the product and still generate a specific level of profit. They also want to determine the optimal price for the product to maximize the company's net income. You will use Excel to help find these answers.

STARTING DATA FILES

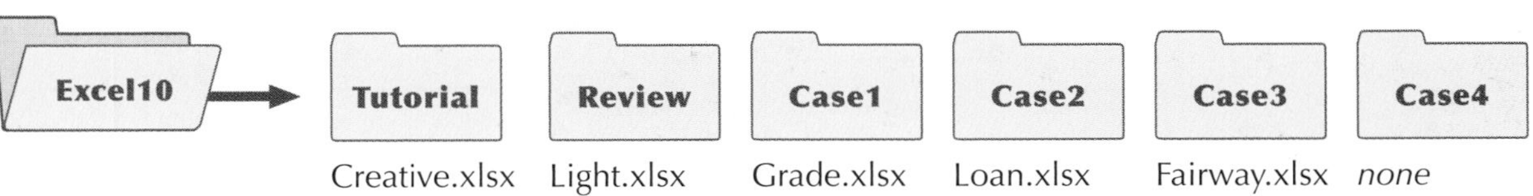

Creative.xlsx Light.xlsx Grade.xlsx Loan.xlsx Fairway.xlsx *none*

SESSION 10.1 VISUAL OVERVIEW

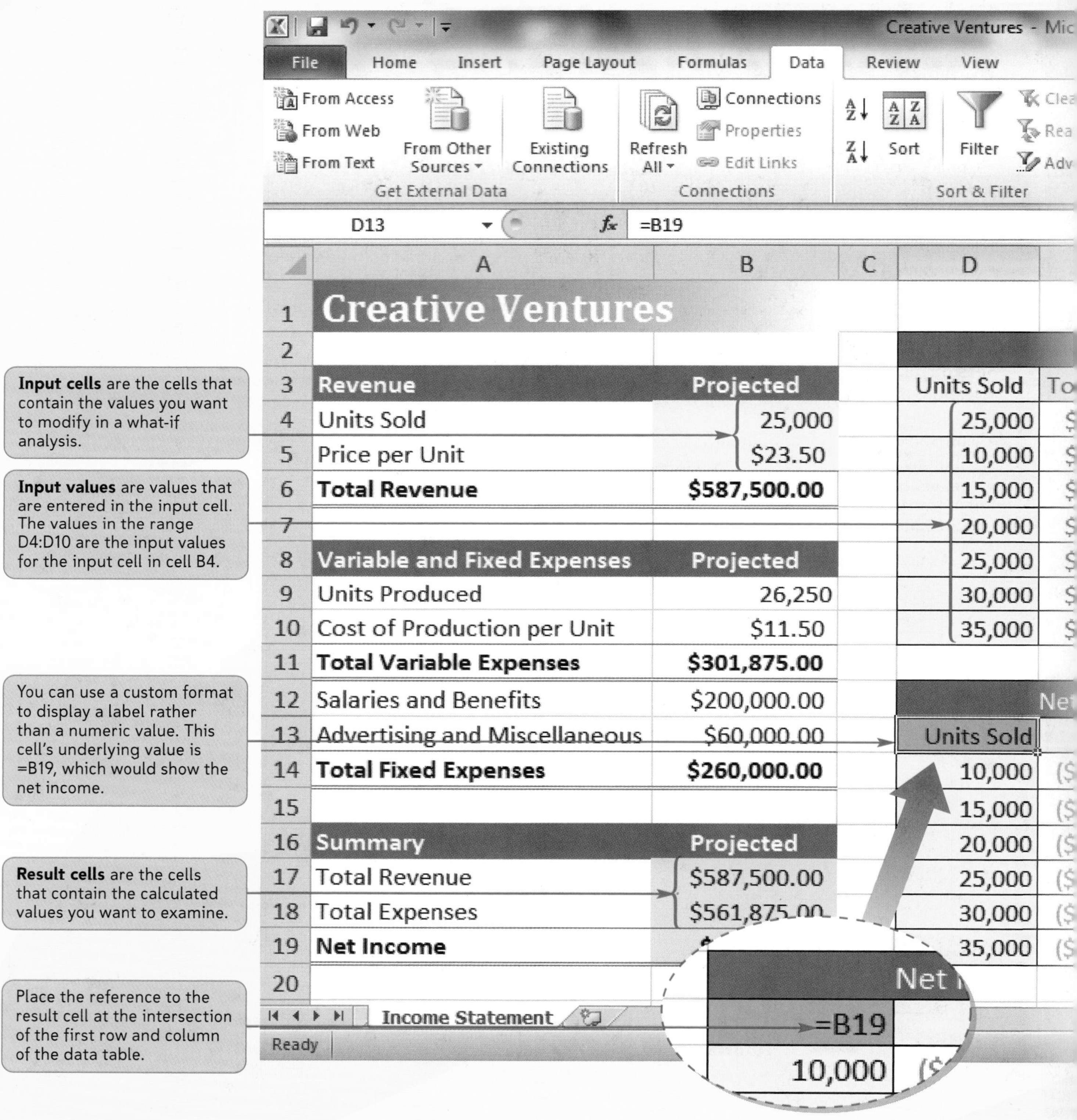

DATA TABLES AND WHAT-IF ANALYSIS

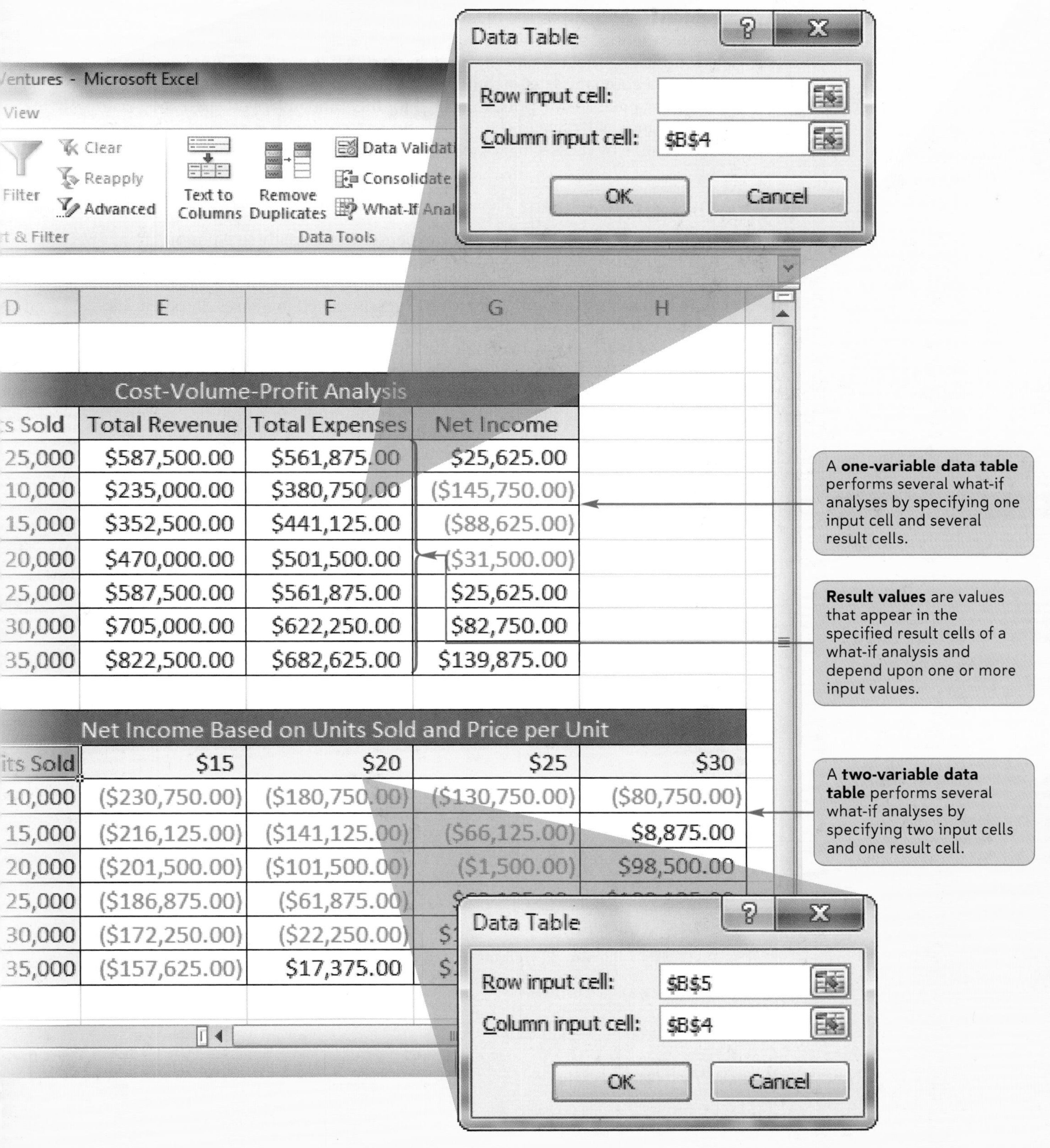

Understanding Cost-Volume-Profit Relationships

Cost-volume-profit (**CVP**) **analysis** is a branch of financial analysis that studies the relationship between expenses, sales volume, and profitability. CVP analysis is an important business decision-making tool because it can help predict the effect of cutting overhead or raising prices on a company's net income. For example, Todd and Brent need to determine what would be a reasonable price to charge for their line of HoverDisks. They need to know how much they will have to charge the consumer to break even, and how much profit they could realize by increasing (or even decreasing) the sales price.

Comparing Expenses and Revenue

The first component of CVP analysis is cost, or expense. There are three types of expenses: variable, fixed, and mixed. **Variable expenses** change in proportion to the amount of business a company does. For example, Creative Ventures has to spend more money on raw materials as the number of HoverDisks produced increases. In other words, as the sales volume increases, the costs associated with production also increase. Each HoverDisk costs $6.20 in raw materials and $4.10 in other production costs, for a total cost of $10.30 per disk. The total variable expenses for the company are equal to the cost per disk multiplied by the total number of disks produced. The line graph in Figure 10-1 plots the total variable expenses based on the production volume. As you can see from this graph, it will cost Creative Ventures more than $200,000 to produce 20,000 disks.

Figure 10-1 Chart of variable expenses

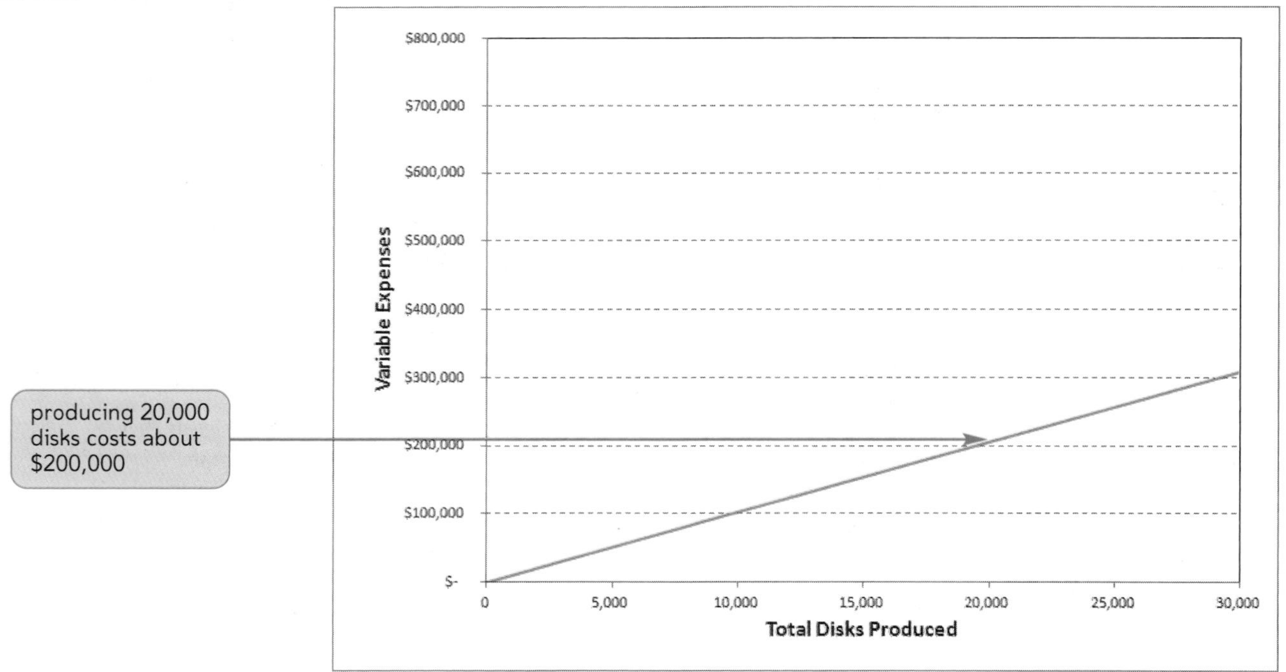

Creative Ventures sells HoverDisks for $24. You can deduct the variable expenses ($10.30) from the sales price ($24) to calculate the company's profit of $13.70 on each sale. That might seem like a lot, but that profit has to cover the company's fixed expenses. A **fixed expense** is an expense that must be paid regardless of sales volume. For example, Creative Ventures needs to pay salaries and benefits for its employees as well as insurance, maintenance fees, and taxes. The company has $260,000 in fixed expenses, which must be paid even if the company doesn't sell a single disk.

You can estimate Creative Ventures' total expenses by adding the variable and fixed expenses. The graph in Figure 10-2 shows the company's total expenses for a given number of disks produced each year. If the company produces 20,000 disks, its total expense would be about $460,000. Of this, $260,000 represents fixed expenses and more than $200,000 represents variable expenses involved in the actual production of the disks.

Figure 10-2 **Chart of total expenses**

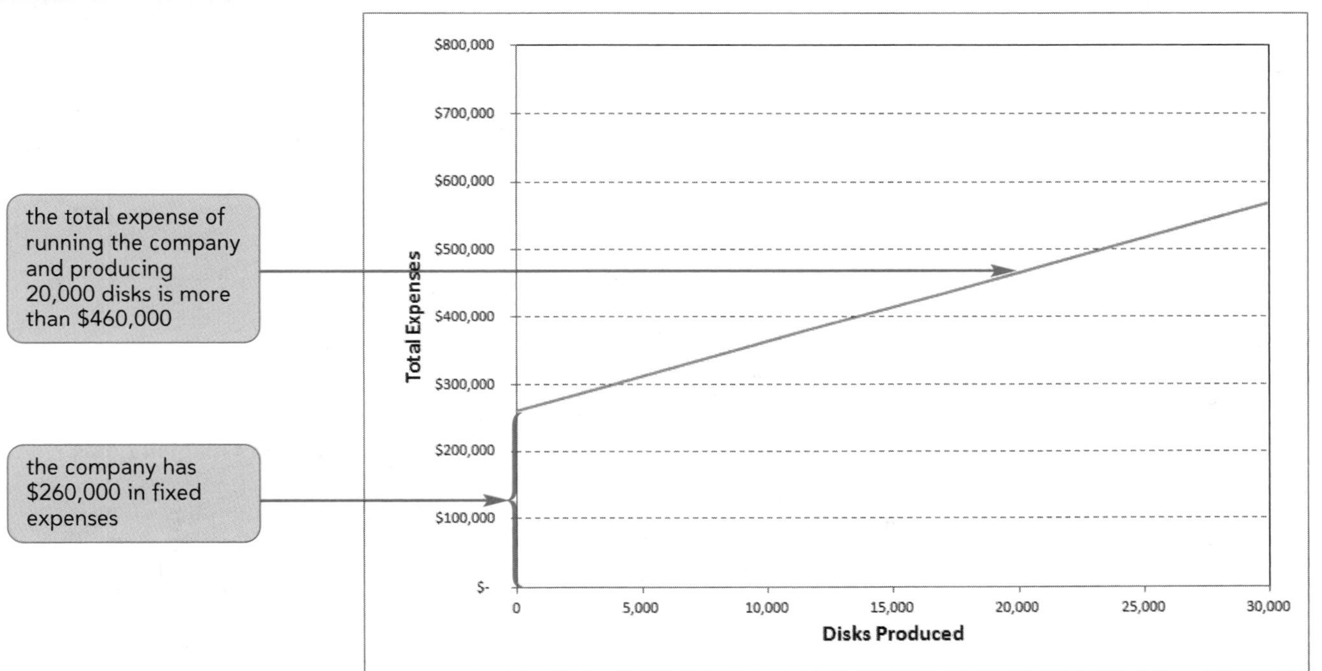

A third type of expense is a **mixed expense**, which is an expense that is part variable and part fixed. For this analysis, you will not consider any mixed expenses.

Creative Ventures is selling most of what it produces, so the company should bring in more revenue as it increases production. Figure 10-3 shows the increase in revenue in relation to the increase in sales volume. Selling 20,000 disks at $24 a piece brings in $480,000 of revenue. This means the company would make a profit of about $20,000 if it sold 20,000 disks.

Figure 10-3 Chart of revenue

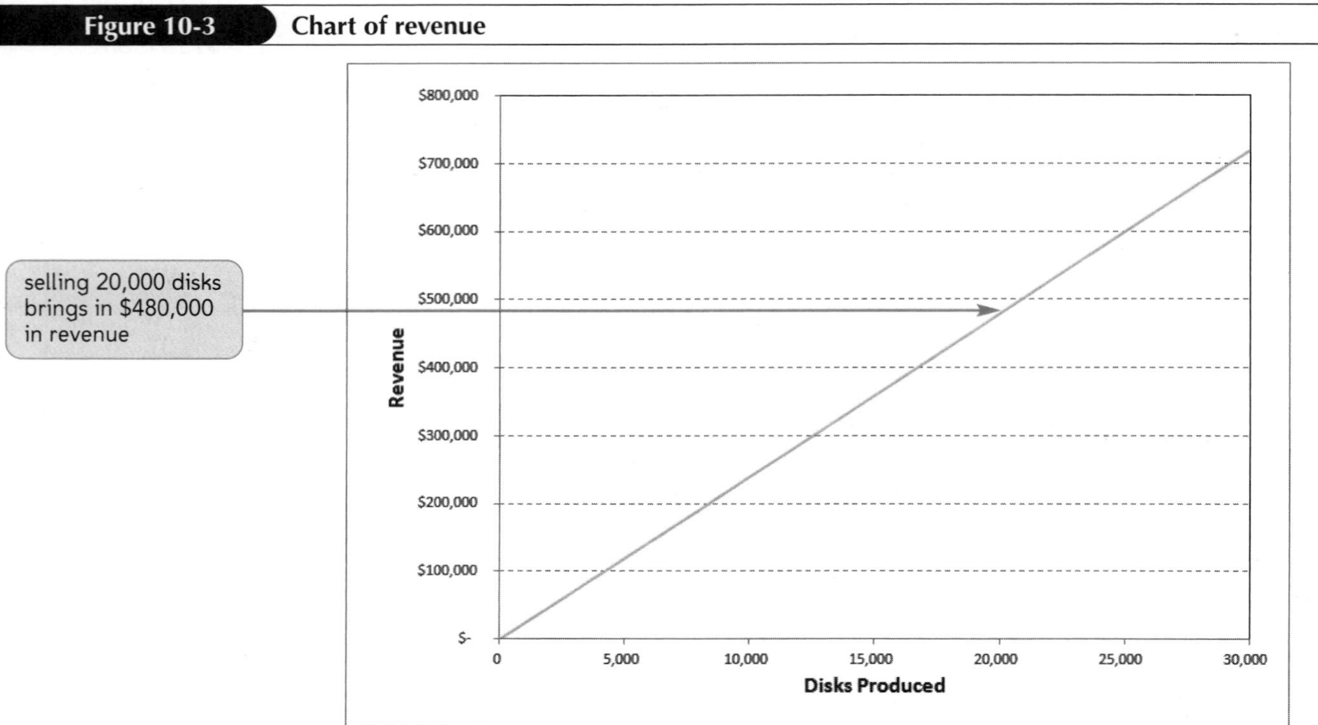

Determining the Break-Even Point

The point where revenue equals expenses is called the break-even point. For this reason, CVP analysis is sometimes called **break-even analysis**. The more disks Creative Ventures sells above the break-even point, the greater its profit. Conversely, sales that fall below the break-even point mean the company is losing money.

You can present a break-even analysis by graphing both revenue and total expenses against sales volume. The point at which the two lines cross is the break-even point. This type of chart is called a **cost-volume-profit (CVP) chart**. As shown in Figure 10-4, a CVP chart shows the relationship between expenses and revenue.

Figure 10-4 Typical CVP chart

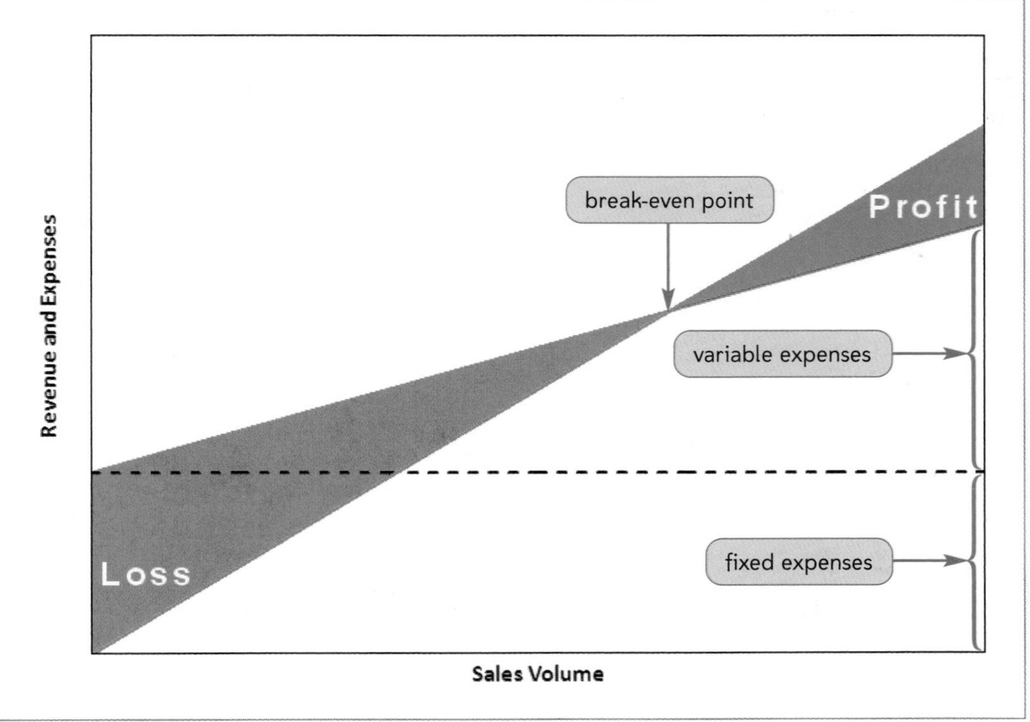

Todd and Brent have prepared an income statement with projected revenue, variable expenses, and fixed expenses based on the previous year's sales of the HoverDisk. You'll review the worksheet with this data. Later, you will use this data to calculate the company's break-even point.

To review the income statement for Creative Ventures:

1. Open the **Creative** workbook located in the Excel10\Tutorial folder included with your Data Files, and then save the workbook as **Creative Ventures** in the same folder.
2. In the Documentation worksheet, enter your name in cell B3 and the date in cell B4.
3. Switch to the **Income Statement** worksheet and review its contents and formulas. See Figure 10-5.

Figure 10-5 Creative Ventures income statement

TIP

In this tutorial, the figures show the entire income statement; you'll need to scroll the worksheet to see all of the content.

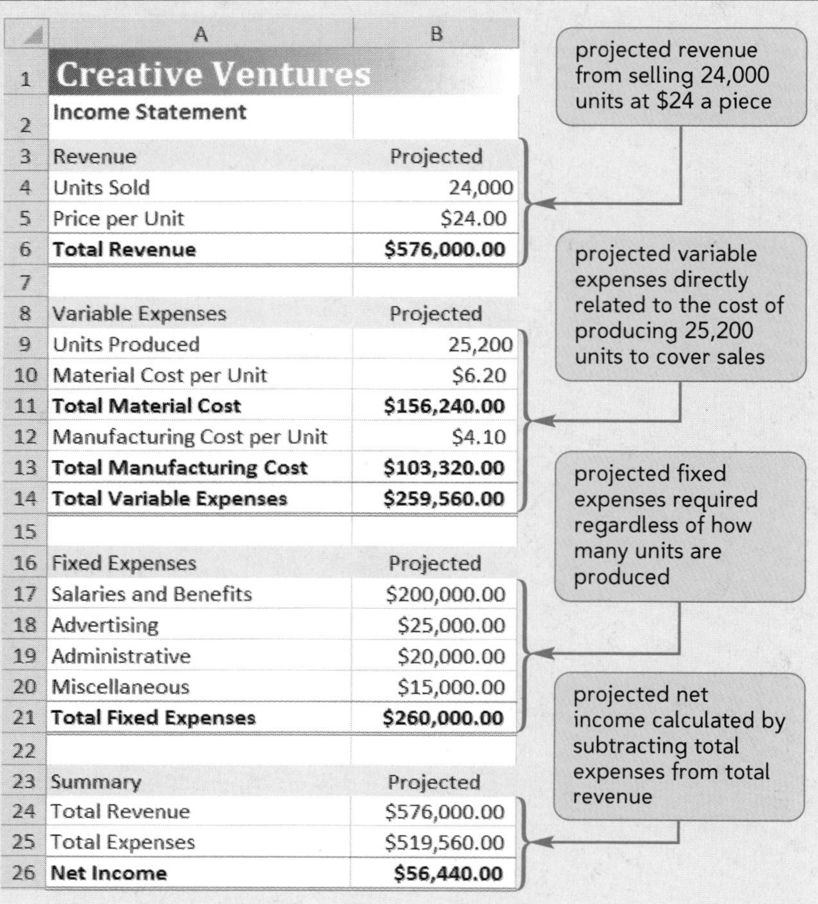

	A	B
1	Creative Ventures	
2	Income Statement	
3	Revenue	Projected
4	Units Sold	24,000
5	Price per Unit	$24.00
6	**Total Revenue**	**$576,000.00**
7		
8	Variable Expenses	Projected
9	Units Produced	25,200
10	Material Cost per Unit	$6.20
11	**Total Material Cost**	**$156,240.00**
12	Manufacturing Cost per Unit	$4.10
13	**Total Manufacturing Cost**	**$103,320.00**
14	**Total Variable Expenses**	**$259,560.00**
15		
16	Fixed Expenses	Projected
17	Salaries and Benefits	$200,000.00
18	Advertising	$25,000.00
19	Administrative	$20,000.00
20	Miscellaneous	$15,000.00
21	**Total Fixed Expenses**	**$260,000.00**
22		
23	Summary	Projected
24	Total Revenue	$576,000.00
25	Total Expenses	$519,560.00
26	**Net Income**	**$56,440.00**

As itemized in the Income Statement worksheet, Todd and Brent hope to sell 24,000 disks at a price of $24 per disk, generating $576,000 in revenue. They plan to produce 5 percent more disks than they expect to sell to create a reasonable inventory. This means the company will produce 25,200 disks at a variable cost of $259,560. The fixed expenses are projected to be $260,000. The net income from the sale of the disks is projected to be $56,440.

Performing a What-If Analysis with Goal Seek

What-if analysis lets you explore the impact of changing different values in a worksheet. You'll use a what-if analysis to investigate what would happen to the company's net income if sales declined to 20,000 units or lower. You'll change the projected values in the income statement.

To calculate the net income for different sales volumes:

1. In cell B4, change the units sold value from 24,000 units to **20,000**. The total revenue drop to $480,000.
2. Scroll down to cell B26. If sales drop to 20,000 units, the net income will fall to $3,700.

3. Change the units sold value in cell B4 to **15,000**. If sales drop to this level, the company will show a net loss of $62,225.
4. Change the value in cell B4 back to **24,000**. The net income returns to $56,440.

Todd and Brent want to know exactly how many disks they must sell to break even, assuming no other factors change in the projections. You could find this value by inserting different values in cell B4, hunting for a units sold value resulting in a net income of zero. A faster approach is to use Goal Seek.

In the what-if analysis you just performed, you changed an input value—Units Sold—to see how it affected a calculated item. **Goal Seek** automates the trial-and-error process by allowing you to specify a value for a calculated item, and then Excel returns the input value needed to reach that goal.

Figure 10-6 illustrates the difference between what-if analysis and Goal Seek. In this example, a what-if analysis might ask *what* would be the total revenue *if* the company sold 15,000 disks. The input value is the number of disks sold and the result is the total revenue, which, in this case, is $360,000. Goal Seek might determine how many disks the company needs to sell to meet the specified goal of $400,000 in revenue. In this case, selling 16,667 disks would be required to reach that revenue goal.

Figure 10-6 What-if analysis and Goal Seek

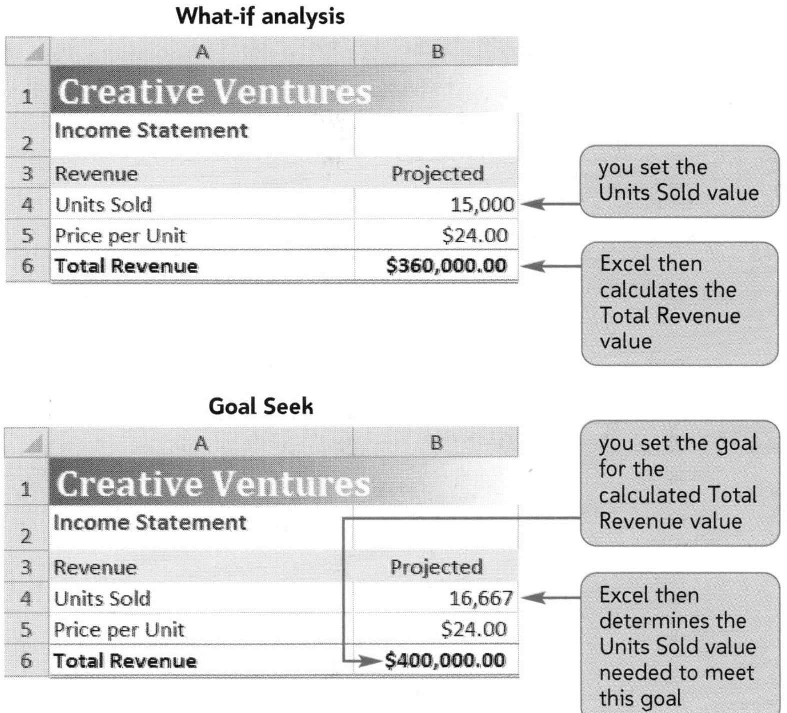

REFERENCE

Performing What-If Analysis and Goal Seek

To perform what-if analysis:
- Change the value of a worksheet cell (the input cell).
- Observe its impact on one or more calculated cells (the result cells).

To perform Goal Seek:
- In the Data Tools group on the Data tab, click the What-If Analysis button, and then click Goal Seek.
- Select the result cell in the Set cell box, and then specify its value (goal) in the To value box.
- In the By changing cell box, specify the input cell.
- Click the OK button. The value of the input cell changes to set the value of the result cell.

You'll use Goal Seek to determine the number of disks that Creative Ventures must sell to break even.

To use Goal Seek to determine the break-even point:

1. Click the **Data** tab on the Ribbon.
2. In the Data Tools group, click the **What-If Analysis** button, and then click **Goal Seek**. The Goal Seek dialog box opens.
3. Make sure the value in the Set cell box is selected, and then click cell **B26** in the Income Statement worksheet. The absolute reference $B$26 indicates that you want to set the value of cell B26 (the net income cell).
4. Press the **Tab** key to move the insertion point to the To value box, and then type **0**. This indicates that you want to set the value of cell B26 (the net income cell) to 0.
5. Press the **Tab** key to move the insertion point to the By changing cell box, and then click cell **B4**. The absolute reference $B$4 indicates that you want to set the total income value to 0 by changing the value in cell B4 (the units sold cell). See Figure 10-7.

Figure 10-7 Goal Seek dialog box

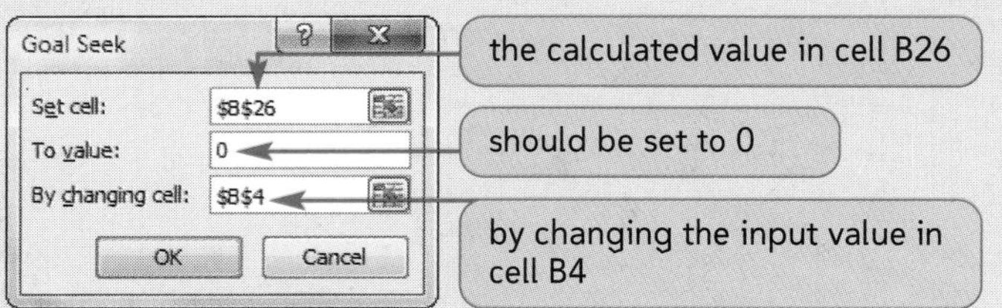

6. Click the **OK** button. The Goal Seek dialog box closes, and the Goal Seek Status dialog box opens, indicating that Goal Seek found a solution.
7. Click the **OK** button. The value 19,719 appears in cell B4. See Figure 10-8.

Figure 10-8 **Annual sales required to break even**

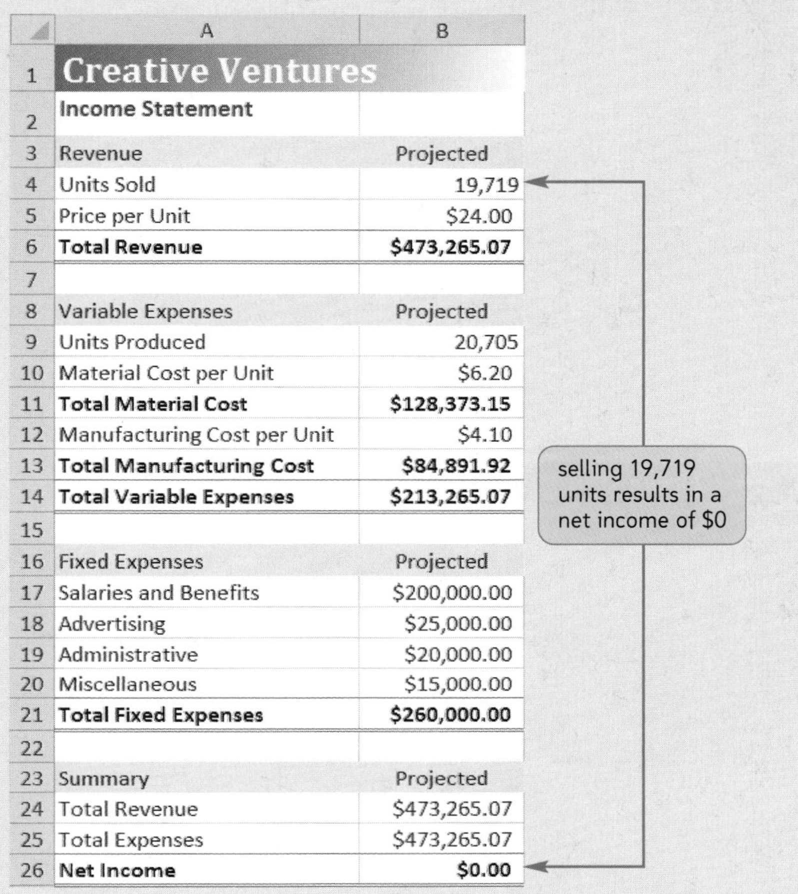

	A	B
1	Creative Ventures	
2	Income Statement	
3	Revenue	Projected
4	Units Sold	19,719
5	Price per Unit	$24.00
6	**Total Revenue**	**$473,265.07**
7		
8	Variable Expenses	Projected
9	Units Produced	20,705
10	Material Cost per Unit	$6.20
11	**Total Material Cost**	**$128,373.15**
12	Manufacturing Cost per Unit	$4.10
13	**Total Manufacturing Cost**	**$84,891.92**
14	**Total Variable Expenses**	**$213,265.07**
15		
16	Fixed Expenses	Projected
17	Salaries and Benefits	$200,000.00
18	Advertising	$25,000.00
19	Administrative	$20,000.00
20	Miscellaneous	$15,000.00
21	**Total Fixed Expenses**	**$260,000.00**
22		
23	Summary	Projected
24	Total Revenue	$473,265.07
25	Total Expenses	$473,265.07
26	**Net Income**	**$0.00**

8. Click cell **B4**. The exact cell value in the formula bar is 19719.3780811528, indicating that the company needs to sell *more than* 19,719 units to break even.
9. Change the value in cell B4 back to **24,000**.

Working with Data Tables

Todd and Brent want to analyze the company's net income under different sales assumptions. For example, what would the company's net income be if sales increased to 30,000 units or 35,000 units or 40,000 units? How many units will the company need to sell to reach a net income of $200,000? You could continue to use Goal Seek to answer these questions, but a more efficient approach is to use a data table.

A data table is an Excel table that displays the results from several what-if analyses. To set up a data table, you first insert references to the input and result cells. The input and result values can be arranged in rows or columns. You should always clearly label the row or column containing the input and result values. You'll work with one-variable and two-variable data tables to answer some of Todd and Brent's questions.

Creating a One-Variable Data Table

In a one-variable data table, you specify one input cell and any number of result cells. The range of possible values for the input cell is entered in the first row or column of the data table, and the corresponding result values appear in the accompanying rows or columns. One-variable data tables are particularly useful in business to explore how changing a single input cell can impact several result cells.

For example, a one-variable data table can be used to determine the impact of different interest rates on the monthly payment and total cost of a mortgage, as shown in Figure 10-9. The interest rate in cell C4 is the input cell, and the values in the range E4:E12 are input values; that is, possible values for the input cell. Cells C7 and C8 are the result cells, and the values in the range F4:G12 are the result values. The results from nine different what-if analyses appear in this single table. Using the table, you can quickly see that a 7% interest rate results in a $1,663.26 monthly payment and a total mortgage cost of $598,772.25. You can also observe how quickly the total payments rise with an increasing interest rate. When the annual interest rate increases two percentage points from 6% to 8%, the total cost of the mortgage increases about $120,000.

Figure 10-9 One-variable data table example

	A	B	C	D	E	F	G
2		Loan Conditions				One-Variable Data Table	
3		Down Payment	$0		Rates	Monthly Payments	Totals
4		Rate	6.00%		6.00%	($1,498.88)	($539,595.47)
5		Term (months)	360		6.25%	($1,539.29)	($554,145.48)
6		Loan	$250,000		6.50%	($1,580.17)	($568,861.22)
7		Monthly Payment	($1,498.88)		6.75%	($1,621.50)	($583,738.29)
8		Total	($539,595.47)		7.00%	($1,663.26)	($598,772.25)
9					7.25%	($1,705.44)	($613,958.65)
10					7.50%	($1,748.04)	($629,293.06)
11					7.75%	($1,791.03)	($644,771.02)
12					8.00%	($1,834.41)	($660,388.12)

REFERENCE

Creating a One-Variable Data Table

- Insert a formula that references the input cell in the upper-left cell of the table.
- Insert input values in either the first row or first column of the table.
- For input values in the first row, insert formulas referencing result cells in the table's first column; for input values in the first column, insert formulas referencing result cells in the table's first row.
- Select the table (excluding any row or column headings).
- In the Data Tools group on the Data tab, click the What-If Analysis button, and then click Data Table.
- If the input values are in the first row, enter the cell reference to the input cell in the Row input cell box; if the input values are in the first column, enter the cell reference to the input cell in the Column input cell box.
- Click the OK button.

You'll create a one-variable data table to examine the impact of changing sales volume on the company's revenue, total expenses, and net income.

To set up the one-variable data table:

1. In cell E2, enter **Cost-Volume-Profit Analysis**, merge and center the range E2:H2, and then format the text using the **20% - Accent3** cell style.
2. In the range E3:H3, enter the following labels:

   cell E3: **Units Sold** cell G3: **Expenses**
   cell F3: **Revenue** cell H3: **Net Income**
3. In the range E4:H4, enter the following formulas to reference the input cell and the result cells:

   cell E4: **=B4** cell G4: **=B25**
   cell F4: **=B24** cell H4: **=B26**
4. Enter **10,000** in cell E5, enter **15,000** in cell E6, select the range **E5:E6**, and then drag the fill handle to cell **E10** to enter the input values in the data table. In this case, you inserted sales volumes of 10,000 units sold up to 35,000 units sold in increments of 5,000 units.
5. Click cell **E11** to deselect the range. See Figure 10-10.

Figure 10-10 Setup for the one-variable data table

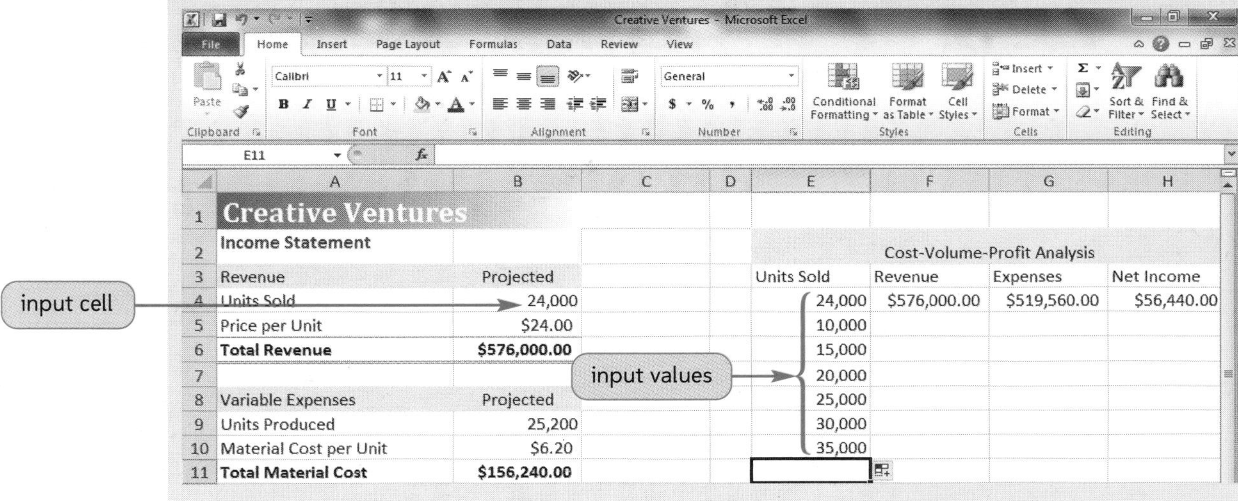

Next, you'll fill the table with the result values. To do this, you select the range that contains the data table (excluding the column headings), and then use the Data Table dialog box to specify the input cell based on whether the input values are arranged in rows or columns. Because your input values are in a column, you'll use the Column input cell option. If you had oriented the table so that the input values were in a single row, you would use the Row input cell option.

To complete the one-variable data table:

1. Select the range **E4:H10**. This is the range of the data table.
2. In the Data Tools group on the Data tab, click the **What-If Analysis** button, and then click **Data Table**. The Data Table dialog box opens.
3. Press the **Tab** key to move the insertion point to the Column input cell box, and then click cell **B4** in the worksheet. See Figure 10-11.

Use the Column input cell box because the input values appear in the first column of the data table.

Figure 10-11 Data Table dialog box

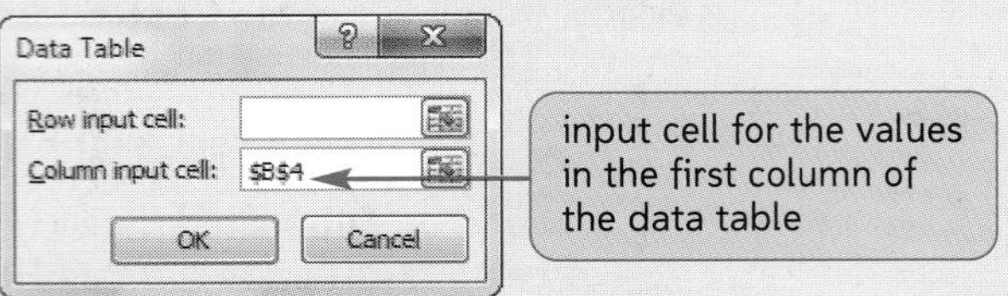

4. Click the **OK** button. The data table displays the expenses and revenue for each of the input values in the range E5:E10.
5. Copy the formats from the range **F4:H4** and apply them to the range **F5:H10**.
6. Click cell **E11** to deselect the range. See Figure 10-12.

Figure 10-12 Completed one-variable data table

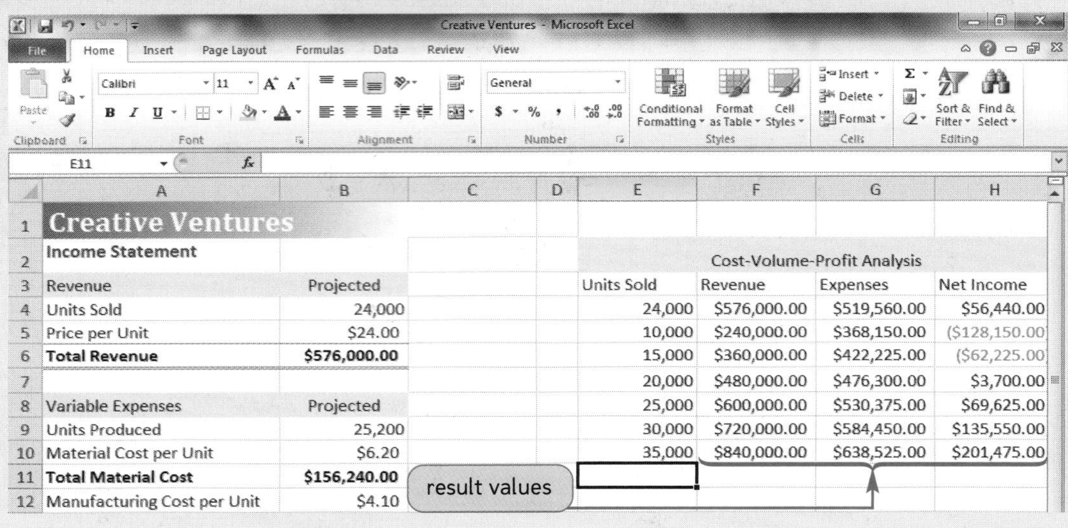

The data table shows the results of several what-if analyses simultaneously. For example, if annual sales increase to 35,000 units, the company's revenue will be $840,000, but the total expenses will be more than $638,000, yielding a net income of more than $201,000.

Charting a One-Variable Data Table

The data table provides the results of several what-if analyses, but the results are often clearer if you include a CVP chart along with the table. The chart gives a better picture of the relationship between sales volume, revenue, and total expenses.

You'll use a scatter chart to chart the revenue and total expenses against the total number of units sold.

To create the CVP chart:

1. Select the range **E3:G10**. This range contains the data you want to chart.
2. Click the **Insert** tab on the Ribbon, click the **Scatter** button in the Charts group, and then click the **Scatter with Smooth Lines** chart type (the left chart in the second row).

3. Move the chart to a new sheet named **CVP Chart**, and then drag the **CVP Chart** sheet after the Income Statement worksheet.
4. Click the **Chart Tools Layout** tab on the Ribbon, and then use the tools on this tab to add the chart title **Cost-Volume-Profit Analysis** above the chart, add a primary vertical axis title rotated with the text **Revenue and Expenses**, and then add a primary horizontal axis title below the axis with the text **Units Sold**.
5. Format the values on the vertical axis as Currency with no decimal places.
6. Set the font size of the axis titles, axis values, and chart legend to **14** points. See Figure 10-13.

Figure 10-13 Completed CVP chart

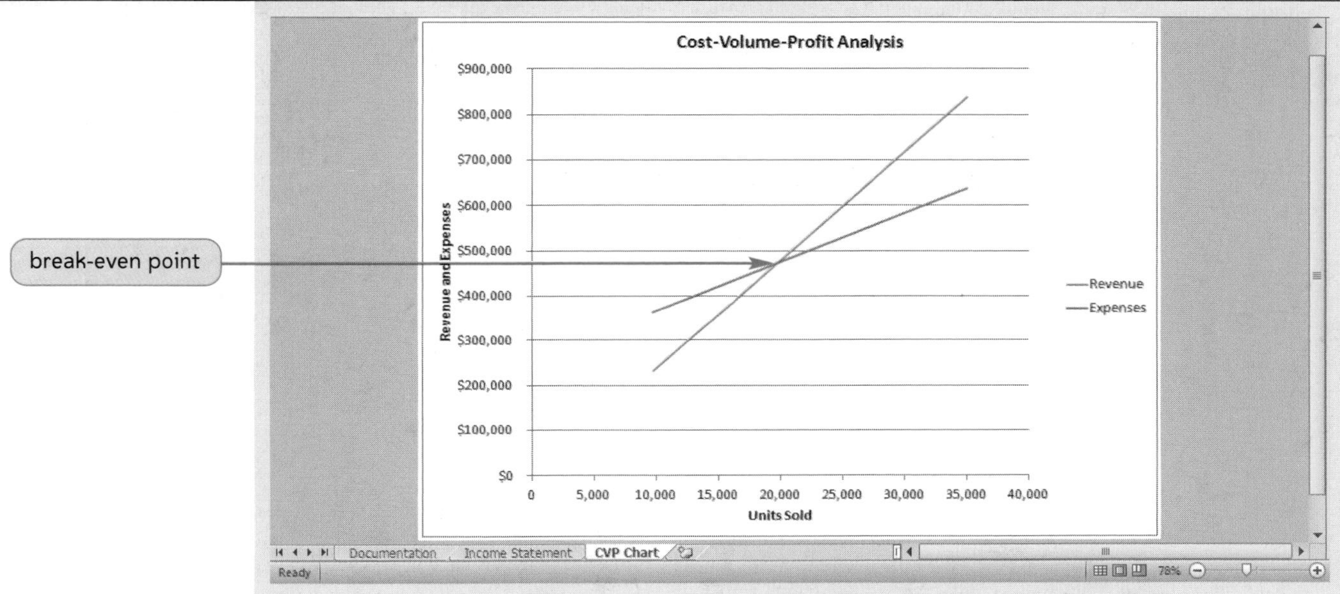

Each point in the data table is plotted on the chart and connected with a line. The blue line represents revenue; the red line represents expenses. The break-even point occurs at a sales volume of about 20,000 units. The data table and CVP chart give a comprehensive picture of the impact of sales volume on total expenses and revenue.

Todd and Brent are considering lowering the price of HoverDisks to be more competitive with other toy manufacturers. You'll perform another what-if analysis using a sales price of $19.95. Because data tables are dynamic, changes in the worksheet are automatically reflected in the data table values.

To view the impact of changing the price per unit:

1. Switch to the **Income Statement** worksheet.
2. Change the value in cell B5 from $24 to **$19.95**. See Figure 10-14.

Figure 10-14 Data table for a $19.95 sales price

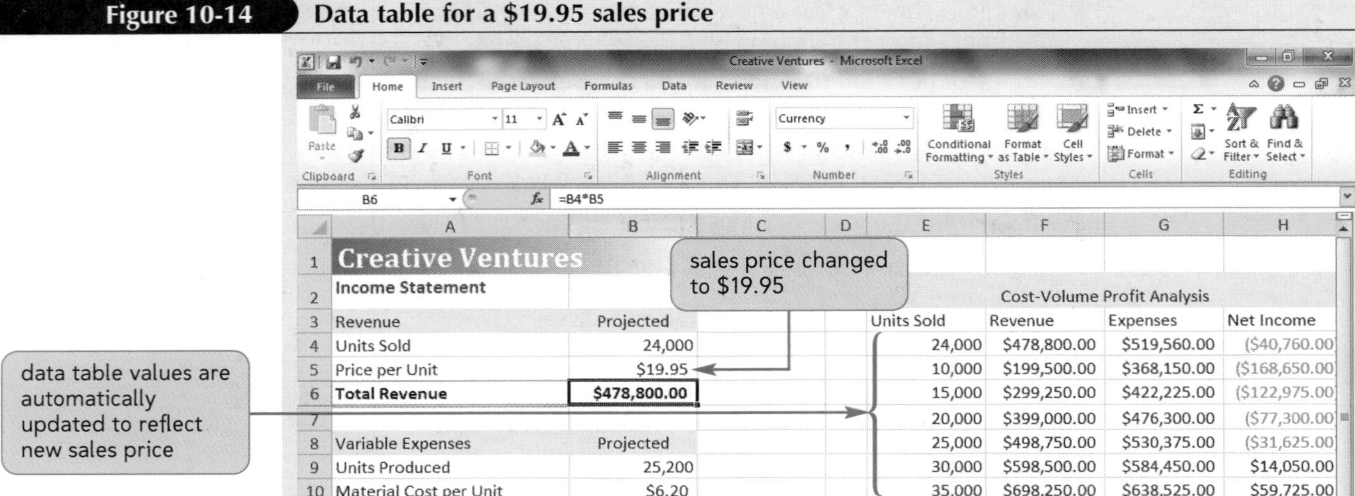

3. Switch to the **CVP Chart** sheet and view the results of the change you made in the price. The break-even point, where the Revenue and Expenses lines intersect, has moved to the right, indicating that Creative Ventures would have to sell between 25,000 and 30,000 units to break even.

4. Return to the **Income Statement** worksheet and change the value in cell B5 back to **$24**.

Creating a Two-Variable Data Table

Rather than repeatedly changing the input values for the one-variable data table, you can analyze a variety of combinations simultaneously with a two-variable data table. As the name implies, a two-variable data table uses two input cells; but unlike a one-variable data table, it can display only a single result value.

Figure 10-15 shows an example of a two-variable data table that examines the impact of the interest rate and the length of the mortgage on the calculated monthly payment. The two input cells are cells C4 and C5, which show the interest rate and the number of months before the loan is repaid. The first column of the data table displays a range of interest values for the first input cell, and the first row of the data table shows a range of possible terms for the second input cell. The result cell in this what-if analysis is cell C7—the monthly payment. Result values in the two-variable data table are displayed at the intersection of each input value. For example, a 240-month loan at 7.25% interest would require a monthly payment of $1,975.94 (cell H10). This two-variable data table quickly shows the results of 36 what-if analyses on different loan conditions.

Figure 10-15 Two-variable data table example

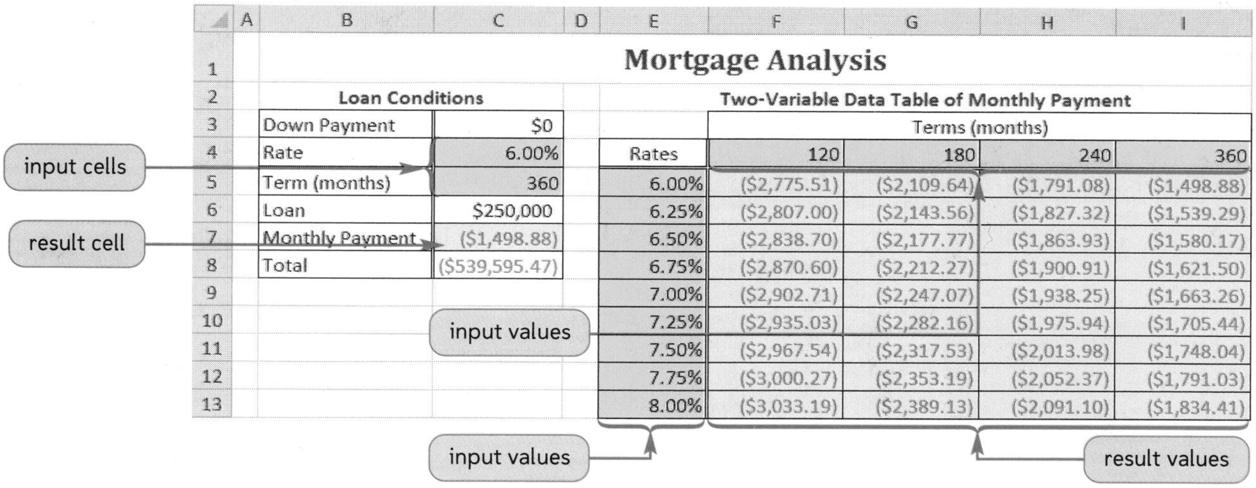

	A	B	C	D	E	F	G	H	I
1					Mortgage Analysis				
2		Loan Conditions			Two-Variable Data Table of Monthly Payment				
3		Down Payment	$0			Terms (months)			
4		Rate	6.00%		Rates	120	180	240	360
5		Term (months)	360		6.00%	($2,775.51)	($2,109.64)	($1,791.08)	($1,498.88)
6		Loan	$250,000		6.25%	($2,807.00)	($2,143.56)	($1,827.32)	($1,539.29)
7		Monthly Payment	($1,498.88)		6.50%	($2,838.70)	($2,177.77)	($1,863.93)	($1,580.17)
8		Total	($539,595.47)		6.75%	($2,870.60)	($2,212.27)	($1,900.91)	($1,621.50)
9					7.00%	($2,902.71)	($2,247.07)	($1,938.25)	($1,663.26)
10					7.25%	($2,935.03)	($2,282.16)	($1,975.94)	($1,705.44)
11					7.50%	($2,967.54)	($2,317.53)	($2,013.98)	($1,748.04)
12					7.75%	($3,000.27)	($2,353.19)	($2,052.37)	($1,791.03)
13					8.00%	($3,033.19)	($2,389.13)	($2,091.10)	($1,834.41)

For Creative Ventures, you'll create a two-variable data table that examines the impact of sales price and the yearly sales volume on net income.

REFERENCE

Creating a Two-Variable Data Table

- Insert a formula that references the result cell in the upper-left cell of the table.
- Insert input values in the first row and first column of the table.
- Select the table (excluding any row or column headings).
- In the Data Tools group on the Data tab, click the What-If Analysis button, and then click Data Table.
- Enter the cell reference corresponding to the input values in the first row in the Row input cell box; enter the cell reference to the input values in the first column in the Column input cell box.
- Click the OK button.

You'll start by entering the labels and input values for the two-variable data table.

To set up the two-variable data table:

1. In cell E12, enter **Net Income Analysis** and then merge and center the range E12:J12.
2. In cell F13, enter **Price per Unit**, merge and center the range F13:J13, and then format the merged cell using the **20% - Accent3** cell style.

3. In the range E15:E20, enter the values **10,000** through **35,000** in increments of 5,000.
4. In the range F14:J14, enter the values **$15** to **$35** in increments of $5. See Figure 10-16.

Figure 10-16 **Setup for the two-variable data table**

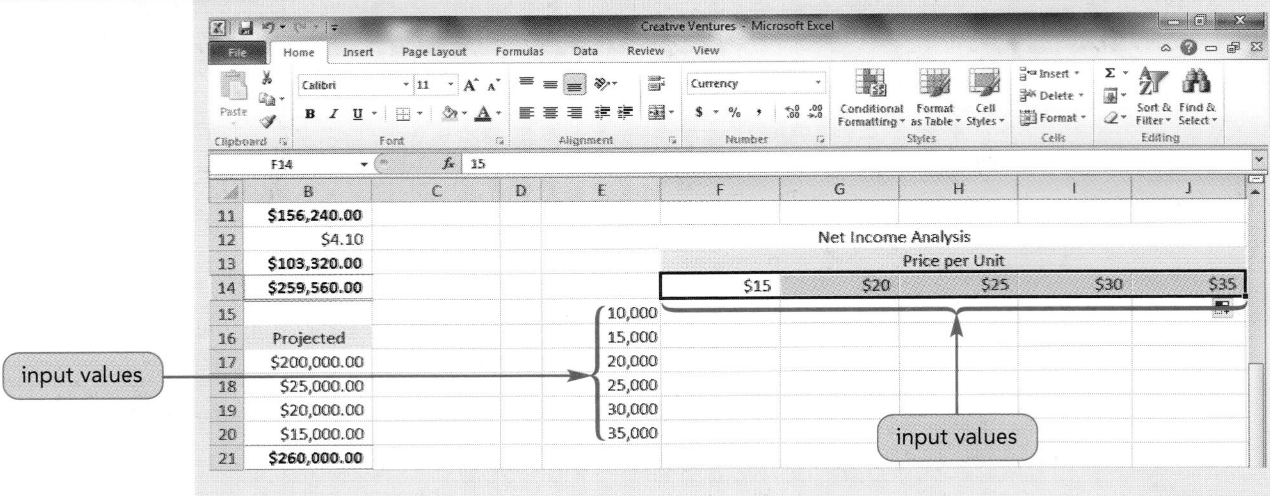

In two-variable data tables, the reference to the result cell is placed in the upper-left corner of the table at the intersection of the row and column input values. In this case, you'll enter a formula in cell E14 that references the company's net income.

To insert the reference to the result cell:

1. Click cell **E14** to select it.
2. In cell E14, enter **=B26**. The formula returns the value $56,440.00, which is the current projected net income.

Because placing a value in this location on the table might confuse some users, you'll use a custom format to replace the cell value with text. You can hide the cell value using the custom format "*text*" where *text* is the text you want to display in place of the cell value. You'll use a custom format now to display "Units Sold" in place of the value in cell E14.

To apply a custom format to cell E14:

1. Right-click cell **E14**, and then click **Format Cells** on the shortcut menu. The Format Cells dialog box opens.
2. Click the **Number** tab if it is not selected, click **Custom** in the Category box, and then type **"Units Sold"** in the Type box. See Figure 10-17.

Figure 10-17 Custom format to display text

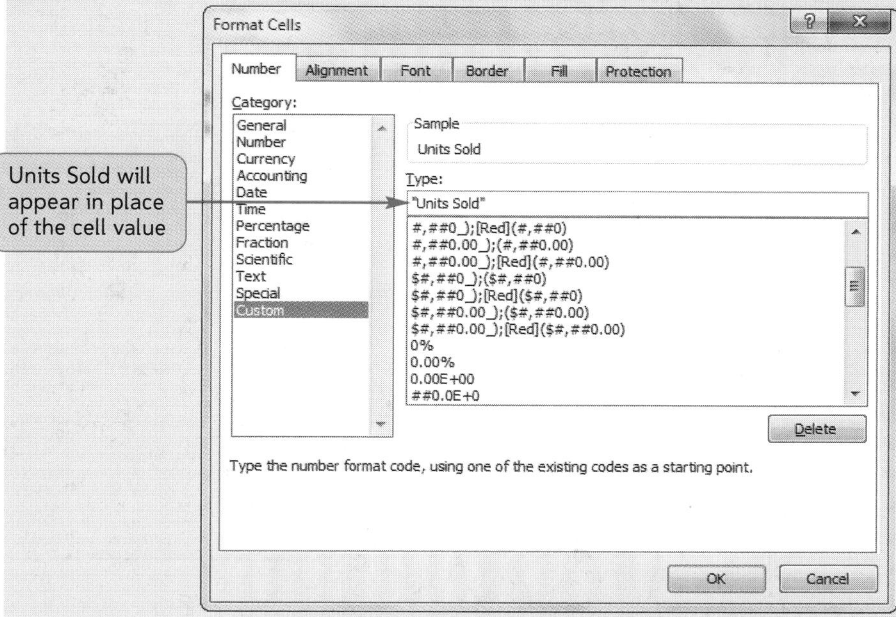

TIP

You can also hide the reference to the result cell by applying the same fill color to the cell text and background.

3. Click the **OK** button. The text *Units Sold* appears in cell E14, even though the cell's underlying content is the formula =B26, which results in the value $56,440.

   Trouble? If *Units Sold* does not appear in cell E14, you probably didn't include the quotation marks in the custom format. Repeat Steps 1 through 3, making sure that you include both the opening and closing quotation marks.

4. Format cell E14 with the **20% - Accent3** cell style.

When creating a two-variable data table, you must identify the row input cell and the column input cell. The **row input cell** is the cell on which you base values placed in the first row of the data table. The first row of the data table contains the unit price, so the row input cell is cell B5—the current unit price of the HoverDisk. Similarly, the **column input cell** is the cell on which values placed in the first column of the data table are based. In this case, cell B4, the number of disks sold by the company, is the column input cell.

You'll complete the two-variable table by identifying the two input cells, which will display the net income for each combination of price and units sold.

To complete the two-variable data table:

1. Select the range **E14:J20**. This range includes input values for both the row and the column input cells as well as the hidden reference to the result cell in cell E14.
2. In the Data Tools group on the Data tab, click the **What-If Analysis** button, and then click **Data Table**. The Data Table dialog box opens.
3. In the Row input cell box, type **B5** to reference the price per unit value from the income statement.
4. In the Column input cell box, type **B4** to reference the number of units sold value from the income statement.
5. Click the **OK** button. The data table values are filled in.

6. Use the Format Painter to copy the format from cell **H10** into the range **F15:J20**.
7. Click cell **E13** to deselect the range. See Figure 10-18.

Figure 10-18 Completed two-variable data table

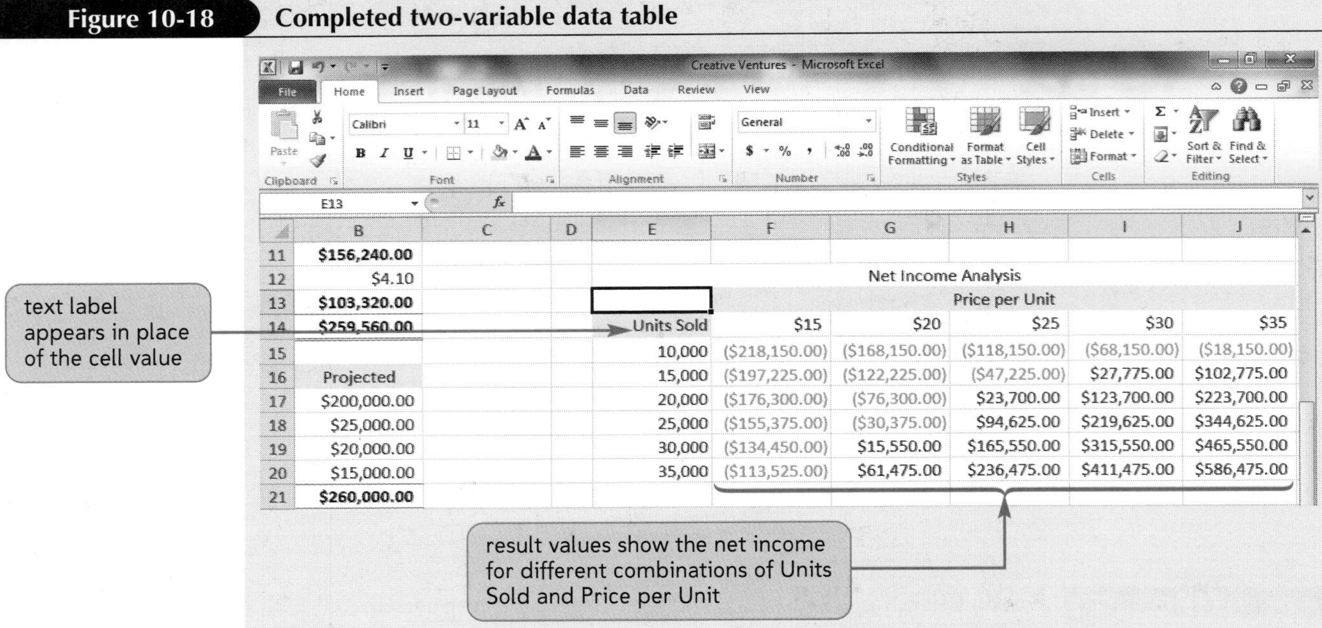

If the unit price drops to $15 per disk, none of the projected sales volume figures would show a net profit. On the other hand, the company will show a profit for most of the projected sales volumes if the sales price of the unit is set to $25 or above.

Charting a Two-Variable Data Table

You will chart the data from the two-variable data table. The chart will plot net income versus sales volume with the data from each unit price displayed on a different line.

To create the chart of the two-variable data table:

1. Select the range **E15:J20**. You'll plot this range on a scatter chart. You did not select the unit prices in row 14 because Excel would interpret these values as data values to be charted, not as labels.
2. Click the **Insert** tab on the Ribbon, click the **Scatter** button in the Charts group, and then click the **Scatter with Straight Lines** chart type (the chart in the third row).
3. In the Data group on the Chart Tools Design tab, click the **Switch Row/Column** button to plot the data values based on a column rather than a row layout.
4. Move the chart to a new sheet named **Net Income Chart**, and then drag the **Net Income Chart** sheet tab to the end of the workbook.

5. Click the **Chart Tools Layout** tab on the Ribbon, and then insert the title **Net Income Analysis** above the chart, insert the primary vertical axis title with the rotated title **Net Income**, and insert the primary horizontal axis title below the axis as **Units Sold**.
6. Format the vertical axis values as Currency with no decimal places. See Figure 10-19.

Figure 10-19 Two-variable table chart

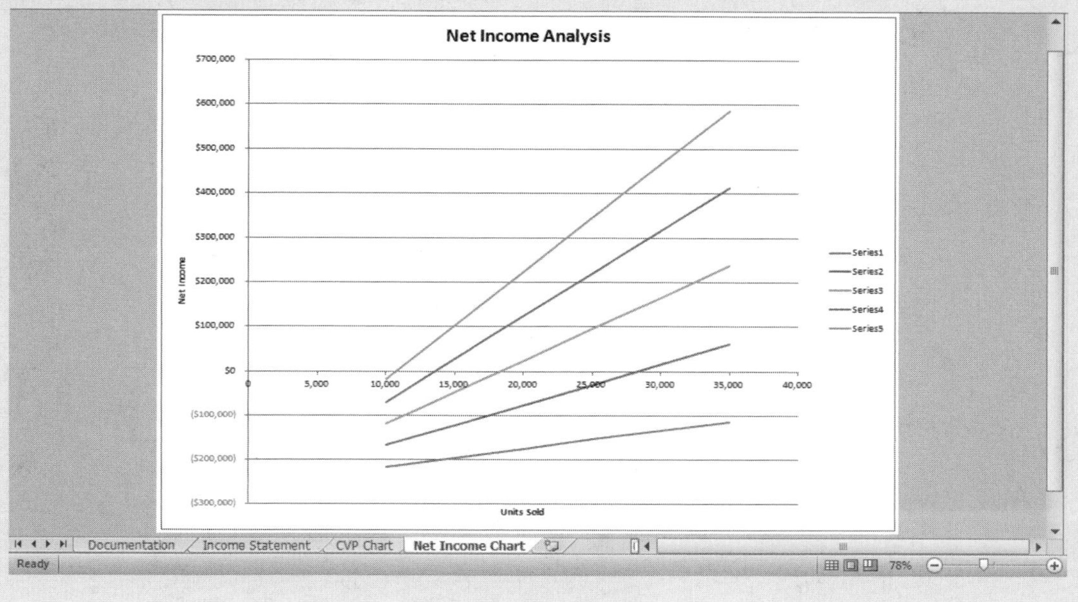

The chart shows a different trend line for each of the five possible values for unit price. However, the prices are not listed in the chart and Excel uses the generic series names Series1, Series2, Series3, Series4, and Series5. To use the unit prices rather than the generic names in the chart, you must edit the name property of each series.

To edit the chart series names:

1. Click the **Chart Tools Design** tab on the Ribbon, and then click the **Select Data** button in the Data Group. The Select Data Source dialog box opens.
2. Click **Series1** in the Legend Entries (Series) box, and then click the **Edit** button. The Edit Series dialog box opens with the Series name box active.
3. Click the **Income Statement** sheet tab, click cell **F14** to insert the reference in the Series name box, and then click the **OK** button. The Select Data Source dialog box reappears, and the Series1 name changes to $15.
4. Repeat Steps 2 and 3 to rename the Series2 chart series using the value in cell **G14**, rename the Series3 chart series using the value in cell **H14**, rename the Series4 chart series using the value in cell **I14**, and rename the Series5 chart series using the value in cell **J14**. See Figure 10-20.

Figure 10-20 Select Data Source dialog box

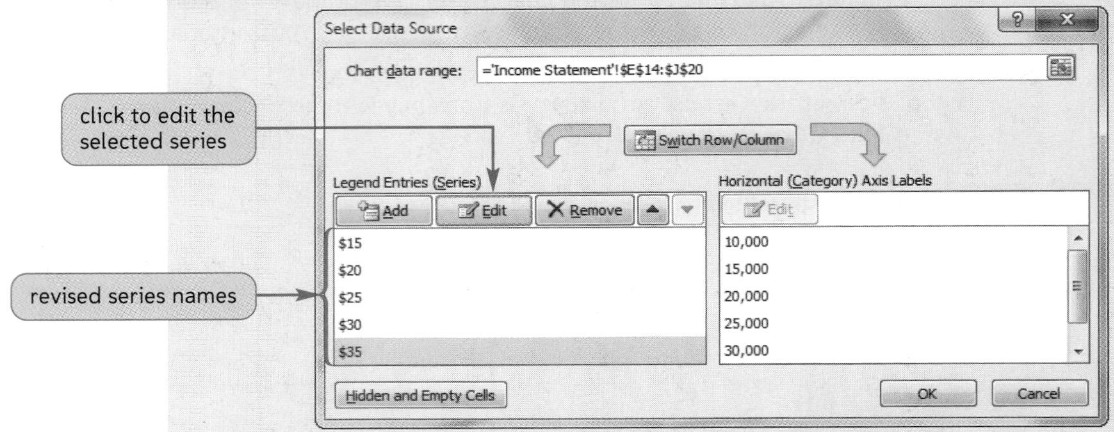

5. Click the **OK** button. The legend shows the renamed series.
6. In the Chart Styles group, click the **More** button to open the Chart Styles gallery, and then click **Style 13** (the fifth style in the second row) to change the line colors to shades of green, reflecting the increasing value of the unit price. The lightest shade is applied to the highest unit price values.
7. Set the font size of the axis titles, axis values, and legend to **14** points. See Figure 10-21.

Figure 10-21 Final chart of net income values

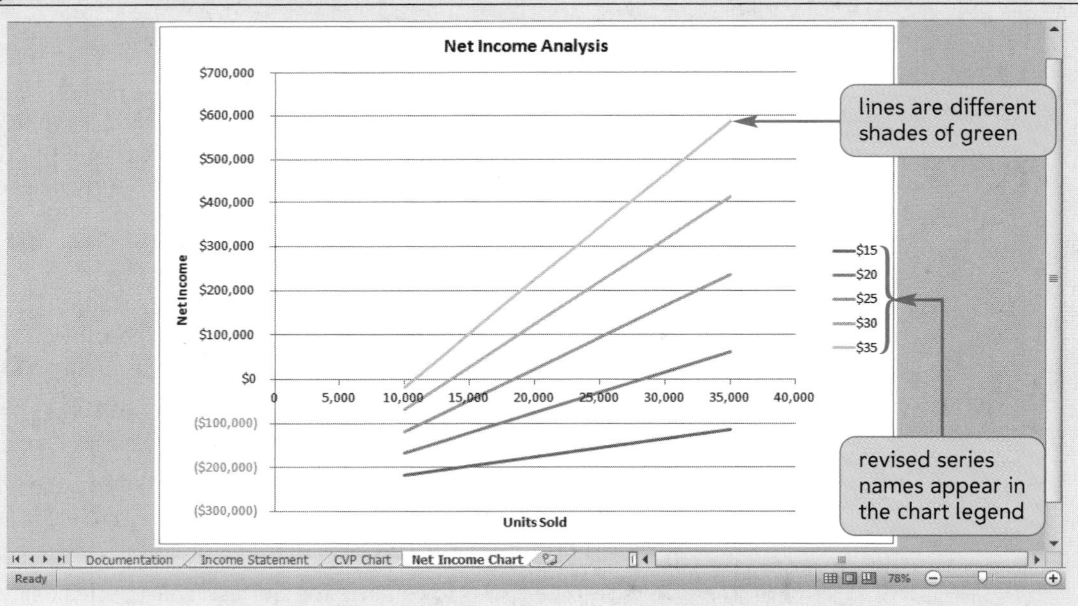

The chart shows how different unit prices will affect the relationship between sales volume and net income. A value of 0 on the vertical axis represents the break-even point. The $15 line doesn't cross 0 in the chart, indicating that Todd and Brent cannot make a profit by charging $15 per disk unless the company has a much higher sales volume than Todd and Brent have specified. On the other hand, at $35 per disk, Creative Ventures will show a profit (albeit a small one) unless the sales drop to about 10,000 units a year.

INSIGHT

Data Tables and Arrays

If you examine the cells in the two-variable data table you just created, you can see that every cell displays a different value even though it has the same formula: `{=TABLE(B5, B4)}`. This formula is an **array formula**, which performs multiple calculations in a single step, returning either a single value to one cell or multiple values to several cells. Array formulas are always enclosed within curly braces.

One example of an array formula that returns a single value is `{=SUM(B1:B10*C1:C10)}`. This formula multiplies each cell in the range B1:B10 by the matching cell in the same row of the range C1:C10. The sum of those 10 products is then calculated and returned. To create this array formula, enter the formula `=SUM(B1:B10*C1:C10)` and then press the Ctrl+Shift+Enter keys. Excel treats the formula as an array formula, adding the curly braces for you.

The **TABLE function** is an array function that returns multiple values to multiple cells. Other such functions include the TREND, MINVERSE, MMULT, and TRANSPOSE functions. To calculate multiple cell values, select the range, type the array formula, and then press the Ctrl+Shift+Enter keys to enter the formula. Excel applies the array formula to all of the selected cells.

Array formulas are a powerful feature of Excel. If used properly, they help you perform complex calculations within a single formula and extend a single formula over a range of cells. Use Microsoft Excel Help to learn more about array formulas and the functions that support them.

So far, you've used what-if analysis with Goal Seek and data tables to analyze how much Todd and Brent can charge for the HoverDisk and what impact sales volume has on Creative Ventures' profitability. In the next session, you will use other what-if analysis tools to examine the impact of more than two factors on an outcome.

REVIEW

Session 10.1 Quick Check

1. Describe the difference between a what-if analysis and Goal Seek.
2. Name the three components of the Goal Seek command.
3. What is a data table? What is an input cell? What is a result cell?
4. What is a one-variable data table? What is a two-variable data table?
5. How many result cells can you display with a one-variable data table? How many result cells can be displayed with a two-variable data table?
6. Cell E5 contains the formula =B10. You want to display the text "Profits" instead of the formula's value. What custom format would you use?
7. What is an array formula?

SESSION 10.2 VISUAL OVERVIEW

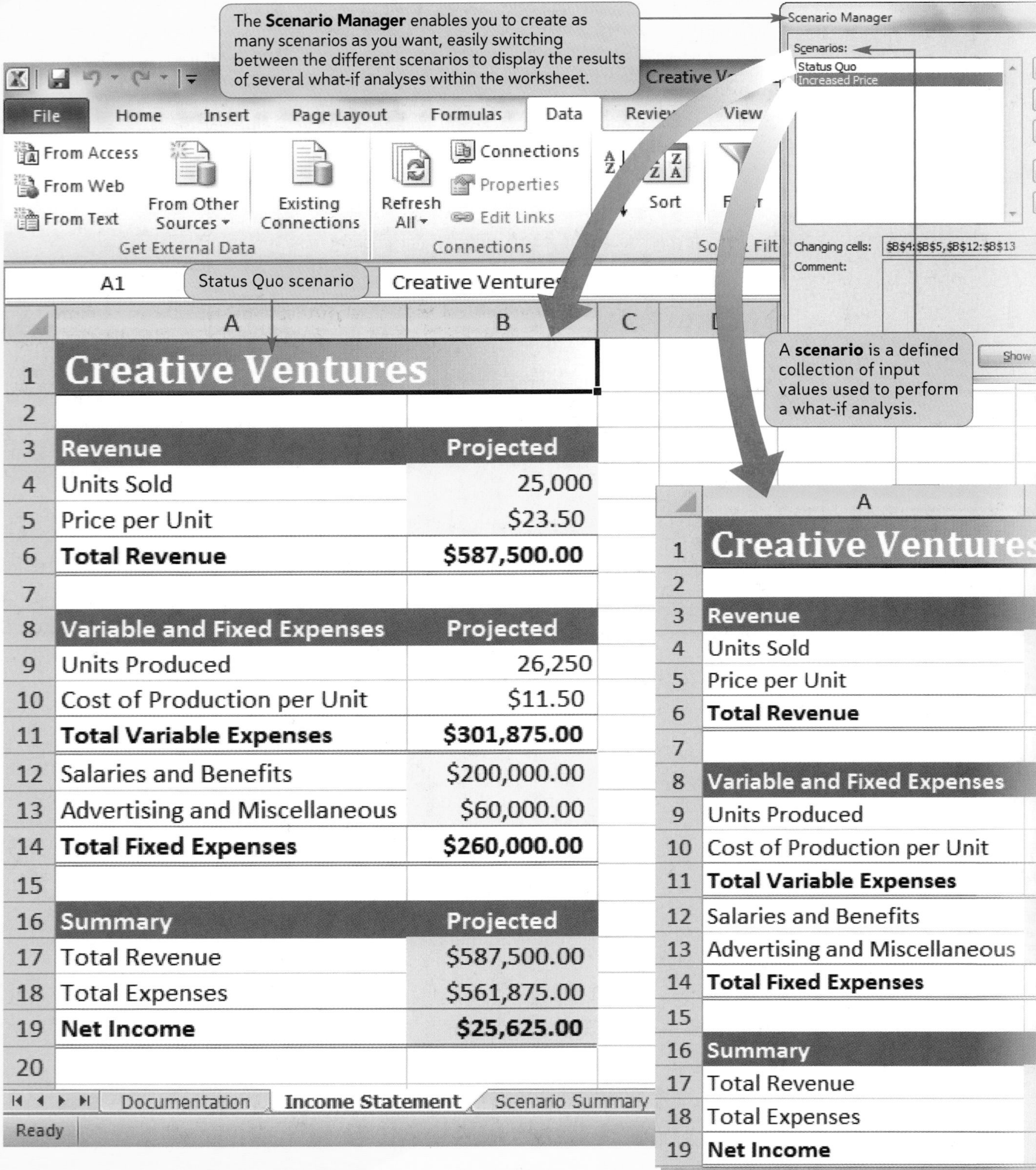

WHAT-IF SCENARIOS

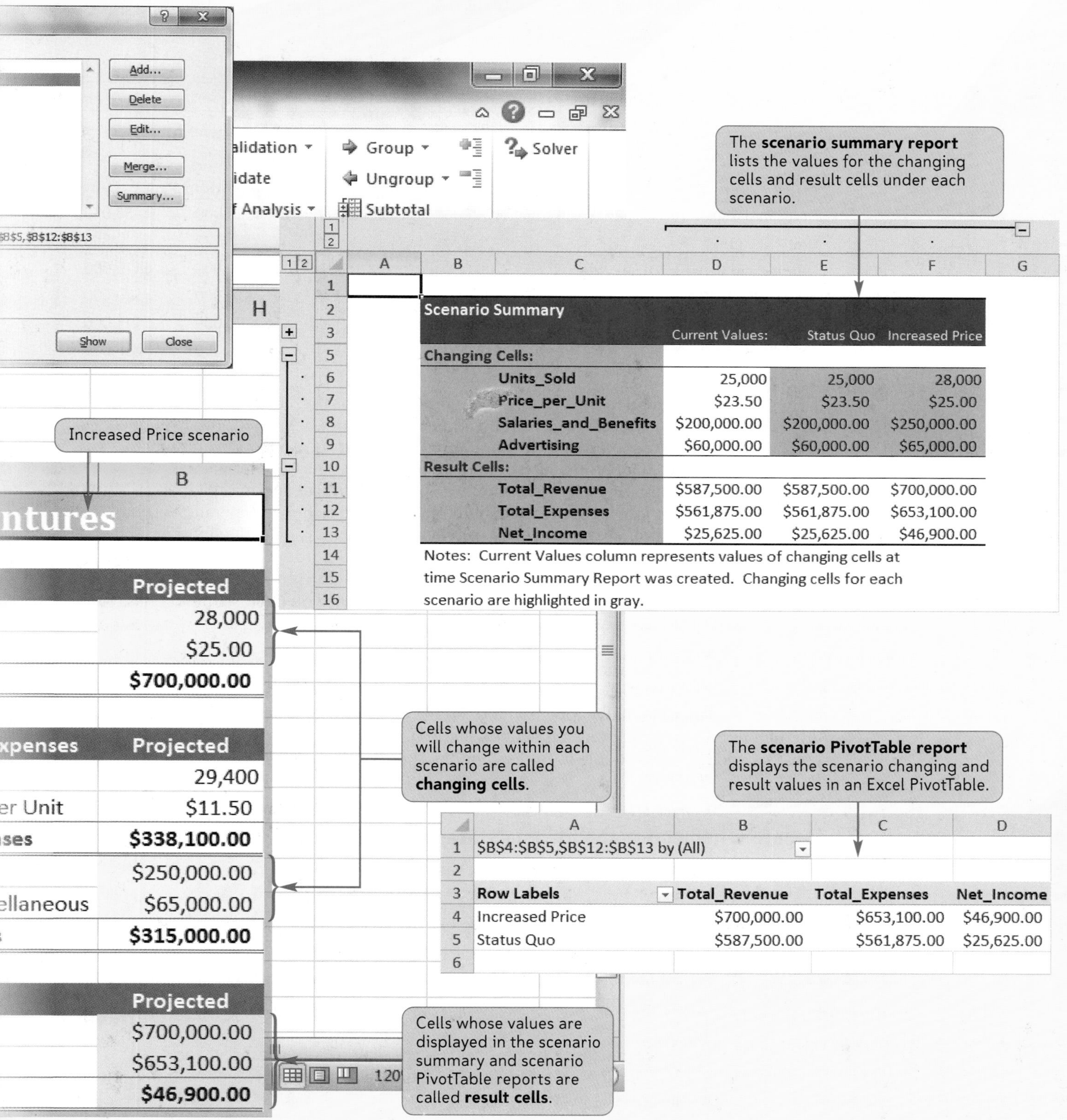

Using the Scenario Manager

Todd and Brent want to change other values in the income statement to see the impact on the company's revenue, expenses, and net income. You will investigate four situations, labeled Status Quo, Expanded Operations, Reduced Operations, and Sale. Figure 10-22 shows the values of the input cells for these four situations.

Figure 10-22 **New what-if analysis scenarios**

Input Cells	Status Quo	Expanded Operations	Reduced Operations	Sale
Units Sold (B4)	24,000	30,000	20,000	33,000
Unit Price (B5)	$24	$27	$22	$20
Salaries and Benefits (B17)	$200,000	$270,000	$180,000	$175,000
Advertising (B18)	$25,000	$50,000	$20,000	$20,000
Administrative (B19)	$20,000	$30,000	$20,000	$15,000
Miscellaneous (B20)	$15,000	$30,000	$15,000	$15,000

The Status Quo situation assumes that everything remains the same for the upcoming year. All of the fixed expenses, units sold, and unit prices are unchanged. The Expanded Operations situation assumes that the company will expand its production and marketing of HoverDisks. Under this proposal, the company will hire additional workers, expand its advertising budget, and spend more on administrative and miscellaneous expenses hoping that sales of HoverDisks will increase. The Reduced Operations situation decreases the amount spent for fixed expenses and assumes a decline in sales. The Sale situation assumes the unit price for HoverDisks will drop from $24 to $20 per unit. To cover the loss in revenue, the company will also reduce its fixed expenses.

You cannot generate this report using a data table because you need six input cells. To perform a what-if analysis with more than two input cells, you create scenarios using the Scenario Manager.

Before using the Scenario Manager, you should define names for all the input and result cells that you intend to use in the analysis. As you'll see later in this tutorial, the defined names automatically appear in the reports generated by the Scenario Manager. Although not a requirement, using defined names makes it easier for you to work with scenarios and for other people to understand the scenario reports.

To define names for the income statement values:

1. If you took a break after the previous session, make sure the Creative Ventures workbook is open.
2. Switch to the **Income Statement** worksheet, and then select the nonadjacent range **A4:B5;A17:B20;A24:B26**. You'll define names for each of these cells.
3. Click the **Formulas** tab on the Ribbon, and then click the **Create from Selection** button in the Defined Names group. The Create Names from Selection dialog box opens.
4. Click the **Left column** check box to insert a check mark, if necessary, and then click the **OK** button. The selected cells in column B are named using the labels in the corresponding cells in column A.
5. Click cell **A1** to deselect the range.

Select only the Left column check box to generate the names from the text labels in the left column.

Defining a Scenario

You use the Scenario Manager to define the scenarios. Each scenario includes a scenario name, input or changing cells, and the values for each input cell. The number of scenarios you can create is limited only by your computer's memory.

REFERENCE

Defining a Scenario

- Enter the data values in the worksheet for the scenario.
- In the Data Tools group on the Data tab, click the What-If Analysis button, and then click Scenario Manager.
- Click the Add button in the Scenario Manager dialog box.
- In the Scenario name box, type a name for the scenario.
- In the Changing cells box, specify the changing cells.
- Click the OK button.
- In the Scenario Values dialog box, specify values for each of the input cells, clicking the Add button after each.
- Click the OK button.

You'll start by creating the Status Quo scenario, whose values match those currently entered in the workbook.

To add the Status Quo scenario:

1. Click the **Data** tab on the Ribbon, click the **What-If Analysis** button in the Data Tools group, and then click **Scenario Manager**. The Scenario Manager dialog box opens. No scenarios are defined yet.
2. Click the **Add** button. The Add Scenario dialog box opens.
3. In the Scenario name box, type **Status Quo** and then press the **Tab** key. The range in the Changing cells box is selected.

The Scenario Manager refers to input cells as changing cells because these worksheet cells contain values that are changed under the scenario. Changing cells can be located anywhere in the worksheet. You can type the range names or locations of changing cells, but it's faster and more accurate to select them with the mouse. To select nonadjacent changing cells, press and hold the Ctrl key as you click each cell. The changing cells for each of the four scenarios are:

- Cell B4: Units Sold
- Cell B5: Price per Unit
- Cell B17: Salaries and Benefits
- Cell B18: Advertising
- Cell B19: Administrative
- Cell B20: Miscellaneous

You'll specify the changing cells for the Status Quo scenario.

To specify the changing cells for the Status Quo scenario:

1. With the Changing Cells box still active, select the nonadjacent range **B4:B5;B17:B20**. The range appears in the Changing cells box. These are the input cells.
2. Press the **Tab** key to select the default text in the Comment box, and then type **Scenario assuming current values.** in the Comment box. See Figure 10-23.

Figure 10-23 Edit Scenario dialog box

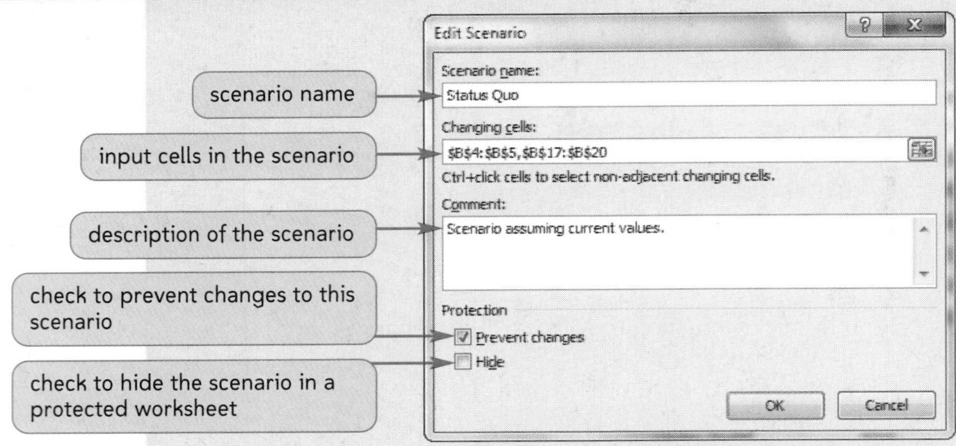

3. Click the **OK** button. The Scenario Values dialog box opens so you can specify values for each of the input cells you entered in the Changing cells box in the Add Scenario dialog box. Because the Status Quo scenario values are the current values in the workbook, you can accept the values displayed in the Scenario Values dialog box. See Figure 10-24.

Figure 10-24 Scenario Values dialog box

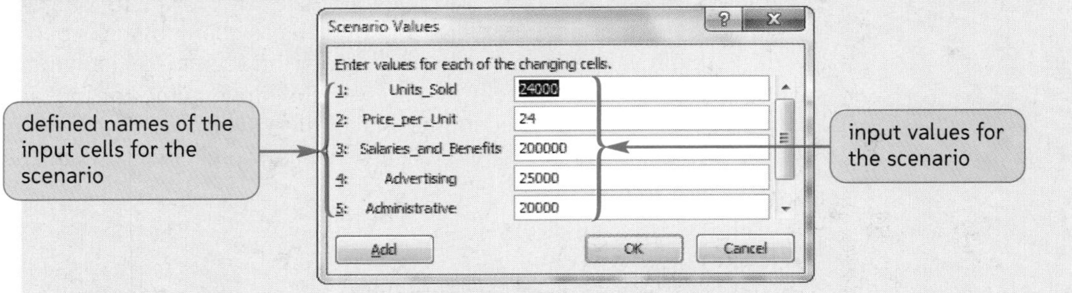

4. Click the **OK** button. The Scenario Manager dialog box reopens. The Status Quo scenario is listed in the Scenarios box.

You'll use the same process to add the remaining three scenarios that Todd and Brent are interested in.

To add the remaining scenarios:

1. Click the **Add** button. The Add Scenario dialog box opens. You need to enter the scenario name.

2. In the Scenario name box, type **Expanded Operations** and then press the **Tab** key. The nonadjacent range you selected for the Status Quo scenario is selected in the Changing cells box. You want to use the same set of changing cells, so you won't make any edits to the range. You will modify the scenario comment.
3. Press the **Tab** key to select the text in the Comment box, type **Scenario assuming expanded operations.** in the Comment box, and then click the **OK** button. The Scenario Values dialog box opens. This scenario uses different values for the changing cells, which you'll enter now.
4. Enter the following values for the Expanded Operations scenario, pressing the **Tab** key to move from one input box to another:

Units_Sold	**30,000**
Price_per_Unit	**27**
Salaries_and_Benefits	**270,000**
Advertising	**50,000**
Administrative	**30,000**
Miscellaneous	**30,000**

Trouble? If the Scenario Manager dialog box reopens, you probably pressed the Enter key instead of the Tab key. Make sure that the Expanded Operations scenario is selected in the Scenarios box, click the Edit button, and then click the OK button to return to the Scenario Values dialog box. Enter the remaining values in the scenario, being sure to press the Tab key to move to the next input box.

5. Click the **Add** button. The Add Scenario dialog box reopens. You'll create the third scenario now. As with the second scenario, you need to enter a new name and comment. The changing cells are the same.

Trouble? If the Scenario Manager dialog box reappeared, you clicked the OK button instead of the Add button. Click the Add button in the Scenario Manager dialog box to return to the Add Scenario dialog box, and then continue with Step 6.

6. Type **Reduced Operations** in the Scenario name box, press the **Tab** key twice, type **Scenario assuming reduced operations.** in the Comment box, and then click the **OK** button.
7. Enter the following values for the Reduced Operations scenario in the Scenario Values dialog box, pressing the **Tab** key to move between input boxes:

Units_Sold	**20,000**
Price_per_Unit	**22**
Salaries_and_Benefits	**180,000**
Advertising	**20,000**
Administrative	**20,000**
Miscellaneous	**15,000**

8. Click the **Add** button to open the Add Scenario dialog box and create the fourth scenario.
9. Type **Sale** in the Scenario name box, press the **Tab** key twice, type **Scenario assuming a sale of HoverDisks.** in the Comment box, and then click the **OK** button.

10. Enter the following values for the Sale scenario in the Scenario Values dialog box, pressing the **Tab** key to move between input boxes:

Units_Sold	**33,000**
Price_per_Unit	**20**
Salaries_and_Benefits	**175,000**
Advertising	**20,000**
Administrative	**15,000**
Miscellaneous	**15,000**

11. Click the **OK** button. The Scenario Manager dialog box lists the four scenarios you created. See Figure 10-25.

Figure 10-25 **Scenario Manager dialog box**

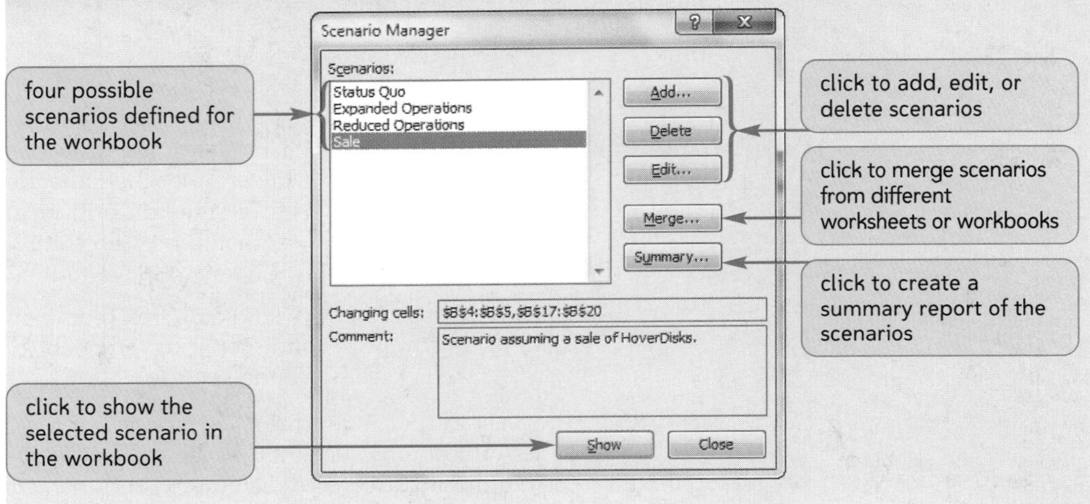

Viewing Scenarios

Now, you can view the effect of each scenario by selecting the scenario in the Scenario Manager dialog box. You switch from one scenario to another by clicking the Show button in the Scenario Manager dialog box. You do not have to close the dialog box to switch between scenarios.

You'll start by viewing the impact of the Expanded Operations scenario on the company's income statement.

TIP

You can also double-click a scenario name in the Scenarios box in the Scenario Manager dialog box to view that scenario.

To view the impact of the Expanded Operations scenario:

1. In the Scenarios box in the Scenario Manager dialog box, click **Expanded Operations**. The changing cells and comment for the selected scenario appear in the bottom of the Scenario Manager dialog box.
2. Click the **Show** button. The values in the Income Statement worksheet change to reflect the scenario.
3. Click the **Close** button. The Scenario Manager dialog box closes. The income statement for Creative Ventures is updated to show expanded operations with increased fixed expenses. See Figure 10-26.

Figure 10-26 **Income statement under the Expanded Operations scenario**

	A	B
1	Creative Ventures	
2	Income Statement	
3	Revenue	Projected
4	Units Sold	30,000
5	Price per Unit	$27.00
6	**Total Revenue**	**$810,000.00**
7		
8	Variable Expenses	Projected
9	Units Produced	31,500
10	Material Cost per Unit	$6.20
11	**Total Material Cost**	**$195,300.00**
12	Manufacturing Cost per Unit	$4.10
13	**Total Manufacturing Cost**	**$129,150.00**
14	**Total Variable Expenses**	**$324,450.00**
15		
16	Fixed Expenses	Projected
17	Salaries and Benefits	$270,000.00
18	Advertising	$50,000.00
19	Administrative	$30,000.00
20	Miscellaneous	$30,000.00
21	**Total Fixed Expenses**	**$380,000.00**
22		
23	Summary	Projected
24	Total Revenue	$810,000.00
25	Total Expenses	$704,450.00
26	**Net Income**	**$105,550.00**

Trouble? If the values in your income statement do not match those in the figure, you might have entered the values for the scenario incorrectly. You'll learn how to edit a scenario shortly.

Excel automatically changes the values of the six input cells to match the scenario. Under the Expanded Operations scenario, the company's net income increases from the current value of $56,440 to $105,550. You'll review the other scenarios.

To view the impact of the remaining scenarios:

1. In the Data Tools group on the Data tab, click the **What-If Analysis** button, and then click **Scenario Manager**. The Scenario Manager dialog box opens.
2. Double-click **Reduced Operations** in the Scenarios box to update the worksheet, and then click the **Close** button to close the Scenario Manager dialog box. Under the Reduced Operations scenario, the net income value shown in cell B26 becomes a deficit of $11,300.
3. Open the Scenario Manager dialog box, double-click **Sale** in the Scenarios box to update the worksheet, and then click the **Close** button to close the Scenario Manager dialog box. Under the Sale scenario, with the reduced unit price of each disk, the company would show a net income of $78,105. Figure 10-27 shows the income statements for the Reduced Operations and Sale scenarios.

Figure 10-27 Income statements for the Reduced Operations and Sale scenarios

	A	B
1	Creative Ventures	
2	Income Statement	
3	Revenue	Projected
4	Units Sold	20,000
5	Price per Unit	$22.00
6	**Total Revenue**	**$440,000.00**
7		
8	Variable Expenses	Projected
9	Units Produced	21,000
10	Material Cost per Unit	$6.20
11	**Total Material Cost**	**$130,200.00**
12	Manufacturing Cost per Unit	$4.10
13	**Total Manufacturing Cost**	**$86,100.00**
14	**Total Variable Expenses**	**$216,300.00**
15		
16	Fixed Expenses	Projected
17	Salaries and Benefits	$180,000.00
18	Advertising	$20,000.00
19	Administrative	$20,000.00
20	Miscellaneous	$15,000.00
21	**Total Fixed Expenses**	**$235,000.00**
22		
23	Summary	Projected
24	Total Revenue	$440,000.00
25	Total Expenses	$451,300.00
26	**Net Income**	($11,300.00)

Reduced Operations scenario

	A	B
1	Creative Ventures	
2	Income Statement	
3	Revenue	Projected
4	Units Sold	33,000
5	Price per Unit	$20.00
6	**Total Revenue**	**$660,000.00**
7		
8	Variable Expenses	Projected
9	Units Produced	34,650
10	Material Cost per Unit	$6.20
11	**Total Material Cost**	**$214,830.00**
12	Manufacturing Cost per Unit	$4.10
13	**Total Manufacturing Cost**	**$142,065.00**
14	**Total Variable Expenses**	**$356,895.00**
15		
16	Fixed Expenses	Projected
17	Salaries and Benefits	$175,000.00
18	Advertising	$20,000.00
19	Administrative	$15,000.00
20	Miscellaneous	$15,000.00
21	**Total Fixed Expenses**	**$225,000.00**
22		
23	Summary	Projected
24	Total Revenue	$660,000.00
25	Total Expenses	$581,895.00
26	**Net Income**	**$78,105.00**

Sale scenario

Editing a Scenario

After you create a scenario, you can edit its assumptions to view other possibilities. When you edit a scenario, the worksheet calculations are automatically updated to reflect the new scenario.

The most profitable scenario, the Expanded Operations scenario, relies on the company selling 30,000 units at $27. Todd and Brent are unsure whether the company can meet that sales goal. They want you to modify the Expanded Operations scenario, reducing the total sales to 27,000 units and reducing salaries and benefits to $230,000.

To edit the Expanded Operations scenario:

1. In the Data Tools group on the Data tab, click the **What-If Analysis** button, and then click **Scenario Manager**. The Scenario Manager dialog box opens.
2. Click **Expanded Operations** in the Scenarios box, and then click the **Edit** button. The Edit Scenario dialog box opens. You don't need to make any changes in this dialog box.
3. Click the **OK** button. The Scenario Values dialog box opens. You'll change values in some of these cells.
4. Change the Units_Sold value from 30,000 to **27,000** and then change the Salaries_and_Benefits value from 270,000 to **230,000**.

5. Click the **OK** button. The Scenario Manager dialog box reopens.
6. Click the **Show** button. The Income Statement worksheet updates to reflect the revised scenario, which results in net income decreasing from $105,550 to $96,995.
7. Click the **Close** button. The Scenario Manager dialog box closes. The income statement reflects the edited Expanded Operations scenario. See Figure 10-28.

Figure 10-28 **Income statement for the revised Expanded Operations scenario**

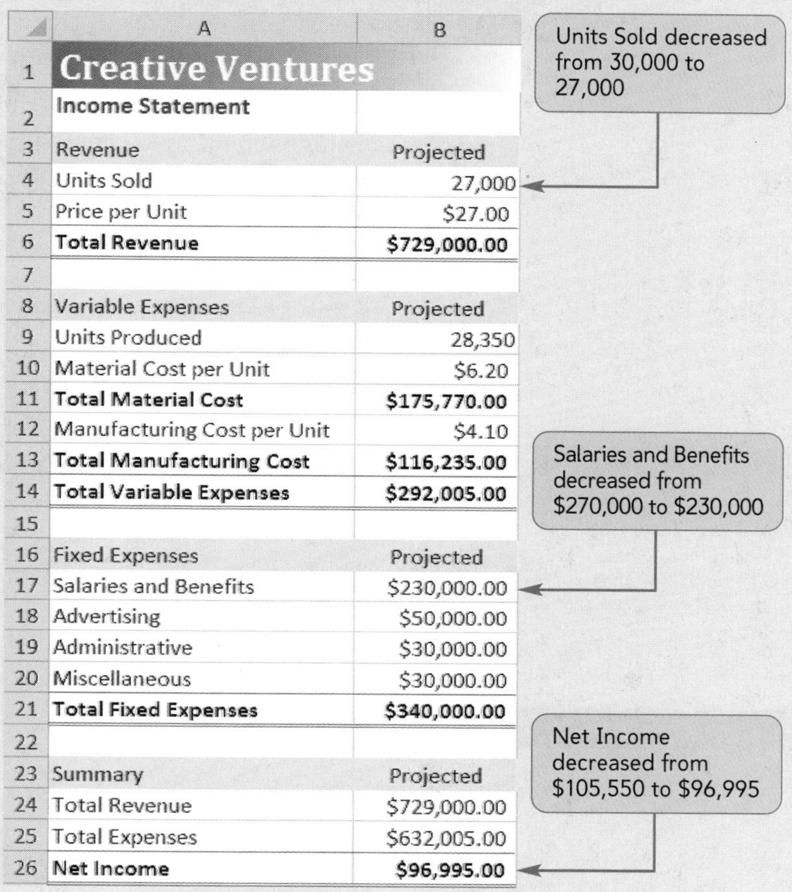

	A	B
1	Creative Ventures	
2	Income Statement	
3	Revenue	Projected
4	Units Sold	27,000
5	Price per Unit	$27.00
6	**Total Revenue**	**$729,000.00**
7		
8	Variable Expenses	Projected
9	Units Produced	28,350
10	Material Cost per Unit	$6.20
11	**Total Material Cost**	**$175,770.00**
12	Manufacturing Cost per Unit	$4.10
13	**Total Manufacturing Cost**	**$116,235.00**
14	**Total Variable Expenses**	**$292,005.00**
15		
16	Fixed Expenses	Projected
17	Salaries and Benefits	$230,000.00
18	Advertising	$50,000.00
19	Administrative	$30,000.00
20	Miscellaneous	$30,000.00
21	**Total Fixed Expenses**	**$340,000.00**
22		
23	Summary	Projected
24	Total Revenue	$729,000.00
25	Total Expenses	$632,005.00
26	**Net Income**	**$96,995.00**

8. In the Data Tools group on the Data tab, click the **What-If Analysis** button, and then click **Scenario Manager** to open the Scenario Manager dialog box.
9. Double-click **Status Quo** in the Scenarios box to show the income statement with the original values. You'll leave the Scenario Manager dialog box open.

Creating a Scenario Summary Report

Although scenarios can help you make important business decisions, switching between scenarios can become time-consuming. Another option is to create a single table that contains the results from all of the scenarios. You can do this with a scenario summary report. The report's tabular layout makes it simpler to compare the results of each scenario, and the automatic formatting makes it useful for reports and meetings.

REFERENCE

Creating a Scenario Summary Report or a Scenario PivotTable Report

- In the Data Tools group on the Data tab, click the What-If Analysis button, and then click Scenario Manager.
- Click the Summary button.
- Click the Scenario summary option button to create a scenario summary report.

or

- Click the Scenario PivotTable report option button to create a PivotTable describing the scenarios.
- Select the result cells to display in the report.
- Click the OK button.

To create a scenario summary report, you must identify the result cells. Todd and Brent are interested in the following result cells: cell B24 (Total Revenue), cell B25 (Total Expenses), and cell B26 (Net Income). You'll display these values, along with the values of the input cells, in your report.

TIP

The scenario summary report has outline tools that allow you to hide and expand different parts of the report, so you can concentrate on only a few key cells.

To create the scenario summary report:

1. Click the **Summary** button in the Scenario Manager dialog box. The Scenario Summary dialog box opens, allowing you to create a scenario summary report or a scenario PivotTable report. You want to create a scenario summary report.
2. Verify that the **Scenario summary** option button is selected.
3. Make sure that the Result cells box is active, and then select the range **B24:B26**. This range references the result cells that you want to display in the report.
4. Click the **OK** button. The Scenario Summary report is inserted in the workbook.
5. Move the **Scenario Summary** report to the end of the workbook. See Figure 10-29.

Figure 10-29 Scenario summary report

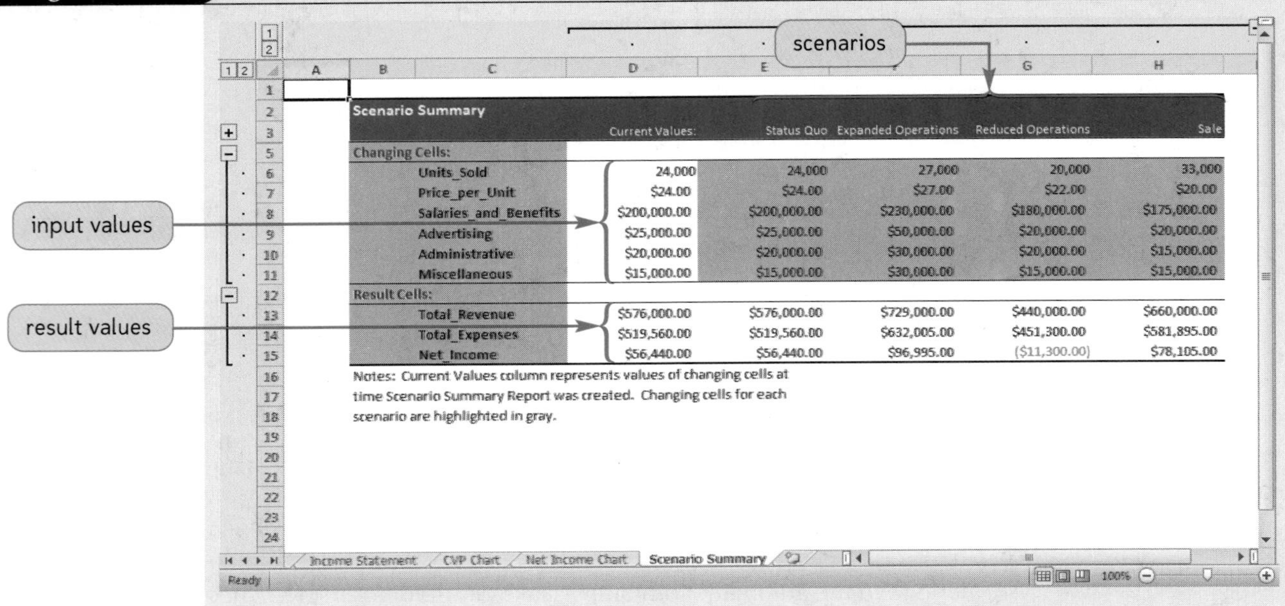

Scenario Summary

	Current Values:	Status Quo	Expanded Operations	Reduced Operations	Sale
Changing Cells:					
Units_Sold	24,000	24,000	27,000	20,000	33,000
Price_per_Unit	$24.00	$24.00	$27.00	$22.00	$20.00
Salaries_and_Benefits	$200,000.00	$200,000.00	$230,000.00	$180,000.00	$175,000.00
Advertising	$25,000.00	$25,000.00	$50,000.00	$20,000.00	$20,000.00
Administrative	$20,000.00	$20,000.00	$30,000.00	$20,000.00	$15,000.00
Miscellaneous	$15,000.00	$15,000.00	$30,000.00	$15,000.00	$15,000.00
Result Cells:					
Total_Revenue	$576,000.00	$576,000.00	$729,000.00	$440,000.00	$660,000.00
Total_Expenses	$519,560.00	$519,560.00	$632,005.00	$451,300.00	$581,895.00
Net_Income	$56,440.00	$56,440.00	$96,995.00	($11,300.00)	$78,105.00

Notes: Current Values column represents values of changing cells at time Scenario Summary Report was created. Changing cells for each scenario are highlighted in gray.

The scenario summary report displays the values of the input cells and result cells under each scenario. Each scenario is listed by name, and the current worksheet values are also displayed. Note that the report uses the defined names you created earlier to identify the changing and result cells. The defined names make the report simpler to interpret.

Creating a Scenario PivotTable Report

Another way to display the results of scenarios is with a PivotTable report. As the name implies, a **Scenario PivotTable report** displays the results from each scenario as a pivot field in a PivotTable. You'll create a Scenario PivotTable report.

To create the Scenario PivotTable report:

1. Return to the **Income Statement** worksheet.
2. In the Data Tools group on the Data tab, click the **What-If Analysis** button, and then click **Scenario Manager**. The Scenario Manager dialog box opens.
3. Click the **Summary** button to open the Scenario Summary dialog box, and then click the **Scenario PivotTable report** option button.
4. Click the **OK** button. The Scenario PivotTable sheet is inserted in the workbook and contains the scenario values in PivotTable form.
5. Move the **Scenario PivotTable** worksheet to the end of the workbook. See Figure 10-30.

Figure 10-30 Scenario PivotTable report

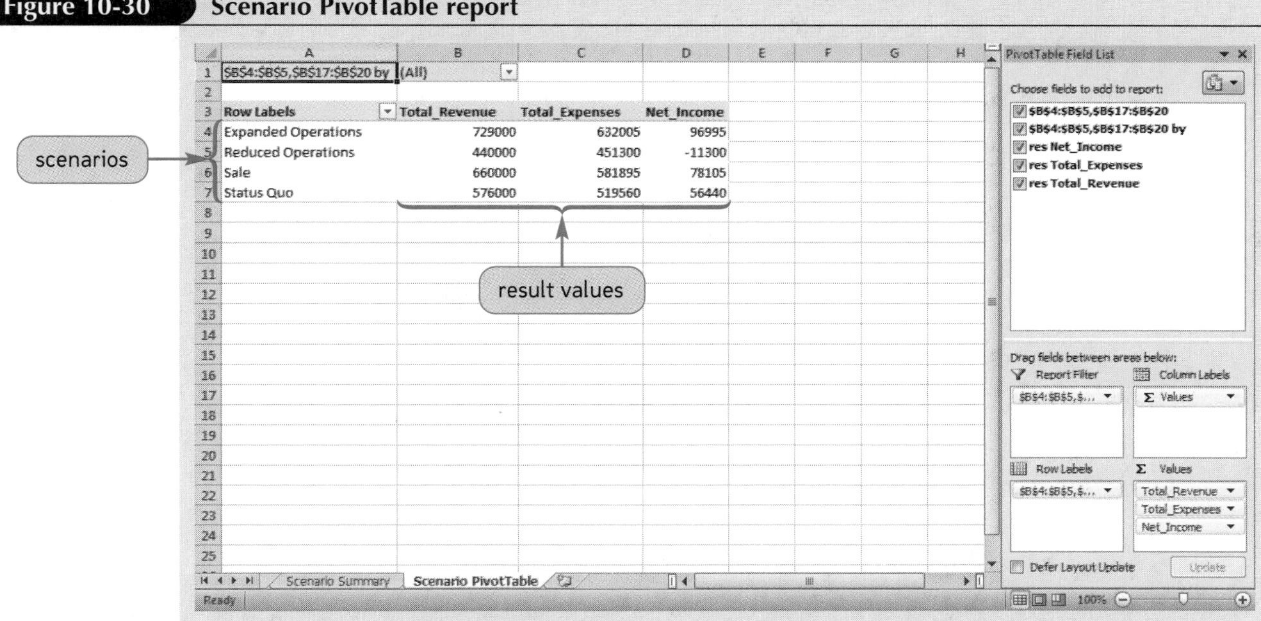

You'll edit the scenario PivotTable to make it easier to read, but you will not filter it. Then, you'll generate a PivotChart of revenue, expenses, and net income under each scenario.

To edit the PivotTable report:

1. In the Values box of the PivotTable Field List, click the **Total Revenue** button, and then click **Value Field Settings**. The Value Field Settings dialog box opens.
2. Click the **Number Format** button to open the Format Cells dialog box, click **Currency** in the Category box, and then click the last entry **($1,234,10)** in the Negative numbers box to display negative currency values in a red font enclosed in parentheses.
3. Click the **OK** button in the Format Cells dialog box, and then click the **OK** button in the Value Field Settings dialog box. The number format is applied to the Total_Revenue cells.
4. Repeat Steps 1 through 3 for the **Total_Expenses** and the **Net_Income** buttons in the Values box to apply the same number format.
5. In the Report Filter box, click the **$B$4:$B$5,$...** button, and then click **Remove Field**. The field is removed from the PivotTable because you do not need to filter the PivotTable.
6. In cell A1, enter **Scenario PivotTable** and then format the text using the **Title** cell style. See Figure 10-31.

Figure 10-31 **Formatted scenario PivotTable**

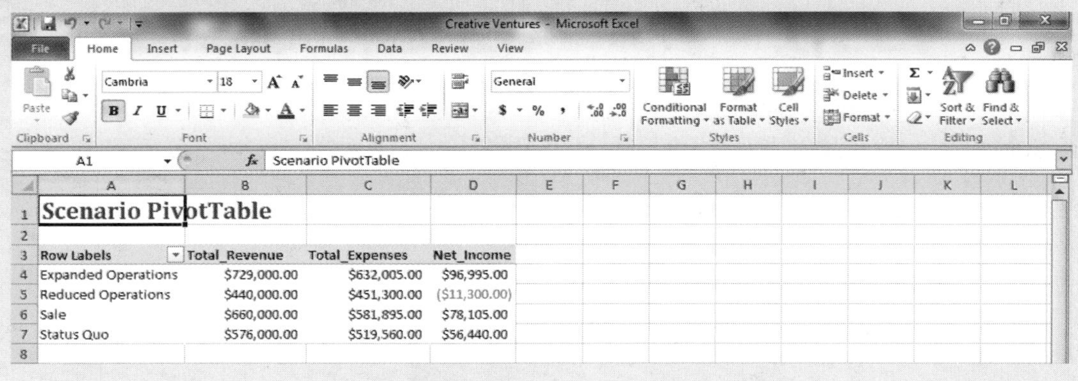

Scenario PivotTable

Row Labels	Total_Revenue	Total_Expenses	Net_Income
Expanded Operations	$729,000.00	$632,005.00	$96,995.00
Reduced Operations	$440,000.00	$451,300.00	($11,300.00)
Sale	$660,000.00	$581,895.00	$78,105.00
Status Quo	$576,000.00	$519,560.00	$56,440.00

Finally, you'll display the results of this table in a PivotChart.

To create the PivotChart:

1. Click cell **A4** to select the PivotTable, click the **PivotTable Tools Options** tab on the Ribbon, and then click the **PivotChart** button in the Tools group. The Insert Chart dialog box opens.
2. Click the **Clustered Column** chart type (the first chart type in the Column section), and then click the **OK** button.
3. Move and resize the embedded chart so that it covers the range **A9:F23**, and then click cell **C1** to deselect the PivotTable and PivotChart. See Figure 10-32.

Figure 10-32 Scenario PivotChart

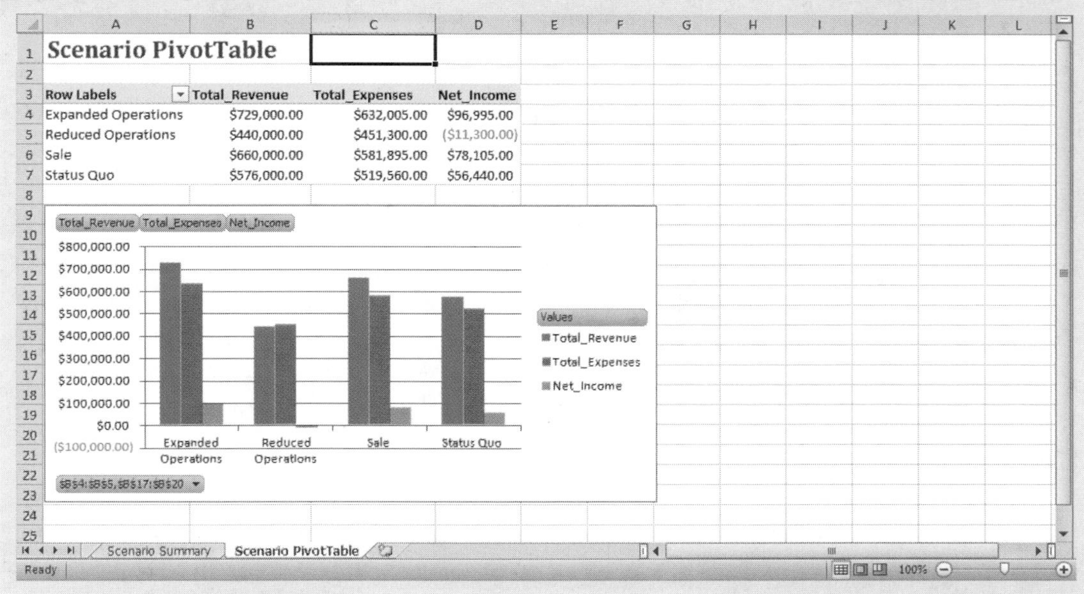

Based on the income statements from the different scenarios, Todd and Brent can expect a net income for the company that ranges from more than $56,000 to nearly $97,000 per year. However, they shouldn't pursue the Reduced Operations scenario because of the risk of losing money.

PROSKILLS

Teamwork: Merging Scenarios

In a business, several workbooks often track the same set of figures and evaluate the same set of scenarios. Colleagues can share scenarios by merging the scenarios from multiple workbooks into one workbook. The Scenario Manager dialog box includes a Merge button that you can use to merge scenarios from different workbooks. The scenarios merge into the active sheet. It's easier to merge scenarios if all of the what-if analyses on the different worksheets and workbooks are identical. All of the changing cells from the merged scenario must correspond to changing cells in the active workbook and worksheet. By sharing your scenarios, a team can more easily explore the impact of different financial situations, ensuring that the entire team is always working from a common set of assumptions and goals.

REVIEW

Session 10.2 Quick Check

1. What is one advantage of scenarios over data tables?
2. What should you do before creating a scenario report to make the entries on the report easier to interpret?
3. What are changing cells?
4. What are result cells?
5. Where do you define result cells in the Scenario Manager?
6. How do you display a scenario in the active worksheet?
7. How do you create a scenario PivotTable report?

SESSION 10.3 VISUAL OVERVIEW

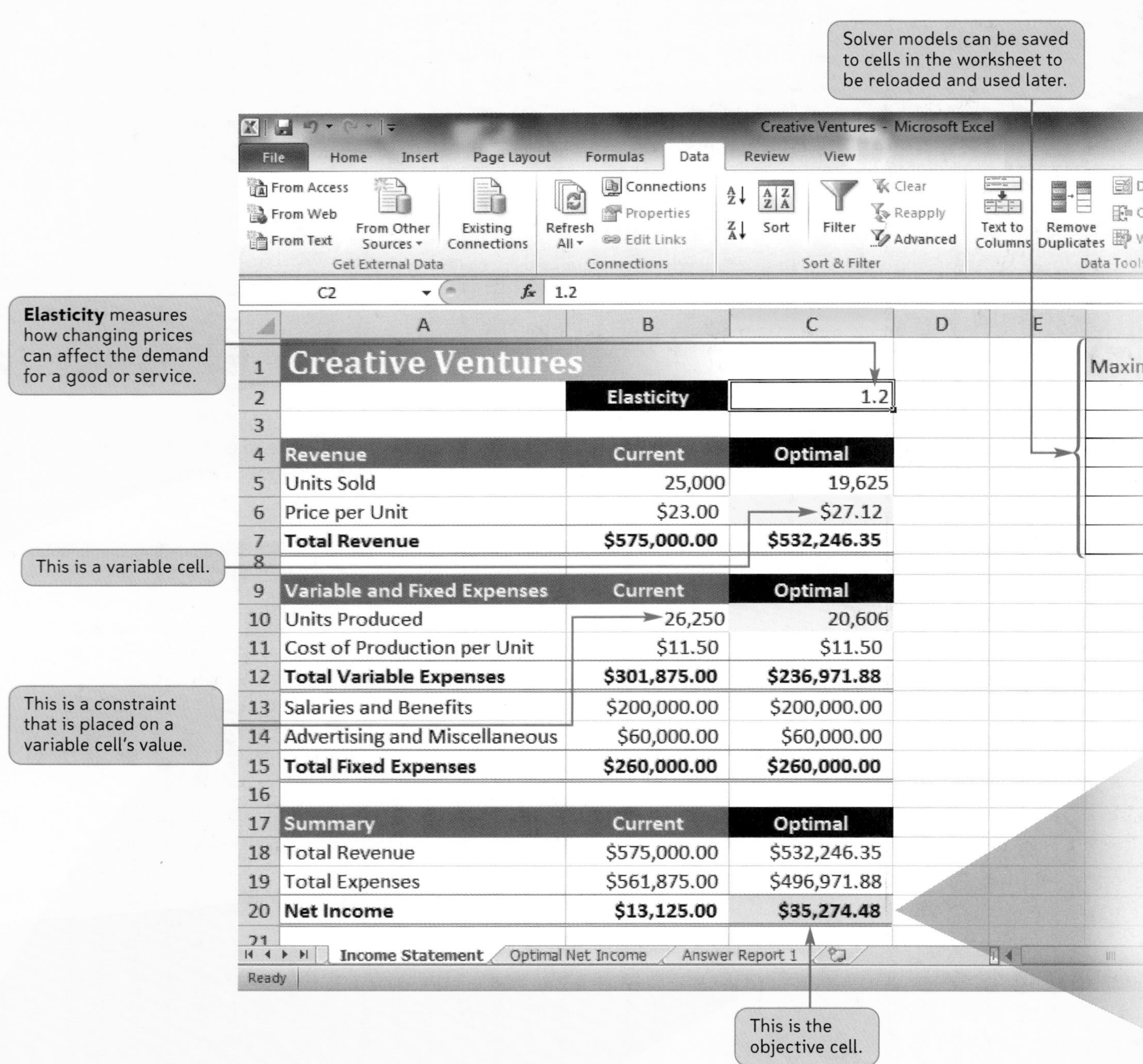

USING SOLVER

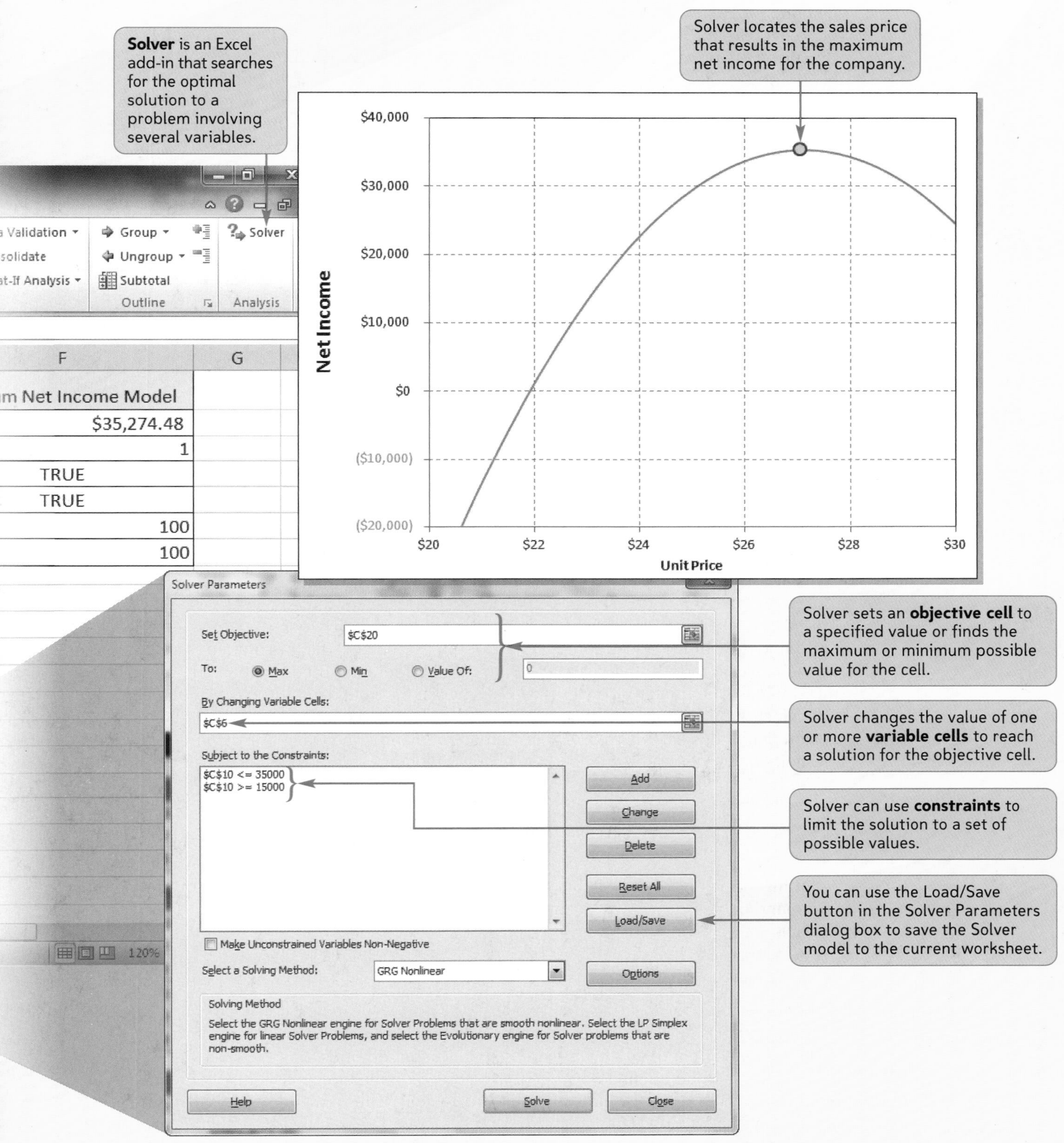

Understanding Price Elasticity of Demand

Any analysis of the relationship between cost, sales volume, and profit needs to take into account the impact of price on demand. The scenarios you analyzed show that demand for HoverDisks would go down as the price increased and would rise as the price decreased. This relationship between sales price and demand affects revenue. By raising the price, the company might generate more revenue; but at a certain point, higher prices will generate less revenue as customers stop buying the product. On the other hand, lower prices might actually increase revenue if enough new customers are attracted to the product; but at a certain point, the price will be so low that there will simply not be enough customers to allow the company to make a profit. The point of maximum revenue occurs somewhere between the lowest sales price and the highest sales price, as illustrated by the charts in Figure 10-33.

Figure 10-33 **Demand and revenue as functions of price**

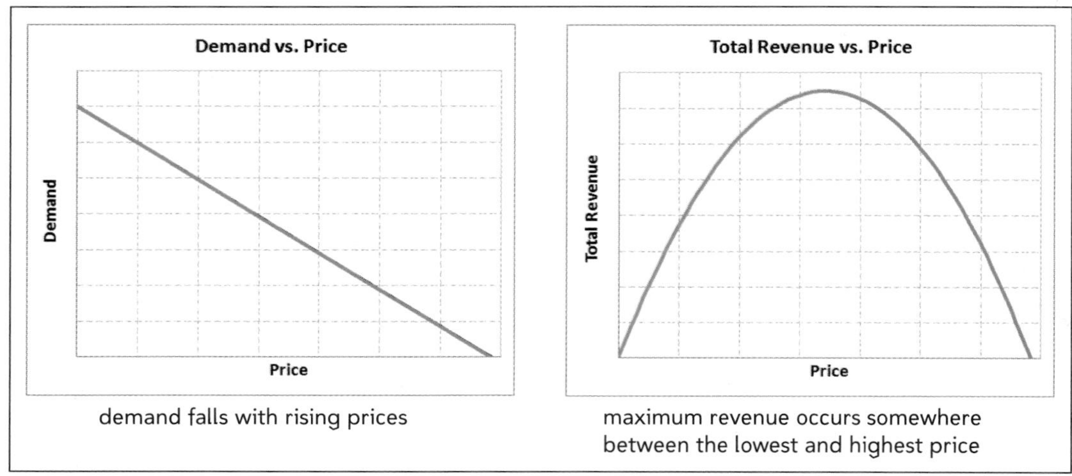

demand falls with rising prices

maximum revenue occurs somewhere between the lowest and highest price

To find the point of maximum revenue, you must make certain assumptions about how changes in price affect demand. For example, Todd and Brent might assume that if they increase the price of HoverDisks by 10 percent, demand will drop by 15 percent. The effect of one financial variable upon another is called elasticity. The effect that price has on demand is called the **price elasticity of demand**. One way of measuring the price elasticity of demand is to calculate the change in demand divided by the change in price. The formula is:

$$elasticity = \left| \frac{\%\ change\ in\ demand}{\%\ change\ in\ price} \right|$$

In this formula, *elasticity* is the value of the price elasticity of demand. For example, if demand decreases by 15 percent when the price increases by 10 percent, the price elasticity of demand would be:

$$elasticity = \left| \frac{-15\%}{10\%} \right| = |-1.5| = 1.5$$

Note that elasticity measures are always expressed as positive values because it is assumed that demand will never increase with increased price.

Products are often defined by their elasticity. When the price elasticity of demand is less than 1, the product is **relatively inelastic**, which means that large changes in price will cause small changes in demand. For example, if the elasticity is 0.1, then increasing the price of the product by 10 percent decreases demand by only 1 percent. If elasticity equals 0, then changes in price have *no* impact on demand. This situation is referred to as **perfectly inelastic** and occurs when the item being sold is rare or essential, such as a life-saving drug for which people are willing to spend whatever necessary to procure it.

When the price elasticity of demand is greater than 1, the product is **relatively elastic**, indicating that demand is very responsive to changes in price. For example, if the elasticity equals 2.0, then increasing the object's price by 10 percent decreases demand by 20 percent. For large elasticity values, any change in price causes a huge change in demand, resulting in a **perfectly elastic** relationship between price and demand. This can occur when consumers have to choose between two products that are exactly equal in all respects other than price. So, raising the price of one would cause a huge decrease in demand (because consumers will opt for the cheaper though identical product). For example, if neighboring gas stations are competing for business selling the same quality of gas, the station that raises its price might see a considerable drop in demand because motorists will simply purchase the less expensive gas at the nearby station.

Finally, when elasticity equals 1.0, the product is referred to as **unit elastic** because any change in price is met by an equal and opposite change in demand.

Todd and Brent want you to add another what-if analysis to the workbook, one that includes the price elasticity of demand as a factor in calculating sales volume. First, you must determine the elasticity value.

Maximizing Net Income Through Trial and Error

Determining a value for the price elasticity of demand involves a shrewd examination of the market, the product itself, and the desires of consumers. A review of historical trends and the relationship between demand and price for similar products can also be helpful. The relationship between price and demand for a novelty item such as the HoverDisk is relatively elastic because the product is of interest to the public, but the novelty will quickly wear off if the price is set too high. Todd and Brent settle on an elasticity value of 1.2; in other words, for every 10 percent increase in the price of HoverDisks, they expect that the demand will decrease by 12 percent.

Because you are dealing with percentage increases and decreases, you need to establish a baseline of price and demand. You'll assume the Status Quo scenario, which indicates that 24,000 HoverDisks can be sold at a price of $24 per disk. If the price increased 10 percent, or by $2.40, to $26.40, but the demand decreased by 12 percent, or by 2,880 units, the sales volume would be 21,120 disks per year. What would the net income be under this scenario? To find out, you can perform a what-if analysis with the company's Income Statement worksheet.

Because you will be exploring other possible changes in price, you'll insert a formula into the worksheet to calculate the sales volume for different prices. The general formula for determining the change in demand for a product based on a new price is:

$$\textit{New Demand} = \textit{Old Demand} \times \left[1 + \textit{elasticity} \times \left(1 - \frac{\textit{New Price}}{\textit{Old Price}}\right)\right]$$

In this formula, *Old Demand* is the current demand for the product, *elasticity* is the price elasticity of demand, *New Price* is the proposed price for the product, *Old Price* is the current price of the product, and *New Demand* is the demand for the product at its new price. You'll add this formula to the workbook to project the revenue, expenses, and net income that would result from raising the price of HoverDisks by 10 percent.

To project the effect of raising the price of HoverDisks:

1. If you took a break at the end of the previous session, make sure the Creative Ventures workbook is open.
2. Switch to the **Income Statement** worksheet, select the range **A3:B26**, and move it down to the range **A6:B29**.

You need to add a new column to the workbook for revenue and expense calculations on the price elasticity model.

3. Copy the range **B6:B29**, paste it into the range **C6:C29**, and then, in cells C6, C11, C19, and C26, enter **New Price**.
4. In cell A3, enter **Price Elasticity of Demand**, format cell A3 with the **20% - Accent3** cell style, and then, in cell B3, enter **1.2**.

   In the new column, you'll make the Units Sold value a calculated item based on the elasticity value and the ratio of the new price to the old price. You'll use the general formula described above with the Old Demand value from cell B7, the elasticity value from cell B3, the New Price value from cell C8, and the Old Price value from cell B8. The New Demand value will be placed in cell C7.

5. In cell C7, enter the formula **=B7*(1+B3*(1–C8/B8))**. The formula returns the value 24,000, which is what we would expect if the new sales price remained unchanged at $24.
6. In cell C8, enter the new sales price of **$26.40**. As discussed earlier, the demand for disks at this price drops to 21,120. Review the income statement under this new price. See Figure 10-34.

Figure 10-34 **Price elasticity of demand used to calculate net income**

for every 10 percent increase in price, sales drop by 12 percent

Units Sold is calculated based on the sales price and the price elasticity of demand

	A	B	C	D	E	F	G	H
1	Creative Ventures							
2	Income Statement				Cost-Volume-Profit Analysis			
3	Price Elasticity of Demand	1.2			Units Sold	Revenue	Expenses	Net Income
4					24,000	$576,000.00	$519,560.00	$56,440.00
5					10,000	$240,000.00	$368,150.00	($128,150.00)
6	Revenue	Projected	New Price		15,000	$360,000.00	$422,225.00	($62,225.00)
7	Units Sold	24,000	21,120		20,000	$480,000.00	$476,300.00	$3,700.00
8	Price per Unit	$24.00	$26.40		25,000	$600,000.00	$530,375.00	$69,625.00
9	**Total Revenue**	**$576,000.00**	**$557,568.00**		30,000	$720,000.00	$584,450.00	$135,550.00
10					35,000	$840,000.00	$638,525.00	$201,475.00
11	Variable Expenses	Projected	New Price					
12	Units Produced	25,200	22,176				Net Income Analysis	
13	Material Cost per Unit	$6.20	$6.20					Price per Unit
14	**Total Material Cost**	**$156,240.00**	**$137,491.20**		Units Sold	$15	$20	$25
15	Manufacturing Cost per Unit	$4.10	$4.10		10,000	($218,150.00)	($168,150.00)	($118,150.00)
16	**Total Manufacturing Cost**	**$103,320.00**	**$90,921.60**		15,000	($197,225.00)	($122,225.00)	($47,225.00)
17	**Total Variable Expenses**	**$259,560.00**	**$228,412.80**		20,000	($176,300.00)	($76,300.00)	$23,700.00
18					25,000	($155,375.00)	($30,375.00)	$94,625.00
19	Fixed Expenses	Projected	New Price		30,000	($134,450.00)	$15,550.00	$165,550.00
20	Salaries and Benefits	$200,000.00	$200,000.00		35,000	($113,525.00)	$61,475.00	$236,475.00

Documentation | Income Statement | CVP Chart | Net Income Chart | Scenario Summ

Ready 120%

Based on these calculations, the total revenue under this new price drops by about $19,000 from $576,000 to $557,568. However, variable expenses also decrease under this plan because the company will not be manufacturing as many disks as before. The result is that the company's net income actually increases by almost $13,000 from $56,440 under the current price to $69,155.20 under the new price. If Todd and Brent's assumptions regarding the relationship between price and demand for the HoverDisk are correct, they can actually increase the company's net income by increasing the sales price even if they sell fewer disks. You'll examine the effect of other prices on net income.

To calculate net income for other prices:

1. Change the value in cell C8 from $26.40 to **$30**. At this price, the net income changes to $62,308 which is still an improvement over the status quo values but not as high as projected when the sales price was $26.40.
2. Change the value in cell C8 to **$35**. At this price, the company sells 10,800 disks per year and the net income drops to $1,198. At that high price, the company sells so few disks that it's barely profitable to produce the product.
3. Change the value in cell C8 back to **$24.00**.

Clearly, increasing the price doesn't always mean increasing the profit. Todd and Brent want to find the best price for the HoverDisks: one that results in the maximum net income for the company. You could continue entering different price values, zeroing in on the one value that produces the highest net income. This process, known as **trial and error**, can be very time-consuming if you have a large range of possible values. In this case, you've already determined that you cannot increase the price of the HoverDisk much past $35 per disk without losing money, but it's not immediately clear what the best price would be. To determine the answer to that question, you can use Solver.

Finding an Optimal Solution Using Solver

Solver searches for the optimal solution to a problem involving several variables. For example, Solver can find the curve or line that best fits a set of data or minimizes production costs for a product or service. You'll use Solver to determine the unit price that maximizes net income from the sales of HoverDisks.

Activating Solver

Solver is an **add-in**, a program that adds customized commands and features to Microsoft Office programs such as Excel. Because Solver is an added feature of Excel, it might not be activated in your version of Excel. Before running Solver, you might have to activate it.

REFERENCE

Activating Solver

- Check whether Solver appears in the Analysis group on the Data tab. If it does, Solver is already active. If not, continue with the rest of these steps.
- Click the File tab, and then click the Options button in the navigation bar.
- Click Add-Ins in the left pane, click the arrow next to the Manage box, and then click Excel Add-ins.
- Click the Go button to open the Add-Ins dialog box.
- Click the Solver Add-in check box, and then click the OK button.
- Follow the remaining prompts to install Solver, if it is not already installed.

You'll check whether Solver is already active on your version of Excel by checking whether the Solver button appears on the Data tab. If the Solver button does not appear on the Data tab, the Solver add-in needs to be activated. If you are working on a network, you might need your instructor or network administrator to activate Solver for you. If you are working on a stand-alone PC, you can activate Solver yourself. You'll make sure Solver is active for your installation of Excel.

To activate the Solver add-in:

1. Click the **Data** tab on the Ribbon, and then look to see if the Solver button appears in the Analysis group on the right side of the tab, as shown in Figure 10-35. If you see the Solver button, Solver is active and you should read but not perform the rest of the steps in this section. If you don't see the Solver button, continue with Step 2.

Figure 10-35 Solver button in the Analysis group on the Data tab

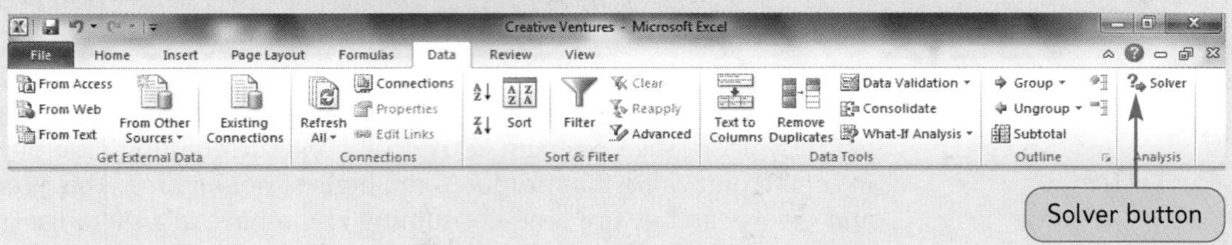

2. Click the **File** tab, and then click the **Options** button in the navigation bar. The Excel Options dialog box opens.
3. In the left pane, click **Add-Ins**. Information about all of the add-ins currently installed on your computer appears in the right pane.
4. If necessary, click the arrow next to the Manage box, and then click **Excel Add-ins**.
5. Click the **Go** button. The Add-Ins dialog box opens and displays a list of all of the installed add-ins. A check box appears before each add-in name that has been activated and is ready for use.
6. Click the **Solver Add-in** check box to insert a check mark. See Figure 10-36.

Figure 10-36 Add-Ins dialog box

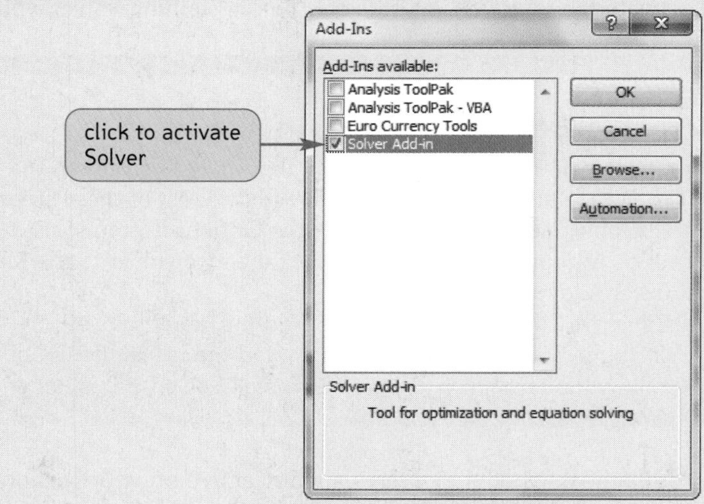

7. Click the **OK** button. The Solver button is added to the Data tab.

Solver is active and ready to use.

INSIGHT

Excel Add-Ins

Solver is only one of a collection of Excel add-ins. Other add-ins provide the ability to perform statistical analyses, generate business reports, and retrieve financial data from the Internet. You can also create your own add-in using the Visual Basic for Applications (VBA) macro language. The process activating add-ins is the same as the process you used to activate the Solver add-in. Most third-party add-ins provide detailed instructions for their installation and use.

Setting Up Solver to Find a Solution

To use Solver, you must specify three items, or **Solver parameters**: the objective cell, the variable (or changing) cells, and the constraints on the problem. The objective cell is a cell that you want to maximize, minimize, or change to a specific value. In this case, the company's net income is your objective cell, whose value you want to maximize. A variable cell is a cell that Excel changes to produce the desired result in the objective cell. In this case, the adjustable cell is the sales price of each HoverDisk. Finally, a constraint is a limit that is placed on the problem's solution. For example, Creative Ventures might have a physical limit on the number of HoverDisks it can produce in a given year (no matter how profitable it would be to produce extra disks), so this would be a constraint that Solver would have to include when finding the maximum net income.

REFERENCE

Setting Solver Parameters

- In the Analysis group on the Data tab, click the Solver button.
- In the Set Objective box, specify the cell whose value you want to set to match a specific objective.
- Click the Max, Min, or Value Of option buttons to maximize, minimize, or set the objective cell to a specified value, respectively.
- In the By Changing Variable Cells input box, specify the changing cells.

You'll set up the Solver parameters.

To define the objective cell and changing cells:

1. In the Analysis group on the Data tab, click the **Solver** button. The Solver Parameters dialog box opens.
2. With the Set Objective box active, click cell **C29** on the Income Statement worksheet. The absolute reference to the cell appears in the Set Objective box.
3. Verify that the **Max** option button is selected. This defines the objective of Solver to find the maximum value that can be calculated for cell C29 (the company's net income from the HoverDisk sales).
4. Click the **By Changing Variable Cells** box, and then click cell **C8** in the Income Statement worksheet. The absolute reference to cell C8, which contains the unit price, appears in the input box, specifying the cell you want to change to locate the maximum possible net income. See Figure 10-37.

Figure 10-37 **Solver Parameters dialog box**

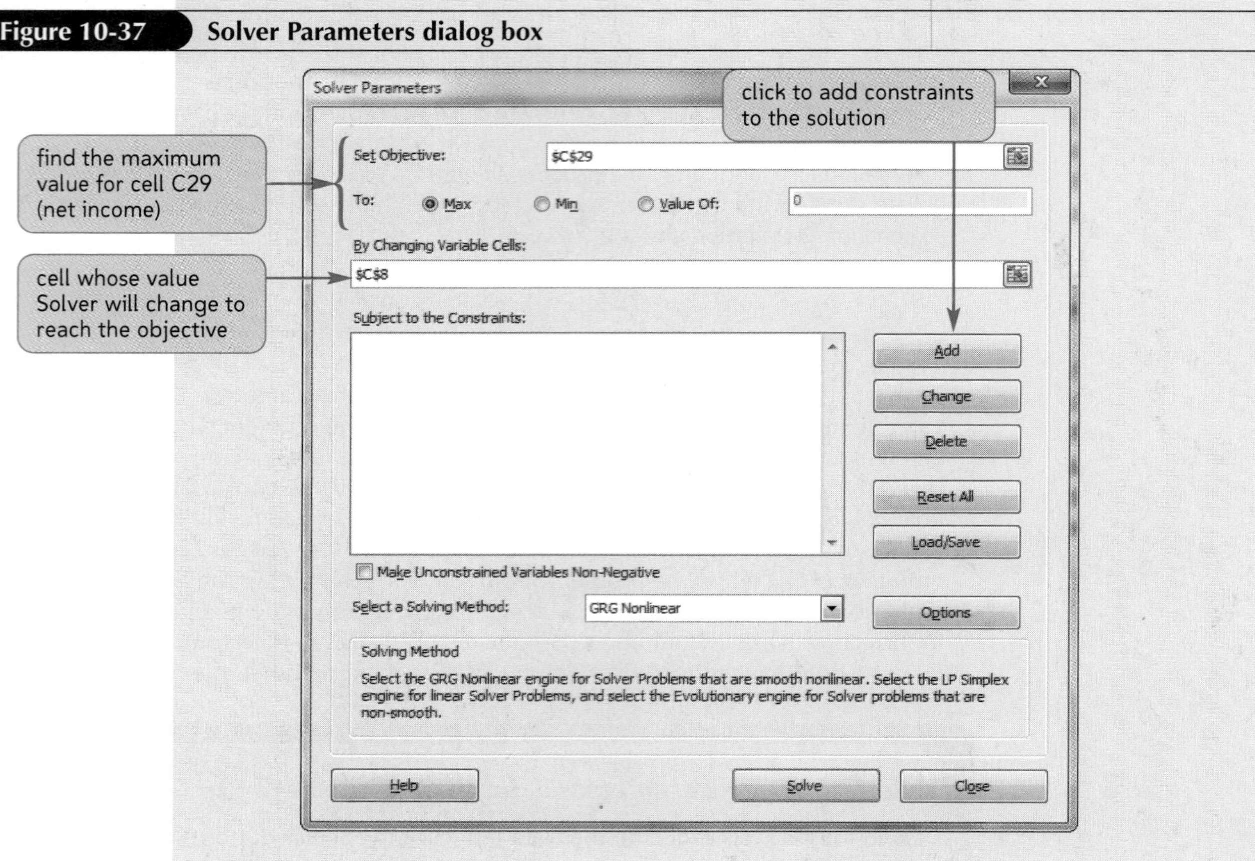

Next, you'll add constraints, or limits, for the solution. Constraints are important because they confine the solution within a reasonable set of limits that you define. Solver supports six possible constraints. The <=, >=, and = constraints are used when you want to set a cell's value to always be less than or equal to, greater than or equal to, or equal to a specified value. You can also use an integer or int constraint, which forces a cell value to always be a whole number, and you can apply a binary or bin constraint that forces a cell value to always be either 0 or 1. Finally, you can apply the dif or AllDifferent constraint, which forces all values within the selected cell range to have different integer values.

REFERENCE

Setting Constraints on the Solver Solution

- In the Solver Parameters dialog box, click the Add button.
- Enter the cell reference of the cell or cells containing the constraint.
- Specify the nature of the constraint (<=, =, >=, int, bin, or dif).
- Enter the constraint value in the Constraint box.
- Click the OK button to add the constraint and return to the Solver Parameters dialog box.
- Repeat for each constraint you want to add.

Todd and Brent know that the company cannot produce more than 35,000 disks per year, even if it were more profitable to do so. They also know that to keep their staff, they must produce at least 15,000 disks each year. You'll add a >= and a <= constraint to ensure that the production always falls between those two limits, even if it means accepting less profit. You do not have to add an = constraint, integer constraint, or binary constraint to the Solver model.

To add constraints to Solver:

1. Click the **Add** button to open the Add Constraint dialog box.
2. With the Cell Reference box active, click cell **C12**. This is the number of units the company will produce annually.
3. Click the arrow next to the center box, and then click **>=** to set the constraint to greater than or equal to.
4. Type **15000** in the Constraint box. See Figure 10-38.

Figure 10-38 Add Constraint dialog box

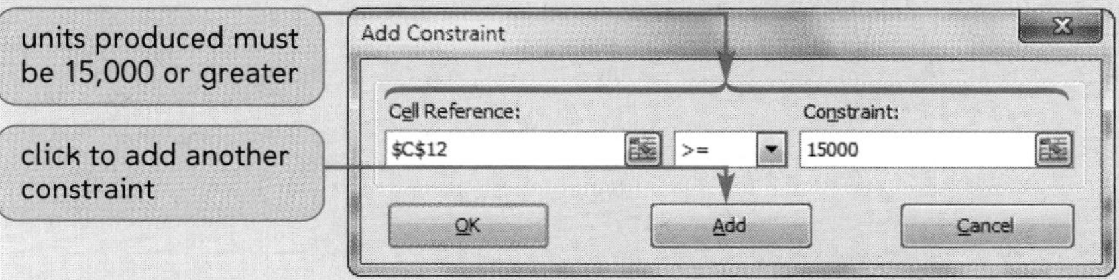

5. Click the **Add** button. The constraint is saved, and the Add Constraint dialog box is cleared so you can enter another constraint.
6. With the Cell Reference box active, click cell **C12**, verify that <= is selected in the center box, and then type **35000** in the Constraint box. The constraint is that the number of units produced must be less than or equal to 35,000.
7. Click the **OK** button to return to the Solver Parameters dialog box because you do not need to enter any more constraints at this time. See Figure 10-39.

TIP

You can apply the same constraint to a range of cells. Select the range in the Cell Reference box of the Add Constraint dialog box, and then specify the constraint to apply to each cell in the range.

Figure 10-39 Completed Solver Parameters dialog box

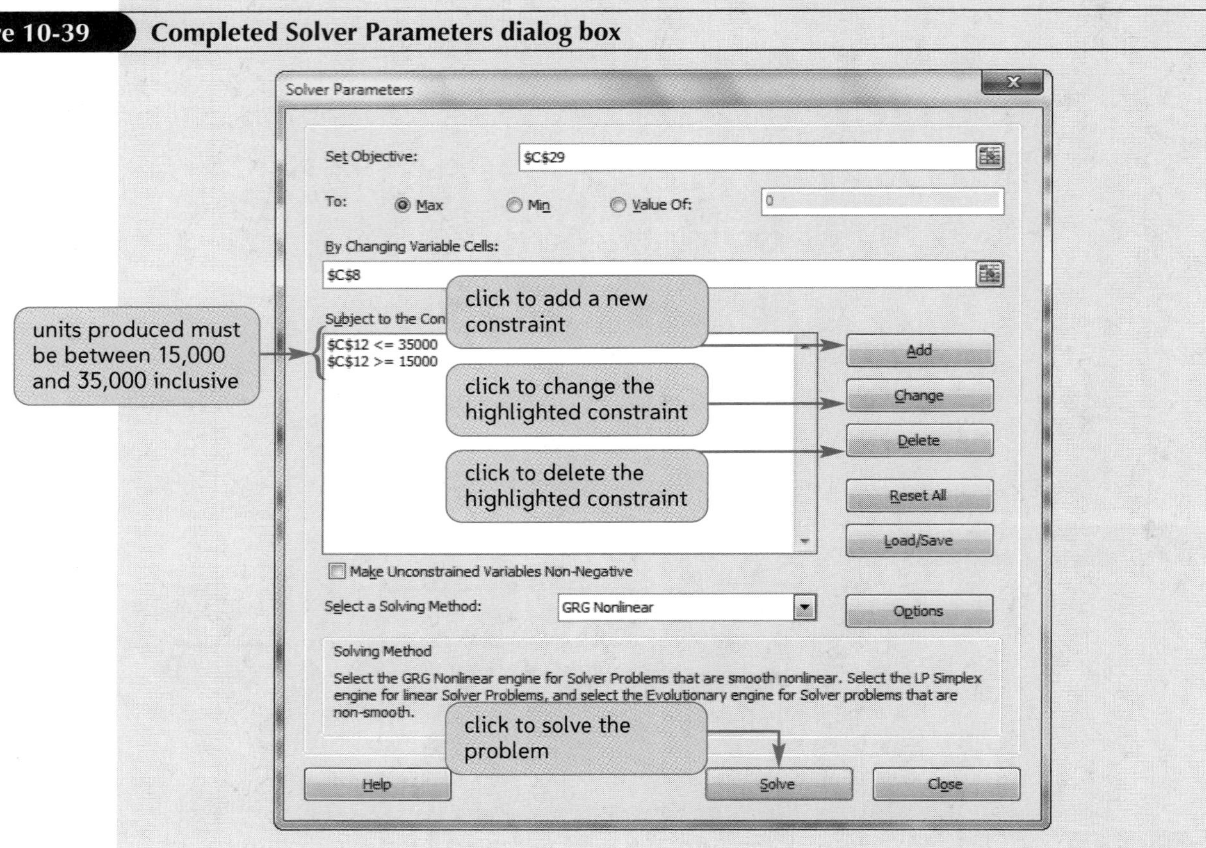

Now that you've specified all of the parameters for the model, you can run Solver to determine what unit price will result in the maximum net income to the company.

To calculate the maximum net income:

1. In the Solver Parameters dialog box, click the **Solve** button to run Solver. The status bar shows Solver rapidly "trying out" solutions. In a moment, the Solver Results dialog box opens and indicates that Solver has found a solution that satisfies the constraints. See Figure 10-40.

Figure 10-40 Solver Results dialog box

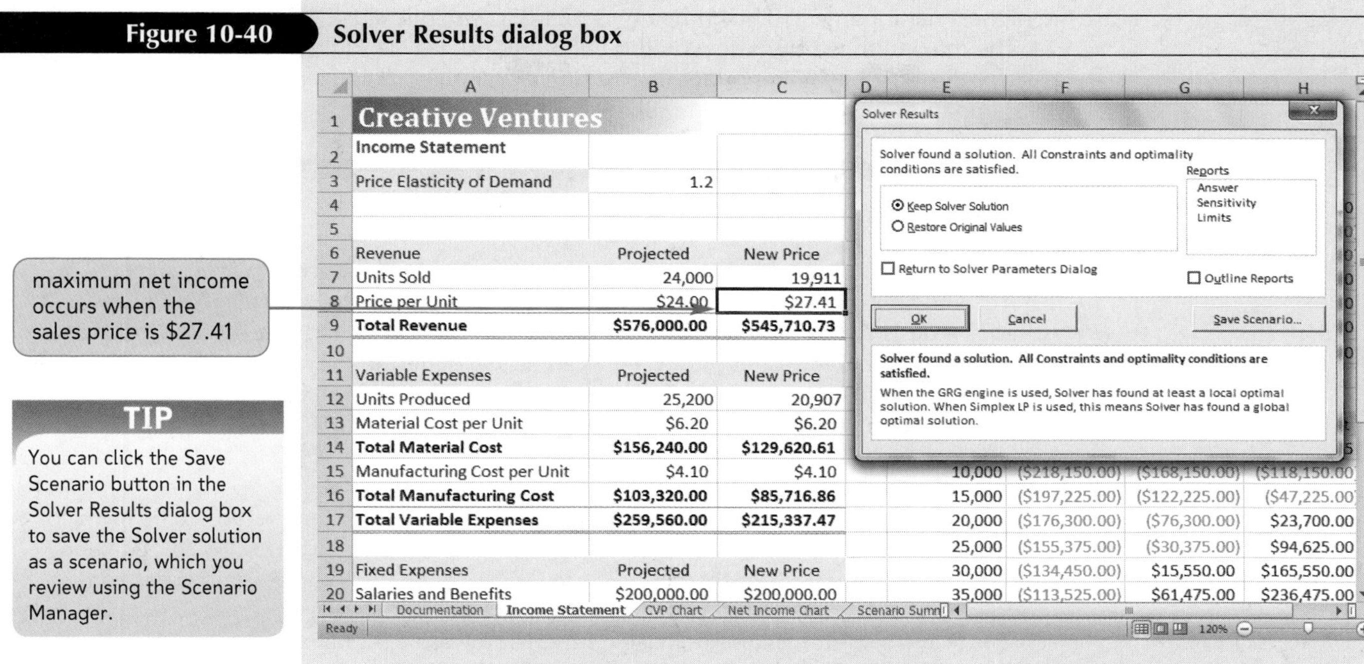

TIP

You can click the Save Scenario button in the Solver Results dialog box to save the Solver solution as a scenario, which you review using the Scenario Manager.

Trouble? If Solver fails to find a solution, check your Solver parameters against those shown in Figure 10-39. Make sure that all of your constraints match the constraints in that figure.

2. In the Solver Results dialog box, verify that the **Keep Solver Solution** option button is selected, and then click the **OK** button. The Solver solution is saved with the workbook.

Based on the Solver results, Creative Ventures will maximize its net income by selling HoverDisks for $27.41 each. Under this plan, the company will sell 19,911 units yearly for a net income of $70,373.27. This assumes that the price elasticity of demand for the product is equal to 1.2. However, it's quite possible that Todd and Brent's assumptions are inaccurate and that the elasticity value is considerably higher, which would mean a greater drop-off in sales if they increase the price. You can explore this possibility and use Solver to determine a new "best" price for the product.

To rerun Solver to determine a new "best" price:

1. Change the value in cell B3 from 1.2 to **1.8**. This elasticity value assumes that a 10 percent increase in the sales price causes demand to fall by 18 percent.
2. Look at the units sold value in cell C7. If the elasticity value is 1.8 rather than 1.2, the company will sell only 17,867 HoverDisks per year rather than 19,911.
3. Look at the net income value in cell C29. The net income under this scenario drops from about $70,000 down to $36,449.90. If Todd and Brent's estimate of elasticity is incorrect and it is actually 1.8 rather than 1.2, the company will lose a lot of revenue trying to sell the disks for $27.41.

   You'll use Solver to determine the best price when the elasticity value is equal to 1.8.
4. In the Analysis group on the Data tab, click the **Solver** button to open the Solver Parameters dialog box.
5. Click the **Solve** button to run Solver. The Solver Results dialog box opens.
6. Click the **OK** button to keep the Solver solution.

If the elasticity value is as high as 1.8, then the price for HoverDisks that results in the highest net income for the company is $24.07, which is close to the current price of $24. The maximum net income would be $56,449.90. It's clear that knowing the correct value for the elasticity is important in ensuring a company remains profitable, which is why companies invest so much in market analysis.

INSIGHT

Understanding the Iterative Process

Solver arrives at optimal solutions through an **iterative procedure**, in which Solver starts with an initial solution (usually the current values from the worksheet) and uses that as a basis to calculate a new set of values. If those values improve the value of the objective cell, the new values are used as a basis to generate the next set of values. If they don't improve the solution, Solver tries a different set of values. Each step, or iteration, in this process improves the solution until Solver reaches the point where the new solutions are not significantly better than the solution from the previous step. At that point, Solver will stop and indicate that it has found an answer.

What does "significantly better" mean? The default convergence value is 0.001, which means that if the change in the value of the objective cell between the new solution and the previous solution is less than or equal to 0.001, Solver will consider that it has converged to the solution and stop the iterative process.

Solver will also stop if it is not making progress toward a solution. The default length of time that Solver will spend on the iterative process is 100 seconds or 100 total iterations (whichever comes first). If 100 seconds or 100 iterations have passed and Solver has not found a solution, it will report this fact. At that point, you can have Solver continue the iterative process or stop the process without finding a solution. If Solver is taking too long to find a solution, you can halt the program at any time by pressing the Esc key. If you want to see the iterative process in action, click the Show Iteration Results check box in the Options dialog box, and Excel will pause after each iteration and show the intermediate solution.

Creating a Solver Answer Report

How do you evaluate the solution that Solver produced? Solver can create three different reports—an answer report, a sensitivity report, and a limits report. The **answer report** may be the most useful of the three because it summarizes the results of a successful solution by displaying information about the objective cell, changing cells, and constraints. This report includes the original and final values for the objective and changing cells, as well as the constraint formulas. The **sensitivity report** and **limits report** are often used in science and engineering environments when the user wants to investigate the mathematical aspects of the Solver solution. These reports allow you to quantify the reliability of the solution. You cannot use these reports when the problem contains integer constraints.

As part of the cost-volume-profit analysis, you will create an answer report, which will provide information on the process used to determine the optimal price for the product. To ensure that the answer report includes information on the entire process, you'll set the quantities back to their original values, and then you will solve the problem again.

To create an answer report:

1. Change the value in cell B3 to **1.2**. Change the value in cell C8 to **$24**.
2. In the Analysis group on the Data tab, click the **Solver** button to open the Solver Parameters dialog box, and then click the **Solve** button to run Solver.
3. In the Solver Results dialog box, click **Answer** in the Reports box, and then verify that the **Keep Solver Solution** option button is selected. See Figure 10-41.

Figure 10-41 Solver Results dialog box for an answer report

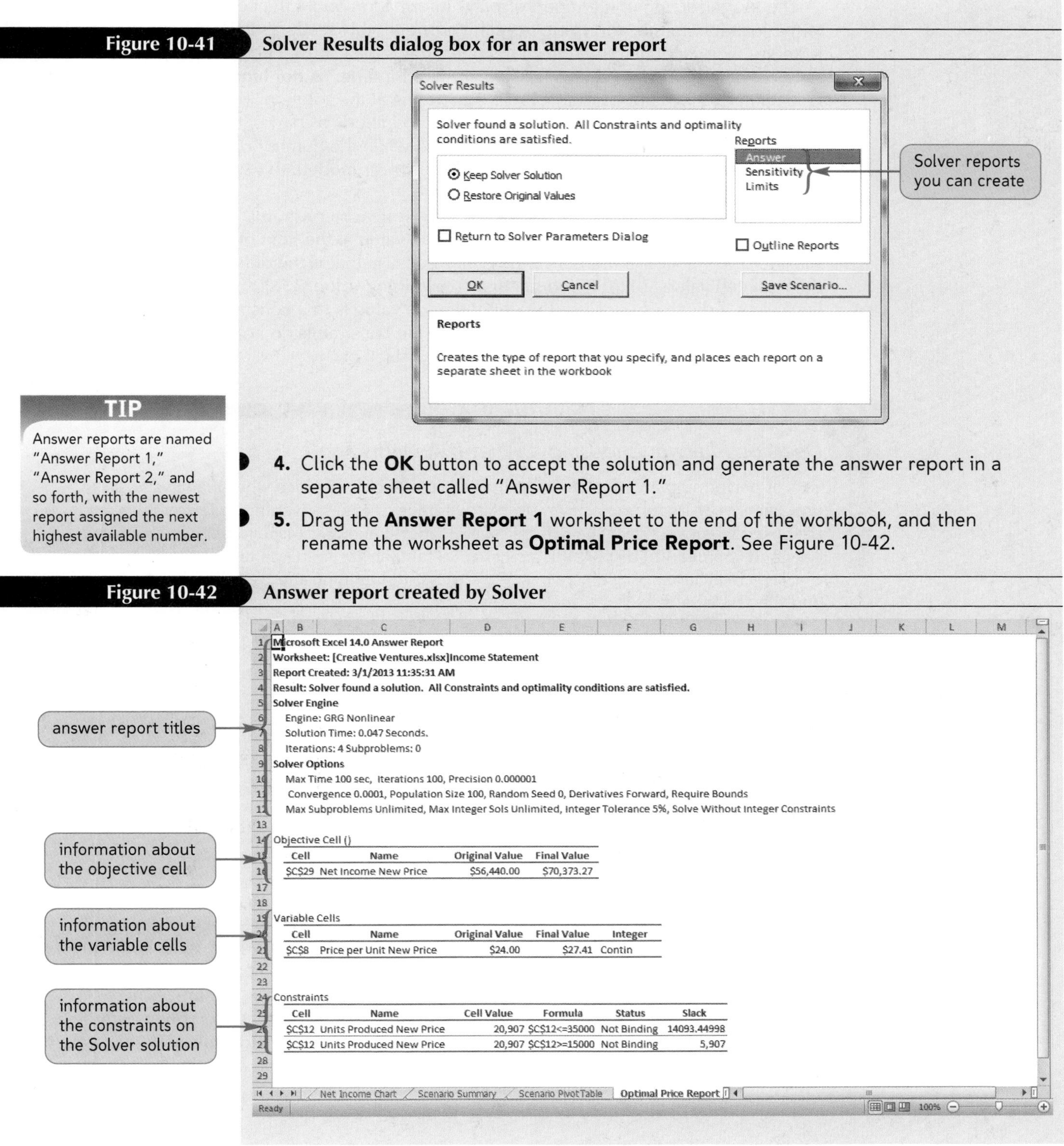

TIP

Answer reports are named "Answer Report 1," "Answer Report 2," and so forth, with the newest report assigned the next highest available number.

4. Click the **OK** button to accept the solution and generate the answer report in a separate sheet called "Answer Report 1."
5. Drag the **Answer Report 1** worksheet to the end of the workbook, and then rename the worksheet as **Optimal Price Report**. See Figure 10-42.

Figure 10-42 Answer report created by Solver

The answer report is divided into four sections. The first section includes titles that indicate that this is an Excel answer report created from the Income Statement worksheet in the Creative Ventures workbook on the day and at the time specified. The second section displays information about the objective cell, its location, the cell label, and the cell's original value and final values. The third section displays information about the changing cells, which the report calls variable cells. This section of the report shows the location, column and row label, original value, and final value of each cell.

The fourth section of the report displays information about the constraints. In addition to the location, name, and value of each constraint, this section shows the constraint formulas. The second column from the right shows the status of each constraint. The status of both of the constraints is listed as "Not Binding." A **not binding constraint** is a constraint that was not a limiting factor in arriving at the solution. The other possibility is a **binding constraint**, which Solver was forced to include as part of the final solution. For example, if the maximum net income occurred when the number of units produced was equal to 15,000 (one of the constraints in your Solver model), this would be a binding constraint.

The last column on the right shows the slack for each constraint. The **slack** is the difference between the value in the cell and the value at the limit of the constraint. The slack for the first constraint is 14,093.44998 because that is the difference between the final cell value, 20,907, and the first constraining value, 35,000. The slack is useful because it indicates how close the optimal price value is to a constraining point. In this case, the slack for both constraints is large, so the constraints do not have any impact on the solution. Binding constraints always show a slack of 0.

PROSKILLS

Decision Making: Choosing a What-If Analysis Tool

Part of performing an effective what-if analysis is deciding which what-if analysis tool to use. Each what-if tool has its own set of advantages and disadvantages. Data tables are best used when you want to perform several what-if analyses involving one or two input cells and you need to display the analysis in a tabular format. Data tables can also be easily displayed as charts, providing a visual picture of the relationship between your input values and the result values.

For what-if analyses involving more than two input cells, you must create a scenario. Scenario summary tables and scenario PivotTables can be used to obtain a quick snapshot of several possible outcomes, and scenarios can be merged and shared among several workbooks.

Data tables and scenarios can give a lot of information, but they can't easily provide a single solution or "best outcome." If you need to maximize or minimize a value, you must use Solver. You can also use Solver to set a calculated cell to a specific value. However, if you don't need to specify any constraints on your solution, it is generally quicker and easier to use Goal Seek.

Saving and Loading Solver Models

Todd and Brent are looking at ways to reduce the cost of producing HoverDisks. Until they have a final proposal in place, they want to know what unit price results in the highest revenue for the company, but not necessarily the highest net income.

They want the workbook to include two Solver models: one that maximizes net income and another that maximizes revenue. Rather than reentering the Solver parameters for each model, you can save the parameters in cells in the worksheet. Then, if you want to rerun a particular problem, you can reload the parameters from the worksheet cells without having to reformulate the problem. You'll store the parameters for both models in empty cells in the Income Statement worksheet.

REFERENCE

Saving and Loading a Solver Model

To save a Solver model:
- Open the Solver dialog box.
- Click the Load/Save button, and then select an empty range containing the number of cells specified in the dialog box.
- Click the Save button.

To load a Solver model:
- Open the Solver dialog box.
- Click the Load/Save button, and then select the cell range containing the saved model.
- Click the Load button.

You'll start by saving the current Solver model.

To save the current model:

1. Switch to the **Income Statement** worksheet, and then click the **Solver** button in the Analysis group on the Data tab. The Solver Parameters dialog box opens.
2. Click the **Load/Save** button. The Load/Save dialog box opens and indicates that you need to select an empty range containing six cells to store the model.
3. Select the range **A32:A37** in the worksheet. See Figure 10-43.

Figure 10-43 **Load/Save Model dialog box**

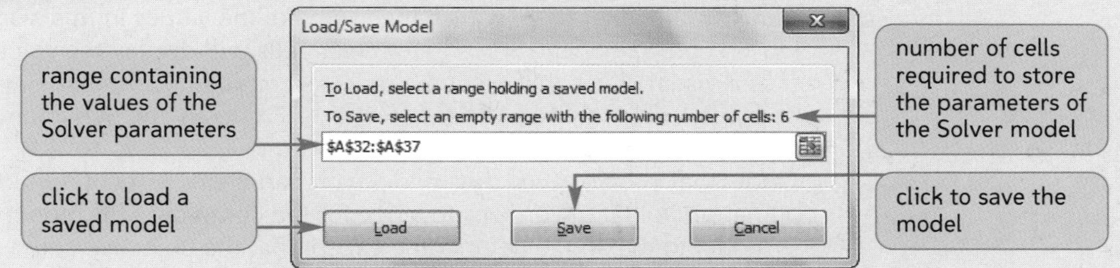

4. Click the **Save** button. The information about the Solver model is entered in the range A32:A37, and the Solver Parameters dialog box reappears.
5. Click the **Close** button to close the Solver Parameters dialog box.
6. In cell A31, enter **Maximum Net Income Model** and then format the text using the **20% - Accent3** cell style. See Figure 10-44.

Figure 10-44 Saved Solver model

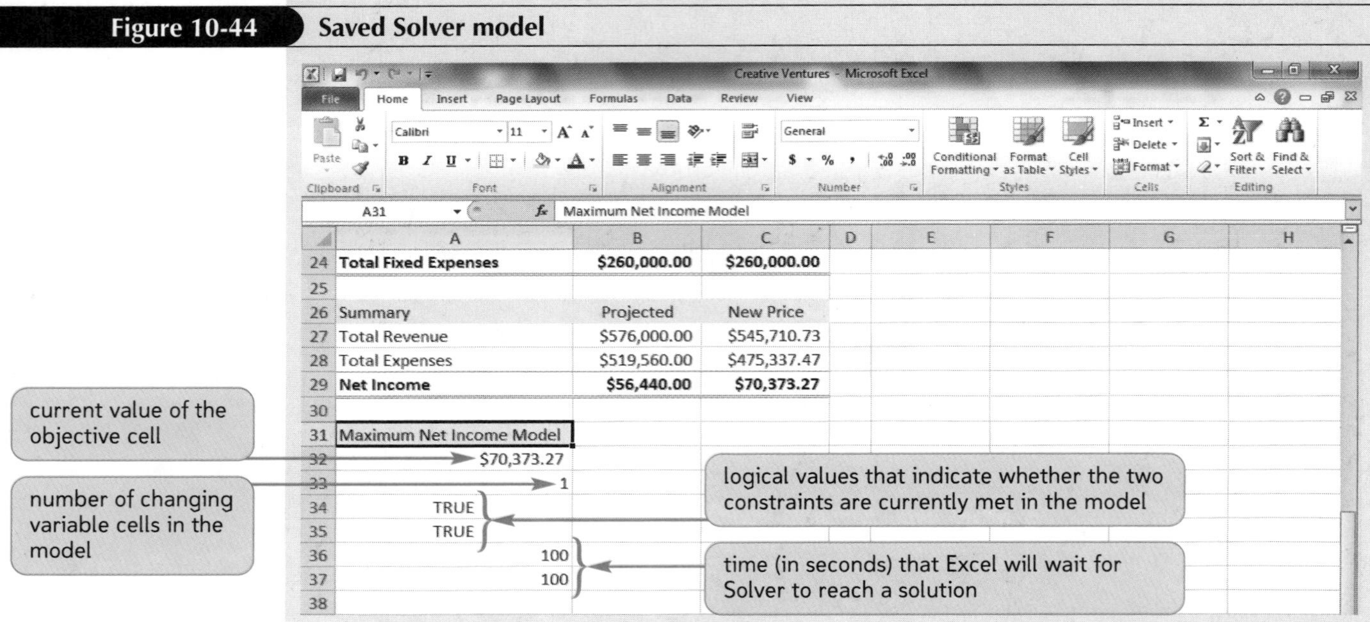

The first parameter in cell A32 displays the value $70,373.27, which is the value of the objective cell under this model. The second parameter in cell A33 displays the value 1, indicating the number of changing cells in the model. The next two cells display the value TRUE. Those cells correspond to the constraints in the model. The fact that they both display the value TRUE indicates that all of the values in the worksheet must satisfy the constraints. If, at a later date, you change some of the values in this worksheet, violating one of those constraints, the Solver parameter cells will display the value FALSE. The cells can act as a visual check that all of the model's conditions are still being met as the worksheet is modified. The final two cells, A36 and A37, specify the maximum time in seconds that Excel will wait for Solver to reach a solution.

Now that you've saved this model, you can create a second model to determine the optimal price that maximizes revenue for the company. This model will be the same as the model to maximize net income except that the objective cell will be cell C9 rather than C29.

To calculate the price to maximize the company's revenue:

1. In the Analysis group on the Data tab, click the **Solver** button. The Solver Parameters dialog box opens.
2. With the Set Objective cell box active, click cell **C9** in the Income Statement worksheet. The objective cell changes to cell C9.
3. Click the **Solve** button to find a solution, and then click the **OK** button in the Solver Results dialog box to accept the Solver solution. See Figure 10-45.

Figure 10-45 **Price that results in the maximum revenue for the company**

The maximum revenue that the company can generate is $580,800 based on a sales volume of 26,400 units per year at $22 per unit. If Todd and Brent can find a way to reduce the cost of production, this might be the most profitable sales price for the company. You will save this new Solver model to the worksheet and then reload the model that maximizes net income.

To save the maximum revenue model:

1. In cell A39, enter **Maximum Revenue Model** and then format the text using the **20% - Accent3** cell style.
2. In the Analysis group on the Data tab, click the **Solver** button to open the Solver Parameters dialog box, and then click the **Load/Save** button to open the Load/Save Model dialog box.
3. Select the range **A40:A45**, and then click the **Save** button. The Solver parameters are pasted in the A40:A45 range.

Next, you'll reload the Solver model that maximizes net income for the company and rerun it.

To load the maximum net income model and rerun it:

1. In the Solver Parameters dialog box, click the **Load/Save** button.
2. Select the range **A32:A37** in the Income Statement worksheet. This range contains the parameters of the Maximum Net Income model.

3. Click the **Load** button. The Load Model dialog box opens so you can select whether to merge these parameters with the current model or to replace the current model with these new parameters.
4. Click the **Replace** button. The Maximum Net Income model is loaded.
5. Click the **Solve** button to rerun Solver under this model, and then click the **OK** button to accept Solver's solution.
6. Save the Creative Ventures workbook, and then close it.

By saving the Solver model parameters to cells on the worksheet, you can create dozens of models that you can load and apply to your analysis as new data is entered.

You've finished analyzing the cost-volume-profit relationship for Creative Ventures' HoverDisk. Your analysis explored the relationship between unit price, sales volume, and profit. By using Solver, you were able to provide Todd and Brent with several pricing options for the upcoming year.

REVIEW

Session 10.3 Quick Check

1. What is an add-in?
2. What are three options for the objective cell using Solver?
3. What are the six types of constraints you can put on a cell in a Solver model?
4. Define the following terms: *not binding constraint, binding constraint,* and *slack.*
5. How would you save several Solver models on a single worksheet?
6. What is an iterative procedure?

Practice the skills you learned in the tutorial using the same case scenario.

PRACTICE

Review Assignments

Data File needed for the Review Assignments: Light.xlsx

Creative Ventures has another product that it has been selling called a Light Styk. Todd and Brent have used last year's sales data to project next year's income statement. They want you to analyze the cost-volume-profit relationship of the Light Styk product. They also want you to determine the price for Light Styks that maximizes the company's net income. Complete the following:

1. Open the **Light** workbook located in the Excel10\Review folder included with your Data Files, and then save the workbook as **Light Styks** in the same folder. In the Documentation sheet, enter your name in cell B3 and the date in cell B4.
2. In the Income Statement worksheet, create a one-variable data table to calculate the revenue, expenses, and net income for sales volume ranging from 0 units sold up to 30,000 units sold in increments of 5000 units. Format the table so that it is easy to read.
3. Use the data table you created in Step 2 to create a scatter chart with straight lines displaying the revenue and total expenses plotted against units sold. Store the chart in a chart sheet named **CVP Chart**. Based on the chart, project the break-even point for the company's sale of Light Styks. Add appropriate titles to the chart and chart axes.
4. Create a two-variable data table that calculates net income based on different units sold and sales price values. Assume that the units sold values range from 0 to 30,000 units in increments of 5000 units, and that the possible sales price values are \$10, \$12, \$14, and \$16. Format the table so that it is easy to read and interpret.
5. Plot the results of the two-variable data table in a scatter chart with straight lines. Save the chart in a chart sheet named **Net Income Chart**. Edit the chart series so that the series names, \$10, \$12, \$14, and \$16, are displayed in the legend for each chart. Add appropriate titles to the chart and chart axes. Based on the results of the chart, estimate the amount of units that must be sold for each price in order for the company to break even.
6. Create range names for the values in the nonadjacent range B7:B8;B12:B16;B20:B22;B26:B28 based on the corresponding labels in column A.
7. Todd and Brent want to study the four scenarios shown below. Add these scenarios to the Light Styks workbook.

Input Cells	Status Quo	Expanded	Reduced	Sale
Units Sold (B7)	14,000	12,000	16,000	18,000
Price per Unit (B8)	\$11	\$15	\$10	\$8
Advertising (B20)	\$10,000	\$30,000	\$10,000	\$10,000
Administrative (B21)	\$10,000	\$25,000	\$5,000	\$5,000
Miscellaneous (B22)	\$5,000	\$20,000	\$5,000	\$5,000

8. Create a scenario summary report on the four scenarios you created, reporting their effect on total revenue, total expenses, and net income.
9. Create a Scenario PivotTable based on the four scenarios. Format the values in the PivotTable as currency.
10. Create a Scenario PivotChart based on the four scenarios. Place the PivotChart in a chart sheet named **Scenario PivotChart**. Add an appropriate chart title and axes titles.
11. Todd and Brent want to calculate the optimal price for their Light Styks product, assuming a price elasticity of demand value of 1.4. With the Status Quo scenario displayed in the worksheet, copy the values in the range B6:B28 into the range C6:C28. Change the label in cells C6, C11, C19, and C25 to **Optimal Price**.
12. In cell C7, project the units sold based on the sales price by entering the formula **=B7*(1+B4*(1–C8/B8))**. Verify that with the price of \$12.97 in cell C8, the units sold value in C7 is 10,486.

13. Use Solver to calculate the sales price that results in the maximum net income subject to the following constraints: units produced (cell C12) must be less than or equal to 30,000 and greater than or equal to 5,000.
14. Save the Solver answer report to a worksheet named **Net Income Answer Report**.
15. In cell A30 of the Income Statement worksheet, enter **Maximum Net Income** and then format the cell using the 20% - Accent3 cell style. Save the parameters of the Solver model to the range A31:A36.
16. Save and close the workbook. Submit the finished workbook to your instructor, either in printed or electronic form, as requested.

Apply the skills you've learned to create a grading curve for an instructor.

APPLY

Case Problem 1

Data File needed for this Case Problem: Grade.xlsx

High Desert University Professor Karen Reynolds teaches calculus at High Desert University in Tempe, Arizona. The class has 220 students who are distributed among dozens of sections and discussion groups. Professor Reynolds wants to use Excel to determine appropriate cutoff points for her grading curve. Generally, she wants to set the cutoff points so that the following distribution of grades is observed in the student body:

F	5%
D	10%
C	35%
B	35%
A	15%

Professor Reynolds has five possible grading curves. For example, in Grading Curve 1, she will assign As to test scores from 80 to 100. She wants you to evaluate each one and determine which one results in a distribution of grades closest to her proposed distribution. After you choose which of the five scenarios fits the data the best, she wants you to use Solver to determine whether there is a grading curve that is even closer than any of her proposed scenarios to the desired distribution of grades. Complete the following:

1. Open the **Grade** workbook located in the Excel10\Case1 folder included with your Data Files, and then save the workbook as **Grade Curve** in the same folder. In the Documentation worksheet, enter your name in cell B3 and the date in cell B4.
2. The Test Score worksheet contains a table of individual student scores and a table for the grading curve. In the Test Score worksheet, the range F4:G8 will contain the lower and upper ranges for each letter grade. Add the missing upper range values in the range G4:G7 by inserting formulas in those cells so that the upper range for each letter grade is one point lower than the lower range of the next letter grade.
3. In cell D4, enter the VLOOKUP function to return the letter grade for the first student in the list. (*Hint*: The lookup value is the student's final score, the table array is the cell range $F$4:$H$8, the column index number is 3, and the lookup should find the closest match in the first column of the lookup table.) Copy the formula in cell D4 into the range D5:D223 to calculate the grades for the rest of the students' scores.
4. In cell I4, use the COUNTIF function to count the total number of letter grades in the range $D$4:$D$223 equal to "F". Copy your formula into the range I5:I8 to count the total number of the other letter grades assigned under the current grading scale. In cell I9, calculate the total number of all letter grades, verifying that the total equals 220.
5. In the range J4:J8, calculate the percent of each letter grade assigned to the student body. In cell J9, calculate the total percentage of all letter grades, verifying that the total percentage is 100 percent.

6. In the range L4:L8, use the ABS function to calculate the absolute value of the difference between the observed percentage of each letter grade and Professor Reynolds' optimal percentage. In cell L9, calculate the total value of these absolute differences.
7. Assign the range names **LowF** through **LowA** for the values in the range F4:F8. Assign the range names **HighF** through **HighA** for the values in the range G4:G8. Assign the range names **PercentF** through **PercentA** for the values in the range J4:J8. Assign the range name **DifferenceFromCurve** to the value in cell L9.
8. Enter the five grading curve scenarios shown below into scenarios named **Grading Curve 1** through **Grading Curve 5**. Use the range F4:F8 as your changing cells. Create a scenario summary report evaluating the results from each of the five scenarios, displaying the values from the range J4:J8;L9 as your result cells.

Scenario	F	D	C	B	A
Grading Curve 1	0 – 19	20 – 39	40 – 59	60 – 79	80 – 100
Grading Curve 2	0 – 29	30 – 49	50 – 69	70 – 89	90 – 100
Grading Curve 3	0 – 49	50 – 64	65 – 79	80 – 94	95 – 100
Grading Curve 4	0 – 39	40 – 59	60 – 74	75 – 84	85 – 100
Grading Curve 5	0 – 59	60 – 69	70 – 79	80 – 89	90 – 100

9. The closeness of each grading curve to Professor Reynolds' optimal grading curve is expressed in the value of cell L9. If there was perfect correspondence, the value of cell L9 would be 0. Pick the grading curve that has the lowest value for cell L9 and show that grading curve in the Test Score worksheet.

EXPLORE

10. Using the scenario values you selected in the last step as a starting point, create a Solver model to minimize the value in cell L9 by changing the values in the range F5:F8, subject to the constraint that all of the values in the range F5:F8 must be integers.

EXPLORE

11. Store the grading curve returned by Solver as a new scenario named **Optimal Grading Curve**. Create a second scenario summary report displaying this grading curve along with the five others you've investigated.
12. Save and close the workbook. Submit the finished workbook to your instructor, either in printed or electronic form, as requested.

Use the skills you've learned to create a data table describing a home loan.

APPLY

Case Problem 2

Data File needed for this Case Problem: Loan.xlsx

Mortgage Analysis Kevin Webber is considering taking out a second mortgage for an addition on his home. He decides to use Excel to analyze several possibilities for the loan, including the size of the loan, the interest rate, and the number of years required to pay back the loan. He wants your help in developing a two-variable data table and scenarios to examine how varying these factors affects the required monthly payment and the total cost of the loan. Complete the following:

1. Open the **Loan** workbook located in the Excel10\Case2 folder included with your Data Files, and then save the workbook as **Loan Table** in the same folder. In the Documentation sheet, enter your name in cell B3 and the date in cell B4.
2. In the Mortgage worksheet, define names for the values in the range B3:B8 based on the name values in the left column.

3. Enter **Monthly Payment** in cell D1. Enter **Years** in cell E2, and then merge and center the range E2:I2. Enter the values **10** through **30** in increments of 5 in the range E3:I3. Enter the values **4.5%** through **6.0%** in increments of 0.1% in the range D4:D19.
4. In cell D3, enter a reference to the value in cell B7. Format the cell to display the text string **Interest Rate**.
5. Create a two-variable data table in the range D3:I19 using cells B5 and B4 as the column and row input cells, respectively.
6. Format the resulting two-variable data table so that the result values appear as currency, and the row and column labels appear on a light yellow background. Add gridlines to the table.
7. Format the sheet so that it prints in landscape orientation on a single page with your name, the filename, and the date in the right footer.
8. Add scenarios to the worksheet to display all combinations of the loan assuming that the number of years required for payment is 30; the interest rate is 5.5%, 6.0%, or 6.5%; and the amount of the loan is $200,000, $250,000, or $300,000. (*Hint*: There will be nine scenarios.)
9. Create a scenario summary report that displays the value of the monthly payment and total cost of the loan for each of the scenarios you created.
10. Format the scenario summary report so that it prints in landscape orientation on a single page with your name, the filename, and the date in the right footer.
11. Save and close the workbook. Submit the finished workbook to your instructor, either in printed or electronic form, as requested.

Explore how to use Solver to aid in the scheduling of conference center rooms.

CHALLENGE

Case Problem 3

Data File needed for this Case Problem: Fairway.xlsx

Fairway Convention Center Patrick Ross is the resource manager at the Fairway Convention Center in Atlanta, Georgia. One of his tasks is to determine who reserves which of the 10 conference rooms. To best match the individual with the room, Patrick asks applicants to list their room preferences from 1 (the most desirable) to 10 (the least desirable). Patrick then tries to allocate the rooms so that the sum of the preference scores is minimized. If an applicant requires a particular room, Patrick can reserve that room for the applicant. You'll help Patrick by setting up a Solver solution for one of his scheduling problems. Complete the following:

1. Open the **Fairway** workbook located in the Excel10\Case3 folder included with your Data Files, and then save the workbook as **Fairway Convention Center** in the same folder. In the Documentation worksheet, enter your name in cell B3 and the date in cell B4.
2. Switch to the Rooms worksheet. The Rooms sheet has two tables. The first table indicates each applicant's preference for the 10 conference rooms. The second table indicates the assignment of the room to the applicant. A value of 1 in the table indicates that the conference room has been assigned to an applicant. A value of 0 indicates that the room has not been assigned. Only one conference room can be assigned to each applicant and each applicant can only reserve one room; thus, each row and column of the table will have one cell containing the value 1 and the rest of the cells will contain the value 0. Cells N18:N27 display the preference score for each applicant's assigned conference room. Cell B31 displays the sum of the 10 preference scores. This is the value you seek to minimize for Patrick.
3. Start Solver and indicate that the objective cell, cell B31, should be set to its minimal value by changing the values in the range B18:K27.

EXPLORE

4. Add the following constraints in the following order to the problem:
   - The values in the range B18:K27 must be binary.
   - The values in the range B29:K29 must all equal 1 (indicating that each room has a single occupant).
   - The values in the range M18:M27 must all equal 1 (indicating that each applicant receives a single room).
   - The values in the range N18:N27 must be less than or equal to 6 (indicating that each applicant will receive no worse than their sixth-best choice).
   - Yvonne Sprague needs a large space that can be found only in the Canyon Room. Constrain the value of cell D22 so that it equals 1 and that all of the other cells in row 22 and column D of the Room Assignments table are equal to 0.
   - Edith Dillion needs to use the Oak View Room. Constrain the value of cell I25 so that it equals 1 and that all of the other cells in row 25 and column I of the Room Assignments table are equal to 0.

EXPLORE

5. Run Solver (it might take a while for Solver to arrive at a solution). Verify that all of the constraints have been satisfied.
6. Enter the text **Room Assignment Model** in cell A33 displayed on a yellow background. Save your Solver model to the range A34:A43.
7. Format the page layout of the Rooms worksheet, limiting the print area to the range A1:N32. Format the worksheet to print on a single page in landscape orientation. Add your name, the date, and the filename to the right section of the footer of the printout.
8. Save and close the workbook. Submit the finished workbook to your instructor, either in printed or electronic form, as requested.

Create an Excel workbook to analyze the cost-volume-profit relationship of a new product.

RESEARCH

Case Problem 4

There are no Data Files needed for this Case Problem.

NewGen Robotics Wesley Lee is a marketing manager at NewGen Robotics in Greenville, Oregon. The company is introducing a new line of household robots capable of performing basic vacuuming and cleanup tasks. Wesley needs you to examine a projected income statement for the company's operations, calculate the break-even point for the product, and determine the optimal price point. Complete the following:

1. Create a workbook named **NewGen Robotics** located in the Excel10\Case4 folder included with your Data Files. Add a Documentation worksheet that describes the workbook and includes your name and the date.
2. Complete the income statement based on the values shown below. Assume that the company produces enough cleaning robots to have a 1 percent surplus over units sold.

Revenue	Units Sold	85,300
	Price per Unit	$185
Variable Expenses	Material Cost per Unit	$90.50
	Manufacturing Cost per Unit	$62.20
Fixed Expenses	Salaries and Benefits	$950,000
	Advertising	$390,000
	Administrative	$280,000
	Miscellaneous	$240,000

3. Based on your income statement, calculate the number of units the company would have to sell at its current price to break even.

4. Use a one-variable data table to calculate the total revenue, expenses, and net income if the company sells from 75,000 to 200,000 units in increments of 25,000. Create a CVP chart based on your results.
5. Use a two-variable data table to calculate the net income for units sold from 50,000 to 200,000 units in increments of 25,000 with sales prices of $180 up to $200 in increments of $5. Plot your results.
6. Create scenarios based on the possibilities shown below. Report the net income, revenue, and total expenses for each scenario in a scenario summary report.

Changing Values	Status Quo	Scenario 1	Scenario 2	Scenario 3
Units Sold	85,300	60,000	100,000	125,000
Price per Unit	$185	$200	$175	$172
Salaries and Benefits	$950,000	$950,000	$1,000,000	$1,000,000
Advertising	$390,000	$350,000	$470,000	$525,000
Administrative	$280,000	$250,000	$350,000	$375,000
Miscellaneous	$240,000	$220,000	$300,000	$325,000

7. Wesley assumes that for the product, the price elasticity of demand is 2.0 (for every 10 percent increase in sales price, he expects sales to drop by 20 percent). Using the values from the Status Quo scenario as a basis, run Solver to calculate the optimal price for the company's product to maximize net income. Assume that the company must manufacture at least 60,000 units but no more than 150,000.
8. Because this is a new market, the company is willing to build the market for cleaning robots in exchange for losing money. Use Solver to calculate the sales price the company can charge for its product in order to lose no more than $300,000 in net income. Assume an initial value of $185 for the product and a price elasticity of demand of 2.0. What is the sales price under this scenario and how many units would the company sell?
9. Save and close the workbook. Submit the finished workbook to your instructor, either in printed or electronic form, as requested.

SAM

ASSESS

SAM: Skills Assessment Manager

For current SAM information, including versions and content details, visit SAM Central (http://samcentral.course.com). If you have a SAM user profile, you may have access to hands-on instruction, practice, and assessment of the skills covered in this tutorial. Because various versions of SAM are supported throughout the life of this text, check with your instructor for the correct instructions and URL/Web site for accessing assignments.

ENDING DATA FILES

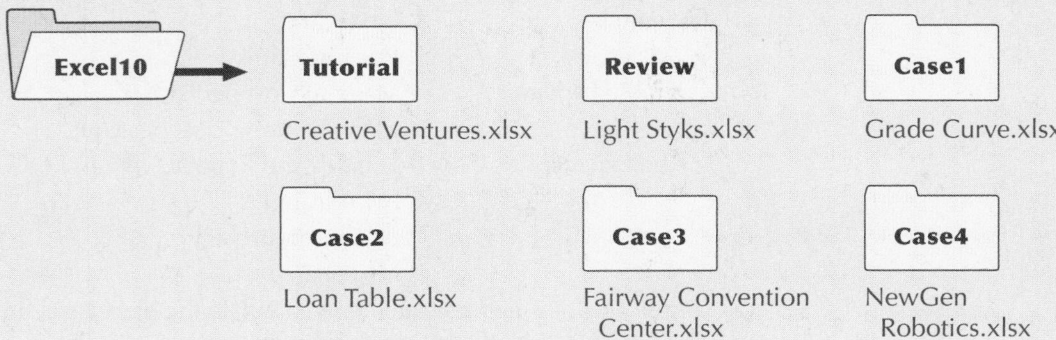

TUTORIAL 11

Connecting to External Data

Retrieving Financial Information from Different Data Sources

EXCEL

OBJECTIVES

Session 11.1
- Import data from a text file
- Work with connections and external data ranges
- Define a trusted location

Session 11.2
- Understand databases and queries
- Use the Query Wizard to import data from several tables
- Edit a query
- Import data into a PivotTable and PivotChart

Session 11.3
- Create a Web query
- Retrieve data from the Web
- Use hyperlinks in a workbook
- Access data from an XML document
- Work with XML data maps

Case | *Union Financial*

Union Financial is a brokerage firm in Moline, Illinois. As part of its investment services business, the company advises clients on their investment portfolios. The investment counselors at the company need current financial data and reports, but they also must examine information on long-term trends in the market.

Some of this information comes from Excel workbooks, but other information is stored in specialized financial packages and statistical programs. In addition, the company maintains a database with detailed financial information about a variety of stocks, bonds, and funds. Company employees also use the Internet to receive up-to-the-minute market reports. Because much of the information that the counselors need comes from outside the company, they must retrieve information to analyze it and make decisions.

Carol Hill is an investment counselor at Union Financial. She wants you to help her manage the different types of data available as she works on the Horizons Fund, one of the company's most important stock portfolios. You'll retrieve sample data from different sources and include them in a workbook.

STARTING DATA FILES

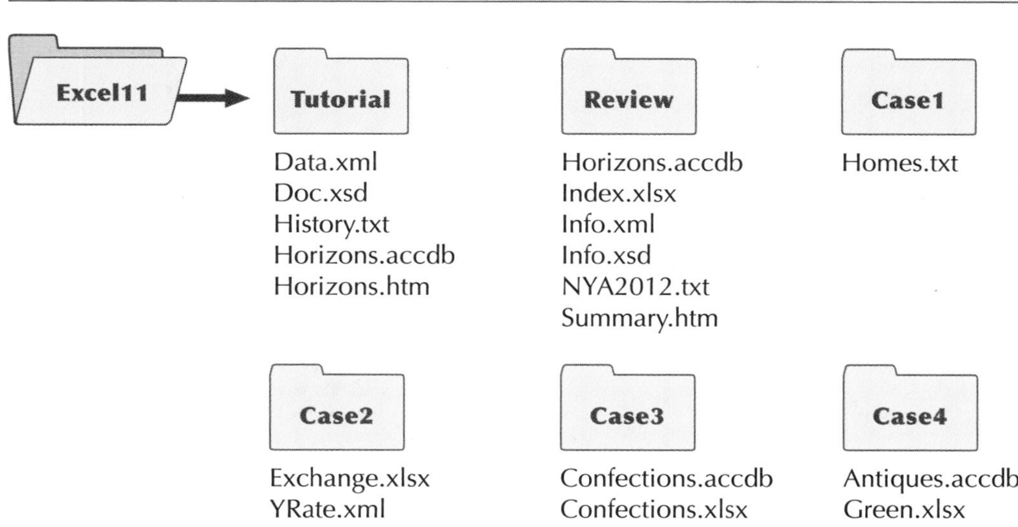

SESSION 11.1 VISUAL OVERVIEW

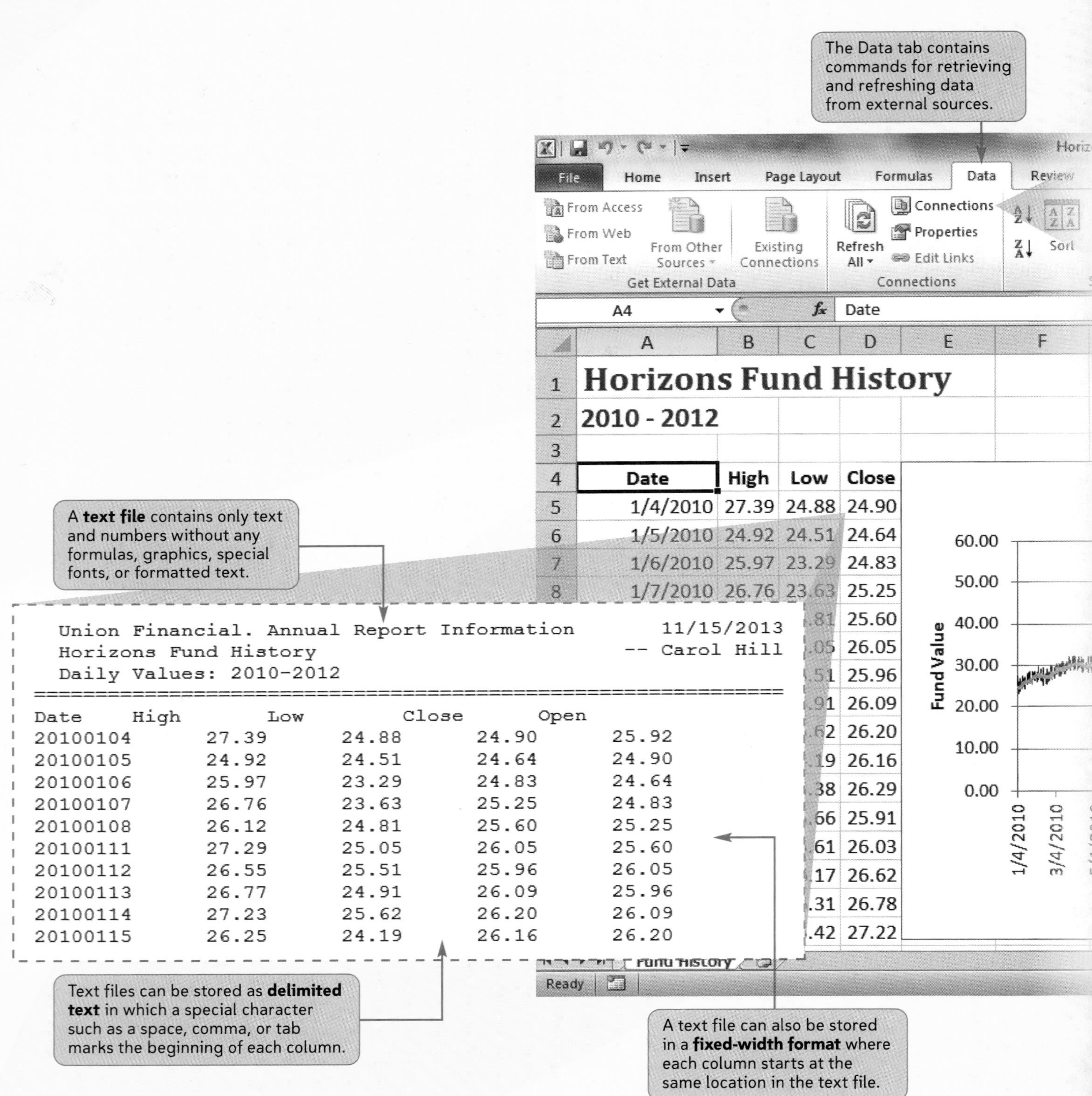

RETRIEVING TEXT DATA

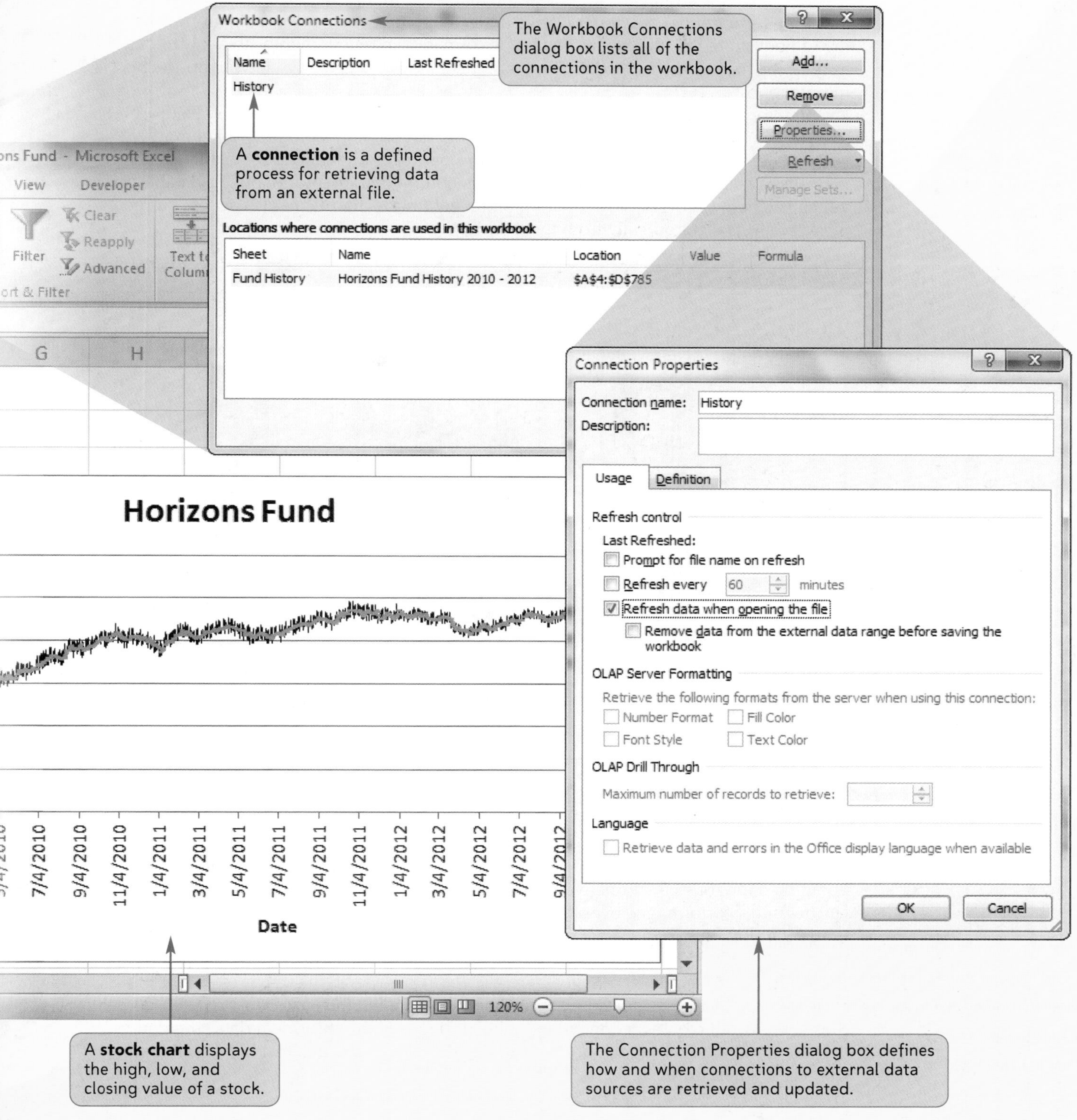

Exploring External Data Sources

As an investment counselor, Carol helps her clients plan their investment strategies. To do her job well, Carol needs to look at the market from a variety of angles. She examines long-term trends so that her clients understand the benefits of creating long-term investment strategies. She tracks market performance in recent months to analyze current trends. She also assesses the daily mood of the market by regularly viewing up-to-the-minute reports.

The information that Carol needs comes from many sources. As shown in Figure 11-1, long-term and historical stock information from the company's old record-keeping system has been retrieved from financial software packages and placed in text files that all counselors can use. Union Financial stores its current market information in databases, which is where Carol finds information on recent trends. Carol can also access current market reports electronically from the Internet.

Figure 11-1 **Carol's data sources**

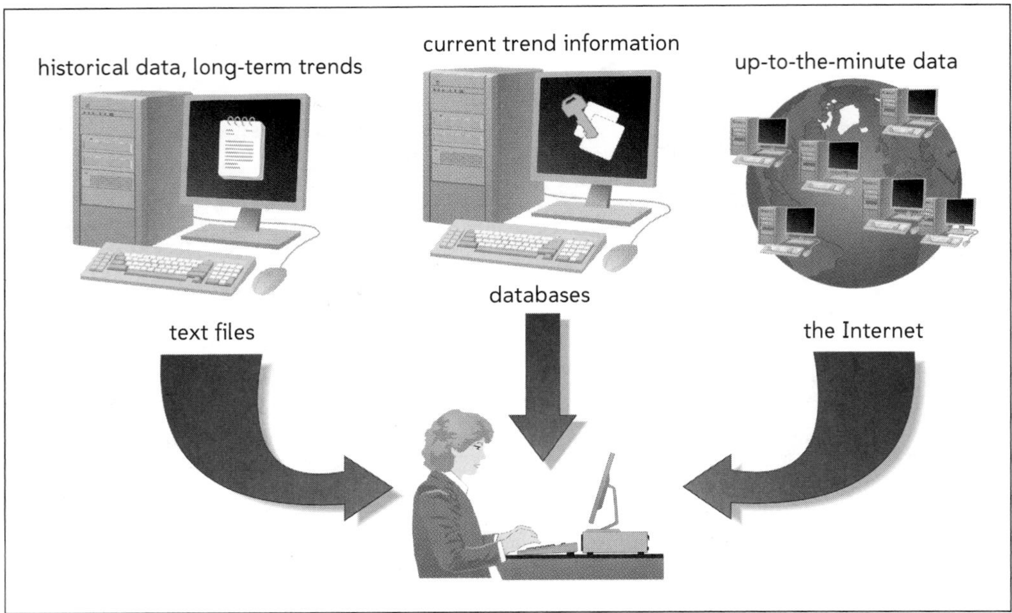

Carol is responsible for tracking the performance of the Horizons Fund, one of the company's investment vehicles. The Horizons Fund, one of Union Financial's oldest and most successful funds, is composed of several stocks on the New York Stock Exchange (NYSE). Carol asks you to develop a workbook that summarizes essential information about the Horizons Fund. She wants the workbook to connect to sources containing (1) the fund's performance over the past few years, (2) more recent information on the fund's performance in the last year as well as the last few days, and (3) up-to-the-minute reports on the fund's current status. Figure 11-2 shows Carol's strategy for the workbook she wants you to create.

To gather data from three sources, you need to connect the workbook to external data files. First, you'll create a connection to the Horizons Fund's historical data. The daily values for the fund during the previous three years are stored in a text file. You'll import this text file into Excel.

Figure 11-2 Carol's plan for the Horizons Fund workbook

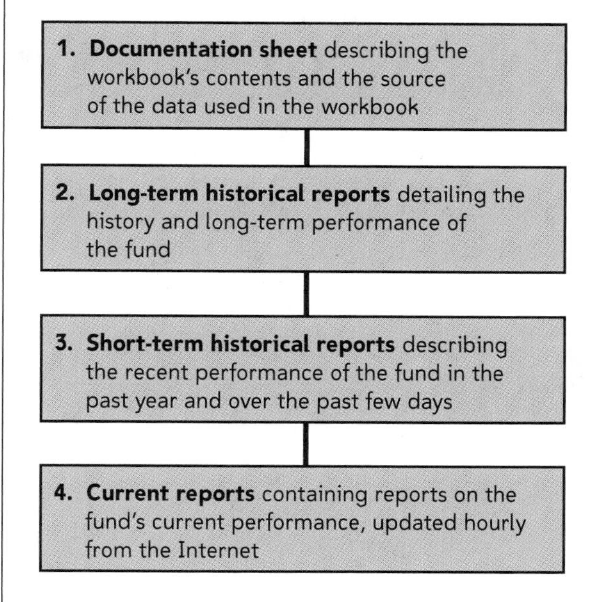

Importing Data from Text Files

A text file contains only text and numbers without any formulas, graphics, special fonts, or formatted text. Text files are one of the simplest and most widely used formats for storing data because most software programs can save and retrieve data in a text file format. For example, Excel can open a text file in a worksheet, where you can format it as you would any data. Excel can also save a workbook as a text file, preserving only the data values without any of its formats. In addition, many types of computers can read text files. So, although text files contain only raw, unformatted data, they are very useful when you want to share data across software programs and computer systems such as between a PC and a Macintosh.

REFERENCE

Connecting to a Text File

- In the Get External Data group on the Data tab, click the From Text button, and then select the text file containing the data.
- In the first step of the Text Import Wizard, choose how the data is organized, and then specify the row in which to start the import.
- In the second step, set the column breaks by clicking a location in the Data preview box to insert a column break, double-clicking a column break to delete it, and dragging a column break to move it to a new location.
- In the third step, specify the data format for each column by clicking the column and then selecting the appropriate data format option button, or skip importing a column by clicking the column in the Data preview box and then clicking the Do not import (skip) option button.
- Click the Finish button.
- Specify where to insert the imported text, and then click the OK button to import the text file into the worksheet.

Understanding Text File Formats

Because a text file doesn't contain formatting codes to give it structure, a program needs another way to understand the file contents. If a text file contains only numbers, how does the importing program know where one group of values ends and another begins? You must distinguish how that data is organized within the file. One way to structure a text file is to use a **delimiter**, which is a symbol—usually a space, a comma, or a tab—that separates one column of data from another.

Figure 11-3 shows the same four columns of stock market data delimited by spaces, commas, and tabs. Columns in delimited text files are not always vertically aligned as they would be in a spreadsheet, but this is not a problem for a program that recognizes the delimiter. A tab delimiter is often the best way to separate text columns because tab-delimited text can include spaces or commas within each column.

Figure 11-3 **Delimited text**

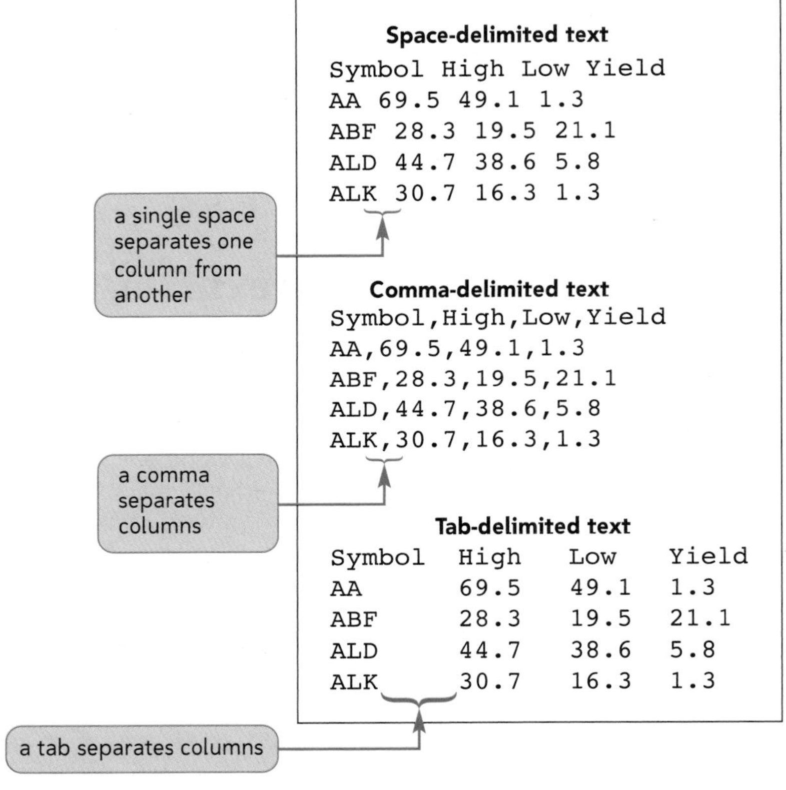

The other way to organize textual data is with a fixed-width text file in which each column starts at the same location in the file. For example, the first column starts at the first space in the file, the second column starts at the tenth space, and so forth. Figure 11-4 shows columns arranged in a fixed-width format. In this example, all the columns line up visually because each one must start at the same location.

Figure 11-4 **Fixed-width text**

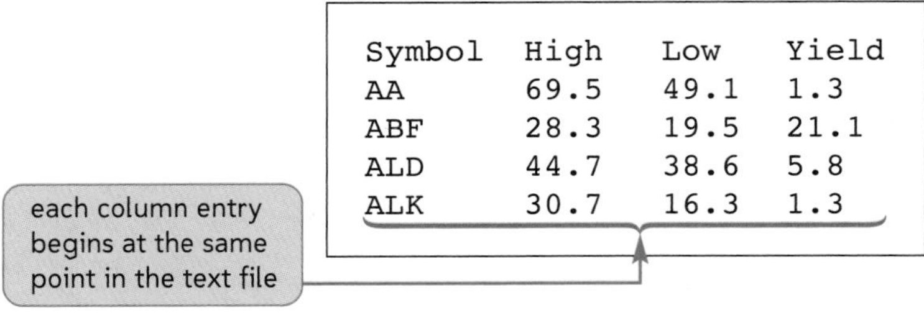

Starting the Text Import Wizard

When you use Excel to connect to a text file, the Text Import Wizard determines whether the data is in a fixed-width format or a delimited format—and if it's delimited, what delimiter is used. You can also tell Excel how to interpret the text file.

The text that Carol wants you to import into Excel is stored in the file named History.txt. The .txt file extension identifies it as a text file. (Other common text file extensions are .dat, .prn, and .csv.) Although you know nothing about the file's structure, you can easily determine how the data is arranged by using the Text Import Wizard. You'll begin by creating a connection to the text file.

TIP

You can also open a text file using the Open dialog box. When Excel detects the data in the text file, the Text Import Wizard opens.

To connect to the History text file:

1. Create a new workbook, and then save the workbook as **Horizons Fund** in the Excel11\Tutorial folder included with your Data Files.
2. Change the zoom level of the Sheet1 worksheet to **120%**.
3. With cell A1 selected in the Sheet1 worksheet, click the **Data** tab on the Ribbon, and then click the **From Text** button in the Get External Data group. The Import Text File dialog box opens.
4. Click the **History** text file located in the Excel11\Tutorial folder included with your Data Files, and then click the **Import** button. The Text Import Wizard – Step 1 of 3 dialog box opens. In the Original data type section, the Fixed width option button is already selected, indicating that the Text Import Wizard has determined the data is arranged in a fixed-width format. See Figure 11-5.

Figure 11-5 Text Import Wizard – Step 1 of 3

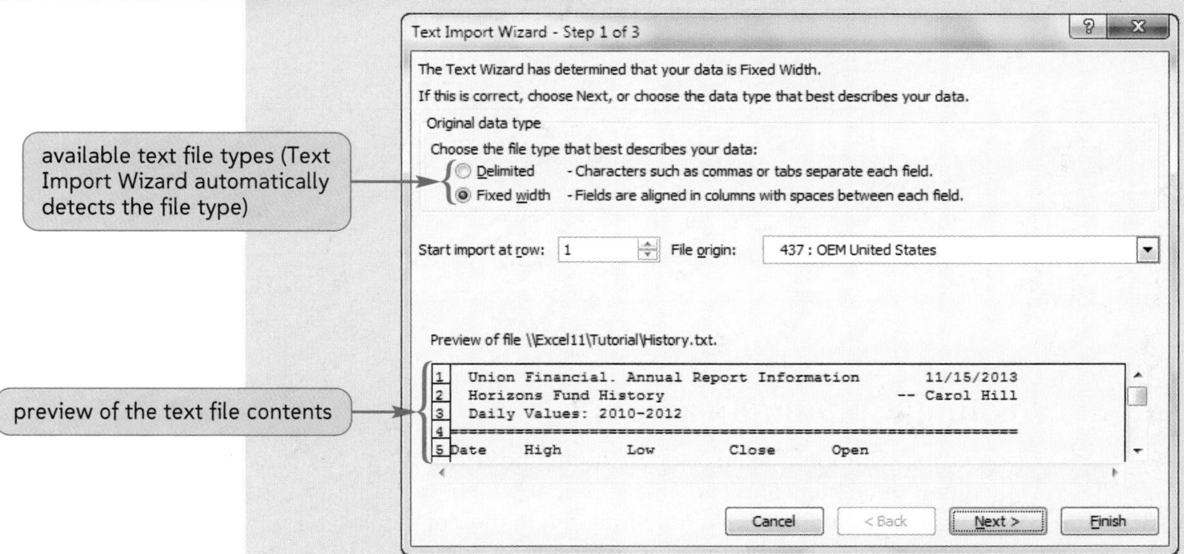

5. Scroll the preview box to view the data in the text file. The column titles for the data are in row 5, and the data list begins at row 6.

Specifying the Starting Row

By default, the Text Import Wizard starts importing text at the first row of the file. You can specify a different starting row, as needed. In this case, you want the Text Import Wizard to skip the first four lines of the file, which contain titles and a description of the text file's contents. Because you're only interested in the data, you'll start importing at row 5, which contains the labels for each column of numbers—Date, High, Low, Close, and Open—that correspond to the date, the fund's high and low values on that date, and the fund's opening and closing values.

To specify row 5 as the starting row:

1. Click the **Start import at row** up arrow to change the value to 5.
2. Click the **Next** button to display the second step of the Text Import Wizard.
3. Scroll the Data preview box. The data to import from the text file starts with the column titles. See Figure 11-6.

Figure 11-6 **Text Import Wizard – Step 2 of 3**

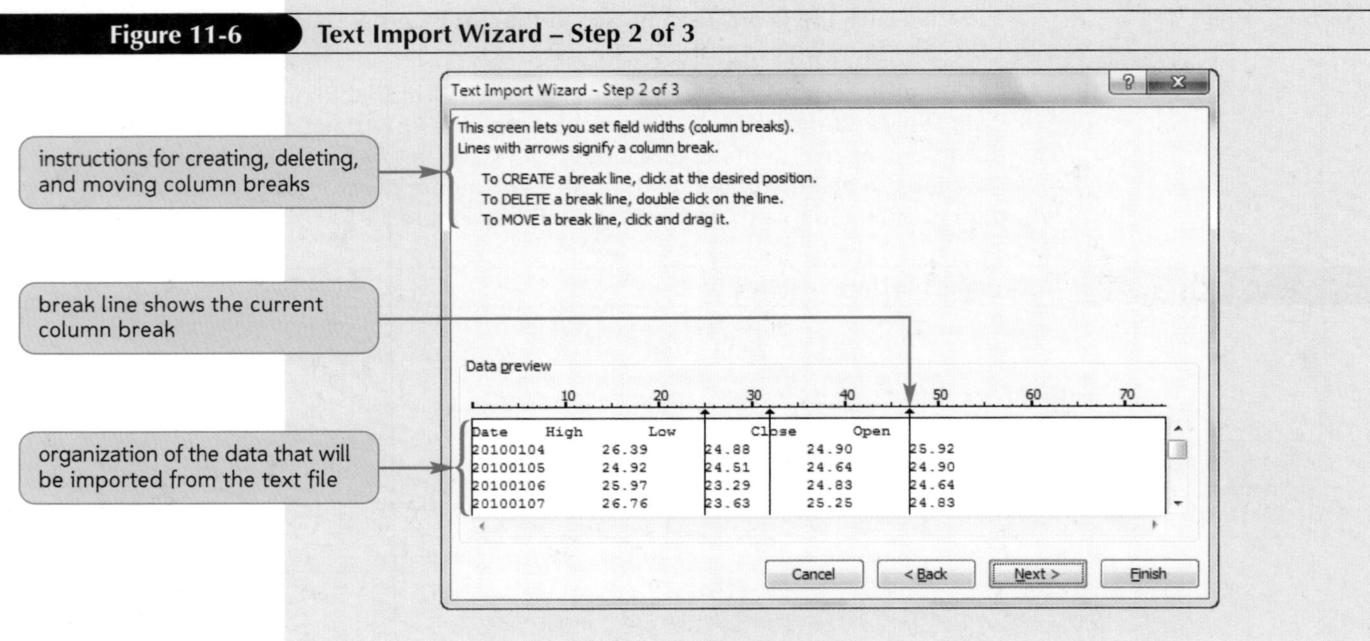

Editing Column Breaks

To correctly import a fixed-width text file, the Text Import Wizard needs to know where each column begins and ends. The point at which one column ends and another begins is called a **column break**. In a delimited file, the delimiter determines the column breaks, whereas in a fixed-width file, the wizard guesses the locations of the column breaks. Sometimes, the wizard incorrectly defines the number and location of columns, so you should always check the Data preview box and edit the columns as needed.

You insert a new column break by clicking the position in the Data preview box where you want the break to appear. If a break is in the wrong location, you click and drag the break line to a new location in the Data preview box. You can delete an extra column break by double-clicking its break.

You'll edit the column breaks in the History text file.

To edit the column breaks in the History text file:

1. Click the blank space between the Date and High columns to insert a column break, and then drag the break line as needed so that it does not intersect either column title or any value in the two columns.
2. Drag the second break line to between the High and Low columns. The column break moves to the new location.
3. Drag the third column line to the left of the Close column title. The column break moves to separate the Low and Close columns.
4. Drag the fourth column break to the left of the Open column title. The column break moves to separate the Open and Close columns. See Figure 11-7.

Figure 11-7 **Revised column breaks**

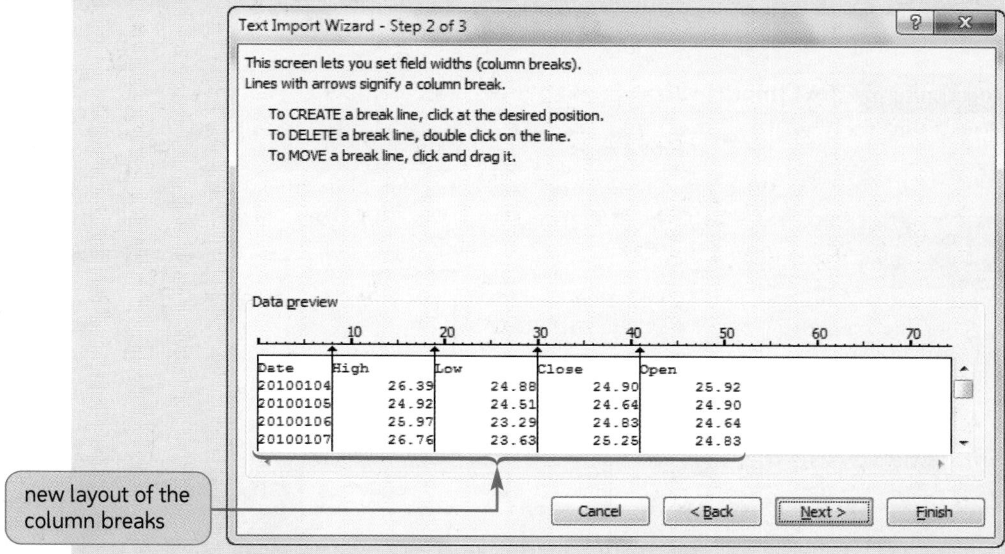

5. Click the **Next** button to proceed to the third step of the Text Import Wizard.

Formatting and Trimming Incoming Data

In the third and final step of the Text Import Wizard, you format the data in each column. Unless you specify a format, the General format style is applied to all of the columns. To specify a format, you select a column in the Data preview box, and then click the appropriate option button in the Column data format section. You can also indicate whether a column should not be imported. Eliminating columns is useful when you want to import only a few items from a large text file containing many columns.

The Date column in the text file displays the year, followed by the month and the day with no separators. This is not a common date format. To make sure that the Text Import Wizard correctly interprets these values, you'll change the General format style to a date format. To reduce the amount of data in the workbook, you will import only the date and the high, low, and closing values of the fund for each day, and not the fund's daily opening value, which is the same as its closing value from the previous day.

To specify a date format and remove the Open column:

1. Verify that the first column is selected in the preview box, and then click the **Date** option button in the Column data format section. The first column heading changes from General to MDY.

   Trouble? If the first column is not selected, click anywhere within the column to select it.

2. Click the **Date button arrow** to display a list of date formats, and then click **YMD**. The column heading for the first column changes to YMD, indicating the values in this column will be interpreted as dates formatted with the year followed by the month and day.

3. In the Data preview box, click anywhere within the **Open** column to select it, and then click the **Do not import column (skip)** option button. The column heading for the Open column changes from General to Skip Column, indicating the data from this column will not be imported. See Figure 11-8.

TIP

If you're importing international data from a text file, click the Advanced button in Step 3 of the Text Import Wizard to specify a different character for the decimal point and thousands separator.

Figure 11-8 Text Import Wizard – Step 3 of 3

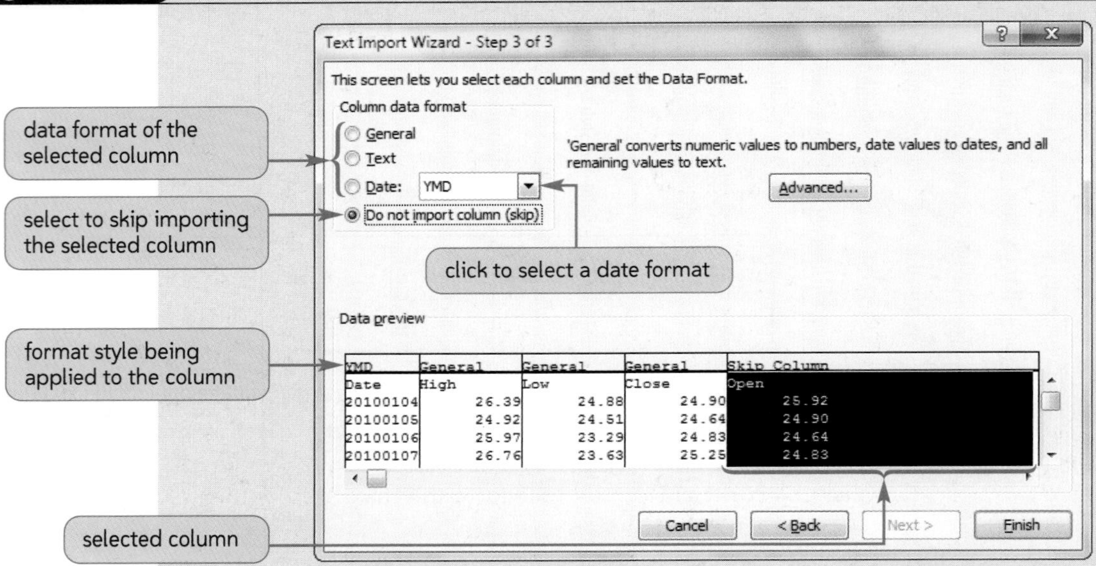

4. Click the **Finish** button. The Import Data dialog box opens so you can specify where to place the imported data in the worksheet.

5. Click cell **A4** in the Sheet1 worksheet to leave the first three rows blank in which to enter a worksheet title, and then click the **OK** button.

The data appears in the worksheet in the range A4:D785. You'll add a descriptive title to the worksheet and format the column headings in the blank rows you left above the data.

To title and format the worksheet:

1. In cell A1, enter **Horizons Fund History** and then format the title using the **Title** cell style.

2. In cell A2, enter **2010 – 2012**, format the text with the **Heading 1** cell style, and then remove the bottom border from cell A2.

3. Bold and center the headings in the range A4:D4, and then increase the width of column A to **13** characters.

4. Click cell **B5**, and then press **Ctrl+Shift+End** to select the range B5:D785. The High, Low, and Close data are selected.
5. Apply the **Number** format to the selected data, and then click cell **A3** to deselect the range.
6. Rename the worksheet as **Fund History**. See Figure 11-9.

Figure 11-9 **Fund History worksheet**

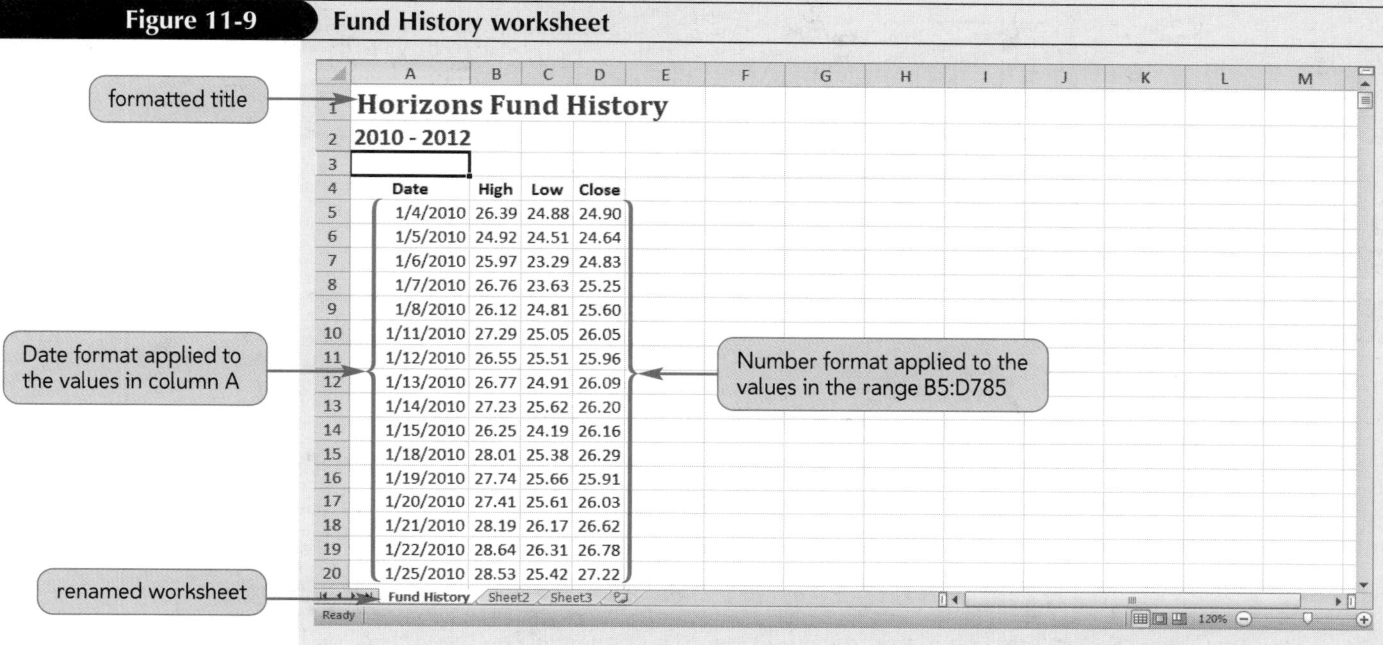

Date	High	Low	Close
1/4/2010	26.39	24.88	24.90
1/5/2010	24.92	24.51	24.64
1/6/2010	25.97	23.29	24.83
1/7/2010	26.76	23.63	25.25
1/8/2010	26.12	24.81	25.60
1/11/2010	27.29	25.05	26.05
1/12/2010	26.55	25.51	25.96
1/13/2010	26.77	24.91	26.09
1/14/2010	27.23	25.62	26.20
1/15/2010	26.25	24.19	26.16
1/18/2010	28.01	25.38	26.29
1/19/2010	27.74	25.66	25.91
1/20/2010	27.41	25.61	26.03
1/21/2010	28.19	26.17	26.62
1/22/2010	28.64	26.31	26.78
1/25/2010	28.53	25.42	27.22

In addition to the fund values themselves, Carol wants you to include a high-low-close chart in the workbook displaying the fund's recent history. You will use a Stock chart type designed to compare the high, low, and closing prices of a stock.

To create a high-low-close chart for the fund data:

1. Click cell **A4**, and then press the **Ctrl+Shift+End** keys to select the range A4:D785. All of the fund data is selected.
2. Scroll to the top of the worksheet without deselecting the range.
3. Click the **Insert** tab on the Ribbon, click the **Other Charts** button in the Charts group, and then click the **High-Low-Close** stock chart type (the first stock chart in the Chart gallery). The High-Low-Close chart is embedded in the Fund History worksheet.
4. Move the chart so that its upper-left corner covers cell **E4**, and then hold down the **Shift** key as you drag a corner of the chart to cover the range **E4:M20**. The chart is resized proportionally.
5. Add the chart title **Horizons Fund** above the chart, add the horizontal axis title **Date**, add the rotated vertical axis title **Fund Value**, and then remove the legend.

TIP

You can quickly move a chart by cutting the chart, clicking the cell in which you want to place the chart, and then clicking the Paste button.

6. Click cell **A3** to deselect the chart. See Figure 11-10.

Figure 11-10 **Formatted chart on the worksheet**

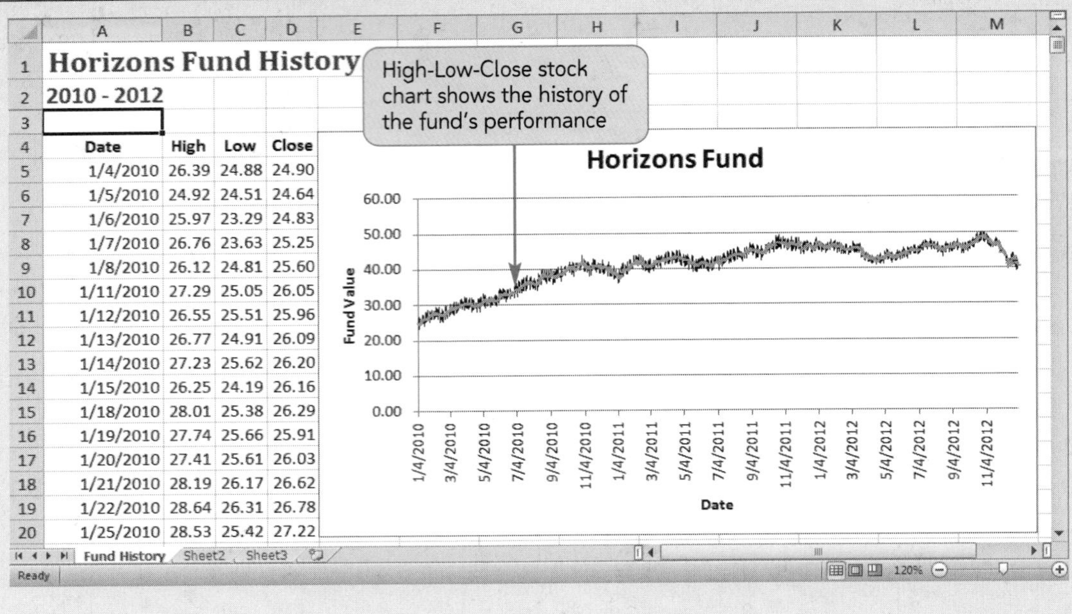

Exploring Connections and Data Ranges

When you import data, you create a connection between the workbook and the text file. A connection is a defined process of retrieving data from an external file. In this case, the process involves importing the data columns from the History text file. All of the connections used in the current workbook are listed in the Workbook Connections dialog box.

Carol wants to know what happens to the workbook if data is added or edited in the History text file. To answer that question, you'll examine the connections currently established in the Horizons Fund workbook.

TIP

To delete a connection to its data source, select the connection in the Workbook Connections dialog box, and then click the Remove button.

To view the Horizons Fund workbook connections:

1. Click the **Data** tab on the Ribbon, and then click the **Connections** button in the Connections group. The Workbook Connections dialog box opens. Only one connection is listed—the connection you created to the History text file.
2. Click the **Click here to see where the selected connections are used** link. The Workbook Connections dialog box shows where the connection to the History text file is used. See Figure 11-11.

Figure 11-11 Workbook Connections dialog box

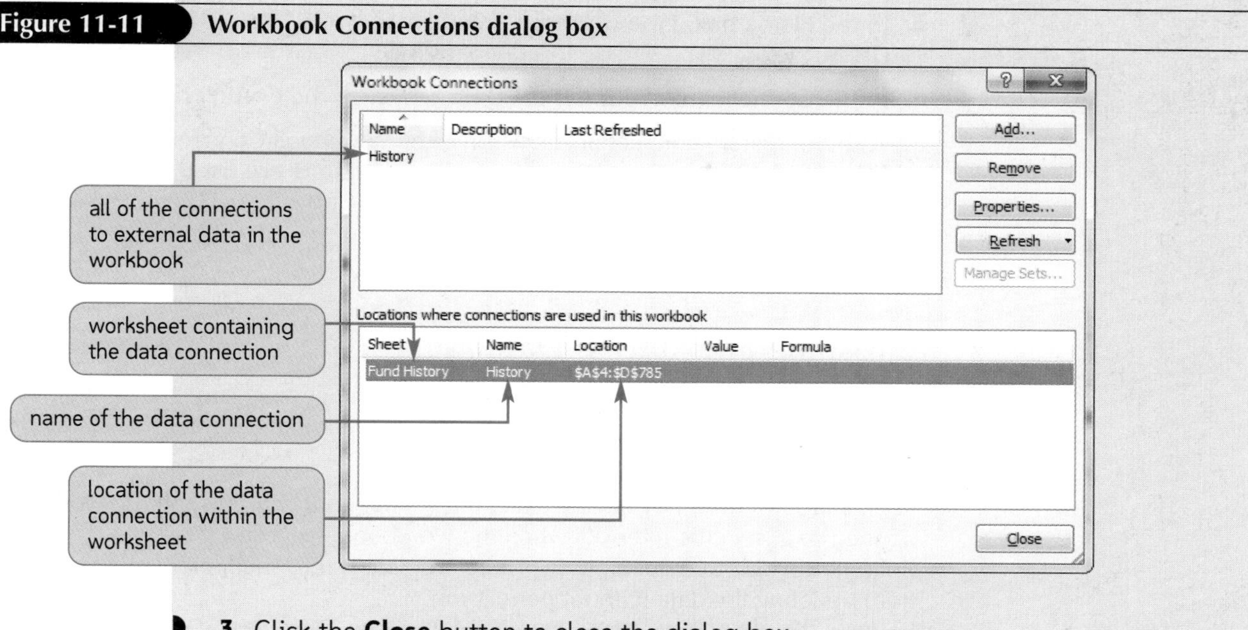

3. Click the **Close** button to close the dialog box.

Understanding External Data Ranges

The same connection might be used in several locations in the workbook, freeing Excel from having to establish a connection to the same file every time the data is imported. Each location in which a connection is applied is called an **external data range**. Excel gives each external data range a name. You can create a more descriptive range name by editing the properties of the external data range.

REFERENCE

Editing the Properties of an External Data Range

- Click any cell in the range containing the external data.
- In the Connections group on the Data tab, click the Properties button.
- To define a name for the data range, enter the name in the Name box.
- To specify how the external data is refreshed in the workbook, check the appropriate check boxes in the External Data Range Properties dialog box.
- Click the OK button.

The external data range in the range A4:D785 of the Fund History worksheet is named "History"—the same name given to the connection. This is the only external data range in the workbook at the moment. Because you'll soon add more connections and external data ranges to this workbook, you'll use a more descriptive title for the data range.

To edit the properties of an external data range:

1. Click cell **A4** to select one cell within the History external data range.
2. In the Connections group on the Data tab, click the **Properties** button. The External Data Range Properties dialog box opens.

3. In the Name box, type **Horizons Fund History: 2010 – 2012** and then click the **OK** button.
4. In the Connections group on the Data tab, click the **Connections** button.
5. With the History connection selected in the Workbook Connections list, click the **Click here to see where the selected connections are used** link. The name of this location is now "Horizons Fund History: 2010 – 2012," as you entered in Step 3.
6. Click the **Close** button to close the Workbook Connections dialog box.

Refreshing an External Data Range

In addition to setting the name of an external data range, you can also define how Excel updates, or **refreshes**, the data. From the External Data Range Properties dialog box, you can:

- Keep a report current by having Excel refresh the connection when the workbook is opened or at specific intervals when the workbook is in use.
- Require the user to enter a password before data is refreshed, preventing other users from updating the data without permission.
- Remove the connection to the external data range, freezing the data so that it cannot be refreshed.
- Refresh the connection in the background, so you can work on other portions of the workbook as you wait for the data to be retrieved; this is helpful if you are retrieving large amounts of data.
- Define whether the refreshed data retains the formatting and layout you've already defined for the location or replaces the current format and layout.
- Define whether Excel inserts or overwrites cells when new rows are added to the data range.

REFERENCE

Refreshing External Data

To manually refresh a data range:
- In the Connections group on the Data tab, click the Refresh All button arrow.
- Click Refresh to refresh the currently selected data range or click Refresh All to refresh all of the connections in the workbook.

To automatically refresh a data range:
- Select any cell in the data range, and then click the Properties button in the Connections group on the Data tab.
- Click the Refresh every check box, and then enter a minutes value to refresh the data range at regular intervals.
- Click the Refresh data when opening the file check box to refresh the data when the user opens the workbook.

To manually refresh a connection:
- In the Connections group on the Data tab, click the Connections button.
- Select the connection in the Workbook Connections list, and then click the Refresh button.

To automatically refresh a connection:
- In the Connections group on the Data tab, click the Connections button, and then click the Properties button.
- Click the Usage tab in the Connection Properties dialog box, and then select the Refresh options.

The History text file is periodically updated as recent fund values are transferred from current documents into historic documents. Carol wants the workbook to always display the most current values from the History text file, so she asks you to ensure that the connection to the file is updated whenever the workbook is opened. You can define how Excel refreshes this data by editing the properties of the connection or the properties of the external data range. The advantage of editing the connection is that your choices are applied to all of the external data ranges that use that connection. Because the History connection is only used in one location, it doesn't matter which property you choose to change. You'll edit the property of the external data range rather than the connection.

To define how external data is refreshed:

1. Verify that cell **A4** is still selected so that at least one cell within the data range is selected.
2. In the Connections group on the Data tab, click the **Properties** button. The External Data Range Properties dialog box opens.
3. Click the **Prompt for file name on refresh** check box to remove the check mark. Now, Carol will not be prompted for the filename each time the data is refreshed.
4. Click the **Refresh data when opening the file** check box to insert a check mark so that Excel automatically refreshes the data connection when the file is initially opened.
5. Click the **Adjust column width** check box to remove the check mark because you've already set the column widths. See Figure 11-12.

Figure 11-12 External Data Range Properties dialog box

TIP

Check the Remove external data from worksheet before closing check box to remove the external data when the file is closed, which reduces the file size, and retrieve the data when the file is reopened.

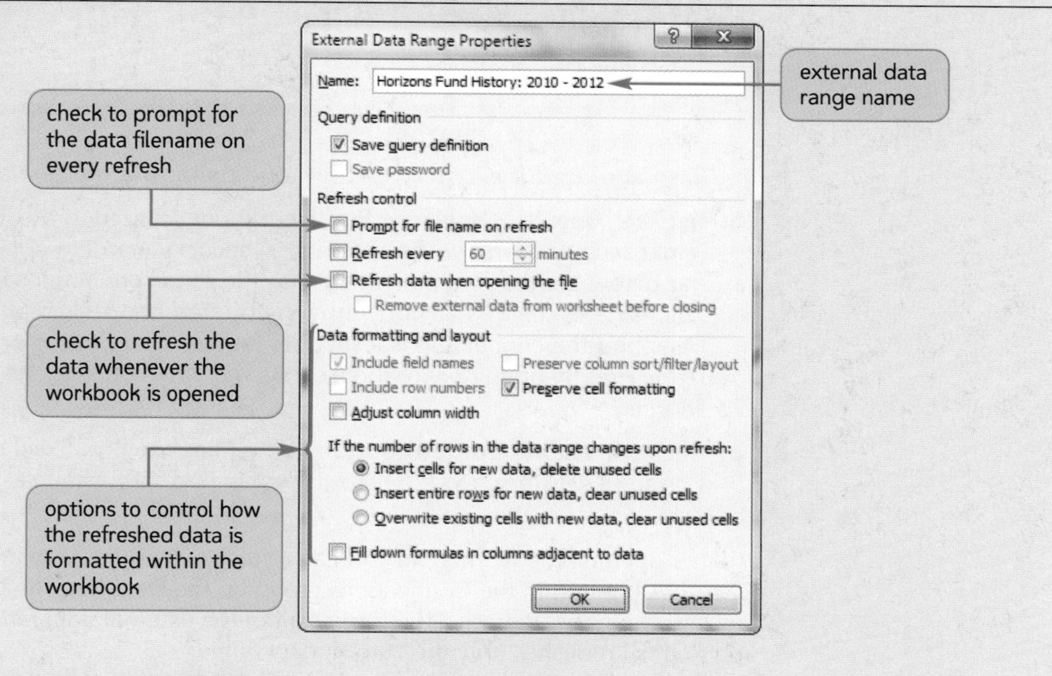

6. Click the **OK** button.

Carol discovered an error in the History text file. The first value in the High column was entered incorrectly. You'll fix the error and verify that the workbook will be automatically updated to reflect the edit.

To edit the text file and refresh external data:

1. Save and close the Horizons Fund workbook.
2. In Notepad or another text editor, open the **History** text file located in the Excel11\Tutorial folder included with your Data Files.
3. Change the High value in the first row from 26.39 to **27.39**. See Figure 11-13.

Figure 11-13 History text file in Notepad

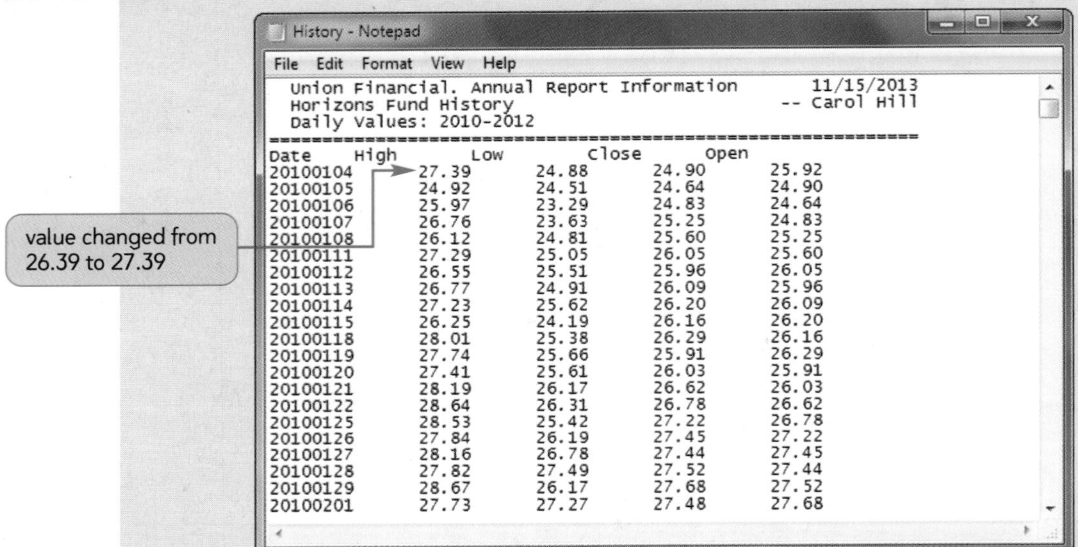


```
  Union Financial. Annual Report Information          11/15/2013
  Horizons Fund History                             -- Carol Hill
  Daily Values: 2010-2012
=================================================================
Date      High       Low         Close       Open
20100104   27.39      24.88       24.90       25.92
20100105   24.92      24.51       24.64       24.90
20100106   25.97      23.29       24.83       24.64
20100107   26.76      23.63       25.25       24.83
20100108   26.12      24.81       25.60       25.25
20100111   27.29      25.05       26.05       25.60
20100112   26.55      25.51       25.96       26.05
20100113   26.77      24.91       26.09       25.96
20100114   27.23      25.62       26.20       26.09
20100115   26.25      24.19       26.16       26.20
20100118   28.01      25.38       26.29       26.16
20100119   27.74      25.66       25.91       26.29
20100120   27.41      25.61       26.03       25.91
20100121   28.19      26.17       26.62       26.03
20100122   28.64      26.31       26.78       26.62
20100125   28.53      25.42       27.22       26.78
20100126   27.84      26.19       27.45       27.22
20100127   28.16      26.78       27.44       27.45
20100128   27.82      27.49       27.52       27.44
20100129   28.67      26.17       27.68       27.52
20100201   27.73      27.27       27.48       27.68
```

4. Save and close the History text file, and then close the text editor.
5. In Excel, open the **Horizons Fund** workbook located in the Excel11\Tutorial folder included with your Data Files. A security warning appears in the Message Bar below the Ribbon, indicating that the data connections have been disabled. The value in cell B5 has not yet been updated and still displays the value 26.39. Disabling the connection is a security feature designed to prevent users from inadvertently opening workbooks infected with connections to invalid data sources.
6. Click the **Enable Content** button in the Message Bar. Excel refreshes the connection to the History text file, and the value in cell B5 changes from 26.39 to 27.39.

After opening the workbook, you can refresh external data manually by clicking the Refresh All button in the Connections group on the Data tab. The Refresh All button provides two options: Refresh All refreshes all of the external data ranges in the workbook, and Refresh refreshes only the current data range.

PROSKILLS

Teamwork: Maintaining Data Security

Database security is essential for any business to maintain the integrity of its data and retain the trust of its colleagues and customers. Securing a database may be even more critical for small businesses because they have so much more to lose from lapses in security. If you are using a database for storing data with your Excel workbooks, keep in mind the following tips:

- Enable your database security controls. Make sure your new databases are set up with password controls to prohibit unauthorized access.
- Keep your database software updated with the latest security patches.
- Do not allow database copying. There should be one source of your data. When multiple copies of the database are allowed, data security, consistency, and integrity are compromised.
- Use your database software to encrypt your database to prevent hackers from gaining unauthorized access to your information.

Maintaining database security requires that everyone with access to the database know how to retrieve and process data appropriately. In the end, a database will only be as secure as the work habits of the people who access it.

Defining a Trusted Location

Carol is concerned about Excel automatically disabling external data and forcing the user to enable it before the data can be refreshed. She asks you to override the default settings so that it always enables her data sources. You do this by defining the location of Carol's data sources as a **trusted location**, which means that Excel will access the connection to this data source without prompting you to confirm that the connection is secure.

REFERENCE

Defining a Trusted Location

- Click the File tab, and then click Options in the navigation bar.
- Click Trust Center in the Excel Options list, and then click the Trust Center Settings button.
- Click Trusted Locations in the Trust Center list, and then click the Add new location button.
- Click the Browse button to locate the trusted location, and then specify whether to include subfolders.
- Click the OK button in each dialog box.

A trusted location is defined in the Trust Center. You'll define all of the subfolders in the Excel11 folder as trusted locations.

To set up a trusted location:

1. Click the **File** tab, and then click **Options** on the navigation bar. The Excel Options dialog box opens.
2. Click **Trust Center** in the left pane, and then click the **Trust Center Settings** button in the right pane. The Trust Center dialog box opens.

3. Click **Trusted Locations** in the left pane to display the list of locations that are trusted by Microsoft Office.
4. If your data files are located in a network folder, click the **Allow Trusted Locations on my network** check box.
5. Click the **Add new location** button. The Microsoft Office Trusted Location dialog box opens.
6. Click the **Browse** button, and then navigate to the **Excel11** folder included with your Data Files.
7. Double-click the **Excel11** folder icon to open it, and then click the **OK** button to return to the Microsoft Office Trusted Location dialog box.
8. Click the **Subfolders of this location are also trusted** check box to insert a check mark. This option allows all of the subfolders in the Excel11 folder to be trusted.
9. Type **Data sources for Tutorial 11** in the Description box. See Figure 11-14.

Figure 11-14 Microsoft Office Trusted Location dialog box

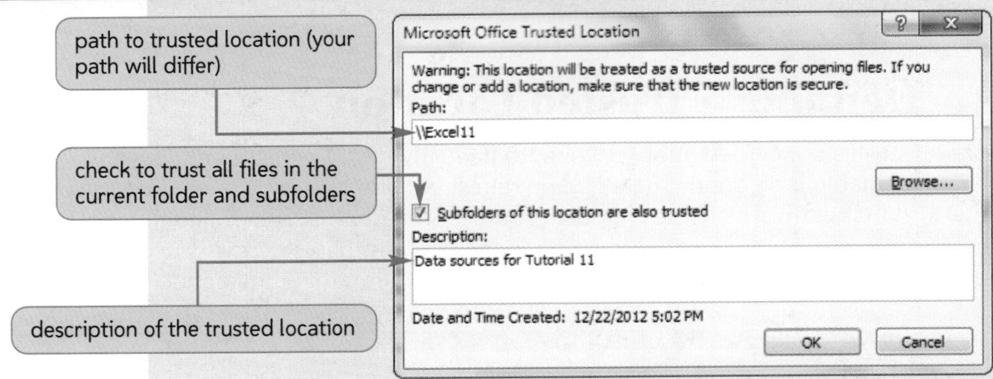

10. Click the **OK** button in each of the three dialog boxes to return to the Excel workbook. Excel now trusts your data source and will refresh the data from the History text file without prompting.
11. Save and close the Horizons Fund workbook, and then reopen the workbook, verifying that you are not prompted to enable the data connections in the workbook when you reopen it.

INSIGHT

Moving a Data Source

When an Excel project is copied to another computer, the path names to the external data sources might change and become unusable. To fix this problem, you must modify the properties of the connections established in the workbook. When you move or copy a workbook that is connected to external data, you must change the path to the external data. To update the connection, you modify the path on the Definition tab in the Connection Properties dialog box, which you open by clicking the Connections button in the Connections group on the Data tab, selecting the connection, and then clicking the Properties button. With the definition established for the connection, other users can access and refresh the data from the external data source.

You've set up the connection from the Horizons Fund workbook to the History text file. In the process, you've worked with connections, external data ranges, and trusted locations. In the next session, you'll learn about databases and how to connect an Excel workbook to a database.

REVIEW

Session 11.1 Quick Check

1. What is the difference between a fixed-width and a delimited text file?
2. Name three delimiters that can be used to separate data in a delimited text file.
3. How do you insert column breaks when importing a text file using the Text Import Wizard?
4. What is the relationship between a connection and an external data range?
5. Name two ways in which Excel automatically refreshes a connection.
6. What is a trusted location?

SESSION 11.2 VISUAL OVERVIEW

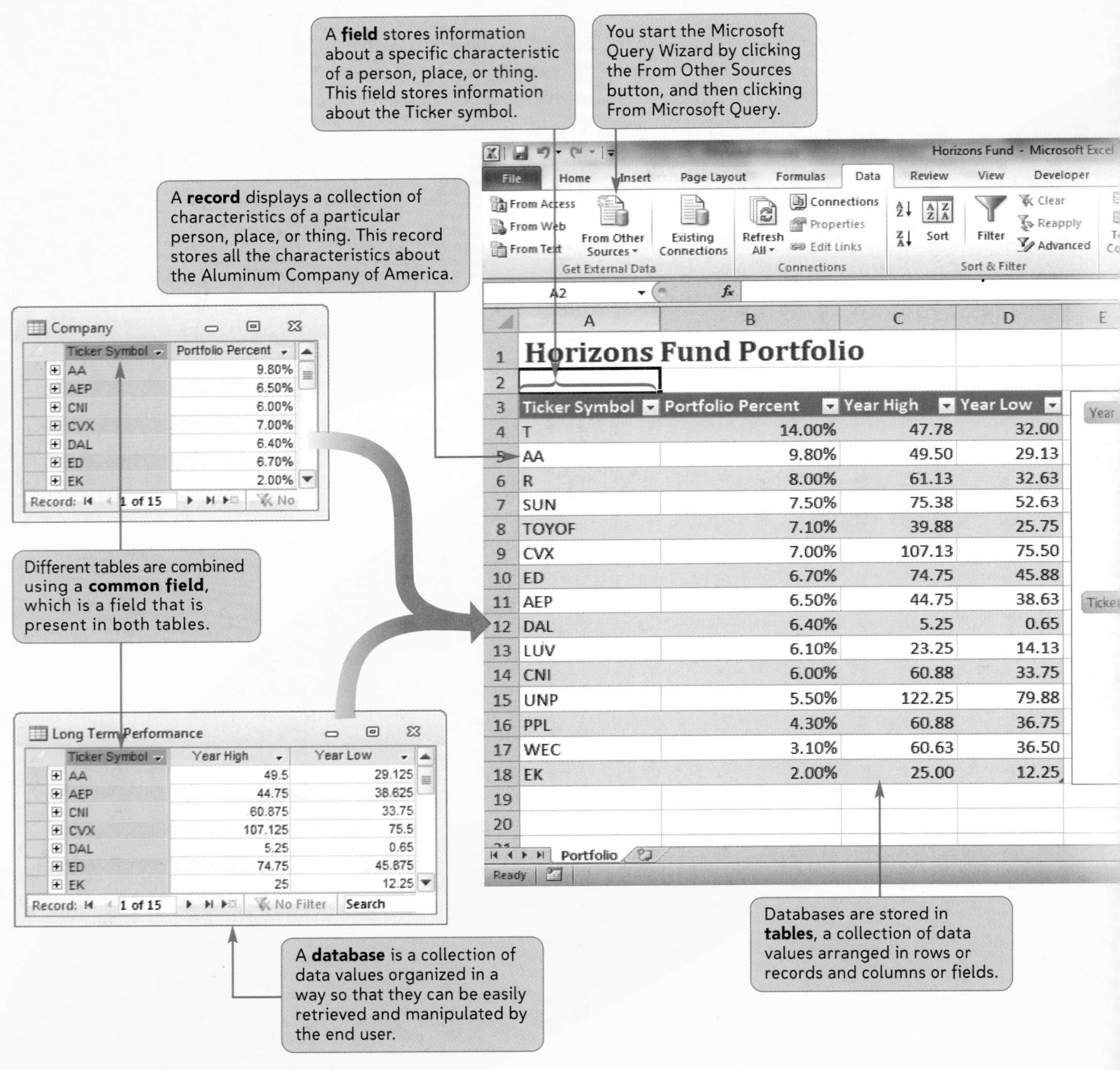

EXCEL DATABASES AND QUERIES

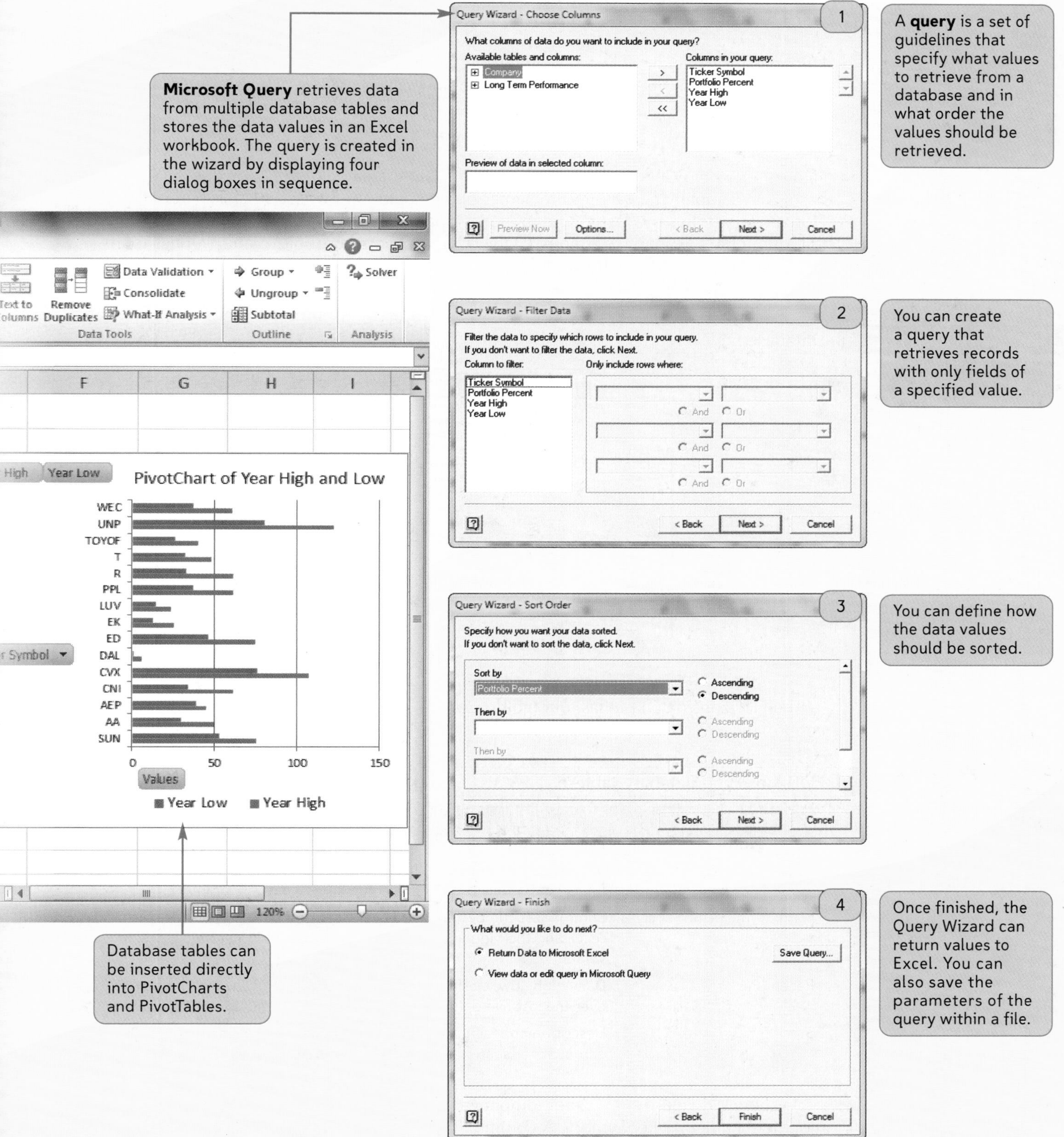

Introducing Databases and Queries

Excel can retrieve data directly from most database programs, including Microsoft Access, the database program that is part of the Microsoft Office software suite. As in many financial firms, much of the information Union Financial analysts work with is stored in databases. Information on the stocks in the Horizons Fund is stored in the Horizons database, which was created using Access. Before establishing a connection to the information in this database, you need to understand how databases are organized.

Understanding Tables, Fields, and Records

Figure 11-15 shows the Company table, which Carol created in the Horizons database. The Company field stores the names of the companies whose stock is part of the Horizons portfolio. The first record in the Company table displays stock information for the Aluminum Company of America, which has the ticker symbol AA and belongs to the group of industrial stocks. To simplify the workbook, Carol included only a selection of 15 stocks in her sample database.

Figure 11-15 **Database table**

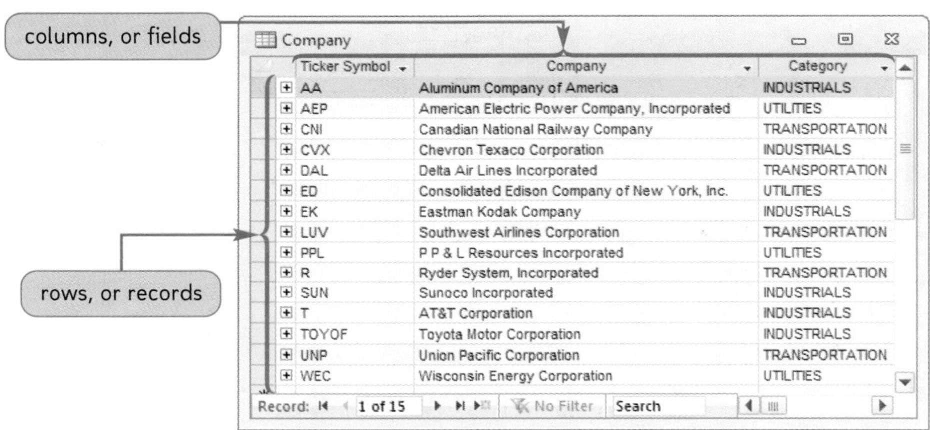

The Horizons database has four tables: Company, Long Term Performance, Recent Performance, and Stock Info. Figure 11-16 describes the contents of each table.

Figure 11-16 **Horizons Fund database tables**

Table Name	Description
Company	Includes data about each company in the fund and the percentage of the fund that is allocated to purchasing stocks for that company
Long Term Performance	Summarizes the performance over the last 52 weeks for each stock, recording the high and low values over that period of time, and its volatility
Recent Performance	Daily high, low, closing, and volume values for each stock in the portfolio over the last five days
Stock Info	Description of each stock, including the yield, dividend amount and date, earnings per share, and number of outstanding shares

As shown in Figure 11-17, the Company table and the Stock Info table share a common field named Ticker Symbol. A common field can be used to match information from both tables into a single table.

Figure 11-17 **Combining tables based on a common field**

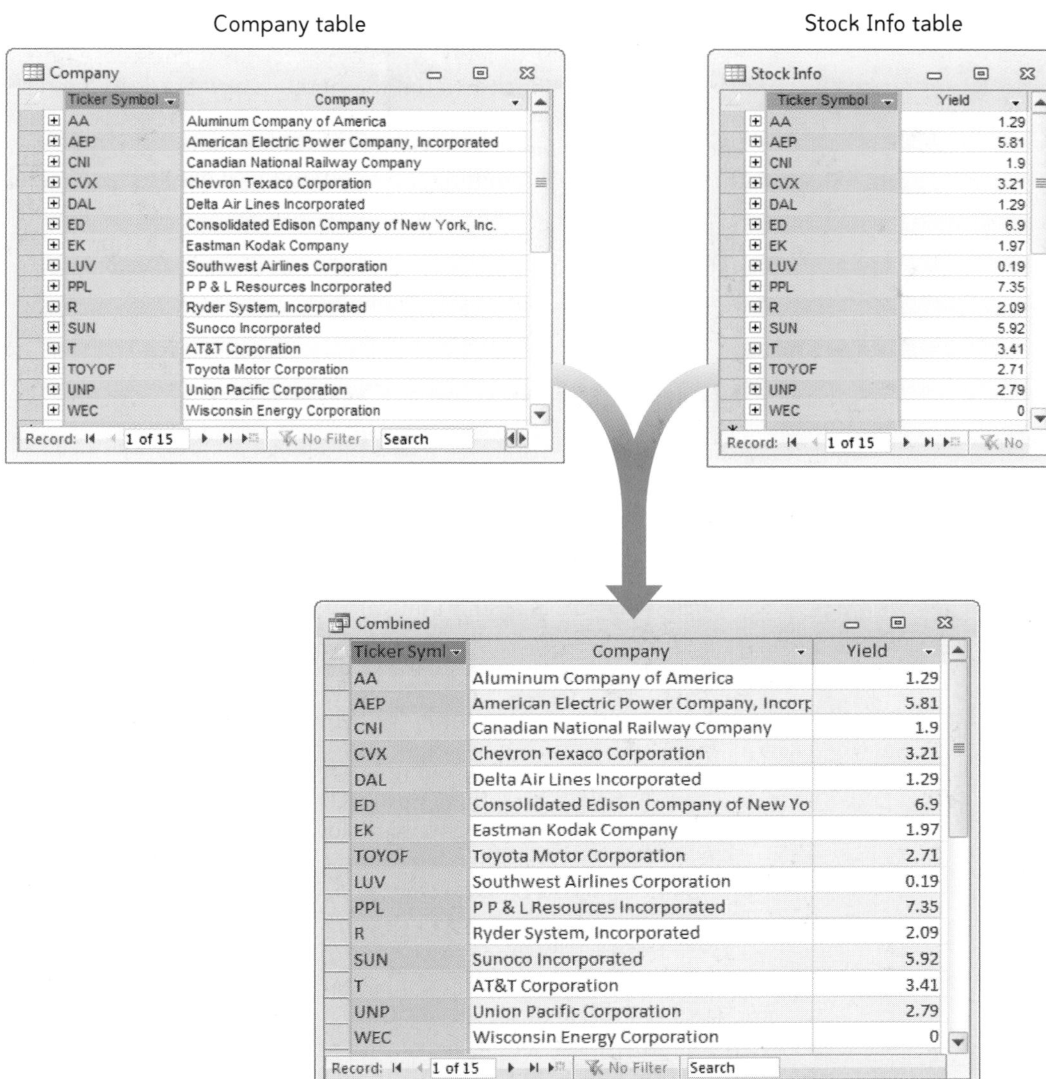

Company

Ticker Symbol	Company
AA	Aluminum Company of America
AEP	American Electric Power Company, Incorporated
CNI	Canadian National Railway Company
CVX	Chevron Texaco Corporation
DAL	Delta Air Lines Incorporated
ED	Consolidated Edison Company of New York, Inc.
EK	Eastman Kodak Company
LUV	Southwest Airlines Corporation
PPL	P P & L Resources Incorporated
R	Ryder System, Incorporated
SUN	Sunoco Incorporated
T	AT&T Corporation
TOYOF	Toyota Motor Corporation
UNP	Union Pacific Corporation
WEC	Wisconsin Energy Corporation

Record: 1 of 15 No Filter Search

Stock Info

Ticker Symbol	Yield
AA	1.29
AEP	5.81
CNI	1.9
CVX	3.21
DAL	1.29
ED	6.9
EK	1.97
LUV	0.19
PPL	7.35
R	2.09
SUN	5.92
T	3.41
TOYOF	2.71
UNP	2.79
WEC	0

Record: 1 of 15 No

Combined

Ticker Syml	Company	Yield
AA	Aluminum Company of America	1.29
AEP	American Electric Power Company, Incorp	5.81
CNI	Canadian National Railway Company	1.9
CVX	Chevron Texaco Corporation	3.21
DAL	Delta Air Lines Incorporated	1.29
ED	Consolidated Edison Company of New Yo	6.9
EK	Eastman Kodak Company	1.97
TOYOF	Toyota Motor Corporation	2.71
LUV	Southwest Airlines Corporation	0.19
PPL	P P & L Resources Incorporated	7.35
R	Ryder System, Incorporated	2.09
SUN	Sunoco Incorporated	5.92
T	AT&T Corporation	3.41
UNP	Union Pacific Corporation	2.79
WEC	Wisconsin Energy Corporation	0

Record: 1 of 15 No Filter Search

When retrieving information from two tables, such as the Company table and the Stock Info table, the value of the ticker symbol in one table is matched with the value of the ticker symbol in the other table, displaying information about both the company and the stock itself. Without this common field, you cannot match the company information from one table with the yield information from the other.

Understanding Queries

A large database can contain dozens or hundreds of tables, and each table can have several fields and thousands of records, so you need a way to choose only the information that you most want to see. When you want to look at only specific information from a database, you create a query. In response to the query, the database displays the records and fields that meet the requirements of that question. A query might ask, "What are the names of all the stocks in the portfolio, and what are their corresponding ticker symbols?" To answer this question, you submit the query to the database in a form that the database can read. The database then extracts the relevant information, displaying the stock names alongside their ticker symbols.

A query might extract only specific records. In this case, the query contains **criteria**, which are conditions that limit the number of records in the results. Excel then extracts only those records that match the specified conditions. For example, you might want to know the names and ticker symbols of only the top five performing stocks from the past three months. In submitting the query to the database, you include criteria to limit the results to only the top five performing stocks from that time period in the portfolio. In a query, you can also specify how you want the data to appear. If you want the names and ticker symbols of the top five performing stocks arranged alphabetically by ticker symbol, you include that in the query definition.

Using Microsoft Query

Carol wants the workbook to list the stocks in the Horizons Fund and describe their performance in the last year. According to the worksheet plan (refer to Figure 11-2), you can extract this information from the Horizons database. Excel supports two ways of importing database data. One way is to create a connection to the database and retrieve all of the information from a single table. However, if you want to retrieve data from multiple tables, you use Microsoft Query.

REFERENCE

Using Microsoft Query with an Access Database

- In the Get External Data group on the Data tab, click the From Other Sources button, and then click From Microsoft Query.
- In the Choose Data Source dialog box, specify MS Access Database as the data source, select a database file, and then click the OK button.
- In the first step of the Query Wizard, select the columns from the different tables to include in your query, and then click the Next button.
- In the second step of the wizard, filter the data by selecting the columns to filter, specifying the nature of the filter in the Only include rows where list boxes, and then click the Next button.
- In the third step of the wizard, specify the sort order for the data values in the query, and then click the Next button.
- In the last step of the wizard, specify whether to return the query data to Excel, view or edit the data in Microsoft Query, or save the written query to a permanent file for use later.

Microsoft Query is an application included with Microsoft Office to write database queries. Like the Text Import Wizard you used in the previous session, Microsoft Query uses a wizard containing a collection of dialog boxes that guide you through the entire query-writing process. The first step in the Microsoft Query Wizard is to create a data source. A **data source** is any file that contains the data you want to retrieve. Data sources can be databases, text files, or other Excel workbooks. In this tutorial, you'll use the wizard only with databases because Excel supports newer and better tools to deal with other types of data sources.

To start the Microsoft Query Wizard:

1. If you took a break at the end of the previous session, make sure the Horizons Fund workbook is open.
2. Switch to the **Sheet2** worksheet.
3. Click the **Data** tab on the Ribbon, if necessary.
4. In the Get External Data group, click the **From Other Sources** button, and then click **From Microsoft Query**. The Choose Data Source dialog box opens. See Figure 11-18.

Figure 11-18 Choose Data Source dialog box

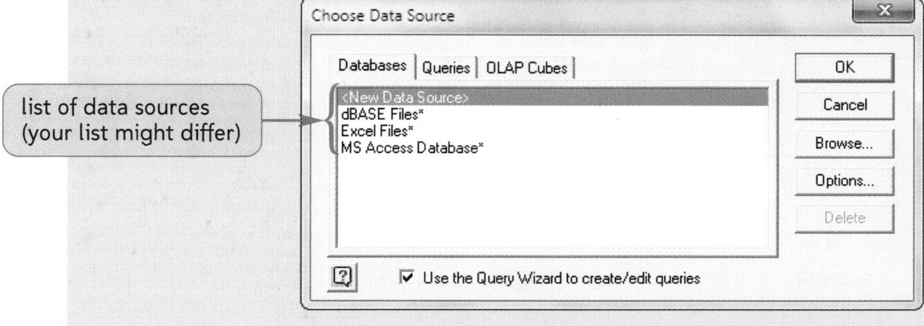

Connecting to a Data Source

The Choose Data Source dialog box lists several data sources from which you can retrieve data. You can also define your own data source by clicking <New Data Source> in the list of databases. In this case, because you're trying to connect to a Microsoft Access database, you'll use the MS Access Database data source.

To connect to an Access data source:

1. Click **MS Access Database*** in the list of data sources.
2. Verify that the **Use the Query Wizard to create/edit queries** check box is checked, and then click the **OK** button. The Select Database dialog box opens.
3. Navigate to the **Excel11\Tutorial** folder included with your Data Files, and then click the **Horizons.accdb** database file.

   Trouble? Microsoft Query does not support the use of network folders. If your data source is located on a network folder, you must map the folder to a drive letter. To do so, click the Network button in the Select Database dialog box to open the Map Network Drive dialog box.
4. Click the **OK** button. Excel connects to the data source, the Horizons database, and then opens the Query Wizard – Choose Columns dialog box. See Figure 11-19.

Figure 11-19 Query Wizard – Choose Columns dialog box

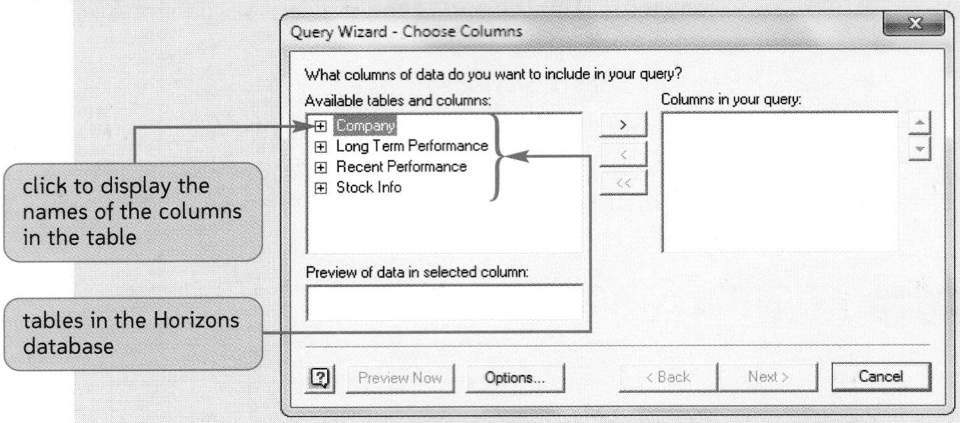

click to display the names of the columns in the table

tables in the Horizons database

Choosing Tables and Columns

The next step in retrieving data from the Horizons database is to choose the table and fields (columns) to include in the query. The Query Wizard lets you preview the structure of the database and its contents. You'll start by examining the fields in the Company table.

To view a list of fields in the Company table:

1. Click the **Expand** button [+] next to Company.
2. Verify that the columns (or fields) in the Company table are displayed in the Available tables and columns list box. See Figure 11-20.

Figure 11-20 Columns in the Company table

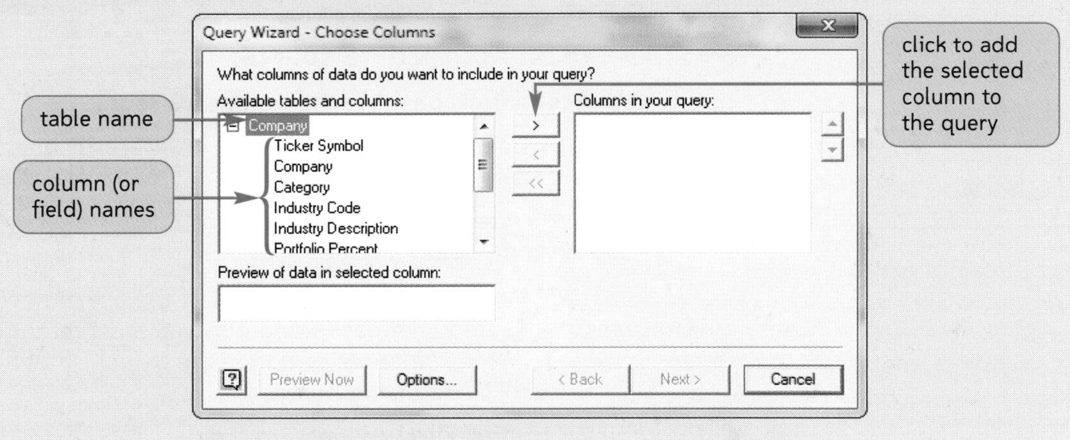

Carol wants to include the ticker symbol, the company, and the portfolio percent from the Company table in the query. The portfolio percent is the percentage of the portfolio that is invested in each particular stock. Carol also wants to include the Year High and Year Low fields from the Long Term Performance table so that she can identify the high and low points in the previous year for each stock in the portfolio. Because the two tables share Ticker Symbol as a common field, you'll select data from both tables with the Query Wizard.

To select the columns to import into Excel:

1. Click **Ticker Symbol** in the Available tables and columns box, and then click the **Select Field** button [>]. The Ticker Symbol column moves to the Columns in your query box, indicating that it will be included in the query.
2. In the Available tables and columns list box, double-click the **Company** column name (not the Company table name) to move the field into the query, and then double-click **Portfolio Percent**. These columns now appear in the Columns in your query box.
3. Click the **Expand** button [+] next to Long Term Performance to display the list of columns in that table.
4. Double-click the **Year High** and **Year Low** column names. The five fields that Carol wants to include in the query are selected. See Figure 11-21.

Figure 11-21 Columns selected for the query

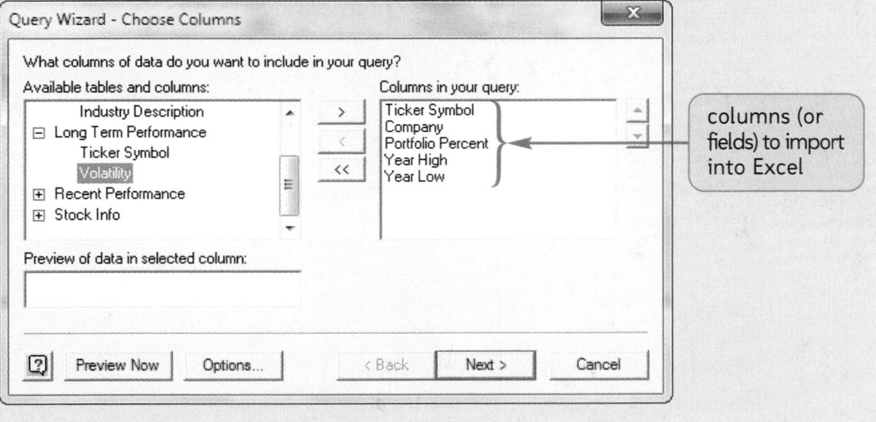

You can preview the contents of each field in the table by selecting the field in either the Available tables and columns box or the Columns in your query box of the Query Wizard – Choose Columns dialog box, and then clicking the Preview Now button. You will preview the contents of the Company field to see the types of entries it contains.

To preview the contents of the Company field:

1. Click **Company** in the Columns in your query box.
2. Click the **Preview Now** button. Some of the values in the selected column appear in the Preview of data in selected column box. See Figure 11-22. You can scroll to see more of the values.

Figure 11-22 **Preview of the company data**

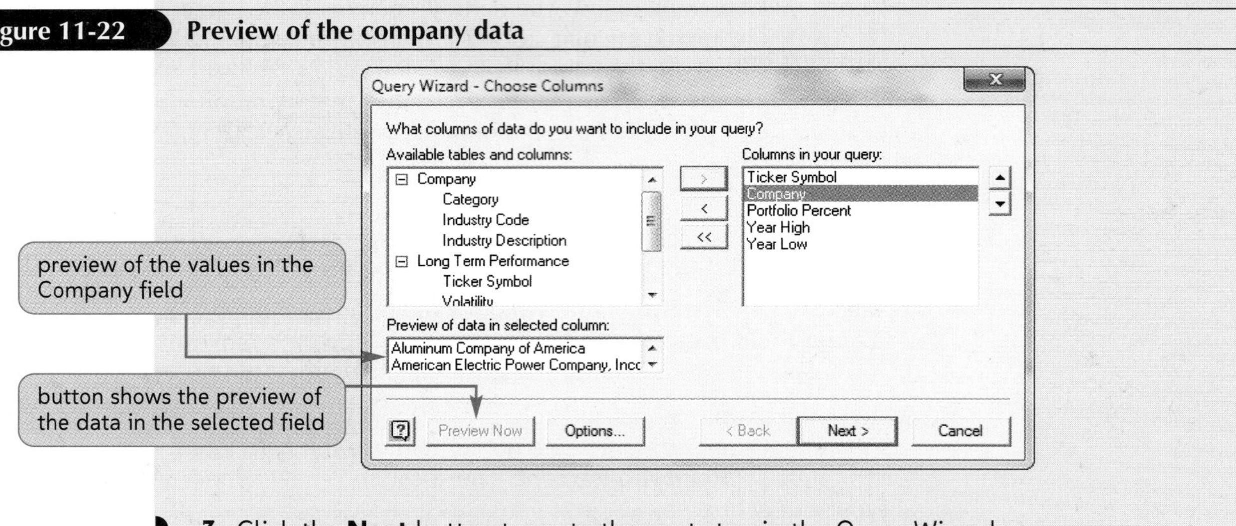

3. Click the **Next** button to go to the next step in the Query Wizard.

Filtering and Sorting Data

Now that you've selected the five columns for the Portfolio worksheet, you must determine whether to retrieve all of the records in the tables or to filter the data to retrieve only records that satisfy particular criteria. When you filter data, you specify which records you want to retrieve using specific criteria. In this query, you can filter the data to remove particular stocks or to retrieve only those stocks that perform at a certain level. You do so using the Query Wizard – Filter Data dialog box. You specify the type of comparison you want to make in the filter, such as equals, greater than, or less than. Then, you enter a value for the comparison.

You'll use the Query Wizard – Filter Data dialog box to create a filter that retrieves stock information only for stocks from the Eastman Kodak Company or from the Toyota Motor Corporation.

To create a filter that retrieves stocks for only two companies:

1. Click **Company** in the Column to filter box. You want to retrieve the Eastman Kodak stock.
2. Click the **arrow** button in the left column of the first row of the Only include rows where section, and then click **equals** to select the type of comparison.
3. Click the **arrow** button in the right column of the first row of the Only include rows where section, and then click **Eastman Kodak Company** to select the value for the comparison.
4. Click the **Or** option button. You have completed the first row and indicated that you want to include another filter. The second row becomes available so you can add a second set of conditions to the query.
5. Click the **arrow** button in the left column of the second row, and then click **equals**.
6. Click the **arrow** button in the right column of the second row, and then click **Toyota Motor Corporation**. The query includes two sets of conditions. See Figure 11-23.

Figure 11-23 Query Wizard – Filter Data dialog box

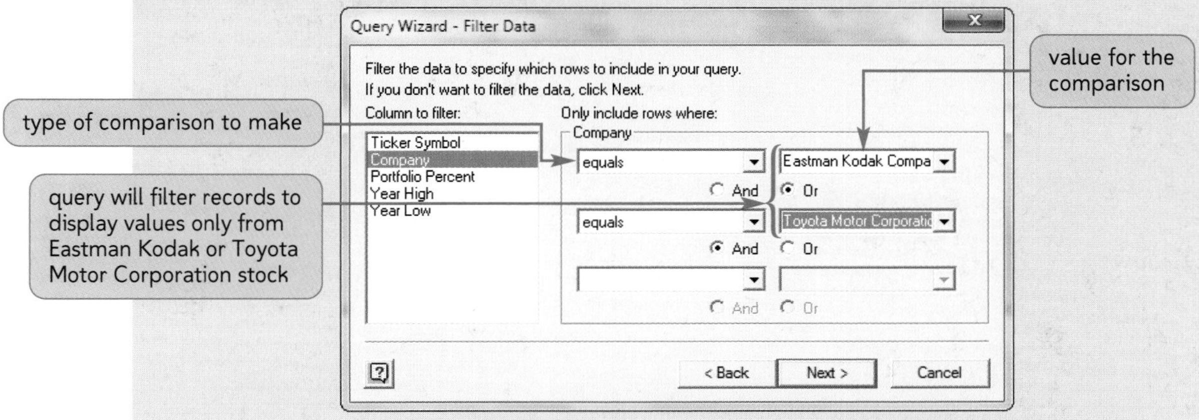

The filter you created retrieves only those records for Eastman Kodak or Toyota. The Query Wizard will not retrieve stock information for other companies in the Horizons Fund. Although only three rows of criteria are shown in the Query Wizard – Filter Data dialog box, the dialog box expands to provide additional rows as you specify requirements for your filter.

Carol wants information on all the companies in the portfolio, so you'll remove the data filter you just created.

To remove the filter from the query:

1. Click the **equals arrow** button in the second row, scroll to the top of the list, and then click the blank space above equals. The second condition is cleared.
2. Repeat Step 1 for the box in the first row. The first condition is cleared. The query doesn't contain a filter.
3. Click the **Next** button to continue to the next step of the Query Wizard without filtering the data.

In the last part of writing a query, you specify how to sort the data. You select the sort field and then specify either ascending or descending order. Microsoft Query allows you to specify up to three sort fields.

Carol wants to display the portfolio information showing the stocks in which the Horizons Fund has the largest capital investment and then showing the stocks with the smallest capital investment. The Portfolio Percent field tells you how much of the fund is invested in each stock, so you'll sort the data by the values in that field in descending order (from highest percentage to lowest).

To sort the data in the query:

1. Click the **Sort by arrow** button, and then click **Portfolio Percent** to select the sort field.
2. Click the **Descending** option button to sort the values from highest percentage to lowest percentage. See Figure 11-24.

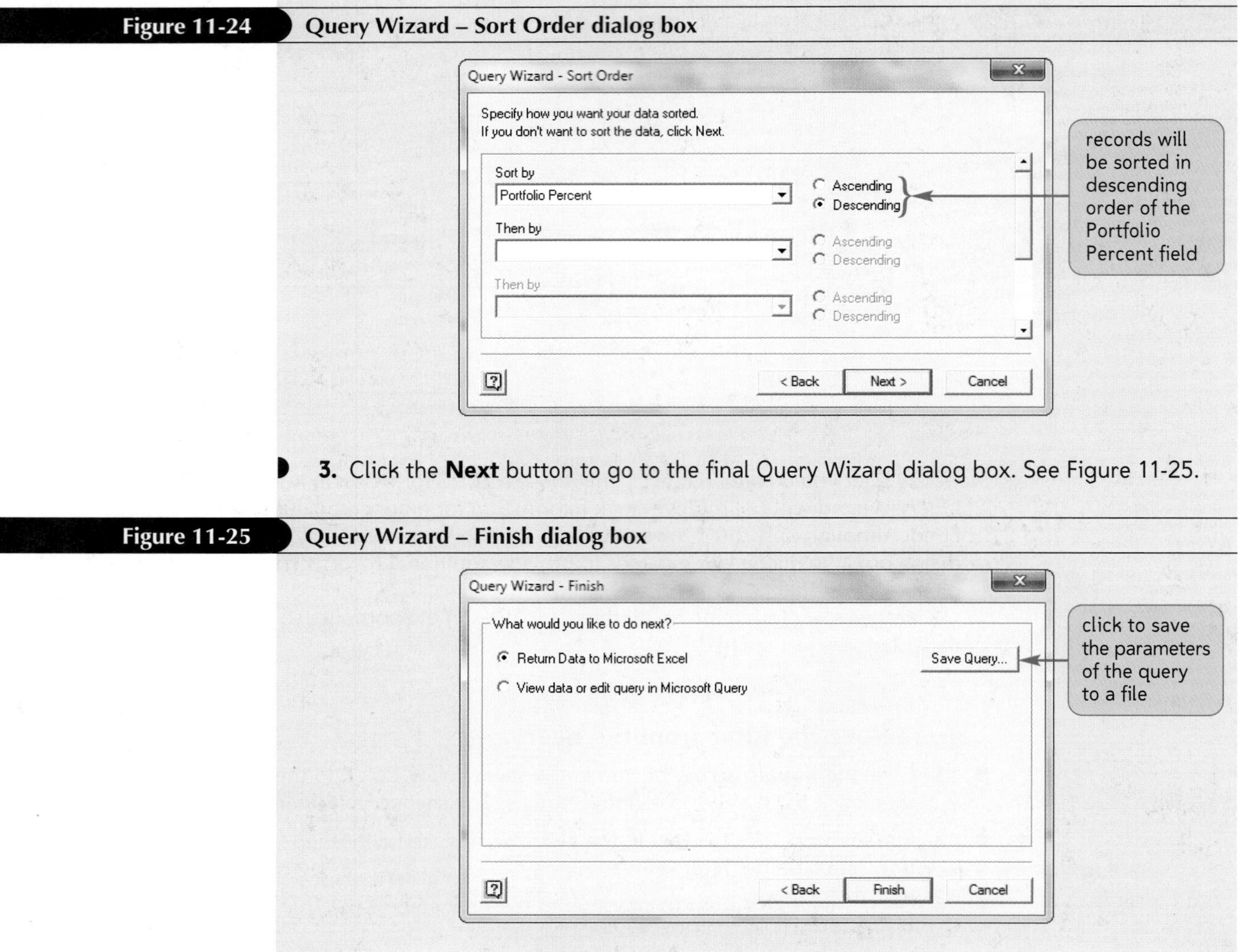

Figure 11-24 Query Wizard – Sort Order dialog box

3. Click the **Next** button to go to the final Query Wizard dialog box. See Figure 11-25.

Figure 11-25 Query Wizard – Finish dialog box

Saving a Query

When you save a query, you are placing into a file the query choices you made when you defined the query. You can later open the file and run the query without having to spend time redefining the query. You can also share the query with others who might want to extract the same information from the data source.

You can store query files in any folder you choose. You should save query files to trusted locations so that Excel can update the queries when the workbook is opened. The default folder for queries is the Queries folder located on your computer's hard drive. Saving the query file to this folder has some advantages. If you are running Excel on a network, you can make the query file accessible to other network users. Also, query files in this folder appear on the Queries tab of the Choose Data Source dialog box (refer to Figure 11-18), giving you quick access to saved queries. Query files have the .dqy file extension. After saving a query as a file, you return to the final dialog box of the Query Wizard, where you can import the data from the database into your workbook.

You have finished defining the query. Before you run the query and produce the information Carol requested, you will save the query with the name "Horizons Portfolio" because it displays a list of stocks in the Horizons Fund. You'll save the query with your other Data Files because you might not have access to the default Queries folder.

To save the query:

1. Click the **Save Query** button in the Query Wizard – Finish dialog box. The Save As dialog box opens and displays the contents of the Queries folder.
2. Navigate to the **Excel11\Tutorial** folder included with your Data Files, and then save the query as **Horizons Portfolio**. The query file is saved with your Data Files, and you return to the final step of the Query Wizard.

INSIGHT

Relational Databases and SQL

Databases such as those created in Access are examples of relational databases in which data is organized as a collection of tables with rows and columns. Relationships are also defined between the tables so that the data can be stored in smaller, more manageable chunks. Relational databases reduce data redundancy and increase data integrity.

One way to interact with a relational database is with a query language. The most popular query language is Structured Query Language (SQL). SQL consists of a series of statements that you use to define exactly how to extract data from the relational database.

Microsoft Query supports SQL. In fact, the Microsoft Query Wizard puts a friendly interface on the process of writing the SQL statement for you through your actions in the different dialog boxes in the wizard. You can view the SQL statement that the Query Wizard generates by viewing the definition of the connection for the query.

Importing Data from Microsoft Query

The Query Wizard – Finish dialog box provides two options. You can return (import) the data into the Excel workbook, or you can display the results of the query in Microsoft Query, where you can further edit the data and the query definition. Microsoft Query is an Office program that includes several tools that allow you to create even more complex queries. Because you don't need to refine the query, you won't open it in Microsoft Query. Instead, you'll import the data into the Horizons Fund workbook. With Microsoft Query, you can import the query data in the form of an Excel table, a PivotTable, or a PivotTable and PivotChart, or you can simply create the connection to the query without actually importing the data. You'll import the query data into an Excel table.

To import the query data into an Excel table:

1. Make sure the **Return Data to Microsoft Excel** option button is selected, and then click the **Finish** button. The Import Data dialog box opens so you can select where to insert the imported data.
2. Click cell **A3** in the Sheet2 worksheet to specify the location to create the Excel table.
3. Verify that the **Table** option button is selected so that the data is stored as an Excel table, and then click the **OK** button. The data from the query is imported into the worksheet at cell A3.
4. In cell A1, enter **Horizons Fund Portfolio** and then format it using the **Title** cell style.

5. Format the data in the range C4:C18 using the **Percentage** format displayed to two decimal places, and then format the data in the range D4:E18 using the **Number** format.
6. Click cell **A2** to deselect the range, rename the worksheet as **Portfolio** and then move it to the beginning of the workbook.
7. Change the zoom level of the Portfolio worksheet to **120%**. See Figure 11-26.

Figure 11-26 **Formatted Portfolio worksheet**

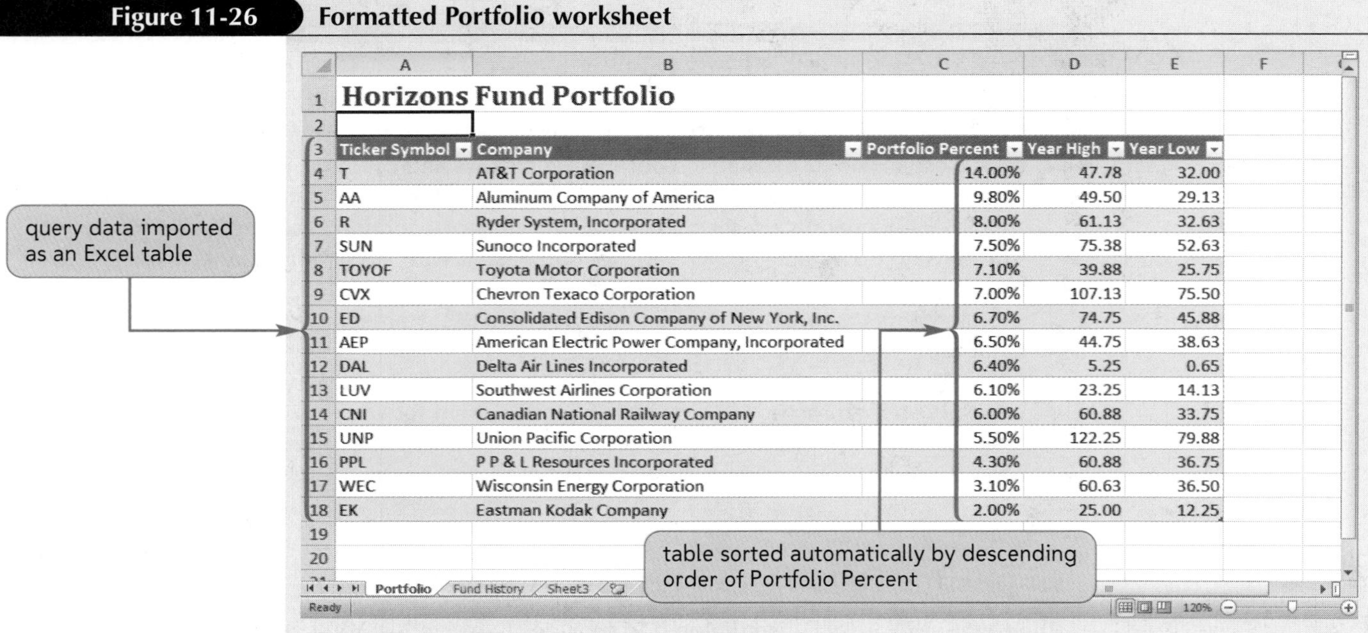

Horizons Fund Portfolio

Ticker Symbol	Company	Portfolio Percent	Year High	Year Low
T	AT&T Corporation	14.00%	47.78	32.00
AA	Aluminum Company of America	9.80%	49.50	29.13
R	Ryder System, Incorporated	8.00%	61.13	32.63
SUN	Sunoco Incorporated	7.50%	75.38	52.63
TOYOF	Toyota Motor Corporation	7.10%	39.88	25.75
CVX	Chevron Texaco Corporation	7.00%	107.13	75.50
ED	Consolidated Edison Company of New York, Inc.	6.70%	74.75	45.88
AEP	American Electric Power Company, Incorporated	6.50%	44.75	38.63
DAL	Delta Air Lines Incorporated	6.40%	5.25	0.65
LUV	Southwest Airlines Corporation	6.10%	23.25	14.13
CNI	Canadian National Railway Company	6.00%	60.88	33.75
UNP	Union Pacific Corporation	5.50%	122.25	79.88
PPL	P P & L Resources Incorporated	4.30%	60.88	36.75
WEC	Wisconsin Energy Corporation	3.10%	60.63	36.50
EK	Eastman Kodak Company	2.00%	25.00	12.25

The contents of the portfolio show that 14 percent of the fund is invested in AT&T Corporation and that the value of that stock has ranged from a high of 47.78 points to a low of 32 points. The table is sorted in descending order by the percentage of each stock in the portfolio, placing the most heavily invested stocks at the top of the list. This worksheet will help Carol understand the financial makeup of the Horizons fund.

As with the connection to the History text file, Carol wants to refresh the connection to the Horizons database whenever the workbook is opened.

To edit the properties of the connection to the Horizons database:

1. Click cell **A3** to select the Excel table, click the **Data** tab on the Ribbon, and then click the **Connections** button in the Connections group. The Workbook Connections dialog box opens, listing the two connections—History and Horizons Portfolio—active in the workbook.
2. Click **Horizons Portfolio** in the list, and then click the **Properties** button. The Connection Properties dialog box opens.
3. Type **Portfolio data imported from the Horizons database using Microsoft Query** in the Description box.
4. Verify that the **Refresh data when opening the file** check box is checked. See Figure 11-27.

Figure 11-27 Connection Properties dialog box

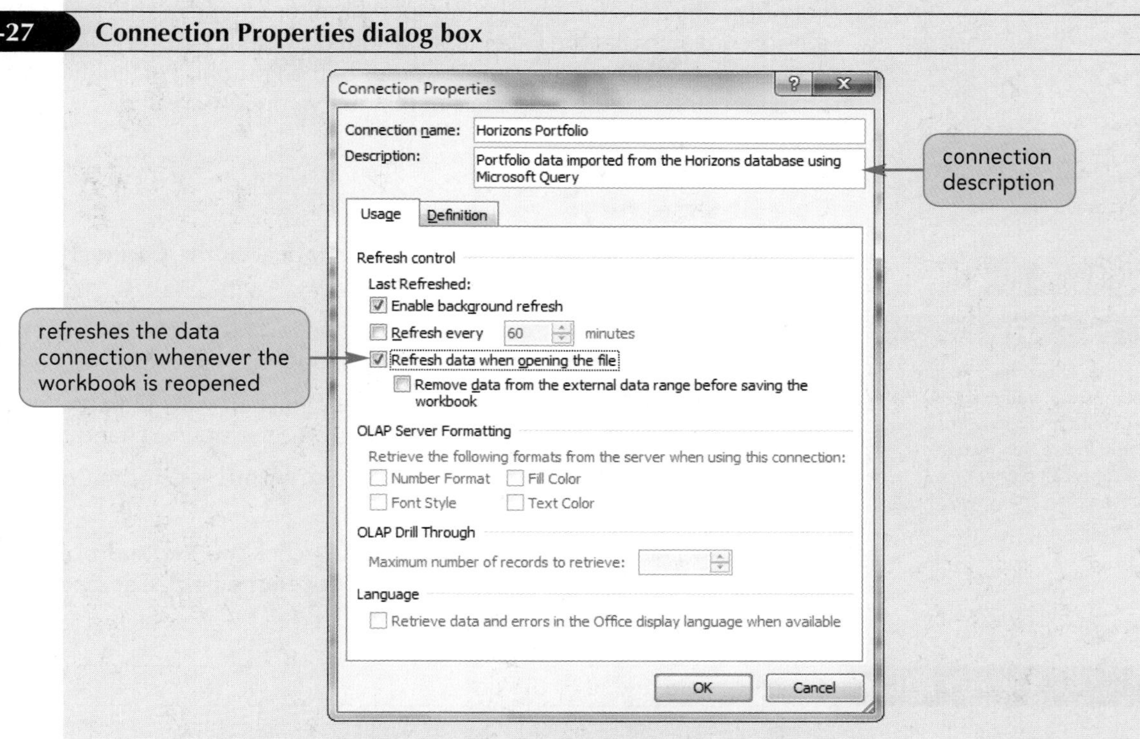

5. Click the **OK** button to close the Connection Properties dialog box, and then click the **Close** button to close the Workbook Connections dialog box.

TIP

To detach an Excel table from its data source, select a cell in the table, click the Table Tools Design tab, and then, in the External Table Data group, click the Unlink button.

The external data range for the Horizons Portfolio connection covers the Excel table in the range A3:E18 of the Portfolio worksheet. You can edit the properties of this table by clicking any cell in the table and then clicking the Properties button in the Connections group on the Data tab. Carol is pleased with the layout format and does not want you to make any changes.

Editing a Query

By editing a query, you can add new columns to your worksheet, change the sort order options, or specify a filter. You edit a query by editing the definition of the connection. When you edit the connection, Excel recognizes that the Query Wizard was used to define the parameters of the connection and restarts the Query Wizard. You can then walk through the steps of the wizard, modifying the query definition as you go.

REFERENCE

Editing a Database Query

- In the Connections group on the Data tab, click the Connections button.
- Select the connection used by the database query, and then click the Properties button.
- Click the Definition tab in the Connection Properties dialog box, and then click the Edit Query button.
- Change the query definition using the dialog boxes provided by the Query Wizard.

Carol wants you to add the Category field to the query so that she can see the category of each stock (Industrials, Transportation, or Utilities). She also wants you to change the sort order so that the Excel table is sorted by stock category first, and then within each stock category by descending order of the Portfolio Percent field. To make this change, you'll edit the properties of the query you just created.

To edit the query:

1. In the Connections group on the Data tab, click the **Connections** button. The Workbook Connections dialog box opens.
2. Click the **Horizons Portfolio** connection, and then click the **Properties** button. The Connection Properties dialog box opens.
3. Click the **Definition** tab. From this tab, you can view the current definition of the Horizons Portfolio query. You can also edit the query, changing its definition.
4. Click the **Edit Query** button. The Query Wizard – Choose Columns dialog box opens.
5. In the Available tables and column box, click the **Expand** button [+] next to Company, and then double-click the **Category** field. Category is added to the list of columns in the query. See Figure 11-28.

TIP

If you know the SQL query language, you can edit the definition directly from within the Connection Properties dialog box, bypassing the Query Wizard.

Figure 11-28 Category field added to the query

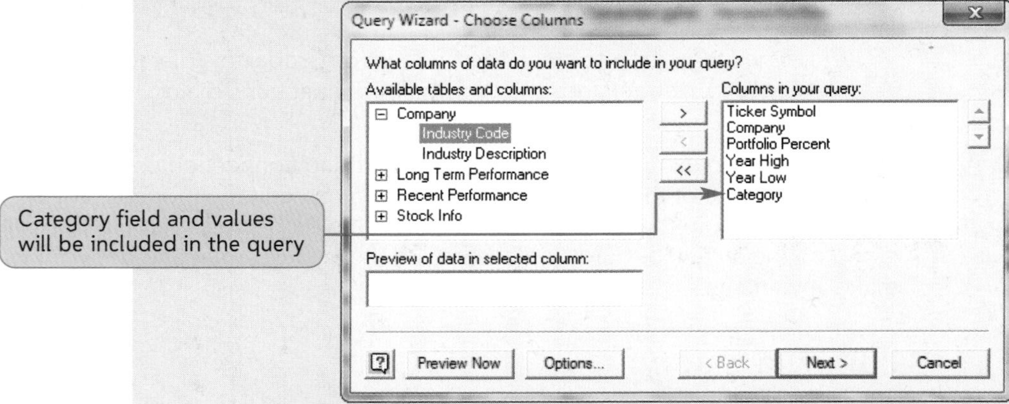

6. Click the **Next** button twice to go to the Query Wizard – Sort Order dialog box.
7. Click the **Sort by arrow** button, click **Category**, and then click the **Ascending** option button. The sort order for the query is modified.
8. Click the **Then by arrow** button, click **Portfolio Percent**, and then click the **Descending** option button. See Figure 11-29.

Figure 11-29 Modified sort order of the query

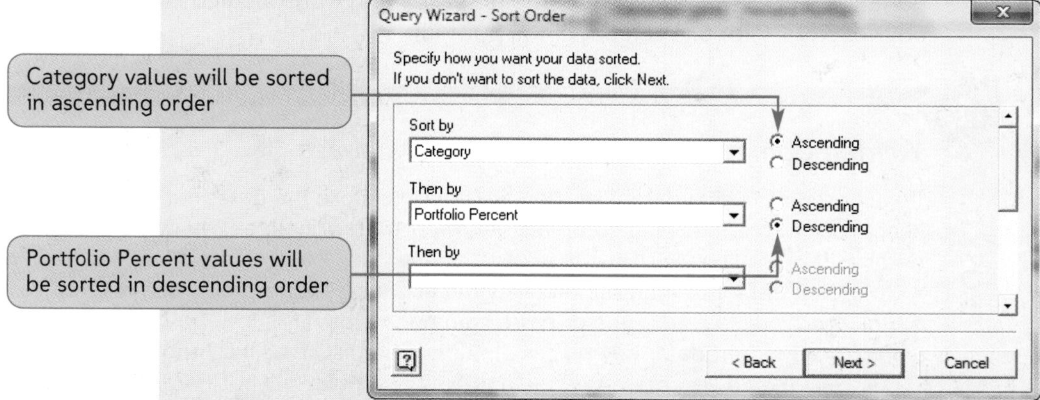

9. Click the **Next** button, and then click the **Finish** button to close the Query Wizard.
10. Click the **OK** button in the Connection Properties dialog box, and then click the **Close** button in the Worksheet Properties dialog box to return to the Portfolio worksheet. See Figure 11-30.

Figure 11-30 Revised portfolio table

Horizons Fund Portfolio

Ticker Symbol	Company	Portfolio Percent	Year High	Year Low	Category
T	AT&T Corporation	14.00%	47.78	32.00	INDUSTRIALS
AA	Aluminum Company of America	9.80%	49.50	29.13	INDUSTRIALS
SUN	Sunoco Incorporated	7.50%	75.38	52.63	INDUSTRIALS
TOYOF	Toyota Motor Corporation	7.10%	39.88	25.75	INDUSTRIALS
CVX	Chevron Texaco Corporation	7.00%	107.13	75.50	INDUSTRIALS
EK	Eastman Kodak Company	2.00%	25.00	12.25	INDUSTRIALS
R	Ryder System, Incorporated	8.00%	61.13	32.63	TRANSPORTAT
DAL	Delta Air Lines Incorporated	6.40%	5.25	0.65	TRANSPORTAT
LUV	Southwest Airlines Corporation	6.10%	23.25	14.13	TRANSPORTAT
CNI	Canadian National Railway Company	6.00%	60.88	33.75	TRANSPORTAT
UNP	Union Pacific Corporation	5.50%	122.25	79.88	TRANSPORTAT
ED	Consolidated Edison Company of New York, Inc.	6.70%	74.75	45.88	UTILITIES
AEP	American Electric Power Company, Incorporated	6.50%	44.75	38.63	UTILITIES
PPL	P P & L Resources Incorporated	4.30%	60.88	36.75	UTILITIES
WEC	Wisconsin Energy Corporation	3.10%	60.63	36.50	UTILITIES

Portfolio / Fund History / Sheet3

Ready

Category column added to the query results

data is sorted by Category and then by descending Portfolio Percent within each category

The fund is composed of 15 stocks—with six industrial stocks, five transportation stocks, and four utility stocks. The most heavily invested stocks within each category are AT&T, an industrial stock with 14 percent of the portfolio; Ryder System, Inc., a transportation stock with 8 percent of the portfolio; and Consolidated Edison of New York, a utilities stock with 6.7 percent of the portfolio.

PROSKILLS

Written Communication: Designing a Database

If you intend to use a database such as Access to store the data that you'll view in Excel, keep in mind the following common, yet important, principles when designing your database:

- Split your data into multiple tables with each table focused on a specific topical area. Link the tables through one or more common fields.
- Avoid redundant data. Key pieces of information, such as a customer's address or phone number, should be entered in one and only one place in your database.
- Use understandable field names. Avoid using acronyms or abbreviations that may confuse your users.
- Maintain consistency in data entry. For example, if you abbreviate titles (such as Mr. instead of Mister), include data entry checks that ensure this rule is always followed.
- Avoid the occurrence of blank field values. A blank field can be subject to misinterpretation as to whether the field value is really blank or it has not been entered yet. Identify missing field values with a code word or symbol.
- Avoid the use of field dividers such as commas, semicolons, and tabs in your field values. If you export your database table to a text file, such characters can be erroneously interpreted as representing new or separate columns within the field.
- Test your database on a small subset of your data before committing your entire data. The more errors you weed out early, the easier it will be to manage your database.

Databases are great tools to organize information, track statistics, and generate reports. When used in conjunction with Excel, a properly designed database can provide valuable information and help you make informed financial decisions. However, like any tool, they must be used correctly. A badly designed or improperly used database will end up creating more problems rather than solving them.

Importing Data into PivotTables and PivotCharts

The Recent Performance table in the Horizons database contains a record of the last five days of stock market activity for each of the 15 stocks in the Horizons Fund. Figure 11-31 shows the contents of the Recent Performance table.

Figure 11-31 Recent Performance table

Recent Performance

Ticker Symbol	Date	Volume	High	Low	Closing
AA	09/16/2013	364300	38.75	38	38.25
AA	09/17/2013	412300	38.625	37.125	37.25
AA	09/18/2013	650100	37.25	36	36.75
AA	09/19/2013	891200	39.25	36.75	37.625
AA	09/20/2013	459500	38	36.625	36.625
AEP	09/16/2013	134100	41.625	41.125	41.25
AEP	09/17/2013	1481100	41.625	40.75	41.125
AEP	09/18/2013	1761000	40.875	40.5	40.625
AEP	09/19/2013	459300	41.375	40.75	41.375
AEP	09/20/2013	494100	41.75	41.25	41.75
CNI	09/16/2013	339900	47.75	47	47.75
CNI	09/17/2013	297900	47.25	46.75	47
CNI	09/18/2013	120800	46.875	46	46.25
CNI	09/19/2013	58100	46.625	46	46.625
CNI	09/20/2013	161500	46.875	46.375	46.625
CVX	09/16/2013	590600	75.5	73	75.5
CVX	09/17/2013	796700	76.5	74.625	75.375
CVX	09/18/2013	1140000	76	72.75	73.875
CVX	09/19/2013	964000	73.875	71	72
CVX	09/20/2013	1310000	73	71.625	72.5

Record: 1 of 75 No Filter Search

Carol wants to connect the Horizons Fund workbook to this data, creating a chart and table that show the recent activity of each stock. You could create 15 charts and tables, one for each stock in the fund. However, this approach would result in a workbook that would be difficult to manage. Besides, Carol wants to create similar workbooks for other databases that contain records of hundreds of stocks and funds.

Another option is to create a PivotTable and PivotChart that display market values from the past five days. You can use the PivotTable and PivotChart tools to select and display values from only one stock at a time, adding only a single table and chart to the workbook rather than 15. A second advantage of a PivotTable and PivotChart is that the data used in the table and chart can be stored in an external data source. As the user interacts with the table and chart, the needed data is retrieved from the data source, freeing your workbook from having to store data that is not immediately required.

TIP

Always document your connections to external data so that users can see what the data is used for and where it came from.

All of the five-day stock data you need for the report is stored in the Recent Performance table, so your first step is to establish a connection to the table. Because you'll be working with only this one table and not several tables from the Horizons database, you don't have to use the Query Wizard. Instead, you can import the table's contents directly. As you establish the connection, you can use the Connection Properties dialog box to provide a name and description of the connection.

To import data into a PivotTable and PivotChart:

1. Rename the Sheet3 worksheet as **Recent Performance**, move the worksheet between the Portfolio and Fund History worksheets, and then change the zoom level to **120%**.
2. In cell A1, enter **Horizons Fund Recent History** and then format the text using the **Title** cell style.

3. In cell A2, enter **5-Day Stock Report** as the report title, format cell A2 with the **Heading 1** cell style, and then remove the border from cell A2.
4. Click cell **A6**, click the **Data** tab on the Ribbon, and then click the **From Access** button in the Get External Data group. The Select Data Source dialog box opens.
5. Select the **Horizons** database file located in the Excel11\Tutorial folder included with your Data Files, and then click the **Open** button. The Select Table dialog box opens.
6. Click **Recent Performance** in the Name column, and then click the **OK** button. The Import Data dialog box opens. Before importing the recent performance data, you'll change the properties of this connection.
7. Click the **Properties** button to open the Connection Properties dialog box, and then type **Horizons Fund Recent History** in the Connection name box.
8. Type **Retrieves data from the Recent Performance table in the Horizons database** in the Description box, and then click the **Refresh data when opening the file** check box so that Excel refreshes the data in this connection whenever the workbook is opened.
9. Click the **OK** button to return to the Import Data dialog box.
10. Click the **PivotChart and PivotTable Report** option button, and then click the **OK** button. An empty PivotTable and PivotChart are added to the Recent Performance worksheet. See Figure 11-32.

Figure 11-32 PivotTable and PivotChart added to the worksheet

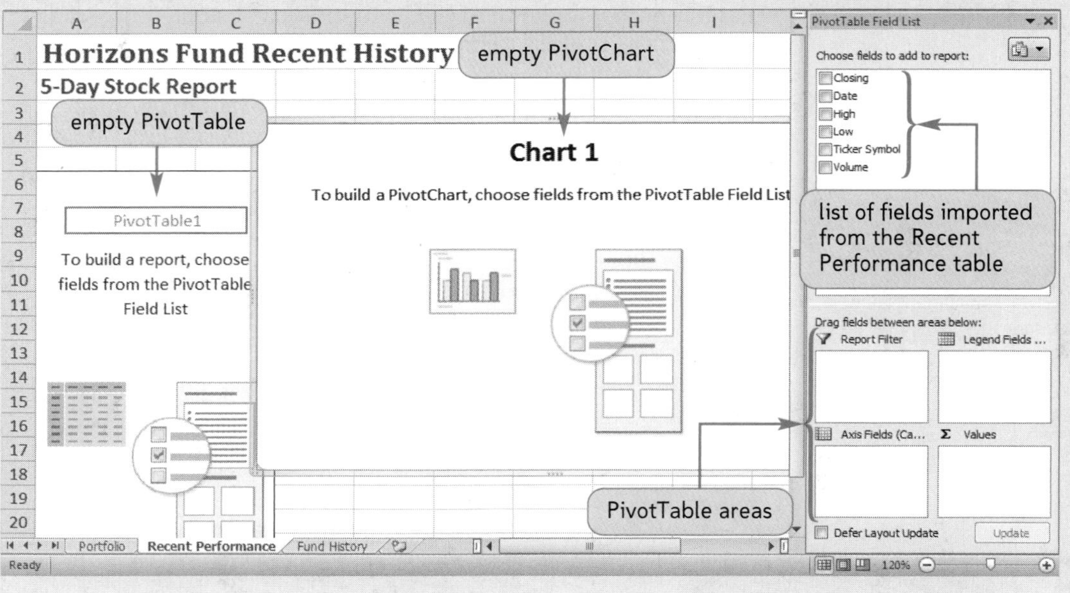

When Excel imports external data into a PivotTable or PivotChart, the initial table and chart are empty because you have not defined yet where to place the different fields from the data source. The fields of the Recent Performance table are all displayed in the PivotTable Field List. You'll create the PivotTable for Carol.

To set the PivotTable layout:

1. Drag the **Ticker Symbol** field from the PivotTable Field List to the Report Filter area. The Ticker Symbol field is the report filter, allowing you to display stocks from one company—or ticker symbol—at a time.
2. Drag the **Date** field to the Axis Fields area. The Date field from the five-day data will appear as an axis or category field in the PivotTable.
3. Drag the **High**, **Low**, and **Closing** fields into the Values area in that order. The High, Low, and Closing fields will be the values displayed in the table and chart. You won't use the Volume field in this table and chart. See Figure 11-33.

Figure 11-33 PivotTable and PivotChart area set

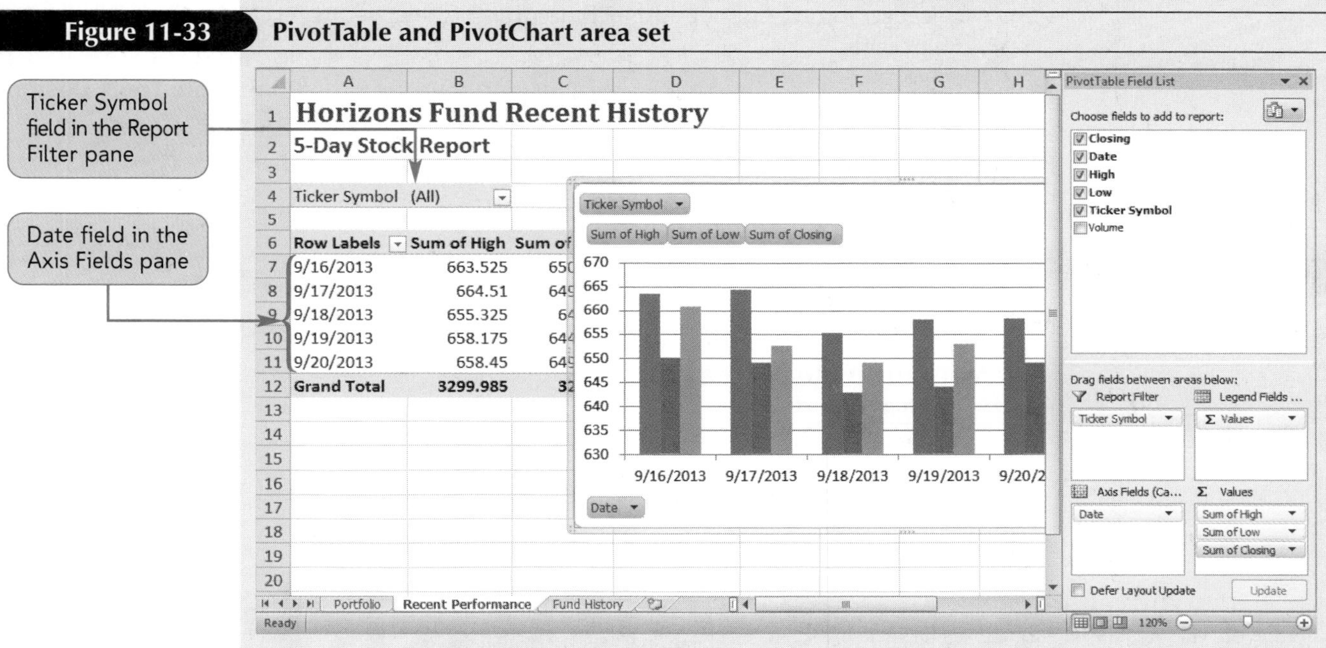

The Data area labels read "Sum of" before the name of each field. This label is misleading because only one value appears for these items for each stock on each day, so the PivotTable shows a "sum" of only one record. The table will display individual volume and stock values, so you will change the labels to prevent others from interpreting them as the sum of many values. You'll also specify the format for these values.

To change the labels and format the data values in the PivotTable:

1. Click the **Sum of High** button in the Values area, and then click **Value Field Settings**. The Value Field Settings dialog box opens.
2. Type **High Value** in the Custom Name box.
3. Click the **Number Format** button to open the Number tab in the Format Cells dialog box, and then click **Number** in the Category list. You'll use this default number format.
4. Click the **OK** button in both dialog boxes.
5. Repeat Steps 1 through 4 for the Sum of Low and Sum of Closing entries in the Values pane, renaming Sum of Low as **Low Value** and Sum of Closing as **Closing Value**.
6. Close the PivotTable Field List pane to display more of the worksheet containing the PivotTable and PivotChart.

   Because you do not need to include grand totals, you can remove them from the PivotTable.
7. Click cell **A4** to select the PivotTable, and then click the **PivotTable Tools Design** tab on the Ribbon.
8. In the Layout group, click the **Grand Totals** button, and then click **Off for Rows and Columns**. See Figure 11-34.

Figure 11-34 Formatted PivotTable data

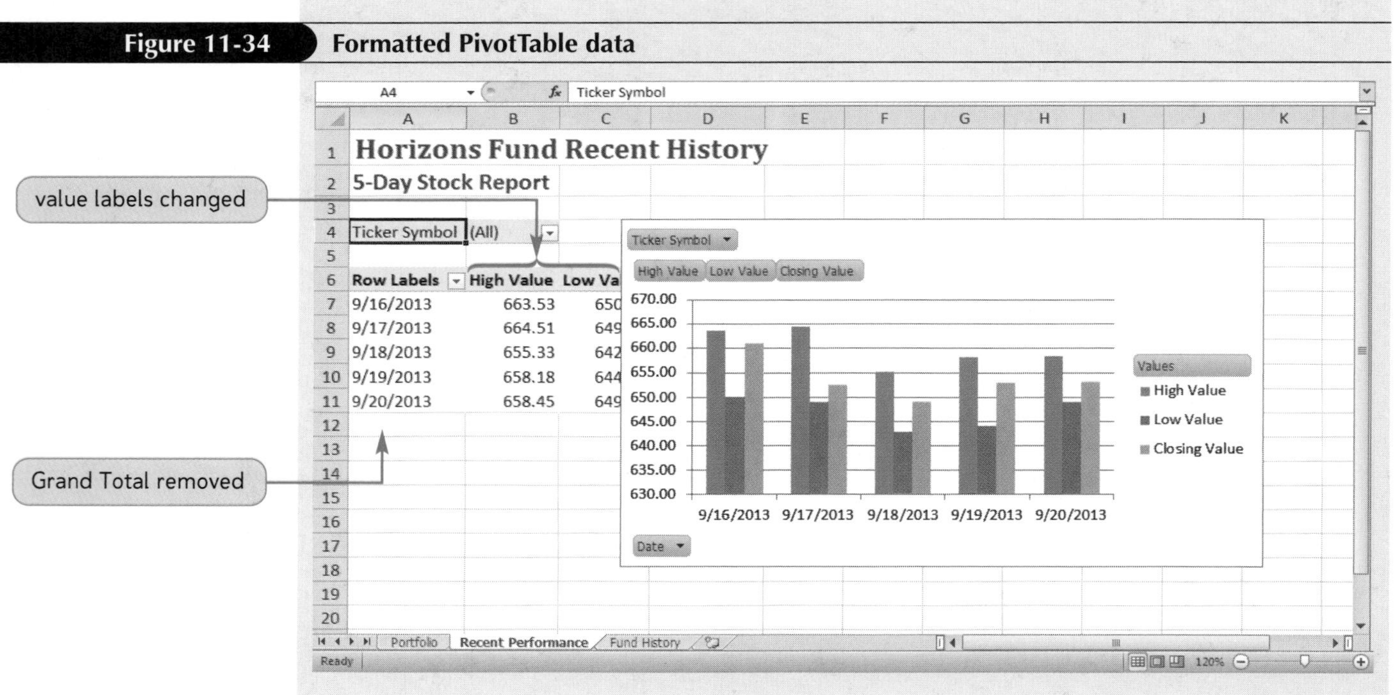

Finally, you need to format the PivotChart. Carol wants you to resize the chart smaller and move it closer to the PivotTable. She also wants you to change the chart type from a column chart to a line chart. Finally, she wants you to add an appropriate title to the chart.

To format the PivotChart:

1. Move and resize the PivotChart so that it covers the range **E4:K19**.
2. Insert the chart title **Recent Performance** above the chart, and change the font size of the title to **12** points.
3. Change the chart type from Column to **Line**.
4. Click cell **A3** to deselect the PivotTable and PivotChart. See Figure 11-35.

Figure 11-35 Formatted PivotChart

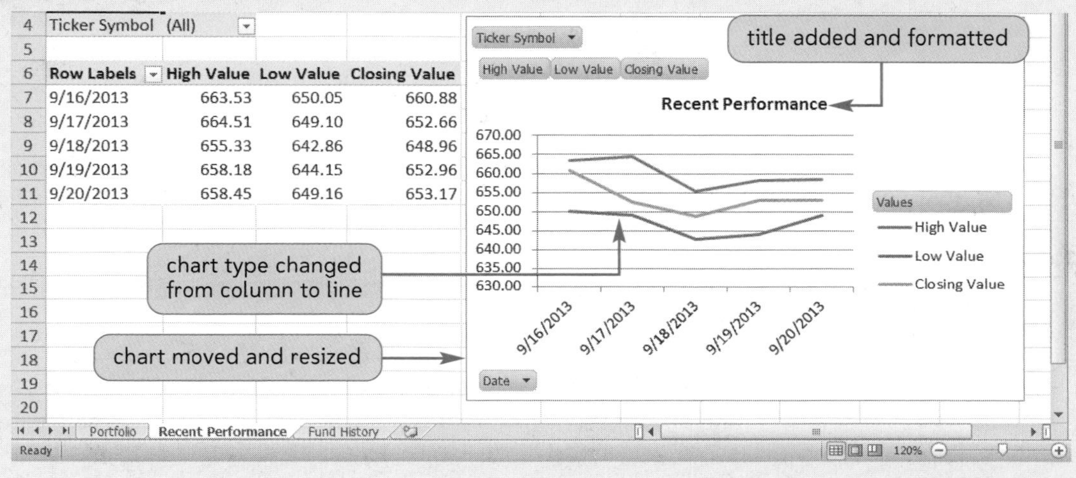

The line chart gives you a quick view of each stock's low, high, and closing values. By default, the PivotTable and PivotChart show the sum of these values over all of the stocks in the portfolio. Those values are not very useful. However, by clicking the Ticker Symbol arrow button, you can quickly view the daily values from the last five days for any individual stock in the portfolio.

To view the recent performance of the Toyota stock:

1. Click the **Ticker Symbol arrow** button in cell B4 of the PivotTable.
2. Click **TOYOF** in the list of ticker symbols, and then click the **OK** button. See Figure 11-36.

Figure 11-36 Recent performance of the Toyota stock

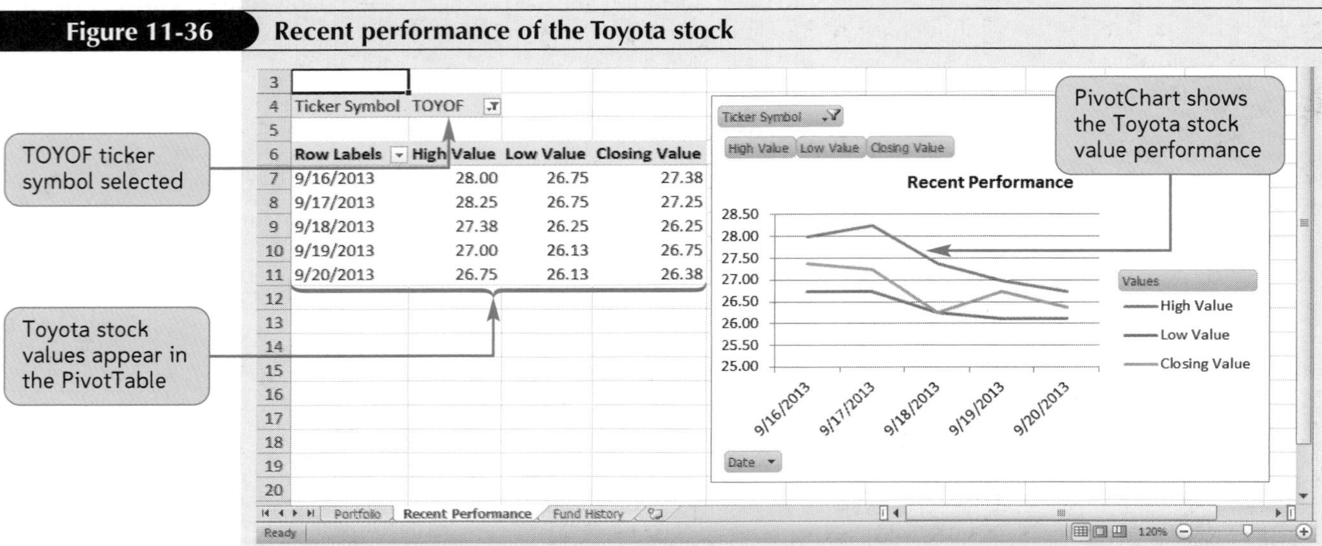

3. Click the **Ticker Symbol arrow** button and select other stocks, verifying that you can view the five-day history for any stock from the Recent Performance table.

INSIGHT

Working with Connection Files

Connection information is stored within the workbook, allowing users to interact with their connections as they design their Excel project. For more extensive projects, you can store connections in an external file such as an Office Data Connection (ODC) file or a Universal Data Connection (UDC) file. It's a good idea to use connection files when you want to share information about a connection with other users, use the same connection in multiple workbooks, or create a library of connection files for use with large database structures.

To manually save a connection to an ODC file, use the Export Connection File button on the Definition tab of the Connection Properties dialog box to specify the name and location of your Office Data Connection file. The default location for ODC files is the My Data Sources subfolder of the Documents folder (or the My Documents folder in Windows Vista and Windows XP). ODC files are added to the My Data Sources subfolder whenever you create a connection to an Access database table. UDC files are not created within Excel. To create a UDC file, you can use Microsoft InfoPath for creating and designing XML-based data entry forms for businesses.

To access a connection file, click the Existing Connections button in the Get External Data group on the Data tab to select the connection file from your workbook, your network, or your computer.

In this session, you explored how to connect an Excel workbook to an Access database. You used the Query Wizard to retrieve data from several database tables, and you connected directly to the Access database when you wanted only one table. From the database, you created an Excel table, a PivotTable, and a PivotChart for Carol's report. Carol is pleased with your progress and wants to look for more sources of data that she can use in the Horizons Fund workbook.

REVIEW

Session 11.2 Quick Check

1. Define the following terms: (a) *database,* (b) *table,* (c) *field,* (d) *record,* (e) *common field.*
2. What is a query?
3. How do you edit a query?
4. How do you create a PivotTable and PivotChart based on an external data source?
5. What is the advantage of using external data in a PivotTable rather than importing data into the workbook and creating a PivotTable from the imported data?
6. What is SQL?
7. List two places that connection information can be stored.

SESSION 11.3 VISUAL OVERVIEW

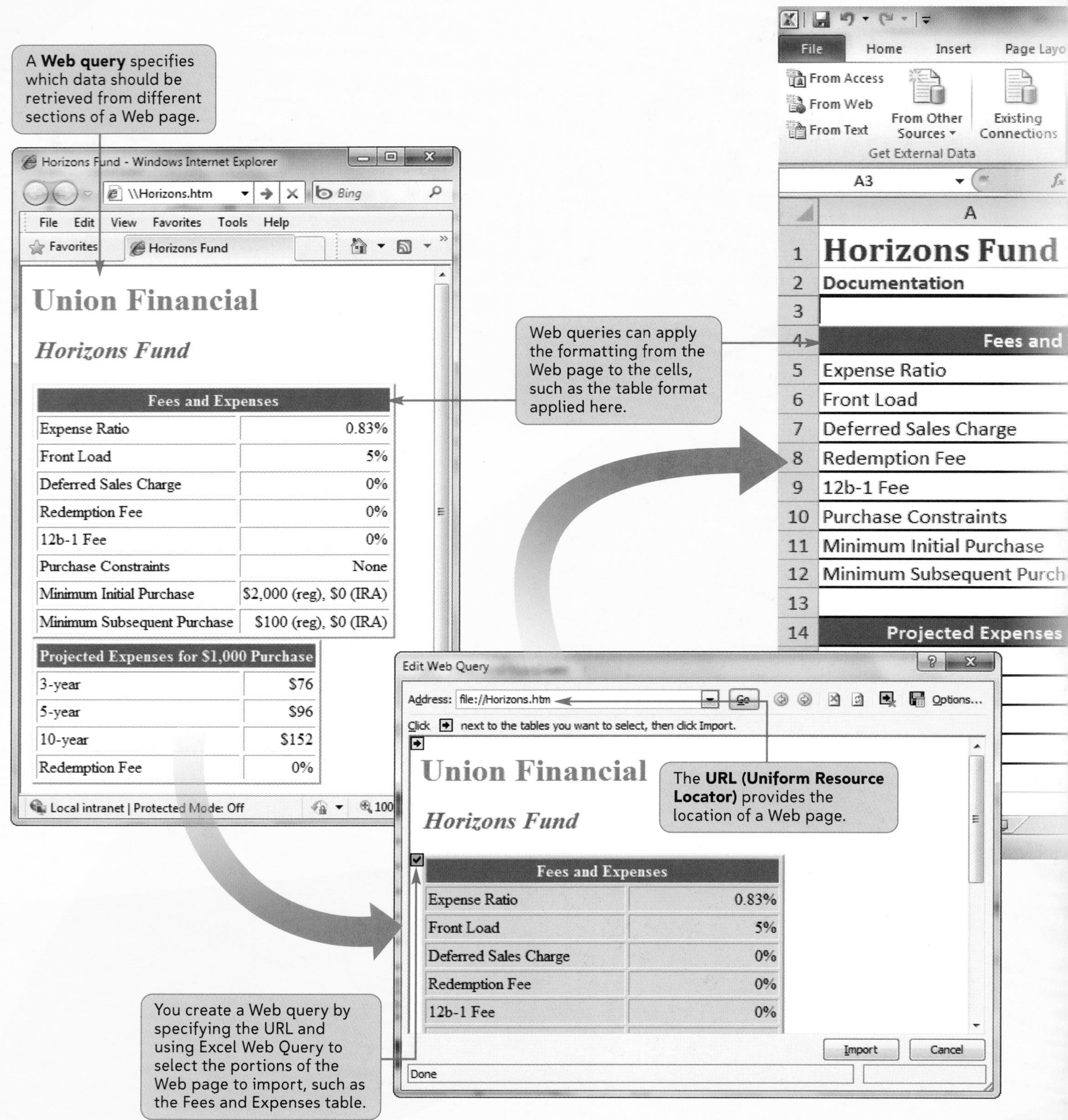

WEB AND XML CONNECTIONS

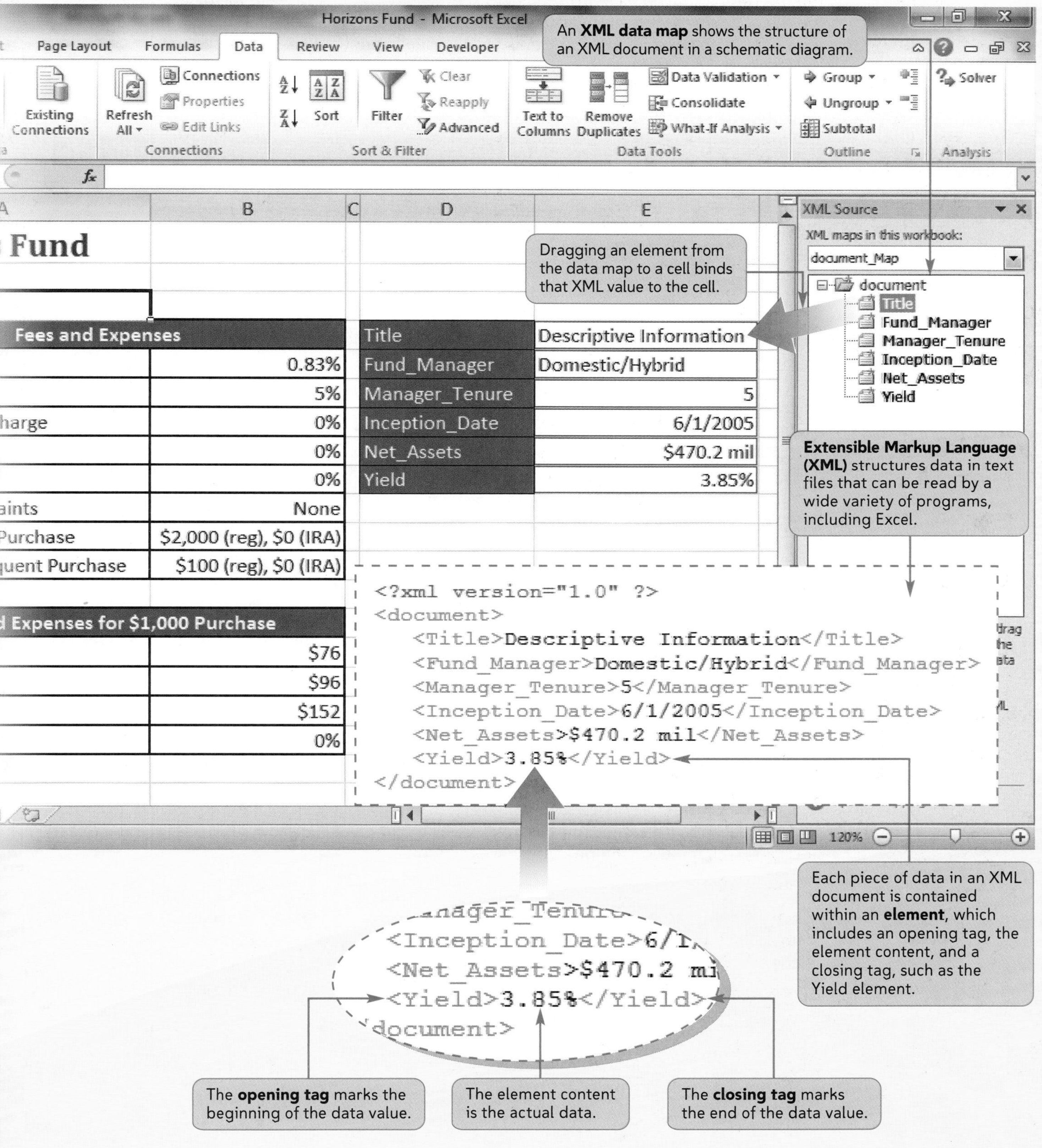

Creating a Web Query

Union Financial often stores corporate information on its Web server to be displayed on the company Web page. To keep her Excel workbooks in sync with the data stored on the company's Web site, Carol wants to create a query that retrieves data from the company Web page. The Union Financial Web site includes pages that describe the various funds the company supports. The Horizons Fund Web page shown in Figure 11-37 provides descriptive information about the fund, such as the fund's manager and its inception date.

Figure 11-37 Horizons Fund Web page

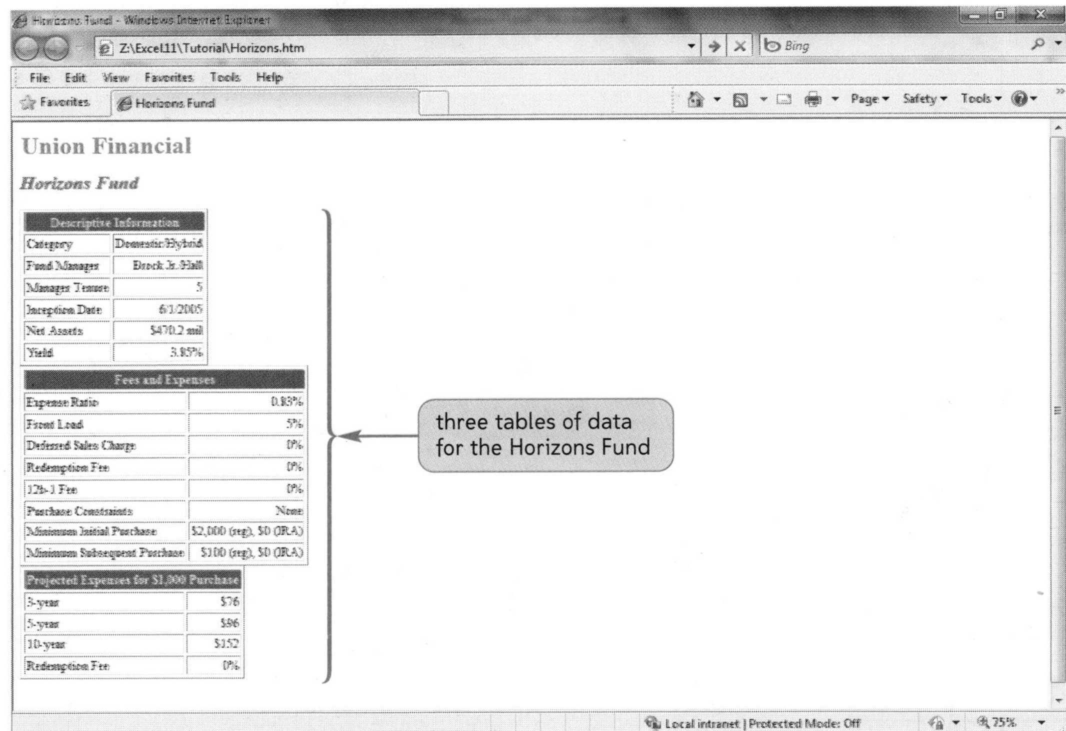

You could copy and paste the data from the Web page into the workbook, but Carol wants to create a query between the Web page and the workbook so that the workbook always matches the material on the company's Web site. To create this Web query, you need to know the URL of the page you're accessing. A copy of the Horizons Fund's information Web page, Horizons.htm, is included with your Data Files. If the file is stored on a Web server, the URL will probably have the form

`http://`*`server/path/filename`*

where *server* is the name of the computer or Web server storing the page, *path* is the path to the folder on the server in which the page is stored, and *filename* is the name of the Web page file. For Union Financial, the URL for the Horizons HTML file is:

`http://www.ufcompany.com/docs/History.htm`

When a file is stored locally and not on a Web server, the general form of a URL is

`file:///`*`drive:/path/filename`*

where *drive* is the letter of the drive containing the file, *path* is the full path name of the folder containing the file, and *filename* is the filename of the Web page. For example, if the Data Files are on drive Z and Horizons.htm is located in the Excel11\Tutorial folder, the URL is:

```
file:///Z:/Excel11/Tutorial/Horizons.htm
```

If you don't include the "file:" prefix for the URL, your computer will attempt to locate the file on the Web and not in a folder stored locally on your computer. If you don't want to enter this long string of text, you can also enter the path to the folder and Web page file in the more standard form:

```
Z:\Excel11\Tutorial\Horizons.htm
```

The Web query will replace this text with the URL form.

REFERENCE

Working with Web Queries

To create a Web query:
- In the Get External Data group on the Data tab, click the From Web button.
- Enter the URL of the Web site or the folder path to a local file in the Address box of the New Web Query dialog box.
- Click the selection arrows for the parts of the Web page you want to retrieve.
- Click the Import button.

To set the Web query format options:
- Open the Connection Properties dialog box for the query.
- Click the Edit Query button on the Definition tab.
- Click the Options button and select the format options in the Web Query Options dialog box.

To save a Web query:
- Open the Connection Properties dialog box for the query.
- Click the Edit Query button on the Definition tab.
- Click the Save Query button in the Edit Web Query dialog box and specify the filename and location of the Web query file.

You'll create a connection to the Horizons HTML file from the Horizons Fund workbook.

To create a Web query to import the Horizons Web page:

1. If you took a break at the end of the previous session, make sure the Horizons Fund workbook is open.
2. Insert a new worksheet named **Horizons Fund** at the beginning of the workbook, and then change the zoom level of the worksheet to **120%**.
3. In cell A1, enter **Horizons Fund** and then format the text using the **Title** cell style.
4. In cell A2, enter **Summary**, format the cell using the **Heading 1** cell style, and then remove the border from cell A2.
5. Click cell **A4**, click the **Data** tab on the Ribbon, and then click the **From Web** button in the Get External Group. The New Web Query dialog box opens.
6. In the Address box, enter the path to the Horizons.htm file located in the Excel11\Tutorial folder included with your Data Files, and then press the **Enter** key. For example, if the file is located in the Documents\Data\Excel11\Tutorial folder of drive E, enter E:\Documents\Data\Excel11\Tutorial\Horizons.htm. The contents of the Web page appear in the dialog box. See Figure 11-38.

TIP

To find the exact path to the Horizons.htm file, open the file in your Web browser and copy the path from the browser's Address box into the Address box of the New Web Query dialog box.

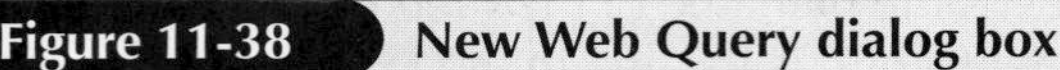

Figure 11-38 New Web Query dialog box

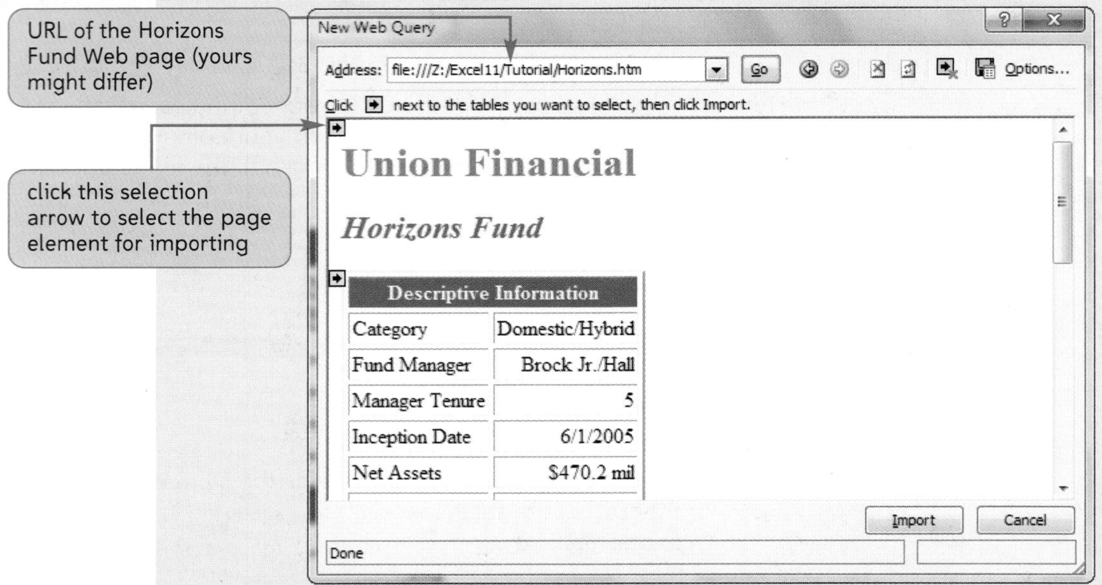

7. Click the **selection arrow** next to the Descriptive Information table to select the table. The selection arrow changes to a check mark to indicate that this table is selected.
8. Scroll down, click the **selection arrow** next to the Fees and Expenses table, and then click the **selection arrow** next to the Projected Expenses for $1,000 Purchase table. The check marks indicate that these sections of the Web page are selected.
9. Click the **Import** button. The Import Data dialog box opens.
10. Verify that the data will be placed starting in cell A4 of the existing worksheet, and then click the **OK** button. The Web content is imported into the Horizons Fund worksheet. See Figure 11-39.

Figure 11-39 Horizons Fund Web page content imported into the workbook

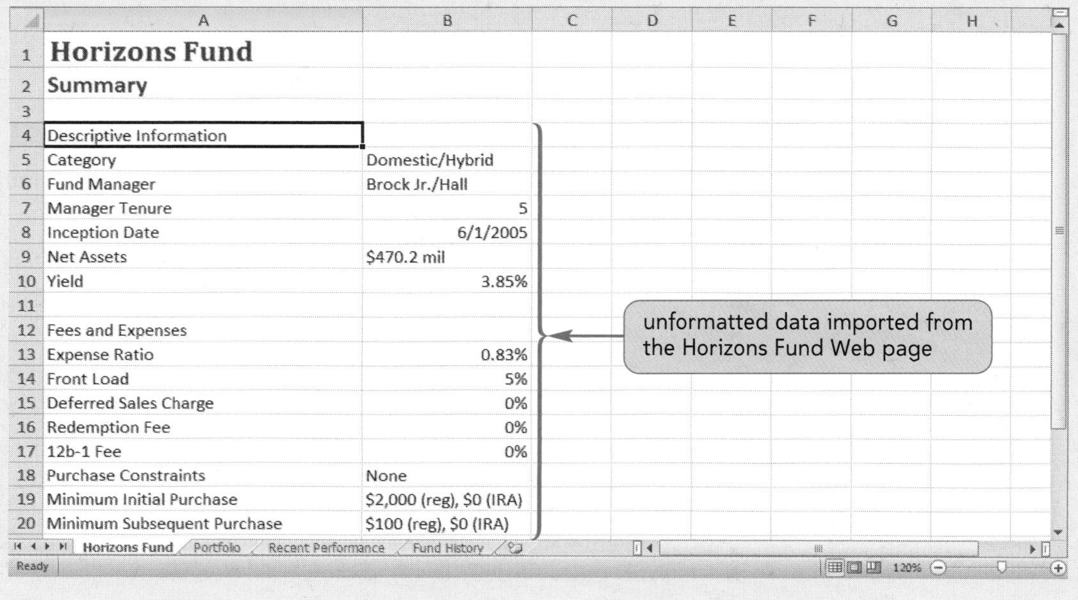

Formatting a Web Query

The text from the Web query has been placed into the worksheet as unformatted text. If you format this text, the formatting is preserved when Excel refreshes the data later. Another option is to retrieve both the Web page data and the styles used on the Web page.

You can retrieve the Web page format using None (the default, which imports the text but not the formatting), Rich text formatting only, or Full HTML formatting. **Rich Text Format** (**RTF**) is a file format that allows for text formatting styles including boldface, italic, and color, but not advanced features such as hyperlinks or complicated table structures. The Full HTML formatting option retrieves all simple as well as advanced HTML formatting features, including hyperlinks. Full HTML formatting results in imported data that most closely resembles the appearance of the Web page.

Carol wants the text on this page to resemble the Web page. You'll format the Web query you just created to use full HTML formatting by modifying the connection properties.

To format the Web query:

1. In the Connections group on the Data tab, click the **Connections** button. The Workbook Connections dialog box opens.
2. Click **Connection** in the Name column, if necessary, and then click the **Properties** button. The Connection Properties dialog box opens.
3. Type **Horizons Fund Web Page** in the Connection name box, type **Retrieves summary information from the Horizons Fund Web page** in the Description box, and then click the **Refresh data when opening the file** check box.
4. Click the **Definition** tab, and then click the **Edit Query** button. The Edit Web Query dialog box opens and displays the contents of the Horizons HTML file.
5. Click the **Options** button on the Edit Web Query toolbar. The Web Query Options dialog box opens.
6. Click the **Full HTML formatting** option button to specify that this Web query should retrieve the HTML formatting along with the Web page text, and then click the **OK** button.
7. Click the **Import** button, click the **OK** button, and then click the **Close** button. The worksheet is updated, reflecting the full HTML formatting of the original Web page. See Figure 11-40.

Figure 11-40 **Formatted Horizons Fund worksheet**

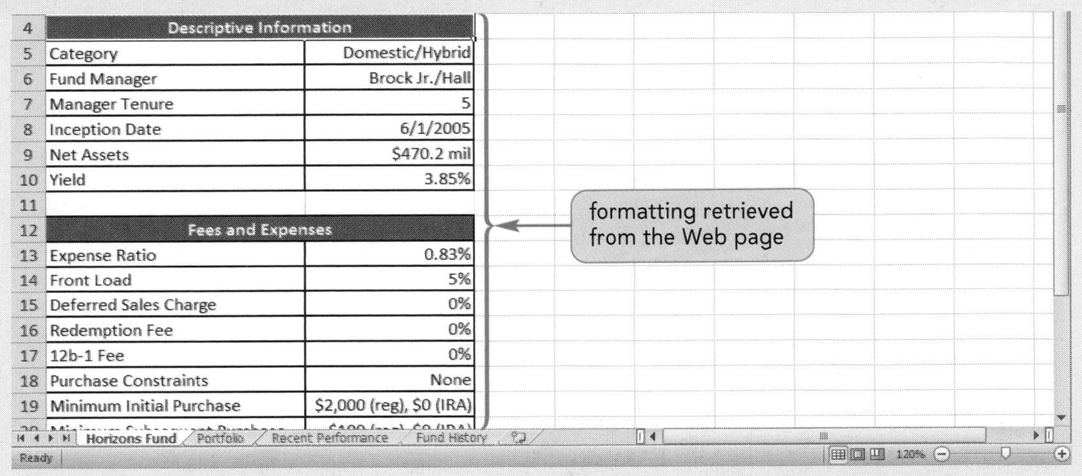

Saving a Web Query

You can save the Web query to a permanent file that you share among other Office documents. The saved connection file can then be loaded in any Office program. For example, after saving the Horizons Fund Web Page Web query, Carol can retrieve the contents of the Horizons Fund Web page and display it in a Word document. Because Carol wants to place the Horizons Fund information in other workbooks, you'll save the Horizons Fund Web Page Web query in a permanent file.

To save the Horizons Fund Web Page Web query:

1. In the Connections group on the Data tab, click the **Connections** button. The Workbook Connections dialog box opens.
2. Click **Horizons Fund Web Page** in the Name column, and then click the **Properties** button. The Connection Properties dialog box opens.
3. Click the **Definition** tab, and then click the **Edit Query** button. The Edit Web Query dialog box opens.
4. Click the **Save Query** button on the Edit Web Query toolbar. The contents of the Microsoft\Queries folder are listed in the Save Workspace dialog box. This is the default folder in which all queries are placed. In this case, you'll save the query file in the Excel11\Tutorial folder.
5. Navigate to the **Excel11\Tutorial** folder included with your Data Files, type **Horizons Web Query** in the File name box, and then click the **Save** button to save the Web query.
6. Click the **Import** button, click the **OK** button, and then click the **Close** button to return to the workbook.

TIP

Web query files are simple text files that you can view and edit in Notepad. If you understand the Web query language, you can create sophisticated programs to retrieve and process Web data.

Importing Data from the Web

Carol often needs to know how the stocks in the Horizons Fund portfolio are doing at each moment. That information is available on the Web, where up-to-the-minute stock values are posted for online traders and brokers. You can use a Web query to retrieve online data and import it into a workbook. Excel has several Web query files stored in a library of built-in Web queries. These files are similar to the query file you just created and saved, except that they define how to retrieve data from a page on the Web.

Retrieving Multiple Stock Quotes

Carol's sample database includes 15 stocks, and she wants to be able to view current information on all of them. One of the Web query files that Excel supplies is the MSN MoneyCentral Investor Stock Quotes query. You can enter up to 20 **ticker symbols** (abbreviations for the stock names used by the market) in the query, and then the query retrieves the current market values of those stocks and places the information into a table in the workbook. Some of the built-in queries include parameters that you can enter to specify exactly what information is imported. For the MSN MoneyCentral Investor Stock Quotes query, you have to specify the stock values to be imported by entering their ticker symbols. This information has already been entered in the Portfolio worksheet.

You will begin by creating a new worksheet for the current stock values, and then opening the query file for the MSN MoneyCentral Investor Stock Quotes query.

To retrieve current stock quotes:

1. Insert a new worksheet named **Current Values** to the right of the Portfolio worksheet, and then change the zoom level of the worksheet to **120%**.
2. In cell A1, enter **Horizons Fund Stocks** and then format the text using the **Title** cell style.
3. In cell A2, enter **Current Quotes**, format the text using the **Heading 1** cell style, and then remove the border from cell A2.
4. Click cell **A4**.
5. In the Get External Data group on the Data tab, click the **Existing Connections** button. The Existing Connections dialog box opens, listing all of the connections available to the workbook. See Figure 11-41.

TIP

To list your connection file in the Existing Connections dialog box, place it in your My Data Sources folder.

Figure 11-41 **Existing Connections dialog box**

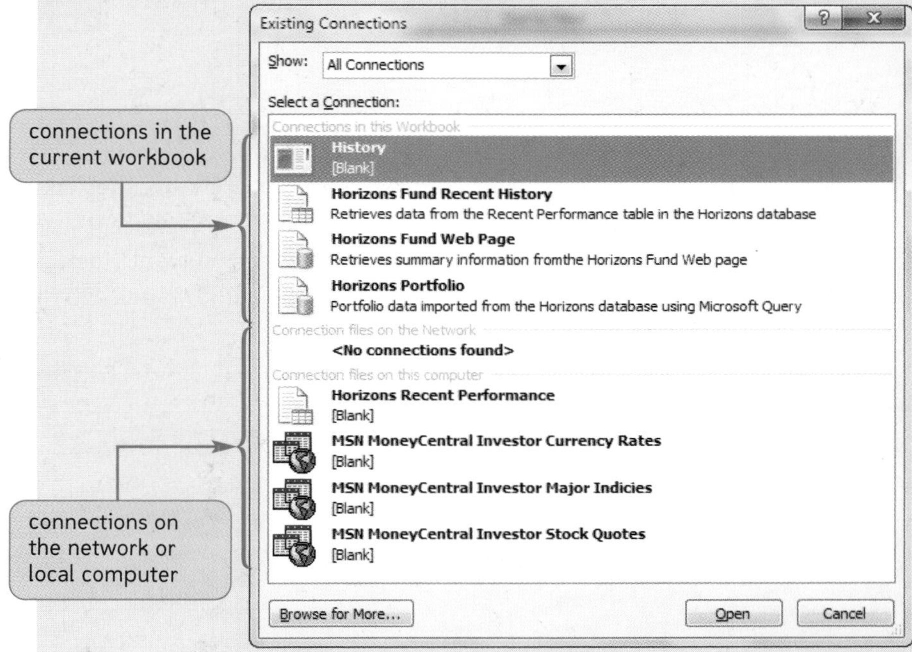

6. Click **MSN MoneyCentral Investor Stock Quotes**, and then click the **Open** button. The Import Data dialog box opens.
7. Verify that Excel will place the data in cell A4 of the existing worksheet, and then click the **OK** button. The Enter Parameter Value dialog box opens.
8. Click the **Portfolio** sheet tab, and then select the range **A4:A18**, which includes the ticker symbols for the stocks whose values you want to import. The range reference =Portfolio!$A$4:$A$18 appears in the dialog box. See Figure 11-42.

Figure 11-42 **Enter Parameter Value dialog box**

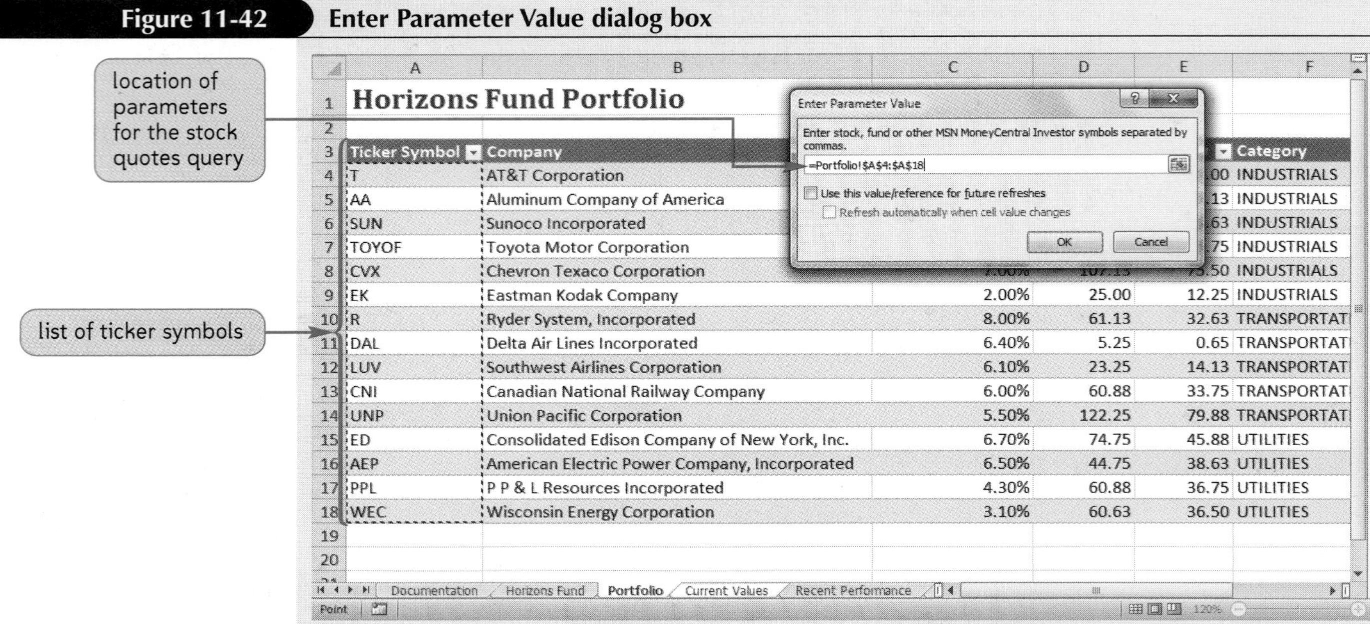

9. Click the **Use this value/reference for future refreshes** check box to insert a check mark. Excel will always use the ticker symbols from the Portfolio worksheet.

10. Click the **OK** button. Excel retrieves the most current stock information on the 15 stocks in the Horizons Fund portfolio and displays that data in the Current Values worksheet. See Figure 11-43.

Figure 11-43 **Stock quotes imported from the Web**

TIP

The MSN MoneyCentral Web page stock values are at least 20 minutes old because the service is free. If you need real-time stock reports, you must pay for that capability from an online investment firm.

Horizons Fund Stocks

Current Quotes

Stock Quotes Provided by MSN Money

Click here to visit MSN Money

			Last	Previous Close	High	Low
AT&T Inc	Chart	News	24.3	24.63	24.73	24.29
Alcoa Inc	Chart	News	11.64	11.82	11.79	11.54
Sunoco Inc	Chart	News	29.87	29.88	30.16	29.21
TOYOTA MOTOR CORP	Chart	News	36.6	36.73	36.6	36.41
Chevron Corp	Chart	News	73.87	74.36	74.4	73.04
Eastman Kodak Co	Chart	News	5.64	5.89	5.92	5.6
Ryder System Inc	Chart	News	44.94	45.47	45.54	44.4
Delta Air Lines Inc	Chart	News	13.58	13.95	13.91	13.4
Southwest Airlines Co	Chart	News	12.44	12.64	12.64	12.31
Canadian National Railway Co	Chart	News	57.37	57.92	58.98	57.27
Union Pacific Corp	Chart	News	71.43	71.55	72.13	70.56
Consolidated Edison Inc	Chart	News	42.59	42.74	42.98	42.44
American Electric Power Co Inc	Chart	News	31.96	31.99	32.28	31.78

Horizons Fund | Portfolio | Current Values | Recent Performance | Fund History

Ready

Trouble? If your screen looks different from Figure 11-43, some of the ticker symbols are no longer listed on the stock exchange due to the changing nature of the stock market.

Based on the Web query results, Carol has a good idea of how the stocks in the database are doing at the moment. Because stock values can change a great deal from the time she first opens the workbook, you can manually refresh the data connections in the workbook at any time.

To manually refresh the Web query:

1. In the Connections group on the Data tab, click the **Refresh All button arrow**. A menu of refresh commands opens.
2. Click **Refresh**. Excel updates the stock values on the Current Values worksheet.

   Trouble? If you don't have access to the Internet, you cannot refresh the data in the Web query. Continue with the tutorial.

Another way to ensure current stock results is to have Excel periodically refresh the stock quotes for you by editing the properties of the connection to the Web site. Carol wants the data refreshed every 10 minutes while the workbook is open.

To periodically update the stock quotes:

1. In the Connections group on the Data tab, click the **Connections** button. The Workbook Connections dialog box opens.
2. Click the **MSN MoneyCentral Investor Stock Quotes** connection, and then click the **Properties** button. The Connection Properties dialog box opens.
3. Enter **Retrieves current quotes for stocks in the Horizons Fund** in the Description box.
4. Click the **Refresh data when opening the file** check box to insert a check mark. Excel will update the stock values automatically when opening the workbook.
5. Click the **Refresh every** check box to insert a check mark, and then type **10** in the minutes box. Excel will update the stock values every 10 minutes while the workbook is open.
6. Click the **OK** button in the Connection Properties dialog box, and then click the **Close** button in the Workbook Connections dialog box to return to the workbook.

The Web query results in the Current Values worksheet include hyperlinks to documents that contain additional information about the stocks in the portfolio. Carol can click a hyperlink when she wants more detailed information about a particular stock. She can even use a hyperlink to access the home page of each company listed in the fund. You will try the hyperlink associated with AT&T.

To use the AT&T hyperlink:

1. Point to the **AT&T Inc.** hyperlink in cell A7. The URL appears in a ScreenTip.

   Trouble? If the AT&T hyperlink does not appear in your workbook, point to a different hyperlink and continue with Step 2.

2. Click the link. Your default Web browser starts and displays a Web page describing the current financial status of AT&T stock. See Figure 11-44.

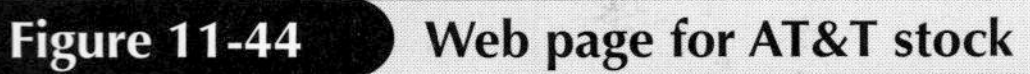

Figure 11-44 Web page for AT&T stock

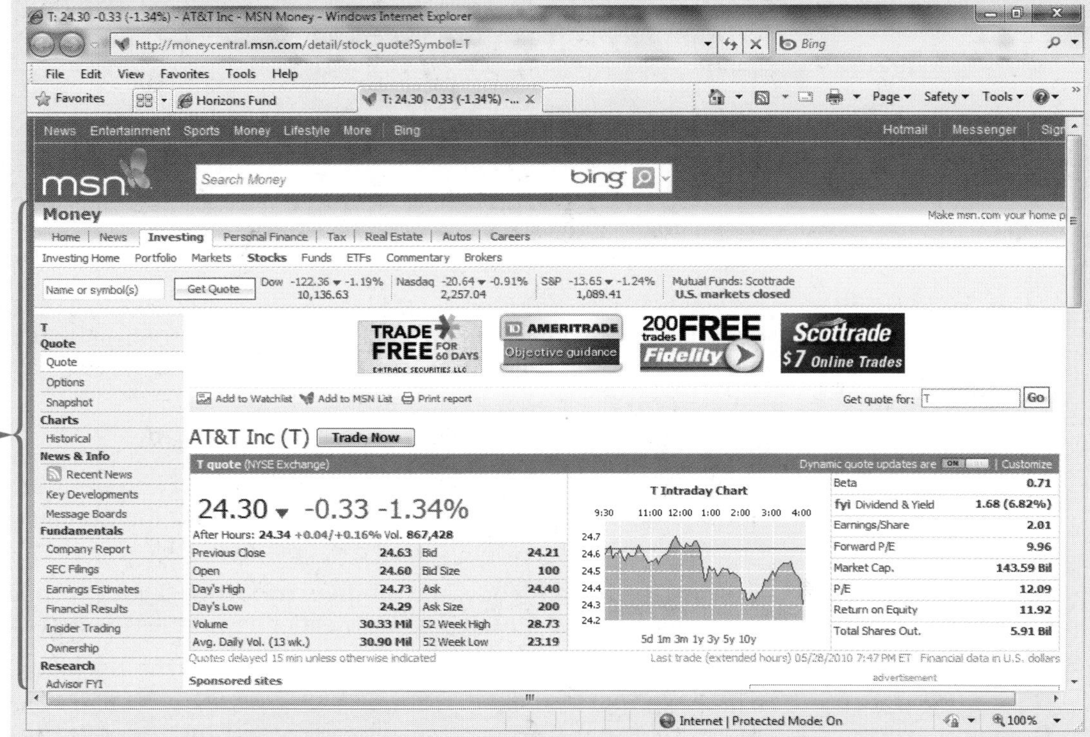

your Web page and stock information might differ

Trouble? If your screen looks different from Figure 11-44, you are probably using a Web browser other than Internet Explorer, such as Firefox. The numeric values of the Web page you retrieve will be different because the values change rapidly over time. If the links do not open any Web pages, ask your instructor or technical support person for help.

3. Review the Web page, and then close your Web browser and return to the Horizons Fund workbook.

Importing Data from XML

The final data source you will examine for Carol's workbook involves an XML document. XML has been widely used in database programs, Web programming, and word processing. Office 2010 files are stored in an XML-based file format called **Office Open XML format**. Union Financial stores much of its data in XML documents that can be read and processed by a wide range of XML-based programs.

A programmer at Union Financial has created an XML document that contains information on the workbook you've been using. Figure 11-45 shows the contents of this XML document, named Data.xml.

Figure 11-45 **Contents of the Data.xml file**

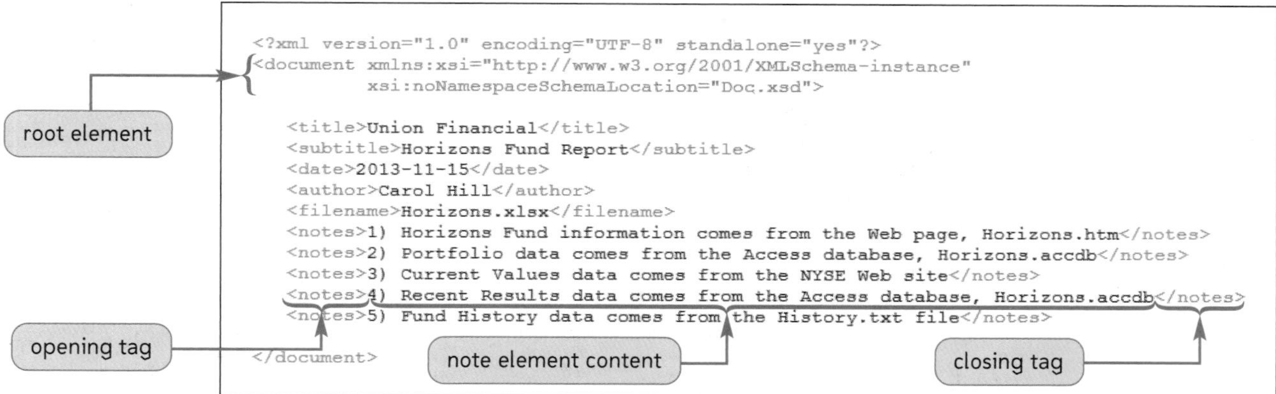

```
<?xml version="1.0" encoding="UTF-8" standalone="yes"?>
<document xmlns:xsi="http://www.w3.org/2001/XMLSchema-instance"
          xsi:noNamespaceSchemaLocation="Doc.xsd">

   <title>Union Financial</title>
   <subtitle>Horizons Fund Report</subtitle>
   <date>2013-11-15</date>
   <author>Carol Hill</author>
   <filename>Horizons.xlsx</filename>
   <notes>1) Horizons Fund information comes from the Web page, Horizons.htm</notes>
   <notes>2) Portfolio data comes from the Access database, Horizons.accdb</notes>
   <notes>3) Current Values data comes from the NYSE Web site</notes>
   <notes>4) Recent Results data comes from the Access database, Horizons.accdb</notes>
   <notes>5) Fund History data comes from the History.txt file</notes>

</document>
```


In Figure 11-45, the opening and closing tags are highlighted in red to make it easier to differentiate the element tags from the data they contain. For example, the following code contains the data marked by the author element. In this case, the value is the text string *Carol Hill.*

```
<author>Carol Hill</author>
```

An XML document is structured like a tree in which elements are placed within one another, descending from a common **root element**. In the XML document shown in Figure 11-45, the root element is called document and contains six elements named title, subtitle, date, author, filename, and notes. Figure 11-46 shows a data map for the root element and nested elements from the Data.xml file.

Figure 11-46 **Data map of the Data.xml document**

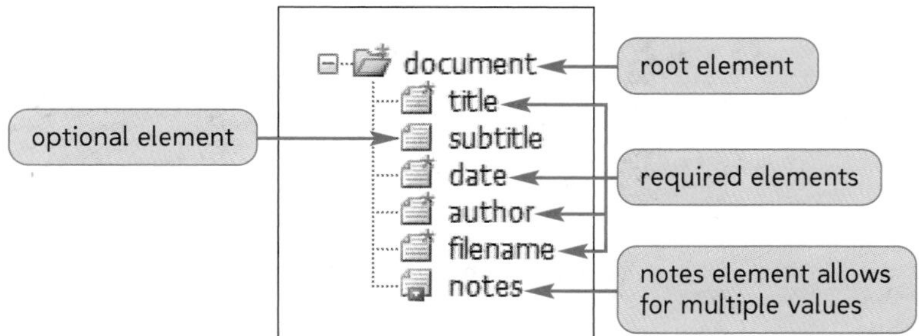

One advantage of XML is that the XML author defines what makes up a valid document, indicating which elements are required and which are optional. The document author can also indicate what type of values each element can contain. Documents that fail to meet these rules can be rejected by an XML program as invalid, ensuring data integrity. Information about the requirements for a valid XML document is also displayed in the data map. Required elements are shown with a red star. The required elements in the Data.xml file are document, title, date, author, and filename. An element containing other elements is displayed using a folder icon, whereas an element that only contains data is displayed with a document icon. In the Data.xml file, only the document element contains other elements. Finally, an element can allow for multiple values. This is indicated with a document icon containing an arrow. Only the notes element in the Data.xml file allows for multiple values, with each note specifying a different piece of information about the data sources for Carol's workbook.

The rules about which elements are required and which are not, as well as which elements support multiple values and which only allow for a single value, are stored in a second document called a **schema**. Schemas are not required in XML, but they are useful in ensuring that any data inserted into an XML document follows predefined rules for both content and structure. Carol has created a schema for the Data.xml file, which she stored in a text file named Doc.xsd. Like the data file, schema files are also stored as text files.

When you connect to an XML document, Excel creates a data map of the document's structure and contents. If a schema is present, Excel uses it to create the data map; otherwise, it creates the map based on the contents of the XML document. After the data map is created, you can use it to place XML elements anywhere within the workbook.

Loading an XML Data Map

The commands to access the data map of an XML document are part of the Excel Developer tools. To work with an XML data map, you must show the Developer tab on the Ribbon. If the XML document has a schema file attached to it, you can load a data map without actually importing the data into the Excel workbook.

REFERENCE

Loading an XML Data Map

- In the XML group on the Developer tab, click the Source button.
- In the XML Source task pane, click the XML Maps button.
- Locate and select the XML document file.
- Click the Rename button within the XML Maps dialog box to define a name for the map.

To see how you can load a data map without importing the data, you'll load the data map for the Data.xml file.

To load the data map for the Data.xml file:

1. If the Developer tab is not on the Ribbon, use the Excel Options dialog box to customize the Ribbon to show the Developer tab.
2. Click the **Developer** tab on the Ribbon, and then click the **Source** button in the XML group. The XML Source task pane opens on the right side of the workbook window. From this pane, you can load the data map for the Data.xml file.
3. Click the **XML Maps** button at the bottom of the XML Source task pane. The XML Maps dialog box opens.
4. Click the **Add** button to add an XML data map to the workbook. The Select XML Source dialog box opens.

5. Click the **Data** file located in the Excel11\Tutorial folder included with your Data Files, and then click the **Open** button. The document map for the Data.xml file is added to the list of XML maps in the current workbook and assigned the default name document_map.
6. Click the **Rename** button, type **Horizons Fund XML Data**, and then press the **Enter** key to give the data map a more descriptive name.
7. Resize the **Name** column to display the entire name. See Figure 11-47.

Figure 11-47 XML Maps dialog box

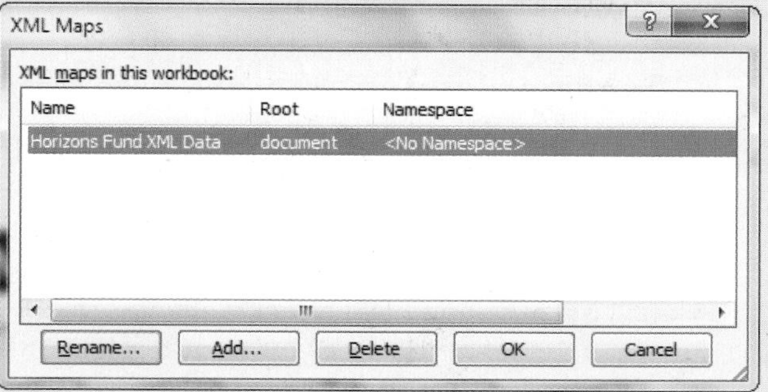

8. Click the **OK** button. The Horizons Fund XML Data map is loaded into Excel and appears in the XML Source task pane. See Figure 11-48.

Figure 11-48 Data map in the XML Source task pane

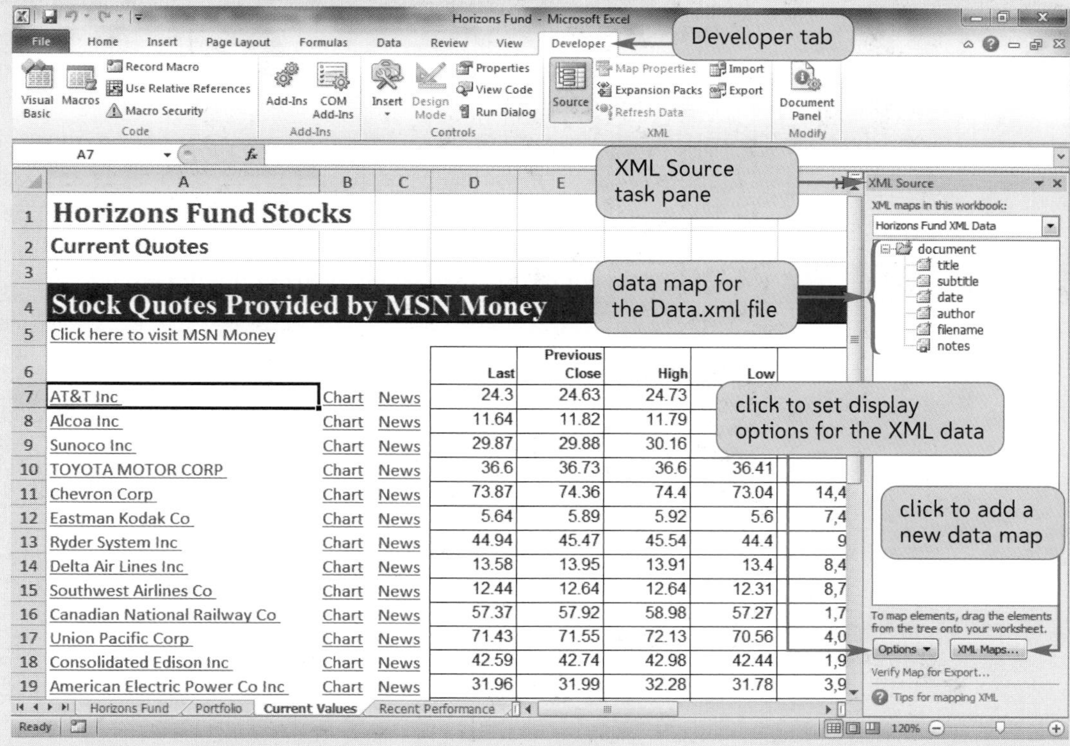

Binding XML Elements to a Worksheet

One advantage of using XML as a data source is that it allows you to attach, or **bind**, elements to specific cells in the workbook, providing you with greater freedom in designing a worksheet layout. To bind an element to a cell, you drag the element name from the XML map and drop it into the cell. After you drop the element, you can place the element name above or to the right of the cell (if those locations are available). If a Header Options button appears next to a cell, you can click the button to define where you want to place an element's name (if you want it displayed at all). The Header Options button does not appear for elements you place in the leftmost column of the worksheet because no room is available to place the element name to the left of or above the element data.

You'll bind the elements of the Data.xml file to cells in a Documentation worksheet.

To place elements from the data map into the workbook:

1. Insert a new worksheet named **Documentation** at the beginning of the workbook, and then change the zoom level of the worksheet to **120%**.
2. In the XML Source task pane, click **title** in the Horizons Fund XML Data map and drag it to cell A1 in the Documentation worksheet. No data appears in the cell because you have not actually imported the contents of the Data.xml file. You've only defined where you want to place the contents of the title element.
3. Drag **subtitle** from the data map to cell A2 of the Documentation sheet.
4. Drag **author** from the data map to cell B4. When you drop the author element into cell B4, the Header Options button appears to the right of cell B4. You can select the Header Options button to determine where to place the author element name.
5. Click the **Header Options** button, and then click the **Place XML Heading to the Left** option button.
6. Repeat Steps 4 and 5 to place the **date** and **filename** elements in cells B5 and B6, respectively.
7. Drag the **notes** element from the data map to cell B8. Because this element can contain multiple values, Excel places it into the cell as an Excel table. The element name is placed above the table in cell B8. See Figure 11-49.

TIP

To map an XML document directly into an Excel table, click the From Other Sources button in the Get External Data group on the Data tab, and then click From XML Data Import.

Figure 11-49 Completed layout of the XML elements from the data map

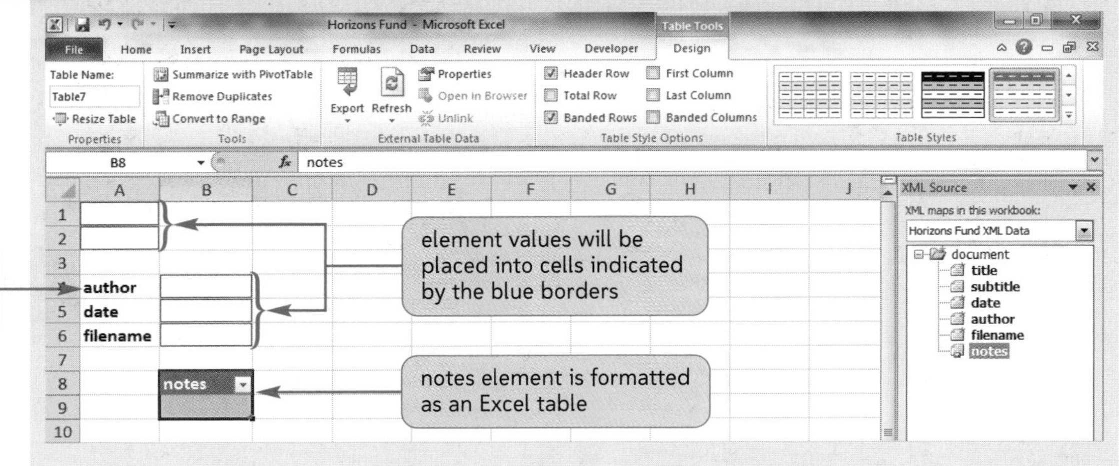

Importing XML Data

By using XML and the data map, you placed the elements in specific locations in the Documentation worksheet. Because these cells are now bound with elements from the XML file, you can import the XML data directly into the worksheet cells.

To retrieve the XML data, you refresh the connection to the data source. Excel will automatically place the data in the correct worksheet cells. You can also format the Documentation worksheet. Formatting the worksheet does not affect Excel's ability to retrieve and display the data from the XML document.

To import data from the Data.xml file:

1. Click the **Data** tab on the Ribbon, and then click the **Connections** button in the Connections group. The connection you made to the Data.xml file is listed as Data in the Workbook Connections dialog box.
2. Verify that **Data** is selected in the list of workbook connections, click the **Refresh button arrow**, and then click **Refresh**. Excel refreshes the connection to the Data.xml file, importing the data into the Documentation worksheet.
3. Click the **Properties** button to open the Connection Properties dialog box, type **Horizons Fund Report** in the Connection name box, and then type **Retrieves information about the Horizons Fund Report from the Data.xml file** in the Description box to provide descriptive information about the connection established to the Data.xml file.
4. Click the **OK** button, and then click the **Close** button.
5. Format cell A1 with the **Title** cell style, format cell A2 with the **Heading 4** cell style, and then click cell **A3**. See Figure 11-50.

Figure 11-50 Binding XML data to cells in the Documentation sheet

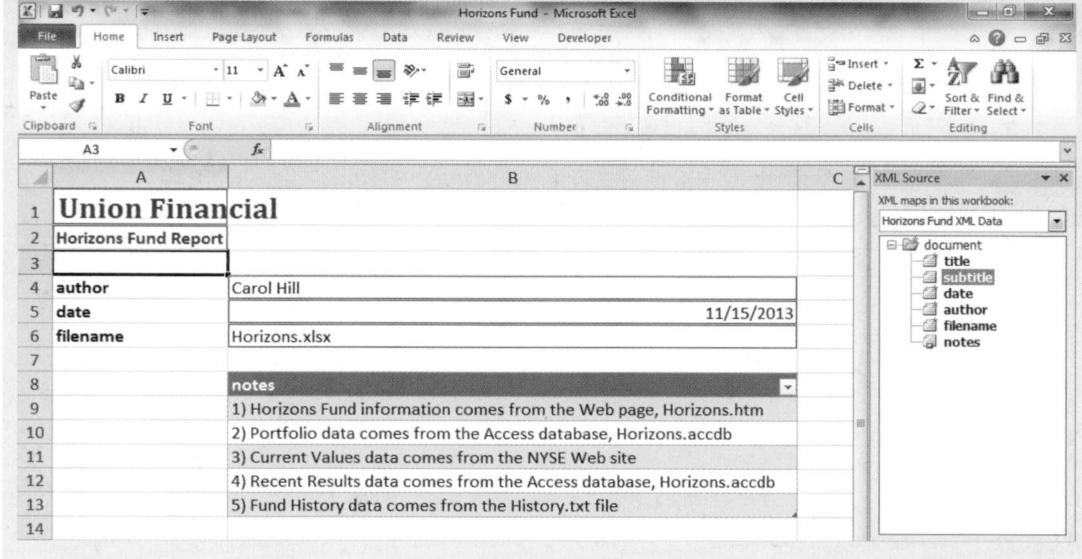

As with database and Web page queries, you can automatically update the XML data in a workbook to reflect changes to the source XML document. You'll change the values in the Data.xml file to include information about the source of the data for the Documentation sheet and add your name as the document author.

To modify the Data.xml data file:

1. Use your text editor to open the **Data** file located in the Excel11\Tutorial folder included with your Data Files.
2. Delete the text **Carol Hill** from between the <author> and </author> tags, and then type your name.
3. Directly below the fifth notes element, insert the following text: **<notes>6) Documentation sheet data comes from the Data.xml file</notes>**
4. Save the file, and then close it.
5. Return to the **Documentation** worksheet in the Horizons Fund workbook.
6. Click cell **A1** to select an element from the data map, click the **Data** tab on the Ribbon, click the **Refresh All button arrow** in the Connections group, and then click **Refresh** to refresh the data in the Documentation sheet.
7. Close the XML Source task pane. See Figure 11-51.

Figure 11-51 **Completed Documentation worksheet**

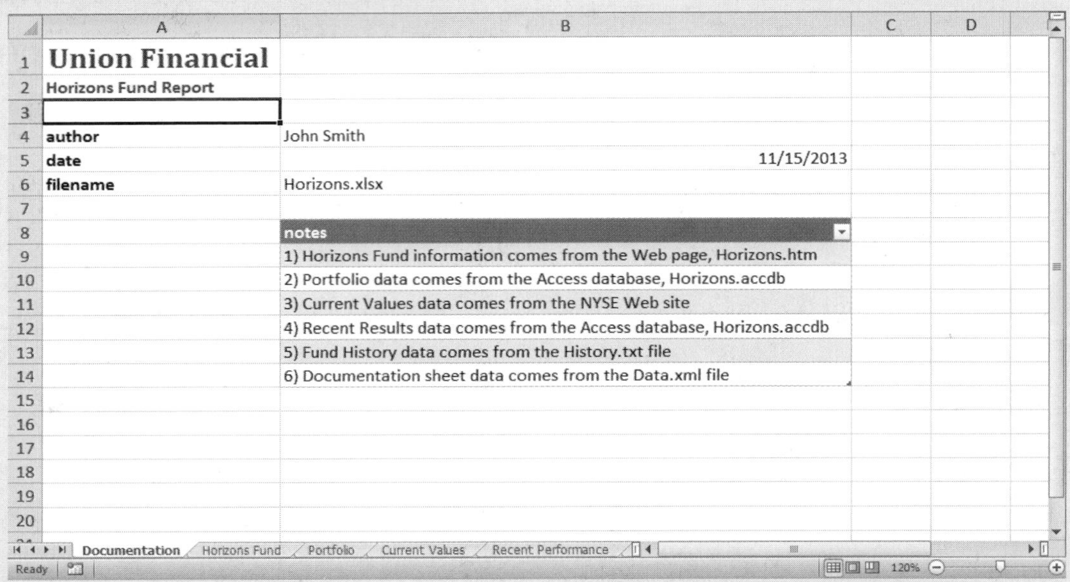

8. Save the Horizons Fund workbook, and then close it.
9. Remove the Developer tab from the Ribbon.

You can also use a data map to export data from your worksheet to an XML document. After cells have been mapped to XML elements, save the worksheet as an XML document. The contents of the cells will be placed into elements in the XML file.

The Horizons Fund workbook is complete. By tapping into a variety of data sources, you've created a file that Carol can use to get current information on the fund as well as examine long-term and short-term data to look for important trends. She expects to find many ways to incorporate this new information into her daily work as an investment counselor at Union Financial.

INSIGHT

Excel and the Office Open XML Format

Starting with Office 2007, Microsoft moved its file from binary formats to formats based on the XML language. Changing the file formats gave developers access to a wealth of tools for working with XML files. The new format improved file and data management, data recovery, and interoperability with line-of-business systems. Any program that supports XML can access and work with data in the new file format. The program does not need to be part of Microsoft Office.

The Office Open XML format stores the XML code in a compressed file, not as a text file. However, you can open an Office file using compression programs such as WinZip to view the underlying XML files. A single Excel workbook might consist of several XML files, including a file to contain the workbook data and another file to contain the document's schema. The schema file allows developers to ensure the integrity of Excel data. You can extract the compressed XML files as text files and then view or manipulate the contents of the workbook from outside of Excel.

Understanding Real-Time Data Acquisition

For Carol's workbook, you imported data from four sources: simple text files, databases, Web pages, and XML documents. Scientists and researchers have a fifth possible data source: **real-time data** values from measuring devices and scientific equipment. A scientist might connect a computer to a temperature sensor, for example, and import temperature values at one-minute intervals directly into a workbook. If you want to use real-time data acquisition, you usually need to purchase an add-in to work with Excel and the device. To facilitate importing data from an external device, Excel provides the RTD function. The syntax of the RTD function is

```
RTD(ProgID, server,topic1 [, topic2] [, topic3] ...)
```

where *ProgID* is the program ID of the add-in that has been installed on the computer to retrieve the real-time data, *server* is the name of the server where the add-in is run (leave the server parameter blank if the add-in is being run on your computer), and *topic1*, *topic2*, and so forth are names assigned to the real-time data values. You can insert up to 28 different topics. After you insert the RTD function into a cell, the value of the cell displays the latest value retrieved from the measuring device. You can also write a VBA macro to run the RTD function in a range of cells, recording the last several values from the measuring device.

By using the RTD function along with an add-in program, the scientist or researcher can save hours of data entry time and concentrate on analysis.

PROSKILLS

Problem Solving: Best Practices for Data Storage

In the past, it was generally accepted that the solution to the ever-increasing need for data was to simply increase the amount of data storage. However, this is no longer the case as the cost of managing the stored data is outstripping the cost of purchasing and upgrading the physical data storage medium. In order to reduce costs and improve data quality, many information managers are looking at different ways to improve their data storage practices. Whether you are storing your data in text files, databases, Web servers, or XML documents, keep in mind the following practices:

- Maintain an inventory of your data, including where it is located and how it is stored. Know what you have.
- Develop a system to regularly purge unwanted data. Don't become buried under a pile of useless or outdated information.
- Develop a system that searches for and removes duplicated data.
- Develop a policy for handling stale data. For example, many businesses will regularly purge records that are more than five years old or move them to offsite storage.

By developing a data storage policy, you can help ensure that the data you want to analyze can be easily retrieved and imported into your Excel workbooks. It also ensures that more of your time is spent understanding the data rather than trying to locate it.

REVIEW

Session 11.3 Quick Check

1. Describe how to import data from a Web page into a workbook.
2. What are the three options for retaining the format styles found within an imported Web page?
3. How would you import the most current stock market data into a workbook?
4. How current are the stock market quotes retrieved from Excel's built-in Web queries?
5. What is XML?
6. What is an XML data map?
7. What Excel function would you use to retrieve real-time data from a measuring device connected to your computer?

Practice the skills you learned in the tutorial using the same case scenario.

PRACTICE

Review Assignments

Data Files needed for the Review Assignments: Index.xlsx, NYA2012.txt, Horizons.accdb, Summary.htm, Info.xml, Info.xsd

Carol wants you to create a new workbook that analyzes the performance of the stocks in the Horizons database by the three NYSE categories: industrials, transportation stocks, and utilities. You'll import a text file that contains the daily indexes of these subgroups for the year 2012 into the workbook. Then, you'll create a table of yield and price/earnings, or P/E ratio values, for the stocks in the Horizons database, sorted by category. Next, you'll create a PivotTable and a PivotChart that display the average closing values of the industrial, transportation, and utility stocks in the Horizons Fund during the past five days. In addition, you'll create a worksheet that displays a table of current Dow Jones stock quote data retrieved from the Web. Finally, you'll import data about the workbook from an XML file, binding the XML data to cells in the workbook. Complete the following:

1. Open the **Index** workbook located in the Excel11\Review folder included with your Data Files, and then save the workbook as **Index Report** in the same folder.
2. In cell A3 of the Historical Data worksheet, get the external data stored in the **NYA2012** text file located in the Excel11\Review folder. The data type is fixed width; start the import at row 4 of the text file. Adjust the column breaks to match the layout of the columns of text in the file. Import the Date column in YMD format. Import the Date, Composite, Industrial, Transport, and Utility columns. Do not import the Finance column.
3. Resize the columns to completely display all of the data. Format the values in the Composite, Industrial, Transport, and Utility columns using the Number format.
4. Set the connection properties of the external data range containing the imported text to refresh the connection whenever the workbook is opened.
5. Go to the Yield and PE Ratios worksheet and select cell A3. Use the Microsoft Query Wizard get the external data stored in the following fields from the **Horizons** database located in the Excel11\Review folder:
   - Company table: Ticker Symbol, Company, and Category fields
   - Stock Info table: Yield and P/E Ratio fields
6. Sort the data in ascending order by the values of the Category field.
7. Save the query as a permanent file named **Index Query** in the Excel11\Review folder.
8. Import the results of the query into the Yield and PE Values worksheet as an Excel table starting in cell A3.
9. Set the connection properties of the query so that it is refreshed whenever the workbook is opened. Add the description **Retrieves yield and PE ratios from the Horizons database** to the connection.
10. Click cell A5 in the Five-Day Averages worksheet. Use the Microsoft Query Wizard to get the external data stored in the Category field from the Company table, and in the Date and Closing fields from the Recent Performance table in the Horizons database. Import the data from this query into cell A5 as a PivotChart and PivotTable Report.

11. Format the PivotTable so that the Category field is displayed as the report filter, the Date field is displayed as an axis field, and the Closing field is displayed as a PivotTable value. Edit the field settings of the Closing field so that it summarizes the values using the average rather than the sum. Display the average values with the Number format. Remove the Grand Total row from the PivotTable.
12. Move and resize the PivotChart so that it covers the range C3:I17. Change the chart type to a line chart and remove the legend from the chart. Change the text of the chart title to **Five-Day Averages** in a 12-point font. Display the values from the Utilities category.
13. Name this connection **Five-Day Averages** with the description **Retrieves five days of closing values from the Horizons database**. Set the connection to refresh whenever the workbook is opened.
14. In the Summary worksheet, get external data from the Web by creating a Web query that accesses the **Summary** file located in the Excel11\Review folder. Retrieve only the four tables located at the bottom of the page and preserve their formats using Rich text formatting. Place the imported data into cell A3.
15. Name the Web query connection you just created **NYSE Summary Web page** with the description **Retrieves financial tables from the Summary.htm file**. Set the connection to refresh whenever the workbook is opened.
16. In the Dow Jones worksheet, use the MSN MoneyCentral Major Indices query to import current index values. Place the imported data into the worksheet starting at cell A3. (*Note*: The MSN MoneyCentral Major Indices query might display invalid ticker symbols in some of the cells.)
17. Edit the properties of the connection to the MSN MoneyCentral Web site so that it refreshes every 10 minutes and whenever the workbook is opened. Name the connection **Current Index Values** and add the description **Retrieves current financial indices using the MSN MoneyCentral Web Query**.
18. Use a text editor to open the **Info.xml** file located in the Excel11\Review folder. Substitute your name for Carol Hill as the document author. Also add the following line directly below the last notes tag, and then close the file, saving your changes:

    <notes>6) Documentation data comes from the Info.xml file</notes>
19. In the Index Report workbook, add a data map to the workbook based on the contents of the Info.xml file. (*Hint*: Customize the Ribbon to show the Developer tab if it is not already displayed.)
20. In the Documentation worksheet, bind the title element to cell A1; the subtitle element to cell A2; the author, date, and filename elements to cells in the range B4:B6; and the notes element to cell B8. Display the headings for the date, author, and filename elements to the left of the element values. Format cell A1 using the Title cell style. Format cell A2 using the Heading 4 cell style.
21. Refresh the connections in the Documentation worksheet to display the text from the Info.xml file. Edit the properties of the Info connection, changing the name to **Document Information** and adding the description **Retrieves document titles from the Info.xml file**.
22. Save and close the workbook. Submit the finished workbook to your instructor, either in printed or electronic form, as requested.

Use the skills you learned to import home sales data from a delimited text file.

APPLY

Case Problem 1

Data File needed for this Case Problem: Homes.txt

Kroft Realty Tim Kroft is the owner of Kroft Realty, a large real estate agency in Ames, Iowa. Tim wants to create tables of comparable sales prices for homes listed in the area. He downloaded a text file containing the most recent sales listings that includes details such as the price, age, and size of the home and its location within the city of Ames. You'll import the data from this text file into Excel, and then use that data to create a PivotTable. The text file uses a delimited format in which one column is separated from another using the forward slash (/) character. Complete the following:

1. Use Excel to open the **Homes** text file located in the Excel11\Case1 folder included with your Data Files.
2. In the Text Import Wizard, set the original data type to Delimited and start the text import at row 5.
3. EXPLORE In the second step of the wizard, set the delimiter as /, the forward slash character. (*Hint*: Select the Other check box in the Text Import Wizard dialog box, and then enter the forward slash character.)
4. Do not import the Offer Pending and Annual Tax columns. Use the General format for all of the columns in the file except the Age column, which uses the Text format.
5. Import the data, and then save the workbook in Excel Workbook format as **Home Sales Analysis** in the Excel11\Case1 folder.
6. Resize the columns to fit the data. Rename the worksheet as **Home Listings**.
7. Insert a new worksheet named **Home Summary** at the end of the workbook. In the Home Summary worksheet, create a PivotTable using the data on the Home Listings sheet to show the average sales price of each home. Format the sales data as currency with no decimal places. Display Square Feet as a row label in the table, Age as a column label, and NE Sector as a report filter.
8. Insert a new worksheet named **Documentation** at the beginning of the workbook containing your name, the date, the purpose of the workbook, and a description of the data source used in the analysis.
9. Save and close the workbook. Submit the finished workbook to your instructor, either in printed or electronic form, as requested.

Import data for a financial consultant tracking currency exchange rates.

APPLY

Case Problem 2

Data Files needed for this Case Problem: Exchange.xlsx, YRate.xml

Brooks and Beckman Henry Sanchez is a financial consultant at Brooks and Beckman. He is developing a workbook to calculate money values in different currencies based on the current exchange rate. He has already created the part of the workbook that performs the calculations, but he needs your help in determining the current exchange rate between U.S. dollars and foreign currencies. Henry is paying particular attention to the exchange rate between U.S. dollars and Japanese yen. So, he also wants you to insert the contents of an XML document that has the last 120 days of exchange rate information into the workbook. One of the built-in Web queries links to a Web page that displays current exchange rates. You'll use this query to complete Henry's workbook.

Complete the following:

1. Open the **Exchange** workbook located in the Excel11\Case2 folder included with your Data Files, and then save the workbook as **Exchange Rate Calculator** in the same folder. In the Documentation worksheet, enter your name in cell B3 and the date in cell B4.
2. Insert a new worksheet named **Exchange Rates** at the end of the workbook.
3. EXPLORE Create a connection to the built-in MSN MoneyCentral Investor Currency Rates Web query. Place the data in cell A1 of the Exchange Rates worksheet.
4. Modify the properties of the MSN MoneyCentral connection so that currency rate data is refreshed every 10 minutes and whenever the workbook is opened.
5. Assign the defined name **currency_names** to the names of the currency exchanges in column A of the Exchange Rates worksheet. Assign the defined name **currency_rates** to the three columns of currency data in the Exchange Rates worksheet. Do not include the column headings in either of these ranges.
6. In cell C3 of the Calculator worksheet, insert a data validation rule that only allows values from a list. The source of the list is the range of values returned by the currency_names range reference.
7. In cell C5, use the VLOOKUP function to retrieve the exchange rates between a selected currency and U.S. dollars. (*Hint*: The lookup value is the currency value in cell C3; the lookup table is the table of currency rates referenced by the currency_rates range reference. Use the second column of the table and instruct Excel to return only exact matches.) Multiply the lookup value by whatever value the user enters into cell C4.
8. Repeat Steps 7 and 8 for the exchange rate calculator in cells C8 and C10. However, use the third column from the lookup table to return the exchange rate and multiply the value returned by the VLOOKUP function by the value entered by the user in cell C9.
9. Determine the current value of 15,000 yen in U.S. dollars by entering **15,000** in cell C4 and then choosing the Japanese Yen currency exchange rate from the list in cell C3.
10. Determine the current value of $75 in Japanese yen by entering **75** in cell C9 and then choosing the Japanese Yen currency exchange rate from the list in cell C8.
11. Insert a new worksheet named **Japanese Yen Recent History** at the end of the workbook.
12. EXPLORE Create a connection to the **YRate.xml** file located in the Excel11\Case2 folder. (*Hint*: In the Get External Data group on the Data tab, click the From Other Sources button, and then click From XML Data Import.) Import the data from this file as an XML table.
13. Create a line chart in the Japanese Yen Recent History worksheet based on the exchange rate data you imported. Add the title **Value of Yen per U.S. $** above the chart. Remove the chart legend.
14. Edit the properties of the connection you just created, changing the name of the connection to **Recent value of the Yen**.
15. Save and close the workbook. Submit the finished workbook to your instructor, either in printed or electronic form, as requested.

Expand the skills you learned to query and summarize data for an online candy company.

CHALLENGE

Case Problem 3

Data Files needed for this Case Problem: Confections.accdb, Confections.xlsx

Kate's Confections Kate Amundsen is the owner of Kate's Confections, an online company that sells delicious candies and chocolates. Kate has been storing orders in an Access database and wants to import a subset of its data into an Excel worksheet. The database, named Confections.accdb, contains five tables. The Customers table lists the names and contact information for customers who have ordered during the past several weeks. The Orders table lists each order and the date it was submitted. The Products table lists products sold by Kate's Confections. The Customers_Orders table matches each order with the customer who ordered it. Finally, the Orders_Products table matches each order with the products on the order. You'll import the data from the Customers and Products tables into separate worksheets. You'll also create a PivotTable that displays details on each order. Complete the following:

1. Open the **Confections** workbook located in the Excel11\Case3 folder included with your Data Files, and then save the workbook as **Kate's Confections** in the same folder. In the Documentation worksheet, enter your name in cell B3 and the date in cell B4.
2. Insert a new worksheet named **Customers** at the end of the workbook. In cell A1, enter **Kate's Confections** and format the text with the Title cell style. In cell A2, enter **Customer List** and format the text with the Heading 4 cell style.
3. Create a connection to the Customers table of the **Confections** database located in the Excel11\Case3 folder. Place the data as an Excel table starting in cell A4 of the Customers worksheet.
4. Edit the properties of the connection you just created. Name the connection **Customer List** and add the description **Data retrieved from the Customers table in the Confections database**. Refresh the connection whenever the workbook is opened.
5. Insert a worksheet named **Products** at the end of the workbook. Enter **Kate's Confections** in cell A1 and **Product List** in cell A2. Format cells A1 and A2 to match the title and subtitle in the Customers worksheet.
6. Establish a connection to the Products table of the **Confections** database located in the Excel11\Case3 folder, importing the data as an Excel table starting in cell A4. Format the Price values in column C using the Currency format.
7. Edit the properties of the connection, naming the connection **Product List** and entering the description **Data retrieved from the Products table in the Confections database**. Refresh the connection whenever the workbook is opened.
8. Insert a worksheet named **Product Orders** at the end of the workbook. Enter **Kate's Confections** in cell A1 and **Product Orders** in cell A2. Format cells A1 and A2 to match the titles and subtitles in the previous two worksheets.
9. Use the Query Wizard to create a query based on the tables in the Confections database. The query should extract the following fields:
   - Name from the Customers table
   - CID and OID from the Customers_Orders table
   - Date from the Orders table
   - PID from the Orders_Products table
   - Product and Price from the Products table
10. Save the query as a permanent file named **Order Query** in the Excel11\Case3 folder.
11. Import the data from the query into cell A5 of the Product Orders sheet as a PivotTable Report.

12. Place the Name, Date, and Product fields as row labels in the PivotTable. Display the sum of the Price field in the Values section of the table. Format the Sum of Price values using the Currency format.
13. Name this connection **Product Orders** with the description **Retrieves product orders from Kate's Confections customers recorded in the Confections database**. Refresh the connection whenever the workbook opens.
14. **EXPLORE** Kate wants to save the connections you've created as Office Data Connection (ODC) files for use in other projects. To save the connections as permanent files, open the Connection Properties dialog box for each of the three connections you've created, and then click the Export Connection File button on the Definition tab. Save the ODC files as **Customer List**, **Product List**, and **Product Orders** in the Excel11\Case3 folder.
15. **EXPLORE** Test the connection files you created in Step 14. Open a new blank workbook, click the Connections button in the Connections group on the Data tab, and then click the Add button. Click the Browse for More button in the Existing Connections dialog box, and then locate and open the three connection files you created in Step 14.
16. **EXPLORE** Click the Existing Connections button in the Get External Data group on the Data tab, and then verify that the three connections you added to this workbook are listed. Select the Customer List connection and click the Open button. Confirm that you can get external data from this connection and place that data into your workbook as an Excel table. Close the workbook without saving; you do not need to submit this workbook to your instructor.
17. Submit the completed files to your instructor, either in printed or electronic form, as requested.

Create a sales report with data imported from an Access database.

CREATE

Case Problem 4

Data Files needed for this Case Problem: Antiques.accdb, Green.xlsx

Green Cove Antiques Green Cove Antiques, located in Burlington, Vermont, is an online reseller of antiques and fine arts. Karl Umhoefer is a sales manager at the store. One of his jobs is to maintain reports on customer orders to help the company find trends in sales and product interest. The customer order data is stored in an Access database, which contains five tables: Products, Customer, Orders, Item, and Staff. Each table shares a common field with at least one other table in the database. The Products table stores information about products in the company's catalog. The Customer table records personal information about people who have bought products from Green Cove Antiques. The Orders table contains information about each order, including the date, who placed the order, and who recorded the transaction. The Item table records the items purchased in each order. Finally, the Staff table contains information about the sales personnel who take the orders. You'll extract this information and place it into an Excel workbook. Complete the following:

1. Open the **Green** workbook located in the Excel11\Case4 folder included with your Data Files, and then save the workbook as **Green Cove Antiques** in the same folder. In the Documentation worksheet, enter your name in cell B3 and the date in cell B4.
2. Create a worksheet named **Staff** containing an Excel table listing the sales staff at Green Cove Antiques. Connect to the STAFF table in the **Antiques** database located in the Excel11\Case4 folder. Name this connection **Green Cove Staff** and refresh the connection whenever the workbook opens.
3. Insert a worksheet named **Products** containing an Excel table listing the products in the company database. Display the price of each item in currency format. Connect to the PRODUCTS table in the Antiques database located in the Excel11\Case4 folder. Name this connection **Green Cove Products** and refresh the connection whenever the workbook is opened.

4. Create a worksheet named **Customers** containing an Excel table listing the customers. Connect to the CUSTOMER table in the Antiques database located in the Excel11\Case4 folder. Name this connection **Customer List** and refresh the connection whenever the workbook is opened.
5. Create a worksheet named **Orders**. Use the Query Wizard to import the following fields from the different tables in the Antiques database:
   - LAST_NAME, FIRST_NAME, and COMPANY from the CUSTOMER table
   - QUANTITY from the ITEM table
   - DATE from the ORDERS table
   - SELLER, TYPE, DESCRIPTION, and ITEM PRICE from the PRODUCTS table
6. Save the query in a permanent file named **Orders Query** in the Excel11\Case4 folder.
7. Import the data into cell A1 of the Orders worksheet as an Excel table. Name this connection **Customer Orders** and refresh the connection whenever the workbook is opened.
8. Add a new column to the table you created in the previous step that calculates the total price of each order (equal to the item price multiplied by the quantity). Use **Sales** as the heading text for the new column. Format its values and the values of the ITEM PRICE column as Currency. Add a Total row to the table that calculates the total income from all of the orders in the database.
9. Add a worksheet named **Sales Types** at the end of the workbook. Use the Query Wizard to import the following fields from the tables in the Antiques database:
   - QUANTITY and ITEM_ID# from the ITEM table
   - ORDER_ID# from the ORDERS table
   - TYPE from the PRODUCTS table
   - STAFF_ID# and LAST_NAME from the STAFF table
10. Save the definition of this query as a permanent file named **Sales Types Query** in the Excel11\Case4 folder. Import the query data into cell A1 of the Sales Types worksheet as a PivotTable Report. Rename the connection for this query as **Sales Types** and refresh the query whenever the workbook is opened.
11. Display the quantity of each order broken down by the staff person's last name and the type of product sold.
12. Save and close the workbook. Submit the finished files to your instructor, either in printed or electronic form, as requested.

ASSESS

SAM: Skills Assessment Manager

For current SAM information, including versions and content details, visit SAM Central (http://samcentral.course.com). If you have a SAM user profile, you may have access to hands-on instruction, practice, and assessment of the skills covered in this tutorial. Because various versions of SAM are supported throughout the life of this text, check with your instructor for the correct instructions and URL/Web site for accessing assignments.

ENDING DATA FILES

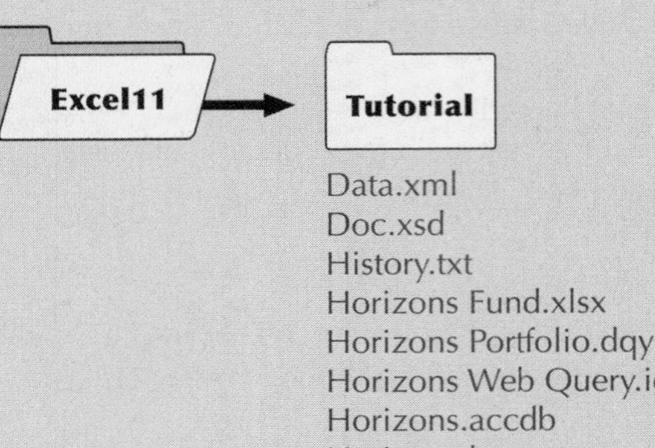

Tutorial

Data.xml
Doc.xsd
History.txt
Horizons Fund.xlsx
Horizons Portfolio.dqy
Horizons Web Query.iqy
Horizons.accdb
Horizons.htm

Review

Horizons.accdb
Index Query.dqy
Index Report.xlsx
Info.xml
Info.xsd
NYA2012.txt
Summary.htm

Case1

Home Sales Analysis.xlsx

Case2

Exchange Rate Calculator.xlsx
YRate.xml

Case3

Confections.accdb
Customer List.odc
Kate's Confections.xlsx
Product List.odc
Product Orders.odc

Case4

Antiques.accdb
Green Cove Antiques.xlsx
Orders Query.dqy
Sales Types Query.dqy

TUTORIAL 12

OBJECTIVES

Session 12.1
- Create a macro using the macro recorder
- Work with the Project Explorer and Properties window of the VBA Editor
- Edit a sub procedure
- Run a sub procedure

Session 12.2
- Work with VBA objects, properties, and methods
- Create an input box to retrieve information from the user

Session 12.3
- Create and run If-Then control structures
- Work with comparison and logical operators
- Create message boxes
- Customize the Quick Access Toolbar
- Customize Excel

Enhancing Excel with Visual Basic for Applications

Creating a Climate Report Application

EXCEL

Case | *Center for Atmospheric Science*

David Faducci is a researcher at the Midwest Center for Atmospheric Science in Council Bluffs, Iowa. One of his research areas involves tornadoes. He has collected data on the yearly occurrence of tornadoes in the United States from 1950 to 1999 to analyze a possible relationship between the prevalence of tornadoes and climate change. David is curious whether the occurrence of tornadoes increased in the last 25 years of the twentieth century. To investigate this, David compiled statistics on the rate of tornado occurrence and created charts that display the annual number of tornadoes in the country. The research has revealed some interesting results. He is planning to use this information in a kiosk to be run in the public entrance at the center. He wants visitors to be able to interact with the data, choosing which charts or tables of statistics to display. Because David doesn't expect visitors to know how to use Excel, he wants the workbook to contain custom dialog boxes, macro buttons, and menus more suited to his users.

STARTING DATA FILES

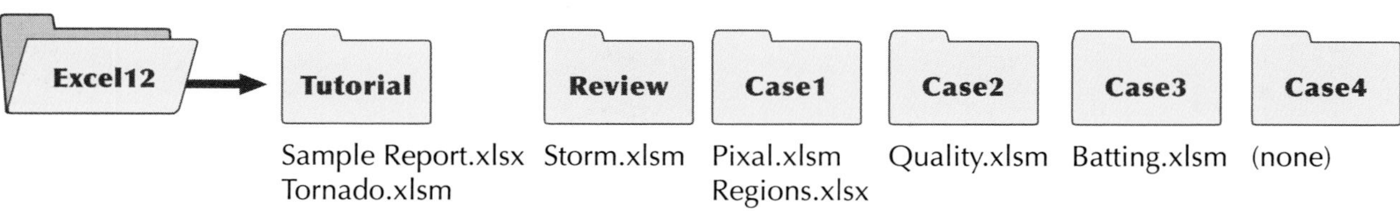

Tutorial	Review	Case1	Case2	Case3	Case4
Sample Report.xlsx Tornado.xlsm	Storm.xlsm	Pixal.xlsm Regions.xlsx	Quality.xlsm	Batting.xlsm	(none)

SESSION 12.1 VISUAL OVERVIEW

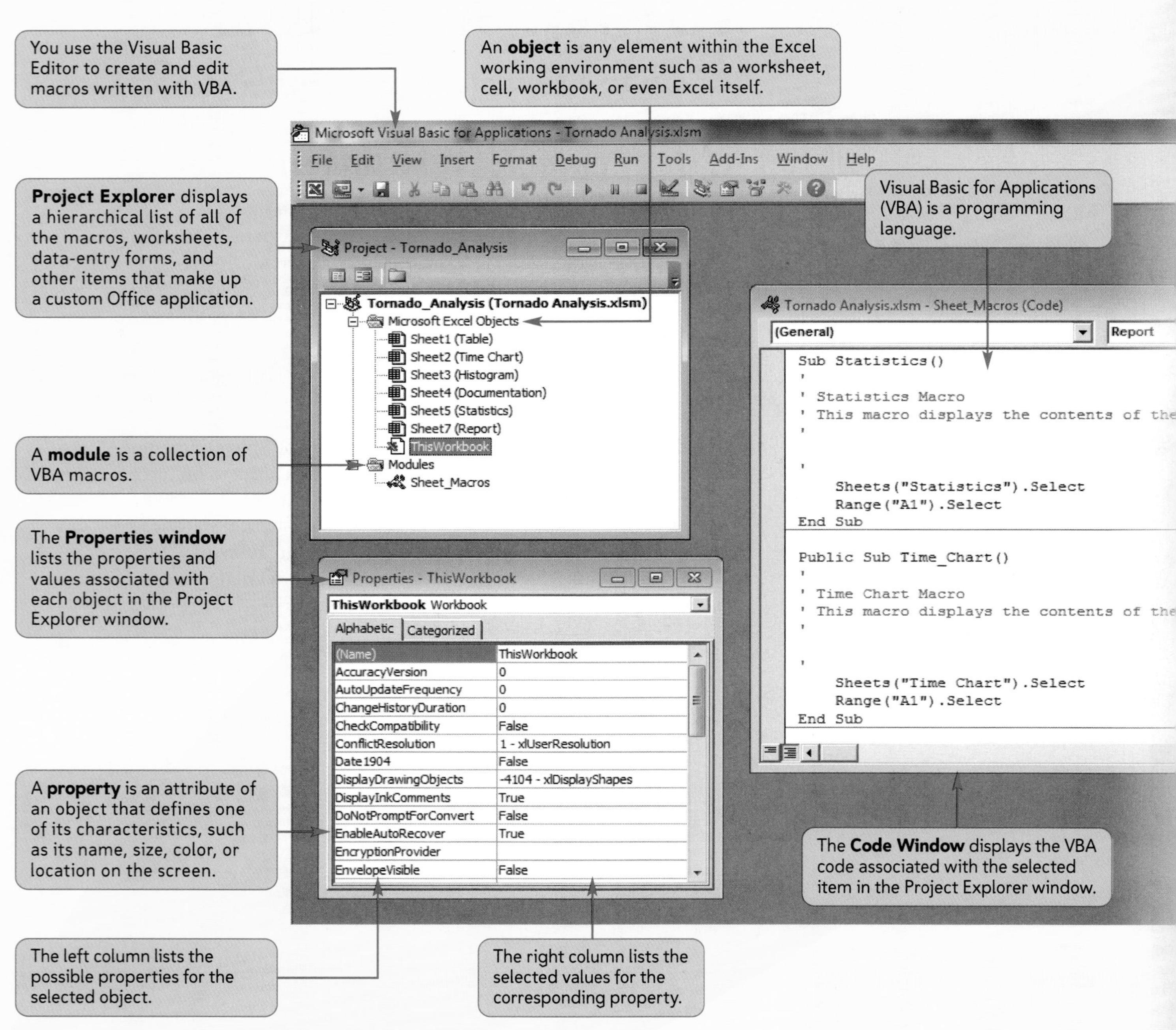

THE VISUAL BASIC EDITOR

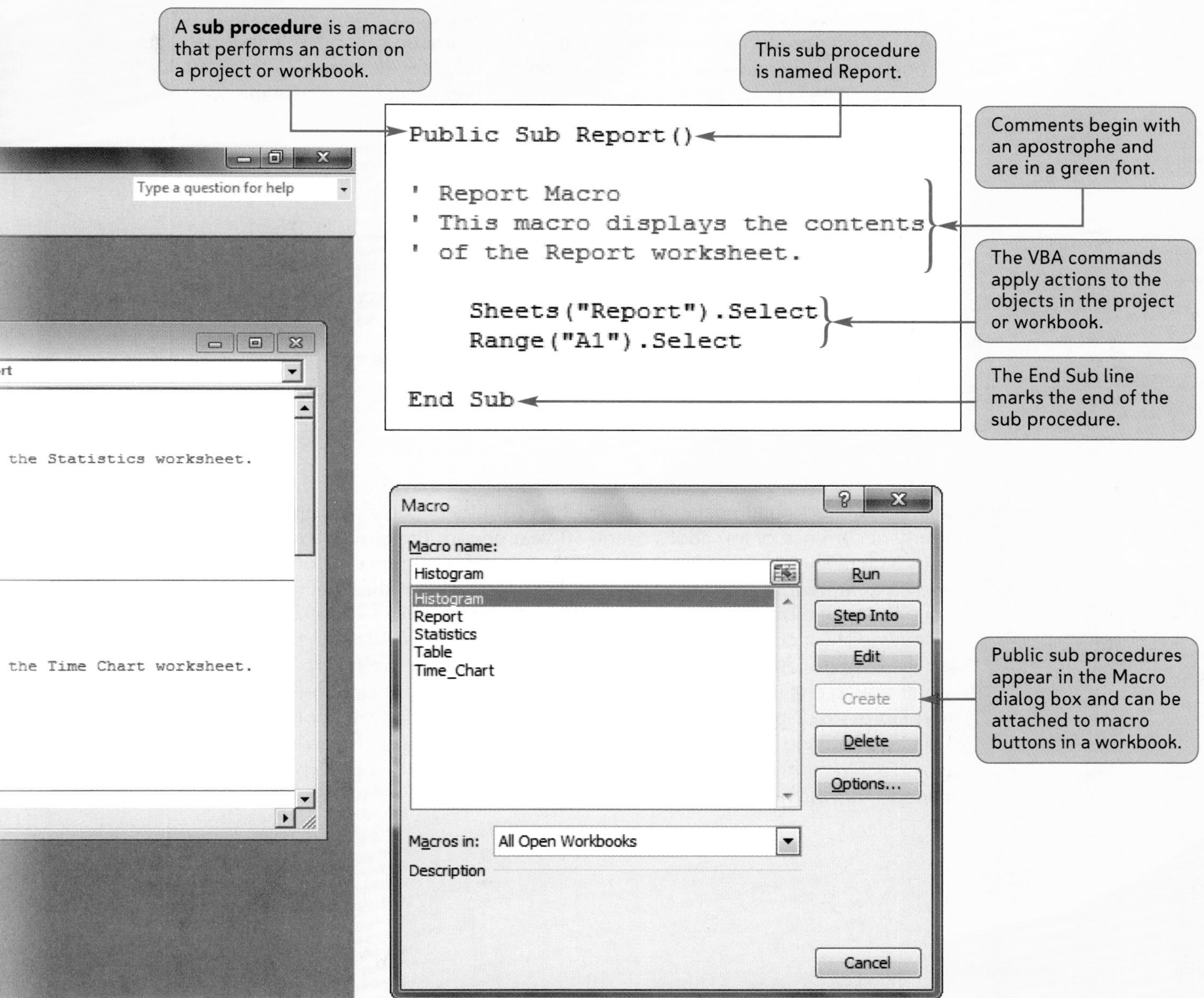

Developing an Excel Application

An **Excel application** is an application that uses Excel commands, tools, and functions to perform an action. The application itself is stored as an Excel file and can only be opened from within Excel. David wants you to create an Excel application based on the workbook in which he has stored information on the yearly occurrence of tornadoes classified as F0, F1, and F2 or higher.

Historically, the intensity of tornadoes was classified according to the Fujita Tornado Scale, which rates tornadoes from F0 (a gale-force tornado capable of minor damage) through F6 (an inconceivably strong tornado capable of widespread destruction). David has also created charts and statistical tables based on his data. Because this workbook will be used by the general public, he wants it to be easy for non–Excel users to operate.

You'll open and review David's workbook.

To open and review David's workbook:

1. Open the **Tornado** workbook located in the Excel12\Tutorial folder included with your Data Files, and then save it as a macro-enabled workbook named **Tornado Analysis** in the same folder.
2. In the Documentation worksheet, enter your name and the date.
3. Review the **Report**, **Time Chart**, **Histogram**, **Statistics**, and **Raw Data** worksheets.

The Report worksheet contains macro buttons that David wants to use to display analyses of his tornado data. The Time Chart worksheet contains a line chart showing the yearly occurrence of tornadoes over a 50-year period. The Histogram worksheet contains a chart showing the distribution of the annual occurrence of tornadoes divided into two 25-year periods. The Statistics worksheet contains statistics that describe the annual occurrence of tornadoes from 1950 to 1974 and from 1975 to 1999. Finally, the Raw Data worksheet contains a table of the actual data that David collected for this report.

The Report worksheet, shown in Figure 12-1, contains five macro buttons. David wants you to create macros for the first four buttons—Statistics, Time Chart, Histogram, and Table—to display the corresponding worksheets in the workbook. The fifth button, Specify a Tornado Type, will be used to display charts and statistics on a different tornado type. Each remaining worksheet in the workbook contains a macro button, Return to Report Tab, which David wants to use to return to the Report worksheet.

Figure 12-1 **Proposed report application**

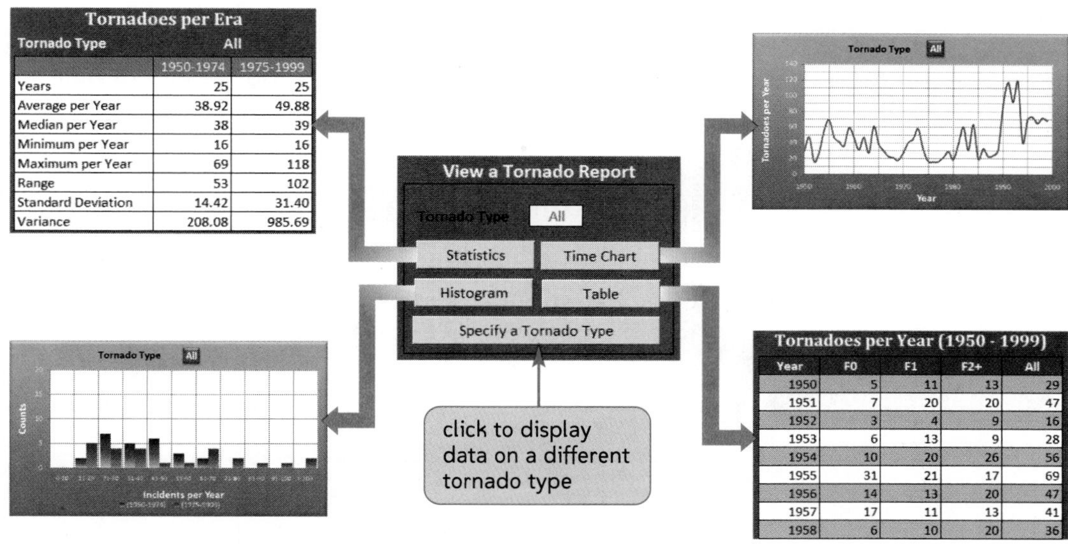

The fastest way to create macros is to use the Excel macro recorder. After recording a macro, you can edit it as needed. First you'll record a macro to display the contents of the Statistics worksheet. You already saved the workbook with macro capability enabled, in preparation for recording macros.

To record the Statistics macro:

1. Display the **Developer** tab on the Ribbon, if necessary.
2. Click the **Developer** tab on the Ribbon, and then click the **Record Macro** button in the Code group. The Record Macro dialog box opens.
3. Create a macro named **Statistics** stored in **This Workbook** with **This macro displays the contents of the Statistics worksheet.** as the description, and then click the **OK** button. The dialog box closes, and you can begin to record the macro.
4. Click the **Statistics** sheet tab, and then press the **Ctrl+Home** keys to select cell A1.
5. Stop recording the macro. The Statistics macro is complete.

You'll run the Statistics macro to verify that it makes the Statistics worksheet active.

To test the Statistics macro:

1. Click cell **C2** in the Statistics worksheet to make it the active cell, and then switch to the **Report** worksheet.
2. Run the **Statistics** macro. The Statistics worksheet becomes active and cell A1 is selected.

   Trouble? If the Statistics macro does not make the Statistics worksheet active and select cell A1, open the Macro dialog box, click Statistics in the Macro name box, and then click the Delete button to delete the macro. Repeat the previous set of steps to record the macro again, and then repeat this set of steps to test the macro.
3. When you are sure that the macro runs correctly, save the workbook.

Working with the Visual Basic Editor

TIP

You can quickly switch to the Visual Basic Editor by pressing the Alt+F11 keys.

Excel macros are written in the Visual Basic for Applications (VBA) programming language. VBA is the common language used by all Microsoft Office programs. So after you learn how to use VBA in Excel, you can also use VBA to write and edit macros in other Office programs. You'll use the Visual Basic Editor to review and edit the Statistics macro.

To start the Visual Basic Editor:

1. In the Code group on the Developer tab, click the **Macros** button.
2. Click **Statistics** in the Macro name box, if necessary, and then click the **Edit** button. The Visual Basic Editor opens. See Figure 12-2.

Figure 12-2 **Visual Basic Editor**

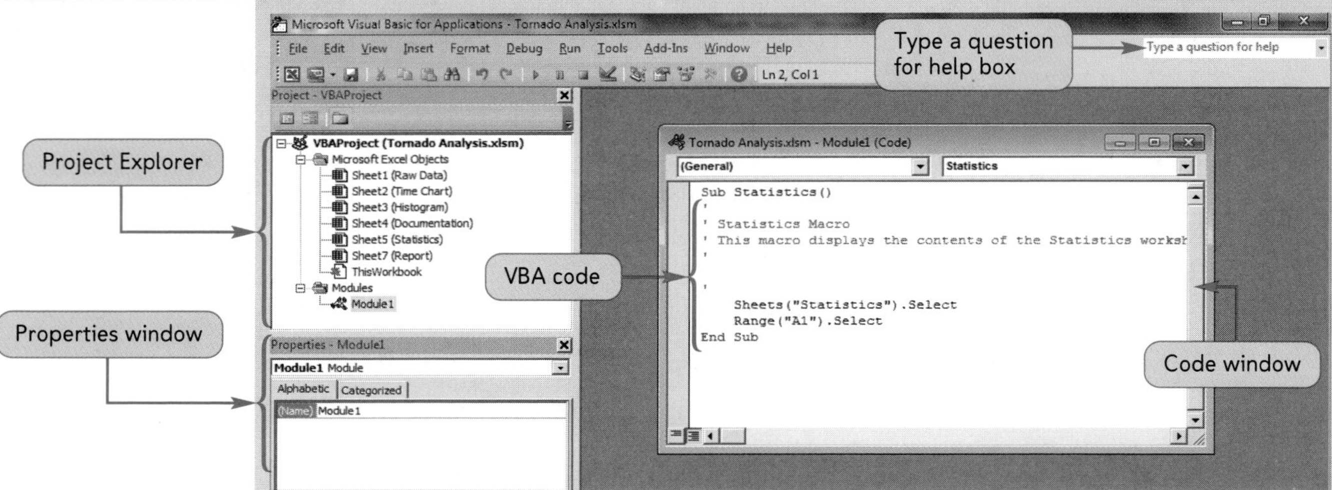

Trouble? If the Visual Basic Editor on your screen does not look like the one shown in Figure 12-2, it might be set up differently on your computer. You'll change the appearance of the Visual Basic Editor shortly.

The Visual Basic Editor usually displays three windows: the Project Explorer window, the Properties window, and the Code window. You can use these windows to examine the structure and content of workbooks as well as macros. You might see other windows, depending on how the Editor was installed on your system. You'll close these windows and then reopen them one at a time.

To clear the Visual Basic Editor:

1. Close all the open windows in the Visual Basic Editor, including the Project Explorer, Properties, and Code windows.

Examining Project Explorer

One important use of the Visual Basic Editor is to manage projects. A **project** is a collection of macros, worksheets, data-entry forms, and other items that make up a customized application. The Project Explorer window contains a hierarchical list of all of these objects.

The Project Explorer window is **dockable**, meaning that you can drag it to the edge of the screen, and the window stays on top of other windows. Docking a window is useful when you want the contents of that window to always remain in view. The drawback of docking a window is that the window takes up screen space. The alternative is to let the window float free within the Visual Basic Editor. You can resize or minimize a floating window as you would other windows. You'll display Project Explorer and float the window to make it easier to view the other windows you'll open.

To view and undock Project Explorer:

1. Click **View** on the menu bar, and then click **Project Explorer**. The Project Explorer window opens, and Project – VBAProject appears in its title bar.
2. Right-click the title bar of the Project Explorer window, and then click **Dockable** to remove the Dockable check mark. Project Explorer floats in the Visual Basic Editor window. See Figure 12-3.

Figure 12-3 **Undocked Project Explorer window**

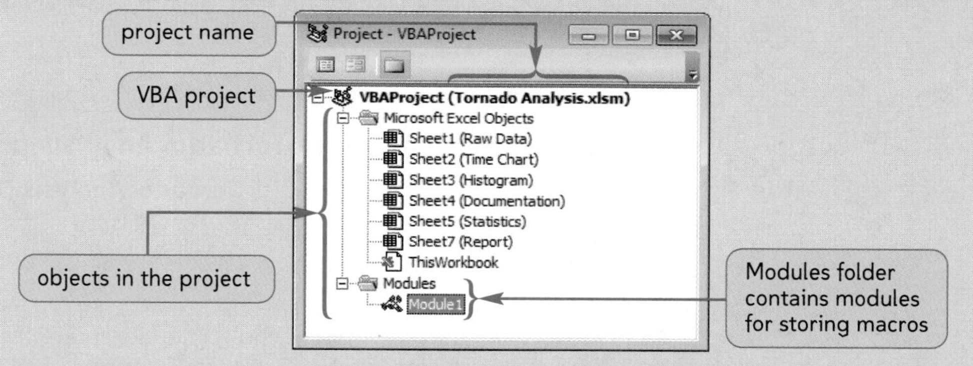

Trouble? If the shortcut menu does not appear when you right-click the title bar, Project Explorer is already undocked. Continue with Step 3.

3. If the Project Explorer window is maximized to fill the Visual Basic Editor window, click the **Restore Window** button to resize the Project Explorer window.

Project Explorer allows you to view your project components in a tree structure. At the top of the tree is the project itself. Each project is identified by a project icon, followed by the project name and the filename in parentheses. The default project name given to new projects is VBAProject. You might see other projects listed in Project Explorer, including projects for Excel add-ins such as Solver. Within each project are various objects. As shown in Figure 12-3, some of the objects listed for the Tornado Analysis workbook include each worksheet and ThisWorkbook, which refers to the open workbook—in this case, the Tornado Analysis workbook itself. To help you manage and organize projects, you can rename a project with a meaningful and easily recognized name. You can also enter a description of the project, so you can recall its purpose or goal and provide others a clear understanding of the project. You can rename a project in the Project Explorer window.

You'll change the default project name, VBAProject, to a more informative name and enter a description of the project in the Project Properties dialog box.

To rename the project and add a description:

1. If necessary, click the title bar of the Project Explorer window to make it the active window.
2. Click **Tools** on the menu bar, and then click **VBAProject Properties**. The VBAProject – Project Properties dialog box opens.
3. On the General tab, type **Tornado_Analysis** in the Project Name box, and then press the **Tab** key.
4. In the Project Description box, type **Application to review tornado annual occurrence data.**
5. Click the **OK** button. Project Explorer displays the new project name.

TIP

Because project names cannot include spaces, you can use an underscore (_) to separate the words in the name.

Using the Properties Window

When you entered the name and description of your project, you were actually modifying two of its properties. All objects have properties that define its characteristics, such as its name, size, color, or location on the screen. You can view a list of properties for any object in the Properties window. You'll display the Properties window for the Tornado_Analysis project.

To view the properties for the Tornado_Analysis project:

1. In the Project Explorer window, click **Tornado_Analysis (Tornado Analysis.xlsm)** to select the project.
2. Click **View** on the menu bar, and then click **Properties Window**. The Properties window opens.
3. If any of the windows overlap, drag the windows by their title bars until all the windows are visible.
4. Right-click the title bar of the Properties window, and then click **Dockable** on the shortcut menu to remove the check mark. The Properties window floats in the Visual Basic Editor. See Figure 12-4.

Figure 12-4 Undocked Properties window

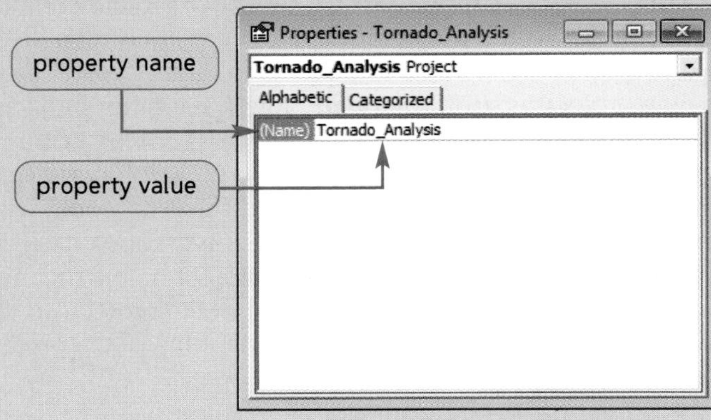

Trouble? If you don't see a shortcut menu when you right-click the title bar, the Properties window is already undocked, and you can continue with the tutorial.

The Properties window displays each property's name in the left column and its value in the right column. You can view the list of properties in alphabetical order and by category. Figure 12-4 lists only one property, the Name property, which has the value Tornado_Analysis.

You'll change the name of the Raw Data worksheet in the Tornado Analysis workbook to "Table." You could do this in Excel, but changing the name from within VBA will give you practice with Project Explorer and the Properties window.

To rename the Raw Data worksheet in the Project Explorer window:

1. Click **Sheet1 (Raw Data)** in the Project Explorer window. The Properties window shows a list of properties associated with the Raw Data worksheet.
2. In the Properties window, click the **Alphabetic** tab, if necessary, to show its contents. The Properties window has two columns. The left column contains the name of the property and the right column contains the property value.
3. In the left column, click the **Name** property in the alphabetical list of properties, and then press the **Tab** key. The property value, Raw Data, is selected in the right column.
4. Type **Table** as the property value, and then press the **Enter** key. The name of the worksheet displayed in the Project Explorer window changes to Table. As you'll see when you return to the Tornado Analysis workbook in Excel, the worksheet name has changed there as well.

Many properties can be listed in the Properties window. The meaning of some of them is clear (such as the Name property); others might require further explanation. You can use Excel Help to obtain more information about a particular property in the Properties window. In general, if you are not sure what a VBA button, command, or object does, or if you don't know the meaning of an element in the VBA programming language, you can enter a description of the item in the Type a question for help box to view documentation on it. You'll use Excel Help to learn more about the ScrollArea property.

To view information about the ScrollArea property:

1. In the upper-right corner of the Visual Basic Editor window, type **ScrollArea** in the Type a question for help box, and then press the **Enter** key. The Excel Help window opens and displays the search results.
2. Click **Worksheet.ScrollArea Property** in the search results list. The Help topic opens in the Help window.
3. Read the topic, and then close the Excel Help window.

Naming Modules

In Project Explorer, the Modules folder appears at the bottom of the object list. A module is a collection of VBA macros. A project might contain several modules, with each module containing macros that accomplish a common set of tasks. For example, you might group all the macros that handle printing tasks in one module and group all the macros that format worksheets in another.

When you recorded the Statistics macro, the Visual Basic Editor placed the macro in a new module with the default name Module1. A good practice is to rename the module with a descriptive name that describes the type of macros it will contain. You'll rename Module1 as Sheet_Macros because the macros in this module will be used to display different worksheets in the workbook.

To rename the macro module:

1. Click **Module1** in Project Explorer. The module is selected.
2. If necessary, click the **title bar** of the Properties window to make the window active.
3. Double-click **Module1** in the (Name) row to select it, type **Sheet_Macros** and then press the **Enter** key. The name of the module in the Project Explorer window and the Properties window changes to Sheet_Macros. See Figure 12-5.

Figure 12-5 Renamed project module

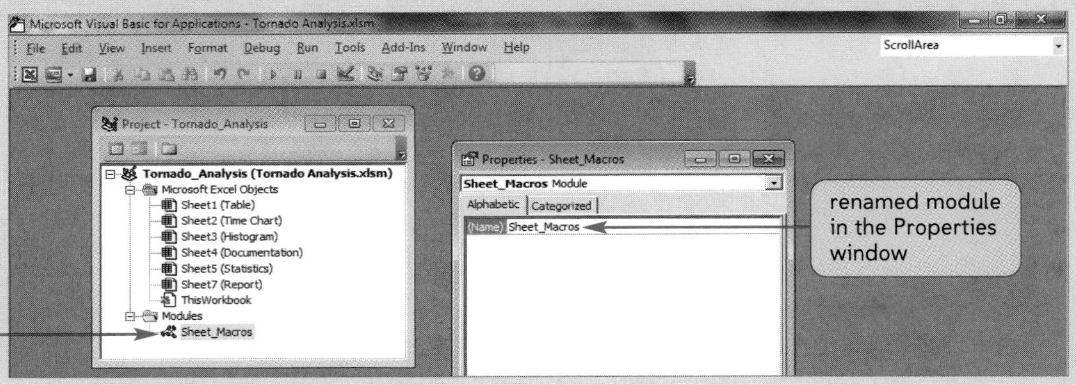

Viewing the Code Window

When you want to view the contents of the macros in your project modules, you use the Code window. You saw the Code window when you first opened the Visual Basic Editor. You'll reopen it now.

TIP

To open the Code window to the contents of a specific module, select the module in the Project Explorer window, and then press the F7 key.

To view the Code window:

1. Click **View** on the menu bar, and then click **Code**. The Code window opens, floating in the Visual Basic Editor. The Code window displays the lines of VBA code that make up the Statistics macro. See Figure 12-6.

Figure 12-6 Floating Code window

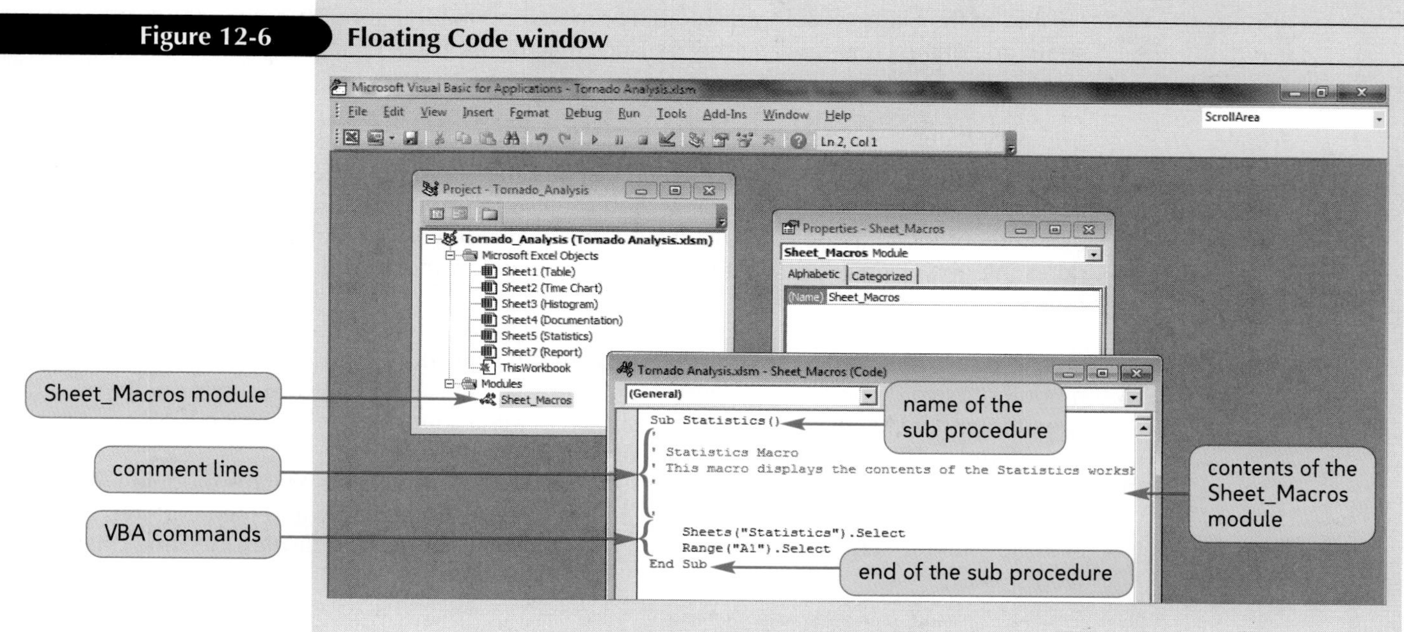

Working with Sub Procedures

The macro you recorded earlier is a special example of a procedure. Visual Basic supports three kinds of procedures: sub procedures, function procedures, and property procedures. A sub procedure performs an action on your project or workbook, such as formatting a cell or displaying a chart. You created a sub procedure when you recorded the Statistics macro. A **function procedure** returns a value. Function procedures are often used to create custom functions that can be entered in worksheet cells. A **property procedure** is used to create custom properties for the objects in your project.

Because the Tornado_Analysis project deals with displaying different worksheets within the Tornado Analysis workbook, you'll work only with sub procedures in this project.

Introducing Sub Procedures

To create a sub procedure without using the macro recorder, you need to understand the basics of VBA syntax. If you use improper syntax, Excel cannot run the macro. However, the Visual Basic Editor will highlight the error in the command.

All sub procedures follow the general syntax

```
Sub Procedure_Name(parameters)
      VBA commands and comments
End Sub
```

where `Procedure_Name` is the name of the macro, and `parameters` are values passed to the sub procedure that control the operation of the procedure.

TIP

Use comment lines to explain the purpose of the macro and how it works without affecting the code.

Review the code generated by the macro recorder when it created the Statistics macro shown in Figure 12-6. The Statistics macro has the sub procedure name *Statistics*. Although the Statistics sub procedure has no parameter values, the parentheses are still required. After the name of the sub procedure, the description you entered in the Record Macro dialog box appears as a comment. A **comment** is a statement that describes the behavior or purpose of a procedure, but does not perform any action. Comments must begin with an apostrophe ('). In the Code window, comments appear in a green font to distinguish them from other statements. After the comments are the commands to select the Statistics worksheet and to select cell A1 on that worksheet. The `End Sub` line signals the end of the Statistics sub procedure. For more information about sub procedures or about any of the commands in the Statistics macro, use Excel Help.

Creating a Sub Procedure Using Copy and Paste

The Statistics sub procedure you created displays the Statistics worksheet. You need additional procedures to display the other worksheets in the workbook. You could use the macro recorder to create these other sub procedures, or you can enter new sub procedures into the Code window either by typing the VBA commands directly or by using the Insert Procedure command.

Sub procedures can be public or private in scope. A **public sub procedure** is available to other modules in the project. A **private sub procedure** is hidden from other modules to avoid conflicts in procedure names. The Statistics sub procedure is public, even though the keyword Public is not shown in the Code window. All procedures are considered public unless specified as Private.

Because the code for the remaining sub procedures in the Sheet_Macros module will be very similar to the Statistics sub procedure, you can simply copy and then edit the Statistics sub procedure. You'll start by creating a sub procedure to display the Time Chart worksheet.

TIP

Use descriptive names for sub procedures. Procedure names can contain as many as 255 characters and cannot contain spaces.

To begin creating a new procedure:

1. If necessary, click the title bar of the Code window to make it the active window.
2. Click **Insert** on the menu bar, and then click **Procedure**. The Add Procedure dialog box opens.
3. Type **Time_Chart** in the Name box to assign a title to the sub procedure.
4. Click the **Sub** and **Public** option buttons to select them, if necessary. You have entered the name, type, and scope of the procedure. See Figure 12-7.

Figure 12-7 Add Procedure dialog box

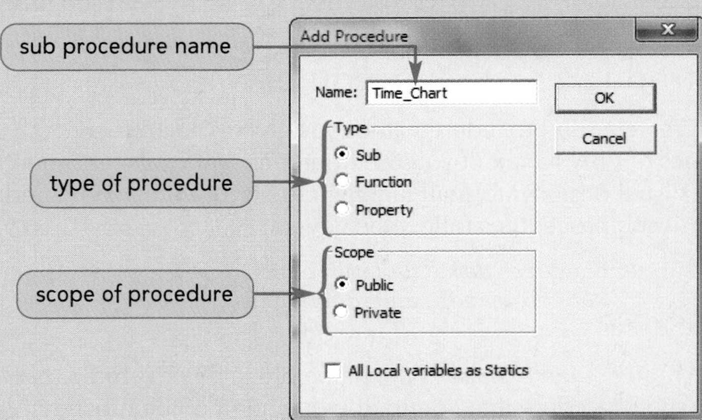

5. Click the **OK** button. The Code window displays the beginning and ending lines of the new sub procedure. A horizontal line separates the new procedure from the Statistics sub procedure. See Figure 12-8.

Figure 12-8 Inserted sub procedure

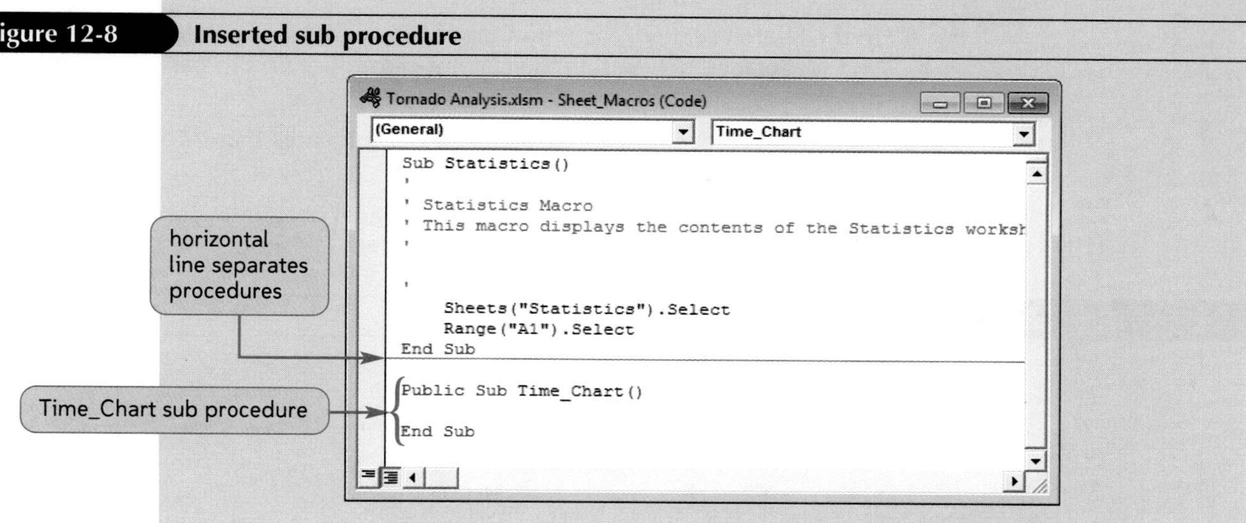

You add, delete, and replace text in the Code window the same way you do in any text editor. Next, you'll copy the VBA code from the Statistics sub procedure into the Time_Chart sub procedure. If you had not already recorded the Statistics macro, you would have to enter the code manually.

To copy and paste the VBA code from the Statistics sub procedure:

1. If necessary, scroll up the Code window until you can see the entire Statistics sub procedure.
2. Click to the left of the apostrophe for the first comment line located directly below the `Sub Statistics()` line of code.
3. Select all the comment lines and VBA commands, beginning with the first apostrophe and ending with the `Range("A1").Select` line. Do not select either the `Sub Statistics()` or the `End Sub` line.
4. On the Standard toolbar, click the **Copy** button. The selected code is copied to the Clipboard.
5. Scroll down the Code window, if necessary, and then click the blank line below the Time_Chart sub procedure name.
6. On the Standard toolbar, click the **Paste** button. The Statistics sub procedure code is pasted into the Time_Chart sub procedure.

You need to edit the pasted code. You'll replace all occurrences of "Statistics" with "Time Chart." You could do this by selecting the text and typing the new text. But it is faster and more efficient to use the Replace command to replace all the occurrences at once.

TIP

To replace text throughout the current procedure, current module (across several procedures), or current project (across several modules), click the corresponding option button in the Replace dialog box.

To replace text in the Time_Chart sub procedure:

1. Click **Edit** on the menu bar, and then click **Replace**. The Replace dialog box opens.
2. Type **Statistics** in the Find What box, and then press the **Tab** key.
3. Type **Time Chart** in the Replace With box.

Select Current Procedure so the Visual Basic Editor doesn't replace text throughout the project.

4. In the Search section, click the **Current Procedure** option button to specify that text is replaced only within the current procedure (in this case, the Time_Chart procedure).
5. Click the **Replace All** button. A dialog box indicates that three replacements of the Statistics text were made.
6. Click the **OK** button, and then click the **Cancel** button to close the Replace dialog box. The Time_Chart sub procedure is edited. See Figure 12-9.

Figure 12-9 Edited Time_Chart sub procedure

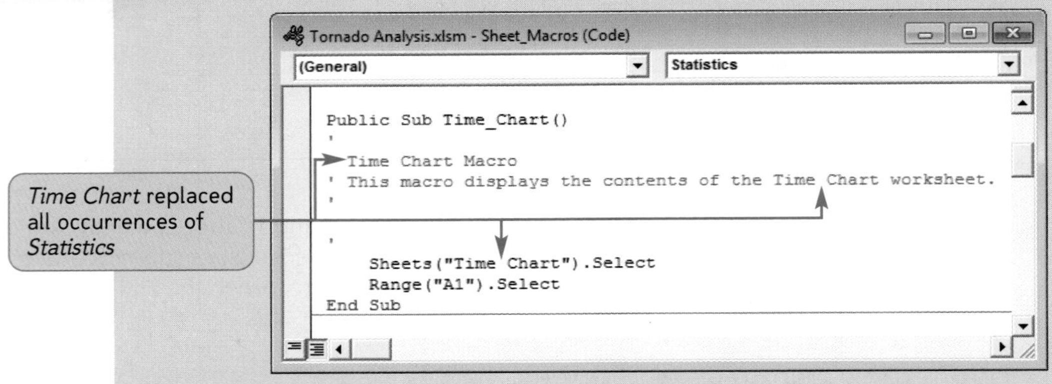

Running a Sub Procedure

After creating a procedure, you should test it to ensure that it works as intended. You can test a macro by running it from the workbook or from within the Visual Basic Editor. You'll test the new procedure you created in the Tornado Analysis workbook. You'll run the Time_Chart sub procedure in the Visual Basic Editor to verify that it opens the Time Chart worksheet.

To run the Time_Chart sub procedure in the Visual Basic Editor:

1. Make sure the insertion point is still within the Time_Chart sub procedure.
2. Click **Run** on the menu bar, and then click **Run Sub/UserForm**. The Visual Basic Editor runs the current sub procedure selected in the Code window—in this case, the Time_Chart sub procedure.

   Trouble? If the Visual Basic Editor displays an error message, you probably made a mistake while creating the Time_Chart sub procedure. Click the End button in the dialog box, check your code against the code in Figure 12-9, correct any errors you find, and then repeat Steps 1 and 2.

TIP

To step through the sub procedure one line at a time, click in the code, and then repeatedly press the F8 key. To run the entire sub procedure, press the F5 key.

3. Switch to Excel and the Tornado Analysis workbook so you can make sure that running the sub procedure actually selected the Time Chart worksheet. The Time Chart worksheet is the active sheet in the workbook and cell A1 is selected on the sheet.

   Trouble? If the macro doesn't work properly, return to the Visual Basic Editor and compare your code to that shown in the earlier figures. Correct any differences that you find, and then repeat Steps 1 through 3.

4. Save the workbook, and then return to the Visual Basic Editor.

You'll use the same process to create macros that display the remaining worksheets in the Tornado Analysis workbook. You'll copy and edit the sub procedure to display the contents of the Histogram, Table, and Report worksheets.

To create the remaining sub procedures:

1. Make sure the Code window in the Visual Basic Editor is active.
2. Click **Insert** on the menu bar, and then click **Procedure**. The Add Procedure dialog box opens.
3. Type **Histogram** in the Name box, verify that the **Sub** and **Public** option buttons are selected, and then click the **OK** button.
4. On the Standard toolbar, click the **Paste** button. The lines of code you copied from the Statistics sub procedure are pasted into the new sub procedure.
5. Click **Edit** on the menu bar, and then click **Replace**. The Replace dialog box opens.
6. Type **Statistics** in the Find What box, type **Histogram** in the Replace With box, verify that the **Current Procedure** option button is selected, and then click the **Replace All** button.
7. Click the **OK** button to confirm that three replacements of the word *Statistics* were made, and then click the **Cancel** button to close the Replace dialog box.
8. With the insertion point still within the Histogram sub procedure, click **Run** on the menu bar, and then click **Run Sub/UserForm**.
9. Go to the **Tornado Analysis** workbook in the Excel window and verify that the Histogram worksheet is selected.

   Trouble? If the Histogram sub procedure fails to run correctly, delete the code and repeat Steps 2 through 9 to recreate the macro with the correct code.
10. Return to the Visual Basic Editor.
11. Repeat Steps 2 through 10 to create a sub procedure named **Table**, replacing all occurrences of the word *Statistics* with *Table*.
12. Repeat Steps 2 through 10 to create a sub procedure named **Report**, replacing all occurrences of the word *Statistics* with *Report*.

You've created five sub procedures to display each of the worksheets in the Tornado Analysis workbook. You'll return to Excel and assign those macros to macro buttons in the workbook. You do not need to save the code within the Visual Basic Editor because macro code is part of the Excel workbook. When you save the workbook, you are also saving the macro code.

To assign the sub procedures to macro buttons:

1. Click **File** on the menu bar, and then click **Close and Return to Microsoft Excel**. The Visual Basic Editor closes and you return to the Tornado Analysis workbook.
2. Switch to the **Report** worksheet, right-click the **Statistics** macro button, and then click **Assign Macro** on the shortcut menu. The Assign Macro dialog box opens.
3. Click **Statistics** in the Macro name box, and then click the **OK** button to assign the macro to the button.

4. Repeat Steps 2 and 3 for the **Time Chart**, **Histogram**, and **Table** macro buttons, assigning the corresponding macros to them, and then click any cell to deselect the buttons.
5. Click the **Statistics** macro button and verify that the Statistics worksheet opens.

   Trouble? If the worksheet doesn't open, the macro button might be selected (indicated by selection handles around the button). If the button is selected, click any cell to deselect the macro button, and then click the button again.
6. In the Statistics worksheet, right-click the **Return to Report Tab** macro button, click **Assign Macro** on the shortcut menu, and then double-click **Report** to assign that macro to the button.
7. Click any cell to deselect the button, and then click the **Return to Report Tab** macro button and verify that the Report worksheet opens.
8. Repeat Steps 5 through 7 to test the **Time Chart**, **Histogram**, and **Table** macro buttons and assign the **Report** macro to the Return to Report Tab macro button on each worksheet.
9. Test the workbook to ensure that you can move through it using only the macro buttons.
10. Save and close the workbook.

The macro buttons provide a quick way to move between the worksheets.

PROSKILLS

Problem Solving: Learning VBA

The best way to learn VBA is by doing. Start with the macro recorder to generate VBA code. The code is guaranteed to be free of syntax errors, so you can identify the key elements of the VBA language. However, the macro recorder does not write the most efficient code. It also records commands and actions that you might not want or need in a finished project. Experienced programmers might use the macro recorder as a starting point, but quickly edit the generated code to remove the extraneous material. As you learn more about VBA, you'll likely rely on the macro recorder less often.

The next source of information for a new programmer is the Microsoft Visual Basic for Applications Help. The online Help contains descriptions of all of the VBA commands and operations. It also includes code samples you can often apply to your own projects.

After becoming familiar with the VBA Help, try writing some code. The interactive tools guide you to use the correct syntax by identifying syntax errors as you type them rather than after the program is run. You often learn more from overcoming mistakes than by reading many programming manuals.

Finally, examine what other programmers are doing. In many cases, program code is password-protected, but not always. You can learn from others' techniques, and the Web is a great source of VBA code samples. However, if you do use code from another programmer, be sure to obtain permission first and to cite the programmer's work in any publication.

So far, you have created macros that allow users to easily move between sheets in the workbook and assign them to macro buttons. In the next session, you'll create a sub procedure to display information on different tornado types. In the process, you'll learn how to write and interpret VBA sub procedures.

REVIEW

Session 12.1 Quick Check

1. Describe each of the following VBA elements: (a) Project Explorer, (b) Properties window, and (c) Code window.
2. Define the following terms: (a) *project*, (b) *object*, (c) *property*, and (d) *module*.
3. How can you get help with a property listed in the Properties window?
4. What are the three types of procedures in VBA?
5. Write the general syntax of a sub procedure.
6. Why would a project contain several modules?
7. How do you enter a comment into a sub procedure?

SESSION 12.2 VISUAL OVERVIEW

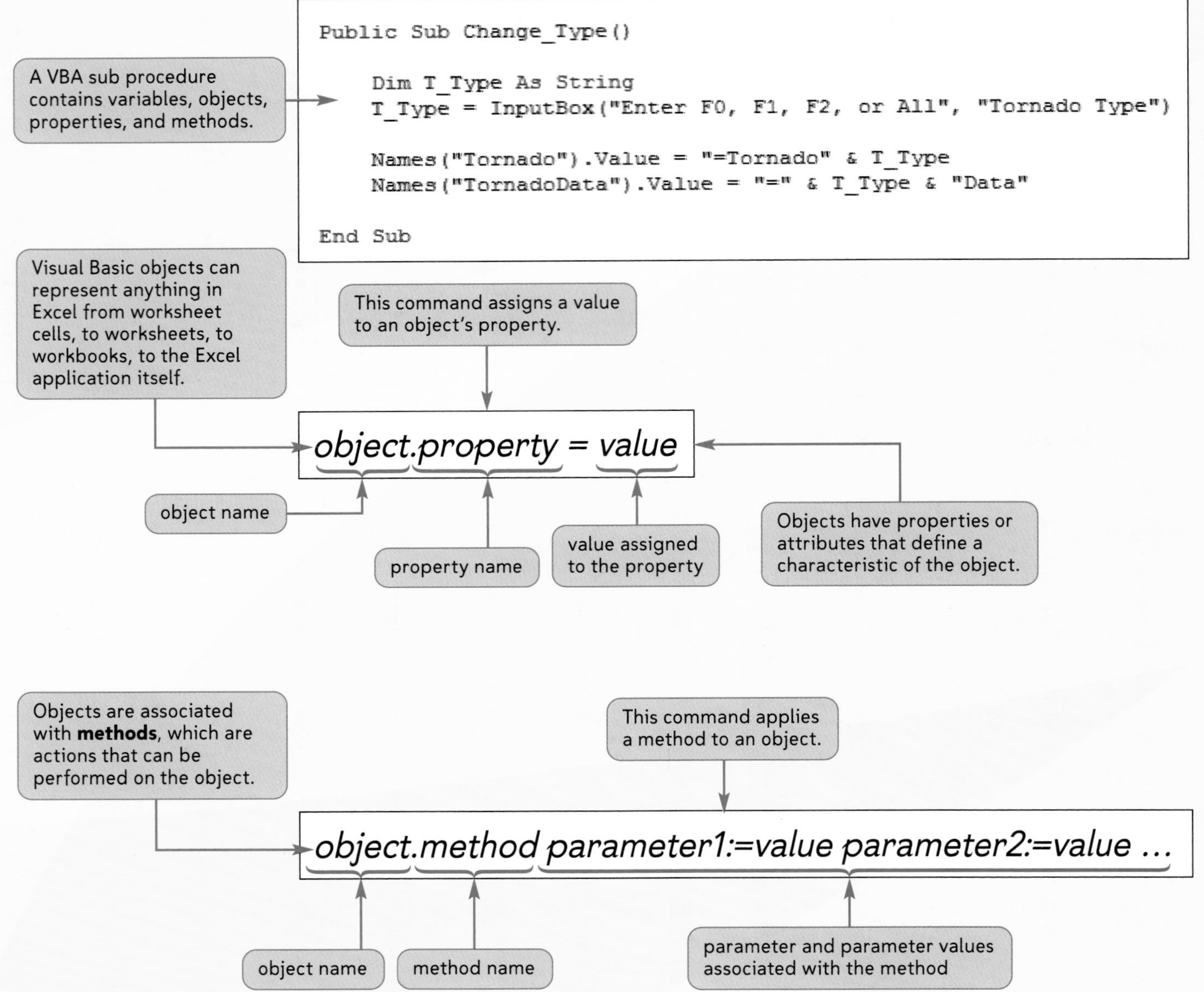

VISUAL BASIC OBJECTS

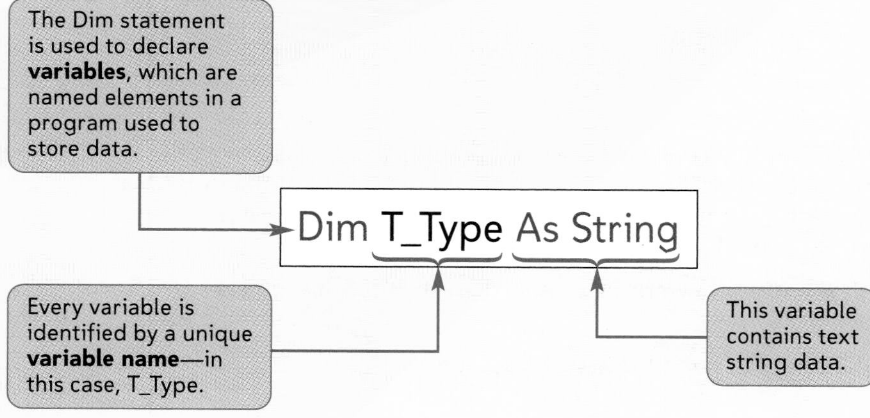

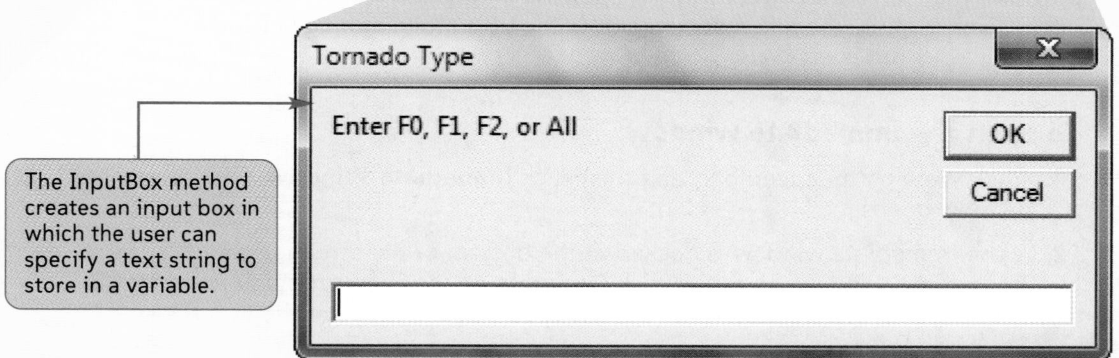

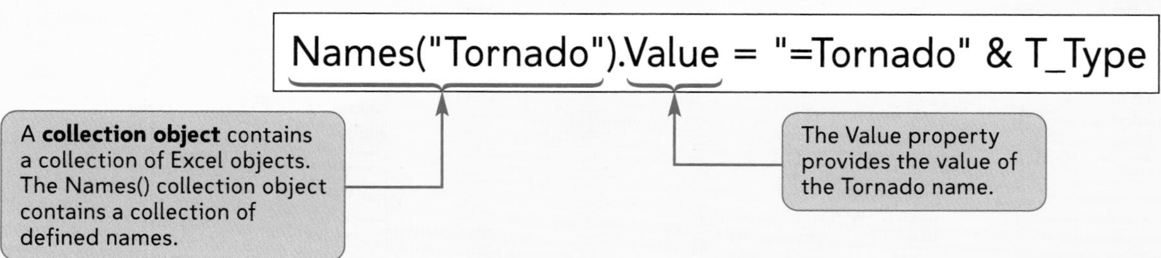

Introducing Visual Basic for Applications

The following discussion provides an overview of some concepts involved in writing a VBA program. You'll use a sample workbook as you explore the syntax of the Visual Basic for Applications language.

To open the sample workbook:

1. Open the **Sample Report** workbook located in the Excel12\Tutorial folder included with your Data Files.
2. Review the contents of the **Yearly Counts**, **Incidents**, and **Statistics** worksheets. Each worksheet describes the prevalence of tornadoes in the latter half of the twentieth century. You have already seen a variation of these pages in the Tornado Analysis workbook.
3. Switch to the **Yearly Counts** worksheet, and then click cell **A1**, if necessary, to make it the active cell.
4. Press the **Alt+F11** keys to open the Visual Basic Editor.

Using the Immediate Window to Learn VBA

As you work in VBA, you might want to see the effects of a single command rather than an entire sub procedure. You can run single command lines in the Visual Basic Editor **Immediate window**. As you enter a command in the Immediate window, its effects are instantly applied to the workbook, making it an ideal way to learn VBA syntax and debug programs that don't run correctly. You'll open the Immediate window, and then use it to interactively explore the different elements of the VBA programming language.

TIP

You can also open the Immediate window by pressing the Ctrl+G keys in the Visual Basic Editor.

To open the Immediate window:

1. Click **View** on the menu bar, and then click **Immediate Window**. The Immediate window opens.
2. If the Immediate window is docked at the bottom of the screen, right-click the **Immediate** window, and then click **Dockable** on the shortcut menu to undock the window, and then resize the window so that it does not fill up the entire Visual Basic Editor window.
3. If the Immediate window displays command lines, select the command lines, and then press the **Delete** key to delete them. See Figure 12-10 (the size and position of your windows might differ).

Figure 12-10 **Immediate window in the Visual Basic Editor**

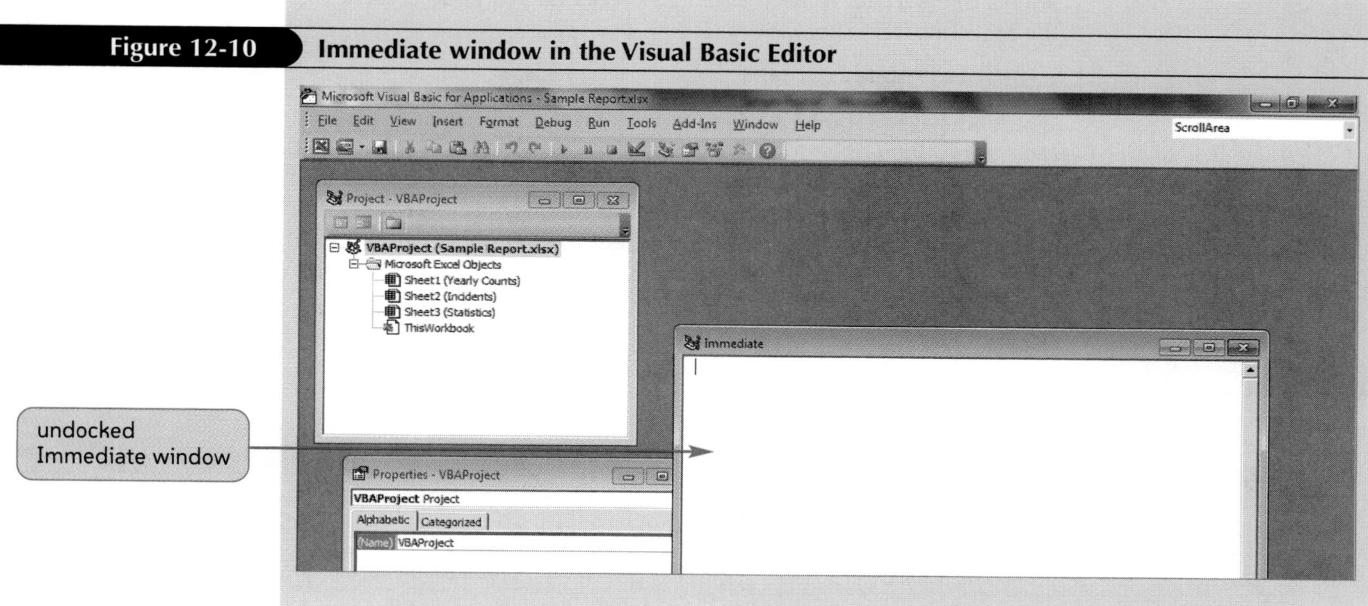

Referring to VBA Objects

VBA is an **object-oriented programming language**, in which tasks are performed by manipulating objects. Almost anything in Excel, from a single cell, to an entire worksheet, to the Excel application itself, is considered a Visual Basic object. You can perform any task on these objects that you can perform in Excel, such as creating charts, moving worksheets, or entering formulas into cells. Figure 12-11 describes some of the common Excel objects you'll use to create VBA programs.

Figure 12-11 **VBA objects in Excel**

Excel Object	Description
Range	A range in a worksheet
Name	A defined name in a workbook
Chart	A chart in a workbook (either embedded within a worksheet or stored as a chart sheet)
ChartObject	A chart embedded within a worksheet
Worksheet	A worksheet in a workbook
Workbook	An Excel workbook
VBAProject	A VBA project
Application	The Excel program itself

Objects are often grouped into collection objects, which are themselves objects. For example, a sheet in a workbook is an object, but the collection of all the sheets in a workbook is also an object. To refer to a specific object in a collection, use the syntax

```
object_collection(id)
```

where *object_collection* is the name of the object collection and *id* is either a name or number that identifies an object in the collection. For example, the object collection

Sheets refers to all of the sheets in a particular workbook. The VBA code that references the Statistics worksheet is

```
Sheets("Statistics")
```

where `Sheets` is the object collection and `"Statistics"` is the name of a specific member in the collection. You could also use the object reference `Sheets(5)` because the Statistics worksheet is the fifth object in the collection of worksheets. Note that the number does not indicate the sheet's location in the workbook. For example, the Statistics worksheet is the fifth worksheet in the collection, but it might be placed anywhere within the workbook. Figure 12-12 provides other examples of VBA code that use object collections.

Figure 12-12 **Object collection examples**

Object Collection	Description
Range("A1:B10")	The collection of cells in the range A1:B10
Names("F1Data")	The F1Data defined name
ChartObjects(3)	The third embedded chart in a worksheet
Charts(3)	The third chart sheet in a workbook
Sheets("Statistics")	The Statistics worksheet
Workbooks("Tornado Analysis")	The Tornado Analysis workbook
Windows(2)	The second open Excel workbook window

VBA organizes objects and object collections in a hierarchy with Excel at the top and the individual cells of a workbook at the bottom. This hierarchy is often referred to as the **Excel Object Model**. Figure 12-13 shows a small portion of the hierarchy that the Excel Object Model follows. You can view the complete listing of the hierarchy using Excel Help in the Visual Basic Editor.

Figure 12-13 **Partial Excel Object Model**

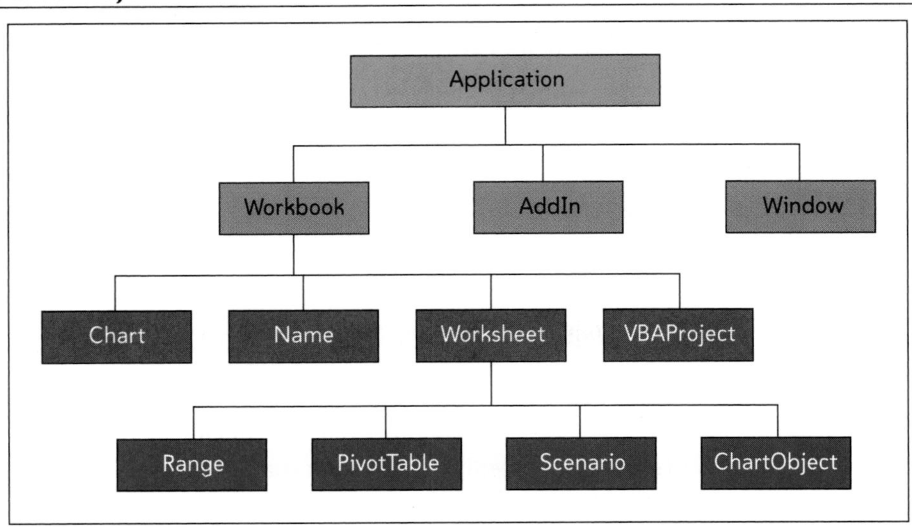

Sometimes you'll refer to an object by indicating its place within the Excel Object Model. The general syntax for expressing an object's location within this hierarchy is

```
object1.object2.object3
```

where *object1* is an object at the upper level of the hierarchy, *object2* is the object at the next lower level in the hierarchy, *object3* is the next lower-level object, and so forth. For example, the complete object reference to cell A1 in the Statistics worksheet of the Tornado workbook within the Excel application is:

```
Application.Workbooks("Tornado").Sheets("Statistics").Range("A1")
```

This object reference starts at the top level in the Excel Object Model (the Excel application) and drills down to a specific cell in a worksheet (cell A1). If you don't include the complete object hierarchy, the object is assumed to be based in the active application, workbook, and worksheet. For example, the following object reference refers to cell A1 of the Statistics worksheet, and the workbook is assumed to be the active workbook:

```
Sheets("Statistics").Range("A1")
```

Similarly, the following object reference refers to cell A1 of the active sheet in the active workbook:

```
Range("A1")
```

To help you work with the hierarchy of objects in the Excel Object Model, VBA provides special object names to refer directly to certain objects. For example, `ActiveSheet` refers to the worksheet currently displayed in the workbook. Figure 12-14 describes some of these special object names.

Figure 12-14 **Special object names**

Object Name	Description
ActiveCell	The currently selected cell
ActiveChart	The currently selected chart
ActiveSheet	The currently selected sheet
ActiveWindow	The currently selected window
ActiveWorkbook	The current workbook
ThisCell	The cell from which a custom function is being run
ThisWorkbook	The workbook containing the macro code that is currently running

TIP

The `ActiveWorkbook` is the workbook selected when the macro is running; the `ThisWorkbook` object refers to the workbook in which the macro code has been stored.

As far as VBA is concerned, the following two lines are equivalent because they both reference cell A1 of the active sheet and workbook:

```
Range("A1")
ActiveWorkbook.ActiveSheet.Range("A1")
```

Modifying Properties

The VBA language alters objects by either modifying the object's properties or applying a method to the object. Properties are the attributes that characterize the object. For example, a worksheet cell supports several properties, such as the value or formula contained in the cell, the formatting applied to the cell's appearance, and the text of the comment that might be attached to the cell. Figure 12-15 describes some Excel objects and the properties associated with them. Note that some properties are themselves objects.

Figure 12-15 **Objects and their properties**

Object	Property	Description
Range	Address	The cell reference of the range
	Comment	A comment attached to the cell
	Formula	The formula entered into the cell
	Value	The value of the cell
Name	RefersTo	The cell(s) that the defined name refers to
	Value	The value of the cell referred to by the defined name
Worksheet	Name	The name of the worksheet
	Visible	Whether the worksheet is visible or hidden
Chart	ChartTitle	The text of the chart's title
	ChartType	The type of the chart
	HasLegend	Whether the chart has a legend
Workbook	HasPassword	Whether the workbook has a password
	Name	The name of the workbook
	Path	The folder and drive in which the workbook is stored
	Saved	Whether the workbook has been saved

This list is only a small sample of the vast number of objects and properties available in VBA programs. Literally everything contained in Excel can be expressed in terms of an object or a property.

TIP

Property values containing text strings and formulas must be placed within quotation marks; property values containing numeric values or Boolean values (true or false) do not.

To change the property of an object, you enter the statement

```
object.property=expression
```

where ***object*** is the object name, ***property*** is the name of the property, and ***expression*** is a value that you want to assign to the property. For example, to change the value of cell A2 in the active sheet to 395, you would use the following command:

```
Range("A2").Value=395
```

Figure 12-16 shows other examples of VBA statements that use this syntax. The fourth example changes the Name property of the Raw Data worksheet object to Table. You did this in the previous session when you changed the worksheet name in the Properties window. This shows the command to do the same thing in VBA.

Figure 12-16 Examples of changing a property's value

VBA Code	Description
ActiveCell.Value=23	Changes the value of the active cell to 23
Range("A5").Formula="SUM(A1:A4)"	Changes the formula of cell A5 to add the values in the range A1:A4
Range("A5").Font.Italic=true	Displays the text of cell A5 in an italic font
Worksheets("Raw Data").Name="Table"	Changes the name of the Raw Data worksheet to *Table*
ActiveWorkbook.Password="weather"	Changes the password of the current workbook to *weather*
Application.StatusBar="Running macro"	Changes the status bar text to *Running macro*
Application.StatusBar=false	Resets the status bar text to its default value
Application.ScreenUpdating=false	Turns off screen updating within Excel
Application.ScreenUpdating=true	Turns on screen updating within Excel

You can also use an object property statement to turn a property on or off. The following VBA command hides the Documentation worksheet from the user by setting the sheet's Visible property to false; to make the worksheet visible again, you switch the value to true:

```
Sheets("Documentation").Visible=false
```

You'll work with objects and properties as you write VBA commands to modify the contents of the Sample Report workbook. You'll write a VBA command in the Immediate window to change the value of a worksheet cell. When you type a VBA command in the Immediate window (and, as you'll see later, in the Code window), ScreenTips describe how to correctly enter the command.

To write an object property statement:

1. With the insertion point in the Immediate window, type **Range(** to begin the command. A ScreenTip indicates that to complete the Range object, you need to enter one or two cell addresses. See Figure 12-17.

Figure 12-17 Command entered in the Immediate window

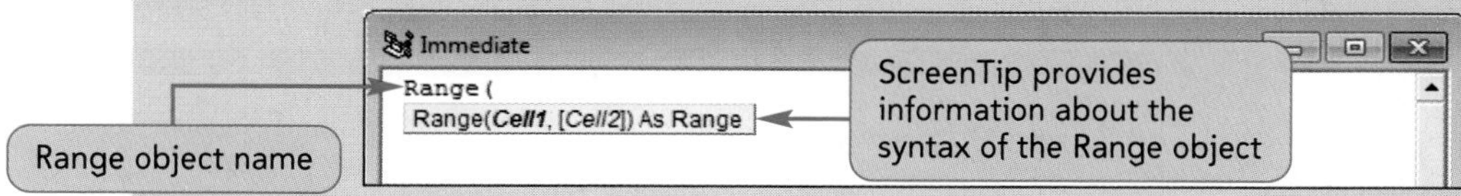

2. Type **"F6").** (including the period) to continue entering the command. A list of properties and methods associated with the Range object opens. (You'll learn about methods shortly.) From this list, you can select the appropriate property for the object. See Figure 12-18.

Figure 12-18 **List of properties and methods**

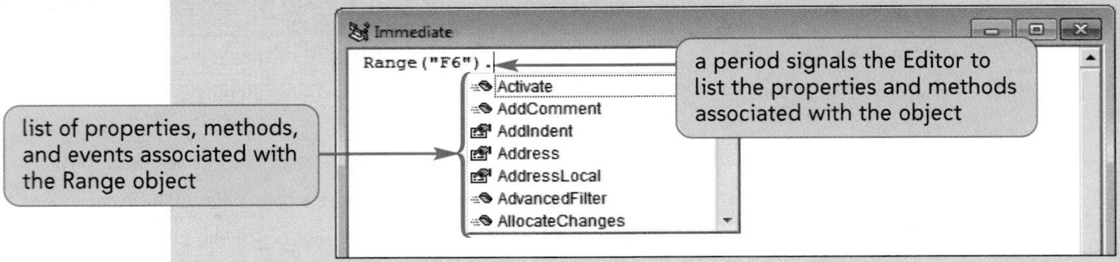

3. Press the **V** key to scroll to the properties that begin with the letter *v*, and then double-click **Value** to insert the property into the command.
4. Type `=49` to complete the command line, and then press the **Enter** key. The command `Range("F6").Value=49` is entered into the Immediate window. See Figure 12-19.

Figure 12-19 **Completed VBA command to set the cell value**

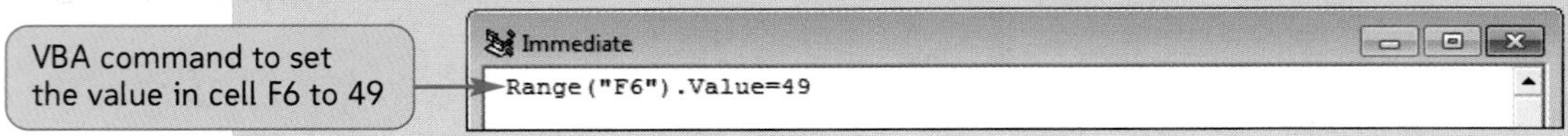

When you pressed the Enter key, the Editor ran the command, changing the value of cell F6 in the active worksheet to 49.

TIP

To save time when running similar commands, press the ↑ key to go to the previous command, edit the command, and then press the Enter key to run the revised command.

5. Return to the **Sample Report** workbook, and then verify that the value in cell F6 is 49. The original value in the cell was 29. You'll change it back with another VBA command.
6. Return to the Visual Basic Editor, type **Range("F6").Value=29** in the Immediate window, and then press the **Enter** key. The completed command is entered in the Immediate window and runs.
7. Return to the **Sample Report** workbook, verify that the value in cell F6 is 29, and then return to the Visual Basic Editor.

The completed VBA command sets the cell value as intended.

INSIGHT

The Undo Button and VBA

You cannot use the Undo button on the Quick Access Toolbar in the Excel workbook to return cell F6 to its original value. The Undo and Redo buttons record the keystrokes and commands you made within the Excel window. They do not record the effect of VBA commands, which are applied to the objects found in the workbook.

Applying Methods

Next, you'll apply a method to an object. A method is an action that can be performed on an object, such as closing a workbook or printing the contents of a worksheet. The syntax to apply a method is

```
object.method
```

where *object* is the name of the object and *method* is the name of the VBA method.

One method you can apply to a worksheet is to select it. The following command selects the Statistics worksheet in the active workbook:

```
Sheets("Statistics").Select
```

Figure 12-20 describes methods associated with different VBA objects.

Figure 12-20 Objects and their methods

Object	Method	Description
Range	Clear	Clears all formulas and values in the range
	Copy	Copies the values in the range to the Clipboard
	Merge	Merges the cells in the range
Worksheet	Delete	Deletes the worksheet
	Select	Selects (and displays) the worksheet
Workbook	Close	Closes the workbook
	Protect	Protects the workbook
	Save	Saves the workbook
Chart	Copy	Copies the chart to the Clipboard
	Select	Selects the chart
	Delete	Deletes the chart
Charts	Select	Selects the chart sheets in the workbook
Worksheets	Select	Selects the worksheets in the workbook

You'll apply the Select method to select the Statistics worksheet, making it the active sheet in the workbook.

TIP

You can also apply the Select method to cells to select them.

To apply the Select method to the Statistics worksheet:

1. Press the **Enter** key to move the insertion point to a new line in the Immediate window, type **Sheets("Statistics").Select** and then press the **Enter** key. The Statistics worksheet is active.
2. Type **Range("D13").Select** in the Immediate window, and then press the **Enter** key. Cell D13 is the active cell in the worksheet.
3. Return to the **Sample Report** workbook, and then verify that the Statistics worksheet is the active sheet and cell D13 is the active cell.

Methods often have parameters that govern how they are applied. A workbook object has the SaveAs method for saving the workbook to a file; but to run the SaveAs method, you need to supply a filename. The statement to apply parameter values to a method is

```
object.method parameter1:=value1 parameter2:=value2...
```

where `object` is the name of an object, `method` is a method that can be applied to that object, `parameter1` and `parameter2` are the names of parameters associated with the method, and `value1` and `value2` are the values assigned to those parameters. For example, to save the active workbook using the filename Budget.xlsx, you would run the following VBA command:

```
ActiveWorkbook.SaveAs Filename:="Budget.xlsx"
```

Figure 12-21 describes other ways of applying methods with parameter values to an object.

Figure 12-21 **Code to apply a method with parameters**

VBA Code	Description
Range("A1").Copy Destination:=Range("A5")	Copies the contents of cell A1 into cell A5
Range("A1").AddComment Text:="Total Assets"	Adds the comment *Total Assets* to cell A1
Sheets("Sheet 1").Move After:=Sheets("Sheet 3")	Moves the Sheet 1 worksheet after the Sheet 3 worksheet
ActiveWorkbook.SaveAs Filename:="Tornado Analysis"	Saves the active workbook as *Tornado Analysis*
ActiveWorkbook.Protect Password:="tornado"	Protects the current workbook using the password *tornado*
Workbooks.Open Filename:="Budget.xlsx"	Opens the Budget.xlsx file, adding it to the collection of open workbooks

You'll write a VBA command to move the Statistics worksheet directly before the Yearly Counts worksheet. You'll apply the Move method and set the Before parameter, which defines before which sheet in the workbook to place the worksheet.

To apply the Move method to move a worksheet:

1. Return to the Visual Basic Editor.
2. Click in the Immediate window, and then press the **Enter** key.
3. Type **Sheets("Statistics").Move Before:=Sheets("Yearly Counts")** and then press the **Enter** key. See Figure 12-22.

Figure 12-22 Select and Move methods

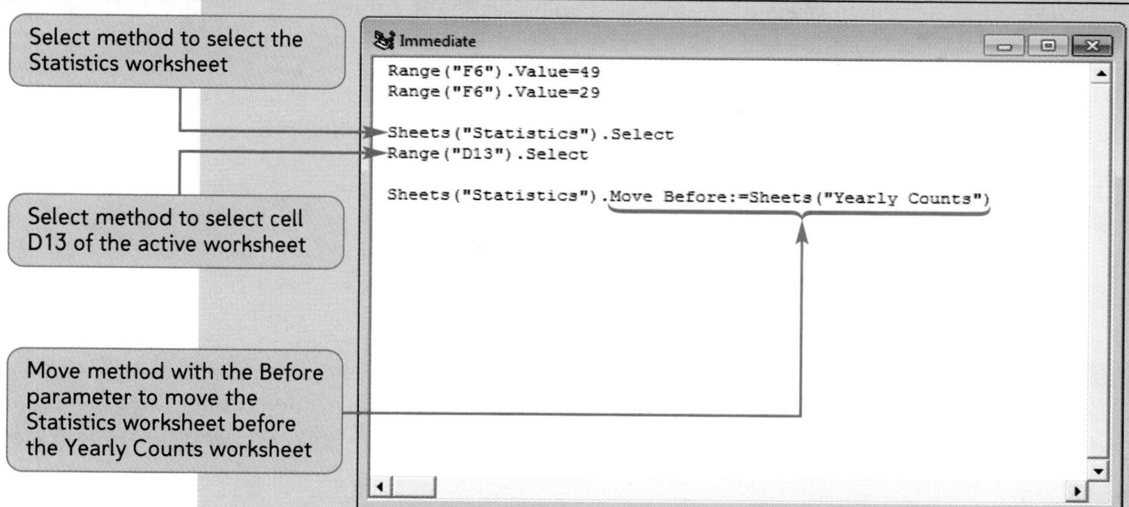

Trouble? If the Immediate window displays an error message, you might have entered the code incorrectly. Close the dialog box and then compare your code to the code shown in Figure 12-22, editing as needed.

4. Return to the **Sample Report** workbook, and then verify that the Statistics worksheet is before the Yearly Counts worksheet at the front of the workbook.
5. Return to the Visual Basic Editor.

Another way of entering an object method is to use the following syntax, which requires that the parameter values be entered in a specific order as determined by the syntax for the method that is being applied:

```
object.method(value1, value2, ...)
```

However, you must know exactly what parameters are required for the method and in what order they need to be entered. For example, to save the active workbook in the Budget.xlsx file, you could run the following VBA command:

```
ActiveWorkbook.SaveAs("Budget.xlsx")
```

The SaveAs method has only one required parameter value: the filename. The filename must be entered before the other parameters, which are optional.

Working with Variables and Values

So far, you've written code for tasks that represent what you could have done directly within Excel using your mouse and keyboard. The power of VBA really begins when you start using variables. For example, you could declare a variable named *tornado_type* and use it to store the type of tornado data displayed in the Tornado Analysis workbook. Variables are case sensitive, so VBA distinguishes between variables named *WBook* and *wbook*.

Declaring a Variable

When you declare a variable, you need to allocate storage space for it, which is referred to as "dimensioning" a variable. Dimensioning is abbreviated as "Dim" in the commands for declaring variables. To declare a variable, you use the command

```
Dim variable
```

where *variable* is the variable name. You can also define exactly what type of data can be stored in a variable with the command

```
Dim variable as type
```

where *type* is the data type. For example, the following command declares a variable named SheetName that will contain text strings:

```
Dim SheetName as String
```

TIP

Declare all variables and their data types at the start of sub procedures to document exactly what variables are used in the procedure and the type of data each variable stores.

VBA supports a wide range of data types. For example, it supports several data types for numeric values, including the Integer data type for whole numbers and the Single data type for decimal values. In David's project, you'll only use the String data type. You can learn more about data types using VBA Help.

INSIGHT

Determining a Data Type

It is not strictly required to specify a data type or declare a variable in Visual Basic. If you don't specify a data type, Excel determines the data type by what is stored in the variable. Likewise, if you don't declare a variable, Excel creates the variable when you first attempt to store data in it. However, good programming practice is to declare variables and their data types as a way of catching errors that might creep into the code.

Assigning a Value to a Variable

After you declare a variable, you store data in it using the command

```
variable=expression
```

where *expression* is the initial value or text string that is assigned to the variable. For example, the following command stores the text string *Budget* in the variable SheetName. If you have not declared the SheetName variable beforehand, this command creates the variable for you:

```
SheetName="Budget"
```

Variables can also store objects such as worksheets, workbooks, or cell ranges. The command

```
Set variable = object
```

stores an object in a variable, where *object* is an object in Excel. So, the command that stores the Statistics worksheet in the ReportSheet variable is:

```
Set ReportSheet=Sheets("Statistics")
```

You can use a VBA property or method with the ReportSheet variable in the same way you would use it with the object itself. For example, the following command uses the ReportSheet variable to select the Statistics worksheet:

```
ReportSheet.Select
```

Figure 12-23 shows VBA statements in which variables are assigned values or are used to store objects.

Figure 12-23 Code to set the value of a variable

VBA Code	Description
Year=2013	Stores the value 2013 in the Year variable
Type="F2"	Stores the text string *F2* in the Type variable
Type=Range("A2").Value	Stores the value entered in cell A2 of the active worksheet in the Type variable
Set WSheet=Sheets("Statistics")	Stores the Statistics worksheet in the WSheet variable
Set WBook=Workbooks("Tornado Analysis")	Stores the Tornado Analysis workbook in the WBook variable

You can use variables to create general procedures that apply to several objects. For example, to select a worksheet, you could create a variable named *SheetName* that contains the name of a sheet you want to select. The general sub procedure might look as follows:

```
Sub SelectSheet()
    Dim SheetName
    SheetName="Statistics"
    Sheets(SheetName).Select
    Range("A1").Select
End Sub
```

TIP

To display the value of a variable, type ?*variable* (where *variable* is the variable name) in the Immediate window, and then press the Enter key.

Later in this session, you'll learn how to set variable values with user input as the program is running to create a general program, but this code shows how the variable is used within the procedure.

In the Sample Report workbook, you'll enter code to change the name of a worksheet to the value stored in the SheetName variable. Because of how memory is allocated in the Immediate window, you cannot run the Dim statement to declare the variable. Instead, you'll assign a value to the SheetName variable, which creates the variable without declaring it.

To create and apply the SheetName variable:

1. In the Immediate window, press the **Enter** key, type **SheetName=Range("B4").Value** and then press the **Enter** key. Excel creates the SheetName variable, assigning it the value entered into cell B4 of the active worksheet.
2. Type **ActiveSheet.Name=SheetName** and then press the **Enter** key. Excel uses the Name property of the ActiveSheet object to change the sheet's name to the value stored in the SheetName variable. See Figure 12-24.

Figure 12-24 SheetName variable created and applied

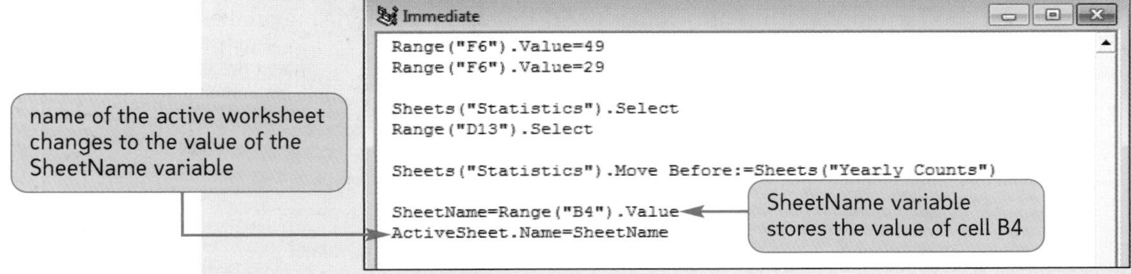

3. Return to the Sample Report workbook, and then verify that the name of the Statistics worksheet (the active sheet) changed to *Tornadoes per Era*, which is the value in cell B4 of that sheet.
4. Close the Sample Report workbook without saving changes.

Writing a Sub Procedure

You'll use the basic concepts of the VBA programming language you just reviewed to create a sub procedure in which you can display the atmospheric data for different tornado types in David's workbook. To create a program to display data on different tornado types, you first must understand how David organized the data in the Tornado Analysis workbook. David defined names to the values he collected and stored in the Table worksheet. All of the charts and statistics in the Tornado Analysis workbook are based on defined names rather than cell references. Figure 12-25 lists the defined names he used in the Tornado Analysis workbook.

Figure 12-25 **Defined names in the Tornado Analysis workbook**

Defined Name	Definition	Refers to
AllData	=Table!$F$7:$F$56	All tornado data regardless of type
F0Data	=Table!$C$7:$C$56	Data on the occurrence of F0 tornadoes
F1Data	=Table!$D$7:$D$56	Data on the occurrence of F1 tornadoes
F2Data	=Table!$E$7:$E$56	Data on the occurrence of F2+ tornadoes
TornadoData	=AllData	Data from the currently selected tornado type
TornadoAll	=Table!$F$6	A cell containing the text "All"
TornadoF0	=Table!$C$6	A cell containing the text "F0"
TornadoF1	=Table!$D$6	A cell containing the text "F1"
TornadoF2	=Table!$E$6	A cell containing the text "F2+"
Tornado	=TornadoAll	The name of the selected tornado type

Range C6:F6 in the Table worksheet contains the names of the different tornado types, and each of these cells has been assigned a name. For example, the TornadoF1 name points to cell D6, which displays the text *F1*. The type of tornado displayed in the workbook's charts and statistics has the defined name *Tornado*. The current definition of the Tornado name is "=TornadoAll", which means that it points to the TornadoAll range (cell F6 in the Table worksheet). Similarly, F0Data, F1Data, and F2Data point to the data values detailing the number of occurrences per year of each tornado type.

To switch from one tornado type to another, David simply changes the definition of the Tornado and TornadoData names. For example, to display data about F1 tornadoes, he changes the definition of the Tornado name from "=TornadoAll" to "=TornadoF1" and changes the definition of the TornadoData name from "=AllData" to "=F1Data". All of the charts and statistics are then updated and display data on F1 tornadoes only.

Creating a Sub Procedure to Switch Defined Names

David wants to automate this process because other users might not be familiar with names or know how to use them. Instead of using the Name Manager dialog box, he wants Excel to prompt the user for the tornado type to display and then automatically switch to the type indicated by the user. You can create such a dialog box using VBA. First, you'll write a sub procedure to display data on F1 tornadoes. To do that, you'll use some of the objects, properties, and methods you used with the Sample Report workbook.

Defined names are stored in the Names object collection. To modify the definition of a particular name, you use either the Value property or the RefersTo property. The command to change the definition of the Tornado name to point to "=TornadoF1" is:

```
Names("Tornado").Value="=TornadoF1"
```

The command to change the definition of the TornadoData name is:

```
Names("TornadoData").Value="=F1Data"
```

Both commands assume that the Names collection is contained within the currently active workbook.

To write the Change_Type sub procedure:

1. Open the **Tornado Analysis** workbook.
2. Return to the Visual Basic Editor, and then close the Immediate window.
3. Click in the Code window, click **Insert** on the menu bar, and then click **Procedure**. The Add Procedure dialog box opens.
4. Type **Change_Type** in the Name box, and then click the **OK** button. The Visual Basic Editor inserts a new sub procedure in the Code window named *Change_Type*. The insertion point is below the Public Sub Change_Type() line.
5. Press the **Tab** key to indent the line where you will type the command.
6. Type **Names("Tornado").Value = "=TornadoF1"** and then press the **Enter** key. This command changes the value of the Tornado name from "=TornadoAll" to "=TornadoF1".
7. Type **Names("TornadoData").Value = "=F1Data"** into the next line of the sub procedure. See Figure 12-26.

TIP

Inserting tabs into command lines makes the code easier to read by emphasizing the structure of the sub procedure.

Figure 12-26 Initial Change_Type( ) sub procedure

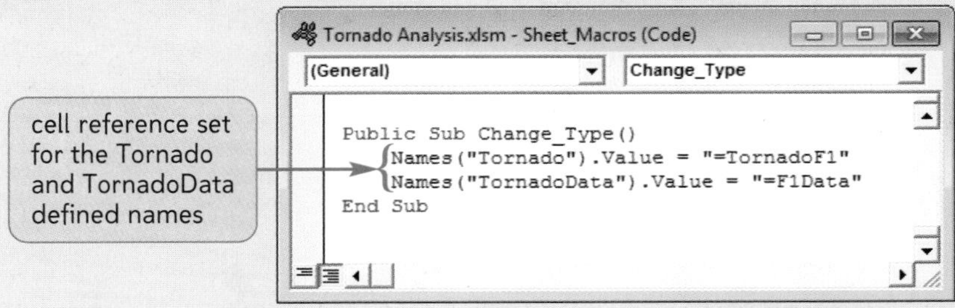

Trouble? If you have problems running this macro, you might have mistyped the code. Review the code for misspellings and other errors, making sure you included the equal sign in "=TornadoF1", as shown in Figure 12-26.

Next, you'll test the Change_Type sub procedure by running the procedure from within the Visual Basic Editor.

To test the Change_Type sub procedure:

1. With the insertion point within the Change_Type sub procedure, click **Run** on the menu bar, and then click **Run Sub/UserForm**.
2. Return to the **Tornado Analysis** workbook, switch to the **Report** worksheet, and then verify that the tornado type in cell C6 is *F1*.
3. Switch to each of the other worksheets in the workbook, verifying that the layout of the charts and tables changed to reflect the new data source. Figure 12-27 shows the revised histogram chart.

Figure 12-27 Histogram of the yearly occurrence of F1 tornadoes

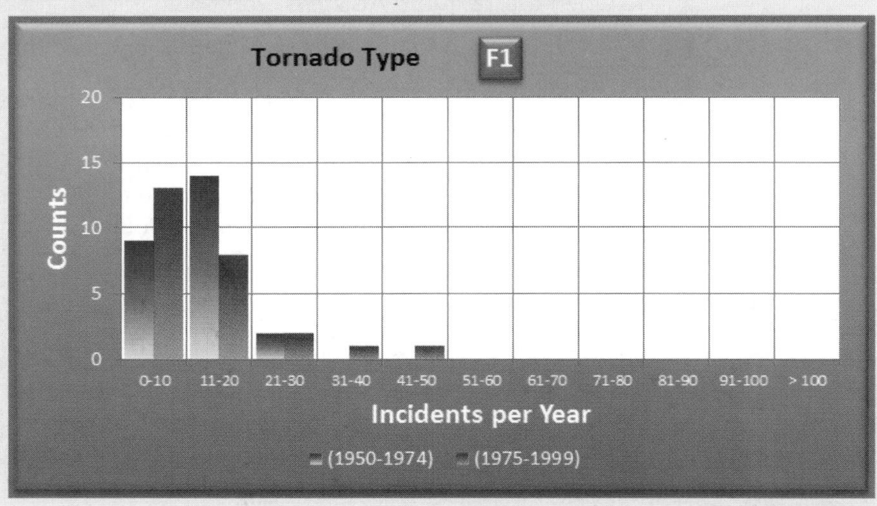

PROSKILLS

Problem Solving: Common Sources of Program Errors

When you write VBA programs, you can encounter three types of errors: syntax errors, run-time errors, and logical errors. Syntax errors occur when a line of VBA code is entered improperly. The Visual Basic Editor catches such errors before you get a chance to run the program and usually provides ScreenTips to help you fix the error.

Run-time errors occur when the program is running. At that point, the code has no known syntax errors, but something in the code keeps it from running successfully. For example, Excel does not recognize a mistyped worksheet name as a programming error, but the code will fail when it cannot locate the sheet object the program references. You can use the debugging tools in Excel to run the program up to a certain spot in the code. By running only part of the code, you can quickly locate the command line that is causing the program to fail. After you identify the command, you can use Excel Help to determine the reason for the error.

Logical errors can be the most difficult to resolve. With these errors, the program is free of syntax errors and it runs without failing, but the results are incorrect. To fix a logical error, run the program one line at a time, confirming the correctness of each operation until you find the command that results in an incorrect value or operation. If you still cannot find the source of the error, consider a different approach to solving the problem. VBA often provides several different ways of performing the same task.

Creating a Variable to Store a Defined Name

The kiosk application must be able to display data on different tornado types. For example, one user might want to display data from F1 tornadoes while another user might want to see the data for F2 tornadoes. You could edit the code, changing "TornadoF1" and "F1Data" to "TornadoF2" and "F2Data", but a more general approach is to create a variable that stores the tornado type you want to display in the workbook. You'll create such a variable named *T_Type*, setting its initial value to the text string *F2*.

To create the T_Type variable:

1. Return to the Visual Basic Editor.
2. Click at the end of the Public Sub Change_Type() line, and then press the **Enter** key to insert a new line at the top of the procedure.
3. Press the **Tab** key, type **Dim T_Type As String**, and then press the **Enter** key to insert a new line.
4. Type **T_Type = "F2"** and then press the **Enter** key. The T_Type variable is defined.

TIP

All VBA commands are read on a single line of code. To break a line to make your code easier to read, type a space followed by the underscore character (_), at the end of the line.

Next, you'll use the T_Type variable to change the cell references of the two defined names. Currently, the Tornado name has the reference "=TornadoF1". You'll replace this value with the expression "=Tornado" & T_Type. The ampersand symbol (&) is used to combine two text strings into a single text string. Because the T_Type variable has a value of "F2", the value of "=Tornado" & T_Type is "=TornadoF2". Similarly, the reference for the TornadoData name changes from "=F1Data" to "=" & T_Type & "Data". In this case, you'll use the ampersand symbol twice to connect three text strings.

To edit the range reference names:

1. In the next line of the sub procedure, change "=TornadoF1" to **"=Tornado" & T_Type**.
2. In the next line of the sub procedure, change "=F1Data" to **"=" & T_Type & "Data"**. See Figure 12-28.

Figure 12-28 T_Type variable defined

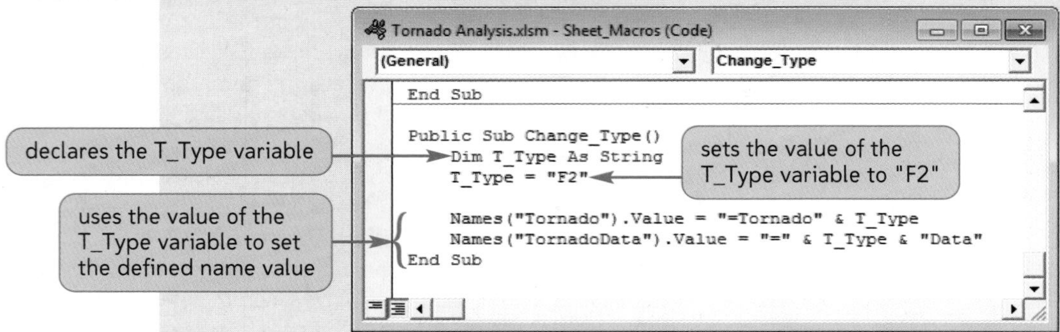

Next, you'll test the program to confirm that it switches from displaying information on F1 type tornadoes to F2 type tornadoes.

3. With the insertion point within the Change_Type sub procedure, click **Run** on the menu bar, and then click **Run Sub/UserForm**. The program runs.
4. Return to the Tornado Analysis workbook, and then verify that the workbook displays data on F2+-type tornadoes in all of the charts and tables.

   Trouble? If an error message appears, you probably made an error entering the code. Check your code against the code shown in Figure 12-28, paying close attention to the use of uppercase and lowercase letters, and verifying that you have closed all quotation marks.

Retrieving Information from the User

The macro works, but you want to prompt users for the value of the T_Type variable rather than entering it directly into the VBA code. You can do this using the InputBox method with the statement

```
variable = InputBox(Prompt, Title)
```

where ***variable*** is a variable whose value is set based on what the user enters in the input box, ***Prompt*** is the message you want to appear in the input box, and ***Title*** is the text that appears in the title bar of the input box. Figure 12-29 shows the VBA code that produces the input box, storing the result from the input box in a variable named *user*.

Figure 12-29 **InputBox function**

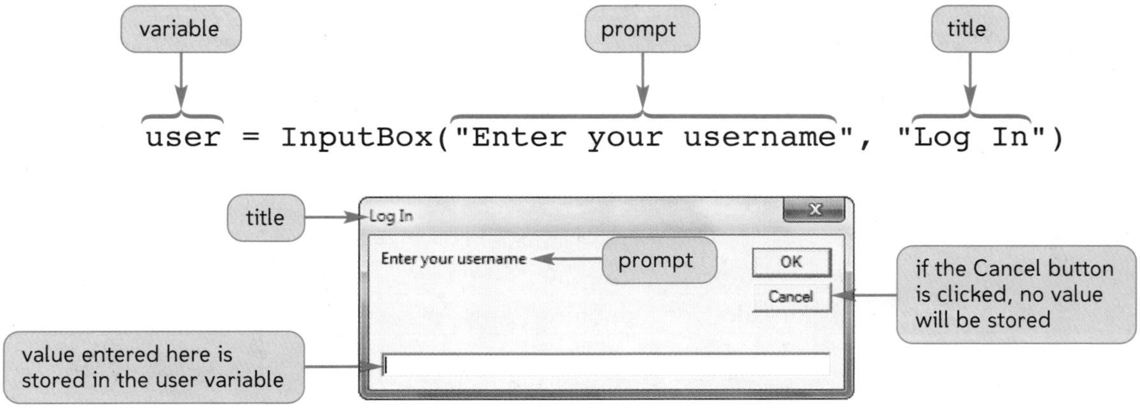

variable

prompt

title

```
user = InputBox("Enter your username", "Log In")
```

title

Log In

Enter your username

prompt

OK

Cancel

if the Cancel button is clicked, no value will be stored

value entered here is stored in the user variable

You'll create an input box to prompt the user for the value of the T_Type variable.

To create the input box:

1. Return to the Visual Basic Editor.
2. Change the second line of the Change_Type() sub procedure from T_Type = "F2" to **T_Type = InputBox("Enter F0, F1, F2, or All", "Tornado Type")**. See Figure 12-30.

Figure 12-30 **InputBox command to set the value of the T_Type variable**

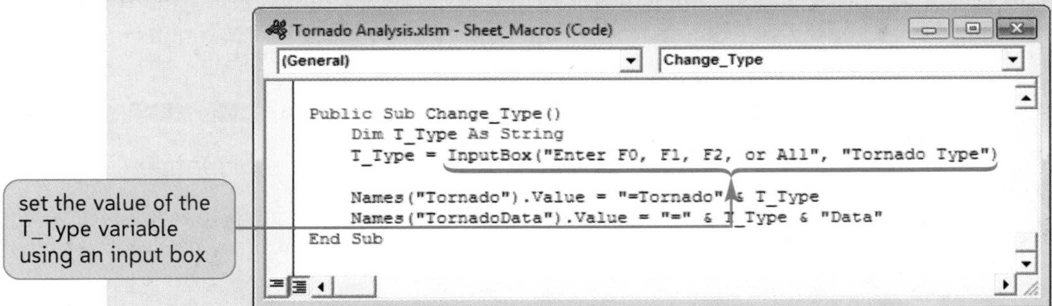

3. Close the Visual Basic Editor, and return to the **Report** worksheet of the Tornado Analysis workbook.

Next, you'll apply the Change_Type macro to the Specify a Tornado Type macro button on the Report worksheet, and then run the macro, changing the type from F2 to F0.

To assign the Change_Type macro to a button and test it:

1. On the Report worksheet, right-click the **Specify a Tornado Type** button, and then click **Assign Macro** on the shortcut menu.
2. Select **Change_Type** in the Macro name box, and then click the **OK** button.
3. Click any cell in the worksheet to deselect the macro button, and then click the **Specify a Tornado Type** button. The Tornado Type dialog box opens.
4. Type **F0** to enter a test value. See Figure 12-31.

Figure 12-31 **Tornado Type input box**

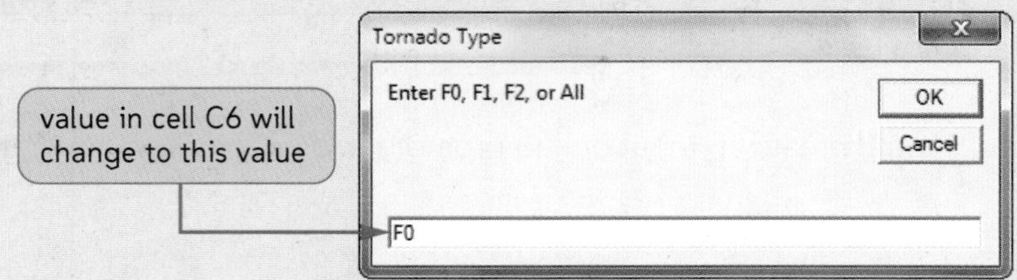

5. Click the **OK** button. The value in cell C6 changes from F2+ to F0.
6. View the other worksheets, verifying that the charts and tables changed to display data on F0 tornadoes, and then save the workbook.

Using VBA, you created a macro that makes it easier to display data on different tornado types. In the next session, you'll create procedures called control structures that "make decisions" based on the type of information the user enters.

PROSKILLS

Written Communication: Writing Clear and Informative Code

When writing VBA programs, good coding practices help to avoid bugs and errors that cause the program to return incorrect values or to not run at all. Keep in mind these general tips:

- Add comment lines to programs to document exactly what the program is doing at each step in the process and why.
- Declare all variables at the top of the sub procedure with comments describing the purpose of each variable. Use descriptive variable names.
- Assign data types to all of your variables.
- Indent the code to make it easier to read.
- Write code in lowercase text. If the spelling is correct, the Visual Basic Editor automatically capitalizes the letters to fit the syntax.

Writing clear and concise VBA code makes your programs easier for your colleagues to read and interpret. Remember that your application must be readable to your coworkers long after you have moved on to other jobs.

REVIEW

Session 12.2 Quick Check

1. Define the following terms: (a) *object-oriented programming language,* (b) *collection object,* (c) *method,* (d) *parameter,* and (e) *variable.*
2. What VBA command would you enter to change the name of the Histogram worksheet to *Histogram Chart*? (*Hint*: The object name is Sheets("Histogram") and the name of the worksheet is contained in the Name property.)
3. What VBA command would you enter to select the Histogram worksheet?
4. What VBA command would you enter to store the name of the active worksheet in a variable named *SheetName*?
5. What VBA command would you enter to change the text of the Excel status bar to *Program Running*?
6. What VBA command would you enter to turn off screen updating in Excel?
7. What VBA command would you enter to display an input box containing the prompt "Enter your last name", display the text "Log In" in the title bar, and then save whatever the user entered into a variable named *Lastname*?

SESSION 12.3 VISUAL OVERVIEW

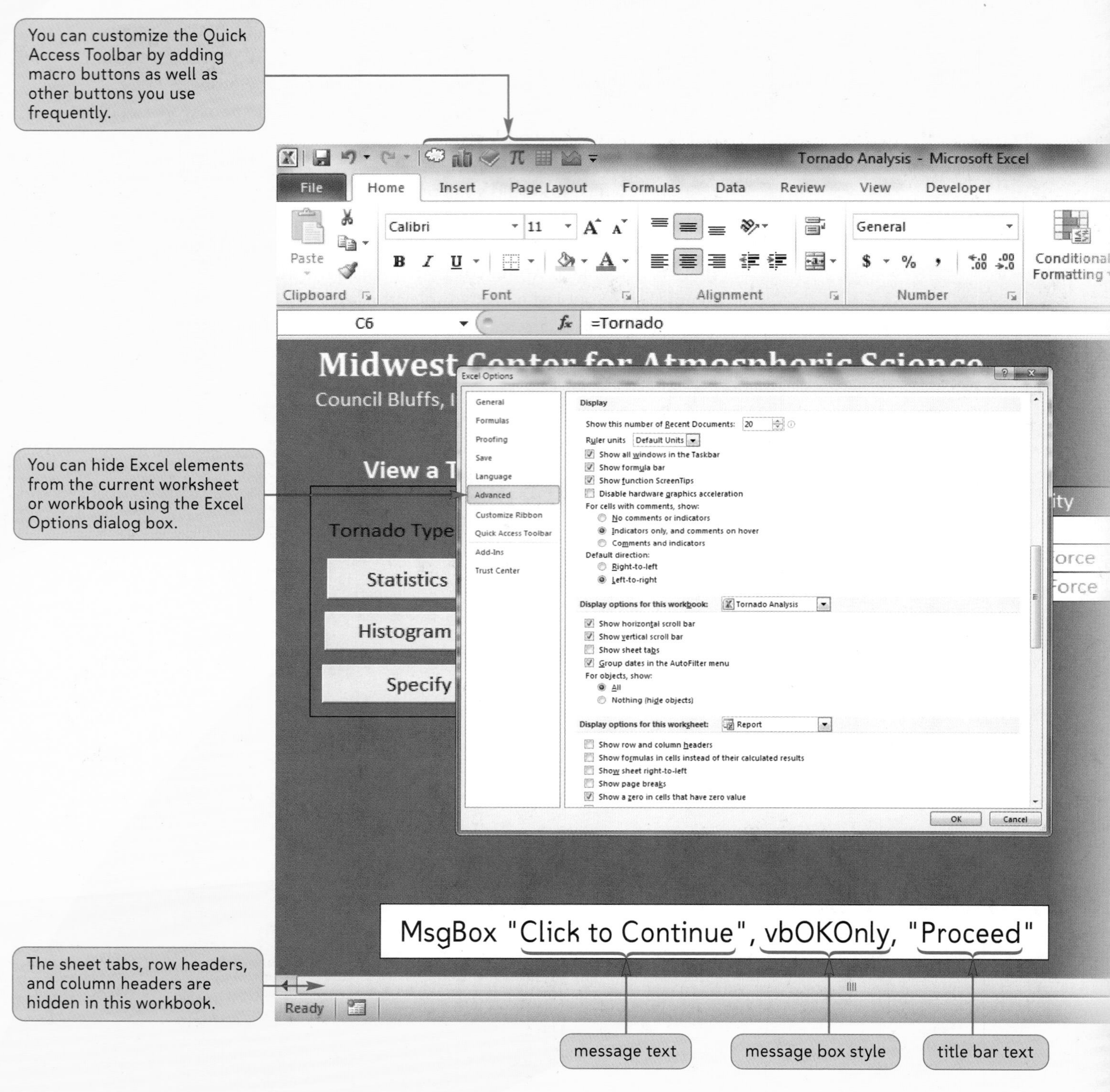

IF STATEMENTS AND CUSTOMIZATION

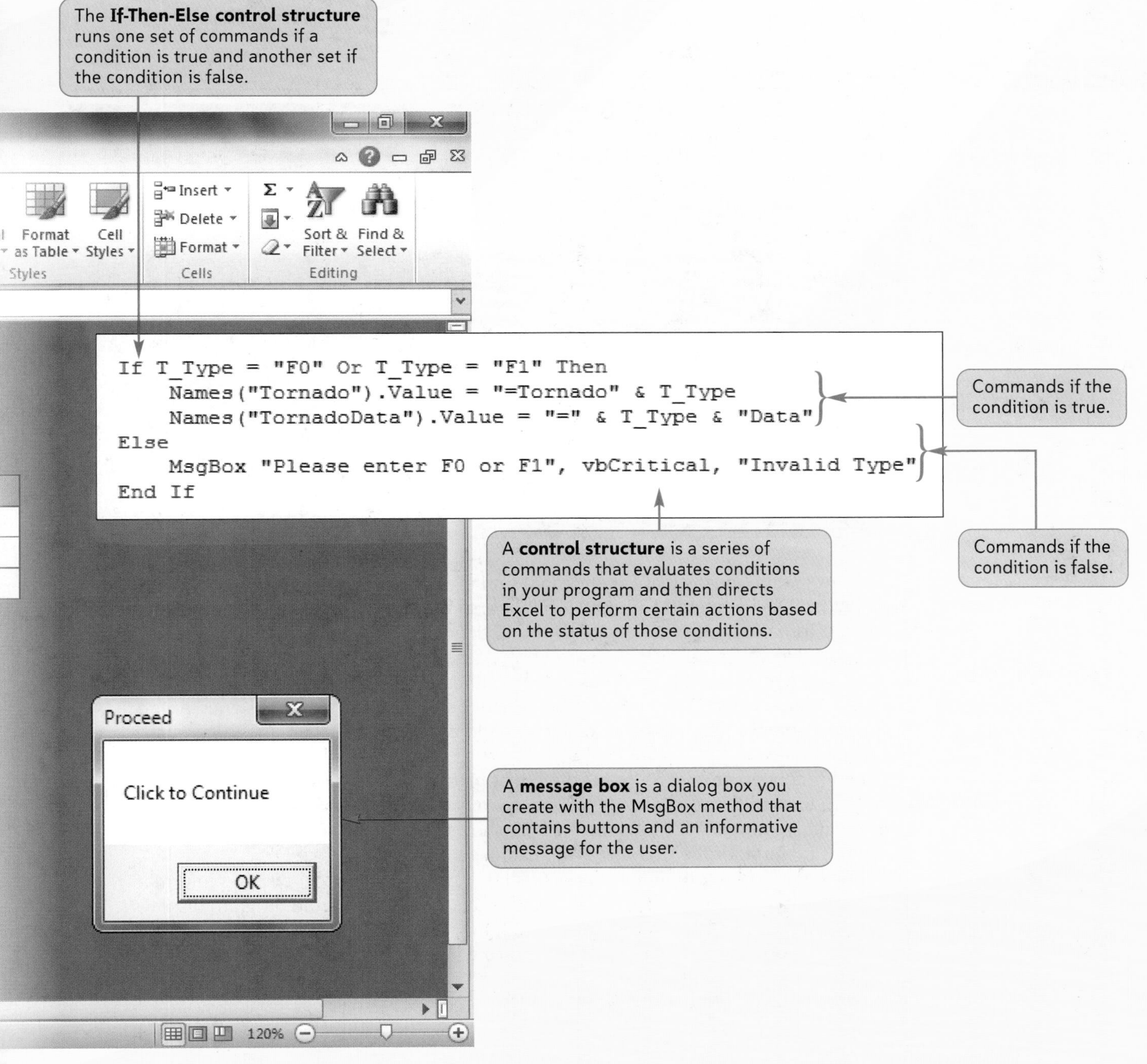

Working with Conditional Statements

David has been testing the macro buttons in the Tornado Analysis workbook and he found that the Change_Type macro does not accept any entry other than F0, F1, F2, and All without resulting in an error. Once, David mistakenly typed *F3* in the input box; when he pressed the OK button, the error value shown in Figure 12-32 appeared in cell C6. Another time, he mistakenly typed F3 again but clicked the Cancel button. However, the error value still appeared.

Figure 12-32 **Report worksheet after specifying an incorrect type**

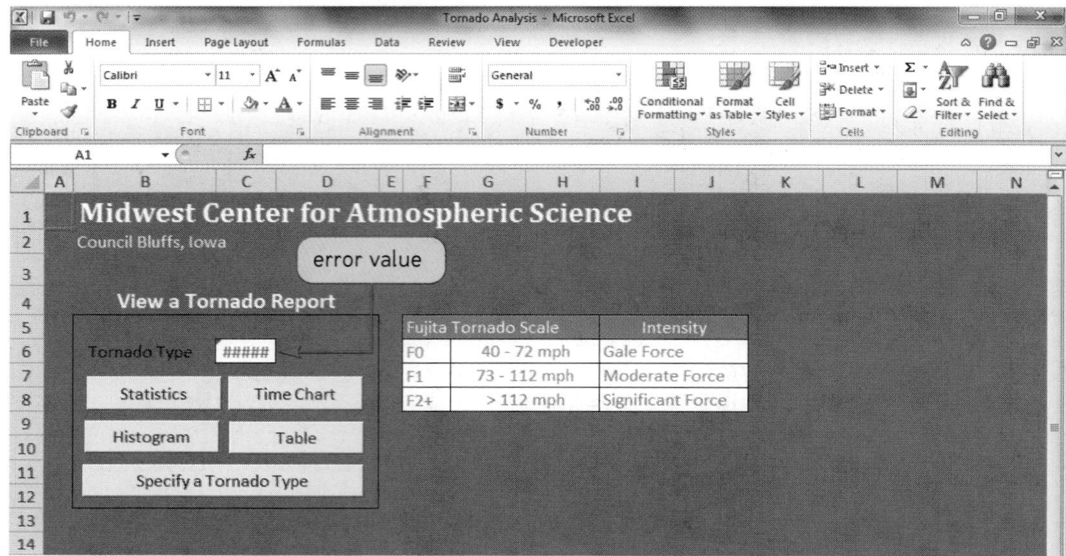

The error value means that Excel cannot find the defined name used in the formula. When David entered F3 in the input box, the Change_Type macro attempted to assign the Tornado and TornadoData names to the cell references "=TornadoF3" and "=F3Data". However, because the workbook does not contain these defined names, an error value appeared for formulas that use either the Tornado or TornadoData name. Similarly, when David clicked the Cancel button, no value was assigned to the T_Type variable, so the definitions of the Tornado and TornadoData names again had improper values.

David is concerned that other people might be confused if this happens to them. He wants you to modify the Change_Type macro to handle this problem. To do this, you must create a control structure. Figure 12-33 shows the kind of control structure that David has in mind for the Change_Type macro.

In this control structure, if the user enters F0, F1, F2, or All, Excel displays information on the selected tornado type. If the user enters different text, the program displays a message indicating the acceptable entries. If the user clicks the Cancel button instead of entering a tornado type, the input box closes without doing anything, and the user returns to the Report worksheet.

Figure 12-33 Control structure for the Change_Type macro

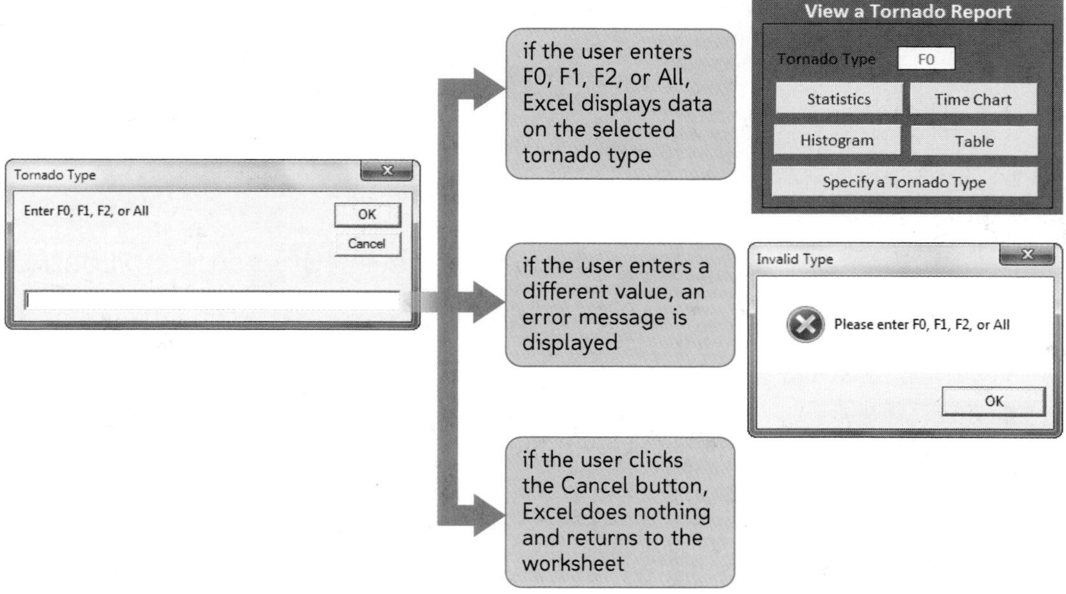

Using the If Statement

The most basic way to run a VBA command in response to a particular condition is the If statement. In this type of control structure, if a certain condition is met, such as the user entering F0, F1, F2, or All, the program executes a specified command. The If statement has the syntax

```
If Condition Then Command
```

where *Condition* is a VBA expression that is either true or false, and *Command* is a command that the macro will run if *Condition* is true. For example, the following statement sets the value of cell B10 to "Loan Approved" if the Savings variable has a value greater than 20,000:

```
If Savings > 20000 Then Range("B10").Value = "Loan Approved"
```

Using the If-Then-Else Control Structure

When the condition of the If statement is not true, the macro does nothing. For the macro to run an alternate command when the condition is false, you need to use an If-Then-Else statement. In an If-Then-Else control structure, one set of commands is run if the condition is true and a different set of commands is run if the condition is false. The If-Then-Else control structure has the syntax

```
If Condition Then
     Commands if Condition is true
Else
     Commands if Condition is false
End If
```

where *Condition* is a VBA expression that is either true or false. If the condition is true, then the first set of commands is run; otherwise, the second set of commands is run.

Figure 12-34 shows an example of an If-Then-Else control structure. This macro has two possible outcomes based on whether the user has more than $20,000 in savings. If the value of the Savings variable is greater than 20,000, "Loan Approved" is displayed in cell B10; otherwise, "Loan Denied" is displayed.

Figure 12-34 Sample If-Then-Else control structure

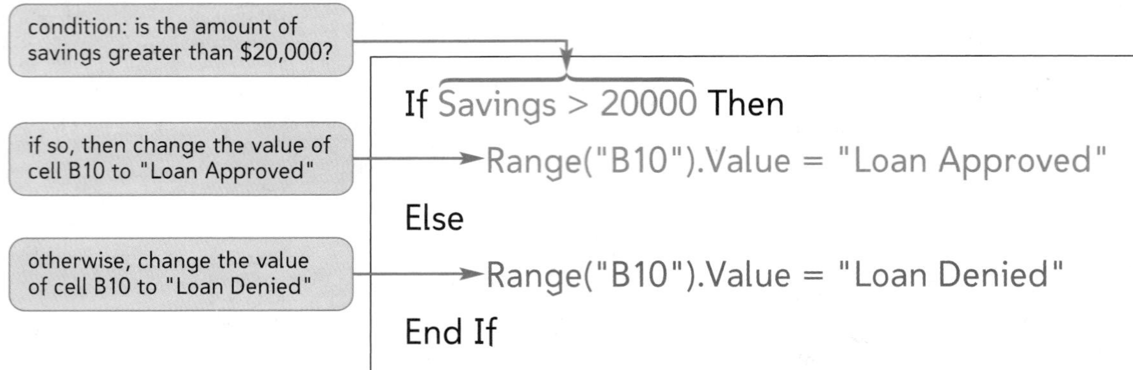

TIP

The If-Then-ElseIf control structure can be unwieldy with many conditions. To test several conditions in a macro, use the VBA Select Case statement instead.

If a control structure has several conditions, you need to use an **If-Then-ElseIf control structure** to run commands in response to each condition. This control structure in VBA has the syntax

```
If Condition1 Then
     Commands if Condition1 is true
ElseIf Condition2 Then
     Commands if Condition2 is true
ElseIf Condition3 Then
     Commands if Condition3 is true
Else
     Commands if none of the conditions are true
End If
```

where `Condition1`, `Condition2`, `Condition3`, and so forth are expressions that represent distinct conditions. You can specify an unlimited number of conditions. Visual Basic analyzes the conditions in sequence, bypassing any remaining conditions when it finds a condition that is true. There should be no overlap between the conditions so that one, and only one, condition is true for any If statement.

Figure 12-35 shows an example of VBA code using multiple conditions in a control structure that evaluates whether a user qualifies for a loan. This example presents three conditions: (1) the person applying for the loan could have more than $20,000 in savings; (2) the person could have from $15,000 to $20,000; or (3) the person could have less than $15,000. Based on which condition is true, the text *Loan Approved, Loan Pending*, or *Loan Denied* is entered into cell B10.

Figure 12-35 Sample If-Then-ElseIf control structure

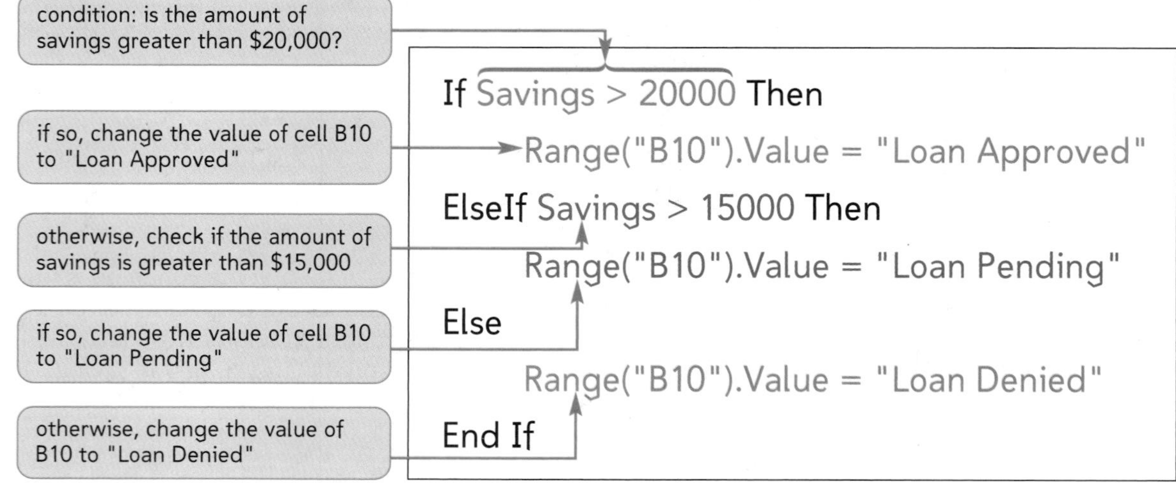

Using Comparison and Logical Operators

To determine whether the expression used in the condition is true or false, the expression must contain a comparison operator. Recall that a comparison operator is a symbol used to compare one value with another, such as <, >, =, <=, >=, and <>. Figures 12-34 and 12-35 used > in the expression that determined whether the value of the Savings variable was greater than 20,000. You'll use these comparison operators frequently in VBA control structures. Another common comparison operator—*is*—tests whether one object is the same as another.

As you write conditions for control structures, you'll also use logical operators. **Logical operators** combine expressions within a condition. The most common logical operators are the And operator and the Or operator. The And operator requires both expressions to be true before the procedure acts on them; the Or operator requires only one expression to be true. Figure 12-36 shows a condition that uses the And logical operator. In this example, the text *Loan Approved* is displayed in cell B10 only if the Savings variable has a value greater than 20,000 and the Credit variable has the value "Good". Otherwise, the value displayed in cell B10 is *Loan Denied*.

Figure 12-36 **Condition with the And logical operator**

```
If Savings > 20000  And Credit = "Good" Then
        Range("B10").Value = "Loan Approved"
Else
        Range("B10").Value = "Loan Denied"
End If
```

And logical operator combines two expressions

Figure 12-37 shows a similar condition that uses the Or logical operator. In this example, the loan is approved if either the Savings variable is greater than 20,000 or the value of the equity in a home mortgage is greater than or equal to 10,000.

Figure 12-37 **Condition using the Or logical operator**

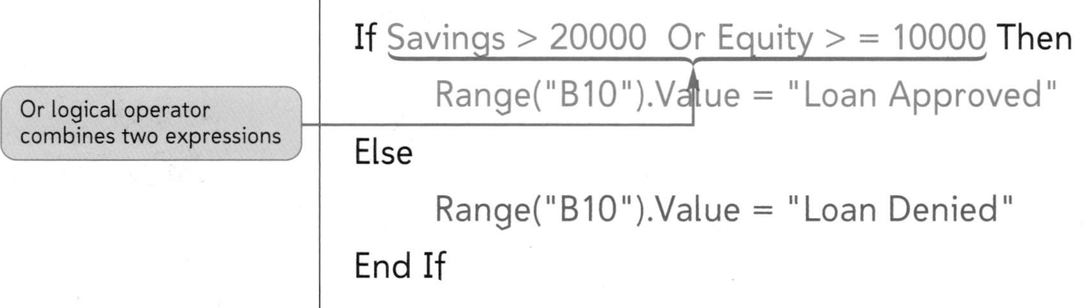

VBA supports other control structures as well. These include the For-Next control structure, which allows you to repeat a series of commands a set number of times, and the Do-While control structure, which repeats a series of commands as long as a particular condition is true. Finally, the Do-Until control structure repeats a series of commands until a particular condition is true. You can learn more about these control structures in Excel Help.

INSIGHT

Using the NOT Logical Operator

Every VBA logical operator is matched by a logical function. You can simplify program code by inserting logical tests within the worksheet and then referencing those worksheet values in your program. One advantage of using logical functions is that the worksheet will then display the logical conditions under which the program is being run. For example, the Not operator, which reverses the logical value of an expression, could be used in the following statement in the VBA code:

```
If Not(Savings>2000) Then
```

This statement tests whether the value of the Savings variable is not greater than 2000.

To perform the same type of test in your worksheet, you could use the NOT function. The syntax of the NOT function is

```
=NOT(logical)
```

where *`logical`* is an expression that can be true or false. The NOT function returns the value FALSE if the *`logical`* expression is true, and it returns the value TRUE if the *`logical`* expression is false.

Using the If-Then-ElseIf Control Structure

You are ready to write the control structure to make the Change_Type macro work under the following three possible conditions:

- The user enters a valid tornado type (the T_Type variable is equal to F0, F1, F2, or All).
- The user enters an invalid tornado type.
- The user clicks the Cancel button (the T_Type variable has no value).

Because you have three conditions, you must use an If-Then-ElseIf control structure. Also, because the first condition (the user enters a valid type) has four valid answers, it will contain several expressions linked with the Or operator.

You want the control structure to work for both uppercase and lowercase letters so that it treats entries such as f0 and F0 the same way. To do this, you'll use VBA's UCase() function to convert the text the user enters in the input box into uppercase letters. Then, you can test only uppercase letters.

You'll start by editing the Change_Type macro to specify the conditions necessary for the macro to work properly. The first line you'll add to the sub procedure will convert the text string entered by the user into all uppercase letters. You'll then enter the first condition to test whether the user has entered F0, F1, F2, or All.

TIP

You can nest If statements to handle complicated situations involving several conditions. Make sure that each If statement is matched with an End If statement.

To start creating the If-Then-ElseIf control structure:

1. If you took a break at the end of the previous session, make sure the Tornado Analysis workbook is open in Excel and the Visual Basic Editor is open.
2. Switch to the Visual Basic Editor and make sure the Code window is active.
3. In the Change_Type sub procedure, click at the end of the line containing the InputBox function, and then press the **Enter** key to insert a new blank line.
4. Type **T_Type = UCase(T_Type)** and then press the **Enter** key twice. This command converts any text entered in the T_Type variable to uppercase letters.
5. Type **If T_Type = "F0" or T_Type = "F1" or T_Type = "F2" or T_Type = "ALL" Then** and then press the ↓ key. This condition checks whether the T_Type variable is equal to F0, F1, F2, or All.

6. Use the **Tab** key to indent the next two lines of code, which set the value of the Tornado and TornadoData names.

After the If statement, the next two lines set the reference values for the Tornado and TornadoData names. Because these definitions apply only if the user enters F0, F1, F2, or All, you must account for the two remaining possibilities in the next part of the control structure: The user enters an invalid tornado type in the input box, or the user clicks the Cancel button and does not enter any value. First, you'll enter a condition that determines whether a value is entered into the input box, and, if so, display an error message if an incorrect type is entered.

To enter the second condition of the If-Then-ElseIf control structure:

1. Click at the beginning of the End Sub line, press the **Enter** key, and then press the ↑ key to move the insertion point to the new blank line.
2. Press the **Tab** key to indent the line, type **ElseIf T_Type <> "" Then** and then press the **Enter** key. This second condition tests whether the T_Type variable is not equal to an empty text string. In other words, as long as something is entered in the input box, this condition will be true.

   Next, you'll enter a comment statement as a placeholder for the error message, which you will create later in this tutorial.
3. Press the **Tab** key to indent the line, type **'Display an error message** and then press the **Enter** key. You'll replace this VBA comment with a command to create a message box later.

The only remaining possibility is that the user has entered nothing at all, which occurs when the user clicks the Cancel button in the input box. In this case, you want the macro to do nothing, so you'll simply end the If-Then-ElseIf structure without entering any commands for this condition.

To complete the control structure:

1. Press the **Backspace** key to remove the indent.
2. Type **EndIf** and then press the **Enter** key. The control structure is complete. See Figure 12-38.

Figure 12-38 Change_Type sub procedure

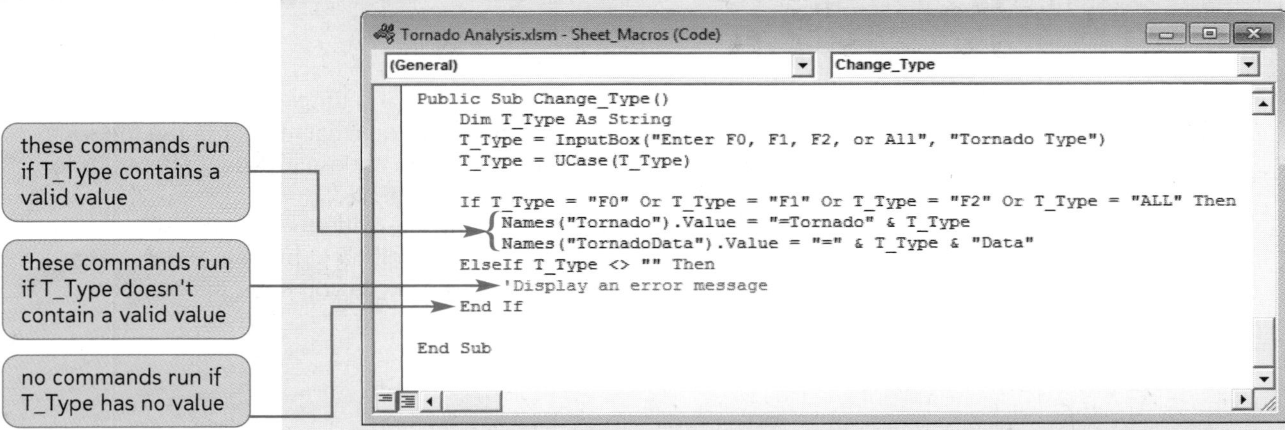

Next, you'll test the Change_Type macro and make sure that no errors are generated when you click the Cancel button in the input box.

To test the Cancel button:

1. Return to the **Tornado Analysis** workbook, and then switch to the **Report** worksheet.
2. Click the **Specify a Tornado Type** macro button. The Tornado Type dialog box opens.
3. Click the **Cancel** button. The Tornado Type dialog box closes and nothing changes in the workbook.

   Trouble? If an error message opens or ### appears in cell C6 in the Report worksheet, the code probably contains a typing error. Press the Alt+Tab keys to switch to the Visual Basic Editor, compare your code with the code shown in Figure 12-38, make any necessary changes to the code, and then repeat Steps 1 through 3.

INSIGHT

Hiding the Operation of a Macro

In a finished Excel application, you might want to hide the operation of macros as they run, showing only the end result to the user. You can hide a macro's operation by inserting the command `Application.ScreenUpdating = false` at the beginning of the sub procedure. As the macro runs, the screen will not be updated and the user will not be distracted by the intermediate results. After the macro has finished, you can turn screen updating back on by running the command

```
Application.ScreenUpdating = true
```

at the end of the program. Note that you should only turn off screen updating after you have thoroughly tested the macro and know that it contains no errors.

Creating a Message Box

A message box is a dialog box that you create that includes buttons and an informative message for the user. You use a message box when you simply want to send the user a message. Although similar to an input box, the message box does not contain a text box for the user to enter values. To create a message box, you use the MsgBox function, which has the syntax

```
MsgBox Prompt, Buttons, Title
```

where *`Prompt`* is the message in the dialog box, and *`Title`* is the text that appears in the title bar. The *`Buttons`* parameter specifies the kind of buttons that appear in the message box, as well as the style of the message box itself. You can choose a variety of options for the Buttons parameter, some of which are shown in Figure 12-39.

Some button styles merely inform, some ask a question, and others provide an alert to a problem. You don't need to learn the names of these different buttons and message styles; the Visual Basic Editor will display a description box as you enter the MsgBox function.

Figure 12-39 **Button parameters**

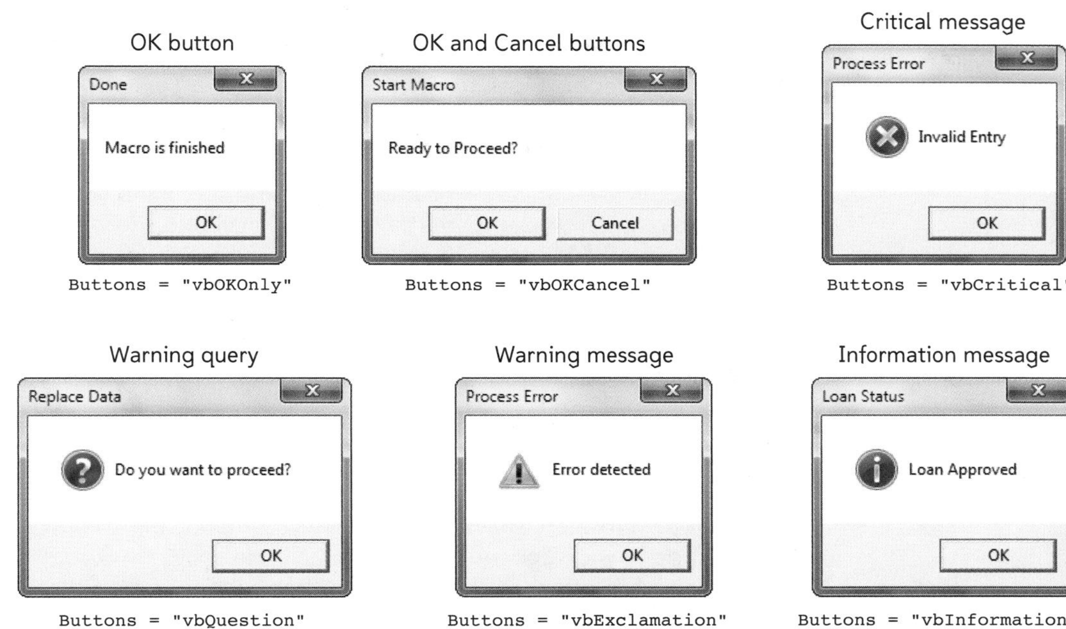

You'll use the MsgBox function in the Change_Type macro. Because the message box will be reporting a user error, you'll use the vbCritical button style, which indicates an invalid entry.

To create the message box with the vbCritical button style:

1. Return to the Visual Basic Editor.
2. In the Change_Type sub procedure in the Code window, select the **'Display an error message** comment line you entered as a placeholder, and then press the **Delete** key to delete the line, leaving a blank line in its place.
3. Press the **Tab** key to indent the line of code, if necessary, and then type **MsgBox "Please enter F0, F1, F2, or All",** to begin the MsgBox function and enter the prompt. After you type the comma, a list of the possible values for the Buttons parameter appears.
4. Double-click **vbCritical** to select the Buttons parameter.
5. Type **, "Invalid Type"** to enter the title. The macro is completed. See Figure 12-40.

Figure 12-40 **Completed Change_Type sub procedure**

TIP

To display the message box prompt on more than one line, enter the text as `"line1" & vbCrLf & "line2"`, where *line1* is the text of the first line and *line2* is the text of the second line.

Tornado Analysis.xlsm - Sheet_Macros (Code)

(General) | Statistics

```
Public Sub Change_Type()
    Dim T_Type As String
    T_Type = InputBox("Enter F0, F1, F2, or All", "Tornado Type")
    T_Type = UCase(T_Type)

    If T_Type = "F0" Or T_Type = "F1" Or T_Type = "F2" Or T_Type = "ALL" Then
        Names("Tornado").Value = "=Tornado" & T_Type
        Names("TornadoData").Value = "=" & T_Type & "Data"
    ElseIf T_Type <> "" Then
        MsgBox "Please enter F0, F1, F2, or All", vbCritical, "Invalid Type"
    End If

End Sub
```

MsgBox function to display a critical message box

6. Close the Visual Basic Editor, and then return to Excel and the Tornado Analysis workbook.
7. In the Report worksheet, click the **Specify a Tornado Type** macro button. The Tornado Type dialog box opens. You'll verify that the macro identifies errors by intentionally entering an invalid value in the input box.

   Trouble? If an error message opens, the command you entered probably contains a typing error. Compare the command in your Code window to the code shown in Figure 12-40, and make any necessary corrections to the MsgBox command.
8. Type **F3** in the input box, and then click the **OK** button. The Invalid Type message box opens.
9. Click the **OK** button to close the dialog box and return to the workbook.
10. Test whether the macro works properly by changing the tornado type displayed in the workbook to **F0**, **F1**, **F2**, and **All**.

    Trouble? If the macro does not work, your code probably contains a typing error. Return to the Visual Basic Editor and compare the complete Change_Type macro code in your Code window with the code shown in Figure 12-40. Make any necessary corrections to the code, and then repeat Steps 6 through 10.

INSIGHT

Customized Dialog Boxes and VBA

The simplest way to create a dialog box in VBA is with the InputBox() or MsgBox() methods. However, both dialog boxes are limited in the amount of information they can present to and receive from the user. If these dialog boxes do not meet your needs, you can create custom dialog boxes, known as user forms. You create user forms in the Visual Basic Editor by clicking UserForm on the Insert menu. You can then insert controls on a blank form to create a custom dialog box. User forms support a wide range of controls, including input boxes, option buttons, check boxes, and list boxes. Information entered into these controls can be retrieved and stored in variables used in your VBA programs. After designing a custom dialog box, you can display it using the `*userform*.Show` command, where `*userform*` is the name of the user form. See Excel Help for more information and tutorials on creating custom dialog boxes.

Customizing the Quick Access Toolbar

David is pleased with how simple it is to switch between tornado types in the Tornado Analysis workbook and how the Change_Type macro prevents users from entering invalid data. However, to switch between the Statistics, Time Chart, and Histogram worksheets or to choose a different tornado type, users must return to the Report worksheet. David wants users to be able to run these macro commands no matter which worksheet is active. You could copy the macro buttons on the Report worksheet to the other worksheets, but David thinks this will make the other sheets too cluttered. Instead, he wants you to make the macros accessible from any sheet in the workbook.

Adding Commands to the Quick Access Toolbar

The Quick Access Toolbar, by default, includes three commands: the Save command, the Undo command, and the Redo command. However, you can add or remove buttons from the Quick Access Toolbar. When you customize the Quick Access Toolbar, you specify whether the changes affect all workbooks or a specific workbook. This way, you can create a different Quick Access Toolbar for each workbook.

You'll add the six macros to the Quick Access Toolbar for the Tornado Analysis workbook.

To add the six macros to the Quick Access Toolbar:

1. Click the **Customize Quick Access Toolbar** button next to the Quick Access Toolbar, and then click **More Commands**. The Excel Options dialog box with the Quick Access Toolbar options is displayed.
2. Click the **Choose commands from** arrow, and then click **Macros**. A list of all the macros in the current workbook, other workbooks, or add-ins installed in Excel appears in the left box.
3. Click the **Customize Quick Access Toolbar** arrow, and then click **For Tornado Analysis.xlsm**. Only the Quick Access Toolbar in the Tornado Analysis workbook will be customized.
4. Click **Change_Type** in the list of macros, and then click the **Add** button. The macro will be added to the Quick Access Toolbar. See Figure 12-41.

Figure 12-41 Quick Access Toolbar options

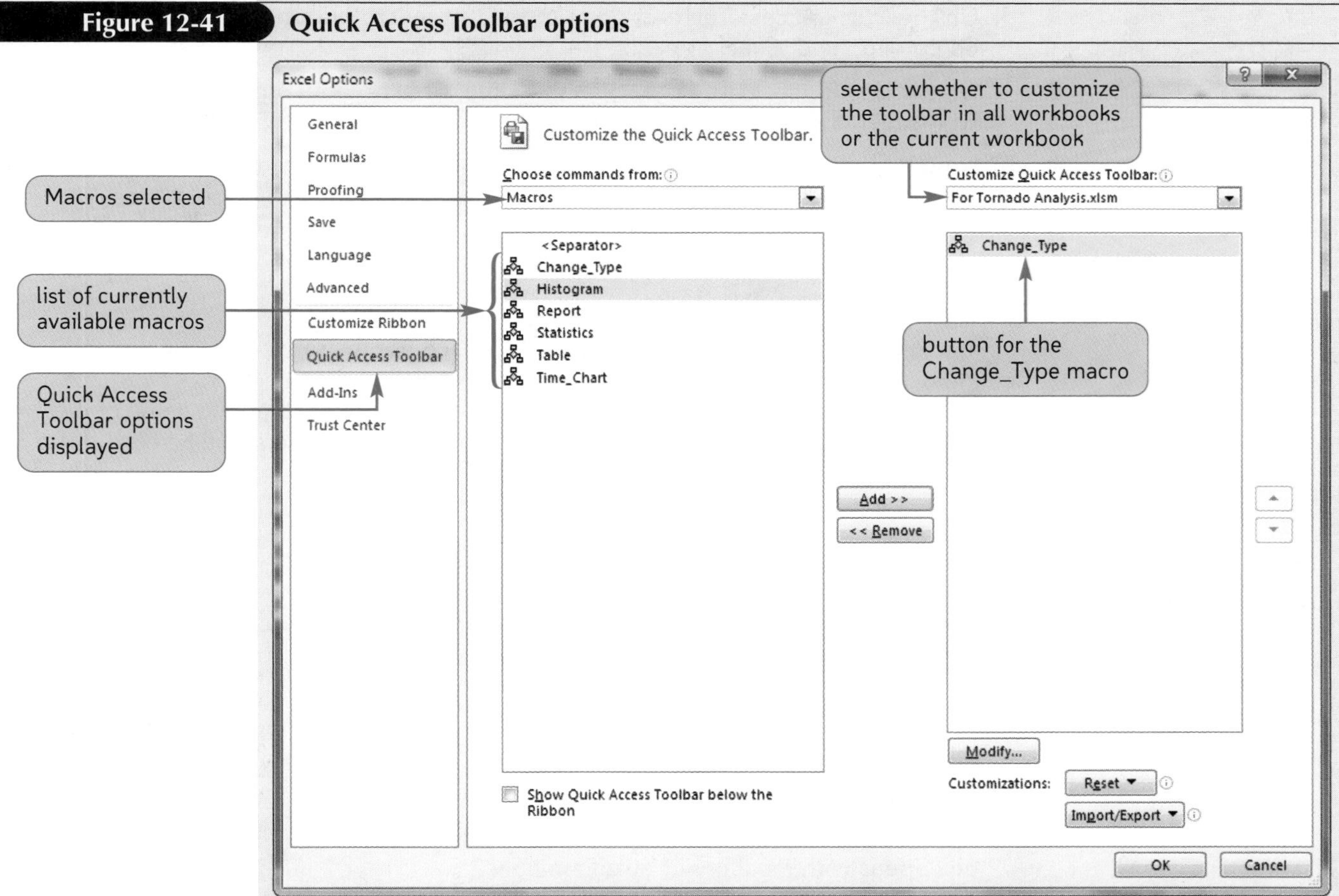

5. Add the macros **Histogram**, **Report**, **Statistics**, **Table**, and **Time_Chart** to the Quick Access Toolbar.
6. Click the **OK** button. The Excel Options dialog box closes, and six macro buttons appear on the Quick Access Toolbar. See Figure 12-42.

Figure 12-42 **Macro buttons added to the Quick Access Toolbar**

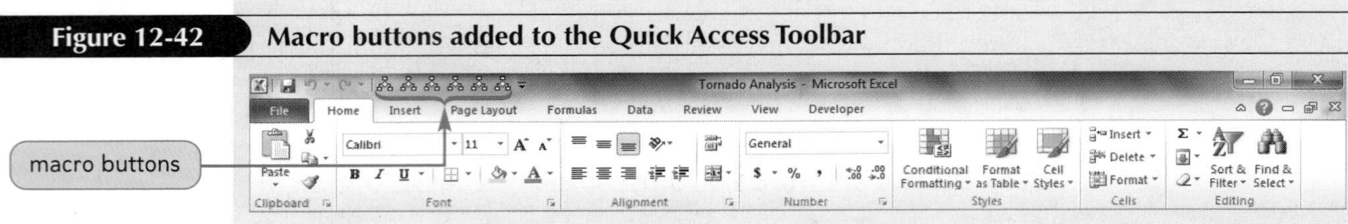

Each macro button on the Quick Access Toolbar uses the same icon or symbol. However, the different macro names appear in each button's ScreenTip. You'll test the customized Quick Access Toolbar.

To test the macro buttons on the Quick Access Toolbar:

1. On the Quick Access Toolbar, point to the second macro button and verify that the ScreenTip *Histogram* appears.
2. On the Quick Access Toolbar, click the **Histogram** macro button. The Histogram worksheet is active.
3. On the Quick Access Toolbar, point to the last macro button and verify that the ScreenTip *Time_Chart* appears.
4. On the Quick Access Toolbar, click the **Time_Chart** macro button. The Time Chart worksheet is active.
5. On the Quick Access Toolbar, click the **Report** macro button (the third macro button). The Report worksheet is active.

Customizing a Quick Access Toolbar Button

The macro buttons on the Quick Access Toolbar each use the same icon, making it difficult to distinguish between them. You can modify the buttons so each has a distinct image. You can also enter ScreenTip text that is more descriptive than the name of the macro command. David wants you to use different icons and descriptive ScreenTips for each macro button.

To modify the appearance of the macro buttons:

1. On the Quick Access Toolbar, click the **Customize Quick Access Toolbar** button, and then click **More Commands**. The Quick Access Toolbar options are displayed in the Excel Options dialog box.
2. Click the **Customize Quick Access Toolbar** arrow, and then click **For Tornado Analysis.xlsm**. The commands on the Quick Access Toolbar in the Tornado Analysis workbook appear in the right box.
3. Click **Change_Type**, and then click the **Modify** button. The Modify Button dialog box opens with a gallery of button images.
4. Scroll to the bottom of the gallery, and then click the **Cloud** icon. This is the image you'll use for the Change_Type macro button.
5. Select **Change_Type** in the Display name box, and then type **Select a Tornado Type**. This is the descriptive text for the ScreenTip. See Figure 12-43.

Figure 12-43 Modify Button dialog box

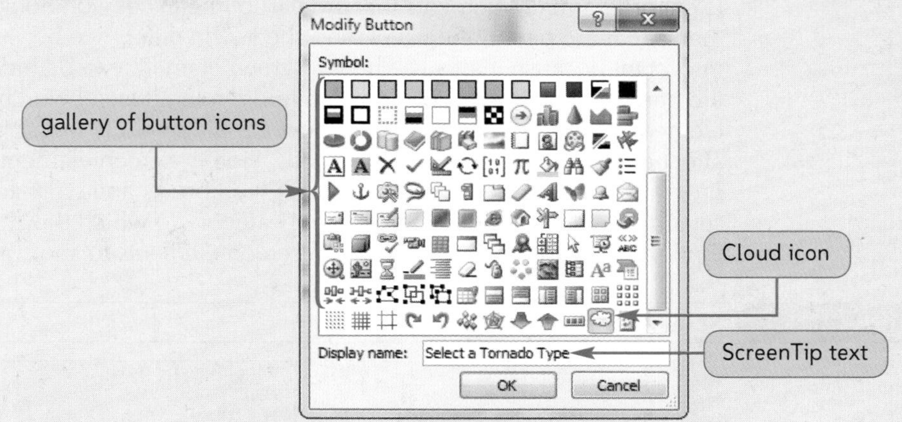

6. Click the **OK** button. The button image and the descriptive text for the Change_Type macro command change.
7. Repeat Steps 3 through 6 for the other five macro commands.

Command	Symbol	Display name
Histogram	**Column Chart**	**Display a Histogram**
Report	**Book**	**Display the Report Sheet**
Statistics	**Pi**	**Display Statistics on Tornadoes**
Table	**Table**	**Display Tornado Data**
Time_Chart	**Line Chart**	**Display a Time Chart**

Figure 12-44 shows the list of edited macro buttons.

Figure 12-44 New images and text for the macro buttons

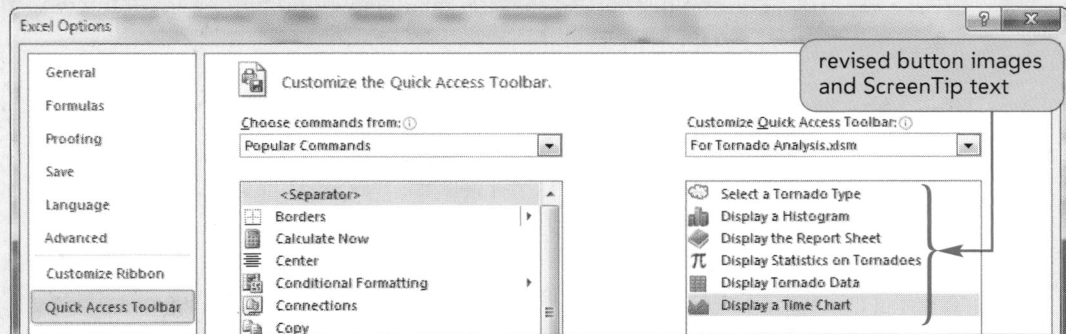

8. Click the **OK** button. The six macro buttons on the Quick Access Toolbar have new icons and ScreenTips.
9. For each macro button on the Quick Access Toolbar, verify that the ScreenTip shows the descriptive text and that clicking the button makes the correct worksheet active.

Customizing Excel Screen Elements

Excel screen elements fall into three general categories: (1) elements that are part of the Excel program; (2) elements that are part of the Excel workbook window; and (3) elements that are part of the Excel worksheet. The difference between these categories is important because it affects where a screen element can be hidden. Screen elements that are part of the workbook window are hidden in all Excel workbooks you open. Screen elements that are part of the worksheet are hidden only in that worksheet and do not affect other worksheets and workbooks. Finally, screen elements that are part of the Excel program will be hidden across all open workbooks and worksheets. Figure 12-45 lists the screen elements you can hide and the category to which they belong. You use the Excel Options dialog box to specify which screen elements to show and hide.

Figure 12-45 **Screen elements that can be hidden**

Displayed in the	Screen Element
Excel window	Formula bar
	ScreenTips
	Chart element names on hover
Workbook	Horizontal scroll bar
	Vertical scroll bar
	Sheet tabs
Worksheet	Row and column headers
	Gridlines

David does not want unneeded Excel elements to distract users when the program is displayed in the kiosk. You'll modify the Excel workbook and worksheet window to display only the Tornado Analysis workbook, the Ribbon, the Quick Access Toolbar, and a few other Excel screen elements. You'll group the worksheets before hiding the row and column headers so that the headers will be hidden in all the worksheets.

To hide the row and column headers in the worksheets:

1. Click the **Documentation** sheet tab, hold down the **Shift** key, click the **Table** sheet tab, and then release the **Shift** key. All of the sheets in the workbook are selected.
2. Click the **File** tab on the Ribbon, and then click the **Options** command in the navigation bar. The Excel Options dialog box opens.
3. Click **Advanced** in the list of options.
4. Scroll down to the **Display options for this worksheet** section, and verify that **Multiple Selected** appears in the Display options for this worksheet box.
5. Click the **Show row and column headers** check box to remove the check mark. See Figure 12-46.

Figure 12-46 Advanced Excel options

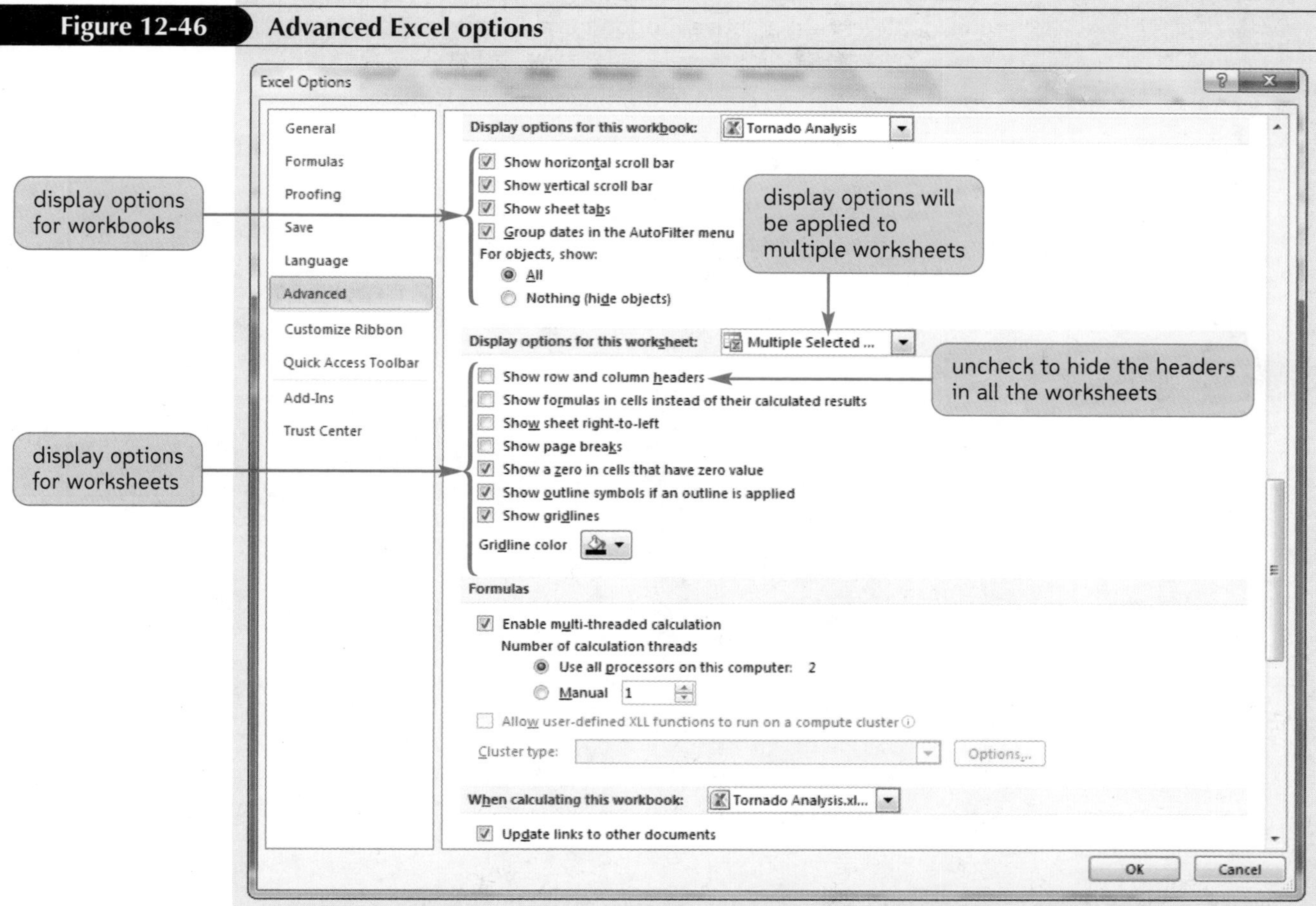

6. Click the **OK** button. The column headings are hidden on the selected worksheets.
7. Verify that the row and column headings are hidden on each worksheet.

Next, David wants you to hide the sheet tabs, which are a display option for the entire workbook. He also wants you to remove the formula bar, which is a display option for the Excel program, and then minimize the Ribbon.

To edit the workbook and Excel display options, and minimize the Ribbon:

1. Click the **File** tab on the Ribbon, click the **Options** command in the navigation bar to open the Excel Options dialog box, and then click **Advanced** in the list of Excel options.
2. Scroll down to the **Display options for this workbook** section, and then verify that **Tornado Analysis** appears in the Display options for this workbook box.
3. Click the **Show sheet tabs** check box to remove the check mark.
4. Scroll up to the Display section, and then click the **Show formula bar** check box to remove the check mark.
5. Click the **OK** button. The sheet tabs are hidden in the workbook and the formula bar is hidden for all workbooks.

6. Double-click the active Ribbon tab to minimize the Ribbon. See Figure 12-47.

Figure 12-47 Tornado Analysis workbook with hidden Excel elements

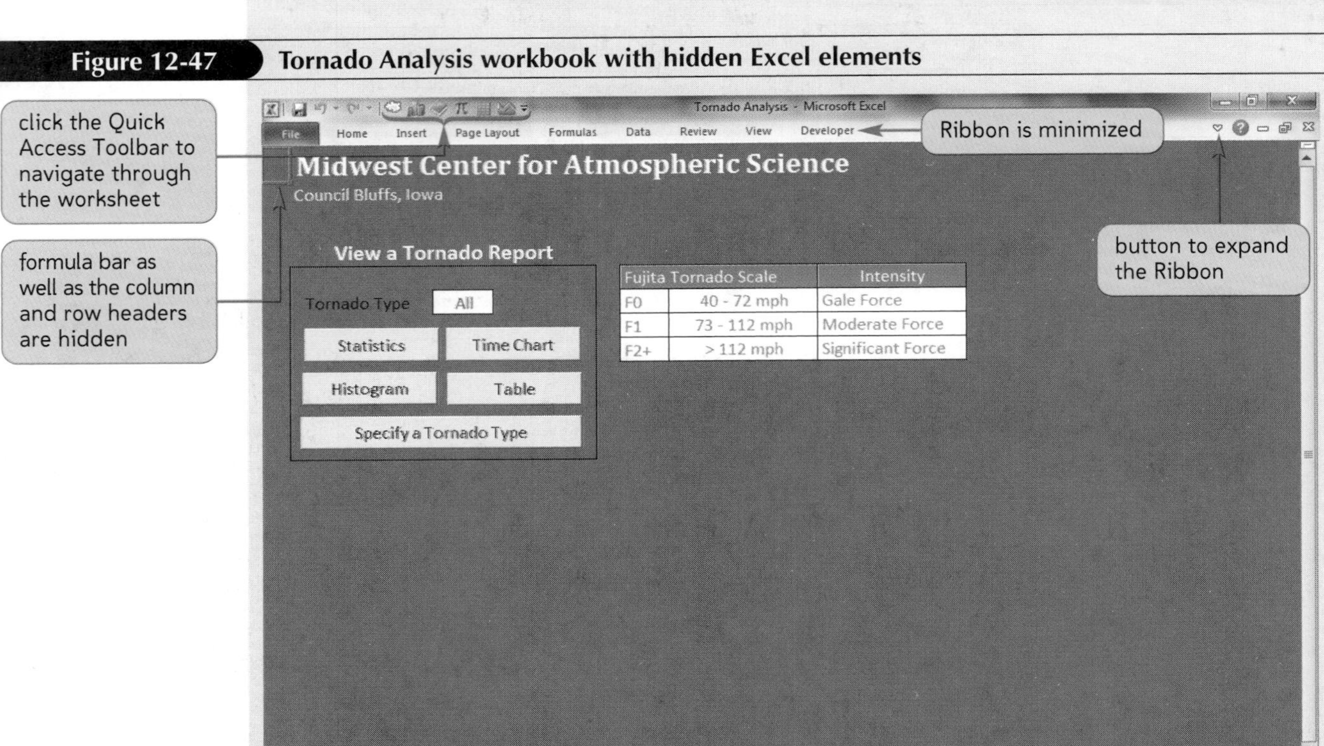

Hiding the formula bar affects every Excel workbook. David wants you to redisplay the formula bar so he can use it in other workbooks. You'll also expand the Ribbon.

To show the formula bar and expand the Ribbon:

1. Click the **File** tab on the Ribbon, click the **Options** command in the navigation bar to open the Excel Options dialog box, and then click **Advanced** in the list of Excel options.
2. Scroll down to the Display section, click the **Show formula bar** check box to insert a check mark, and then click the **OK** button. The formula bar reappears in all workbooks.
3. Click the **Expand the Ribbon** button on the Ribbon to maximize the Ribbon.

The Excel Options dialog box provides many customization options for controlling how Excel works on your computer. For example, you can change the default font setting, which is 11-point Calibri. Or, you can change the default number of worksheets in new workbooks from three to another number. Figure 12-48 lists other features you can customize.

Figure 12-48 Excel customization options

Customization Option	Location in Excel Options dialog box
Turn on and off Formula AutoComplete	Formulas options
Select the default file format for saving workbooks	Save options
Set the length of time in minutes to create an AutoRecover file	Save options
Set the default location for Excel workbook files	Save options
Set the number of recent documents to show in the Office menu	Advanced options, Display section
Show all workbook windows as separate icons on the Windows taskbar	Advanced options, Display section
Automatically format percent values in the Percent style	Advanced options, Editing options section
Turn on or off AutoComplete for cell values	Advanced options, Editing options section

Saving a Worksheet as a PDF

PDF (**Portable Document Format**) is a file format developed by Adobe Systems that supports all of the elements of a printed document in an electronic format that is easily shared. To display a PDF file, you need only the free Adobe Reader software. Many documents are available as PDFs because of the format's popularity. Excel provides two options for publishing PDFs. The Standard option optimizes the PDF for use with online publishing and printing. The Minimum size option is used strictly for online publishing, but not for printing.

One of David's colleagues asked for a copy of the Histogram worksheet for all types of tornadoes in PDF format. You'll save the Histogram worksheet as a PDF document using the Standard option.

To save the Histogram worksheet as a PDF file:

1. Click the **Select a Tornado Type** button on the Quick Access Toolbar. The Tornado Type dialog box opens.
2. Type **All** in the box, and then click the **OK** button.
3. Click the **Display a Histogram** button on the Quick Access Toolbar to make the Histogram worksheet active.
4. Click the **File** tab on the Ribbon, and then click the **Save As** command in the navigation bar to open the Save As dialog box.
5. Click the **Save as type** button, and then click **PDF**. The dialog box expands to show additional options for saving a file as a PDF.
6. Verify that the **Standard (publishing online and printing)** option button is selected.
7. Type **Tornado History (1950 – 1999)** in the File name box, and then click the **Save** button. The worksheet is saved as a PDF file and opens in Adobe Reader. See Figure 12-49.

TIP

To publish multiple worksheet pages, select multiple sheets from the workbook and then save the selected sheet range as a PDF file.

Figure 12-49 Tornado History PDF document

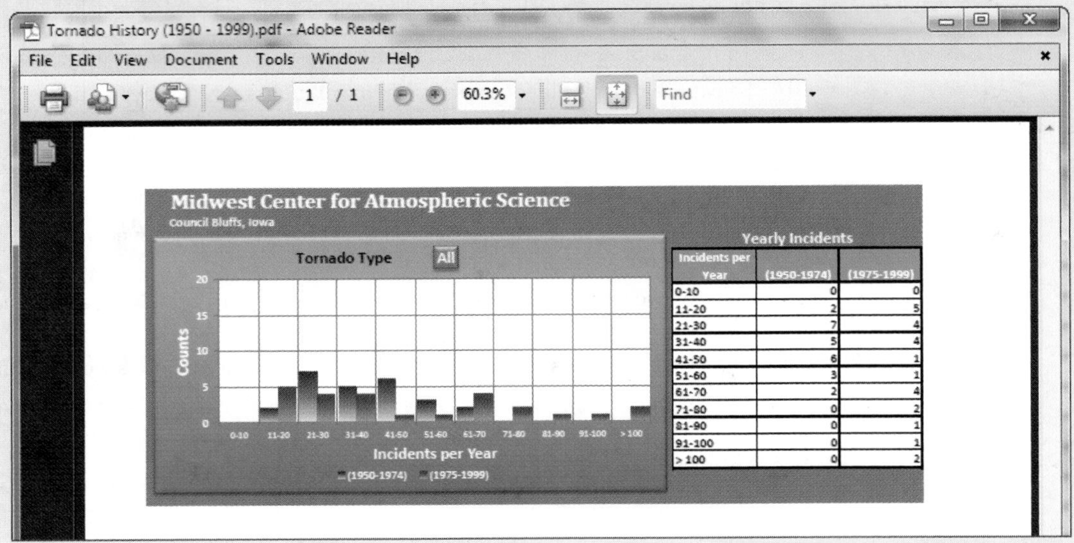

Trouble? If you don't have Adobe Reader, you can download a free version from the Adobe Web site at *www.adobe.com*.

8. Close Adobe Reader, and then save and close the Tornado Analysis workbook.

Introducing Custom Functions

All of the programming you've done for David's project involved creating sub procedures that perform actions in the Tornado Analysis workbook. David could also use a function procedure that returns a value rather than performing an action. Function procedures have the syntax

```
Function function_name(parameters)
     VBA commands
     function_name = expression
End Function
```

where *function_name* is the name of the custom function, and *parameters* is a list of parameters (separated by commas) required by the function. Note that *function_name* is listed twice: once in the Function statement that starts the function procedure, and again in the last statement of the function procedure in which a value is assigned to the function. It is this last value that is returned by VBA to Excel.

The following TaxesDue function has two parameters—income and taxrate—and returns the amount of taxes due by multiplying the income value by the taxrate value (taxrate is assumed to be a percentage):

```
Function TaxesDue(income, taxrate)
     TaxesDue = income * taxrate
End Function
```

You can run the TaxesDue function just like any of the Excel built-in functions. For example, to calculate the taxes due for an income of $45,000 at a 33% tax rate, you enter the formula =TaxesDue(45000, 33%) and Excel returns the value 14850 or $14,850.

The following is a slightly more complex custom function that uses an If-Then structure to apply one of two tax rates, depending on whether the value of the income parameter is less than 30,000:

```
Function TaxesDue(income, lowtax, hightax)
   If income < 30000 Then
      TaxesDue = income * lowtax
   Else
        TaxesDue = income * hightax
   End If
End Function
```

Running this function, the formula =TaxesDue(45000, 20%, 33%) would return a value of 14,850 (using the higher tax rate), whereas the formula =TaxesDue(25000, 20%, 33%) would return a value of 5000 (using the lower tax rate).

David does not need you to create custom functions for the Tornado Analysis workbook. The Tornado Analysis workbook is now an application that others can use easily and efficiently.

INSIGHT

Turning a Workbook into an Add-In

After you become more familiar with VBA, you might want to store favorite macros and custom functions in an add-in file, making them available to other workbooks. To convert an Excel workbook into an add-in file, save the workbook in the Excel Add-In file format. If you need to support earlier versions of Excel, save it in the Excel 97-2003 Add-In file format. Add-in files are not displayed in the Excel workbook window; their contents can be viewed only from within the Visual Basic Editor.

To load a customized add-in, go to the Add-Ins options in the Excel Options dialog box, and then click the Go button to manage your Excel add-ins. Within the Add-Ins dialog box, click the Browse button to locate and select the add-in file. The selected add-in will be available to everything you run in Excel.

REVIEW

Session 12.3 Quick Check

1. What is a control structure, and why might you need one in a VBA procedure?
2. Define the terms *comparison operator* and *logical operator*.
3. What is the syntax of the If-Then-Else control structure?
4. What control structure would you use if you had multiple conditions from which to choose?
5. What is the syntax of the MsgBox function?
6. What command would you enter to display a message box with the following elements: the text *File Status* in the title bar, the message *File Saved*, and an OK button?
7. What can you customize to insert macro buttons that can be used from anywhere within a workbook?
8. What is the difference between a sub procedure and a function procedure?

Practice the skills you learned in the tutorial using the same case scenario.

PRACTICE

Review Assignments

Data File needed for the Review Assignments: Storm.xlsm

David has a new version of his workbook for which he wants you to create macros. In this version, he moved all charts to chart sheets. He also added a new chart describing the number of tornadoes occurring each decade. Finally, he expanded the scope of the report, including information on F3, F4, and F5 type tornadoes. David wants you to create macros to move among the different sheets and to select the tornado type to display. He wants these macros to be run either from macro buttons on the chart sheets and worksheets, or from the Quick Access Toolbar. Complete the following:

1. Open the **Storm** workbook located in the Excel12\Review folder included with your Data Files, and then save the file as a macro-enabled workbook named **Storm Report**. In the Documentation worksheet, enter your name and the date.
2. Use the macro recorder to record a macro named **Yearly_Chart** that completes the action of going to the Yearly Chart sheet by clicking the Yearly Chart sheet tab.
3. Open the Visual Basic Editor and change the name of the project associated with the Storm Report workbook to **Storm_Report_Project**. Rename Module 1 as **Storm_Report_Module**.
4. Using the Yearly_Chart sub procedure as a guide, create the following four sub procedures:
   - In the Decades_Chart sub procedure, display the contents of the Decades Chart sheet.
   - In the Comparison_Chart sub procedure, display the Comparison Chart sheet.
   - In the Stat_Sheet sub procedure, display the contents of the Statistics worksheet and select cell B6 on the worksheet.
   - In the Report_Sheet sub procedure, display the Report worksheet and select cell C6 on the sheet.
5. Create a sub procedure named **Change_Type** that does the following:
   - Declare a variable named **Tornado** and a variable named **PromptTxt** both of the String data type.
   - Set the value of the PromptTxt variable to **"Please enter F0, F1, F2, F3, F4, F5, or All"**.
   - Set the value of the Tornado variable based on the value returned from an input box. The prompt of the input box should be equal to the value of the PromptTxt variable. The title of the input box should be **Tornado Type**.
   - Change the value of the Tornado variable to uppercase letters.
   - Create an If-Then-ElseIf control structure that first tests whether the Tornado variable equals F0, F1, F2, F3, F4, F5, or ALL. If it does, then change the reference of the TornadoLabel name to **"=*Tornado*Label"**, where *Tornado* is the value of the Tornado variable, and change the references of the TornadoData name to **"=*Tornado*Data"**; else if the Tornado variable does not equal an empty text string, display a critical message box with a prompt equal to the value of the PromptTxt variable and the title **Invalid Type**.
6. In the Storm Report workbook, assign the sub procedures you created to the appropriate macro buttons in the workbook. Test each macro to verify that it works correctly.
7. Customize the Quick Access Toolbar, adding buttons for the six macros in the workbook. For each button, choose an appropriate image and add a descriptive ScreenTip.
8. Hide the row and column headings as well as the gridlines on the Report worksheet.

9. Hide the gridlines on the Statistics worksheet.
10. Hide the sheet tabs on the Storm Report workbook.
11. Go to the chart of yearly tornado occurrence, and set the margin size of the sheet to Narrow and the page orientation to Landscape. Publish the chart for F0 tornadoes as a PDF file named **F0 Tornadoes by Year**.
12. Save and close the workbook. Submit the finished workbook and the PDF file to your instructor, either in printed or electronic form, as requested.

Use the skills you learned to create an Excel application that retrieves sales data.

APPLY

Case Problem 1

Data Files needed for this Case Problem: Pixal.xlsm, Regions.xlsx

Pixal Printing, Inc. Frances York is a sales manager at Pixal Printing, Inc., and tracks sales figures from 20 sales regions. She has placed sales data for these regions during the last 12 months in a workbook named Regions. The information for each region is stored in a separate worksheet named after the region (Region 1, Region 2, and so on).

Because navigating 20 worksheets is cumbersome, Frances created a second workbook to display summary information on a single region. Currently, the workbook displays information on Region 1. All of the sales values in the workbook are linked to source data in the Regions workbook. If Frances wants to display information on a different region, she must use the Find and Replace command to replace the text in a selected range with the text of the region she wants to view. The updated formulas then display information on the specified region.

Frances wants to automate this process. She added a list box that displays 20 region names. She wants to be able to select a region from the list and have Excel automatically perform the Find and Replace command, replacing the current region with data from the region selected in the list box. To do this, you'll need to use the Replace method of the Range object, which has the syntax

```
Range.Replace OldText, NewText
```

where `Range` is a cell range, `OldText` is text within that range to be replaced, and `NewText` is the new text you want to substitute for the old text.

Complete the following:

1. Open the **Pixal** workbook located in the Excel12\Case1 folder included with your Data Files, and then save it as a macro-enabled workbook named **Pixal Sales Report** in the same folder. In the Documentation worksheet, enter your name and the date.
2. Review the formulas and contents of the Sales worksheet. Note that all of the data values in the range E3:F19 are formulas linked to the cells in the Regions workbook. For example, cell F3 is linked to cell B2 in the Region 1 worksheet. The list of regions that Frances can choose from is contained in the list box in cell C4.
3. In the Sales worksheet, assign a new macro named **Retrieve_Sales** to the Go macro button. (*Hint*: Click the New button in the Assign Macro dialog box to create the sub procedure and open the Visual Basic Editor.) Within the Retrieve_Sales sub procedure, add the commands outlined in Steps 4 through 8 that follow.
4. Declare the following variables:
   - **OldRegion** with the String data type. Set OldRegion equal to the value of cell E2.
   - **NewRegion** with the String data type. Set NewRegion equal to the value of cell C4.

EXPLORE

5. Change the text of the status bar to **Retrieving data on *NewRegion***, where *NewRegion* is the value of the NewRegion variable. Turn off screen updating to hide the action running the Replace method. (*Hint*: Refer to Figure 12-16 for code samples to modify the status bar text and turn screen updating on and off.)

EXPLORE

6. Use the Replace method of the Range object to replace all occurrences of *OldRegion* with *NewRegion* in the range E2:F19, where *OldRegion* is the value of the OldRegion variable and *NewRegion* is the value of the NewRegion variable.
7. Turn screen updating back on.
8. Reset the text of the status bar to its default value.
9. Close the Visual Basic Editor and return to the Pixal Sales Report workbook.
10. Hide the gridlines on the Sales worksheet.
11. Select Region 15 from the list in cell C4, and then click the Go button. The workbook displays information on sales from Region 15.
12. Save and close the workbook. Submit the finished workbook to your instructor, either in printed or electronic form, as requested.

Create an Excel application that enters data into a quality control chart.

APPLY

Case Problem 2

Data File needed for this Case Problem: Quality.xlsm

Steel Crafters Uwe Vandenbloom is the quality control manager for Steel Crafters of Van Buren, Washington. His job is to monitor the quality of steel ingots produced by the company's machine presses. Each ingot must be manufactured with a tensile strength within a certain range of values. A press that is starting to show the effects of overuse and wear will begin to produce ingots out of the specified tolerance. To save money, malfunctioning presses are taken offline and fixed or replaced.

Uwe wants to use Excel to enter press samples to determine whether the machine is working properly or "in-control." To help decide whether a manufacturing process is in-control, engineers create quality control charts that display the sample values. Upper- and lower-control limits are displayed on the chart. Values outside of the control limits indicate a process that is out of control and might need to be shut down.

Uwe created a workbook to generate the quality control chart and calculate the upper- and lower-control limits. He entered sample data in the QC Data sheet and created a quality control chart based on the data in the QA Chart sheet. He wants you to automate the process with a macro so he can enter sample values in the worksheet with an input box. The macro should place the value from the input box in the correct cell and then update the quality control chart. The macro should also report any quality control failures with a message box. Eventually, Uwe will replace the input box with a process in which the data values are retrieved directly from the machinery, but this is a good first step. Complete the following:

1. Open the **Quality** workbook located in the Excel12\Case2 folder included with your Data Files, and then save it as a macro-enabled workbook named **Quality Control Report** in the same folder. In the Documentation worksheet, enter your name and the date.
2. In the QC Chart sheet, add a new observation to the sample by doing the following:
   a. Turn on the macro recorder with the Use Relative References button *not* selected, and then create a macro named **Add_Data** and the macro description **Adds an observation to the quality control chart**.
   b. Click the QC Data sheet tab, select the range A3:E3, and then click the Insert button in the Cells group on the Home tab to insert new cells, shifting the existing cells down one row.
   c. In cell A3, enter **26** and then in cell B3, enter **64**.
   d. Copy the range C4:E4 and paste it into the range C3:E3.
   e. Click the QC Chart sheet tab to return to the chart sheet, and then turn off the macro recorder.

EXPLORE

3. Go to the Add_Data sub procedure in the Visual Basic Editor. Below the comments at the top of the sub procedure, enter the following statements:
   a. Declare the **new_obs** variable. This variable will store the observation number of the quality control sample. Set the data type of the variable to Integer because it will store only whole numbers.
   b. Declare the **new_data** variable. This variable will store the actual quality control values. Set the data type of the variable to Single because it will store decimal values.
   c. Set the value of the new_obs variable equal to one plus the value of cell A3 in the QC Data worksheet. (*Hint*: Use an object reference that includes the object hierarchy from the Sheets collection to the range object.)
   d. Set the value of the new_data variable equal to the numeric value returned from an input box. The input box prompt should read **Enter tensile strength value** and the input box title should be **Add Data**.
4. Turn off screen updating for Excel.
5. Within the code generated by the macro recorder, replace the text string "26" with the new_obs variable. Replace the text string "64" with the new_data variable. (*Hint*: Replace the values including the quotation marks with the variable names for the new_obs and new_data variables.)
6. At the bottom of the sub procedure, directly above the End Sub statement, declare two variables named **lcl** and **ucl**. These variables will store the lower- and upper-control limit values used in the quality control chart. Set the data type of both variables to Single.
7. Set the value of the lcl variable equal to the value of cell D3 in the QC Data worksheet. Set the value of the ucl variable equal to the value of cell E3 in the QC Data worksheet.
8. If the value of the new_data variable is less than the lcl variable, display a critical message box with the message **Value below control limits**. The message box title should read **Out of Control**.
9. If the value of the new_data variable is greater than the ucl variable, display a critical message box with the message **Value above control limits**. Again, the message box title should read **Out of Control**.
10. Turn screen updating back on.
11. Return to the Quality Control Report workbook and assign the Add_Data macro to the corresponding macro button on the QC Chart sheet.
12. Use the Add New Data macro button to add the following sample values to the quality control chart: **65**, **67**, **64**, **66**, and **68**. Verify that the new data is added to the control chart and to the QC Data worksheet. Also verify that the sample values 67 and 68 are reported by the macro as being out of control.
13. Return to the QC Chart sheet, if necessary. Use the macro recorder to record another macro named **Remove_Data** with the description **Removes the last data sample from the chart**. With the macro recording running, do the following:
   a. Click the QC Data sheet tab.
   b. Select the range A3:E3, and then click the Delete button in the Cells group on the Home tab, deleting the cells and shifting the other cells up one row.
   c. Click the QC Chart sheet tab to return to the control chart and turn off the macro recorder.
14. Edit the code for the Remove_Data sub procedure, adding a line at the top of the procedure to turn off screen updating and another line at the end of the procedure to turn screen updating back on.
15. Return to the workbook and assign the Remove_Data macro to the Remove Last Value macro button on the chart sheet.

16. Test the Remove_Data macro by removing the last three values from the Quality Control chart.
17. Save and close the workbook. Submit the finished workbook to your instructor, either in printed or electronic form, as requested.

Explore how to use Visual Basic for Applications to create a custom function.

CHALLENGE

Case Problem 3

Data File needed for this Case Problem: Batting.xlsm

Stats, Inc. Hiroshi Suzuki works at Stats, Inc., a repository of sports facts and statistics. One of Hiroshi's jobs is to maintain an Excel workbook of baseball batting statistics. Two statistics that Hiroshi needs to calculate on a regular basis are batting average and slugging percentage. The following formula calculates the batting average:

```
BA = Hits / AB
```

In this formula, *BA* is the batting average, *Hits* is the total number of hits by the player, and *AB* is the total number of at bats. The following formula calculates the slugging percentage:

```
SLG = (Hits + Doubles + 2 * Triples + 3 * Home Runs) / AB
```

In this formula, *SLG* is the slugging percentage, *Hits* is the total number of hits, *Doubles* is the total number of doubles, *Triples* is the total number of triples, Home Runs is the total number of home runs, and AB is the total number of at bats.

Hiroshi wants to use VBA to calculate these kinds of values rather than always entering the formulas. He asks you to create two custom functions named *BA* and *SLG*. The BA function will have two parameters: hits and ab. The SLG function will have five parameters: hits, doubles, triples, homeruns, and ab. Complete the following:

1. Open the **Batting** workbook located in the Excel12\Case3 folder included with your Data Files, and then save it as a macro-enabled workbook named **Batting Statistics** in the same folder. In the Documentation worksheet, enter your name and the date. Review the Stats worksheet contents; the values in the columns will be used to calculate the values of the batting average and slugging percentage statistics.
2. Go to the Visual Basic Editor and change the name of the project for the Batting Statistics workbook from VBAProject to **Baseball_Stats**.
3. Insert a new module into the Baseball_Stats project named **Functions**. Open the Functions module in the Code window.
4. **EXPLORE** Use the Insert menu to insert a function procedure named **BA**. Add the following parameters to the BA() function: **hits** and **ab**.
5. **EXPLORE** Insert a line in the function procedure to return the value of the BA() function. The value should be equal to the value of the hits parameter divided by the value of the ab parameter.
6. **EXPLORE** Insert another function procedure into the Code window with the name **SLG**. The SLG() function should have the following parameters: **hits**, **doubles**, **triples**, **homeruns**, and **ab**.
7. **EXPLORE** Add a line to the SLG() function procedure to return the value of the SLG statistic.
8. Close the Visual Basic Editor and return to the Batting Statistics workbook.
9. Select cell J5 in the Stats worksheet, and then insert the BA function located in the User Defined category. Calculate the batting average for the first place in the list.
10. Click cell K5, and then insert the SLG function to calculate the slugging percentage for the first place.
11. Fill the formulas from the range J5:K5 into the range J6:K44.

12. Sort the baseball statistics in the table in descending order of slugging percentage.
13. Format the page layout of the Stats sheet to print in portrait orientation with narrow margins.
14. Save the Stats worksheet as a PDF file named **Baseball Report**.
15. Save and close the workbook. Submit the finished workbook and the PDF file to your instructor, either in printed or electronic form, as requested.

Test your knowledge of VBA by creating an accounting program.

CREATE

Case Problem 4

There are no Data Files needed for this Case Problem.

The Brass Broker Linda Greenwood has a small home business called The Brass Broker, in which she purchases brass instruments from online auctions, reconditions the instruments, and then resells them at a profit. Linda wants to create an Excel workbook to track her purchases and sales from the online auctions she participates in. The workbook will essentially be an interactive checking account. She will enter the cost of the purchases she makes or the income from her sales in one worksheet. Another worksheet will contain a running list of the transactions, including the cost of the purchase or the income it generated, the item purchased, the date, and the current balance in her auction account.

Linda wants to automate this process in Excel so that she enters the data in a form in one worksheet and the data is automatically transferred to the list in another sheet. She also wants the application to check her running balance, displaying an error message if she attempts to make a purchase for which there are insufficient funds in the auction account. You'll design a VBA program to create this interactive checking account. Complete the following:

1. Create a macro-enabled workbook named **The Brass Broker** and save it in the Excel12\Case4 folder included with your Data Files. Add a Documentation worksheet containing a title, your name, the date, and a brief statement describing the purpose of the workbook.
2. Create a worksheet named **Auction Account** that contains a range of columns with the following labels: the date, the transaction description (purchase or sale), the item being purchased or sold, the transaction amount (enter purchases as negative cash flows and sales as positive cash flows), the starting balance (before the transaction), and the ending balance (after the transaction).
3. Enter the information shown below as the starting point for the auction account. The most recent transactions are at the top of the table. Use a formula to calculate the starting and ending balances (aside from the initial starting balance of $345).

Date	Description	Item	Amount	Starting Balance	Ending Balance
3/31/2013	Purchase	Brass Band Trumpet	–$135	$616	$481
3/24/2013	Sale	Dolnet Alto Saxophone	$115	$501	$616
3/22/2013	Sale	Bach TR155 Trumpet	$215	$286	$501
3/21/2013	Purchase	Brass Bugle Army Horn	–$59	$345	$286

4. Create a worksheet named **Transaction** that contains cells in which you'll enter the details of new transactions. The worksheet should contain places to enter the date of the transaction, the transaction type, the item being sold or purchased, and the cost of or the income generated from the transaction.

5. Write a macro named **Insert_Transaction** to copy the transaction data from the Transaction worksheet and insert it at the top of the list of transactions in the Auction Account worksheet. (*Hint*: You can use the macro recorder to record the steps to copy sample data from the Transaction sheet to the Auction Account sheet.) The macro should include the following:
   - An If statement that verifies that there is enough money in the auction account to cover the transaction. If there is not enough money, the macro should prevent the transaction from being entered into the auction account and notify the user with a message box, indicating how much money is in the account.
   - If the transaction is covered by the account, copy the values from the Transaction worksheet into the Auction Account worksheet. After the values have been copied, use a message box to notify the user of a successful transaction along with the current account balance. Replace the values in the Transaction worksheet with blanks.
6. Test the macro by entering the data shown below in the order shown. Sales are entered as positive values and purchases are entered as negative values.

Date	Description	Item	Amount
4/2/2013	Purchase	Bach Trumpet with Mouth Piece	–$165
4/4/2013	Sale	King 1250 Flugelhorn	$210
4/7/2013	Purchase	Schiller Lightweight Trumpet	–$350

7. Add any final formatting to your workbook to give it a professional look.
8. Save and close the workbook. Submit the finished workbook to your instructor, either in printed or electronic form, as requested.

ASSESS

SAM: Skills Assessment Manager

For current SAM information, including versions and content details, visit SAM Central (http://samcentral.course.com). If you have a SAM user profile, you may have access to hands-on instruction, practice, and assessment of the skills covered in this tutorial. Because various versions of SAM are supported throughout the life of this text, check with your instructor for the correct instructions and URL/Web site for accessing assignments.

ENDING DATA FILES

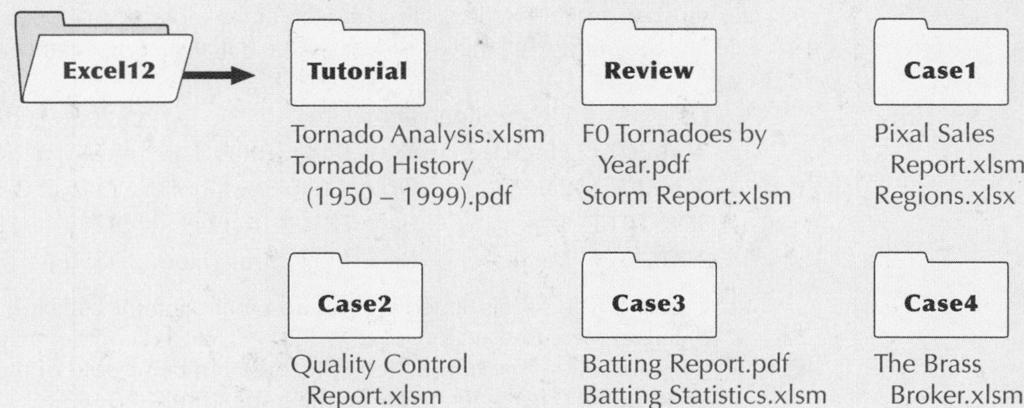

ProSkills

Teamwork

Working in a Team to Analyze Data

Teamwork involves the collaborative process by which managers and non-managers work together to achieve a common goal or outcome. Teamwork usually involves setting aside individual success for the greater good of the team's collective work. It might also involve collaboration with customers, suppliers, or other organizations.

Characteristics of Teams

Team members get to know how their teammates work, so each member can make contributions where they will count most. For example, on a football team, not everyone plays the role of quarterback; the team needs other positions working with him if touchdowns are to be scored. However, before the first play is ever made, members bring their skills to the group and spend time learning each others' moves. The best teams have members whose background, skills, and abilities complement each other.

Team Diversity

Team diversity comes in a variety of forms. Gender, race, ethnicity, and age are certainly part of it. But diversity can also be expressed in terms of experience, culture, and personality. A team that is too homogenous might lead to average solutions. A team that is too diverse might require extra effort just to get everyone heading in the same direction. Yet research concludes a good mix can lead to greater performance and creativity.

Roles You Might Play

If a team is to be successful for any length of time, members must see the value in both their contribution and what the team gets out of it. This means meeting two important requirements: task performance and social satisfaction. Task performance is usually handled by one or more members who are specialists. Task specialists spend a lot of time and effort ensuring that the team achieves its goals. Often, they initiate ideas, give opinions, gather information, sort and cull details, and provide the spark that keeps the team on track. The socioemotional role is handled by people who strengthen the team's social bonds. This is often done through encouragement, empathy, conflict resolution, compromise, and tension reduction. In a group that has conflict, the person who steps in to tell a joke or soften the blow of criticism holds the socioemotional role.

Most teams will have other roles as well, including team leaders, work coordinators, idea people, and critics. These roles are not mutually exclusive. On a team, no single role is more or less important than the others. The progress and results the team achieves depend on how well the roles mesh in getting the work done.

PROSKILLS

Develop a Financial Report

Excel is a powerful program for analyzing financial data, projecting future income and expenses, and organizing information from a wide variety of sources. With the Excel support for Visual Basic for Applications, experienced users and programmers can expand Excel's capability to accommodate a wide range of problems and challenges. In this exercise, you will work with a team to prepare a financial report. Your team should talk to instructors, colleagues, and business leaders about obtaining some real-world financial data, if possible. You'll want to obtain accounting data that

ProSkills

you can use to perform a financial analysis, including a balance sheet, an income statement, a cash flow report, and sales data for a product or service that indicates the level of sales volume for a given price or fee. Your team will then use Excel to create a workbook that contains the information of your choice, using the Excel skills and features presented in Tutorials 9 through 12. **Note:** Please be sure *not* to include any personal information of a sensitive nature in the workbooks you create to submit to your instructor. Later, you can update the worksheets with such information for your personal use.

1. Prepare a working schedule and a list of responsibilities for your team. Select an individual to act as team leader who will coordinate the efforts of the members.
2. One or more team members should work on assembling the financial data in external data files. Those members should be ready to consolidate several sources of data from text files and databases to Web queries and other workbooks.
3. The team should develop a new workbook to contain the business information the group intends to collect. Use the first worksheet to document the scope and purpose of the workbook, including a listing of all data sources you intend to use and a description of the team members and their responsibilities.
4. The workbook should contain connections to the financial data you have accumulated and stored in external files.
5. On the next several sheets in the workbook, use the connections in the workbook to import and display the data. Format the data so it is easy to read and interpret. If your team has collected financial reports from a company, examine how the reports interrelate. Replace the data values with formulas whenever possible.
6. Assign a team member to perform a what-if analysis on your financial data. He or she should determine what would happen to the company's balance sheets, cash flow, or net income if certain key variables were changed.
7. The workbook should contain a worksheet with either a one- or a two-variable table. Use the data table to explore the financial impact of several what-if analyses.
8. Extrapolate the company's income and expenses three years into the future assuming first a linear trend and then a growth trend. Discuss with your colleagues and advisors what would constitute a realistic trend line.
9. Include charts and tables in the financial report that clearly explain the projections and assumptions the team made.
10. Investigate the sales data. Assuming different values for price elasticity, calculate the company's break-even point. Investigate market information to determine which value for price elasticity is the most appropriate for the sale item.
11. Select one value for price elasticity, and then calculate the price that would result in maximum revenue. Calculate the price that would result in maximum net income. Save both Solver models in the workbook.
12. Prepare a report that documents your conclusions and methods.
13. Assign a team member to create VBA sub procedures to automate the process of displaying the different charts and tables from your report. The application should contain macro buttons users can click to quickly navigate the workbook, displaying the chief items of interest.
14. Modify the Quick Access Toolbar for the workbook so the macros can be run from either the toolbar or the worksheet.
15. Save and close the workbook, and then submit the completed workbook to your instructor, in printed or electronic form, as requested.

ADDITIONAL CASE 1

EXCEL

Creating a Grading Workbook

OBJECTIVES

- Create a connection to a text file
- Create defined names
- Apply data validation based on a list of values
- Use the VLOOKUP function to retrieve data from a list
- Use the SUMPRODUCT function to calculate the sum from multiplying two lists of numbers
- Use the COUNTIF function to count totals corresponding to a query
- Display data values using data bars
- Display an array of data values with freeze panes
- Save a workbook as a template file

Case | *High Plains School*

Fran Lewis teaches math and science at High Plains School in Lane, Kansas. She's been asked to develop a grading workbook for the staff at the school. The workbook needs to allow teachers to submit final grades based on a weighted average of homework, projects, quizzes, and exams. The workbook should also contain sheets for entering absences and tardiness as well as any special notes about student performance and behavior. The school uses a special database system in which homework, quiz, and exam scores are entered automatically during class. The scores are then exported to text files. The workbook needs to be able to connect to these text files and extract the student scores.

Fran already developed a prototype workbook that contains the formatting and some of the text needed for the final workbook. You'll complete the workbook for Fran and then save it as a template file that other staff members can use.

Complete the following:

1. Open the **Grading** workbook located in the AddCases folder included with your Data Files, and then save the workbook as **Grading Sheet** in the same folder. In the Documentation worksheet, enter your name and the date.
2. In the Class Summary worksheet, which will show basic information about a course, enter **Algebra II** for the course title, **Fran Lewis** for the instructor, and **IV** for the quarter. Assign the following weights to the grading components: Homework (**20%**), Quizzes (**40%**), and Exams (**40%**).
3. Assign the defined name **Grade_Scale** to the range B13:C26 with the workbook as its scope because the grading scale is set by the school.

STARTING DATA FILES

AddCases

Exam Grades.txt
Grading.xlsx
Homework Grades.txt
Quiz Grades.txt
Student List.txt

4. In the Student List worksheet, which will list students in the class and their grades, create a connection to the student list stored in the tab-delimited **Student List** text file. Import the data starting at the seventh row. Set the properties of the import so that Excel does not adjust the column widths. Place the imported data in the range B6:C25.
5. Assign the defined name **Student_List** to the range B6:B25. Set the scope of the range name to the workbook.
6. In the Student Notes worksheet, which will store notes about a student's progress and behavior, add data validation to the range B5:B40, confining entries to the list of students from the Student_List range. In the Resolved? column, confine entries to either Yes or No.
7. Add the following notes to the worksheet:

Boyd, Jason	**3/1/2013**	**Missing homework**	**Yes**
Jared, Lynn	**3/3/2013**	**Talking in class, disruptive behavior**	**No**

8. In the Attendance worksheet, which will store attendance records, confine the entries in the Student column to the student names from the Student_List range. Limit the entries in the Attendance Issue column to either Absent or Tardy. Limit the entries in the Excused? column to either Yes or No.
9. Add the following attendance issues to the worksheet:

Trout, Jay	**3/2/2013**	**Absent**	**Yes**
Trout, Jay	**3/3/2013**	**Absent**	**Yes**
Benjamin, Andrea	**3/4/2013**	**Tardy**	**No**

10. In the Homework worksheet, which will record homework scores, insert a reference in the range A9:A28 to each of the student names in the Student List worksheet.
11. Create a connection to the homework scores from the **Homework Grades** text file located in the AddCases folder. Import the data starting at row 6, excluding the first column. Set the import properties so that Excel does not adjust the column width when importing the data. Import the data into the range B9:O28.
12. Freeze the worksheet at cell B9.
13. Repeat Steps 10 through 12 for the Quizzes worksheet. In Step 11, import the grades from the **Quiz Grades** text file, placing the imported data in the range B9:E28.
14. Repeat Steps 10 through 12 for the Exams worksheet. In Step 11, import the grades from the **Exam Grades** text file, placing the imported data into the range B9:C28.
15. In the Grades worksheet, which will calculate each student's final grade, insert references in the range B6:D6 to the three component percentages in the Class Summary worksheet in the range C9:C11. In cell E6, calculate the total of the percentages.
16. In the range A7:A26, insert a reference to each student name in the Student List worksheet.
17. In cell B7, create a formula to calculate the first student's percentage score on homework by adding all of the values in that student's row in the Homework worksheet and then dividing the sum by the total number of homework points in row 7 of the Homework worksheet. Fill the formula into the rest of the column to calculate each student's homework percentage.
18. Repeat Step 17 to calculate each student's quiz percentage and exam percentage.
19. In cell E7, use the SUMPRODUCT function to calculate the weighted percentage of each component score multiplied by the weight assigned to that component. Copy the formula into the rest of the column to calculate each student's final overall grade percentage.
20. In cell F7, calculate the student's final grade using the VLOOKUP function with grades taken from the Grade_Scale range. Use an approximate match to the scores from the Grade_Scale range.

21. In the Student List worksheet, insert references to the Grades worksheet to display each student's average score and grade.
22. In the Class Summary worksheet, in the range D14:D26, use the COUNTIF function with the grades from the Student List worksheet to calculate the total number of each grade in the class.
23. Add tan data bars to the values in the range D14:D26 to indicate the frequency of each grade in the class. Save the workbook.
24. Delete the class data from the range C4:C6;C9:C11 in the Class Summary worksheet. Delete the student name data from the range B6:C25 in the Student List worksheet, but do not delete the query. Delete the student notes data and the attendance data from the Student Notes and Attendance worksheets.
25. In the Homework worksheet, delete the homework descriptions in row 5, the homework points in row 7, and the homework scores in the range B9:O28. Do not delete the query associated with the homework data.
26. Repeat Step 25 for the quiz and exam data in the Quizzes and Exams worksheets.
27. Save the workbook as a template file named **Grading Template** in the AddCases folder. Do not have Excel automatically refresh the external data before saving the workbook nor when the workbook is opened.
28. Submit the finished workbooks to your instructor, either in printed or electronic form, as requested.

ENDING DATA FILES

AddCases

Exam Grades.txt
Grading Sheet.xlsx
Grading Template.xltx
Homework Grades.txt
Quiz Grades.txt
Student List.txt

ADDITIONAL CASE 2

Calculating the Optimal Price

EXCEL

OBJECTIVES

- Calculate revenue assuming price elasticity of demand
- Format a scatter plot chart
- Add new data series to a chart
- Use Solver to determine an optimal price point
- Add constraints to a Solver model
- Save a Solver model
- Add headers and footers to a page layout
- Publish a worksheet as a PDF file

Case | *StarDust Scopes*

Kevin Falk owns StarDust Scopes, which manufactures telescopes, binoculars, and spotting scopes. Kevin wants to determine a sales price for the StarDust 8 telescope to maximize the company's revenue. Raising the price too much will greatly decrease sales. Lowering it will sell more scopes, but requires the inventory to cover production. Complete the following:

1. Open the **StarDust** workbook located in the AddCases folder included with your Data Files, and then save the workbook as **StarDust Scopes**. In the Documentation worksheet, enter your name and the date.
2. Based on the past year's sales, Kevin estimates that the company can sell 2,800 scopes at a price of $1,400 per telescope. In the Price Point Analysis worksheet, enter these values in the range D5:D6, and then calculate the revenue from the sales in cell D7. Format the values appropriately.
3. In cell D10, enter the price elasticity value of **1.6** (for every 10 percent increase in price, sales will decline by 16 percent). Enter the sales price of **$1,400** in cell D12. Calculate the estimated units sold assuming elasticity in cell D11; use the INT function to truncate the value to limit the units sold to an integer. (*Hint*: Use the formula from Tutorial 10 to calculate the units sold value.)
4. Enter **Price Elasticity Curve** in cell B15, and then enter the column labels **Price** and **Revenue** in cells B16 and C16, respectively. Insert a formula that references the values of cells D12 and D13 in the range B17:C17.
5. In the range B18:C38, create a one-variable data table for price values ranging from $500 to $2,500 in increments of $100. Format the text and data appropriately.
6. Create a scatter plot with smooth lines of the range B18:C38 to show how changing the sales price affects revenue.
   a. Resize the chart to cover the range D16:H36.
   b. Change the name of the data series from Series1 to **Price Elasticity Curve**.

STARTING DATA FILES

AddCases

StarDust.xlsx

c. Move the chart legend to the bottom of the chart.
d. Change the color of the scatter plot line to Olive Green.
e. Set the range of the horizontal axis to $500 up to $2,500.
f. Set the range of the vertical axis to $3,000,000 up to $4,500,000 in increments of $250,000. Do not show the display units label on the chart. Edit the axis number format to display the axis values in the custom format **$#.0 "mil"**.
g. Add **Price** as the horizontal axis title and **Revenue** as the vertical axis title. Rotate the vertical axis title. Format the titles appropriately.
h. Add the title **Price Point Analysis**.

7. Add the data values from the range D6:D7 to the plot as a single point in a new data series. Name this series **Current Price Point**.
   a. Do not display a line for the point. (*Hint*: You can select the data series with the Selection box in the Current Selection group on the Chart Tools Layout tab.)
   b. Change the marker to a dark tan circle that is 7 points in size.

Kevin could increase the company's revenue by decreasing the price of the telescope.

8. Use Solver to find the maximum revenue in cell D13 by changing the value of cell D12. Constrain cell D12 to integer values greater than or equal to $500.
9. Enter **Optimal Price Point** in cell I15. Enter **Price** in cell I16. Enter **Revenue** in cell I17. Copy the values (not the formulas) from the range D12:D13 into the range J16:J17, and format them appropriately.
10. Add the values from the range J16:J17 as a new data series into the chart. Name the series **Optimal Price Point**. Format it to have no lines, but a 7-point blue circle.
11. Enter **Solver Model Parameters** in cell I19. Save the parameters of the current Solver model into the range I20:I25. Format the cells appropriately.
12. In the range I6:I12, calculate the number of parts Kevin would need in order to create the number of units produced and sold indicated in cell D11. Kevin can make only as many scopes for which he has parts.
13. In the range J6:J12, calculate the number of parts remaining after completing the orders indicated by the optimal price point. Does Kevin have enough parts to fill the order? Format all negative values in a red font enclosed in parentheses.
14. Edit the Solver model to include the constraint that you cannot produce more telescopes than allowed by the amount of available parts. Change the price value in cell D12 back to **$1,400** and rerun the model.
15. Enter **Optimal Price Point with Inventory** in cell I27. Enter **Price** in cell I28. Enter **Revenue** in cell I29. Copy the values (not the formulas) from the range D12:D13 into the range J28:J29, and format them appropriately.
16. Add the values from the range J28:J29 as a new data series named **Optimal Price Point with Inventory** formatted to have no lines, but have a 7-point red circle.
17. Enter **Solver Model Parameters** in cell I31. Save the parameters of the current Solver model into the range I32:I38. Format the cells appropriately.
18. Change the Price Point Analysis worksheet to landscape; scale it to fit on a single page.
19. Center the header, **Price Point Analysis**, on the printed page. Add a right footer containing your name, the date, and the name of the workbook on separate lines.
20. Save the workbook, and then publish the Price Point Analysis worksheet as a PDF file named **Price Point Analysis**.
21. Submit the finished files to your instructor, in printed or electronic form, as requested.

ENDING DATA FILES

AddCases

Price Point Analysis.pdf
StarDust Scopes.xlsx

ADDITIONAL CASE 3

Creating an Interactive Order Form

OBJECTIVES

- Import data from an XML document
- Use the IF and VLOOKUP functions
- Load an XML map
- Map XML elements to worksheet cells
- Export a worksheet to an XML document
- Record a macro and assign it to a macro button
- Edit a VBA sub procedure
- Unlock worksheet cells and protect a worksheet

Case | *The Mustard Hut*

Helen Jankowski works at The Mustard Hut, a novelty shop in Sanford, Maine, that sells a wide variety of mustards ranging from common American deli mustards like brown Dijon and classic yellow to exotic mustards like maple walnut. The company is starting to transfer its order data and inventory reports to XML files. Helen wants to use an Excel application to easily enter customer orders and then export the order data into an XML document. Because this application will be used by other employees, she wants to make it as simple to use as possible. You'll include macros to help simplify the process. The finished product should export data to a single XML document by clicking a macro button on the workbook. Helen has already created the initial workbook. Complete the following:

1. Open the macro-enabled **Mustard** workbook located in the AddCases folder included with your Data Files, and then save it as a macro-enabled workbook named **Mustard Hut**. In the Documentation worksheet, enter your name and the date.
2. In the Mustard Products worksheet, enter a list of products sold by the Mustard Hut, which is stored in an XML document. Create a connection to the **Product List.xml** document in the AddCases folder, and insert the contents of the file as an XML table into the worksheet starting at cell B4.
3. Name the XML table **Product_List**. Assign the defined name **Item_IDs** to the item ID values in the first column of the Product_List table. Format the item price values as currency.
4. In the Order Form worksheet, all customer orders should be based on products in the Product_List table. In the range B17:B22, add a data validation check to ensure that item IDs come from the list of values in the Item_IDs range.

STARTING DATA FILES

AddCases

Mustard.xlsm
Mustard Orders.xsd
Product List.xml

5. In cell C17, insert an IF function that tests whether the value in cell B17 is equal to an empty text string (" "). If so, display an empty text string; otherwise, use the VLOOKUP function to look up the name of the item corresponding to the item ID in cell B17 in the Product_List table. Specify an exact match. Copy the formula in cell C17 to the range C18:C22.
6. In cell D17, insert an IF function that tests whether the value in cell C17 is equal to an empty text string. If so, display an empty text string; otherwise, use the VLOOKUP function to look up the price of the item in the Product_List table. Again, specify an exact match and copy the formula in cell D17 to the range D18:D22.
7. In cell F17, insert an IF function that tests whether the value in cell B17 is equal to an empty text string. If so, display an empty text string; otherwise, multiply the item price in cell D17 by the quantity in cell E17. Copy the formula in cell F17 to the range F18:F22.
8. In cell F24, calculate the total charges from the range F17:F22.
9. The Mustard Hut gives a 4 percent discount for sales over $125. Insert an IF function in cell F25 that calculates the discount (if any) for the order. In cell F26, calculate the cost of the order minus the discount.
10. There is a 5 percent sales tax on all orders. Calculate the sales tax in cell F28. Calculate the total cost of the order (charge after discount plus the sales tax) in cell F30.
11. Test the worksheet by inserting the following sample customer order:

Customer	**Paul Nichols**
Date	**3/10/2013**
Order No.	**17871**
Shipping Address	**1500 Palm Drive**
	Clearwater, FL 33755
Customer Order	**EX004** (1 item)
	HVM015 (2 item)
	HVM018 (3 items)
	FM013 (2 items)
	FM010 (3 items)
	HD011 (1 item)

12. Verify that the subtotal is $145, the discount is $5.80, the cost after discount is $139.20, the 5 percent sales tax is $6.96, and the total cost of the order is $146.16.
13. To export this order to an XML document, you must map each value in the order sheet to an element in the XML file. Load the XML map based on the file **Mustard Orders.xsd**.
14. Drag each element from the data map into the corresponding cell in the Order Form worksheet. You do not need to display any element headers because they already appear in the worksheet. Because the customer_order element contains the table of order items, drag the customer_order element to cell B16. You do not have to match any of the item elements within the customer_order element to cells in the worksheet.
15. Start the macro recorder. Name the macro **Export_Order** and add the description **This macro exports the customer order to the Order.xml file.**
16. Click the Export button in the XML group on the Developer tab. Export the contents of the document to a new XML file named **Order**. Stop the macro recorder.
17. View the code for the Export_Order sub procedure in the Visual Basic Editor. Edit the text string of the Export method so that it reads:

```
ActiveWorkbook.XmlMaps("order_Map").Export URL:= _
ActiveWorkbook.Path + Application.PathSeparator + "Order.xml",Overwrite:=True
```

Close the Editor and return to the Mustard Hut workbook.

18. Using Notepad or another text editor, open the **Order.xml** file. Verify that the XML document contains the order details you entered in Step 11, and then save the file as **First Order.xml**.
19. In the Order Form worksheet in the Mustard Hut workbook, add a macro button with the label **Export Order to XML** directly below the Customer Order table. Assign the Export_Order macro to the button.
20. Record a second macro named **Erase_Order** with the description **This macro erases the current customer order**.
21. Select the nonadjacent range C5:C7;C10:C13;B17:B22;E17:E22, press the Delete key to clear the contents of the order, click cell C5, and then stop the macro recorder.
22. Add a second macro button with the label **Erase Order from Worksheet** below the Customer Order table. Assign the Erase_Order macro to the button.
23. Enter the following customer order to your worksheet:

Customer	**Jane Reynolds**
Date	**3/11/2013**
Order No.	**17872**
Shipping Address	**31 West Lincoln**
	Laurel, MD 20707
Customer Order	**FM015** (1 item)
	FM013 (3 items)

24. Click the Export Order to XML button to export the order, and then click the Erase Order from Worksheet button to erase the order.
25. Select the range C5:C7;C10:C13;B17:B22;E17:E22, and remove the Locked protection from the selected cells.
26. Protect the worksheet, allowing users to select only unlocked cells. Do not specify a password for the protected worksheet. Save and close the workbook.
27. Locate the **Order.xml** file that was created for the second order you entered and change the filename to **Second Order.xml**.
28. Submit the finished files to your instructor, either in printed or electronic form, as requested.

ENDING DATA FILES

AddCases

First Order.xml
Mustard Hut.xlsm
Mustard Orders.xsd
Product List.xml
Second Order.xml

ADDITIONAL CASE 4

Analyzing Housing Prices

OBJECTIVES

- Create a connection to an Access database
- Insert a PivotTable
- Add fields to a PivotTable
- Group PivotTable row and column labels
- Format PivotTable data
- Create and format a 3-D chart
- Modify the properties of a connection
- Save a worksheet to SkyDrive and download a file from Windows Live

Case | *Premier Realty*

Janice Carson works at Premier Realty in Loveland, Colorado, analyzing the housing market. Janice wants to use Excel to create a report that describes the average price of houses in different sectors of the city. She wants to compare homes in the northeast sector against homes in other sectors, and she wants to break down the data by the age of the home and the size of the home in square feet. The company keeps daily records of home sales and prices in an Access database. Janice asks you to retrieve the data from the database and place it in a PivotTable and a PivotChart. She also wants to save the final version of the worksheet to SkyDrive. Janice has not done any work on this project, so you'll have to create the workbook yourself.

Complete the following:

1. Create a workbook named **Home Prices** in the AddCases folder included with your Data Files. Create a Documentation worksheet that includes the name of the company, your name, the date, and a purpose statement formatted appropriately.
2. Create a worksheet named **Home Price Analysis**. In cell B1, enter **Premier Realty** as the title. In cell B2, enter **An analysis of prices in the Loveland area** as the subtitle.
3. Insert a PivotTable based on a connection to the **Loveland Homes** Access database file in the AddCases folder.
4. Use NE Sector field, which indicates whether a home is located in the northeast sector of the city, as a report filter.
5. Display the Square Feet field as a row label, grouped into the following categories: Less than 1200 sq. ft., 1200 to 2000 sq. ft., and Greater than 2000 sq. ft. Name the row labels **Home Size**.
6. Display the Age field as a column label grouped into the following categories: 1 to 10 Years, 11 to 20 Years, and Greater than 20 Years. Name the column labels **Home Age**.

STARTING DATA FILES

AddCases

Loveland Homes.accdb

7. Display the average price of the homes in the Loveland area. Format the values as currency with no decimal places.
8. Create a 3-D column chart of the data from the PivotTable. Format the chart as follows:
   a. Remove the chart legend.
   b. Add the chart title **Home Price Analysis**.
   c. Rotate the chart 210 degrees in the x-direction and 20 degrees in the y-direction, with a perspective value of 25 degrees.
   d. Format the size of the axis titles and the chart area so that the chart is easy to read.
9. Apply an appropriate built-in PivotTable style to the PivotTable.
10. Apply an appropriate built-in chart style to the PivotChart.
11. Edit the properties of the connection to the Loveland Homes database so that the data is refreshed whenever the workbook is opened. Change the name of the connection to **Loveland Housing Prices** and add the description **Data from the Loveland Homes Access database containing housing prices in the Loveland area**.
12. Export the ODC connection file to the **Loveland Housing Connection.odc** file in the AddCases folder so Janice can use this connection in another Office file.
13. Delete any unused worksheets, and then save the workbook.
14. Save the contents of the Home Price Analysis worksheet to the My Documents folder on your SkyDrive. Name the file as **Loveland Housing Prices**.
15. Close the **Home Prices** workbook and exit Excel.
16. Go to **www.windowslive.com** using your Web browser, and then log in to your Windows Live account.
17. Locate and open the **Loveland Housing Prices** workbook and edit the workbook in your Web browser.
18. Change the text of the subtitle in cell B2 to **An analysis of housing prices in the Loveland, Colorado area**.
19. Click the File tab on the Ribbon in the Excel Web App, click the Download a Copy command, and then save the edited file to the AddCases folder.
20. Submit the finished files to your instructor, either in printed or electronic form, as requested.

ENDING DATA FILES

AddCases

Home Prices.xlsx
Loveland Homes.accdb
Loveland Housing Connection.odc
Loveland Housing Prices.xlsx

APPENDIX A

Working with Text Functions and Creating Custom Formats

Cleaning Data in a Spreadsheet

EXCEL

OBJECTIVES

- Open a workbook in Compatibility Mode
- Use the LEN function
- Use the LEFT function
- Use the Paste Values command
- Use the PROPER function
- Use the & operator
- Use the Text to Columns command
- USE the UPPER function
- Use the SUBSTITUTE function
- Use a special format for phone numbers
- Create custom formats for numbers and dates
- Using the Compatibility Checker

Case | *Zeus Engineering*

Growth in the town of Bayville has strained the capacity of local roads. Traffic increases have created delays, vehicular hazards, and pedestrian safety concerns. To address these issues, the town has contracted Zeus Engineering to develop a Transportation Improvement Program (TIP).

Myron Londale, traffic analyst at Zeus Engineering, will analyze data on private homes and commercial buildings located along the route being analyzed. He received the data from the Bayville Assessor's Office, which transferred the data to Excel. Before Myron begins his analysis, he needs to "clean" the data, and has asked for your help.

STARTING DATA FILES

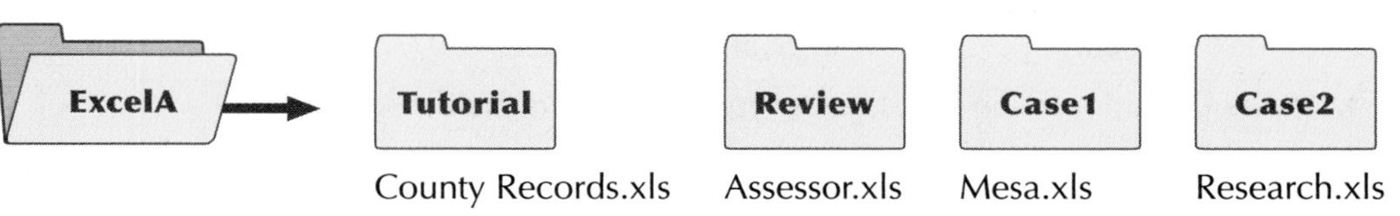

County Records.xls Assessor.xls Mesa.xls Research.xls

Opening and Saving Workbooks Created in Earlier Versions of Excel

TIP

In the Open dialog box, point to a workbook file; the ScreenTip "Microsoft Excel Worksheet" appears for Excel 2007/2010 files and "Microsoft Excel 97-2003 Worksheet" appears for earlier files.

When you open a workbook that was created in an earlier version of Excel (Excel 2003 or earlier), Excel 2010 opens the workbook in Compatibility Mode. **Compatibility Mode** keeps the workbook in the older file format, making the workbook accessible for users who do not have the current version of Excel installed. The words "[Compatibility Mode]" appear in the title bar, indicating the file is not in the latest Excel format. You can work in Compatibility Mode, which keeps the workbook in the older file format with the .xls file extension. However, to have access to all the latest features and tools in Excel 2010, the workbook must be converted to the current file format, which has the .xlsx file extension. This is the file format you have used to save all workbooks in the tutorials.

The workbook Myron received from the Bayville Assessor's Office was created in Excel 2003. Myron wants you to convert the workbook to the current format.

To save the workbook in the Excel 2007/2010 file format:

1. Open the **County Records** workbook located in the ExcelA\Tutorial folder included with your Data Files. The workbook opens in Compatibility Mode because the workbook was created in an earlier version of Excel. See Figure A-1.

Figure A-1 Workbook in Compatibility Mode

workbook was created in an earlier version of Excel

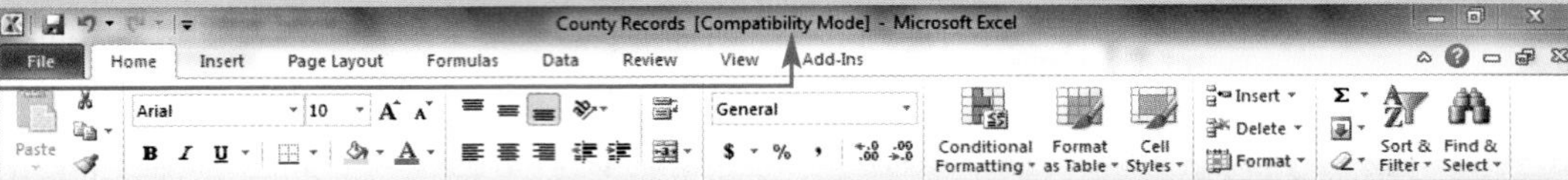

2. Click the **File** tab on the Ribbon to open Backstage view, and then click the **Save As** command in the navigation bar. The Save As dialog box opens.
3. In the File name box, type **Bayville County**. The Save as type box shows that the current file format is Excel 97-2003 Workbook, which is the earlier file format. You'll change this to the latest file format.
4. Click the **Save as type** button, and then click **Excel Workbook**. This is the file format for Excel 2007 and 2010.
5. Click the **Save** button. The workbook is saved with the new name and file type.

The workbook remains in Compatibility Mode, as you can see from the title bar. You can continue to work in Compatibility Mode, or you can close and then reopen the workbook in the new file format. You will open the workbook in the current file format.

To open the Bayville County workbook in the current file format:

1. Close the **Bayville County** workbook.
2. Open the **Bayville County** workbook. The title bar no longer has "[Compatibility Mode]", indicating that the workbook is in the Excel 2007/2010 file format.
3. In the Documentation sheet, enter your name and the date.

The Data worksheet contains data obtained from the county assessor's office. Myron wants you to convert this data to an Excel table.

To create an Excel table from the county records:

1. Switch to the **Data** worksheet.
2. Click the **Insert** tab on the Ribbon, and then click the **Table** button in the Tables group. The Create Table dialog box opens with the range A1:H51 selected.
3. Click the **OK** button to create the Excel table.
4. In the Properties group on the Table Tools Design tab, enter **TIPData** in the Table Name box to rename the table.
5. Click the **Data** tab on the Ribbon, and then click the **Filter** button in the Sort & Filter group. The filter arrows are removed from the column headers.
6. Click any cell in the Excel table.

Using Text Functions

If you receive a workbook from a coworker or obtain data from other software packages, you often have to edit (sometimes referred to as *clean* or *scrub*) and manipulate the data before it is ready to use. Many Text functions help users edit and correct the text values in their workbooks. Text, also referred to as a *text string* or *string*, contains one or more characters and can include spaces, symbols, and numbers as well as uppercase and lowercase letters. For example, Text functions are used to return the number of characters, remove extra spaces, and change the case of text strings. Figure A-2 reviews some of the common Text functions available in Excel.

Figure A-2 **Text functions**

Function	Syntax	Description	Example
LEFT	=LEFT(*text,nbr chars*)	Returns a specified number of characters at the left of the string	=LEFT("Michael",3) returns Mic
RIGHT	=RIGHT(*text,nbr chars*)	Returns a specified number of characters at the right of the string	=RIGHT("Michael",3) returns ael
MID	=MID(*text,start nbr, nbr chars*)	Returns a specified number of characters from a string, starting at a position you specify	=MID("Net Income",5,3) returns Inc
UPPER	=UPPER(*text*)	Converts all lowercase characters in a string to uppercase	=UPPER("kim") returns KIM
LOWER	=LOWER(*text*)	Converts all uppercase characters in a string to lowercase	=LOWER("KIM") returns kim
PROPER	=PROPER(*text*)	Capitalizes the first letter of each word in a string	=PROPER("JASON BAKER") returns Jason Baker
LEN	=LEN(*text*)	Returns the number of characters in a string	=LEN("Judith Tinker") returns 13
SEARCH	=SEARCH(*find_text, within_text, start_nbr*)	Returns the number of the character at which the find_text is first found reading from left to right	=SEARCH("Main", "1234 Main St",1) returns 6
TEXT	=TEXT(*value, format_text_code*)	Formats numbers within text using a specific number format	="Total Revenue " & TEXT(SUM(D5:D75),"$#,0.00") returns Total Revenue $1,052.00
TRIM	=TRIM(*text*)	Removes all spaces from a string except for single spaces between words	=TRIM(" Mary Eck") returns Mary Eck

Using the LEN and LEFT Functions

The Zip column includes zip codes in both five-digit and 10-digit formats. Myron wants only the five-digit component of the zip code. You will use the LEN and LEFT functions to convert all of the zip codes to the shorter form.

The **LEN function** returns the number of characters (length) of the specified string. Cell D4 stores the text *Narragansett, ri* so the formula =LEN(D4) returns the value 16, the number of characters, including spaces, in *Narragansett, ri*. You will use the LEN function to determine how many characters are in each cell of the Zip column.

The **LEFT function** returns a specified number of characters from the beginning of the string. To extract the five-digit zip code from the zip code 92975-0999 stored in cell G3, you use the formula =LEFT(G3,5) to return 92975.

You can use the IF function in the formula =IF(LEN([Zip])=10,LEFT([Zip],5),[Zip]) to display a five-digit zip code. The IF function uses the LEN function to test whether the zip code has 10 digits. If true (the zip code is 10 digits), the LEFT function displays the first five digits in the cell. If false (the code is not 10 digits), all the digits in the cell are displayed.

You'll insert a new column to the left of the Phone column in which to display the results.

To extract the five-digit zip code from the Zip column:

1. Click cell **F2**. You'll insert the table column to the left of this column.
2. Click the **Home** tab on the Ribbon.
3. In the Cells group, click the **Insert button arrow**, and then click **Insert Table Columns to the Left**. A new column named Column1 is inserted with the Text number format, which is the same format as the Zip column (column E).
4. Select the range **F2:F51**. This range is formatted as Text.
5. In the Number group on the Home tab, click the **Number Format arrow**, and then click **General**. Now, you can enter the formula in cell F2.
6. Make sure cell **F2** is the active cell, and then click the **Insert Function** button *fx* on the formula bar. The Insert Function dialog box opens.
7. Click **Logical** in the Or select a category list, click **IF** in the Select a function box, and then click the **OK** button. The Function Arguments dialog box opens.
8. In the Logical_test box, type **LEN([Zip])=10**. The logical test tests whether the number of characters in the current cell of the Zip column equals 10.
9. In the Value_if_true box, type **LEFT([Zip],5)**. This argument specifies that if the condition is true, the first five characters from the cell are displayed.
10. In the Value_if_false box, type **[Zip]**. This argument specifies that if the condition is false, all the characters from the cell are displayed. See Figure A-3.

TIP

You cannot enter a formula in a cell formatted as Text.

Figure A-3 IF function with the LEN and LEFT functions

Function Arguments

IF

Logical_test LEN([Zip])=10 = {FALSE;TRUE;FALSE;TRUE;FALSE;TRUE

Value_if_true LEFT([Zip],5) = {"02975";"02975";"02895";"02895";"02

Value_if_false [Zip] = {"02975";"02975-0999";"02895";"02895

= {"02975";"02975";"02895";"02895";"02

Checks whether a condition is met, and returns one value if TRUE, and another value if FALSE.

Value_if_false is the value that is returned if Logical_test is FALSE. If omitted, FALSE is returned.

Formula result = 02975

Help on this function

OK Cancel

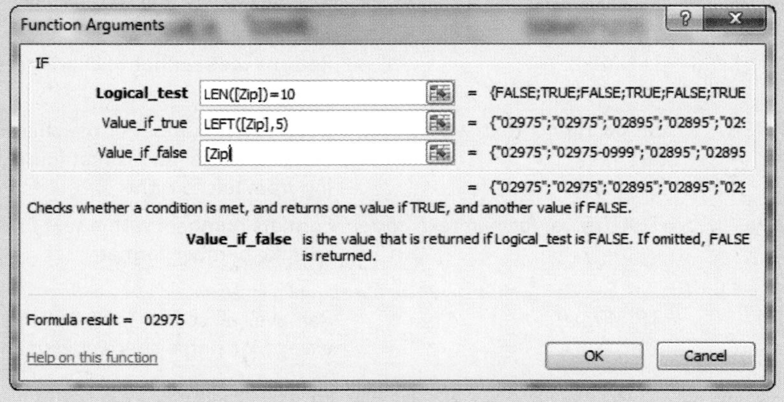

11. Click the **OK** button. The formula =IF(LEN([Zip])=10,LEFT([Zip],5),[Zip]) appears in the formula bar, and the value 02975 appears in cell F2 because the condition is false. The results are automatically copied to all rows in column F of the table. Each cell in column F displays the five-digit zip code. See Figure A-4.

Figure A-4 **Table column with five-digit zip codes**

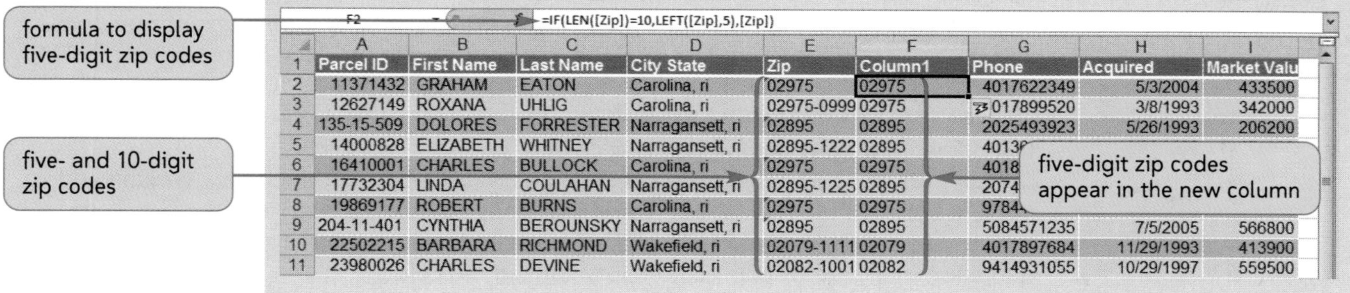

formula to display five-digit zip codes

five- and 10-digit zip codes

five-digit zip codes appear in the new column

F2 =IF(LEN([Zip])=10,LEFT([Zip],5),[Zip])

	A	B	C	D	E	F	G	H	I
1	Parcel ID	First Name	Last Name	City State	Zip	Column1	Phone	Acquired	Market Valu
2	11371432	GRAHAM	EATON	Carolina, ri	02975	02975	4017622349	5/3/2004	433500
3	12627149	ROXANA	UHLIG	Carolina, ri	02975-0999	02975	017899520	3/8/1993	342000
4	135-15-509	DOLORES	FORRESTER	Narragansett, ri	02895	02895	2025493923	5/26/1993	206200
5	14000828	ELIZABETH	WHITNEY	Narragansett, ri	02895-1222	02895	4013		
6	16410001	CHARLES	BULLOCK	Carolina, ri	02975	02975	4018		
7	17732304	LINDA	COULAHAN	Narragansett, ri	02895-1225	02895	2074		
8	19869177	ROBERT	BURNS	Carolina, ri	02975	02975	9784		
9	204-11-401	CYNTHIA	BEROUNSKY	Narragansett, ri	02895	02895	5084571235	7/5/2005	566800
10	22502215	BARBARA	RICHMOND	Wakefield, ri	02079-1111	02079	4017897684	11/29/1993	413900
11	23980026	CHARLES	DEVINE	Wakefield, ri	02082-1001	02082	9414931055	10/29/1997	559500

Using the Paste Values Command

You now have two columns with zip codes (columns E and F). You need to keep only the column that displays the five-digit zip code. However, the data in column F is dependent on column E. If you delete column E, column F displays the #REF! error value. Therefore, before you delete column E, you need to convert the data in column F, which is based on a formula, to values. The easiest way to do that is to copy and paste the formula results, but not the actual formula, to a new column using the Paste Values command. Then, you can delete columns E and F.

To convert the five-digit zip code formula results to values:

1. Click cell **G2**. In the Cells group on the Home tab, click the **Insert button arrow**, and then click **Insert Table Columns to the Left**. A new column named Column2 is inserted to the left of the Phone column.
2. Select the range **F2:F51**, which contains the formula results you want to convert to values.
3. In the Clipboard group on the Home tab, click the **Copy** button, and then click cell **G2**.
4. In the Clipboard group, click the **Paste button arrow**, and then click the **Values** button in the Paste gallery. The values from Column1 are pasted into Column2. The error button that appears indicates that the numbers in column G are stored as text; you want this to display leading zeros for zip codes.
5. Press the **Esc** key, and then click cell **F2**. The formula appears in the formula bar and the formula results appear in the cell.
6. Click cell **G2**. Both the formula bar and the cell display values because you pasted the range using the Paste Values command.
7. Select columns **E** and **F**, right-click the selected columns, and then click **Delete**. The two columns are removed.
8. In cell E1, enter **Zip**. Column E, which stores the five-digit zip code values, now has a descriptive column header.
9. Autofit the Zip column to fit the five-digit length.

Using the PROPER Function and the & Operator

The **PROPER function** converts the first letter of each word to uppercase, capitalizes any letter that does not follow another letter, and changes all other letters to lowercase. The formula =PROPER("BOOTH") changes the word *BOOTH* to *Booth*.

The **& operator**, also called the Concatenation operator, concatenates or joins two or more text values. The syntax of the & operator is

```
Value1 & Value2 [& Value3 …]
```

where *Value1*, *Value2*, and *Value3* are string constants or cells storing text or numbers, and the & operator joins (or concatenates) these values to produce a single string. For example, if the last name "Eaton" is in cell B2 and the first name "Graham" is in cell C2, you can use the formula =B2 & C2 to join the contents of the two cells (last name and first name) to display the full name in cell D2.

However, this formula returns "EatonGraham" in cell D2. To include a comma and a space between the two names, you must change the formula to `=B2 & ", " & C2` which uses two & operators and a string constant (a comma and a space enclosed in quotation marks) to display "Eaton, Graham" in the cell.

Myron wants to combine the First Name and Last Name columns into one column. Because the names were entered in all uppercase letters, you need to combine the PROPER function and the & operator into the formula `=PROPER(B2)& ", " & PROPER(C2)`.

To combine the names in one column with standard capitalization:

1. Click cell **D2**, and then insert a table column to the left. A new column named Column1 is inserted to the left of the Zip column.
2. In cell D2, type **=PR** and then double-click **PROPER** in the list of functions. The beginning of the formula, =PROPER(, appears in the cell and the formula bar, and a ScreenTip shows the function's syntax.
3. Type **[** to begin the column specifier, double-click **Last Name** in the list of the column qualifiers, type **]** to end the column specifier, and then type **)** to complete the PROPER function that converts the last name to uppercase and lowercase letters.
4. Type **&** to enter the operator, and then type **", "** to join the contents of cell D2 with a comma and space.
5. Type **&** to enter the operator, type **PR** and then double-click **PROPER** in the list of functions to begin the second PROPER function.
6. Type **[** to begin the column specifier, double-click **First Name** in the list of the column qualifiers, type **]** to end the column specifier, and then type **)** to complete the second PROPER function. The complete formula =PROPER([Last Name]) & ", "& PROPER([First Name]) appears in the cell and the formula bar.
7. Press the **Enter** key. Each cell in column D displays the owner's name in the form *Last name, First name* with the first letter of each name capitalized. See Figure A-5.

Figure A-5 **Owner's name displayed in one column**

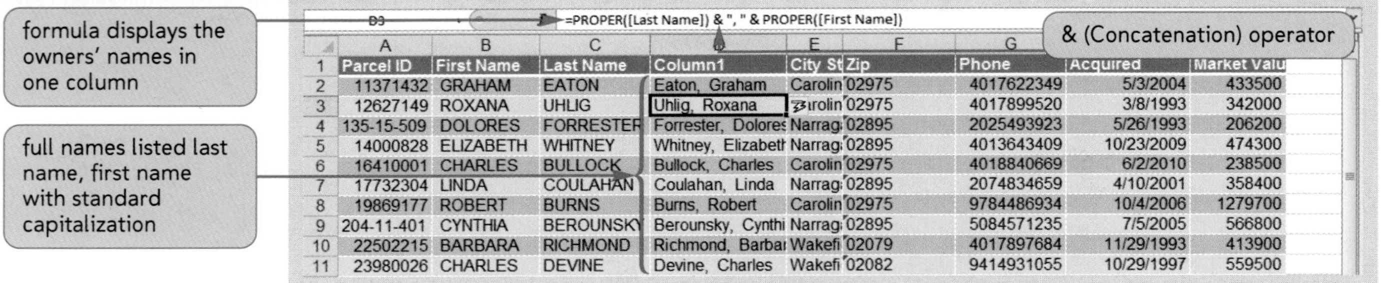

formula displays the owners' names in one column

full names listed last name, first name with standard capitalization

& (Concatenation) operator

D3 =PROPER([Last Name]) & ", " & PROPER([First Name])

	A	B	C	D	E	F	G	H	I
1	Parcel ID	First Name	Last Name	Column1	City St	Zip	Phone	Acquired	Market Valu
2	11371432	GRAHAM	EATON	Eaton, Graham	Carolin	02975	4017622349	5/3/2004	433500
3	12627149	ROXANA	UHLIG	Uhlig, Roxana	Carolin	02975	4017899520	3/8/1993	342000
4	135-15-509	DOLORES	FORRESTER	Forrester, Dolores	Narrag	02895	2025493923	5/26/1993	206200
5	14000828	ELIZABETH	WHITNEY	Whitney, Elizabeth	Narrag	02895	4013643409	10/23/2009	474300
6	16410001	CHARLES	BULLOCK	Bullock, Charles	Carolin	02975	4018840669	6/2/2010	238500
7	17732304	LINDA	COULAHAN	Coulahan, Linda	Narrag	02895	2074834659	4/10/2001	358400
8	19869177	ROBERT	BURNS	Burns, Robert	Carolin	02975	9784486934	10/4/2006	1279700
9	204-11-401	CYNTHIA	BEROUNSKY	Berounsky, Cynthi	Narrag	02895	5084571235	7/5/2005	566800
10	22502215	BARBARA	RICHMOND	Richmond, Barbai	Wakefi	02079	4017897684	11/29/1993	413900
11	23980026	CHARLES	DEVINE	Devine, Charles	Wakefi	02082	9414931055	10/29/1997	559500

Now that the owners' names data is stored in column D, you no longer need the data in column B (Last Name) and column C (First Name). Because the results in column D are based on a formula, you need to convert the formula in column D to values before you delete columns B and C.

To paste the formula results as values and delete the original data:

1. Click cell **E2**, and then insert a table column to the left. A new column named Column2 is added to the table.
2. Select the range **D2:D51**, and then copy the range to the Clipboard.
3. Click cell **E2**, and then paste the values from the Clipboard to Column2.
4. Press the **Esc** key, and then autofit column E so you can see the owners' full names.
5. In cell E1, enter **Owners** as the column header.
6. Delete columns **B**, **C**, and **D**. The Owner column remains in the Excel table.

Using the Text to Columns Command

When multiple pieces of data are stored in one cell, you can separate each piece of data into a different column using the Text to Columns command. This command starts the Convert Text to Column Wizard. You specify how to split the data based on how the data is stored. You can select what **delimits**, or separates, the data, such as a tab, a semicolon, a comma, or a space. For fixed-width data, you specify break locations. Each entry in a fixed-width field is the same length no matter how many characters are entered in the field. For example, a Last Name field with a fixed width of 20 characters always takes up 20 spaces in the record even though some last names contain a few characters and others contain many characters.

You'll split the city and state data into different columns.

To split the city and state data into separate columns:

1. Click cell **D2**, and then insert a table column to the left. A new column named Column1 is inserted to the left of the Zip column.
2. Select the range **C2:C51**. These cells contain the values you want to split.
3. Click the **Data** tab on the Ribbon, and then click the **Text to Columns** button in the Data Tools group. The Convert Text to Columns Wizard - Step 1 of 3 dialog box opens. You select how the data is organized in this step—delimited or a fixed width.
4. In the Original data type area, verify that the **Delimited** option button is selected, and then click the **Next** button. The Convert Text to Columns Wizard - Step 2 of 3 dialog box opens. You select the delimiter character in this step.
5. Click any check box with a check mark in the Delimiters section to remove the check mark, and then click the **Comma** check box. The data in the City State column is separated by a comma. The Data preview box shows the City and State data in separate columns. See Figure A-6.

Figure A-6 Convert Text to Columns Wizard – Step 2 of 3 dialog box

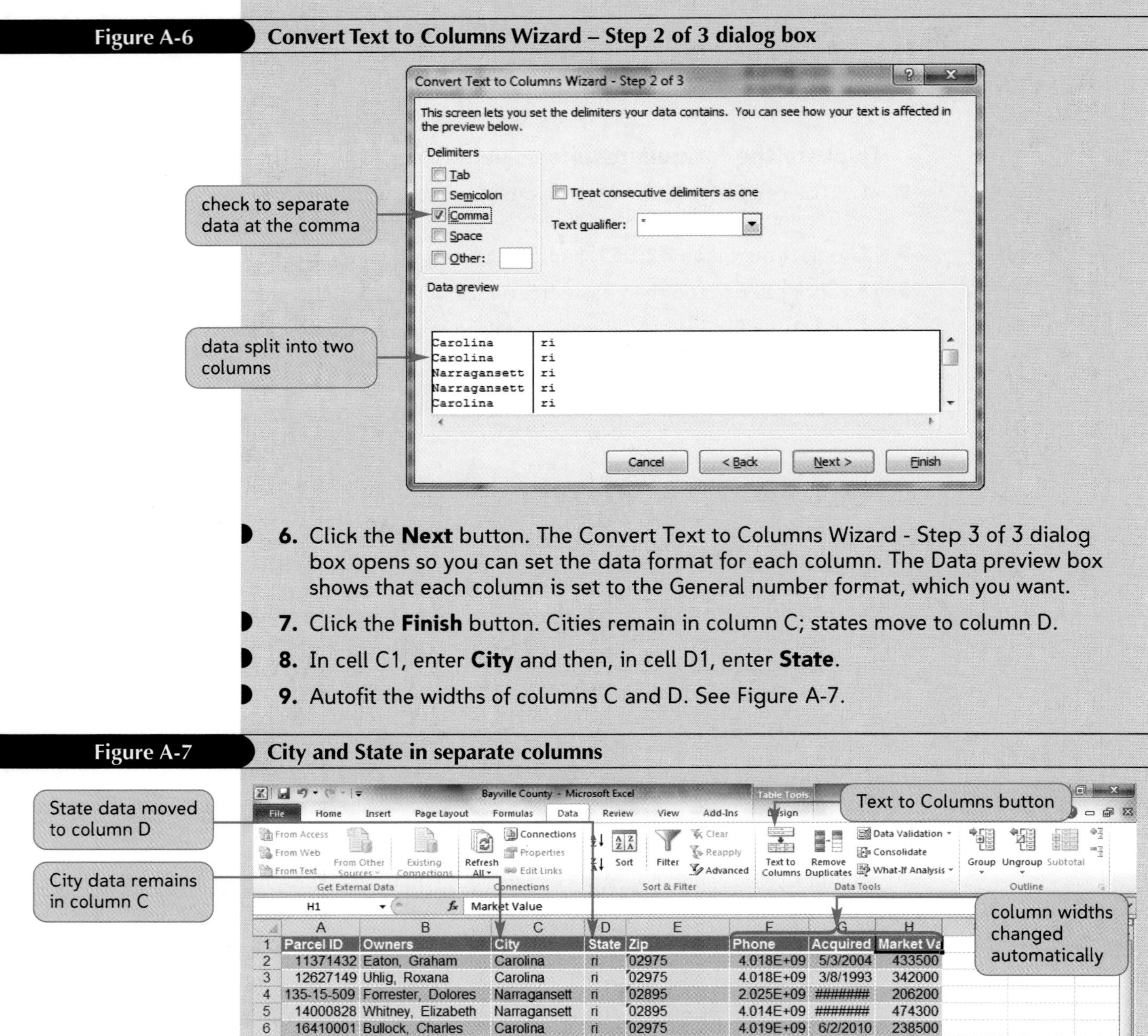

6. Click the **Next** button. The Convert Text to Columns Wizard - Step 3 of 3 dialog box opens so you can set the data format for each column. The Data preview box shows that each column is set to the General number format, which you want.
7. Click the **Finish** button. Cities remain in column C; states move to column D.
8. In cell C1, enter **City** and then, in cell D1, enter **State**.
9. Autofit the widths of columns C and D. See Figure A-7.

Figure A-7 City and State in separate columns

Using the UPPER Function to Convert Case

The **UPPER function** converts all letters of each word in a text string to uppercase. The formula =UPPER("ri") returns RI. You'll use the UPPER function to change state abbreviations in column D from lowercase to uppercase.

To use the UPPER function to capitalize the state abbreviations:

1. Click cell **E2**, and then insert a table column to the left. A new column named Column1 is inserted to the left of the Zip column.
2. In cell E2, type **=U** and then press the **Tab** key to select the UPPER function in the list. The beginning of the formula =UPPER(is in the cell and the formula bar.

3. Type **[** to begin the column specifier, double-click **State** in the list of the column qualifiers, type **]** to end the column specifier, and then type**)**. The formula =UPPER([State]) appears in the formula bar.
4. Press the **Enter** key. The state abbreviation appears in all uppercase letters in column E. See Figure A-8.

Figure A-8 **UPPER function converted state abbreviations to uppercase**

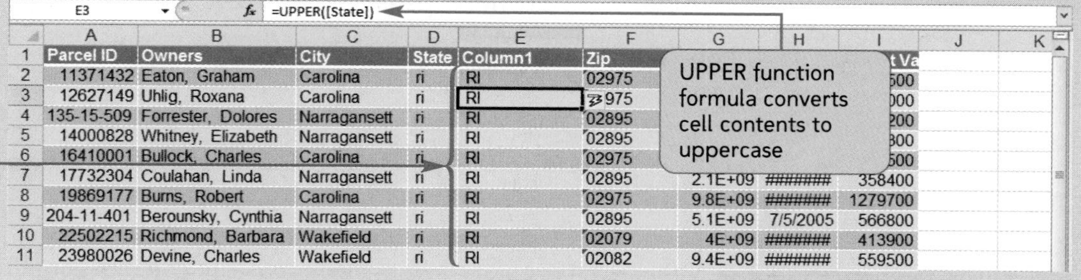

E3 =UPPER([State])

	A	B	C	D	E	F	G	H	I
1	Parcel ID	Owners	City	State	Column1	Zip			
2	11371432	Eaton, Graham	Carolina	ri	RI	'02975			
3	12627149	Uhlig, Roxana	Carolina	ri	RI				
4	135-15-509	Forrester, Dolores	Narragansett	ri	RI	'02895			
5	14000828	Whitney, Elizabeth	Narragansett	ri	RI	'02895			
6	16410001	Bullock, Charles	Carolina	ri	RI	'02975			
7	17732304	Coulahan, Linda	Narragansett	ri	RI	'02895	2.1E+09	#######	358400
8	19869177	Burns, Robert	Carolina	ri	RI	'02975	9.8E+09	#######	1279700
9	204-11-401	Berounsky, Cynthia	Narragansett	ri	RI	'02895	5.1E+09	7/5/2005	566800
10	22502215	Richmond, Barbara	Wakefield	ri	RI	'02079	4E+09	#######	413900
11	23980026	Devine, Charles	Wakefield	ri	RI	'02082	9.4E+09	#######	559500

You want to keep only the data in column E. Because the results of column E are based on a formula, you again will convert the formula in column E to values before you delete columns D and E.

To paste the state abbreviations as values:

1. Click cell **F2**, and then insert a table column to the left. A new column named Column2 is inserted to the left of the Zip column.
2. Select the range **E2:E51**, and then copy the range to the Clipboard.
3. Click cell **F2**, and then paste the values from the Clipboard. Verify that the formula bar displays a value and not a formula.
4. Delete columns **D** and **E**. Column D remains in the Excel table.
5. In cell D1, enter **State**. The column is renamed with a more descriptive header.

Using the SUBSTITUTE Function

The **SUBSTITUTE function** replaces existing text with new text. The SUBSTITUTE function has the syntax

```
SUBSTITUTE (text,old_text,new_text,instance_num)
```

where *text* is a string constant or reference to a cell containing text you want to replace, *old_text* is the existing text you want to replace, *new_text* is the text you want to replace *old_text* with, and *instance_num* specifies which occurrence of *old_text* you want to replace. If you omit *instance_num*, every instance of *old_text* is replaced. The formula =SUBSTITUTE("164-45-890","-","") returns 16445890.

The entries in Parcel ID, column A, are inconsistent. Sometimes they are an eight-digit value, and other times hyphens separate the components of the Parcel (Book No., Map No., and Parcel No.). Myron wants you to remove the hyphens from the Parcel ID. You'll enter a formula with the SUBSTITUTE function to remove the hyphens from the Parcel ID data.

To remove hyphens from the Parcel ID data and paste the values:

1. Click cell **B2**, and then insert a table column to the left. A new column named Column1 is inserted to the left of the Owners column.
2. Click the **Insert Function** button [fx] on the formula bar. The Insert Function dialog box opens.
3. Click the **Or select a category** arrow, click **Text** to display the Text functions, and then double-click **SUBSTITUTE** in the Select a function box. The Function Arguments dialog box opens.
4. In the Text box, type **A2**. The text in cell A2 is displayed.
5. In the Old_text box, type **"-"**. The hyphen is the text you want to remove.
6. In the New_text box, type **""**. You want to replace the old text with nothing. You do not need to enter anything in the Instance_num box because you want to replace every instance of a hyphen.
7. Click the **OK** button. All of the Parcel IDs are changed to eight-digit numbers. The hyphens were replaced with an empty string (a blank, or nothing).
8. Click cell **B2**. See Figure A-9.

Figure A-9 SUBSTITUTE function removed hyphens from the Parcel IDs

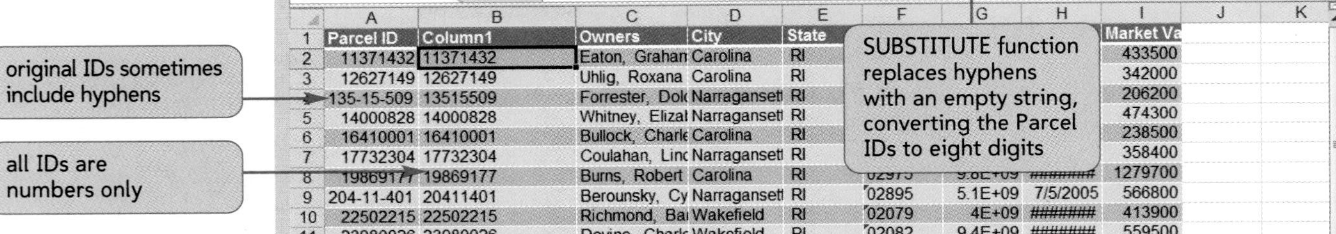

9. Click cell **C2**, and then insert a table column to the left. A new column named Column2 is inserted to the left of the Owners column.
10. Select the range **B2:B51**, and then copy this range to the Clipboard.
11. Click cell **C2**, and then paste the values from the Clipboard.
12. Delete columns **A** and **B**. The Parcel ID column remains in the Excel table.
13. In cell A1, enter **Parcel ID**.
14. Autofit the Parcel ID, Owners, City, State, Zip, Phone, Acquired, and Market Value columns.

Using Special Formats

Four commonly used formats, referred to as special formats, are available: two zip code formats (five-digit and 10-digit), a phone number format (with the area code in parentheses and a hyphen between the prefix and the last four digits), and a Social Security number format. Using these special formats allows you to type a number without punctuation, yet still display that number in its common format.

Myron wants you to display the phone number using the common format of area code in parentheses and a hyphen between the prefix and the last four digits.

To format the phone number with the Phone Number format:

1. Select the range **F2:F51**. In the Number group on the Home tab, click the **Dialog Box Launcher**. The Format Cells dialog box opens with the Number tab active.
2. In the Category box, click **Special**. Four special formats appear in the Type list: Zip Code, Zip Code + 4, Phone Number, and Social Security Number.
3. In the Type box, click **Phone Number**. See Figure A-10.

Figure A-10 Special category on the Number tab

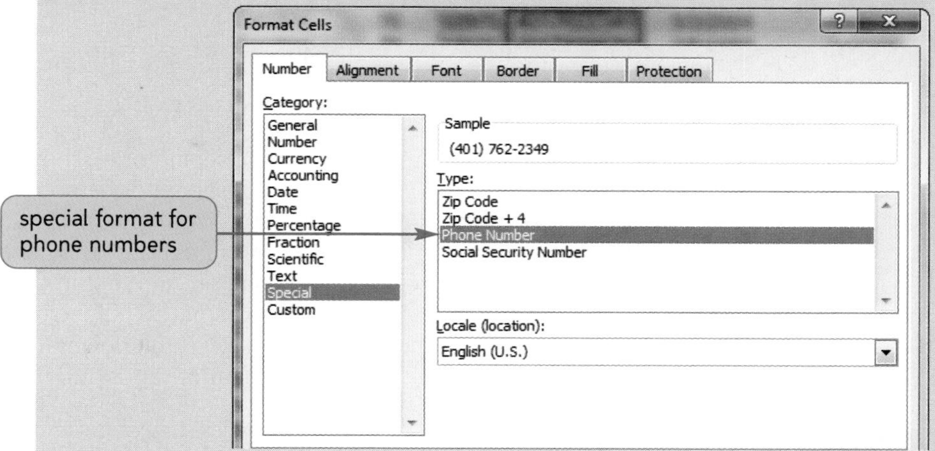

4. Click the **OK** button. The phone numbers are formatted in a standard format.

Creating Custom Formats

TIP

Any custom format you create is stored only in the workbook in which it was created. To use it in another workbook, you must reenter it.

Excel supplies a generous collection of formats and styles to improve the appearance and readability of worksheets. However, sometimes you will need a format and style to accommodate a specific requirement. In these cases, you can create your own formats, called **custom formats**. Custom formats use **format codes**, a series of symbols, to describe exactly how Excel should display a number, date, time, or text string. You can use format codes to display text strings and spaces, and determine how many decimal places to display in a cell.

Creating a Custom Number Format

Each number is composed of digits. In displaying these digits, Excel makes special note of **insignificant zeros**, which are zeros whose omission from the number does not change the number's value. For example, the number 0.1 is displayed in the General number format but changes to 0.10 when the cell is formatted as a number. To format a value, Excel uses the **placeholders** shown in Figure A-11 to represent individual digits.

Figure A-11 Description of digit placeholders

Placeholder	Description
#	Displays only significant digits; insignificant zeros are omitted.
0 (zero)	Displays significant digits as well as insignificant zeros.
?	Replaces insignificant zeros with spaces on either side of the decimal point so that decimal points align when formatted with a fixed-width font, such as Courier.

A custom format can use combinations of these placeholders. For example, the custom format #.00 displays the value 8.9 as 8.90. If a value has more digits than placeholders in the custom format, Excel rounds the value to match the number of placeholders. Thus, the value 8.938 formatted with the custom format #.## is displayed as 8.94. Figure A-12 shows how the same series of numbers appears with different custom number formats.

Figure A-12 **Examples of digit placeholders**

	Custom Formats			
Cell Value	**#.##**	**0.00**	**?.??**	**#.#0**
0.57	.57	0.57	.57	.57
123.4	123.4	123.40	123.4	123.40
3.45	3.45	3.45	3.45	3.45

Number formats also include the decimal point separator (.), the thousands separator (,), and the fraction separator (/). The thousands separator can be used to separate the number in groups of 1000 or to scale a number by a multiple of 1000.

The fraction separator displays decimal values as fractions. The general syntax is *placeholder/placeholder*, where *placeholder* is one or more of the custom format placeholders. Excel displays the fraction that best approximates the decimal value. You can also specify the denominator for the fraction to convert the decimals to halves, quarters, and so forth. Figure A-13 provides examples of the thousands and fraction separators.

Figure A-13 **Examples of thousands and fraction separators**

Value	**Custom Format**	**Appearance**
12000	#,###	12,000
12000	#,	12
12200000	0.0,,	12.2
5.4	# #/#	5 2/5

All of the numeric format codes can be combined in a single custom format. If you don't specify a numeric code for data values, Excel uses the General format code, which hides all insignificant zeros.

You'll create a custom format to display the market values to the nearest thousand.

To create a custom format for the market values:

1. Select the range **H2:H51**.
2. In the Number group on the Home tab, click the **Dialog Box Launcher**. The Format Cells dialog box opens with the Number tab active.
3. In the Category box, click **Custom**. You will enter a custom format to display the numbers to the nearest thousand.
4. In the Type box, double-click **General** to select it, and then type **#,###,** as the custom format code. See Figure A-14.

Be sure to type a comma at the end of the format code so that the numbers will be displayed to the nearest thousand.

Figure A-14 Custom category on the Number tab

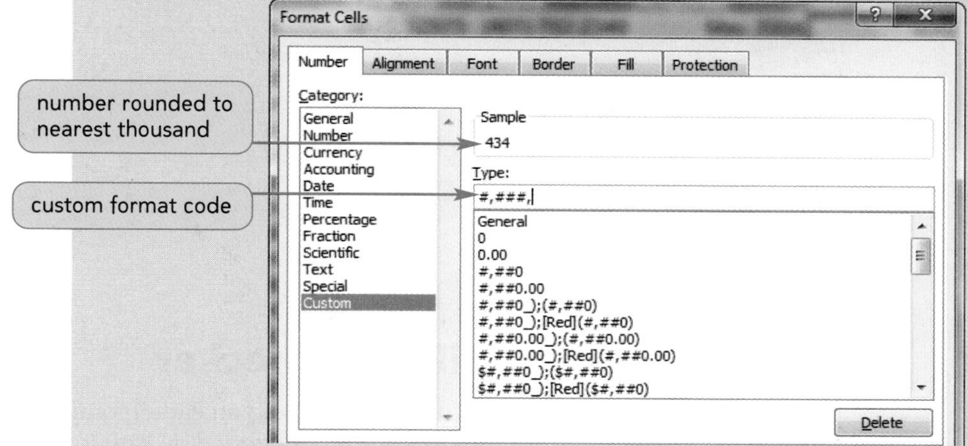

5. Click the **OK** button. The market values are displayed to the nearest thousand.

Creating a Custom Date Format

When you have dates, times, or both in a workbook, you can use a predefined date and time format to display this information in a readable format. Although the predefined time and date formats are usually fine, you can also create your own custom date formats. Figure A-15 describes the format codes used for dates and times.

Figure A-15 Date and Time format codes

Symbol	To Display	Symbol	To Display
m	Months as 1 through 12	dddd	Days as Sunday through Saturday
mm	Months as 01 through 12	yy	Years as 00 through 99
mmm	Months as Jan through Dec	yyyy	Years as 1900 through 9999
mmmm	Months as January through December	h	Hours as 1 through 24
d	Days as 1 through 31	mm	Minutes as 01 through 60 (when immediately following h, mm signifies minutes; otherwise, months)
dd	Days as 01 through 31		
ddd	Days as Sun through Sat	ss	Seconds as 01 through 60

Myron wants the date values in the Acquired column to show the name of the month followed by the year (for example, 7/22/2013 should be displayed as July, 2013). You need to apply the custom format code *mmmm, yyyy* to do this.

To apply a custom date format to the Acquired dates:

1. Select the range **G2:G51**.
2. In the Number group on the Home tab, click the **Dialog Box Launcher**. The Format Cells dialog box opens with the Number tab active.
3. In the Category box, click **Custom**.
4. In the Type box, select the current format, and then type **mmmm, yyyy**. The Sample box shows an example of the custom format you entered.
5. Click the **OK** button, and then click cell **A1** to deselect the range. See Figure A-16.

Figure A-16 **Final formatted workbook**

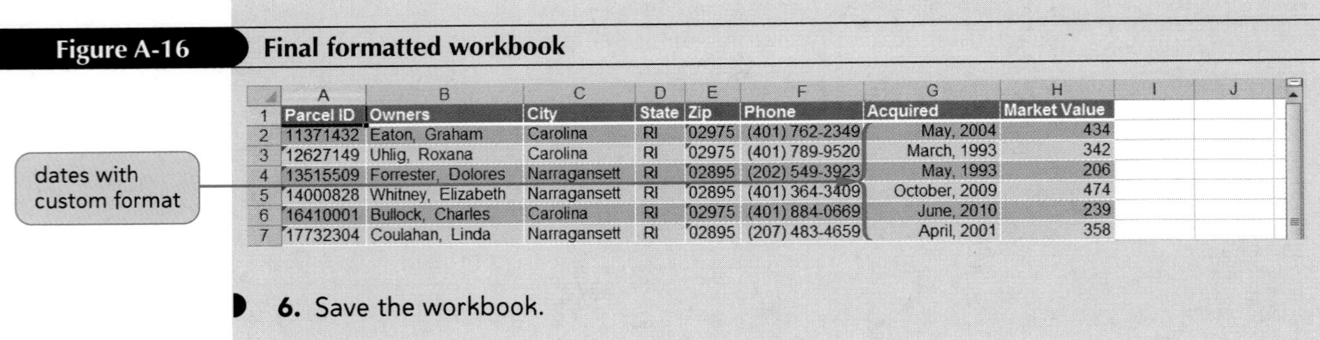

	A	B	C	D	E	F	G	H	I	J
1	Parcel ID	Owners	City	State	Zip	Phone	Acquired	Market Value		
2	11371432	Eaton, Graham	Carolina	RI	02975	(401) 762-2349	May, 2004	434		
3	12627149	Uhlig, Roxana	Carolina	RI	02975	(401) 789-9520	March, 1993	342		
4	13515509	Forrester, Dolores	Narragansett	RI	02895	(202) 549-3923	May, 1993	206		
5	14000828	Whitney, Elizabeth	Narragansett	RI	02895	(401) 364-3409	October, 2009	474		
6	16410001	Bullock, Charles	Carolina	RI	02975	(401) 884-0669	June, 2010	239		
7	17732304	Coulahan, Linda	Narragansett	RI	02895	(207) 483-4659	April, 2001	358		

6. Save the workbook.

Using the Compatibility Checker

When you save an Excel 2007 or 2010 workbook to an earlier format, the **Compatibility Checker** alerts you to any features that are not supported by earlier versions of Excel. You can click the Cancel button and redo the worksheet using a different approach, or you can click the Continue button to save the workbook in the earlier format. If you save the workbook in an earlier format, unsupported features will be lost.

You'll save a copy of the workbook in the Excel 2003 format.

To convert the workbook to the Excel 2003 file format:

1. Open the Save As dialog box, and then change the filename to **Bayville County 2003**.
2. Click the **Save as type** button, and then click **Excel 97-2003 Workbook**. This is the earlier Excel file format you want to use.
3. Click the **Save** button. The Compatibility Checker dialog box opens, alerting you to features not supported by earlier versions of Excel. See Figure A-17.

Figure A-17 **Compatibility Checker**

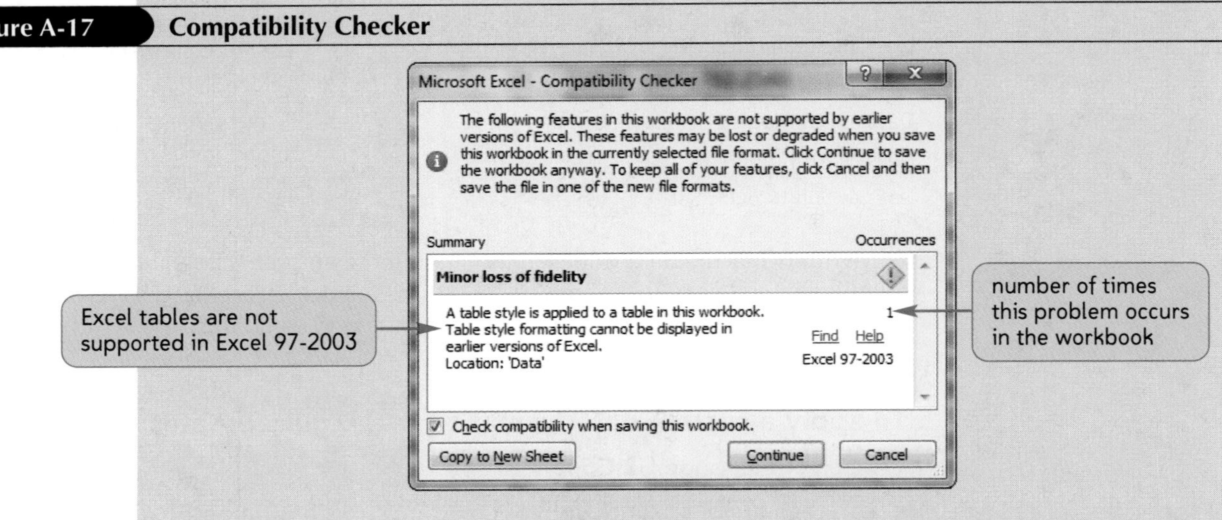

4. Read the message, and then click the **Continue** button. The workbook is saved in the earlier file format with the .xls file extension. Close the workbook.

The workbook data is clean and formatted in the best way for Myron. He'll analyze this data as he comes up with a proposal to address Bayville's traffic concerns.

Practice the skills you learned by using the same case scenario.

PRACTICE

Review Assignments

Data File needed for the Review Assignments: Assessor.xls

As part of the Transportation Improvement Program (TIP) study, Myron Londale obtained a second workbook from the Bayville Assessor's Office containing data on private homes and commercial buildings located along the route being reviewed. Myron asks you to clean and format the data. Complete the following:

1. Open the **Assessor** workbook located in the ExcelA\Review folder, and then save the workbook in the Excel Workbook (2007-2010) format as **Owners**.
2. Insert a new worksheet. Enter your name, the date, and a purpose statement in the worksheet, and then rename the worksheet as **Documentation**.
3. In the Owners worksheet, create an Excel table for the data in the range A1:G51. Apply the Table Style Medium 10 table style to the Excel table.
4. Use the Text to Columns command to split the Owner column into two columns named **Last Name** and **First Name**. Insert a blank column to the left of column C to store the first name, and leave the last name in column B.
5. In cell I1, enter the column header **Status**. In the Status column, use the IF and LEFT functions to display the word **Discard** if the address is a PO Box; otherwise, leave the cell blank.
6. In cell J1, enter the column header **Twn**. In cell J2, enter a formula to convert the data in the Town column to proper case.
7. In cell K1, enter the column header **St**. In column K, enter a formula to convert the data in the State column to uppercase.
8. In cell L1, enter the column header **Town State**. In column L, combine the town and state data from columns J and K into one column using the format *town, state*.
9. Format the data in the SSN column (column A) with the Social Security Number format.
10. Save and close the workbook. Submit the finished workbook to your instructor, either in printed or electronic form, as requested.

Apply the skills you learned to clean and format data.

APPLY

Case Problem 1

Data File needed for this Case Problem: Mesa.xls

Mesa Senior Center Elliot Turner, director of the Mesa Senior Center, has begun compiling a list of its members. He's asked you to clean and format the data in the worksheet before he continues working on the project. Complete the following:

1. Open the **Mesa** workbook located in the ExcelA\Case1 folder, and then save the workbook in Excel Workbook (2007-2010) format as **Senior Center**.
2. Insert a new worksheet. Enter the company name, your name, the date, and a purpose statement in the worksheet, and then rename the worksheet as **Documentation**.
3. In the Members worksheet, apply the Social Security Number format to the data in the SSN column.
4. Split the Name data into two columns. Store the first name in column B and the last name in column C. Change the column headers to **First Name** and **Last Name**.
5. Insert two columns to the left of the CSZ column. In column D, apply the proper case to the first name data, and change the column header to **F Name**. In column E, apply the proper case to the last name data, and change the column header to **L Name**.
6. In the Member Since column, apply a custom format that displays only the year.
7. Split the CSZ column into three columns named **City**, **State**, and **Zip**. (*Hint*: Repeat the split twice.)

8. Sort the data by City and then within City by L Name.

EXPLORE

9. Name column J **UniqueID**. The senior center uses an ID that consists of the first three letters of the last name (L Name) followed by the first letter of first name (F Name). If the last name is fewer than three characters, the letter "Z" replaces each missing character. Use the LEN and LEFT functions and the & operator to display the proposed UniqueID.
10. Save the workbook. Submit the finished workbook to your instructor, either in printed or electronic form, as requested.

Apply the skills you learned to calculate overhead.

APPLY

Case Problem 2

Data File needed for this Case Problem: Research.xls

Steuben Institute Every two weeks, Elli Pjster processes payroll information for employees whose salaries are paid fully or partially from research grants. She downloads an Excel workbook from the Steuben Institute's Research and Grant Accounting system to calculate overhead. The overhead rate varies depending on the research grant. She asks you to clean and format the data in the worksheet. Complete the following:

1. Open the **Research** workbook located in the ExcelA\Case2 folder, and save the workbook in the Excel 2007/2010 format as **Grants**.
2. Insert a new worksheet. Enter the company name, your name, the date, and a purpose statement in the worksheet, and then rename the worksheet as **Documentation**.
3. In the Pay Period 10 worksheet, create an Excel table for the range A1:C51. Hide the filter arrows.
4. Split the data in column A into separate columns for the first name and the last name. Change the column headers to **First Name** and **Last Name**. Autofit the two columns, and then sort the table by the Last Name data.

EXPLORE

5. Use the MID function to extract the grant number from the ChartString column and display it in column E. Name the new column **Grant Nbr**. The Grant Nbr is a four-digit number that begins in position 10 of the ChartString column. (*Hint*: Research the MID function in the Help system.)
6. In the column to the right of the Grant Nbr column (column F), enter a VLOOKUP function to find the grant number in the lookup table in the Overhead Rates worksheet and display the grant name from the second column in the lookup table. Change the column header to **Grant Name**. Autofit the column.
7. In column G, enter the formula to calculate overhead (the Overhead Rate in the third column of the Overhead Rates worksheet multiplied by Salary). Use a VLOOKUP function to find the correct overhead rate for the grant. Name the column **Overhead**.
8. Format the Salary and Overhead columns using the Accounting number format.
9. Save and close the workbook. Submit the finished workbook to your instructor, either in printed or electronic form, as requested.

ENDING DATA FILES

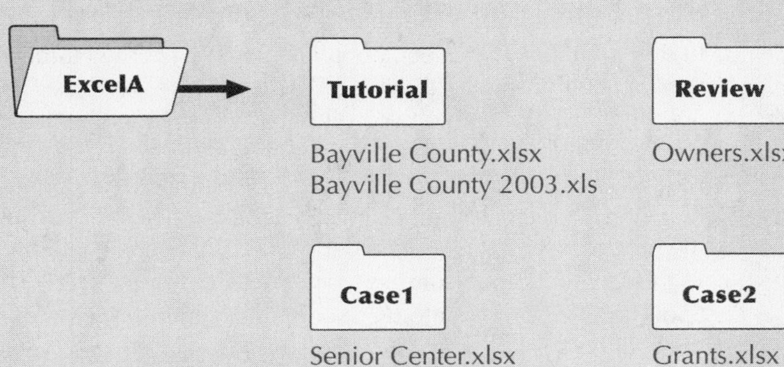

EXCEL

APPENDIX B

Advanced Filters, Database, and Summary IFS Functions

Generating a List of Eligible Employee Candidates

OBJECTIVES

- Use advanced filters
- Create a criteria range
- Use Database functions
- Summarize data using the COUNTIFS, SUMIFS, and AVERAGEIFS functions

Case | *Talent Tracs*

Talent Tracs is growing rapidly and plans to hire additional full-time employees. Before searching outside the company, Rita Corvales wants to give preference to part-time employees and consultants at Talent Tracs who want to apply for the new full-time positions. Rita has established the following criteria to determine which part-time employees and consultants will be considered for full-time employment:

- Part-time employees who have worked for Talent Tracs for two or more years
- Consultants who have worked for Talent Tracs for more than three years earning less than $55,000

You will use advanced filters to generate the list of candidates who are eligible for the new positions.

STARTING DATA FILES

TracEmployees.xlsx TracReview.xlsx World.xlsx Gifts.xlsx

Using Advanced Filters

Advanced filtering displays a subset of the rows in an Excel table or a range of data that match the criteria you specify. With advanced filtering, you specify the filter criteria in a separate range, called the criteria range. Advanced filtering enables you to perform OR conditions across multiple fields, such as the criteria Rita wants you to use to find eligible candidates within Talent Tracs for the new full-time positions. You can also use advanced filtering to create complex criteria using functions and formulas. For example, Rita could use advanced filtering to find all female salaried employees whose salary falls below the median salary for all employees.

Rita created a workbook that contains data for each employee. You will open this workbook and filter the employee information to identify employees who are eligible for the new positions.

To open the Talent Tracs workbook:

1. Open the **TracEmployees** workbook located in the ExcelB\Tutorial folder included with your Data Files, and then save the workbook as **TracSearch**.
2. In the Documentation worksheet, enter your name and the date.
3. Switch to the **Employee Data** worksheet. See Figure B-1.

Figure B-1 **Employee table**

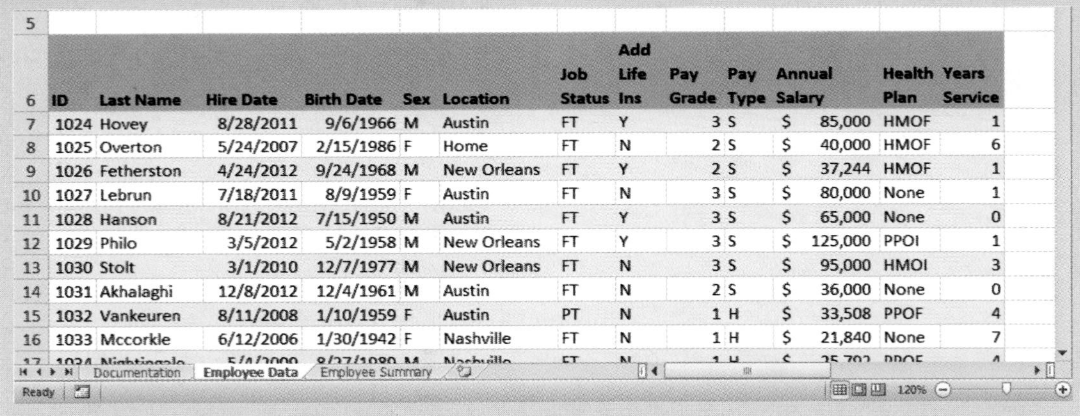

ID	Last Name	Hire Date	Birth Date	Sex	Location	Job Status	Add Life Ins	Pay Grade	Pay Type	Annual Salary	Health Plan	Years Service
1024	Hovey	8/28/2011	9/6/1966	M	Austin	FT	Y	3	S	$ 85,000	HMOF	1
1025	Overton	5/24/2007	2/15/1986	F	Home	FT	N	2	S	$ 40,000	HMOF	6
1026	Fetherston	4/24/2012	9/24/1968	M	New Orleans	FT	Y	2	S	$ 37,244	HMOF	1
1027	Lebrun	7/18/2011	8/9/1959	F	Austin	FT	N	3	S	$ 80,000	None	1
1028	Hanson	8/21/2012	7/15/1950	M	Austin	FT	Y	3	S	$ 65,000	None	0
1029	Philo	3/5/2012	5/2/1958	M	New Orleans	FT	Y	3	S	$ 125,000	PPOI	1
1030	Stolt	3/1/2010	12/7/1977	M	New Orleans	FT	N	3	S	$ 95,000	HMOI	3
1031	Akhalaghi	12/8/2012	12/4/1961	M	Austin	FT	N	2	S	$ 36,000	None	0
1032	Vankeuren	8/11/2008	1/10/1959	F	Austin	PT	N	1	H	$ 33,508	PPOF	4
1033	Mccorkle	6/12/2006	1/30/1942	F	Nashville	FT	N	1	H	$ 21,840	None	7

Understanding the Criteria Range

The **criteria range** is an area in a worksheet, separate from a range of data or an Excel table, used to specify the criteria for the data to be displayed after the filter is applied to the range or Excel table. The criteria range consists of a header row that lists field names from the table's header row, and at least one row with the specific filtering criteria for each field. The criteria range specifies which records from the data range will be included in the filtered data.

Criteria placed on the same row are considered to be connected with the logical operator AND. That means all criteria in the same row must be met before a record is included in the filtered data. Figure B-2 shows an AND criteria range filter to retrieve all employees from Nashville who earn more than $55,000.

Figure B-2 **Example of an AND filter specified in a criteria range**

	A	B	C	D	E	F	G	H	I	J	K	L	M
1	ID	Last Name	Hire Date	Birth Date	Sex	Location	Job Status	Add Life Ins	Pay Grade	Pay Type	Annual Salary	Health Plan	Years Service
2						Nashville					>55000		

Criteria placed on separate rows of the criteria range are treated as being connected by the logical operator OR. That means records that meet all the criteria on either row in the criteria range will be displayed. Figure B-3 shows an example of the OR filter to retrieve female employees or employees who are working in Austin and earning less than $50,000.

Figure B-3 **Example of an OR filter specified in a criteria range**

	A	B	C	D	E	F	G	H	I	J	K	L	M
1	ID	Last Name	Hire Date	Birth Date	Sex	Location	Job Status	Add Life Ins	Pay Grade	Pay Type	Annual Salary	Health Plan	Years Service
2					F								
3						Austin					<50000		

To specify criteria between a range of values in the same field, you use the same field name repeated in separate cells within the same row to match a range of values (BETWEEN criteria). Figure B-4 shows a criteria range to retrieve all employees who were hired between 1/1/2008 and 12/31/2012.

Figure B-4 **Example of a Between filter specified in a criteria range**

	A	B	C	D	E	F	G	H	I	J	K	L	M
1	ID	Last Name	Hire Date	Hire Date	Sex	Location	Job Status	Add Life Ins	Pay Grade	Pay Type	Annual Salary	Health Plan	Years Service
2			>=1/1/2008	<=12/31/2012									

Creating a Criteria Range

Typically, you place a criteria range above the data range to keep it separate from the data. If you place a criteria range next to the data range, the criteria might be hidden when the advanced filtering causes rows to be hidden. You can also place a criteria range in a separate worksheet, particularly if you need to use several criteria ranges in different cells to perform calculations based on various sets of filtered records.

You will place the criteria range in rows 1 to 4 of the Employee Data worksheet to make it easier to locate. Because the field names in the criteria range must exactly match the field names in the Excel table or range except for capitalization, you should copy and paste the field names instead of retyping them. In row 2, you will enter an AND criteria range with the criteria for consultants (code CN) who earn less than $55,000 and have worked at Talent Tracs for more than three years. In row 3, you will enter the criteria for part-time employees who have more than two years of service.

To create the criteria range to find eligible candidates:

1. Point to the left side of cell **A6** until the pointer changes to ➡, and then click the mouse button. The column headers in row 6 are selected.

2. Copy the field names to the Clipboard.
3. Click cell **A1**, and then paste the field names. The field names for the criteria range appear in row 1.
4. Press the **Esc** key to remove the copied data from the Clipboard.
5. In cell G2, enter **CN**. The condition specifies the criteria to retrieve all consultants (Pay Type code beginning with CN).
6. In cell K2, enter **<55000**. This condition specifies the criteria to retrieve all employees whose salaries are less than $55,000.
7. In cell M2, enter **>3**. This condition specifies the criteria to retrieve all employees who have more than 3 years of service. The criteria in row 2 select all consultants who earn less than $55,000 and have more than three years of service at Talent Tracs.
8. In cell G3, enter **PT**.
9. In cell M3, enter **>=2**. The criteria in row 3 select all employees who are part-time (Job Status is equal to PT) and who have two or more years of service at Talent Tracs (Years Service is greater than or equal to 2). See Figure B-5.

Figure B-5 Criteria range to filter records

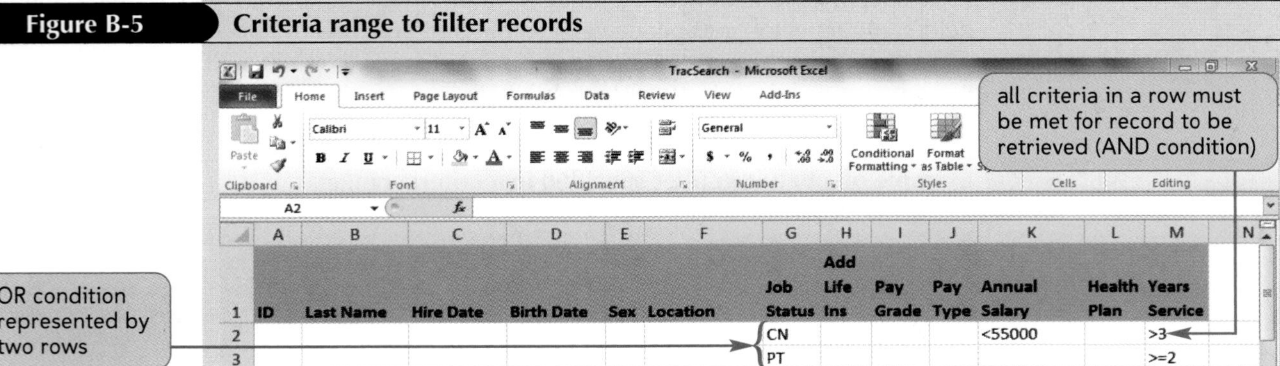

Now that the criteria range is established, you can use the Advanced Filter command to filter the Employee table. You can filter the records in their current location by hiding rows that don't match your criteria, as you have done with the Filter command. Or, you can copy the records that match your criteria to another location in the worksheet. Rita wants you to filter the records in their current location.

To filter the Employee table in its current location:

1. Click any cell in the Employee table to make the table active.
2. Click the **Data** tab on the Ribbon.
3. In the Sort & Filter group, click the **Advanced** button. The Advanced Filter dialog box opens.
4. Make sure the **Filter the list, in-place** option button is selected and the range **$A$6:$M$106** appears in the List range box. The range $A$6:$M$106 is the current location of the Employee table, which is the table you want to filter.
5. Make sure the Criteria range box displays **$A$1:$M$3**. This range references the criteria range. See Figure B-6.

Figure B-6 Completed Advanced Filter dialog box

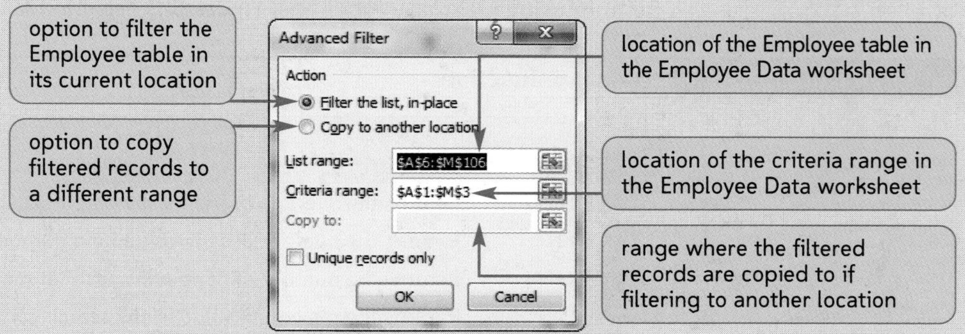

6. Click the **OK** button, and then scroll to the top of the worksheet. The list is filtered in its current location, and nine employee records match the criteria (as shown in the status bar). See Figure B-7.

Figure B-7 Filtered employee data

6	ID	Last Name	Hire Date	Birth Date	Sex	Location	Job Status	Add Life Ins	Pay Grade	Pay Type	Annual Salary	Health Plan	Years Service
15	1032	Vankeuren	8/11/2008	1/10/1959	F	Austin	PT	N	1	H	$ 33,508	PPOF	4
41	1058	Myette	5/4/2009	6/28/1967	M	Home	PT	N	2	S	$ 33,000	HMOF	4
65	1082	Steyerl	3/13/2008	5/12/1969	M	Austin	CN	N	3	S	$ 54,000	None	5
75	1092	Sherman	11/26/2010	3/2/1955	M	Austin	PT	N	1	H	$ 33,280	HMOI	2
76	1093	Mulcahey	8/25/2001	5/13/1964	F	Austin	PT	N	2	S	$ 45,000	None	11
79	1096	Silver	9/6/2005	6/26/1967	F	Austin	PT	N	3	S	$ 93,000	None	7
82	1099	Reels	6/15/2009	7/31/1963	F	Austin	PT	N	1	H	$ 26,520	None	4
89	1106	Tucker	3/11/2007	3/3/1958	F	Nashville	PT	N	1	H	$ 22,880	PPOF	6
100	1117	Zunjic	10/12/2010	1/17/1970	F	Austin	PT	N	1	H	$ 36,004	HMOI	2

employees eligible to apply for the full-time position

Trouble? If all of the data in the table is filtered, the list range or criteria range might be incorrect. Click the Clear button in the Sort & Filter group on the Data tab, and then repeat Steps 1 through 6, making sure the list range is $A$6:$M$106 and the criteria range is $A$1:$M$3 in the Advanced Filter dialog box.

After providing the list of eligible employees to Rita, you remove the filter to display all of the records in the Employee table.

To show all of the records in the table:

1. In the Sort & Filter group on the Data tab, click the **Clear** button. All of the records in the Employee table reappear.

Using Database Functions to Summarize Data

Database functions (or **Dfunctions**) perform summary data analysis, such as sum, average, and count, on an Excel table or data range based on criteria specified in a criteria range. Although you can often use the SUMIF, AVERAGEIF, and COUNTIF functions;

the Total row of an Excel table; and PivotTables to achieve the same results as Database functions, some situations require Database functions. For example, the type of summary analysis, the placement of the summary results, or the complexity of the criteria might require using Database functions. Figure B-8 lists the Database functions.

Figure B-8 **Database functions**

Function	Description
DAVERAGE	Returns the average of the values that meet specified criteria
DCOUNT	Returns the number of cells containing numbers that meet specified criteria
DCOUNTA	Returns the number of nonblank cells that meet specified criteria
DMAX	Returns the maximum value in the search column that meets specified criteria
DMIN	Returns the minimum value in the search column that meets specified criteria
DSTDEV	Returns the estimate of standard deviation based on a sample of entries that meet the specified criteria
DSUM	Returns the sum of the values in the summary column that meet specified criteria

Rita needs to prepare a report comparing the average salaries paid to employees by pay type (hourly and salaried) and by gender. To create this report, you must set up a criteria range to retrieve the appropriate records for each calculation. Consequently, a Database function is a good approach.

Database functions use a criteria range to specify the records to summarize. In a Database function, the criteria range is used as one of the arguments of the function. The general syntax for any Database function is

```
DatabaseFunctionName(table range, column to summarize, criteria range)
```

where *table range* refers to the cells where the data to summarize is located, including the column header, *column to summarize* is the column name of the field to summarize entered within quotation marks, and *criteria range* is the range where the criteria that determine which records are used in the calculation are specified.

You will use Database functions to complete the Employee Summary worksheet, summarizing the average salaries for employees by pay type and gender. First, you will set up a criteria range. Although the criteria range often includes all fields from the table, even those not needed to select records, you do not have to include all field names from the table when setting up a criteria range. In this case, you will use only the fields needed to specify the criteria.

You will create two criteria ranges for the Employee Pay Comparison report.

To create criteria ranges for the Employee Pay Comparison report:

1. Switch to the **Employee Summary** worksheet. The column headers for the criteria range have already been copied from the Employee Data worksheet.
2. In cell G6, enter **F** and then, in cell H6, enter **S**. These are the criteria to find all salaried females.
3. In cell J6, enter **M** and then, in cell K6, enter **S**. These are the criteria to find all salaried males.
4. In cell G10, enter **F** and then, in cell H10, enter **H**. These are the criteria to find all hourly females.
5. In cell J10, enter **M** and then, in cell K10, enter **H**. These are the criteria to find all hourly males. See Figure B-9.

Figure B-9 **Criteria ranges for the report**

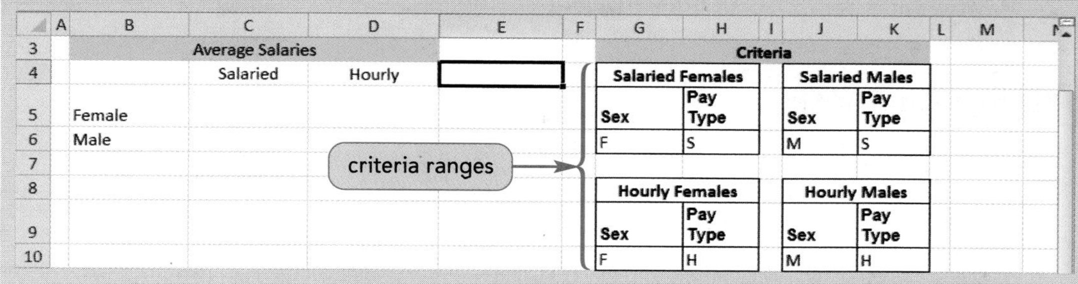

The criteria ranges are complete, so you can enter the formulas for the employee salary comparison. You will enter the DAVERAGE function to calculate the average salary in each group. In each function, the first two arguments are identical. The third argument, the criteria range, is different for each function so you can average a different subset of employees each time.

To find average salaries for salaried males and salaried females:

1. Click cell **C5**, and then click the **Insert Function** button on the formula bar. The Insert Function dialog box opens.
2. Click the **Or select a category arrow**, and then click **Database**.
3. In the Select a function box, select **DAVERAGE**, if necessary, and then click the **OK** button. The Function Arguments dialog box opens.
4. In the Database box, type **'Employee Data'!$A$6:$M$106** to enter the range to search, and then press the **Tab** key. In this case, 'Employee Data'!$A$6:$M$106 refers to all data values in the range A6:M106 of the Employee Data worksheet.

   Trouble? If the error "Invalid" appears to the right of the Database box, you probably mistyped the range to search. Make sure you typed apostrophes (') and not quotation marks (") around the Employee Data worksheet name, included a space in the Employee Data worksheet name, and typed ! (an exclamation mark) before the criteria range.
5. In the Field box, type **"Annual Salary"** and then press the **Tab** key. The field specifies the table column that contains the data to be averaged.
6. In the Criteria box, type **G5:H6** to specify the criteria for salaried females. See Figure B-10.

Figure B-10 **DAVERAGE Function Arguments dialog box**

Function Arguments

DAVERAGE

Database 'Employee Data'!$A$6:$M$106 = {"ID","Last Name","Hire Date","Birth Dat

Field "Annual Salary" = "Annual Salary"

Criteria G5:H6 = G5:H6

= 61793.91304

Averages the values in a column in a list or database that match conditions you specify.

Criteria is the range of cells that contains the conditions you specify. The range includes a column label and one cell below the label for a condition.

Formula result = $ 61,794

Help on this function

OK Cancel

7. Click the **OK** button. The formula =DAVERAGE('Employee Data'!$A$6:$M$106, "Annual Salary",G5:H6) appears in the formula bar and $61,794 appears in cell C5, indicating the average salary paid to salaried females. See Figure B-11.

Figure B-11 DAVERAGE function

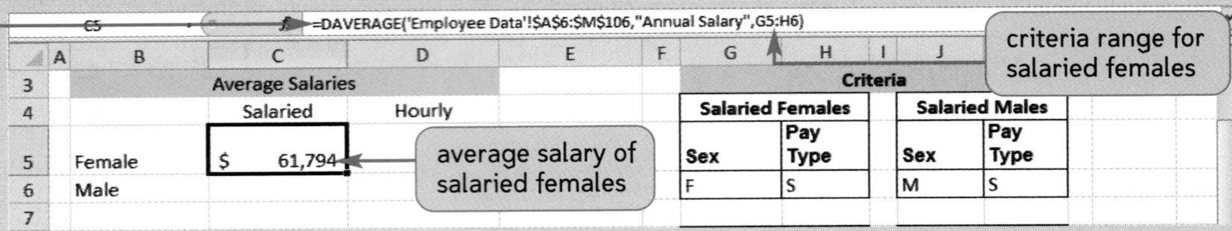

8. Click cell **C6**, and then click the **Insert Function** button on the formula bar.
9. Repeat Steps 2 through 5 to enter the first two arguments for the DAVERAGE function to calculate the average salary paid to male employees.
10. In the Criteria box, type **J5:K6** to specify the criteria for salaried males.
11. Click the **OK** button. The formula =DAVERAGE ('Employee Data'!$A$6:$M$106, "Annual Salary",J5:K6) appears in the formula bar and $95,081 appears in cell C6, indicating the average salary paid to salaried males.

For the last two cells in the salary comparison, you will copy the formulas in cells C5:C6 to cells D5 and D6 to calculate the average salaries paid to hourly females and hourly males.

To find the average salaries for male and female hourly employees:

1. Copy the formula in cell **C5** to cell **D5**.
2. Click cell **D5**, and then change the criteria range (the third argument) from H5:I6 to **G9:H10**. The formula =DAVERAGE('Employee Data'!$A$6:$M$106,"Annual Salary",G9:H10) appears in the formula bar and $27,213 appears in cell D5, indicating the average salary paid to hourly females.
3. Copy the formula from cell **C6** to cell **D6**.
4. Click cell **D6**, and then change the criteria range (the third argument) from K5:L6 to **J9:K10**. The formula =DAVERAGE('Employee Data'!$A$6:$M$106,"Annual Salary",J9:K10) appears in the formula bar and $26,707 appears in cell D6, indicating the average salary paid to salaried males. See Figure B-12.

Figure B-12 Completed Average Salaries report

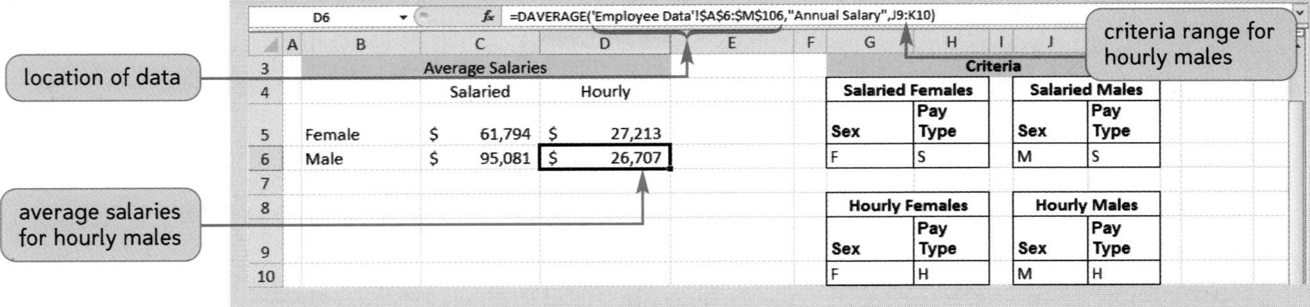

Summarizing Data Using the COUNTIFS, SUMIFS, and AVERAGEIFS Functions

The COUNTIFS, SUMIFS, and AVERAGEIFS functions are similar to the COUNTIF, SUMIF, and AVERAGEIF functions except the latter functions enable you to specify only one condition to summarize the data, whereas the former functions enable you to summarize the data using several conditions.

The **COUNTIFS function** counts the number of cells within a range that meet multiple criteria. Its syntax is

```
COUNTIFS(,criteria_range1,criteria1[,criteria_range2,criteria2,…])
```

where *criteria_range1*, *criteria_range2*, and up represent up to 127 ranges (columns of data) in which to evaluate the associated criteria, and *criteria1*, *criteria2*, and up represent 127 criteria in the form of a number, an expression, a cell reference, or text that define which cells will be counted. Criteria can be expressed as a number such as 50 to find a number equal to 50, the expression ">10000" to find an amount greater than 10000, text such as "FT" to find a text value equal to FT, or the cell reference B4 to find the value equal to the value stored in cell B4. Each cell in a range is counted only if all of the corresponding criteria specified in the COUNTIFS function are true.

To count the number of full-time (FT) employees who are female (F) and earn more than $50,000, you can use the following function to count the full-time employees (Employee[Job Status],"FT") who are female (Employee[Sex],"F") and have a salary greater than 50,000 (Employee[Annual Salary],">50000"). The criteria are treated as if they are connected by an AND function, so all conditions must be true for a record to be counted.

```
=COUNTIFS(Employee[Job Status],"FT",Employee[Sex],"F",
Employee[Annual Salary],">50000")
```

The SUMIFS and AVERAGEIFS functions have a slightly different syntax. The **SUMIFS function** adds values in a range that meet multiple criteria using the syntax

```
SUMIFS(sum_range,criteria_range1,criteria1[,criteria_range2,
criteria2,…])
```

where *sum_range* is the range you want to add; *criteria_range1*, *criteria_range2*, and so on represent up to 127 ranges (columns of data) in which to evaluate the associated criteria; and *criteria1*, *criteria2*, and so on up to 127 criteria in the form of a number, expression, cell reference, or text define which cells will be added.

To calculate the total salary paid to full-time (FT) employees hired after 2012 who are living in Austin, you can use the following SUMIFS function to add the salaries (Employee[Annual Salary]) of employees located in Austin (Employee[Location],"Austin") who have a hire date on or later than 1/1/2012 (Employee[Hire Date],">=1/1/2012") and are full-time employees (Employee[Job Status],"FT"):

```
=SUMIFS(Employee[Annual Salary],Employee [Location],"Austin",
Employee[Hire Date],">=1/1/2012",Employee[Job Status],"FT")
```

The **AVERAGEIFS function** calculates the average of values within a range of cells that meet multiple conditions. Its syntax is

```
AVERAGEIFS(average_range,criteria_range1,criteria1[,criteria_range2,
criteria2,…])
```

where *average_range* is the range to average; *criteria_range1*, *criteria_range2*, and so on represent up to 127 ranges in which to evaluate the associated criteria; and *criteria1*, *criteria2*, and so on up to 127 criteria in the form of a number, an expression, a cell reference, or text define which cells will be averaged.

To calculate the average salary paid to males (M) who have worked at Talent Tracs for more than five years, you can use the following AVERAGEIFS function to average the salaries (Employee[Annual Salary]) of male employees (Employee[Sex],"M"), having more than five years of service (Employee[Years Service],">5"):

```
=AVERAGEIFS(Employee[Annual Salary],Employee[Sex],"M",
Employee[Years Service],">5")
```

Rita wants you to complete the Years' Service Summary report using the COUNTIFS, SUMIFS, and AVERAGEIFS functions to compute statistical information for Talent Tracs employees excluding employees working from home.

To calculate employees with years of service between 0 and 4 years:

1. Click cell **C16**, and then click the **Insert Function** button *fx* on the formula bar. The Insert Function dialog box opens.
2. Click the **Or select a category arrow**, and then click **Statistical**.
3. In the Select a function box, click **COUNTIFS**, and then click the **OK** button. The Function Arguments dialog box opens.
4. In the Criteria_range1 box, enter **Employee[Location]** and then press the **Tab** key. This criterion selects employees not working from home.
5. In the Criteria1 box, type **"<>Home"** to specify employees not working from home, and then press the **Tab** key. The first condition is complete, and 93 appears as the total count in the middle of the Function Arguments dialog box.
6. In the Criteria_range2 box, enter **Employee[Years Service]** to enter the range referencing the number of years the employee has worked at Talent Tracs, and then press the **Tab** key.
7. In the Criteria2 box, type **">=0"** to select employees whose years of service are greater than or equal to 0, and then press the **Tab** key. The second condition is complete, and 93 appears as the total count.
8. In the Criteria_range3 box, enter **Employee[Years Service]** to enter the range referencing the number of years the employee has worked at Talent Tracs, and then press the **Tab** key.
9. In the Criteria3 box, type **"<=4"** to enter the criterion that employees' years of service are less than or equal to 4. The third condition is complete, and 57 appears as the total count. See Figure B-13.

Figure B-13 **Function Arguments box for the COUNTIFS function**

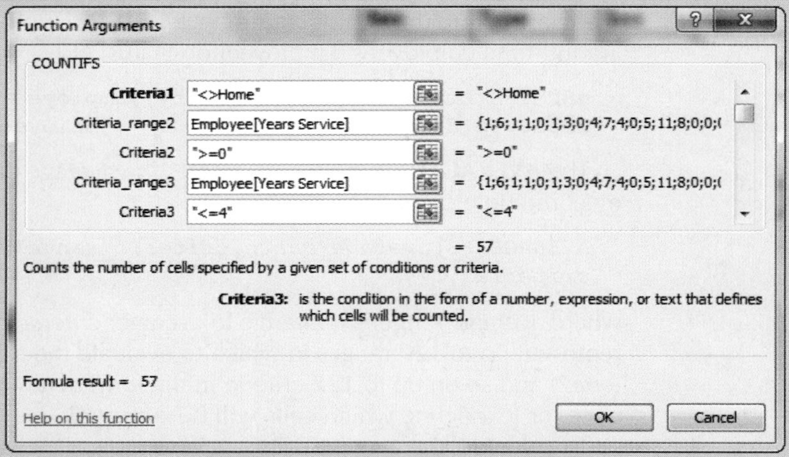

Function Arguments

COUNTIFS

Criteria1 "<>Home" = "<>Home"

Criteria_range2 Employee[Years Service] = {1;6;1;1;0;1;3;0;4;7;4;0;5;11;8;0;0;(

Criteria2 ">=0" = ">=0"

Criteria_range3 Employee[Years Service] = {1;6;1;1;0;1;3;0;4;7;4;0;5;11;8;0;0;(

Criteria3 "<=4" = "<=4"

= 57

Counts the number of cells specified by a given set of conditions or criteria.

Criteria3: is the condition in the form of a number, expression, or text that defines which cells will be counted.

Formula result = 57

Help on this function

OK Cancel

10. Click the **OK** button. The formula =COUNTIFS(Employee[Location],"<>Home", Employee[Years Service],">=0",Employee[Years Service],"<=4") appears in the formula bar and the value 57 appears in cell C16. See Figure B-14.

Figure B-14 **Years' Service Summary report in process**

COUNTIFS function to calculate the number of employees who have worked 4 or fewer years

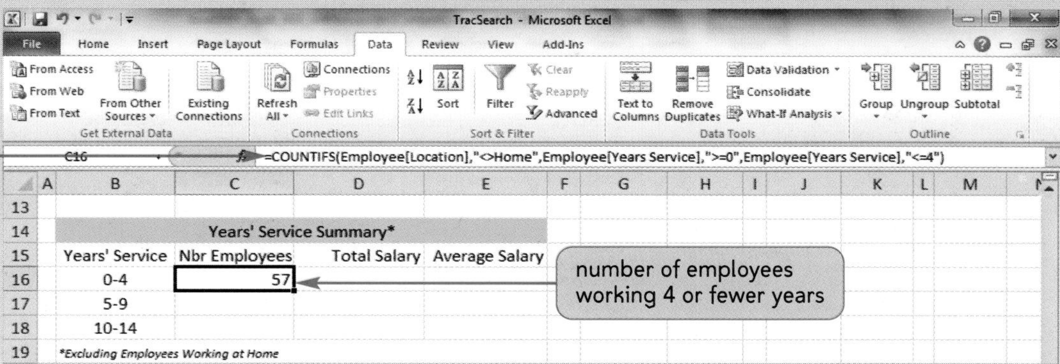

11. Copy the formula from cell **C16** to the range **C17:C18**.

12. In cell C17, change the second criteria argument from ">=0" to **">=5"** and change the third criteria argument from "<=4" to **"<=9"**. The criteria specify years of service greater than or equal to 5 and less than or equal to 9. The formula =COUNT IFS(Employee[Location],"<>Home",Employee[Years Service],">=5",Employee[Years Service],"<=9") appears in the formula bar and 26 appears in cell C17.

13. In cell C18, change the second criteria argument from ">=0" to **">=10"** and change the third criteria argument from "<=4" to **"<=14"**. The criteria specify years of service greater than or equal to 10 and less than or equal to 14. The formula =COUNTIFS(Employee[Location],"<>Home",Employee[Years Service], ">=10",Employee[Years Service],"<=14") appears in the formula bar and 10 appears in cell C18.

Next, you will calculate the total salary paid to employees based on years of service. To do this, you will use the SUMIFS function.

To calculate the total salary paid to employees:

1. Click cell **D16**, and then click the **Insert Function** button on the formula bar. The Insert Function dialog box opens.
2. Click the **Or select a category arrow**, and then click **Math & Trig**.
3. In the Select a function box, click **SUMIFS**, and then click the **OK** button. The Function Arguments dialog box opens.
4. In the Sum_range box, type **Employee[Annual Salary]** to enter the range of data to sum, and then press the **Tab** key. In this case, a structured reference was used to reference all data values in the Annual Salary column.
5. In the Criteria_range1 box, enter **Employee[Location]** and then press the **Tab** key.

TIP

You could also have used the worksheet reference 'Employee Data'!K6:K106 to reference the annual salaries for all employees.

6. In the Criteria1 box, type **"<>Home"** to specify employees not working from home, and then press the **Tab** key. The first condition is complete. See Figure B-15.

Figure B-15 **Function Arguments dialog box for the SUMIFS function**

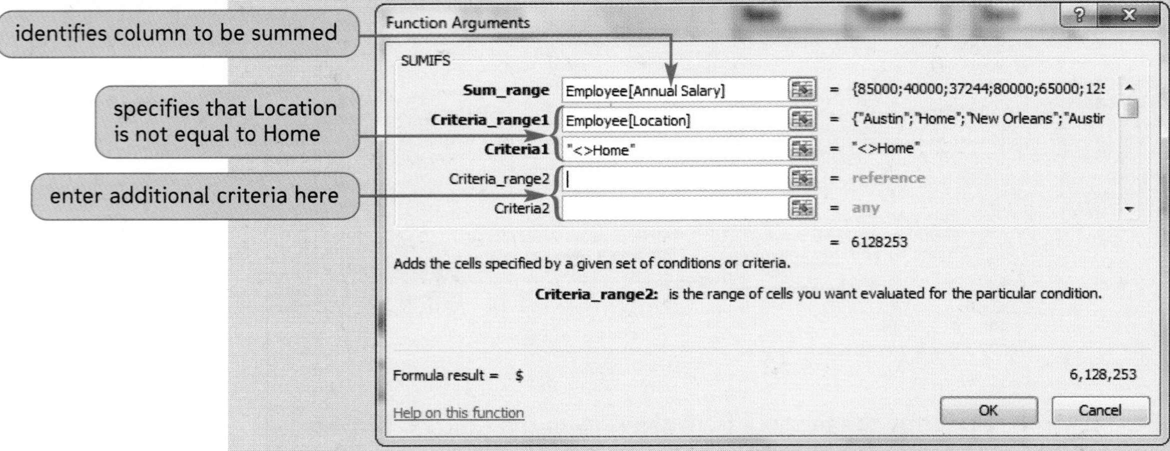

7. In the Criteria_range2 box, enter **Employee[Years Service]** for the range referencing the number of years the employee has worked at Talent Tracs, and then press the **Tab** key.
8. In the Criteria2 box, type **">=0"** to specify years of service that are greater than or equal to 0, and then press the **Tab** key.
9. In the Criteria_range3 box, type **Employee[Years Service]** for the range referencing the number of years the employee has worked at Talent Tracs, and then press the **Tab** key.
10. In the Criteria3 box, type **"<=4"** to specify years of service that are less than or equal to 4, and then press the **Tab** key.
11. Click the **OK** button. The formula =SUMIFS(Employee[Annual Salary],Employee[Location],"<>Home",Employee[Years Service],">=0",Employee[Years Service],"<=4") appears in the formula bar and 3,868,395 appears in cell D16.
12. Copy the formula from cell **D16** to the range **D17:D18**.
13. In cell D17, change the second criteria argument from ">=0" to **">=5"** and change the third criteria argument from "<=4" to **"<=9"**. The criteria specify years of service greater than or equal to 5 and less than or equal to 9. The formula =SUMIFS(Employee[Annual Salary],Employee[Location],"<>Home", Employee[Years Service],">=5",Employee[Years Service],"<=9") appears in the formula bar and 1,517,799 appears in cell D17.
14. In cell D18, change the second criteria argument from ">=0" to **">=10"** and then change the third criteria argument from "<=4" to **"<=14"**. The criteria specify years of service greater than or equal to 10 and less than or equal to 14. The formula =SUMIFS(Employee[Annual Salary],Employee[Location],"<>Home", Employee[Years Service],">=10",Employee[Years Service],"<=14") appears in the formula bar and 742,059 appears in cell D18.

Next, you will calculate the average salary paid to employees based on years of service. You will use the AVERAGEIFS function to do this.

To calculate the average salary paid to employees:

1. Click cell **E16**, and then click the **Insert Function** button on the formula bar. The Insert Function dialog box opens.
2. Click the **Or select a category arrow**, and then click **Statistical**.
3. In the Select a function box, click **AVERAGEIFS**, and then click the **OK** button. The Function Arguments dialog box opens.
4. In the Average_range box, type **Employee[Annual Salary]** to enter the range to be averaged, and then press the **Tab** key.
5. In the Criteria_range1 box, enter **Employee[Location]** and then press the **Tab** key.
6. In the Criteria1 box, type **"<>Home"** to specify employees not working from home, and then press the **Tab** key. The first condition is complete.
7. In the Criteria_range2 box, enter **Employee[Years Service]** for the range referencing the number of years the employee has worked at Talent Tracs, and then press the **Tab** key.
8. In the Criteria2 box, type **">=0"** to specify years of service greater than or equal to 0, and then press the **Tab** key.
9. In the Criteria_range3 box, enter **Employee[Years Service]** for the range referencing the number of years the employee has worked at Talent Tracs, and then press the **Tab** key.
10. In the Criteria3 box, type **"<=4"** to specify years of service less than or equal to 4, and then press the **Tab** key.
11. Click the **OK** button. The formula =AVERAGEIFS(Employee[Annual Salary], Employee[Location],"<>Home",Employee[Years Service],">=0",Employee[Years Service],"<=4") appears in the formula bar and 67,867 appears in cell E16.
12. Copy the formula from cell E16 to the range **E17:E18**.
13. In cell E17, change the second criteria argument from ">=0" to **">=5"** and change the third criteria argument from "<=4" to **"<=9"**. The criteria specify years of service greater than or equal to 5 and less than or equal to 9. The formula =AVERAGEIFS(Employee[Annual Salary],Employee[Location],"<>Home", Employee[Years Service], ">=5",Employee[Years Service],"<=9") appears in the formula bar and 58,377 appears in cell E17.
14. In cell E18, change the second criteria argument from ">=0" to **">=10"** and change the third criteria argument from "<=4" to **"<=14"**. The criteria specify years of service greater than or equal to 10 and less than or equal to 14. The formula =AVERAGEIFS(Employee[Annual Salary],Employee[Location],"<>Home", Employee[Years Service],">=10",Employee[Years Service],"<=14") appears in the formula bar and 74,206 appears in cell E18.
15. Click cell **E18**, and then expand the formula bar. See Figure B-16.

Figure B-16 Completed Years' Service Summary report

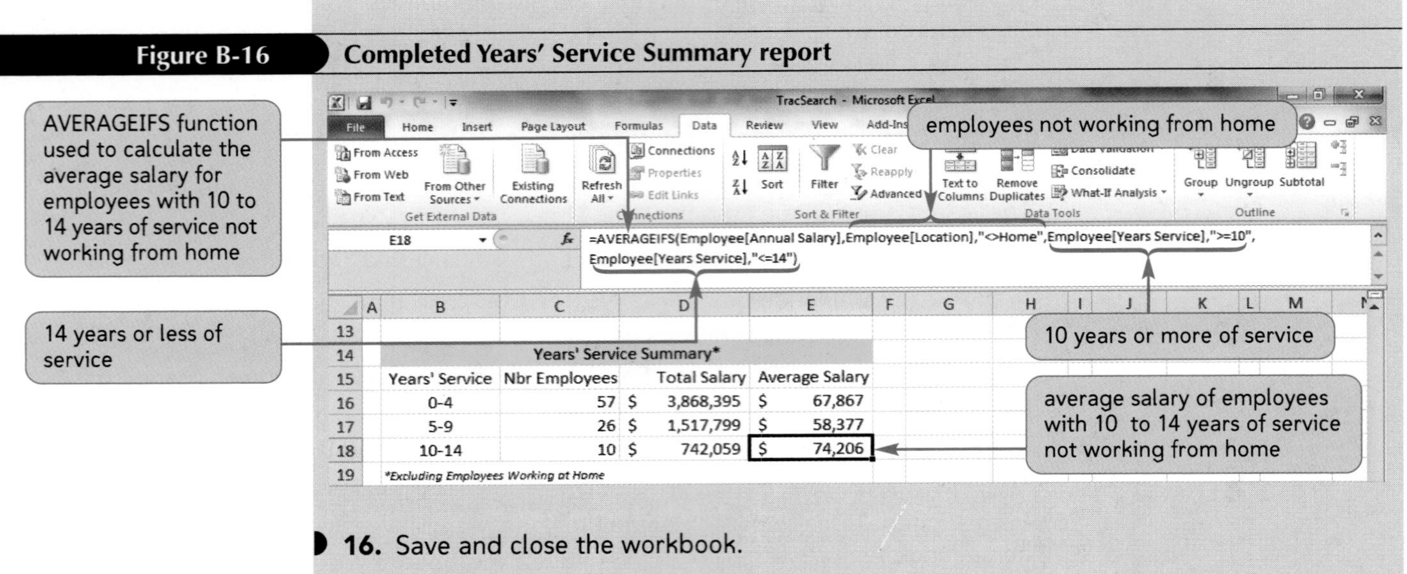

16. Save and close the workbook.

The Years' Service Summary report is complete. In this session, you used advanced filtering techniques to find potential candidates for a new full-time position. You also used the DAVERAGE and AVERAGEIFS functions to prepare a report calculating the average salary of employees broken down by pay type and gender.

Practice the skills you learned in the tutorial using the same case scenario.

PRACTICE

Review Assignments

Data File needed for the Review Assignments: TracReview.xlsx

Rita wants you to perform advanced filtering tasks to create a report about employee compensation and benefits. You need to set up a criteria range to generate the report. Complete the following:

1. Open the **TracReview** workbook located in the ExcelB\Review folder included with your Data Files, and then save the workbook as **TracReviewReport**. In the Documentation sheet, enter your name and the date.
2. Make a copy of the Employee Data worksheet, and then rename the copied worksheet as **Q2**. Complete the criteria range located in the range A1:M3 of the Q2 worksheet, and then use advanced filtering to display all part-time (PT) employees who have worked 2 or more years and earned more than $60,000 or consultants (CN). Filter the Employee table.
3. Make a copy of the Employee Data worksheet, and then rename the copied worksheet as **Q3**. Complete the criteria range located in the range A1:M3 of the Q3 worksheet so you can use advanced filtering to display all part-time (PT) employees working in Austin as well as all full-time (FT) employees working at home and earning $40,000 or more. Filter the Employee table.
4. Complete the Number of Employees by Sex and Health Plan report in the Employee Summary worksheet. Complete the criteria ranges (G4:K22) and then use the DCOUNT Database function to count the number of employees found in the range C5:D9 of the report. For example, in cell C5 count the number of employees with Health Plan PPOI that are female, in cell D5 count the number of employees with Health Plan PPOI that are male, and so on. Calculate totals in row 10 and column E to complete the report.
5. Complete the Total Salaries by Years Service and Sex in the Employee Summary worksheet. Use the SUMIFS function to calculate the total salary for each cell in the range C14:D16 of the Total Salaries by Years Service and Sex report. For example, in cell C14 calculate the total salary for female employees who have worked 0 to 4 years.
6. Save and close the workbook. Submit the finished workbook to your instructor, either in printed or electronic form, as requested.

Apply the skills you learned by summarizing order data.

APPLY

Case Problem 1

Data File needed for this Case Problem: World.xlsx

World Foods Kerry Jeffries is analyzing orders from last year. She has already summarized orders by month for all customers. Complete the following:

1. Open the **World** workbook located in the ExcelB\Case1 folder included with your Data Files, and then save the workbook as **World Foods**.
2. In the Documentation worksheet, enter your name and the date.
3. Make a copy of the Orders worksheet, and then rename the copied worksheet as **Q3**. In the Q3 worksheet, use advanced filtering to display sales in the Scandinavian countries (Denmark, Finland, Norway, and Sweden). Set up the criteria range beginning in row 1 and use the filter the list in place option.
4. Make a copy of the Orders worksheet, and then rename the copied worksheet as **Q4**. In the Q4 worksheet, use advanced filtering to display all records for Laura Callahan with sales over $1,500 in September. Set up the criteria range beginning in row 1 and use the filter the list in place option.

5. In the Summary worksheet, complete the analysis for the South American countries (Argentina and Brazil). Use Database functions to count and sum orders totaling $150 or more in March for Argentina. Set up an appropriate criteria range in rows 1 and 2, and then build the formulas in row 11 for Argentina.
6. In the Summary worksheet, complete the analysis for the South American country Brazil. Use the COUNTIFS and SUMIFS functions to enter formulas in row 12 to count and sum orders that total $150 or more in March in Brazil.
7. Save and close the workbook. Submit the finished workbook to your instructor, either in printed or electronic form, as requested.

Apply the skills you learned by analyzing donor gift data.

APPLY

Case Problem 2

Data File needed for this Case Problem: Gifts.xlsx

College Fund Raising Elliot Fastchow, the controller at ABC University, is analyzing gifts from several hundred donors. Complete the following:

1. Open the **Gifts** workbook located in the ExcelB\Case2 folder included with your Data Files, and then save the workbook as **ABC Gifts**.
2. In the Documentation worksheet, enter your name and the date.
3. Make a copy of the FundGifts worksheet, and then rename the copied worksheet as **Q3**. In the Q3 worksheet, use advanced filtering to display records from the current operating fund (FundType C) created after the year 2000 in the College of Nursing that have gifts totaling more than $1,000.
4. Make a copy of the FundGifts worksheet, and then rename the copied worksheet as **Q4**. In the Q4 worksheet, use advanced filtering to display records for funds in the College of Engineering with gifts of either $500 or less, or more than $50,000.
5. Sort the filtered data in the Gifts column from highest to lowest, and then format the Gifts column appropriately.
6. In the Summary worksheet, complete the analysis for Gifts from Endowment Funds. Use FundType E with Gifts over $1,000 to compare the gifts to the College of Arts & Science with gifts to the College of Pharmacy. Use Database functions to calculate the results for the college of Arts & Science. Use COUNTIFS, SUMIFS, and AVERAGEIFS to calculate the results for the College of Pharmacy.
7. Save and close the workbook. Submit the finished workbook to your instructor, either in printed or electronic form, as requested.

ENDING DATA FILES

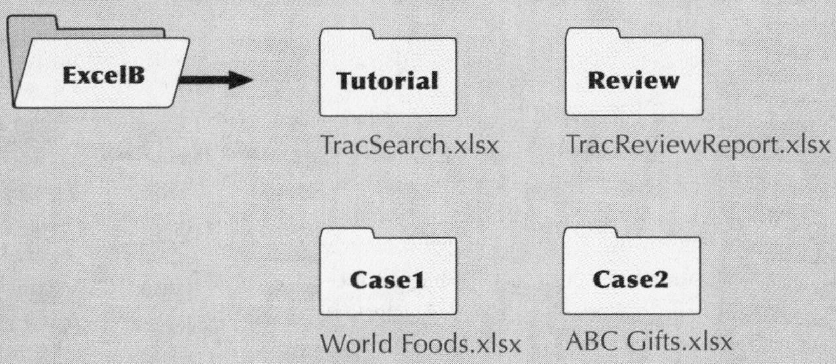

APPENDIX C

Creating a Shared Workbook

Collaborating on a Financial Report

EXCEL

OBJECTIVES

- Create a shared workbook
- Review edits to a shared workbook
- Merge two workbooks into one
- Inspect a document for hidden data
- Encrypt a workbook
- Digitally sign a finished workbook
- Understand linking and embedding
- Integrate Excel with other Office products

Case | *DataSafe*

DataSafe, a company based in Mobile, Alabama, specializes in data storage and recovery. Each year the company publishes a financial report for its stockholders. Jennifer Inwe and her team in the financial department are responsible for creating and publishing this year's report. In the process of developing this report, different employees will review and edit the workbook's content, which will go through several drafts and revisions. Jennifer asks you to help manage this collaborative process of development from initial draft to final form. Jennifer is aware that the final version of the workbook should be error-free. You'll be the first reviewer, and then send the workbook to other employees to review. The finished report will be distributed to the rest of the company and presented to the stockholders in time for the annual meeting. As part of the finished report, you will integrate the Excel workbook with other Office documents, including Word and PowerPoint.

STARTING DATA FILES

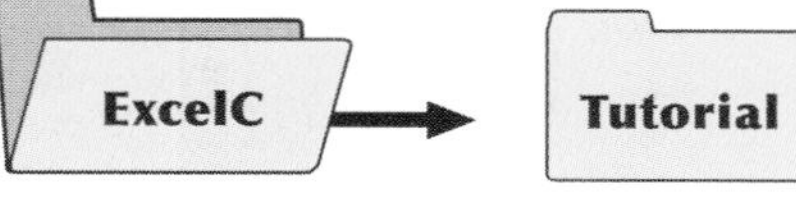

Tutorial	Review	Case1	Case2
Financial.xlsx	Cash Flow.xlsx	Budget.docx	Contributor.docx
Group.xlsx	Notes.docx	Covey.xlsx	Mailing.xlsx
Income Statement.xlsx	Projected.xlsx	Kao.xlsx	Student.xlsx
Linde Edits.xlsx	SL Comments.xlsx	Roper.xlsx	
Memo.docx	Stockholders.xlsx		
Merge.xlsx	Team.xlsx		

Sharing a Workbook with Multiple Users

To enable several users to view and modify the same workbook, you can share the workbook. A **shared workbook** can be edited simultaneously by more than one user when it is placed on a shared network folder, making it accessible to multiple users. A shared workbook can also be edited sequentially by users who work on the file in turns. One advantage of sharing a workbook is that you can track the changes made by different people and the time that each change was made.

In a shared workbook, you can enter numbers and text, edit cells, move data, insert new rows and columns, and perform other usual editing tasks. However, you cannot delete worksheets and ranges, insert ranges, merge and split cells, edit charts, or use the drawing tools. In general, you can do anything in the workbook that does not drastically change the layout or content to such an extent that Excel can no longer reconcile your edits with the edits from other users.

Jennifer has saved the first draft of her financial report in an Excel workbook. The workbook contains four worksheets describing DataSafe's financial status during the prior three years as well as the Documentation sheet. You'll open this workbook now.

To open the financial report workbook:

1. Open the **Financial** workbook located in the ExcelC\Tutorial folder included with your Data Files, and then save the workbook as **Financial Report**.
2. In the Documentation worksheet, enter your name and the date.

Setting Privacy Options

By default, Excel does not enable workbook sharing in order to prevent malicious software from opening and sharing personal information and sensitive data with the outside world. Before you can share a workbook, you must reset the privacy options. You set the privacy options for each workbook you wish to share, not the entire Excel program.

To enable sharing for the Financial Report workbook:

1. Click the **File** tab on the Ribbon, and then click **Options** in the navigation bar. The Excel Options dialog box opens.
2. Click **Trust Center** in the left pane, and then click the **Trust Center Settings** button in the right pane. The Trust Center dialog box opens.
3. Click **Privacy Options** in the left pane, and then uncheck the **Remove personal information from file properties on save** check box in the Document-specific settings section.
4. Click the **OK** button in each dialog box to return to the workbook.

Enable Workbook Sharing

You need to share a workbook to make it possible for several users to access and edit the same data simultaneously. You do this from the Share Workbook dialog box. You can also use this dialog box to monitor who has access to the shared workbook. For example, after sharing the Financial Report workbook and placing it in a network folder, both Jennifer and Alberto Conti can open the workbook at the same time, as shown in Figure C-1.

Figure C-1 Share Workbook dialog box

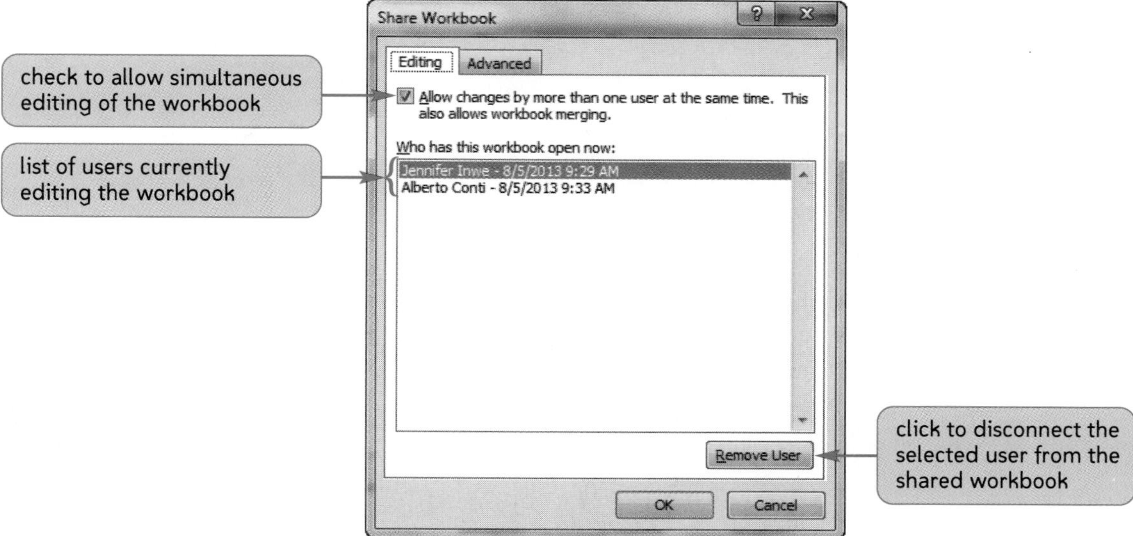

TIP

To add a password to a shared workbook so only approved users can edit it, click the Protect and Share Workbook button in the Changes group on the Review tab.

You'll enable workbook sharing for the Financial Report workbook.

To enable workbook sharing:

1. Click the **Review** tab on the Ribbon, and then click the **Share Workbook** button in the Changes group. The Share Workbook dialog box opens with the Editing tab active.
2. Click the **Allow changes by more than one user at the same time** check box to insert a check mark. This allows others to access and edit this workbook.
3. Click the **OK** button. A dialog box opens indicating the workbook will be saved, which changes its status to shared.
4. Click the **OK** button. The workbook is saved and [Shared] appears on the title bar next to the workbook name.
5. Close the workbook.

Resolving Conflicts

When people make changes to different cells, Excel marks those edits into the shared workbook and notifies current users of the change. Consider the situation shown in Figure C-2, in which Jennifer and Alberto are working on the same document. Alberto changes the value in cell B7, and then saves the workbook. When Jennifer saves the shared workbook, any changes made by other users appear as comments attached to the edited cells. Excel will remove these comments automatically when Jennifer reopens the workbook at a later date. However, it will preserve that information if you want to track the changes at a later date.

Figure C-2 **Two users simultaneously edit a shared workbook**

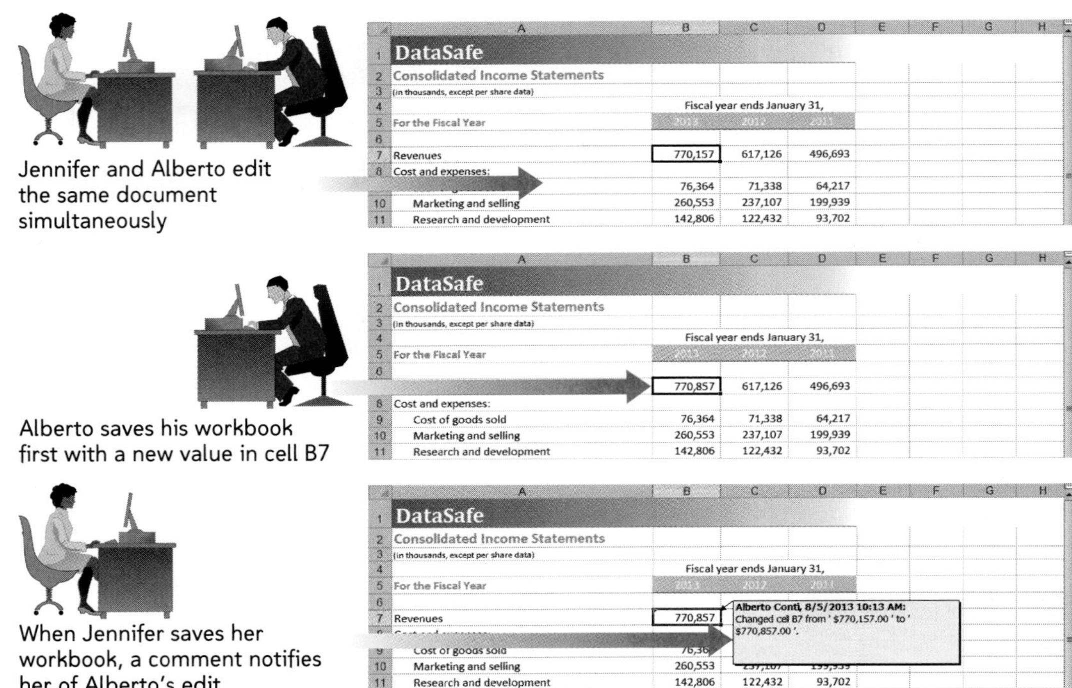

Conflicts occur when users try to save *different* changes to the same cell. Suppose Jennifer and Alberto make different edits to cell B7. Alberto saves his workbook first and stores $770,857 in cell B7. However, Jennifer is working at the same time and enters $770,457 in cell B7. When Jennifer saves her workbook, the Resolve Conflicts dialog box opens, notifying her of the conflict in cell B7, as shown in Figure C-3. From this dialog box, Jennifer can choose which edit to accept. She can repeat this process for each conflict. The Resolve Conflicts dialog box appears only when conflicts arise in the edits that the coworkers make while working on the document simultaneously.

Figure C-3 **Resolve Conflicts dialog box**

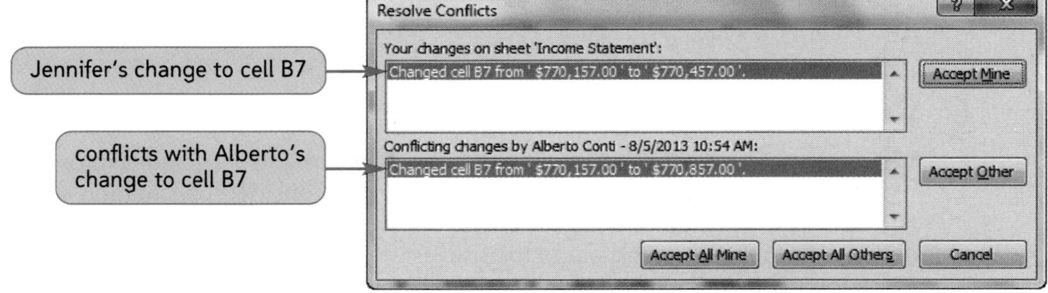

All users have equal authority to resolve conflicts. The last user to save the document is the one who sees the Resolve Conflicts dialog box. Rejected edits are stored in a tracking log so any user can review and retrieve them. This feature is particularly useful when a large group is editing a workbook and more control over the final content is needed. In the financial report for DataSafe, Jennifer will review the tracking log before signing off on the final report.

Tracking Changes in a Workbook

Alberto Conti, Thomas Uecker, and Mai Le of the finance group have reviewed the Financial Report workbook and added comments and edits. You'll open the shared workbook and help Jennifer resolve the different changes made to the report.

To open and review the shared workbook:

1. Open the **Group** workbook located in the ExcelC\Tutorial folder included with your Data Files, and then save the workbook as **Group Edit**.

   Trouble? If Excel reports that the file is locked, click the Notify button, wait until Excel notifies you that the file is no longer locked for editing, and then click the Read/Write button in the next dialog box that opens.

2. In the Documentation worksheet, enter your name and the date.
3. In the Comments group on the Review tab, click the **Next** button. The next—or, in this case, the first—comment is selected. It contains the responses to Jennifer's query about whether to expand the report to five years. Alberto and Mai suggest leaving the report as is; Tom prefers the five-year report. See Figure C-4.

Figure C-4 Shared workbook with user comments

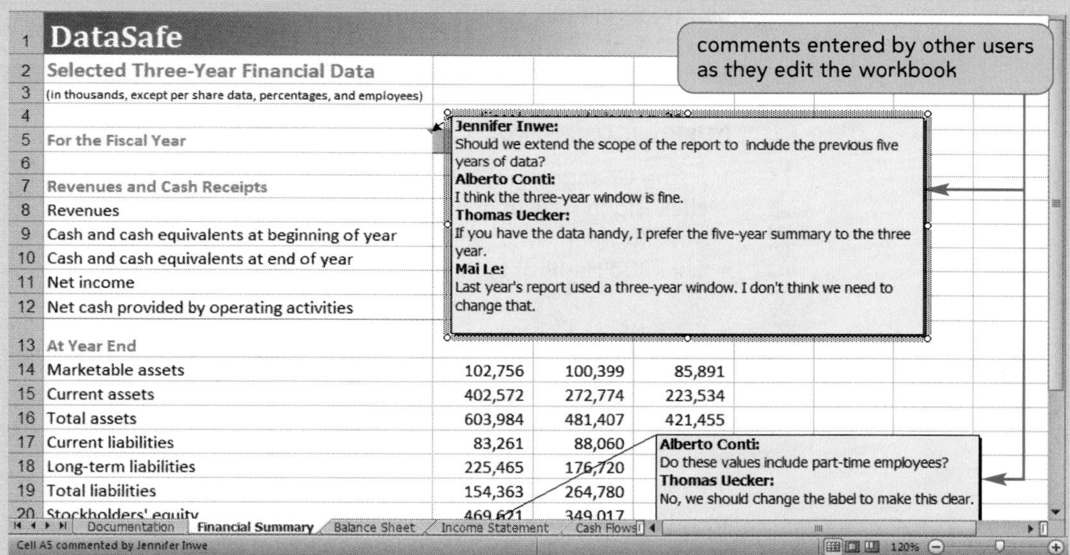

4. Click the **Next** button again. The comment in cell A22 is selected, in which Alberto asks whether the number of employees reported in the worksheet includes part-time employees. Thomas responds that it doesn't and suggests changing the label.
5. Click the **Next** button again to view the comments for cell B25, and then click the **Next** button again to confirm that there are no more comments in the workbook.
6. Click the **Cancel** button to end the comment review.

Because you have reviewed all of the comments in the workbook, Jennifer wants you to delete them.

To delete the comments:

1. In the Financial Summary worksheet, click cell **A1**. You want to review the comments, starting at the beginning of the worksheet.
2. In the Comments group on the Review tab, click the **Next** button to go to the first comment in the workbook.
3. In the Comments group, click the **Delete** button. The comment in cell A5 is deleted.
4. Repeat Steps 2 and 3 for the other two comments in the workbook.
5. Click cell **A1** to return to the beginning of the report.

TIP

When no comments remain in the workbook, the Delete, Previous, and Next buttons in the Comments group are grayed out.

Reviewing Changes Using the Tracking Log

Having reviewed and deleted the comments in the workbook, you will examine the edits made to the contents of the workbook. The tracking log, by default, stores all edits made to the workbook during the previous 30 days. However, inserted or deleted worksheets and style changes are not tracked. To review the tracked edits, you can use the Track Changes feature to highlight each edit. When Track Changes is enabled, edits appear in a comment box next to the cell that describes the change, who made it, and when. Each cell with an edit has a color border added to it.

REFERENCE

Reviewing Tracked Changes in a Shared Workbook

- In the Changes group on the Review tab, click the Track Changes button, and then click Highlight Changes.
- Specify when, who, and where in the Highlight which changes section.
- Click the Highlight changes on screen check box to see edits in comments.

or

- Click the List changes on a new sheet check box to view the tracking log.
- Click the OK button.
- Point to the highlighted cells to see the edits and/or view the tracking log in the History worksheet.

You'll use Track Changes to highlight the edits to the Group Edit workbook.

To highlight and review the changes to the shared workbook:

1. In the Changes group on the Review tab, click the **Track Changes** button, and then click **Highlight Changes**. The Highlight Changes dialog box opens. You'll review all the changes made by everyone but yourself.
2. Click the **When** arrow, and then click **All**. This specifies that you'll review all the changes.
3. Click the **Who** arrow, and then click **Everyone but Me**. The Who check box is automatically checked, and you'll see everyone else's edits.
4. Verify that the **Highlight changes on screen** check box is checked and the **List changes on a new sheet** check box is unchecked. See Figure C-5.

Figure C-5 **Highlight Changes dialog box**

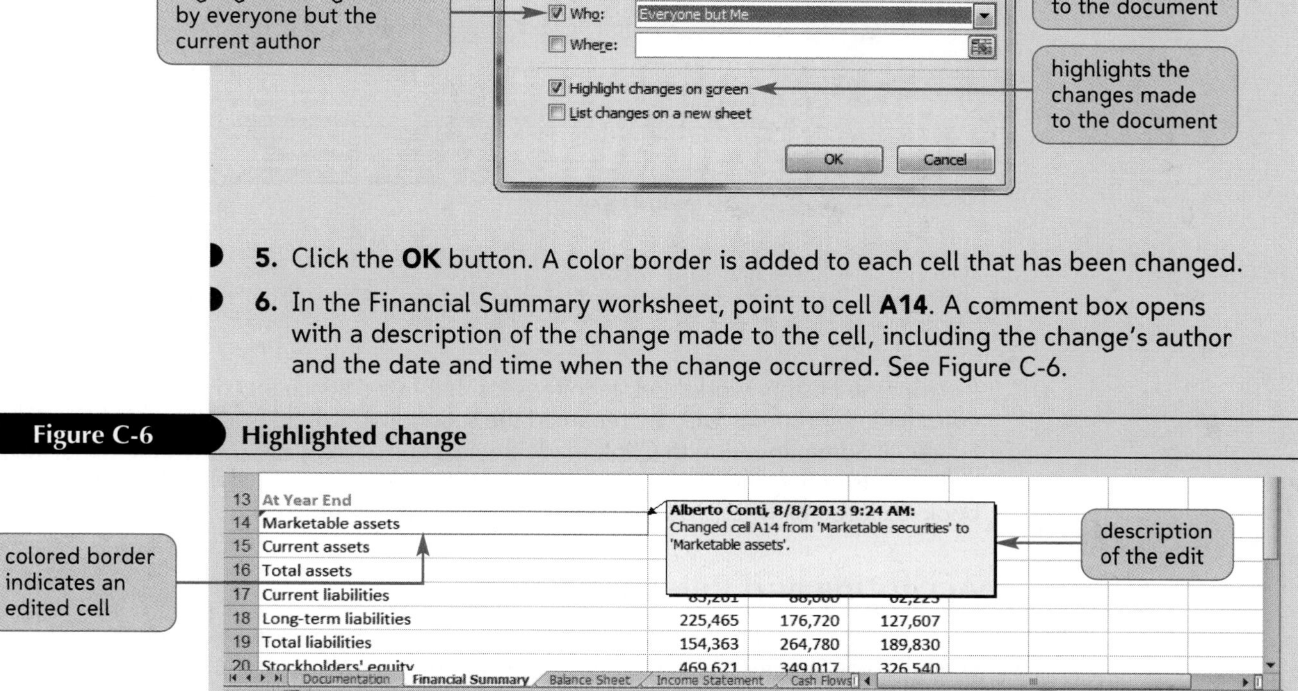

5. Click the **OK** button. A color border is added to each cell that has been changed.
6. In the Financial Summary worksheet, point to cell **A14**. A comment box opens with a description of the change made to the cell, including the change's author and the date and time when the change occurred. See Figure C-6.

Figure C-6 **Highlighted change**

Examining all the sheets in a workbook to find the highlighted changes can be time consuming, especially in workbooks with many worksheets. The tracking log provides a faster method to review the changes. When you create a tracking log, which appears on the History worksheet, it lists all the changes made to the workbook along with information about the date and time each change was made, the person who made the change, the location of the change, and the change itself. You'll review the tracking log for the Financial Reports workbook.

To show the contents of the tracking log:

1. In the Changes group on the Review tab, click the **Track Changes** button, and then click **Highlight Changes**. The Highlight Changes dialog box opens.
2. Click the **List changes on a new sheet** check box to insert a check mark.
3. Click the **OK** button. The History worksheet is created, detailing the history of the six changes made to the workbook in chronological order along with who made each change, where it was made, and what kind of change it was. See Figure C-7.

Figure C-7 History worksheet with tracking log

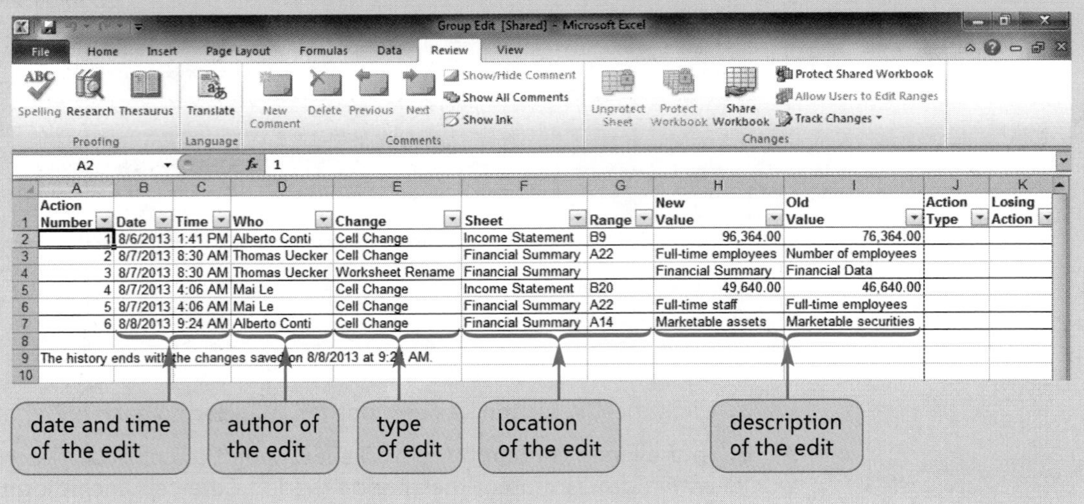

From the History worksheet, Jennifer sees that five edits changed cell values, and one edit, made by Thomas Uecker, renamed the second worksheet from Financial Data to Financial Summary. Alberto Conti made the last edit at 9:24 AM. Note that the History sheet exists only for the current Excel session. It is automatically deleted when the workbook is closed or when you start rejecting or accepting the changes from the tracking log.

Accepting and Rejecting Edits

You can accept or reject edits using commands on the Review tab. As with tracking changes, you specify which changes you want to examine for accepting and rejecting. The changes are reviewed in chronological order, just as they appeared in the tracking log.

REFERENCE

Accepting and Rejecting Edits

- In the Changes group on the Review tab, click the Track Changes button, and then click Accept/Reject Changes.
- Specify when, by whom, and where changes are to be reviewed.
- Click the OK button.
- Proceed through the list of changes, clicking the Accept, Reject, Accept All, Reject All, or Close buttons.

Jennifer wants to keep some edits but not others.

To accept or reject edits in the workbook:

1. In the Changes group on the Review tab, click the **Track Changes** button, and then click **Accept/Reject Changes**.
2. Click the **OK** button if prompted by Excel to save the workbook. The Select Changes to Accept or Reject dialog box opens. You'll use the settings shown in Figure C-8.

Figure C-8 Select Changes to Accept or Reject dialog box

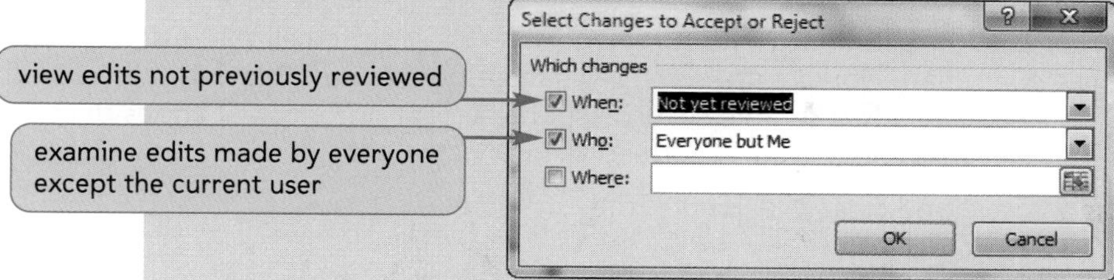

3. Verify that the settings in your dialog box match the ones shown in Figure C-8, and then click the **OK** button. The first change is in cell B9 of the Income Statement worksheet. Alberto Conti changed the value from 76,364 to 96,364. See Figure C-9.

Figure C-9 Accept or Reject Changes dialog box

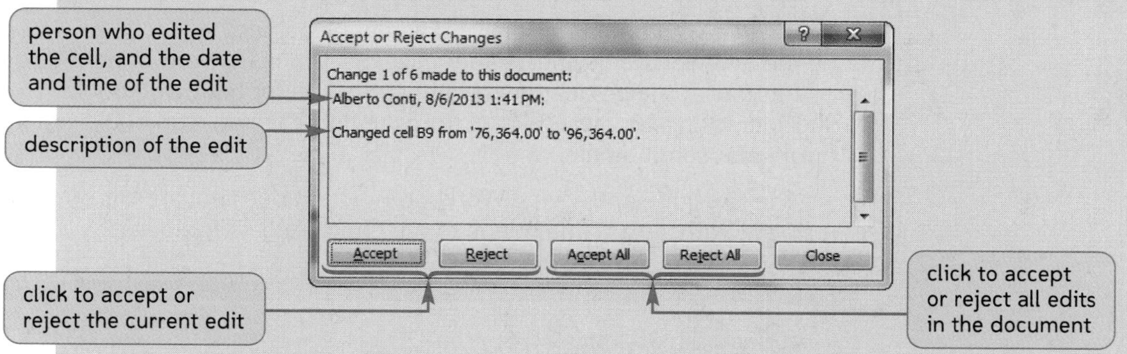

4. Click the **Accept** button to accept this edit. The next change is in the Financial Summary worksheet in cell A22, which contains two conflicting edits. See Figure C-10.

Figure C-10 Multiple edits for the same cell

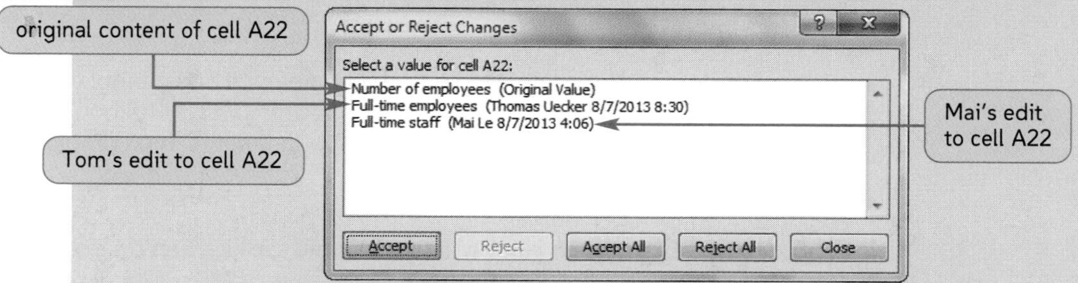

TIP

You can accept or reject all changes to the workbook at one time by clicking the Accept All or Reject All button.

5. In the Select a value for cell A22 box, click **Full-time employees**, and then click the **Accept** button. This accepts Thomas's edit, rejecting the original text and Mai's subsequent edit.

6. Click the **Accept** button to accept Thomas's edit to rename the second worksheet from Financial Data to Financial Summary.

7. Click the **Accept** button to accept Mai's edit of the value of cell B20 in the Income Statement worksheet from 46,640 to 49,640.
8. Click the **Reject** button to reject Alberto's edit to cell A14 of the Financial Summary worksheet, which reverses Alberto's edit, leaving the cell with its original value: Marketable securities. The Accept or Reject Changes dialog box closes because there are no more edits to review.
9. Save and close the Group Edit workbook.

Merge and Compare Workbooks

When two (or more) copies of the same workbook have different edits, you can merge the workbooks to create a single workbook that combines the edits from both files. The following conditions must be met to merge two workbooks:

- The two workbooks must be copies of the same file, which must also be a shared workbook.
- The two workbooks must have different filenames.
- The two workbooks must either have the same password or not be password-protected.
- The Track Changes feature must be turned on for both workbooks.
- The tracking log must be kept from the time the two workbooks are made from the original common file.

The Compare and Merge Workbooks button does not appear on the Ribbon. Before using it, you can add the button to the Quick Access Toolbar.

REFERENCE

Merging Workbooks

- Customize the Quick Access Toolbar to display the Compare and Merge Workbooks button.
- Open the workbook into which you want to merge the workbooks.
- Click the Compare and Merge Workbooks button on the Quick Access Toolbar.
- Select the workbook that you want to merge into the current document, and then click the OK button.

Jennifer's supervisor, Steve Linde, is at a conference and cannot access the shared file on the company network. Instead, he edited a copy of the workbook and emailed it to Jennifer. You'll set up Excel so you can perform the merge and compare the workbooks.

To add the Compare and Merge Workbooks button to the Quick Access Toolbar:

1. On the Quick Access Toolbar, click the **Customize Quick Access Toolbar** button, and then click **More Commands**.
2. Click the **Choose commands from** arrow, and then click **Commands Not in the Ribbon** to display a list of all the Excel commands that do not appear on the Ribbon.

TIP

You can also add the Compare and Merge Workbooks button to the Ribbon by selecting Customize Ribbon from the list of Excel options.

3. Click **Compare and Merge Workbooks** from the list of commands, and then click the **Add** button. The Compare and Merge Workbooks command button is added to the commands on the Quick Access Toolbar.
4. Click the **OK** button.

Now you can merge two workbooks. First, you open the workbook into which you want to merge the two files—in this case, Jennifer's workbook. Then, you use the Compare and Merge command to open the other workbook—in this case, Steve's workbook—and merge it with Jennifer's workbook.

To merge Jennifer's workbook with Steve's workbook:

1. Open the **Merge** workbook located in the ExcelC\Tutorial folder included with your Data Files, and then save it as **Merged Report** in the same folder.

   Trouble? If a dialog box opens indicating that the file is locked for editing, click the Notify button, proceed to the workbook, and then click the Read/Write button in the next dialog box that opens.
2. In the Documentation worksheet, enter your name and the date.
3. On the Quick Access Toolbar, click the **Compare and Merge Workbooks** button. A dialog box opens indicating the workbook will be saved.
4. Click the **OK** button to save the current workbook. The Select Files to Merge Into Current Workbook dialog box opens.
5. Select the **Linde Edits** workbook located in the ExcelC\Tutorial folder included with your Data Files, and then click the **OK** button. The two workbooks are merged, and all the edits and comments from both workbooks appear in the Merged Report workbook.
6. Switch to the **Financial Summary** worksheet. Steve inserted a comment in cell A2.
7. Click cell **A2**, and then read the comment indicating that Steve thinks the workbook is in good shape.
8. Click the **Review** tab on the Ribbon, and then click the **Delete** button in the Comments group. The comment in cell A2 is deleted. There are no other comments in the workbook.

Next, you'll review the edits in the merged workbook. You've already reviewed the changes in Jennifer's workbook, so you'll review only the changes that Steve made.

To review Steve's changes in the merged workbook:

1. In the Changes group on the Review tab, click the **Track Changes** button, and then click **Accept/Reject Changes**. The Select Changes to Accept or Reject dialog box opens.
2. Click the **Who arrow**, and then click **Steve Linde** to set the changes to review to only those that Steve made.
3. Click the **OK** button. Steve made four changes. The first change is in cell A2 of the Financial Summary worksheet, where Steve changed the subtitle.

4. Click the **Accept** button to accept the change. You could continue to review each change one at a time, or you could accept or reject all of the changes. Jennifer wants you to accept all of Steve's edits.
5. Click the **Accept All** button. All of Steve's edits are accepted, and the dialog box closes.
6. Save the workbook.

Preparing the Final Workbook

Jennifer is ready to send the workbook to the company's department heads. She doesn't want the department heads to edit the workbook, so you will remove the sharing features.

To save the final workbook and remove workbook sharing:

1. Save the workbook as **Financial Report Final Draft**.
2. In the Changes group on the Review tab, click the **Share Workbook** button. The Share Workbook dialog box opens.
3. Click the **Allow changes by more than one user at the same time** check box to remove the check mark.
4. Click the **OK** button, and then click the **Yes** button in the dialog box that opens to confirm that you want to remove the workbook from shared use.

Setting Document Properties

The Documentation worksheet includes a description of the final workbook, its contents, and its purpose. You can also make this information available by modifying the workbook's **document properties**, or **metadata**, which are the descriptive details about a file, including its author, title, and subject. The five types of document properties are:

- Standard properties, which are properties associated with all Office files and include the author, title, and subject.
- Automatically updated properties, which are properties usually associated with the file itself, such as the file size or the date the file was last edited. You cannot modify the automatically updated properties.
- Custom properties, which are properties you define and create specifically for your workbook.
- Organization properties, which are properties created for organizations using the Document Information Panel available with Microsoft InfoPath.
- Document library properties, which are properties associated with documents in a document library on a Web site or in a public network folder.

TIP

You can create a document library with Microsoft SharePoint, a group of services that support document collaboration and information sharing.

Users can access document properties without opening the workbook, making it easier to find key files. For example, in a network folder with hundreds of files, Jennifer's colleagues can quickly locate workbooks she authored or workbooks about a specific topic, such as the stockholders' meeting.

You'll add document properties that describe the workbook.

TIP

You can insert multiple values for a document property by typing a semicolon between the property values.

To add document properties to the workbook:

1. Click the **File** tab on the Ribbon, and then click **Info** in the navigation bar, if necessary, to display information about the workbook in Backstage view.
2. Click the **Show All Properties** link in the right pane.
3. Enter the following document properties, as shown in Figure C-11:

Field	Click	Type
Tags	Add a tag	**stockholders; yearly meeting**
Comments	Add comments	**Final draft of the 2013 financial report to be presented at the September meeting in Atlanta.**
Status	Add text	**Final Draft**
Categories	Add a category	**Financial Statements**
Subject	Specify the subject	**DataSafe Financial Report**
Author	Add an author	your name

Figure C-11 **Document properties**

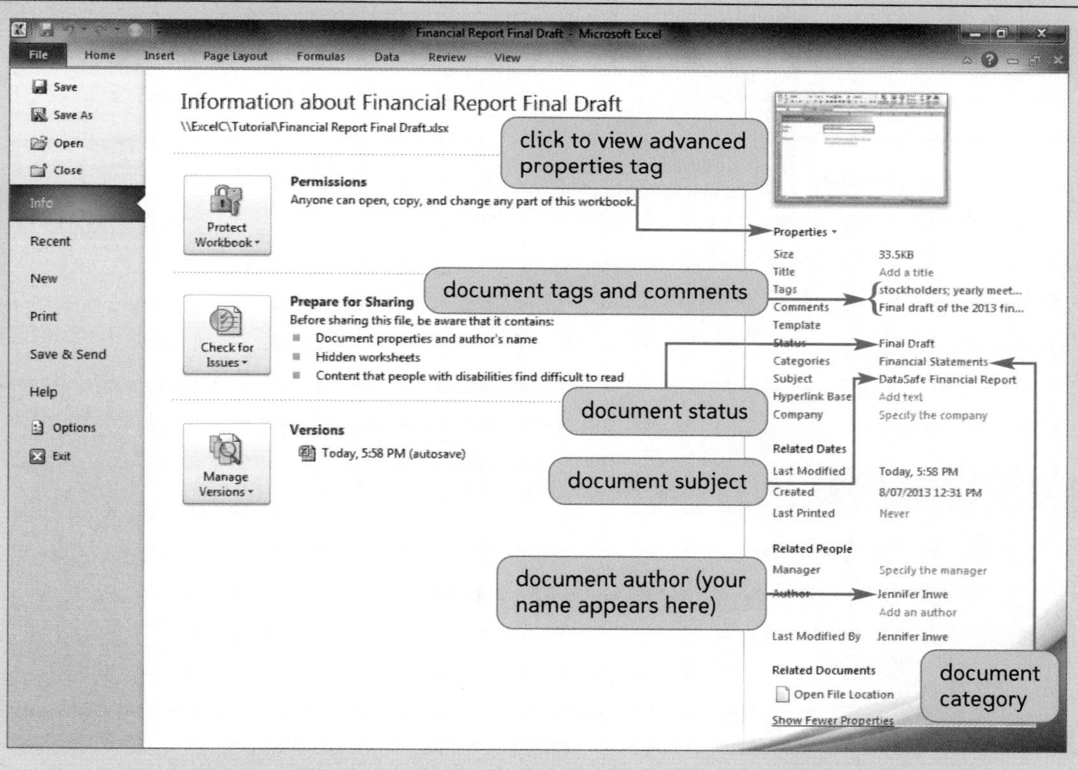

Jennifer needs to identify the department that created this workbook. Because no department tag appears in the document properties list, you'll add a custom property. After you save and close the workbook, its properties are available to other programs, including the Windows operating system.

To enter a custom property:

1. At the top of the right pane of the Info tab in Backstage view, click the **Properties** button, and then click **Advanced Properties**. The Financial Report Final Draft Properties dialog box opens.
2. Click the **Custom** tab, and then click **Department** in the Name box. The data type is correctly set as Text.
3. Type **Finance** in the Value box, and then click the **Add** button. The Department property is added to the Properties box. See Figure C-12.

Figure C-12 Custom document properties

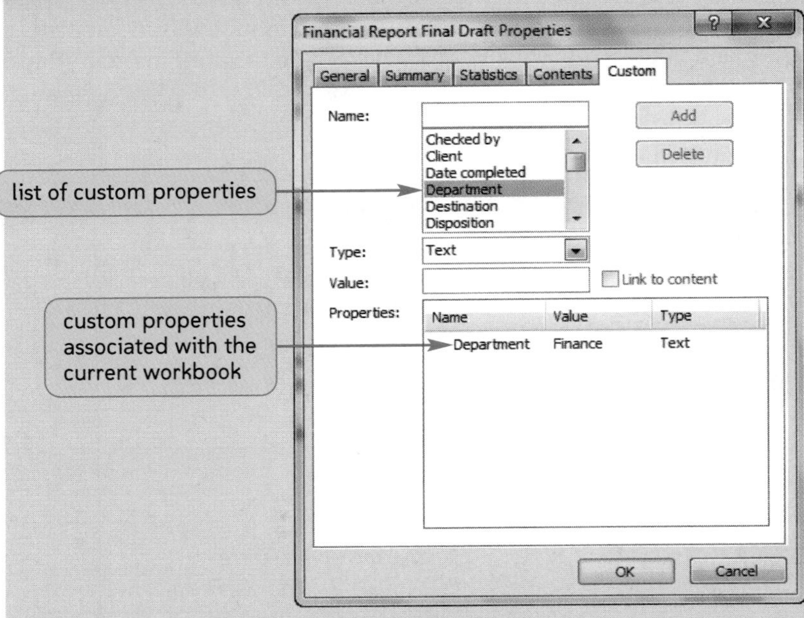

4. Click the **OK** button to close the dialog box.

TIP

You can display the document properties in a panel above the workbook window by clicking the Properties button and then clicking Show Document Panel.

Inspecting a Workbook

Before distributing the workbook, Jennifer wants to ensure it doesn't contain sensitive or personal information. Personal information can come from comments and annotations, document properties and metadata attached to the workbook, custom XML data stored within the XML code for the workbook file, headers and footers, hidden worksheets and cells, cells whose display styles make them invisible to the user, and server information inserted by saving a workbook on the Document Workspace site or within a Document Library. To determine whether a workbook contains sensitive or personal information, you can use the **Document Inspector**, which searches the workbook to locate data and text that fit these categories. You can then remove any personal information, if necessary, with the Document Inspector.

To inspect the workbook:

1. In the left pane of the Info tab in Backstage view, click the **Check for Issues** button, and then click **Inspect Document**.
2. Click the **Yes** button in the dialog box that opens prompting you to save the file. The Document Inspector dialog box opens.
3. Leave all of the check boxes checked, and then click the **Inspect** button. The inspection results appear in the dialog box. See Figure C-13.

Figure C-13 Document Inspector

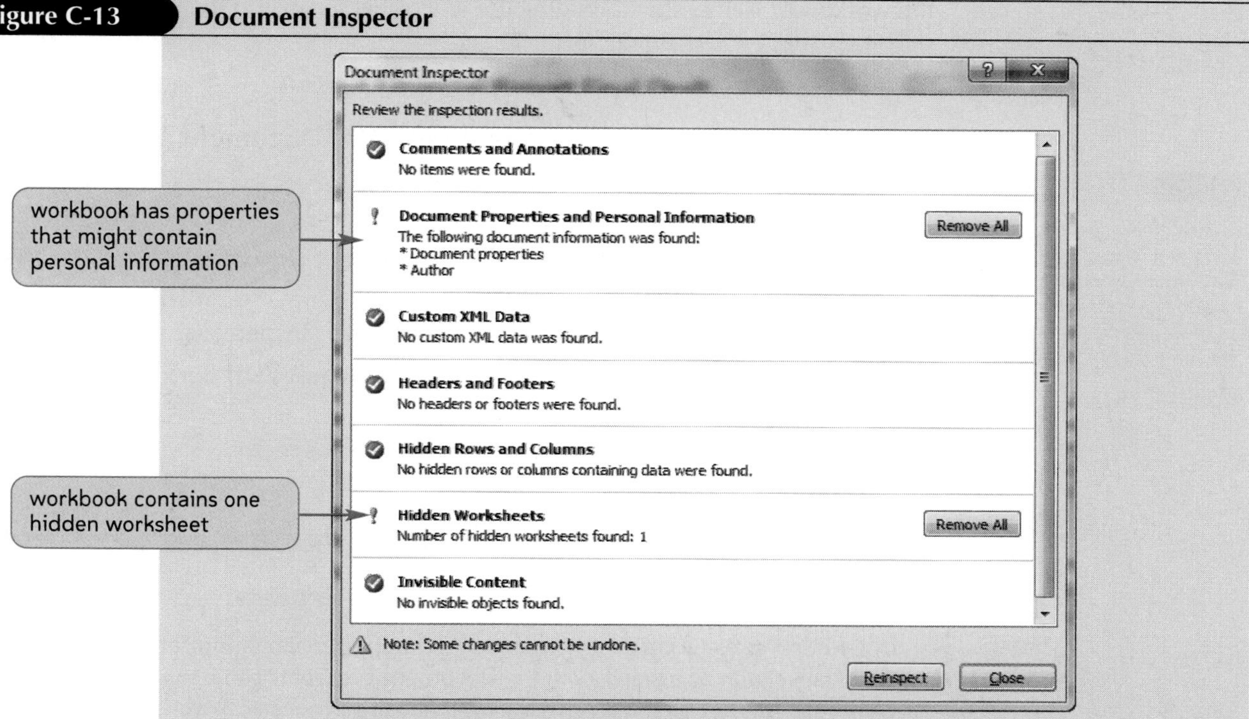

The Document Inspector indicates two instances where personal or sensitive information might appear in the workbook. The first is your name, which you entered as the author in the document properties; you want that information to appear in the workbook. The second is a **hidden worksheet,** which is a worksheet that is removed from the user's view. Hidden worksheets are often used to conceal source data and documentation that is useful to the author but is distracting or confusing to other users. Before Jennifer distributes the workbook, you'll find out what the hidden sheet contains.

To show and hide the hidden worksheet:

1. Click the **Close** button to close the Document Inspector dialog box.
2. Click the **Home** tab to return to the Financial Summary worksheet.
3. Right-click any sheet tab in the workbook, and click **Unhide** on the shortcut menu. The Unhide dialog box opens, displaying a list of all the hidden sheets in the workbook. In this case, the only hidden sheet is the Notes on the Report worksheet.

4. With the sheet name selected, click the **OK** button. The Notes on the Report worksheet appears between the Documentation and Financial Summary worksheets. The worksheet contains Jennifer's to-do list for the project, which is not relevant for her colleagues.
5. Right-click the **Notes on the Report** sheet tab, and then click **Hide** on the shortcut menu. The worksheet is again hidden from view.

Jennifer asks you to delete the Notes on the Report worksheet before she distributes the workbook. Rather than unhiding the worksheet again and then deleting it, you'll delete it using the Document Inspector.

To remove the hidden worksheet with the Document Inspector:

1. Click the **File** tab on the Ribbon, and then, if necessary, click **Info** in the navigation bar.
2. Click the **Check for Issues** button, click **Inspect Document**, and then click the **Yes** button when prompted to save the file.
3. Click the **Inspect** button to rerun the Document Inspector.
4. In the Hidden Worksheets section, click the **Remove All** button to delete the hidden worksheet.
5. Click the **Close** button to close the Document Inspector.

TIP

Use caution when you remove information and data from a workbook with the Document Inspector because you cannot undo the removal.

INSIGHT

Using the Document Inspector to Detect Viruses

In addition to ensuring that no personal or inappropriate information is included in the final version of a workbook, the Document Inspector can be used to verify that the workbook has not been corrupted by a malicious program. A workbook virus might be signaled by a hidden worksheet or hidden code attached to the XML code in the file.

Encrypting a Workbook

You can encrypt a workbook to help secure its contents. **Encryption** is the process by which a file is encoded so that it cannot be opened without the proper password. The encryption password is different from the passwords to prevent users from editing a worksheet or the entire workbook. An encryption password prevents unauthorized users from even opening the file. Passwords can be up to 255 characters in length and can include numbers, symbols, and upper- and lowercase letters. Jennifer wants to encrypt the workbook before sending it to the department heads to ensure that only authorized users can view the data.

To encrypt the workbook:

1. Save the workbook as **Financial Report Final Draft Encrypted**.
2. Click the **File** tab on the Ribbon, and then click **Info** in the navigation bar, if necessary.
3. Click the **Protect Workbook** button, and then click the **Encrypt with Password** button.
4. Type **datasafe** (in all lowercase letters) in the Password box, and then click the **OK** button.
5. Type **datasafe** in the Reenter password box, and then click the **OK** button. A password is now required to open this workbook.
6. Save and close the workbook, and then reopen the workbook. The Password dialog box opens, preventing the workbook from opening without the password.
7. Type **datasafe** in the Password box, and then click the **OK** button. The workbook opens.

   Trouble? If the workbook doesn't open, you might have mistyped the password. Repeat Step 7. If the workbook still doesn't open, you might have mistyped the password in Steps 4 and 5. There is no simple way to recover a mistyped password from an encrypted document. Open the Financial Report Final Draft workbook, and then repeat Steps 1 through 7 to re-create the encrypted version of the workbook.

Type your password carefully to avoid a misspelling, which will make the file difficult or impossible to open later.

Marking a Workbook as Final

Jennifer wants the department heads to know that the workbook they receive is the final version of the report. She can do this by marking the workbook as final, which makes the workbook read-only, preventing any additional changes to it. A final workbook has the editing, typing, and proofing commands disabled or turned off. The user can only view the contents of the file, not change it. Also, the Status document property value changes to Final.

The Mark as Final command informs others that this workbook is intended to be the final version of the workbook. However, anyone can remove the Mark as Final status from the workbook by reapplying the Mark as Final command to deselect it.

TIP

To ensure a workbook cannot be edited, password-protect the workbook using the Protect Workbook button in the Changes group on the Review tab.

To mark the financial report workbook as final:

1. Click the **File** tab on the Ribbon, and then click **Info** in the navigation bar, if necessary.
2. Click the **Protect Workbook** button, and then click **Mark as Final**. A dialog box opens indicating that the workbook will be marked as final and then saved.
3. Click the **OK** button. A second dialog box opens indicating that the file has been marked as final.
4. Click the **OK** button. A marked-as-final workbook is displayed with [Read-Only] in the title bar.
5. Click a blank cell in the active worksheet to confirm that you cannot edit the workbook.

Providing a Digital Signature

A **digital signature** is an electronic version of a written signature and provides a way to authenticate a workbook. Digital signatures cannot be forged. Also, a workbook signed with a digital signature cannot be altered without removing the signature, ensuring that the workbook received is the one that the user intended to send. With a digital signature, other users know that the workbook comes from a trusted source and has not been altered since it was originally signed, and that its origin is accepted by all parties and can't be repudiated by the signer.

To add a digital signature, you need a **digital ID** or **digital certificate**, which authenticates the source of the signature. If you do not have a digital certificate, you can get one from a third-party source or you can create your own. The third-party source, also known as a **certificate authority** (**CA**), is a trusted entity that issues certificates as a service for companies and individuals. The CA may be a commercial service that requires payment. If you create your own certificate, it authenticates the file only for that computer and not for other users on other computers.

REFERENCE

Adding a Digital Signature to a Workbook

- Click the File tab on the Ribbon, and then click Info in the navigation bar.
- Click the Protect Workbook button, and then click Add a Digital Signature.
- If requested, specify whether to create a third-party digital ID or a local digital ID. Provide descriptive information for the digital ID.
- If no digital IDs are made, specify whether to create a third-party digital ID or a local digital ID. Provide descriptive information for the digital ID, and then click the Create button.
- Enter a purpose for the digital signature, click the Sign button, and then click the OK button.

DataSafe uses digital signatures to monitor and authenticate files as they travel between departments. Jennifer does not have a third-party digital certificate, so you'll create one as you add the digital signature.

To add a digital signature:

1. Click the **File** tab on the Ribbon, and then click **Info** in the navigation bar, if necessary.
2. Click the **Protect Workbook** button, and then click **Add a Digital Signature**.
3. If a dialog box opens, describing digital signatures, click the **OK** button. The Get a Digital ID dialog box opens.
4. Click the **Create your own digital ID** option button, and then click the **OK** button. The Create a Digital ID dialog box opens.

   Trouble? If you see the Sign dialog box rather than the Create a Digital ID dialog box, a digital ID is already registered on your computer. You can enter a purpose for signing the document and click the Sign button (see Step 6 below). You can remove a digital ID using the Certificate Manager. To run the Certificate Manager, click the Windows Start button, and then type certmgr.msc in the Search box.
5. Type your name in the Name box, type your email address in the E-mail address box, type the name of your school or organization in the Organization box, and then type your city or location in the Location box. See Figure C-14.

Figure C-14 Create a Digital ID dialog box

Create a Digital ID

Enter the information to be included in your digital ID.

Name: Jennifer Inwe

E-mail address: JenniferInwe@datasafealabama.com

Organization: DataSafe

Location: Mobile, AL

Create Cancel

information describing the digital ID (your information will differ)

6. Click the **Create** button. The Sign dialog box opens prompting you to enter a purpose for the digital signature.
7. Type **Authenticating the final version of the DataSafe financial report** in the Purpose for signing this document box, and then click the **Sign** button. The Signature Confirmation dialog box opens.
8. Click the **OK** button. The Info tab in Backstage view reappears, and the View Signatures button appears in the left pane.
9. Click the **View Signatures** button. The Financial Summary worksheet reappears, and then the Signatures pane opens, listing the valid signatures applied to the file. The digital certificate icon appears in the status bar. See Figure C-15.

Figure C-15 Digitally signed workbook

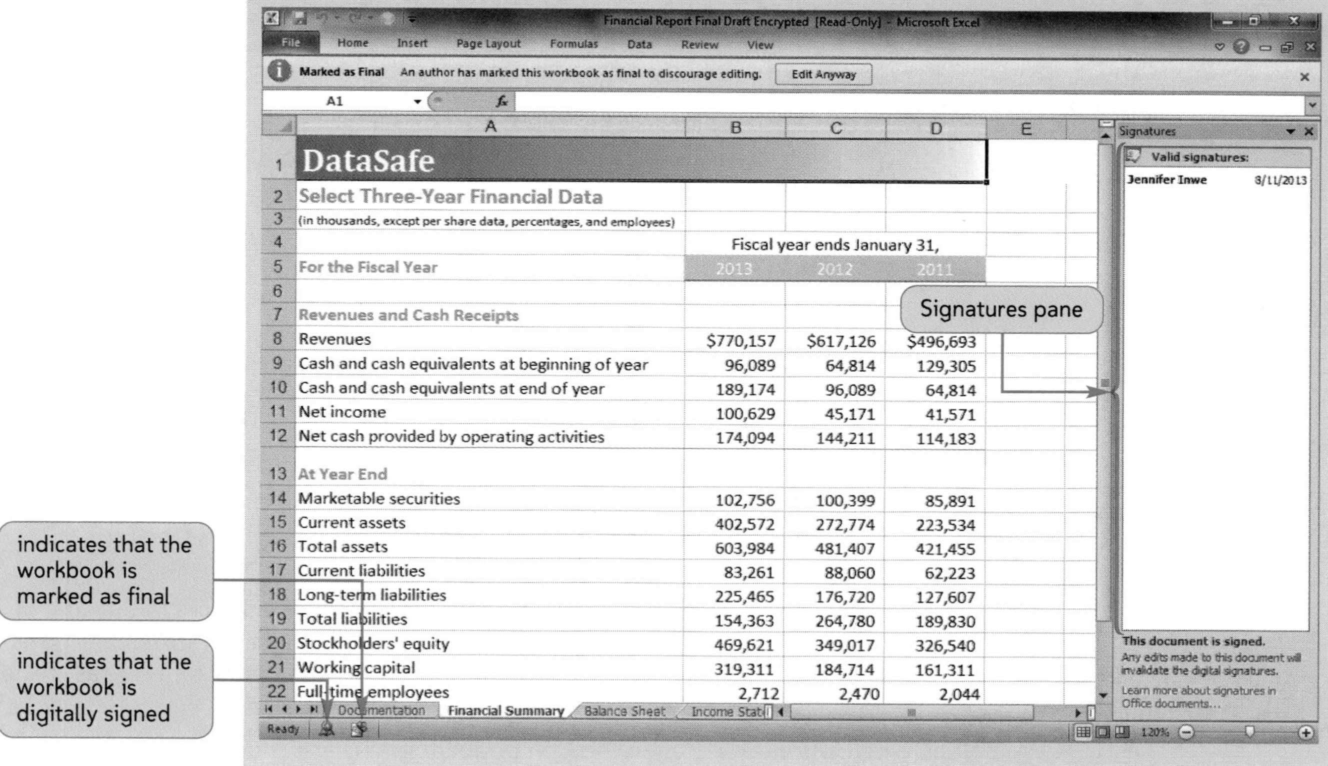

If any edits are made to the digitally signed workbook document, or if the marked-as-final status is changed, the digital signature will be removed, providing another protection against unapproved edits.

Ensuring Backward Compatibility in a Workbook

You will sometimes need to create a copy of a workbook that is compatible with earlier Excel versions to share with other users who are not using Excel 2010. The Compatibility Checker flags any content, formatting, or element in the workbook that cannot be transferred to earlier versions of Excel. Jennifer wants you to ensure that no critical features or content in the financial report are lost when you save the workbook in the Excel 2003 format.

To run the Compatibility Checker on Jennifer's workbook:

1. Click the **File** tab on the Ribbon, and then click **Info** in the navigation bar, if necessary.
2. Click the **Check for Issues** button, and then click **Check Compatibility**. The Compatibility Checker dialog box opens. See Figure C-16.

Figure C-16 **Compatibility Checker dialog box**

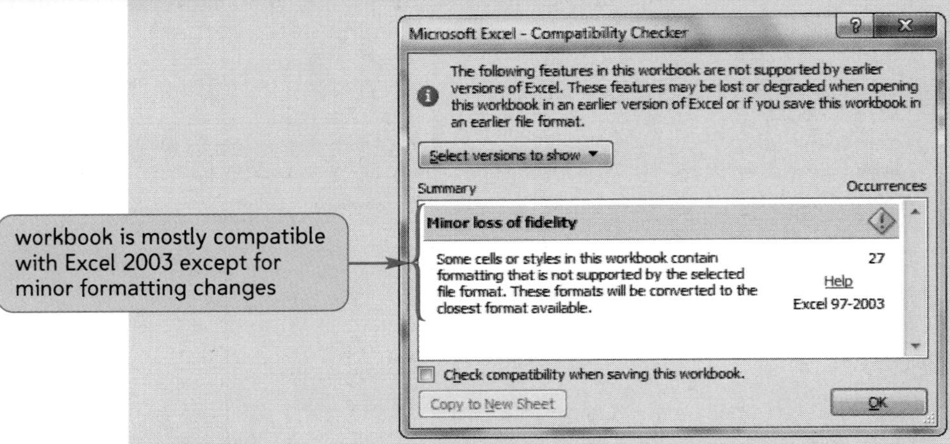

3. Read the summary of features not supported in the earlier versions of Excel, and then click the **OK** button. You'll save the financial report workbook in the Excel 97-2003 file format.
4. Save the workbook as **Financial Report Excel 2003** with the save as type set to **Excel 97-2003 Workbook**. Saving a workbook in an earlier file format is considered an edit, so a dialog box notifies you that Excel will remove the digital signature.
5. Click the **Yes** button to continue saving the file, and then click the **No** button when prompted to convert the file to an Office Open XML format. Excel performs a last compatibility check, again finding that there will be minor differences in the format styles.
6. Click the **Continue** button in the Compatibility Checker dialog box. The Excel 2003 version of the workbook is saved.
7. Save and close the workbook.

Teamwork: Improving the Collaborative Process

The collaborative tools in Excel make it simpler for groups to share the work of writing, editing, and finishing a financial report. But no tool, however useful, can overcome problems associated with colleagues who cannot work together effectively. Keep in mind the following to improve the collaborative process:

- Project goals should be stated in advance with all team members clearly understanding what is expected of them. Team members should feel comfortable requesting clarification of those goals at any time in the process.
- Identify the strengths and weaknesses of each team member and adjust the project accordingly.
- Start work on the project at the earliest possible date.
- Constantly monitor the progress of the project, staying up to date on what has been done and what needs to be done. Communicate the status of the project with progress reports to each team member.
- Make it easy for team members to suggest new ideas and voice objections.
- Finish your tasks on time and meet your project goals.
- Treat each team member with respect. Do not allow personal grudges or differences to influence the successful completion of the project.

By successfully managing the group dynamic, you can make Excel's collaborative tools even more effective and useful.

Integrating Excel with other Office Applications

A file that relies on data from more than one program is called a **compound file**. The **source file** (or files) supplies the data to be shared. The **destination file** (or files) displays the data from the source file (or files). Compound files are easy to create in Office because all Office programs share a common interface and can read each other's file formats.

As described in Figure C-17, there are three ways to insert data from one program into another program: copying and pasting, linking, and embedding. All of these techniques can be used to create a compound file.

Figure C-17 **Integration methods**

Method	Description	When to Use
Copying and pasting	Inserts an object into a file	You want to exchange the data between the two files only once. If the source file changes, the change is not reflected in the destination file.
Linking	Displays an object in the destination file but only stores the location of the source file	You need to ensure that the data will be current and identical in both the source and destination files. Any changes made to the source file will be reflected in the destination file.
Embedding	Displays and stores an object in the destination file	You want the source data to become a permanent part of the destination file, or the source data will no longer be available to the destination file. Any changes made to either the destination or the source file are not reflected in the other.

Copying and Pasting Data

You can copy text, values, cells and ranges, or even charts and graphics from one program and paste them in another program using the Windows copy and paste features. The item being copied and pasted is referred to as an **object**. When you paste an object from the source file into the destination file, you are inserting the object so that it is part of the destination file. The pasted object is static, having no connection to the source file. If you want to change the pasted object, you must do so in the destination file. For example, a range of cells pasted into a Word document can be edited only within the Word document. Any changes made in the original Excel workbook have no impact on the Word document. For this reason, pasting is used only for one-time exchanges of information.

Object Linking and Embedding

If you want to create a live connection between two files, so that changes in the source file are automatically reflected in the destination file, you must use object linking and embedding. **Object linking and embedding** (**OLE**) refers to the technology that allows you to copy and paste objects, such as graphic files, cell and ranges, or charts, so that information about the program that created the object is included with the object itself.

The objects are inserted into the destination file as either linked objects or embedded objects. A **linked object** is actually a separate file that is connected to the source file. If you make a change to the source file, the destination file can automatically reflect the change. On the other hand, an **embedded object** is stored in the destination file (Word, in this example) and is no longer part of the source file. In the case of Office programs, embedded objects include their Ribbon, tabs, and buttons. This means you can edit an Excel worksheet or chart embedded in a Word document using Excel tools and commands to modify the worksheet or chart content. Because embedded objects have no link to the source file, changes made to the embedded object are not reflected in the source file.

The main difference between linked and embedded objects lies in where the data is stored and how the data is updated after being inserted into the destination file. Figure C-18 illustrates the difference between linking and embedding.

Figure C-18 **Embedding contrasted with linking**

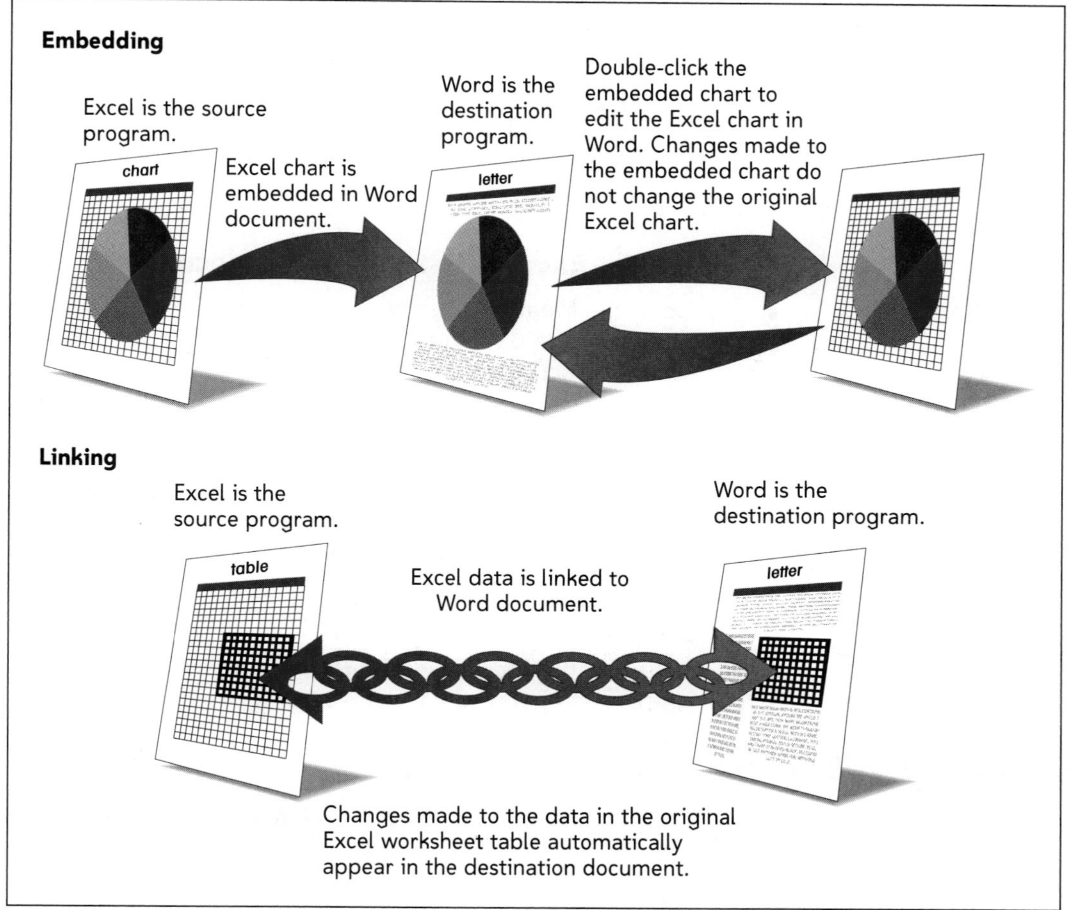

INSIGHT

Inserting a Screenshot

A final way to share content between files is by taking a screenshot of the open file. Office 2010 includes a built-in tool to capture and insert images from your computer screen. To capture a screen image, click the Insert tab on the Ribbon, and then click the Screenshot button in the Illustrations group. A gallery opens displaying thumbnails of all the open windows on your desktop. You can choose to take a screenshot of one of these open windows or you can click the Screen Clipping button to select a portion of an open window for the screenshot.

Unlike linking and embedded, inserting a screenshot does not insert the actual data from the document. Instead, it inserts only the image of that document as a picture. Therefore, screenshots are best used for content that is not going to change. For data that will be edited or to allow users to access Microsoft Office tools to manipulate the data, choose linking or embedding the data rather than inserting a screenshot.

Linking Excel and Word Files

Jennifer wants you to insert some financial data from her workbook into a report she is writing in a Word document. Rather than pasting the data each time she modifies the report, you'll create a link between her Excel workbook and her Word document, so that any subsequent edits she makes to the workbook are automatically reflected in the document. You will open both files, copy the Excel data, and then paste the data as a link in the Word document.

To link the Excel data to the Word document:

1. Open the **Memo** Word document located in the ExcelC\Tutorial folder, enter your name and the date in the From: and To: entries at the top of the page, and then save the document as **Memo Destination**.
2. Open the **Income Statement** workbook located in the ExcelC\Tutorial folder included with your Data Files, and then save the workbook as **Income Statement Source**.
3. In the Documentation worksheet, enter your name and the date, and then switch to the **Income Statement** worksheet.
4. Select the range **A5:D13**, and then click the **Copy** button in the Clipboard group on the Home tab.
5. Return to the **Memo Destination** document, and then click to the left of the paragraph mark below the letter's second paragraph, as shown in Figure C-19.

Figure C-19 Memo Destination document

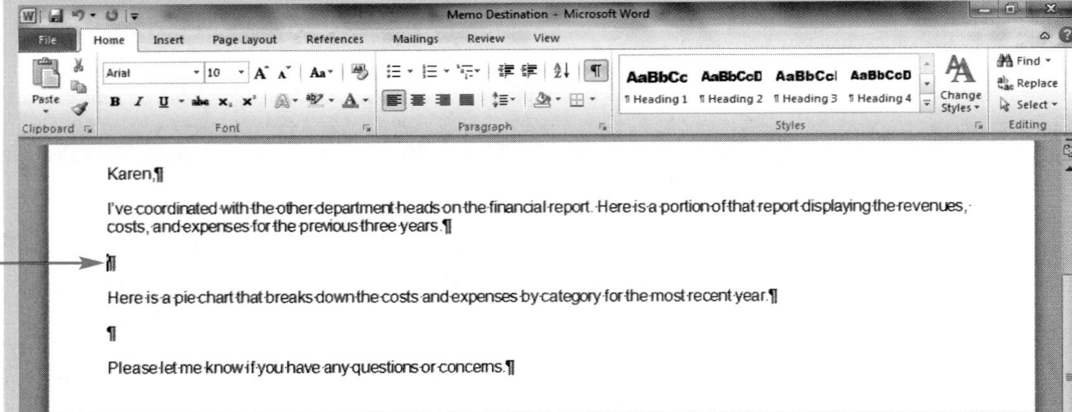

TIP

You can click Paste Special from the Paste button to have more control over the format of the pasted worksheet cells.

Trouble? If your document does not show paragraph marks at the end of each paragraph, you need to show the nonprinting characters. In the Paragraph group on the Home tab, click the Show/Hide button.

6. In the Clipboard group on the Home tab, click the **Paste button arrow**, and then click **Link & Keep Source Formatting (F)**. The selected cell range is linked and pasted into the Word document. See Figure C-20.

Figure C-20 Financial data pasted into the Memo Destination document

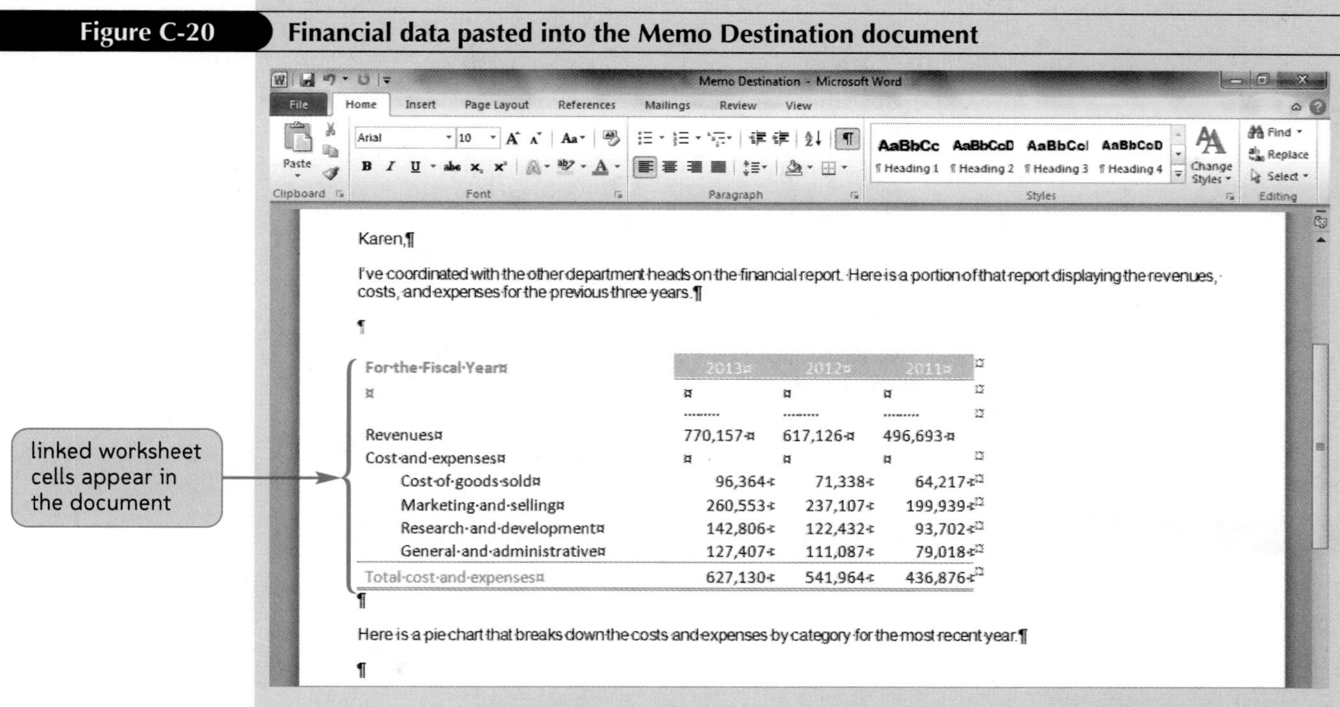

Updating a Linked Object

Linked objects are updated automatically. In this case, Word updates the linked information every time you open the Word document or any time the Excel source file changes while the Word document is open. Jennifer wants to edit one of the cell titles in the Income Statement worksheet. Because the workbook is linked with the Word document, any changes made to the workbook will be automatically reflected in the document.

To update the linked object:

1. Return to the **Income Statement Source** workbook, and then press the **Esc** key to deselect the range A5:D13.
2. Change the text in cell A7 from Revenues to **Revenue**.
3. Return to the **Memo Destination** document, right-click the table, and then click **Update Link** on the shortcut menu.

TIP

You can also double-click an Excel object in Word to return to Excel and edit the Excel worksheet. The linked object in Word is automatically updated.

Embedding an Object

Jennifer wants the memo to include the pie chart from the Income Statement Source workbook that details the source of the company's costs and expenses. Jennifer is confident that the pie chart is accurate, so you will embed the chart in the memo. Keep in mind that you can use the Excel chart-editing tools directly from the Word document to modify the chart's appearance and data before printing the memo. You will embed the pie chart in the document.

To embed an Excel chart in a Word document:

1. Switch to the **Income Statement Source** workbook, and then click the **Cost and Expenses Pie Chart** chart sheet to select it.
2. Click the **chart area**, and then click the **Copy** button in the Clipboard group on the Home tab.
3. Switch to the **Memo Destination** document, and then click to the left of the paragraph mark above the next-to-last paragraph in the memo (above the sentence that begins "Please let me know...").
4. In the Clipboard group on the Home tab, click the **Paste button arrow**, and then click the **Keep Source Formatting & Embed Workbook (K)** button. A copy of the chart is embedded as an object into the document.
5. Click the chart to select it, and then drag the resizing handles to resize the chart so that it fits into the first page as shown in Figure C-21.

Figure C-21 Chart embedded in the Memo Destination document

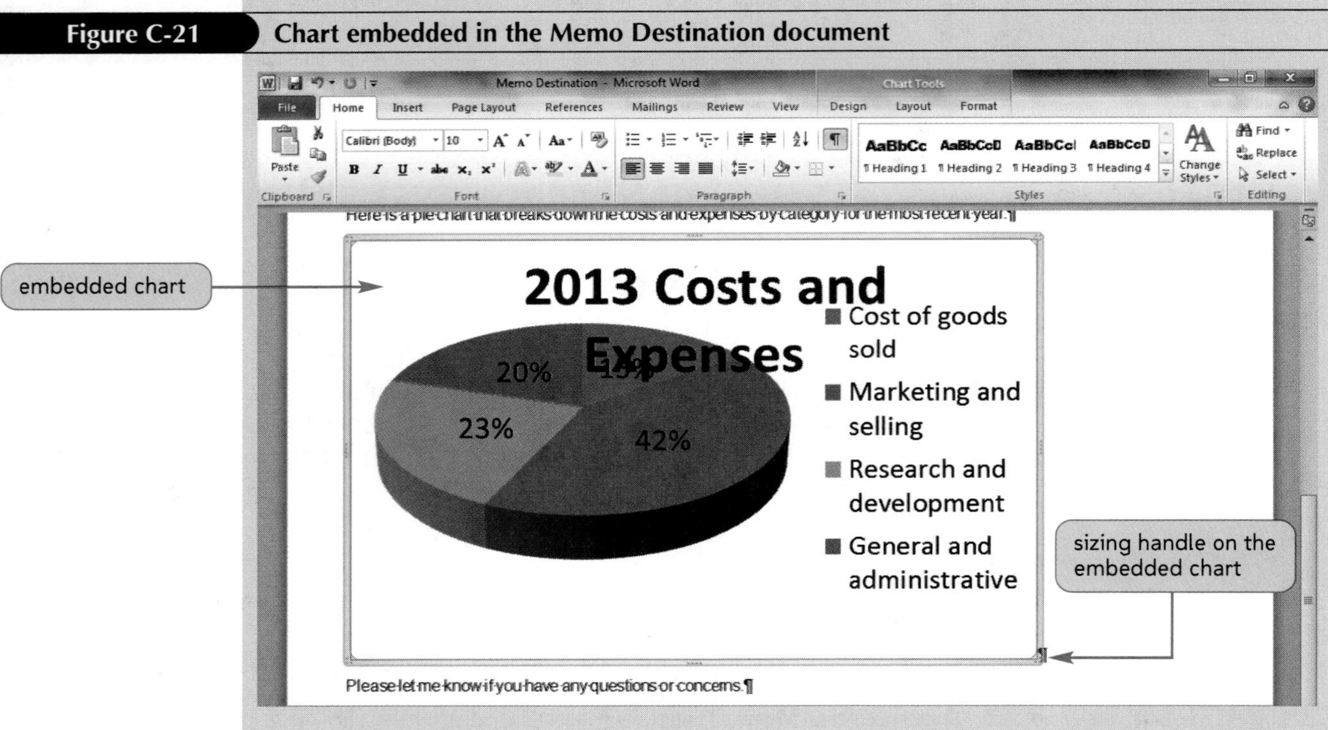

Modifying an Embedded Object

Embedded objects become part of the destination file after they are inserted; they are no longer linked to the source file. For example, if you change the chart in the Excel workbook, the embedded chart object in Word does not change. Conversely, if you change the embedded object, the source file is not modified.

You need to change the font size of the chart labels of the embedded chart so that they can be easily read.

To edit the embedded chart:

1. With the embedded chart still selected, click the **chart title** and change the font size to **18** points.
2. Click the **chart legend** and change the font size to **10** points.
3. Click the **pie chart labels** and change the font size to **14** points.
4. Click the **Chart Tools Design** tab on the Ribbon, and then click **Style 5** (the fifth style in the first row) in the Chart Styles gallery.
5. Click the outside of the chart to deselect it. See Figure C-22.

Figure C-22 **Edited chart object**

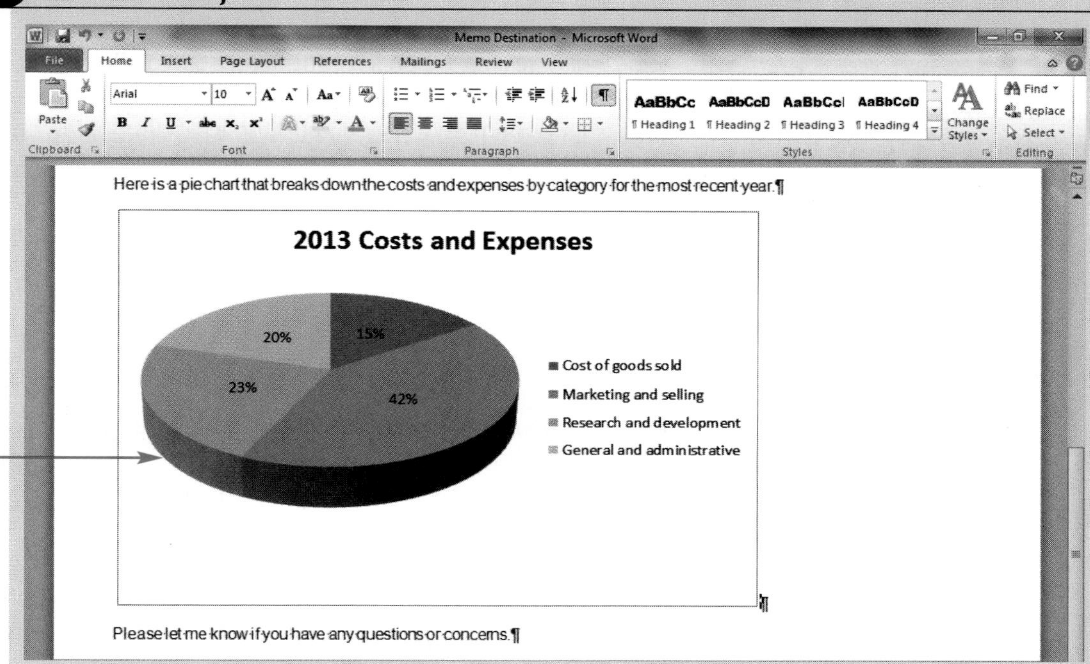

6. Save and close the **Memo Destination** document.
7. Return to the **Income Statement Source** workbook, and note that the pie chart in the source document has not been changed because you edited the embedded chart, which is not linked to the Excel workbook.
8. Save and close the workbook.

INSIGHT

Embedding versus Linking

An embedded object such as a chart includes not only the chart sheet but also the other worksheets in the workbook. One disadvantage of embedded objects is that they tend to greatly increase the size of the destination file. You should embed objects only when file size is not an issue and when you need the entire contents of the document to be embedded in the destination file.

Practice the skills you learned in the appendix using the same case scenario.

PRACTICE

Review Assignments

Data Files needed for the Review Assignments: Cash Flow.xlsx, Notes.docx, Projected.xlsx, SL Comments.xlsx, Stockholders.xlsx, Team.xlsx

Jennifer needs to provide a projected income statement and project cash flow schedule for the upcoming year for the stockholders' meeting. She created the initial workbook, but wants your help with sending it out for review and then reconciling the edits made by her colleagues. After Jennifer has a final draft, she wants you to add document properties, encrypt the workbook, mark it as final, and add a digital signature. She also wants you to create a copy of the workbook for employees who are using an earlier version of Excel. Finally, Jennifer wants you to embed some of the financial information in a Word document to be shared with her supervisor. Complete the following:

1. Open the **Projected** workbook located in the ExcelC\Review folder included with your Data Files, and then save the workbook as **Projected Statements**. In the Documentation worksheet, enter your name and the date.
2. In the Projected Income worksheet, add the following comment to cell B7: **Do you think that $840,000 is a reasonable estimate for next year's revenue?**
3. Share the workbook, enabling changes by more than one user at a time. Save and close the Projected Statements workbook.
4. Open the **Team** workbook located in the ExcelC\Review folder, and then save the workbook as **Team Edits**. In the Documentation worksheet, enter your name and the date.
5. In the Projected Income Statement worksheet, delete the comments that were added to cell B7.
6. Review the changes in the workbook by everyone but you, accepting them or rejecting the changes as follows:
   - Accept Alberto Conti's recommended projection for the 2013 net revenue of $850,000 in cell B7 of the Projected Income Statement worksheet.
   - Accept the rest of Alberto Conti's edits.
   - Accept Tom Uecker's edit of cell B19 in the Income Projections worksheet.
   - Reject Mai Le's edit of cell B13 in the Income Projections worksheet.
   - Reject all of Tom Uecker's edits.
7. Save and close the workbook. Open the **Stockholders** workbook located in the ExcelC\Review folder, and then save the workbook as **Stockholders Report**. In the Documentation worksheet, enter your name and the date.
8. Merge the contents of the **SL Comments** workbook with the current workbook. Delete Steve's comment on the Pro forma Cash Flow Schedule worksheet. Accept all of Steve's edits to the workbook, and then save the workbook.
9. Save the workbook as **Stockholders Report Final**. Remove the workbook from shared use.
10. Add the following document properties to the workbook:
    - your name as the author
    - **Financial Projections** as the title
    - **Stockholders' Report** as the subject
    - **projections; stockholders** as tags
    - **Conference Reports** as the category
    - **Final Draft** as the status
11. Click the Show All Properties link in the Properties pane, and then add the following comments tag: **Financial projections for the 2013 Stockholders' Conference**.

12. Insert the Department custom property using Text as the type and **Finance** as the value.
13. Use the Document Inspector to determine whether Jennifer left any notes hidden in a cell or column. If so, remove the hidden row or column from the workbook.
14. Encrypt the document using the password **datasafe**.
15. Mark the document as final.
16. Digitally sign the document using a digital certificate supplied by your instructor or one you create. Save the workbook.
17. Resave the workbook as **Stockholders Report Final for Excel 2003** in the Excel 97-2003 Workbook file format. Confirm that there are no major compatibility issues, and then reapply the digital signature to this version of the workbook.
18. Open the **Cash Flow** workbook located in the ExcelC\Review folder, enter your name and the date on the Documentation worksheet, and then save the file as **Cash Flow Source**.
19. Open the **Notes** document located in the ExcelC\Review folder, enter your name and the date in the memo heading, and then save the file as **Notes on Cash Flow**.
20. Copy the range A5:E9 from the Pro forma Cash Flow Schedule in the Cash Flow Source workbook, and then paste a link to the copied range as a Picture (Windows Metafile) after the opening paragraph in the Notes on Cash Flow document. Resize the picture to fit within the page margins.
21. Save the Excel workbook and the linked Word document.
22. Submit the finished workbooks and document to your instructor, either in printed or electronic form, as requested.

Use the skills you learned to merge data and prepare a final budget workbook.

APPLY

Case Problem 1

Data Files needed for this Case Problem: Budget.docx, Covey.xlsx, Kao.xlsx, Roper.xlsx

City of Covey Pines Dale Jaffa, an assistant to the treasurer of the town of Covey Pines, Iowa, is helping to prepare the annual budget forecast. He emailed his budget workbook to different department heads to get their budget projections. Norma Roper is responsible for budgeted and actual expenses in the general fund. Mary Kao is responsible for budgeted and actual expenses for special funds. Dale received their workbooks and needs to merge them into one workbook that he can prepare for final distribution to other city leaders. Complete the following:

1. Open the **Covey** workbook located in the ExcelC\Case1 folder included with your Data Files, and then save the workbook as **Covey Pines Budget**. In the Documentation worksheet, enter your name and the date.
2. Merge the workbook with both the **Roper** and **Kao** workbooks located in the ExcelC\Case1 folder. (*Hint*: You must select both files in the dialog box.)
3. Remove the workbook from shared use.
4. Add the following document properties to the workbook:
   - your name as the author
   - **Covey Pines Budget** as the title
   - **budget;general fund;special funds** as tags
   - **Proposed 2012 – 2013 budget for the general fund and special funds** as the comment
   - **proposed** as the status
   - **budget** as the category
   - **Annual Budget Forecast** as the subject

EXPLORE

5. Insert the Date Completed advanced property using Date as the type and the current date for the value.
6. Inspect the workbook for hidden data or content, and then remove any hidden comments or annotations. Save the workbook.
7. In Word, open the **Budget** document located in the ExcelC\Case1 folder. Replace [Your Name] with your name at the top and bottom of the document, and then save the document as **Budget Memo**.
8. Copy the range A18:D23 from the Budget worksheet in the Covey Pines Budget workbook, and then paste it as a link in the Picture (Enhanced Metafile) format into the second paragraph of the Budget Memo document.

EXPLORE

9. Dale wants you to insert a screenshot of a pie chart showing the budgeted values for the Special Fund. To insert the screenshot:
   a. Select the range A18:A22;D18:D22 from the Budget worksheet in the Covey Pines Budget workbook, and then insert a 2-D pie chart into the worksheet. Resize the pie chart so that it covers the range F5:K22. Click cell A5 to deselect the chart.
   b. Go to the Budget Memo document, and insert a new blank line below the picture of the Special Funds table.
   c. Click the Insert tab on the Ribbon, click the Screenshot button in the Illustrations group, and then click Screen Clipping.
   d. From the Excel window for the Covey Pines Budget workbook, drag the cursor over the pie chart, capturing the screen image of the pie chart and inserting it into the Word document.
10. Save and close the Budget Memo document.
11. Return to Excel and save an encrypted version of the Covey Pines Budget workbook as **Covey Pines Budget Encrypted** with the encryption password **coveypines** (in all lowercase letters), and then close the workbook.
12. Submit the finished files to your instructor, either in printed or electronic form, as requested.

Use the skills you learned to share a workbook and reconcile edits.

APPLY

Case Problem 2

Data Files needed for this Case Problem: Contributor.docx, Mailing.xlsx, Student.xlsx

Templeton University Foundation Tim Stoddard is in charge of fund-raising for the Templeton University Foundation (TUF) of Madison, Wisconsin. As TUF's spring fund-raising drive approaches, Tim needs to compile a mailing list of past contributors. He created a workbook with names and addresses, and wants several student assistants to review the workbook and correct errors they find. You'll set up the shared workbook and reconcile the edits made by his assistants. Tim will send a final draft of the workbook to TUF members who are creating the form letters and mailing labels. Complete the following:

1. Open the **Mailing** workbook located in the ExcelC\Case2 folder included with your Data Files, and then save the workbook as **Mailing List Shared**. In the Documentation worksheet, enter your name and the date.

EXPLORE

2. Share the workbook, making it available for editing. (*Hint*: Excel cannot share the workbook because of the Excel table in the Mailing List worksheet. Convert the table to a range, and then share the workbook.)
3. Open the **Student** workbook located in the ExcelC\Case2 folder, and then save the workbook as **Student Edits** in the same folder. In the Documentation worksheet, enter your name and the date.

4. Display the tracking log for all edits made to the workbook except yours. Print the History worksheet with the tracking log in landscape orientation scaled to fit on a single page.
5. Review the changes made by Tim's student assistants. Accept all of their edits except for Sandy Lopez's edit of cell B54 in the Mailing List worksheet. In cell B16, accept Alvaro Sanchez's edit over those made by Sandy Lopez and Gary Weiss.
6. Remove the workbook from shared use.
7. Add the following document properties to the workbook:
   - **Templeton University Foundation** as the title
   - **Mailing list for the 2013 appeal** as the comment
   - **final** as the status
   - **fundraiser** as the category
   - **Mailing List** as the subject
   - your name as the author
8. In the advanced properties, add the Checked by property using Text as the type and **Sandy Lopez**;**Alvaro Sanchez**;**Gary Weiss** as the value.
9. Inspect the document for hidden or personal data. If you find a hidden worksheet, print it in portrait orientation on two pages and then remove it from the workbook.
10. Create a local digital ID for the workbook, using your name for the Name element, your email for the E-mail address, your school or organization for the Organization element, and your city or location for the Location element.
11. Enter **To ensure the integrity of the mailing list** as the purpose of the digital signature, and then sign the workbook.
12. In Word, open the **Contributor** document located in the ExcelC\Case2 folder, and then save the document as **Contributor Memo**.
13. Return to the **Student Edits** workbook, and then copy the range A6:F16.

EXPLORE

14. Paste the selected range at the bottom of the Contributor Memo document using the Link & Use Destination Style (L) option.
15. Save and close the Student Edits workbook and the Contributor Memo document.
16. Submit the finished files to your instructor, either in printed or electronic form, as requested.

ENDING DATA FILES

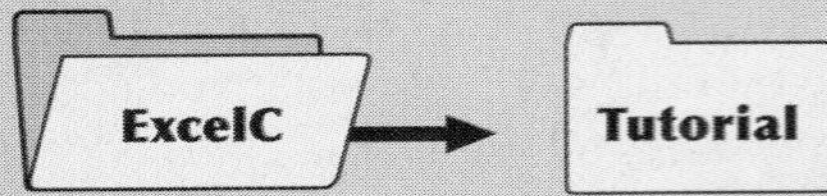

Tutorial

Financial Report Excel 2003.xlsx
Financial Report Final Draft Encrypted.xlsx
Financial Report Final Draft.xlsx
Financial Report.xlsx
Group Edit.xlsx
Income Statement Source.xlsx
Memo Destination.docx
Merged Report.xlsx

Review

Cash Flow Source.xlsx
Notes on Cash Flow.xlsx
Projected Statements.xlsx
Stockholders Report Final for Excel 2003.xlsx
Stockholders Report Final.xlsx
Stockholders Report.xlsx
Team Edits.xlsx

Case1

Budget Memo.docx
Covey Pines Budget Encrypted.xlsx
Covey Pines Budget.xlsx

Case2

Contributor Memo.docx
Mailing List Shared.xlsx
Student Edits.xlsx

APPENDIX **D**

Working with Enhanced Formatting Tools

Formatting a Chemistry Report

EXCEL

OBJECTIVES

- Create a custom cell style
- Create a custom table style
- Create a conditional format to highlight cells
- Create a color scale conditional format
- Create an icon set conditional format
- Insert and modify a SmartArt graphic
- Modify the image properties of a picture
- Create and save a theme

Case | *Online Interactive Chemistry*

Dr. Charles Scott is an award-winning high school chemistry teacher with 30 years of teaching experience. In recent years, he's turned his attention to creating a collection of interactive chemistry tutorials called Online Interactive Chemistry (OIC). Charles knows from his classroom experience and discussions with other professionals that Excel is a useful tool for recording and analyzing chemistry experiments. He wants to create a series of Excel chemistry workbooks to allow students to work with chemical concepts, perform what-if analyses, and generate reports.

The first set of workbooks he wants to create is based on the chemical properties described in the periodic table. Rather than provide students with raw data values, he wants the periodic table to present these values graphically with custom symbols and colors. You'll help him develop the first prototypes for his project.

STARTING DATA FILES

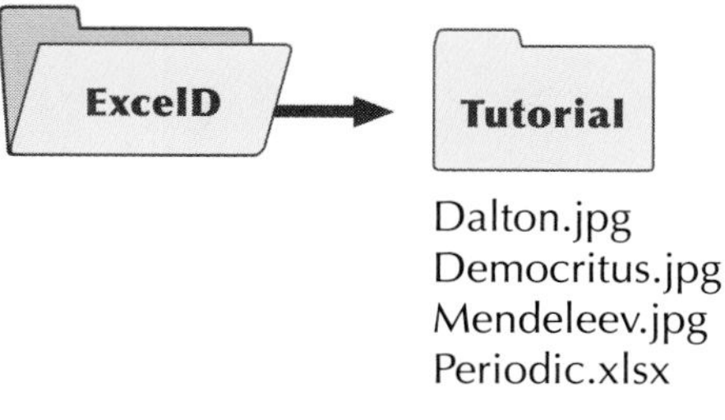

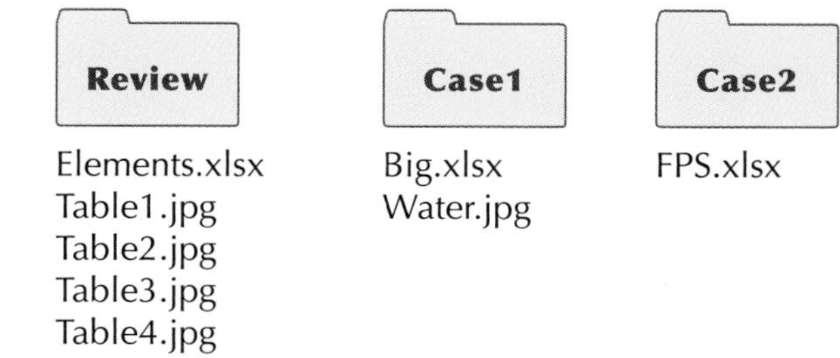

Tutorial	Review	Case1	Case2
Dalton.jpg	Elements.xlsx	Big.xlsx	FPS.xlsx
Democritus.jpg	Table1.jpg	Water.jpg	
Mendeleev.jpg	Table2.jpg		
Periodic.xlsx	Table3.jpg		
	Table4.jpg		

Creating a Custom Cell Style

Charles created a sample workbook that contains four worksheets in addition to the Documentation sheet. The Element Families worksheet contains the periodic table with each element labeled according to its element family. The Ionization Energy worksheet contains the periodic table listing each element's ionization energy. The Radioactive Elements worksheet contains the periodic table identifying radioactive elements. The Element Data worksheet contains the raw data about each element from which the other worksheets draw their information.

To open and review the periodic table workbook:

1. Open the **Periodic** workbook located in the ExcelD\Tutorial folder included with your Data Files, and then save the workbook as **Periodic Table**.
2. In the Documentation worksheet, enter your name and the date.
3. Review the workbook contents, reducing the zoom percentage to see the entire periodic tables in the worksheets.

A custom cell style is a cell style you create with the exact formatting you want that can be applied to other cells. To create a custom cell style, you select a cell that has the formatting you want to use in the new style. When you save the cell formatting as a style, you select which formatting elements to include in the final cell style definition. The new cell style then appears in the Cell Styles gallery, ready to be applied to other worksheet cells and shared with other workbooks.

REFERENCE

Creating a Cell Style

- Select a cell that contains the formatting you want to use in the custom cell style.
- In the Styles group on the Home tab, click the Cell Styles button, and then click New Cell Style.
- In the Style name box, type a name for the style.
- In the Style Includes (By Example) section, check the style elements that you want to be part of the custom style.
- Click the Format button, and then select any other formatting options you want to include in the custom style.
- Click the OK button in each dialog box to add the custom cell style to the Cell Styles gallery.

Charles wants you to use custom styles to create a unifying look for the workbook. You'll create a custom cell style named PTitle that formats the title in a large bold font centered over a double bottom border.

To create the PTitle cell style:

TIP

Apply the Normal cell style to the cell you want to use to create a custom cell style, and then apply the formatting you want to ensure that the new style has only the formatting you intended.

1. Switch to the **Element Families** worksheet, and then click cell **B4** to select it.
2. In the Styles group on the Home tab, click the **Cell Styles** button to open the Cell Styles gallery, and then click **New Cell Style**. The Style dialog box opens.
3. In the Style name box, type **PTitle**.
4. Click the **Number**, **Fill**, and **Protection** check boxes to remove the check marks, leaving the Alignment, Font, and Border style elements checked. The checked elements are included in the custom style. See Figure D-1.

Figure D-1 **Style dialog box**

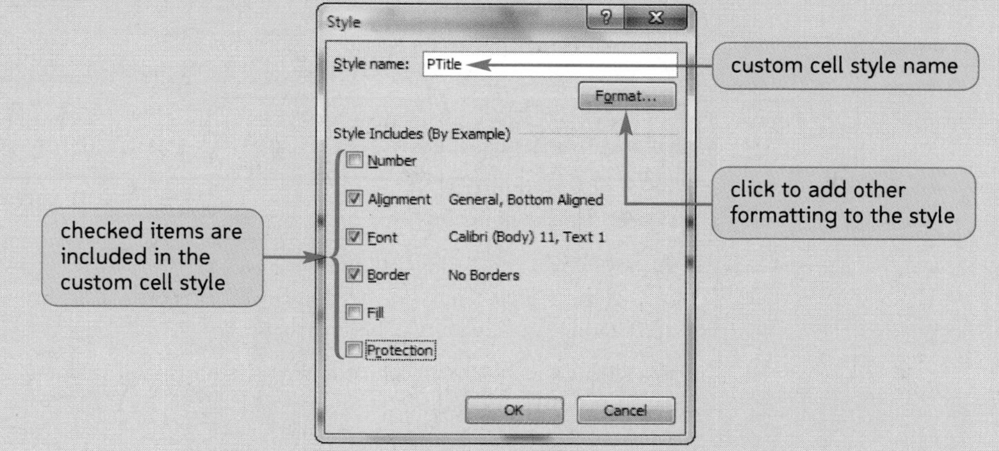

5. Click the **Format** button. The Format Cells dialog box opens.
6. Click the **Alignment** tab, click the **Horizontal** arrow, and then click **Center**.
7. Click the **Font** tab, click **Bold** in the Font style box, and then click **20** in the Size box.
8. Click the **Border** tab, click the **double line** in the Style box, and then click the **bottom border** of the Border preview.
9. Click the **OK** button in each dialog box to return to the workbook.

The PTitle cell style appears in the Cell Styles gallery and is ready to be applied to the active cell, which is cell B4, in this case. Custom styles appear at the top of the Cell Styles gallery.

To apply the PTitle cell style:

1. In the Styles group on the Home tab, click the **Cell Styles** button to open the Cell Styles gallery.
2. In the Custom section, click **PTitle** to apply the style to the selected cell.
3. Click cell **A1** to deselect the cell with the formatted title. See Figure D-2.

Figure D-2 PTitle cell style applied to cell B4

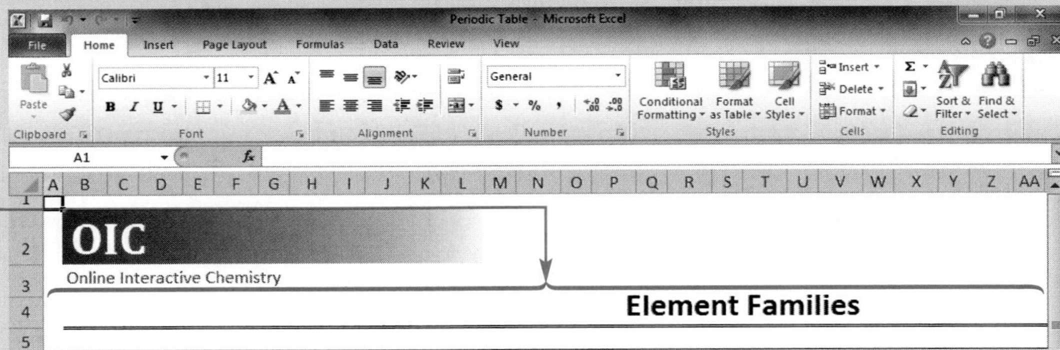

4. Apply the **PTitle** cell style to cell B4 in the Ionization Energy, Radioactive Elements, and Element Data worksheets.
5. Switch to the **Element Families** worksheet. Cell B4 in the four worksheets is formatted with the PTitle cell style.

After you have defined and applied a cell style, you can modify it. Modifying a cell style affects any cell with that style. In a large workbook, you can use styles to make global changes to the workbook's appearance without having to select and reformat individual cells. Charles wants you to modify the PTitle cell style, changing the font color to a dark olive green.

To modify the PTitle cell style:

1. In the Styles group on the Home tab, click the **Cell Styles** button. The Cell Styles gallery opens.
2. In the Custom section, right-click **PTitle**, and then click **Modify** on the shortcut menu. The Style dialog box for the PTitle cell style opens.
3. Click the **Format** button. The Format Cells dialog box opens.
4. Click the **Font** tab, click the **Color** box, and then, in the Theme Colors section of the palette, click **Olive Green, Accent 3, Darker 50%** (the seventh color in the last row).
5. Click the **OK** button in each dialog box. The PTitle cell style is updated, and the font color in cell B4 of each worksheet is dark olive green.

The PTitle style is part of the Periodic Table workbook, but not other workbooks.

INSIGHT

Sharing Styles

You can copy styles from one workbook to another to create workbooks with a common look and feel. To copy a style, open the workbook with the styles you want to copy, switch to the workbook in which you want to copy the styles, click the Cell Styles button in the Styles group on the Home tab, click Merge Styles, select the workbook with the cell styles to copy to the active workbook, and then click the OK button.

Creating a Custom Table Style

Charles wants you to format the tabular data in the Element Data worksheet. The data is already formatted with cell styles, but Charles wants you to use a table style.

To apply a table style to the data in the Element Data worksheet:

1. Switch to the **Element Data** worksheet, click cell **B6**, and then press the **Ctrl+Shift+End** keys. The entire data range of the elements list is selected.
2. In the Styles group on the Home tab, click the **Format as Table** button to open the gallery, and then click **Table Style Medium 4** (the fourth table style in the first row of the Medium section). The Format As Table dialog box opens.
3. Make sure the range $B$6:$I$124 is selected as the data for your table and that the My table has headers check box is checked, and then click the **OK** button. The table style is applied to the selected data.
4. In the Table Style Options group on the Table Tools Design tab, click the **First Column** check box to insert a check mark. The first column of the table (in column B) is formatted with bold.
5. Click cell **A1** to deselect the table. See Figure D-3.

Figure D-3 Element Data table

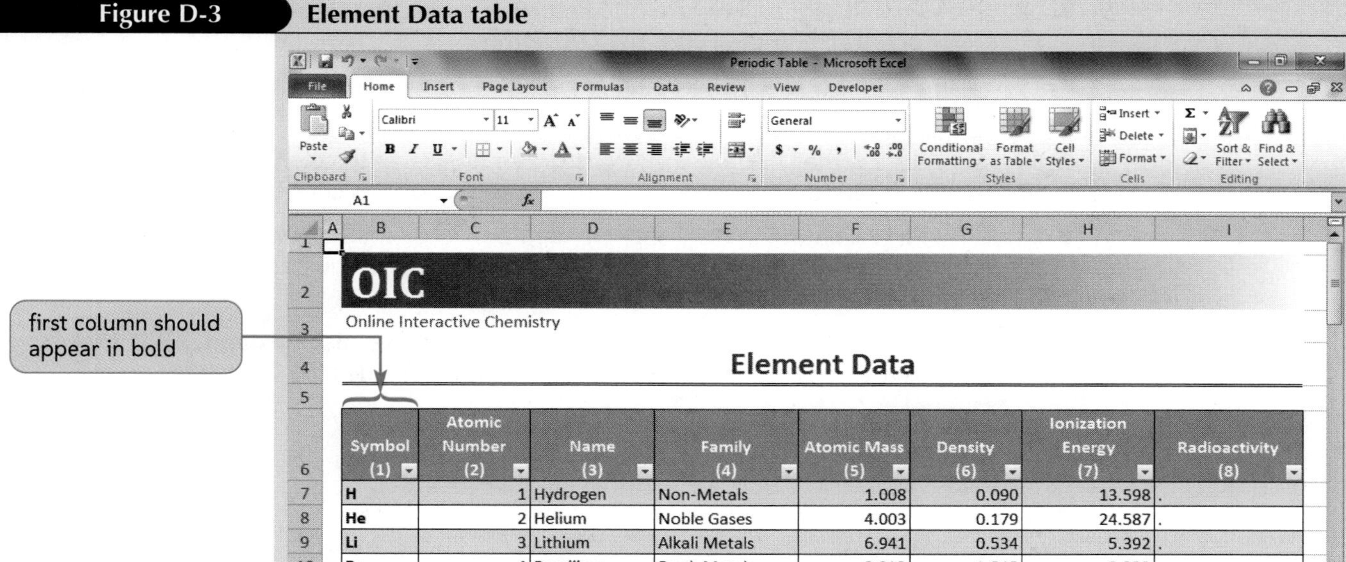

As you did with cell styles, you can create custom table styles. A table style has parts that correspond to different elements of the table structure. To create a table style, you must specify the format for each element. Each table style has 13 elements, including the header row, the first and last columns, the first and last rows, and the stripes used in banded rows or columns. Any element left unformatted in a custom table style uses its default style.

Charles wants to make the following changes to the table style:

1. Change the table headers to have a dark green fill.
2. Start the banded rows fill color with white, not light green.
3. Change the first column to have a dark green fill.

You'll modify the table style to create this custom style, and then you'll apply the custom style to the Element Data table.

To modify and apply the custom table style:

1. In the Styles group on the Home tab, click the **Format as Table** button, and then click **New Table Style**. The New Table Quick Style dialog box opens. The Table Element box shows the 13 table elements you can format. The Preview box shows the formatted table.
2. In the Name box, type **ElemTable**.
3. Click **Header Row** in the Table Element box, and then click the **Format** button. The Format Cells dialog box opens.
4. Click the **Fill** tab, and then click **dark green** (the seventh color in the sixth row in the Background Color palette).
5. Click the **Font** tab, click the **Color** arrow, and then click **White, Background 1** (the first color in the first row in the Color palette).
6. Click the **OK** button to return to the New Table Quick Style dialog box.
7. Click **First Row Stripe** in the Table Element box, verify that 1 is entered in the Stripe Size box, and then click the **Format** button.
8. Click the **Fill** tab, click **white** (the first color in the first row in the Background Color palette), and then click the **OK** button.
9. Click **Second Row Stripe** in the Table Element box, and then verify that the stripe size value is 1.
10. Click the **Format** button, click **light green** (the seventh color in the second row in the Background Color palette) on the Fill tab, and then click the **OK** button.
11. Click **First Column** in the Table Element box, click the **Format** button, and then click **dark green** (the seventh color in the sixth row in the Background Color palette) on the Fill tab.
12. Click the **Font** tab, click the **Color** arrow, click **White, Background 1** (the first color in the first row in the Color palette), and then click the **OK** button. See Figure D-4.

TIP

You can create banded rows covering more than one row with a color by increasing the value of the Stripe Size.

Figure D-4 New Table Quick Style dialog box

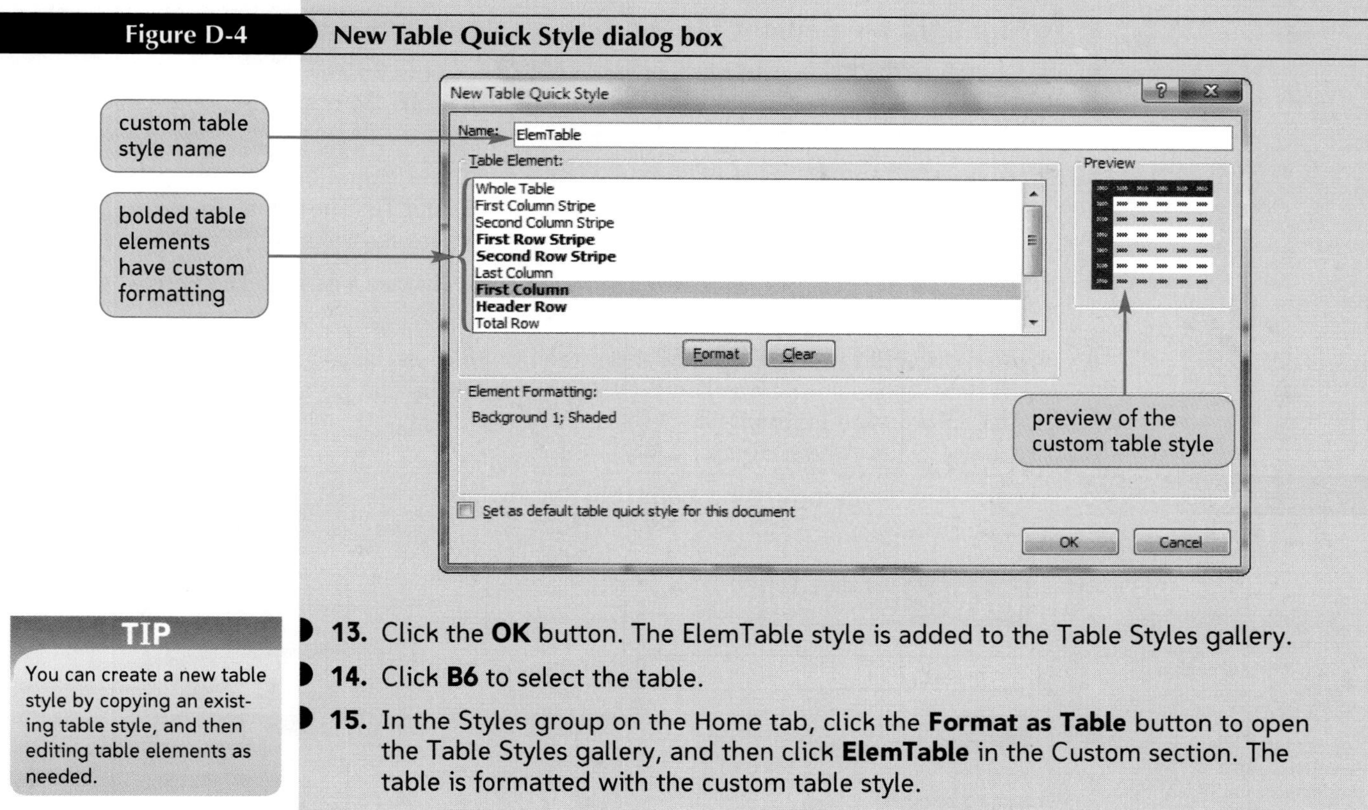

TIP

You can create a new table style by copying an existing table style, and then editing table elements as needed.

13. Click the **OK** button. The ElemTable style is added to the Table Styles gallery.
14. Click **B6** to select the table.
15. In the Styles group on the Home tab, click the **Format as Table** button to open the Table Styles gallery, and then click **ElemTable** in the Custom section. The table is formatted with the custom table style.

Charles wants to use this custom table style in other workbooks. To make a table style available to every workbook you open, create the custom table style in a blank workbook, and then save the workbook as an Excel template named book.xltx in the xlStart folder.

Working with Conditional Formats

Charles wants to present the information in the three periodic table worksheets in a visually interesting and informative way. The periodic table in the Element Families worksheet lists each element along with its atomic number and family. All of this information is stored in the Element Data worksheet.

Highlighting Cells

Charles added a legend to the worksheet that indicates how he wants the different cells colored. Although you could edit the fill colors of selected cells to match the legend, it is more efficient to highlight the cells using conditional formats. Charles defined a name for the periodic table cells, which you can use with the highlight cells rules to quickly format them.

To highlight an element family:

1. Switch to the **Element Families** worksheet, press the **F5** key to open the Go To dialog box, and then double-click **Family_Data** in the Go to box. All of the cells in the periodic table containing the element names are selected.
2. In the Styles group on the Home tab, click the **Conditional Formatting** button, point to **Highlight Cells Rules**, and then click **Equal To**. The Equal To dialog box opens. Instead of typing text, you'll use the element family entry from the legend.
3. Click cell **H6**, click the **with** box, and then click **Custom Format**. The Format Cells dialog box opens.
4. Click the **Fill** tab, click **light orange** (the last color in the second row) in the Background Color palette, and then click the **OK** button to return to the Equal To dialog box. See Figure D-5.

Figure D-5 Custom conditional formatting applied to non-metals

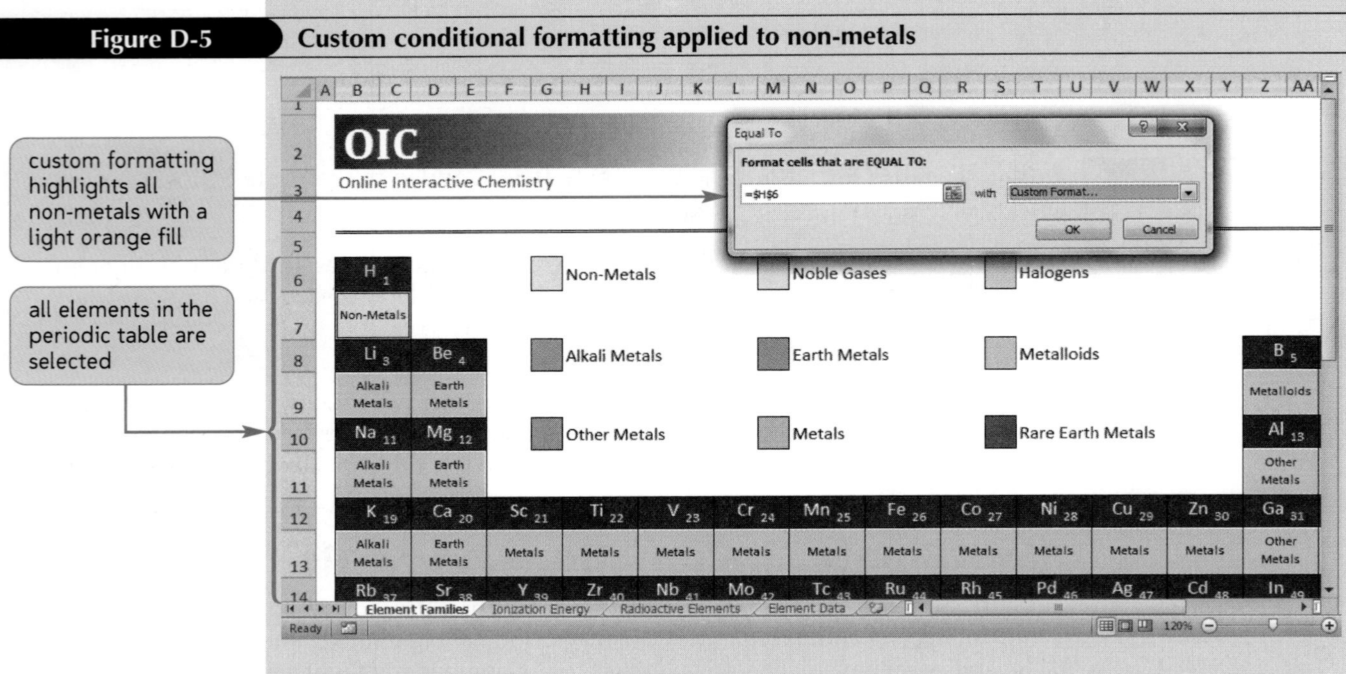

5. Click the **OK** button to accept the highlighting rule.
6. Click cell **A1** to deselect the range, and then scroll the worksheet to verify that the only cells with a light orange fill are Hydrogen (H_1), Carbon (C_6), Nitrogen (N_7), Oxygen (O_8), Phosphorus (P_{15}), Sulfur (S_{16}), and Selenium (Se_{34}). The background color of the other cells remains white color.

To highlight the other eight element families, you'll repeat this process for the remaining entries in the legend.

To highlight the remaining element families:

1. Press the **F5** key to open the Go To dialog box, and then double-click **Family_Data** in the Go to box to select all of the elements in the periodic table.
2. In the Styles group on the Home tab, click the **Conditional Formatting** button, point to **Highlight Cells Rules**, and then click **Equal To**. The Equal To dialog box opens.
3. Click cell **N6**, click the **with** box, and then click **Custom Format**. The Format Cells dialog box opens.
4. On the Fill tab, click **light blue** (the ninth color in the second row) in the Background Color palette, and then click the **OK** button in each dialog box.
5. Repeat Steps 2 through 4 for the remaining legend entries, using the following cell references and colors:

Halogens	cell T6	light purple (eighth color in the second row)
Alkali Metals	cell H8	blue (fifth color in the fourth row)
Earth Metals	cell N8	rose (sixth color in the fourth row)
Metalloids	cell T8	medium orange (last color in the fourth row)
Other Metals	cell H10	gray (first color in the fourth row)
Metals	cell N10	tan (third color in the second row)
Rare Earth Metals	cell T10	medium tan (third color in the fourth row)

6. Click cell **A1** to deselect the range, and then zoom out as needed to view the entire table. See Figure D-6.

Figure D-6 All element families conditionally formatted

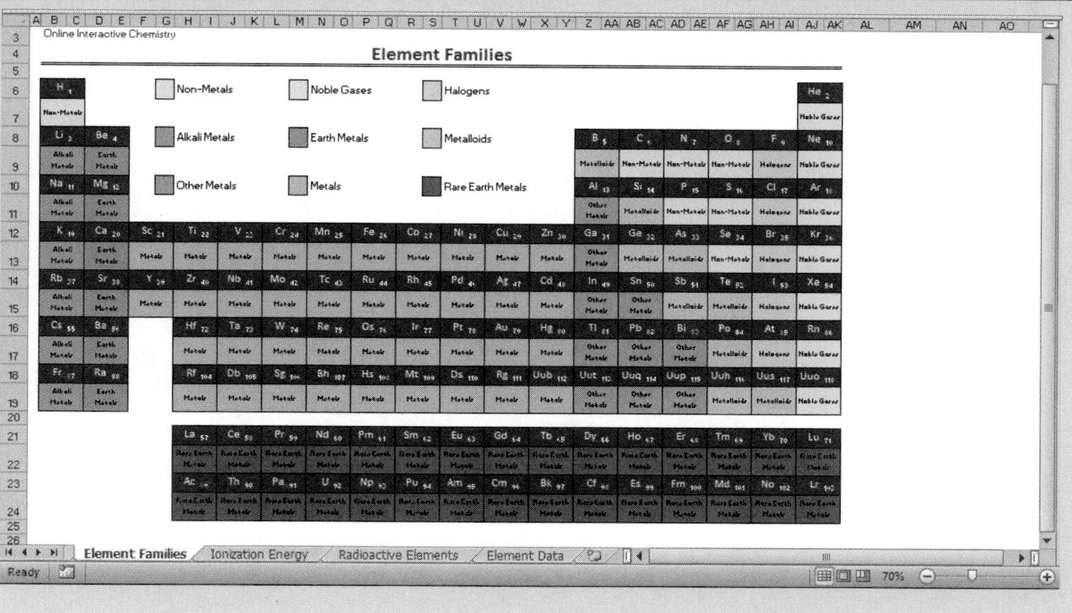

TIP

To clear all conditional formatting rules, click the Conditional Formatting button in the Styles group on the Home tab, point to Clear Rules, and then click Clear Rules from Selected Cells or Clear Rules from Entire Sheet.

Charles wants you to hide the element family names. Instead of changing the font color to match the background color to hide the text, you'll apply a custom format that prevents Excel from displaying a cell's value.

To hide the element family names:

1. Press **F5** and then double-click **Family_Data** to select all of the elements in the periodic table.
2. In the Number group on the Home tab, click the **Dialog Box Launcher**. The Format Cells dialog box appears with the Number tab displayed.
3. In the Category box, click **Custom**, type **;;;** in the Type box, and then click the **OK** button.
4. Click cell **A1** to deselect the range. All of the family names in the periodic table are hidden.

Modifying a Conditional Formatting Rule

Charles wants you to change the color of the Metals family elements to a dark red fill color. You can do this by editing the properties of the conditional formatting rule applied to those cells.

To modify a conditional formatting rule:

1. In the Styles group on the Home tab, click the **Conditional Formatting** button, and then click **Manage Rules**. The Conditional Formatting Rules Manager dialog box opens.
2. Click the **Show formatting rules for** arrow, and then click **This Worksheet** to display all of the formatting rules for the current worksheet.
3. Click **Cell Value = $N$10** in the Rule list to select the rule for the Metals family elements, and then click the **Edit Rule** button. The Edit Formatting Rule dialog box opens.
4. Click the **Format** button to open the Format Cells dialog box, click the **Fill** tab, and then click **dark red** (the sixth color in the fifth row) in the Background Color palette.
5. Click the **OK** button in each dialog box to return to the worksheet.
6. Click cell **M10** to select the Metals legend entry.
7. In the Font group on the Home tab, click the **Fill Color button arrow** in the Theme Colors section, and then click **Red, Accent 2, Darker 25%**. When you change the formatting of the cell on which the rule is based, all cells that fit that rule change as well. See Figure D-7.

TIP

To delete a rule, select the rule in the Rule list, and then click the Delete Rule button.

Figure D-7 Final periodic table of element families

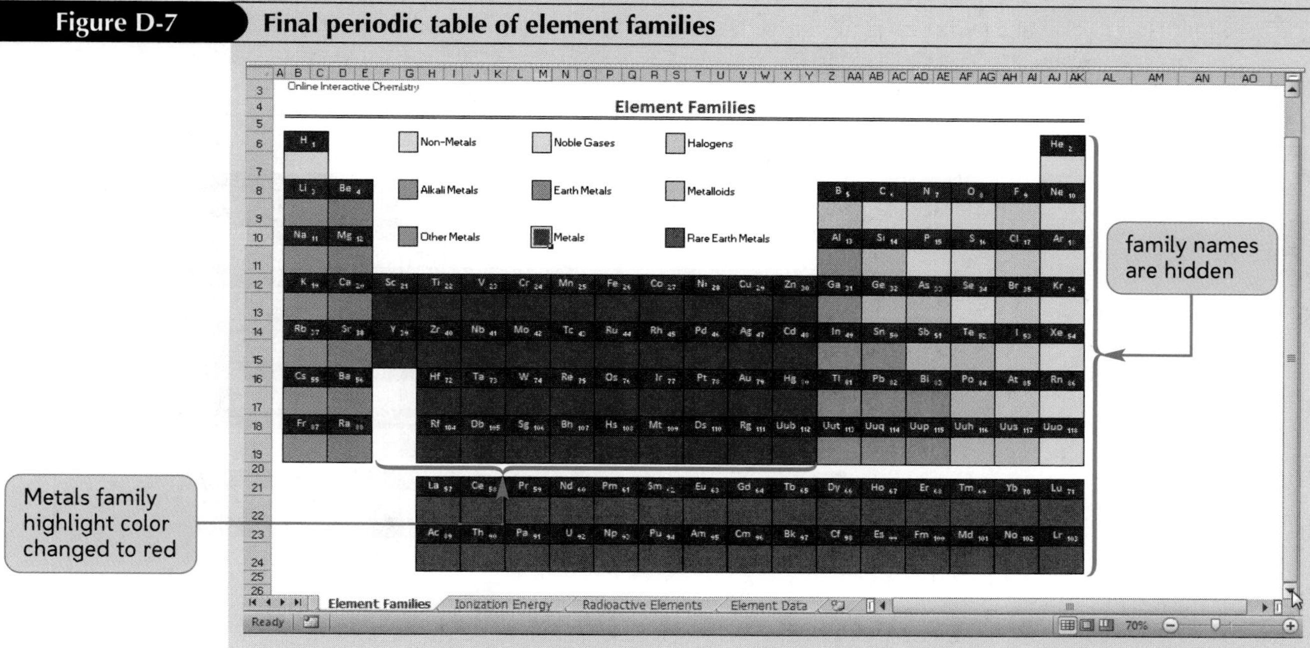

Working with Color Scales

Ionization energy is the energy required to remove an electron from an element, which indicates the element's ability to form bonds with atoms from other elements. The higher the ionization energy, the more difficult it is for the element to bond. For example, noble gases (Helium, Argon, Neon, Krypton, etc.) have the highest ionization energy and are the most difficult to bond with other elements.

To illustrate this concept clearly in the Ionization periodic table, Charles wants to base the fill color of each element on its ionization energy. The color shade should grow increasingly darker as the ionization energy increases so that elements with the lowest ionization energy have the lightest fill and elements with the highest ionization energy have the darkest fill. You can do this by applying a **color scale**, which is conditional formatting that determines the color shade of a cell based on its value.

To apply a color scale to the elements based on their ionization energy:

1. Switch to the **Ionization Energy** worksheet, press the **F5** key, and then double-click **Ionization_Data** to select the cells with the ionization data values.
2. In the Styles group on the Home tab, click the **Conditional Formatting** button, point to **Color Scales**, and then click **Green – Yellow – Red Color Scale** (the first color scale in the first row). The color scale is applied to the ionization data values.
3. Click cell **A1** to deselect the range, and then zoom out the worksheet to view the entire table. See Figure D-8.

Figure D-8 Color scale added to the ionization energy data values

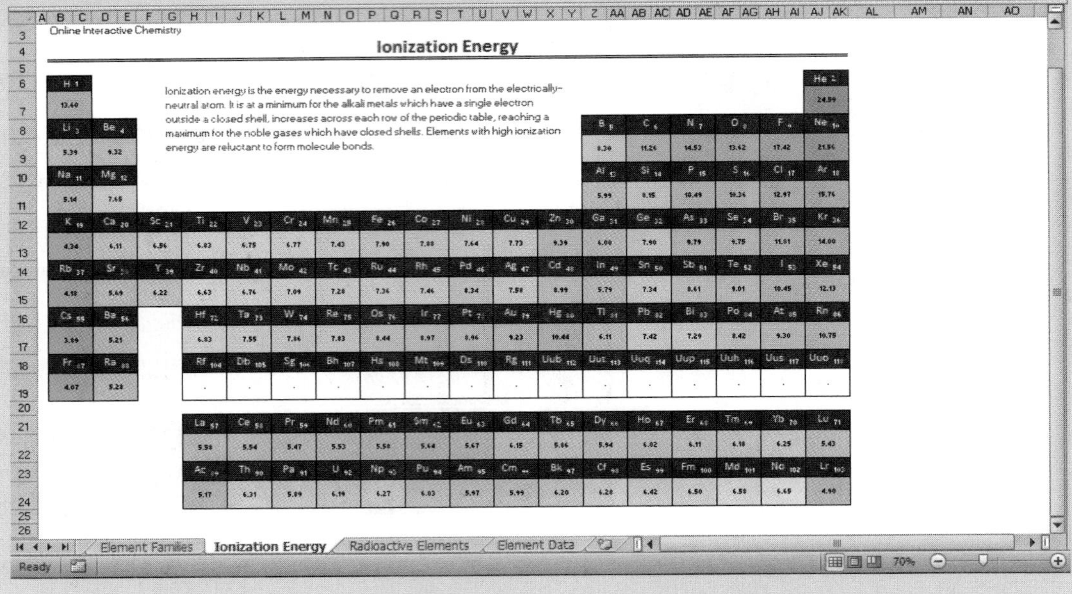

The color scale displays cells with the highest values in dark green, the lowest values in dark red, and the middle values in orange and yellow. The cells that remain white are unstable synthetic elements that do not exist long enough to have their ionization energies determined, and Charles entered a period (.) for these values, which cannot be placed on a color scale.

Charles doesn't think the default color scale presents the data clearly. He wants all of the cells to be orange, growing increasingly darker for higher ionization values. To do this, you'll change the conditional formatting rule for the color scale.

To modify the color scale:

1. In the Styles group on the Home tab, click the **Conditional Formatting** button, and then click **Manage Rules**. The Conditional Formatting Rules Manager dialog box opens.
2. Click the **Show formatting rules for** box, and then click **This Worksheet** to display all of the conditional formatting rules for the current worksheet.
3. Click **Graded Color Scale** in the Rule list, and then click the **Edit Rule** button. The Edit Formatting Rule dialog box opens, showing the three colors used in the color scale and a Preview box with the color gradation.
4. Click the **Minimum Color** arrow to open a color palette, and then click **Orange, Accent 6, Lighter 80%** in the Theme Colors section.
5. Click the **Midpoint Color** arrow to open a color palette, and then click **Orange, Accent 6, Lighter 40%** in the Theme Colors section.
6. Click the **Maximum Color** arrow to open a color palette, and then click **Orange, Accent 6, Darker 50%** in the Theme Colors section. See Figure D-9.

Figure D-9 Edit Formatting Rule dialog box

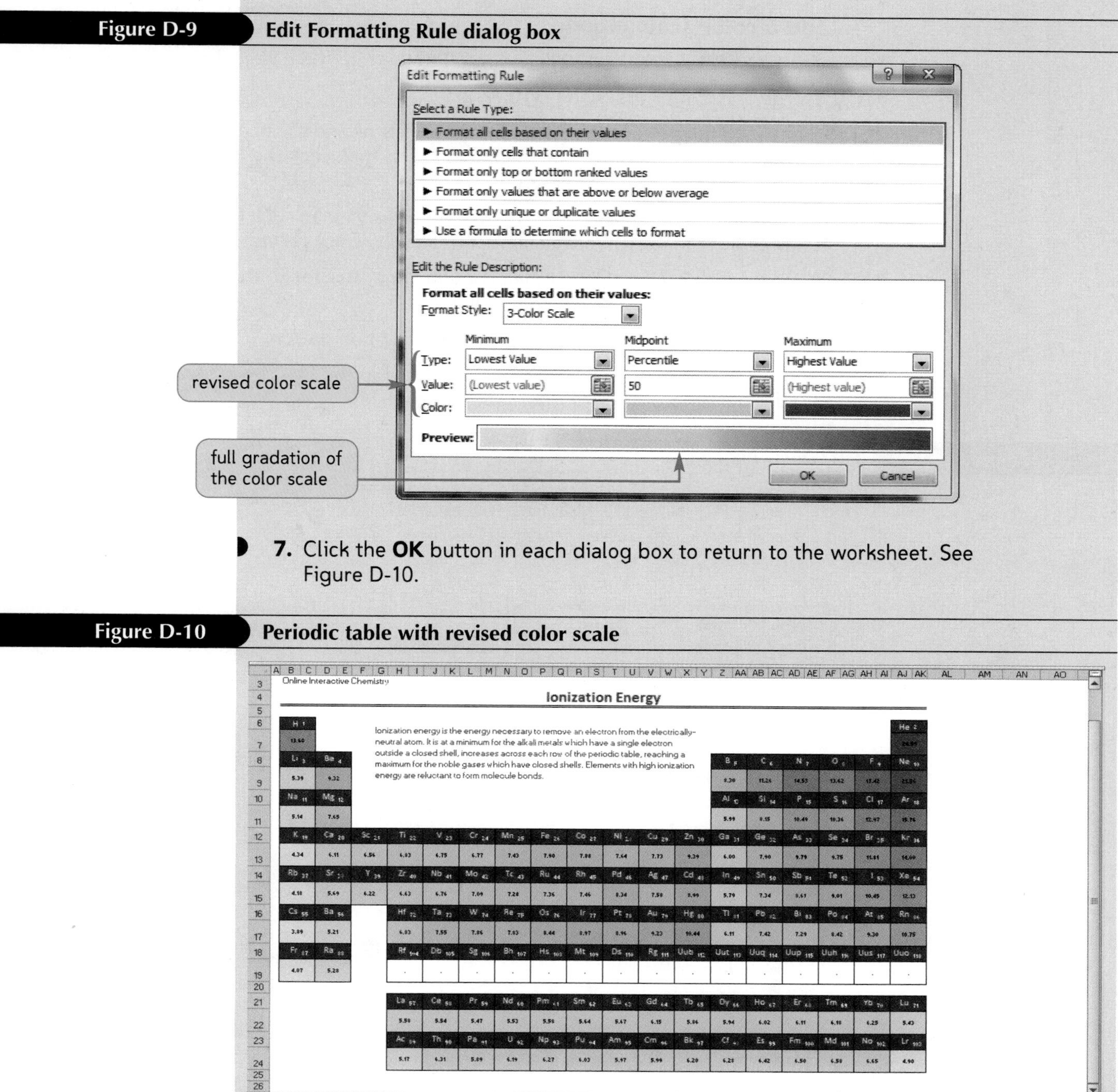

7. Click the **OK** button in each dialog box to return to the worksheet. See Figure D-10.

Figure D-10 Periodic table with revised color scale

The revised color scale more clearly shows how the ionization energies generally increase as you move across the table to the right, and the highest values occur for elements of the Noble Gases family. You'll add a legend to the worksheet to make this clear.

To add a color scale legend:

1. Zoom the worksheet to **120%** and scroll to the top of the worksheet.
2. Merge and center the range **G10:X10**.
3. Right-click the merged cell, click **Format Cells** on the shortcut menu to open the Format Cells dialog box, click the **Fill** tab, and then click the **Fill Effects** button. The Fill Effects dialog box opens.
4. In the Colors section, click the **Color 1** arrow, and then click **Orange, Accent 6, Lighter 80%** in the Theme Colors section of the color palette.
5. Click the **Color 2** arrow, and then click **Orange, Accent 6, Darker 50%** in the Theme Colors section of the color palette.
6. In the Shading styles box, click the **Vertical** option button.
7. In the Variants box, click the first color variant in the first row, in which the color shades darken from left to right. See Figure D-11.

Figure D-11 **Fill Effects dialog box**

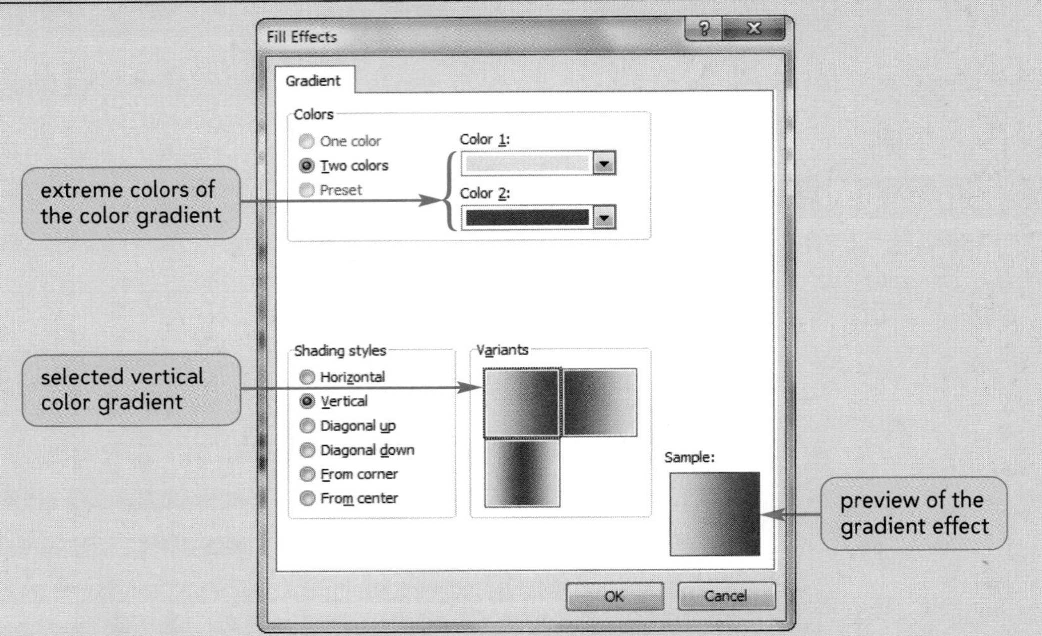

8. Click the **OK** button in each dialog box to return to the worksheet. The vertical gradient fill effect appears in the merged cell G10.
9. In cell G11, enter **lower energy** and then top-align the text.
10. In cell X11, enter **higher energy** and then right-align and top-align the text.
11. Click cell **A1**, and then scroll up to row 5. Figure D-12 shows the completed energy scale.

Figure D-12 Color scale legend

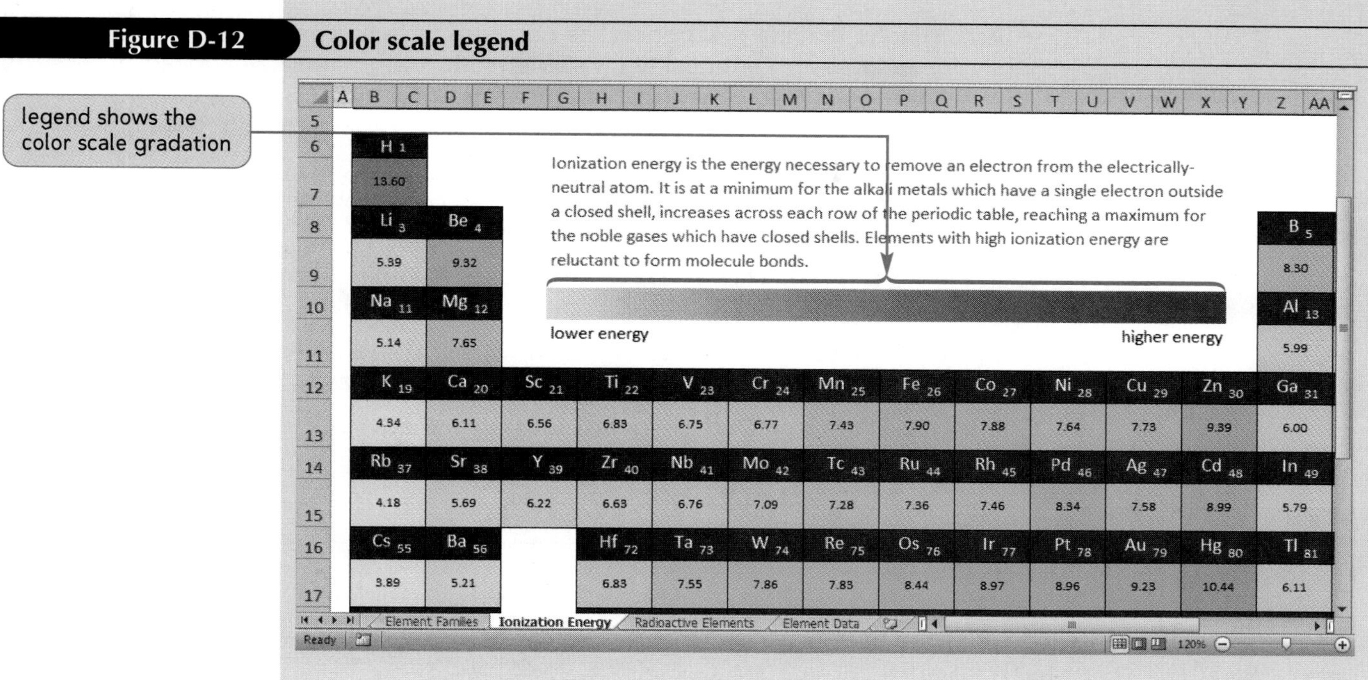

Working with Icon Sets

The Radioactive Elements worksheet lists elements that are considered radioactive. Radioactive elements have the value 1; non-radioactive elements have a period (.) as their value. Charles wants the values replaced with a red circle indicating a radioactive element. You'll add a conditional format called an **icon set**, which displays a symbol based on a cell's value.

To apply and modify an icon set:

1. Switch to the **Radioactive Elements** worksheet, press the **F5** key to open the Go To dialog box, and then double-click **Radioactivity_Data** in the Go to box to select the cells with the radioactivity data values.
2. In the Styles group on the Home tab, click the **Conditional Formatting** button, point to **Icon Sets**, and then click **3 Traffic Lights (Rimmed)**, the second icon set in the Shapes section. The periodic table has green traffic lights in all cells with the value 1.
3. In the Styles group on the Home tab, click the **Conditional Formatting** button, and then click **Manage Rules**. The Conditional Formatting Rules Manager dialog box opens.
4. Click **This Worksheet** in the Show formatting rules for box, click **Icon Set** in the Rule list, and then click the **Edit Rule** button. The Edit Formatting Rule dialog box opens.

According to the rule description, the green traffic light icon appears in cells with a value greater than or equal to 67%. The yellow traffic light icon appears in cells with a value less than 67% but greater than or equal to 33%. The red traffic light icon appears in all other cells in the range. In this case, you want to display a red traffic light icon for cells with a value equal to 1.

5. Click the **Reverse Icon Order** button. The red icon is now first and the green icon is now last.
6. In the red icon row, click the **Type** arrow, click **Number**, and then type **1** in the Value box.
7. In the yellow icon row, click the **Type** arrow, and then click **Number**. The value changes to 0 and the types are consistent, although it has no effect in this case.
8. Click the **Show Icon Only** check box to insert a check mark, which hides the cell values. See Figure D-13.

Figure D-13 **Edited icon set rule**

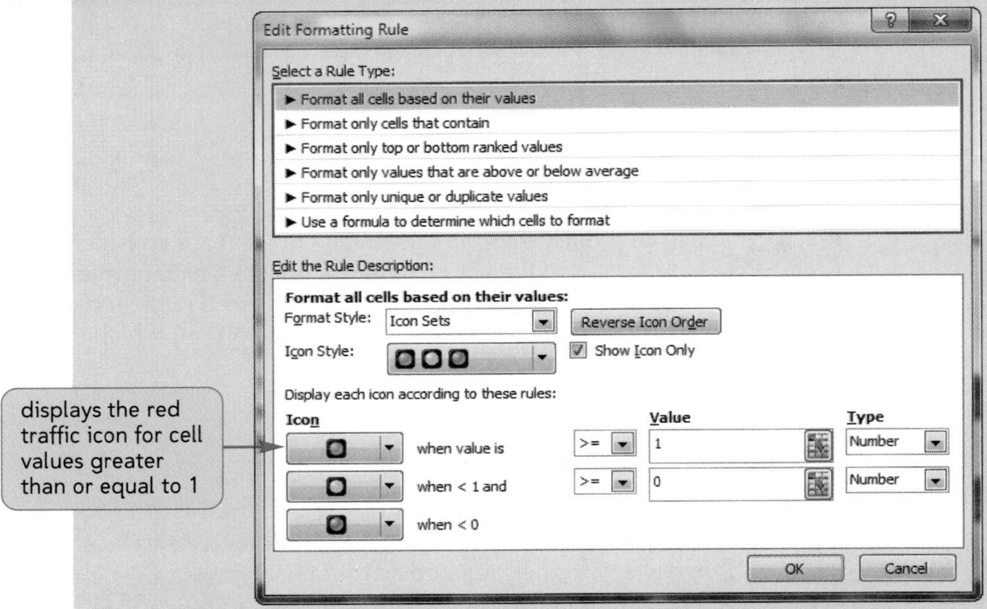

9. Click the **OK** button in each dialog box to return to the worksheet.
10. Scroll down to see that the red traffic light icon appears in 37 elements in the periodic table. The non-radioactive elements still show periods because the icon set rule applies only to number value.

TIP

When possible, use one conditional formatting rule for the legend and the cell values so any edits you make affect both.

Charles wants you to add a legend to this table, making it clear that the red traffic light icon identifies the radioactive elements. You'll create the legend by editing the conditional formatting rule you used in the table to include the legend text. This ensures that if you change the icon style in the icon set rule, both the periodic table and the legend are automatically updated.

To create a legend for the icon set:

1. In cell J10, enter **1** and then center and middle-align the value.
2. In the Styles group on the Home tab, click the **Conditional Formatting** button, and then click **Manage Rules**. The Conditional Formatting Rules Manager opens.
3. Click **This Worksheet** in the Show formatting rules for box, click after the = symbol in the Applies to box, click cell **J10** in the worksheet to insert an absolute reference to the legend cell, and then type **,** (a comma). The range =$J$10,$H$24:$AK$24,$H$22:$AK$2 is visible in the Applies to box.
4. Click the **OK** button. The red traffic light icon appears in cell J10, matching the icon for radioactive elements in the periodic table.
5. In cell K10, enter **Radioactive Element** and then middle-align the text.
6. Click cell **A1**, and then zoom the worksheet to view the entire periodic table. See Figure D-14.

Figure D-14 **Final radioactive element table**

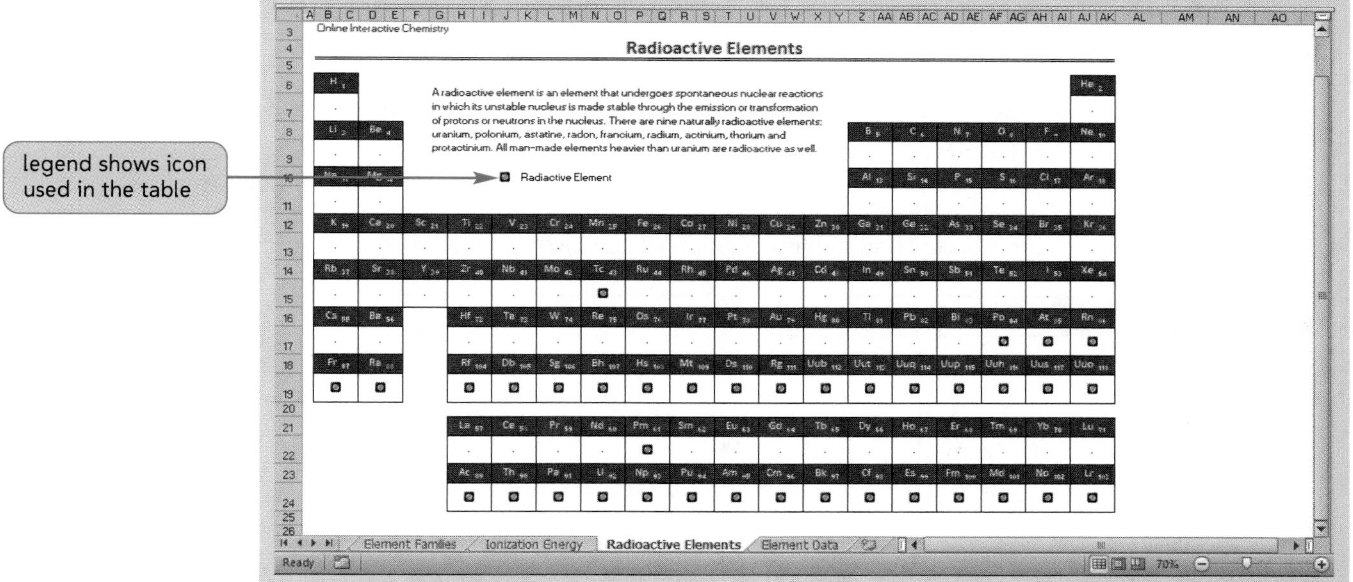

legend shows icon used in the table

Conditional Formatting with Formulas

All of the conditional formats you have used so far are based on the cell's value. You can also base the format on a function of the cell's value. For example, you can highlight cells with dates that fall on a weekend differently from cells with dates that fall on a weekday. To highlight a cell based on a formula, click the Conditional Formatting button in the Styles group on the Home tab, click New Rule to open the New Formatting Rule dialog box, and then click "Use a formula to determine which cells to format" in the Select a Rule Type box. In the Edit the Rule Description section of the dialog box, enter a formula that begins with an equal sign and uses a logical function that returns a true or false value. If the formula's value is true, the conditional formatting is applied; if the value is false, the formatting is not applied. For example, the following formulas will format the cell only if the value in cell A3 is less than the value in cell A4 (the first formula uses the IF function; the second formula is a briefer format of the first formula):

```
=IF(A3<A4, true, false)
=A3<A4
```

Conditional formatting formulas can use relative, absolute, and mixed references. When applying a conditional format formula to a range of cells, write the formula for the active cell in the selected range. Excel will modify the references to match the new location of each cell in the range.

You can use formulas when defining conditional formatting rules for data bars, color scales, and icon sets. Enter the formula as a function of the selected cell using a logical function. For example, to display an icon in comparison to the average value in the range A1:A10, in the rule description select Formula in the Type box, and then enter the following formula:

```
=AVERAGE(A1:A10)
```

As with formulas stored within cells, Excel will adjust the relative references as the format is copied across the selected range.

Working with Pictures and SmartArt Graphics

Charles wants you to create a logo for Online Interactive Chemistry based on the idea he sketched in Figure D-15. You'll create this logo as a **SmartArt graphic**, which is a professionally designed business diagram, such as a flow chart, organization chart, or production cycle chart. SmartArt graphics can also be used to create graphic logos.

Figure D-15 **Charles' proposed logo**

You'll insert the SmartArt graphic in the Documentation worksheet.

To insert the SmartArt graphic logo:

1. Switch to the **Documentation** worksheet, click the **Insert** tab on the Ribbon, and then click the **SmartArt** button in the Illustrations group. The Choose a SmartArt Graphic dialog box opens.
2. Click **Cycle** in the left pane, and then click **Gear** (the second graphic in the last row) as the layout. See Figure D-16.

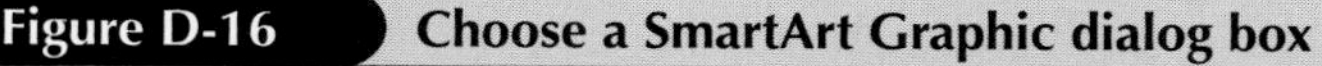

Figure D-16 Choose a SmartArt Graphic dialog box

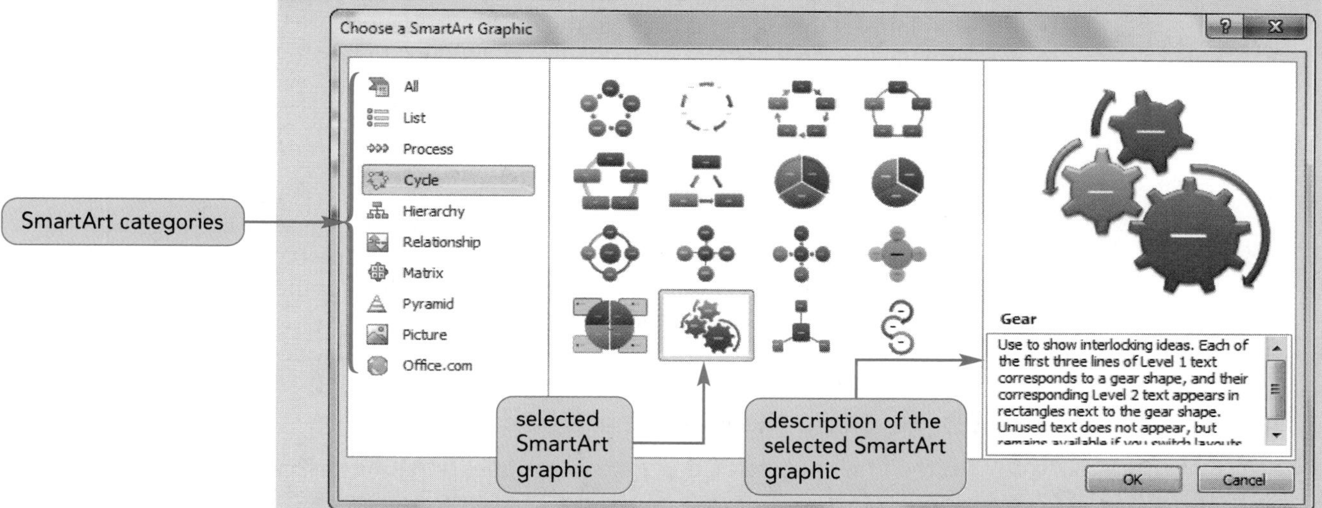

3. Click the **OK** button. The gear SmartArt graphic is inserted in the Documentation worksheet. See Figure D-17.

Figure D-17 SmartArt graphic inserted into the worksheet

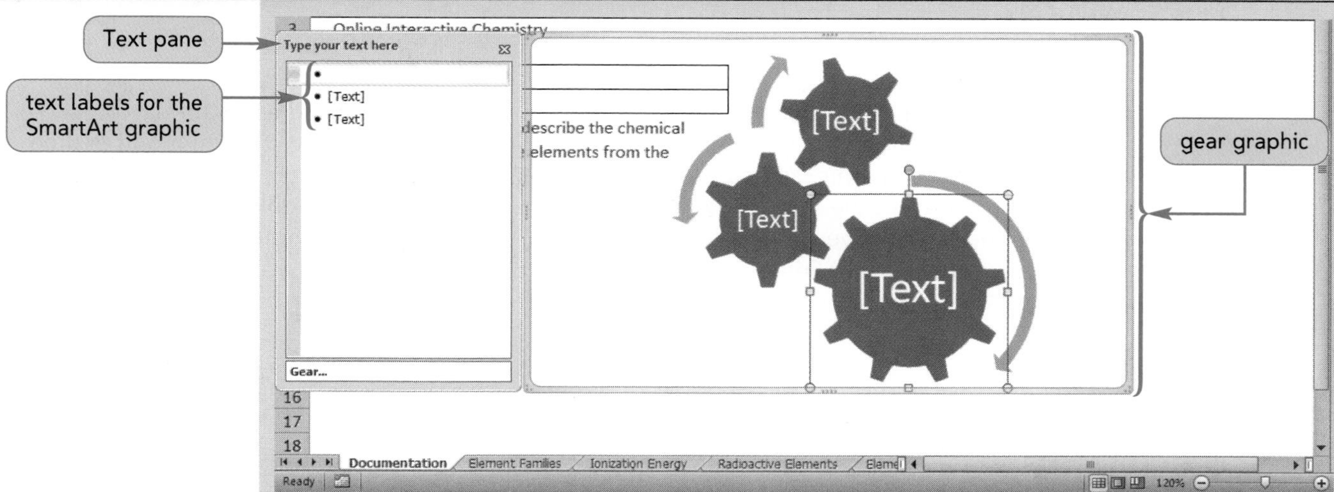

Trouble? If you do not see the Text pane, you need to display it. Click the Text Pane button in the Create Graphic group on the SmartArt Tools Design tab.

Inserting Text Labels

You enter or edit text for each element of the SmartArt graphic in the Text pane. Most SmartArt graphics support several levels of text. The gear graphic has three rows of text by default. The first level of text will appear in the largest gear, in the lower-right corner of the graphic. As you type the text, the font size changes so that the labels fit within the graphic elements. Font sizes also increase or decrease as needed when the SmartArt graphic is resized. The Text pane uses the following rules for editing the SmartArt graphic text:

- Press the Enter key to add a new row of text to the Text pane and a new element to the SmartArt graphic.
- Press the Tab key to demote the text to the next lower level.
- Press the Backspace key to promote the text to the next higher level.
- Hold down the Shift key as you press the Enter key to insert text on a new line at the same level.
- Press the ↑ and ↓ keys to move between the entries in the Text pane without inserting new text.

Charles wants you to insert the label "Online Interactive Chemistry" in the gear SmartArt graphic. Because the most prominent and largest graphic element is listed first in the Text pane but appears in the last gear graphic, you'll enter the label text in reverse order so that it reads correctly on the screen.

To enter text into the gear SmartArt graphic:

1. With the first entry selected in the Text pane, type **Chemistry** and then click the second text label entry.
2. Type **Interactive** for the second text label, and then click the third text label entry.
3. Type **Online** for the third text label. The three text labels appear in the gear graphic.

Applying SmartArt Quick Styles

Quick Styles are a collection of styles you can use to quickly and easily format a SmartArt graphic's appearance. With Quick Styles you can change the color and outline style of the graphic. You can also rotate the graphic elements to give them a 3-D look. Charles wants the SmartArt graphic to have a 3-D or "chiseled" look, and the gear color to match the olive green color used elsewhere in the workbook. You'll use a Quick Style to format the gear SmartArt graphic.

To apply a Quick Style to the SmartArt graphic:

1. In the SmartArt Styles group on the SmartArt Tools Design tab, click the **More** button, and then click **Inset** (the style in the first row and second column of the 3-D section of the gallery). The style is applied to the gear graphic.
2. In the SmartArt Styles group, click the **Change Colors** button, and then click **Gradient Loop – Accent 3** in the Accent 3 section. The graphic color changes to shades of olive green.
3. Click cell **A1** to deselect the graphic. The formatted SmartArt image is shown in Figure D-18.

Figure D-18 Formatted SmartArt graphic

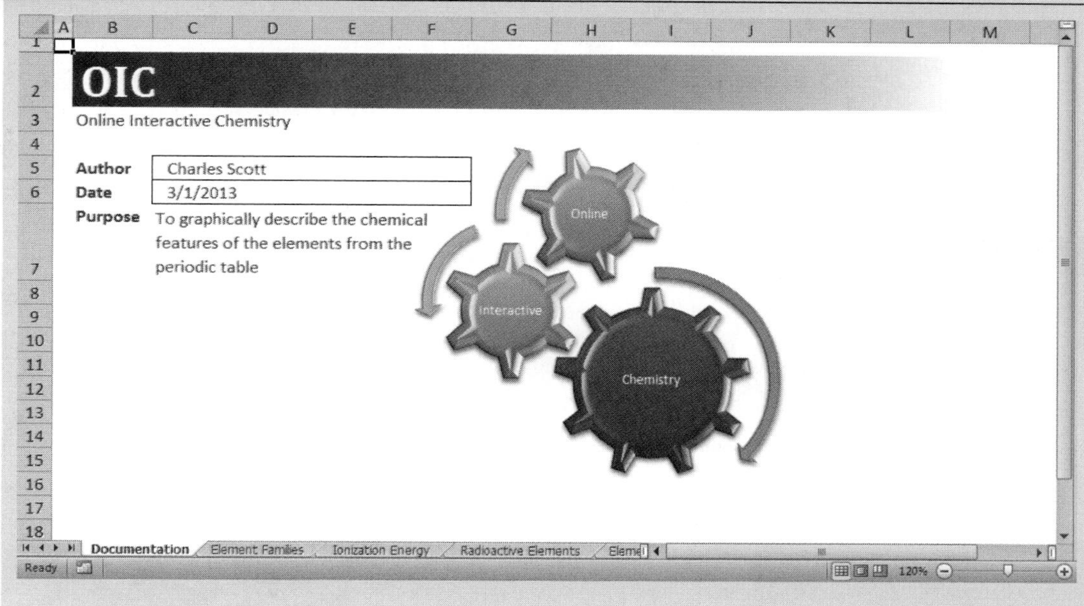

TIP

To restore a SmartArt graphic to its original appearance, click the Reset Graphic button in the Reset group on the SmartArt Tools Design tab.

Charles has graphic images of three famous chemists from history: Democritus, the Greek philosopher who first proposed that all matter is composed of atoms; John Dalton, the English chemist and physicist who proposed a modern interpretation of the atomic theory; and Dmitri Mendeleev, the Russian chemist who was the primary creator of the first periodic table of elements. Charles wants you to insert these images into the three gears of the logo.

To fill the gear elements of the logo with clip art images:

1. Click the **Chemistry** gear in the SmartArt graphic. A selection box appears around the selected element.

   Trouble? If the selection box is dotted, only the Chemistry label is selected. Click the gear element but not its label to select the entire gear element.

2. Click the **SmartArt Tools Format** tab on the Ribbon, click the **Shape Fill button arrow** in the Shape Styles group, and then click **Picture**. The Insert Picture dialog box opens.
3. Click the **Mendeleev** image file located in the ExcelD\Tutorial folder included with your Data Files, and then click the **Insert** button. The fill style of the Chemistry gear displays a portion of the Mendeleev image, and the Chemistry label is difficult to read.
4. Click the **Home** tab on the Ribbon, click the **Bold** button **B** in the Font group, and then change the font color to **Yellow** in the Standard Colors section. The Chemistry label changes to bold yellow.
5. Click the **Interactive** gear in the SmartArt graphic, repeat Steps 2 and 3 to fill the background with the **Dalton** image file, and then repeat Step 4 to change the Interactive label to **bold yellow**.
6. Click the **Online** gear in the SmartArt graphic, repeat Steps 2 and 3 to fill the background with the **Democritus** image file, and then repeat Step 4 to change the Online label to **bold yellow**.
7. Click cell **A1** to deselect the graphic. See Figure D-19.

Figure D-19 Gear SmartArt graphic with pictures used for the background fill

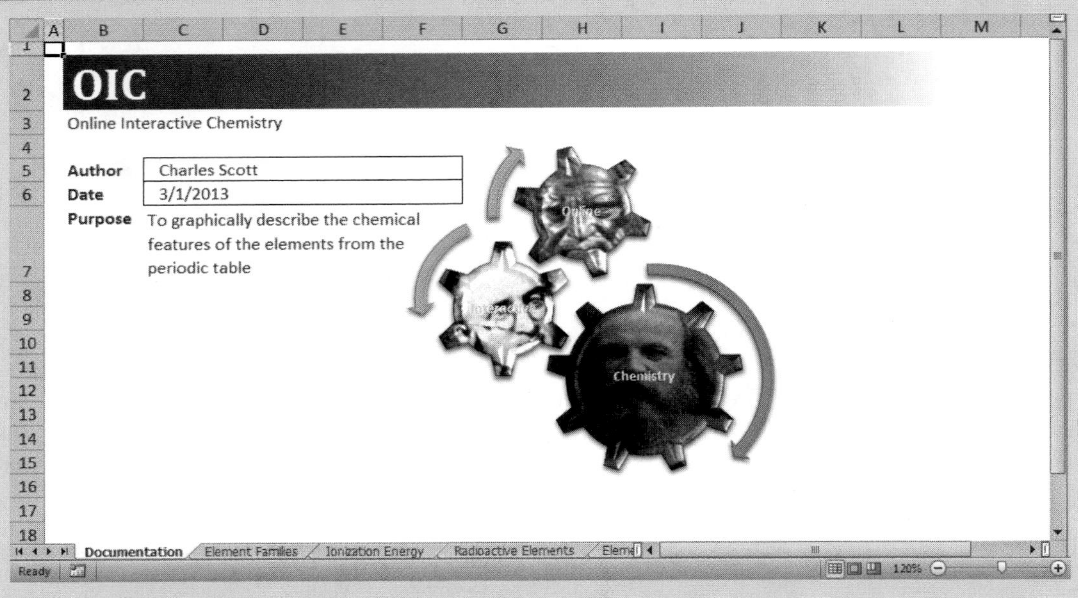

Editing a Picture

Imaging tools enable you to modify the appearance of pictures in a workbook. You can recolor pictures and change the picture's contrast and brightness level. For pictures inserted into a workbook as separate graphic objects (as opposed to fills), you can change the picture's shape, add a graphical border, and apply special effects such as rotating the picture in three dimensions and adding a drop shadow.

REFERENCE

Editing a Picture

- Select the picture image, and then click the Picture Tools Format tab on the Ribbon.
- To change the color tint, brightness, or contrast of the picture, click the Color button or the Corrections button in the Adjust group.
- To add an artistic effect to the picture, click the Artistic Effects button in the Adjust group.
- To apply a style to the picture, select an effect in the Styles gallery in the Picture Styles group.
- To add a graphical border or a special effect, click the Picture Border or Picture Effects button, respectively, in the Pictures Styles group.
- To crop or resize the picture, click the Crop button or enter values in the Size boxes in the Size group.
- To restore the picture to its original appearance, click the Reset Picture button in the Adjust group.

Charles wants you to recolor the graphic images to make them darker, which would make the labels more readable. You'll give the Mendeleev image a green tint, the Dalton image a red tint, and the Democritus image a blue tint, and then increase the contrast to make the labels stand out.

To edit the pictures:

1. Click the **Mendeleev** image in the Chemistry gear to select it.
2. Click the **Picture Tools Format** tab, click the **Color** button in the Adjust group, and then click **Olive Green, Accent color 3 Dark** located in the second row and fourth column of the Recolor section of the gallery to change the gear color to olive green.
3. In the Adjust group, click the **Corrections** button and then click **Brightness: -20% Contrast 0% (Normal)** located in the third row and second column of the Brightness and Contrast section of the Corrections gallery.
4. Click the **Dalton** image in the Interactive gear to select it, repeat Step 2 to apply the **Red, Accent color 2 Dark** color (located in the second row and third column of the Recolor section of the gallery) to change the gear color to red.
5. With the Dalton image still selected, click the **Corrections** button, and then click **Brightness: -40% Contrast +40%** (located in the fifth row and first column of the Brightness and Contrast section).
6. Click the **Democritus** image in the Online gear to select it, repeat Step 2 to apply the **Blue, Accent color 1 Dark** color located in the second row and second column of the Recolor section of the color gallery.
7. Click cell **A1** to deselect the SmartArt graphic. See Figure D-20.

Figure D-20 Adjusted SmartArt graphic

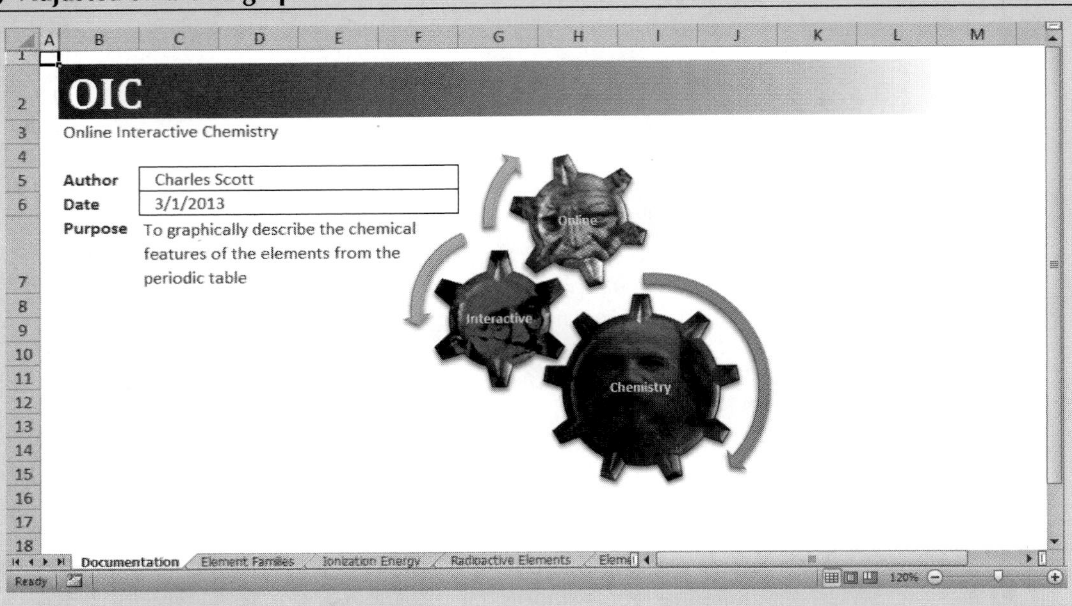

PROSKILLS

Decision Making: Choosing a Graphic Image Type

Excel supports most graphic file formats, so you have a choice of formats for the pictures you import into workbooks. The most common picture format is the **Joint Photographic Experts Group** format, commonly known as **JPEG**. JPEGs are produced by most digital cameras and can support up to 16.7 million colors (which is more colors than the human eye can distinguish). JPEGs can also be compressed to save file space without greatly affecting image quality. You will most often use JPEGs with photo images.

Another popular format is the **Portable Network Graphics** format, or **PNG**. Like JPEGs, PNG graphics allow for picture compression for smaller file sizes. PNG is a better choice than JPEG for storing images that contain line art or text. PNG also supports transparency, allowing graphic images in which sections of the background will appear through the graphic. You will use PNGs for photo images, line art images, and images that require the use of transparency.

For better quality photos, choose the **Tagged Image File Format**, or **TIFF**. Although TIFFs provide higher quality photos, the image files tend to be much larger as well, which increases the workbook's size.

Finally, you can also import logos and formatted documents in **Encapsulated PostScript** format, or **EPS**. Written in the PostScript language, EPS files provide perhaps the highest quality format for clip art files, but require access to a PostScript printer to view the results; otherwise, EPS files are not viewable.

Working with Themes

Charles wants his Periodic Table workbook to apply a consistent design. For example, the various shades of olive green provide the workbook's visual effects, and the text is either Cambria or Calibri font. Charles wants you to look at other design themes.

Applying a Theme

Office supports a library of built-in themes. If a workbook uses only theme colors and fonts, you can switch between themes without editing the styles of individual cells and ranges. You'll change the theme to see its impact on the workbook's appearance.

To apply a different theme:

1. Click the **Page Layout** tab on the Ribbon, click the **Themes** button in the Themes group to open the Themes gallery, and then click **Apex**. The workbook's theme changes from the default Office theme to the Apex theme.
2. View each worksheet in the workbook to see the impact of the Apex theme on the workbook, and note that the fonts and colors changed to reflect the Apex theme.
3. Switch to the **Element Families** worksheet. See Figure D-21.

Figure D-21 Element Families worksheet under the Apex theme

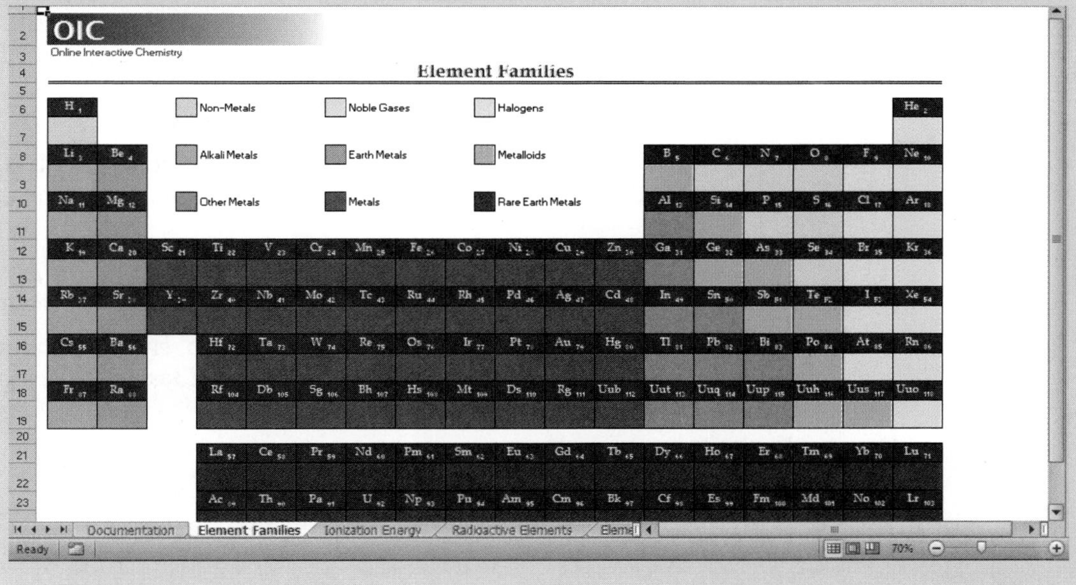

Creating and Saving a Custom Theme

TIP

All theme files have the .thmx file extension.

If the built-in themes do not meet your needs, you can create a custom theme by selecting different fonts, colors, and effects. You can choose from a list of built-in theme fonts, colors, and effects, or you can create your own collection. After the custom theme is complete, you can save it as a permanent file to format other workbooks. You can save theme files in the default theme folders on your computer or in another folder you choose. Files stored in the default theme folders appear in the Themes gallery, which is not the case when you save the theme file elsewhere.

Word and PowerPoint use the same file format for theme files, so you can share custom themes that you create in Excel with other Office files. For example, Charles could create a consistent look and feel for all of his Office files by designing a theme with the fonts, colors, and effects he wants. If Charles later modifies and resaves the custom theme file, the changes will be automatically reflected in every Excel, PowerPoint, and Word document that uses the theme.

REFERENCE

Creating and Saving a Theme

- In the Themes group on the Page Layout tab, click the Themes button, and then click a theme to apply it.
- In the Themes group on the Page Layout tab, click the Fonts button, the Colors button, or the Effects button, and then click the theme fonts, colors, or effects you want to use in the custom theme.
- In the Themes group on the Page Layout tab, click the Themes button arrow, and then click Save Current Theme.
- Type a filename in the File name box, and then click the Save button.

Charles likes the Apex theme's effects, but not its fonts or colors. You'll change the font to Arial and the colors to Metro. Then, you'll save the current theme.

To modify the Apex theme and save the custom theme:

1. In the Themes group on the Page Layout tab, click the **Fonts** button to open the Built-In Fonts gallery, and then click **Office Classic 2**. All of the text in the workbook changes to Arial.
2. In the Themes group, click the **Colors** button to open the Built-In Colors gallery, and then click **Metro**. See Figure D-22.

Figure D-22 **Custom theme applied to the Element Families worksheet**

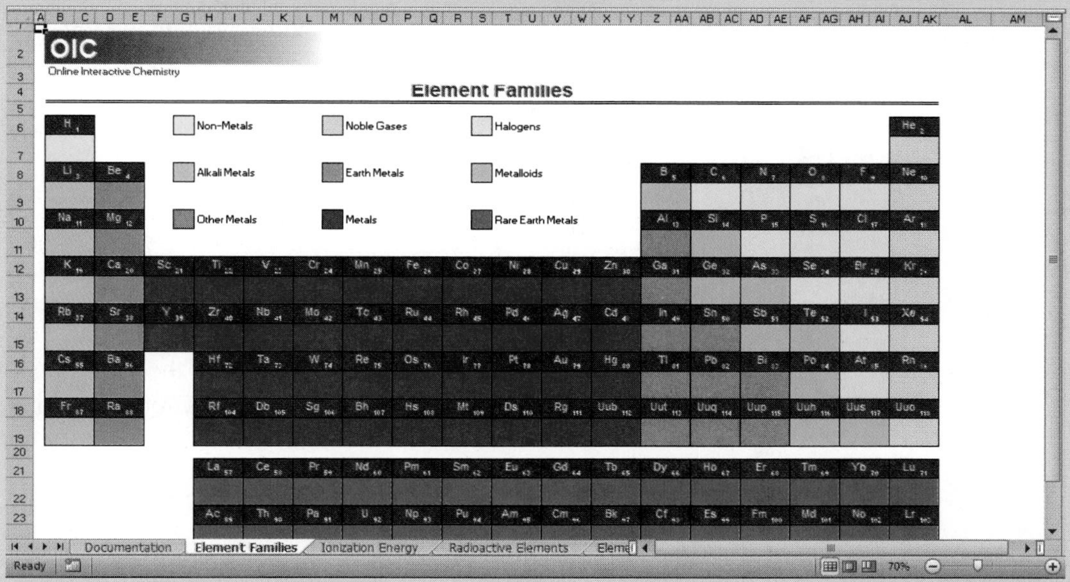

3. View all of the worksheets in the workbook with the custom theme.
4. In the Themes group on the Page Layout tab, click the **Themes** button, and then click **Save Current Theme**. The Save Current Theme dialog box opens, displaying the default Office theme folders.
5. Save the custom theme with the filename **OIC** in the ExcelD\Tutorial folder included with your Data Files.
6. Save and close the Periodic Table workbook.

The Periodic Table workbook is complete. Charles is pleased with the design and graphic elements you added. He plans to produce other workbooks for students to use in their explorations of chemistry concepts.

Practice the skills you learned in the appendix using the same case scenario.

PRACTICE

Review Assignments

Data Files needed for the Review Assignments: Elements.xlsx, Table1.jpg, Table2.jpg, Table3.jpg, Table4.jpg

Charles created another workbook of chemistry information based on the periodic table. This workbook contains charts of the periodic table describing the orbital group of each element, each element's melting and boiling point, and a list of the elements present in the human body. He wants you to add graphical elements to the workbook and create a unified design theme. Complete the following:

1. Open the **Elements** workbook located in the ExcelD\Review folder included with your Data Files, and then save the workbook as **Elements Table**. In the Documentation worksheet, enter your name and the date.
2. Create a new cell style named **ETitle** that uses the following formatting:
   - Font size of 18 point bold with the Olive Green, Accent 3, Darker 50% theme color
   - Text centered horizontally
   - Single thick bottom border in Olive Green, Accent 3, Darker 50% theme color
3. Apply the ETitle cell style to cell B4 in the last five worksheets of the workbook.
4. In the Data worksheet, create a custom table style named **ETable** that uses the following formatting, and then apply it to the Element Data table:
   - A header row with white text on a dark olive background (use the theme color) and a double bottom border
   - Banded rows five stripes high—the first set of stripes has a light green background fill (using the theme colors); the next set of stripes has a white background
5. Switch to the Sub-Orbital Blocks worksheet, which indicates to which of four electron sub-orbital groups each element belongs: S, D, P, and F. The defined name Sub_Orbital_Blocks_Data references all of the data in the table and the entries in the legend. Create the following conditional formatting rules to highlight the values in this range:
   - Highlight cells that contain the "S" character with a medium orange fill color (the tenth theme color).
   - Highlight cells that contain the "D" character with a medium turquoise fill color (the ninth theme color).
   - Highlight cells that contain the "P" character with a medium lavender fill color (the eighth theme color).
   - Highlight cells that contain the "F" character with a medium olive green fill color (the seventh theme color).
   - Hide the cell text of all values in the selected range.
6. Go to the Melting Point worksheet, which contains the melting points of the elements from the periodic table. Display the values from this table using a color scale ranging from a light red theme color for the lowest melting points to a dark red theme color for the highest melting points. Use the defined name Melting_Point to quickly select the data values from the table. Use a gradient fill in cell H9 to indicate the range of colors used in the table.

7. Go to the Boiling Point worksheet and repeat Step 6, using the orange theme color to indicate low to high boiling points.
8. Go to the Human Body worksheet and create a conditional formatting rule that displays a green circle with a white check mark for all cells in the table and legend in place of the value 1. Use the Human_Body_Data defined name to select the appropriate cells in the worksheet.
9. Go to the Documentation worksheet and then insert the Picture Caption List SmartArt graphic (located in the first row and third column of the List category). Add the text labels **Sub-Orbital Blocks**, **Melting Point**, **Boiling Point**, and **Human Body** to the four blocks in the list.
10. Change the Quick Style of the graphic to the Brick Scene style located in the second row and second column of the 3-D section of the Quick Style gallery.
11. Insert the graphic image files **Table1.jpg**, **Table2.jpg**, **Table3.jpg**, and **Table4.jpg** located in the ExcelD\Review folder into the four blocks from the SmartArt graphic.
12. Create a custom theme for the workbook using the Module color theme combined with fonts from the Foundry theme. Save the custom theme with the filename **ETheme** in the ExcelD\Review folder.
13. Apply the following colors to the four graphic images:
    - Display the Sub-Orbital Blocks picture using the Gold, Accent color 1 Light variation located in the third row and second column of the Recolor section in the Color gallery.
    - Display the Melting Point picture using the Aqua, Accent color 2 Dark variation located in the second row and third column of the Recolor section of the color gallery.
    - Display the Boiling Point picture using the Rose, Accent color 3 Dark variation located in the second row and fourth column of the Recolor section.
    - Display the Human Body picture using the Green, Accent color 4 Dark variation located in the second row and fifth column of the Recolor section.
14. Save and close the workbook. Submit the finished workbook and theme file to your instructor, either in printed or electronic form, as requested.

Use the skills you learned to format an attendance report for a water park.

APPLY

Case Problem 1

Data Files needed for this Case Problem: Big.xlsx, Water.jpg

Big Wave Water Park Robert Tru is an operations manager at Big Wave Water Park, a popular indoor/outdoor water park located outside of Greenville, South Carolina. He is preparing an annual report that contains the daily attendance figures at the park and compares the total annual attendance to that of previous years. He wants you to format the workbook. Complete the following:

1. Open the **Big** workbook located in the ExcelD\Case1 folder included with your Data Files, and then save the workbook as **Big Wave** in the same folder. In the Documentation sheet, enter your name and the current date.
2. In the 2013 Attendance worksheet, create a color scale for the daily attendance figures in the range C7:AG18 that displays the days of lowest attendance with a light blue fill and the days of highest attendance with a dark blue fill.

3. Add conditional formatting to the daily attendance figures that highlights the day of highest attendance with a bold font, a white background, and a solid black border.
4. Add a color scale to the monthly totals in the range AH7:AH18 that displays the months of lowest attendance with a light aqua fill and the months of highest attendance with a dark aqua fill.
5. Add conditional formatting to the monthly attendance figures that highlights the month of highest attendance with a white background and a solid black border.
6. In the Yearly Attendance worksheet, replace the values in the change column with an icon set that displays a green up arrow for years the attendance increased compared to the previous year, a yellow horizontal arrow when the attendance was unchanged, and a red down arrow for years the attendance decreased. Center the arrows in the cells.
7. Format the contents with a new table style named **Attendance**. The header row should be displayed in a white font on a dark blue background with a double bottom border. The contents of the table should be displayed in banded rows, starting with a light blue fill color on the first row and alternating with rows with a white fill color.

EXPLORE

8. Insert the picture file **Water.jpg** located in the ExcelD\Case1 folder next to the yearly attendance table. Make the following edits to the picture:
   - Change the picture size to 2.67 inches high by 4 inches wide.
   - Recolor the picture with the Blue, Accent color 1 Light color located in the third row and second column of the Recolor section in the Color gallery.
   - Apply the Reflected Rounded Rectangle picture style (located in the first row and fifth column of the Pictures Styles gallery) to the graphic.
9. Save and close the workbook. Submit the finished workbook to your instructor, either in printed or electronic form, as requested.

Expand on the skills you learned to create a Gantt chart for a video production company.

CHALLENGE

Case Problem 2

Data File needed for this Case Problem: FPS.xlsx

FPS Productions Linda Thomas owns FPS Productions, a video production company located in St. Charles, Missouri, that specializes in creating short videos for local businesses and government agencies. The company just received a contract to create a promotional video for the St. Charles Civic Center. The video must be ready for distribution in four weeks. To keep the project on schedule, Linda wants to create a Gantt chart (a graphical representation of a project with each phase represented as a horizontal bar, with vertical lines often superimposed to indicate the current date to show the progress of the project versus time). Linda asks you to create the Gantt chart. Complete the following:

1. Open the **FPS** workbook located in the ExcelD\Case2 folder included with your Data Files, and then save the workbook as **FPS Productions**. In the Documentation worksheet, enter your name and the date.

2. In the Production Schedule worksheet, you'll create the Gantt chart. Linda already entered the start and stop dates of the eight tasks involved in producing the video. In the range B7:B14, enter formulas to calculate the percentage of each task that has been completed given the task's start and stop dates and the current date in cell E5. (*Hint*: The percentage equals the number of days from the current date shown in cell E5 to the task's start date in column D divided by the number of days allotted to complete each task.)

EXPLORE

3. Replace the percentages in the range B7:B14 with the 5 Quarters icon set. Modify the icon set to display the full circle when the cell's value is greater than or equal to 1; display the three-quarter circle when the cell's value is from 0.75 up to 1; display the half circle when the cell's value is from 0.5 up to 0.75; display the quarter circle when the cell's value is from 0.25 up to 0.5; and display an empty circle when the cell's value is less than 0.25.

EXPLORE

4. Create a conditional formatting rule that places a red right border in the Gantt chart cells that fall on the current date as specified in cell E5. To create the rule, select the range F7:AG14 and create a highlight rule for the cells in the range using a formula. The formula should test whether the value in the cell F$4 (a date from the Gantt chart) is equal to the value in cell $E$5 (the current date). If the function returns the value true, the cell should display a red right border.

EXPLORE

5. Create another conditional formatting rule that highlights the cells in the Gantt chart corresponding to the dates in which the task is performed. To create this rule, add a second highlight rule for the cells in the range F7:AG14 using another formula. The formula should test whether the value in cell F$4 is greater than or equal to the value in cell $D7 (the start date), and whether the value in cell F$4 is less than or equal to the value in cell $E7 (the stop date). If the formula returns a value of true, the cell should have a horizontal gradient fill starting with a white color at the top and ending with a purple color at the bottom. (*Hint*: Use the IF function and the AND function in the formula.)
6. In the Production Tasks worksheet, insert the Continuous Block Process SmartArt graphic (located in the third row and first column of the Process category), and then type the eight task names from the Production Schedule worksheet into the eight blocks on the SmartArt graphic.
7. Format the SmartArt graphic by setting its size to 3.75 inches high by 7 inches wide, changing its color to Colored Fill – Accent 4, and changing its style to the Cartoon Style located in the first row and third column of the 3-D section of the SmartArt Styles gallery.
8. Save and close the workbook. Submit the finished workbook to your instructor, either in printed or electronic form, as requested.

ENDING DATA FILES

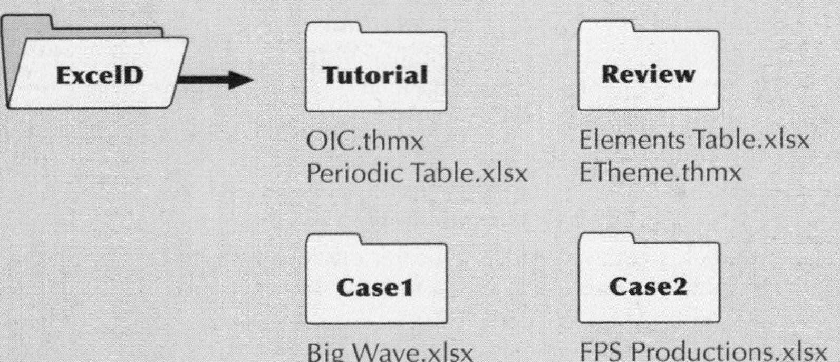

APPENDIX E

Microsoft Office Specialist Certification Skills

EXCEL

OBJECTIVES

- Learn about the Microsoft Office Specialist certification program
- Print cell gridlines and row and column headers
- Set columns to repeat on each printed page
- Work with advanced header and footer print options
- Create a custom view
- Edit a defined name
- Hide and unhide worksheets
- Customize the Excel environment
- Enable and disable automatic workbook calculation
- Set the iterative calculations option
- Apply trendlines in a chart
- Use dual axes in a chart
- Use slicers with data sets from external data connections
- Restrict permissions to a workbook
- Understand CUBE functions
- Insert and modify a screenshot

This appendix provides information about the Microsoft Office Specialist certification program and the benefits of achieving certification. The appendix also presents coverage of additional skills related to the Microsoft Office Specialist Expert exam for Microsoft Excel 2010 that are not covered in the main tutorials and appendices of this text. Finally, the appendix includes a grid showing where the skills for both the Excel 2010 Specialist (Core) exam and the Excel 2010 Expert exam are covered in this text.

STARTING DATA FILES

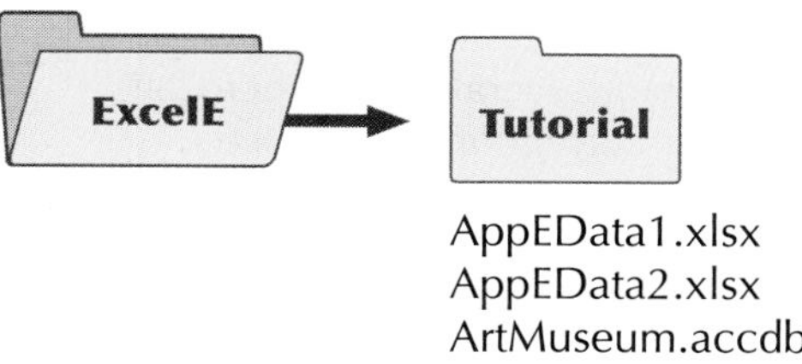

AppEData1.xlsx
AppEData2.xlsx
ArtMuseum.accdb

What Is Microsoft Office Specialist Certification?

Certification is a growing trend in the Information Technology industry whereby a software or hardware company devises and administers exams for users that enable them to demonstrate their ability to use the software or hardware effectively. By passing a certification exam, users prove their competence and knowledge of the software or hardware to prospective employers and colleagues.

The Microsoft Office Specialist program is the only comprehensive, performance-based certification program approved by Microsoft to validate desktop computer skills using the Microsoft Office 2010 programs, including Microsoft Excel. The program provides computer program literacy, measures proficiency, and identifies opportunities for skill enhancement. Successful candidates receive a certificate that sets them apart from their peers in the competitive job market. The certificate is a valuable credential, recognized worldwide as proof that an individual has the desktop computing skills needed to work productively and efficiently. Certification is a valuable asset to individuals who want to begin or advance their computer careers.

The Microsoft Office Specialist exams are developed, marketed, and administered by Certiport, Inc., a company that has an exclusive license from Microsoft. Exams must be taken at an authorized Certiport Center, which administers exams in a quiet room with the proper hardware and software and has trained personnel to manage and proctor the exams.

Go to www.microsoft.com/learning/en/us/certification/mos.aspx#certifications to access the Microsoft Office Specialist Certification page, as shown in Figure E-1.

Figure E-1 **Microsoft Office Specialist Certification page**

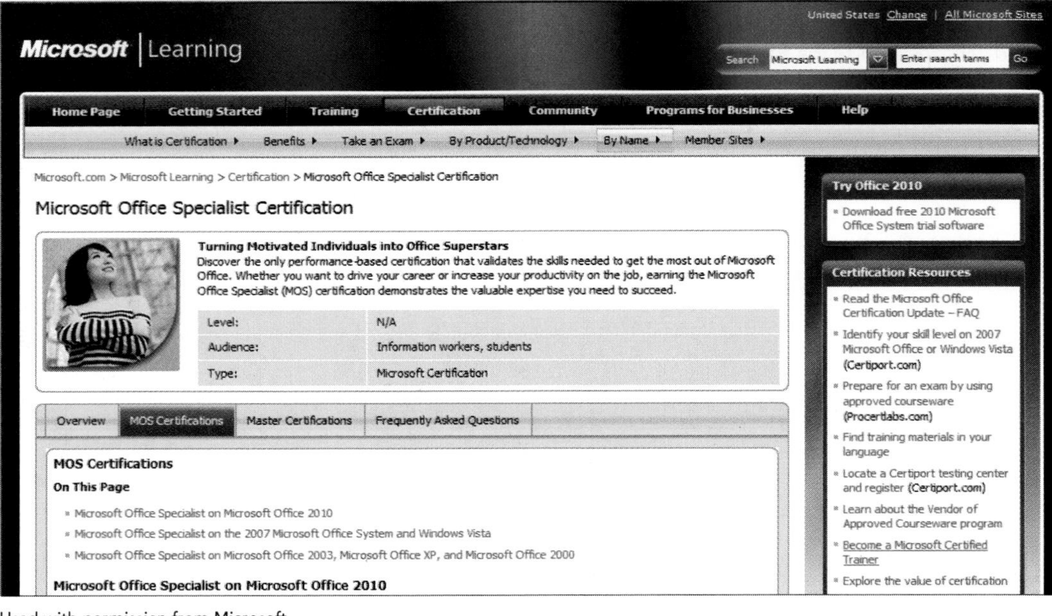

Used with permission from Microsoft.

> **TIP**
> For more information about the exams, view the FAQ documents at www.microsoft.com/certification or www.certiport.com/portal.

Benefits of Achieving Certification

Achieving Microsoft Office Specialist certification in one or several of the Microsoft Office 2010 programs can be beneficial to you and your current or prospective employer. Earning certification acknowledges that you have the expertise to work with Microsoft Office programs. Individuals who are Microsoft Office Specialist certified report increased competence and productivity with Microsoft Office programs, as well as increased credibility with their employers, coworkers, and clients. Certification sets you apart in today's competitive job market, bringing employment opportunities, greater earning potential and career advancement, and increased job satisfaction.

Certification can help you increase your productivity within your current job and is a great way to enhance your skills without taking courses to obtain a new degree. Another benefit of Microsoft certification is that you gain access to a member website, career-building tools, and training. More information about the certification series can be located on the Certiport web site at www.certiport.com/portal, as shown in Figure E-2.

Figure E-2 **Certification information on the Certiport site**

Courtesy of Certiport, Inc. www.certiport.com

Certification Process

> **TIP**
> Course Technology publishes a multitude of Microsoft Office 2010 products that you can use for self-study. Visit www.cengagebrain.com to view the options. You can also purchase the texts directly from this site.

The steps to successfully completing Microsoft Office Specialist Expert Certification for Microsoft Excel are outlined below. The expert-level user should be able to perform many of the advanced skills in the program. Note that the Web addresses shown throughout might change. If you cannot find what you're looking for, go to the main site (www.microsoft.com or www.certiport.com) to search for a topic.

1. Find an authorized testing center near you using the Certiport Center locator at www.certiport.com/Portal/Pages/LocatorView.aspx.
2. Prepare for the exam by selecting the method that is appropriate for you, including taking a class or purchasing self-study materials.
3. Take a practice test (recommended) before taking the exam. To view the practice tests available, go to www.certiport.com/portal. Follow the online instructions for purchasing a voucher and taking the practice test.
4. Contact the Certiport Center and make an appointment for the exam you want to take. Check the organization's payment and exam policies. Purchase an exam voucher at www.certiport.com/portal. Go to the Certiport Center to take the test, and bring a printout of the exam voucher, your Certiport username and password, and a valid picture ID.
5. You will find out your results immediately. If you pass, you will receive your certificate two to three weeks after the date of the exam.

If you do not pass, refunds will not be given. But keep in mind that the exams are challenging and do not become discouraged. If you purchased a voucher with a retake, a second chance to take the exam might be all you need to pass. Check your Certiport Center's exam retake policies for more information.

Inserting Multiple Worksheets at One Time

Although you can insert multiple new worksheets into a workbook one at a time, it's possible to insert multiple worksheets at the same time.

To insert multiple worksheets at the same time:

1. Open the **AppEData1** workbook located in the ExcelE\Tutorial folder included with your Data Files, click the **Enable Editing** button if necessary to remove the workbook from Protected View, and then save the workbook as **AppESolutions1** in the same folder.
2. Click the **Gridlines** worksheet, press and hold the **Shift** key, and then click the **Sales** worksheet.
3. On the Home tab, in the Cells group, click the **Insert button arrow**, and then click **Insert Sheet**. Two worksheets are added to the left of the Gridlines worksheet.
4. Rename the new Sheet1 **PasteSpc**, and then rename the new Sheet2 **Logo**.
5. Save your changes to the workbook.

You can delete multiple sheets at the same time by selecting the sheets you want to delete, clicking the Delete button arrow in the Cells group on the Home tab, and then clicking Delete Sheet.

Printing Cell Gridlines

Normally cell gridlines, the grid of lines separating rows and columns you see on worksheets, are not printed. If you want your printout to include gridlines, you choose the Print option in the Gridlines section of the Sheet Options group on the Page Layout tab.

To print gridlines in printed output of the Gridlines worksheet:

1. Switch to the **Gridlines** worksheet. The worksheet contains a comparison between budgeted and actual cash flow for a budget.
2. Click the **Page Layout** tab on the Ribbon.
3. In the Sheet Options group, click the **Print** check box in the Gridlines section.
4. Click the **File** tab, and then click the **Print** tab to display the print options in Backstage view. The cash budget appears with gridlines in the print preview. See Figure E-3.

Figure E-3 Print preview of budget with gridlines

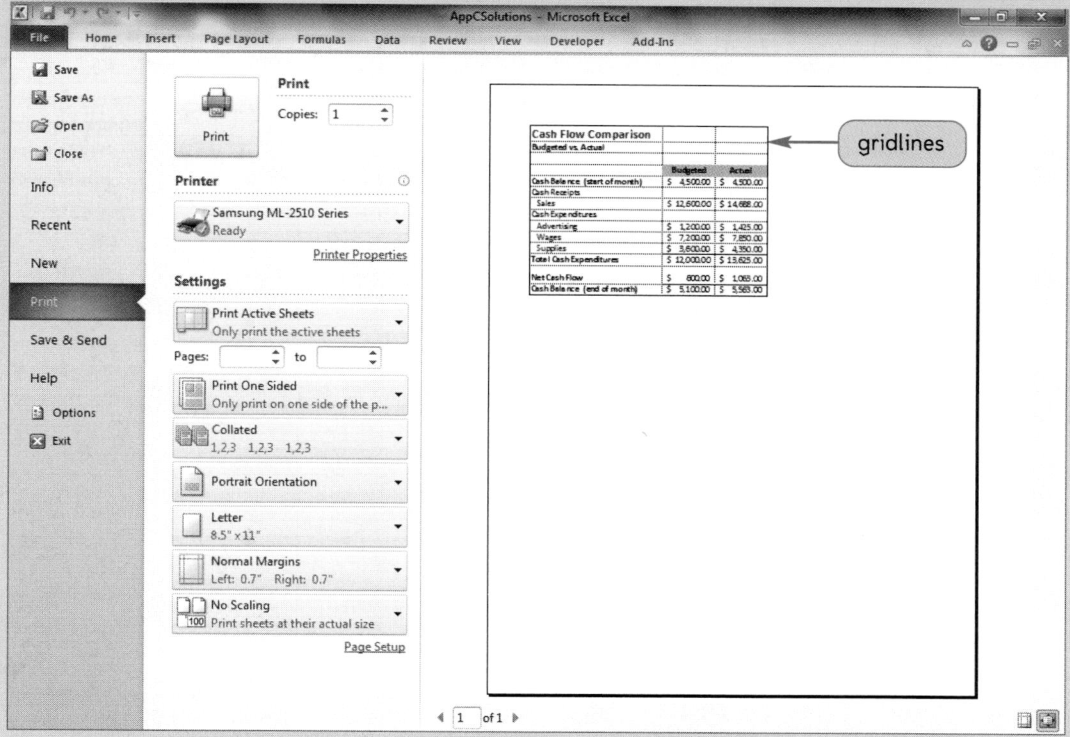

5. Click the **Print** button to print the result, and then click the **Home** tab to return to the Gridlines worksheet.

Printing Row and Column Headers

Normally the row and column headers (column letters and row numbers) for a worksheet are not printed. If you want your printout to include these headers, you select the Print check box in the Headings section of the Sheet Options group on the Page Layout tab.

You will print the formulas used to calculate the cash budget. You will include column and row headers as part of the printout so you can see where on the worksheet these formulas are entered.

To print row and column headers in the Gridlines worksheet:

1. In the Gridlines worksheet, press the **Ctrl+`** keys. The worksheet changes to formula view.
2. If necessary, change the column width of column A to **14**, and then click cell **A1**.
3. Click the **Page Layout** tab on the Ribbon.
4. In the Sheet Options group, click the **Print** check box in the Headings section of the tab.
5. Click the **File** tab and then click the **Print** tab to display the print options. Notice the cash budget formulas appear in the print preview with column and row headings. See Figure E-4.

Figure E-4 Row and column headers in print preview

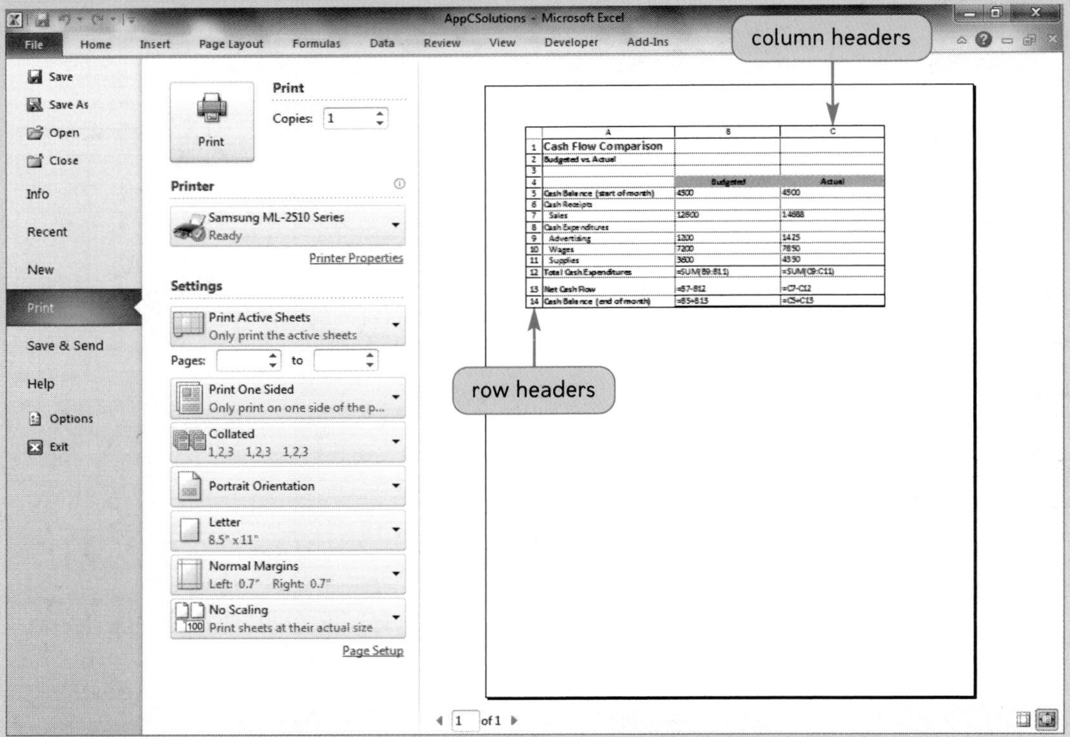

6. Click the **Print** button to print the result.
7. Click the **Home** tab to return to the Gridlines worksheet.

Printing Columns to Repeat on Each Printed Page

Sometimes a large worksheet has too many columns to fit on one printed page. If the first column in the worksheet (which will print on the first page only) contains the row labels for the worksheet, it can make the second and subsequent pages of the printed worksheet hard to interpret. In Excel, you can set the print options to include the first column of the worksheet on each page of the printed output.

To include column A on each page of the printed output of the Sales worksheet:

1. Switch to the **Sales** worksheet. Notice the Sales worksheet has sales data in columns A through Y for various sales representatives. Column A contains the row labels identifying the sales representatives whose sales data appears in each row.
2. Click the **File** tab, and then click the **Print** tab to display print options in Backstage view. The first page of the worksheet appears in the print preview.

3. Click the **Next Page** button ▶ to view the second page of the worksheet. Notice on page 2 the sales rep names do not appear in the first column of this page of the printed output, making it difficult to know which rep is responsible for the sales units in each row. You want to print column A on both pages 1 and 2 of the worksheet.
4. Click the **Page Layout** tab, and then in the Page Setup group, click the **Print Titles** button. The Page Setup dialog box opens.
5. If necessary, click the **Sheet** tab, click the **Columns to repeat at left** box, and then in the Sales worksheet, click the **column A** row header. The reference $A:$A appears in the Columns to repeat at left box.
6. Click the **Print Preview** button to return to the Print tab in Backstage view, and then navigate to the second page in the print preview to verify that the sales rep names appear in the first column of the second page of the worksheet. See Figure E-5.

Figure E-5 **Preview of printed output with repeated first column on page 2**

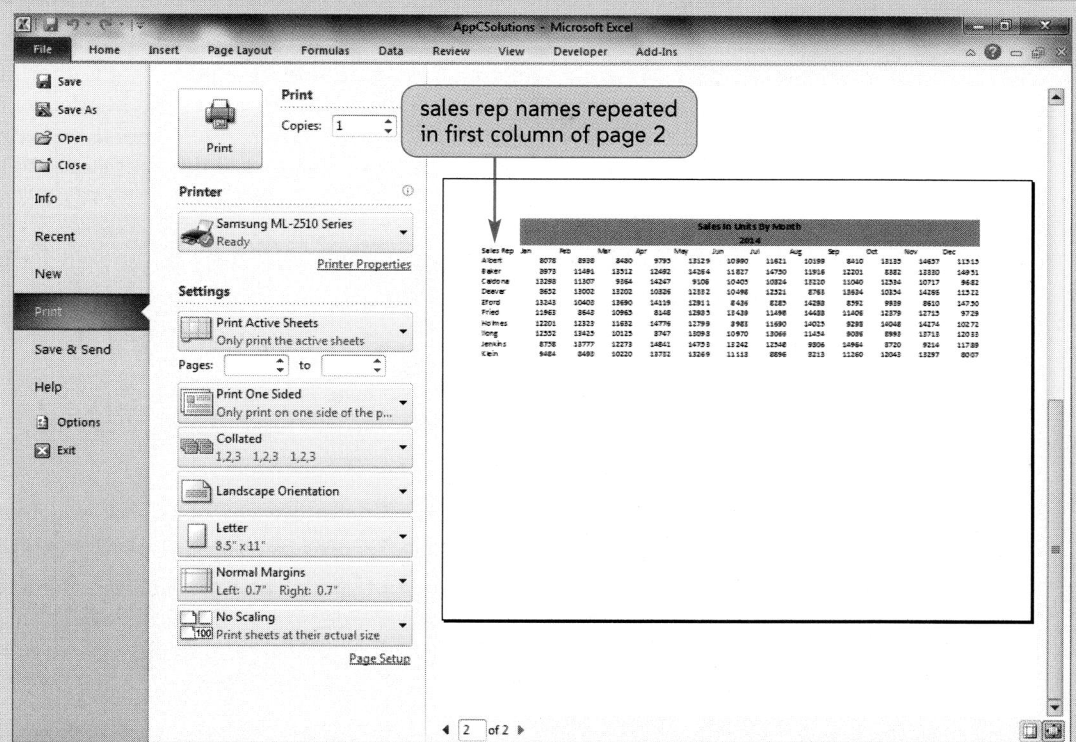

7. Click the **Print** button to print the worksheet, and then click the **Home** tab to return to the Sales worksheet.

Working with Advanced Header and Footer Print Options

In the last set of steps, you worked with the Page Setup dialog box. There are several advanced printing options available in the Page Setup dialog box on the Header/Footer tab that provide flexibility when printing headers and footers in worksheets. These include:

- **Different first page check box** – This option lets you display a different header and footer on the first page of your worksheet than on the other pages in the worksheet. Once you check this option, edit the first page's header and footer as you want. Then, edit any header or footer other than the one on the first page to display what you want on subsequent pages.
- **Different odd and even pages check box** – This option lets you create one header and footer for all even-numbered pages and one for all odd-numbered pages. This is useful if you want to print your worksheet book style and want page numbers, for example, to be at the left and right edges of the paper.
- **Scale with document check box** – This option automatically increases and decreases the size of the header and footer to properly fit the page.
- **Align with page margins check box** – As you change the page margins, this option changes the location of the header and footer so they are centered in relation to the margins.

The TOC worksheet contains an outline for a book that will print over multiple pages. You will print it with the title "Table of Contents" as the header on the first page. On subsequent even-numbered pages, the text "New Perspectives Series" will appear in the header; and on odd-numbered pages, the text "Microsoft Excel 2010" will appear.

To create a separate header for the first page, and different odd- and even-numbered page headers:

1. Switch to the **TOC** worksheet.
2. Click the **Page Layout** tab on the Ribbon, and then click the **Print Titles** button in the Page Setup group. The Page Setup dialog box opens.
3. If necessary, click the **Header/Footer** tab.
4. Click the **Different odd and even pages** check box, and then click the **Different first page** check box. Check marks appear in both check boxes.
5. Click the **Custom Header** button to open the Header dialog box, and then click the **First page header** tab (if necessary). See Figure E-6. Three tabs appear in this dialog box. You want the text "Table of Contents" to appear centered in the header on the first page of the printed worksheet.

Figure E-6 Header dialog box

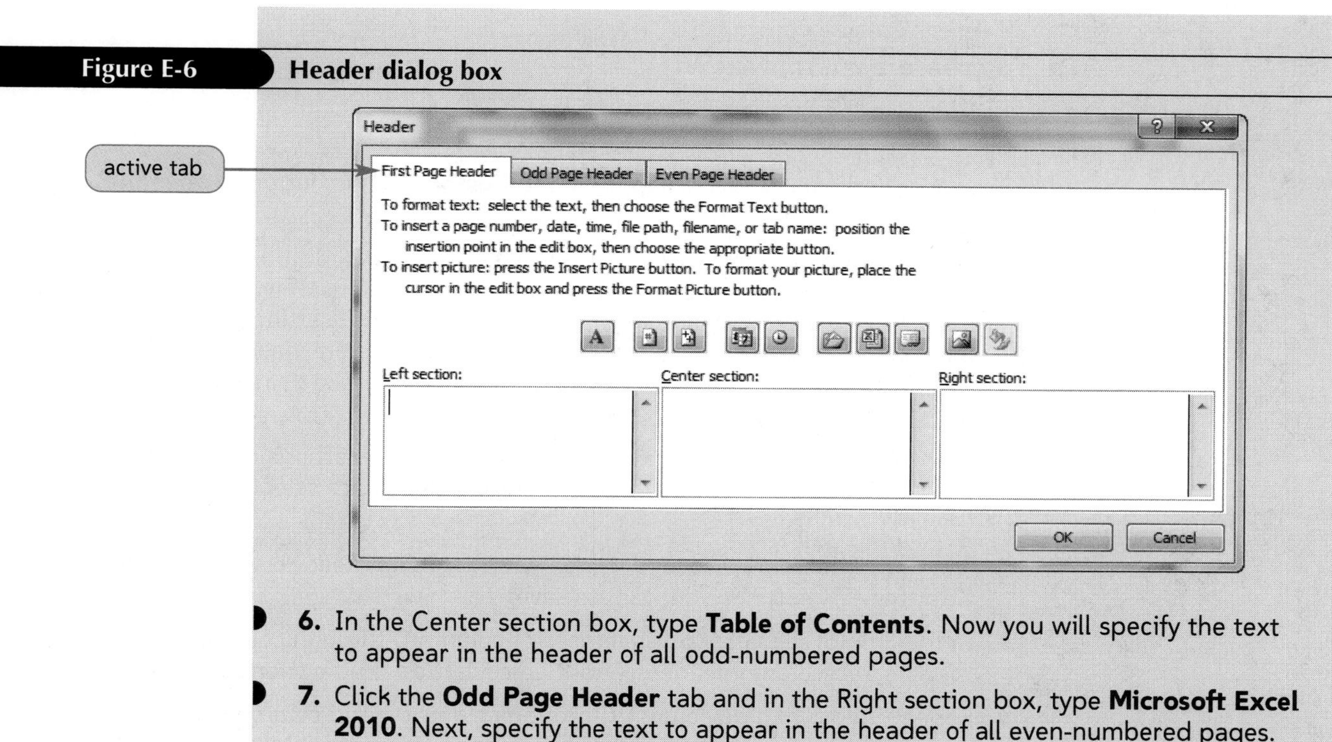

6. In the Center section box, type **Table of Contents**. Now you will specify the text to appear in the header of all odd-numbered pages.
7. Click the **Odd Page Header** tab and in the Right section box, type **Microsoft Excel 2010**. Next, specify the text to appear in the header of all even-numbered pages.
8. Click the **Even Page Header** tab and in the Left section box, type **New Perspectives Series**.
9. Click the **OK** button to close the Header dialog box and then click the **Print Preview** button in the Page Setup dialog box to display a preview of the worksheet on the Print tab in Backstage view. "Table of Contents" appears as the header at the top of page 1.
10. Navigate to the second page. The header on the even-numbered page includes the text "New Perspectives Series."
11. Navigate to the third page. The header on the odd-numbered page is "Microsoft Excel 2010."
12. Click the **Home** tab to return to the TOC worksheet, and then save your changes to the workbook.

TIP

To print the entire workbook, select the Print Entire Workbook option in the Settings section on the Print tab in Backstage view.

Creating a Custom View

Custom views let you save a combination of view settings in a workbook, such as zoom, visible columns, and filters, so that when you want to use a particular view you select it from a list in the Custom Views dialog box, and Excel applies it to the active worksheet.

In the Employee Data worksheet, you want to view and edit all columns in the worksheet, but you want to be able to exclude several columns when you print this data. You will hide columns C to F, I to K, and O to T and create a custom view. Before you modify your view settings for a particular purpose, you should save the current default settings as a custom view. This provides you with an easy way to return to the unmodified default view.

To create a custom view:

1. Switch to the **Employee Data** worksheet, and then click the **View** tab on the Ribbon.
2. In the Workbook Views group, click the **Custom Views** button to open the Custom Views dialog box.
3. Click the **Add** button to open the Add View dialog box. In this dialog box, you can specify a name for the custom view, and what types of settings will be saved in the custom view. For example, you can check the Print settings check box to save the print settings for the workbook as part of the custom view. You also can click the Hidden rows, columns, and filter settings check box to save these types of settings as part of the custom view.
4. In the Name box, type **Normal**, make sure the Print settings check box and the Hidden rows, columns, and filter settings check box are selected, and then click the **OK** button.

   Now you will create a second custom view. You first need to set up the worksheet with the view settings you want to save.
5. In the Employee Data worksheet, select column **C** through column **F**, right-click the selected column headers, and then click **Hide** on the shortcut menu.
6. Repeat Step 5 to hide column **I** through column **K**, and column **O** through column **T**. Now only columns A, B, G, H, L, M, and N are visible with data.
7. In the Workbook Views group on the View tab, click the **Custom Views** button to open the Custom Views dialog box, and then click the **Add** button to open the Add View dialog box.
8. In the Name box, type **HideColumns**, make sure the Print settings check box and the Hidden rows, columns, and filter settings check box are selected, and then click the **OK** button.

Now apply the custom views you created.

To apply a custom view:

1. In the Workbook Views group on the Views tab, click the **Custom Views** button to open the Custom Views dialog box.
2. In the Views box, click **Normal**, and then click the **Show** button. The default view settings are applied and all columns are now displayed.

   Now apply the HideColumns custom view.
3. In the Workbook Views group, click the **Custom Views** button to open the Custom Views dialog box.
4. In the Views box, click **HideColumns**, and then click the **Show** button. The columns C to F, I to K, and O to T are hidden.

Using the Percent Symbol in a Formula

How does Excel perform calculations when the percent (%) symbol is encountered in a formula? Recall that if a formula contains more than one arithmetic operator, Excel performs the calculations using an order of precedence. Excel first calculates any value within parentheses, next the percent (%) operator is calculated, then the ^ operator (exponentiation) is performed, then multiplication (*) and division (/) are calculated, and finally addition (+) and subtraction (-) are calculated.

For example, the following formula

=10^2*3%

returns the value 3. First, the percent operation 3% is calculated (.03). Next, exponentiation, 10^2, is performed (100). In the final calculation, the two values (.03 and 100) are multiplied to produce the final result of 3.

Editing a Defined Name

You have learned how to create and assign defined names to cells and ranges. You also can edit the defined name if the range reference changes.

In the Extension worksheet, the VLOOKUP function uses the employee ID to retrieve the employee name and phone extension from a list of employees. The data for the lookup table is referenced using the defined range name *EmployeeExt*.

To use the employee ID to search for an employee name and phone extension:

1. Switch to the **Extension** worksheet.
2. In cell A2, enter **3**. The employee name Charl appears in cell B2 and extension 309 appears in cell C2.
3. Click cell **B2** and review the VLOOKUP formula in the formula bar. The defined name EmployeeExt is used to reference the employee data in the range A5:C11.

You need to add two employees to the employee list.

To add new employees to the employee list:

1. In cell A12, enter **8**; in cell B12, enter **Howard**; and then in cell C12, enter **678**.
2. In A13, enter **9**; in cell B13, enter **Ireland**; and then in cell C13, enter **876**.

   Now test the application.

3. In cell A2, enter **2**. The employee name Byter appears in cell B2 and the phone extension 567 appears in cell C2.
4. In cell A2, enter **8**. The error value, #N/A, is displayed in cells B2 and C2.

The error values appear in cells B2 and C2 because the defined name EmployeeExt references the range A5:C11. It needs to be modified to reference the range A5:C13, which includes the information for the two employees you added to the employee list.

To edit the range reference of a defined name:

1. Click the **Name Box arrow** and then click **EmployeeExt**. The range A5:C11 is highlighted in the worksheet. The defined name only references the range A5:C11; it does not reference all the employee data.
2. Click cell **A1** to deselect the selected range, and then click the **Formulas** tab.
3. In the Defined Names group, click the **Name Manager** button. The Name Manager dialog box opens.
4. If necessary, select the **EmployeeExt** defined name.
5. In the Refers to box, change =Extension!$A$5:$C$11 to **=Extension!$A$5:$C$13** and then click the **Close** button.
6. Click the **Yes** button in the message box to confirm the changes made to the name reference. The error values in cells B2 and C2 are replaced by the employee name Howard and the phone extension 678.
7. Click the **Name Box arrow** and then click **EmployeeExt**. The range A5:C13 is highlighted in the worksheet. The defined name now references all the employee data in the list.
8. Click cell **A1** to deselect the range.

Hiding and Unhiding Worksheets

There are times when information is needed in a worksheet for calculation purposes but you prefer that the worksheet is not seen by other users of the workbook. You can hide a worksheet, and when you do so, its tab is hidden but the worksheet remains within the workbook file.

Next you will hide the Extension worksheet.

To hide and unhide the Extension worksheet:

1. Right-click the Extension sheet tab, and then click **Hide** on the shortcut menu. The Extension tab is no longer visible. Now restore the Extension worksheet.
2. Right-click any sheet tab, and then click **Unhide** on the shortcut menu to display the Unhide dialog box.
3. In the Unhide box, click **Extension** if necessary to select it, and then click the **OK** button. The Extension sheet tab is visible again.

Changing the Default Font and Font Size

You can change the default font type, style, size, color, and other font effects using the options in the Excel Options dialog box, which you open by clicking the Options command in Backstage view. Once the new font style settings are set as default, all new workbooks created by Excel will use the new font settings. Workbooks created before the settings were changed will still use the previous setting.

For example, you change the default font type and font size by doing the following:

1. Click the File tab on the Ribbon to open Backstage view, and then click the Options command to open the Excel Options dialog box.
2. If necessary, click General in the left pane of the dialog box.
3. In the When creating new workbooks section of the right pane, click the Use this font arrow and select the desired font from the menu.
4. Click the Font size arrow and select the desired font size.
5. Click the OK button, and then click the OK button again in the message box informing you that you need to restart Excel so that the changes take effect. You will need to restart Excel to allow changes for default font and font size to take effect.

Customizing Ribbon Groups

In Excel you can change the Ribbon to suit your work style. Among many other customization features, you can minimize the Ribbon, create or remove tabs and groups, hide tabs or commands, and rename tabs or commands.

Next you will remove the Symbols group from the Insert tab.

To remove the Symbols group from the Insert tab:

1. Click the **File** tab on the Ribbon to open Backstage view, and then click the **Options** command to open the Excel Options dialog box.
2. In the left pane, click **Customize Ribbon**. The right pane of the dialog box displays options for customizing the Ribbon. See Figure E-7.

Figure E-7 Customize Ribbon options

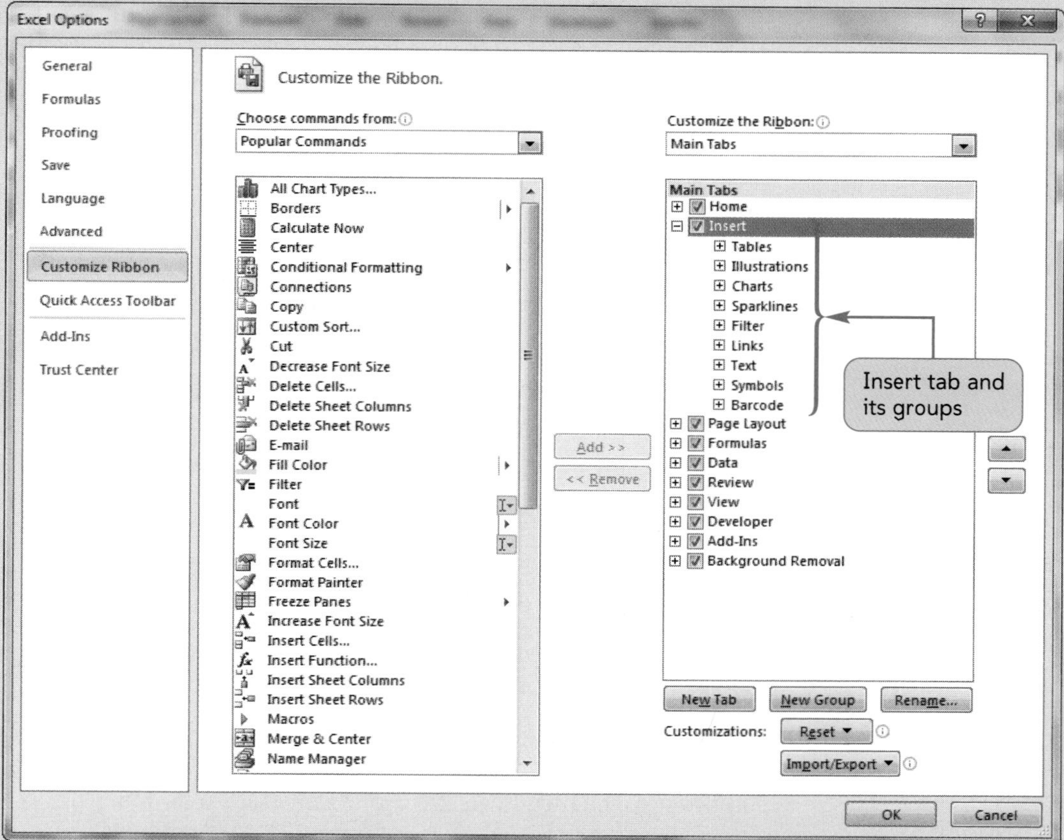

3. In the right pane, click the plus symbol to the left of **Insert tab** in the list on the right. The numerous groups included on the Insert tab are displayed.
4. Click **Symbols** and then click the **Remove** button. The Symbols group is removed from the list of groups for the Insert tab.
5. Click the **OK** button, and then click the **Insert** tab. Notice the Symbols group no longer appears as a group on the Insert tab.

You can return the Ribbon to its default state or restore a tab you have removed or modified to its original state.

To restore the Symbols group to the Insert tab:

1. Click the **File** tab on the Ribbon to open Backstage view, and then click the **Options** command to open the Excel Options dialog box.
2. In the left pane, click **Customize Ribbon**.
3. If necessary, click the **Insert** tab in the list on the right to select it.
4. Click the **Reset** button at the bottom of the dialog box, and then click **Reset only selected Ribbon tab**.
5. Click the **OK** button to return to the worksheet. Notice the Symbols group appears on the Insert tab again.

Setting AutoSave and Managed Version

It is now easier to recover an Excel file if you close your file without saving, or you want to review or return to an earlier version of the file you're currently working in.

As with earlier versions of Office, enabling *AutoRecover Excel 2010* will save versions while you are working in your file at the time interval you set. You can also choose to keep the last AutoSaved version of a file in case you accidentally close that file without saving, so that you can restore it the next time that you open the file. Also, while you are working in your file, you can access a listing of the AutoSaved files from Backstage view.

You will confirm that the AutoRecover and AutoSave features of Excel are enabled.

To check AutoRecover and AutoSave settings:

1. Click the **File** tab on the Ribbon to open Backstage view, and then click the **Options** command to open the Excel Options dialog box.
2. In the left pane, click **Save** to display the Customize how workbooks are saved options. See Figure E-8.

Figure E-8 Customizing how workbooks are saved

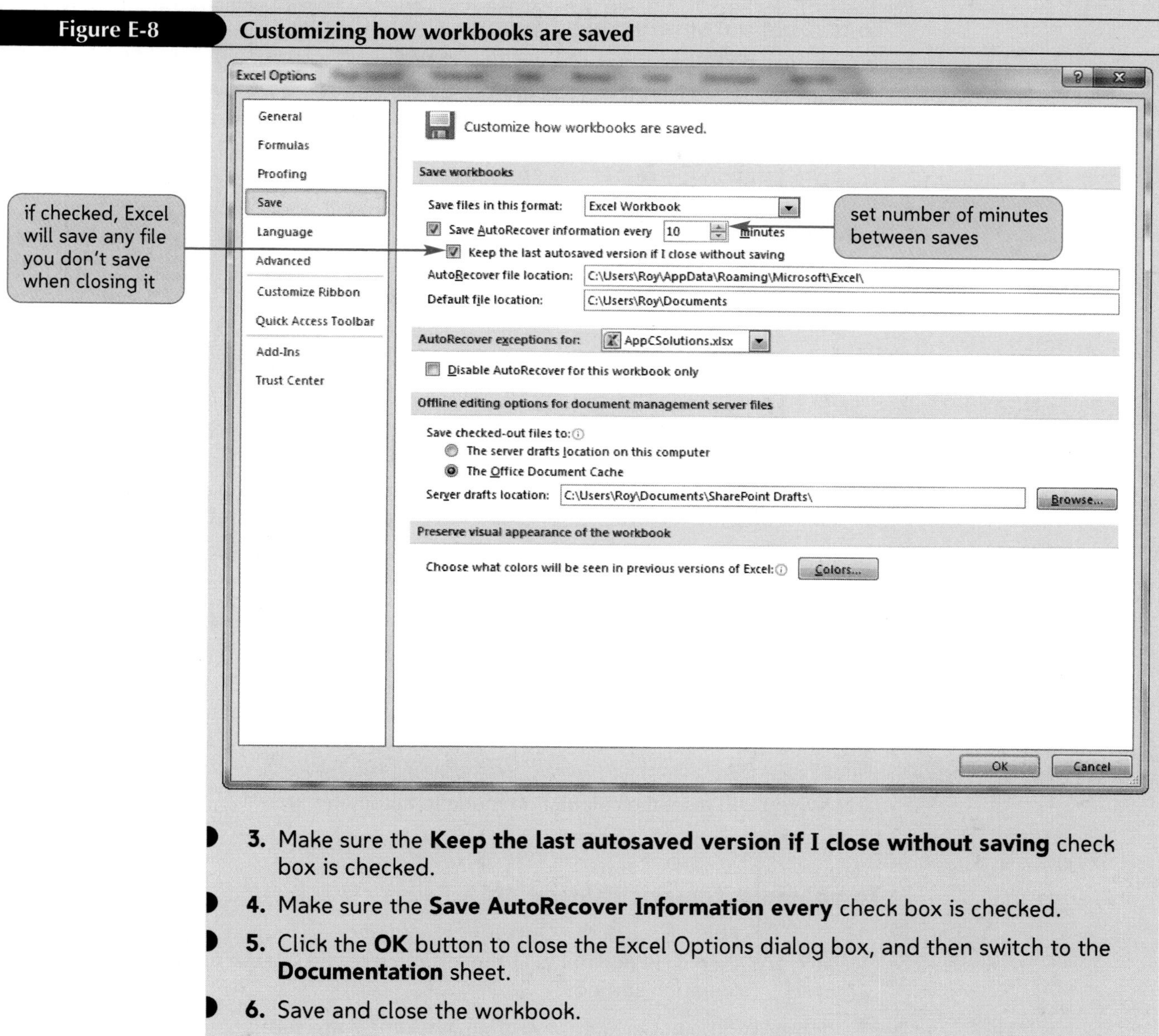

3. Make sure the **Keep the last autosaved version if I close without saving** check box is checked.
4. Make sure the **Save AutoRecover Information every** check box is checked.
5. Click the **OK** button to close the Excel Options dialog box, and then switch to the **Documentation** sheet.
6. Save and close the workbook.

Enabling or Disabling Automatic Workbook Calculation

Excel has two main calculation modes, manual and automatic, which let you control when calculation occurs:

- **Automatic calculation**–Formulas and their dependent cells that have changes are automatically recalculated whenever you make a change.
- **Manual calculation**–Formulas are only recalculated when you request it by pressing the F9 key.

Automatic recalculation is the default setting when you open a new workbook and when you are editing an existing workbook. However, you can control when and how Excel recalculates formulas by changing to manual calculation mode.

To disable automatic calculation in a workbook:

1. Open the **AppEData2** workbook located in the ExcelE\Tutorial folder included with your Data Files, click the **Enable Editing** button if necessary to remove the workbook from Protected View, and then save the workbook as **AppESolutions2** in the same folder. The workbook contains five worksheets that you will use as you work through the rest of this appendix.
2. In the Documentation worksheet, enter your name in cell B3 and the date in cell B4, and then switch to the **ManualRecalc** worksheet. The worksheet contains a cash flow comparison for a cash budget.
3. In cell C5, type **5000**, and then press the **Enter** key. When you changed the start of month actual cash balance value in this cell from $4,500 to $5,000, the cash balance for the month's end that appears in cell C14 is immediately changed to $6,063. The calculation occurred automatically.

   Now, disable automatic calculation.
4. Click the **File** tab to open Backstage view, click the **Options** command in the navigation bar, and then click **Formulas** in the left pane of the Excel Options dialog box to display the options for changing Excel's calculation settings.
5. In the Workbook Calculation section, click the **Manual** option button, and then click the **OK** button to return to the worksheet. Now test the manual calculation.
6. In cell C5, type **6000**, and then press the **Enter** key. Notice the end of month cash balance in cell C14 remains $6,063. No calculations have occurred. Now you will manually calculate the formulas in the worksheet.
7. Press the **F9** key. Excel calculates the formulas in the worksheet and the end of the month cash balance in cell C14 changes to $7,063.

Now you will reset the calculation mode to automatic.

To enable automatic calculation:

1. Click the **File** tab, click the **Options** command to open the Excel Options dialog box, and then click **Formulas** in the left pane to display the options for changing Excel's calculation settings.
2. In the Workbook Calculation section, click the **Automatic** option button, and then click the **OK** button.

Setting the Iterative Calculations Option

When a formula refers back to the cell into which it is entered, either directly or indirectly, it creates a circular reference. A circular reference can have a significant impact on performance because it can iterate indefinitely. **Iteration** is the repeated recalculation of a worksheet until a specific numeric condition is met. By default, iterative calculations are turned off in Excel. You can handle a circular reference by doing one of the following: remove the circular reference or enable iterative calculations.

If you want to keep the circular reference, you can enable iterative calculations but you must determine how many times the formula should recalculate. When you turn on iterative calculations without changing the values for maximum iterations or maximum change, Excel stops calculating after 100 iterations or after all values in the circular reference change by less than 0.001 between iterations, whichever comes first. However, you can control the maximum number of iterations and the amount of acceptable change.

To allow iterative calculations you do the following:

1. Click the File tab to open Backstage view, click the Options command in the navigation bar, and then click Formulas in the left pane of the Excel Options dialog box.
2. In the Calculation options section in the right pane, select the Enable iterative calculation check box.
3. To set the maximum number of times that Excel will recalculate, type the number of desired iterations in the Maximum Iterations box. The higher the number of iterations, the more time that Excel needs to calculate a worksheet.
4. To set the maximum amount of change you will accept between calculation results, type the desired amount in the Maximum Change box. The smaller the number, the more accurate the result and the more time that Excel needs to calculate a worksheet.
5. Click the OK button to close the Excel Options dialog box.

Applying Advanced Chart Features Using Trendlines

One reason for creating charts is to reveal patterns in the data. In Excel you can add a trendline to a chart to help interpret the data. Instead of connecting every point in a data series, as you do with a line chart, a **trendline** shows a line that best represents all the data on the chart.

You will use a trendline in an XY scatter chart.

To create an XY scatter chart and add a trendline to it:

1. Switch to the **Trendline** worksheet, and then select the range **A4:B13**.
2. Click the **Insert** tab on the Ribbon, click the **Scatter** button in the Charts group, and then click the **Scatter with only Markers** chart (first chart in the gallery). The scatter chart appears to the right of the chart data in the worksheet.
3. Click the **Chart Tools Layout** tab, click the **Legend** button in the Labels group, and then click **None** to remove the legend from the chart. Now add the trendline.
4. In the Analysis group on the Chart Tools Layout tab, click the **Trendline** button.
5. Click the **Linear Trendline** option to add a linear trendline for the selected data. A solid black line appears on the chart, following the general path of the scattered points in the chart.
6. Move the chart so its upper-left corner is aligned with cell D4. See Figure E-9.

Figure E-9 XY scatter chart with trendline

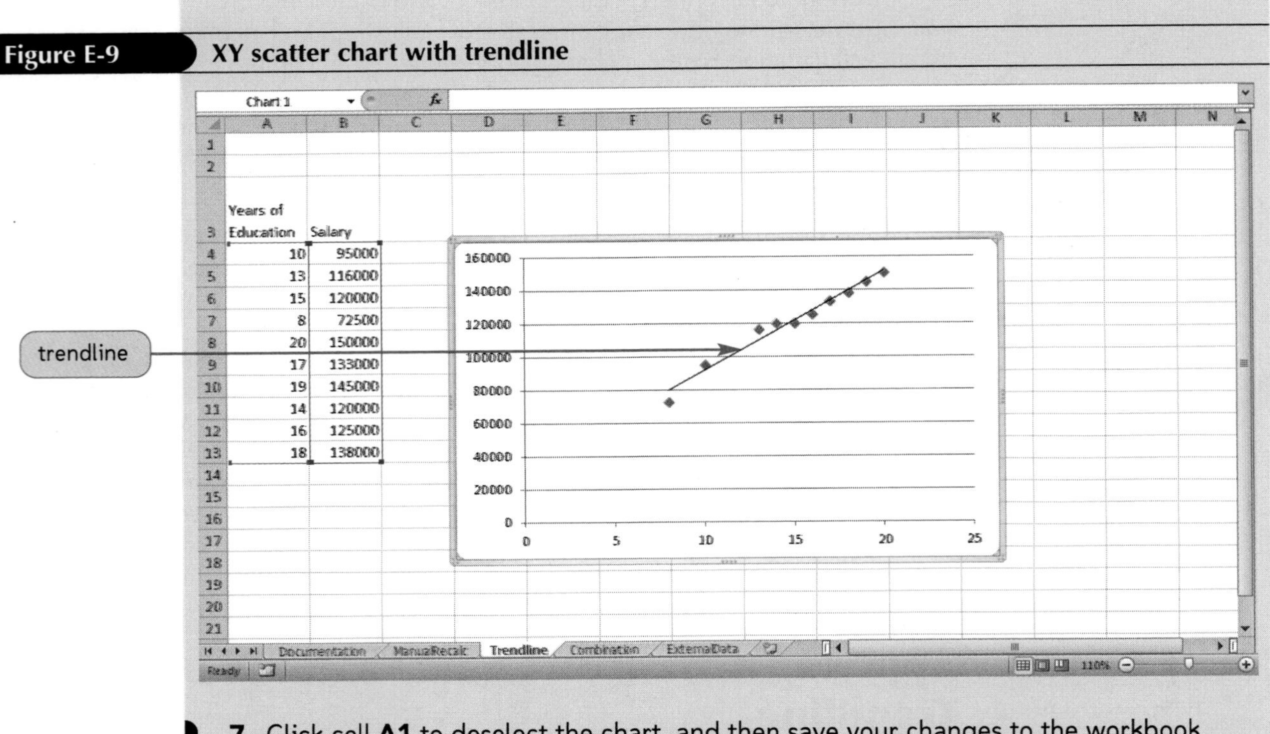

7. Click cell **A1** to deselect the chart, and then save your changes to the workbook.

Applying Advanced Chart Features Using Dual Axes

When the range of values for different data series in your chart varies widely, or when you have mixed types of data, you can plot one or more data series from a different chart type on a secondary vertical (value) axis of the chart. For example, you can combine a column chart with a line chart for a visual effect that might make the chart easier to understand.

You will combine the monthly average high temperatures and average precipitation for Beijing, China in a dual axis chart.

To create a dual axis chart:

1. Switch to the **Combination** worksheet, and then select the range **A4:C16**.
2. Click the **Insert** tab on the Ribbon, click the **Column** button in the Charts group, and then click the **Clustered Column** chart (first chart in the 2-D Column section). The column chart is inserted to the right of the chart data in the worksheet.

   Notice that the Rainfall data series (the red bars) is difficult to see using one axis for both sets of data. To emphasize the different types of information in this chart, you will display the rainfall data series on a secondary vertical axis.

3. Right-click any bar in the **Rainfall** data series, and then click **Change Series Chart Type** on the shortcut menu to open the Change Chart Type dialog box.
4. Click the **Line** chart type (the first chart in the Line section), and then click the **OK** button. The Rainfall data series is now displayed as a red line in the chart.
5. Right-click the **Rainfall** data series (the red line), and then click **Format Data Series** on the shortcut menu to open the Format Data Series dialog box.
6. Click the **Secondary Axis** option button in the Plot Series On section, and then click the **Close** button. See Figure E-10. Excel creates a new axis scale on the right side of the chart and uses this scale to plot the rainfall data.

Figure E-10 Temperature and rainfall data series on a dual axis chart

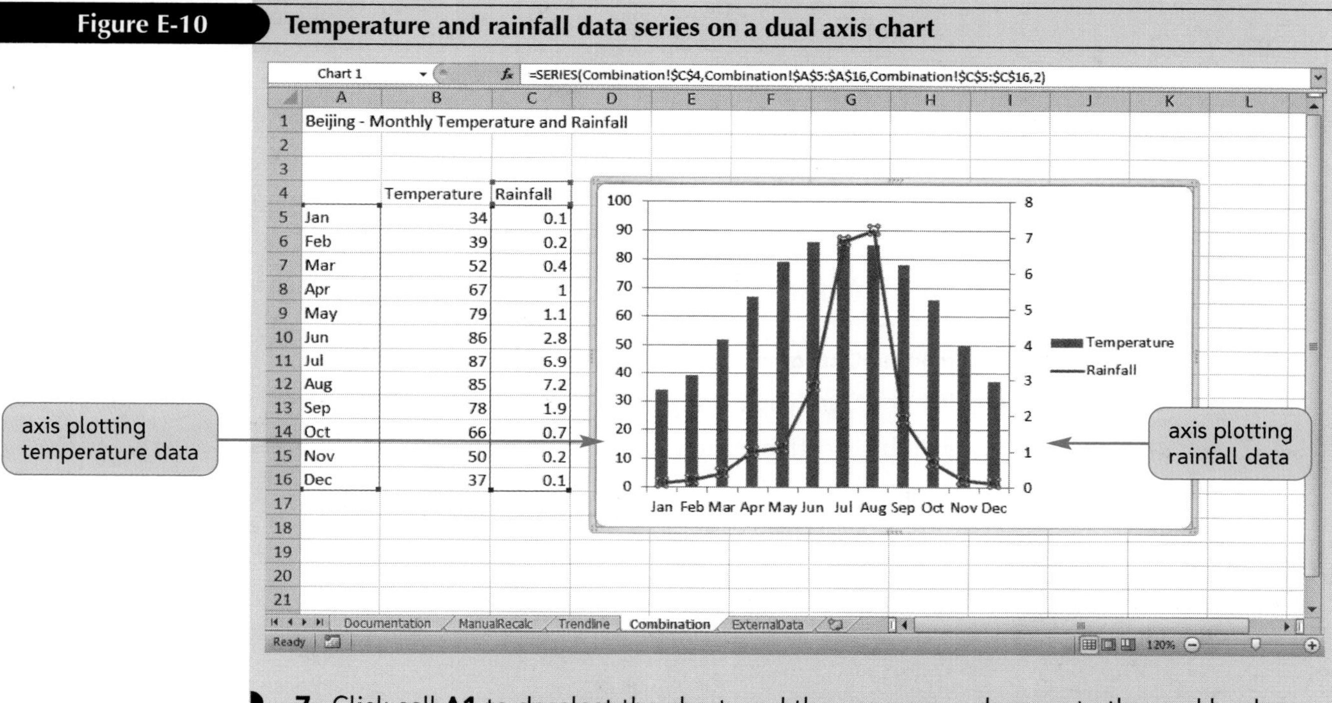

7. Click cell **A1** to deselect the chart, and then save your changes to the workbook.

Using Slicers with Data Sets from External Data Connections

In addition to creating a PivotTable from data within a workbook, you can build a PivotTable based on records you select from an external database.

You'll create a PivotTable using data from an Access database. First you will connect to the Access database.

To connect to an Access database:

1. Switch to the **ExternalData** worksheet, click cell **A1** if necessary to make it the active cell, and then click the **Data** tab on the Ribbon.
2. In the Get External Data group, click the **From Access** button to open the Select Data Source dialog box. This dialog box is similar to the Open dialog box.

3. Navigate to the ExcelE\Tutorial folder included with your Data Files, click the **ArtMuseum** Access database file, and then click the **Open** button. The Select Table dialog box opens.
4. Click the **ArtCollection** table, and then click the **OK** button to open the Import Data dialog box.
5. Click the **PivotTable Report** option button. Selecting this option ensures the data from the database will not be imported; only a PivotTable report will be created.
6. If necessary, click the **Existing worksheet** option button to place the PivotTable in the ExternalData worksheet, and then click the **OK** button. The framework for creating a PivotTable appears in the worksheet.

Now create a PivotTable.

To create the PivotTable:

1. In the PivotTable Field List, click the **Location** check box. The Location field appears in the Row Labels box.
2. Click the **Appraised Value** check box. The Sum of Appraised Value appears in the Values box.
3. Click the **Category** check box. The Category field appears in the Row Labels box.
4. Click the **Condition** check box. The Condition field appears in the Row Labels box.
5. Drag the Location button from the Row Labels box to the Report Filter box.
6. Format the PivotTable report so the Sum of Appraised Value column is formatted with Accounting Number format with no decimal places. See Figure E-11.

Figure E-11 PivotTable using external data

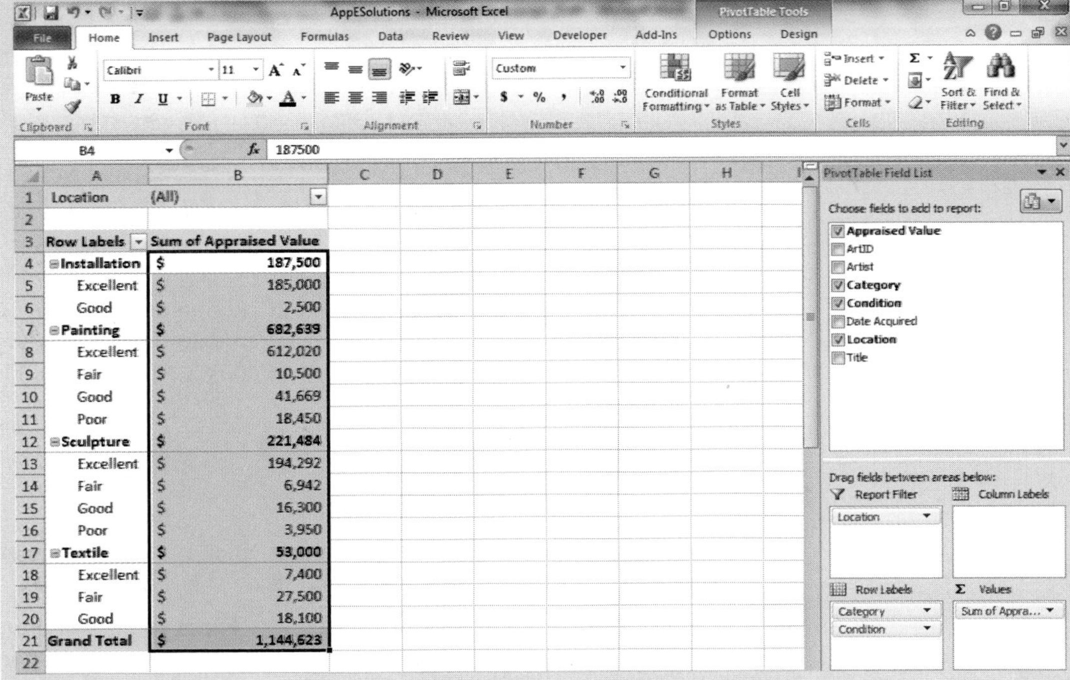

Now add slicers to make it easier to filter the PivotTable.

To add Location, Category, and Condition slicers to the PivotTable:

1. If necessary, click the **PivotTable Tools Options** tab on the Ribbon. In the Sort & Filer group, click the **Insert Slicer** button to open the Insert Slicers dialog box. The PivotTable fields are listed in this dialog box.
2. Click the **Location** check box, the **Category** check box, and the **Condition** check box, and then click the **OK** button.
3. Size and place the three slicer controls in the worksheet as shown in Figure E-12.

Figure E-12 **PivotTable with resized and relocated slicer controls**

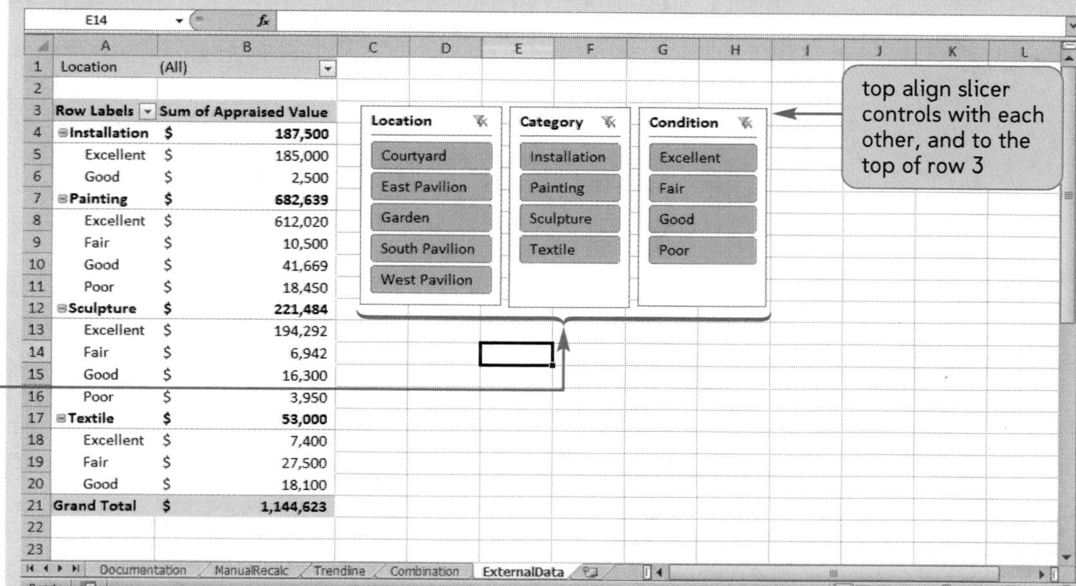

resize slicer controls to be the same size and to remove excess white space below the buttons

4. In the Location slicer control, click the **East Pavilion** button, press and hold the **Ctrl** key, click the **South Pavilion** button, click the **West Pavilion** button, and then release the Ctrl key.
5. In the Category slicer control, click the **Painting** button.
6. In the Condition slicer control, click the **Excellent** button, press the **Ctrl** key, click the **Good** button, and then release the Ctrl key. See Figure E-13.

Figure E-13 Filtered PivotTable

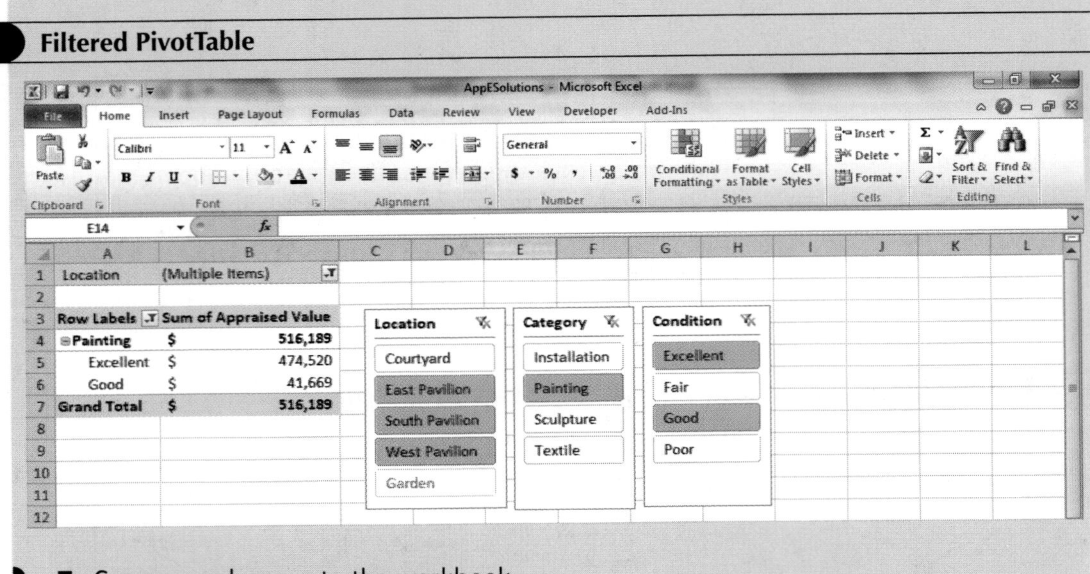

7. Save your changes to the workbook.

Restricting Permissions to a Workbook

You can add advanced restrictions to your workbook using the Information Rights Management (IRM) add-in. Authors can restrict permission for workbooks on a user and/or file basis.

Authors using this add-in can set the following permission levels:

- **Read**–Users with Read permission can view (read) a workbook, but they don't have permission to edit, print, or copy it.
- **Change**–Users with Change permission can read, edit, and save changes to a workbook, but they don't have permission to print it.
- **Full Control**–Users with Full Control permission have full authoring permissions and can do anything with the workbook that an author can do, such as set expiration dates for content, prevent printing, and give permissions to users. After permission for a workbook has expired for authorized users, the workbook can be opened only by the author or by users with Full Control permission. Authors always have Full Control permission.

Authors use the Permission dialog box to give users Read and Change access, and to set expiration dates for content. For example, if you are the author of a workbook, you can give a coworker permission to read an Excel worksheet but not change it. You can give another coworker permission to change the workbook and allow this individual to save the workbook. You can also decide to limit user access to this workbook for a set number of days before the permission to use the workbook expires.

To set the Restrict Permission options you do the following:

1. Click the File tab on the Ribbon to open Backstage view, and then click the Info tab in the navigation bar to display information about the workbook.

2. In the Permissions section, click the Protect Workbook button, and then point to Restrict Permission by People.
   Note: If you do not see the Restrict Permission by People option, your computer might not be configured to use IRM. To use IRM in Office 2010, the minimum required software is Windows Rights Management Services (RMS) Client Service Pack 1 (SP1). Also, if this is the first time you are using the feature, you might be prompted to install the Information Rights Management add-in and sign up for this free service.
3. Click the Restricted Access or Manage Credentials options on the Restrict Permission by People menu. If you select Restricted Access, the Permission dialog box opens and you can then assign the appropriate access levels you want for each user. If you select Manage Credentials, the Select User dialog box opens, and you can add appropriate credentials for each user.

Introducing CUBE Functions

OLAP (online analytical processing) cubes can be thought of as extensions to the two-dimensional spreadsheet. For example, a company might wish to analyze some financial data by product, by time-period, by city, by type of revenue and cost, and by comparing actual data with a budget. These additional methods of analyzing the data are known as dimensions. Because there can be more than three dimensions in an OLAP system, the term *cube* is sometimes used.

In Excel, Microsoft provides seven spreadsheet functions that return information from cubes. Figure E-14 explains the purpose of Excel's CUBE functions:

Figure E-14 **CUBE function**

Function Name and Arguments	Description
CUBEKPIMEMBER(connection,kpi_name,kpi_property)	Returns key performance indicator (KPI) and displays KPI name in cell
CUBEMEMBER(connection,member_expression)	Returns member from cube
CUBEMEMBERPROPERTY(connection,member_expression,property)	Returns value of member property from cube
CUBERANKEDMEMBER(connection,Set_expression,Rank)	Returns n^{th} or ranked member in cube
CUBESET(connection,Set_expression)	Defines a calculated set of members by sending a set expression to the cube on the server, creates the set, and then returns the set to Excel
CUBESETCOUNT(Set)	Returns the number of items in a set
CUBEVALUE(connection,member_expression1,member_expression2,...)	Returns an aggregated value from the cube

Here is an example using the CUBE function, CUBEVALUE. Assume you are looking for the Sum of the Sales Amount (SumofSalesAmount) of Bikes (Category) for Fiscal Year 2012 (FiscalYear) for Australia (Country).

The CUBEVALUE() function to get this value for "Bikes" in Australia for Fiscal Year 2012:

=CUBEVALUE("PowerPivot Data","[SumofSalesAmount]","[Country].[Australia]","[Category].[Bikes]","[FiscalYear].[2012]")

The CUBEVALUE function returns a single total value.

Inserting and Modifying a Screenshot

Office 2010 includes a built-in tool to capture and insert images from your computer screen. To capture a screen image, click the Insert tab on the Ribbon and then click the Screenshot button in the Illustrations group. A gallery opens displaying thumbnails of all open windows on your desktop. You can choose to take a screenshot of one of these open windows or you can click the Screen Clipping button to select a portion of an open window for the screenshot. When the screenshot is inserted into your worksheet, it is inserted as a picture. You can then modify the screenshot using the tools on the Picture Tools Format tab.

ENDING DATA FILES

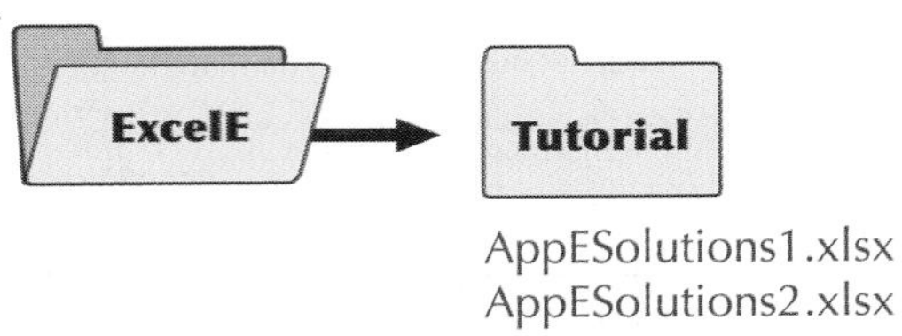

AppESolutions1.xlsx
AppESolutions2.xlsx

Microsoft Office Specialist: Excel 2010 Core Certification Skills Reference

Managing the Worksheet Environment

Skill	Pages Where Covered
Navigate through a worksheet	
Use hot keys	EX 6-EX 7
Use the Name box	EX 424-EX 425
Print a worksheet or workbook	
Print only selected worksheets	EX 317
Print an entire workbook	EX E9
Construct headers and footers	EX 105
Apply printing options	
Scale	EX 47
Print titles	EX 104
Page setup	EX 101-EX 107
Print area	EX 102
Gridlines	EX E4-EX E5
Personalize the environment using Backstage	
Manipulate the Quick Access Toolbar	EX 732-EX 735
Customize the Ribbon	
Tabs	EX 454, EX 472-EX 473
Groups	EX E13-EX E14
Manipulate Excel default settings (Excel Options)	EX 736-EX 739, EX E12-EX E13
Manipulate workbook properties (document panel)	EX C12-EX C21
Manipulate workbook files and folders	
Manage versions	EX E14-EX E15
AutoSave	EX E14-EX E15

Creating Cell Data

Skill	Pages Where Covered
Construct cell data	
Use paste special	
Formats	EX 81
Formulas	EX 81
Values	EX 81, EX A5
Preview icons	EX 80-EX 81
Transpose rows	EX 81
Transpose columns	EX 81
Operations	
Add	EX 81
Divide	EX 81
Comments	EX 81
Validation	EX 81
Paste as a link	EX 81
Cut	EX 28
Move	EX 26
Select cell data	EX 24
Apply AutoFill	
Copy data	EX 141-EX 147
Fill a series	EX 143-EX 147
Preserve cell format	EX 143
Apply and manipulate hyperlinks	
Create a hyperlink in a cell	EX 338
Modify hyperlinks	EX 340
Modify hyperlinked cell attributes	EX 340
Remove a hyperlink	EX 340

Formatting Cells and Worksheets

Skill	Pages Where Covered
Apply and modify cell formats	
Align cell content	EX 72-EX 73
Apply a number format	EX 68-EX 71
Wrapping text in a cell	EX 11-EX 12
Use Format Painter	EX 79-EX 80
Merge or split cells	
Use Merge & Center	EX 74
Merge Across	EX 74
Merge cells	EX 74-EX 75
Unmerge cells	EX 74
Create row and column titles	
Print row and column headings	EX E5-EX E6
Print rows to repeat with titles	EX 104
Print columns to repeat with titles	EX E6-EX E7
Configure titles to print only on odd or even pages	EX E8
Configure titles to skip the first worksheet page	EX E8
Hide or unhide rows and columns	
Hide or unhide a column	EX 101
Hide or unhide a row	EX 101
Hide a series of columns	EX E9-EX E10
Hide a series of rows	EX 101
Manipulate Page Setup options for worksheets	
Configure page orientation	EX 44
Manage page scaling	EX 47
Configure page margins	EX 107
Change header and footer size	EX 107
Create and apply cell styles	
Apply cell styles	EX 84-EX 85
Construct new cell styles	EX D2-EX D5

Managing Worksheets and Workbooks

Skill	Pages Where Covered
Create and format worksheets	
Insert worksheets	
Single	EX 37
Multiple	EX E4
Delete worksheets	
Single	EX 38
Multiple	EX E4
Reposition worksheets	EX 38
Copy worksheets	EX 38
Move worksheets	EX 38
Rename worksheets	EX 38
Group worksheets	EX 304
Apply color to worksheet tabs	EX 64
Hide worksheet tabs	EX E12
Unhide worksheet tabs	EX E12
Manipulate window views	
Split window views	EX 261
Arrange window views	EX 324
Open a new window with contents from the current worksheet	EX 324
Manipulate workbook views	
Use Normal workbook view	EX 43
Use Page Layout workbook view	EX 43-EX 44
Use Page Break workbook view	EX 43-EX 44
Create custom views	EX E9-EX E10

Applying Formulas and Functions

Skill	Pages Where Covered
Create formulas	
Use basic operators	EX 30
Revise formulas	EX 390, EX 396
Enforce precedence	
Order of evaluation	EX 30-EX 31
Precedence using parentheses	EX 31
Precedence of operations for percent vs. exponentiation	EX E11
Apply cell references in formulas	
Relative and absolute references	EX 118-EX 127

Skill	Pages Where Covered
Apply conditional logic in a formula	
Create a formula with values that match conditions	EX 367
Edit defined conditions in a formula	EX 384, EX 396
Use a series of conditional logic values in a formula	EX 382
Apply named ranges in formulas	
Define ranges in formulas	EX 423, EX 429
Edit ranges in formulas	EX C15
Rename a named range	EX 427
Apply cell ranges in formulas	
Enter a cell range definition in the formula bar	EX 431-EX 432
Define a cell range	EX 431-EX 432

Presenting Data Visually

Skill	Pages Where Covered
Create charts based on worksheet data	EX 172-EX 175
Apply and manipulate illustrations	
Insert	EX D19
Position	EX D19
Size	EX D23
Rotate	EX D21-EX D25
Modify Clip Art SmartArt	EX D21-EX D25
Modify Shape	EX D21-EX D25
Modify Screenshots	EX E24
Create and modify images by using the Image Editor	
Make corrections to an image	
Sharpen or soften an image	EX D23
Change brightness	EX D23
Change contrast	EX D23
Use picture color tools	EX D21
Change artistic effects on an image	EX D23
Apply Sparklines	
Use Line chart types	EX 211-EX 214
Use Column chart types	EX 212
Use Win/Loss chart types	EX 212
Create a Sparkline chart	EX 211-EX 214
Customize a Sparkline	EX 214-EX 215
Format a Sparkline	EX 214-EX 215
Show or hide data markers	EX 215

Sharing Worksheet Data with Other Users

Skill	Pages Where Covered
Share spreadsheets using Backstage	
Send a worksheet via E-mail or Skydrive	EX 348
Change the file type to a different version of Excel	EX A14
Save as PDF or XPS	EX 460
Manage comments	
Insert	EX 449
View	EX 450
Edit	EX 450
Delete comments	EX 450

Analyzing and Organizing Data

Skill	Pages Where Covered
Filter data	
Define a filter	EX 252-EX 253
Apply a filter	EX 253-EX 255
Remove a filter	EX 255
Filter lists using AutoFilter	EX 255-EX 256
Sort data	
Use sort options	
Values	EX 244-EX 249
Font color	EX 246
Cell color	EX 246
Apply conditional formatting	
Apply conditional formatting to cells	EX 400-EX 404
Use the Rule Manager to apply conditional formats	EX 402
Use the IF function to apply conditional formatting	EX 400
Clear rules	EX D9
Use icon sets	EX D15
Use data bars	EX 216-EX 218

Microsoft Office Specialist: Excel 2010 Expert Certification Skills Reference

Sharing and Maintaining Workbooks

Skill	Pages Where Covered
Apply workbook settings, properties, and data options	
Set advanced properties	EX C12-EX C14
Save a workbook as a template	EX 340-EX 348
Import and export XML data	EX 666-EX 673
Apply protection and sharing properties to workbooks and worksheets	
Protect the current sheet	EX 445-EX 446
Protect the workbook structure	EX 447-EX 448
Restrict permissions	EX E22-EX E23
Require a password to open a workbook	EX 446
Maintain shared workbooks	
Merge workbooks	EX C10-EX C12
Set Track Changes options	EX C5-EX C8

Applying Formulas and Functions

Skill	Pages Where Covered
Audit formulas	
Trace formula precedents	EX 535-EX 538
Trace dependents	EX 535-EX 538
Trace errors	EX 535-EX 538
Locate invalid data	EX 438-EX 442, EX 444
Locate invalid formulas	EX 536
Correct errors in formulas	EX 538-EX 540
Manipulate formula options	
Set iterative calculation options	EX E16-EX E17
Enable or disable automatic workbook calculations	EX E16-EX E17
Perform data summary tasks	
Use an array formula	EX 573
Use a SUMIFS function	EX 407-EX 411, EX B9-EX B14
Apply functions in formulas	
Find and correct errors in functions	EX 538-EX 540
Apply arrays to functions	EX 573
Use Statistical functions	EX 407-EX 411, EX B9-EX B14
Use Date functions	EX 155-EX 156
Use Time functions	EX 155-EX 156

Skill	Pages Where Covered
Use Financial functions	EX 492-EX 504
Use Text functions	EX A3-EX A10
Cube functions	EX E23-EX E24

Presenting Data Visually

Skill	Pages Where Covered
Apply advanced chart features	
Use Trend lines	EX E17-EX E18
Use Dual axes	EX E18-EX E19
Use chart templates	EX 177-EX 179
Use Sparklines	EX 211-EX 215
Apply data analysis	
Use automated analysis tools	EX 438-EX 444
Perform What-If analysis	EX 558-EX 561
Apply and manipulate PivotTables	
Manipulate PivotTable data	EX 270-EX 295
Use the slicer to filter and segment your PivotTable data in multiple layers	EX 285-EX 287
Apply and manipulate PivotCharts	
Create PivotChart	EX 291-EX 292
Manipulate PivotChart data	EX 292-EX 293
Analyze PivotChart data	EX 292-EX 293
Demonstrate how to use the slicer	
Choose data sets from external data connections	EX E19-EX E22

Working with Macros and Forms

Skill	Pages Where Covered
Create and manipulate macros	
Run a macro	EX 460-EX 462
Run a macro when a workbook is opened	EX 461
Run a macro when a button is clicked	EX 468-EX 470
Record an action macro	EX 462-EX 463
Assign a macro to a command button	EX 469
Create a custom macro button on the Quick Access Toolbar	EX 732-EX 734
Apply modifications to a macro	EX 464-EX 467
Insert and manipulate form controls	
Insert form controls	EX 468-EX 471
Set form properties	EX 468-EX 471

GLOSSARY/INDEX

Note: Boldface entries include definitions.

SPECIAL CHARACTERS

< (left angle bracket), EX 152
> (right angle bracket), EX 152
<> (not equal to operator), EX 152
(number sign), EX 394
& (ampersand), EX A6
* (asterisk), EX 30, EX 31
+ (plus sign), EX 30, EX 31
- (minus sign), EX 30, EX 31
/ (slash), EX 30, EX 31
= (equal sign), EX 33, EX 152
>= (greater than or equal to operator), EX 152
<= (less than or equal to operator), EX 152
^ (caret), EX 30, EX 31

A

absolute reference A cell reference that remains fixed when the cell formula is copied to a new location. EX 116, EX 118, EX 121–125, EX 126

accent A theme color variation. EX 62

Accept or Reject Changes dialog box, EX C9

Access. *See* Microsoft Access 2010

Accounting style, EX 58

active cell The cell currently selected in the active worksheet. EX 3
  changing, EX 6

active sheet The sheet currently displayed in the workbook window. EX 2

ActiveCell object, EX 705

ActiveChart object, EX 705

ActiveSheet object, EX 705

ActiveWindow object, EX 705

ActiveWorkbook object, EX 705

Add Constraint dialog box, EX 597

Add Procedure dialog box, EX 694

add-in A program that adds customized commands and features to Microsoft Office programs such as Excel. EX 593–595

Add-Ins dialog box, EX 594

addition, formulas to calculate totals, EX 66–67, EX 88–89

addition operator (+), EX 30, EX 31

Address bar, FM 7

adjacent range A group of cells in a single rectangular block of cells. EX 23
  selecting, EX 25

Advanced Filter dialog box, EX B4–B5

advanced filtering A filter that displays a subset of the rows in an Excel table or range of data based on the criteria in the criteria range. EX B2–B5

aligning cell contents, EX 72–73

alignment button list, EX 73

Alignment group, EX 58, EX 74–75

Alignment option, Format Cells dialog box, EX 77

amortization schedule A table that specifies how much of each loan payment is devoted toward interest and toward repaying the principal. EX 491, EX 500–502

ampersand (&), Concatenation operator, EX A6

AND function A logical function that returns a TRUE value if all of the logical conditions are true, and a FALSE value if any or all of the logical conditions are false. EX 364, EX 365, EX 370–373

And logical operator, EX 727

answer report A report created by Solver that summarizes the results of a successful solution by displaying information about the objective cell, changing cells, and constraints. EX 600–602

Application object, EX 703

Apply names dialog box, EX 434

approximate match lookup A lookup that occurs when the value entered falls within a range of values in the first column of the lookup table. EX 388, EX 390–393

area chart, EX 174

argument The numbers, text, or cell references used by the function to return a value. EX 117

arithmetic operator An mathematical symbol representing the operations of addition, subtraction, multiplication, division, or exponentiation. EX 30–31

Arrange All button, EX 321

array formula A formula that performs multiple calculations in a single step, returning either a single value to one cell or multiple values to several cells. EX 573

arrow button, FM 2

ascending order The arrangement of text alphabetically from A to Z, numbers from smallest to largest, and dates from oldest to newest. EX 244

Assign Macro dialog box, EX 469

asterisk (*), multiplication operator, EX 30, EX 31

audition a workbook, EX 534–542
  evaluating formulas, EX 538–540
  tracing errors, EX 536–538
  Watch Window, EX 540–542

Auto Fill Options button, EX 143

AutoComplete The feature that helps make entering repetitive text easier; as you type text into the active cell, Excel displays text that begins with the same letters as a previous entry in the same column. EX 11

AutoFill A feature that copies content (text, values, or formulas) and formats from a cell or range into an adjacent cell or range. EX 139, EX 140–147
  Auto Fill Options button, EX 143
  fill handle, EX 141–142
  filling a series, EX 143–147

autofit To eliminate empty space by matching the row height or column width to its tallest or longest cell entry. EX 17–18

automatic color A color choice option based on your Windows default text and background colors, usually represented as black text on a white background. EX 62

automatic page break A page break Excel inserts automatically after fitting as much of the content on single page as possible without resizing the text. EX 103

AutoSum A button that inserts Excel functions to sum, average, or count all the values in a column or row, or display the minimum or maximum value in a column or row. EX 23, EX 35–36

AVERAGE function A function that returns the average value of the range. EX 117, EX 129, EX 132–134

AVERAGEIF function A function that calculates the average of values in a range that match criteria you specify. EX 399, EX 408–411

AVERAGEIFS function A function that calculates the average of values within a range that meet multiple criteria. EX B9–B10, EX B13–B14

axis, chart
  editing, EX 187–189
  horizontal, EX 171
  labels, EX 192, EX 195–199
  primary, EX 187
  secondary, EX 187
  3-D charts, EX 209
  titles, EX 201–202
  vertical (value), EX 170

B

Back A button that takes you back to your previous location in your sequence of opened locations; appears next to the Address bar in a folder window. FM 2, FM 7

background
  fill color, EX 59, EX 64–65
  images, EX 59, EX 65

Backstage view The File tab of the Ribbon, which provides access to file-level options and program settings. EX 22, OFF 2
  printing workbooks, EX 45–46
  saving files, OFF 20
  saving workbooks to SkyDrive, EX 349–350

backup A duplicate copy of a file. FM 6

backward compatibility, workbooks, EX C20

Banded Columns option, table styles, EX 93

banded rows A table style in which different fill colors are applied to adjacent rows in an Excel table. EX 82, EX 91–92, EX 93

Banded Rows option, table styles, EX 93

bar chart A column chart turned on its side so that the length of each bar is proportional to its value. EX 174, EX 184

bind The process by which an XML element is attached to a specific cell in the workbook. EX 670

binding constraint A constraint that Solver is forced to include as part of the final solution. EX 602

border A line you add along an edge of a cell to improve readability of the data. EX 59
  cells, EX 76–77
  column labels, setting color, EX 78–79

Border option, Format Cells dialog box, EX 77

break-even analysis. *See* cost-volume-profit (CVP) analysis

bubble chart, EX 174

budget, planning and presenting, EX 161

button An icon you click to access a command. OFF 2
  appearance on Ribbon, OFF 12
  clicking, OFF 12
  macros, EX 468–471
  parameters, EX 730–731
  removing from PivotTables, EX 284–285
  using on Ribbon, OFF 12–13

C

CA. *See* certificate authority

calculated column A column in an Excel table that Excel automatically fills with a formula after you enter or edit a formula in one cell of that column. EX 365
- inserting in Excel tables, EX 366–367

calculation. *See* formula

caret (^), exponentiation operator, EX 30, EX 31

cascade workbook layout, EX 324

case, converting using UPPER function, EX A8–A9

cash inflow. *See* positive cash flow

cash outflow. *See* negative cash flow

category axis. *See* horizontal, or category, axis

category field A field that groups the values in a PivotTable; appears in PivotTables as a row label, a column label, and a report filter. EX 269

category value The group or category that a series value belongs to. EX 170

cell The intersection of a single row and a single column. EX 3
- active, EX 6
- borders, EX 76–77
- contents. *See* cell content
- highlighting, EX D7–D10
- highlighting with conditional formats, EX 95–100
- inserting comments, EX 449–451
- locking and unlocking, EX 445
- merging, EX 74–75
- in other worksheets, referencing, EX 310–312

cell content
- aligning, EX 72–73
- centering, EX 74–75
- formatting text, EX 60–64
- indenting, EX 73–74
- number of decimal places, EX 59
- rotating, EX 58, EX 75–76

cell range A group of cells, which can be either adjacent or nonadjacent. EX 22
- deleting, EX 29
- inserting, EX 28–29
- moving and copying, EX 26–28
- in other worksheets, referencing, EX 310–312
- selecting, EX 24–26

cell reference The column and row location that identifies a cell within a worksheet; for example, the cell reference B6 refers to the cell located where column B intersects row 6. EX 6, EX 118–127
- absolute, EX 116, EX 118, EX 121–125, EX 126
- entering, EX 118
- entering using mouse, EX 33
- mixed, EX 117, EX 118, EX 125–127
- relative, EX 116, EX 118, EX 120–121, EX 126

cell style, EX 84–85
- custom, EX D2–D5

Cell Styles gallery, EX 84–85

centering cell content, EX 74–75

certificate authority (CA) A trusted entity that issues certificates as a service for companies and individuals. EX C18

Change your view button, FM 3

changing cell A cell whose value is changed within each scenario, also referred to as an input cell. EX 575

chart A visual representation of a set of data values; used to show trends or relationships that may not be readily apparent from numbers alone. EX 170
- adding data series, EX 203–205
- adding dual axes, EX E18
- adding trendlines, EX E17
- axes. *See* axis, chart
- bar, EX 185
- choosing style, EX 177–178
- choosing type, EX 209
- color, EX 183–184
- column. *See* column chart
- combination, EX 193, EX 205–209
- creating, EX 172–177
- data labels, EX 171, EX 182–183
- data source, EX 170, EX 173
- effective, EX 191
- embedded, EX 170
- embedding in chart sheet, EX 219
- horizontal (data) axis, EX 171
- inserting, EX 172
- layout, EX 178–179
- legend, EX 171, EX 180–181
- line. *See* line chart
- moving, EX 176–177
- moving to different worksheet, EX 175–176
- pie. *See* pie chart
- resizing, EX 176–177
- retaining proportions when resizing, EX 176
- 3-D, EX 209–211
- title, EX 171, EX 179–180
- types, list, EX 174
- vertical (value) axis, EX 170
- XY scatter charts, EX 209

chart area The chart and all of the other chart elements. EX 171

chart column, formatting, EX 189–190

chart junk, EX 219

Chart object, EX 703, EX 706, EX 709

chart sheet A sheet that contains only the chart and no worksheet cells. EX 5
- creating, EX 219–222
- embedding charts, EX 219

chart title A descriptive label or name displayed at the top of the chart area. EX 171
- formatting, EX 179–180, EX 186–187, EX 221–222
- overlaying, EX 221–222

ChartObject object, EX 703

Choose a SmartArt Graphic dialog box, EX D19

clear To remove, such as data from a worksheet (leaving blank cells where the data had been) or a filter. EX 20–21, EX 255

Clipboard A temporary storage area for files and information that you have copied or moved from one place and plan to use somewhere else. FM 13–14

Close button, OFF 8

closing a file, OFF 22

closing tag An XML tag that marks the end of a data value. EX 657

cloud computing Data, applications, and even resources that are stored on servers that you access over the Internet rather than on your own computer. EX 348

code, writing, EX 720

Code window The window in the Visual Basic Editor that displays the VBA macro code associated with the selected item in the Project Explorer window. EX 684
- viewing, EX 692–693

Collapse button, PivotTables, EX 282

Collapse Dialog Box button, EX 131

collection object An object that contains a collection of Excel objects. EX 701

color
- automatic, EX 62
- column label borders, EX 78–79
- conditional formats with, EX 100
- custom, EX 62
- enhancing workbooks, EX 66
- fill, EX 59, EX 64–65
- fonts, EX 62–63
- pie chart slices, EX 183–184
- sparklines, EX 214
- standard, EX 62
- theme, EX 62

color scale A conditional format that bases the color shade of a cell on its value. EX D11–D15

column. *See* chart column; table column; worksheet column

column break The point at which one column ends and another begins. EX 620–621

column chart A chart that displays values in different categories as columns; the height of each column is based on its value. EX 174, EX 184–191
- axis scale and text, EX 187–189
- chart title, EX 186–187
- formatting columns, EX 189–190
- inserting, EX 185–186
- legend, EX 186–187

column header. *See* field name

column heading The letters along the top of the worksheet that identify the different columns in the worksheet. EX 3

column input cell The cell that the values from the first column of a data table are based upon. EX 569

column label, setting border color, EX 78–79

column sparkline, EX 212

combination chart A chart that combines two or more Excel chart types into a single graph. EX 193, EX 205–209

Comma style, EX 58

command, adding to Quick Access toolbar, EX 732–734

comment (Excel) A text box that is attached to a specific cell in a worksheet in which you can enter notes. EX 437
- inserting, EX 449–451

comment (VBA) A VBA statement that describes the behavior or purpose of a procedure, but does not perform any action. EX 693

common field A field that is present in more than one table in a database; used to relate tables. EX 632

compare value A category for a lookup table that is located in the table's first column or row. EX 380

comparing shared workbooks, EX C10–C12

comparison operator A symbol that indicates the relationship between two values. EX 152, EX 727

compatibility, backward, workbooks, EX C20

Compatibility Checker A dialog box that alerts you to any features that are not supported by earlier versions of Excel when you save a workbook to an earlier format. EX A14

Compatibility Checker dialog box, EX C20

Compatibility Mode The mode that keeps a workbook in the older file format, making the workbook accessible for users who do not have the current version of Excel installed. EX A2–A3

compound file A file that relies on data from more than one program. EX C21

compound interest Interest that is applied not only to the principal but also to any accrued interest. EX 157

compressed file, FM 17–19

compressed (zipped) folder A folder that reduces the size of the files it contains so they take up less disk space. FM 3, FM 18–19

Computer icon An icon in the Navigation pane of a folder window that shows the drives on your computer. FM 2

Computer window A tool that shows the drives on your computer, making it easy to perform system tasks, such as viewing system information. FM 6

Concatenation operator (&), EX A6

conditional count. *See* COUNTIF function

conditional format Formatting that is applied only when a cell's value meets a specified condition. EX D7–D18, EX 83, EX 95–100, EX 400–404
- clearing, EX 97–98
- color scales, EX D11–D15
- effective use, EX 100
- formulas, EX D17–D18
- hiding duplicate values, EX 400–401
- highlighting cells, EX D7–D10
- icon sets, EX D15–D17
- legends, EX 99–100
- modifying conditional formatting rules, EX D10–D11

conditional formatting rule A rule that specifies the condition, the formatting, and the cell or range to apply the rule to. EX 398
- editing, EX 402–403

Conditional Formatting Rules Manager dialog box, EX 402

conditional statement, EX 724–730

conditional sum. *See* SUMIF function

conflict, shared workbooks, resolving, EX C3–C4

connection A defined process for retrieving data from an external file. EX 615

connection file, EX 654

Connection Properties dialog box, EX 615

constraint A limit that is placed on the solution to a set of possible values. EX 589
- Solver, EX 596–598, EX 602

contextual tab A Ribbon tab that contains commands related to the selected object so you can manipulate, edit, and format that object; appears to the right of the standard Ribbon tabs below a title label. OFF 16

control structure A series of commands that evaluates conditions in a program and then directs Excel to perform certain actions based on the status of those conditions. EX 723

copy To place a file in a new location that you specify without removing it from its current location. FM 12–15
- AutoFill, EX 141–142
- cell formatting, EX 79–81
- cell ranges, EX 26–28
- COUNTIF formula, EX 407
- creating sub procedures using copy and paste, EX 694–696
- formats using AutoFill, EX 141–142
- formulas, EX 33–34, EX 141–142
- integrating files using copy and paste, EX C22
- worksheets, EX 38, EX 309–310

cost of goods sold Any expenses directly related to production. EX 506
- projecting, EX 511–512

cost-volume-profit (CVP) analysis A branch of financial analysis that studies the relationship between expenses, sales volume, and profitability; sometimes called break-even analysis. EX 554–558
- break-even point, EX 556–558
- comparing expenses and revenue, EX 554–556

cost-volume-profit (CVP) chart A chart that plots revenue and total expenses against sales volume; the point at which the two lines cross is the break-even point. EX 556–557

COUNT function, EX 129

COUNTA function, EX 129

COUNTIF function A function that calculates the number of cells in a range that match criteria you specify; also referred to as a conditional count. EX 399, EX 405–407

COUNTIFS function A function that counts the number of cells within a range that meet multiple criteria. EX B9, EX B10–B11

Create a Digital ID dialog box, EX C18–C19

Create Names from Selection dialog box, EX 426

Create PivotTable dialog box, EX 272–273

Create Sparklines dialog box, EX 213–214

criteria Conditions that limit the number of records in the results. EX 636

criteria filter Conditions you specify for a filter. EX 256–259

criteria range An area in a worksheet, separate from a range of data or an Excel table, used to specify the criteria for the data to be displayed after the filter is applied to the range or Excel table. EX B2–B5

cube function, EX 128

CUMIPNT function, EX 503

CUMPRINC function, EX 503–504

Custom AutoFilter dialog box, EX 257–258

custom color A color created by specifying a mixture of red, blue, and green color values. EX 62

custom format A format and style you create to accommodate a specific requirement. EX A11–A14
- dates, EX A13–A14
- numbers, EX A11–A13

custom function, EX 740–741

custom list The sequence you specify to sort data. EX 247–249

Custom Lists dialog box, EX 248–249

custom template A workbook template you create that is ready to run with the formulas for all calculations included as well as all formatting and labels. EX 344–346

custom view, EX E9

customizing
- cell styles, EX D2–D5
- dialog boxes, EX 732
- Quick Access toolbar, EX 732–735
- screen elements, EX 736–739
- table styles, EX D5–D7
- themes, EX D26–D27

cut To place cell contents into computer memory or on the Clipboard; the contents can then be pasted from the Clipboard into a new location in the worksheet. EX 28

CVP. *See* cost-volume-profit analysis; cost-volume-profit chart

D

data
- analyzing with PivotTables. *See* PivotTable
- chart, editing and revising, EX 202–205
- date. *See* date data
- entering using AutoFill, EX 140–147
- Excel tables, maintaining, EX 241–244
- hiding and unhiding worksheet data, EX 101
- number. *See* number data
- structured range, EX 236–239
- text. *See* entering text; text data

data bar A conditional format that adds a horizontal bar to the background of a cell proportional in length to the cell's value. EX 192
- creating, EX 216–217
- modifying rules, EX 217–218
- negative values, EX 217

data definition table Documentation that lists the fields to be maintained for each record and a description of the information each field will include. EX 236–237

data label Text associated with an individual data marker, such as a pie slice. EX 171
- formatting, EX 182–183

data marker A graphical representation of a value in a chart such as a column or pie slice. EX 171, EX 193
- sparklines, EX 214–215

data security, EX 629

data series A range of values plotted on a chart. EX 170
- adding to existing chart, EX 203–205
- selecting, EX 189

data source A range that contains the data displayed in a chart, or any file that contains the data you want to retrieve. EX 170, EX 636
- selecting, EX 173

data storage, EX 674

Data tab, EX 614

data table, EX 561–573
- one-variable, EX 562–566
- two-variable, EX 566–573

Data Table dialog box, EX 564

data type, variables, EX 711

data validation A set of rules that determine what users can enter in a specific cell or range. EX 436, EX 438–444
- creating error alert style and message, EX 440–442
- creating input messages, EX 440
- creating list validation rules, EX 442–444
- existing data, EX 444
- specifying validation criteria, EX 438–439

Data Validation dialog box, EX 439, EX 441

database A file that stores a collection of data values organized in a way so that they can be easily retrieved and manipulated. OFF 4, EX 632
- fields, EX 634–635
- queries. *See* Microsoft Query
- records, EX 634–635
- relational, EX 643
- tables, EX 634–635

Database function Function that performs summary data analysis, such as sum, average, and count, on an Excel table or data range based on criteria specified in a criteria range; also called Dfunction. EX B5–B8, EX 128

date, custom formats, EX A13–A14

date data A value in a recognized date format. EX 9
- entering, EX 12–13
- formatting, EX 71–72
- international date formats, EX 13
- storage by Excel, EX 72

DATE function, EX 155

date function A function that inserts or calculates dates and times. EX 128, EX 138, EX 155–156

date label, line charts, formatting, EX 195–198

DATEDIF function A function that calculates the difference between two dates and shows the result in months, days, or years. EX 374

DAVERAGE function, EX B6, EX B8

DAY function, EX 155

DB function, EX 507, EX 515

DCOUNT function, EX B6

DCOUNTA function, EX B6

DDB function, EX 515

decimal place, number in cell value, EX 59

decision making, IF function to explore financial options, EX 155

declining balance depreciation The depreciation of an asset by a constant percentage each year rather than a constant amount. EX 517–519

default A setting that is preset by the operating system or program. OFF 12

default template The template on which the blank Book1 workbook that opens when you start Excel is based; contains no text or formulas, but includes all the formatting available in every new workbook. EX 341

defined name A word or string of characters associated with a single cell or a range; also called a range name. EX 420, EX 423–435
- adding to existing formulas, EX 433–435
- creating, EX 424–428
- Paste Names command, EX 428
- using in formulas, EX 429–433

delete To remove both the data and the cells from the worksheet. EX 20–21
- cell ranges, EX 29
- columns, EX 20–21
- records, EX 244
- rows, EX 20–21
- worksheets, EX 38

deleting
- files, FM 17
- folders, FM 17

delimit To separate. EX A7

delimited text A text file in which a special character such as a space, comma, or tab marks the beginning of each column. EX 614, EX 618

delimiter A symbol-usually a space, a comma, or a tab-that separates one column of data from another in a text file. EX 618

demand, price elasticity of, EX 590–593

dependent cell A cell whose value depends on the value in the active cell for its result. EX 525

depreciation The process of allocating the original cost of an asset over the lifetime of the asset. EX 506, EX 514–522
- choosing schedule, EX 519
- declining balance, EX 517–519
- on income statement, EX 520
- straight-line, EX 516–517

descending order The arrangement of text in reverse alphabetical order from Z to A, numbers from largest to smallest, and dates from newest to oldest. EX 244

destination file The workbook that receives data from another workbook when two workbooks are linked; sometimes referred to as the dependent file, or a file that displays data from a source file. EX 320, EX C21
- updating with source workbooks closed, EX 330–334
- updating with source workbooks open, EX 329–330

Details pane, FM 3

Dfunctions. *See* Database functions

dialog box A window from which you enter or choose settings for how you want to perform a task. OFF 15. *See also* message box; *specific dialog boxes*
- customized, EX 732
- opening, OFF 14–15

Dialog Box Launcher A button in the lower-right corner of a group on a Ribbon tab that opens a task pane or dialog box that provides additional options for that group of tasks. OFF 3, OFF 15

digital certificate. *See* digital ID

digital ID A file that authenticates the source of a digital signature; also called a digital certificate. EX C18

digital signature An electronic version of a signature that provides a way to authenticate a workbook; also called a digital certificate. EX 457, EX C18–C20

discount rate. *See* rate of return

division, formulas, EX 67–68

division operator (/), EX 30, EX 31

DMAX function, EX B6

DMIN function, EX B6

dockable A window you can drag to the edge of the screen have it stay on top of other windows. EX 689

document The files you create in Word, although many people use the term document to refer to any file created on a computer. OFF 4

Document Inspector A feature that searches the workbook to locate sensitive or personal information and then removes any personal information, if necessary. EX C14

document property The descriptive details about a file, including its author, title, and subject; also called metadata. EX C12–C14

doughnut chart, EX 174

drag and drop The technique to move a cell or range by selecting it, positioning the pointer over the bottom border of the selection, and then dragging the selection to a new location. EX 27–28

drive, FM 2

DSTDEV function, EX B6

DSUM function, EX B6

duplicate values, highlighting, EX 400–401

E

Edit Formatting Rule dialog box, EX D8–D9, EX 217–218, EX 403

Edit Links dialog box, EX 332–333

Edit mode The mode in which you can edit cell contents. EX 39, EX 58

Edit Name dialog box, EX 427

Edit Scenario dialog box, EX 578

editing
- accepting/rejecting edits in shared workbooks, EX C8–C109
- chart axis scale and text, EX 187–189
- column breaks in text files, EX 620–621
- conditional formatting rules, EX 402–403
- grouped worksheets, EX 307
- hyperlinks, EX 340
- macros, EX 464, EX 466–467
- pictures, EX D22–D24
- queries, EX 645–648
- records, EX 243
- Scenario PivotTable reports, EX 586
- scenarios, EX 582–583
- sparklines, EX 213
- workbooks with Excel Web App, EX 350–352
- worksheet content, EX 38–42

elasticity A measure of how changing prices can affect the demand for a good or service. EX 588. *See also* price elasticity of demand

element The unit that stores a piece of data in an XML document; roughly analogous to the fields used in databases. EX 657

embedded chart A chart object placed in a worksheet. EX 170

embedded object A document object stored within the destination file. EX C22, EX C23, EX C25–C27
- modifying, EX C26–C27

embedding, EX C22
- linking versus, EX C27

Encapsulated PostScript (EPS) format Written in the PostScript language, provide perhaps the highest quality format for clip art files, but require access to a PostScript printer to view the results. EX D24

encryption The process by which a file is encoded so that it cannot be opened without the proper password. EX C16
- worksheets, EX C16–C17

engineering function, EX 128

Enter Parameter Value dialog box, EX 663–664

entering text, EX 9–11
- multiple lines of text within a cell, EX 11–12

EPS. *See* Encapsulated PostScript format

equal sign (=)
- equal to operator, EX 152
- formulas, EX 33

error
- program, common sources, EX 717
- tracing, EX 535–538

error alert A message that appears if a user tries to enter a value in the cell that does not meet the validation rule. EX 436
- data validation, EX 440–442

error correction
- formulas, EX 384
- macros, EX 464

error indicator A green triangle in the upper-left corner of a cell that identifies a cell with an error or potential error. EX 525

error value Text displayed in a cell that indicates some element in a formula or a cell referenced in that formula is preventing Excel from returning a calculated value. EX 394

Evaluate Formula dialog box, EX 539–540

exact match lookup A lookup that occurs when the value entered must match one of the values in the first column of the lookup table. EX 388–390

Excel. *See* Microsoft Excel 2010

Excel application A spreadsheet written or tailored to meet the user's specific needs; typically includes reports and charts, a data entry area, a custom interface, as well as instructions and documentation. EX 420
- defined names. *See* defined names
- planning, EX 422–423

Excel application An application that uses Excel commands, tools, and functions to perform an action. EX 686
- developing, EX 686–687

Excel Object Model The hierarchy that VBA uses to organize objects and object collections, beginning with the Excel application at the top and the individual cells of a workbook at the bottom. EX 704–705

Excel table A range of data that is treated as a distinct object in a worksheet. EX 83, EX 235
- calculating summary statistics using Total row, EX 259–263
- creating, EX 239–240
- creating fields, EX 367
- formatting, EX 241
- inserting calculated columns, EX 366–367
- inserting page breaks between, EX 103–104
- maintaining data, EX 241–244
- making active, EX 93
- records. *See* record
- renaming, EX 240–241
- savings plan development, EX 147–148
- sorting data, EX 244–249
- structured references, EX 364, EX 376–379
- style. *See* table style
- subtotals, EX 263–267

Excel Web App, editing workbooks, EX 350–352

Excel window, EX 4–5

Existing Connections dialog box, EX 663

exiting a program, OFF 30

Expand button, PivotTables, EX 282

Expand Dialog Box button, EX 131, EX 378

expanding the Ribbon, EX 473–474

expense
- fixed, EX 555
- mixed, EX 555
- variable, EX 554

exploded pie chart A pie chart that moves one slice away from the others as if someone were taking the piece away from the pie. EX 184

exponentiation operator (^), EX 30

Extensible Markup Language (XML) A language that structures data in text files that can be read by a wide variety of programs, including Excel. EX 657
- binding XML elements to a worksheet, EX 670
- importing data from, EX 671–673
- loading XML data maps, EX 668

extension A dot followed by three or more characters in a filename that identifies the file's type. FM 16

external data range A cell range containing data retrieved from an external data source. EX 625–626
- refreshing, EX 626–628

External Data range Properties dialog box, EX 627

external data source, EX 613–674
- data ranges, EX 624–628
- data security, EX 629
- databases. *See* database; query
- moving, EX 630
- text files. *See* text file
- trusted locations, EX 629–630
- Web. *See* Web; Web query
- XML, EX 666–673

external reference A reference to cells or ranges in a worksheet from another workbook. EX 320, EX 325–239

extract To create an uncompressed copy of a file in a folder you specify. FM 18

extrapolation The process used to extend series from an initial value or values in order to project future values. EX 507, EX 512–514

F

field A characteristic or a person, place, or thing (such as a last name, address, city, or state); in Excel, each column represents a field. EX 234
- adding to PivotTables, EX 274–276
- category, EX 269
- creating, EX 367
- PivotTable, filtering, EX 281
- PivotTable, grouping, EX 290
- PivotTable, sorting, EX 283
- removing from PivotTables, EX 284–285
- sort. *See* sort field
- value. *See* value field

field Information about a specific characteristic of a person, place, or thing. EX 632
- common, EX 632

field header, removing from PivotTables, EX 284–285

field name A unique label that describes the contents of the data in a column; also called a column header. EX 235

file A collection of data that has a name and is stored on a computer. FM 4
- closing, OFF 22
- compound, EX C21
- compressed, FM 17–19
- connection, EX 654
- copying by right-dragging, FM 15
- deleting, FM 17
- destination, EX C21
- determining location for storing, FM 15
- extracting, FM 18
- moving, FM 12–15
- naming, FM 15–16
- need for organizing, FM 4–5
- opening, OFF 22–24
- printing, OFF 28–30
- renaming, FM 16–17
- saving. *See* saving a file
- sharing using Windows Live SkyDrive, OFF 24–25
- source, EX C21
- strategies for organizing, FM 5–6
- text. *See* text file

file extension A period followed by several characters that Office adds to the title you give a file to identify the program in which that file was created; the default file extensions for Office 2010 are .docx for Word, .xlsx for Excel, .pptx for PowerPoint, and .accdb for Access. OFF 19

file icon An icon that indicates a file's type. FM 3

file path A notation that indicates a file's location on your computer. FM 2

file system The organization of files and folders in a hierarchy in Windows 7. FM 4

filename A title you select and a file extension assigned by Office to indicate the file type; identifies the file's contents. FM 3, FM 13–14, OFF 19

fill color A background color that can be added to cells to help differentiate parts of a worksheet or highlight data. EX 59, EX 64–65

Fill Effects dialog box, EX D14

fill handle A small black square in the lower-right corner of a selected cell or range that you drag over an adjacent cell or range to copy the original content and formatting into the selected range. EX 139, EX 141–142

Fill option, Format Cells dialog box, EX 77

filter The process of displaying a subset of rows in an Excel table that meets the specified criteria. EX 251, EX 252–259
- advanced, EX B2–B5
- clearing filters, EX 255
- criteria, EX 256–259
- criteria filters, EX 256–259
- PivotChart items, EX 292–293
- PivotTable, using a slicer, EX 285–287
- PivotTable fields, EX 281
- queries, EX 640–641
- report filters in PivotTables, EX 279–281
- selecting multiple filter items, EX 255–256
- text filters, EX 254
- using multiple columns, EX 254–255
- using one column, EX 252–254

financial function A function related to monetary calculations, such as loans and payments. EX 128, EX 138, EX 156–161
- list, EX 157
- managing personal finances, EX 158

financial workbook, writing, EX 504

Find & Select button, EX 23

Find and Replace dialog box, EX 40–41

Find command, EX 23, EX 40–41

finding
- errors in formulas, EX 384
- records, EX 243

First Column option, table styles, EX 93

fixed disk. *See* hard disk

fixed expense An expense that must be paid regardless of sales volume. EX 555

fixed-width format A text file in which each column starts at the same location in the file. EX 614, EX 618

folder A container for files. FM 3, FM 7–8, OFF 19
- compressed (zipped), FM 3, FM 18–19
- creating, FM 11–12
- deleting, FM 17
- duplicating folder organization, FM 6
- moving, FM 12–15
- naming, FM 11

need for organizing, FM 4–5
strategies for organizing, FM 5–6

folder window A window that displays the files and subfolders in a folder. FM 6
copying folders, FM 14–15
creating folders, FM 11–12
moving folders, FM 12–14

font A set of characters that employ the same typeface, such as Arial, Times New Roman, and Courier. EX 58
color, EX 62–63
non-theme, EX 61
sans serif, EX 61
serif, EX 61
theme, EX 61

Font option, Format Cells dialog box, EX 77

font size The size of the text. EX 58
changing, EX 62

font style Formats that can applied to a font such as *italic*, **bold**, or ***bold italic*** and special effects such as underline, strikethrough, and color. EX 58, EX 61–62

footer Information that appears in the bottom margin of each printed page; it often includes summary information such as the current page number and the number of pages in the printout. EX 82
creating, EX 105–106

format
conditional. *See* conditional format
fixed-width, EX 614, EX 618

Format Axis dialog box, EX 187–188

Format Cells dialog box, EX 77–79
opening, EX 72

Format Chart Area dialog box, EX 210

format code A series of symbols used to describe exactly how Excel should display a number, date, time, or text string. EX A11

Format Data Labels dialog box, EX 182–183

Format Data Series dialog box, EX 190, EX 207

Format Painter A feature that copies and pastes formatting from one cell or range to another without copying and pasting the data. EX 58, EX 79–80, EX 84

formatting
incoming data from text files, EX 621–624
Web queries, EX 661

formatting The process of changing a workbook's appearance by defining the fonts, styles, colors, and decorative features. EX 60
calculated values, EX 66–72
cell background, EX 64–66
cell styles, EX 84–85, EX 87
cell text, EX 60–64
chart columns, EX 189–190
chart date labels, EX 195–198
chart labels, EX 180–181
chart legend, EX 180–181
chart titles, EX 179–180, EX 186–187
conditional formats, EX 83, EX 95–100
copying and pasting formats, EX 79–81
copying using AutoFill, EX 141–142
custom formats. *See* custom format
data labels, EX 182–183
dates, EX 71–72
Excel tables, EX 241
Format Cells dialog box, EX 77–79
formulas. *See* formula
hiding worksheet data, EX 101
legends, EX 186–187
number formats, EX 68–71
PivotTable values fields, EX 276–277
row and column titles, EX 90–91
special formats, EX A10–A11
table styles, EX 91–95
themes, EX 60, EX 86–87
times, EX 71–72
workbooks, EX 60
worksheet cells, EX 72–77
worksheet groups, EX 308
worksheets, for printing, EX 101–107

formula A mathematical expression that returns a value. EX 22, EX 30–34
to calculate totals, EX 66–67, EX 88–89
checking for matching parentheses, EX 386
conditional formatting, EX D17
copying and pasting, EX 33–34
copying using AutoFill, EX 141–142
defined name use, EX 429–433
defining complEX validation criteria, EX 442
to divide values, EX 67–68
effective, EX 37
entering, EX 30–33
entering in worksheet groups, EX 306–307
entering using AutoFill, EX 140–147
evaluating, EX 538–540
existing, adding defined names, EX 433–435
external references, EX 325–239
finding and fixing errors, EX 384
number formats, EX 68–71
printing, EX 46–48
with references to another worksheet, EX 311
savings plan development, EX 148, EX 150–151
to subtract values, EX 67–68, EX 89–91
viewing, EX 46–48

Formula Auditing group, EX 524

formula bar The bar located below the Ribbon that displays the value or formula entered in the active cell. EX 2

formula view A view of the worksheet that displays formulas instead of the resulting values. EX 46

Forward A button that takes you to the next location in your sequence of opened locations; appears next to the Address bar in a folder window. FM 2, FM 7

freeze The process of keeping rows and/or columns you select visible as you scroll the worksheet. EX 238–239

Full Screen button, EX 43

function A named operation that returns a value; used to simplify formulas. EX 34–37, EX 127–137
categories, EX 128
custom, EX 740–741
entering, EX 34–36
inserting, EX 131–134
list, EX 129
lookup. *See* lookup function
nested, EX 130
summary, choosing, EX 130
syntax, EX 127–130
typing, EX 134–137

Function Arguments dialog box, EX 131–132, EX 153–154, EX 160, EX 364
AND function, EX 372–373
AVERAGEIF function, EX 409
COUNTIF function, EX 405–406
IF function, EX 368–369
IF function with OR function, EX 378
SUMIF function, EX 408
SUMIFS function, EX B12
VLOOKUP function, EX 389, EX 393

Function Library group, EX 116

function procedure A procedure that returns a value. EX 693

future value. *See* FV function

FV function The financial function to calculate the future value of a loan or an investment. EX 157, EX 490, EX 494–495, EX 528

G

gallery A menu or grid that shows a visual representation of the options available when you click a button. OFF 14

general expenses Expenses that are not directly related to production. EX 506

General number format The number format that, for the most part, displays values exactly as they are typed. EX 68

Go To dialog box, EX 7

Goal Seek An Excel analysis tool that automates the trial-and-error process using a value you specify for a calculated item and then returning the input value needed to reach that goal. EX 558–561
determining break-even point, EX 560–561

Goal Seek dialog box, EX 560

graph. *See* chart

graphic
file formats, EX D24
SmartArt. *See* SmartArt graphic

greater than or equal to operator (>=), EX 152

gridline
charts, EX 193, EX 201
worksheets, printing, EX 76

gross profit The difference between a company's sales revenue and the cost of goods sold. EX 511–512

group A collection of buttons for related commands organized on a Ribbon tab. OFF 2
appearance on Ribbon, OFF 12

grouping
date fields, EX 290
PivotTable items, EX 288–291
worksheets. *See* worksheet group

growth trend A series in which values change by a constant percentage; when plotted, a growth trend appears as a curve with the greatest increases occurring near the end of the series. EX 507, EX 509

H

hard disks A storage device permanently housed inside the computer case. FM 4

header Information that appears in the top margin of each printed page; it often includes summary information such as the filename and the date. EX 82
creating, EX 105–106

header row The first row of the range or Excel table that contains field names. EX 234

Header Row option, table styles, EX 93

heading
columns, EX 3
rows, EX 2
worksheet, printing, EX 76, EX E5

Help (Office) Information on a feature or how to perform a task in an Office program. OFF 25–28
  Help window, OFF 26–28
  ScreenTips, OFF 12, OFF 13, OFF 25–26

Help window A window that provides access to all the Help topics, templates, and training installed on your computer with Office and available on Office.com. OFF 26–28

hidden worksheet A worksheet that is removed from the user's view but is still stored in the workbook. EX C15–C16

hiding worksheet data, EX 101

Highlight Changes dialog box, EX C6–C7, EX C7

highlighting
  cells, EX D7–D10
  cells, conditional formats, EX 95–100
  duplicate values, EX 400–401

HLOOKUP function A lookup function that searches horizontally across the top row of the lookup table and retrieves the value in the column you specify. EX 394

horizontal, or category, axis The axis that displays the category values from each data series. EX 171

horizontal workbook layout, EX 324

hyperlink A link in a file, such as a workbook, to information within that file or another file. EX 337, EX 338–340. *See also* link; linking workbooks
  editing, EX 340
  inserting, EX 338–340

I

icon set A conditional format that displays a symbol based on a cell's value. EX D15–D17

IF function A logical function that tests a condition and then returns one value if the condition is true and another value if the condition is false. EX 138, EX 151–155, EX 365, EX 367–369
  nested, EX 380, EX 382–387

If statement, EX 725

IFERROR function A function that can determine if a cell contains an error value and then display the message you choose rather than the default error value. EX 381, EX 394–397

If-Then-Else control structure A control structure that runs one set of commands if the condition is true and a different set of commands if the condition is false. EX 723, EX 725–726

If-Then-ElseIf control structure A control structure that runs commands in response to each of several conditions. EX 726, EX 728–729

image, background, EX 59, EX 65

Immediate window The Visual Basic Editor window in which you enter a command and *see* its effect immediately applied to the workbook, making it an ideal way to learn VBA syntax and debug programs that fail to run correctly. EX 702–703

importing
  data from Microsoft Query, EX 643–645
  data from text files. *See* text file
  data from Web, EX 662–666
  data from XML, EX 671–673
  data into PivotTables and Pivot Charts, EX 647–654

income statement A file that shows how much money a person or business makes or loses over a specified period of time; also called a profit and loss statement. EX 506, EX 508
  completing, EX 520–522
  depreciation, EX 520

indenting cell content, EX 73–74

information function, EX 128

input cell A cell containing a value that will be changed within a what-if analysis. EX 552, EX 569

input message A message that appears when the cell becomes active; can be used to specify the type of data the user should enter in that cell. EX 436
  data validation, EX 440

input value A value that is entered in an input cell. EX 552

InputBox method, EX 701

Insert Function button, EX 116, EX 132

Insert Function dialog box, EX 132–133

Insert Hyperlink dialog box, EX 339

Insert Worksheet tab, EX 22

insertion point A nonprinting marker that shows where characters will appear when you start to type. OFF 2

insignificant zero A zero whose omission from a number does not change the number's value. EX A11

inspecting a workbook, EX C14–C16

INT function, EX 129

integrating Excel with other Office applications, EX C21–C27
  copying and pasting data, EX C22
  embedding objects, EX C22, EX C25–C26
  embedding versus linking, EX C27
  inserting screenshots, EX C23
  linking, EX C22
  modifying embedded objects, EX C26–C27
  OLE, EX C22–C23
  updating linked objects, EX C25
  Word files, EX C24–C25

integration The ability to share information between programs. OFF 5

interest The amount added to the principal by the lender. EX 157
  calculating payments, EX 157
  edit EX 502–504

interest rate on investments, calculating, EX 497–498

internal rate of return (IRR) The return rate for a series of future cash flows that will result in a net present value of zero. EX 524, EX 530–534
  comparing investments, EX 533
  IRR function, EX 524, EX 531–533
  XIRR function, EX 533, EX 534
  XNPV function, EX 533–534

international date format, EX 13

interpolation The process used to fill in unknown values located between the starting and ending values of a data series. EX 507, EX 509–511

investment
  comparing investments using net present value and internal rate of return, EX 533
  future value calculation, EX 157, EX 490, EX 494–495
  interest rate calculation, EX 157, EX 491, EX 497–498
  IRR. *See* internal rate of return (IRR)
  length calculation, EX 157, EX 491, EX 495–496
  payback period calculation, EX 526–527
  periodic payments, EX 138, EX 139, EX 492–494
  present value calculation, EX 157, EX 490, EX 496–497

IPMT function The financial function to calculate the amount of a loan payment that is used to pay OFF the interest. EX 157, EX 491
  creating amortization schedules, EX 500

IRR. *See* internal rate of return

IRR function The financial function to calculate the internal rate of return for an investment. EX 524, EX 531–533

iterative procedure The approach by which Solver starts with an initial solution (usually the current values from the worksheet) and uses that as a basis to calculate a new set of values to arrive at an optimal solution. EX 600

J

Joint Photographic Experts Group (JPEG) format The most common picture format; can support up to 16.7 million colors (more colors than the human eye can distinguish) and can be compressed to save file space without greatly affecting image quality. EX D24

JPEG. *See* Joint Photographic Experts Group format

K

Key Tip, OFF 13

keyboard shortcut A key or combination of keys you press to access a feature or perform a command. OFF 13

L

landscape orientation The page orientation where the page is wider than it is tall. EX 44, EX 102

Last Column option, table styles, EX 93

layout
  charts, EX 178–179
  multiple workbooks, EX 324–325
  multiple worksheets with identical layouts, EX 309
  PivotTable reports, EX 278–279
  PivotTables, EX 277–278

leader line Lines that connect each data label to its corresponding data marker. EX 182

left angle bracket (<), less than operator, EX 152

LEFT function A text function that returns a specified number of characters from the beginning of a specified string. EX A3, EX A4–A5

legend A chart element that identifies the data markers associated with each data series in the chart. EX 99, EX 171
  conditional formatting, EX 99–100
  formatting, EX 180–181, EX 186–187
  overlaying, EX 199–200

LEN function A text function that returns the number of characters (length) of a specified string. EX A3, EX A4–A5

less than or equal to operator (<=), EX 152

library A central place to view and organize files and folders stored anywhere that your computer can access, such as your hard disk, removable drives, and network. FM 2, FM 7–8

limits report A report used to quantify the reliability of the solution provided by Solver; often used in science and engineering environments when the user wants to investigate the mathematical aspects of the Solver solution. EX 600

line chart A chart that displays data values using a connected line rather than columns or bars. EX 174, EX 192, EX 194–202
  axis titles, EX 201–202
  data labels, EX 195–198
  gridlines, EX 201
  label units, EX 198–199
  overlaying chart legends, EX 199–200

line sparkline, EX 212

linear trend A series in which values change by a constant amount; when plotted, a linear trend appears as a straight line. EX 507, EX 509

link A connection between files that allows data to be transferred from one file to the other. EX 321. *See also* hyperlink; linking workbooks

linked object A document object within the destination file that is connected to a source file. EX C22, EX C23
- updating, EX C25

linking, EX C22
- embedding versus, EX C27
- Excel and Word files, EX C24–C25
- workbooks. *See* linking workbooks

linking workbooks, EX 322–333
- arranging multiple workbooks, EX 324–325
- deciding when to link, EX 323
- formulas with external references, EX 325–239
- managing links, EX 332–333
- navigating multiple workbooks, EX 323–324
- updating linked workbooks, EX 329–332

list, custom, EX 247–249

list validation rule, EX 442–444

Live Preview An Office feature that shows the results that would occur in your file, such as the effects of formatting options on a document's appearance, if you clicked the option to which you are pointing. OFF 14, OFF 16

loading a Solver model, EX 605–606

Load/Save Model dialog box, EX 603

loan or mortgage, EX 498–505
- amortization schedules, EX 500–502
- calculating cumulative interest and principal payments, EX 502–504
- calculating payments, EX 499–500

locked property A setting that determines whether changes can be made to a cell. EX 445

logical condition An expression that returns either a TRUE value or a FALSE value. EX 365

logical error, EX 717

logical function A function that works with statements that are either true or false. EX 128, EX 138, EX 151–155, EX 364–376. *See also* AND function; DATEDIF function; IF function; OR function
- inserting calculated columns in Excel tables, EX 366–367

logical operator An operator that combines expressions within a condition; used when writing conditions for control structures. EX 727–728

lookup function A function that allows you to use tables of data to "look up" values and insert them in another worksheet location. EX 128, EX 380, EX 387–394
- finding approximate matches, EX 390–393
- finding exact matches, EX 388–390
- looking up values, EX 394

lookup table A table that organizes data that you want to retrieve into different categories. EX 380

lookup value The value you are trying to find in a lookup table. EX 380

M

macro A series of stored commands that can be run whenever you need to perform that task. EX 453–472
- creating, EX 462–464
- creating macro buttons, EX 468–471
- digital signatures with, EX 457
- editing, EX 466–467
- error correction, EX 464
- opening workbooks with, EX 472
- planning, EX 458
- recording, EX 457–460
- running, EX 460–464
- saving workbooks with, EX 471–472
- security settings, EX 455–457
- structure, EX 466
- Visual Basic Editor, EX 464–467

macro security setting A setting that controls what Excel will do about macros in a workbook when you open that workbook. EX 452

macro virus A type of virus that uses a program's own macro programming language to distribute the virus. EX 455
- protecting against, EX 455–457

manual page break A page break inserted by the user to specify the exact location of the page break. EX 103–104

margin The space between the page content and the edges of the page. EX 107

math function, EX 128

MAX function A function that returns the maximum value of the values in a range. EX 117, EX 129, EX 130, EX 135–136

Maximize button, OFF 8

median The middle value in data. EX 130

MEDIAN function, EX 129

menu, shortcut, OFF 17–18

merge To combine, such as several cells into one cell. EX 58, EX 74–75

merging
- scenarios, EX 587
- shared workbooks, EX C10–C11

message box A dialog box you create with the MsgBox method that contains buttons and an informative message for the user. EX 723, EX 730–732

metadata. *See* document property

method A action that can be performed on an object, such as closing a workbook or printing the contents of a worksheet. EX 700, EX 709
- applying, EX 709–711

Microsoft Access 2010 A computer program used to enter, maintain, and retrieve related information (or data) in a format known as a database; is often referred to as a database or relational database program. EX 1, OFF 4
- starting, EX 5, OFF 7

Microsoft Excel 2010 A computer program you use to enter, calculate, analyze, and present numerical data; often called a spreadsheet program. OFF 4
- linking Excel files, EX C24–C25
- starting, EX 1, EX 5, OFF 7

Microsoft Live SkyDrive. *See* SkyDrive

Microsoft Office 2010 A collection of Microsoft programs, such as Word, Excel, PowerPoint, Access, Outlook, Publisher, and OneNote. OFF 4–5
- integrating programs, OFF 5

Microsoft Office Help button, OFF 3

Microsoft Office Specialist Certification, EX E2

Microsoft Office Trusted Location dialog box, EX 630

Microsoft Outlook 2010 A computer program you use to send, receive, and organize email; plan your schedule; arrange meetings; organize contacts; create a to-do list; and record notes; as well as print schedules, task lists, phone directories, and other documents; often referred to as an information management program. OFF 4

Microsoft PowerPoint 2010 A computer program you use to create a collection of slides that can contain text, charts, pictures, sound, movies, multimedia, and so on; often called a presentation graphics program. OFF 4

Microsoft Query A program included with Microsoft Office that retrieves data from multiple database tables and stores the data values in an Excel workbook. EX 633, EX 636–648
- choosing tables and columns, EX 638–640
- connecting to data source, EX 637–638
- editing queries, EX 645–648
- filtering and sorting data, EX 640–642
- importing data from, EX 643–645
- saving queries, EX 642–643

Microsoft Word 2010 A computer program you use to enter, edit, and format text; often called a word-processing program. OFF 4
- linking Excel files, EX C24–C25
- starting, OFF 6

MID function, EX A3

MIN function A function that returns the minimum value in the range. EX 117, EX 129, EX 134–135

Mini toolbar A toolbar that appears next to the pointer whenever you select text; contains buttons for the most commonly used formatting commands, such as font, font size, styles, color, alignment, and indents. OFF 16–17

minimizing the Ribbon, EX 473

minus sign (-), subtraction operator, EX 30, EX 31

mixed expense An expense that is part variable and part fixed. EX 555

mixed reference A cell reference that contains an absolute row (such as $D6) or an absolute column (such as D$6). EX 117, EX 118, EX 125–127

mode The most common value in data. EX 130

Modify Button dialog box, EX 734–735

module In VBA, a collection of sub procedures. EX 466, EX 684
- naming, EX 692

MONTH function, EX 155

More button, OFF 14

mortgage. *See* loan or mortgage

move To remove a file from its current location and place it in a new location. FM 12–15

moving
- cell ranges, EX 26–28
- charts, EX 176–177
- charts between worksheets, EX 175–176
- data sources, EX 630
- worksheets, EX 38

multiplication operator (*), EX 30, EX 31

N

Name box The box located at the left side of the formula bar that displays the cell reference of the active cell. EX 2

Name Manager dialog box, EX 427–428

Name object, EX 703, EX 706

naming a module, EX 692

navigating
- to data files, FM 9–11
- multiple workbooks, EX 323–324
- between worksheets, EX 5
- within worksheets, EX 6–7

navigation key, EX 6

Navigation pane, FM 6–7

negative cash flow A negative value that represents money going away from the investor; also called cash outflow. EX 490

negative value, setting format, EX 78

nest To place one function inside another function. EX 130

nested IF function One IF function is placed inside another IF function to test an additional condition. EX 380, EX 382–387

net income The income after all expenses and taxes have been paid. EX 521
- maximizing through trial and error, EX 591–593

net present value (NPV) The difference between the present value of a series of future cash flows from an investment and the initial expenditure on that investment. EX 524
- calculation, EX 527–530
- comparing investments, EX 533

New Table Quick Style dialog box, EX D6–D7

New Web Query dialog box, EX 660

nonadjacent range The combination of two or more distinct adjacent ranges. EX 23
- selecting, EX 25–26

non-theme font A font that is not associated with a particular design; non-theme fonts retain their appearance no matter what theme is used with the workbook. EX 61

Normal view The default Excel view that shows the contents of the worksheet. EX 43

not binding constraint A constraint that was not a limiting factor in Solver arriving at a solution. EX 602

not equal to operator (<>), EX 152

NOT logical operator, EX 728

NOW function, EX 155

NPER function The financial function to calculate the number of payments required to pay OFF a loan or reach an investment goal. EX 157, EX 491, EX 495–496

NPV. *See* net present value

NPV function The financial function to calculate the present value of a series of future cash flows. EX 524, EX 528–529, EX 530

number data Any numerical value that can be used in a mathematical calculation. EX 9
- entering, EX 13–15
- truncating, EX 13

number format Formatting that displays values in a way that makes it easy for the reader to understand and interpret them. EX 68–71
- custom, EX A11–A13

Number option, Format Cells dialog box, EX 77

number sign (#), error values, EX 394

O

object Anything that appears on your screen that can be selected and manipulated, such as a table, a picture, a shape, a chart, or an equation; in Excel, any element within the working environment, such as a cell, worksheet, workbook, or even Excel itself. OFF 16,EX C22, EX 700
- collections, EX 701, EX 704
- embedded, EX C22, EX C23, EX C25–C27
- linked, EX C22, EX C23, EX C24–C25, EX C27
- pasted, EX C22
- properties. *See* property
- referring to, EX 703–705

Object linking and embedding (OLE) The technology used to copy and paste objects, such as graphic files, cell and ranges, or charts, so that information about the program that created the object is included with the object itself. EX C22–C23

objective cell The cell that Solver sets to a specified value or sets to its maximum or minimum possible value. EX 589

object-oriented programming language A programming language, such as VBA, in which tasks are performed by manipulating objects. EX 703

ODC. *See* Office Data Connection (ODC) file

Office. *See* Microsoft Office 2010

Office Data Connection (ODC) file, EX 654

Office Open XML Format The XML-based file format in which Office 2010 files are stored. EX 666, EX 673

Office Web Apps Web-based versions of Microsoft Excel, Word, PowerPoint, and OneNote that allow you to create, view, and edit Office files directly from a Web browser as well as share files and collaborate with other users online. EX 348

Office.com A Web site maintained by Microsoft that provides access to the latest information and additional Help resources. OFF 26

OLE. *See* Object linking and embedding

one-variable data table A data table used to perform several what-if analyses by specifying one input cell and several result cells. EX 553, EX 562–566
- charting, EX 564–566
- creating, EX 562–564

Open dialog box, OFF 24

opening
- dialog boxes, OFF 14–15
- files, OFF 22–24
- Format Cells dialog box, EX 72
- task panes, OFF 14–15
- workbooks created in earlier versions of Excel, EX A2–A3
- workbooks with macros, EX 472

opening tag An XML tag that marks the beginning of a data value. EX 657

operating profit, EX 520

operator A mathematical symbol used in a formula to combine different values, resulting in a single value that is displayed within the cell. EX 30–31
- comparison, EX 152
- order of precedence, EX 30–31

& operator The operator that concatenates or joins the contents of two or more cells; also called the Concatenation operator. EX A6

optional argument An argument that is not required for the function to return a value. EX 117

OR function A logical function that returns a TRUE value if any of the logical conditions are true, and a FALSE value if none of the logical conditions are true. EX 365, EX 374–376

Or logical operator, EX 727

order of precedence A set of predefined rules used to determine the sequence in which operators are applied in a calculation. EX 30–31

Outlook. *See* Microsoft Outlook 2010

P

page break
- automatic, EX 103
- manual, EX 103–104

Page Break Preview The view of the worksheet that displays the location of each page break. EX 43, EX 44, EX 102, EX 103

Page Layout tab, EX 22, EX 82

Page Layout view The view that shows how the worksheet will appear when printed. EX 43, EX 83

Page Setup dialog box, OFF 15

pane A section of a window; In Excel, you can split the worksheet window into two or four resizable panes. EX 251
- splitting worksheet window into panes, EX 261–263

password protection, EX 446

Paste Names command, EX 428

Paste Options button, copying formats, EX 80

Paste Special command, copying formats, EX 81

Paste Values command, EX A5

pasted object, EX C22

pasting
- cell formatting, EX 79–81
- formulas, EX 33–34

payback period The length of time before an investment recovers its initial cost. EX 524

PDF (Portable Document Format) A file format developed by Adobe Systems that supports all of the elements of a printed document but in an electronic format that is easily shared. EX 739–740

Percentage style, EX 59

perfectly elastic The price elasticity of demand when any change in price causes a huge change in demand. EX 591

perfectly inelastic The price elasticity of demand when changes in price have no impact on demand. EX 591

Personal Macro workbook A hidden workbook named Personal.xlsb that opens whenever you start Excel, making the macros you stored there available any time you use Excel. EX 458

perspective The setting that controls how fast a three-dimensional chart appears to recede from the viewer's eye. EX 210

picture, SmartArt. *See* SmartArt graphic

pie chart A chart in the shape of a circle (like a pie) that shows data values as a percentage of the whole. EX 174, EX 177–184
- chart style, EX 177–178
- chart title, EX 179–180
- colors, EX 183–184
- data labels, EX 182–183
- exploding, EX 184
- inserting, EX 174–175
- layout, EX 178–179
- legend, EX 180–181

PivotChart A graphical representation of the data in a PivotTable. EX 268, EX 291–293
- creating, EX 291–292
- filtering, EX 292–293
- importing data into, EX 647–654

PivotTable An interactive table used to group and summarize either a range of data or an Excel table into a concise, tabular format for easier reporting and analysis. EX 268, EX 270–291. *See also* Scenario PivotTable report
- adding fields, EX 274–276
- adding report filters, EX 279–281
- adding values fields, EX 283–284
- applying styles, EX 276

changing report layout options, EX 278–279
collapsing and expanding items, EX 282
creating, EX 272–274
filtering fields, EX 281
filtering using slicers, EX 285–287
formatting values fields, EX 276–277
grouping items, EX 288–291
importing data into, EX 647–654
layout, EX 277–278
rearranging, EX 277–278
refreshing, EX 287–288
removing fields, field headers, and buttons, EX 284–285
reports. *See* PivotTable report
sorting fields, EX 283
summarizing data, EX 271

PivotTable report
layout, EX 278–279
report filters, EX 279–281
types, EX 291

pixel A single point on a computer monitor or printout. EX 16

placeholder A special character used to represent individual digits. EX A11–A12

planning
budgets, EX 161
importance, EX 236
macros, EX 458

planning analysis sheet A series of questions that help you think about the workbook's purpose and how to achieve the desired results. EX 8

plot area The part of a chart that contains the graphical representation of the data series. EX 171

plus sign (+), addition operator, EX 30, EX 31

PMT function A financial function that calculates the monthly payment required in each period to pay back a loan or reach an investment goal. EX 138, EX 139, EX 157, EX 158–161, EX 491
calculating loan payments, EX 499–500
calculating periodic payments, EX 492–494

PNG. *See* Portable Network Graphics format

point A unit of measure equal to approximately 1/72 of an inch. EX 17, EX 58

Portable Document Format. *See* PDF

Portable Network Graphics (PNG) format A popular picture format that allows for picture compression for smaller file sizes. EX D24

portrait orientation The page orientation where the page is taller than it is wide. EX 44

positive cash flow A positive value that represents money coming to the investor; also called cash inflow. EX 490

PowerPoint. *See* Microsoft PowerPoint 2010

PPMT function The financial function to calculate the amount of a loan payment that is applied to the principal. EX 157, EX 491
creating amortization schedules, EX 500–502

precedent cell A cell that supplies a data value to the formula in the active cell. EX 525

present value. *See* PV function

presentation The file you create in PowerPoint. OFF 4

price elasticity of demand The effect that price has on demand. EX 590–593

primary axis The axis that usually appears along the left side of a chart. EX 187

primary sort field The first sort field. EX 245

principal The amount of money being loaned or that is still unpaid. EX 157, EX 500
calculating payments, EX 502–504

print area The region that is sent to the printer from the active sheet. EX 102–103

print title Information that appears on every printed page; specified as rows or columns to repeat on the top or left of each page. EX 82, EX 104–105

printing
files, OFF 28–30
formatting worksheets for, EX 101–107
gridlines, EX 76, EX E4
headings, EX 76, EX E5
workbooks, EX 45–46
worksheet formulas, EX 46–48
worksheet groups, EX 317–318

privacy option, shared workbooks, EX C2

private sub procedure A procedure that is hidden from other modules in a project. EX 694

profit
gross, EX 511–512
operating, on income statement, EX 520

profit and loss statement. *See* income statement

program. *See also specific program names*
exiting, OFF 30
integrating, OFF 5
open, switching between, OFF 2, OFF 7–8
starting, OFF 5–8

program window, OFF 8–11
resizing, OFF 8–9
scrolling, OFF 11
switching views, OFF 9
zooming, OFF 9–11

project A collection of macros, worksheets, data-entry forms, and other items that make up the customized application. EX 689

Project Explorer The window in the Visual Basic Editor that displays a hierarchical list of all the macros, worksheets, data-entry forms, and other items that make up a custom Office application. EX 684, EX 689–690

PROPER function A text function that converts the first letter of each word to uppercase, capitalizes any letter that does not follow another letter, and changes all other letters to lowercase. EX A3, EX A6–A7

Properties window The window in the Visual Basic Editor that lists the properties and values associated with each object in the Project Explorer window. EX 684, EX 690–691

property An attribute of an object that defines one of its characteristics, such as its name, size, color, or location on the screen; all objects have properties. EX 684, EX 700
modifying, EX 705–708

property procedure A procedure that is used to create custom properties for the objects in a project. EX 693

Protect Sheet dialog box, EX 446

Protected View A read-only format in which any file downloaded from the Internet, accessed from a shared network, or received as an email attachment may open where you can *see* the file's contents, but you cannot edit, save, or print them until you enable editing. OFF 23

Protection option, Format Cells dialog box, EX 77

public sub procedure A procedure that is available to other modules in a project. EX 694

PV function The financial function to calculate the present value of a loan or an investment. EX 157, EX 490, EX 496–497

Q

query A set of guidelines that specify what values to retrieve from a database and in what order the values should be retrieved. EX 633, EX 635–648. *See also* Microsoft Query
criteria, EX 636

Query Wizard—Choose Columns dialog box, EX 638

Query Wizard—Finish dialog box, EX 642

Query Wizard—Sort Order dialog box, EX 642

Quick Access Toolbar A collection of buttons that provides one-click access to commonly used commands, such as Save, Undo, and Repeat. OFF 2
adding commands, EX 732–734
customizing buttons, EX 734–735

Quick Style A built-in style you can use to quickly and easily format a SmartArt graphic's appearance. EX D20–D22

R

radar chart, EX 174

RAND function, EX 129

range. *See* cell range; worksheet range

range name. *See* defined name

Range object, EX 703, EX 706, EX 709

range reference The location and size of a cell range. EX 24

RATE function The financial function to calculate the per period interest rate required to pay OFF a loan or reach an investment goal. EX 157, EX 491, EX 497–498

rate of return An interest rate that compares the value of current dollars to future dollars from a series of cash flows, also known as the discount rate. EX 524
choosing, EX 529–530

real-time data Values from measuring devices and scientific equipment. EX 673

Recent Pages A button that displays a list of recent locations; appears next to the Address bar in a folder window. FM 2, FM 7

record A collection of related fields that are grouped together, such as the characteristics of a particular person, place, or thing; in Excel, each row in an Excel table or range represents a record. EX 234, EX 632
adding, EX 242–243
deleting, EX 244
editing, EX 243
finding, EX 243

recording a macro, EX 457–460

Recycle Bin An area on your hard disk that holds deleted files until you remove them permanently. FM 17

redoing an action, EX 40

reference function, EX 128

refresh To update. EX 287, EX 626
external data, EX 626–628
PivotTables, EX 287–288

relational database, EX 643

relative reference A cell reference that is interpreted in relation to the location of the cell containing the formula. EX 116, EX 118, EX 120–121, EX 126

relatively elastic The price elasticity of demand when demand is very responsive to changes in price. EX 591

relatively inelastic The price elasticity of demand when large changes in price will cause small changes in demand. EX 590

removing. *See also* delete
  tabs from Ribbon, EX 473

renaming
  Excel tables, EX 240–241
  files, FM 16–17
  worksheets, EX 38

Replace command, EX 23, EX 40–41

replacement string A string of characters to use in place of the search string. EX 40

report, PivotTable. *See* PivotTable report

required argument An argument that is needed for the function to return a value. EX 117

resizing
  chart titles, EX 179–180
  charts, EX 176–177

Resolve Conflicts dialog box, EX C4

Restore Down button, OFF 8

result cell A cell containing the calculated value from a what-if analysis and depending on one or more input cells. EX 552, EX 575

result value The value stored in the result cell from a what-if analysis. EX 553

Ribbon The main set of commands organized into tabs and groups that you click to execute tasks. OFF 2, OFF 11–15
  clicking buttons, OFF 12–13
  expanding, EX 473–474
  galleries, OFF 14
  key tips, OFF 13
  keyboard shortcuts, OFF 13
  Live Preview, OFF 14
  minimizing, EX 473
  opening dialog boxes and task panes, OFF 14–15
  removing a tab, EX 473
  tabs, OFF 2, OFF 11

Rich Text Format (RTF) A file format that allows text formatting styles including boldface, italic, and color, but not advanced features such as hyperlinks or complicated table structures. EX 661

right angle bracket (>), greater than operator, EX 152

RIGHT function, EX A3

right-dragging, copying files, FM 15

risk The possibility that an entire transaction will fail, resulting in a loss of the initial investment. EX 529

root directory The location at the top of the file system hierarchy where Windows stores folders and important files that it needs when you turn on the computer. FM 4

root element The common element on which an XML document is structured and which contains all other XML elements. EX 667

rotating
  cell contents, EX 58, EX 75–76
  3-D charts, EX 210–211

ROUND function, EX 129

row. *See* worksheet row

row heading The numbers along the left side of the worksheet that identify the different rows in the worksheet. EX 2

row height, setting, EX 15, EX 17–18

row input cell The cell that the values from the first row of a data table are based upon. EX 569

RTF. *See* Rich Text Format

running a macro, EX 460–464

run-time error, EX 717

S

salvage value The value of an asset at the end of its useful life. EX 515

sans serif font A font that does not include decorative strokes, such as Arial. EX 61

Save As command, EX 21, OFF 20–21

saving
  files. *See* saving a file
  queries, EX 642–643
  Solver models, EX 602–605
  themes, EX D26
  Web queries, EX 662
  workbooks created in earlier versions of Excel, EX A2–A3
  workbooks to SkyDrive, EX 349–350
  workbooks with macros, EX 471–472

saving a file, OFF 19–22
  before closing, OFF 22
  earlier formats, OFF 19
  first time, OFF 20–21
  new name or location, OFF 19
  same location and same name, OFF 19
  to SkyDrive, OFF 25
  workbooks, EX 21

savings plan development, EX 147–151

scale (n.) The range of values displayed on a chart axis. EX 187
  editing scale and text, EX 187–189

scale (v.) To reduce the width and the height of the printout to fit the number of pages you specify by shrinking the text size as needed. EX 47

scatter chart, EX 174

scenario A defined collection of input values used to perform a what-if analysis. EX 574
  defining, EX 577–580
  editing, EX 582–583
  merging scenarios, EX 587
  viewing, EX 580–582

Scenario Manager An Excel feature used create multiple scenarios, save them, and then switch between them to display the results of several what-if analyses within the worksheet. EX 574, EX 576–583
  defining scenarios, EX 577–580
  editing scenarios, EX 582–583
  viewing scenarios, EX 580–582

Scenario PivotTable report A PivotTable report generated by the Scenario Manager that displays the scenario changing and result values in an Excel PivotTable. EX 575, EX 585–587

scenario summary report A report generated by the Scenario Manager that lists the values for the changing cells and result cells under each scenario. EX 575, EX 583–585

Scenario Values dialog box, EX 578

schema A document that stores the rules about which elements in an XML document are required and which elements support multiple values and which only allow for a single value. EX 668

screen element, customizing, EX 736–739

screenshot, inserting, EX C23

ScreenTip A box with descriptive text about an object or button you are pointing to. OFF 12, OFF 13, OFF 25–26

scroll To move a different part of the workspace into view. OFF 3, OFF 11

Search box, FM 7

SEARCH function, EX A3

search string A string of characters to locate. EX 40

secondary axis A second or alternate chart axis that usually appears on the right side of a chart. EX 187

secondary sort field The second sort field. EX 245

security, data, EX 629

Select All button The button used to select all of the cells in the active worksheet. EX 2

Select Changes to Accept or Reject dialog box, EX C8–C9

Select Data Source dialog box, EX 204, EX 572

selecting
  cell ranges, EX 24–26
  multiple columns, EX 17
  multiple filter items, EX 255–256

selection box A box surrounding an object such as a chart that is used to move or resize the object. EX 176

sensitivity report A report used to quantify the reliability of the solution provided by Solver; often used in science and engineering environments when the user wants to investigate the mathematical aspects of the Solver solution. EX 600

series
  extrapolating from, EX 512–514
  filling, EX 143–147
  interpolating within, EX 509–511

Series dialog box, EX 510

SERIES function, EX 205

series name The first row of the data range, which identifies the data series. EX 170

series value The data that is displayed in a chart. EX 170

serif font A font that has extra decorative strokes at the end of each character, such as Times New Roman. EX 61

Share Workbook dialog box, EX C2–C3

shared workbook A workbook that can be edited simultaneously by more than one user when it is placed on a shared network folder or edited sequentially by users who edit the file in turns. EX C1–C21
  accepting and rejecting edits, EX C8–C10
  backward compatibility, EX C20
  digital signatures, EX C18–C20
  enabling workbook sharing, EX C2–C10
  encrypting, EX C16–C17
  inspecting, EX C14–C16
  marking as final, EX C17
  merging and comparing, EX C10–C12
  privacy options, EX C2
  resolving conflicts, EX C3–C4
  reviewing changes using tracking log, EX C6–C8
  setting document properties, EX C12–C14
  tracking changes, EX C5–C6

sharing
  files using Windows Live SkyDrive, OFF 24–25
  styles, EX D5

sheet. *See* chart sheet; worksheet

sheet tab The area at the bottom of the worksheet that identifies the sheet by name. EX 2

sheet tab scrolling button Button used to scroll the list of sheet tabs in the worksheet. EX 2

shortcut menu A list of commands related to a selection that opens when you click the right mouse button. OFF 17–18

simple interest Interest that is equal to a percentage of principal for each period that the money has been lent. EX 157

sizing button Buttons in the upper-right corner of the title bar that you click to resize and close the program window; Excel has a second set that resizes the workspace. OFF 3, OFF 8

sizing handle A square or dot on the selection box that is used to change the object's width and height. EX 176

SkyDrive An online workspace provided by Microsoft that you can use to make a file available to others for review and collaboration. OFF 24–25
- saving workbooks to, EX 349–350

slack The difference between the value in the cell and the value at the limit of the constraint. EX 602

slash (/), division operator, EX 30, EX 31

slicer An object used to filter a PivotTable or PivotChart. EX 269, EX 285–287

SLN function, EX 515

SmartArt graphic A professionally designed business diagram, such as a flow chart, organization chart, or production cycle chart. EX D18–D24
- editing pictures, EX D22–D24
- inserting text labels, EX D20
- Quick Styles, EX D20–D22

Solver An Excel add-in that searches for the optimal solution to a problem involving several variables. EX 588, EX 589, EX 593–606
- activating, EX 593–595
- answer reports, EX 600–602
- constraints, EX 596–598, EX 602
- saving and loading models, EX 602–606
- setting parameters, EX 595–596

Solver parameter One of three items you must specify: the objective cell, the variable (or changing) cells, and the constraints on the problem. EX 595–600

Solver Parameters dialog box, EX 595–596, EX 597–598

Solver Results dialog box, EX 599, EX 600–601

sort The process of rearranging data such as the records in an Excel table or range based on one or more fields; data can be sorted in ascending or descending order. EX 234, EX 244–249
- ascending/descending order, EX 244
- multiple columns using Sort dialog box, EX 245–247
- one column using sort buttons, EX 244–245
- PivotTable fields, EX 283
- queries, EX 641–642
- using custom list, EX 247–249

Sort dialog box, sorting multiple columns, EX 245–247

sort field A field that you use to order data. EX 235
- multiple, EX 245–247
- primary, EX 245
- secondary, EX 245

source file A file that supplies data to be displayed within the destination file, such as when two or more workbooks are linked. EX 321, EX C21
- closed, updating destination workbook with, EX 330–334
- open, updating destination workbook with, EX 329–330

sparkline A mini-chart that is displayed within a cell, displaying values from a selected range. EX 192, EX 193, EX 211–219
- creating, EX 211–214
- editing, EX 213
- groups, EX 215
- inserting, EX 213–214
- markers, EX 214–215
- types, EX 212

special format, EX A10–A11

spelling checker A feature that verifies the words in the active worksheet against the program's dictionary; you can replace or ignore the words it flags as misspelled. EX 22, EX 41–42

split bar A moveable bar that indicates the division between panes and that can be dragged to resize the panes. EX 251

spreadsheet A collection of text and numbers laid out in a rectangular grid. EX 4. *See also* workbook
- documenting, EX 451

standard color The 10 colors-dark red, red, orange, yellow, light green, green, light blue, blue, dark blue, and purple-that are always available regardless of the workbook's theme. EX 62

starting a program, OFF 5–8
- Microsoft Excel, EX 5

starting VBE, EX 688

statistical function, EX 128

status bar An area at the bottom of the program window that provides information about the program, open file, or current task or selection; it also contains buttons and other controls for working with the file and its content. EX 22, OFF 2

stock chart A chart that displays the high, low, and closing value of a stock. EX 174, EX 615

stock quote, retrieving from Web, EX 662–666

straight-line depreciation The depreciation of an asset by equal amounts each year of its lifetime until it reaches the salvage value. EX 516–517

Structured Query Language (SQL), EX 643

structured reference The Excel table name or column header that you can use in a formula in place of its cell or range reference. EX 364, EX 376–379

style
- cells, EX 84–85
- charts, EX 177–178
- PivotTables, EX 276
- sharing, EX D5, EX 87
- table. *See* table style

Style dialog box, EX D3

sub procedure In VBA, a macro that performs an action on a project or workbook. EX 466, EX 685, EX 693–698, EX 700, EX 714–718
- creating using copy and paste, EX 694–696
- private, EX 694
- public, EX 694
- running, EX 696–698
- to store defined names, EX 717–718
- to switch defined names, EX 715–716

subfolder A folder contained within another folder. FM 5

SUBSTITUTE function A text function that replaces existing text with new text. EX A9–A10

subtotal, inserting in Excel table, EX 263–267

subtraction, formulas, EX 67–68, EX 89–91

subtraction operator (-), EX 30, EX 31

Sum button. *See* AutoSum

SUM function A function that returns the sum of the values in the range. EX 117, EX 129, EX 131–132

SUMIF function A function that adds the values in a range that match criteria you specify. EX 399, EX 407–408

SUMIFS function A function that adds values in a range that meet multiple criteria. EX B9, EX B11–B12

surface chart, EX 174

Switch Windows button, EX 321, EX 324

switching
- between open programs, OFF 2, OFF 7–8
- views, OFF 9
- worksheet views, EX 43–44

SYD function, EX 515

syntax A set of rules that specifies how the function should be written. EX 127–130

syntax error, EX 717

T

tab The part of the Ribbon that includes commands related to particular activities or tasks. OFF 2, OFF 11. *See also* contextual tab
- removing, EX 473

table
- Excel. *See* Excel table
- lookup, EX 380

table A collection of data values arranged in rows (or records) and columns (or fields). EX 632, EX 634–635
- choosing for queries, EX 638–640

table column
- calculated, inserting, EX 366–367
- filtering using multiple columns, EX 254–255
- filtering using one column, EX 252–254

TABLE function An array function that returns multiple values to multiple cells. EX 573

Table Name box, EX 241

table style A single style that formats all of the table elements within an Excel table. EX 83, EX 91–95, EX 235
- applying, EX 92
- custom, EX D5–D7
- selecting options, EX 93–95

Table Tools tab, EX 83

Tagged Image File Format (TIFF) A picture format that provides higher quality photos, but much larger image files, increasing the workbook's size. EX D24

tangible asset A long-lasting material asset not intended for sale, such as equipment, land, buildings and delivery trucks. EX 514
- depreciation. *See* depreciation

task pane A window that helps you navigate through a complEX task or feature in Office programs. OFF 14–15

teamwork, OFF 32
- improving collaborative process, EX C21

template A workbook with labels, formats, and formulas already built into it and with variable data removed. EX 336, EX 340–348
- creating new workbook from, EX 346–348
- custom, EX 344–346
- default, EX 341
- existing, creating workbooks based on, EX 341–344

text
cells, formatting, EX 60–64
chart axis, editing, EX 187–189
converting case using UPPER function, EX A8–A9
delimited, EX 614, EX 618
existing, replacing with new text, EX A9–A10
inserting into SmartArt graphics, EX D19

text data A any combination of letters, numbers, and symbols that form words and sentences. EX 9
entering. *See* entering text
wrapping within cell, EX 12

text file A file type that contains only text and numbers without any formulas, graphics, special fonts, or formatted text. EX 614, EX 617–624
connecting to, EX 617
connections, EX 624–625
editing column breaks, EX 620–621
formats, EX 618
formatting and trimming data, EX 621–624
importing data, EX 619–620
specifying starting row, EX 620

text filter, EX 254

TEXT function, EX A3

text function, EX A3–A10, EX 128

Text Import Wizard, EX 619–620

text string Two or more text characters. EX 9

Text to Columns command, EX A7–A8

theme A collection of formats for text, colors, images, and graphical effects applied throughout a workbook. EX D25–D27, EX 60, EX 86–87
applying, EX D25
custom, EX D26–D27
saving, EX D26
sharing, EX 87

theme color The 12 colors that belong to the workbook's theme. EX 62

theme font A font associated with a particular theme and used for headings and body text in the workbook; theme fonts change automatically when you change the theme applied to the workbook. EX 61

ThisCell object, EX 705

ThisWorkbook object, EX 705

3-D chart, EX 209–211
effective, EX 211

3-D reference A reference to the same cell or range in multiple worksheets in the same workbook. EX 303
adding values across worksheets, EX 312–317
managing, EX 313

thumbnail, Word document, OFF 8

thumbnail image A small graphic that previews a file's contents for certain file types. FM 2

tick mark A line that identifies the units at regular intervals on a chart axis. EX 171

ticker symbol An abbreviation for a stock name used by the stock market. EX 662

TIFF. *See* Tagged Image File Format

tiled workbook layout, EX 3240–235

time data A value in a recognized time format. EX 9
formatting, EX 71–72
storage by Excel, EX 72

time function, EX 128, EX 155

time value of money The observation that money received today is worth more than the same amount received later. EX 527–528

title
charts. *See* chart title
columns, formatting, EX 90–91
print titles, EX 82, EX 104–105
rows, formatting, EX 90–91

title bar The area at the top of the program window that displays the name of the open file and the program. OFF 3

TODAY function A date function that displays the current date. EX 138, EX 155–156

toggle A type of button that you click to turn the feature both on and off; while the feature is on, the button remains colored or highlighted. OFF 12

Total row A row at the end of an Excel table that is used to calculate summary statistics (such as sum, average, count, maximum, and minimum) for each column in the Excel table. EX 250, EX 259–263

Total Row option, table styles, EX 93

tracer arrow An arrow used to track an error to its source by pointing from the precedent cell to the dependent cell. EX 525

tracing an error, EX 535–538

tracking changes in workbook, EX C5–C6

tracking log, EX C6–C8

trial and error An approach to finding the optimal solution by exploring different possible values at random. EX 593
maximizing net income, EX 591–593

trig function, EX 128

TRIM function, EX A3

truncate To hide from the view. EX 10

Trust Center A central location for all of the security settings in Office 2010. EX 456

Trust Center dialog box, EX 456

trusted location A connection to a data source that Excel will access without prompting you to confirm that the connection is secure. EX 629–630

Tufte, Edward, EX 219

two-variable data table A data table used to perform several what-if analyses by specifying two input cells and one result cell. EX 553, EX 566–573
charting, EX 570–573
creating, EX 566–570

typeface The specific design of a set of characters, including letters, numbers, punctuation marks, and symbols. EX 58

U

Undo button, VBA, EX 708

undoing an action, EX 40

ungrouping worksheets, EX 308–309

unhiding worksheet data, EX 101

Uniform Resource Locator (URL) The location of a Web page. EX 656

unit elastic The price elasticity of demand when any change in price is met by an equal and opposite change in demand. EX 591

updating a linked workbook, EX 329–332

UPPER function A text function that converts all letters of each word in a text string to uppercase. EX A3, EX A8–A9

URL. *See* Uniform Resource Locator

user
multiple, sharing workbooks. *See* shared workbook
retrieving information from, EX 718–720

V

validation rule A statement that defines criteria for the data that can be stored in a cell or range. EX 438–444

value axis. *See* vertical, or value, axis

value field A field that contains summary data in a PivotTable. EX 268
adding, EX 283–284
formatting, EX 276–277

Value Field Settings dialog box, EX 277

variable A named element in a program used to store data. EX 701, EX 711–714
assigning values, EX 712–714
data types, EX 711
declaring, EX 712

variable cell A cell whose values Solver changes in order to reach a solution. EX 589

variable expense An expense that changes in proportion to the amount of business a company does. EX 554

variable name A unique name that identifies a variable. EX 701

VBA. *See* Visual Basic for Applications

VBAProject object, EX 703

VBE. *See* Visual Basic Editor

VDB function, EX 515

vertical, or **value, axis** The axis that displays the series values from the data series. EX 170

vertical workbook layout, EX 324

view, switching, OFF 9

view button The buttons that change how the worksheet content is displayed-Normal view, Page Layout view, or Page Break Preview. EX 23, OFF 3

viewing
Code window, EX 692–693
more workspace, OFF 11
scenarios, EX 580–582
worksheet formulas, EX 46–48

virus A computer program designed to copy itself into other programs with the intention of causing mischief or harm. EX 455
macros, protecting against, EX 455–457

Visual Basic Editor (VBE) An application that works with Excel and all of the Office programs to view, debug, edit, and manage VBA code. EX 453, EX 464–467, EX 688–693
clearing, EX 688
starting, EX 688

Visual Basic for Applications (VBA) A programming language. EX 457, EX 702–720
Immediate window, EX 702–703
learning, EX 688, EX 702–703
objects. *See* object
sub procedures. *See* sub procedure
Undo button, EX 708
VBE. *See* Visual Basic Editor

VLOOKUP function A lookup function that searches vertically down the first column of the lookup table (where the compare values are stored) and retrieves the appropriate value from the table. EX 381
- finding an approximate match, EX 390–394
- finding an exact match, EX 388–390

W

Watch Window A dialog box that displays values of cells located throughout the workbook so the user can view the impact of changing a cell's value on widely scattered dependent cells. EX 540–542

Web query A set of guidelines that specifies how data should be retrieved from different sections of a Web page. EX 656, EX 658–662
- formatting, EX 661
- saving, EX 662

WEEKDAY function, EX 155

what-if analysis An approach in which you change one or more values in a spreadsheet and then assess the effect those changes have on the calculated values. EX 4, EX 551–606
- choosing tool, EX 602
- CVP analysis, EX 554–558
- data tables. *See* data table
- Goal Seek, EX 558–561
- price elasticity of demand, EX 590–593
- Scenario PivotTable reports, EX 585–587
- scenarios. *See* scenario *entries*
- Solver. *See* Solver

window. *See* program window; worksheet window

Windows Explorer A tool that shows the contents of the default libraries on your computer, making it easy to find the files you work with often, such as documents and pictures. FM 6

Windows Live A collection of services and Web applications that you can use to be more productive. EX 348–352
- obtaining a Windows Live ID, EX 349
- SkyDrive. *See* SkyDrive

win/loss sparkline, EX 212

Word. *See* Microsoft Word 2010

workbook The file you create in Excel; commonly referred to as a spreadsheet. OFF 4
- auditing. *See* auditing a workbook
- automatic calculation, EX E15
- backward compatibility, EX C20
- created in earlier versions of Excel, opening and saving, EX A2–A3
- creating from template, EX 346–348
- digital signatures, EX C18–C20
- editing from Excel Web App, EX 350–352
- encrypting, EX C16–C17
- enhancing using color, EX 66
- formatting, EX 60
- linking. *See also* linking workbooks
- marking as final, EX C17
- planning, EX 8
- printing, EX 45–46
- restricting permissions, EX E22
- saving, EX 21
- saving to SkyDrive, EX 349–350
- shared. *See* shared workbook
- unprotecting, EX 448–449
- with macros, opening, EX 472
- with macros, saving, EX 471–472

Workbook Connections dialog box, EX 615, EX 625

Workbook object, EX 703, EX 706, EX 709

workbook protection A setting that limits users' ability to make changes to the workbook's structure and windows. EX 437, EX 447–449

worksheet A grid of rows and columns in which the contents of the spreadsheet are laid out. EX 2, EX 3, EX 37–38
- active, EX 2
- background images, EX 59
- binding XML elements to a worksheet, EX 670
- changing views, EX 43–44
- columns. *See* worksheet column
- copying, EX 38
- deleting, EX 38
- editing content, EX 38–42
- entering formulas, EX 30–33
- formatting for printing, EX 101–107
- grouping. *See* worksheet group
- hidden, EX C15–C16
- hiding data, EX 101
- inserting, EX 37–38
- inserting macro buttons, EX 468–469
- inserting multiple, EX E4
- moving, EX 38
- moving charts between, EX 175–176
- multiple. *See* worksheet group
- navigating between, EX 5
- navigating within, EX 6–7
- page breaks, EX 103–104
- renaming, EX 38
- rows. *See* worksheet row
- scrolling through, EX 7
- unprotecting, EX 448–449

worksheet column
- clearing, EX 20–21
- deleting, EX 20–21
- freezing, EX 238–239
- inserting, EX 18–20
- multiple, selecting, EX 17
- setting width, EX 15–17

worksheet group A collection of two or more selected worksheets. EX 302, EX 304–309, EX 309–318
- adding references across using 3-D references, EX 312–317
- copying worksheets, EX 309–310
- editing grouped worksheets, EX 307
- entering formulas, EX 306–307
- formatting, EX 308
- multiple worksheets with identical layouts, EX 309
- printing, EX 317–318
- referencing cells and ranges in other worksheets, EX 310–312
- ungrouping worksheets, EX 308–309

Worksheet object, EX 703, EX 706, EX 709

worksheet protection A setting that limits users' ability to modify the worksheet's contents, structure, or formatting. EX 437, EX 445–447, EX 448–449

worksheet row
- banded, EX 82, EX 91–92, EX 93
- clearing, EX 20–21
- deleting, EX 20–21
- freezing, EX 238–239
- hiding, EX 101
- inserting, EX 18–20

worksheet window, splitting into panes, EX 261–263

workspace (Excel) An Excel file that saves information about all of the currently opened workbooks, such as their locations, window sizes, zoom level, and other settings. EX 321
- creating, EX 333–335

workspace (Office) The area that displays the file you are working on (a Word document, an Excel workbook, an Access database, or a PowerPoint slide). OFF 2
- resizing, OFF 8–9
- viewing more, OFF 11

Wrap Text button, EX 12

writing code, EX 720

X

x-axis The axis that represents the length of the object. EX 209

XML. *See* Extensible Markup Language

XML data map A schematic diagram that shows the structure of an XML document. EX 657

XML Maps dialog box, EX 669

XY scatter chart A chart that shows the pattern or relationship between two or more sets of values. EX 209

Y

y-axis The axis that represents the height of the object. EX 209

YEAR function, EX 155

Z

z-axis In a three-dimensional chart, the axis that represents the object's depth. EX 209

zipped folder. *See* compressed folder

zoom To magnify or shrink the display of content in the workspace. OFF 3, OFF 9–11

Zoom control, EX 3

Zoom dialog box, OFF 10–11

TASK REFERENCE

TASK	PAGE #	RECOMMENDED METHOD
3-D Pie chart, rotate	EX 210	Select chart, click 3-D Rotation button in Background group on Chart Tools Layout tab, set rotation, click Close
3-D reference, use	EX 313	*See* Reference box: Entering a Function That Contains a 3-D Reference
Access database, retrieve data	EX 649	Click From Access button in Get External Data group on Data tab, locate and select Access database file, select database table with data to retrieve
Action, undo or redo	EX 40	Click [undo] or [redo] on Quick Access Toolbar
Advanced filter, clear	EX B7	Click Clear button in Sort & Filter group on Data tab
Advanced filter, create	EX B4	Click Advanced button in Sort & Filter group on Data tab, set filter options, data, and criteria ranges in Advanced Filter dialog box, click OK
AutoFill, copy formulas	EX 142	Select cell with formula, click and drag fill handle over adjacent range
AutoFill, create series	EX 143	Enter first few entries in series, drag fill handle over adjacent range
AutoSum feature, enter function with	EX 35	Click cell, click [Σ] in Editing group on Home tab, click function, verify range, press Enter
Axis title, add	EX 201	Select chart, click Axis Titles button in Labels group on Chart Tools Layout tab, point to axis, select options
Background image, add to worksheet	EX 65	Click Background button in Page Setup group on Page Layout tab, click image file, click Insert
Border, add to cell	EX 76	Select range, click [border] in Font group on Home tab, click border
Cell, change fill color	EX 64	Click [fill color] in Font group on Home tab, click color
Cell, clear contents of	EX 20	Right-click cell, range, column, or row; click Clear Contents
Cell, delete	EX 20	Select cell or range, click Delete button in Cells group on Home tab
Cell, edit	EX 38	Double-click cell, enter changes
Cell, go to	EX 7	Click Find & Select button in Editing group on Home tab, click Go To
Cell, move or copy	EX 26	*See* Reference box: Moving or Copying a Cell or Range
Cell contents, align horizontally in cell	EX 72	Click [align left], [center], or [align right] in Alignment group on Home tab
Cell contents, change indent of	EX 73	Click [decrease indent] or [increase indent] in Alignment group on Home tab
Cell contents, rotate	EX 75	Click [orientation] in Alignment group on Home tab, click rotation angle
Cell or range, select by defined name	EX 426	Click Name box arrow, click defined name
Cell reference, change	EX 118	*See* Reference box: Entering Relative, Absolute, and Mixed References
Cell style, create	EX D2	*See* Reference box: Creating a Cell Style
Cell value, hide	EX D10	Select cell, open Format Cells dialog box, click Number tab, click Custom category, type ;;; in Type box, click OK
Cells, lock or unlock	EX 445	Select cell or range, click Dialog Box Launcher in Font group on Home tab, click Protection tab, check or uncheck Locked check box, click OK
Cells, merge and center	EX 74	Select adjacent cells, click [merge and center] in Alignment group on Home tab
Cells, reference in other worksheets	EX 310	Enter reference in the format =*SheetName!CellRange*
Cells, select all in worksheet	EX 24	*See* Reference box: Selecting Ranges

TASK	PAGE #	RECOMMENDED METHOD
Chart, add axis title to	EX 201	Select chart, click Axis Titles button in Labels group on Chart Tools Layout tab, point to axis, select option
Chart, add data label	EX 182	Select chart, click Data Labels button in Labels group on Chart Tools Layout tab, Click More Data Label Options, select options, click Close
Chart, add data series	EX 203	*See* Reference box: Adding a Data Series to a Chart
Chart, add gridlines	EX 201	Select chart, click Gridlines button in Axes group on Chart Tools Layout tab, select option
Chart, change data	EX 202	Enter new values in chart's data source
Chart, change layout	EX 178	Select chart, click layout in Chart Layout group on Chart Tools Design tab
Chart, change style	EX 177	Select chart, click chart style in Chart Styles group on Chart Tools Design tab
Chart, change to 3-D	EX 209	Select chart, click Change Chart Type button in Type group on Chart Tools Design tab, select 3-D chart type
Chart, create	EX172	*See* Reference box: Inserting a Chart
Chart, format data marker	EX 207	Click data marker, click Format Selection in Current Selection group on Chart Tools Layout tab, format as needed
Chart, move within worksheet	EX 176	Select chart, drag to new location
Chart, move to another sheet	EX 175	Select chart, click Move Chart button in Location group on Chart Tools Design tab
Chart, resize	EX 176	Select chart, drag sizing handle
Chart, select	EX 176	Click empty area of chart ("Chart Area" ScreenTip appears)
Chart axis, change scale	EX 187	Select chart, click Axes button in Axes group on Chart Tools Layout tab, click option
Chart legend, add or remove	EX 186	Select chart, click Legend button in Labels group on Chart Tools Layout tab, click option
Chart legend, format	EX 180	Select chart, click Legend button in Labels group on Chart Tools Layout tab, click legend format
Chart legend, overlay	EX 199	Double-click legend, uncheck Show the legend without overlapping the chart check box, click Close
Chart sheet, create	EX 219	Select chart, click Move Chart button in Location group on Chart Tools Design tab, click New sheet option button, enter name, click OK
Chart title, change	EX 179	Click chart title, type new chart title, press Enter
Code window, view	EX 692	In Visual Basic Editor, click View, click Code
Color scale, apply	EX D11	Click Conditional Formatting button in Styles group on Home tab, click Color Scales, select scale type
Column, change width	EX 15	*See* Reference box: Changing the Column Width or Row Height
Column, insert	EX 19	*See* Reference box: Inserting a Column or Row
Column, select	EX 17	Click column heading
Column chart, format columns	EX 189	Select all columns in data series, click Format Selection button in Current Selection group on Chart Tools Layout tab, specify column format
Columns, select	EX 17	Click first column heading, hold down Shift, click last column heading

TASK	PAGE #	RECOMMENDED METHOD
Comment, delete	EX 450	Click cell with comment, click Delete button in Comments group on Review tab
Comment, insert	EX 449	*See* Reference box: Inserting a Comment
Combination chart, create	EX 206	*See* Reference box: Creating a Combination Chart
Compressed folder, create	FM 18	In a folder window, select files and folders to compress, right-click selection, point to Send to, click Compressed (zipped) folder, type folder name, press Enter
Compressed folder, extract all files and folders from	FM 19	Right-click compressed folder, click Extract All
Compressed folder, open	FM 18	Double-click compressed folder
Conditional format, clear	EX 97	Select cell, click Conditional Formatting button in Styles group on Home tab, point to Clear Rules, click Clear Rules from Selected Cells
Conditional format, use to highlight cells	EX 96	*See* Reference box: Highlighting a Cell Based on Its Value
Conditional formatting rule, edit	EX 402	*See* Reference box: Entering a Conditional Formatting Rule
Conditional formatting rule, modify	EX D10	Click Conditional Formatting button in Styles group on Home tab, click Manage Rules, click Show formatting rules for box, click This Worksheet, click rule to modify, click Edit Rule, change format, click OK
Connection, edit	EX 644	Click Connections button in Connections group on Data tab, select connection to edit, click Properties button
Criteria filter, specify complex criteria	EX 256	Click filter arrow, point to Number Filters, Text Filters, or Date Filters, specify filter criteria, click OK
Custom format, create	EX A11	Select range, click Dialog Box Launcher in Number group on Home tab, click Number tab, click Custom in Category box, enter format codes in Type box, click OK
Data, create input message, error alert message, or validation rule	EX 438	*See* Reference box: Validating Data
Data, split from one column into separate columns	EX A7	Select range, click Text to Columns button in Data Tools group on Data tab, follow steps in wizard.
Data bars, create	EX 216	Select range, click Conditional Formatting button in Styles group on Home tab, point to Data Bars, select data bar style
Data series, add to chart	EX 203	*See* Reference box: Adding a Data Series to a Chart
Database query, create	EX 636	*See* Reference box: Using Microsoft Query with an Access Database
Date, enter into cell	EX 12	Click cell, type date, press Enter or Tab
Defined name, create for cell or range	EX 424	*See* Reference box: Creating a Defined Name for a Cell or Range
Defined name, edit or delete	EX 427	Click Name Manager button in Defined Names group on Formulas tab, select name, click Edit and modify or click Delete, click OK
Defined names, add to formulas	EX 433	*See* Reference box: Adding Defined Names to Existing Formulas
Defined names, paste list in worksheet	EX 428	Click cell, click Use in Formula button in Defined Names group on Formulas tab, click Paste Names, click Paste List button
Depreciation, calculate	EX 516	*See* Reference box: Calculating Depreciation
Developer tab, display or hide	EX 454	Click File tab, click Options button, click Customize Ribbon, check or uncheck Developer check box, click OK

TASK	PAGE #	RECOMMENDED METHOD
Document Inspector, run	EX C14	Click the File tab, click Info, click Check for Issues button, click Inspect Document
Duplicate values, highlight	EX 400	*See* Reference box: Highlighting Duplicate Values
Embedded object, modify	EX C25	Click embedded object, select editing tools on contextual tabs
Error Alert message, create	EX 438	*See* Reference box: Validating Data
Error value, trace	EX 536	*See* Reference box: Tracing Error Values
Excel screen elements, customize	EX 736	Click File tab, click Options, click Advanced, select element to customize
Excel table, add a record	EX 242	*See* Reference box: Adding a Record to an Excel Table
Excel, start	EX 5	Click [Start button], click All Programs, click Microsoft Office, click Microsoft Excel 2010
Excel table, add a record	EX 242	*See* Reference box: Adding a Record to an Excel Table
Excel table, create	EX 239	Click Table button in Tables group on Insert tab, verify range of data, click OK
Excel table, format	EX 241	Click options in Table Style Options group on Table Tools Design tab
Excel table, rename	EX 240	Click Excel table, select name in Table Name box in Properties group on Table Tools Design tab, type name
External data, refresh	EX 626	*See* Reference box: Refreshing External Data
External data range, set properties	EX 625	*See* Reference box: Editing the Properties of an External Data Range
External reference formula, create	EX 325	Click cell in destination file, type =, click cell in source file, complete formula as usual
File, close	OFF 22	Click File tab, click Close
File, copy	FM 14	*See* Reference box: Copying a File or Folder in a Folder Window
File, delete	FM 17	Right-click file, click Delete
File, move	FM 13	*See* Reference box: Moving a File or Folder in a Folder Window
File, open	OFF 22	*See* Reference box: Opening an Existing File
File, print	OFF 29	*See* Reference box: Printing a File
File, save	OFF 19	*See* Reference box: Saving a File
File, save to SkyDrive	OFF 24	*See* Reference box: Saving a File to SkyDrive
File, switch between open	OFF 7	Point to program button on taskbar, click thumbnail of file to make active
Files, select multiple	FM 14	Hold down Ctrl key and click files
Fill handle, use	EX 141	*See* Reference box: Copying Formulas and Formats with AutoFill
Filter, clear from column	EX 255	Click filter arrow, click Clear Filter From *column*
Filter, clear from Excel table	EX 259	Click Clear button in Sort & Filter group on Data tab
Filter, select multiple items	EX 255	Click filter arrow, check two or more items, click OK
Filter, use multiple columns	EX 254	Filter for one column, repeat to filter for additional columns
Filter, use one column	EX 252	Click filter arrow, check item to filter by, click OK
Filter arrows, display or hide	EX 252	In Sort & Filter group on Data tab, click Filter button
Financial data, retrieve	EX 662	Click Existing Connections button in Get External Data group on Data tab, select a built-in MSN MoneyCentral Investor financial query
Folder, copy	FM 14	*See* Reference box: Copying a File or Folder in a Folder Window
Folder, create	FM 11	*See* Reference box: Creating a Folder in a Folder Window

TASK	PAGE #	RECOMMENDED METHOD
Folder, move	FM 13	*See* Reference box: Moving a File or Folder in a Folder Window
Font, change color	EX 62	Click [Font Color button] in Font group on Home tab, click color
Font, change size	EX 61	Click Font Size arrow in Font group on Home tab, click point size
Font, change style	EX 61	In Font group on Home tab, click **B**, *I*, or U
Font, change typeface	EX 61	Click Font arrow in Font group on Home tab, click font
Format, copy using Format Painter	EX 79	Select range with original formatting, click [Format Painter button] in Clipboard group on Home tab, select range to format
Format, find and replace	EX 40	Click Find & Select in Editing group on Home tab, click Replace
Format Cells dialog box, open	EX 77	Click Dialog Box Launcher in Number group on Home tab
Formula, enter	EX 31	*See* Reference box: Inserting a Formula
Formula, evaluate a	EX 538	Select cell containing formula, click Evaluate Formula button in Formula Auditing group on Formulas tab
Formula, reference another worksheet	EX 311	*See* Reference box: Entering a Formula with References to Another Worksheet
Formula results, copy and paste as values	EX A5	Copy range with formula results, click first cell in paste location, click Paste button arrow in Clipboard group on Home tab, click Values button
Formula view, switch to	EX 46	Press Ctrl+`
Function, insert	EX 131	Click function category in the Function Library group on Formulas tab, click a function, enter arguments, click OK
Goal Seek, perform	EX 558	Click What-If Analysis button in Data Tools group on Data tab, click Goal Seek, enter parameters
Gridlines, add to chart	EX 201	Select chart, click Gridlines button in Axes group on Chart Tools Layout tab, select option
Header or footer, create	EX 105	Click Header & Footer button in Text group on Insert tab
Help, get in Office	OFF 27	*See* Reference box: Getting Help
Hyperlink, create	EX 338	*See* Reference box: Inserting a Hyperlink
Hyperlink, edit	EX 340	Right-click cell with hyperlink, click Edit Hyperlink, make edits in Edit Hyperlink dialog box, click OK
Icon set, apply	EX D15	Click Conditional Formatting button in Styles group on Home tab, click Icon Sets, select icon set type
Immediate window, open	EX 702	In Visual Basic Editor, click View, click Immediate Window
Input message, create	EX 438	*See* Reference box: Validating Data
Internal rate of return, calculate	EX 532	*See* Reference box: Calculating the Value of an Investment
Invalid data, circle	EX 444	Click Data Validation button arrow in Data Tools group on Data tab, click Circle Invalid Data
Link, embed	EX C24	Copy range or chart, go to destination Office file, click Paste button arrow, click Keep Source Formatting & Embed Workbook
Link, paste	EX C24	Copy range or chart, go to destination Office file, click Paste button arrow, click Link & Keep Source Formatting
Link, update	EX C25	Right-click linked object, click Update Link
Linked workbooks, update	EX 329	Click in source file, edit as usual

TASK	PAGE #	RECOMMENDED METHOD
Links, manage	EX 332	Click Edit Links button in Connections group on Data tab, select option, click OK
Macro, edit	EX 464	*See* Reference box: Editing a Macro
Macro, record	EX 458	*See* Reference box: Recording a Macro
Macro, run	EX 461	*See* Reference box: Running a Macro
Macro, set security level for	EX 456	*See* Reference box: Setting Macro Security in Excel
Macro button, create	EX 468	*See* Reference box: Creating a Macro Button
Macro button, move	EX 470	Right-click macro button, press Esc, drag button by its selection box to new location
Macro button, resize	EX 470	Right-click macro button, press Esc, drag sizing handle
Margins, set	EX 107	Click Margins button in Page Setup group on Page Layout tab, select margin size
Module, change name	EX 692	Select module from Project Explorer, type new name in Properties window in (Name) row
My Documents folder, open	FM 8	In a folder window, click ▷ next to Libraries in Navigation pane, click ▷ next to Documents, click My Documents
Net present value, calculate	EX 532	*See* Reference box: Calculating the Value of an Investment
Number format, apply	EX 68	Click $, %, , in Number group on Home tab
Number format, apply long date	EX 71	Click Number Format arrow in Number group on Home tab, click Long Date
Number format, increase or decrease decimal places	EX 68	Click or in Number group on Home tab
Office program, exit	OFF 30	Click X
Office program, start	OFF 5	*See* Reference box: Starting an Office Program
Office program, switch between open	OFF 7	Click program button on taskbar to make active
One-variable data table, create	EX 562	*See* Reference box: Creating a One-Variable Data Table
Page break, insert or remove	EX 103	*See* Reference box: Inserting and Removing Page Breaks
Picture, edit	EX D23	*See* Reference box: Editing a Picture
Pie chart, change slice color	EX 183	Click pie, click slice, click in Font group on Home tab, click color
PivotChart, create	EX 291	Click PivotTable button arrow in Tables group on Insert tab, click PivotChart, select options, click OK
PivotTable, create	EX 272	*See* Reference box: Creating a PivotTable
PivotTable, filter using slicer	EX 286	Click slicer button
PivotTable, rearrange	EX 277	Drag field buttons in PivotTable Field List
PivotTable, refresh	EX 287	click Refresh button in Data group on PivotTable Tools Options tab
PivotTable field, remove	EX 284	Uncheck items in field area of PivotTable Field List
PivotTable fields, filter	EX 281	Click the column or row label filter arrow in PivotTable for data to filter, check and uncheck items
PivotTable items, group	EX 288	Click Group Field button in Group group on PivotTable Tools Options tab, select options in Grouping dialog box, click OK

TASK	PAGE #	RECOMMENDED METHOD
PivotTable report filter, add	EX 279	Drag field button from PivotTable Field List to Report Filter box
PivotTable report filter, modify	EX 280	Click report filter arrow, click filter items
PivotTable report layout, change	EX 278	Click Report Layout button in Layout group on PivotTable Tools Design tab, click layout
PivotTable slicer, create	EX 285	Click Insert Slicer button in Sort & Filter group on PivotTable Tools Options tab, click field check box, click OK
PivotTable style, apply	EX 276	Click More button in PivotTable Styles group on PivotTable Tools Design tab, click style
PivotTable value fields, format	EX 276	Click cell in PivotTable, click Field Settings button in Active Field group on PivotTable Tools Options tab, click Number Format button, select format, click OK in each dialog box
Present value, calculate	EX 496	Use the function =PV(*rate*, *nper*, *pmt* [, *fv*=0] [, *type* = 0])
Preview pane, open	FM 17	In a folder window, click
Print area, clear	EX 102	Click Print Area button in Page Setup group on Page Layout tab, click Clear Print Area
Print area, set	EX 102	Select range, click Print Area button in Page Setup group on Page Layout tab, click Set Print Area
Print titles, add to printout	EX 104	Click Print Titles button in Page Setup group on Page Layout tab, click in Rows to repeat at top box, select range, click OK
Program window, resize	OFF 8	Click , ,
Project Explorer, view	EX 689	In Visual Basic Editor, click View, click Project Explorer
Properties window, view	EX 690	In Visual Basic Editor, click View, click Properties Window
Query Wizard, start	EX 637	Click From Other Sources button in Get External Data group on Data tab, click From Microsoft Query
Query, edit	EX 645	See Reference box: Editing a Database Query
Query, save	EX 643	In the last step of the Query wizard, click Save Query button, specify filename and location for the query file
Quick Access Toolbar, customize	EX 732	Click Customize Quick Access Toolbar button, click More Commands, select commands to display
Range, insert or delete	EX 29	*See* Reference box: Inserting or Deleting a Range
Range, move or copy	EX 26	*See* Reference box: Moving or Copying a Cell or Range
Range, select adjacent or nonadjacent	EX 24	*See* Reference box: Selecting Ranges
Record, delete from Excel table	EX 244	Select the record, click Delete button arrow in Cells group on Home tab, click Delete Table Rows
Ribbon, minimize or maximize	EX 473	Click or , or double-click any tab
Row, change height	EX 15	*See* Reference box: Changing the Column Width or Row Height
Row, hide	EX 101	Select rows to hide, click Format button in Cells group on Home tab, point to Hide & Unhide, click Hide Rows
Row, insert	EX 19	*See* Reference box: Inserting a Column or Row
Row, select one or more	EX 20	Click row heading, hold down Shift and click last row heading

TASK	PAGE #	RECOMMENDED METHOD
Row, unhide	EX 101	Select rows above and below hidden rows, click Format button in Cells group on Home tab, point to Hide & Unhide, click Unhide Rows
Rows, repeat in printout	EX 104	Click Print Titles button in Page Setup group on Page Layout tab, click in Rows to repeat at top box, select range, click OK
Row(s) and column(s), freeze	EX 238	Click cell below and to right of row(s) and column(s) to freeze, click Freeze Panes button in Window group on View tab, click option
Row(s) and column(s), unfreeze	EX 239	Click Freeze Panes button in Window group on View tab, click Unfreeze Panes
Scenario, define	EX 577	*See* Reference box: Defining a Scenario
Scenario, edit	EX 584	*See* Reference box: Creating a Scenario Report or Scenario PivotTable Report
Scenario Summary or PivotTable report, create	EX 584	*See* Reference box: Creating a Scenario Report or Scenario PivotTable Report
Screenshot, insert	EX C23	Click Screenshot button in Illustrations group on Insert tab
Series, create with AutoFill	EX 144	*See* Reference box: Creating a Series with AutoFill
Shared workbook, accept changes	EX C8	*See* Reference box: Accepting and Rejecting Edits
Shared workbook, review edits	EX C6	*See* Reference box: Reviewing Tracked Changes in a Shared Workbook
SmartArt graphic, insert	EX D19	Click SmartArt button in Illustrations group on Insert tab, click graphic type, select graphic, click OK
Solver, activate	EX 593	*See* Reference box: Activating Solver
Solver, create Answer Report	EX 600	Run Solver, click Answer button in Reports box, click Keep Solver Solution option button, click OK
Solver, run	EX 598	Click Solver button in Analysis group on Data tab, enter parameters and constraints, click Solve
Solver, set constraints	EX 596	*See* Reference box: Setting Constraints on the Solver Solution
Solver, set parameters	EX 595	*See* Reference box: Setting Solver Parameters
Solver model, save and load	EX 603	*See* Reference box: Saving and Loading a Solver Model
Sort, create a custom list	EX 248	*See* Reference box: Creating a Custom List
Sort, multiple columns	EX 245	*See* Reference box: Sorting Data Using Multiple Sort Fields
Sort, one column	EX 244	Click Sort & Filter button in Editing group on Home tab, click AZ↓ or ZA↓
Sparklines, add markers	EX 214	Select range with sparklines, click marker check boxes in Show group on Sparklines Tools Design tab
Sparklines, create	EX 213	*See* Reference box: Creating and Editing Sparklines
Special format, apply to data	EX A10	Select range, click Dialog Box Launcher in Number group on Home tab, click Special in Category box, click special format, click OK
Spelling, check in worksheet	EX 41	Click Spelling button in Proofing group on Review tab
Split panes, create or remove	EX 261	Click Split button in Window group on View tab
Style, apply to cell	EX 84	*See* Reference box: Applying a Cell Style
Sub procedure, insert	EX 694	Open Code window in Visual Basic Editor, click Insert, clic enter procedure name, type, and scope, click OK
Sub procedure, run	EX 696	Click within sub procedure in Visual Basic Editor, click Run, click Run Sub/UserForm.

TASK	PAGE #	RECOMMENDED METHOD
Subtotal Outline view, use	EX 266	Click outline button to show or hide the selected outline level
Subtotals, insert	EX 263	*See* Reference box: Calculating Subtotals for a Range of Data
Subtotals, remove	EX 266	Click Subtotal button in Outline group on Data tab, click Remove All button
Table, apply style	EX 91	Select range, click Format as Table button in Styles group on Home tab, click style, verify range for table, click OK
Table, remove filter	EX 93	Click in table, click Filter button in Sort & Filter group on Data tab
Table, select style options	EX 93	Click table, select options in Table Style Options group on Table Tools Design tab
Table style, create	EX D5	Click Format as Table button in Styles group on Home tab, click New Table Style, type style name, format table elements, click OK
Template, create custom	EX 344	*See* Reference box: Creating a Custom Template
Text, enter multiple lines in a cell	EX 11	Type first line of entry, press Alt+Enter, type next line
Text, format selection	EX 63	Double-click cell, select text, format as needed
Text file, connect	EX 617	*See* Reference box: Connecting to a Text File
Theme, create and save	EX D26	*See* Reference box: Creating and Saving a Theme
Theme, change for workbook	EX 86	Click Themes button in Themes group on Page Layout tab, click theme
Total row, add or remove from Excel table	EX 259	Check or uncheck Total Row check box in Table Style Options group on Table Tools Design tab
Total row, select summary statistics	EX 260	Click arrow button in Total row cell, click summary function
Trend, interpolate or extrapolate	EX 512	*See* Reference box: Interpolating and Extrapolating a Series
Trusted Location, define	EX 629	*See* Reference box: Defining a Trusted Location
Two-variable data table, create	EX 567	*See* Reference box: Creating a Two-Variable Data Table
Validation circle, clear from a cell	EX 444	Enter valid data
Validation circles, create or clear	EX 444	Click Data Validation button arrow in Data Tools group on Data tab, click Circle Invalid Data or Clear Validation Circles
Validation rule, create	EX 438	*See* Reference box: Validating Data
VBA code, view	EX 454	*See* Reference box: Editing a Macro
Visual Basic Editor, open or close	EX 454	*See* Reference box: Editing a Macro
Visual Basic Editor, start	EX 688	Click Macros button in Code group on Developer tab, click macro name, click Edit
Watch Window, open	EX 540	Click Watch Window button in Formula Auditing group on Formulas tab, click Add Watch button
Web query, create, save, or format	EX 659	*See* Reference box: Working with Web Queries
Workbook, add digital signature to	EX C18	*See* Reference box: Adding a Digital Signature to a Workbook
Workbook, check backward compatibility	EX C20	Click File tab, click Info tab, click Check for Issues button, click Check Compatibility
Workbook, create from template	EX 342	*See* Reference box: Creating a Workbook Based on a Template
Workbook, encrypt	EX C16	Click File tab, click Info, click Protect Workbook button, click Encrypt with Password
Workbook, mark as final	EX C17	Click File tab, click Info tab, click Protect Workbook button, click Mark as Final

TASK	PAGE #	RECOMMENDED METHOD
Workbook, protect	EX 448	*See* Reference box: Protecting a Workbook
Workbook, save to SkyDrive	EX 349	*See* Reference box: Saving a Workbook to SkyDrive
Workbook, save with macros	EX 471	In Save As dialog box, select save location, enter filename, click the Save as type button, click Excel Macro-Enabled Workbook, click Save
Workbook, share	EX C2	Click Share Workbook button in Changes group on Review tab
Workbooks, arrange	EX 324	*See* Reference box: Arranging Workbooks
Workbooks, merge	EX C10	*See* Reference box: Merging Workbooks
Workbooks, switch between	EX 324	Click Switch Windows button in Window group on View tab, click workbook to make active
Worksheet, add background image	EX 65	Click Background button in Page Setup group on Page Layout tab, click image file, click Insert
Worksheet, change orientation	EX 44	Click Orientation button in Page Setup group on the Page Layout tab, click Landscape or Portrait
Worksheet, change view	EX 43	Click , , or on status bar
Worksheet, copy	EX 38	Hold down Ctrl and drag sheet tab to new location
Worksheet, delete	EX 37	Right-click sheet tab, click Delete, click Delete button
Worksheet, hide or unhide	EX C15	Right-click sheet tab, click Hide or click Unhide, select worksheet, click OK
Worksheet, insert	EX 37	Click
Worksheet, move	EX 38	Drag sheet tab to new location
Worksheet, protect	EX 446	*See* Reference box: Protecting a Worksheet
Worksheet, rename	EX 38	Double-click sheet tab, type new name, press Enter
Worksheet, scale for printing	EX 47	Set width and height in Scale to Fit group on Page Layout tab
Worksheet, unprotect	EX 449	Make worksheet active, click Unprotect Sheet button in Changes group on Review tab
Worksheet group, print	EX 317	Create worksheet group, apply page layout settings, print as usual
Worksheets, move between	EX 5	Click sheet tab; or click tab scrolling button and then click sheet tab
Worksheets, copy to another workbook	EX 310	*See* Reference box: Copying Worksheets to Another Workbook
Worksheets, group or ungroup	EX 305	*See* Reference box: Grouping and Ungrouping Worksheets
Workspace, create	EX 333	Open and arrange workbooks as desired, click Save Workspace button in Window group on View tab, save as usual
Workspace, scroll	OFF 9	Click arrow button on scroll bar or drag scroll box
Workspace, zoom	OFF 9	Drag the Zoom slider
XML data, bind to cells	EX 670	Click Source button in XML group on Developer tab to display XML Source task pane, drag XML elements from XML data map to cells
XML map, load	EX 668	*See* Reference box: Loading an XML Data Map